Education at a Glance 2011

OECD INDICATORS

This work is published on the responsibility of the Secretary-General of the OECD. The opinions expressed and arguments employed herein do not necessarily reflect the official views of the Organisation or of the governments of its member countries.

Please cite this publication as:
OECD (2011), *Education at at Glance 2011: OECD Indicators*, OECD Publishing.
http://dx.doi.org/10.1787/eag-2011-en

ISBN 978-92-64-11420-3 (print)
ISBN 978-92-64-11705-1 (PDF)

Photo credits:
Stocklib Image Bank © Cathy Yeulet
Fotolia.com © Feng Yu
Getty Images © blue jean images

Corrigenda to OECD publications may be found on line at: *www.oecd.org/publishing/corrigenda*.

Foreword

Governments are paying increasing attention to international comparisons as they search for effective policies that enhance individuals' social and economic prospects, provide incentives for greater efficiency in schooling, and help to mobilise resources to meet rising demands. As part of its response, the OECD Directorate for Education devotes a major effort to the development and analysis of the quantitative, internationally comparable indicators that it publishes annually in *Education at a Glance*. These indicators enable educational policy makers and practitioners alike to see their education systems in the light of other countries' performances and, together with OECD's country policy reviews, are designed to support and review the efforts that governments are making towards policy reform.

Education at a Glance addresses the needs of a range of users, from governments seeking to learn policy lessons to academics requiring data for further analysis to the general public wanting to monitor how its nation's schools are progressing in producing world-class students. The publication examines the quality of learning outcomes, the policy levers and contextual factors that shape these outcomes, and the broader private and social returns that accrue to investments in education.

Education at a Glance is the product of a long-standing, collaborative effort between OECD governments, the experts and institutions working within the framework of the OECD's Indicators of Education Systems (INES) programme and the OECD Secretariat. The publication was prepared by the Indicators and Analysis Division of the OECD Directorate for Education with input from the Centre for Educational Research and Innovation, under the responsibility of Andreas Schleicher, in co-operation with Etienne Albiser, Eric Charbonnier, Pedro Lenin Garcia de Léon, Bo Hansson, Corinne Heckmann, Estelle Herbaut, Karinne Logez, Koji Miyamoto and Jean Yip. Administrative support was provided by Sandrine Meireles and Rebecca Tessier, editing of the report was undertaken by Marilyn Achiron and additional advice as well as analytical and editorial support were provided by Marika Boiron, Ji Eun Chung, Anaïs Dubreucq-Le Bouffant, Maciej Jakubowski, Manal Quota, Giannina Rech and Elisabeth Villoutreix. Production of the report was co-ordinated by Corinne Heckmann and Elisabeth Villoutreix. The development of the publication was steered by member countries through the INES Working Party and facilitated by the INES Networks. The members of the various bodies as well as the individual experts who have contributed to this publication and to OECD INES more generally are listed at the end of the book.

While much progress has been accomplished in recent years, member countries and the OECD continue to strive to strengthen the link between policy needs and the best available internationally comparable data. In doing so, various challenges and trade-offs are faced. First, the indicators need to respond to educational issues that are high on national policy agendas, and where the international comparative perspective can offer important added value to what can be accomplished through national analysis and evaluation. Second, while the indicators need to be as comparable as possible, they also need to be as country-specific as is necessary to allow for historical, systemic and cultural differences between countries. Third, the indicators need to be presented in as straightforward a manner as possible, while remaining sufficiently complex to reflect multi-faceted educational realities. Fourth, there is a general desire to keep the indicator set as small as possible, but it needs to be large enough to be useful to policy makers across countries that face different educational challenges.

The OECD will continue to address these challenges vigorously and to pursue not just the development of indicators in areas where it is feasible and promising to develop data, but also to advance in areas where a considerable investment still needs to be made in conceptual work. The further development of the OECD Programme for International Student Assessment (PISA) and its extension through the OECD Programme for the International Assessment of Adult Competencies (PIAAC), as well as OECD's Teaching and Learning International Survey (TALIS) are major efforts to this end.

TABLE OF CONTENTS

Number of the indicator in the 2010 edition

Editorial ... 13

Introduction ... 21

Reader's Guide ... 25

CHAPTER A THE OUTPUT OF EDUCATIONAL INSTITUTIONS AND THE IMPACT OF LEARNING ... 29

Indicator A1 To what level have adults studied? ... **30** A1

Table A1.1a Educational attainment: Adult population (2009) ... 38

Table A1.2a Population with at least upper secondary education (2009) ... 39

Table A1.3a Population with tertiary education (2009) ... 40

Table A1.4 Trends in educational attainment: 25-64 year-olds (1997-2009) ... 41

Indicator A2 How many students finish secondary education? ... 44 A2

Table A2.1 Upper secondary graduation rates (2009) ... 54

Table A2.2 Trends in graduation rates (first-time) at upper secondary level (1995-2009) ... 55

Table A2.3 Post-secondary non-tertiary graduation rates (2009) ... 56

Table A2.4 Successful completion of upper secondary programmes, by gender and programme orientation ... 57

Indicator A3 How many students finish tertiary education? ... **60** A3

Table A3.1 Graduation rates at tertiary level (2009) ... 68

Table A3.2 Trends in tertiary graduation rates (1995-2009) ... 69

Table A3.3 Graduation rate at different tertiary levels, impact of international/foreign students (2009) ... 70

Table A3.4 Structure of tertiary education: Main programme blocks (2009) ... 71

Indicator A4 To which fields of education are students attracted? ... **72**

Table A4.1a Distribution of upper secondary vocational graduates, by field of education and gender (2009) ... 82

Table A4.2a Distribution of new entrants into tertiary programmes, by field of education (2009) ... 83

Table A4.3a Percentage of tertiary qualifications awarded to women in tertiary-type A and advanced research programmes, by field of education (2000, 2009) ... 84

Table A4.4 Distribution of enrolment in tertiary programmes, by field of education (2009) ... 85

Table A4.5 Distribution of international and foreign students enrolled in tertiary programmes, by field of education (2009) ... 86

Table A4.6 Science-related graduates among 25-34 year-olds in employment, by gender (2009) ... 87

		Number of the indicator in the 2010 edition
Indicator A5	**Does student background affect student performance? 88**	
Table A5.1	Socio-economic background and reading performance 95	
Table A5.2	Percentage of students by immigrant status and their reading performance 97	
Table A5.3	Percentage of resilient students and disadvantaged low achievers among all students, by gender 99	
Indicator A6	**Are students who enjoy reading better readers? 100**	
Table A6.1	Index of enjoyment of reading and reading performance, by national quarters of this index 109	
Table A6.2	Percentage of students and reading performance, by time spent reading for enjoyment 111	
Table A6.3	Reading diverse materials and performance 113	
Table A6.4	Percentage of students and reading performance, by whether students spend any time reading for enjoyment and gender 114	
Indicator A7	**How does educational attainment affect participation in the labour market? 116**	A6
Table A7.1a	Employment rates and educational attainment, by gender (2009) 125	
Table A7.2a	Unemployment rates and educational attainment, by gender (2009) 127	
Table A7.3a	Trends in employment rates of 25-64 year-olds, by educational attainment (1997-2009) 129	
Table A7.4a	Trends in unemployment rates of 25-64 year-olds, by educational attainment (1997-2009) 131	
Table A7.5	Proportion of individuals with earnings from employment working on a full-time basis (2009 or latest available year) 133	
Table A7.6	Size and labour outcomes of vocational education and training (2009) 135	
Indicator A8	**What are the earnings premiums from education? 138**	A7
Table A8.1	Relative earnings of the population with income from employment (2009 or latest available year) 147	
Table A8.2a	Trends in relative earnings: Total population (1999-2009) 149	
Table A8.2b	Trends in relative earnings: Men (1999-2009) 151	
Table A8.2c	Trends in relative earnings: Women (1999-2009) 153	
Table A8.3a	Differences in earnings between women and men (2009 or latest available year) 155	
Table A8.3b	Trends in differences in earnings between women and men (1999-2009) 156	
Indicator A9	**What are the incentives to invest in education? 158**	A8
Table A9.1	Private net present value and internal rate of return for an individual obtaining upper secondary or post-secondary non-tertiary education as part of initial education, ISCED 3/4, in equivalent USD (2007 or latest available year) 170	
Table A9.2	Public net present value and internal rate of return for an individual obtaining upper secondary or post-secondary non-tertiary education as part of initial education, ISCED 3/4, in equivalent USD (2007 or latest available year) 172	

Number of the indicator in the 2010 edition

Table A9.3 Private net present value and internal rate of return for an individual obtaining tertiary education as part of initial education, ISCED 5/6, in equivalent USD (2007 or latest available year) 174

Table A9.4 Public net present value and internal rate of return for an individual obtaining tertiary education as part of initial education, ISCED 5/6, in equivalent USD (2007 or latest available year) 175

Indicator A10 How expensive are graduates to hire? 176 A10

Table A10.1 Annual labour costs, full-time gross earnings and annual net income, by ISCED levels in equivalent USD, 25-64 year-olds (2009 or latest available year) 185

Table A10.2 Annual labour costs, full-time gross earnings and annual net income, by ISCED levels in equivalent USD, 25-34 year-olds (2009 or latest available year) 187

Table A10.4 Annual labour costs, full-time gross earnings and annual net income, by ISCED levels in equivalent USD, 45-54 year-olds (2009 or latest available year) 189

Indicator A11 What are the social outcomes of education? 192 A9

Table A11.1 Proportion of adults voting, volunteering and satisfied with life, by level of education (2008) 200

Table A11.2 Civic engagement, by students' level of civic knowledge (2009) 201

Table A11.3 Incremental differences in adult voting, volunteering and life satisfaction associated with an increase in the level of educational attainment (2008) (with and without adjustments for age, gender and income) 202

CHAPTER B FINANCIAL AND HUMAN RESOURCES INVESTED IN EDUCATION 203

Indicator B1 How much is spent per student? 206 B1

Table B1.1a Annual expenditure per student by educational institutions for all services (2008) 218

Table B1.2 Annual expenditure per student, by educational institutions on core services, ancillary services and R&D (2008) 219

Table B1.3a Cumulative expenditure per student by educational institutions for all services over the average duration of tertiary studies (2008) 220

Table B1.4 Annual expenditure per student by educational institutions for all services relative to GDP per capita (2008) 221

Table B1.5 Change in expenditure per student by educational institutions for all services relative to different factors, by level of education (1995, 2000, 2008) 222

Table B1.6 Annual expenditure per student by educational institutions for all services, by type of programme, at the secondary level (2008) 223

Indicator B2 What proportion of national wealth is spent on education? 224 B2

Table B2.1 Expenditure on educational institutions as a percentage of GDP, by level of education (1995, 2000, 2008) 229

Table B2.2 Expenditure on educational institutions as a percentage of GDP, by level of education (2008) 230

Table B2.3 Expenditure on educational institutions as a percentage of GDP, by source of fund and level of education (2008) 231

			Number of the indicator in the 2010 edition
Indicator B3	**How much public and private investment in education is there?**	**232**	**B3**
Table B3.1	Relative proportions of public and private expenditure on educational institutions for all levels of education (2000, 2008)	242	
Table B3.2a	Relative proportions of public and private expenditure on educational institutions, as a percentage, by level of education (2000, 2008)	243	
Table B3.2b	Relative proportions of public and private expenditure on educational institutions, as a percentage, for tertiary education (2000, 2008)	244	
Table B3.3	Trends in relative proportions of public expenditure on educational institutions and index of change between 1995 and 2008 (2000 = 100), for tertiary education (1995, 2000, 2005, 2006, 2007 and 2008)	245	
Table B3.4	Annual public expenditure on educational institutions per student, by type of institution (2008)	246	
Indicator B4	**What is the total public spending on education?**	**248**	**B4**
Table B4.1	Total public expenditure on education (1995, 2000, 2008)	254	
Table B4.2	Sources of public educational funds, before and after transfers, by level of government for primary, secondary and post-secondary non-tertiary education (2008)	255	
Indicator B5	**How much do tertiary students pay and what public subsidies do they receive?**	**256**	**B5**
Table B5.1	Estimated annual average tuition fees charged, by tertiary-type A educational institutions for national students (academic year 2008-09)	266	
Table B5.2	Distribution of financial aid to students compared to the amount of tuition fees charged in tertiary-type A education (academic year 2008-09)	268	
Table B5.3	Public subsidies for households and other private entities as a percentage of total public expenditure on education and GDP, for tertiary education (2008)	269	
Indicator B6	**On what resources and services is education funding spent?**	**270**	**B6**
Table B6.1	Expenditure on educational institutions by service category as a percentage of GDP (2008)	276	
Table B6.2a	Expenditure by educational institutions, by resource category in primary and secondary education (2008)	277	
Table B6.2b	Expenditure by educational institutions, by resource category and level of education (2008)	278	
Indicator B7	**Which factors influence the level of expenditure?**	**280**	**B7**
Table B7.1	Contribution, in USD, of various factors to salary cost per student at the primary level of education (2008)	288	
Table B7.2	Contribution, in USD, of various factors to salary cost per student at the lower secondary level of education (2008)	289	
Table B7.3	Contribution, in USD, of various factors to salary cost per student at the upper secondary level of education (2008)	290	
CHAPTER C	**ACCESS TO EDUCATION, PARTICIPATION AND PROGRESSION**	**291**	
Indicator C1	**Who participates in education?**	**292**	**C1**
Table C1.1a	Enrolment rates, by age (2009)	303	

		Number of the indicator in the 2010 edition
Table C1.2	Trends in enrolment rates (1995-2009) 304	
Table C1.3	Secondary enrolment patterns (2009) 305	
Table C1.4	Students in primary and secondary education, by type of institution or mode of enrolment (2009) 306	
Table C1.5	Students in tertiary education, by type of institution or mode of enrolment (2009) 307	
Indicator C2	**How many students will enter tertiary education? 308**	A2
Table C2.1	Entry rates into tertiary education and age distribution of new entrants (2009) 316	
Table C2.2	Trends in entry rates at the tertiary level (1995-2009) 317	
Indicator C3	**Who studies abroad and where? 318**	C2
Table C3.1	International and foreign students in tertiary education (2000, 2004, 2009) 333	
Table C3.2	Distribution of international and foreign students in tertiary education, by country of origin (2009) 334	
Table C3.3	Citizens studying abroad in tertiary education, by country of destination (2009) 336	
Table C3.4	Distribution of international and foreign students in tertiary education, by level and type of tertiary education (2009) 338	
Table C3.5	Trends in the number of foreign students enrolled outside their country of origin, by region of destination (2000 to 2009) 339	
Indicator C4	**Transition from school to work: Where are the 15-29 year-olds? 340**	C3
Table C4.1a	Expected years in education and not in education for 15-29 year-olds (2009) 348	
Table C4.2a	Percentage of young people in education and not in education, by age group (2009) 349	
Table C4.2d	Percentage of 15-29 year-olds in education and not in education, by level of education (2009) 352	
Table C4.3	Percentage of the cohort population not in education and unemployed (2009) 355	
Table C4.4a	Trends in the percentage of young people in education and not in education (1997-2009) 357	
Indicator C5	**How many adults participate in education and learning? 364**	
Table C5.1a	Participation rate, hours of instruction per participant, per adult and expected hours in all non-formal education (NFE) and in job-related NFE, annual hours actually worked, and ratio of hours in job-related NFE to hours worked, 2008 373	
Table C5.1b	Participation rate and expected hours in job-related non-formal education, by educational attainment, 2007 374	
Table C5.2a	Hours of instruction per participant and per adult, in all non-formal education (NFE) and in job-related NFE, by educational attainment and labour force status, 2007 375	
Table C5.3a	Participation in formal and non-formal education, by type of education and educational attainment, 2007 377	
Table C5.4a	Proportion of individuals who have looked for and found information, by educational attainment, 2007 378	

			Number of the indicator in the 2010 edition
CHAPTER D	**THE LEARNING ENVIRONMENT AND ORGANISATION OF SCHOOLS**	**379**	
Indicator D1	**How much time do students spend in the classroom?**	**380**	D1
Table D1.1	Compulsory and intended instruction time in public institutions (2009)	389	
Table D1.2a	Instruction time per subject as a percentage of total compulsory instruction time for 9-11 year-olds (2009)	390	
Table D1.2b	Instruction time per subject as a percentage of total compulsory instruction time for 12-14 year-olds (2009)	391	
Indicator D2	**What is the student-teacher ratio and how big are classes?**	**392**	D2
Table D2.1	Average class size, by type of institution and level of education (2009)	402	
Table D2.2	Ratio of students to teaching staff in educational institutions (2009)	403	
Table D2.3	Ratio of students to teaching staff, by type of institution (2009)	404	
Indicator D3	**How much are teachers paid?**	**406**	D3
Table D3.1	Teachers' salaries (2009)	415	
Table D3.2	Teachers' salaries and pre-service teacher training requirements (2009)	417	
Table D3.3	Trends in teachers' salaries between 1995 and 2009 (2005 = 100)	418	
Table D3.4	Trends in the ratio of salaries to GDP per capita (2000-09)	419	
Table D3.5a	Decisions on payments for teachers in public institutions (2009)	420	
Indicator D4	**How much time do teachers spend teaching?**	**422**	D4
Table D4.1	Organisation of teachers' working time (2009)	428	
Table D4.2	Number of teaching hours per year (2000, 2005-09)	429	
Indicator D5	**How are schools held accountable?**	**430**	
Table D5.1a	National examinations at the lower secondary level (2009)	441	
Table D5.2a	National assessments at the lower secondary level (2009)	443	
Table D5.3	Regulatory accountability: Domains in which public schools are expected to submit compliance-oriented reports (2009)	445	
Table D5.4a	School inspection at the lower secondary level (2009)	446	
Table D5.5	Existence of school choice options and financial incentives for school choice (2009)	448	
Indicator D6	**How equal are educational outcomes and opportunities?**	**450**	
Table D6.1	Percentage of potentially vulnerable students, age 15 (PISA 2009)	459	
Table D6.2	Index of social inclusion (PISA 2009)	460	
Table D6.3	Reading scores below PISA proficiency Level 3, age 15 (PISA 2009)	461	
Table D6.4	Reading scores below PISA proficiency Level 2, age 15 (PISA 2009)	462	
Table D6.5	Student does not value schooling outcomes (PISA 2009)	463	
Table D6.6	Student attends a school with negative student-teacher relations (PISA 2009)	464	
ANNEX 1	**CHARACTERISTICS OF EDUCATIONAL SYSTEMS**	**465**	
Table X1.1a	Upper secondary graduation rate: Typical graduation ages and method used to calculate graduation rates (2009)	466	
Table X1.1b	Post-secondary non-tertiary graduation rates: Typical graduation ages and method used to calculate graduation rates (2009)	468	

Number of the indicator in the 2010 edition

Table X1.1c Tertiary graduation rate: Typical graduation ages and method used to calculate graduation rates (2009) ... 469

Table X1.1d Tertiary entry rate: Typical age of entry and method used to calculate entry rates (2009) ... 471

Table X1.2a School year and financial year used for the calculation of indicators, OECD countries ... 472

Table X1.2b School year and financial year used for the calculation of indicators, other G20 countries ... 473

Table X1.3 Summary of completion requirements for upper secondary programmes ... 474

ANNEX 2 REFERENCE STATISTICS ... 475

Table X2.1 Overview of the economic context using basic variables (reference period: calendar year 2008, 2008 current prices) ... 476

Table X2.2a Basic reference statistics (reference period: calendar year 2008, 2008 current prices) ... 477

Table X2.2b Basic reference statistics (reference period: calendar year 1995 and 2000, current prices) ... 478

Table X2.3a Teachers' salaries in national currency (2009) ... 479

Table X2.3b Teachers' salaries in equivalent euros (2009) ... 480

Table X2.3c Trends in teachers' salaries in national currency, by level of education ... 481

Table X2.3d Reference statistics used in the calculation of teachers' salaries (1995, 2000, 2005-2009) ... 483

ANNEX 3 SOURCES, METHODS AND TECHNICAL NOTES ... 487

References ... 489

Contributors to this publication ... 491

Related OECD publications ... 495

Editorial

Fifty years of change in education

Since its early days, the OECD has emphasised the role of education and human capital in driving economic and social development; and in the half century since its founding, the pool of human capital in its member countries has developed dramatically. Access to education has expanded to the extent that the majority of people in OECD countries is now enrolled in education beyond basic, compulsory schooling. At the same time, countries have transformed the ways they look at educational outcomes, moving beyond a simplistic "more is better" perspective that simply measures investment and participation in education to one that encompasses the quality of the competencies that students ultimately acquire. In an increasingly global economy, in which the benchmark for educational success is no longer improvement by national standards alone, but the best performing education systems internationally, the role of the OECD has become central, providing indicators of educational performance that not only evaluate but also help shape public policy.

Growth in educational attainment from the 1950s to the 2000s

During the past 50 years, the expansion of education has contributed to a fundamental transformation of societies in OECD countries. In 1961, higher education was the privilege of the few, and even upper secondary education was denied to the majority of young people in many countries. Today, the great majority of the population completes secondary education, one in three young adults has a tertiary degree and, in some countries, half of the population could soon hold a tertiary degree.

It hasn't always been possible to quantify such changes over time: for most of the past half-century, a lack of consistent data made it virtually impossible to track the pace of change. Data on educational attainment was not sufficiently standardised until the 1990s. However, age-based attainment levels can be used to estimate how many people earned education qualifications over their lifetimes. For example, the number of people aged 55-64 who have a degree is a proxy for the number of people who graduated three or four decades ago. This method somewhat overestimates the qualification rates among older compared to younger groups of people, because it measures the attainment of the latter group after those individuals have had a chance to acquire qualifications later in life. However, now that consistent attainment data have been around for over a decade, we can also chart this "lifelong learning" effect by comparing the qualifications held by the same cohort at different times during their lives.

Chart 1 offers a broad estimate based on this method. It provides information on qualifications held by adults born as far apart as 1933 (now aged 78) and 1984 (now aged 27). The oldest among them completed their initial education in the 1950s, the youngest in the 2000s. These data show clearly that the rise in attainment both at upper secondary and tertiary levels has not only been large but it has been continuous over the entire half-century, spurred by strong and generally rising economic and social outcomes for the better qualified. Among the 34 OECD countries, most of those in which college enrolment expanded the most over the past decades still see rising earnings differentials for college graduates, suggesting that an increase in the supply of highly educated workers does not lead to a decrease in their pay, as is the case among low-skilled workers.

On average across OECD countries, the proportion of people with at least an upper secondary education has risen from 45% to 81%, and the proportion of those with tertiary qualifications has risen from 13% to 37%. The chart suggests that about 7% of the cohort now aged 35-44 have gained tertiary qualifications that they did not have at age of 25-34, and that 4% of individuals have these qualifications at age 45-54 but did not have them at age 35-44. If people now aged 25-34, 37% of whom already have tertiary qualifications, make similar progress in the next two decades, half of this cohort could have tertiary qualifications by the time they reach their middle age.

Chart 1. Educational attainment, by age and birth cohort (OECD average)

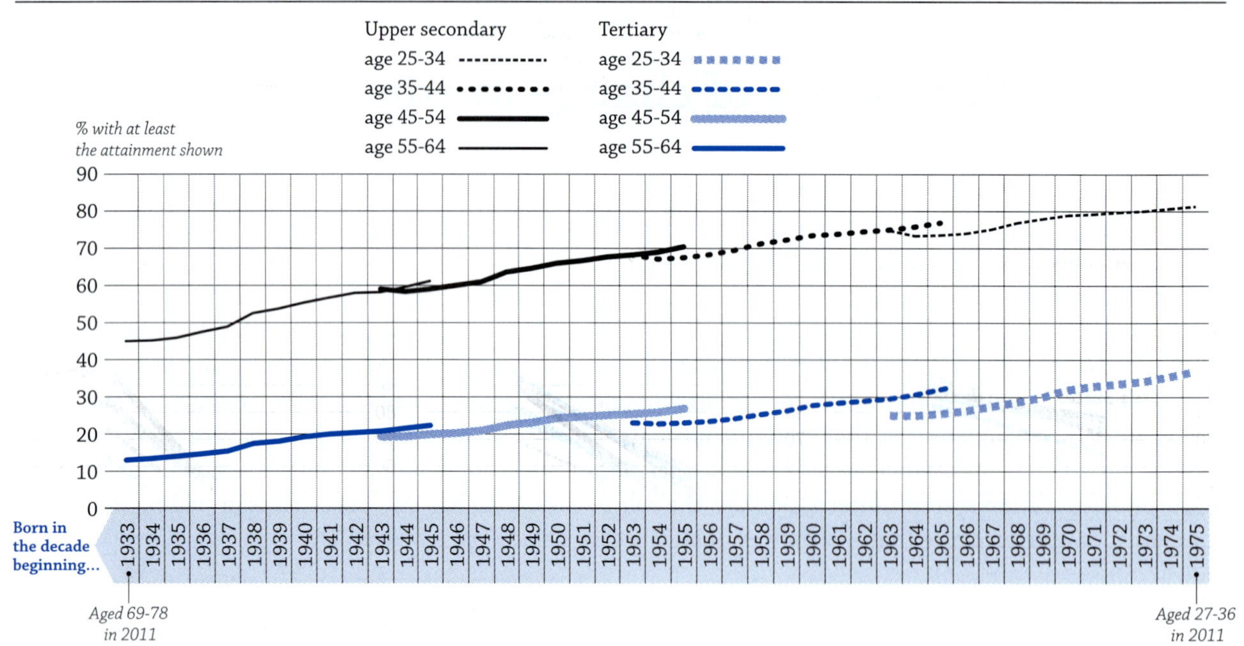

Source: OECD. See Annex 3 for notes (*www.oecd.org/edu/eag2011*).
StatLink http://dx.doi.org/10.1787/888932478964

How to read this chart

This chart shows the percentage of adults born during a certain time period who have attained a given level of attainment by a particular age – based on reported attainment between 1997 and 2009. Each year shown represents an age cohort in a ten-year period starting with that year: for example 1933 represents people born from 1933 to 1942, inclusive. As a result, the age cohorts shown for successive starting years overlap.

The chart shows that cohorts born in later years have progressively higher levels of attainment, regardless of the age at which this is measured. Measuring attainment at a later age allows for the acquisition of qualifications later in life. However, in most cases where the same cohort reports attainment at different ages (i.e. where the lines overlap), the result is similar. The greatest apparent increase is shown on the bottom right of the chart, for the cohort born in the decade starting in 1965 (now aged 37-46). Of this cohort, 25% reported having a tertiary education in 1999 when they were 25-34, but 32% had this level of education in 2009, when they were ten years older.

(Note, however, that these results do not measure the educational progress of cohorts precisely, because the composition of the age groups changed due to migration and mortality.)

These data also tell us that rates of educational expansion have varied greatly among countries over recent decades. Charts 2 and 3 show the attainment rates for the oldest and youngest cohorts of those shown in Chart 1, by individual countries. Chart 2 shows a general increase in upper secondary education, with those countries that had low attainment levels "catching up" with those that had higher levels of attainment. Now, at least 80% of young adults in all OECD countries complete an upper secondary education. Within this general pattern, the United States has seen only a small improvement, having started out from the highest high-school completion rate, while Finland and Korea transformed themselves from countries where only a minority of students graduated from secondary school to those where virtually all students do.

Attainment at the tertiary level varies more by country (Chart 3). The growth rate has been relatively slow in the United States, for example, where attainment was originally relatively high, and in Germany, which had lower levels of attainment. In contrast, Japan and Korea have made higher education dramatically more accessible. In both countries, among the cohort who were of graduation age in the late 1950s and early 1960s (born 1933-42), only about one in ten had tertiary qualifications by late in their working lives. Among younger Japanese and Koreans, who reached graduation age around the turn of the millennium, most now have tertiary degrees. On this measure, Korea has moved from the 21st to the first rank among 25 OECD countries with comparable data.

Chart 2. Progress in attainment of upper secondary education over half a century, by country

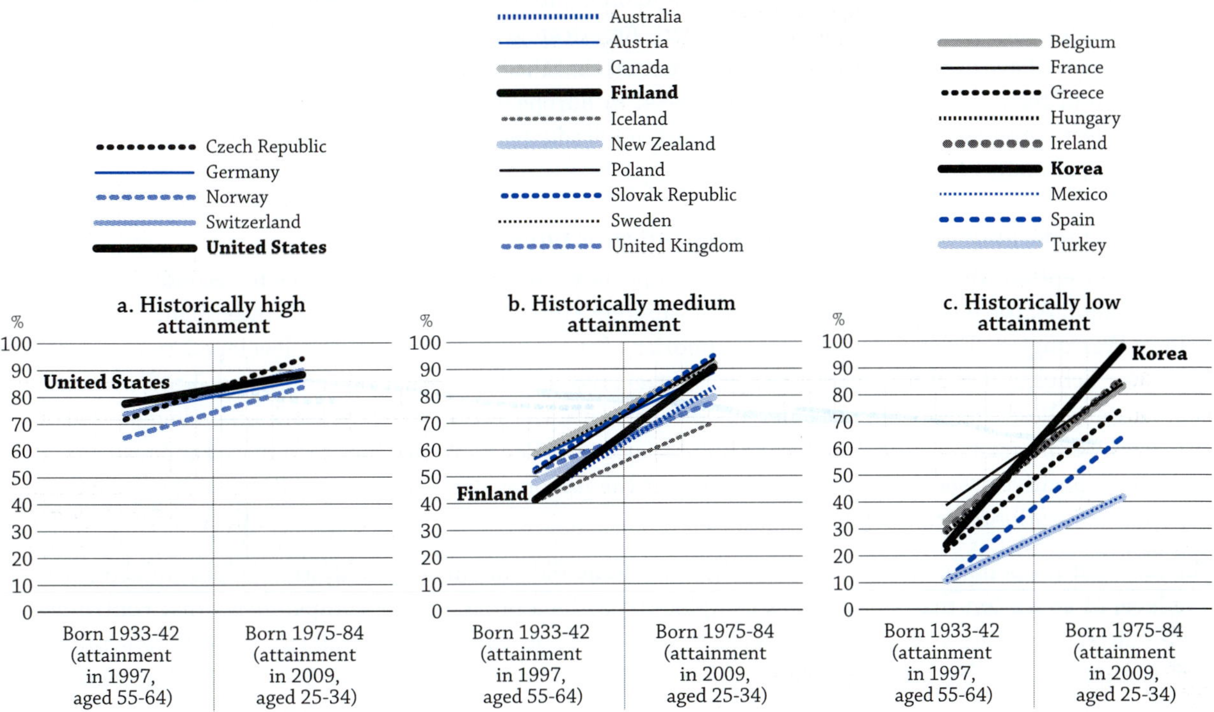

Source: OECD. See Annex 3 for notes (*www.oecd.org/edu/eag2011*).
StatLink http://dx.doi.org/10.1787/888932478983

Chart 3. Progress in attainment of tertiary education over half a century, by country

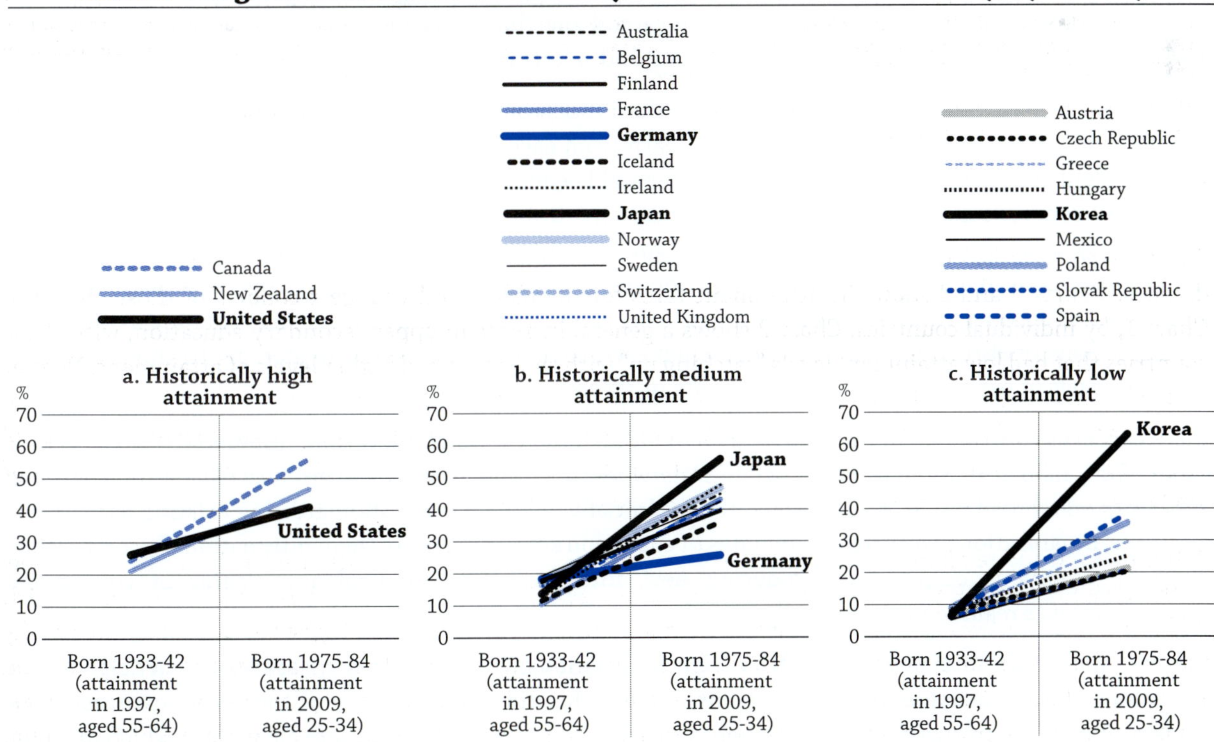

Source: OECD. See Annex 3 for notes (*www.oecd.org/edu/eag2011*).
StatLink http://dx.doi.org/10.1787/888932479002

Half a century ago, employers in the United States and Canada recruited their workforce from a pool of young adults, most of whom had high school diplomas and one in four of whom had degrees – far more than in most European and Asian countries. Today, while North American graduation rates have increased, those of some other countries have done so much faster, to the extent that the United States now shows just over the average proportion of tertiary-level graduates at age 25-34. In Europe, Germany stands out as the country that has made the least progress: it has a population of tertiary graduates only around half the size, relative to its total population, of many of its neighbours'.

The OECD and education: An evolving narrative of human capital

From its inception, the OECD has stressed the importance of human competencies for economic and social development. At the new organisation's Policy Conference on Economic Growth and Investment in Education, held in Washington, DC in 1961, emerging theories of human capital then being developed by Gary Becker, Theodore Schultz and others were brought centre-stage in the international dialogue. Hard evidence to substantiate these theories did not emerge, however, until the 1980s, with the work on endogenous growth theories by economists such as Paul Romer, Robert Lucas and Robert Barro. They formulated and tested models measuring positive associations between growth at the national level and crude indicators of human capital, especially educational attainment.

The fact that these measured associations remained weak did not surprise analysts of educational outcomes. The level of education that an adult has completed may be a proxy for the competencies that contribute to economic success, but it is a highly imperfect measure. First, each country has its own different processes and standards for accrediting completion of secondary or tertiary education. Second, the knowledge and skills acquired in education are by no means identical to those that enhance economic potential. And third, it has become increasingly evident that to realise human potential in today's societies and economies, lifelong learning is required, not just an initial period of formal schooling.

Once the association between education and development was made, countries were keen to better understand the nature of education outcomes and to compare them internationally. From the 1970s onwards, the OECD has been in the vanguard of those promoting lifelong learning as a paradigm. More recently, it has formulated broad interpretations of what comprises human capital and the related concept of social capital. It has also developed a comprehensive framework for defining and selecting necessary competencies.

The development of indicators has been central to this process of improved understanding about the outcomes of education, and to the ability of countries to learn from each other about what works. By the mid-1980s, it was evident that the lack of internationally comparable education data was greatly hindering the ability to make valid comparisons or to develop policy conclusions from the experiences of countries with successful education systems. This was a time when national governments were starting to ask themselves new questions about the direction and outcomes of their education systems. The idea that simply getting more people through high school or university was an end in itself was being challenged. Issues of quality and value-for-money arose during periods of shrinking public budgets, when early international tests were starting to show markedly different levels of performance between students in different countries.

These concerns contributed to the 1988 launch of OECD's Indicators of Education Systems (INES) project – a major effort, managed through a series of OECD networks of national experts, to produce reliable international indicators on a broad range of educational topics. Initially, INES involved standardising existing data on the resources, organisation and participation rates of education systems to make them internationally comparable. Its more ambitious objective of producing new, internationally comparable measures of educational performance was realised more gradually.

The first indicators to emerge from INES were internationally standardised measures of participation in education, such as students enrolled at different levels of education, graduation rates and resources invested per student. But it was only when more direct measures of educational outcomes were developed, which involved testing students and adults, that the effectiveness of investment in education and educational processes could start to be evaluated.

The International Adult Literacy Survey (IALS) in the mid-1990s showed that although adults who have attained higher levels of education have, on average, greater levels of literacy, those with a given level of educational attainment have very different ranges of literacy skills from one country to another. This showed that direct measures of human capital could produce different results from proxy measures based on people's educational experiences and qualifications. Subsequently, IALS was analysed to consider the economic effect of countries' stock of human capital, and identified a substantially stronger relationship between measured literacy levels and economic growth than previous studies had found (Coulombe, *et al.*, *Literacy scores, human capital and growth across fourteen OECD countries*, Statistics Canada, 2004). This confirmed that the effectiveness of education systems should not just be considered in terms of the rate at which they award qualifications, but could be related to the acquisition of measurable competencies.

But it is the OECD's Programme for International Student Assessment (PISA) survey, which tests young people's acquisition of knowledge and skills for life, that is the most powerful and extensive tool for considering educational outcomes and transforming public policy. The triennial PISA surveys, which began in 2000, have shown large differences between what students know and can do in different countries as they near the end of compulsory education.

One of the most common ways of comparing educational quality before PISA existed, spending per student, is shown to be positively associated with outcomes, but explains only about a quarter of the differences among countries. PISA results show that no single aspect of the educational process provides the key to success; but a combination of a range of policies and practices measured in PISA can jointly account for 80% of the variation in school performance among countries. Such findings, combined with existing research in education, have begun to shape policy development. Indeed, the world of education has moved a long way from 1961, when the standards guiding education policy relied principally on national beliefs, based only on precedent and tradition, about what constituted a good education.

Indicators as a catalyst for change

As the quality of international indicators improves, so does their potential for influencing the development of education systems. At one level, indicators are no more than a metric for gauging progress towards goals. Yet increasingly, they are performing a more influential role. Indicators can prompt change by raising national concern over weak educational outcomes compared to international benchmarks; sometimes, they can even encourage stronger countries to consolidate their positions. When indicators build a profile of high-performing education systems, they can also inform the design of improvements for weaker systems.

The "shock" effect of international comparisons on educational reform is nothing new. Reforms in the United States following the publication of *A Nation at Risk* in 1983 were partly triggered by evidence from international tests showing that American students were lagging behind. However, while such early international comparisons acted as a "wake-up call", they offered few clues about solutions, and reforms were designed mainly against national analyses of what was wrong with the education system. In contrast, when PISA published its first results in 2001 showing that German students were performing below the OECD average, the initial shock in Germany was swiftly followed by an outward-looking response: a determination to emulate successful practices that work elsewhere. The education system was reviewed in light of internationally comparable data, internationally benchmarked national standards were introduced, and evidence-based practices were emphasised.

More systematic analysis suggests that the uses and impact of the OECD's education indicators are varied:

- By showing what is possible in education, the indicators have helped countries not just to optimise existing policies but also to reflect on what lies behind them. This involves questioning, and sometimes changing, the paradigms and beliefs that underlie current policies.
- The indicators have helped countries to set policy targets as measurable goals achieved by other systems, identify policy levers and establish trajectories for reform.
- Using the indicators as a reference, countries can better gauge the pace of progress in education and review how education is delivered at the classroom level. The indicators show that while educational reform may be politically difficult to initiate, the benefits almost inevitably accrue to successive governments if not generations.

Opening eyes and minds to new possibilities

Indicators have a particularly powerful impact when they contradict the self-perception of a national education system, and therefore challenge the beliefs and assumptions that guide it. The impact of the PISA survey in Germany was strong not just because the country's initial performance in the survey was below average, but also because those results prompted a rethink of the assumption that the system produced socially equitable outcomes (Box 1). Governments in a number of countries have used PISA results showing their relative standing internationally as a starting point for a peer review to study the policies and practices of countries in similar circumstances that achieve better results.

Box 1. Germany rethinks its assumptions about education and social equity

Before PISA, equity in learning opportunities across schools in Germany had often been taken for granted, as significant efforts were devoted to ensuring that schools were adequately and equitably resourced. The PISA 2000 results, however, revealed large socio-economic disparities in educational outcomes between schools. Further analysis linked this in large part to the tendency for students from more privileged social backgrounds to attend more prestigious academic schools and those from less privileged social backgrounds to attend less prestigious vocational schools, even when their performance on the PISA assessment was similar. This raised concern that the education system was reinforcing rather than moderating the influence of socio-economic background on student performance. These results, and the ensuing public debate, inspired a wide range of equity-related reform efforts in Germany, some of which have been transformational in nature. These include: giving an educational orientation to early childhood education, which had hitherto been considered largely an aspect of social welfare; establishing national educational standards in a country where regional and local autonomy had long been the overriding paradigm; and enhancing support for disadvantaged students, such as students from immigrant backgrounds.

For many educators and experts in Germany, the socio-economic disparities that PISA had revealed had not been surprising. That disadvantaged children would do less well in school was often taken for granted and outside the scope of public policy discussions. The fact that PISA revealed that the influence of socio-economic background on students and school performance varies so considerably across countries, and that other countries appeared to moderate socio-economic disparities so much more effectively, showed that improvement was possible and provided the momentum for policy change.

As international benchmarks, such as PISA, are disseminated more widely, the debate about improving education moves from a circle of specialised experts to a larger public. Indicators make international comparisons both accessible and powerful. As students will now compete in a global economy, people realise that their country's educational performance must exceed average levels if their children are to earn above-average wages later on.

Putting national targets into a broader perspective

The OECD education indicators have also played an important role in putting national performance targets into perspective. If the percentage of students who perform well in school increases, some will claim that the school system has improved; others will claim that standards must have been lowered. Behind the suspicion that better results reflect lowered standards is often a belief that overall performance in education cannot be improved. International benchmarks enable countries to relate those perceptions to a wider reference framework by allowing schools and education systems to look at themselves through the prism of the performance of schools and education systems in other countries. Some countries have actively embraced this perspective and, for example, established PISA-based performance targets for their education systems.

Assessing the pace of change in educational improvement

International comparisons also provide a frame of reference to assess the pace of change in educational development. While a national framework allows countries to assess progress in features such as expanded participation in absolute terms, the OECD's education indicators have allowed countries to assess whether that progress matches the pace of change observed elsewhere. Indeed, as noted earlier, all education systems in the OECD area have seen quantitative growth in attainment over past decades; but international comparisons reveal that the pace of change in educational output has varied markedly, such that the relative standing of countries on many indicators is now very different from that two decades ago.

Helping to make reform happen

Last but not least, international benchmarks can help make reform happen. At its most straightforward, this can take the form of creating a public clamour for improved standards that politicians and administrators cannot ignore. However, the pressure to improve systems does not always come via public opinion. In Mexico, the PISA results contradicted the view of parents that the education system was serving their children well, by showing how far standards lag behind OECD norms (Box 2). In Japan, PISA has shown weaknesses in a generally strong system, and thus helped justify to parents and the public why the existing style of education in Japan needs to be adapted (Box 3).

Box 2. **Mexican reform based on PISA benchmarks**

In the 2007 Mexican national survey of parents, 77% of those interviewed reported that the quality of education services provided by their children's school was good or very good even though, measured by OECD's PISA 2006 assessment, roughly half of the Mexican 15-year-olds who were then enrolled in school performed at or below the lowest level of proficiency established by PISA (IFIE-ALDUCIN, 2007; OECD, 2007a). There may be many reasons for such a discrepancy between perceived educational quality and performance on international benchmarks. For example, the education services that Mexican children receive are significantly better than those that their parents received. Still, justifying the investment of public resources into areas for which there seems no public demand poses challenges to reform. One response by the Mexican President has been to include a "PISA performance target" in the new Mexican reform plan. This internationally benchmarked performance target, which is to be reached by 2012, will highlight the gap between national performance and international standards and monitor how educational improvement can help close that gap. It is associated with the introduction of support systems, incentive structures and improved access to professional development to assist school leaders and teachers in meeting the target. Much of the reform draws on the experience of other countries. Brazil has taken a similar route, providing each secondary school with information on the amount of progress that is needed to perform at the OECD average level on PISA by 2021.

Box 3. **Japan adapts assessment style to mirror PISA**

Japan is one of the best-performing education systems. However, PISA revealed that while students tended to do very well on tasks that require reproducing subject content, they did much less well on open-ended tasks requiring them to demonstrate their capacity to extrapolate from what they know and apply their knowledge in novel settings. Convincing parents and a general public who are used to certain types of tests is difficult. One policy response in Japan has been to incorporate "PISA-type" open-constructed tasks into the national assessment, coupled with corresponding changes in curriculum and instructional practices. The aim of doing so is to ensure that skills that are considered important become valued in the education system. And indeed, a decade later, PISA outcomes in these areas had improved markedly. Like Japan, Korea has made PISA tasks part of national assessments, incorporating them into university entrance examinations, in order to build the capacity of its students to access, manage, integrate and evaluate written material. In both countries, these are fundamental changes that would have been much harder to imagine, much less achieve, without evidence from PISA.

Unfinished business

The OECD education indicators and related analyses cannot provide a blueprint for educational reform: the OECD's analysis is always careful not to imply that any one factor associated with strong performance can provide the single key to improvement. However, as the evidence base grows, the combination of factors indicative of strong education systems is becoming clearer. More fundamentally, the emergence of international standards has stopped education from being delivered in largely "closed" national systems. International indicators have made education systems more outward-looking. Moreover, as countries compete to excel in a knowledge-oriented global economy, international benchmarks allow them to track the evolution of the level of skills and knowledge of their own populations compared to those of their competitors.

As a result, the past 50 years have brought a fundamental transformation, not just in the level of educational activity but in how educational outcomes are monitored. The size of the investment in education is now too big, and its benefits too central to the success of economies and societies, for the design of effective education systems to take place in the dark. With economic competition now global, countries can no longer afford to measure their education systems against national standards. The OECD has recognised from the outset that education plays a central role in economic development; today, the Organisation is better equipped than ever to both track and support that role.

Angel Gurría
OECD Secretary-General

Further references

Coulombe, S., J.F. Tremblay and S. Marchand (2004), *Literacy Scores, Human Capital and Growth across Fourteen OECD Countries,* Statistics Canada, 2004.

IFIE-ALDUCIN (2007), *Mexican National Survey to Parents Regarding the Quality of Basic Education,* IFIE- ALDUCIN, Mexico City.

OECD (2007a), *PISA 2006: Science Competencies for Tomorrow's World: Volume I: Analysis,* OECD, Paris.

Introduction: the Indicators and their Framework

The organising framework

Education at a Glance: OECD Indicators 2011 offers a rich, comparable and up-to-date array of indicators that reflect a consensus among professionals on how to measure the current state of education internationally. The indicators provide information on the human and financial resources invested in education, on how education and learning systems operate and evolve, and on the returns to educational investments. The indicators are organised thematically, and each is accompanied by information on the policy context and the interpretation of the data. The education indicators are presented within an organising framework that:

- distinguishes between the actors in education systems: individual learners and teachers, instructional settings and learning environments, educational service providers, and the education system as a whole;
- groups the indicators according to whether they speak to learning outcomes for individuals or countries, policy levers or circumstances that shape these outcomes, or to antecedents or constraints that set policy choices into context; and
- identifies the policy issues to which the indicators relate, with three major categories distinguishing between the quality of educational outcomes and educational provision, issues of equity in educational outcomes and educational opportunities, and the adequacy and effectiveness of resource management.

The following matrix describes the first two dimensions:

	1. Education and learning outputs and outcomes	2. Policy levers and contexts shaping educational outcomes	3. Antecedents or constraints that contextualise policy
I. Individual participants in education and learning	1.I. The quality and distribution of individual educational outcomes	2.I. Individual attitudes, engagement, and behaviour to teaching and learning	3.I. Background characteristics of the individual learners and teachers
II. Instructional settings	1.II. The quality of instructional delivery	2.II. Pedagogy, learning practices and classroom climate	3.II. Student learning conditions and teacher working conditions
III. Providers of educational services	1.III. The output of educational institutions and institutional performance	2.III. School environment and organisation	3.III. Characteristics of the service providers and their communities
IV. The education system as a whole	1.IV. The overall performance of the education system	2.IV. System-wide institutional settings, resource allocations, and policies	3.IV. The national educational, social, economic, and demographic contexts

The following sections discuss the matrix dimensions in more detail:

Actors in education systems

The OECD Indicators of Education Systems (INES) programme seeks to gauge the performance of national education systems as a whole, rather than to compare individual institutional or other sub-national entities. However, there is increasing recognition that many important features of the development, functioning and impact of education systems can only be assessed through an understanding of learning outcomes and their relationships to inputs and processes at the level of individuals and institutions. To account for this, the indicator framework distinguishes between a macro level, two meso-levels and a micro-level of education systems. These relate to:

- the education system as a whole;
- the educational institutions and providers of educational services;
- the instructional setting and the learning environment within the institutions; and
- the individual participants in education and learning.

To some extent, these levels correspond to the entities from which data are being collected but their importance mainly centres on the fact that many features of the education system play out quite differently at different levels of the system, which needs to be taken into account when interpreting the indicators. For example, at the level of students within a classroom, the relationship between student achievement and class size may be negative, if students in small classes benefit from improved contact with teachers. At the class or school level, however, students are often intentionally grouped such that weaker or disadvantaged students are placed in smaller classes so that they receive more individual attention. At the school level, therefore, the observed relationship between class size and student achievement is often positive (suggesting that students in larger classes perform better than students in smaller classes). At higher aggregated levels of education systems, the relationship between student achievement and class size is further confounded, e.g. by the socio-economic intake of schools or by factors relating to the learning culture in different countries. Past analyses which have relied on macro-level data alone have therefore sometimes led to misleading conclusions.

Outcomes, policy levers and antecedents

The second dimension in the organising framework further groups the indicators at each of the above levels:

- indicators on observed outputs of education systems, as well as indicators related to the impact of knowledge and skills for individuals, societies and economies, are grouped under the sub-heading *output and outcomes of education and learning;*
- the sub-heading *policy levers and contexts* groups activities seeking information on the policy levers or circumstances which shape the outputs and outcomes at each level; and
- these policy levers and contexts typically have *antecedents* – factors that define or constrain policy. These are represented by the sub-heading antecedents and constraints. It should be noted that the antecedents or constraints are usually specific for a given level of the education system and that antecedents at a lower level of the system may well be policy levers at a higher level. For teachers and students in a school, for example, teacher qualifications are a given constraint while, at the level of the education system, professional development of teachers is a key policy lever.

Policy issues

Each of the resulting cells in the framework can then be used to address a variety of issues from different policy perspectives. For the purpose of this framework, policy perspectives are grouped into three classes that constitute the third dimension in the organising framework for INES:

- quality of educational outcomes and educational provision;
- equality of educational outcomes and equity in educational opportunities; and
- adequacy, effectiveness and efficiency of resource management.

In addition to the dimensions mentioned above, the time perspective as an additional dimension in the framework also allows dynamic aspects in the development of education systems to be modelled.

The indicators that are published in *Education at a Glance 2011* fit within this framework, though often they speak to more than one cell.

Most of the indicators in **Chapter A** *The output of educational institutions and the impact of learning* relate to the first column of the matrix describing outputs and outcomes of education. Even so, indicators in **Chapter A** measuring educational attainment for different generations, for instance, not only provide a measure of the output of the educational system, but also provide context for current educational policies, helping to shape polices on, for example, lifelong learning.

Chapter B *Financial and human resources invested in education* provides indicators that are either policy levers or antecedents to policy, or sometimes both. For example, expenditure per student is a key policy measure which most directly impacts on the individual learner as it acts as a constraint on the learning environment in schools and student learning conditions in the classroom.

Chapter C *Access to education, participation and progression* provides indicators that are a mixture of outcome indicators, policy levers and context indicators. Internationalisation of education and progression rates are, for instance, outcome measures to the extent that they indicate the results of policies and practices in the classroom, school and system levels. But they can also provide contexts for establishing policy by identifying areas where policy intervention is necessary to, for instance, address issues of inequity.

Chapter D *The learning environment and organisation of schools* provides indicators on instruction time, teachers' working time and teachers' salaries that not only represent policy levers which can be manipulated but also provide contexts for the quality of instruction in instructional settings and for the outcomes of learners at the individual level. This chapter also presents data on school accountability and educational equality and equity.

The reader should note that, for the first time, *Education at a Glance* covers a significant amount of data from China, India and Indonesia (please refer to the Reader's Guide for details).

Reader's Guide

Coverage of the statistics

Although a lack of data still limits the scope of the indicators in many countries, the coverage extends, in principle, to the entire national education system (within the national territory), regardless of who owns or sponsors the institutions concerned and regardless of how education is delivered. With one exception (described below), all types of students and all age groups are included: children (including students with special needs), adults, nationals, foreigners, and students in open-distance learning, in special education programmes or in educational programmes organised by ministries other than the Ministry of Education, provided that the main aim of the programme is to broaden or deepen an individual's knowledge. However, children below the age of 3 are only included if they participate in programmes that typically cater to children who are at least 3 years old. Vocational and technical training in the workplace, with the exception of combined school- and work-based programmes that are explicitly deemed to be parts of the education system, is not included in the basic education expenditure and enrolment data.

Educational activities classified as "adult" or "non-regular" are covered, provided that the activities involve the same or similar content as "regular" education studies, or that the programmes of which they are a part lead to qualifications similar to those awarded in regular educational programmes. Courses for adults that are primarily for general interest, personal enrichment, leisure or recreation are excluded (except in the indicator on adult learning, C5).

Country coverage

This publication features data on education from the 34 OECD member countries, two non-OECD countries that participate in the OECD Indicators of Education Systems programme (INES), namely Brazil and the Russian Federation, and the other G20 countries that do not participate in INES (Argentina, China, India, Indonesia, Saudi Arabia and South Africa). When data for these latter six countries are available, data sources are specified below the tables and charts.

The statistical data for Israel are supplied by and under the responsibility of the relevant Israeli authorities. The use of such data by the OECD is without prejudice to the status of the Golan Heights, East Jerusalem and Israeli settlements in the West Bank under the terms of international law.

Calculation of international means

For many indicators, an OECD average is presented; for some, an OECD total is shown.

The **OECD average** is calculated as the unweighted mean of the data values of all OECD countries for which data are available or can be estimated. The OECD average therefore refers to an average of data values at the level of the national systems and can be used to answer the question of how an indicator value for a given country compares with the value for a typical or average country. It does not take into account the absolute size of the education system in each country.

The **OECD total** is calculated as a weighted mean of the data values of all OECD countries for which data are available or can be estimated. It reflects the value for a given indicator when the OECD area is considered as a whole. This approach is taken for the purpose of comparing, for example, expenditure charts for individual countries with those of the entire OECD area for which valid data are available, with this area considered as a single entity.

Both the OECD average and the OECD total can be significantly affected by missing data. Given the relatively small number of countries, no statistical methods are used to compensate for this. In cases where a category is not applicable (code "a") in a country or where the data value is negligible (code "n") for the corresponding calculation, the value zero is imputed for the purpose of calculating OECD averages. In cases where both the numerator and the denominator of a ratio are not applicable (code "a") for a certain country, this country is not included in the OECD average.

For financial tables using 1995 and 2000 data, both the OECD average and OECD total are calculated for countries providing 1995, 2000 and 2008 data. This allows comparison of the OECD average and OECD total over time with no distortion due to the exclusion of certain countries in the different years.

For many indicators, an **EU21 average** is also presented. It is calculated as the unweighted mean of the data values of the 21 OECD countries that are members of the European Union for which data are available or can be estimated. These 21 countries are Austria, Belgium, the Czech Republic, Denmark, Estonia, Finland, France, Germany, Greece, Hungary, Ireland, Italy, Luxembourg, the Netherlands, Poland, Portugal, Slovenia, the Slovak Republic, Spain, Sweden and the United Kingdom.

For some indicators, a **G20 average** is presented. The G20 average is calculated as the unweighted mean of the data values of all G20 countries for which data are available or can be estimated (Argentina, Australia, Brazil, Canada, China, France, India, Indonesia, Italy, Japan, Korea, Mexico, the Netherlands, the Russian Federation, Saudi Arabia, South Africa, Spain, Turkey, the United Kingdom and the United States; the European Commission is not included in the calculation). The G20 average is not computed if the data for China or India are not available.

Classification of levels of education

The classification of the levels of education is based on the revised International Standard Classification of Education (ISCED 1997).The biggest change between the revised ISCED and the former ISCED (ISCED 1976) is the introduction of a multi-dimensional classification framework, allowing for the alignment of the educational content of programmes using multiple classification criteria. ISCED is an instrument for compiling statistics on education internationally and distinguishes among six levels of education.

Term used in this publication	**ISCED classification** (and subcategories)
Pre-primary education The first stage of organised instruction designed to introduce very young children to the school atmosphere. Minimum entry age of 3.	**ISCED 0**
Primary education Designed to provide a sound basic education in reading, writing and mathematics and a basic understanding of some other subjects. Entry age: between 5 and 7. Duration: 6 years.	**ISCED 1**
Lower secondary education Completes provision of basic education, usually in a more subject-oriented way with more specialist teachers. Entry follows 6 years of primary education; duration is 3 years. In some countries, the end of this level marks the end of compulsory education.	**ISCED 2** (subcategories: 2A prepares students for continuing academic education, leading to 3A; 2B has stronger vocational focus, leading to 3B; 2C offers preparation of entering workforce)
Upper secondary education Stronger subject specialisation than at lower secondary level, with teachers usually more qualified. Students typically expected to have completed 9 years of education or lower secondary schooling before entry and are generally 15 or 16 years old.	**ISCED 3** (subcategories: 3A prepares students for university-level education at level 5A; 3B for entry to vocationally oriented tertiary education at level 5B; 3C prepares students for workforce or for post-secondary non-tertiary education at level ISCED 4)

Post-secondary non-tertiary education Internationally, this level straddles the boundary between upper secondary and post-secondary education, even though it might be considered upper secondary or post-secondary in a national context. Programme content may not be significantly more advanced than that in upper secondary, but is not as advanced as that in tertiary programmes. Duration usually the equivalent of between 6 months and 2 years of full-time study. Students tend to be older than those enrolled in upper secondary education.	**ISCED 4** (subcategories: 4A may prepare students for entry to tertiary education, both university level and vocationally oriented; 4B typically prepares students to enter the workforce)
Tertiary education	**ISCED 5** (subcategories: 5A and 5B; see below)
Tertiary-type A education Largely theory-based programmes designed to provide sufficient qualifications for entry to advanced research programmes and professions with high skill requirements, such as medicine, dentistry or architecture. Duration at least 3 years full-time, though usually four or more years. These programmes are not exclusively offered at universities; and not all programmes nationally recognised as university programmes fulfil the criteria to be classified as tertiary-type A. Tertiary-type A programmes include second-degree programmes, such as the American master's degree.	**ISCED 5A**
Tertiary-type B education Programmes are typically shorter than those of tertiary-type A and focus on practical, technical or occupational skills for direct entry into the labour market, although some theoretical foundations may be covered in the respective programmes. They have a minimum duration of two years full-time equivalent at the tertiary level.	**ISCED 5B**
Advanced research programmes Programmes that lead directly to the award of an advanced research qualification, e.g. Ph.D. The theoretical duration of these programmes is 3 years, full-time, in most countries (for a cumulative total of at least seven years full-time equivalent at the tertiary level), although the actual enrolment time is typically longer. Programmes are devoted to advanced study and original research.	**ISCED 6**

The glossary available at *www.oecd.org/edu/eag2011* also describes these levels of education in detail, and Annex 1 shows the typical age of graduates of the main educational programmes, by ISCED level.

Symbols for missing data and abbreviations

These symbols and abbreviations are used in the tables and charts:

- a Data is not applicable because the category does not apply.
- c There are too few observations to provide reliable estimates (e.g. in PISA, there are fewer than 30 students or fewer than five schools with valid data). However, these statistics were included in the calculation of cross-country averages.
- m Data is not available.
- n Magnitude is either negligible or zero.
- P.A.R. Population Attributable Risk.
- R.R. Relative Risk.
- S.E. Standard Error.
- w Data has been withdrawn at the request of the country concerned.
- x Data included in another category or column of the table (e.g. x(2) means that data are included in column 2 of the table).
- ~ Average is not comparable with other levels of education.

Further resources

The website *www.oecd.org/edu/eag2011* is a rich source of information on the methods used to calculate the indicators, on the interpretation of the indicators in the respective national contexts, and on the data sources involved. The website also provides access to the data underlying the indicators and to a comprehensive glossary for technical terms used in this publication.

All post-production changes to this publication are listed at *www.oecd.org/edu/eag2011*.

The website *www.pisa.oecd.org* provides information on the OECD Programme for International Student Assessment (PISA), on which many of the indicators in this publication are based.

Education at a Glance uses the OECD's StatLinks service. Below each table and chart in *Education at Glance 2011* is a URL that leads to a corresponding Excel workbook containing the underlying data for the indicator. These URLs are stable and will remain unchanged over time. In addition, readers of the *Education at a Glance* e-book will be able to click directly on these links and the workbook will open in a separate window.

Codes used for territorial entities

These codes are used in certain charts. Country or territorial entity names are used in the text. Note that throughout the publication, the Flemish Community of Belgium and the French Community of Belgium may be referred to as "Belgium (Fl.)" and "Belgium (Fr.)", respectively.

ARG Argentina
AUS Australia
AUT Austria
BEL Belgium
BFL Belgium (Flemish Community)
BFR Belgium (French Community)
BRA Brazil
CAN Canada
CHE Switzerland
CHL Chile
CHN China
CZE Czech Republic
DEU Germany
DNK Denmark
ENG England
ESP Spain
EST Estonie
FIN Finland
FRA France
GRC Greece
HUN Hungary
IDN Indonesia
IND India
IRL Ireland
ISL Iceland
ISR Israel
ITA Italy
JPN Japan
KOR Korea
LUX Luxembourg
MEX Mexico
NLD Netherlands
NOR Norway
NZL New Zealand
POL Poland
PRT Portugal
RUS Russian Federation
SAU Saudi Arabia
SCO Scotland
SVK Slovak Republic
SVN Slovenia
SWE Sweden
TUR Turkey
UKM United Kingdom
USA United States
ZAF South Africa

Chapter

The Output of Educational Institutions and the Impact of Learning

TO WHAT LEVEL HAVE ADULTS STUDIED?

- In almost all countries, the proportion of 25-34 year-olds who attained tertiary levels of education is greater than that among the generation about to leave the labour market (55-64 year-olds).
- On average across OECD countries, the proportion of 25-34 year-olds with at least upper secondary education is 20 percentage points higher than that among 55-64 year-olds.

Chart A1.1. Percentage of population that has attained tertiary education, by age group (2009)

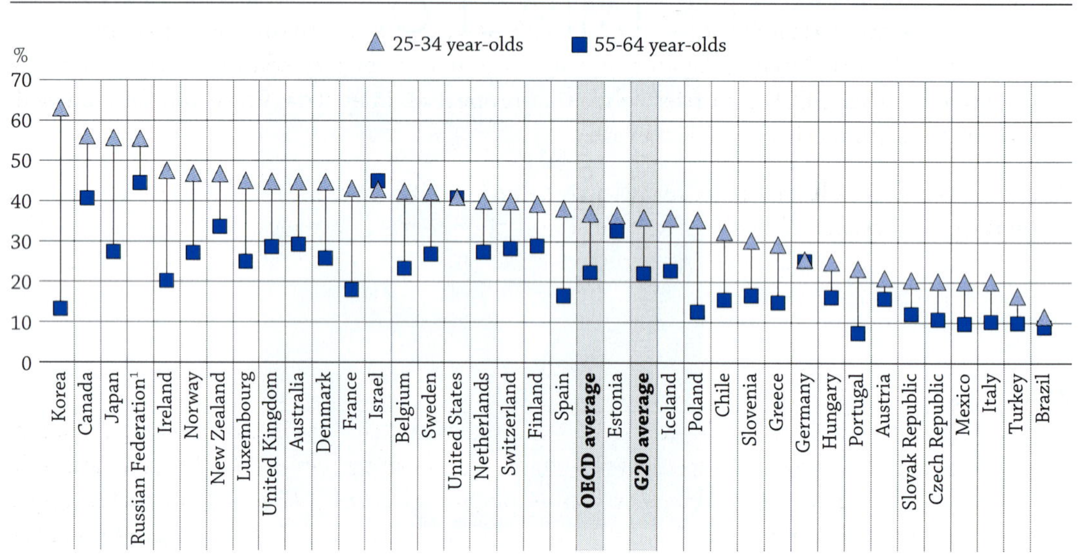

1. Year of reference 2002.

Countries are ranked in descending order of the percentage of 25-34 year-olds who have attained tertiary education.

Source: OECD. Table A1.3a. See Annex 3 for notes (*www.oecd.org/edu/eag2011*).

StatLink http://dx.doi.org/10.1787/888932459831

Context

In this publication, different indicators show the level of education among individuals, groups and countries. Indicator A1 shows the level of attainment, i.e. the percentage of a population that has reached a certain level of education. Graduation rates in Indicators A2 and A3 measure the estimated percentage of young adults who graduate from this level of education during their lifetimes. Successful completion of upper secondary programmes in Indicator A2 estimates the proportion of students who enter a programme and complete it successfully (see Box A2.1). Educational attainment is a commonly used proxy for the stock of human capital – that is, the skills available in the population and the labour force. Following a decline in demand for manual labour and for basic cognitive skills that can be replicated by computers, recent trends show sharp increases in the demand for complex communication and advanced analytical skills. These trends generally favour a more educated labour force, and the demand for education is thus increasing at a rapid pace in many countries. While the economic crisis increased the speed of change, it is also bolstering incentives for individuals to invest in education, as worsening prospects in the labour market lower some of the costs of education, such as earnings foregone while studying.

Other findings

- The big change in the educational attainment of the adult population over the past decade has been at the **low and high ends of the attainment distribution**. On average across OECD countries, 27% of adults now have only primary or lower secondary levels of education, 44% have upper secondary education and 30% have a tertiary qualification.
- **Upper secondary education** has become the norm among younger people in almost all OECD countries. The change has been particularly dramatic in Chile, Greece, Ireland, Italy, Korea, Portugal and Spain, all of which have seen an increase of 30 percentage points or more between the younger (25-34 year-olds) and older (55-64 year-olds) age cohorts who have at least an upper secondary education.
- **If current tertiary attainment rates among 25-34 year-olds are maintained**, the proportion of adults in France, Ireland, Japan and Korea who have a tertiary education will grow more than that of other OECD countries, while that proportion in Austria, Brazil and Germany will fall further behind other OECD countries.
- **More than 255 million people in OECD and G20 countries with available data now have a tertiary education**. While the level of tertiary attainment in China is still low, because of the size of its population, China still holds some 12% of all tertiary graduates, compared with 11% in Japan and 26% in the USA.

Trends

Efforts to raise people's level of education have led to significant changes in attainment, particularly at the top and bottom ends of the spectrum. In 1998, on average across OECD countries, 37% of 25-64 year-olds had not completed upper secondary education, 42% had completed upper secondary and post-secondary non-tertiary education, and another 21% had completed tertiary education. By 2009, the proportion of adults who had not attained an upper secondary education had fallen by 10 percentage points, the proportion with a tertiary degree had risen by 9 percentage points, and the proportion with upper secondary and post-secondary non-tertiary education had increased marginally, by 2 percentage points.

Analysis

Attainment levels in OECD countries

While, in general, there have been important changes in educational attainment over the past decade, there are wide differences among countries in how educational attainment is distributed across their populations (Table A1.1a).

In 28 out of 33 OECD countries, 60% or more of 25-64 year-olds have completed at least upper secondary education. However, in Brazil, Mexico, Portugal and Turkey, more than half of that age group have not completed upper secondary education (Table A1.2a).

A comparison of educational attainment among younger (25-34 year-olds) and older (55-64 year-olds) age groups indicates marked progress in attaining an upper secondary education in most countries (Chart A1.2).

Chart A1.2. Percentage of population that has attained at least upper secondary education,[1] by age group (2009)

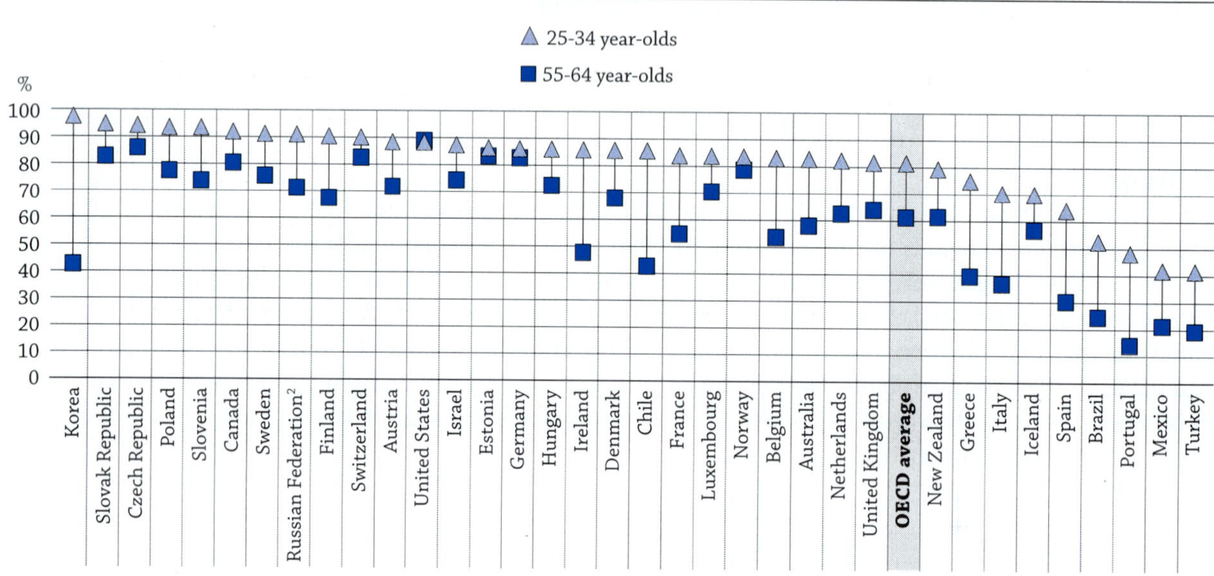

1. Excluding ISCED 3C short programmes.
2. Year of reference 2002.

Countries are ranked in descending order of the percentage of 25-34 year-olds who have attained at least upper secondary education.

Source: OECD. Table A1.2a. See Annex 3 for notes (*www.oecd.org/edu/eag2011*).

StatLink http://dx.doi.org/10.1787/888932459850

In countries where the adult population generally has a high level of educational attainment, differences among age groups are less pronounced (Table A1.2a). In the 15 OECD countries in which 80% or more of 25-64 year-olds have at least an upper secondary education, there is an 11 percentage point difference, on average, between 25-34 year-olds and 55-64 year-olds with this level of education.

In Germany and the United States, the proportion of the population with at least an upper secondary education is almost the same for all age groups. For countries where a smaller percentage of the population has attained upper secondary education, the average gain in attainment between age groups is typically large, but differs widely. In Iceland, the difference between 25-34 year-olds and 55-64 year-olds is 13 percentage points; in Korea, the difference is 55 percentage points.

Box A1.1. Vocational education

Being able to distinguish labour market outcomes between general and vocational education can help to identify the supply of and demand for education. To this end, the OECD/INES Network on Labour Market, Economic and Social Outcomes of Learning, together with Eurostat and Cedefop, developed a pilot data-collection at upper secondary and post-secondary non-tertiary levels (ISCED 3/4) of education.

Vocational or **technical education** is defined as education that is mainly designed to offer participants the opportunity to acquire the practical skills, know-how and understanding necessary for employment in a particular occupation or trade, or class of occupations or trades. Successful completion of such programmes leads to a labour market-relevant vocational qualification recognised by the competent authorities in the country in which it is obtained (e.g. Ministry of Education, employers' associations, etc.) (ISCED-97 paragraph 59).

Some countries have used their own national codifications to distinguish between general and vocational education in this pilot, while others have used, to various degrees, aggregated fields of education to derive vocational education. Given these differences in the operational definition of vocational education, some caution is needed in interpreting the results. The chart below shows the proportion of 25-64 year-olds and 25-34 year-olds with an upper secondary vocational education (ISCED 3/4) as their highest level of education.

Percentage of 25-64 year-olds and 25-34 year-olds whose highest level of education is vocational upper secondary and post-secondary non-tertiary, ISCED 3/4 (2009)

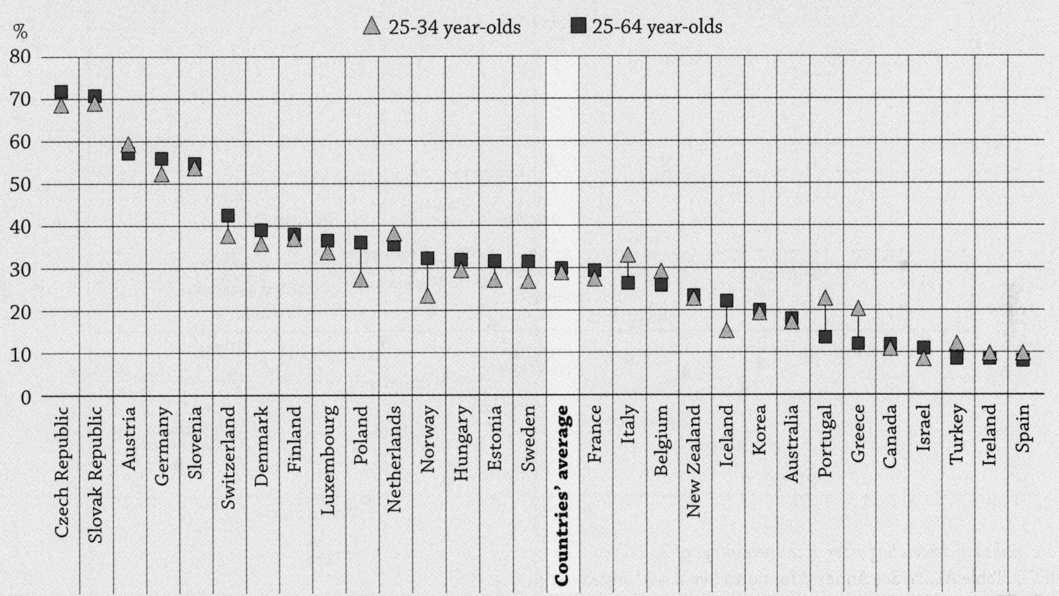

Countries are ranked in descending order of the percentage of 25-64 year-olds whose highest level of education is vocational upper secondary and post-secondary non-tertiary, ISCED 3/4.

Source: OECD, LSO network special data collection on vocational education, Learnings and Labour Transitions Working Group, Table A7.6. See Annex 3 for notes (*www.oecd.org/edu/eag2011*).

StatLink http://dx.doi.org/10.1787/888932459907

Vocational education appears to be particularly important in those countries where a large proportion of the population has an upper secondary education (ISCED 3/4). In Austria, the Czech Republic, Germany, the Slovak Republic and Slovenia, more than 50% of 25-64 year-olds have an upper secondary education (ISCED 3/4), and over 90% of them have a vocational qualification (Table A1.1a). Vocational education has increased in importance among 25-34 year-olds in Greece, Italy and Portugal, while fewer young people in Iceland, Norway and Poland have chosen a vocational upper secondary education as compared to the population as a whole (the difference exceeds five percentage points). Further analysis of this data collection is provided in Indicator A7.

Tertiary attainment levels have increased considerably over the past 30 years. On average across OECD countries, 37% of 25-34 year-olds have completed tertiary education, compared with 22% of 55-64 year-olds. Japan and Korea, together with Canada and the Russian Federation, have the highest proportion of young adults with a tertiary education. Over 50% of young adults in these countries have attained a tertiary education (Chart A1.1). In France, Ireland, Japan and Korea there is a difference of 25 percentage points or more between the proportion of young adults and older adults who attain this level of education (Table A1.3a).

Chart A1.3 provides an overview of the influence that tertiary education among 25-34 year-olds will have on overall tertiary attainment (25-64 year-olds) if current levels among young people are maintained.

Chart A1.3. Proportion of population with tertiary education and potential growth (2009)

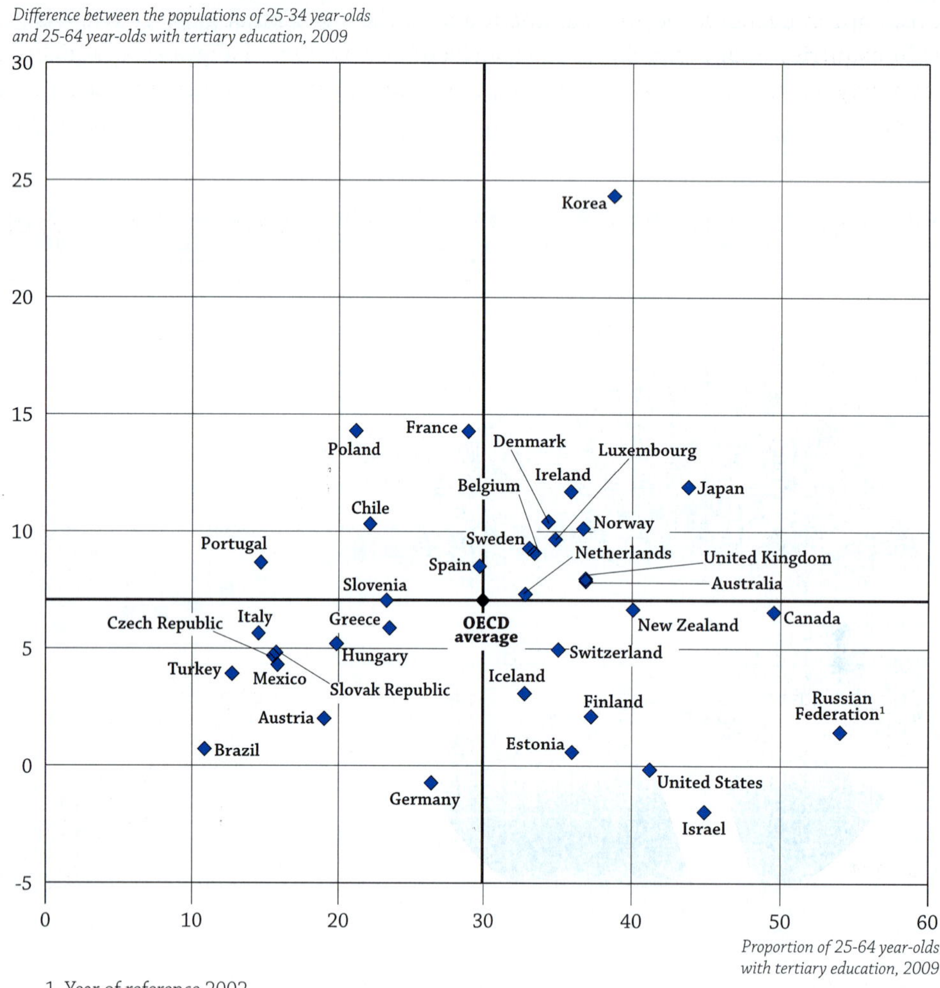

1. Year of reference 2002.

Source: OECD. Table A1.3a. See Annex 3 for notes (*www.oecd.org/edu/eag2011*).

StatLink http://dx.doi.org/10.1787/888932459869

The upper-right quadrant includes countries with already-high levels of tertiary attainment that may increase their advantage over time. France, Ireland, Japan and Korea belong to this category. The lower-right quadrant of the chart includes countries, such as Estonia, Finland, Iceland, Israel, the Russian Federation, Switzerland and the United States, that have high levels of attainment, but that will find that an increasing number of countries approach or surpass their levels of tertiary attainment in the coming years.

Some countries, such as Chile and Poland, have lower tertiary attainment levels than the OECD average but, given the current attainment rates among 25-34 year-olds, overall levels will move closer to other OECD countries over time. Countries with low tertiary attainment that will fall further behind are grouped in the lower-left quadrant of the chart. This disadvantage is particularly marked in Austria, Brazil and Germany. Note that tertiary graduation rates provide more recent data on the possible evolution of educational attainment (see Indicator A3).

Table A1.3a also provides the total number of 25-64 year-olds with tertiary education. Both Japan and the United States, which, together, have nearly half of all tertiary-educated adults in the OECD area (47%), enjoyed high levels of tertiary attainment before most other countries had started to expand their higher-education systems. Having a more educated work force gave these countries a head-start in many high-skill areas. This advantage is likely to have been particularly important for innovation and the adoption of new technologies.

However, the expansion of tertiary education in many countries has narrowed the advantage of Japan and the United States both in overall levels of attainment and in the sheer number of individuals with tertiary education. If G20 countries with available data are included, the picture changes substantially. Chart A1.4 illustrates the country shares of the OECD and G20 population, roughly 255 million people, who have a tertiary education.

Chart A1.4. Countries' share in the total 25-64 year-old population with tertiary education, percentage (2009)

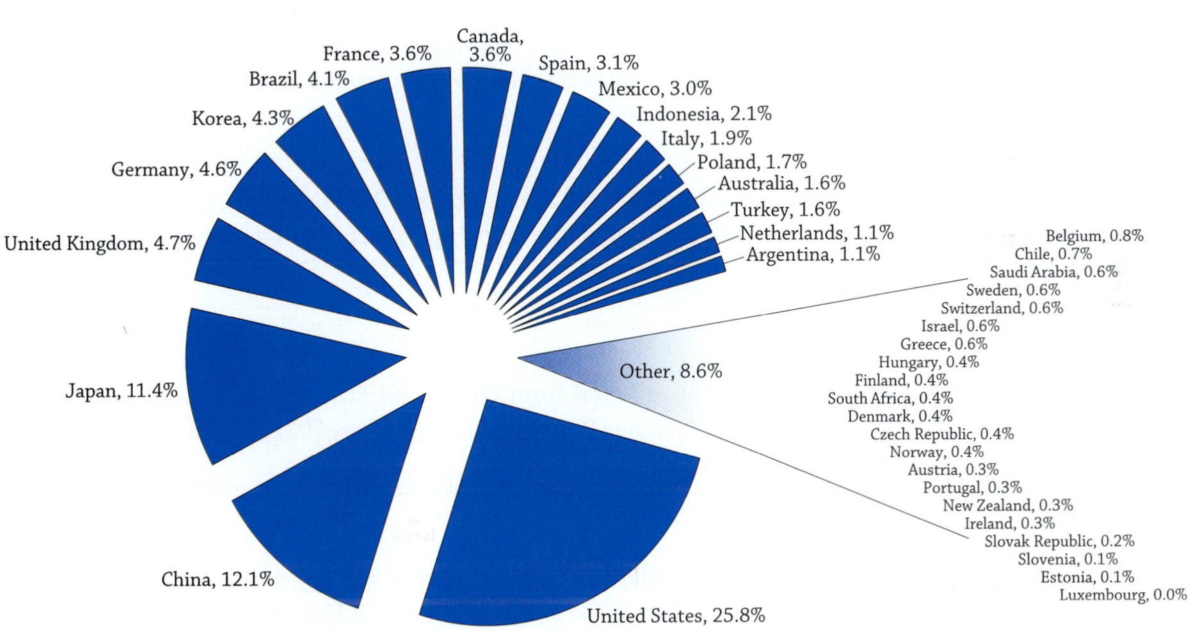

Note: Argentina refers to year 2003, China refers to year 2000, Saudi Arabia refers to year 2004, Indonesia and South Africa refer to 2007.
Source: OECD. Table A1.3a. See Annex 3 for notes (*www.oecd.org/edu/eag2011*).
StatLink http://dx.doi.org/10.1787/888932459888

While the proportion of adults with tertiary education is still low (5%), China ranks second, behind the United States and ahead of Japan, in the percent of the OECD and G20 population with tertiary attainment because of the size of its population. Brazil holds a further 4.1% of this overall share. The combined population with tertiary education in the 6 G20 countries that are not members of the OECD amounts to approximately 53 million people, less than 12 million short of the total tertiary-educated population in EU21 countries (65 million).

Below the top three countries, the United Kingdom has 4.7% of the international pool of tertiary educated individuals, Germany has 4.6% and Korea, with its rapid expansion of higher education, is ranked in sixth place with a 4.3% share. Brazil (4.1%), Canada (3.6%), France (3.6%), and Spain (3.1%) make up the other top 10 countries.

Trends in attainment rates in OECD countries

Table A1.4 shows how levels of educational attainment among 25-64 year-olds have evolved from 1997 to 2009. Average annual growth in the proportion of those with a tertiary education has exceeded 5% in Ireland, Korea, Luxembourg, Poland and Portugal. The proportion of the population that had not attained upper secondary education decreased by 5% or more per year in Hungary, Luxembourg, the Netherlands, Poland and the Slovak Republic. No country has seen growth above 5% for upper secondary and post-secondary non-tertiary attainment. Only Portugal and Spain have seen growth rates above 4% (Table A1.4).

On average across OECD countries, the proportion of 25-64 year-olds who have not attained an upper secondary education has decreased by 3.4% on average per year since 1999, the proportion with an upper secondary and post-secondary non-tertiary education has increased by 0.9% on average per year since 1999, and the proportion with tertiary education has increased by 3.7% on average per year since 1999. Most of the changes in educational attainment have occurred at the low and high ends of the skill distribution, largely because older workers with low levels of education are moving out of the labour force and as a result of the expansion of higher education in many countries in recent years (Table A1.4).

This expansion has generally been met by an even more rapid shift in the demand for skills in most OECD countries. The demand side is explored in labour-market indicators on employment and unemployment (see Indicator A7), earnings (see Indicator A8), incentives to invest in education (see Indicator A9), labour costs and net income (see Indicator A10) and transition from school to work (see Indicator C4).

Definitions

Levels of education are defined according to the International Standard Classification of Education (ISCED-97). See Annex 3 (*www.oecd.org/edu/eag2011*) for a description of the mapping of ISCED-97 education programmes and attainment levels for each country.

Methodology

Data on population and educational attainment are taken from OECD and Eurostat databases, which are compiled from National Labour Force Surveys. See Annex 3 (*www.oecd.org/edu/eag2011*) for national sources.

Attainment profiles are based on the percentage of the population aged 25 to 64 that has completed a specified level of education.

The statistical data for Israel are supplied by and under the responsibility of the relevant Israeli authorities. The use of such data by the OECD is without prejudice to the status of the Golan Heights, East Jerusalem and Israeli settlements in the West Bank under the terms of international law.

References

OECD (2004a), *OECD Handbook for Internationally Comparative Education Statistics: Concepts, Standards, Definitions and Classifications*, OECD, Paris.

The following additional material relevant to this indicator is available on line:

- ***Table A1.1b. Educational attainment: Men (2009)***
  StatLink http://dx.doi.org/10.1787/888932462187
- ***Table A1.1c. Educational attainment: Women (2009)***
  StatLink http://dx.doi.org/10.1787/888932462206

- ***Table A1.2b. Population of men with at least upper secondary education (2009)***
  StatLink http://dx.doi.org/10.1787/888932462244
- ***Table A1.2c. Population of women with at least upper secondary education (2009)***
  StatLink http://dx.doi.org/10.1787/888932462263
- ***Table A1.3b. Population of men with tertiary education (2009)***
  StatLink http://dx.doi.org/10.1787/888932462301
- ***Table A1.3c. Population of women with tertiary education (2009)***
  StatLink http://dx.doi.org/10.1787/888932462320

Table A1.1a. Educational attainment: Adult population (2009)

		Pre-primary and primary education	Lower secondary education	ISCED 3C (short programme)	Upper secondary education: ISCED 3C (long programme) /3B	Upper secondary education: ISCED 3A	Post-secondary non-tertiary education	Tertiary education: Type B	Tertiary education: Type A	Tertiary education: Advanced research programmes	All levels of education
		(1)	(2)	(3)	(4)	(5)	(6)	(7)	(8)	(9)	(10)
OECD	Australia	7	22	a	14	16	4	10	26	1	100
	Austria	x(2)	17	1	48	6	10	8	11	x(8)	100
	Belgium	13	17	a	10	24	2	16	17	1	100
	Canada	4	9	a	x(5)	26	12	24	25	x(8)	100
	Chile	x(2)	30	x(5)	13	34	a	6	17	x(8)	100
	Czech Republic	n	8	a	40	36	a	x(8)	16	x(8)	100
	Denmark	n	22	1	36	6	n	7	26	1	100
	Estonia	1	10	a	4	43	6	13	23	n	100
	Finland	8	10	a	a	44	1	15	22	1	100
	France	12	18	a	29	12	n	12	17	1	100
	Germany	3	11	a	49	3	7	9	16	1	100
	Greece	25	11	3	4	26	8	7	17	n	100
	Hungary	1	18	a	30	29	2	n	19	n	100
	Iceland	2	26	6	13	11	9	4	28	1	100
	Ireland	12	16	n	x(5)	23	12	15	20	1	100
	Israel	11	7	a	9	28	a	15	28	1	100
	Italy	13	33	1	7	32	1	n	14	n	100
	Japan	x(5)	x(5)	x(5)	x(5)	56	a	19	25	x(8)	100
	Korea	9	11	a	20	21	a	12	24	3	100
	Luxembourg	9	8	6	20	19	3	15	17	3	100
	Mexico	43	21	a	x(5)	19	a	x(8)	16	x(8)	100
	Netherlands	7	19	x(4)	15	22	3	3	29	1	100
	New Zealand	x(2)	21	7	12	9	11	17	23	x(8)	100
	Norway	1	19	a	30	11	3	2	34	1	100
	Poland	x(2)	12	a	32	31	4	x(8)	21	x(8)	100
	Portugal	51	19	x(5)	x(5)	15	1	x(8)	13	1	100
	Slovak Republic	1	8	x(4)	35	40	x(5)	1	15	n	100
	Slovenia	2	15	a	27	33	a	11	10	2	100
	Spain	20	28	a	8	14	n	10	20	1	100
	Sweden	5	9	a	x(5)	46	6	9	24	x(8)	100
	Switzerland	3	8	1	44	5	3	10	22	3	100
	Turkey	58	10	a	8	10	a	x(8)	13	x(8)	100
	United Kingdom	n	11	15	30	7	n	10	26	1	100
	United States	4	7	x(5)	x(5)	47	x(5)	10	30	1	100
		Below upper secondary education			Upper secondary level of education			Tertiary level of education			
	OECD average	27			44			30			
	EU21 average	25			48			27			
Other G20	Argentina	m	m	m	m	m	m	m	m	m	m
	Brazil	45	14	x(5)	x(5)	30	a	x(8)	11	x(8)	100
	China	m	m	m	m	m	m	m	m	m	m
	India	m	m	m	m	m	m	m	m	m	m
	Indonesia	m	m	m	m	m	m	m	m	m	m
	Russian Federation[1]	3	8	x(4)	16	18	x(4)	34	20	n	100
	Saudi Arabia	m	m	m	m	m	m	m	m	m	m
	South Africa	m	m	m	m	m	m	m	m	m	m

Note: Due to discrepancies in the data, averages have not been calculated for each column individually.
1. Year of reference 2002.
Source: OECD. See Annex 3 for notes *(www.oecd.org/edu/eag2011)*.
Please refer to the Reader's Guide for information concerning the symbols replacing missing data.
StatLink http://dx.doi.org/10.1787/888932462168

Table A1.2a. Population with at least upper secondary education[1] (2009)

Percentage, by age group

		Age group				
		25-64	25-34	35-44	45-54	55-64
		(1)	(2)	(3)	(4)	(5)
OECD	Australia	**71**	83	73	67	58
	Austria	**82**	88	85	80	72
	Belgium	**71**	83	78	67	54
	Canada	**88**	92	91	87	80
	Chile	**69**	86	75	66	43
	Czech Republic	**91**	94	94	91	86
	Denmark	**76**	86	81	71	68
	Estonia	**89**	86	92	93	83
	Finland	**82**	90	88	84	67
	France	**70**	84	77	64	55
	Germany	**85**	86	87	86	83
	Greece	**61**	75	69	57	40
	Hungary	**81**	86	83	80	72
	Iceland	**66**	70	71	64	57
	Ireland	**72**	86	77	65	48
	Israel	**82**	87	84	78	74
	Italy	**54**	70	58	50	37
	Japan	**m**	m	m	m	m
	Korea	**80**	98	94	71	43
	Luxembourg	**77**	84	79	74	70
	Mexico	**35**	42	37	32	21
	Netherlands	**73**	82	78	71	63
	New Zealand	**72**	79	75	70	62
	Norway	**81**	84	83	77	79
	Poland	**88**	93	92	88	77
	Portugal	**30**	48	31	22	14
	Slovak Republic	**91**	95	94	90	83
	Slovenia	**83**	93	85	80	74
	Spain	**52**	64	58	46	30
	Sweden	**86**	91	91	85	76
	Switzerland	**87**	90	88	86	83
	Turkey	**31**	42	28	25	19
	United Kingdom	**74**	82	76	72	64
	United States	**89**	88	88	89	89
	OECD average	**73**	81	77	71	61
	EU21 average	**75**	83	79	72	63
Other G20	Argentina	**m**	m	m	m	m
	Brazil	**41**	53	42	34	25
	China	**m**	m	m	m	m
	India	**m**	m	m	m	m
	Indonesia	**m**	m	m	m	m
	Russian Federation[2]	**88**	91	94	89	71
	Saudi Arabia	**m**	m	m	m	m
	South Africa	**m**	m	m	m	m

1. Excluding ISCED 3C short programmes.
2. Year of reference 2002.
Source: OECD. See Annex 3 for notes *(www.oecd.org/edu/eag2011)*.
Please refer to the Reader's Guide for information concerning the symbols replacing missing data.
StatLink http://dx.doi.org/10.1787/888932462225

Table A1.3a. Population with tertiary education (2009)

Percentage of the population that has attained tertiary education, by age group. Column 16 refers to absolute numbers (in thousands).

		Tertiary-type B education				Tertiary-type A and advanced research programmes					Total tertiary					
		25-64	25-34	35-44	45-54	55-64	25-64	25-34	35-44	45-54	55-64	25-64	25-34	35-44	45-54	55-64	25-64 in thousands
		(1)	(2)	(3)	(4)	(5)	(6)	(7)	(8)	(9)	(10)	(11)	(12)	(13)	(14)	(15)	(16)
OECD	Australia	**10**	10	11	10	9	**27**	35	27	24	20	**37**	45	38	34	29	4 125
	Austria	**8**	6	8	9	8	**11**	15	12	10	8	**19**	21	20	18	16	875
	Belgium	**16**	18	18	15	12	**17**	24	19	15	11	**33**	42	37	30	23	1 943
	Canada	**24**	26	27	24	20	**25**	30	29	21	21	**50**	56	56	45	41	9 187
	Chile	**8**	11	10	7	3	**16**	24	14	14	14	**24**	35	24	20	17	2 004
	Czech Republic	**x(11)**	x(12)	x(13)	x(14)	x(15)	**16**	20	15	16	11	**16**	20	15	16	11	948
	Denmark	**7**	9	8	7	6	**27**	36	31	22	20	**34**	45	39	28	26	978
	Estonia	**13**	15	11	15	11	**23**	22	25	22	21	**36**	37	36	38	33	256
	Finland	**15**	3	19	20	15	**23**	36	25	17	14	**37**	39	44	37	29	1 076
	France	**12**	17	13	10	6	**17**	26	19	13	12	**29**	43	32	22	18	9 263
	Germany	**9**	7	10	10	10	**17**	19	18	16	16	**26**	26	28	26	25	11 721
	Greece	**7**	10	8	5	3	**17**	19	19	16	12	**24**	29	26	22	15	1 435
	Hungary	**n**	1	n	n	n	**19**	24	19	18	16	**20**	25	19	18	16	1 104
	Iceland	**4**	2	6	4	3	**29**	33	33	27	20	**33**	36	38	32	23	53
	Ireland	**15**	19	17	12	9	**21**	29	23	16	11	**36**	48	39	28	20	848
	Israel	**15**	13	16	16	17	**29**	30	31	29	28	**45**	43	47	45	45	1 511
	Italy	**n**	n	n	n	n	**14**	20	15	11	10	**15**	20	15	12	10	4 836
	Japan	**19**	24	23	19	11	**25**	32	25	26	16	**44**	56	49	45	27	29 230
	Korea	**12**	25	12	5	1	**27**	38	33	21	12	**39**	63	44	26	13	11 042
	Luxembourg	**15**	20	15	11	11	**20**	24	23	18	14	**35**	44	38	29	25	93
	Mexico	**1**	1	1	1	1	**16**	20	15	15	10	**16**	20	15	15	10	7 789
	Netherlands	**3**	2	3	3	2	**30**	38	30	28	25	**33**	40	34	31	27	2 922
	New Zealand	**17**	16	16	18	18	**23**	31	26	20	16	**40**	47	41	38	34	851
	Norway	**2**	1	2	3	3	**34**	45	38	30	24	**37**	47	40	33	27	915
	Poland	**x(11)**	x(12)	x(13)	x(14)	x(15)	**21**	35	21	13	13	**21**	35	21	13	13	4 469
	Portugal	**x(11)**	x(12)	x(13)	x(14)	x(15)	**15**	23	15	11	7	**15**	23	15	11	7	873
	Slovak Republic	**1**	1	1	1	1	**15**	20	14	13	11	**16**	21	15	14	12	489
	Slovenia	**11**	12	12	10	9	**13**	19	14	9	7	**23**	30	26	19	17	272
	Spain	**10**	13	11	7	4	**20**	25	22	18	12	**30**	38	34	25	17	7 844
	Sweden	**9**	8	8	9	9	**24**	34	26	19	18	**33**	42	35	29	27	1 592
	Switzerland	**10**	9	12	11	9	**25**	31	26	22	19	**35**	40	38	33	28	1 512
	Turkey	**x(11)**	x(12)	x(13)	x(14)	x(15)	**13**	17	11	10	10	**13**	17	11	10	10	4 065
	United Kingdom	**10**	9	11	11	9	**27**	36	28	23	19	**37**	45	39	34	29	11 992
	United States	**10**	9	10	11	9	**31**	32	33	29	32	**41**	41	43	40	41	66 148
	OECD average	**10**	11	11	10	8	**21**	28	23	19	16	**30**	37	32	27	22	
	OECD total (in thousands)																204 262
	EU21 average	**10**	10	11	10	8	**19**	26	21	16	14	**27**	34	29	24	20	
Other G20	Argentina[1]	**x(11)**	m	m	m	m	**x(11)**	m	m	m	m	**14**	m	m	m	m	2 909
	Brazil	**x(11)**	x(12)	x(13)	x(14)	x(15)	**11**	12	11	11	9	**11**	12	11	11	9	10 502
	China[2]	**x(11)**	x(12)	x(13)	x(14)	x(15)	**x(11)**	x(12)	x(13)	x(14)	x(15)	**5**	6	5	3	3	31 137
	India	**m**	m	m	m	m	**m**	m	m	m	m	**m**	m	m	m	m	m
	Indonesia[3]	**x(11)**	m	m	m	m	**x(11)**	m	m	m	m	**4**	m	m	m	m	5 447
	Russian Federation[4]	**33**	34	37	34	26	**21**	21	21	20	19	**54**	55	58	54	44	m
	Saudi Arabia[5]	**x(11)**	m	m	m	m	**x(11)**	m	m	m	m	**15**	m	m	m	m	1 594
	South Africa[3]	**x(11)**	m	m	m	m	**x(11)**	m	m	m	m	**4**	m	m	m	m	1023
	G20 average	**14**	16	16	13	10	**21**	26	22	18	16	**25**	36	32	27	22	
	G20 total (in thousands)																222 012

1. Year of reference 2003. Source: UNESCO/UIS, educational attainment of 25-year-olds and older.
2. Year of reference 2000. Source: 2000 census, Chinese National Bureau of Statistics, education level (college, university and master's and above) of 25-64 year-olds.
3. Year of reference 2007. Source: UNESCO/UIS, educational attainment of 25-year-olds and older.
4. Year of reference 2002.
5. Year of reference 2004. Source: UNESCO/UIS, educational attainment of 25-year-olds and older.

Source: OECD. See Annex 3 for notes *(www.oecd.org/edu/eag2011)*.

Please refer to the Reader's Guide for information concerning the symbols replacing missing data.

StatLink http://dx.doi.org/10.1787/888932462282

Table A1.4. [1/2] Trends in educational attainment: 25-64 year-olds (1997-2009)

OECD

	Percentage, by educational level	1997	1998	1999	2000	2001	2002	2003	2004	2005	2006	2007	2008	2009	Average annual growth rate 2009/1999
Australia	Below upper secondary	47	44	43	41	41	39	38	36	35	33	32	30	**29**	-3.8
	Upper secondary and post-secondary non-tertiary	29	31	31	31	30	30	31	33	33	34	34	34	**34**	1.1
	Tertiary education	24	25	27	27	29	31	31	31	32	33	34	36	**37**	3.3
Austria	Below upper secondary	26	26	25	24	23	22	21	20	19	20	20	19	**18**	-3.1
	Upper secondary and post-secondary non-tertiary	63	61	61	62	63	64	64	62	63	63	63	63	**63**	0.2
	Tertiary education	11	14	14	14	14	15	15	18	18	18	18	18	**19**	3.4
Belgium	Below upper secondary	45	43	43	41	41	39	38	36	34	33	32	30	**29**	-3.6
	Upper secondary and post-secondary non-tertiary	30	31	31	31	32	33	33	34	35	35	36	37	**37**	1.9
	Tertiary education	25	25	27	27	28	28	29	30	31	32	32	32	**33**	2.3
Canada	Below upper secondary	22	21	20	19	18	17	16	16	15	14	13	13	**12**	-4.9
	Upper secondary and post-secondary non-tertiary	40	40	40	41	40	40	40	40	39	39	38	38	**38**	-0.5
	Tertiary education	37	38	39	40	42	43	44	45	46	47	48	49	**50**	2.3
Chile	Below upper secondary	m	m	m	m	m	m	m	m	m	m	32	32	**31**	
	Upper secondary and post-secondary non-tertiary	m	m	m	m	m	m	m	m	m	m	44	44	**45**	
	Tertiary education	m	m	m	m	m	m	m	m	m	m	24	24	**24**	
Czech Republic	Below upper secondary	15	15	14	14	14	12	14	11	10	10	9	9	**9**	-4.7
	Upper secondary and post-secondary non-tertiary	74	75	75	75	75	76	74	77	77	77	77	76	**76**	0.1
	Tertiary education	11	10	11	11	11	12	12	12	13	14	14	14	**16**	3.7
Denmark	Below upper secondary	m	21	20	21	19	19	19	19	19	18	25	25	**24**	1.5
	Upper secondary and post-secondary non-tertiary	m	53	53	52	52	52	49	48	47	47	43	42	**42**	-2.3
	Tertiary education	m	25	27	26	28	30	32	33	34	35	32	32	**34**	2.6
Estonia	Below upper secondary	m	m	m	m	m	12	12	11	11	12	11	12	**11**	
	Upper secondary and post-secondary non-tertiary	m	m	m	m	m	57	58	57	56	55	56	54	**53**	
	Tertiary education	m	m	m	m	m	30	31	31	33	33	33	34	**36**	
Finland	Below upper secondary	32	31	28	27	26	25	24	22	21	20	19	19	**18**	-4.5
	Upper secondary and post-secondary non-tertiary	39	39	40	41	42	42	43	43	44	44	44	44	**45**	1.1
	Tertiary education	29	30	31	32	32	33	33	34	35	35	36	37	**37**	1.8
France	Below upper secondary	41	39	38	37	36	35	35	34	33	33	32	30	**30**	-2.4
	Upper secondary and post-secondary non-tertiary	39	40	40	41	41	41	41	41	41	41	42	42	**41**	0.2
	Tertiary education	20	21	21	22	23	24	24	24	25	26	27	27	**29**	3.0
Germany	Below upper secondary	17	16	19	18	17	17	17	16	17	17	16	15	**15**	-2.5
	Upper secondary and post-secondary non-tertiary	61	61	58	58	59	60	59	59	59	59	60	60	**59**	0.1
	Tertiary education	23	23	23	23	23	23	24	25	25	24	24	25	**26**	1.4
Greece	Below upper secondary	56	54	52	51	50	48	47	44	43	41	40	39	**39**	-2.9
	Upper secondary and post-secondary non-tertiary	29	29	30	32	32	33	34	35	36	37	37	38	**38**	2.2
	Tertiary education	16	17	17	18	18	19	19	21	21	22	23	23	**24**	3.1
Hungary	Below upper secondary	37	37	33	31	30	29	26	25	24	22	21	20	**19**	-5.1
	Upper secondary and post-secondary non-tertiary	51	50	54	55	56	57	59	59	59	60	61	61	**61**	1.2
	Tertiary education	12	13	14	14	14	14	15	17	17	18	18	19	**20**	3.9
Iceland	Below upper secondary	44	45	44	45	43	41	40	39	37	37	36	36	**34**	-2.5
	Upper secondary and post-secondary non-tertiary	35	34	34	32	32	33	31	32	32	34	34	33	**33**	-0.1
	Tertiary education	21	21	22	23	25	26	29	29	31	30	30	31	**33**	3.9
Ireland	Below upper secondary	50	49	45	54	45	40	38	37	35	34	32	31	**28**	-4.5
	Upper secondary and post-secondary non-tertiary	27	30	35	28	32	35	35	35	35	35	35	36	**36**	0.3
	Tertiary education	23	21	20	19	24	25	26	28	29	31	32	34	**36**	5.8
Israel	Below upper secondary	m	m	m	m	m	20	18	21	21	20	20	19	**18**	
	Upper secondary and post-secondary non-tertiary	m	m	m	m	m	38	39	34	33	34	37	37	**37**	
	Tertiary education	m	m	m	m	m	42	43	45	46	46	44	44	**45**	
Italy	Below upper secondary	m	59	58	58	57	56	52	51	50	49	48	47	**46**	-2.3
	Upper secondary and post-secondary non-tertiary	m	32	33	33	33	34	38	37	38	38	39	39	**40**	1.9
	Tertiary education	m	9	9	9	10	10	10	12	12	13	14	14	**15**	4.6
Japan	Below upper secondary	20	20	19	17	17	m	m	m	m	m	m	m	**m**	
	Upper secondary and post-secondary non-tertiary	49	49	49	49	49	63	63	61	60	60	59	57	**56**	
	Tertiary education	31	31	32	34	34	37	37	39	40	40	41	43	**44**	3.2
Korea	Below upper secondary	38	34	33	32	30	29	27	26	24	23	22	21	**20**	-4.7
	Upper secondary and post-secondary non-tertiary	42	44	44	44	45	45	44	44	44	44	43	43	**41**	-0.7
	Tertiary education	20	22	23	24	25	26	29	30	32	33	35	37	**39**	5.3
Luxembourg	Below upper secondary	m	m	44	44	47	38	41	37	34	34	34	32	**23**	-6.4
	Upper secondary and post-secondary non-tertiary	m	m	38	38	35	43	45	40	39	42	39	40	**43**	1.3
	Tertiary education	m	m	18	18	18	19	14	24	27	24	27	28	**35**	6.6

Note: Norway revised the education attainment criteria in 2005; this created a major break in the time series. See Annex 3 for other breaks in time series.
Source: OECD. See Annex 3 for notes *(www.oecd.org/edu/eag2011)*.
Please refer to the Reader's Guide for information concerning the symbols replacing missing data.

StatLink http://dx.doi.org/10.1787/888932462339

A1

Table A1.4. [2/2] Trends in educational attainment: 25-64 year-olds (1997-2009)

		Percentage, by educational level	1997	1998	1999	2000	2001	2002	2003	2004	2005	2006	2007	2008	2009	2009/1999 Average annual growth rate
OECD	Mexico	Below upper secondary	72	72	73	71	70	70	70	69	68	68	67	66	**65**	-1.2
		Upper secondary and post-secondary non-tertiary	15	15	14	14	15	15	14	15	18	18	18	19	**19**	3.3
		Tertiary education	13	13	13	15	15	15	16	17	14	14	15	15	**16**	1.9
	Netherlands	Below upper secondary	m	36	45	35	35	32	31	29	28	28	27	27	**27**	-5.2
		Upper secondary and post-secondary non-tertiary	m	40	32	41	42	43	42	41	42	42	42	41	**41**	2.4
		Tertiary education	m	24	23	23	23	25	28	30	30	30	31	32	**33**	3.8
	New Zealand	Below upper secondary	40	39	38	37	36	34	33	33	32	31	29	28	**28**	-3.1
		Upper secondary and post-secondary non-tertiary	33	34	33	34	36	35	35	32	29	31	30	32	**32**	-0.4
		Tertiary education	27	28	28	29	29	30	32	35	39	38	41	40	**40**	3.5
	Norway	Below upper secondary	17	15	15	15	14	14	13	12	23	21	21	19	**19**	
		Upper secondary and post-secondary non-tertiary	57	57	57	57	55	55	56	56	45	46	45	45	**44**	
		Tertiary education	26	27	28	28	30	31	31	32	33	33	34	36	**37**	
	Poland	Below upper secondary	23	22	22	20	19	19	17	16	15	14	14	13	**12**	-5.6
		Upper secondary and post-secondary non-tertiary	67	67	67	69	69	69	68	68	68	68	68	68	**67**	-0.1
		Tertiary education	10	11	11	11	12	13	14	16	17	18	19	20	**21**	6.5
	Portugal	Below upper secondary	m	82	81	81	80	79	77	75	74	72	73	72	**70**	-1.5
		Upper secondary and post-secondary non-tertiary	m	10	10	11	11	11	12	13	14	14	14	14	**15**	4.1
		Tertiary education	m	8	9	9	9	9	11	13	13	13	14	14	**15**	5.4
	Slovak Republic	Below upper secondary	21	20	18	16	15	14	13	13	12	11	11	10	**9**	-6.4
		Upper secondary and post-secondary non-tertiary	68	70	72	73	74	75	75	74	74	74	75	75	**75**	0.4
		Tertiary education	10	10	10	10	11	11	12	13	14	15	14	15	**16**	4.6
	Slovenia	Below upper secondary	m	m	m	m	m	23	22	20	20	18	18	18	**17**	
		Upper secondary and post-secondary non-tertiary	m	m	m	m	m	62	60	61	60	60	60	59	**60**	
		Tertiary education	m	m	m	m	m	15	18	19	20	21	22	23	**23**	
	Spain	Below upper secondary	69	67	65	62	60	59	57	55	51	50	49	49	**48**	-2.9
		Upper secondary and post-secondary non-tertiary	13	13	14	16	16	17	18	19	21	21	22	22	**22**	4.6
		Tertiary education	19	20	21	23	24	24	25	26	28	28	29	29	**30**	3.5
	Sweden	Below upper secondary	25	24	24	21	20	19	18	18	17	17	16	16	**14**	-4.4
		Upper secondary and post-secondary non-tertiary	54	54	54	54	55	54	54	54	54	54	54	53	**53**	-0.2
		Tertiary education	21	22	22	25	26	26	27	28	29	30	30	31	**33**	3.7
	Switzerland	Below upper secondary	16	16	16	16	15	15	15	15	15	15	14	13	**13**	
		Upper secondary and post-secondary non-tertiary	61	61	60	60	59	60	58	57	56	56	55	53	**52**	
		Tertiary education	22	23	24	24	25	25	27	28	29	30	31	34	**35**	
	Turkey	Below upper secondary	79	78	78	77	76	75	74	73	72	71	70	70	**69**	-1.2
		Upper secondary and post-secondary non-tertiary	13	14	14	15	15	16	17	18	18	18	18	18	**18**	2.5
		Tertiary education	8	7	8	8	8	9	10	10	10	11	11	12	**13**	4.6
	United Kingdom	Below upper secondary	41	40	38	37	37	36	35	34	33	32	32	30	**26**	-3.7
		Upper secondary and post-secondary non-tertiary	37	36	37	37	37	37	37	37	37	38	37	37	**37**	0.0
		Tertiary education	23	24	25	26	26	27	28	29	30	31	32	33	**37**	4.0
	United States	Below upper secondary	14	14	13	13	12	13	12	12	12	12	12	11	**11**	-1.4
		Upper secondary and post-secondary non-tertiary	52	52	51	51	50	49	49	49	49	48	48	48	**47**	-0.8
		Tertiary education	34	35	36	36	37	38	38	39	39	39	40	41	**41**	1.4
	OECD average	Below upper secondary	36	37	37	36	35	33	32	30	30	29	29	28	**27**	-3.4
		Upper secondary and post-secondary non-tertiary	43	42	42	43	43	45	45	44	44	44	44	44	**44**	0.9
		Tertiary education	21	21	21	22	22	24	25	26	27	27	28	29	**30**	3.7
	EU 21 average	Below upper secondary	36	38	37	36	35	32	31	30	29	28	28	27	**25**	-3.7
		Upper secondary and post-secondary non-tertiary	46	44	44	45	45	47	48	47	48	48	48	48	**48**	1.0
		Tertiary education	18	18	19	19	20	21	21	23	24	24	25	25	**27**	3.9
Other G20	Argentina		m	m	m	m	m	m	m	m	m	m	m	m	**m**	
	Brazil	Below upper secondary	m	m	m	m	m	m	m	m	m	m	63	61	**59**	
		Upper secondary and post-secondary non-tertiary	m	m	m	m	m	m	m	m	m	m	27	28	**30**	
		Tertiary education	m	m	m	m	m	m	m	m	m	m	10	11	**11**	
	China		m	m	m	m	m	m	m	m	m	m	m	m	**m**	
	India		m	m	m	m	m	m	m	m	m	m	m	m	**m**	
	Indonesia		m	m	m	m	m	m	m	m	m	m	m	m	**m**	
	Russian Federation		m	m	m	m	m	m	m	m	m	m	m	m	**m**	
	Saudi Arabia		m	m	m	m	m	m	m	m	m	m	m	m	**m**	
	South Africa		m	m	m	m	m	m	m	m	m	m	m	m	**m**	

Note: Norway revised the education attainment criteria in 2005; this created a major break in the time series. See Annex 3 for other breaks in time series.
Source: OECD. See Annex 3 for notes *(www.oecd.org/edu/eag2011).*
Please refer to the Reader's Guide for information concerning the symbols replacing missing data.
StatLink http://dx.doi.org/10.1787/888932462339

INDICATOR A2

HOW MANY STUDENTS FINISH SECONDARY EDUCATION?

- Based on current patterns of graduation, it is estimated that an average of 82% of today's young people in OECD countries will complete upper secondary education over their lifetimes. For G20 countries, the rate is lower, at 75%.
- In some countries, it is common for students to graduate from upper secondary programmes after the age of 25. At least 10% of upper secondary graduates in Denmark, Finland, Iceland, New Zealand, Norway and Portugal are 25 or older.

Chart A2.1. Upper secondary graduation rates (2009)

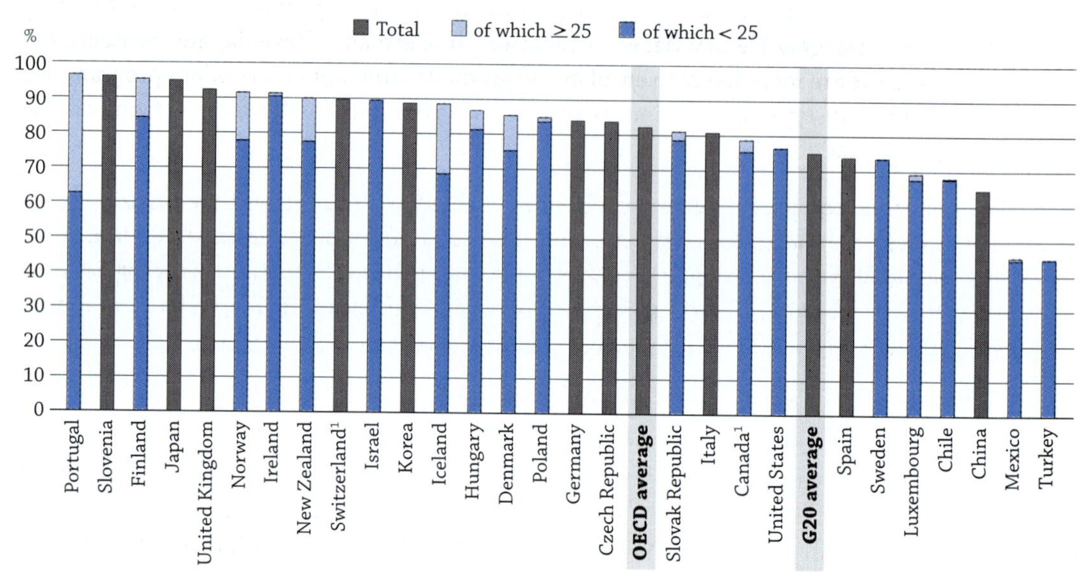

1. Year of reference 2008.

Countries are ranked in descending order of the upper secondary graduation rates in 2009.

Source: OECD. China: UNESCO Institution for Statistics (World Education Indicators Programme). Table A2.1. See Annex 3 for notes (*www.oecd.org/edu/eag2011*).

StatLink http://dx.doi.org/10.1787/888932459926

Context

Upper secondary education provides the basis for advanced learning and training opportunities and prepares some students for direct entry into the labour market. Graduation rates discussed here do not assume that an education system has adequately equipped its graduates with the basic skills and knowledge necessary to enter the labour market, because this indicator does not capture the quality of educational outcomes. However, these rates do give an indication of the extent to which education systems succeed in preparing students to meet the labour market's minimum requirements.

Although many countries allow students to leave the education system after completing lower secondary education, those students in OECD countries who leave without an upper secondary qualification tend to face severe difficulties entering – and remaining in – the labour market. Leaving school early is a problem, both for individuals and society. Policy makers are examining ways to reduce the number of early school-leavers, defined as those students who do not complete their upper secondary education. Internationally comparable measures of how many students successfully complete upper secondary programmes – which also imply how many students don't complete those programmes – can assist efforts to that end. For the first time, this edition of *Education at a Glance* presents just such an indicator.

Other findings

- **In 21 of 28 countries with available data, first-time upper secondary graduation rates exceed 75%.** In Finland, Ireland, Japan, New Zealand, Norway, Portugal, Slovenia, Switzerland and the United Kingdom, graduation rates equal or exceed 90%.

- **Young women are now more likely than young men to complete upper secondary education in almost all OECD countries, a reversal of the historical pattern.** Only in Germany and Switzerland are graduation rates for young women below those for young men. Young women are also graduating from vocational programmes more often than in the past; consequently, their graduation rates from these programmes are catching up with young men's graduation rates.

- **In most countries, upper secondary education is designed to prepare students to enter tertiary-type A (largely theory-based) education.** In Germany, Slovenia, and Switzerland, however, students are more likely to enrol in and graduate from upper secondary programmes that lead to tertiary-type B education, where courses are typically shorter and focus on the development of practical, technical or occupational skills.

- For the first time, comparable data have been published on 20 countries that participated in a special survey on successful completion of upper secondary programmes. The data show that **68% of students who begin upper secondary education complete the programmes they entered** within the theoretical duration of the programme. However, there are large differences in completion rates, depending on gender and type of programme.

Trends

Since 1995, the upper secondary graduation rate has increased by an average of 8 percentage points among OECD countries with comparable data, which represents an annual growth rate of 0.7%. The greatest growth occurred in Chile and Portugal, both of which showed an annual growth rate of more than twice the OECD average between 1995 and 2009.

Analysis

Graduation from upper secondary programmes

Even if completing upper secondary education is considered the norm in most OECD and other G20 countries and economies, the proportion of graduates outside the typical age of graduation varies. First-time graduates are generally between 17 and 20 years old (Table X1.1a in Annex 1); but some countries also offer second-chance/adult-education programmes. In the Nordic countries, for example, students can leave the education system relatively easily and re-enter it later on; that is why graduation rates for students 25 years or older are relatively high in Denmark, Finland, Iceland and Norway (at least 10% of graduates). Indeed, graduation rates do not imply that all young people have graduated from secondary school by the time they enter the labour market; some students graduate after some time spent in work. Policy makers could thus encourage students to complete their upper secondary education before they look for a job, as this is often considered to be the minimum credential for successful entry into the labour market (Chart A2.1). In Portugal, the "New Opportunities" programme, launched in 2005, was introduced to provide a second opportunity to those individuals who left school early or are at risk of doing so, and to assist those in the labour force who want to acquire further qualifications. As a result of the programme, graduation rates in 2009 averaged 96% (34 percentage points higher than in 2008), of which more one-third of concerned students were older than 25.

In most countries, men and women do not share the same level of educational attainment. Women, who often had fewer opportunities and/or incentives to attend higher levels of education, have generally been over-represented among those who had not attained an upper secondary education and were thus under-represented at higher levels of education. But this has changed over the years, and the education gap between men and women has narrowed significantly, and even been reversed in some cases, among young people (see Indicator A1).

Upper secondary graduation rates for young women exceed those for young men in nearly all countries for which total upper secondary graduation rates can be compared by gender. The gap is greatest in Denmark, Iceland, Portugal, Slovenia, and Spain, where graduation rates among young women exceed those of young men by 10 percentage points or more. The exceptions are Switzerland and Germany, where graduation rates are significantly higher for young men (Table A2.1).

Most upper secondary programmes are designed primarily to prepare students for tertiary studies, and their orientation may be general, pre-vocational or vocational (see Indicator C1). In 2009, an estimated 49 % of young people will graduate from general programmes compared to 45% from pre-vocational or vocational programmes.

In 2009, more young women graduated from general programmes than young men. The average OECD graduation rate from general programmes was 55% for young women and 43% for young men. In Austria, the Czech Republic, Estonia, Italy, Poland, the Slovak Republic and Slovenia, young women outnumber young men as graduates by at least three to two. Only in China, Ireland and Korea is there no, or an extremely narrow, gender gap in graduates from general upper secondary programmes.

Young women are also graduating from vocational programmes in increasing numbers. In 2009, on average among OECD countries, 44% of graduates from pre-vocational and vocational programmes were young women; 47% were young men. This pattern may influence entry rates into tertiary vocational programmes in subsequent years (Table A2.1).

In addition, pre-vocational and vocational graduation rates are affected by the proportion of students outside the typical age of graduation, which differs markedly across countries. In Australia, Canada, Finland, Iceland, and New Zealand, some 40% or more of all graduates are adults. In these countries, part-time or evening programmes at this level may be designed especially for adults (Table A2.1).

Graduation from post-secondary non-tertiary programmes

Various kinds of post-secondary, non-tertiary programmes are offered in OECD countries. These programmes straddle upper secondary and post-secondary education but may be considered either as upper secondary or post-secondary programmes, depending on the country concerned. Although the content of these programmes may not be significantly more advanced than upper secondary programmes, they broaden the knowledge of individuals who have already attained an upper secondary qualification. Students in these programmes tend to be older than those enrolled in upper secondary schools. These programmes usually offer trade and vocational certificates, and include, for example, nursery-teacher training in Austria and vocational training for those who have attained general upper secondary qualifications in the dual system in Germany. Apprenticeships designed for students who have already graduated from an upper secondary programme are also included among these programmes (Table A2.3).

Transitions following upper secondary education or post-secondary non-tertiary programmes

The vast majority of students who graduate from upper secondary education graduate from programmes designed to provide access to tertiary education (ISCED 3A and 3B). Programmes that facilitate direct entry into tertiary-type A education (ISCED 3A) are preferred by students in all countries except Germany, Slovenia and Switzerland, where more young people graduate from upper secondary programmes that lead to tertiary-type B programmes. In 2009, graduation rates from long upper secondary programmes (ISCED 3C) averaged 17% in OECD countries (Table A2.1).

It is interesting to compare the proportion of students who graduate from programmes designed as preparation for entry into tertiary-type A programmes (ISCED 3A and 4A) with the proportion of students who actually enter these programmes. Chart A2.2 shows significant variation in patterns among countries. For instance, in Belgium, Chile, China, the Czech Republic, Finland, Ireland, Israel, Italy and Japan, the difference between these two groups is relatively large, at more than 20 percentage points. This suggests that many students who attain qualifications that would allow them to enter tertiary-type A programmes do not do so; but upper secondary programmes in Belgium, Israel and Japan also prepare students for tertiary-type B programmes. In addition, Japan has "junior colleges" that offer programmes that are similar to university-type programmes, but are classified as vocationally oriented because they are of shorter duration than most academic programmes at the tertiary level and include more practical courses (based on ISCED 97).

Chart A2.2. Access to tertiary-type A education for upper secondary and post-secondary non-tertiary graduates (2009)

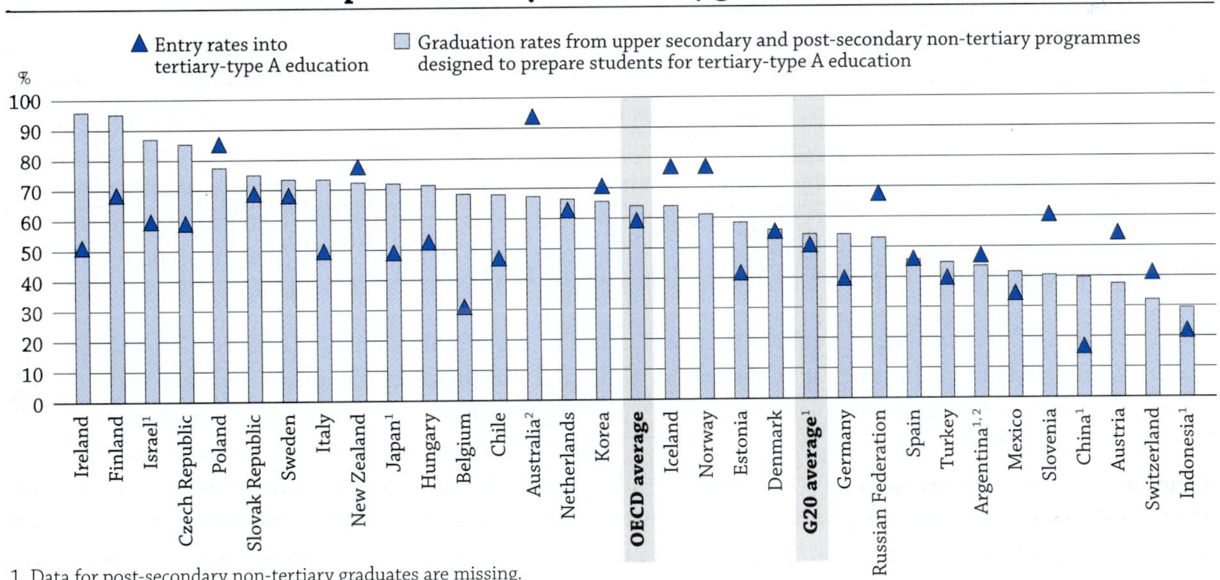

1. Data for post-secondary non-tertiary graduates are missing.

2. Year of reference for graduation rates 2008.

Countries are ranked in descending order of graduation rates from upper secondary and post-secondary non-tertiary programmes designed to prepare students for tertiary-type A education in 2009.

Source: OECD. Argentina, China, Indonesia: UNESCO Institute for Statistics (World Education Indicators Programme). Tables A2.1 and C2.1. See Annex 3 for notes (*www.oecd.org/edu/eag2011*).

StatLink http://dx.doi.org/10.1787/888932459945

In Israel, the difference may be explained by the wide variation in the age of entry to university, which is partly due to the two to three years of mandatory military service students undertake before entering higher education. In Finland, upper secondary education includes vocational training, and many graduates enter the labour market immediately after completing this level, without any studies at the tertiary level. There is also a *numerus clausus* system in Finnish higher education, which means that the number of entry places is restricted. In addition, graduates from upper secondary general education may have to take a break of two to three years before obtaining a place in a university or polytechnic institution. In Ireland, the majority of secondary students take the "Leaving Certificate Examination" (ISCED 3A). Although this course is designed to allow entry into tertiary education, not all of the students who take this examination intend to do so. Until recently, school-leavers in Ireland also had the opportunity to participate in a strong labour market, and this also may have had an impact on the difference.

In contrast, in Australia, Austria, Iceland, Norway, the Russian Federation and Slovenia, the upper secondary and post-secondary non-tertiary graduation rate is markedly lower – by more than 10 percentage points – than entry rates into tertiary-type A programmes. The large gap for Australia, Austria, Iceland and Norway is linked to the high proportion of adults entering tertiary-type A programmes and also to the high proportions of international/foreign students in these programmes (see Indicator C2). Although many students in Slovenia and, to a lesser extent, in the Russian Federation are more likely to graduate from upper secondary programmes leading to tertiary-type B programmes, some may later choose to pursue university studies, and can do so thanks to pathways between the two types of tertiary programmes.

Depending on the country and the relative flexibility of the education system, pathways between the upper secondary/post-secondary non-tertiary and tertiary programmes are either common or non-existent. Switching from vocational to academic programmes, or vice versa, can also occur at the upper secondary level. For the first time, *Education at a Glance* is presenting a new indicator to measure the successful completion of upper secondary programmes and, thus, the pathways between programmes. The indicator discusses the time needed to complete these programmes and the proportion of students still in education after the theoretical duration of programmes. It allows for an estimation of the number of students who drop out and a comparison of completion rates by gender and programme orientation.

Successful completion of upper secondary programmes

The majority of students who start upper secondary education complete the programmes they entered. It is estimated that 68% of boys and girls who begin an upper secondary programme graduate within the theoretical duration of the programme. However, in some countries, it is relatively common for students and apprentices to take a break from their studies and leave the educational system temporarily. Some return quickly to their studies, while others stay away for longer periods of time. In other countries, it is also common to repeat a grade or to change programmes; by doing so, their graduation is delayed. Around 81% of students have successfully completed their upper secondary programmes two years after the stipulated time of graduation – 13 percentage points more than the proportion of students who complete their programmes within the theoretical duration.

The proportion of students who complete their education in the stipulated time varies considerably among countries, with Ireland having the highest share, at 87%, and Luxembourg the lowest share, at 41%. Giving two extra years to students to complete the programmes slightly changes the ranking of the countries, with Estonia and the United States, both are around 87%, and Iceland in last place, at 58% (among countries with available data). In most OECD countries, students may attend regular education institutions for additional years to complete their upper secondary education whereas, in some other countries, students above that age must attend special programmes designed for older students. The difference in the proportion of students who completed their programmes within the stipulated time and that of students who completed after two additional years is more than 30 percentage points in Luxembourg, where it is common for students to repeat one or more years of school. In contrast among countries with available data, in New Zealand and the United States, the difference is as low as three and five percentage points, respectively (Chart A2.3). In the United States, it is highly unusual for students over the age of 20 to still be enrolled in a regular high school programme.

Box A2.1. Completion and graduation: Two different measures

How is completion measured in *Education at a Glance*? The completion rate describes the percentage of students who enter an upper secondary programme for the first time and who graduate from it. **It represents the relationship between the graduates of and the new entrants into the same level of education.** The calculation is made in the amount of time normally allocated for completing the programme and also after an additional two years (for students who had to repeat a grade or individual courses, who studied part-time, etc.). This indicator also includes the percentage of students who do not graduate from an upper secondary programme but are still in education. These might include part-time students who need more time to complete their studies and adults who decide to return to school, perhaps while they are working. However, only initial education programmes are covered by this indicator.

This measure should not be confused with upper secondary graduation rates. The graduation rate is a snapshot of who is estimated to graduate from upper secondary education. **It represents the relationship between all the graduates in a given year and a particular population.** For each country, for a given year, the number of students who graduate is broken down into age groups. For example, the number of 15-year-old graduates will then be divided by the total number of 15-year-olds in the country; the number of 16-year-old graduates will be divided by the total number of 16-year-olds in the country, etc. The graduation rate is the sum of all the age groups.

A third indicator in *Education at a Glance* uses the notion of educational attainment (see Indicator A1). Attainment measures the percentage of a population that has reached a certain level of education, in this case, those who graduated from upper secondary education. It represents the relationship between all graduates (of the given year and previous years) and the total population.

Chart A2.3. Successful completion of upper secondary programmes

Ratio of graduates to new entrants based on cohorts

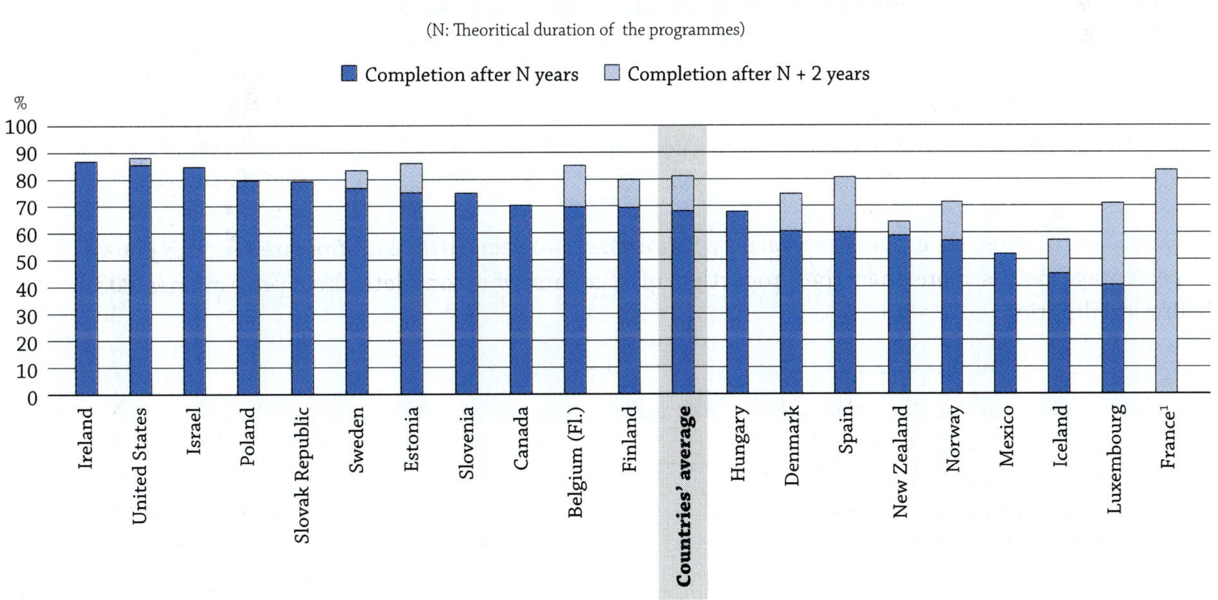

Note: Data presented in this chart come from a special survey in which 20 countries participated. Please refer to Annex 3 for details concerning this indicator, including methods used, programmes included/excluded, year of entry, etc.

1. Time frame N + 3 instead of N + 2.

Countries are ranked in descending order of the successful completion of upper secondary programmes (after N years).

Source: OECD. Table A2.4. See Annex 3 for notes (*www.oecd.org/edu/eag2011*).

StatLink http://dx.doi.org/10.1787/888932459964

In contrast, in New Zealand and the United States, the difference is as low as three and five percentage points, respectively (Chart A2.3). In the United States, it is highly unusual for students over the age of 20 to still be enrolled in a regular high school programme.

Successful completion of upper secondary education also depends on how accessible these programmes are. In most of the countries with available data, upper secondary entry rates for students younger than 20 are over 90%, except in Israel, Luxembourg and Mexico. It is reasonable to expect that students in countries with limited access to upper secondary education are a select group with, on average, higher achievement compared to students in countries with nearly universal access to upper secondary education (Table A2.4).

Successful completion by programme orientation

In several countries, general and vocational programmes are organised separately and students have to opt for one or the other. In other countries, general and vocational programmes are offered in the same structure and sometimes in the same establishment.

Students who enter general programmes are more likely to graduate than those who are enrolled in vocational programmes. Among the 14 countries with available data, 76% of students completed their general programme within the theoretical duration of the programme, and that proportion increased by 13 percentage points two years after the stipulated time of the programme. In contrast, 55% of students completed their vocational programme within the theoretical duration and that proportion increased by 17 percentage points two years after the stipulated time. This average difference of 21 percentage points between completion rates for upper secondary general and vocational programmes is more than 40 percentage points in Denmark and Estonia, and less than 10 percentage points in Israel, Spain and Sweden (Chart A2.4).

The choice between general and vocational studies is made at different stages in a student's career, depending on the country. In countries with a highly comprehensive system, students follow a common core curriculum until the age of 16 (e.g. Nordic countries), while in countries with a highly differentiated system, the choice of a particular programme or type of school can be made from the age of 10-12 onwards (e.g. Luxembourg).

Chart A2.4. Successful completion of upper secondary programmes, by programme orientation

Ratio of graduates to new entrants based on cohorts

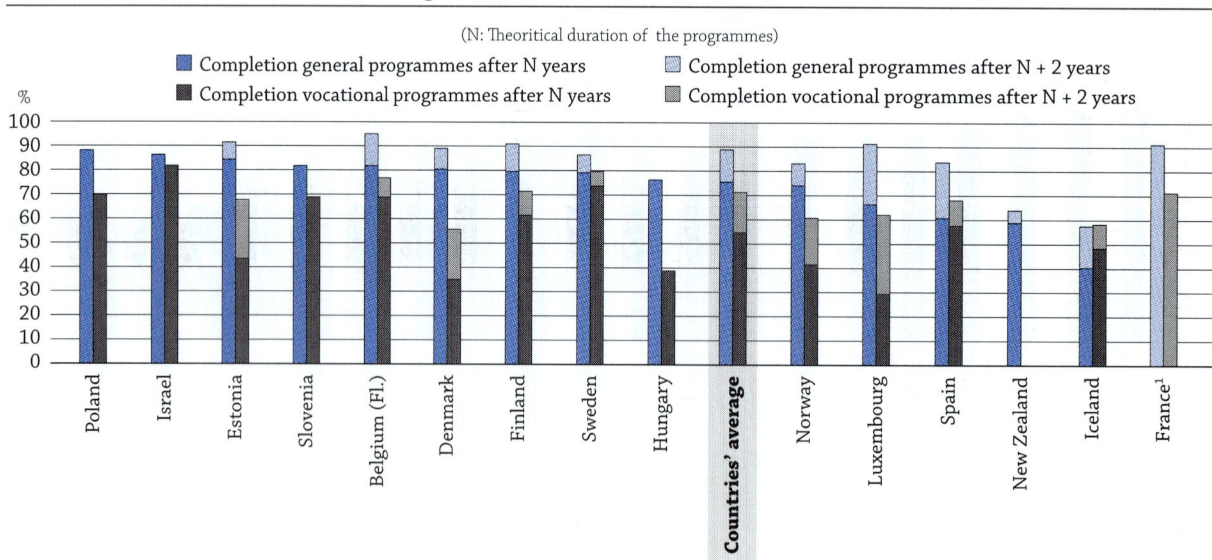

Note: Data presented in this chart come from a special survey in which 20 countries participated. Please refer to Annex 3 for details concerning this indicator, including methods used, programmes included/excluded, year of entry, etc.

1. Time frame N + 3 instead of N + 2.

Countries are ranked in descending order of the successful completion of upper secondary general programmes (after N years).

Source: OECD. Table A2.4. See Annex 3 for notes (*www.oecd.org/edu/eag2011*).

StatLink http://dx.doi.org/10.1787/888932459983

The large difference between completion of upper secondary general or vocational programmes among countries can be explained by the fact that in some countries low achievers may be oriented (or re-oriented) into vocational programmes while high achievers go into general programmes. Some students may also have difficulty determining which programme is best for them and thus may have to repeat one or more grades at this level of education.

Pathways between these two types of education are well developed in some countries. In Norway, for example, among the 42% of students who entered a vocational programme and graduated within the stipulated time, 51% graduated from a general programme and 49% from a vocational programme. In Belgium (Flemish Community), among the 92% of students who entered a general programme and graduated within the stipulated time, 12% graduated from a vocational programme (Table A2.4).

Some students who begin a vocational programme may leave the educational system to enter the labour market directly. Access to employment for people with low educational attainment could also affect successful completion rates and the incidence of dropping out.

Among students who do not complete their programmes within the stipulated time, 61% of those who follow a general programme are still in education compared to only 50% of those who follow a vocational programme. There is large variation among countries: in Belgium (Flemish Community), 90% of students who had not graduated after the theoretical duration of general programmes are still in education, compared to 26% in Israel.

Successful completion by gender

In all countries with available data, boys are more likely than girls to drop out of upper secondary school without a diploma. On average, 73% of girls complete their upper secondary education within the stipulated time compared to 63% of boys. Only in Finland, the Slovak Republic and Sweden is the difference in the proportions of boys and girls who leave school early less than five percentage points. In Israel and Norway, girls outnumbered boys who successfully completed upper secondary education by more than 15 percentage points (Chart A2.5).

Chart A2.5. Successful completion of upper secondary programmes, by gender

Ratio of graduates to new entrants based on cohorts

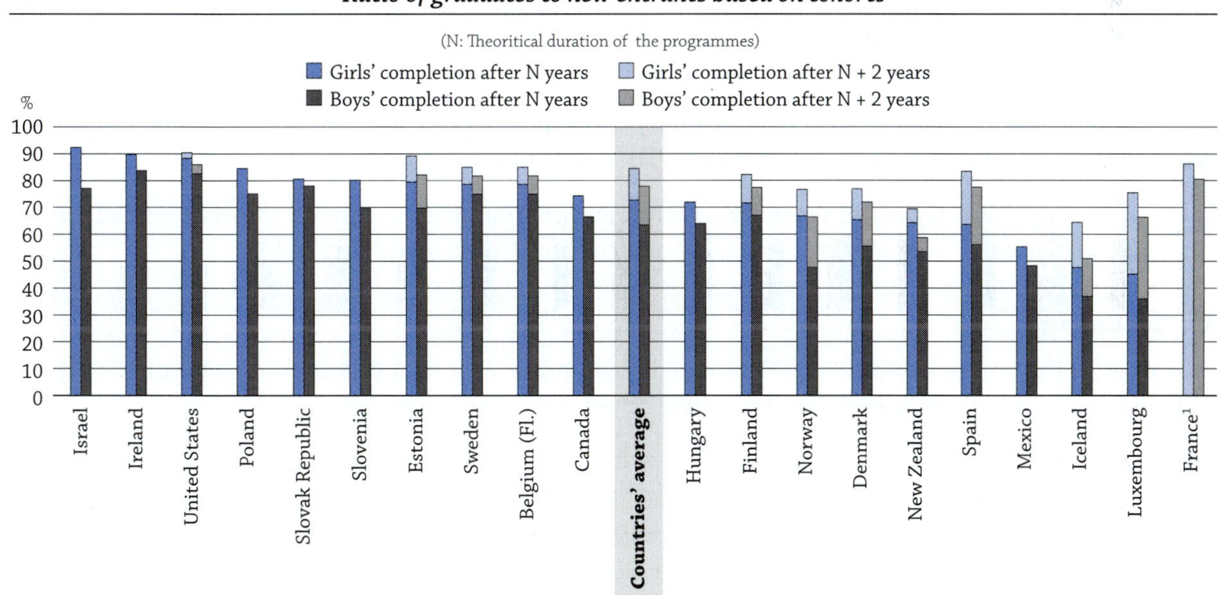

Note: Data presented in this chart come from a special survey in which 20 countries participated. Please refer to Annex 3 for details concerning this indicator, including methods used, programmes included/excluded, year of entry, etc.

1. Time frame N + 3 instead of N + 2.

Countries are ranked in descending order of the successful completion of girls in upper secondary programmes (after N years).

Source: OECD. Table A2.4. See Annex 3 for notes (*www.oecd.org/edu/eag2011*).

StatLink http://dx.doi.org/10.1787/888932460002

The gender differences seen in Norway are due to the fact that girls tend to have better marks than boys in lower secondary school. Controlling for marks in lower secondary school, there is no gender difference – or just a small advantage for boys (Falch, T., *et al.*, 2010).

The gender gap narrowed slightly, to an average of seven percentage points, when completion was delayed by two years because of grade repetition or transfer to a different programme.

The gender gap also varies depending on the programme: 79% of girls complete general programmes compared to 72% of boys; 59% of girls complete vocational programmes compared to 51% of boys. In Norway, this gender gap widens to more than 20 percentage points, in favour of girls, in vocational programmes. In Estonia, girls in vocational programmes are not as successful as boys in completing their upper secondary education within the normal duration of the programmes (Table A2.4).

As PISA reports, many studies confirm that girls are less likely than boys to leave school early. That said, those young women who did leave school early had poorer outcomes than their male counterparts despite their higher average attainment (see Indicators A1 and C4).

The rate of successful completion of upper secondary programmes is also linked to many other issues, such as parental education and immigrant background. The number of countries that completed the part of the survey on parental education and immigrant background was not sufficient to provide publishable data in this year's edition of *Education at a Glance*.

Definitions

Graduates in the reference period can be either first-time graduates or repeat graduates. A **first-time graduate** is a student who has graduated for the first time at a given level of education in the reference period. So, if a student has graduated multiple times over the years, he or she is counted as a graduate each year, but as a first-time graduate only once.

Net graduation rates represent the estimated percentage of an age group that will complete upper secondary education, based on current patterns of graduation.

Successful completion of upper secondary programmes represents the ratio of graduates to new entrants based on cohorts.

Successful completion of upper secondary general programmes represents the ratio of "all" upper secondary graduates to "general programmes" new entrants (based on cohorts).

Successful completion of upper secondary vocational programmes represents the ratio of "all" upper secondary graduates to "vocational programmes" new entrants (based on cohorts).

Methodology

Data refer to the academic year 2008-09 and are based on the UOE data collection on education statistics administered by the OECD in 2010 (for details, see Annex 3 at *www.oecd.org/edu/eag2011*).

Upper secondary graduation rates (Tables A2.1 and A2.2) are calculated as net graduation rates (i.e. as the sum of age-specific graduation rates) for the years 2005-09. Gross graduation rates are presented for the years 1995 and 2000-04. Gross graduation rates are presented for 2005-09 for countries that are unable to provide such detailed data. In order to calculate gross graduation rates, countries identify the age at which graduation typically occurs. The number of graduates, regardless of their age, is divided by the population at the typical graduation age. The graduation rates take into account students graduating from upper secondary education at the typical graduation ages, as well as older students (e.g. those in "second chance" programmes) or younger students. Information on the methods used to calculate graduation rates–gross versus net rates–are presented for each level of education in Annex 1.

The count of first-time graduates (columns 1-4 in Table A2.1 and columns 1-3 in Table A2.3) is calculated by netting out students who graduated from another upper secondary programme in a previous year (or another post-secondary non-tertiary programme). As for the others columns of the tables, the net rate is calculated when data are available.

Graduates of ISCED 3A, 3B and 3C (or 4A, 4B, 4C) programmes are not considered as first-time counts. Therefore, gross graduation rates cannot be added, as some individuals graduate from more than one upper secondary programme and would be counted twice. The same applies for graduation rates according to programme orientation, i.e. general or vocational. In addition, the typical graduation ages are not necessarily the same for the different types of programmes (see Annex 1). Pre-vocational and vocational programmes include both school-based programmes and combined school- and work-based programmes that are recognised as part of the education system. Entirely work-based education and training that are not overseen by a formal education authority are not included.

In Table A2.2 (trends in graduation rates at upper secondary level), data for the years 1995, 2000, 2001, 2002, 2003 and 2004 are based on a special survey carried out in January 2007.

In Table A2.4, data are based on a special survey carried out in December 2010. Successful completion of upper secondary programmes is estimated using different methods: true cohort, longitudinal survey, proxy cohort data. A large description of the method used for each country is included in the Annex 3 (years of new entrants, years of graduates, programmes taken into account, etc.).

The statistical data for Israel are supplied by and under the responsibility of the relevant Israeli authorities. The use of such data by the OECD is without prejudice to the status of the Golan Heights, East Jerusalem and Israeli settlements in the West Bank under the terms of international law.

References

Falch, T., *et al.* (2010), *Completion and Dropout in Upper Secondary Education in Norway: Causes and Consequences*, Centre for Economic Research at Norges Teknisk-Naturvitenskapelige Universitet, Trondheim, October 2010.

The following additional material relevant to this indicator is available on line:

- ***Table A2.2a. Trends in graduation rates (general and pre-vocational/vocational programmes) at upper secondary level (2005-2009)***
  StatLink http://dx.doi.org/10.1787/888932462396

Table A2.1. Upper secondary graduation rates (2009)

Sum of graduation rates for single year of age, by programme destination, programme orientation and gender

		Total (first-time graduates)				General programmes				Pre-vocational/vocational programmes				ISCED 3A[1]	ISCED 3B[1]	ISCED 3C (long)[1]	ISCED 3C (short)[1]
		M + W	of which < 25 years[2]	Men	Women	M + W	of which < 25 years[2]	Men	Women	M + W	of which < 25 years[2]	Men	Women	M + W	M + W	M + W	M + W
		(1)	(2)	(3)	(4)	(5)	(6)	(7)	(8)	(9)	(10)	(11)	(12)	(13)	(16)	(19)	(22)
OECD	Australia[3]	**m**	*m*	m	m	**67**	*67*	62	73	**44**	*21*	43	45	67	a	44	a
	Austria	**m**	*m*	m	m	**18**	*18*	14	22	**74**	*69*	85	63	18	53	1	20
	Belgium	**m**	*m*	m	m	**37**	*m*	32	42	**70**	*m*	64	77	61	a	20	26
	Canada[3]	**79**	*75*	75	83	**76**	*74*	72	81	**3**	*1*	4	2	76	a	3	a
	Chile	**68**	*68*	63	73	**38**	*38*	34	42	**30**	*30*	30	31	68	a	a	a
	Czech Republic	**84**	*m*	81	87	**22**	*m*	17	28	**61**	*m*	63	59	59	n	24	a
	Denmark	**85**	*75*	80	91	**55**	*54*	46	64	**47**	*29*	45	48	55	a	47	n
	Estonia	**m**	*m*	m	m	**58**	*57*	46	72	**20**	*20*	27	14	58	19	a	1
	Finland	**95**	*84*	92	98	**48**	*47*	39	56	**94**	*50*	89	100	95	a	a	a
	France	**m**	*m*	m	m	**50**	*50*	43	58	**62**	*55*	63	61	50	12	4	46
	Germany	**84**	*m*	85	83	**39**	*m*	35	44	**45**	*m*	50	40	39	44	a	1
	Greece	**m**	*m*	m	m	**m**	*m*	m	m	**m**	*m*	m	m	m	m	m	m
	Hungary	**87**	*81*	82	92	**71**	*66*	63	80	**16**	*16*	20	13	71	a	16	x(19)
	Iceland	**89**	*68*	79	98	**68**	*59*	56	80	**54**	*32*	59	50	64	2	37	19
	Ireland	**91**	*90*	89	94	**70**	*68*	70	69	**62**	*48*	48	76	96	a	6	30
	Israel	**89**	*89*	86	93	**57**	*57*	51	63	**32**	*32*	34	30	87	a	2	a
	Italy	**81**	*m*	78	84	**35**	*m*	25	46	**59**	*m*	66	52	73	1	a	19
	Japan	**95**	*m*	94	96	**72**	*m*	69	75	**23**	*m*	25	21	72	1	22	x(19)
	Korea	**89**	*m*	88	89	**66**	*m*	65	66	**23**	*m*	24	23	66	a	23	a
	Luxembourg	**69**	*68*	65	74	**28**	*28*	24	34	**43**	*42*	44	42	41	9	20	2
	Mexico	**45**	*45*	41	49	**42**	*41*	38	45	**4**	*3*	4	4	42	a	4	a
	Netherlands	**m**	*m*	m	m	**39**	*39*	36	42	**71**	*58*	71	70	66	a	44	a
	New Zealand	**90**	*77*	85	95	**77**	*71*	72	82	**49**	*19*	43	54	66	14	34	11
	Norway	**91**	*78*	87	96	**60**	*58*	49	72	**38**	*23*	46	29	60	a	38	m
	Poland	**85**	*84*	80	89	**55**	*52*	43	68	**35**	*35*	44	27	77	a	13	a
	Portugal	**96**	*63*	86	107	**65**	*38*	57	74	**31**	*25*	29	33	x(1)	x(1)	x(1)	x(1)
	Slovak Republic	**81**	*79*	78	84	**24**	*24*	19	30	**64**	*60*	66	62	72	a	16	1
	Slovenia	**96**	*m*	90	102	**37**	*37*	28	46	**76**	*m*	80	71	40	47	23	2
	Spain	**74**	*m*	69	80	**46**	*m*	39	53	**41**	*m*	40	42	46	19	10	11
	Sweden	**74**	*74*	71	76	**31**	*31*	26	37	**42**	*42*	45	40	73	n	n	n
	Switzerland[3]	**90**	*m*	92	88	**30**	*m*	25	35	**71**	*m*	76	66	26	69	6	x(13)
	Turkey	**45**	*45*	42	48	**30**	*30*	27	33	**15**	*15*	15	15	45	a	a	m
	United Kingdom	**92**	*m*	90	94	**m**	*m*	m	m	**m**	*m*	m	m	m	m	70	22
	United States	**76**	*76*	73	80	**x(1)**	*x(2)*	x(3)	x(4)	**x(1)**	*x(2)*	x(3)	x(4)	x(1)	x(1)	x(1)	x(1)
	OECD average	**82**	*m*	79	86	**49**	*m*	43	55	**45**	*m*	47	44	61	10	17	8
	EU21 average	**85**	*m*	81	89	**44**	*m*	38	51	**52**	*m*	54	51	62	11	16	10
Other G20	Argentina[3]	**m**	*m*	m	m	**9**	*8*	7	10	**35**	*34*	30	40	44	a	a	a
	Brazil	**m**	*m*	m	m	**65**	*55*	54	77	**9**	*6*	7	11	65	9	a	a
	China	**65**	*m*	62	67	**38**	*m*	38	39	**45**	*m*	43	48	40	x(13)	25	19
	India	**m**	*m*	m	m	**m**	*m*	m	m	**m**	*m*	m	m	m	m	m	m
	Indonesia	**m**	*m*	m	m	**29**	*29*	28	31	**17**	*17*	20	13	29	17	a	a
	Russian Federation	**m**	*m*	m	m	**53**	*m*	x(5)	x(5)	**41**	*m*	x(9)	x(9)	53	15	23	4
	Saudi Arabia	**m**	*m*	m	m	**m**	*m*	m	m	**m**	*m*	m	m	m	m	m	m
	South Africa	**m**	*m*	m	m	**m**	*m*	m	m	**m**	*m*	m	m	m	m	m	m
	G20 average	**75**	*m*	73	77	**48**	*m*	43	52	**30**	*m*	30	29	54	8	14	9

Note: Columns showing men's/women's graduation rates at upper secondary level by programme orientation (i.e. columns 14-15, 17-18, 20-21, 23-24) are available for consultation on line (see StatLink below).

Refer to Annex 1 for information on the method used to calculate graduation rates (gross rates versus net rates) and the corresponding typical ages.

Mismatches between the coverage of the population data and the graduate data mean that the graduation rates for those countries that are net exporters of students may be underestimated (for instance Luxembourg) and those that are net importers may be overestimated.

1. ISCED 3A (designed to prepare for direct entry to tertiary-type A education).
   ISCED 3B (designed to prepare for direct entry to tertiary-type B education).
   ISCED 3C (long) similar to duration of typical 3A or 3B programmes.
   ISCED 3C (short) shorter than duration of typical 3A or 3B programmes.
2. Sum of graduation rates for single year of age for men and women until the age of 25.
3. Year of reference 2008 (for Switzerland, only for first-time graduates).

Source: OECD. Argentina, China, Indonesia: UNESCO Institute for Statistics (World Education Indicators Programme). See Annex 3 for notes (*www.oecd.org/edu/eag2011*).

Please refer to the Reader's Guide for information concerning the symbols replacing missing data.

StatLink http://dx.doi.org/10.1787/888932462358

Table A2.2. **Trends in graduation rates (first-time) at upper secondary level (1995-2009)**

		1995	2000	2001	2002	2003	2004	2005	2006	2007	2008	2009	Average annual growth rate 1995-2009[1]
OECD	Australia	m	m	m	m	m	m	m	m	m	m	**m**	m
	Austria	m	m	m	m	m	m	m	m	m	m	**m**	m
	Belgium	m	m	m	m	m	m	m	m	m	m	**m**	m
	Canada	m	m	77	79	83	79	78	78	77	79	**m**	m
	Chile	46	63	m	61	64	66	73	71	71	69	**68**	2.9
	Czech Republic	78	m	84	83	88	87	89	90	88	87	**84**	0.5
	Denmark	80	90	91	93	87	90	82	84	85	83	**85**	0.5
	Estonia	m	m	m	m	m	m	m	m	m	m	**m**	m
	Finland	91	91	85	84	90	95	94	94	97	93	**95**	0.3
	France	m	m	m	m	m	m	m	m	m	m	**m**	m
	Germany[2]	100	92	92	94	97	99	99	100	100	97	**84**	m
	Greece	80	54	76	85	96	93	99	100	94	93	**m**	m
	Hungary	m	m	83	82	87	86	82	85	84	78	**87**	m
	Iceland	80	67	70	79	81	87	79	87	86	89	**89**	0.8
	Ireland	m	74	77	78	91	92	91	87	90	88	**91**	*2.3*
	Israel	m	m	m	90	89	93	90	90	92	90	**89**	m
	Italy	m	78	81	78	m	82	81	86	86	84	**81**	*0.4*
	Japan	91	94	93	92	91	91	93	93	93	95	**95**	0.3
	Korea	88	96	100	99	92	94	94	93	91	93	**89**	0.1
	Luxembourg	m	m	m	69	71	69	75	71	75	73	**69**	m
	Mexico	m	33	34	35	37	39	40	42	43	44	**45**	*3.5*
	Netherlands	m	m	m	m	m	m	m	m	m	m	**m**	m
	New Zealand[2]	72	80	79	77	78	75	73	75	77	78	**90**	m
	Norway	77	99	105	97	92	100	89	88	92	91	**91**	1.2
	Poland	m	90	93	91	86	79	85	81	84	83	**85**	*-0.7*
	Portugal[3]	52	52	48	50	60	53	51	54	65	63	**96**	4.4
	Slovak Republic	85	87	72	60	56	83	83	84	85	81	**81**	-0.4
	Slovenia	m	m	m	m	m	m	85	97	91	85	**96**	m
	Spain	62	60	66	66	67	66	72	72	74	73	**74**	1.3
	Sweden	62	75	71	72	76	78	76	75	74	74	**74**	1.2
	Switzerland	86	88	91	92	89	87	89	89	89	90	**m**	m
	Turkey	37	37	37	37	41	55	48	52	58	26	**45**	1.4
	United Kingdom	m	m	m	m	m	m	86	88	89	91	**92**	m
	United States	69	70	71	73	74	75	76	75	75	76	**76**	0.7
	OECD average	74	75	77	77	78	81	80	81	82	80	**82**	m
	OECD average for countries with 1995 and 2009 data	*74*	*76*									**82**	0.7
	EU21 average	77	77	77	77	78	78	81	83	84	84	**86**	m
Other G20	Argentina	m	m	m	m	m	m	m	m	m	m	**m**	m
	Brazil	m	m	m	m	m	m	m	m	m	m	**m**	m
	China	m	m	m	m	m	m	m	m	m	m	**65**	m
	India	m	m	m	m	m	m	m	m	m	m	**m**	m
	Indonesia	m	m	m	m	m	m	m	m	m	m	**m**	m
	Russian Federation	m	m	m	m	m	m	m	m	m	m	**m**	m
	Saudi Arabia	m	m	m	m	m	m	m	m	m	m	**m**	m
	South Africa	m	m	m	m	m	m	m	m	m	m	**m**	m
	G20 average	m	m	m	m	m	m	m	m	m	m	**75**	m

Note: Up to 2004, graduation rates at upper secondary level were calculated on a gross basis. From 2005 and for countries with available data, graduation rates are calculated as net graduation rates (i.e. as the sum of age-specific graduation rates).

Refer to Annex 1 for information on the method used to calculate graduation rates (gross rates versus net rates) and the corresponding typical ages.

1. For countries that do not have data for the year 1995, the 2000-2009 average annual growth rate is indicated in italics.

2. Break in the series between 2008 and 2009 due, in Germany, to a partial reallocation of vocational programmes into ISCED 2 and ISCED 5B, and in New Zealand, to the inclusion of ISCED 3C short programmes.

3. Year of reference 1997 instead of 1995.

Source: OECD. China: UNESCO Institute for Statistics (World Education Indicators Programme). See Annex 3 for notes (*www.oecd.org/edu/eag2011*).

Please refer to the Reader's Guide for information concerning the symbols replacing missing data.

StatLink http://dx.doi.org/10.1787/888932462377

Table A2.3. Post-secondary non-tertiary graduation rates (2009)

Sum of graduation rates for single year of age, by programme destination and gender

		Total (first-time graduates)			ISCED 4A[1]			ISCED 4B[1]			ISCED 4C		
		M + W	Men	Women	M + W	Men	Women	M + W	Men	Women	M + W	Men	Women
		(1)	(2)	(3)	(4)	(5)	(6)	(7)	(8)	(9)	(10)	(11)	(12)
OECD	Australia[1]	**18.6**	15.7	21.6	**a**	a	a	**a**	a	a	**20.2**	17.0	23.5
	Austria	**m**	m	m	**19.4**	16.3	22.7	**2.7**	0.9	4.5	**3.1**	1.9	4.3
	Belgium	**m**	m	m	**7.3**	7.4	7.1	**3.2**	2.8	3.6	**11.7**	9.9	13.5
	Canada	**m**	m	m	**m**	m	m	**m**	m	m	**m**	m	m
	Chile	**a**	a	a	**a**	a	a	**a**	a	a	**a**	a	a
	Czech Republic	**26.2**	25.4	27.0	**25.9**	25.0	26.9	**a**	a	a	**0.2**	0.3	0.1
	Denmark	**1.0**	1.5	0.6	**1.1**	1.5	0.6	**a**	a	a	**a**	a	a
	Estonia	**m**	m	m	**a**	a	a	**15.7**	10.7	20.8	**a**	a	a
	Finland	**3.7**	3.8	3.5	**a**	a	a	**a**	a	a	**7.5**	6.8	8.2
	France	**m**	m	m	**0.6**	0.5	0.8	**a**	a	a	**0.7**	0.4	1.1
	Germany	**17.6**	19.2	16.0	**15.1**	16.4	13.9	**2.5**	2.8	2.1	**a**	a	a
	Greece	**m**	m	m	**a**	a	a	**a**	a	a	**m**	m	m
	Hungary	**17.6**	17.8	17.4	**a**	a	a	**a**	a	a	**20.0**	19.7	20.3
	Iceland	**9.3**	10.9	7.7	**n**	n	n	**n**	n	n	**10.0**	11.9	8.0
	Ireland	**10.4**	17.0	4.1	**a**	a	a	**a**	a	a	**10.4**	17.0	4.1
	Israel	**m**	m	m	**m**	m	m	**m**	m	m	**a**	a	a
	Italy	**4.0**	3.1	5.0	**a**	a	a	**a**	a	a	**4.0**	3.1	5.0
	Japan	**m**	m	m	**m**	m	m	**m**	m	m	**m**	m	m
	Korea	**a**	a	a	**a**	a	a	**a**	a	a	**a**	a	a
	Luxembourg	**2.1**	3.2	1.0	**a**	a	a	**a**	a	a	**2.1**	3.2	1.0
	Mexico	**a**	a	a	**a**	a	a	**a**	a	a	**a**	a	a
	Netherlands	**m**	m	m	**a**	a	a	**a**	a	a	**1.0**	1.4	0.6
	New Zealand	**27.1**	21.7	32.2	**6.6**	5.1	8.1	**6.4**	5.1	7.7	**20.1**	17.8	22.2
	Norway	**7.3**	8.6	5.9	**1.1**	1.7	0.5	**a**	a	a	**6.6**	7.4	5.7
	Poland	**12.0**	9.6	14.5	**a**	a	a	**a**	a	a	**12.0**	9.6	14.5
	Portugal	**1.9**	2.5	1.3	**x(1)**	x(2)	x(3)	**x(1)**	x(2)	x(3)	**x(1)**	x(2)	x(3)
	Slovak Republic	**3.2**	4.0	2.3	**3.2**	4.0	2.3	**a**	a	a	**a**	a	a
	Slovenia	**3.1**	2.6	3.6	**1.0**	0.8	1.2	**2.1**	1.8	2.3	**a**	a	a
	Spain	**a**	a	a	**a**	a	a	**a**	a	a	**a**	a	a
	Sweden	**3.1**	2.3	4.0	**n**	n	n	**n**	n	n	**3.2**	2.3	4.0
	Switzerland	**m**	m	m	**6.0**	6.3	5.6	**5.9**	4.8	7.1	**a**	a	a
	Turkey	**a**	a	a	**a**	a	a	**a**	a	a	**a**	a	a
	United Kingdom	**n**	n	n	**n**	n	n	**n**	n	n	**n**	n	n
	United States	**m**	m	m	**m**	m	m	**m**	m	m	**m**	m	m
	OECD average	**7.3**	7.3	7.3	**3.0**	2.9	3.1	**1.3**	1.0	1.7	**4.6**	4.5	4.7
	EU21 average	**7.1**	7.5	6.7	**3.7**	3.6	3.8	**1.3**	0.9	1.7	**3.8**	3.8	3.8
Other G20	Argentina	**m**	m	m	**m**	m	m	**m**	m	m	**m**	m	m
	Brazil	**a**	a	a	**a**	a	a	**a**	a	a	**a**	a	a
	China	**m**	m	m	**m**	m	m	**m**	m	m	**m**	m	m
	India	**m**	m	m	**m**	m	m	**m**	m	m	**m**	m	m
	Indonesia	**m**	m	m	**m**	m	m	**m**	m	m	**m**	m	m
	Russian Federation	**m**	m	m	**a**	a	a	**a**	a	a	**5.3**	5.8	4.7
	Saudi Arabia	**m**	m	m	**m**	m	m	**m**	m	m	**m**	m	m
	South Africa	**m**	m	m	**m**	m	m	**m**	m	m	**m**	m	m

Note: Refer to Annex 1 for information on the method used to calculate graduation rates (gross rates versus net rates) and the corresponding typical ages. Mismatches between the coverage of the population data and the graduate data mean that the graduation rates for those countries that are net exporters of students may be underestimated (for instance Luxembourg) and those that are net importers may be overestimated.

1. ISCED 4A (designed to prepare for direct entry to tertiary-type A education).
ISCED 4B (designed to prepare for direct entry to tertiary-type B education).

2. Year of reference 2008.

Source: OECD. See Annex 3 for notes *(www.oecd.org/edu/eag2011).*

Please refer to the Reader's Guide for information concerning the symbols replacing missing data.

StatLink http://dx.doi.org/10.1787/888932462415

Table A2.4. [1/2] **Successful completion of upper secondary programmes, by gender and programme orientation**

Ratio of graduates to new entrants based on cohorts

OECD

	Method	Year used for new entrants	Programme duration (G: general, V: vocational)	N = theoretical duration	Completion of upper secondary programmes										
					All programmes			General programmes[1]				Vocational programmes[2]			
					Total	Boys	Girls	Total	Boys	Girls	Proportion of vocational programme graduates[3]	Total	Boys	Girls	Proportion of general programme graduates[4]
Belgium (Fl.)	True cohort	2003-2004	4 years G&V	within N	**70**	63	77	**81**	75	87	*12*	**59**	54	66	*n*
				2 years after N	**85**	82	89	**95**	93	97	*18*	**77**	74	80	*n*
Canada	Proxy cohort data	2005-2006	3 years G&V	within N	**70**	66	74	**m**	m	m	*m*	**m**	m	m	*m*
				2 years after N	**m**	m	m	**m**	m	m	*m*	**m**	m	m	*m*
Denmark	True cohort	2001-2002	2-3 years G & 2-4 years V	within N	**61**	56	65	**80**	78	83	*n*	**35**	34	36	*3*
				2 years after N	**74**	72	77	**89**	88	90	*3*	**56**	57	54	*9*
Estonia	True cohort	2004	3 years G&V	within N	**75**	70	79	**84**	82	86	*n*	**44**	46	38	*1*
				2 years after N	**86**	82	89	**91**	90	93	*3*	**68**	67	69	*3*
Finland	True cohort	2002	3 years G&V	within N	**69**	67	72	**80**	78	81	*n*	**62**	60	63	*1*
				2 years after N	**80**	77	82	**91**	90	92	*3*	**71**	70	73	*1*
France[5]	Longitudinal sample survey	1999-2001	3 years G & 2 years V	within N	**m**	m	m	**m**	m	m	*m*	**m**	m	m	*m*
				2 years after N	**83**	80	86	**91**	90	92	*m*	**71**	69	74	*m*
Hungary	Proxy cohort data	2005-2006	4 years	within N	**68**	64	72	**76**	73	79	*m*	**39**	39	39	*m*
				2 years after N	**m**	m	m	**m**	m	m	*m*	**m**	m	m	*m*
Iceland	True cohort	2002	4 years G&V	within N	**45**	38	51	**43**	36	49	*7*	**49**	42	60	*40*
				2 years after N	**58**	51	64	**58**	51	63	*15*	**58**	51	70	*43*
Ireland	True cohort	2004	2-3 years G&V	within N	**87**	84	90	**m**	m	m	*m*	**m**	m	m	*m*
				2 years after N	**m**	m	m	**m**	m	m	*m*	**m**	m	m	*m*
Israel	True cohort	2005	3 years G&V	within N	**85**	77	92	**86**	78	94	*8*	**82**	76	89	*19*
				2 years after N	**m**	m	m	**m**	m	m	*m*	**m**	m	m	*m*
Luxembourg	True cohort	2000-2001	4 years G & 2-5 years V	within N	**41**	36	45	**66**	63	69	*2*	**29**	26	33	*n*
				2 years after N	**71**	66	75	**91**	89	93	*7*	**62**	58	66	*n*
Mexico	Proxy cohort data	2007	3 years	within N	**52**	48	55	**m**	m	m	*m*	**m**	m	m	*m*
				2 years after N	**m**	m	m	**m**	m	m	*m*	**m**	m	m	*m*
New Zealand	True cohort	2004	3 years G	within N	**59**	53	64	**59**	53	64	*m*	**m**	m	m	*m*
				2 years after N	**64**	59	69	**64**	59	69	*m*	**m**	m	m	*m*
Norway	True cohort	2002	3 years G & 4 years V	within N	**57**	48	67	**74**	69	78	*n*	**42**	31	54	*51*
				2 years after N	**71**	66	77	**83**	79	87	*1*	**61**	57	65	*37*
Poland	True cohort	2005-2006	3 years G & 2-4 years V	within N	**80**	75	85	**88**	85	90	*m*	**70**	67	74	*m*
				2 years after N	**m**	m	m	**m**	m	m	*m*	**m**	m	m	*m*
Slovak Republic	Proxy cohort data	2006	4 years G & 3 years V	within N	**79**	78	81	**m**	m	m	*m*	**m**	m	m	*m*
				2 years after N	**m**	m	m	**m**	m	m	*m*	**m**	m	m	*m*
Slovenia	Proxy cohort data	2006	2 years G&V	within N	**75**	70	80	**82**	80	83	*m*	**69**	63	77	*m*
				2 years after N	**m**	m	m	**m**	m	m	*m*	**m**	m	m	*m*
Spain	True cohort	2001-2002	2 years G&V	within N	**60**	56	64	**61**	57	64	*m*	**58**	54	63	*m*
				2 years after N	**81**	77	83	**84**	81	86	*m*	**68**	67	70	*m*
Sweden	True cohort	2005	3 years G&V	within N	**77**	75	79	**79**	77	81	*1*	**74**	72	75	*3*
				2 years after N	**83**	82	85	**87**	85	88	*4*	**80**	78	81	*4*
United States	Longitudinal sample survey	2002	3 years G&V	within N	**85**	83	88	**m**	m	m	*m*	**m**	m	m	*m*
				2 years after N	**88**	86	90	**m**	m	m	*m*	**m**	m	m	*m*
Countries' average[6]				within N	**68**	63	73	**76**	72	79	*m*	**55**	51	59	*m*
				2 years after N	**81**	78	85	**89**	86	91	*m*	**71**	69	75	*m*

Note: Data presented in this table come from a special survey in which 20 countries participated. Refer to Annex 3 for details concerning this indicator, including methods used, programmes included/excluded, year of entry, etc.

1. ISCED 3 general programmes entrants who graduated from either a general or vocational programme.
2. ISCED 3 vocational programmes entrants who graduated from either a general or vocational programme.
3. ISCED 3 general programmes entrants who graduated from a vocational programme.
4. ISCED 3 vocational programme entrants who graduated from a general programme.
5. N + 3 instead of N + 2.
6. Countries average for N + 2 corresponds to the countries average for N + the difference (in percentage points) of the average for countries with N and N + 2 data.

Source: OECD. See Annex 3 for notes *(www.oecd.org/edu/eag2011).*

Please refer to the Reader's Guide for information concerning the symbols replacing missing data.

StatLink http://dx.doi.org/10.1787/888932466690

Table A2.4. [2/2] Successful completion of upper secondary programmes, by gender and programme orientation

Ratio of graduates to new entrants based on cohorts

		Method	Year used for new entrants	Programme duration (G: general, V: vocational)	N = theoretical duration	Proportion of students who did not graduate and who are still in education: General programmes: Total	General programmes: Boys	General programmes: Girls	Vocational programmes: Total	Vocational programmes: Boys	Vocational programmes: Girls	Net entry rates at upper secondary level for students under 20 years old (2009)
OECD	**Belgium (Fl.)**	True cohort	2003-2004	4 years G&V	within N	**90**	91	89	**72**	73	69	92
					2 years after N	**13**	15	9	**7**	8	6	
	Canada	Proxy cohort data	2005-2006	3 years G&V	within N	**m**	m	m	**m**	m	m	m
					2 years after N	**m**	m	m	**m**	m	m	
	Denmark	True cohort	2001-2002	2-3 years G & 2-4 years V	within N	**73**	75	70	**65**	64	65	95
					2 years after N	**37**	40	34	**34**	31	38	
	Estonia	True cohort	2004	3 years G&V	within N	**54**	51	57	**56**	51	65	100
					2 years after N	**24**	20	27	**15**	13	21	
	Finland	True cohort	2002	3 years G&V	within N	**79**	78	81	**47**	47	48	m
					2 years after N	**41**	36	45	**23**	20	26	
	France[5]	Longitudinal sample survey	1999-2001	3 years G & 2 years V	within N	**m**	m	m	**m**	m	m	m
					2 years after N	**m**	m	m	**m**	m	m	
	Hungary	Proxy cohort data	2005-2006	4 years	within N	**m**	m	m	**m**	m	m	96
					2 years after N	**m**	m	m	**m**	m	m	
	Iceland	True cohort	2002	4 years G&V	within N	**51**	47	54	**39**	35	47	99
					2 years after N	**32**	30	35	**25**	23	29	
	Ireland	True cohort	2004	2-3 years G&V	within N	**m**	m	m	**m**	m	m	100
					2 years after N	**m**	m	m	**m**	m	m	
	Israel	True cohort	2005	3 years G&V	within N	**26**	26	25	**10**	8	15	89
					2 years after N	**m**	m	m	**m**	m	m	
	Luxembourg	True cohort	2000-2001	4 years G & 2-5 years V	within N	**84**	83	85	**67**	65	69	88
					2 years after N	**33**	35	31	**24**	23	26	
	Mexico	Proxy cohort data	2007	3 years	within N	**m**	m	m	**m**	m	m	74
					2 years after N	**m**	m	m	**m**	m	m	
	New Zealand	True cohort	2004	3 years G	within N	**34**	34	35	**m**	m	m	99
					2 years after N	**24**	25	24	**m**	m	m	
	Norway	True cohort	2002	3 years G & 4 years V	within N	**38**	37	39	**38**	41	31	m
					2 years after N	**13**	14	12	**12**	12	12	
	Poland	True cohort	2005-2006	3 years G & 2-4 years V	within N	**m**	m	m	**m**	m	m	91
					2 years after N	**m**	m	m	**m**	m	m	
	Slovak Republic	Proxy cohort data	2006	4 years G & 3 years V	within N	**m**	m	m	**m**	m	m	94
					2 years after N	**m**	m	m	**m**	m	m	
	Slovenia	Proxy cohort data	2006	2 years G&V	within N	**m**	m	m	**m**	m	m	100
					2 years after N	**m**	m	m	**m**	m	m	
	Spain	True cohort	2001-2002	2 years G&V	within N	**m**	m	m	**m**	m	m	m
					2 years after N	**m**	m	m	**m**	m	m	
	Sweden	True cohort	2005	3 years G&V	within N	**55**	55	56	**56**	50	37	98
					2 years after N	**1**	1	2	**2**	1	2	
	United States	Longitudinal sample survey	2002	3 years G&V	within N	**m**	m	m	**m**	m	m	99
					2 years after N	**m**	m	m	**m**	m	m	
	Countries' average[6]				within N	**61**	60	62	**50**	48	49	m
					2 years after N	**m**	m	m	**m**	m	m	

Note: Data presented in this table come from a special survey in which 20 countries participated. Refer to Annex 3 for details concerning this indicator, including methods used, programmes included/excluded, year of entry, etc.

1. ISCED 3 general programmes entrants who graduated from either a general or vocational programme.
2. ISCED 3 vocational programmes entrants who graduated from either a general or vocational programme.
3. ISCED 3 general programmes entrants who graduated from a vocational programme.
4. ISCED 3 vocational programme entrants who graduated from a general programme.
5. N + 3 instead of N + 2.
6. Countries average for N + 2 corresponds to the countries average for N + the difference (in percentage points) of the average for countries with N and N + 2 data.

Source: OECD. See Annex 3 for notes *(www.oecd.org/edu/eag2011).*

Please refer to the Reader's Guide for information concerning the symbols replacing missing data.

StatLink http://dx.doi.org/10.1787/888932466690

INDICATOR A3

HOW MANY STUDENTS FINISH TERTIARY EDUCATION?

- Based on current patterns of graduation, it is estimated that an average of 46% of today's women and 31% of today's men in OECD countries will complete tertiary-type A education (largely theory-based) over their lifetimes. Only 39% of women and 25% of men will do so before the age of 30.
- In some countries, it is common for students older than 30 to graduate from tertiary-type A programmes. More than 30% of women in Iceland and Sweden who graduate from these programmes, and more than 30% of men in Iceland and Israel who do so, are over 30.

Chart A3.1. Tertiary-type A graduation rates in 2009, by gender (first-time graduates)

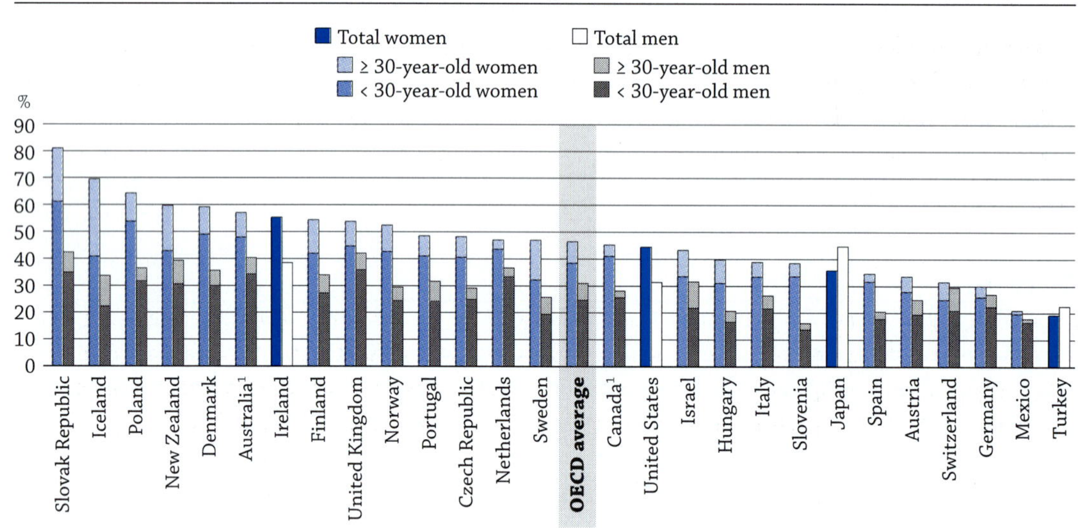

1. Year of reference 2008.

Countries are ranked in descending order of women's graduation rates from tertiary-type A education in 2009.

Source: OECD. Table A3.1. See Annex 3 for notes (*www.oecd.org/edu/eag2011*).

StatLink http://dx.doi.org/10.1787/888932460021

Context

Tertiary graduation rates indicate a country's capacity to produce workers with advanced, specialised knowledge and skills. In OECD countries, there are strong incentives to obtain a tertiary qualification, including higher salaries and better employment prospects. Tertiary education varies widely in structure and scope among countries, and graduation rates are influenced by both the degree of access to these programmes and the demand for higher skills in the labour market. Expanding tertiary education while maintaining quality is likely to create pressures for current levels of tertiary spending to be maintained or increased.

Other findings

- **More than one-third of today's young adults will complete tertiary-type A education.** The proportion ranges from around 20% in Mexico and Turkey to 50% or more in Iceland, New Zealand, Poland and the Slovak Republic.
- Disparities in graduation rates are even greater between women and men. The **gender gap in favour of women is especially wide** in Iceland, Poland and the Slovak Republic (more than 25 percentage points), while in Germany, Mexico and Switzerland, there is practically no gender gap. In contrast, in Japan and Turkey, more men than women graduate from tertiary-type A education.
- **An average of 10% of today's young adults in OECD countries will complete tertiary-type B education** (shorter, vocationally-oriented programmes). Only in Canada, Ireland, Japan, New Zealand and Slovenia do more than 20% of students graduate from these types of programmes.
- **International students make a significant contribution to tertiary graduation rates** in a number of countries. For countries with a high proportion of international students, such as Australia, New Zealand and the United Kingdom, graduation rates are artificially inflated. All international graduates are, by definition, first-time graduates, regardless of their previous education in other countries.

Trends

On average among OECD countries with available data, tertiary-type A graduation rates have risen by 19 percentage points over the past 14 years while rates for tertiary-type B programmes have been stable. While doctorates represent a minor proportion of tertiary programmes, the number of doctoral graduates has been growing at an annual rate of 5% since 2000.

ANALYSIS

Graduation rates for tertiary-type A education

In 2009, graduation rates for tertiary-type A programmes averaged 39% among the 27 OECD countries with comparable data. These programmes are largely theory-based and are designed to provide qualifications for entry into advanced research programmes and professions with high requirements in knowledge and skills. The institutional framework may be universities or other institutions, and the duration of the programmes ranges from three years (e.g. the honours bachelor's degree in many colleges in Ireland and the United Kingdom, and the *licence* in France) to five or more years (e.g. the *Diplom* in Germany).

Many countries make a clear distinction between first and second university degrees (i.e. undergraduate and graduate programmes); however, in some systems, degrees that are internationally comparable to a master's degree are obtained through a single programme of long duration. In order to make accurate comparisons, data presented in this indicator refer to first-time graduates unless otherwise indicated. The Bologna process aims to harmonise programme duration among European countries (see section on the Bologna process below).

Because of increasing harmonisation among the systems of higher education in European countries, some countries have seen rapid rises in their graduation rates. Graduation rates rose sharply in the Czech Republic between 2004 and 2007 and in Finland and the Slovak Republic between 2007 and 2008 for this reason.

In some countries, a large proportion of graduates are older students. Among the 23 countries with available data on students' age, students outside the typical age of graduation represent one-quarter of all graduates in Iceland, Israel, New Zealand, Sweden and Switzerland (Table A3.1). Age differences among graduates may be linked to structural or economic factors, such as the length of tertiary education programmes, the obligation to do military service or the existence of policies to encourage those who have already gained experience in the workplace to enroll in tertiary education.

The proportion of men and women who graduated from tertiary education varies according to country and to age. In Iceland, 41% of women graduates completed tertiary-type A education after the age of 30, compared to 34% of men who did so. In Israel and Switzerland, the reverse is true: 31% and 29% of men, respectively, compared to 23% and 21% of women, respectively, graduated outside the typical age of graduation (Chart A3.1). The fact that these men and women are entering the labour force later has economic repercussions that policy makers should consider, such as higher expenditure per student and foregone tax revenues as a result of shorter working lives.

In 2009, graduation rates for tertiary-type A first-degree programmes (often called a bachelor's degree) averaged 38% among OECD countries. This proportion exceeds 50% in Australia, Iceland, New Zealand, Poland, the Russian Federation and the Slovak Republic. In contrast, fewer than 20% of people in Argentina, Belgium, Indonesia and Mexico graduate from this type of programme. Argentina, Belgium and Slovenia are the only countries in which more people earned their first degree from tertiary-type B programmes than from tertiary-type A programmes (Table A3.3).

An average of 13% of people in OECD countries are expected to receive a second tertiary-type A degree, often called a master's degree, while more than 20% of people in Belgium, Ireland, Poland, the Slovak Republic and the United Kingdom will do so (Table A3.3). With the implementation of the Bologna process, programmes at this level of education have developed considerably.

In every country for which comparable data are available, tertiary-type A graduation rates increased between 1995 and 2009. The increase was particularly steep between 1995 and 2000, then leveled off. During the past three years, graduation rates remained relatively stable at around 38%. The most significant increases since 1995 were reported in Austria, the Czech Republic, the Slovak Republic, Switzerland and Turkey, where the annual growth rate is over 8% (Chart A3.2).

Chart A3.2. First-time graduation rates for tertiary-type A and B programmes (1995 and 2009)

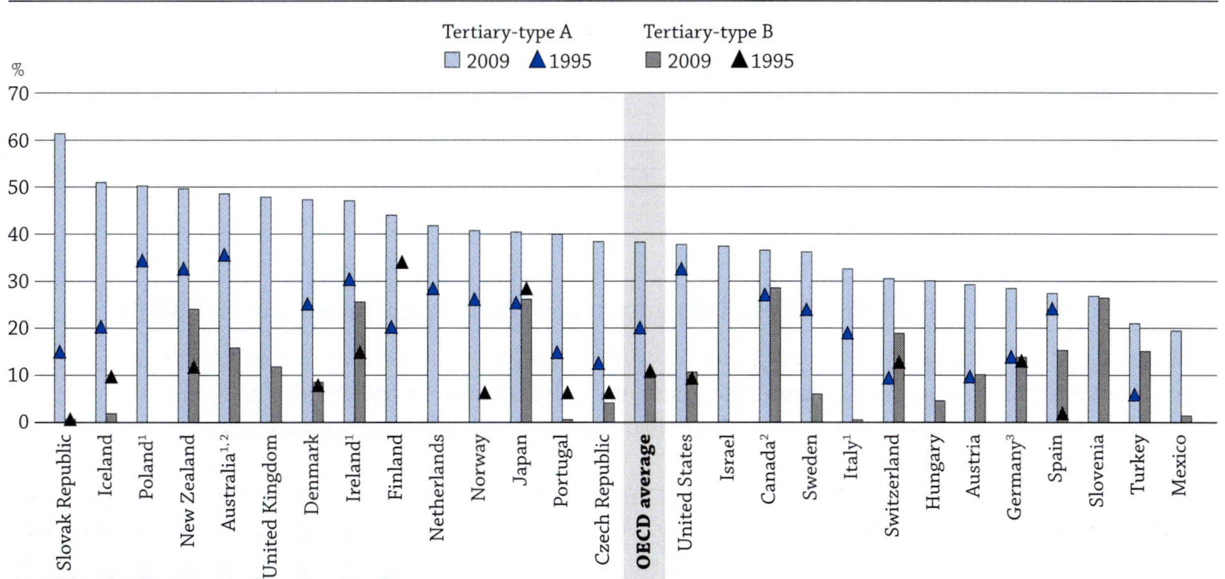

1. Year of reference 2000 instead of 1995.
2. Year of reference 2008 instead of 2009.
3. Break in the series between 2008 and 2009 due to a partial reallocation of vocational programmes into ISCED 2 and ISCED 5B.
Countries are ranked in descending order of first-time graduation rates for tertiary-type A education in 2009.
Source: OECD. Table A3.2. See Annex 3 for notes (*www.oecd.org/edu/eag2011*).
StatLink http://dx.doi.org/10.1787/888932460040

Graduation rates for tertiary-type B education

In 2009, graduation rates for tertiary-type B programmes averaged 10% among the 26 OECD countries with comparable data. These programmes are classified at the same level of competence as those more theory-based programmes, but they are often of shorter duration (usually two to three years) and are generally not intended to lead to university-level degrees, but rather to lead directly to the labour market. Some 12% of women received this type of degree, compared to 9% of men. Among the countries with a large number of first-time graduates from these programmes (namely Canada, Ireland, Japan, New Zealand and Slovenia), New Zealand and Slovenia had the largest proportion of graduates over 30 years old (Table A3.1).

Trends in this type of tertiary education vary, even though the OECD average has been stable between 1995 and 2009. For example, in Spain, the sharp rise in graduate rates from this type of education during this period can be attributed to the development of new advanced-level vocational training programmes. But since these programmes are being phased out in Finland, the rates of graduation from these types of programmes have fallen sharply in favour of more academically oriented tertiary education (Chart A3.2).

Graduation rates for advanced research degrees

Doctoral graduates are those with the highest educational level and thus, as researchers, can help diffuse knowledge in the society. In 2009, graduation rates for advanced research degrees, such as a Ph.D., averaged 1.5% among OECD countries, compared to 1.0% in 2000. This half percentage-point increase in the past nine years represents an annual growth rate of 5%. More than 2.5% of people in Finland, Germany, Portugal, Sweden and Switzerland graduated at this level of education. Some countries promote doctoral education, particularly to international students. In Germany, Sweden and Switzerland, graduation rates at the doctoral level are high compared to the OECD average, while graduation rates for first and second degrees of tertiary-type A programmes are below the OECD average. This is partly due to the high proportion of international students at this level of education in these countries (see the section below on international students' contribution to graduate output) (Table A3.3 and Table A3.5, available on line).

Structure of tertiary education: Main programme blocks

The Bologna process had its origins in the Sorbonne Joint Declaration on Harmonisation of the Architecture of the European Higher Education System, signed in 1998 by France, Germany, Italy and the United Kingdom. Its purpose was to provide a common framework for tertiary education in Europe at the bachelor, master and doctorate levels. Under the new system, the average duration of the bachelor's degree, the master's degree and doctorate have been harmonised in order to improve the comparability of data on European countries and non-European OECD countries, facilitate student mobility among countries, and recognise equivalence between similar programmes.

Chart A3.3. Structure of tertiary education: Main programme blocks (2009)

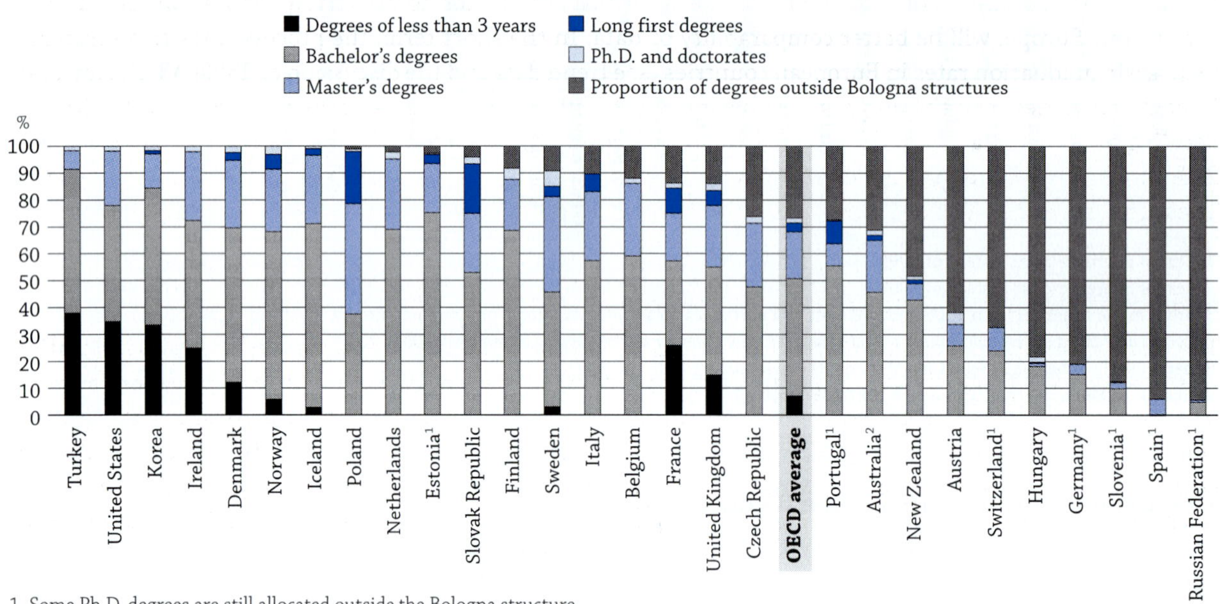

1. Some Ph.D. degrees are still allocated outside the Bologna structure.
2. Year of reference 2008.
Countries are ranked in descending order of the proportion of degrees following the Bologna structures.
Source: OECD. Table A3.4. See Annex 3 for notes (*www.oecd.org/edu/eag2011*).
StatLink http://dx.doi.org/10.1787/888932460059

Table A3.4 presents the main programme blocks in tertiary education and the distribution of graduates from the corresponding blocks. The blocks are organised as follows:

- Programmes that last less than three years but are still considered to be part of tertiary education. In 2009, an average of 7% of all graduates graduated from these programmes; between 12% and 26% of all graduates graduated from these programmes in Denmark, France, Ireland and the United Kingdom; while in Korea, Turkey and the United States, at least 34% of all graduates graduated from these programmes.

- Bachelor's programmes or equivalents, which last three to four years. This is the most common programme block across countries. In 2009, an average of 44% of all graduates graduated from this type of programme. In Estonia, Finland, Iceland, the Netherlands and Norway, more than 60% of all graduates graduated from this type of programme.

- Master's programmes or equivalents, which typically last between one and four years, and usually prepare students for a second degree/qualification following a bachelor's programme. The cumulative duration of studies at the tertiary level is thus four to eight years or even longer. In 2009, an average of 18% of all graduates graduated from this type of programme; in Belgium, Denmark, Iceland, Ireland, Italy, the Netherlands, Poland and Sweden, at least 25% of all graduates did.

- Long programmes and degrees with a single structure and a minimum duration of five years. These are, for the most part, equivalent to master's degrees, but in a few cases, the qualification obtained is equivalent to that of a bachelor's programme. These programmes usually concentrate on medical studies, architecture, engineering and theology. In 2009, an average of only 3% of all graduates graduated from such programmes; but in France and Portugal, 9% did, while in Poland and the Slovak Republic, more than 18% of all graduates did. However, a share of graduates at this level is not counted in this category if the programmes still fall outside the Bologna categories.
- Programmes and degrees at the doctorate/Ph.D. level, which normally corresponds to ISCED 6, usually three to four years' duration, depending on the programme and the country. In 2009, an average of 2% of all graduates graduated from these types of programmes.

One of the beneficial effects of the Bologna process, which aims to harmonise tertiary education programmes throughout Europe, will be better comparability of data. In the short term, the process leads to a structural increase in graduation rates in European countries (see trend data and the discussion of Table A3.2). However, in some countries, certain programmes have not yet shifted to different blocks because of difficulties in deciding which programmes belong in which blocks. In 2009, these programmes represented an average of 27% of all graduates and more than 60% in Austria, Germany, Hungary, Slovenia, Spain and Switzerland. These countries must decide on the appropriate blocks for these programmes if they are to be fully integrated into the Bologna structure, which was scheduled to be operational by 2010.

International students' contribution to graduate output

The term "international students" refers to students who have crossed borders expressly with the intention to study. International students have a marked impact on estimated graduation rates. For example, when international students are excluded, first time tertiary-type A graduation rates for Australia, New Zealand and the United Kingdom drop by 15, 9 and 12 percentage points, respectively. This effect is also evident in second-degree programmes, such as master's degrees, in Australia and the United Kingdom, where graduation rates drop by 11 and 7 percentage points, respectively, when international graduates are excluded (Table A3.3).

Chart A3.4. Graduation rate at tertiary-type A level (first-degree): Impact of international/foreign students (2009)

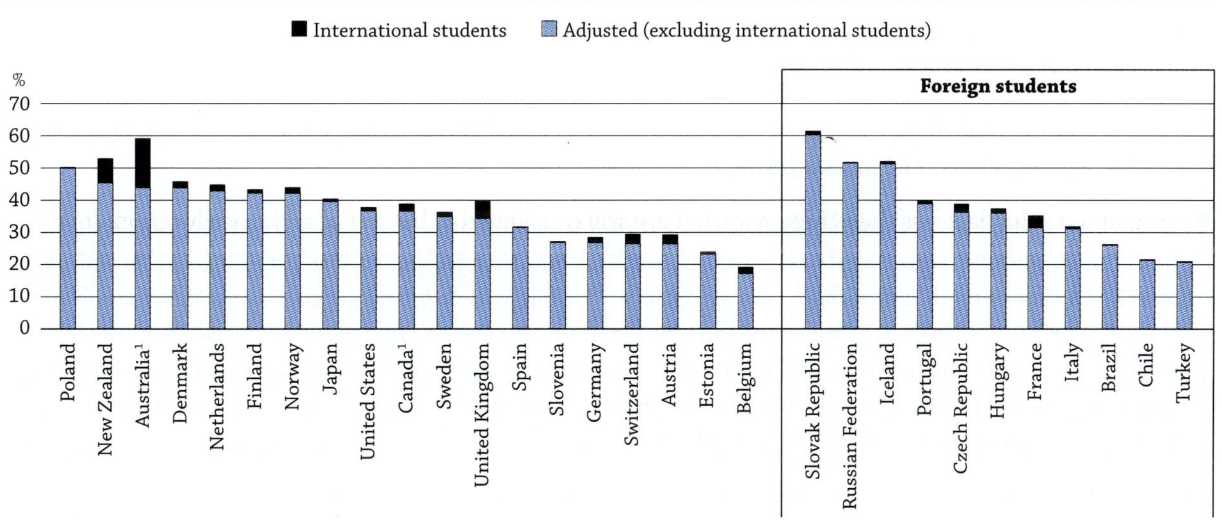

Note: Foreign graduation rates at tertiary-type A first degree level are not comparable with data on international graduation rates and are therefore presented separately.

1. Year of reference 2008.

Countries are ranked in descending order of adjusted graduation rates in tertiary-type A first-degree programmes in 2009.

Source: OECD. Table A3.3. See Annex 3 for notes (*www.oecd.org/edu/eag2011*).

StatLink http://dx.doi.org/10.1787/888932460078

The contribution of international students to graduation rates is also significant at the first stage of tertiary-type A education – although to a lesser extent. In Australia, Austria, New Zealand, Switzerland and the United Kingdom, at least 10% of students graduating with a first degree in tertiary education are international students; while among countries for which data on student mobility are not available, foreign students represent 10% or more of those earning first degrees in Belgium and France (Chart A3.4).

International mobility of doctoral students highlights the attractiveness of advanced research programmes in the host countries. International students at this level of education in Switzerland and the United Kingdom represent more than 40% of graduates in those countries (Table A3.3).

Definitions

A **first degree** at tertiary-type A level has a minimum cumulative theoretical duration of three years, full-time equivalent, e.g. the bachelor's degrees in many English-speaking countries, the *Diplom* in many German-speaking countries, and the *licence* in many French-speaking countries. **Second and higher theory-based programmes** (e.g. master's degree in English-speaking countries and *maîtrise* in French-speaking countries) would be classified in tertiary-type A separately from advanced research qualifications, which would have their own position in ISCED 6.

Graduates in the reference period can be either first-time graduates or repeat graduates. A **first-time graduate** is a student who has graduated for the first time at a given level of education – or in the case of ISCED 5, from a type A or type B programme – in the reference period. So, if a student has graduated multiple times over the years, he or she is counted as a graduate each year, but as a first-time graduate only once.

Net graduation rates represent the estimated percentage of people from a specific age cohort who will complete tertiary education, based on current patterns of graduation.

Tertiary graduates are those who obtain a university degree, vocational qualifications, or advanced research degrees of doctorate standard.

Methodology

Data refer to the academic year 2008-09 and are based on the UOE data collection on education statistics administered by the OECD in 2010 (for details, see Annex 3 at *www.oecd.org/edu/eag2011*).

Data on the impact of international students on tertiary graduation rates are based on a special survey conducted by the OECD in December 2010.

Data on trends in graduation rates at tertiary level for the years 1995 and 2000 through 2004 are based on a special survey carried out in January 2007.

To allow for comparisons that are independent of differences in national degree structures, university-level degrees are subdivided according to the total theoretical duration of study: the standard number of years, established by law or regulations, in which a student can complete the education programme. Degrees obtained from programmes of less than three years' duration are not considered equivalent to completing this level of education and are not included in this indicator. Second-degree programmes are classified according to the cumulative duration of the first- and second-degree programmes. Individuals who already hold a first degree are not included in the count of first-time graduates.

In Tables A3.1, A3.2 (from 2005 onwards) and A3.3, graduation rates are calculated as net graduation rates (i.e. as the sum of age-specific graduation rates). Gross graduation rates are presented for countries that are unable to provide such detailed data. In order to calculate gross graduation rates, countries identify the age at which graduation typically occurs (see Annex 1). The number of graduates, regardless of their age, is divided by the population at the typical graduation age. In many countries, defining a typical age of graduation is difficult, however, because graduates are dispersed over a wide range of ages.

The statistical data for Israel are supplied by and under the responsibility of the relevant Israeli authorities. The use of such data by the OECD is without prejudice to the status of the Golan Heights, East Jerusalem and Israeli settlements in the West Bank under the terms of international law.

References

The following additional material relevant to this indicator is available on line:

- ***Table A3.5. Trends in net graduation rates at advanced research qualification level (1995-2009)***
  StatLink http://dx.doi.org/10.1787/888932462510

Table A3.1. Graduation rates at tertiary level (2009)

Sum of graduation rates for single year of age, by gender and programme destination

		Rates for tertiary-type A programmes (first-time graduates)						Rates for tertiary-type B programmes (first-time graduates)					
					Below the age of 30						Below the age of 30		
		Total	Men	Women	Total	Men	Women	Total	Men	Women	Total	Men	Women
		(1)	(2)	(3)	(4)	(5)	(6)	(7)	(8)	(9)	(10)	(11)	(12)
OECD	Australia[1]	**48.5**	40.4	57.1	**41.0**	34.3	48.0	**15.8**	11.9	19.8	**9.5**	7.0	12.2
	Austria	**29.3**	25.0	33.7	**23.6**	19.4	27.9	**10.1**	10.6	9.6	**6.8**	7.2	6.4
	Belgium	**m**	m	m	**m**	m	m	**m**	m	m	**m**	m	m
	Canada[1]	**36.6**	28.2	45.3	**33.3**	25.7	41.1	**28.6**	23.2	34.1	**21.9**	18.3	25.6
	Chile	**m**	m	m	**m**	m	m	**m**	m	m	**m**	m	m
	Czech Republic	**38.4**	29.2	48.2	**32.5**	25.0	40.6	**4.1**	1.9	6.5	**3.8**	1.8	5.9
	Denmark	**47.3**	35.6	59.2	**39.4**	30.0	49.0	**8.5**	8.5	8.6	**7.0**	6.8	7.2
	Estonia	**m**	m	m	**m**	m	m	**m**	m	m	**m**	m	m
	Finland	**44.0**	34.0	54.4	**34.5**	27.3	42.0	**n**	n	n	**n**	n	n
	France	**m**	m	m	**m**	m	m	**m**	m	m	**m**	m	m
	Germany	**28.5**	27.0	30.0	**24.1**	22.3	26.0	**13.8**	8.6	19.2	**m**	m	m
	Greece	**m**	m	m	**m**	m	m	**m**	m	m	**m**	m	m
	Hungary	**30.1**	20.6	39.8	**23.7**	16.6	31.1	**4.6**	2.4	6.8	**4.1**	2.3	6.0
	Iceland	**51.0**	33.7	69.5	**31.2**	22.2	40.8	**1.9**	1.7	2.1	**0.6**	0.4	0.8
	Ireland	**47.1**	38.5	55.4	**m**	m	m	**25.6**	26.7	24.6	**m**	m	m
	Israel	**37.4**	31.7	43.4	**27.6**	21.8	33.6	**m**	m	m	**m**	m	m
	Italy	**32.6**	26.5	38.9	**27.6**	21.5	33.5	**0.5**	0.5	0.6	**m**	m	m
	Japan	**40.4**	44.7	35.9	**m**	m	m	**26.2**	19.1	33.6	**m**	m	m
	Korea	**m**	m	m	**m**	m	m	**m**	m	m	**m**	m	m
	Luxembourg	**m**	m	m	**m**	m	m	**m**	m	m	**m**	m	m
	Mexico	**19.4**	17.9	20.9	**18.1**	16.5	19.7	**1.4**	1.6	1.3	**1.4**	1.5	1.3
	Netherlands	**41.8**	36.7	47.0	**38.4**	33.4	43.6	**n**	n	n	**m**	m	m
	New Zealand	**49.6**	39.3	59.7	**36.6**	30.6	42.9	**24.0**	21.5	26.3	**14.4**	14.4	14.4
	Norway	**40.7**	29.5	52.5	**33.4**	24.5	42.7	**0.5**	0.4	0.6	**0.2**	0.2	0.3
	Poland	**50.2**	36.5	64.3	**42.6**	31.7	53.8	**0.1**	n	0.2	**m**	m	m
	Portugal	**40.0**	31.7	48.5	**32.5**	24.3	41.1	**0.6**	0.3	0.9	**0.5**	0.2	0.8
	Slovak Republic	**61.4**	42.4	81.1	**47.8**	34.9	61.2	**0.7**	0.5	0.9	**0.6**	0.5	0.7
	Slovenia	**26.8**	16.1	38.5	**23.2**	13.7	33.6	**26.5**	21.5	31.9	**16.0**	12.0	20.5
	Spain	**27.4**	20.5	34.7	**24.5**	17.7	31.7	**15.3**	13.7	16.9	**13.8**	12.5	15.2
	Sweden	**36.2**	25.8	47.0	**25.7**	19.4	32.3	**6.0**	4.9	7.2	**4.1**	3.6	4.7
	Switzerland	**30.5**	29.5	31.6	**22.9**	20.8	24.9	**18.9**	23.4	14.3	**m**	m	m
	Turkey	**20.9**	22.5	19.2	**m**	m	m	**15.1**	16.0	14.1	**12.6**	13.3	11.8
	United Kingdom	**47.8**	42.0	53.8	**40.2**	35.9	44.7	**11.8**	8.8	14.8	**6.9**	5.8	8.1
	United States	**37.8**	31.4	44.5	**m**	m	m	**10.7**	7.7	13.8	**m**	m	m
	OECD average	**38.6**	31.0	46.5	**31.5**	24.8	38.5	**10.4**	9.1	11.9	**6.9**	6.0	7.9
	EU21 average	**39.2**	30.6	48.1	**31.7**	24.7	39.1	**8.0**	6.8	9.3	**5.8**	4.8	6.9
Other G20	Argentina	**m**	m	m	**m**	m	m	**m**	m	m	**m**	m	m
	Brazil	**m**	m	m	**m**	m	m	**m**	m	m	**m**	m	m
	China	**m**	m	m	**m**	m	m	**m**	m	m	**m**	m	m
	India	**m**	m	m	**m**	m	m	**m**	m	m	**m**	m	m
	Indonesia	**m**	m	m	**m**	m	m	**m**	m	m	**m**	m	m
	Russian Federation	**m**	m	m	**m**	m	m	**m**	m	m	**m**	m	m
	Saudi Arabia	**m**	m	m	**m**	m	m	**m**	m	m	**m**	m	m
	South Africa	**m**	m	m	**m**	m	m	**m**	m	m	**m**	m	m

Notes: Refer to Annex 1 for information on the method used to calculate graduation rates (gross rates versus net rates) and the corresponding typical ages. Mismatches between the coverage of the population data and the graduate data mean that the graduation rates for those countries that are net exporters of students may be underestimated, and those that are net importers may be overestimated. The adjusted graduation rates in Table A3.3 seek to compensate for that.

1. Year of reference 2008.

Source: OECD. See Annex 3 for notes *(www.oecd.org/edu/eag2011)*.

Please refer to the Reader's Guide for information concerning the symbols replacing missing data.

StatLink http://dx.doi.org/10.1787/888932462434

Table A3.2. Trends in tertiary graduation rates (1995-2009)

Sum of graduation rates for single year of age, by programme destination

		Tertiary-type A (first-time graduates)							Tertiary-type B (first-time graduates)						
		1995	2000	2005	2006	2007	2008	**2009**	1995	2000	2005	2006	2007	2008	**2009**
OECD	Australia	m	36	50	50	49	49	**m**	m	m	m	m	18	16	**m**
	Austria	10	15	20	21	22	25	**29**	m	m	8	7	7	8	**10**
	Belgium	m	m	m	m	m	m	**m**	m	m	m	m	m	m	**m**
	Canada	27	27	29	31	35	37	**m**	m	m	m	m	30	29	**m**
	Chile	m	m	m	m	m	m	**m**	m	m	m	m	m	m	**m**
	Czech Republic	13	14	23	29	35	36	**38**	6	5	6	6	5	5	**4**
	Denmark	25	37	46	45	47	47	**47**	8	10	10	10	11	11	**9**
	Estonia	m	m	m	m	m	m	**m**	m	m	m	m	m	m	**m**
	Finland	20	41	47	48	48	63	**44**	34	7	n	n	n	n	**n**
	France	m	m	m	m	m	m	**m**	m	m	m	m	m	m	**m**
	Germany[1]	14	18	20	21	23	25	**28**	13	11	11	11	10	10	**14**
	Greece	14	15	25	21	18	m	**m**	5	6	11	12	12	m	**m**
	Hungary	m	m	32	30	29	30	**30**	m	m	4	4	4	4	**5**
	Iceland	20	33	56	63	63	57	**51**	10	5	4	4	2	4	**2**
	Ireland	m	30	38	39	45	46	**47**	m	15	24	27	24	26	**26**
	Israel	m	m	35	36	37	36	**37**	m	m	m	m	m	m	**m**
	Italy	m	19	41	39	35	33	**33**	m	n	n	1	m	1	**1**
	Japan	25	29	37	39	39	39	**40**	28	29	27	28	28	27	**26**
	Korea	m	m	m	m	m	m	**m**	m	m	m	m	m	m	**m**
	Luxembourg	m	m	m	m	m	6	**m**	m	m	m	m	m	n	**m**
	Mexico	m	m	m	m	m	18	**19**	m	m	m	1	1	1	**1**
	Netherlands	29	35	42	43	43	41	**42**	m	m	n	n	n	n	**n**
	New Zealand	33	50	51	52	48	48	**50**	12	17	21	24	20	21	**24**
	Norway	26	37	41	43	43	41	**41**	6	6	2	1	1	1	**n**
	Poland	m	34	47	47	49	50	**50**	m	m	n	n	n	n	**n**
	Portugal	15	23	32	33	43	45	**40**	6	8	9	9	6	2	**1**
	Slovak Republic	15	m	30	35	39	57	**61**	1	2	2	1	1	1	**1**
	Slovenia	m	m	18	21	20	20	**27**	m	m	24	26	25	26	**26**
	Spain[2]	24	29	30	30	30	27	**27**	2	8	14	15	14	14	**15**
	Sweden	24	28	38	41	40	40	**36**	m	4	5	5	5	6	**6**
	Switzerland	9	12	27	30	31	32	**31**	13	14	8	10	18	19	**19**
	Turkey	6	9	11	15	m	20	**21**	m	m	m	11	12	13	**15**
	United Kingdom	m	42	47	47	46	48	**48**	m	7	11	10	10	12	**12**
	United States	33	34	34	36	37	37	**38**	9	8	10	10	10	10	**11**
	OECD average	20	28	35	36	38	38	**38**	11	9	9	9	11	10	**9**
	OECD average for countries with 1995 and 2009 data	*20*						**39**	*11*						**12**
	EU21 average	18	27	34	35	36	38	**39**	9	7	8	8	8	7	**8**
Other G20	Argentina	m	m	m	m	m	m	**m**	m	m	m	m	m	m	**m**
	Brazil	m	10	m	m	m	m	**m**	m	m	m	m	m	m	**m**
	China	m	m	m	m	m	m	**m**	m	m	m	m	m	m	**m**
	India	m	m	m	m	m	m	**m**	m	m	m	m	m	m	**m**
	Indonesia	m	m	m	m	m	m	**m**	m	m	m	m	m	m	**m**
	Russian Federation	m	m	m	m	m	m	**m**	m	m	m	m	m	m	**m**
	Saudi Arabia	m	m	m	m	m	m	**m**	m	m	m	m	m	m	**m**
	South Africa	m	m	m	m	m	m	**m**	m	m	m	m	m	m	**m**

Note: Years 2001, 2002, 2003, 2004 are available for consultation on line (see Statlink below).
Up to 2004, graduation rates at the tertiary-type A or B levels were calculated on a gross basis. From 2005 and for countries with available data, graduation rates are calculated as net graduation rates (i.e. as the sum of age-specific graduation rates). Please refer to Annex 1 for information on the method used to calculate graduation rates (gross rates versus net rates) and the corresponding typical ages.

1. Break in the series between 2008 and 2009 due to a partial reallocation of vocational programmes into ISCED 2 and ISCED 5B.

2. Break in time series following methodological change in 2008.

Source: OECD. See Annex 3 for notes *(www.oecd.org/edu/eag2011)*.

Please refer to the Reader's Guide for information concerning the symbols replacing missing data.

StatLink http://dx.doi.org/10.1787/888932462453

Table A3.3. **Graduation rate at different tertiary levels, impact of international/foreign students (2009)**

Sum of graduation rates for single year of age, by programme destination

		Tertiary-type B programmes (first-time)		Tertiary-type B programmes (first degree)		Tertiary-type A programmes (first-time)		Tertiary-type A programmes (first degree)		Tertiary-type A programmes (second degree)		Advanced research programmes	
		Graduation rate (all students)	Adjusted graduation rate (without international/ foreign students)	Graduation rate (all students)	Adjusted graduation rate (without international/ foreign students)	Graduation rate (all students)	Adjusted graduation rate (without international/ foreign students)	Graduation rate (all students)	Adjusted graduation rate (without international/ foreign students)	Graduation rate (all students)	Adjusted graduation rate (without international/ foreign students)	Graduation rate (all students)	Adjusted graduation rate (without international/ foreign students)
		(1)	(2)	(3)	(4)	(5)	(6)	(7)	(8)	(9)	(10)	(11)	(12)
OECD	Australia[1]	15.8	m	19.8	14.9	48.5	33.9	59.1	43.9	19.1	7.7	1.9	1.4
	Austria	10.1	m	10.1	9.9	29.3	26.4	29.3	26.4	5.9	5.3	2.0	1.6
	Belgium[2]	m	m	29.3	27.4	m	m	19.1	17.1	23.7	20.4	1.3	1.0
	Canada[1]	28.6	28.3	33.0	32.8	36.6	34.3	38.9	36.6	9.0	7.7	1.2	1.0
	Chile[2]	m	m	18.8	18.6	m	m	21.6	21.4	6.6	6.2	0.2	n
	Czech Republic[2]	4.1	m	4.1	4.1	38.4	m	38.8	36.2	19.2	m	1.4	m
	Denmark	8.5	7.8	9.2	8.4	47.3	44.0	45.8	43.8	18.8	17.4	1.6	1.5
	Estonia	m	m	20.5	20.5	m	m	23.9	23.2	11.3	11.0	0.8	0.8
	Finland	n	m	n	m	44.0	m	43.3	42.2	18.0	16.9	2.5	2.3
	France[2]	m	m	25.6	24.7	m	m	35.2	31.5	14.1	10.8	1.5	1.0
	Germany	13.8	m	13.8	11.4	28.5	26.7	28.5	26.7	2.5	1.8	2.5	2.2
	Greece	m	m	m	m	m	m	m	m	m	m	m	m
	Hungary[2]	4.6	m	5.1	5.1	30.1	m	37.4	36.0	5.1	m	0.9	m
	Iceland	1.9	1.9	2.2	2.1	51.0	48.9	52.0	51.2	18.8	17.3	0.7	0.5
	Ireland	25.6	m	25.6	m	47.1	m	47.1	m	22.3	m	1.4	m
	Israel	m	m	m	m	37.4	m	37.1	m	14.3	m	1.3	m
	Italy	0.5	m	0.5	n	32.6	31.9	31.8	31.1	m	m	m	m
	Japan	26.2	25.2	26.2	25.2	40.4	39.6	40.4	39.6	5.7	5.2	1.1	0.9
	Korea	m	m	29.7	m	m	m	44.5	m	9.4	m	1.2	m
	Luxembourg	m	m	m	m	m	m	m	m	a	m	m	m
	Mexico	1.4	m	1.4	m	19.4	m	19.4	m	3.1	m	0.2	m
	Netherlands	n	m	n	m	41.8	39.9	44.8	42.9	16.4	16.1	1.6	m
	New Zealand	24.0	18.7	31.2	25.4	49.6	40.3	52.9	45.4	16.5	13.4	1.4	1.0
	Norway	0.5	0.5	0.6	0.6	40.7	39.0	44.0	42.2	11.2	9.3	1.6	1.2
	Poland	0.1	m	1.0	m	50.2	m	50.2	49.9	34.5	34.4	0.8	m
	Portugal	0.6	0.6	0.6	0.6	40.0	38.9	40.0	38.9	10.6	10.2	2.7	2.4
	Slovak Republic[2]	0.7	m	0.7	m	61.4	60.2	61.4	60.2	21.8	21.5	2.2	2.1
	Slovenia	26.5	26.4	27.7	27.6	26.8	26.5	27.1	26.8	4.8	4.7	1.5	1.4
	Spain	15.3	m	15.3	m	27.4	m	31.7	31.6	3.3	2.8	1.0	m
	Sweden	6.0	6.0	6.1	6.1	36.2	33.0	36.3	34.9	5.7	3.8	3.0	2.4
	Switzerland	18.9	m	24.4	m	30.5	m	29.4	26.4	12.2	9.9	3.4	1.9
	Turkey[2]	15.1	m	15.1	15.1	20.9	m	21.0	20.8	3.0	3.0	0.4	n
	United Kingdom	11.8	11.1	16.2	15.1	47.8	35.6	39.7	34.3	22.3	14.8	2.1	1.2
	United States	10.7	10.5	10.7	10.5	37.8	m	37.8	36.7	17.4	15.5	1.6	1.2
	OECD average	10.4		13.7		38.6		37.8		12.7		1.5	
	EU21 average	11.1		14.2		37.6		36.6		11.8		1.6	
Other G20	Argentina[1]	m	m	20.4	m	m	m	11.7	m	1.1	m	0.1	m
	Brazil[2]	m	m	4.5	4.5	m	m	26.2	26.1	1.3	1.2	0.4	n
	China	m	m	m	m	m	m	m	m	m	m	m	m
	India	m	m	m	m	m	m	m	m	m	m	m	m
	Indonesia	m	m	5.6	m	m	m	12.0	m	1.5	m	0.1	m
	Russian Federation[2]	m	m	28.0	27.9	m	m	51.7	51.5	0.7	m	1.4	m
	Saudi Arabia	m	m	m	m	m	m	m	m	m	m	m	m
	South Africa	m	m	m	m	m	m	m	m	m	m	m	m

Notes: Refer to Annex 1 for information on the method used to calculate graduation rates (gross rates versus net rates) and the corresponding typical ages. Mismatches between the coverage of the population data and the graduate data mean that the graduation rates for those countries that are net exporters of students may be underestimated and those that are net importers may be overestimated. The adjusted graduation rates seek to compensate for that.

1. Year of reference 2008.

2. The graduation rates are calculated for foreign students (defined on the basis of their country of citizenship). These data are not comparable with data on international graduates and are therefore presented separately in Chart A3.4.

Source: OECD. Argentina, Indonesia: UNESCO Institute for Statistics (World Education Indicators Programme). See Annex 3 for notes *(www.oecd.org/edu/eag2011)*.

***Please** refer to the Reader's Guide for information concerning the symbols replacing missing data.*

StatLink http://dx.doi.org/10.1787/888932462472

Table A3.4. **Structure of tertiary education: Main programme blocks (2009)**

Proportion of degrees following the Bologna structures
(or in programmes that lead to a similar degree in non-European countries)

		Of which						
	Proportion of degrees following the Bologna structures[1] 2009	Degrees for less than 3 years but considered to be at tertiary level and part of the Bologna structure[1] (first degree)	Bachelor's degrees 3-4 years of duration (first degree)	Master's degrees 4-8 years of cumulative duration (second degree)	Long first-degrees considered to be part of the Bologna structure[1] (duration 5 or more years)	Ph.D. and doctorates	Proportion of degrees outside the Bologna structures[1] (ISCED levels 5A, 5B and 6)	Proportion of degrees following the Bologna structures[1] 2008
	(1)	(2)	(3)	(4)	(5)	(6)	(7)	(8)
OECD								
Australia[2]	**69**	a	46	19	2	2	**31**	*69*
Austria	**38**	n	26	8	n	4	**62**	*32*
Belgium	**88**	a	59	27	a	2	**12**	*71*
Canada	**m**	m	m	m	m	m	**m**	*m*
Chile	**m**	m	m	m	m	m	**m**	*m*
Czech Republic	**74**	a	48	24	a	2	**26**	*66*
Denmark	**100**	12	57	25	3	2	**m**	*100*
Estonia[3]	**97**	a	75	18	3	n	**3**	*94*
Finland	**92**	a	69	19	n	4	**8**	*56*
France	**86**	26	31	18	9	2	**14**	*87*
Germany[3]	**19**	a	15	4	a	a	**81**	*14*
Greece	**m**	m	m	m	m	m	**m**	*m*
Hungary	**22**	a	18	1	n	2	**78**	*3*
Iceland	**100**	3	68	25	2	1	**n**	*100*
Ireland	**100**	25	47	26	m	2	**a**	*100*
Israel	**m**	m	m	m	m	m	**m**	*m*
Italy	**90**	a	57	26	7	m	**10**	*85*
Japan	**m**	m	m	m	m	m	**m**	*m*
Korea	**100**	34	51	13	1	2	**m**	*100*
Luxembourg	**m**	m	m	m	m	m	**m**	*m*
Mexico	**m**	m	m	m	m	m	**m**	*m*
Netherlands	**98**	a	69	26	a	3	**2**	*96*
New Zealand	**52**	n	43	6	1	1	**48**	*56*
Norway	**100**	6	62	23	5	3	**a**	*100*
Poland	**99**	a	38	41	19	1	**1**	*100*
Portugal[3]	**73**	a	56	8	9	n	**27**	*57*
Slovak Republic	**96**	a	53	22	18	3	**4**	*95*
Slovenia[3]	**13**	a	10	2	n	n	**87**	*5*
Spain[3]	**6**	n	n	6	n	n	**94**	*4*
Sweden	**91**	3	43	36	4	6	**9**	*m*
Switzerland[3]	**33**	n	24	9	n	n	**67**	*26*
Turkey	**100**	38	54	7	m	2	**a**	*m*
United Kingdom	**86**	15	40	23	6	3	**14**	*77*
United States	**100**	35	43	20	a	2	**a**	*100*
OECD average	**73**	7	44	18	3	2	**27**	*68*
EU21 average	**67**	5	42	16	3	2	**33**	*67*
Other G20								
Argentina	**m**	m	m	m	m	m	**m**	*m*
Brazil	**a**	a	a	a	a	a	**a**	*a*
China	**m**	m	m	m	m	m	**m**	*m*
India	**m**	m	m	m	m	m	**m**	*m*
Indonesia	**m**	m	m	m	m	m	**m**	*m*
Russian Federation[3]	**6**	a	5	1	m	a	**94**	*6*
Saudi Arabia	**m**	m	m	m	m	m	**m**	*m*
South Africa	**m**	m	m	m	m	m	**m**	*m*

1. Or in programmes that lead to a similar degree in non-European countries.
2. Year of reference 2008.
3. Some Ph.D. degrees still allocated in Column (7).

Source: OECD. See Annex 3 for notes *(www.oecd.org/edu/eag2011).*

Please refer to the Reader's Guide for information concerning the symbols replacing missing data.

StatLink http://dx.doi.org/10.1787/888932462491

INDICATOR A4

TO WHICH FIELDS OF EDUCATION ARE STUDENTS ATTRACTED?

- Women represent the majority of students and graduates in almost all OECD countries and largely dominate in the fields of education, health and welfare, and humanities and arts. Men dominate in engineering, manufacturing and construction.
- In the vast majority of countries, more than two-thirds of graduates in the field of education and the field of health and welfare in 2009 were women. However, in 26 of the 33 countries, women represented fewer than 30% of graduates in the fields of engineering, manufacturing and construction.

Chart A4.1. Percentage of tertiary degrees awarded to women, by field of education (2009)

Only those fields in which fewer than 30% or more than 70% of women graduated in 2009 are shown in the graph below

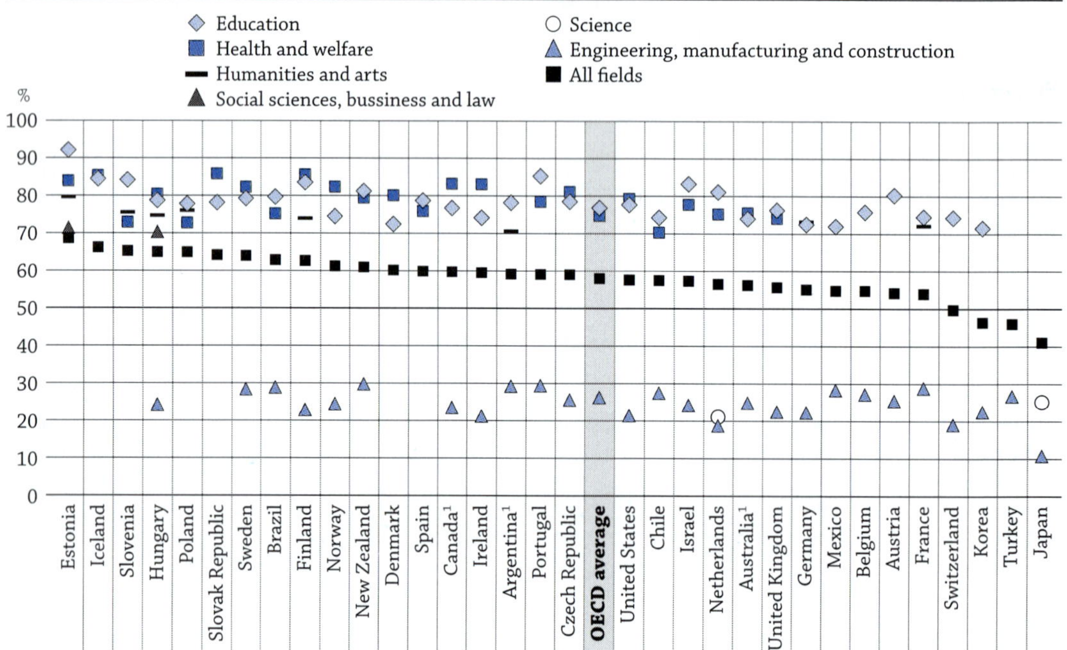

Note: Agriculture and Services are not included in the chart as they account for less than 5% of graduates (on average among OECD countries).

1. Year of reference 2008.

Countries are ranked in descending order of the percentage of tertiary degrees awarded to women in 2009.

Source: OECD. Argentina: UNESCO Institute for Statistics (World Education Indicators Programme). Table A4.3a. See Annex 3 for notes (*www.oecd.org/edu/eag2011*).

StatLink http://dx.doi.org/10.1787/888932460097

Context

Faced with an economic downturn and shrinking budgets, governments need to invest in the fields of education that respond to labour-market needs. Parents and students, too, need to choose prospective fields carefully. The choice is sometimes made early in a child's education, such as when children are directed towards vocational or academic programmes or, later on, if they decide to pursue tertiary studies. Students' preferences and abilities, and the cost, duration and location of higher education can all influence the choice of a field of study, as can changes in the labour market, differences in potential earnings among occupations and sectors, and admissions policies and practices of tertiary education institutions. In turn, the relative popularity of various fields of education affects the demand for programmes and teaching staff, as well as the supply of new graduates.

Other findings

- **Most boys in vocational programmes at the upper secondary level choose to study engineering, manufacturing and construction** while girls in such programmes opt for several different fields of education, notably business, law, social sciences, health and services.
- **Students entering tertiary education overwhelmingly choose social sciences, business and law as their fields of education** in all countries except Finland and Korea.
- **In Germany, more than 60% of students in tertiary-type B (shorter pratically oriented education) choose health and welfare programmes.** Around one-third of students in the Czech Republic, Japan, the Netherlands and the United Kingdom also choose health and welfare programmes; in the United States the proportion is close to 40%.
- **International students prefer social sciences, business and law programmes more than all students in tertiary education** do, particularly in Australia, Estonia, the Netherlands and Portugal. International students in eastern European countries, Belgium, Italy and Spain tend to prefer health programmes.

Trends

The proportion of women graduates has increased from 54% in 2000 to 58% in 2009. During that period, **the proportion of science graduates who are women has been stable at around 40% while the proportion of women in engineering increased slightly from 23% to 26%.**

Analysis

Upper secondary vocational graduates, by field of education

Vocational education and training is chosen by an average of around 50% of students in upper secondary education; the other 50% of students remain in general programmes (see Indicator A2). The priority for many countries is to provide young people with the right skills to find a suitable job and to provide adults with an opportunity to update their skills throughout their working lives. Governments should link the field of study proposed at this level of education with labour-market needs.

The distribution of upper secondary vocational graduates across fields of education sheds light on the relative importance of different fields from country to country. This helps policy makers to ensure that the demand for qualified vocational trainers, who are also adequately prepared to teach, is met. Policies must also ensure that vocational teachers, trainers and training institutions continue to develop and update their skills and equipment to meet current and future labour-market needs. Efficient and effective delivery of vocational education and training is necessary to raise the status of these programmes and can help reduce the number of dropouts (see Indicator A2 on successful completion of upper secondary programmes).

Not all countries offer vocational programmes at this level: pre-vocational and vocational graduation rates are over 70% in Austria, Belgium, Finland, the Netherlands, Slovenia and Switzerland, while in Brazil, Canada, Estonia, Hungary, Indonesia, Japan, Korea, Mexico and Turkey the rates are below 30% (Table A4.1b, available on line).

Chart A4.2. **Distribution of graduates in upper secondary vocational programmes in OECD countries, by field of education and gender (2009)**

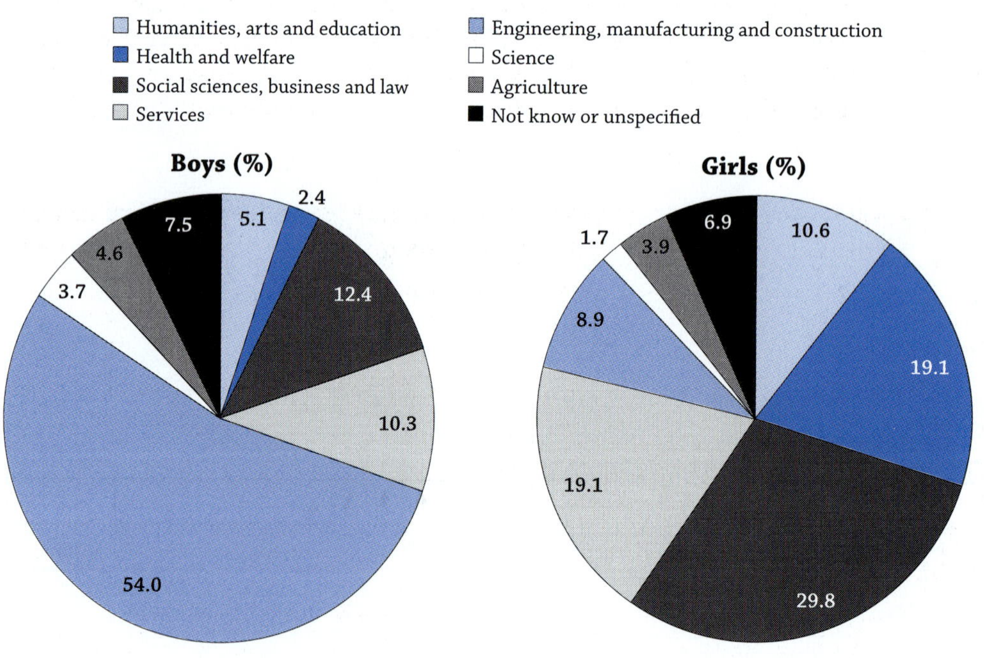

Source: OECD. Table A4.1a. See Annex 3 for notes (*www.oecd.org/edu/eag2011*).
StatLink http://dx.doi.org/10.1787/888932460116

Gender

On average among countries with available data, there is no clear gender trend for pre-vocational and vocational upper secondary graduation rates. Although 47% of boys and 44% of girls in OECD countries graduated from vocational programmes in 2009, graduates who are girls outnumbered those who are boys in Argentina, Australia, Belgium, Brazil, Chile, Denmark, Finland, Ireland, New Zealand, Portugal and Spain. Nevertheless, at this level of education, girls and boys graduate from different fields of education (Table A4.1a).

Differences in young people's choice of study can be attributed to traditional perceptions of gender roles and identities as well as the wide acceptance of the cultural values associated with particular fields of education. For example, while some fields, especially science, engineering, manufacturing and construction, are widely regarded as "masculine" and more suited for men, other fields of study, often care-related fields, such as education and health, are defined as "feminine" and more appropriate for women (Eurydice, 2010).

More than one boy in two graduated from upper secondary vocational education in the fields of engineering, manufacturing and construction (Chart A4.2). In almost all countries with available data, these fields were predominant; and in Estonia and Norway, three-quarters of all graduates in these fields were boys (Table A4.1a).

For girls, the main field of education varied among countries. In Austria, the Czech Republic, France, Germany, Indonesia, Japan, Luxembourg, New Zealand, the Slovak Republic, Slovenia and Switzerland, girls tended to prefer social sciences, business and law. In Australia, Denmark, Finland, the Netherlands and Norway, health and welfare programmes were more popular among girls, while girls in Estonia, Hungary and Poland were more attracted to the service professions, and girls in Iceland, Korea, Spain and Sweden tended to pursue studies in education, humanities and arts (Table A4.1a).

Girls and boys might choose different fields of education because of differences in their personal preferences, differences in performance in reading, mathematics and science, and different expectations about labour-market outcomes, and/or because education policies may lead to gender sorting early in their education. The results from the 2009 PISA reports show that girls outperform boys in reading in every OECD country, with the average gender gap in reading proficiency equivalent to about a year's worth of schooling. While boys score higher in mathematics, there is no gender gap in science (OECD, 2010a).

Entry rate into tertiary programmes, by field of education

In almost all countries, the largest proportion of students chooses tertiary programmes in the fields of social sciences, business and law. In 2009, these fields received the highest share of new entrants in all countries except Finland and Korea. In Finland, the proportion of new entrants was highest in engineering, manufacturing and construction, while in Korea that proportion was highest in education, humanities and arts (Chart A4.3).

Chart A4.3. Distribution of new entrants into tertiary programmes, by field of education (2009)

Only those fields in which more than 20% of students entered a tertiary programme in 2009 are shown in the graph below

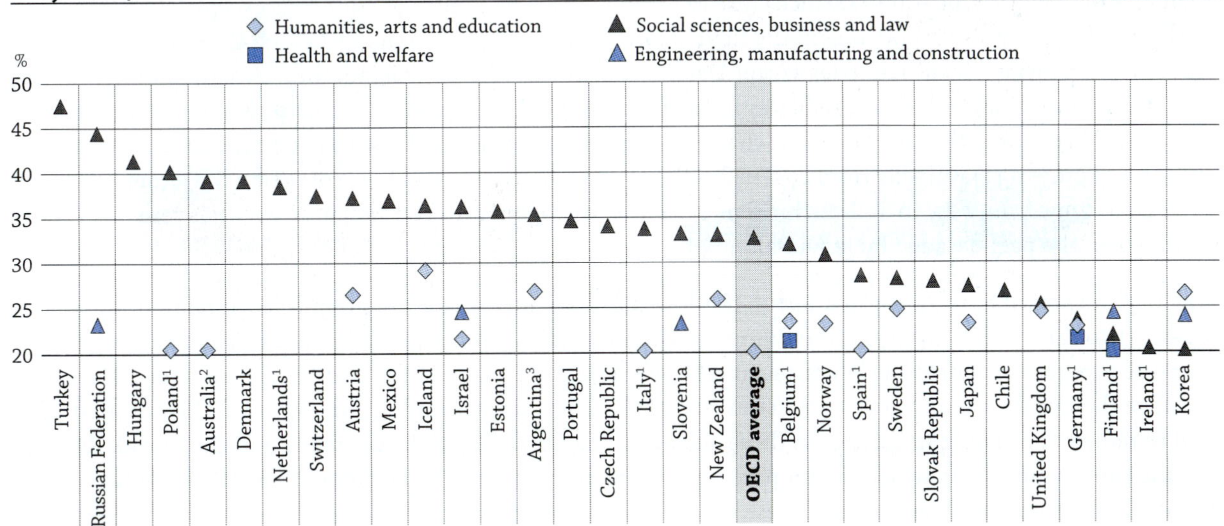

1. Excludes advanced research programmes.
2. Excludes tertiary-type B programmes.
3. Year of reference 2008.

Countries are ranked in descending order of new entrants in social sciences, business and law programmes in 2009.

Source: OECD. Argentina: UNESCO Institute for Statistics (World Education Indicators Programme). Table A4.2a. See Annex 3 for notes (*www.oecd.org/edu/eag2011*).

StatLink http://dx.doi.org/10.1787/888932460135

Science-related fields, which include science and engineering, are less popular: on average, fewer than a quarter of all students enter these fields (Table A4.2a). This low level of participation is partly due to the under-representation of women: on average in 2009, only 13% of new entrants into tertiary education who were young women chose these fields, as compared with 38% of new entrants who were young men. The proportion of women in science-related fields ranged from 5% in Japan and the Netherlands to 20% in Israel, while the proportion of men in these fields ranged from 26% in the Netherlands to 57% in Finland (Table A4.2b, available on line).

The distribution of entrants into advanced research programmes by field of education is very different from that of tertiary education at a whole. In 2009, 22% of new doctoral entrants undertook studies in science compared to the 9% of all new tertiary entrants who chose this field. In Chile, Israel, New Zealand and Norway, more than 30% of advanced research students chose this field (Table A4.2c, available on line).

Tertiary graduates, by field of education

The distribution of graduates by field of education is driven by the relative popularity of these fields among students, the relative number of students admitted to these fields in universities and equivalent institutions, and the degree structure of the various disciplines in a particular country.

In 2009, on average in OECD countries, more than one-third of tertiary-type A (largely theory-based) and advanced research graduates obtained a degree in social sciences, business or law. This ranged from fewer than 25% in Finland, Korea, and Sweden to more than 50% in the Russian Federation and Slovenia. The fields of education, humanities and arts accounted for the largest concentration of tertiary-type A and advanced research qualifications in Germany and Korea, and the field of health and welfare attracted the most students at these levels in Denmark and Sweden. An average of only 21% of tertiary-type A and advanced research students received qualifications in science-related fields (science and engineering) in OECD countries. The proportion varied from less than 15% in Brazil, Iceland, the Netherlands and the United States, to more than 30% in Korea (Table A4.3b, available on line).

Gender

In 2009, the proportion of women among tertiary-type A and advanced research graduates in OECD countries ranged from 41% in Japan to 69% in Estonia. However, the breakdown by gender varied considerably by field of study. Women largely predominated among these graduates in the field of education: they represented more than 70% of tertiary-type A and advanced research students in this field in all countries except Japan (59%) and Turkey (55%). They also dominated in the field of health and welfare, averaging 75% of all degrees awarded in this field. In contrast, in all countries except Denmark, Estonia, Iceland, Poland, the Slovak Republic, Slovenia and Spain, fewer than 30% of all graduates in the fields of engineering, manufacturing and construction were women (Chart A4.1). This situation has changed only slightly since 2000, with the proportion of women in these fields growing marginally from 23% in 2000 to 26% in 2009 – even as the proportion of women graduates in all fields grew from 54% to 58% during that period. The proportion of women in science has remained stable at 40% over the past decade (Table A4.3a).

OECD governments are concerned about the low numbers of women pursuing science-related studies. In an effort to raise those numbers, the European Union established a series of indicators and targets to help measure progress in addressing key issues at all levels of learning. One of the five benchmarks for 2010 was to increase the number of university graduates in mathematics, science and technology (MST) by at least 15%, and to reduce the gender imbalance in these subjects. The Czech Republic, Germany and the Slovak Republic are the three countries in which the proportion of women in science grew by more than 10 percentage points between 2000 and 2009; as a result, these countries are now closer to the OECD average in this respect. In Switzerland, there was an increase in the number of women graduates, to 50% of all graduates in 2009, and an 8-9 percentage point increase in the proportion of women in science-related fields, but that proportion is still below the OECD average. In the Netherlands, the proportion of women graduates in tertiary-type A and advanced research programmes is 57%, around the OECD average; but in 2009, only 19% of graduates in engineering, manufacturing and construction and 21% of graduates in science were women (Table A4.3a).

Enrolment in tertiary programmes leading to direct entry into the labour market, by field of education

Tertiary-type B programmes are conceived with the aim of allowing students to enter directly into the labour market, and the fields of education in which they are concentrated differ markedly from those usually found in tertiary-type A and advanced research programmes. During times of structural readjustments in the labour market, tertiary-type B programmes can help adapt the workforce to new sectors of growth in employment.

For instance, countries show more diversified participation in tertiary-type B programmes than in tertiary-type A and advanced research programmes. As in more academic programmes, most students in tertiary-type B programmes in OECD countries are enrolled in social science, business or law programmes (an average of 25% of all students), but this proportion is 9 percentage points less than the share of students enrolled in the same fields of education in more academic programmes. On the other hand, students in tertiary-type B programmes prefer the fields of services and health – by ten and nine more percentage points, respectively, among students in the EU21 countries – more than do students in more academic programmes, and by eight and six percentage points more, respectively, among students in OECD countries (Chart A4.4).

Chart A4.4. Distribution of students enrolled in tertiary-type B, -type A and advanced research programmes in OECD countries, by field of education (2009)

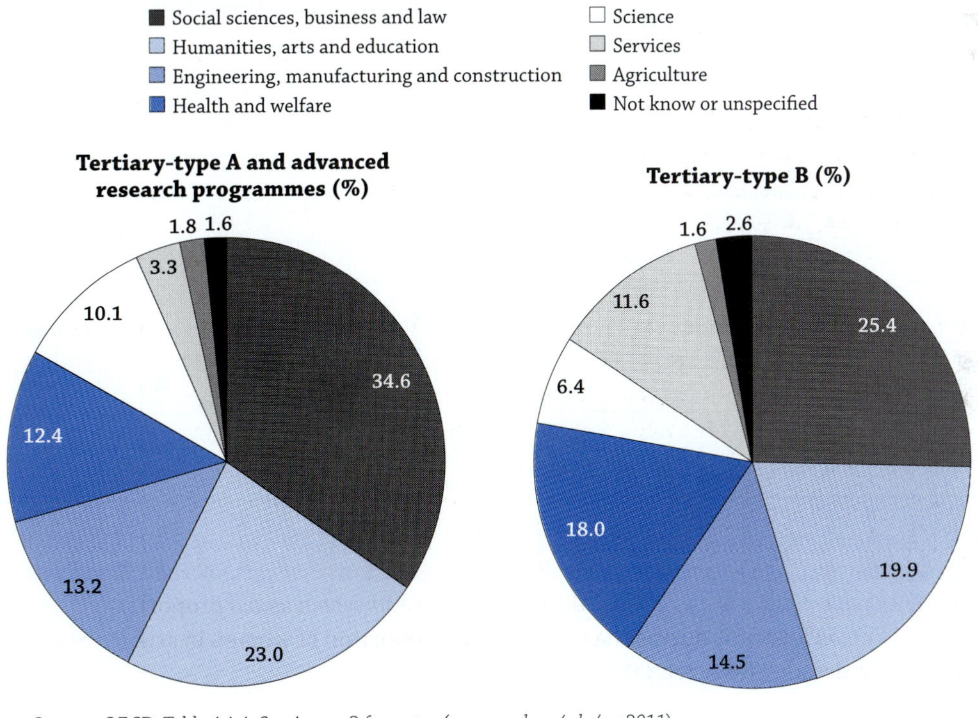

Source: OECD. Table A4.4. See Annex 3 for notes (*www.oecd.org/edu/eag2011*).
StatLink http://dx.doi.org/10.1787/888932460154

Countries also follow more diverse patterns of specialisation in tertiary-type B programmes than in more academic programmes. Some countries restrict tertiary-type B programmes to specific fields, such as services in Finland, humanities and arts in Italy, and education and health in Poland.

Health and welfare is the third most attractive field among tertiary-type B students, with more than 50% of students in Germany (63%) and Portugal (58%) enrolled in this field. It is also the first choice in the Czech Republic (32%), Japan (29%), the Slovak Republic (32%), the United Kingdom (29%) and the United States (38%) (Table A4.4). This preference is partly due to the progressive professionalisation of nursing, given more advanced medical technology, and the growing demand for highly specialised medical care (Table A4.4).

Engineering, manufacturing and construction are the fields of choice for tertiary-type B students in Israel (52%), Korea (33%), Mexico (34%), and the Russian Federation (36%). In Israel, Korea, and the Russian Federation, most of these students are enrolled specifically in engineering; in Mexico, most students are enrolled in manufacturing and processing. As among students in tertiary-type A and advanced research programmes, humanities and arts are the second field of choice for students in tertiary-type B programmes in the OECD area and in EU21 countries. However, these fields are the first choice of study among tertiary-type B students in Belgium (24%), Iceland (56%), Italy (100%) and Poland (89%) (Table A4.4).

Enrolment of international students, by field of education

By using the proportion of international students by field of education as a measure, one can identify magnet centres for student mobility. The distribution is linked to a wide variety of factors ranging from linguistic considerations and the recognition of degrees to the existence of centres of excellence or expertise in countries of destination (see Indicator C3). One pattern is clear: international students are less represented in the humanities and more strongly represented in social sciences, business and law.

Chart A4.5. Distribution of international and foreign students in tertiary programmes, by field of education (2009)

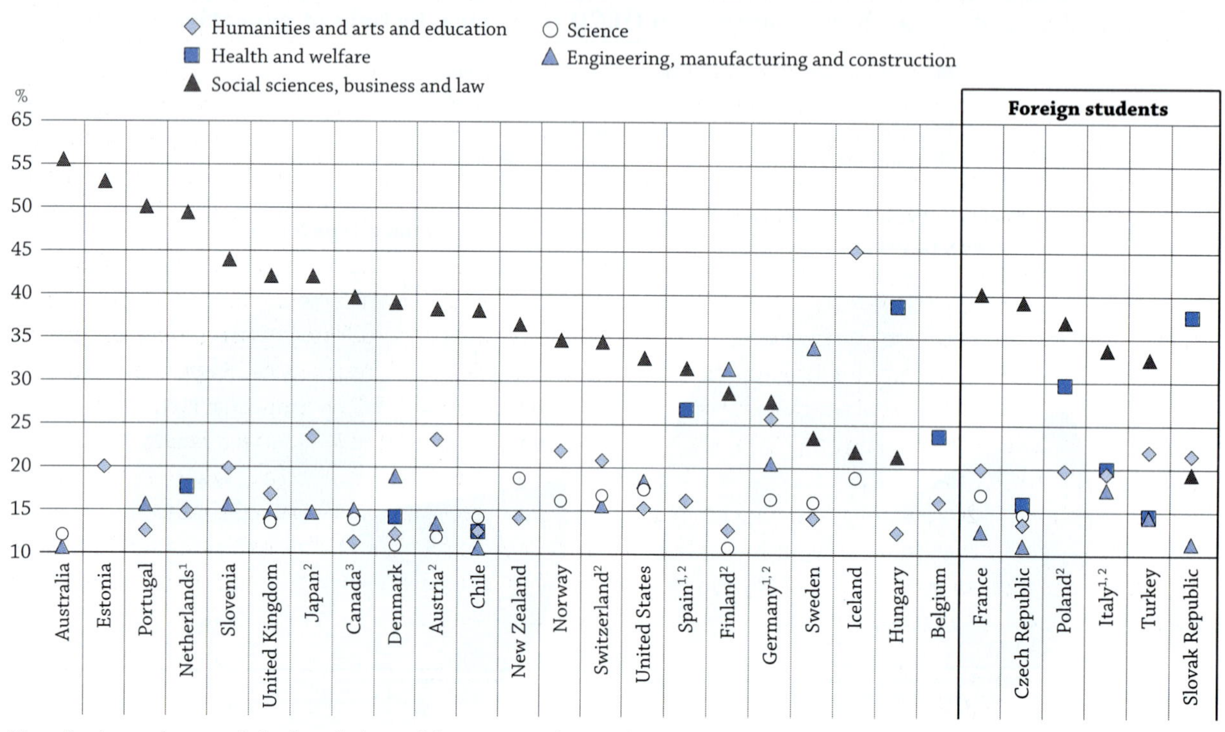

Note: Foreign students are defined on the basis of their country of citizenship; these data are not comparable with data on international students and are therefore presented separately in the table and chart.

1. Excludes advanced research programmes.
2. Excludes tertiary-type B programmes.
3. Year of reference 2008.

Countries are ranked in descending order of the proportion of international students enrolled in Social sciences, business and law in 2009.

Source: OECD. Table A4.5. See Annex 3 for notes (*www.oecd.org/edu/eag2011*).

StatLink http://dx.doi.org/10.1787/888932460173

As shown in Table A4.5, the sciences attract at least 15% of international students in Germany, Iceland, New Zealand, Norway, Sweden, Switzerland and the United States, and a similar proportion of foreign students in France, but fewer than 1 in 50 in Japan. However, the picture changes slightly when agriculture, engineering, manufacturing and construction programmes are also included among scientific disciplines. Some 50% of international students in Sweden are enrolled in these fields of education. The proportion of international students enrolled in agriculture, science or engineering is higher than 20% in 17 of 27 countries and is notably high in Canada (30%), Chile (31%), Denmark (34%), Finland (44%), Germany (39%), Switzerland (33%) and the United States (37%). Similarly, among countries for which data using the preferred definition of international students are not available, agriculture, science and engineering attract at least 20% of students in 4 of 6 countries and the proportion is higher than 25% of foreign students in the Czech Republic (28%) and France (30%). In contrast, few international students are enrolled in agriculture, science and engineering in Estonia, Japan, the Netherlands and Spain (Table A4.5).

Most countries that enrol large proportions of international students in agriculture, science and engineering offer their programmes in English. The large proportion of foreign students in scientific disciplines in Germany may reflect the country's strong tradition in these fields.

Non-English-speaking countries tend to enrol a higher proportion of international students in education, humanities and arts; these areas of study are preferred by 45% of international students in Iceland, and by over 20% in Austria, Germany, Japan, Norway and Switzerland, as well as by foreign students in the Slovak Republic and Turkey (Table A4.5).

International students in tertiary-type A and research programmes prefer business programmes more than all enrolled students do, and this field attracts the largest numbers of international students. This is true in 14 of 22 countries reporting international students and in 2 of 6 countries reporting foreign students. Around half of all international students are enrolled in social sciences, business or law in Australia (56%, 18 percentage points higher than the proportion of total enrolments), Estonia (53%, 16 percentage points higher), the Netherlands (49%, 12 percentage points higher) and Portugal (50%, 18 percentage points higher). Among countries for which data using the preferred definition of international students are not available, France has the largest proportion of foreign students enrolled in these subjects (40%) (Tables A4.4 and A4.5).

Enrolments in health programmes depend to a large extent on national policies relating to recognition of medical degrees. These programmes attract large proportions of international students in EU countries and the proportion is higher than that of total enrolments, especially in Eastern European countries. This is most notable in Belgium (24%, 8 percentage points higher than the proportion of total enrolments), Hungary (39%, 30 percentage points higher) and Spain (27%, 14 percentage points higher). Among countries for which data using the preferred definition of international students are not available, health and welfare programmes are also chosen by around one-third of foreign students in Poland (30%, 23 percentage points higher than the proportion of total enrolments) and the Slovak Republic (38%, 20 percentage points higher). Because many European countries impose quotas that restrict access to educational programmes in medicine, this increases the demand for training in other EU countries, where prospective students can both bypass those quotas and take advantage of EU countries' automatic recognition of medical degrees under the European Medical Directive (Tables A4.4 and A4.5).

Overall, the concentration of international students in various disciplines is due to many factors on both the supply and demand sides.

On the supply side, some destinations offer centres of excellence or traditional expertise that attract students from other countries in large numbers (e.g. Finland and Germany in science and engineering, manufacturing and construction). In humanities and arts, some destinations also have a natural monopoly on some programmes. This is especially obvious for linguistic or cultural studies (e.g. Austria, France, Germany and Japan).

On the demand side, the characteristics of international students can help to explain their concentration in certain fields of tertiary education. For instance, the almost universal use of English in scientific literature may explain why students in scientific disciplines are more likely to study in countries offering education programmes in English and less likely to enrol in countries where these are less common. Similarly, the demand for business training among Asian students may explain the strong concentration of international students in social sciences, business and law in neighbouring Australia and New Zealand and to a lesser extent in Japan. Finally, EU provisions for recognising medical degrees clearly influence the concentration of international students in health and welfare programmes in EU countries.

Graduates in science-related fields among those in employment

Examining the number of graduates in science-related fields (science and engineering, manufacturing and construction), per 100 000 25-34 year-olds in employment, provides another way of gauging the recent output of high-level skills from different education systems. The number of science graduates (all tertiary levels) per 100 000 employed persons ranges from below 1 000 in Hungary to above 2 500 in France, Korea and New Zealand (Chart A4.6).

Chart A4.6. Tertiary graduates in science-related fields among 25-34 year-olds in employment, by gender (2009)

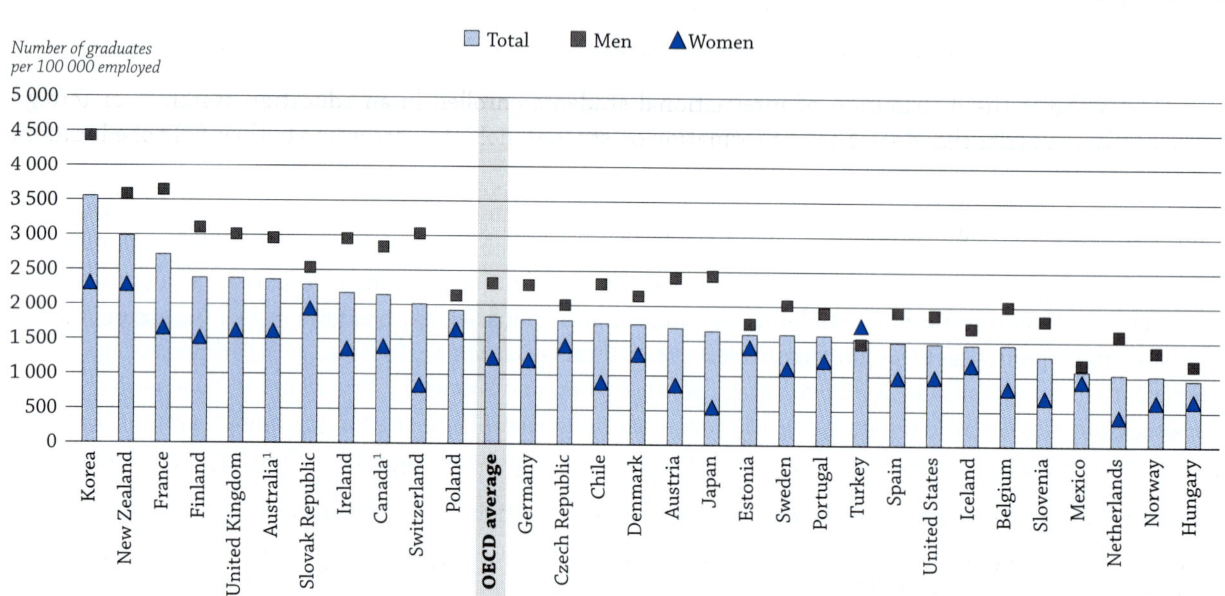

Note: Science-related fields include life sciences; physical sciences, mathematics and statistics, computing; engineering and engineering trades, manufacturing and processing, architecture and building.

1. Year of reference 2008 for the number of graduates.

Countries are ranked in descending order of the percentage of tertiary science-related graduates in tertiary-type A programmes per 100 000 employed 25-34 year-olds.

Source: OECD. Table A4.6. See Annex 3 for notes (*www.oecd.org/edu/eag2011*).

StatLink http://dx.doi.org/10.1787/888932460192

Per 100 000 25-34 year-olds in employment, fewer women than men graduate from science-related tertiary-type A education and advanced research programmes. The number of women science graduates ranges from fewer than 500 in Japan, the Netherlands and Slovenia, to more than 1 500 in Finland, Korea, New Zealand, Poland and the Slovak Republic, while the number of science graduates who are men varies from fewer than 1 000 in Chile, Slovenia and Turkey to around and over 2 500 in Finland, Korea, the Slovak Republic and the United Kingdom. The OECD average is around 1 100 women science graduates per 100 000 25-34 year-olds in employment, compared to approximately 1 800 graduates who are men (Chart A4.6).

This indicator does not provide information on the number of graduates actually employed in scientific fields or, more generally, the number of those using their degree-related skills and knowledge at work.

Definitions

Students are classified as **foreign students** if they are not citizens of the country in which the data are collected. While pragmatic and operational, this classification is inappropriate for capturing student mobility because of differing national policies regarding the naturalisation of immigrants (see Indicator C3 for a more detailed definition of student mobility).

Students are classified as **international students** if they left their country of origin and moved to another country for the purpose of study. Depending on country-specific immigration legislation, mobility arrangements, such as the free movement of individuals within the EU and the EEA, and availability of data, international students may be defined as students who are not permanent or usual residents of their country of study or as students who obtained their prior education in a different country, including another EU country.

Methodology

Data refer to the academic year 2008-09 and are based on the UOE data collection on education statistics administered by the OECD in 2010 (for details, see Annex 3 at *www.oecd.org/edu/eag2011*).

The fields of education used in the UOE data collection instruments follow the revised ISCED classification by field of education. The same classification is used for all levels of education.

Table A4.5 shows the distribution of international students enrolled in an education system – or foreign students for countries that do not have information on student mobility – according to their field of education.

The labour force data used in Table A4.6 are taken from the OECD Labour Force database, compiled from national labour force surveys and the European Labour Force Survey.

The statistical data for Israel are supplied by and under the responsibility of the relevant Israeli authorities. The use of such data by the OECD is without prejudice to the status of the Golan Heights, East Jerusalem and Israeli settlements in the West Bank under the terms of international law.

References

Education, Audiovisual and Culture Executive Agency (Eurydice) (2010), *Gender Differences in Educational Outcomes: Study on the Measures Taken and the Current Situation in Europe,* Eurydice, Brussels.

OECD (2010a), *PISA 2009 Results: What Students Know and Can Do: Student Performance in Reading, Mathematics and Science* (Volume I), OECD, Paris.

The following additional material relevant to this indicator is available on line:

- ***Table A4.1b Distribution of upper secondary vocational graduates, by field of education (2009)***
  StatLink http://dx.doi.org/10.1787/888932462529
- ***Table A4.2b Distribution of tertiary new entrants, by field of education and gender (2009)***
  StatLink http://dx.doi.org/10.1787/888932462586
- ***Table A4.2c Distribution of new entrants into advanced research programmes, by field of education (2009)***
  StatLink http://dx.doi.org/10.1787/888932462605
- ***Table A4.3b Distribution of tertiary-type A and advanced research programmes graduates, by field of education (2009)***
  StatLink http://dx.doi.org/10.1787/888932462643

Table A4.1a. Distribution of upper secondary vocational graduates, by field of education and gender (2009)

		Boys									Girls								
		Pre-vocational/ vocational programmes' graduation rates	Humanities, arts and education	Health and welfare	Social sciences, business and law	Services	Engineering, manufacturing and construction	Science	Agriculture	Not known or unspecified	Pre-vocational/ vocational programmes' graduation rates	Humanities, arts and education	Health and welfare	Social sciences, business and law	Services	Engineering, manufacturing and construction	Science	Agriculture	Not known or unspecified
		(1)	(2)	(5)	(6)	(7)	(8)	(9)	(14)	(15)	(16)	(17)	(20)	(21)	(22)	(23)	(24)	(29)	(30)
OECD	Australia[1]	42	2.2	4.8	13.1	10.8	59.7	2.4	4.9	2.1	44	6.4	32.3	31.0	17.2	4.5	1.5	1.9	5.3
	Austria	85	1.0	1.1	10.2	8.3	43.4	1.3	8.6	26.1	63	2.1	7.8	33.0	21.3	5.5	0.2	8.5	21.7
	Belgium	64	13.3	1.6	9.9	3.8	26.7	2.6	1.3	40.9	77	21.4	9.5	14.9	7.6	1.7	0.3	0.5	44.2
	Canada[1]	4	m	m	m	m	m	m	m	m	2	m	m	m	m	m	m	m	m
	Chile	30	m	m	m	m	m	m	m	m	31	m	m	m	m	m	m	m	m
	Czech Republic	63	2.8	1.2	11.1	13.2	68.7	n	3.0	n	59	6.1	13.6	35.6	28.0	11.3	n	5.5	n
	Denmark	45	2.2	3.4	17.4	10.4	61.1	0.1	5.5	n	48	1.1	46.0	34.8	8.5	6.3	0.2	3.1	n
	Estonia	27	1.4	n	0.7	8.9	82.3	2.3	4.4	n	14	6.9	n	14.7	42.2	29.5	1.7	4.9	n
	Finland	89	4.2	3.3	10.0	16.1	57.1	4.5	4.7	n	100	7.4	28.5	21.3	26.7	10.0	1.1	5.0	n
	France	63	1.9	2.2	14.3	11.3	64.1	n	6.2	n	61	2.1	27.8	34.4	27.6	5.8	n	2.3	n
	Germany	50	2.0	2.4	26.8	9.4	52.5	3.5	3.1	0.3	40	3.0	15.7	52.7	19.7	6.4	0.7	1.3	0.4
	Greece	m	m	m	m	m	m	m	m	m	m	m	m	m	m	m	m	m	m
	Hungary	20	0.8	0.6	5.5	17.7	70.0	n	5.4	n	13	1.9	8.4	30.9	37.7	15.2	n	5.8	n
	Iceland	59	9.2	0.9	9.5	8.5	68.1	1.5	2.3	n	50	27.4	20.5	21.5	20.9	5.9	0.3	3.6	n
	Ireland	48	6.9	5.5	9.5	6.3	3.1	4.3	4.5	59.9	76	5.2	28.5	16.2	5.0	0.2	0.4	1.7	42.9
	Israel	34	m	m	m	m	m	m	m	m	30	m	m	m	m	m	m	m	m
	Italy	66	m	m	m	m	m	m	m	m	52	m	m	m	m	m	m	m	m
	Japan	25	0.1	1.4	17.8	2.5	56.2	0.2	11.1	10.6	21	0.3	9.6	41.3	12.8	8.2	0.2	10.9	16.6
	Korea	24	15.3	0.1	5.5	3.3	63.6	10.4	1.7	n	23	30.9	0.6	20.2	4.9	28.6	13.2	1.7	n
	Luxembourg	44	4.4	2.6	26.0	3.9	52.5	4.1	6.6	n	42	16.4	14.3	52.2	8.0	7.0	0.4	1.7	n
	Mexico	4	m	m	m	m	m	m	m	m	4	m	m	m	m	m	m	m	m
	Netherlands	71	3.8	5.0	18.4	22.2	38.7	7.4	4.6	n	70	6.9	46.5	22.7	18.4	2.6	0.3	2.6	n
	New Zealand	43	14.5	2.0	18.8	12.2	20.9	2.5	9.6	19.6	54	19.5	6.1	39.2	11.9	2.1	3.5	8.0	9.7
	Norway	46	0.7	4.2	1.9	11.3	75.3	4.1	2.5	n	29	4.6	49.1	11.5	23.1	9.0	0.3	2.4	n
	Poland	44	1.1	n	7.8	14.8	63.2	6.5	6.3	0.2	27	2.9	n	37.4	42.5	10.6	1.5	4.6	0.4
	Portugal	29	m	m	m	m	m	m	m	m	33	m	m	m	m	m	m	m	m
	Slovak Republic	66	3.4	1.7	11.5	20.2	60.2	n	3.1	n	62	6.9	10.3	37.9	29.4	11.6	n	3.9	n
	Slovenia	80	2.6	4.5	16.2	10.2	56.6	6.6	3.2	n	71	10.9	18.6	41.8	14.6	8.5	0.1	5.5	n
	Spain	40	18.6	2.3	7.5	13.4	40.4	6.4	2.8	8.7	42	34.2	18.6	23.3	14.5	3.5	1.2	0.9	3.9
	Sweden	47	12.6	5.1	4.2	8.6	63.2	0.1	3.0	3.2	42	33.3	22.4	10.8	13.9	8.5	0.2	7.6	3.3
	Switzerland	76	2.2	2.1	22.5	6.3	57.0	3.6	5.9	0.2	66	4.0	21.9	47.4	14.6	9.0	0.4	2.7	n
	Turkey	15	0.8	1.3	12.5	5.3	45.1	19.2	n	15.8	15	4.3	22.3	17.5	7.6	11.9	13.8	n	22.6
	United Kingdom	m	m	m	m	m	m	m	m	m	m	m	m	m	m	m	m	m	m
	United States	m	m	m	m	m	m	m	m	m	m	m	m	m	m	m	m	m	m
	OECD average	47	5.1	2.4	12.4	10.3	54.0	3.7	4.6	7.5	44	10.6	19.1	29.8	19.1	8.9	1.7	3.9	6.9
	EU21 average	54	4.9	2.5	12.2	11.7	53.2	2.9	4.5	8.2	51	9.9	18.6	30.3	21.5	8.5	0.5	3.8	6.9
Other G20	Argentina[1]	30	m	m	m	m	m	m	m	m	40	m	m	m	m	m	m	m	m
	Brazil	7	m	m	m	m	m	m	m	m	11	m	m	m	m	m	m	m	m
	China	43	m	m	m	m	m	m	m	m	43	m	m	m	m	m	m	m	m
	India	m	m	m	m	m	m	m	m	m	m	m	m	m	m	m	m	m	m
	Indonesia	20	1.7	2.8	49.1	1.6	31.7	n	5.3	7.9	13	2.2	5.7	49.0	n	29.1	n	3.7	10.4
	Russian Federation	37	m	m	m	m	m	m	m	m	14	m	m	m	m	m	m	m	m
	Saudi Arabia	m	m	m	m	m	m	m	m	m	m	m	m	m	m	m	m	m	m
	South Africa	m	m	m	m	m	m	m	m	m	m	m	m	m	m	m	m	m	m

Note: Columns showing the breakdown of humanities, arts and education (3, 4, 18 and 19) and science (10-13 and 25-28) are available for consultation on line (see Statlink below).

1. Year of reference 2008.

Source: OECD. Argentina, China, Indonesia: UNESCO Institute for Statistics (World Education Indicators Programme). See Annex 3 for notes (*www.oecd.org/edu/eag2011*).

Please refer to the Reader's Guide for information concerning the symbols replacing missing data.

StatLink http://dx.doi.org/10.1787/888932462548

Table A4.2a. Distribution of new entrants into tertiary programmes, by field of education (2009)

		Humanities, arts and education	Health and welfare	Social sciences, business and law	Services	Engineering, manufacturing and construction	Science	Agriculture	Not known or unspecified
		(1)	(4)	(5)	(6)	(7)	(8)	(13)	(14)
OECD	Australia[1]	20.5	15.4	39.2	3.7	8.8	11.3	0.9	0.2
	Austria	26.5	6.5	37.2	2.7	16.0	9.9	1.0	0.2
	Belgium[2]	23.4	21.2	32.0	1.9	10.9	6.7	3.1	0.8
	Canada	m	m	m	m	m	m	m	m
	Chile	17.8	19.6	26.8	9.4	16.7	7.4	2.2	0.2
	Czech Republic	17.2	11.4	34.1	6.1	15.5	11.4	4.3	n
	Denmark	15.5	19.4	39.2	2.5	12.0	9.1	2.3	n
	Estonia	18.8	9.4	35.7	9.2	14.1	10.6	2.1	n
	Finland[2]	14.9	20.1	21.9	7.2	24.3	9.1	2.5	n
	France	m	m	m	m	m	m	m	m
	Germany[2]	22.9	21.5	23.6	2.9	15.2	11.7	1.4	0.8
	Greece	m	m	m	m	m	m	m	m
	Hungary	12.7	9.2	41.4	13.3	14.2	7.1	2.2	n
	Iceland	29.2	9.3	36.4	1.6	13.3	9.6	0.6	n
	Ireland[2]	18.2	12.3	20.4	6.0	11.5	12.1	1.4	18.2
	Israel	21.6	5.6	36.3	0.5	24.6	8.6	0.4	2.4
	Italy[2]	20.2	11.8	33.8	3.6	14.9	9.3	2.1	4.4
	Japan	23.2	14.3	27.3	9.1	15.0	2.2	2.1	6.7
	Korea	26.5	13.2	20.2	7.3	24.0	7.9	1.0	n
	Luxembourg	m	m	m	m	m	m	m	m
	Mexico	15.0	9.6	36.9	4.2	19.8	11.7	2.5	0.4
	Netherlands[2]	19.0	18.1	38.5	7.3	9.0	5.9	1.1	1.0
	New Zealand	25.9	11.8	33.1	5.3	6.2	16.4	1.1	0.2
	Norway	23.1	17.5	30.9	6.6	8.1	9.0	0.9	3.8
	Poland[2]	20.5	6.9	40.2	7.8	14.5	8.4	1.7	n
	Portugal	16.0	14.6	34.6	7.0	18.0	8.2	1.6	n
	Slovak Republic	18.5	19.0	27.8	6.9	16.1	9.6	2.1	n
	Slovenia	12.5	8.7	33.2	11.5	23.2	7.4	3.5	n
	Spain[2]	20.2	12.9	28.5	8.0	16.4	8.1	0.9	5.1
	Sweden	24.7	13.9	28.2	3.5	18.5	9.8	1.1	0.2
	Switzerland	17.6	12.4	37.5	7.1	14.8	8.7	1.1	0.8
	Turkey	16.1	6.4	47.5	4.4	13.1	7.6	4.9	n
	United Kingdom	24.4	18.0	25.3	1.4	8.1	13.3	1.0	8.6
	United States	m	m	m	m	m	m	m	m
	OECD average	20.1	13.5	32.7	5.8	15.0	9.2	1.8	1.9
	EU21 average	18.6	13.8	32.5	5.8	15.8	9.4	1.9	2.2
Other G20	Argentina[3]	26.8	12.1	35.4	4.6	7.7	10.1	2.7	0.6
	Brazil	m	m	m	m	m	m	m	m
	China	m	m	m	m	m	m	m	m
	India	m	m	m	m	m	m	m	m
	Indonesia	m	m	m	m	m	m	m	m
	Russian Federation	11.4	5.2	44.4	5.3	23.3	6.1	1.5	2.9
	Saudi Arabia	m	m	m	m	m	m	m	m
	South Africa	m	m	m	m	m	m	m	m

Note: Columns showing the breakdown of humanities, arts and education (2 and 3) and science (9-12) are available for consultation on line (see Statlink below).

1. Exclude tertiary-type B programmes.
2. Exclude advanced research programmes.
3. Year of reference 2008.

Source: OECD. Argentina: UNESCO Institute for Statistics (World Education Indicators Programme). See Annex 3 for notes (*www.oecd.org/edu/eag2011*).

Please refer to the Reader's Guide for information concerning the symbols replacing missing data.

StatLink http://dx.doi.org/10.1787/888932462567

Table A4.3a. Percentage of tertiary qualifications awarded to women in tertiary-type A and advanced research programmes, by field of education (2000, 2009)

		2009									2000								
		All fields	Education	Humanities and arts	Health and welfare	Social sciences, business and law	Services	Engineering, manufacturing and construction	Science	Agriculture	All fields	Education	Humanities and arts	Health and welfare	Social sciences, business and law	Services	Engineering, manufacturing and construction	Science	Agriculture
		(1)	(2)	(3)	(4)	(5)	(6)	(7)	(8)	(13)	(14)	(15)	(16)	(17)	(18)	(19)	(20)	(21)	(26)
OECD	Australia[1]	**56.2**	74.0	64.1	75.6	53.4	54.0	24.8	37.1	57.2	**56.5**	74.8	67.0	75.9	51.9	54.8	21.5	41.1	43.7
	Austria	**54.2**	80.3	65.6	67.1	57.6	38.7	25.5	33.3	62.2	**46.2**	72.1	59.1	59.1	49.3	36.6	18.0	32.9	51.6
	Belgium	**54.8**	75.8	64.2	64.1	57.8	40.7	27.2	38.3	49.2	**50.1**	70.2	62.4	59.2	52.1	43.5	21.1	37.8	40.3
	Canada[1]	**59.8**	76.8	64.6	83.2	57.9	60.4	23.5	49.3	57.7	**57.6**	72.7	62.9	73.6	57.5	61.2	22.7	45.0	50.7
	Chile	**57.5**	74.3	61.3	70.4	52.6	45.5	27.5	35.8	46.4	**m**	m	m	m	m	m	m	m	m
	Czech Republic	**59.0**	78.5	69.7	81.1	66.0	42.4	25.6	39.0	57.6	**50.9**	74.9	63.7	70.1	55.5	27.0	27.2	25.1	38.4
	Denmark	**60.2**	72.5	64.9	80.1	52.4	24.2	31.8	37.2	73.6	**49.2**	59.3	69.2	59.0	43.9	53.8	25.8	41.7	49.9
	Estonia	**68.7**	92.1	79.6	84.0	71.4	68.8	37.6	50.4	53.4	**m**	m	m	m	m	m	m	m	m
	Finland	**62.7**	83.6	74.0	85.6	68.0	77.6	22.8	46.0	59.1	**58.1**	82.2	73.9	83.8	64.4	71.6	18.6	45.8	45.7
	France	**54.0**	74.6	72.2	59.3	59.5	42.3	28.8	38.4	54.4	**56.1**	69.4	74.5	60.0	60.7	41.8	23.8	43.2	54.4
	Germany	**55.1**	72.5	73.3	68.4	52.1	55.9	22.3	43.8	53.4	**44.9**	70.9	67.2	56.2	41.8	58.0	19.6	31.6	46.5
	Greece	**m**	m	m	m	m	m	m	m	m	**m**	m	m	m	m	m	m	m	m
	Hungary	**65.0**	78.7	74.7	80.4	70.4	59.9	24.2	35.0	50.3	**55.1**	71.9	68.9	70.4	54.3	30.8	20.5	31.3	41.7
	Iceland	**66.2**	84.5	63.6	85.4	62.1	84.6	35.3	40.2	26.7	**66.9**	90.6	68.7	81.8	56.6	n	24.5	48.5	n
	Ireland	**59.5**	74.2	65.5	83.1	55.1	54.3	21.2	44.1	51.3	**56.7**	78.2	65.0	74.8	56.1	66.0	23.6	48.2	40.7
	Israel	**57.4**	83.3	60.2	77.8	55.1	76.1	24.2	46.8	56.4	**59.9**	87.7	69.1	67.6	55.9	m	23.7	42.5	48.0
	Italy	**m**	m	m	m	m	m	m	m	m	**m**	m	m	m	m	m	m	m	m
	Japan	**41.1**	59.3	68.1	56.6	34.4	90.6	10.8	25.2	38.7	**35.6**	59.4	69.3	50.1	26.0	m	8.9	24.6	37.7
	Korea	**46.4**	71.6	66.3	63.0	42.1	33.6	22.5	38.6	38.1	**44.6**	73.5	69.1	50.4	40.1	38.7	23.3	47.3	32.8
	Luxembourg	**m**	m	m	m	m	m	m	m	m	**m**	m	m	m	m	m	m	m	m
	Mexico	**54.8**	72.0	58.9	64.1	58.8	59.7	28.3	42.8	34.8	**51.6**	65.6	60.4	60.6	55.0	55.1	22.2	46.0	25.1
	Netherlands	**56.5**	81.1	56.7	75.2	52.4	53.4	18.7	21.1	51.7	**54.8**	75.9	61.0	75.6	48.9	48.5	12.5	28.3	38.4
	New Zealand	**61.0**	81.2	65.0	79.5	57.5	52.2	29.8	44.4	47.8	**60.6**	83.7	66.0	79.2	53.3	50.9	32.8	44.9	41.9
	Norway	**61.3**	74.5	58.7	82.4	55.8	41.9	24.5	36.5	59.5	**61.9**	78.6	62.0	81.5	49.4	36.4	26.6	28.1	46.1
	Poland	**65.0**	77.8	76.1	72.8	68.2	54.9	33.6	44.0	56.3	**64.4**	78.5	77.0	68.4	65.7	50.9	24.3	64.5	57.1
	Portugal	**59.1**	85.3	60.9	78.5	63.4	46.3	29.4	55.9	55.1	**64.5**	83.0	67.3	76.8	64.9	56.6	34.5	46.1	57.6
	Slovak Republic	**64.2**	78.2	66.7	85.9	68.6	45.0	31.1	42.1	42.8	**52.2**	75.1	55.8	69.4	56.4	28.8	29.8	30.2	32.6
	Slovenia	**65.3**	84.2	75.6	72.9	68.3	57.7	31.0	45.5	59.8	**m**	m	m	m	m	m	m	m	m
	Spain	**59.9**	78.7	64.5	75.9	60.7	58.2	33.9	41.5	50.2	**58.5**	77.1	64.3	76.3	59.6	59.9	27.0	46.5	45.7
	Sweden	**64.0**	79.3	61.3	82.3	62.0	59.0	28.4	46.4	61.3	**59.0**	79.1	63.4	78.7	57.8	45.2	24.8	46.8	51.5
	Switzerland	**49.7**	74.3	62.1	68.3	46.8	47.5	19.1	32.8	63.5	**37.8**	62.5	61.3	53.9	33.6	44.5	11.2	24.2	41.8
	Turkey	**46.0**	54.6	60.1	62.6	42.4	32.6	26.7	44.3	34.9	**41.0**	43.3	48.3	53.1	39.8	28.0	24.2	47.0	36.9
	United Kingdom	**55.7**	76.3	62.2	74.1	54.8	60.3	22.5	38.2	63.9	**53.7**	73.1	62.6	70.8	54.5	n	19.6	43.5	52.8
	United States	**57.6**	77.7	58.9	79.3	54.2	55.3	21.4	43.5	49.7	**56.5**	75.8	60.8	75.0	54.2	40.2	21.2	44.4	48.9
	OECD average	**58.0**	76.8	65.8	74.8	57.5	54.0	26.3	40.6	52.2	**53.7**	73.5	65.0	68.3	52.1	43.4	22.6	40.3	42.8
	EU21 average	**60.0**	79.3	67.8	76.2	61.3	53.5	27.4	41.4	55.9	**55.0**	75.2	66.1	69.2	55.4	44.9	23.2	40.4	46.7
Other G20	Argentina[1]	**59.2**	78.2	70.6	69.7	59.3	47.4	29.2	47.8	39.4	**m**	m	m	m	m	m	m	m	m
	Brazil	**62.9**	79.7	58.2	75.2	55.7	70.7	28.8	40.4	39.6	**m**	m	m	m	m	m	m	m	m
	China	**46.7**	m	m	m	m	m	m	m	m	**m**	m	m	m	m	m	m	m	m
	India	**m**	m	m	m	m	m	m	m	m	**m**	m	m	m	m	m	m	m	m
	Indonesia	**m**	m	m	m	m	m	m	m	m	**m**	m	m	m	m	m	m	m	m
	Russian Federation	**m**	m	m	m	m	m	m	m	m	**m**	m	m	m	m	m	m	m	m
	Saudi Arabia	**m**	m	m	m	m	m	m	m	m	**m**	m	m	m	m	m	m	m	m
	South Africa	**m**	m	m	m	m	m	m	m	m	**m**	m	m	m	m	m	m	m	m

Note: Columns showing the breakdown of science (9-12, 22-25) are available for consultation on line (see Statlink below).

1. Year of reference 2008.

Source: OECD. Argentina, China: UNESCO Institute for Statistics (World Education Indicators Programme). See Annex 3 for notes (*www.oecd.org/edu/eag2011*).

Please refer to the Reader's Guide for information concerning the symbols replacing missing data.

StatLink http://dx.doi.org/10.1787/888932462624

Table A4.4. Distribution of enrolment in tertiary programmes, by field of education (2009)

		Tertiary-type B programmes								Tertiary-type A and advanced research programmes							
		Humanities, arts and education	Health and welfare	Social sciences, business and law	Services	Engineering, manufacturing and construction	Science	Agriculture	Not known or unspecified	Humanities, arts and education	Health and welfare	Social sciences, business and law	Services	Engineering, manufacturing and construction	Science	Agriculture	Not known or unspecified
		(1)	(4)	(5)	(6)	(7)	(8)	(13)	(14)	(15)	(18)	(19)	(20)	(21)	(22)	(27)	(28)
OECD	Australia	11.6	19.3	41.3	4.4	15.2	5.3	2.3	0.5	21.3	17.0	37.9	3.3	9.3	9.9	1.0	0.2
	Austria	23.8	10.9	27.6	8.4	26.9	1.9	0.1	0.3	24.8	8.6	37.7	1.8	13.3	12.2	1.4	0.2
	Belgium[1]	23.9	23.7	23.0	2.1	7.4	2.6	1.3	15.9	19.0	15.8	36.0	0.8	12.5	9.1	4.1	2.6
	Canada[2]	12.3	18.5	33.7	7.4	14.1	5.2	1.8	7.1	21.4	11.6	30.7	3.1	9.1	10.2	0.9	12.9
	Chile	12.4	15.8	25.2	14.7	20.8	9.4	1.8	n	24.4	21.0	28.2	1.4	15.5	5.4	3.9	0.2
	Czech Republic	6.8	32.4	26.6	9.9	6.5	4.4	2.2	11.1	22.8	8.4	33.2	4.7	15.4	11.3	3.9	0.4
	Denmark	3.7	2.5	59.6	8.0	10.8	11.9	3.6	n	28.4	24.3	27.2	1.3	9.5	8.2	1.1	n
	Estonia	7.3	15.2	44.9	11.7	14.1	6.4	0.3	n	25.4	4.8	37.0	5.8	12.9	11.1	3.1	n
	Finland[3, 4]	n	n	n	100.0	n	n	n	n	19.3	15.3	22.5	5.1	25.2	10.4	2.2	n
	France	3.4	28.4	35.2	5.1	20.0	4.7	2.4	0.8	22.0	11.7	36.9	2.8	10.5	15.2	0.7	0.2
	Germany	9.5	62.8	8.5	4.5	12.1	0.5	1.3	0.8	24.1	8.4	30.2	2.4	16.1	17.3	1.4	0.1
	Greece	4.4	13.0	29.6	8.1	27.3	8.6	9.1	n	28.4	5.7	34.2	n	11.2	17.1	3.4	n
	Hungary	3.5	7.9	56.1	22.7	3.3	5.9	0.6	n	18.5	9.2	39.7	8.8	14.1	7.1	2.6	n
	Iceland	56.0	n	4.0	n	n	40.0	n	n	29.2	12.9	39.7	1.4	9.4	6.8	0.5	n
	Ireland	11.4	9.1	24.8	13.5	22.0	10.2	2.1	6.8	26.7	17.9	28.3	1.9	9.2	13.9	1.1	1.0
	Israel	32.3	4.9	6.4	a	51.7	a	a	4.7	22.6	7.2	46.0	0.5	12.2	11.0	0.6	n
	Italy[4]	100.0	n	n	n	n	n	n	n	21.3	13.2	34.9	2.8	15.5	7.7	2.2	2.4
	Japan	20.2	29.4	10.7	17.6	13.6	n	0.6	7.9	23.9	8.8	34.0	2.3	16.0	3.7	2.9	8.5
	Korea[3]	19.5	18.8	13.2	10.3	33.1	4.4	0.7	n	25.9	7.2	25.3	5.4	24.6	10.3	1.3	n
	Luxembourg	m	a	a	m	m	m	a	m	m	m	m	m	m	m	m	m
	Mexico	1.7	5.2	31.3	6.9	34.4	19.4	1.1	n	14.6	9.7	38.7	3.3	19.3	11.3	2.4	0.7
	Netherlands[4]	1.9	32.1	53.4	8.1	4.1	0.3	n	n	21.6	17.1	37.7	6.3	8.4	6.1	1.1	1.8
	New Zealand	25.2	10.0	27.6	8.5	7.0	10.4	1.4	10.0	23.9	14.7	36.2	1.5	6.6	15.2	0.9	1.0
	Norway[3, 4]	21.0	26.6	51.7	0.2	0.4	n	n	n	24.6	20.0	32.3	4.7	7.8	8.6	0.7	1.3
	Poland[4]	88.9	11.1	a	a	a	a	a	n	21.7	7.1	41.2	6.3	13.1	8.5	2.0	n
	Portugal[4]	n	57.8	27.9	5.0	0.5	8.8	n	n	13.6	16.7	32.0	6.3	22.2	7.3	1.9	n
	Slovak Republic[4]	25.8	32.2	7.6	25.5	5.3	3.7	n	n	20.3	17.8	30.3	5.8	14.8	8.6	2.3	n
	Slovenia	7.2	10.1	28.4	16.1	28.4	5.9	3.8	n	19.9	7.2	42.4	6.5	14.7	6.3	3.1	n
	Spain	19.3	12.7	22.9	14.5	20.7	9.3	0.6	0.1	20.5	12.5	33.2	3.4	17.0	10.5	2.0	0.9
	Sweden	7.4	10.4	27.6	13.8	25.3	10.4	5.1	n	28.4	18.4	26.3	1.5	15.7	8.8	0.7	0.2
	Switzerland	8.9	20.9	34.9	14.6	16.3	3.2	1.2	n	24.7	12.1	36.5	1.7	11.6	11.5	0.9	0.8
	Turkey	7.9	6.4	43.6	8.0	20.2	6.0	7.9	n	19.4	5.5	55.2	1.6	8.5	7.6	2.3	n
	United Kingdom	22.6	29.0	12.4	1.5	5.6	5.9	1.5	21.4	25.8	14.9	30.9	1.7	9.1	14.9	0.8	1.9
	United States	n	38.3	27.2	13.5	13.5	6.5	0.9	n	30.1	8.2	27.8	4.1	5.4	9.2	0.6	14.6
	OECD average	19.9	18.0	25.4	11.6	14.5	6.4	1.6	2.6	23.0	12.4	34.6	3.3	13.2	10.1	1.8	1.6
	EU21 average	19.6	18.9	24.3	13.6	14.2	4.9	1.6	3.0	22.6	12.5	34.2	3.6	13.9	10.6	2.0	0.6
Other G20	Argentina[2]	42.5	10.4	22.2	6.4	5.4	11.0	2.0	n	14.4	14.2	45.7	1.7	10.6	8.8	4.1	0.4
	Brazil	4.1	2.2	52.0	11.5	11.6	17.2	1.4	n	24.3	15.9	38.9	0.8	8.6	6.3	2.3	3.0
	China	m	m	m	m	m	m	m	m	m	m	m	m	m	m	m	m
	India	m	m	m	m	m	m	m	m	m	m	m	m	m	m	m	m
	Indonesia[3]	16.2	2.7	50.7	n	16.3	8.1	4.8	1.3	15.1	2.6	50.1	n	16.1	8.0	4.9	3.2
	Russian Federation	12.9	10.2	27.5	5.2	36.4	5.9	1.9	n	12.7	3.8	51.6	5.3	18.5	6.7	1.5	n
	Saudi Arabia	m	m	m	m	m	m	m	m	m	m	m	m	m	m	m	m
	South Africa	m	m	m	m	m	m	m	m	m	m	m	m	m	m	m	m

Note: Columns showing the breakdown of humanities, arts and education (2, 3, 16 and 17) and science (9-12, 23-26) are available for consultation on line (see Statlink below).

1. Excludes data for social advancement education in tertiary-type A and advanced research programmes.

2. Year of reference 2008.

3. Excludes advanced research programmes.

4. Net entry rates are below 1% at tertiary-type B level, and not applicable any more in Finland (see Indicator C2).

Source: OECD. Argentina, Indonesia: UNESCO Institute for Statistics (World Education Indicators Programme). See Annex 3 for notes (*www.oecd.org/edu/eag2011*).

Please refer to the Reader's Guide for information concerning the symbols replacing missing data.

StatLink http://dx.doi.org/10.1787/888932462662

Table A4.5. Distribution of international and foreign students enrolled in tertiary programmes, by field of education (2009)

		Humanities, arts and education	Health and welfare	Social sciences, business and law	Services	Engineering, manufacturing and construction	Science	Agriculture	Not known or unspecified
		(1)	(4)	(5)	(6)	(7)	(8)	(13)	(14)
		International students by field of education							
OECD	Australia	9.0	9.9	55.5	2.0	10.6	12.1	0.8	0.1
	Austria[1]	23.2	9.1	38.3	1.5	13.5	11.9	2.2	0.3
	Belgium	16.1	23.7	7.8	1.3	7.3	4.6	1.8	37.5
	Canada[2]	11.3	6.8	39.6	1.5	15.0	13.9	1.1	10.6
	Chile	12.6	12.6	38.2	5.8	10.7	14.2	6.1	n
	Denmark	12.2	14.2	39.0	0.3	18.9	10.9	4.4	n
	Estonia	20.0	9.0	53.0	1.2	2.8	3.6	10.5	n
	Finland[1]	12.8	8.9	28.7	5.8	31.5	10.8	1.6	n
	Germany[1, 3]	25.7	6.2	27.7	1.5	20.5	16.4	1.6	0.4
	Greece	m	m	m	m	m	m	m	m
	Hungary	12.5	38.8	21.4	2.7	9.7	5.6	9.3	n
	Iceland	45.1	4.5	22.0	1.1	7.9	18.9	0.5	n
	Ireland	m	m	m	m	m	m	m	m
	Israel	m	m	m	m	m	m	m	m
	Japan[1]	23.5	2.6	42.1	0.5	14.7	1.5	3.0	12.1
	Korea	m	m	m	m	m	m	m	m
	Luxembourg	m	m	m	m	m	m	m	m
	Mexico	m	m	m	m	m	m	m	m
	Netherlands[3]	14.9	17.6	49.4	8.3	3.6	4.1	1.6	0.5
	New Zealand	14.1	6.1	36.5	4.8	6.5	18.7	1.2	12.0
	Norway	21.9	8.7	34.7	3.1	4.0	16.1	0.9	10.5
	Portugal	12.6	6.8	50.0	6.6	15.6	7.0	1.4	n
	Slovenia	19.8	8.1	44.0	3.1	15.6	7.8	1.7	n
	Spain[1, 3]	16.2	26.7	31.5	3.8	9.3	7.6	1.4	3.4
	Sweden	14.2	9.6	23.6	1.8	33.9	16.0	0.8	0.1
	Switzerland[1]	20.8	7.3	34.5	2.4	15.6	16.8	0.7	1.9
	United Kingdom	16.8	8.9	42.1	2.1	14.6	13.5	0.8	1.1
	United States	15.3	6.6	32.7	2.1	18.4	17.5	0.8	6.6
Other G20	Argentina	m	m	m	m	m	m	m	m
	Brazil	m	m	m	m	m	m	m	m
	China	m	m	m	m	m	m	m	m
	India	m	m	m	m	m	m	m	m
	Indonesia	m	m	m	m	m	m	m	m
	Russian Federation	m	m	m	m	m	m	m	m
	Saudi Arabia	m	m	m	m	m	m	m	m
	South Africa	m	m	m	m	m	m	m	m
		Foreign students by field of education[4]							
OECD	Czech Republic	13.5	15.9	39.3	3.3	11.1	14.6	2.2	n
	France	19.9	8.2	40.2	1.6	12.7	17.0	0.2	0.1
	Italy[1, 3]	19.4	20.0	33.7	1.8	17.6	5.4	1.5	0.6
	Poland[1]	19.8	29.7	36.9	3.5	4.6	4.8	0.7	n
	Slovak Republic	21.5	37.6	19.4	3.5	11.4	3.0	3.6	n
	Turkey	22.0	14.6	32.7	4.2	14.4	10.0	2.2	n

Note : Columns showing the breakdown of humanities, arts and education (2 and 3) and science (9-12) are available for consultation on line (see Statlink below).

1. Excludes tertiary-type B programmes.
2. Year of reference 2008.
3. Excludes advanced research programmes.
4. Foreign students are defined on the basis of their country of citizenship; these data are not comparable with data on international students and are therefore presented separately in the table and chart.

Source: OECD. See Annex 3 for notes *(www.oecd.org/edu/eag2011)*.

Please refer to the Reader's Guide for information concerning the symbols replacing missing data.

StatLink http://dx.doi.org/10.1787/888932462681

Table A4.6. **Science-related graduates among 25-34 year-olds in employment, by gender (2009)**

Number of graduates (science and engineering) divided by the total number of 25-34 year-olds in employment, per 100 000

		Tertiary-type B			Tertiary-type A and advanced research programmes			All tertiary education		
		M + W	Men	Women	M + W	Men	Women	M + W	Men	Women
		(1)	(2)	(3)	(4)	(5)	(6)	(7)	(8)	(9)
OECD	Australia[1]	**438**	612	221	**1 924**	2 349	1 392	**2 362**	2 960	1 613
	Austria	**457**	776	98	**1 227**	1 634	767	**1 684**	2 409	864
	Belgium	**362**	591	107	**1 092**	1 421	726	**1 454**	2 012	833
	Canada[1]	**807**	1 270	305	**1 340**	1 568	1 091	**2 146**	2 838	1 397
	Chile	**913**	1 337	287	**832**	982	609	**1 745**	2 319	896
	Czech Republic	**58**	64	50	**1 726**	1 950	1 373	**1 784**	2 014	1 424
	Denmark	**237**	223	252	**1 498**	1 923	1 049	**1 735**	2 146	1 301
	Estonia	**412**	541	255	**1 184**	1 208	1 155	**1 597**	1 749	1 410
	Finland	**n**	n	n	**2 384**	3 107	1 520	**2 384**	3 107	1 520
	France	**881**	1 363	333	**1 836**	2 285	1 324	**2 717**	3 648	1 658
	Germany	**222**	386	31	**1 574**	1 913	1 179	**1 796**	2 299	1 210
	Greece	**m**	m	m	**m**	m	m	**m**	m	m
	Hungary	**40**	51	25	**918**	1 119	636	**958**	1 170	660
	Iceland	**41**	64	13	**1 414**	1 635	1 154	**1 455**	1 699	1 166
	Ireland	**686**	1 047	311	**1 486**	1 908	1 049	**2 172**	2 954	1 360
	Israel	**m**	m	m	**m**	m	m	**m**	m	m
	Italy	**m**	m	m	**m**	m	m	**m**	m	m
	Japan	**390**	567	146	**1 254**	1 873	404	**1 643**	2 440	550
	Korea	**1 121**	1 420	695	**2 434**	3 012	1 612	**3 555**	4 432	2 307
	Luxembourg	**m**	m	m	**m**	m	m	**m**	m	m
	Mexico	**134**	157	98	**951**	1 022	839	**1 085**	1 179	937
	Netherlands	**m**	m	m	**1 039**	1 597	430	**1 039**	1 597	430
	New Zealand	**955**	1 312	536	**2 032**	2 272	1 749	**2 987**	3 583	2 285
	Norway	**n**	n	n	**1 018**	1 360	643	**1 018**	1 360	643
	Poland	**a**	a	a	**1 920**	2 142	1 644	**1 920**	2 142	1 644
	Portugal	**2**	2	1	**1 582**	1 905	1 219	**1 583**	1 907	1 220
	Slovak Republic	**5**	9	n	**2 285**	2 528	1 941	**2 290**	2 536	1 941
	Slovenia	**663**	1 057	212	**628**	749	489	**1 291**	1 806	701
	Spain	**452**	708	153	**1 036**	1 213	830	**1 488**	1 921	982
	Sweden	**213**	305	109	**1 383**	1 718	1 003	**1 596**	2 023	1 112
	Switzerland	**780**	1 318	165	**1 230**	1 713	679	**2 010**	3 031	844
	Turkey	**712**	736	645	**824**	729	1 084	**1 536**	1 465	1 729
	United Kingdom	**383**	522	216	**1 997**	2 491	1 402	**2 380**	3 013	1 618
	United States	**278**	433	97	**1 194**	1 449	893	**1 472**	1 882	990
	OECD average	**416**	602	191	**1 441**	1 759	1 063	**1 829**	2 321	1 242
	EU21 average	**298**	450	127	**1 489**	1 823	1 096	**1 770**	2 247	1 216
Other G20	Argentina	**m**	m	m	**m**	m	m	**m**	m	m
	Brazil	**m**	m	m	**m**	m	m	**m**	m	m
	China	**m**	m	m	**m**	m	m	**m**	m	m
	India	**m**	m	m	**m**	m	m	**m**	m	m
	Indonesia	**m**	m	m	**m**	m	m	**m**	m	m
	Russian Federation	**m**	m	m	**m**	m	m	**m**	m	m
	Saudi Arabia	**m**	m	m	**m**	m	m	**m**	m	m
	South Africa	**m**	m	m	**m**	m	m	**m**	m	m

Note: Science-related fields include life sciences; physical sciences, mathematics and statistics, computing; engineering and engineering trades, manufacturing and processing, architecture and building.

1. Year of reference 2008 for the number of science-related graduates.

Source: OECD. See Annex 3 for notes *(www.oecd.org/edu/eag2011).*

Please refer to the Reader's Guide for information concerning the symbols replacing missing data.

StatLink http://dx.doi.org/10.1787/888932462700

DOES STUDENT BACKGROUND AFFECT STUDENT PERFORMANCE?

- The difference in reading performance between students from various socio-economic backgrounds is strong, particularly in France and New Zealand.
- Even after adjusting for socio-economic status, students with an immigrant background score an average of 27 points below students who do not have an immigrant background.
- Across OECD countries, nearly one-third of disadvantaged students are identified as "resilient", meaning that they perform better in reading than would be predicted from their socio-economic backgrounds.

Chart A5.1. Difference in reading performance between students from different socio-economic backgrounds

Score point difference in reading performance associated with one unit increase in the **PISA index of economic, social and cultural status (ESCS)**

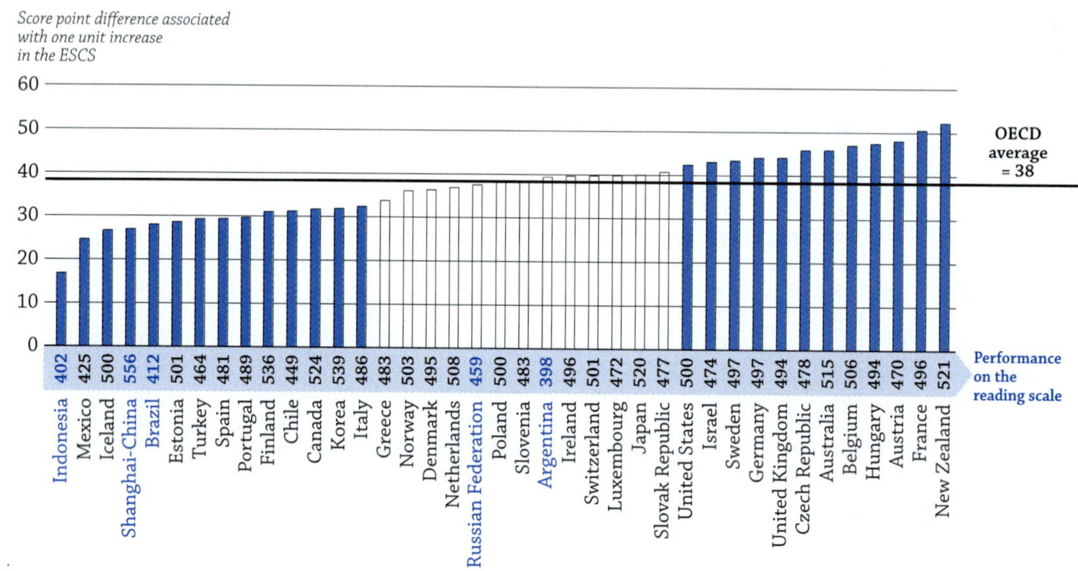

Note: The empty bars indicate that the slope of the socio-economic background is not statistically significantly different from the OECD average slope.

Countries are ranked in ascending order of the difference in performance between students from different socio-economic backgrounds.

Source: OECD, *PISA 2009 Database*, Table A5.1.

StatLink http://dx.doi.org/10.1787/888932460211

Context

In trying to provide students with equitable learning opportunities, education systems aim to reduce the extent to which a student's socio-economic background affects his or her performance in school. Performance differences that are related to student background are evident in every country. But PISA results show that some countries have been more successful than others in mitigating the impact of socio-economic background on students' performance in reading. In general, students with an immigrant background are socio-economically disadvantaged, and this explains part of the performance disadvantage among these students. They face considerable challenges in reading and other aspects of education. In general, they tend to show lower levels of performance even after their socio-economic background is taken into account. However, the differences in performance vary greatly, and in some countries, students with an immigrant background perform just as well as their non-immigrant peers. But despite the strong association between socio-economic status and reading performance, many students from disadvantaged backgrounds confound predictions and perform well. Thus educators must not assume that someone from a disadvantaged background is incapable of high achievement.

Other findings

- Although the relationship between students' background and school performance is evident in all countries, the strength of this relationship varies across school systems. The four top-performers in reading, Canada, Finland, Korea and Shanghai-China, show a below-average impact of socio-economic status on students' reading performance, proving that **it is possible to reduce the strength of the relationship between background and performance**.
- In many countries, **first-generation immigrant students are at a significantly greater risk of being poor performers**. Across OECD countries, they are around twice as likely to perform among the bottom quarter of students when compared to students who do not have an immigrant background.
- Across OECD countries only 23% of boys, but 40% of girls, from disadvantaged backgrounds are considered resilient.

Analysis

Socio-economic background and student performance

Socio-economic background is measured by the *PISA index of social, cultural and economic status*, which is based on information, provided by students, about their parents' education and occupations and their home possessions, such as a desk to use for studying and the number of books in the home. The index is standardised to have an average value of 0 and a standard deviation of 1 across all OECD countries. This means that two-thirds of students are from a socio-economic background that is between one unit above average and one unit below average.

There are two main ways of measuring how closely reading performance is linked to social background. One considers the average difference in performance between students from different socio-economic backgrounds. On average across OECD countries, one unit increase in the *PISA Index of economic, social and cultural status* is associated with 38 score point difference. As shown in Chart A5.1, this gap is greatest in France and New Zealand, where it is at least 30% wider than the OECD average. In these countries, a student's predicted score is most heavily influenced by his or her socio-economic background. This gap is also greater than the OECD average in Australia, Austria, Belgium, the Czech Republic, Germany, Hungary, Israel, Sweden and the United Kingdom and smaller than the OECD average in Brazil, Canada, Chile, Estonia, Finland, Iceland, Indonesia, Italy, Korea, Mexico, Portugal, Shanghai-China, Spain and Turkey (Chart A5.1).

While this measure can be used to predict differences in reading scores among students from different backgrounds, many students confound these predictions. Socio-economically advantaged students perform better, on average, but a number perform poorly, just as a number of disadvantaged students perform well. To show the extent to which levels of student performance conform to a pattern predicted by socio-economic status, PISA also measures the percentage of variation in reading performance than can be explained by a student's background.

Chart A5.2. Strength of the relationship between reading performance and socio-economic background

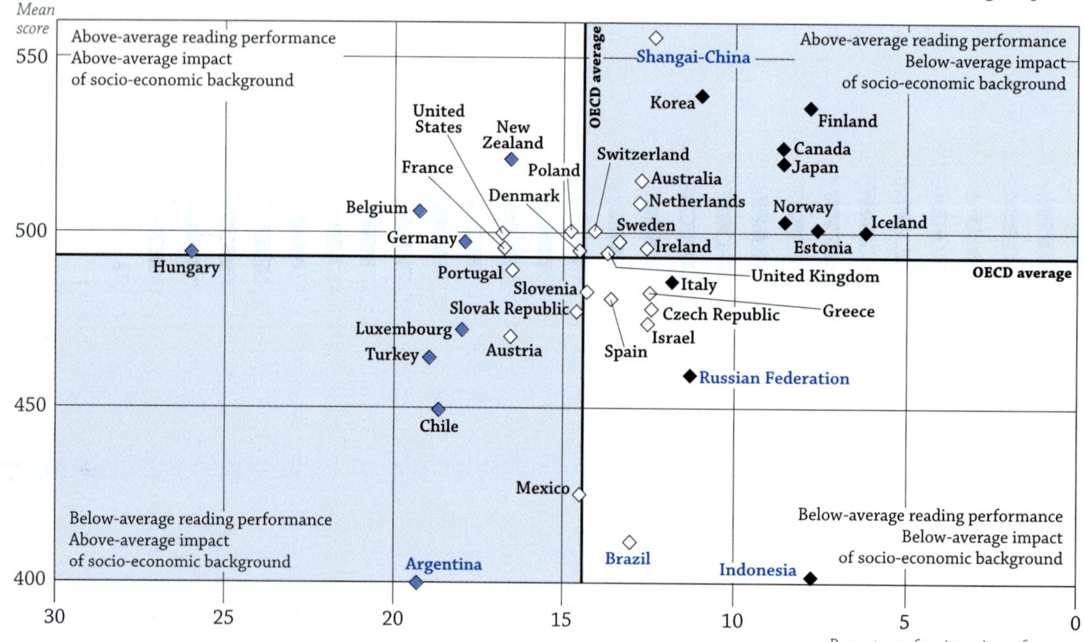

Source: OECD, *PISA 2009 Database*, Table A5.1.

StatLink http://dx.doi.org/10.1787/888932460230

On average across OECD countries, 14% of the variation in students' reading performance can be explained by their socio-economic backgrounds. In Hungary more than 20% of the variation is so explained. In Belgium, Chile, Germany, Luxembourg, New Zealand and Turkey, the strength of the relationship between reading performance and socio-economic background is above the OECD average. In contrast, in Iceland less than 7% of variation in student performance is explained by socio-economic background. In Canada, Estonia, Finland, Indonesia, Italy, Japan, Korea, Norway and the Russian Federation this percentage of variation is below the OECD average (Chart A5.2).

This analysis shows that a student's socio-economic background is associated with his or her reading performance to some extent in all countries. However, among the four countries with the highest reading performance, three of them, namely Canada, Finland and Korea, show a link between student background and performance that is weaker than average for both measures. This indicates that it is possible to achieve the highest levels of performance while providing students with equitable learning opportunities.

Immigrant background and student performance

Chart A5.3 shows the average performance of students with an immigrant background for those countries with significant shares of 15-year-olds who have an immigrant background (see Definitions below). Countries are sorted by the average performance of all students. The figure highlights three main findings. First, students who do not have an immigrant background tend to outperform students with an immigrant background in most countries and economies. The exceptions are Australia and Canada for both first- and second-generation students, and Hungary, where second-generation students significantly outperform students who do not have an immigrant background. Second, the size of the performance gap among these groups of students varies markedly across countries. Third, second-generation students tend to outperform first-generation students.

This analysis defines students with an immigrant background as those who were born in the country of assessment but whose parents are foreign-born (second-generation) and those who are foreign-born whose parents are also foreign-born (first-generation).

Chart A5.3. Reading performance, by immigrant status

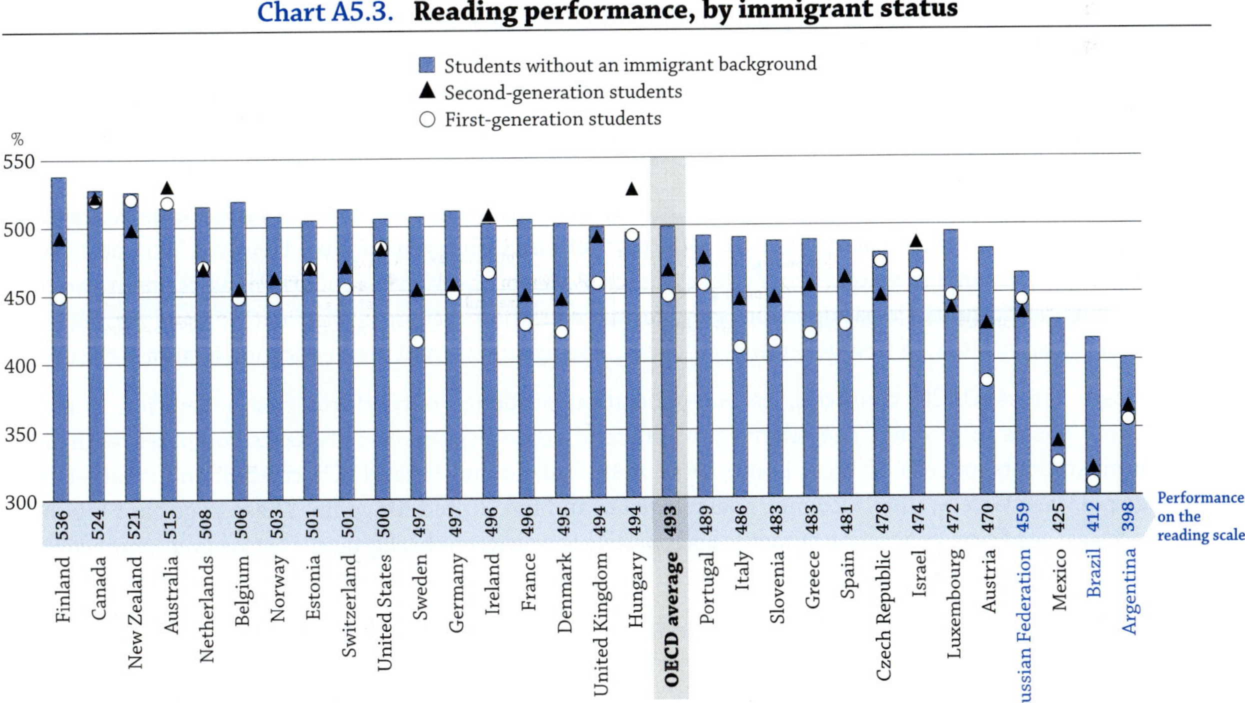

Countries are ranked in descending order of the mean score of all students.
Source: OECD, *PISA 2009 Database*, Table A5.2.
StatLink http://dx.doi.org/10.1787/888932460249

On average across OECD countries, students with an immigrant background scored 44 points below their non-immigrant peers in reading. While this gap shrunk to 27 score points after socio-economic background was taken into account, the difference still amounts to nearly half a proficiency level in reading (Table A5.2).

In many OECD countries, first-generation immigrant students are at a significantly greater risk of being poor performers. They lag 52 score points, on average, behind students who do not have an immigrant background, a difference that exceeds the equivalent of one school year's progress (see Definitions). In Austria, Belgium, Brazil, Denmark, Finland, France, Greece, Iceland, Italy, Mexico, Norway, Slovenia, Spain and Sweden, first-generation immigrant students are at least twice as likely to perform among the bottom quarter of students when compared to students who do not have an immigrant background (Table A5.2).

While the educational experience abroad can help to explain the performance gap for first-generation immigrants, second-generation students were born in the country and therefore benefited from the education system of the host country from the beginning of their previous education. Despite this, second-generation students also lag behind those who are not from immigrant families by an average of 33 score points across OECD countries (Table A5.2).

In general, students with an immigrant background are socio-economically disadvantaged, and this explains part of the performance disadvantage among these students. On average across OECD countries, students with an immigrant background tend to have a socio-economic background that is 0.4 of a standard deviation lower than that of their non-immigrant peers. This relationship is particularly strong in Austria, Denmark, Germany, Iceland, Luxembourg, the Netherlands and the United States. Only in Australia, Brazil, the Czech Republic, Estonia, Hungary, Ireland, New Zealand and Portugal is there no observed difference in the socio-economic background of students by immigrant status (Table A5.2).

The large gaps in performance and socio-economic background suggest that schools and societies face major challenges in realising the potential of students with an immigrant background. However, as Chart A5.3 shows, in some education systems, the gaps are barely noticeable or very narrow, while in others they are significantly above these averages. For example, in Australia, second-generation students, who account for 12% of the student population, outperform students who do not have an immigrant background by 16 score points. In Hungary, second-generation students score 32 points above students who are not from immigrant families, but they account only for 1% of the student population. In Canada, where almost 25% of students have an immigrant background, these students perform as well as students who do not have an immigrant background. Similarly, no statistically significant differences are observed between second-generation students and non-immigrant students in the Czech Republic, Ireland, Israel, Portugal and the United Kingdom, and between first-generation students and non-immigrant students in Australia, the Czech Republic, Hungary and New Zealand.

Without longitudinal data, it is not possible to directly assess to what extent the observed disadvantages of students with an immigrant background are reduced over successive generations. However, it is possible to compare the performance of second-generation students, who were born in the country of assessment and have thereby benefited from participating in the same formal education system as their native peers for the same number of years, with that of first-generation students, who usually started their education in another country.

On average across OECD countries, second-generation students outperform first-generation students by 18 score points in reading. The relative advantage of second-generation students compared with first-generation students exceeds 40 score points in Austria, Finland and Ireland (Chart A5.3) and is larger than 30 score points in Greece, Italy, Slovenia, Spain, Sweden and the United Kingdom. These large gaps highlight the disadvantage of first-generation students and possibly the different backgrounds across immigrant cohorts (Table A5.2). However, they could also signal positive educational and social mobility across generations.

Cross-country comparisons of performance gaps between first- and second-generation immigrant students need to be treated with caution, since they may, in some cases, reflect the characteristics of families participating in different waves of immigration more strongly than the success of integration policies. New Zealand is a case in point. First-generation students perform as well as students without an immigrant background while second-generation students lag behind the former group of students by 22 score points (Table A5.2).

This result signals that there may be important differences in the characteristics of the cohorts of students with an immigrant background. Even students from the same countries of origin, however, show considerable differences in their performance across the different host countries.

In general, a part of these differences persists even after accounting for socio-economic factors. Chart A5.4 shows the size of the performance gap between students with and without an immigrant background before and after accounting for socio-economic status. In Luxembourg, for example, accounting for the socio-economic status of students reduces the performance disadvantage of students with an immigrant background from 52 to 19 score points. On average across OECD countries, the gap is reduced from 44 to 27 score points. The narrowing of the gap after accounting for the socio-economic status of students tends to be similar across countries. The rank order of countries in terms of the performance gap between immigrant and native students remains fairly stable before and after accounting for socio-economic context. This shows the extent to which performance differences between students with varying immigrant backgrounds reflect students' socio-economic status and not necessarily their immigrant background. The fact that the gap is still apparent after accounting for socio-economic status, however, indicates that students from immigrant backgrounds may have difficulties at school that can be attributed directly to their immigrant status.

Chart A5.4. Reading performance by immigrant background, before and after accounting for socio-economic status

Differences in reading performance between native students and students with an immigrant background

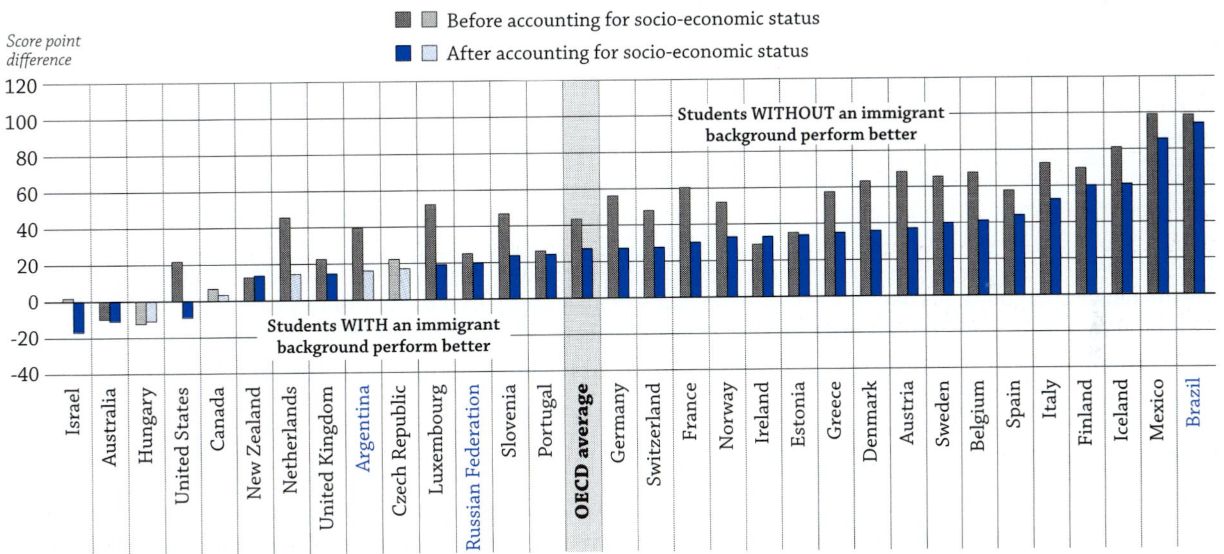

Note: Score point differences that are statistically significant are shown in a darker tone.

Countries are ranked in ascending order of score point differences after accounting for the economic, social and cultural status of students.

Source: OECD, *PISA 2009 Database*, Table A5.2.

StatLink http://dx.doi.org/10.1787/888932460268

Disadvantaged students who succeed

Students' observed performance in reading can be compared to what would be expected of them, given their socio-economic background. Based on the performance of students from different backgrounds across countries, PISA predicts how well a student will perform. Each student's performance can be measured in terms of how much they exceed or fall below this prediction. The quarter of all students across countries who do best relative to those predictions can be seen as the group of students who most exceed expectations. A 15-year-old who is among the 25% most socio-economically disadvantaged students in his or her own country and whose reading performance is ranked among the international group of students who most exceed expectations is described as "resilient". Such a student combines the characteristics of having the weakest prospects and doing the best given those prospects.

On average across OECD countries, 31% of students from disadvantaged backgrounds are resilient. In Korea and Shanghai-China, 56% and 76% of students from such backgrounds, respectively, are resilient, meaning that most students from modest backgrounds do far better in reading than would be expected. In Finland, Japan and Turkey, the proportion of resilient students is between 10 and 15 percentage points higher than the OECD average. In contrast, in Argentina, Austria, Luxembourg and the Russian Federation, this proportion is 10 percentage points lower than the OECD average (Chart A5.5).

Chart A5.5. Percentage of resilient students among disadvantaged students

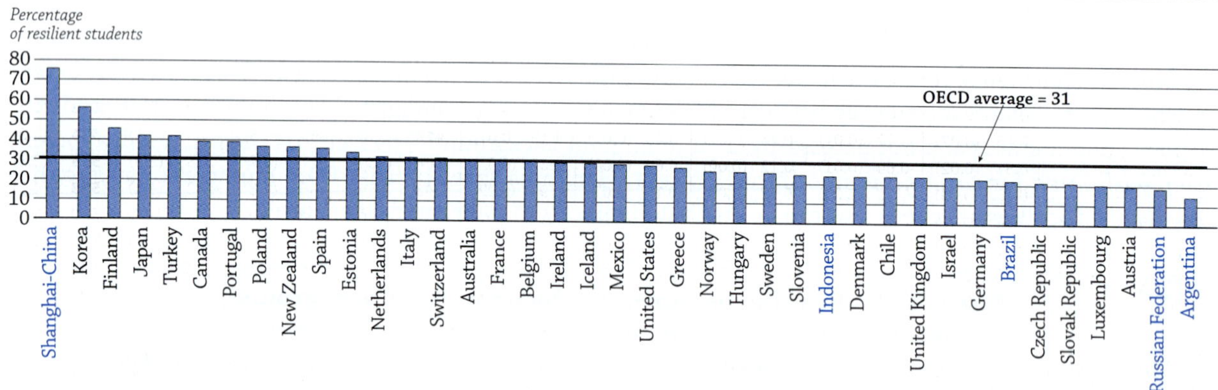

Note: A student is classified as resilient if he or she is in the bottom quarter of the *PISA index of economic, social and cultural status* (ESCS) in the country of assessment and performs in the top quarter across students from all countries after accounting for socio-economic background. The share of resilient students among all students has been multiplied by 4 so that the percentage values presented here reflect the proportion of resilient students among disadvantaged students (those in the bottom quarter of the *PISA index of social, economic and cultural status*).
Countries are ranked in descending order of the percentage of resilient students.

Source: OECD, *PISA 2009 Database*, Table A5.2.

StatLink http://dx.doi.org/10.1787/888932460287

In all countries, girls from disadvantaged backgrounds are far more likely to show resilience in reading performance than boys. Across OECD countries, 39% of girls compared to 22% of boys are considered resilient. The majority of disadvantaged girls in this category are found in Finland, Korea, Poland and Portugal; in Korea, some 65% of disadvantaged girls are resilient. In Poland, Portugal and Slovenia there are 25% more resilient girls than resilient boys.

Definitions

In PISA 2009, **one school year's progress** corresponds to an average of 39 score points on the PISA reading scale. This was determined by calculating the difference in scores among the sizeable number of 15-year-olds in 32 OECD countries who were enrolled in at least two different grade levels.

PISA distinguishes between three types of **student immigrant status**: *i)* students without an immigrant background, also referred to as **native** students, are students who were born in the country where they were assessed by PISA or who had at least one parent born in the country; *ii)* **second-generation students** are students who were born in the country of assessment but whose parents are foreign-born; and *iii)* **first-generation students** are foreign-born students whose parents are also foreign-born. Students with an immigrant background thus include students who are first or second- generation immigrants.

The statistical data for Israel are supplied by and under the responsibility of the relevant Israeli authorities. The use of such data by the OECD is without prejudice to the status of the Golan Heights, East Jerusalem and Israeli settlements in the West Bank under the terms of international law.

References

OECD (2010b), *PISA 2009 Results: Overcoming Social Background: Equity in Learning Opportunities and Outcomes* (Volume II), OECD, Paris.

Table A5.1. [1/2] Socio-economic background and reading performance

Results based on students' self-reports

	PISA index of economic, social and cultural status (ESCS)										Performance on the reading scale, by national quarters of this index							
	All students		Bottom quarter		Second quarter		Third quarter		Top quarter		Bottom quarter		Second quarter		Third quarter		Top quarter	
	Mean index	S.E.	Mean index	S.E.	Mean index	S.E.	Mean index	S.E.	Mean index	S.E.	Mean score	S.E.	Mean score	S.E.	Mean score	S.E.	Mean score	S.E.
OECD Australia	0.34	(0.01)	-0.63	(0.01)	0.09	(0.00)	0.63	(0.00)	1.29	(0.01)	**471**	(2.7)	504	(2.4)	532	(3.0)	**562**	(3.1)
Austria	0.06	(0.02)	-0.97	(0.02)	-0.22	(0.00)	0.28	(0.00)	1.15	(0.01)	**421**	(4.3)	457	(4.2)	482	(3.8)	**525**	(3.9)
Belgium	0.20	(0.02)	-1.00	(0.02)	-0.13	(0.00)	0.54	(0.00)	1.37	(0.01)	**452**	(3.3)	489	(3.3)	525	(2.5)	**567**	(2.6)
Canada	0.50	(0.02)	-0.59	(0.01)	0.25	(0.00)	0.83	(0.00)	1.52	(0.01)	**495**	(2.3)	514	(1.7)	533	(2.1)	**562**	(2.4)
Chile	-0.57	(0.04)	-2.00	(0.01)	-1.00	(0.01)	-0.22	(0.01)	0.95	(0.02)	**409**	(3.5)	435	(3.6)	457	(3.5)	**501**	(3.5)
Czech Republic	-0.09	(0.01)	-0.95	(0.01)	-0.34	(0.00)	0.11	(0.00)	0.85	(0.01)	**437**	(3.3)	467	(3.7)	490	(3.4)	**521**	(4.1)
Denmark	0.30	(0.02)	-0.83	(0.01)	0.00	(0.01)	0.62	(0.01)	1.39	(0.01)	**455**	(2.7)	486	(3.4)	509	(2.9)	**536**	(2.4)
Estonia	0.15	(0.02)	-0.87	(0.01)	-0.16	(0.01)	0.45	(0.01)	1.19	(0.01)	**476**	(3.6)	490	(3.5)	505	(3.1)	**534**	(3.9)
Finland	0.37	(0.02)	-0.64	(0.01)	0.12	(0.00)	0.69	(0.00)	1.32	(0.01)	**504**	(3.2)	527	(2.7)	548	(2.9)	**565**	(2.8)
France	-0.13	(0.03)	-1.19	(0.02)	-0.42	(0.00)	0.15	(0.01)	0.93	(0.02)	**443**	(5.2)	484	(4.6)	513	(4.4)	**553**	(4.8)
Germany	0.18	(0.02)	-0.93	(0.02)	-0.12	(0.00)	0.42	(0.01)	1.36	(0.01)	**445**	(3.9)	494	(2.9)	515	(3.5)	**550**	(3.3)
Greece	-0.02	(0.03)	-1.28	(0.02)	-0.40	(0.01)	0.32	(0.01)	1.27	(0.01)	**437**	(7.1)	475	(5.2)	493	(3.7)	**528**	(3.4)
Hungary	-0.20	(0.03)	-1.38	(0.03)	-0.56	(0.00)	0.06	(0.01)	1.10	(0.02)	**435**	(5.3)	485	(3.4)	505	(4.1)	**553**	(4.1)
Iceland	0.72	(0.01)	-0.46	(0.02)	0.45	(0.01)	1.10	(0.01)	1.79	(0.01)	**470**	(3.1)	494	(3.3)	513	(3.0)	**530**	(2.8)
Ireland	0.05	(0.03)	-1.01	(0.01)	-0.27	(0.01)	0.31	(0.01)	1.15	(0.02)	**454**	(3.8)	486	(4.0)	511	(3.9)	**539**	(3.5)
Israel	-0.02	(0.03)	-1.20	(0.02)	-0.24	(0.01)	0.33	(0.00)	1.01	(0.01)	**423**	(5.4)	465	(4.0)	501	(3.6)	**526**	(4.1)
Italy	-0.12	(0.01)	-1.41	(0.01)	-0.47	(0.00)	0.18	(0.00)	1.21	(0.01)	**442**	(3.0)	477	(2.0)	500	(2.0)	**526**	(2.1)
Japan	-0.01	(0.01)	-0.93	(0.01)	-0.28	(0.00)	0.24	(0.00)	0.93	(0.01)	**483**	(4.8)	510	(4.8)	536	(4.0)	**558**	(3.5)
Korea	-0.15	(0.03)	-1.22	(0.01)	-0.42	(0.01)	0.14	(0.01)	0.88	(0.02)	**503**	(5.1)	534	(2.8)	548	(3.9)	**572**	(4.6)
Luxembourg	0.19	(0.01)	-1.31	(0.02)	-0.09	(0.01)	0.64	(0.01)	1.51	(0.01)	**411**	(2.7)	460	(3.0)	497	(2.8)	**526**	(3.0)
Mexico	-1.22	(0.03)	-2.83	(0.01)	-1.79	(0.00)	-0.81	(0.01)	0.54	(0.02)	**386**	(2.8)	413	(2.3)	434	(2.2)	**469**	(2.2)
Netherlands	0.27	(0.03)	-0.84	(0.03)	0.01	(0.01)	0.61	(0.01)	1.31	(0.01)	**474**	(5.5)	493	(5.8)	519	(4.7)	**553**	(5.9)
New Zealand	0.09	(0.02)	-0.93	(0.01)	-0.17	(0.00)	0.36	(0.01)	1.08	(0.01)	**475**	(3.9)	508	(3.1)	534	(3.3)	**578**	(3.6)
Norway	0.47	(0.02)	-0.47	(0.01)	0.23	(0.00)	0.73	(0.00)	1.40	(0.01)	**468**	(3.4)	495	(3.3)	517	(2.9)	**536**	(3.9)
Poland	-0.28	(0.02)	-1.29	(0.01)	-0.66	(0.00)	-0.15	(0.00)	0.97	(0.01)	**461**	(3.4)	488	(3.1)	507	(2.9)	**550**	(3.8)
Portugal	-0.32	(0.04)	-1.70	(0.01)	-0.87	(0.01)	-0.05	(0.01)	1.35	(0.03)	**451**	(4.2)	472	(3.4)	499	(3.4)	**537**	(3.7)
Slovak Republic	-0.09	(0.02)	-1.04	(0.02)	-0.44	(0.00)	0.04	(0.01)	1.07	(0.02)	**435**	(5.0)	468	(3.4)	488	(3.3)	**521**	(3.6)
Slovenia	0.07	(0.01)	-1.01	(0.01)	-0.31	(0.01)	0.37	(0.01)	1.25	(0.01)	**444**	(2.6)	468	(2.5)	493	(2.7)	**532**	(2.6)
Spain	-0.31	(0.03)	-1.68	(0.02)	-0.74	(0.00)	0.03	(0.01)	1.14	(0.01)	**443**	(3.3)	468	(2.3)	491	(2.2)	**525**	(3.3)
Sweden	0.33	(0.02)	-0.72	(0.02)	0.08	(0.00)	0.63	(0.01)	1.33	(0.01)	**452**	(4.0)	488	(3.3)	515	(3.3)	**543**	(4.1)
Switzerland	0.08	(0.02)	-1.04	(0.01)	-0.22	(0.00)	0.35	(0.00)	1.22	(0.01)	**457**	(3.9)	492	(2.7)	506	(3.0)	**550**	(3.7)
Turkey	-1.16	(0.05)	-2.63	(0.02)	-1.69	(0.01)	-0.82	(0.01)	0.49	(0.03)	**422**	(3.8)	454	(3.5)	469	(3.9)	**514**	(4.6)
United Kingdom	0.20	(0.02)	-0.80	(0.02)	-0.06	(0.00)	0.47	(0.01)	1.21	(0.01)	**451**	(2.9)	483	(3.1)	508	(2.7)	**544**	(3.2)
United States	0.17	(0.04)	-1.05	(0.02)	-0.11	(0.01)	0.52	(0.01)	1.32	(0.02)	**451**	(3.6)	481	(3.6)	512	(3.6)	**558**	(4.7)
OECD average	0.00	(0.00)	-1.14	(0.00)	-0.32	(0.00)	0.30	(0.00)	1.17	(0.00)	**451**	(0.7)	483	(0.6)	506	(0.6)	**540**	(0.6)
Other G20 Argentina	-0.62	(0.05)	-2.17	(0.03)	-1.02	(0.01)	-0.19	(0.01)	0.92	(0.03)	**345**	(4.9)	377	(4.6)	410	(5.5)	**468**	(6.2)
Brazil	-1.16	(0.03)	-2.69	(0.01)	-1.64	(0.01)	-0.76	(0.01)	0.44	(0.02)	**376**	(2.5)	401	(3.0)	413	(3.9)	**460**	(4.1)
Indonesia	-1.55	(0.06)	-2.86	(0.01)	-2.05	(0.01)	-1.26	(0.01)	-0.04	(0.03)	**386**	(3.8)	389	(3.6)	402	(4.5)	**430**	(6.0)
Russian Federation	-0.21	(0.02)	-1.20	(0.01)	-0.56	(0.00)	0.06	(0.00)	0.85	(0.01)	**424**	(3.6)	447	(3.9)	466	(3.5)	**502**	(4.9)
Shanghai-China	-0.49	(0.04)	-1.83	(0.02)	-0.88	(0.01)	-0.11	(0.01)	0.86	(0.01)	**521**	(4.3)	546	(3.3)	564	(2.5)	**594**	(3.4)

Note: Values that are statistically significant are indicated in bold.
1. In these columns values that are statistically significantly different from the OECD average are indicated in bold.
2. Single-level bivariate regression of reading performance on the ESCS, the slope is the regression coefficient for the ESCS.
Source: OECD, *PISA 2009 Database*.
StatLink http://dx.doi.org/10.1787/888932462719

Table A5.1. [2/2] Socio-economic background and reading performance

Results based on students' self-reports

		Slope of the socio-economic gradient[1, 2]		Strength of the relationship between student performance and the ESCS[1]		Increased likelihood of students in the bottom quarter of the ESCS scoring in the bottom quarter of the reading performance distribution		Performance on the reading scale (unadjusted mean score)		Performance on the reading scale if the mean ESCS were equal in all OECD	
		Change in the reading score per unit of this index		Explained variance in student performance (r-squared x 100)							
		Effect	S.E.	%	S.E.	Ratio	S.E.	Mean score	S.E.	Mean score	S.E.
OECD	Australia	**46**	(1.8)	12.7	(0.85)	**2.1**	(0.1)	515	(2.3)	502	(2.0)
	Austria	**48**	(2.3)	16.6	(1.39)	**2.4**	(0.1)	470	(2.9)	468	(2.6)
	Belgium	**47**	(1.5)	**19.3**	(1.01)	**2.4**	(0.1)	506	(2.3)	499	(2.0)
	Canada	**32**	(1.4)	**8.6**	(0.74)	**1.7**	(0.1)	524	(1.5)	510	(1.4)
	Chile	**31**	(1.5)	**18.7**	(1.56)	**2.3**	(0.1)	449	(3.1)	468	(2.6)
	Czech Republic	**46**	(2.3)	12.4	(1.09)	**2.0**	(0.1)	478	(2.9)	483	(2.7)
	Denmark	36	(1.4)	14.5	(1.02)	**2.1**	(0.1)	495	(2.1)	485	(1.8)
	Estonia	**29**	(2.3)	**7.6**	(1.11)	**1.6**	(0.1)	501	(2.6)	497	(2.4)
	Finland	**31**	(1.7)	**7.8**	(0.82)	**1.8**	(0.1)	536	(2.3)	525	(2.2)
	France	**51**	(2.9)	16.7	(1.97)	**2.4**	(0.2)	496	(3.4)	505	(2.9)
	Germany	**44**	(1.9)	**17.9**	(1.29)	**2.6**	(0.2)	497	(2.7)	493	(2.2)
	Greece	34	(2.4)	12.5	(1.43)	**2.2**	(0.1)	483	(4.3)	484	(3.7)
	Hungary	**48**	(2.2)	**26.0**	(2.17)	**3.0**	(0.2)	494	(3.2)	504	(2.5)
	Iceland	**27**	(1.8)	**6.2**	(0.81)	**1.7**	(0.1)	500	(1.4)	483	(2.0)
	Ireland	39	(2.0)	12.6	(1.17)	**2.2**	(0.2)	496	(3.0)	496	(2.6)
	Israel	**43**	(2.4)	12.5	(1.14)	**2.2**	(0.1)	474	(3.6)	480	(2.8)
	Italy	**32**	(1.3)	**11.8**	(0.74)	**2.1**	(0.1)	486	(1.6)	490	(1.4)
	Japan	40	(2.8)	**8.6**	(0.96)	**1.8**	(0.1)	520	(3.5)	522	(3.0)
	Korea	**32**	(2.5)	**11.0**	(1.51)	**2.2**	(0.2)	539	(3.5)	544	(3.0)
	Luxembourg	40	(1.3)	**18.0**	(1.06)	**2.6**	(0.2)	472	(1.3)	466	(1.3)
	Mexico	**25**	(1.0)	14.5	(0.99)	**2.1**	(0.1)	425	(2.0)	456	(1.8)
	Netherlands	37	(1.9)	12.8	(1.20)	**1.8**	(0.1)	508	(5.1)	499	(4.6)
	New Zealand	**52**	(1.9)	**16.6**	(1.08)	**2.2**	(0.1)	521	(2.4)	519	(2.0)
	Norway	36	(2.1)	**8.6**	(0.96)	**2.0**	(0.1)	503	(2.6)	487	(2.4)
	Poland	39	(1.9)	14.8	(1.38)	**2.0**	(0.1)	500	(2.6)	512	(2.2)
	Portugal	**30**	(1.6)	16.5	(1.60)	**2.0**	(0.2)	489	(3.1)	499	(2.3)
	Slovak Republic	41	(2.3)	14.6	(1.48)	**2.1**	(0.2)	477	(2.5)	482	(2.1)
	Slovenia	39	(1.5)	14.3	(1.06)	**2.0**	(0.1)	483	(1.0)	481	(1.1)
	Spain	**29**	(1.5)	13.6	(1.30)	**2.0**	(0.1)	481	(2.0)	491	(1.8)
	Sweden	**43**	(2.2)	13.4	(1.33)	**2.2**	(0.1)	497	(2.9)	485	(2.4)
	Switzerland	40	(2.1)	14.1	(1.38)	**2.1**	(0.1)	501	(2.4)	498	(2.1)
	Turkey	**29**	(1.5)	**19.0**	(1.91)	**2.3**	(0.2)	464	(3.5)	499	(3.5)
	United Kingdom	**44**	(1.9)	13.7	(1.03)	**2.1**	(0.1)	494	(2.3)	488	(1.8)
	United States	42	(2.3)	16.8	(1.65)	**2.2**	(0.1)	500	(3.7)	493	(2.4)
	OECD average	**38**	(0.3)	**14.0**	(0.2)	**2.1**	(0.0)	493	(0.5)	494	(0.4)
Other G20	Argentina	40	(2.3)	**19.6**	(2.23)	**2.2**	(0.2)	398	(4.6)	424	(3.7)
	Brazil	**28**	(1.4)	13.0	(1.27)	**1.7**	(0.1)	412	(2.7)	445	(2.9)
	Indonesia	**17**	(2.4)	**7.8**	(2.23)	**1.4**	(0.1)	402	(3.7)	428	(5.9)
	Russian Federation	37	(2.5)	**11.3**	(1.35)	**1.9**	(0.1)	459	(3.3)	468	(3.0)
	Shanghai-China	**27**	(2.1)	12.3	(1.77)	**2.1**	(0.1)	556	(2.4)	569	(1.9)

Note: Values that are statistically significant are indicated in bold.
1. In these columns values that are statistically significantly different from the OECD average are indicated in bold.
2. Single-level bivariate regression of reading performance on the ESCS, the slope is the regression coefficient for the ESCS.
Source: OECD, *PISA 2009 Database*.
StatLink http://dx.doi.org/10.1787/888932462719

Table A5.2. [1/2] Percentage of students by immigrant status and their reading performance

Results based on students' self-reports

		Native students				Second-generation students				First-generation students				Students with an immigrant background (first- or second-generation)			
		Percentage of students	S.E.	Performance on the reading scale: Mean score	S.E.	Percentage of students	S.E.	Performance on the reading scale: Mean score	S.E.	Percentage of students	S.E.	Performance on the reading scale: Mean score	S.E.	Percentage of students	S.E.	Performance on the reading scale: Mean score	S.E.
OECD	Australia	76.8	(1.1)	515	(2.1)	12.1	(0.7)	530	(6.2)	11.1	(0.6)	518	(6.3)	23.2	(1.1)	524	(5.8)
	Austria	84.8	(1.2)	482	(2.9)	10.5	(0.9)	427	(6.0)	4.8	(0.6)	384	(10.3)	15.2	(1.2)	414	(6.2)
	Belgium	85.2	(1.1)	519	(2.2)	7.8	(0.7)	454	(7.0)	6.9	(0.7)	448	(8.3)	14.8	(1.1)	451	(6.4)
	Canada	75.6	(1.3)	528	(1.5)	13.7	(0.8)	522	(3.6)	10.7	(0.7)	520	(4.6)	24.4	(1.3)	521	(3.4)
	Chile	99.5	(0.1)	452	(3.0)	0.1	(0.0)	c	c	0.4	(0.1)	c	c	0.5	(0.1)	c	c
	Czech Republic	97.7	(0.2)	479	(2.8)	1.4	(0.2)	448	(17.9)	0.8	(0.1)	472	(17.5)	2.3	(0.2)	457	(13.7)
	Denmark	91.4	(0.4)	502	(2.2)	5.9	(0.3)	446	(4.3)	2.8	(0.2)	422	(6.2)	8.6	(0.4)	438	(3.8)
	Estonia	92.0	(0.6)	505	(2.7)	7.4	(0.6)	470	(6.6)	0.6	(0.1)	470	(17.4)	8.0	(0.6)	470	(6.5)
	Finland	97.4	(0.3)	538	(2.2)	1.1	(0.2)	493	(13.9)	1.4	(0.2)	449	(17.7)	2.6	(0.3)	468	(12.8)
	France	86.9	(1.4)	505	(3.8)	10.0	(1.0)	449	(8.9)	3.2	(0.5)	428	(15.9)	13.1	(1.4)	444	(8.5)
	Germany	82.4	(1.0)	511	(2.6)	11.7	(0.8)	457	(6.1)	5.9	(0.4)	450	(5.7)	17.6	(1.0)	455	(4.7)
	Greece	91.0	(0.8)	489	(4.2)	2.9	(0.3)	456	(10.4)	6.1	(0.7)	420	(15.5)	9.0	(0.8)	432	(11.5)
	Hungary	97.9	(0.3)	495	(3.1)	0.9	(0.1)	527	(12.4)	1.2	(0.2)	493	(11.6)	2.1	(0.3)	507	(8.3)
	Iceland	97.6	(0.2)	504	(1.4)	0.4	(0.1)	c	c	1.9	(0.2)	417	(12.4)	2.4	(0.2)	423	(11.7)
	Ireland	91.7	(0.6)	502	(3.0)	1.4	(0.2)	508	(12.8)	6.8	(0.5)	466	(7.6)	8.3	(0.6)	473	(7.1)
	Israel	80.3	(1.1)	480	(3.3)	12.6	(0.7)	487	(6.5)	7.1	(0.7)	462	(9.2)	19.7	(1.1)	478	(6.4)
	Italy	94.5	(0.3)	491	(1.6)	1.3	(0.1)	446	(9.4)	4.2	(0.2)	410	(4.5)	5.5	(0.3)	418	(4.2)
	Japan	99.7	(0.1)	521	(3.4)	0.1	(0.0)	c	c	0.1	(0.0)	c	c	0.3	(0.1)	c	c
	Korea	100.0	(0.0)	540	(3.4)	0.0	(0.0)	c	c	c	c	c	c	0.0	(0.0)	c	c
	Luxembourg	59.8	(0.7)	495	(1.9)	24.0	(0.6)	439	(2.9)	16.1	(0.5)	448	(4.5)	40.2	(0.7)	442	(2.1)
	Mexico	98.1	(0.2)	430	(1.8)	0.7	(0.1)	340	(9.9)	1.1	(0.1)	324	(9.9)	1.9	(0.2)	331	(7.9)
	Netherlands	87.9	(1.4)	515	(5.2)	8.9	(1.1)	469	(8.2)	3.2	(0.5)	471	(12.5)	12.1	(1.4)	470	(7.8)
	New Zealand	75.3	(1.0)	526	(2.6)	8.0	(0.6)	498	(8.3)	16.7	(0.7)	520	(4.5)	24.7	(1.0)	513	(4.7)
	Norway	93.2	(0.6)	508	(2.6)	3.6	(0.4)	463	(8.0)	3.2	(0.3)	447	(7.8)	6.8	(0.6)	456	(5.9)
	Poland	100.0	(0.0)	502	(2.6)	c	c	c	c	0.0	(0.0)	c	c	0.0	(0.0)	c	c
	Portugal	94.5	(0.5)	492	(3.1)	2.7	(0.3)	476	(9.4)	2.8	(0.3)	456	(8.8)	5.5	(0.5)	466	(6.9)
	Slovak Republic	99.5	(0.1)	478	(2.5)	0.3	(0.1)	c	c	0.3	(0.1)	c	c	0.5	(0.1)	c	c
	Slovenia	92.2	(0.4)	488	(1.1)	6.4	(0.4)	447	(5.5)	1.4	(0.2)	414	(8.7)	7.8	(0.4)	441	(4.8)
	Spain	90.5	(0.5)	488	(2.0)	1.1	(0.1)	461	(9.3)	8.4	(0.5)	426	(4.1)	9.5	(0.5)	430	(4.0)
	Sweden	88.3	(1.2)	507	(2.7)	8.0	(0.8)	454	(7.5)	3.7	(0.5)	416	(11.3)	11.7	(1.2)	442	(6.9)
	Switzerland	76.5	(0.9)	513	(2.2)	15.1	(0.7)	471	(4.5)	8.4	(0.5)	455	(6.7)	23.5	(0.9)	465	(4.1)
	Turkey	99.5	(0.1)	466	(3.5)	0.4	(0.1)	c	c	0.1	(0.1)	c	c	0.5	(0.1)	c	c
	United Kingdom	89.4	(1.0)	499	(2.2)	5.8	(0.7)	492	(8.5)	4.8	(0.4)	458	(9.5)	10.6	(1.0)	476	(7.5)
	United States	80.5	(1.3)	506	(3.8)	13.0	(1.1)	483	(6.2)	6.4	(0.5)	485	(7.9)	19.5	(1.3)	484	(5.8)
	OECD average	89.6	(0.1)	499	(0.5)	6.0	(0.1)	467	(1.7)	4.6	(0.1)	448	(2.0)	10.4	(0.1)	457	(1.4)
Other G20	Argentina	96.4	(0.5)	401	(4.6)	2.2	(0.3)	366	(12.6)	1.5	(0.3)	356	(26.5)	3.6	(0.5)	362	(15.2)
	Brazil	99.2	(0.1)	416	(2.7)	0.5	(0.1)	321	(18.7)	0.3	(0.1)	310	(18.6)	0.8	(0.1)	317	(13.5)
	Indonesia	99.7	(0.1)	403	(3.7)	c	c	c	c	0.3	(0.1)	c	c	0.3	(0.1)	c	c
	Russian Federation	87.9	(0.7)	464	(3.2)	7.2	(0.7)	435	(9.4)	4.9	(0.4)	444	(7.1)	12.1	(0.7)	439	(7.0)
	Shanghai-China	99.5	(0.1)	557	(2.3)	0.1	(0.0)	c	c	0.5	(0.1)	c	c	0.5	(0.1)	c	c

Source: OECD, *PISA 2009 Database.*

Please refer to the Reader's Guide for information concerning the symbols replacing missing data.

StatLink http://dx.doi.org/10.1787/888932462738

Table A5.2. [2/2] **Percentage of students by immigrant status and their reading performance**

Results based on students' self-reports

		Difference in reading performance between native and second-generation students		Difference in reading performance between native and first-generation students		Difference in reading performance between second- and first-generation students		Difference in reading performance between native students and students with an immigrant background		Difference in reading performance between native students and students with an immigrant background, after accounting for socio-economic background		Pooled within-country correlations between students' socio-economic status and immigrant status		Pooled within-country correlations between schools' socio-economic status and immigrant status		Difference in the PISA index of economic, social and cultural status between native students and students with an immigrant background		Increased likelihood of first-generation students scoring in the bottom quarter of the reading performance distribution	
		Score dif.	S.E.	Score dif.	S.E.	Score dif.	S.E.	Score dif.	S.E.	Score dif.	S.E.	Corr.	S.E.	Corr.	S.E.	Dif.	S.E.	Ratio	S.E.
OECD	Australia	**-16**	(6.4)	-3	(6.1)	**12**	(4.8)	-10	(5.8)	**-11**	(5.1)	0.01	(0.01)	0.00	(0.07)	0.01	(0.03)	**0.89**	(0.07)
	Austria	**55**	(6.7)	**98**	(10.6)	**43**	(10.7)	**68**	(6.7)	**37**	(6.7)	**-0.30**	(0.02)	**-0.41**	(0.06)	**0.73**	(0.05)	**2.69**	(0.27)
	Belgium	**65**	(7.2)	**71**	(8.0)	6	(8.6)	**68**	(6.3)	**41**	(5.3)	**-0.19**	(0.02)	**-0.39**	(0.05)	**0.56**	(0.06)	**2.18**	(0.17)
	Canada	5	(3.8)	8	(4.7)	3	(4.4)	7	(3.6)	3	(3.1)	-0.02	(0.02)	0.02	(0.05)	**0.08**	(0.04)	**1.27**	(0.09)
	Chile	c	c	c	c	c	c	c	c	c	c	c	c	c	c	c	c	c	c
	Czech Republic	31	(17.7)	7	(16.8)	-24	(23.7)	22	(13.2)	17	(11.4)	-0.01	(0.02)	0.08	(0.10)	0.13	(0.10)	**1.29**	(0.42)
	Denmark	**56**	(4.3)	**79**	(6.5)	**24**	(7.0)	**63**	(3.9)	**36**	(3.7)	**-0.22**	(0.02)	**-0.42**	(0.04)	**0.75**	(0.04)	**2.51**	(0.19)
	Estonia	**35**	(6.5)	**35**	(17.1)	0	(17.1)	**35**	(6.3)	**34**	(5.8)	-0.02	(0.02)	0.01	(0.04)	0.06	(0.06)	**1.49**	(0.34)
	Finland	**45**	(13.9)	**89**	(17.6)	**44**	(21.8)	**70**	(12.7)	**60**	(11.2)	**-0.07**	(0.03)	**0.30**	(0.04)	**0.32**	(0.12)	**2.44**	(0.31)
	France	**55**	(9.6)	**77**	(16.2)	22	(16.6)	**60**	(9.2)	**30**	(8.4)	**-0.23**	(0.03)	**-0.50**	(0.06)	**0.60**	(0.05)	**2.11**	(0.28)
	Germany	**54**	(6.2)	**61**	(6.0)	7	(7.9)	**56**	(4.8)	**27**	(4.3)	**-0.27**	(0.02)	**-0.44**	(0.04)	**0.72**	(0.04)	**1.98**	(0.16)
	Greece	**33**	(10.3)	**69**	(15.2)	**36**	(18.0)	**57**	(11.1)	**35**	(10.9)	**-0.20**	(0.02)	**-0.36**	(0.05)	**0.68**	(0.06)	**2.08**	(0.28)
	Hungary	**-32**	(12.4)	2	(11.7)	34	(17.5)	-12	(8.4)	-11	(7.3)	0.00	(0.02)	**-0.20**	(0.09)	-0.03	(0.11)	**1.10**	(0.31)
	Iceland	c	c	**87**	(12.4)	c	c	**81**	(11.7)	**61**	(11.9)	**-0.14**	(0.02)	**-0.16**	(0.01)	**0.81**	(0.11)	**2.39**	(0.31)
	Ireland	-6	(13.4)	**36**	(7.7)	**42**	(14.6)	**29**	(7.3)	**33**	(6.5)	0.03	(0.02)	0.04	(0.08)	-0.09	(0.06)	**1.80**	(0.19)
	Israel	-7	(6.1)	**18**	(8.9)	**25**	(8.5)	2	(6.1)	**-17**	(4.7)	**-0.15**	(0.02)	**-0.10**	(0.05)	**0.32**	(0.06)	**1.26**	(0.15)
	Italy	**45**	(9.4)	**81**	(4.7)	**36**	(10.3)	**72**	(4.4)	**53**	(4.4)	**-0.14**	(0.01)	**-0.51**	(0.02)	**0.63**	(0.05)	**2.44**	(0.14)
	Japan	c	c	c	c	c	c	c	c	c	c	c	c	c	c	c	c	c	c
	Korea	c	c	c	c	c	c	c	c	c	c	c	c	c	c	c	c	c	c
	Luxembourg	**56**	(3.7)	**47**	(4.9)	-9	(6.0)	**52**	(3.0)	**19**	(3.1)	**-0.34**	(0.01)	**-0.44**	(0.00)	**0.91**	(0.03)	**1.69**	(0.11)
	Mexico	**89**	(9.7)	**105**	(9.5)	16	(12.3)	**99**	(7.5)	**85**	(7.4)	**-0.06**	(0.01)	**-0.28**	(0.03)	**0.57**	(0.08)	**3.15**	(0.17)
	Netherlands	**46**	(9.3)	**44**	(10.9)	-2	(12.3)	**46**	(8.0)	14	(8.0)	**-0.29**	(0.03)	**-0.47**	(0.09)	**0.83**	(0.07)	**1.68**	(0.22)
	New Zealand	**28**	(9.0)	6	(5.0)	**-22**	(8.5)	**13**	(5.3)	**14**	(4.1)	**0.05**	(0.02)	**-0.15**	(0.06)	-0.03	(0.03)	**1.11**	(0.09)
	Norway	**45**	(8.1)	**60**	(7.5)	15	(10.5)	**52**	(5.7)	**33**	(5.5)	**-0.19**	(0.02)	-0.12	(0.09)	**0.54**	(0.06)	**2.11**	(0.19)
	Poland	c	c	c	c	c	c	c	c	c	c	c	c	c	c	c	c	c	c
	Portugal	16	(9.4)	**36**	(8.9)	20	(11.6)	**26**	(7.0)	**24**	(6.0)	-0.01	(0.01)	**-0.12**	(0.05)	0.06	(0.08)	**1.74**	(0.21)
	Slovak Republic	c	c	c	c	c	c	c	c	c	c	c	c	c	c	c	c	c	c
	Slovenia	**41**	(5.6)	**74**	(8.9)	**33**	(10.4)	**47**	(4.9)	**24**	(4.9)	**-0.18**	(0.01)	**-0.29**	(0.01)	**0.62**	(0.05)	**2.06**	(0.29)
	Spain	**26**	(9.2)	**62**	(4.0)	**35**	(9.7)	**58**	(3.9)	**44**	(3.4)	**-0.13**	(0.02)	0.02	(0.06)	**0.47**	(0.05)	**2.17**	(0.11)
	Sweden	**53**	(7.7)	**91**	(11.6)	**38**	(12.2)	**66**	(7.2)	**40**	(6.2)	**-0.23**	(0.03)	**-0.31**	(0.08)	**0.55**	(0.05)	**2.47**	(0.25)
	Switzerland	**42**	(3.9)	**58**	(6.5)	**16**	(7.2)	**48**	(3.5)	**28**	(3.0)	**-0.24**	(0.02)	**-0.34**	(0.06)	**0.56**	(0.04)	**1.98**	(0.12)
	Turkey	c	c	c	c	c	c	c	c	c	c	c	c	c	c	c	c	c	c
	United Kingdom	7	(8.6)	**41**	(9.7)	**34**	(10.7)	**23**	(7.6)	**14**	(5.4)	**-0.08**	(0.03)	**-0.19**	(0.09)	**0.18**	(0.09)	**1.66**	(0.20)
	United States	**22**	(6.1)	**21**	(7.2)	-2	(7.6)	**22**	(5.5)	**-9**	(4.1)	**-0.28**	(0.03)	**-0.49**	(0.06)	**0.70**	(0.07)	**1.30**	(0.13)
	OECD average	**33**	(1.7)	**52**	(1.9)	**18**	(2.4)	**44**	(1.4)	**27**	(1.3)	**-0.14**	(0.00)	**-0.22**	(0.01)	**0.44**	(0.01)	**1.89**	(0.04)
Other G20	Argentina	**35**	(13.3)	46	(26.6)	10	(24.7)	**40**	(15.6)	16	(15.3)	**-0.08**	(0.02)	-0.09	(0.09)	**0.58**	(0.10)	**1.54**	(0.42)
	Brazil	**95**	(19.0)	**106**	(18.8)	11	(27.2)	**99**	(13.8)	**94**	(13.3)	-0.02	(0.02)	-0.02	(0.03)	0.18	(0.24)	**3.07**	(0.51)
	Indonesia	c	c	c	c	c	c	c	c	c	c	c	c	c	c	c	c	c	c
	Russian Federation	**29**	(9.4)	**20**	(6.6)	-9	(10.1)	**25**	(6.8)	**20**	(5.7)	**-0.05**	(0.02)	**-0.27**	(0.05)	**0.13**	(0.04)	**1.27**	(0.20)
	Shanghai-China	c	c	c	c	c	c	c	c	c	c	c	c	c	c	c	c	c	c

Note: Values that are statistically significant are indicated in bold.

Source: OECD, *PISA 2009 Database*.

Please refer to the Reader's Guide for information concerning the symbols replacing missing data.

StatLink http://dx.doi.org/10.1787/888932462738

Table A5.3. Percentage of resilient students and disadvantaged low achievers among all students, by gender

Results based on students' self-reports

		Resilient and disadvantaged low achievers											
		Resilient students[1]						Disadvantaged low achievers[2]					
		All students		Girls		Boys		All students		Girls		Boys	
		%	S.E.	%	S.E.	%	S.E.	%	S.E.	%	S.E.	%	S.E.
OECD	Australia	7.7	(0.3)	9.5	(0.5)	5.8	(0.4)	4.4	(0.3)	2.9	(0.3)	6.0	(0.4)
	Austria	4.9	(0.4)	6.3	(0.5)	3.5	(0.5)	8.2	(0.6)	6.1	(0.8)	10.4	(0.7)
	Belgium	7.6	(0.3)	9.6	(0.5)	5.7	(0.4)	5.1	(0.4)	4.1	(0.5)	6.0	(0.6)
	Canada	9.8	(0.5)	11.6	(0.7)	8.0	(0.5)	2.9	(0.2)	1.8	(0.2)	3.9	(0.3)
	Chile	6.0	(0.5)	7.3	(0.8)	4.7	(0.5)	3.9	(0.5)	2.9	(0.5)	4.9	(0.7)
	Czech Republic	5.3	(0.4)	7.4	(0.6)	3.5	(0.4)	5.8	(0.5)	4.0	(0.5)	7.4	(0.7)
	Denmark	6.0	(0.5)	7.5	(0.8)	4.4	(0.5)	4.2	(0.4)	3.5	(0.4)	4.9	(0.5)
	Estonia	8.5	(0.5)	11.4	(1.0)	5.9	(0.6)	2.9	(0.4)	1.5	(0.4)	4.1	(0.7)
	Finland	11.4	(0.6)	14.4	(0.7)	8.4	(0.8)	2.2	(0.3)	1.0	(0.2)	3.5	(0.4)
	France	7.6	(0.6)	10.1	(0.9)	5.1	(0.7)	5.2	(0.5)	3.6	(0.5)	6.9	(0.8)
	Germany	5.7	(0.4)	7.2	(0.6)	4.2	(0.5)	5.1	(0.5)	3.7	(0.5)	6.5	(0.7)
	Greece	6.9	(0.5)	9.6	(0.9)	4.2	(0.5)	5.2	(0.9)	3.2	(0.6)	7.3	(1.3)
	Hungary	6.4	(0.5)	9.2	(0.9)	3.7	(0.5)	4.2	(0.7)	2.6	(0.8)	5.7	(0.8)
	Iceland	7.4	(0.5)	9.7	(0.7)	5.1	(0.6)	5.1	(0.4)	3.6	(0.5)	6.7	(0.6)
	Ireland	7.4	(0.6)	9.4	(0.8)	5.5	(0.8)	4.1	(0.4)	2.4	(0.4)	5.9	(0.7)
	Israel	6.0	(0.5)	8.4	(0.7)	3.4	(0.5)	6.9	(0.6)	5.6	(0.7)	8.3	(0.7)
	Italy	8.0	(0.3)	10.8	(0.4)	5.3	(0.3)	4.4	(0.3)	2.5	(0.3)	6.1	(0.5)
	Japan	10.5	(0.6)	12.2	(0.8)	9.0	(0.7)	3.3	(0.4)	1.9	(0.4)	4.7	(0.7)
	Korea	14.0	(0.8)	16.3	(1.3)	12.1	(0.9)	1.3	(0.4)	0.5	(0.2)	2.0	(0.6)
	Luxembourg	5.1	(0.4)	7.0	(0.6)	3.2	(0.5)	7.4	(0.4)	5.7	(0.6)	9.1	(0.6)
	Mexico	7.3	(0.4)	9.2	(0.5)	5.3	(0.4)	3.5	(0.3)	2.7	(0.3)	4.2	(0.4)
	Netherlands	8.0	(0.8)	9.2	(1.1)	6.8	(0.8)	2.8	(0.4)	2.1	(0.5)	3.5	(0.6)
	New Zealand	9.2	(0.5)	11.7	(0.7)	6.8	(0.7)	3.6	(0.4)	1.8	(0.4)	5.4	(0.6)
	Norway	6.5	(0.4)	9.3	(0.7)	3.8	(0.5)	5.1	(0.4)	3.6	(0.4)	6.6	(0.7)
	Poland	9.2	(0.5)	12.7	(0.8)	5.7	(0.6)	3.0	(0.4)	1.4	(0.3)	4.6	(0.6)
	Portugal	9.8	(0.5)	12.9	(0.8)	6.6	(0.5)	2.8	(0.3)	1.5	(0.4)	4.2	(0.5)
	Slovak Republic	5.3	(0.4)	7.0	(0.6)	3.5	(0.5)	5.6	(0.6)	3.6	(0.6)	7.7	(0.9)
	Slovenia	6.1	(0.5)	9.4	(0.8)	3.0	(0.4)	5.1	(0.3)	2.8	(0.3)	7.2	(0.5)
	Spain	9.0	(0.6)	10.5	(1.0)	7.6	(0.6)	3.3	(0.4)	2.3	(0.3)	4.3	(0.5)
	Sweden	6.4	(0.5)	8.1	(0.7)	4.6	(0.6)	5.8	(0.5)	3.4	(0.6)	8.1	(0.7)
	Switzerland	7.9	(0.5)	10.4	(0.9)	5.6	(0.4)	4.5	(0.4)	3.0	(0.4)	5.9	(0.6)
	Turkey	10.5	(0.6)	11.5	(0.8)	9.5	(0.8)	1.6	(0.3)	0.7	(0.3)	2.5	(0.5)
	United Kingdom	6.0	(0.4)	7.0	(0.6)	4.8	(0.5)	5.0	(0.4)	4.1	(0.4)	5.9	(0.6)
	United States	7.2	(0.6)	8.6	(0.9)	5.7	(0.5)	4.6	(0.4)	3.0	(0.4)	6.1	(0.6)
	OECD average	7.7	(0.3)	9.8	(0.6)	5.6	(0.3)	4.4	(0.2)	2.9	(0.2)	5.8	(0.5)
Other G20	Argentina	2.7	(0.3)	3.8	(0.5)	1.6	(0.4)	9.9	(0.9)	8.3	(0.8)	11.7	(1.1)
	Brazil	5.5	(0.4)	7.4	(0.6)	3.4	(0.3)	4.6	(0.3)	3.9	(0.4)	5.3	(0.5)
	Indonesia	6.0	(0.7)	8.3	(0.9)	3.7	(0.7)	2.0	(0.4)	1.3	(0.4)	2.8	(0.5)
	Russian Federation	4.7	(0.5)	6.2	(0.7)	3.2	(0.4)	6.0	(0.6)	3.9	(0.6)	8.1	(1.0)
	Shanghai-China	18.9	(1.0)	20.6	(1.2)	17.2	(1.1)	0.3	(0.1)	0.1	(0.1)	0.5	(0.2)

1. A student is classified as resilient if he or she is in the bottom quarter of the *PISA index of economic, social and cultural status* (ESCS) in the country of assessment and performs in the top quarter across students from all countries, after accounting for socio-economic background.

2. A student is classified as a disadvantaged low achiever if he or she is in the bottom quarter of the *PISA index of economic, social and cultural status* (ESCS) in the country of assessment and performs in the bottom quarter across students from all countries, after accounting for socio-economic background.

Source: OECD, *PISA 2009 Database*.

StatLink http://dx.doi.org/10.1787/888932462757

INDICATOR A6

ARE STUDENTS WHO ENJOY READING BETTER READERS?

- Across OECD countries, the quarter of students who most enjoy reading score one-and-a-half proficiency levels higher in reading than the quarter who enjoy reading the least.
- In most countries, students who read fiction for enjoyment are much more likely to be good readers.

Chart A6.1. Relationship between enjoying reading and performance in reading
By national quarters of the **index of enjoyment in reading**

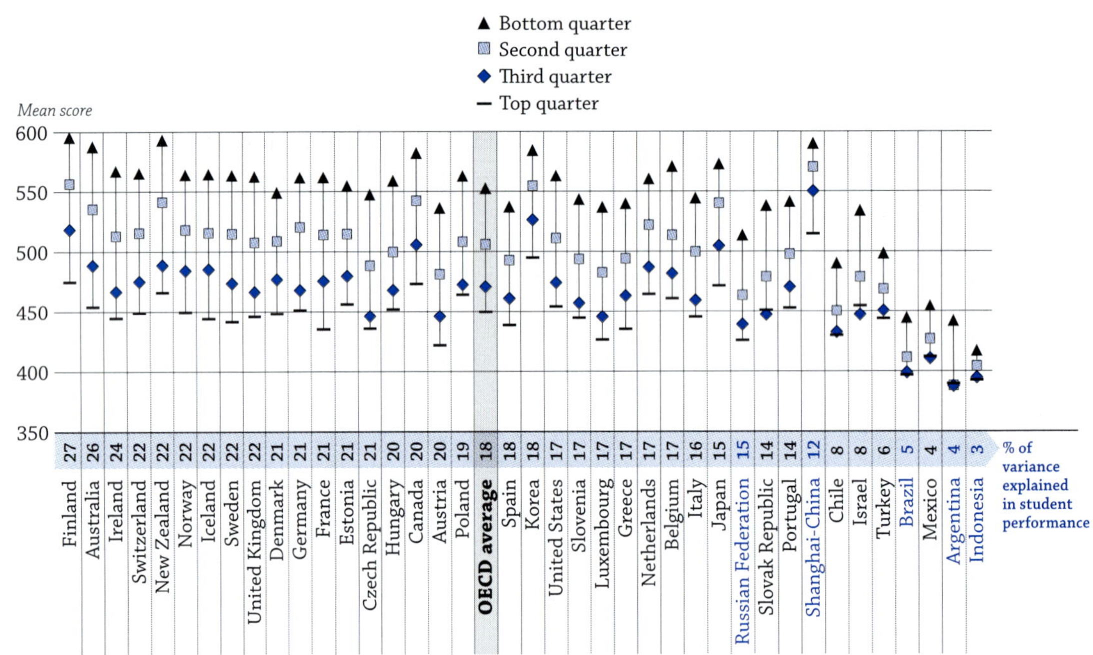

Countries are ranked in descending order of the percentage of explained variance in student performance.
Source: OECD, *PISA 2009 Database*, Table A6.1.
StatLink http://dx.doi.org/10.1787/888932460306

How to read this chart
The chart shows the variation in student reading performance according to the quarter of the *index of enjoyment of reading* in which students are classified (see Definitions below). Countries are ranked according to the percentage of the variation in reading performance explained by the *index of enjoyment of reading* which is indicated next to the name of the country; thus, countries on the left part of the chart are those where a large share of variation in student performance can be explained by how much students reported enjoying reading. Countries where a relatively small share of this variation can be explained by how much students reported enjoying reading are in the right part of this chart.

Context

Students who enjoy reading, and therefore make it a regular part of their lives, are able to build their reading skills through practice. PISA shows strong associations between reading enjoyment and performance. This does not mean that results show that enjoyment of reading has a direct impact on reading scores; rather, the finding is consistent with research showing that such enjoyment is an important precondition for becoming an effective reader. Therefore, to bolster reading performance, schools need to both instruct students in reading techniques and foster an interest in reading.

While the strongest readers are those who read fiction, in practice, many students show a preference for other reading materials that have more direct relevance to their daily lives. Encouraging reading of diverse materials, such as magazines, newspapers and non-fiction books, can help to make reading a habit, especially for some weaker readers who might not be inclined to read a work of fiction.

Other findings

- On average across OECD countries, **37% of students reported that they do not read for enjoyment at all**.
- **Students who read newspapers, magazines and non-fiction books are better readers in many countries**, although the effect of these materials on reading performance is not as much pronounced as the effect of fiction books.
- In every country, **girls read for enjoyment more than boys** (index for enjoyment is 0.31 and -0.31, respectively). Girls also read fiction and magazines more than boys, but boys are more likely to read newspapers and comic books.

Trends

Students in 2009 tended to be less enthusiastic about reading than their counterparts were in 2000. Accross the 26 OECD countries that participated in both assessments, the percentage of students who reported reading for enjoyment fell from 69% to 64%. While the majority of students do read for enjoyment, the growth in the minority who do not should prompt schools to try to engage students in reading activities that they find relevant and interesting.

Analysis

Enjoyment of reading and student performance

The quarter of students who show the highest levels of reading enjoyment attain at least proficiency Level 4, meaning that they have a 50% chance of completing a relatively complex reading task. In Australia and Finland, two of the best-performing countries overall, over 25% of differences in reading performance are associated with how much students enjoy reading. In these countries and in New Zealand, the quarter of students who enjoy reading the most reach exceptionally high levels of reading proficiency, around the middle of Level 4.

In 16 OECD countries, at least 20% of the variation in reading performance is explained by enjoyment of reading. On average in OECD countries, there is a difference of 103 points between the average scores of the top and bottom quarters of students ranked by reading enjoyment. The quarter of students who score the lowest are generally only able to perform relatively simple reading tasks at baseline proficiency Level 2 (see Definitions below).

PISA results show that the group of countries where enjoyment of reading makes the least difference in reading performance tend to have lower reading scores, overall, than those countries where enjoyment of reading makes more of a difference. However, this is not true in Japan, Korea and Shanghai-China (Chart A6.1).

Time spent reading for enjoyment is strongly related to reading performance. Better readers tend to read more because they are more motivated to read, which, in turn, leads to improved vocabulary and comprehension skills.

In all countries and economies that participated in PISA 2009, students who read for enjoyment tend to be more proficient readers than students who do not read for enjoyment. Chart A6.2 shows the average score in the PISA 2009 reading assessment for five groups of students in each country: students who do not read for enjoyment; students who read for enjoyment for up to 30 minutes per day; students who spend between half an hour and one hour daily reading for enjoyment; students who spend between one and two hours; and a group of extremely dedicated readers who reported spending more than two hours per day reading for enjoyment.

Chart A6.2. Relationship between time spent reading for enjoyment and performance in reading

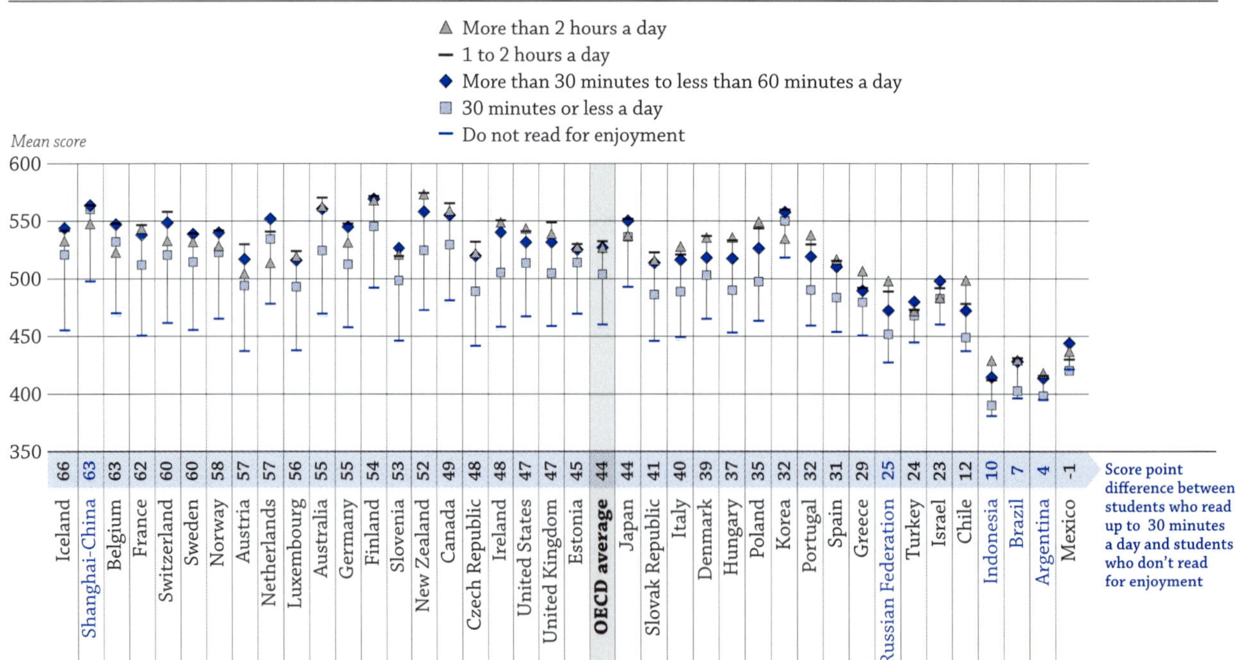

Countries are ranked in descending order of the score point difference between students who read up to 30 minutes a day and students who don't read for enjoyment.
Source: OECD, *PISA 2009 Database*, Table A6.2.
StatLink http://dx.doi.org/10.1787/888932460325

On average across OECD countries, over one-third of students – and 40% or more in Austria, Belgium, the Czech Republic, Germany, Ireland, Japan, Luxembourg, the Netherlands, Norway, the Slovak Republic, Switzerland and the United States – reported that they did not read for enjoyment at all. The average score among these students, 460 points on the PISA reading scale, is well below the OECD average of 493 score points. Another one-third of students across OECD countries read for 30 minutes or less per day. Their mean performance, 504 score points, is in line with the OECD average. A further 17% of students across OECD countries read for between half-an-hour and one hour per day, and achieve an average score of 527 points. Students who reported reading for longer – between one and two hours per day – and assiduous readers, who read for enjoyment for more than two hours daily, achieve scores of 532 and 527 points, respectively (Table A6.2).

In more than two-thirds of countries that participated in PISA, the score point difference associated with at least some daily reading for enjoyment is far greater than the score point difference associated with increasing amounts of time spent reading. The gap in performance between students who read for enjoyment for 30 minutes or less per day and students who do not read for enjoyment at all is more than 30 points in 31 countries; in Belgium, France and Iceland it is more than 60 points. However, the performance gap between students who read for enjoyment between 30 minutes and one hour per day and students who read 30 minutes or less is more than 30 points in only five countries: Australia, the Czech Republic, Germany, Ireland and New Zealand. In no country is the performance gap between students who read for enjoyment between one and two hours per day and students who read between half-an-hour and one hour per day more than 20 points.

The poor reading performance among students who do not read for enjoyment at all demands that education systems encourage reading both in and outside of school. Given that the association between reading daily for enjoyment and reading proficiency is stronger than that between how many hours a day students read and reading proficiency, policy makers should focus on encouraging students to read daily for enjoyment rather than on how much time they spend reading.

Reading material and student performance

PISA 2009 offers a valuable opportunity to explore the association between what students report reading in their free time and reading performance. Although no causal relationship can be established, PISA results offer a glimpse of how reading certain materials is associated with reading proficiency. Chart A6.3 presents the difference in reading performance between students who reported reading regularly, either several times a month or several times a week, and for their enjoyment, different types of material: magazines, comic books, fiction (novels, narratives, stories), non-fiction, and newspapers, and students who reported not reading these materials for enjoyment. Reading fiction for a student's own enjoyment appears to be positively associated with higher performance in the PISA 2009 reading assessment, while reading comic books is associated with little improvement in reading proficiency in some countries, and with lower overall reading performance in other countries (Table A6.3).

In most countries, students who read fiction are particularly likely to be good readers. On average across OECD countries, students who read fiction for their own enjoyment at least several times a month score 53 points above those who do so less frequently. This is equivalent to three-quarters of a proficiency level and more than a year's worth of formal schooling. However, the link between reading fiction and strong reading performance varies greatly across countries. In Argentina, Brazil, Mexico and Turkey there is no positive relationship of this kind. However, in the OECD countries Australia, Austria, Finland, Luxembourg and Sweden, there is a gap of at least one proficiency level between the scores of those 15-year-olds who read fiction frequently and those students who read fiction less often.

Students who read magazines and newspapers regularly for enjoyment also tend to be better readers than those who do not. However, the relationship is less strong than that between performance and reading fiction. Only in Iceland, Israel and Sweden do regular readers of newspapers score at least 35 points more, on average, than other students. Students who read magazines regularly score at least 35 points above those who do not in Finland, Hungary, the Netherlands and the Slovak Republic.

Chart A6.3. [1/2] Relationship between the types of materials students read and performance in reading

Score point difference between students who read these materials and students who do not

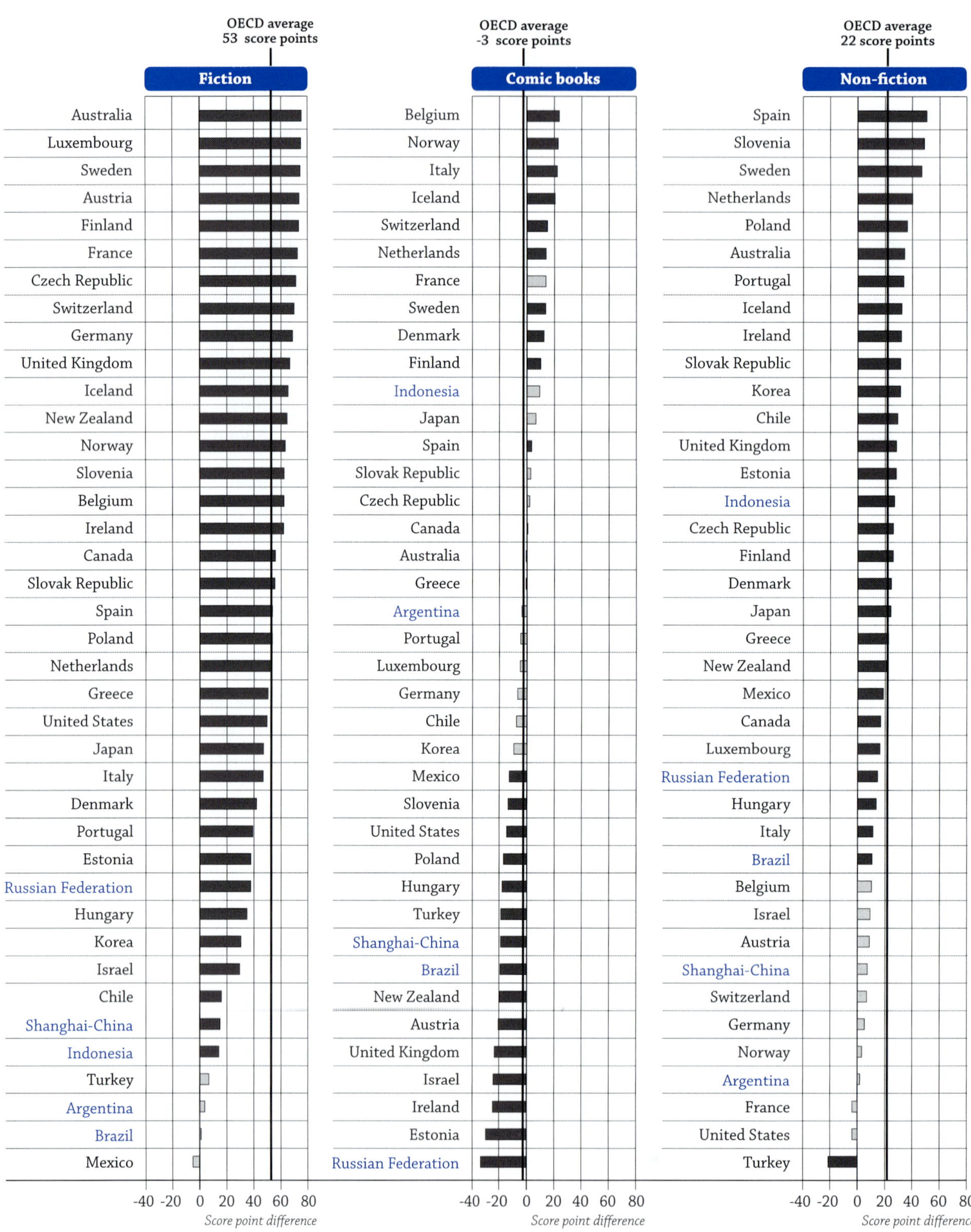

Note: Score point differences that are statistically significant are marked in a darker tone.

Source: OECD, *PISA 2009 Database*, Table A6.3.

StatLink http://dx.doi.org/10.1787/888932460344

Chart A6.3. [2/2] Relationship between the types of materials students read and performance in reading

Score point difference between students who read these materials and students who do not

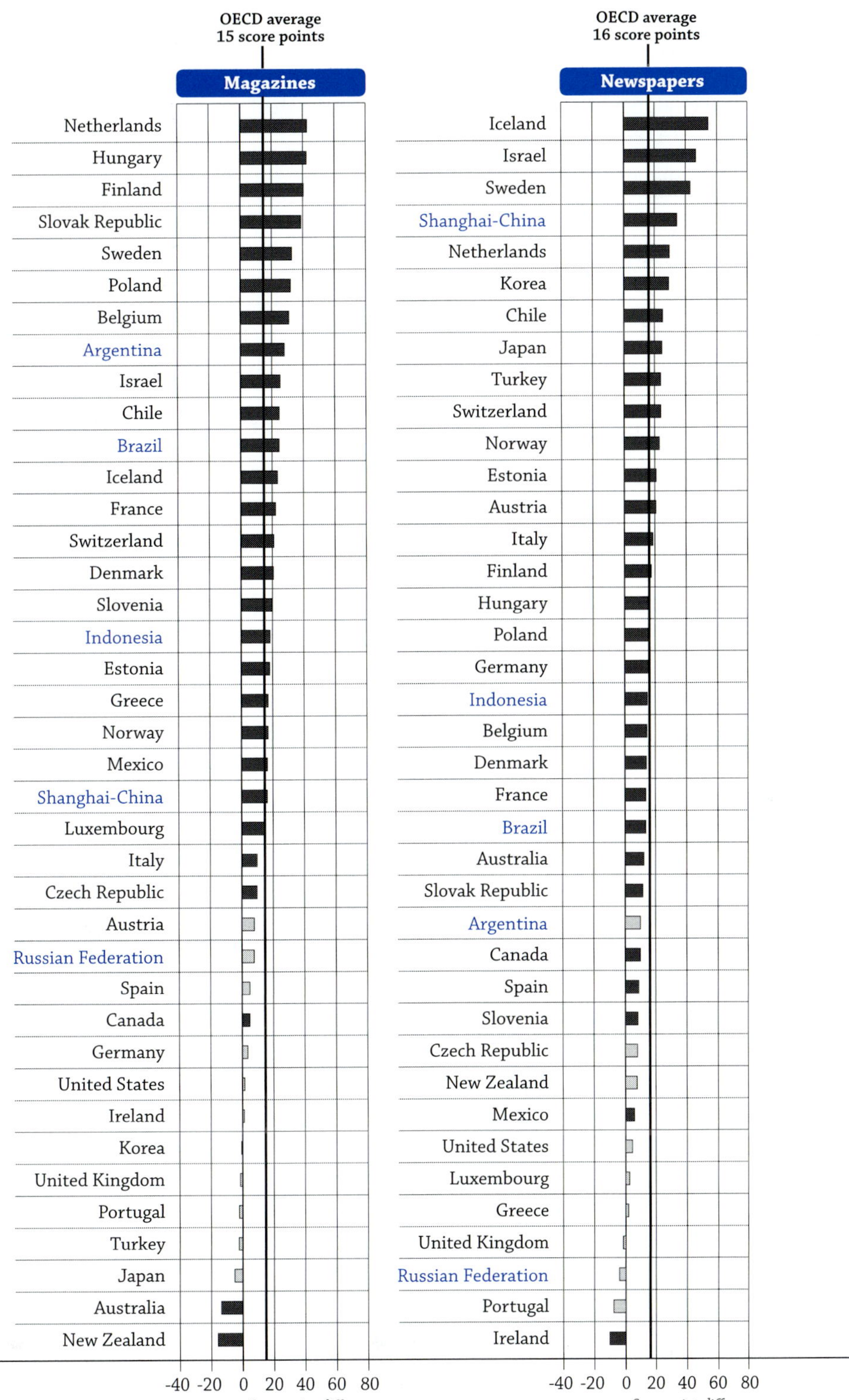

Note: Score point differences that are statistically significant are marked in a darker tone.

Source: OECD, *PISA 2009 Database*, Table A6.3.

StatLink http://dx.doi.org/10.1787/888932460344

Frequent readers of non-fiction read at a higher level than average in some countries, but in most countries, there is no significant positive relationship. The difference is greater than 35 score points in the Netherlands, Poland, Slovenia, Spain and Sweden.

Reading comic books is generally associated with a low level of reading performance. This could well be because weaker readers find comic books more accessible.

These findings need to be set alongside the actual frequency with which students read different materials for enjoyment. On average in OECD countries:

- 62% of students read newspapers at least several times a month;
- 58% read magazines;
- 31% read fiction;
- 22% read comic books; and
- 19% read non-fiction books.

Reading habits of boys and girls

In every country except Korea, girls reported reading for enjoyment more than boys. On average across OECD countries, just over half of boys (52%) but nearly three-quarters of girls (73%) said that they read for enjoyment (Chart A6.4).

The gender gap in reading for enjoyment is greatest in Estonia and the Netherlands, where it is at least 30 percentage points. In 12 countries, only a minority of boys reported that they read for enjoyment. In Austria, Luxembourg and the Netherlands, fewer than 40% of boys said that they read for enjoyment.

Chart A6.4. Percentage of students, by whether they spend any time reading for enjoyment and by gender

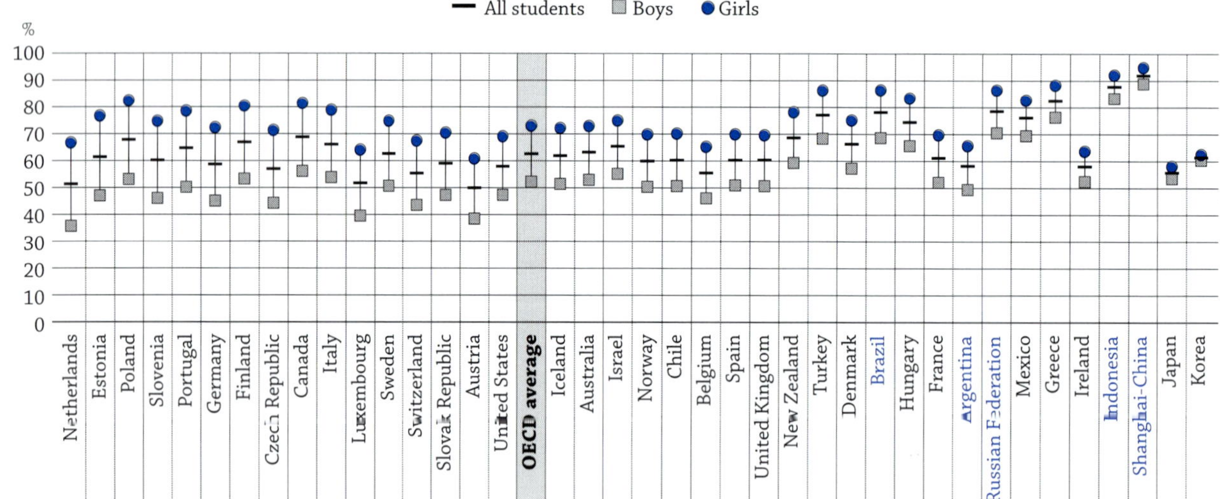

Countries are ranked in descending order of the percentage point difference between girls and boys.
Source: OECD, *PISA 2009 Database*, Table A6.4.
StatLink http://dx.doi.org/10.1787/888932460363

In some of the countries that show small gender differences in enjoyment of reading, both boys and girls are relatively unlikely to report that they enjoy reading. In Japan, for example, only 54% of boys and 58% of girls reported that they enjoy reading. In some countries, the narrow gender gap reflects the opposite: both boys and girls enjoy reading to nearly the same extent. For example, in Indonesia and in Shanghai-China, at least 80% of boys and 90% of girls reported that they read for enjoyment.

Other data from PISA show that girls and boys typically enjoy different kinds of reading. Girls are twice as likely to read fiction for enjoyment, and are more likely than boys to read magazines; boys more commonly read newspapers and comic books. The fact that two in three boys, on average in OECD countries, reported that they read newspapers for pleasure, compared to only one in five who said they read fiction for enjoyment, shows that there could be far more potential for strengthening boys' reading skills by encouraging boys to read other materials in addition to literature (Chart A6.5).

Chart A6.5. What boys and girls read for enjoyment, OECD average

Percentage of boys and girls who reported that they read "several times a month" or "several times a week" the following materials because they want to

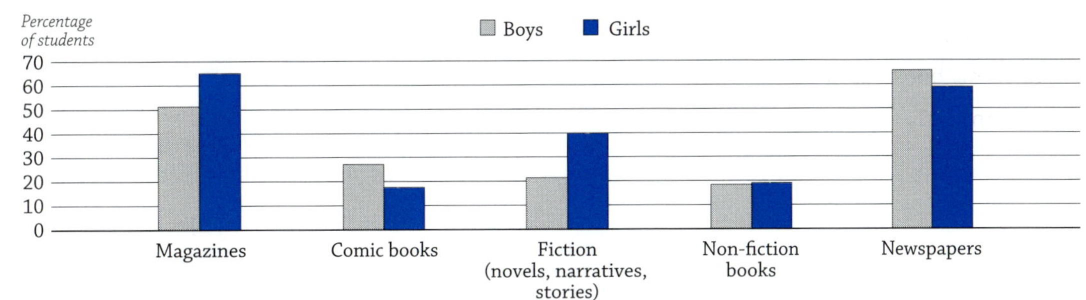

Note: All differences between boys and girls are significant.
Source: OECD, *PISA 2009 Database*, Table A6.5, available on line.
StatLink http://dx.doi.org/10.1787/888932460382

Changes in whether students read for enjoyment

In 18 of the 30 countries for which comparable data are available, the percentage of 15-year-olds who reported that they enjoy reading fell between 2000 and 2009. In nine countries it did not change significantly, and in three the percentage grew (Chart A6.6).

Chart A6.6. Percentage of students who read for enjoyment in 2000 and 2009

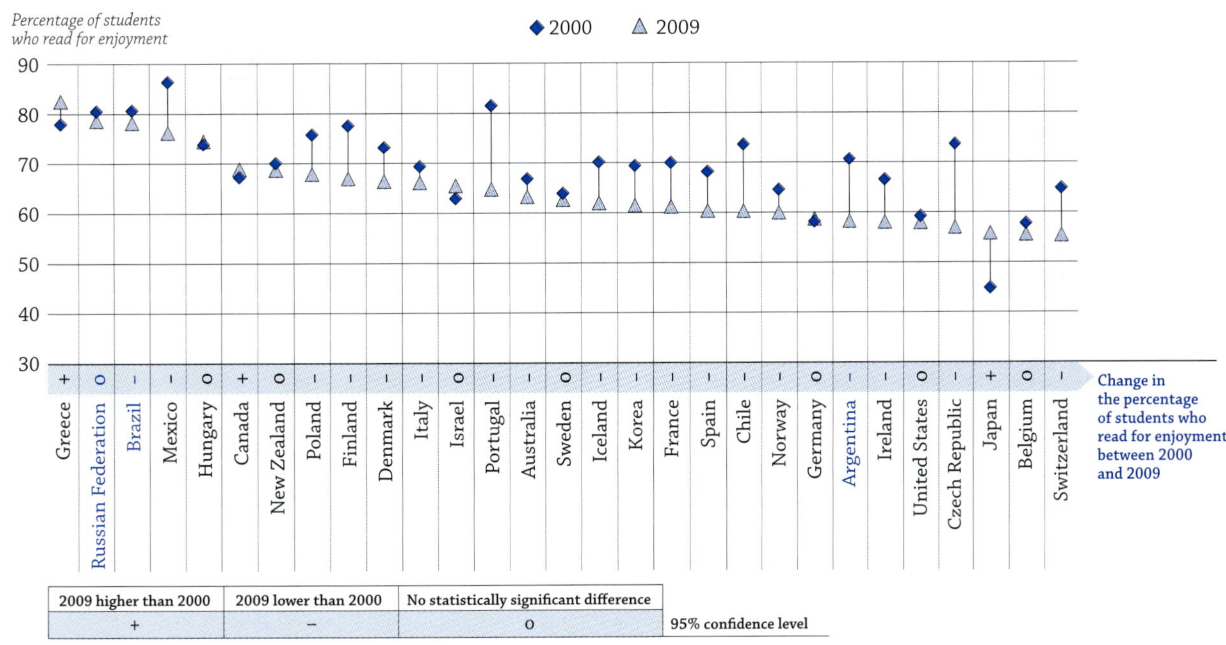

Countries are ranked in descending order of the percentage of students who read for enjoyment in 2009.
Source: OECD, *PISA 2009 Database*, Table A6.2.
StatLink http://dx.doi.org/10.1787/888932460401

The largest declines in reading enjoyment, by at least double the average rate, occurred in Argentina, Chile, the Czech Republic, Finland, Mexico, Portugal. In some cases, students who had been very enthusiastic about reading in 2000 were considerably less so in 2009. For example, in Portugal, more than one student in three did not read for enjoyment in 2009, compared to fewer than one in five in 2000.

In three countries, however, the percentage of students who reported that they read for enjoyment rose. The increase was greatest in Japan, where the smallest proportion of students – just 45% – reported that they read for enjoyment in 2000. By 2009 this proportion had grown to 56%, although this was still well below the OECD average.

Definitions

The **index of enjoyment of reading** was derived from students' level of agreement with the following statements: *i)* I read only if I have to; *ii)* reading is one of my favourite hobbies; *iii)* I like talking about books with other people; *iv)* I find it hard to finish books; *v)* I feel happy if I receive a book as a present; *vi)* for me, reading is a waste of time; *vii)* I enjoy going to a bookstore or library; *viii)* I read only to get information that I need; *ix)* I cannot sit still and read for more than a few minutes; *x)* I like to express my opinions about books I have read; and *xi)* I like to exchange books with my friends.

PISA **reading proficiency levels** summarise student performance on a scale that provides an overall picture of students' accumulated reading skills, knowledge and understanding at age 15. Seven levels of reading proficiency were constructed for PISA 2009, with Level 6 describing very high levels of proficiency and Level 1b describing students with the least proficiency in reading. Level 2 is considered the baseline level of proficiency, at which students begin to demonstrate the reading skills that will enable them to participate effectively and productively in life. Students at that level can locate information that meets several conditions, make comparisons or contrasts around a single feature, work out what a well-defined part of a text means, even when the information is not prominent, and make connections between the text and personal experience. Across OECD countries, some 81% of students are proficient at reading at Level 2 or higher. Students who attain Level 4 proficiency can tackle more difficult reading tasks, such as locating embedded information, construing meaning from nuances of language, and critically evaluating a text. Across OECD countries, 28% of students are proficient at Level 4 or higher.

Methodology

The statistical data for Israel are supplied by and under the responsibility of the relevant Israeli authorities. The use of such data by the OECD is without prejudice to the status of the Golan Heights, East Jerusalem and Israeli settlements in the West Bank under the terms of international law.

References

OECD (2010c), *PISA 2009 Results: Learning to Learn: Student Engagement, Strategies and Practices* (Volume III), OECD, Paris.

The following additional material relevant to this indicator is available on line:

- ***Table A6.5. Percentage of boys and girls who read diverse materials***
  StatLink http://dx.doi.org/10.1787/888932462852

Table A6.1. [1/2] Index of enjoyment of reading and reading performance, by national quarters of this index

Results based on students' self-reports

		Index of enjoyment of reading															
		All students		Boys		Girls		Gender difference (B - G)		Bottom quarter		Second quarter		Third quarter		Top quarter	
		Mean index	S.E.	Mean index	S.E.	Mean index	S.E.	Dif.	S.E.	Mean index	S.E.	Mean index	S.E.	Mean index	S.E.	Mean index	S.E.
OECD	Australia	0.00	(0.02)	-0.33	(0.02)	0.31	(0.02)	**-0.64**	(0.03)	**-1.36**	(0.01)	-0.37	(0.00)	0.31	(0.00)	**1.42**	(0.01)
	Austria	-0.13	(0.03)	-0.55	(0.03)	0.26	(0.03)	**-0.81**	(0.04)	**-1.52**	(0.02)	-0.65	(0.01)	0.16	(0.01)	**1.47**	(0.02)
	Belgium	-0.20	(0.02)	-0.45	(0.02)	0.07	(0.02)	**-0.52**	(0.03)	**-1.42**	(0.01)	-0.58	(0.00)	0.11	(0.01)	**1.11**	(0.01)
	Canada	0.13	(0.01)	-0.28	(0.02)	0.55	(0.02)	**-0.83**	(0.02)	**-1.25**	(0.01)	-0.24	(0.00)	0.45	(0.00)	**1.57**	(0.01)
	Chile	-0.06	(0.01)	-0.28	(0.02)	0.16	(0.02)	**-0.44**	(0.02)	**-1.01**	(0.01)	-0.37	(0.00)	0.10	(0.00)	**1.02**	(0.02)
	Czech Republic	-0.13	(0.02)	-0.44	(0.02)	0.22	(0.02)	**-0.66**	(0.03)	**-1.21**	(0.01)	-0.46	(0.00)	0.10	(0.00)	**1.06**	(0.02)
	Denmark	-0.09	(0.02)	-0.35	(0.02)	0.17	(0.02)	**-0.52**	(0.03)	**-1.17**	(0.01)	-0.40	(0.01)	0.15	(0.01)	**1.07**	(0.02)
	Estonia	-0.03	(0.02)	-0.38	(0.02)	0.33	(0.02)	**-0.71**	(0.03)	**-1.07**	(0.01)	-0.37	(0.00)	0.20	(0.01)	**1.10**	(0.02)
	Finland	0.05	(0.02)	-0.41	(0.02)	0.50	(0.02)	**-0.91**	(0.03)	**-1.25**	(0.02)	-0.28	(0.01)	0.36	(0.01)	**1.35**	(0.02)
	France	0.01	(0.03)	-0.23	(0.03)	0.24	(0.03)	**-0.47**	(0.04)	**-1.26**	(0.01)	-0.33	(0.01)	0.34	(0.01)	**1.30**	(0.02)
	Germany	0.07	(0.02)	-0.38	(0.02)	0.52	(0.03)	**-0.89**	(0.03)	**-1.33**	(0.01)	-0.45	(0.01)	0.42	(0.01)	**1.63**	(0.02)
	Greece	0.07	(0.02)	-0.24	(0.02)	0.36	(0.02)	**-0.60**	(0.03)	**-0.95**	(0.01)	-0.22	(0.00)	0.29	(0.01)	**1.14**	(0.02)
	Hungary	0.14	(0.02)	-0.15	(0.03)	0.43	(0.02)	**-0.58**	(0.04)	**-0.94**	(0.01)	-0.19	(0.01)	0.37	(0.01)	**1.30**	(0.02)
	Iceland	-0.06	(0.02)	-0.38	(0.02)	0.25	(0.02)	**-0.63**	(0.03)	**-1.28**	(0.02)	-0.43	(0.01)	0.18	(0.01)	**1.27**	(0.02)
	Ireland	-0.08	(0.02)	-0.30	(0.03)	0.15	(0.03)	**-0.45**	(0.04)	**-1.30**	(0.02)	-0.44	(0.01)	0.19	(0.01)	**1.23**	(0.02)
	Israel	0.06	(0.02)	-0.26	(0.03)	0.35	(0.03)	**-0.60**	(0.04)	**-1.16**	(0.01)	-0.28	(0.00)	0.31	(0.01)	**1.35**	(0.02)
	Italy	0.06	(0.01)	-0.27	(0.01)	0.41	(0.01)	**-0.68**	(0.02)	**-1.10**	(0.01)	-0.28	(0.00)	0.37	(0.00)	**1.27**	(0.01)
	Japan	0.20	(0.02)	0.02	(0.03)	0.38	(0.02)	**-0.36**	(0.03)	**-1.07**	(0.01)	-0.19	(0.01)	0.48	(0.01)	**1.58**	(0.02)
	Korea	0.13	(0.02)	0.00	(0.02)	0.27	(0.02)	**-0.27**	(0.03)	**-0.82**	(0.01)	-0.15	(0.00)	0.31	(0.00)	**1.17**	(0.02)
	Luxembourg	-0.16	(0.02)	-0.51	(0.02)	0.20	(0.03)	**-0.71**	(0.03)	**-1.43**	(0.02)	-0.58	(0.01)	0.12	(0.01)	**1.25**	(0.02)
	Mexico	0.14	(0.01)	-0.04	(0.01)	0.32	(0.01)	**-0.35**	(0.01)	**-0.77**	(0.01)	-0.13	(0.00)	0.32	(0.00)	**1.15**	(0.01)
	Netherlands	-0.32	(0.03)	-0.66	(0.03)	0.02	(0.03)	**-0.69**	(0.03)	**-1.47**	(0.02)	-0.66	(0.01)	-0.03	(0.01)	**0.88**	(0.02)
	New Zealand	0.13	(0.02)	-0.17	(0.02)	0.44	(0.02)	**-0.61**	(0.03)	**-1.07**	(0.02)	-0.21	(0.01)	0.40	(0.01)	**1.41**	(0.02)
	Norway	-0.19	(0.02)	-0.50	(0.02)	0.13	(0.03)	**-0.63**	(0.03)	**-1.41**	(0.01)	-0.56	(0.01)	0.09	(0.01)	**1.12**	(0.02)
	Poland	0.02	(0.02)	-0.36	(0.02)	0.39	(0.03)	**-0.75**	(0.03)	**-1.21**	(0.01)	-0.43	(0.00)	0.21	(0.01)	**1.49**	(0.02)
	Portugal	0.21	(0.02)	-0.15	(0.02)	0.54	(0.02)	**-0.69**	(0.02)	**-0.87**	(0.02)	-0.09	(0.00)	0.44	(0.00)	**1.35**	(0.02)
	Slovak Republic	-0.10	(0.02)	-0.36	(0.02)	0.15	(0.02)	**-0.51**	(0.03)	**-1.07**	(0.02)	-0.41	(0.00)	0.06	(0.00)	**1.02**	(0.02)
	Slovenia	-0.20	(0.01)	-0.53	(0.02)	0.14	(0.02)	**-0.67**	(0.03)	**-1.35**	(0.01)	-0.55	(0.00)	0.06	(0.01)	**1.04**	(0.02)
	Spain	-0.01	(0.01)	-0.28	(0.02)	0.26	(0.01)	**-0.55**	(0.02)	**-1.15**	(0.01)	-0.35	(0.00)	0.23	(0.00)	**1.22**	(0.01)
	Sweden	-0.11	(0.02)	-0.47	(0.02)	0.26	(0.03)	**-0.72**	(0.03)	**-1.29**	(0.02)	-0.45	(0.01)	0.18	(0.00)	**1.14**	(0.02)
	Switzerland	-0.04	(0.02)	-0.44	(0.02)	0.37	(0.03)	**-0.80**	(0.03)	**-1.46**	(0.02)	-0.50	(0.01)	0.32	(0.01)	**1.48**	(0.02)
	Turkey	0.64	(0.02)	0.34	(0.02)	0.95	(0.02)	**-0.61**	(0.03)	**-0.34**	(0.01)	0.33	(0.00)	0.80	(0.00)	**1.77**	(0.02)
	United Kingdom	-0.12	(0.02)	-0.37	(0.02)	0.13	(0.02)	**-0.50**	(0.03)	**-1.29**	(0.02)	-0.45	(0.00)	0.14	(0.00)	**1.13**	(0.02)
	United States	-0.04	(0.03)	-0.35	(0.03)	0.28	(0.03)	**-0.63**	(0.03)	**-1.27**	(0.01)	-0.41	(0.00)	0.19	(0.01)	**1.33**	(0.02)
	OECD average	0.00	(0.00)	-0.31	(0.00)	0.31	(0.00)	**-0.62**	(0.01)	**-1.17**	(0.00)	-0.36	(0.00)	0.26	(0.00)	**1.27**	(0.00)
Other G20	Argentina	-0.16	(0.02)	-0.34	(0.02)	-0.01	(0.02)	**-0.34**	(0.03)	**-1.02**	(0.01)	-0.43	(0.00)	0.00	(0.00)	**0.81**	(0.02)
	Brazil	0.27	(0.01)	0.05	(0.01)	0.47	(0.01)	**-0.42**	(0.02)	**-0.64**	(0.01)	-0.01	(0.00)	0.45	(0.00)	**1.28**	(0.01)
	Indonesia	0.43	(0.01)	0.32	(0.01)	0.55	(0.01)	**-0.22**	(0.02)	**-0.16**	(0.01)	0.27	(0.00)	0.55	(0.00)	**1.07**	(0.01)
	Russian Federation	0.07	(0.01)	-0.15	(0.02)	0.29	(0.02)	**-0.44**	(0.02)	**-0.73**	(0.01)	-0.19	(0.00)	0.23	(0.00)	**0.99**	(0.01)
	Shanghai-China	0.57	(0.01)	0.39	(0.02)	0.75	(0.01)	**-0.35**	(0.02)	**-0.29**	(0.01)	0.36	(0.00)	0.78	(0.00)	**1.43**	(0.01)

Note: Values that are statistically significant are indicated in bold.
Source: OECD, *PISA 2009 Database.*
StatLink http://dx.doi.org/10.1787/888932462776

Table A6.1. [2/2] **Index of enjoyment of reading and reading performance, by national quarters of this index**

Results based on students' self-reports

		Performance on the reading scale, by national quarters of this index								Change in the reading score per unit of this index		Increased likelihood of students in the bottom quarter of this index scoring in the bottom quarter of the national reading performance distribution		Explained variance in student performance (r-squared x 100)	
		Bottom quarter		Second quarter		Third quarter		Top quarter							
		Mean score	S.E.	Mean score	S.E.	Mean score	S.E.	Mean score	S.E.	Effect	S.E.	Ratio	S.E.	%	S.E.
OECD	Australia	**454**	(2.4)	489	(2.7)	536	(2.7)	**588**	(2.7)	**44.9**	(1.04)	**2.7**	(0.12)	26.0	(0.80)
	Austria	**422**	(3.5)	446	(3.8)	481	(4.2)	**536**	(4.2)	**37.2**	(1.63)	**2.0**	(0.15)	19.8	(1.40)
	Belgium	**461**	(2.4)	482	(3.2)	514	(3.7)	**571**	(2.9)	**40.9**	(1.21)	**1.8**	(0.10)	16.7	(0.93)
	Canada	**473**	(2.0)	506	(2.1)	542	(2.2)	**582**	(1.9)	**35.7**	(0.80)	**2.5**	(0.10)	20.1	(0.83)
	Chile	**430**	(3.3)	433	(4.1)	450	(3.7)	**490**	(3.6)	**29.0**	(1.57)	**1.4**	(0.09)	8.4	(0.84)
	Czech Republic	**436**	(3.3)	446	(3.7)	488	(2.8)	**547**	(3.5)	**46.0**	(1.53)	**2.0**	(0.11)	20.7	(1.10)
	Denmark	**448**	(3.1)	477	(3.4)	509	(2.9)	**549**	(3.1)	**43.2**	(1.46)	**2.5**	(0.16)	21.4	(1.27)
	Estonia	**456**	(3.2)	480	(3.2)	515	(3.3)	**555**	(3.4)	**43.3**	(1.71)	**2.4**	(0.17)	20.7	(1.28)
	Finland	**475**	(2.7)	518	(2.9)	557	(3.0)	**596**	(2.7)	**43.3**	(1.17)	**3.2**	(0.16)	27.0	(1.22)
	France	**435**	(4.9)	475	(3.7)	514	(4.0)	**562**	(4.1)	**47.1**	(2.28)	**2.5**	(0.16)	20.7	(1.55)
	Germany	**451**	(4.0)	468	(3.5)	520	(3.1)	**562**	(3.0)	**36.6**	(1.36)	**2.3**	(0.12)	21.0	(1.13)
	Greece	**435**	(6.2)	463	(6.0)	494	(4.6)	**540**	(3.3)	**46.8**	(2.35)	**2.3**	(0.15)	17.2	(1.36)
	Hungary	**452**	(3.8)	468	(3.5)	500	(4.9)	**559**	(3.4)	**45.1**	(1.92)	**2.1**	(0.16)	20.1	(1.61)
	Iceland	**444**	(2.8)	485	(2.7)	516	(3.3)	**564**	(2.5)	**43.4**	(1.37)	**2.7**	(0.18)	22.2	(1.12)
	Ireland	**445**	(3.9)	467	(3.6)	513	(4.0)	**567**	(3.0)	**45.1**	(1.56)	**2.4**	(0.15)	23.8	(1.36)
	Israel	**455**	(4.5)	447	(4.8)	479	(4.2)	**534**	(3.9)	**30.1**	(1.91)	**1.2**	(0.08)	7.9	(0.90)
	Italy	**445**	(2.3)	459	(2.0)	500	(2.2)	**544**	(2.1)	**40.4**	(1.02)	**1.9**	(0.07)	16.2	(0.71)
	Japan	**471**	(4.3)	505	(4.2)	540	(3.4)	**573**	(3.6)	**35.8**	(1.89)	**2.3**	(0.13)	15.0	(1.12)
	Korea	**495**	(4.5)	526	(3.6)	555	(3.5)	**584**	(3.4)	**40.4**	(2.29)	**2.5**	(0.15)	17.6	(1.35)
	Luxembourg	**426**	(2.7)	445	(2.9)	483	(3.4)	**537**	(2.7)	**39.9**	(1.34)	**1.9**	(0.12)	17.4	(1.09)
	Mexico	**412**	(2.3)	411	(2.4)	427	(2.3)	**454**	(2.4)	**21.6**	(1.12)	**1.2**	(0.04)	4.0	(0.40)
	Netherlands	**464**	(5.1)	487	(5.2)	522	(5.2)	**560**	(5.7)	**38.5**	(1.88)	**2.0**	(0.16)	16.7	(1.46)
	New Zealand	**466**	(3.3)	489	(3.2)	541	(3.8)	**593**	(3.2)	**48.2**	(1.56)	**2.3**	(0.15)	22.3	(1.37)
	Norway	**450**	(3.6)	484	(3.3)	518	(3.3)	**564**	(3.4)	**42.1**	(1.51)	**2.5**	(0.18)	22.2	(1.27)
	Poland	**464**	(3.4)	472	(3.5)	508	(3.3)	**563**	(3.1)	**35.2**	(1.31)	**1.9**	(0.13)	18.7	(1.19)
	Portugal	**453**	(3.4)	470	(3.7)	498	(3.3)	**541**	(3.3)	**35.6**	(1.59)	**1.9**	(0.11)	14.0	(1.00)
	Slovak Republic	**451**	(3.4)	447	(3.8)	479	(3.5)	**538**	(3.9)	**39.8**	(2.42)	**1.5**	(0.09)	14.3	(1.39)
	Slovenia	**445**	(2.3)	457	(2.4)	494	(2.4)	**543**	(2.6)	**39.0**	(1.39)	**1.9**	(0.10)	17.4	(1.09)
	Spain	**439**	(2.6)	461	(2.5)	493	(2.3)	**537**	(1.9)	**38.4**	(0.97)	**2.2**	(0.11)	17.8	(0.74)
	Sweden	**442**	(3.3)	474	(3.8)	515	(3.8)	**563**	(3.6)	**46.8**	(1.54)	**2.4**	(0.18)	21.7	(1.32)
	Switzerland	**449**	(3.1)	475	(2.9)	516	(3.0)	**565**	(3.2)	**37.7**	(1.20)	**2.3**	(0.14)	22.4	(1.13)
	Turkey	**444**	(4.3)	451	(3.8)	469	(3.6)	**498**	(4.7)	**23.5**	(2.03)	**1.5**	(0.11)	6.2	(0.94)
	United Kingdom	**446**	(3.2)	466	(2.6)	508	(3.2)	**562**	(2.7)	**45.0**	(1.52)	**2.2**	(0.13)	21.5	(1.34)
	United States	**454**	(2.8)	474	(4.3)	511	(4.2)	**563**	(5.0)	**38.3**	(1.81)	**2.0**	(0.12)	17.5	(1.30)
	OECD average	**450**	(0.6)	471	(0.6)	506	(0.6)	**553**	(0.6)	**39.5**	(0.28)	**2.1**	(0.02)	18.1	(0.20)
Other G20	Argentina	**390**	(4.9)	388	(5.6)	388	(5.3)	**442**	(6.6)	**27.4**	(3.65)	1.1	(0.07)	3.6	(0.91)
	Brazil	**397**	(2.7)	399	(3.8)	411	(3.0)	**444**	(3.0)	**23.8**	(1.87)	**1.2**	(0.06)	4.6	(0.62)
	Indonesia	**393**	(4.3)	395	(3.8)	404	(4.1)	**417**	(5.1)	**21.2**	(2.89)	**1.3**	(0.09)	2.5	(0.71)
	Russian Federation	**426**	(4.0)	439	(4.5)	464	(3.2)	**514**	(4.6)	**48.6**	(2.70)	**1.8**	(0.12)	14.5	(1.35)
	Shanghai-China	**515**	(3.3)	550	(3.3)	570	(2.9)	**590**	(3.2)	**39.8**	(2.56)	**2.4**	(0.16)	12.2	(1.22)

Note: Values that are statistically significant are indicated in bold.

Source: OECD, *PISA 2009 Database*.

StatLink http://dx.doi.org/10.1787/888932462776

Table A6.2. [1/2] Percentage of students and reading performance, by time spent reading for enjoyment

Results based on students' self-reports

		Percentage of students, by time spent reading for enjoyment											
				I read for enjoyment									
		I do not read for enjoyment		30 minutes or less a day		More than 30 minutes to less than 60 minutes a day		1 to 2 hours a day		More than 2 hours a day		Total	
		%	S.E.	%	S.E.	%	S.E.	%	S.E.	%	S.E.	%	S.E.
OECD	Australia	36.7	(0.6)	30.7	(0.5)	18.0	(0.5)	9.0	(0.3)	5.5	(0.3)	63.3	(0.6)
	Austria	50.0	(0.9)	23.7	(0.6)	14.7	(0.7)	7.2	(0.4)	4.3	(0.3)	50.0	(0.9)
	Belgium	44.4	(0.8)	26.2	(0.5)	17.2	(0.5)	9.1	(0.3)	3.1	(0.2)	55.6	(0.8)
	Canada	31.1	(0.5)	30.5	(0.5)	19.0	(0.4)	13.3	(0.4)	6.0	(0.2)	68.9	(0.5)
	Chile	39.7	(0.8)	35.9	(0.7)	15.5	(0.5)	6.4	(0.4)	2.5	(0.2)	60.3	(0.8)
	Czech Republic	43.0	(0.8)	27.8	(0.7)	14.5	(0.5)	10.2	(0.5)	4.6	(0.3)	57.0	(0.8)
	Denmark	33.6	(0.9)	41.1	(0.8)	15.5	(0.7)	7.4	(0.5)	2.3	(0.2)	66.4	(0.9)
	Estonia	38.6	(1.1)	26.4	(0.8)	18.9	(0.7)	10.5	(0.4)	5.7	(0.4)	61.4	(1.1)
	Finland	33.0	(0.8)	32.4	(0.7)	18.6	(0.6)	12.7	(0.5)	3.2	(0.3)	67.0	(0.8)
	France	38.8	(1.0)	31.1	(0.8)	16.4	(0.6)	9.8	(0.5)	3.9	(0.3)	61.2	(1.0)
	Germany	41.3	(0.9)	24.7	(0.7)	16.8	(0.6)	11.3	(0.5)	5.9	(0.4)	58.7	(0.9)
	Greece	17.5	(0.8)	24.3	(0.8)	21.5	(0.7)	23.6	(0.7)	13.1	(0.6)	82.5	(0.8)
	Hungary	25.5	(0.8)	34.7	(0.8)	22.1	(0.7)	13.6	(0.6)	4.2	(0.3)	74.5	(0.8)
	Iceland	38.0	(0.8)	32.5	(0.8)	16.6	(0.5)	9.6	(0.5)	3.3	(0.3)	62.0	(0.8)
	Ireland	41.9	(1.0)	26.0	(0.7)	16.3	(0.6)	11.7	(0.6)	4.1	(0.3)	58.1	(1.0)
	Israel	34.5	(0.9)	26.5	(0.6)	16.3	(0.5)	15.8	(0.6)	6.9	(0.4)	65.5	(0.9)
	Italy	33.9	(0.6)	28.5	(0.4)	18.9	(0.3)	13.7	(0.3)	5.0	(0.2)	66.1	(0.6)
	Japan	44.2	(0.9)	25.4	(0.9)	16.4	(0.5)	9.6	(0.4)	4.4	(0.3)	55.8	(0.9)
	Korea	38.5	(0.8)	29.8	(0.8)	19.1	(0.6)	8.4	(0.4)	4.2	(0.3)	61.5	(0.8)
	Luxembourg	48.2	(0.8)	24.6	(0.7)	13.9	(0.6)	8.8	(0.5)	4.4	(0.3)	51.8	(0.8)
	Mexico	23.8	(0.4)	44.4	(0.4)	18.6	(0.3)	10.3	(0.2)	2.9	(0.2)	76.2	(0.4)
	Netherlands	48.6	(1.3)	30.8	(0.9)	12.6	(0.6)	6.3	(0.4)	1.8	(0.2)	51.4	(1.3)
	New Zealand	31.3	(0.8)	33.1	(0.8)	19.7	(0.7)	10.2	(0.4)	5.6	(0.3)	68.7	(0.8)
	Norway	40.0	(0.9)	32.9	(0.8)	16.8	(0.7)	6.9	(0.4)	3.4	(0.3)	60.0	(0.9)
	Poland	32.2	(0.8)	30.4	(0.8)	17.6	(0.6)	12.5	(0.6)	7.4	(0.4)	67.8	(0.8)
	Portugal	35.2	(0.7)	32.8	(0.6)	19.2	(0.5)	9.7	(0.4)	3.1	(0.2)	64.8	(0.7)
	Slovak Republic	40.9	(1.1)	32.1	(0.8)	14.1	(0.7)	8.9	(0.5)	3.9	(0.3)	59.1	(1.1)
	Slovenia	39.8	(0.7)	34.5	(0.7)	15.6	(0.5)	8.0	(0.5)	2.2	(0.2)	60.2	(0.7)
	Spain	39.6	(0.7)	25.6	(0.5)	19.5	(0.5)	11.3	(0.4)	3.9	(0.2)	60.4	(0.7)
	Sweden	37.3	(0.9)	34.0	(0.7)	17.4	(0.6)	8.2	(0.4)	3.1	(0.3)	62.7	(0.9)
	Switzerland	44.6	(0.9)	30.1	(0.7)	14.4	(0.6)	8.0	(0.4)	2.9	(0.3)	55.4	(0.9)
	Turkey	22.9	(0.7)	27.5	(0.6)	22.2	(0.6)	21.5	(0.7)	6.0	(0.4)	77.1	(0.7)
	United Kingdom	39.6	(0.9)	31.5	(0.8)	15.5	(0.6)	9.8	(0.4)	3.6	(0.3)	60.4	(0.9)
	United States	42.0	(1.0)	29.3	(0.8)	15.1	(0.5)	8.7	(0.4)	4.9	(0.3)	58.0	(1.0)
	OECD average	37.4	(0.1)	30.3	(0.1)	17.2	(0.1)	10.6	(0.1)	4.5	(0.1)	62.6	(0.1)
Other G20	Argentina	41.7	(1.0)	29.4	(0.8)	14.8	(0.6)	10.4	(0.6)	3.7	(0.3)	58.3	(1.0)
	Brazil	21.8	(0.6)	39.5	(0.5)	20.3	(0.5)	12.9	(0.4)	5.5	(0.3)	78.2	(0.6)
	Indonesia	12.1	(0.6)	37.9	(0.9)	26.7	(0.8)	15.2	(0.6)	8.0	(0.6)	87.9	(0.6)
	Russian Federation	21.4	(0.8)	31.1	(0.9)	27.5	(0.8)	13.2	(0.5)	6.9	(0.4)	78.6	(0.8)
	Shanghai-China	8.0	(0.4)	35.9	(0.8)	36.5	(0.7)	13.2	(0.5)	6.4	(0.3)	92.0	(0.4)

Source: OECD, *PISA 2009 Database*.

StatLink http://dx.doi.org/10.1787/888932462795

Table A6.2. [2/2] Percentage of students and reading performance, by time spent reading for enjoyment

Results based on students' self-reports

		Performance on the reading scale, by time spent reading for enjoyment										Change between 2000 and 2009 in the percentage of students reading for enjoyment (PISA 2009 – PISA 2000)					
		I do not read for enjoyment		30 minutes or less a day		More than 30 minutes to less than 60 minutes a day		1 to 2 hours a day		More than 2 hours a day		All students		Boys		Girls	
		Mean score	S.E.	Mean score	S.E.	Mean score	S.E.	Mean score	S.E.	Mean score	S.E.	% dif.	S.E.	% dif.	S.E.	% dif.	S.E.
OECD	Australia	469	(2.2)	524	(2.6)	560	(3.0)	570	(3.5)	563	(4.0)	**-3.6**	(1.3)	**-6.9**	(1.9)	-1.5	(1.6)
	Austria	437	(3.1)	494	(3.5)	517	(5.7)	530	(5.8)	504	(9.8)	m	m	m	m	m	m
	Belgium	469	(2.7)	532	(2.9)	547	(3.1)	548	(4.2)	523	(8.2)	-2.2	(1.2)	-0.7	(1.7)	**-4.1**	(1.2)
	Canada	481	(1.9)	530	(1.8)	555	(2.2)	565	(2.5)	559	(3.7)	**1.6**	(0.7)	-1.3	(1.0)	**4.5**	(0.7)
	Chile	437	(3.3)	449	(3.5)	472	(4.1)	478	(6.7)	499	(8.3)	**-13.4**	(1.1)	**-16.6**	(1.5)	**-9.0**	(1.3)
	Czech Republic	441	(3.2)	489	(3.5)	520	(4.5)	532	(4.0)	522	(6.7)	**-16.7**	(1.2)	**-17.0**	(1.7)	**-13.4**	(1.4)
	Denmark	464	(2.9)	503	(2.5)	518	(3.0)	537	(3.9)	536	(9.5)	**-6.9**	(1.2)	**-6.8**	(1.7)	**-7.3**	(1.5)
	Estonia	469	(2.8)	514	(3.4)	525	(3.9)	530	(4.8)	527	(6.1)	m	m	m	m	m	m
	Finland	492	(2.5)	545	(2.7)	569	(3.3)	572	(4.0)	568	(9.1)	**-10.7**	(1.0)	**-11.4**	(1.6)	**-9.2**	(1.2)
	France	450	(4.4)	512	(3.8)	538	(4.9)	546	(5.9)	543	(8.8)	**-8.8**	(1.3)	**-8.4**	(1.7)	**-9.0**	(1.6)
	Germany	457	(3.5)	513	(3.3)	545	(3.5)	548	(4.5)	532	(6.8)	0.5	(1.2)	-0.4	(1.6)	1.6	(1.4)
	Greece	450	(7.5)	480	(6.5)	490	(4.6)	492	(4.1)	507	(4.9)	**4.5**	(1.1)	1.0	(1.8)	**7.8**	(1.3)
	Hungary	453	(4.2)	490	(3.5)	517	(4.3)	533	(4.8)	536	(9.1)	0.6	(1.2)	-1.0	(1.7)	2.3	(1.4)
	Iceland	455	(2.5)	521	(2.6)	544	(3.8)	542	(4.5)	533	(9.4)	**-8.2**	(1.0)	**-11.5**	(1.7)	**-5.0**	(1.5)
	Ireland	458	(3.5)	505	(3.9)	540	(3.8)	550	(4.5)	549	(8.2)	**-8.5**	(1.3)	**-5.1**	(1.9)	**-11.7**	(1.6)
	Israel	460	(4.4)	483	(4.1)	498	(4.9)	492	(5.2)	484	(7.8)	2.5	(2.6)	3.3	(2.5)	5.0	(3.0)
	Italy	449	(2.3)	489	(1.8)	516	(2.7)	521	(2.2)	528	(3.5)	**-3.3**	(1.2)	**-8.1**	(1.5)	2.3	(1.3)
	Japan	492	(3.9)	536	(4.2)	550	(4.0)	552	(5.1)	537	(7.1)	**10.9**	(1.6)	**8.8**	(1.9)	**13.1**	(2.0)
	Korea	518	(4.4)	550	(4.0)	558	(3.6)	560	(5.0)	535	(8.8)	**-8.0**	(1.2)	**-8.3**	(1.5)	**-7.7**	(2.0)
	Luxembourg	437	(1.9)	493	(3.3)	516	(3.7)	524	(4.8)	519	(7.2)	m	m	m	m	m	m
	Mexico	421	(2.4)	420	(2.0)	444	(2.4)	430	(3.6)	437	(8.4)	**-10.2**	(0.8)	**-12.1**	(1.3)	**-8.3**	(0.9)
	Netherlands	478	(4.5)	534	(5.9)	552	(5.5)	541	(8.5)	514	(10.6)	m	m	m	m	m	m
	New Zealand	472	(3.4)	525	(3.9)	558	(3.8)	574	(4.8)	573	(6.9)	-1.4	(1.2)	**-3.8**	(1.7)	1.4	(1.4)
	Norway	465	(3.2)	523	(3.0)	540	(4.6)	542	(5.8)	528	(8.8)	**-4.6**	(1.2)	**-4.0**	(1.7)	**-5.3**	(1.6)
	Poland	463	(3.2)	498	(2.9)	526	(3.8)	544	(4.6)	549	(5.4)	**-8.0**	(1.4)	**-14.6**	(2.2)	-1.3	(1.3)
	Portugal	459	(3.0)	490	(3.8)	519	(3.6)	530	(4.9)	538	(5.7)	**-16.8**	(1.1)	**-20.4**	(1.7)	**-13.0**	(1.0)
	Slovak Republic	445	(3.6)	486	(3.1)	514	(4.7)	523	(5.2)	516	(9.3)	m	m	m	m	m	m
	Slovenia	446	(1.7)	499	(2.4)	526	(3.1)	520	(5.3)	521	(10.8)	m	m	m	m	m	m
	Spain	453	(2.4)	484	(2.5)	510	(2.5)	515	(3.1)	517	(4.2)	**-7.9**	(1.1)	**-7.5**	(1.5)	**-7.6**	(1.4)
	Sweden	455	(3.1)	515	(3.8)	539	(4.9)	539	(5.0)	532	(8.2)	-1.3	(1.3)	**-4.5**	(1.6)	2.0	(1.7)
	Switzerland	461	(2.6)	521	(2.8)	548	(4.3)	558	(4.2)	533	(7.6)	**-9.5**	(1.4)	**-7.6**	(1.9)	**-10.9**	(1.5)
	Turkey	444	(4.1)	468	(3.6)	480	(3.9)	473	(4.5)	472	(7.6)	m	m	m	m	m	m
	United Kingdom	458	(2.6)	505	(3.2)	531	(4.3)	549	(4.7)	539	(7.5)	m	m	m	m	m	m
	United States	467	(3.0)	514	(4.8)	532	(6.0)	541	(5.9)	544	(6.6)	-1.3	(1.7)	-2.5	(2.2)	1.2	(2.0)
	OECD average	460	(0.6)	504	(0.6)	527	(0.7)	532	(0.8)	527	(1.3)	**-5.0**	(0.3)	**-6.4**	(0.3)	**-3.2**	(0.3)
Other G20	Argentina	394	(5.5)	398	(5.2)	414	(6.0)	416	(9.0)	418	(10.4)	**-12.4**	(1.3)	**-12.8**	(1.8)	**-11.3**	(1.8)
	Brazil	396	(3.0)	403	(2.5)	428	(3.3)	431	(4.2)	429	(6.3)	**-2.5**	(1.1)	**-4.2**	(1.7)	-0.6	(1.1)
	Indonesia	380	(3.7)	390	(3.2)	414	(4.1)	412	(5.9)	429	(7.8)	1.3	(1.2)	-1.3	(1.4)	**4.1**	(1.6)
	Russian Federation	427	(4.9)	452	(3.4)	472	(3.4)	489	(4.9)	498	(6.6)	-1.9	(1.1)	**-4.4**	(1.5)	0.5	(1.1)
	Shanghai-China	497	(5.5)	560	(2.6)	563	(2.9)	564	(3.7)	548	(4.8)	m	m	m	m	m	m

Note: Changes between 2000 and 2009 that are statistically significant are indicated in bold.
Source: OECD, *PISA 2009 Database.*
Please refer to the Reader's Guide for information concerning the symbols replacing missing data.
StatLink http://dx.doi.org/10.1787/888932462795

Table A6.3. Reading diverse materials and performance

Students who reported that they read the following materials because they want to "several times a month" or "several times a week"

	Performance on the reading scale of students who read different materials																			
	Magazines				Comic books				Fiction (novels, narratives, stories)				Non-fiction books				Newspapers			
	Do not read		Read		Do not read		Read		Do not read		Read		Do not read		Read		Do not read		Read	
	Mean score	S.E.	Mean score	S.E.	Mean score	S.E.	Mean score	S.E.	Mean score	S.E.	Mean score	S.E.	Mean score	S.E.	Mean score	S.E.	Mean score	S.E.	Mean score	S.E.
OECD																				
Australia	524	(2.6)	**510**	(2.5)	517	(2.2)	517	(4.8)	488	(2.0)	**564**	(2.8)	510	(2.3)	**544**	(3.4)	510	(2.2)	**523**	(2.9)
Austria	470	(4.1)	478	(2.8)	478	(2.8)	**458**	(4.8)	456	(2.9)	**530**	(4.0)	474	(3.1)	483	(4.4)	458	(4.6)	**479**	(2.9)
Belgium	492	(3.8)	**523**	(2.2)	505	(2.6)	**529**	(2.7)	499	(2.4)	**561**	(3.1)	512	(2.1)	522	(5.6)	505	(2.9)	**520**	(2.6)
Canada	523	(1.6)	**528**	(1.9)	526	(1.5)	526	(2.6)	502	(1.6)	**558**	(1.7)	522	(1.5)	**539**	(2.5)	521	(1.7)	**531**	(1.9)
Chile	438	(3.7)	**463**	(2.9)	452	(3.2)	444	(3.7)	446	(3.1)	**462**	(3.8)	446	(3.0)	**475**	(4.1)	436	(3.5)	**461**	(3.2)
Czech Republic	476	(3.8)	**485**	(2.9)	482	(2.7)	484	(5.7)	470	(2.9)	**541**	(4.1)	479	(2.9)	**505**	(4.4)	477	(4.0)	485	(2.8)
Denmark	483	(3.4)	**503**	(2.0)	494	(2.4)	**506**	(2.9)	483	(2.3)	**525**	(2.7)	490	(2.2)	**514**	(2.7)	489	(2.5)	**503**	(2.5)
Estonia	488	(3.8)	**506**	(2.7)	506	(2.6)	**476**	(4.5)	493	(2.6)	**531**	(3.5)	493	(2.7)	**521**	(3.3)	485	(4.5)	**506**	(2.6)
Finland	510	(3.5)	**551**	(2.2)	530	(3.0)	**540**	(2.4)	517	(2.2)	**590**	(2.8)	532	(2.2)	**558**	(4.2)	523	(3.2)	**540**	(2.3)
France	483	(4.5)	**505**	(3.3)	493	(3.6)	**507**	(4.5)	477	(3.6)	**549**	(3.9)	497	(3.8)	494	(4.7)	491	(4.0)	**504**	(3.9)
Germany	503	(3.1)	506	(3.1)	506	(2.6)	499	(5.6)	483	(3.0)	**551**	(2.9)	504	(2.9)	509	(4.1)	495	(3.7)	**511**	(2.8)
Greece	473	(5.4)	**490**	(4.3)	483	(4.6)	483	(4.9)	472	(4.9)	**523**	(3.5)	482	(4.4)	**504**	(7.4)	482	(4.7)	484	(4.6)
Hungary	469	(4.6)	**512**	(2.8)	499	(3.1)	**482**	(4.6)	484	(3.1)	**519**	(4.6)	490	(3.3)	**504**	(3.9)	483	(5.0)	**499**	(3.0)
Iceland	488	(2.3)	**511**	(1.7)	495	(1.8)	**516**	(2.6)	484	(1.7)	**549**	(2.8)	496	(1.5)	**528**	(3.6)	457	(4.1)	**511**	(1.6)
Ireland	497	(4.0)	499	(3.1)	500	(3.0)	**476**	(6.7)	480	(3.1)	**542**	(3.5)	494	(3.0)	**526**	(5.1)	505	(4.2)	**495**	(3.0)
Israel	469	(4.1)	**495**	(3.4)	483	(3.6)	**459**	(4.7)	471	(3.6)	**500**	(4.2)	477	(3.5)	486	(4.5)	444	(5.1)	**491**	(3.3)
Italy	482	(1.9)	**492**	(1.7)	483	(1.7)	**505**	(2.5)	471	(1.8)	**517**	(1.9)	486	(1.6)	**497**	(3.9)	477	(1.9)	**496**	(1.7)
Japan	524	(4.5)	519	(3.4)	516	(4.7)	522	(3.4)	501	(4.0)	**548**	(3.3)	518	(3.5)	**542**	(4.8)	506	(4.0)	**531**	(3.5)
Korea	540	(3.5)	539	(4.5)	543	(3.9)	534	(4.1)	526	(4.0)	**556**	(3.1)	530	(3.7)	**562**	(3.6)	527	(3.7)	**556**	(3.6)
Luxembourg	463	(3.1)	**479**	(1.7)	475	(1.4)	470	(3.4)	452	(1.4)	**527**	(2.6)	471	(1.4)	**487**	(3.4)	472	(3.1)	474	(1.7)
Mexico	419	(2.4)	**435**	(1.8)	430	(2.1)	**417**	(1.9)	429	(2.0)	424	(2.2)	423	(1.9)	**442**	(2.6)	424	(2.1)	**429**	(2.0)
Netherlands	487	(5.3)	**530**	(5.0)	509	(5.2)	522	(6.2)	501	(5.5)	**552**	(5.1)	507	(5.3)	**547**	(5.8)	497	(5.8)	**527**	(5.2)
New Zealand	531	(3.2)	**515**	(2.6)	525	(2.3)	**506**	(5.8)	494	(2.6)	**559**	(3.0)	518	(2.5)	**538**	(3.4)	518	(2.9)	526	(2.8)
Norway	494	(3.2)	**511**	(2.7)	495	(2.9)	**517**	(2.8)	487	(2.5)	**551**	(3.4)	503	(2.6)	507	(3.7)	487	(4.0)	**510**	(2.4)
Poland	480	(3.5)	**512**	(2.6)	503	(2.6)	**487**	(5.0)	491	(2.5)	**544**	(4.0)	494	(2.7)	**530**	(3.8)	489	(3.6)	**504**	(2.7)
Portugal	492	(3.8)	489	(3.0)	491	(3.0)	486	(3.9)	479	(3.0)	**518**	(3.8)	485	(2.9)	**519**	(5.1)	494	(3.3)	486	(3.3)
Slovak Republic	448	(5.3)	**487**	(2.3)	478	(2.6)	481	(5.4)	469	(2.6)	**524**	(4.9)	473	(2.5)	**504**	(4.0)	470	(4.2)	**482**	(2.4)
Slovenia	471	(2.6)	**491**	(1.4)	488	(1.2)	**474**	(4.0)	476	(1.2)	**538**	(3.9)	478	(1.1)	**527**	(3.2)	480	(2.5)	**488**	(1.3)
Spain	479	(2.2)	484	(2.3)	482	(2.0)	485	(3.8)	466	(2.1)	**519**	(2.2)	473	(2.1)	**523**	(2.7)	478	(2.2)	**487**	(2.4)
Sweden	480	(3.6)	**513**	(2.9)	496	(2.9)	**510**	(4.0)	475	(2.7)	**549**	(3.3)	495	(2.7)	**541**	(5.5)	468	(3.9)	**511**	(2.8)
Switzerland	487	(3.2)	**508**	(2.4)	498	(2.5)	**513**	(3.2)	480	(2.4)	**550**	(3.3)	500	(2.3)	507	(4.5)	482	(3.4)	**506**	(2.5)
Turkey	467	(4.0)	465	(3.5)	470	(3.5)	**451**	(4.5)	462	(3.7)	468	(3.7)	472	(3.6)	**450**	(4.0)	444	(4.9)	**468**	(3.7)
United Kingdom	496	(3.1)	495	(2.2)	498	(2.2)	**475**	(4.9)	475	(2.3)	**542**	(3.0)	491	(2.3)	**519**	(3.7)	497	(2.6)	495	(2.5)
United States	500	(3.9)	502	(3.9)	502	(3.6)	**488**	(6.4)	483	(3.1)	**532**	(4.8)	502	(3.7)	498	(5.2)	499	(3.9)	504	(4.2)
OECD average	486	(0.6)	**501**	(0.5)	495	(0.5)	**492**	(0.8)	480	(0.5)	**533**	(0.6)	492	(0.5)	**513**	(0.7)	484	(0.6)	**501**	(0.5)
Other G20																				
Argentina	387	(4.8)	**415**	(5.0)	404	(5.2)	400	(4.9)	402	(4.7)	406	(5.8)	402	(4.8)	404	(5.6)	397	(5.1)	407	(4.9)
Brazil	402	(2.7)	**427**	(3.3)	421	(3.1)	**402**	(2.5)	414	(2.8)	416	(3.5)	414	(2.7)	**424**	(4.1)	409	(2.9)	**422**	(3.3)
Indonesia	392	(3.5)	**410**	(4.4)	398	(3.8)	407	(4.0)	394	(4.0)	**408**	(3.9)	393	(3.6)	**420**	(4.3)	393	(3.5)	**407**	(4.2)
Russian Federation	455	(4.6)	463	(3.0)	468	(3.4)	**434**	(4.3)	439	(3.9)	**477**	(3.3)	458	(3.5)	**472**	(3.9)	464	(5.0)	459	(3.0)
Shanghai-China	547	(2.5)	**563**	(2.7)	561	(2.3)	**543**	(3.3)	548	(2.5)	**563**	(2.8)	554	(2.4)	561	(3.3)	531	(3.5)	**566**	(2.6)

Note: Differences between students who read and students who do not that are statistically significant are indicated in bold.

Source: OECD, *PISA 2009 Database.*

StatLink http://dx.doi.org/10.1787/888932462814

Table A6.4. [1/2] Percentage of students and reading performance, by whether students spend any time reading for enjoyment and gender

Results based on students' self-reports

	Percentage of students, by whether they spend any time reading for enjoyment				Percentage of students who read for enjoyment by gender						Reading performance, by whether students read for enjoyment			
	I do not read for enjoyment		I read for enjoyment[1]		Boys		Girls		Difference (B-G)		I do not read for enjoyment		I read for enjoyment	
	%	S.E.	%	S.E.	%	S.E.	%	S.E.	%	S.E.	Mean score	S.E.	Mean score	S.E.
OECD														
Australia	36.7	(0.6)	63.3	(0.6)	53.0	(0.8)	73.1	(0.8)	**-20.1**	(1.1)	469	(2.2)	**545**	(2.5)
Austria	50.0	(0.9)	50.0	(0.9)	38.5	(1.0)	60.9	(1.2)	**-22.4**	(1.6)	437	(3.1)	**507**	(3.5)
Belgium	44.4	(0.8)	55.6	(0.8)	46.2	(1.0)	65.4	(1.0)	**-19.2**	(1.4)	469	(2.7)	**539**	(2.4)
Canada	31.1	(0.5)	68.9	(0.5)	56.2	(0.8)	81.6	(0.5)	**-25.4**	(0.8)	481	(1.9)	**546**	(1.5)
Chile	39.7	(0.8)	60.3	(0.8)	50.7	(1.0)	70.3	(0.9)	**-19.6**	(1.3)	437	(3.3)	**460**	(3.3)
Czech Republic	43.0	(0.8)	57.0	(0.8)	44.3	(1.0)	71.5	(1.2)	**-27.2**	(1.5)	441	(3.2)	**507**	(3.0)
Denmark	33.6	(0.9)	66.4	(0.9)	57.3	(1.1)	75.3	(1.1)	**-18.0**	(1.4)	464	(2.9)	**512**	(2.0)
Estonia	38.6	(1.1)	61.4	(1.1)	47.1	(1.4)	76.8	(1.2)	**-29.8**	(1.7)	469	(2.8)	**521**	(2.7)
Finland	33.0	(0.8)	67.0	(0.8)	53.3	(1.1)	80.6	(1.0)	**-27.3**	(1.5)	492	(2.5)	**558**	(2.3)
France	38.8	(1.0)	61.2	(1.0)	52.1	(1.3)	69.8	(1.3)	**-17.7**	(1.7)	450	(4.4)	**526**	(3.3)
Germany	41.3	(0.9)	58.7	(0.9)	45.1	(1.1)	72.5	(1.1)	**-27.4**	(1.3)	457	(3.5)	**530**	(2.7)
Greece	17.5	(0.8)	82.5	(0.8)	76.4	(1.1)	88.4	(0.9)	**-12.0**	(1.3)	450	(7.5)	**490**	(3.9)
Hungary	25.5	(0.8)	74.5	(0.8)	65.7	(1.2)	83.5	(0.9)	**-17.8**	(1.5)	453	(4.2)	**509**	(3.2)
Iceland	38.0	(0.8)	62.0	(0.8)	51.5	(1.3)	72.3	(1.0)	**-20.8**	(1.7)	455	(2.5)	**531**	(1.6)
Ireland	41.9	(1.0)	58.1	(1.0)	52.5	(1.4)	63.8	(1.3)	**-11.3**	(1.8)	458	(3.5)	**527**	(2.9)
Israel	34.5	(0.9)	65.5	(0.9)	55.2	(1.5)	75.1	(1.0)	**-19.9**	(1.7)	460	(4.4)	**489**	(3.3)
Italy	33.9	(0.6)	66.1	(0.6)	53.9	(0.8)	79.0	(0.6)	**-25.1**	(1.1)	449	(2.3)	**506**	(1.6)
Japan	44.2	(0.9)	55.8	(0.9)	53.6	(1.1)	58.2	(1.3)	**-4.6**	(1.5)	492	(3.9)	**543**	(3.5)
Korea	38.5	(0.8)	61.5	(0.8)	60.5	(1.0)	62.6	(1.4)	-2.2	(1.8)	518	(4.4)	**553**	(3.4)
Luxembourg	48.2	(0.8)	51.8	(0.8)	39.6	(1.1)	64.2	(1.0)	**-24.6**	(1.5)	437	(1.9)	**507**	(2.1)
Mexico	23.8	(0.4)	76.2	(0.4)	69.5	(0.7)	82.8	(0.4)	**-13.3**	(0.7)	421	(2.4)	**428**	(2.1)
Netherlands	48.6	(1.3)	51.4	(1.3)	35.8	(1.5)	66.8	(1.4)	**-31.1**	(1.5)	478	(4.5)	**539**	(5.4)
New Zealand	31.3	(0.8)	68.7	(0.8)	59.4	(1.1)	78.3	(1.0)	**-18.9**	(1.4)	472	(3.4)	**546**	(2.7)
Norway	40.0	(0.9)	60.0	(0.9)	50.4	(1.1)	70.0	(1.1)	**-19.6**	(1.5)	465	(3.2)	**530**	(2.7)
Poland	32.2	(0.8)	67.8	(0.8)	53.1	(1.3)	82.5	(0.9)	**-29.4**	(1.4)	463	(3.2)	**519**	(2.6)
Portugal	35.2	(0.7)	64.8	(0.7)	50.2	(1.0)	78.7	(0.8)	**-28.4**	(1.3)	459	(3.0)	**507**	(3.2)
Slovak Republic	40.9	(1.1)	59.1	(1.1)	47.3	(1.5)	70.5	(1.1)	**-23.2**	(1.8)	445	(3.6)	**500**	(2.7)
Slovenia	39.8	(0.7)	60.2	(0.7)	46.1	(1.2)	74.9	(0.8)	**-28.8**	(1.5)	446	(1.7)	**509**	(1.5)
Spain	39.6	(0.7)	60.4	(0.7)	51.0	(0.9)	70.0	(0.8)	**-19.0**	(1.2)	453	(2.4)	**500**	(2.0)
Sweden	37.3	(0.9)	62.7	(0.9)	50.7	(1.1)	75.0	(1.0)	**-24.3**	(1.3)	455	(3.1)	**525**	(3.1)
Switzerland	44.6	(0.9)	55.4	(0.9)	43.6	(1.1)	67.6	(1.0)	**-24.0**	(1.3)	461	(2.6)	**534**	(2.7)
Turkey	22.9	(0.7)	77.1	(0.7)	68.4	(1.0)	86.5	(1.0)	**-18.1**	(1.5)	444	(4.1)	**473**	(3.4)
United Kingdom	39.6	(0.9)	60.4	(0.9)	50.7	(1.0)	69.7	(1.1)	**-19.0**	(1.4)	458	(2.6)	**521**	(2.6)
United States	42.0	(1.0)	58.0	(1.0)	47.4	(1.2)	69.2	(1.3)	**-21.8**	(1.4)	467	(3.0)	**525**	(4.4)
OECD average	37.4	(0.1)	62.6	(0.1)	52.2	(0.2)	73.1	(0.2)	**-20.9**	(0.2)	460	(0.6)	**517**	(0.5)
Other G20														
Argentina	41.7	(1.0)	58.3	(1.0)	49.4	(1.2)	65.8	(1.3)	**-16.4**	(1.7)	394	(5.5)	407	(4.8)
Brazil	21.8	(0.6)	78.2	(0.6)	68.7	(1.0)	86.6	(0.5)	**-17.9**	(1.0)	396	(3.0)	**416**	(2.5)
Indonesia	12.1	(0.6)	87.9	(0.6)	83.4	(0.9)	92.2	(0.6)	**-8.8**	(1.1)	380	(3.7)	**405**	(3.9)
Russian Federation	21.4	(0.8)	78.6	(0.8)	70.6	(1.2)	86.6	(0.9)	**-16.0**	(1.4)	427	(4.9)	**469**	(3.1)
Shanghai-China	8.0	(0.4)	92.0	(0.4)	89.0	(0.6)	95.0	(0.4)	**-6.1**	(0.6)	497	(5.5)	**561**	(2.3)

Note: Values that are statistically significant are indicated in bold.

1. The "I read for enjoyment" category groups students who: read "30 minutes or less per day", students who read "between 30 minutes and 60 minutes", students who read "between 1 hour and 2 hours" and students who read "more than 2 hours daily".

Source: OECD, *PISA 2009 Database.*

StatLink http://dx.doi.org/10.1787/888932462833

Table A6.4. [2/2] Percentage of students and reading performance, by whether students spend any time reading for enjoyment and gender

Results based on students' self-reports

		Reading performance of boys, by whether they read for enjoyment				Reading performance of girls, by whether they read for enjoyment				Difference between boys and girls, by whether they read for enjoyment			
		I do not read for enjoyment		I read for enjoyment		I do not read for enjoyment		I read for enjoyment		I do not read for enjoyment (B-G)		I read for enjoyment (B-G)	
		Mean score	S.E.	Mean score	S.E.	Mean score	S.E.	Mean score	S.E.	Score dif.	S.E.	Score dif.	S.E.
OECD	Australia	460	(2.9)	**533**	(3.5)	484	(3.1)	**552**	(2.6)	**-25**	(3.9)	**-19**	(3.6)
	Austria	429	(4.2)	**486**	(4.9)	449	(4.3)	**519**	(4.5)	**-20**	(6.1)	**-33**	(6.5)
	Belgium	465	(3.6)	**531**	(3.8)	476	(3.7)	**545**	(2.7)	**-11**	(5.0)	**-14**	(4.3)
	Canada	476	(2.2)	**535**	(2.1)	493	(3.0)	**554**	(1.7)	**-17**	(3.3)	**-19**	(2.2)
	Chile	434	(3.8)	**446**	(4.6)	442	(4.2)	**470**	(3.7)	-8	(4.6)	**-24**	(5.0)
	Czech Republic	433	(3.7)	**485**	(4.5)	459	(4.5)	**523**	(2.9)	**-26**	(5.5)	**-38**	(4.4)
	Denmark	455	(3.6)	**501**	(2.8)	481	(4.1)	**520**	(2.6)	**-26**	(5.1)	**-19**	(3.6)
	Estonia	462	(3.0)	**500**	(3.7)	486	(4.2)	**536**	(2.9)	**-24**	(4.3)	**-36**	(3.7)
	Finland	479	(3.0)	**534**	(3.3)	522	(4.3)	**574**	(2.3)	**-43**	(5.2)	**-40**	(3.1)
	France	439	(5.1)	**511**	(4.5)	467	(5.5)	**537**	(3.5)	**-28**	(6.1)	**-26**	(4.5)
	Germany	452	(4.2)	**516**	(4.0)	467	(4.4)	**540**	(3.0)	**-15**	(5.1)	**-24**	(4.5)
	Greece	437	(8.6)	**466**	(5.0)	475	(7.2)	**510**	(3.5)	**-38**	(7.5)	**-44**	(4.3)
	Hungary	444	(4.9)	**492**	(4.1)	471	(5.3)	**522**	(3.8)	**-28**	(5.9)	**-29**	(4.5)
	Iceland	440	(2.8)	**517**	(3.2)	481	(4.1)	**541**	(2.0)	**-41**	(4.7)	**-24**	(4.1)
	Ireland	445	(5.1)	**509**	(4.3)	475	(3.5)	**543**	(3.2)	**-30**	(5.8)	**-34**	(5.0)
	Israel	450	(5.2)	**467**	(5.2)	475	(5.2)	**504**	(3.7)	**-25**	(5.9)	**-37**	(5.7)
	Italy	440	(2.7)	**487**	(2.3)	470	(3.6)	**520**	(1.9)	**-30**	(4.3)	**-34**	(2.7)
	Japan	476	(5.9)	**524**	(5.3)	512	(3.9)	**562**	(4.8)	**-36**	(7.0)	**-38**	(7.4)
	Korea	499	(6.1)	**538**	(4.8)	540	(5.3)	**569**	(3.8)	**-40**	(7.7)	**-31**	(5.8)
	Luxembourg	429	(2.5)	**493**	(3.7)	451	(2.7)	**516**	(2.1)	**-22**	(3.6)	**-23**	(3.9)
	Mexico	413	(2.9)	414	(2.3)	434	(2.8)	439	(2.2)	**-20**	(3.2)	**-25**	(1.8)
	Netherlands	474	(4.7)	**538**	(5.8)	485	(5.2)	**539**	(5.7)	**-11**	(3.8)	-1	(3.7)
	New Zealand	460	(4.1)	**529**	(4.1)	496	(4.3)	**558**	(3.0)	**-36**	(5.5)	**-29**	(4.6)
	Norway	451	(3.6)	**510**	(3.4)	487	(3.7)	**545**	(3.1)	**-36**	(3.7)	**-35**	(3.5)
	Poland	451	(3.4)	**499**	(3.4)	494	(4.7)	**532**	(2.8)	**-42**	(4.6)	**-33**	(3.3)
	Portugal	451	(3.4)	**490**	(4.1)	476	(3.8)	**517**	(3.1)	**-25**	(4.1)	**-27**	(3.0)
	Slovak Republic	432	(4.4)	**475**	(3.5)	470	(4.3)	**517**	(3.3)	**-38**	(5.1)	**-41**	(3.8)
	Slovenia	433	(2.2)	**486**	(2.5)	474	(3.5)	**524**	(1.7)	**-41**	(4.3)	**-38**	(3.0)
	Spain	446	(2.6)	**489**	(2.6)	466	(3.1)	**509**	(2.2)	**-20**	(3.1)	**-20**	(2.7)
	Sweden	445	(3.8)	**508**	(3.7)	476	(4.0)	**537**	(3.4)	**-31**	(4.7)	**-29**	(3.5)
	Switzerland	452	(3.3)	**522**	(3.4)	476	(3.5)	**542**	(2.7)	**-24**	(4.4)	**-20**	(2.7)
	Turkey	438	(4.5)	**449**	(3.8)	460	(6.6)	**493**	(3.9)	**-22**	(6.9)	**-44**	(3.6)
	United Kingdom	452	(3.4)	**514**	(4.2)	467	(3.0)	**526**	(3.5)	**-15**	(4.0)	**-12**	(5.7)
	United States	462	(3.9)	**517**	(5.2)	474	(4.1)	**530**	(4.5)	**-12**	(5.4)	**-13**	(3.9)
	OECD average	450	(0.7)	**500**	(0.7)	477	(0.7)	**528**	(0.6)	**-27**	(0.9)	**-28**	(0.7)
Other G20	Argentina	380	(6.0)	387	(5.8)	413	(6.2)	419	(5.1)	**-34**	(5.5)	**-32**	(5.0)
	Brazil	393	(3.6)	399	(3.1)	402	(4.6)	**428**	(2.5)	-10	(5.3)	**-29**	(2.1)
	Indonesia	372	(4.2)	**386**	(4.0)	397	(5.4)	**422**	(4.0)	**-25**	(6.3)	**-36**	(3.4)
	Russian Federation	415	(5.0)	**447**	(3.6)	452	(6.5)	**487**	(3.3)	**-37**	(5.7)	**-40**	(3.0)
	Shanghai-China	482	(5.9)	**543**	(2.9)	532	(8.4)	**578**	(2.3)	**-50**	(9.0)	**-35**	(2.9)

Note: Values that are statistically significant are indicated in bold.

1. The "I read for enjoyment" category groups students who: read "30 minutes or less per day", students who read "between 30 minutes and 60 minutes", students who read "between 1 hour and 2 hours" and students who read "more than 2 hours daily".

Source: OECD, *PISA 2009 Database*.

StatLink http://dx.doi.org/10.1787/888932462833

INDICATOR A7

HOW DOES EDUCATIONAL ATTAINMENT AFFECT PARTICIPATION IN THE LABOUR MARKET?

- In all OECD countries, individuals with a tertiary-level degree have a greater chance of being employed than those without such a degree.
- Higher education improves job prospects, in general, and the likelihood of remaining employed in times of economic hardship.
- Differences in employment rates between men and women are wider among less-educated groups.

Chart A7.1. **Percentage of 25-64 year-olds in employment, by level of education (2009)**

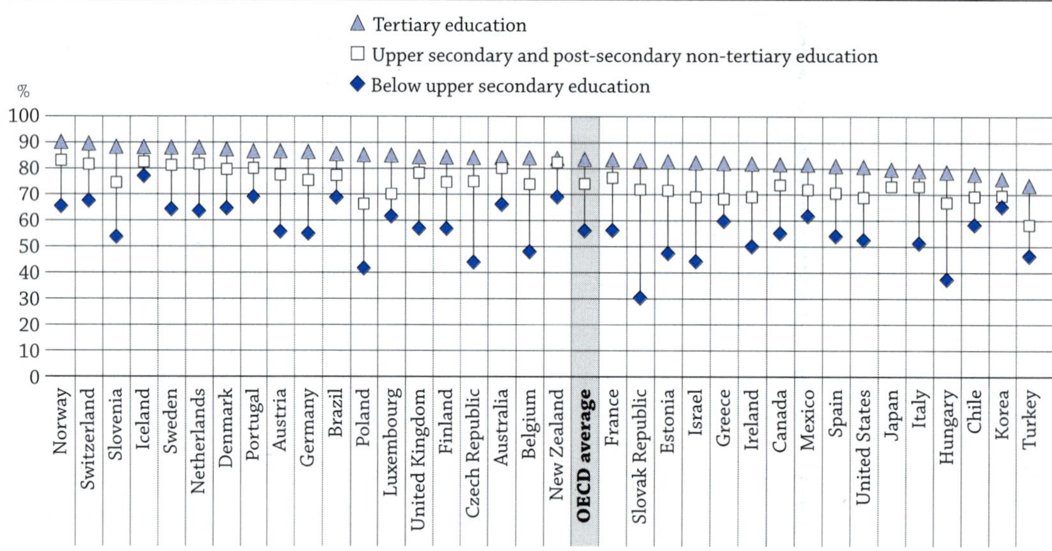

Countries are ranked in descending order of the employment rate for individuals with tertiary education.

Source: OECD. Table A7.3a. See Annex 3 for notes (*www.oecd.org/edu/eag2011*).

StatLink http://dx.doi.org/10.1787/888932460420

How to read this chart

The chart shows the positive relation between education and employment. People who have completed upper secondary education are more likely to be in work than people with below upper secondary education, and people with tertiary education are more likely to be in work than those with upper secondary education. The magnitude of the employment advantage varies across countries.

Context

OECD countries' economies and labour markets depend upon a sufficient supply of well-educated workers. Indicators related to labour-market outcomes by educational attainment show how well the supply of skills matches demand. However, most education programmes have a long time horizon, while shifts in the demand for labour can occur rapidly. The pace of this change has been accentuated by the recent economic downturn.

Labour-force statistics, such as the proportion of individuals in full-time work, employment and unemployment, by educational attainment, mirror this recent shake-up in the demand for skills.

They thus provide important information for policy makers about the supply, and potential supply, of skills available to the labour market and about employers' demand for these skills. Similarly, information on labour-force status over time provides a good basis for assessing the long-term trends and variations in employment and unemployment risks among groups with different levels of educational attainment.

Other findings

- On average across OECD countries, **84% of the population with a tertiary education is employed**. Overall, employment rates are more than 27 percentage points higher for those with a tertiary education than for those who have not completed an upper secondary education.
- **Those adults with low educational attainment are both less likely to be participants in the labour force and are more likely to be unemployed.** On average among OECD countries, men without an upper secondary education are almost twice as likely to be unemployed as men with an upper secondary education and almost three times as likely to be unemployed as men with a tertiary education.
- Among those adults who do not have upper secondary qualifications, men are 21 percentage points more likely to be employed than women; but **among the most highly qualified adults, men are only 9 percentage points more likely than women to be employed**.
- Full-time work generally increases with higher levels of education. **The proportion of individuals working full-time is 10 percentage points higher among those with a tertiary education than among those without an upper secondary education.** Finland, Portugal and the United Kingdom have succeeded in combining high employment levels with a high incidence of full-time work among those with a tertiary education.
- **Young individuals (25-34 year-olds) with a vocational upper secondary education typically do well in the labour market** when compared with the total 25-64 year-old population. Across OECD countries, the unemployment rate is somewhat higher (1.9 percentage points), but the rate of employment is 3.4 percentage points higher than among 25-64 year-olds with the same level of vocational education.

Trends

Education is generally good insurance against unemployment and for staying employed in difficult economic times. On average across OECD countries, unemployment rates of those with tertiary-level education have stayed at or below 4%, unemployment rates of those with an upper secondary education have stayed below 7%, while unemployment rates of those who have not attained an upper secondary education have breached 10% several times between 1997 and 2009. The most recent data suggest that this pattern is not unusual. In 2009, average unemployment rates across OECD countries stood at 4.4% for those with a tertiary education, 6.8% for those with an upper secondary education, and 11.5% for those who have not attained an upper secondary education.

Analysis

Employment

Higher levels of educational attainment typically lead to greater labour participation and higher employment rates. This is principally because adults with more education occupy a more competitive position in the labour market, but also because those adults have made a larger investment in their human capital and need to recoup their investment. Employment rates for men and women across OECD countries increase from an average of 70.1% for men and 48.9% for women with lower secondary qualifications to an average of 88.6% for men and 80.0% for women with tertiary-type A (largely theory-based) qualifications. Employment rates for women with lower secondary education are particularly low: below 40% in Chile, the Czech Republic, Hungary, Poland, the Slovak Republic, Turkey and the United Kingdom. Employment rates for women with tertiary-type A education equal or exceed 75% everywhere except Chile, Italy, Japan, Korea, Mexico and Turkey, but remain below those of men in all countries (Table A7.1a).

Apart from education, variations in women's employment rates contribute to differences in overall employment rates among countries. The countries with the highest overall rate of employment for 25-64 year-olds – Iceland, Norway, Sweden and Switzerland – also have among the highest employment rates among women (Table A7.1a). Nevertheless, employment increases substantially with higher levels of education, and the gap between men's and women's employment rates typically narrows considerably with higher educational attainment. The gap between the employment rates of men and women with tertiary-type A education is five percentage points or less in Canada, Denmark, Iceland, the Netherlands, Norway, Portugal, Slovenia and Sweden.

The employment advantage for women with a tertiary education is particularly pronounced in Belgium, Hungary, Ireland, Israel, Italy, Poland, the Slovak Republic, Slovenia and Turkey and is at least 40 percentage points higher than for those who have not attained an upper secondary education (Table A7.3c, available on line). Similarly, in the Czech Republic and the Slovak Republic, the employment gap is particularly wide between 25-64 year-old men who are upper secondary graduates and those who are not (Table A7.3b, available on line).

The past year saw a large change in employment between different educational groups. Until 2008, overall differences in employment rates between people with different educational qualifications narrowed marginally; but as employment prospects for less-educated individuals are more sensitive to changes in economic conditions, the gap has once again widened. On average across OECD countries, employment rates for those without an upper secondary education dropped by 2.1 percentage points to 56.0%; for those with an upper secondary education the employment rate fell by 1.9 percentage points to 74.2%; and for those with tertiary education the employment rate was 1 percentage point lower in 2009 than in 2008 and stood at 83.6% (Chart A7.1).

Unemployment rates fall with higher educational attainment

An individual's employment prospects depend largely on the requirements of labour markets and on the supply of workers with different skills. Unemployment rates thus indicate the match, or lack of it, between what the education system produces and what skills the labour market demands. Those with lower educational qualifications are at particular risk of economic marginalisation since they are both less likely to participate in the labour force and more likely to be without a job, even if they actively seek one.

Table A7.2a shows unemployment rates for different educational groups, by gender. On average across OECD countries, unemployment rates decrease as educational attainment increases for both men and women. Unemployment rates for those with a tertiary-type A education are still below 4% in many OECD countries (4.1% and 4.4%, on average, for men and women, respectively). Unemployment rates for those with a lower secondary education are above 10% in most countries (on average 12.0% for men and 12.3% for women). In many countries, those rates are above 15%, and both women and men with a lower secondary education are particularly vulnerable in the Czech Republic, Estonia and the Slovak Republic, where the unemployment rate among them is 20% or higher. This is also the case for women in Spain and Turkey and for men in Hungary.

Not only did employment rates drop dramatically for those with low educational attainment in the past year, but unemployment rates also widened substantially between different educational groups. Chart A7.2 illustrates how the economic downturn affected unemployment rates in 2009.

With few exceptions, unemployment rates increased across the board but less so for those with higher education. They increased by 2.8 percentage points for those without an upper secondary education, by 2 percentage points for those with an upper secondary education and by 1.1 percentage points for those with a tertiary education. Individuals with less education were particularly hard hit by the recession in Estonia, Ireland, Spain, and the United States, where unemployment rates among those without an upper secondary education rose by more than five percentage points – more than twice as fast as that for those with a tertiary education.

Chart A7.2. Change in unemployment rates, by level of education (2008-09)

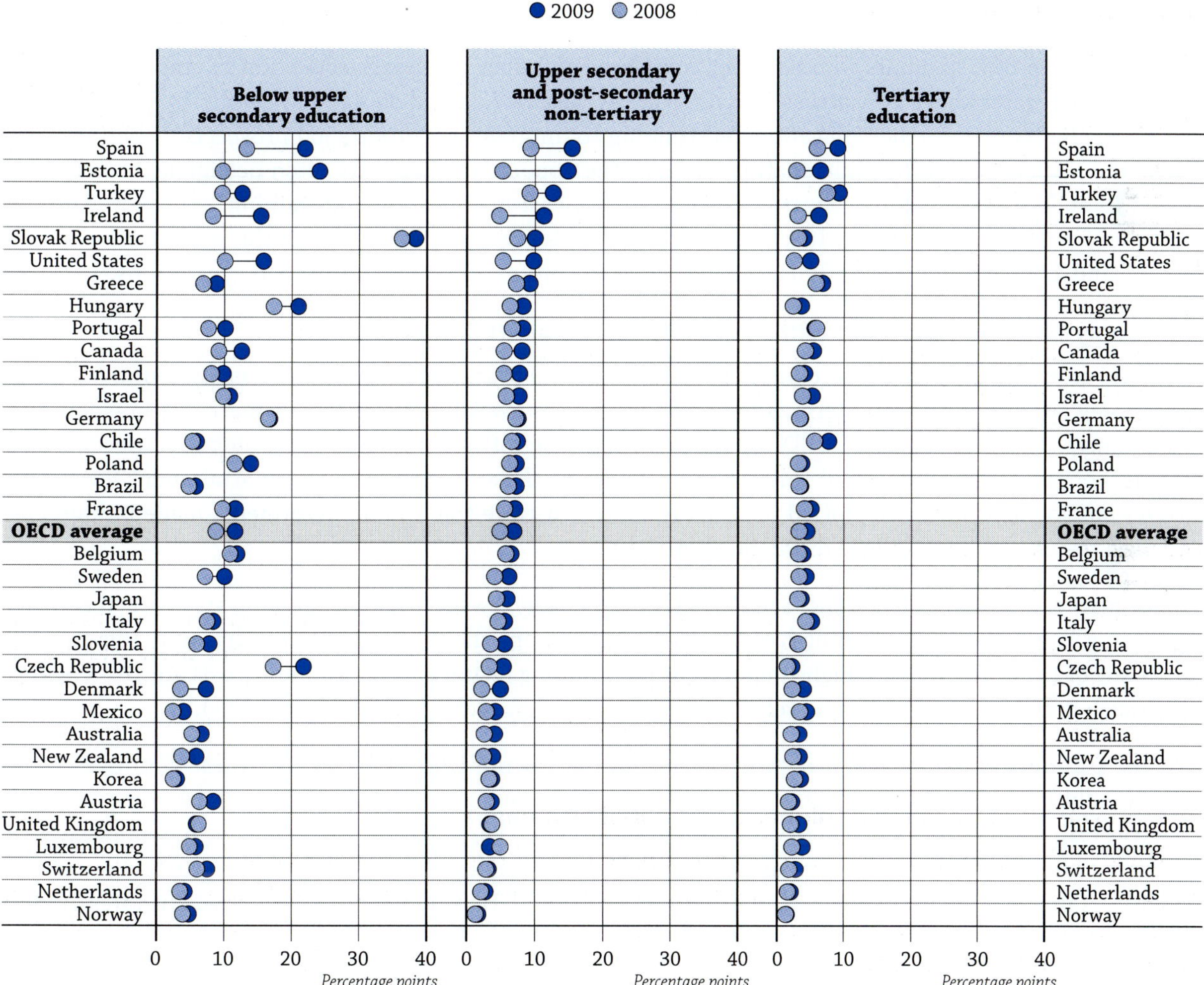

Countries are ranked in descending order of the employment rate in 2009 for individuals with upper secondary and post-secondary non-tertiary education.
Source: OECD. Table A7.4a. See Annex 3 for notes (*www.oecd.org/edu/eag2011*).
StatLink http://dx.doi.org/10.1787/888932460439

Even those individuals with an upper secondary education have seen their job prospects deteriorate between 2008 and 2009. Difficult labour markets pushed unemployment rates among those with an upper secondary education above 10% in Estonia, Ireland, Spain and Turkey. Unemployment rates for those with a tertiary education remained below 10% in all countries.

Still, on average across the OECD area, the rate of unemployment among those who have completed an upper secondary education is close to five percentage points lower than among those who have not completed this level. Only in Brazil, Chile, Greece, Korea and Mexico is the lack of an upper secondary education not associated with a higher risk of unemployment (Table A7.4a).

On average, 25-64 year-old men who have not attained an upper secondary education are nearly twice as likely to be unemployed as those who have, and are almost three times as likely to be unemployed as those who have a tertiary education (Table A7.4b, available on line). The negative association between unemployment and educational attainment is similar, but somewhat less marked, for women (Table A7.4c, available on line).

Countries with high unemployment rates typically also have a large portion of the population out of the labour force (Tables A7.3a and A7.4a). Once individuals are out of the labour force for an extended period, it is often difficult for them to re-enter because their skills no longer match labour-market demands and they are confronted with other barriers to re-entry. Many jobs that have been lost, particularly those in the lower skills segment, will not return.

With fewer than 60% of adults who have not completed an upper secondary education in employment, and unemployment rates above 10% across the OECD area (Tables A7.3a and A7.4a), few countries can afford not to address the issue of further education and training to improve this group's job prospects. When jobs are scarce, the price of retraining individuals is lower, as the opportunity costs are often negligible, both for the individual and society. In many countries, incentives to invest in education and training, and to prepare the workforce for new jobs, are strong. It is thus vital for education systems to respond to this opportunity of high demand and low investment costs by increasing access to and resources for educational institutions.

The supply of labour increases with higher educational attainment

While the economic downturn has made substantial portions of the work force idle in many countries, a key to economic growth in the long term is fully using the skills available to the labour market. In response to demand, over the past decades OECD countries have put significant resources into higher education. It is crucial, then, to take advantage of this lead by fully using these resources. Tertiary attainment levels and tertiary employment rates are plotted in Chart A7.3, to illustrate the overall investments made in high-end skills and the use of these skills in different countries.

Labour markets in Denmark, Iceland, the Netherlands, Norway, Sweden and Switzerland are characterised by high tertiary attainment as well as high employment rates among those with a tertiary education. It is striking that many of the countries with high employment rates among tertiary-educated individuals are also those in which such individuals pay comparatively high income taxes, on average (see Indicator A11).

Tertiary attainments are similarly high in Japan, Korea and the United States, but these countries show substantially lower employment rates among those with a tertiary education than in the top countries. Tertiary attainment is considerably lower in Austria, Germany, Portugal and Slovenia, but individuals with a tertiary education in these four countries are more likely to be employed than in the former group of countries. Tertiary attainment levels are low in Chile, Hungary, Italy, and Turkey, and so are employment rates among those with a tertiary education.

Overall, greater use could be made of the educated population. On average across OECD countries, over 15% of those who have a tertiary education are not employed and, as such, they represent a substantial untapped source of growth. In essence, there is no link between tertiary attainment levels and employment levels among those with a tertiary degree across OECD countries, which suggests that factors other than the supply of higher-educated individuals, such as taxes and social policies, are behind the differences in employment rates.

Information on the proportion of full-time earners is another way of examining the use of labour resources in different countries. Chart A7.4 provides a breakdown of the proportion of full-time earners (among all earners) by educational attainment. The proportion of full-time earners varies considerably between countries and, in most countries, between different educational groups.

Chart A7.3. Skills acquisition and use, 25-64 year-olds with a tertiary education (2009)

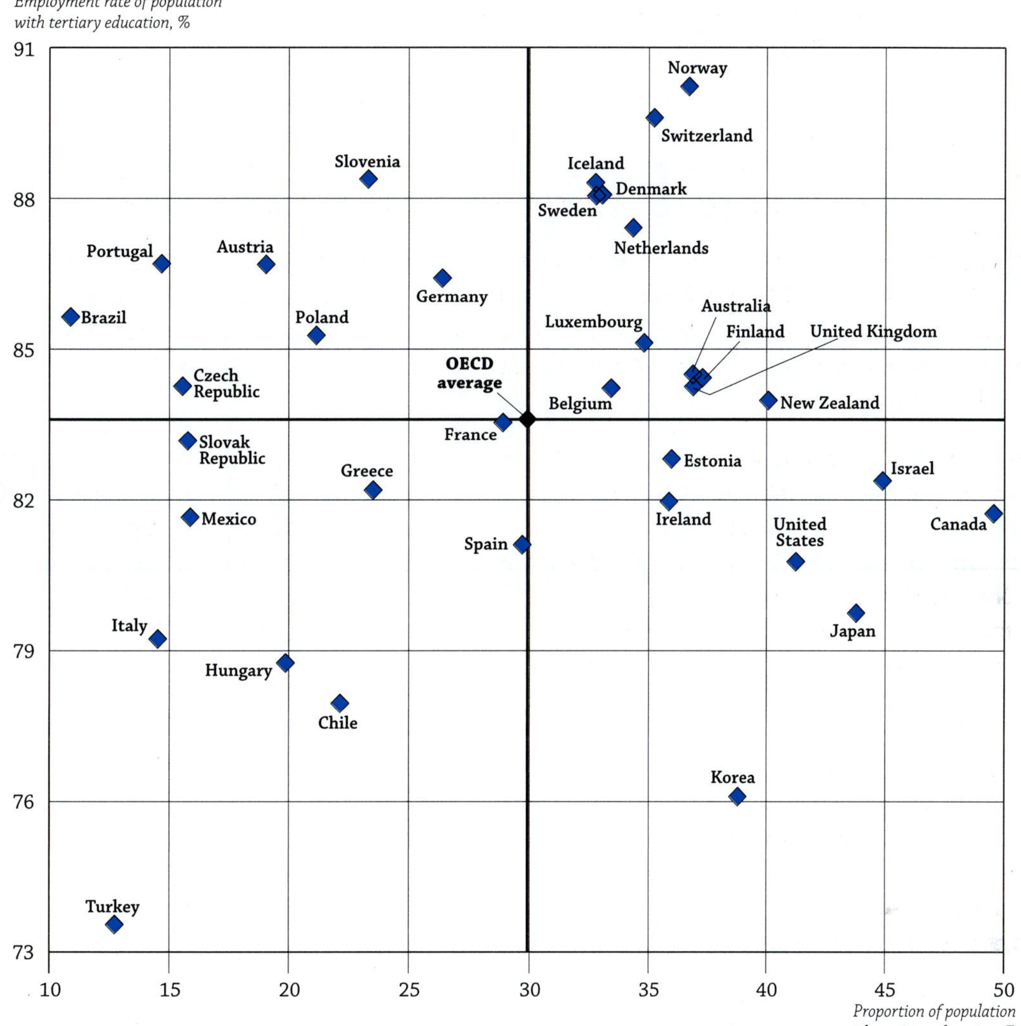

Source: OECD. Tables A7.3a and A1.3a. See Annex 3 for notes (*www.oecd.org/edu/eag2011*).

StatLink http://dx.doi.org/10.1787/888932460458

Full-time work generally increases with higher levels of education. Across OECD countries, 66% of those who have not attained an upper secondary education work full-time, 72% of those with an upper secondary education do, and 75% of those with a tertiary education do. Much of the increase in the proportion of full-time workers is the result of the increasing supply of labour among women with higher educational attainment (Table A7.5).

The largest variation in full-time work is between countries and, to a lesser extent, between educational groups. In Estonia, Finland, Korea and Portugal, almost everyone (90%) works full-time, regardless of their educational attainment. In the Czech Republic and the Netherlands, only half of the population is in full-time work. There is a link between employment rates for those with a tertiary education and the prevalence of full-time work for the same group, suggesting that allowing for more flexibility in working hours might induce more people, particularly women, to take up employment.

However, this association explains 20% of the between-country variation, so other policies and norms are more important in determining the overall supply of labour in the higher skills segments. As a case in point, Finland, Portugal and the United Kingdom have succeeded in combining high employment levels with a high incidence of full-time work among those with a tertiary education (Tables A7.3a and A7.5).

Chart A7.4. Distribution of 25-64 year-olds by earnings categories, by educational attainment (2009 or latest year available)

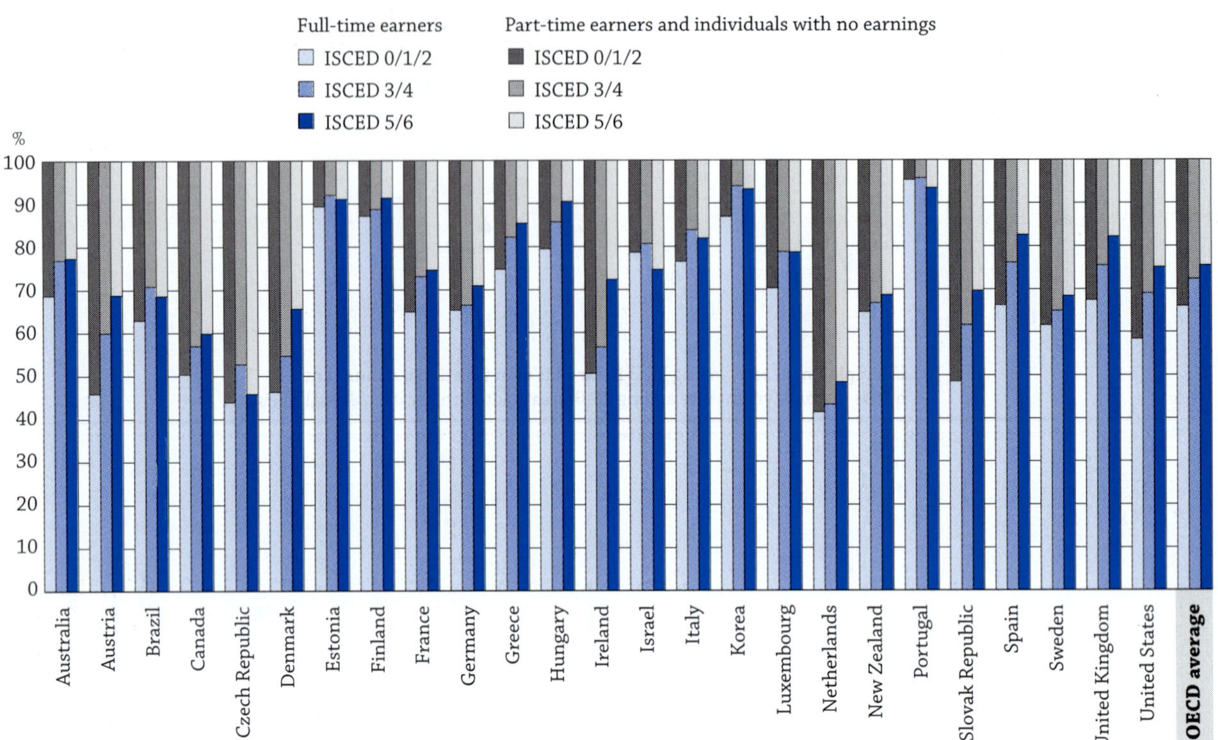

Source: OECD, Table A7.5, LSO Network special data collection on full-time, full-year earnings, Economic Working Group. See Annex 3 for notes (*www.oecd.org/edu/eag2011*).

StatLink http://dx.doi.org/10.1787/888932460477

Labour-force status by vocational and general orientation of education

Matching supply and demand for skills not only concerns the level of education but also the specificity of skills acquired in the educational system. Vocational education and training (VET) is geared towards giving students labour market-relevant skills for a particular occupation or industry. This type of specialisation has the advantage of ensuring a closer match between employer needs for specific skills; as such, it reduces the need for initial on-the-job training and increases immediate, and potentially also long-term, productivity of new hires. The drawback is that the versatility of skills acquired might be limited in times of changing demand. Therefore, vocational education and training is, in many instances, developed in close co-operation with employers and other labour-market participants.

VET systems vary widely among countries, as do the perceptions of what is considered vocational education. Cross-country comparability is thus somewhat less stringent than in other areas of the ISCED classification, and this needs to be kept in mind when comparing the prevalence and outcomes of VET in different OECD countries (see also Box A1.1 in Indicator A1 for additional discussions on comparability). Table A7.6 provides, for the first time, a breakdown of labour-market outcomes by vocational and general education at upper secondary and post-secondary non-tertiary (ISCED 3/4) levels of education.

The proportion of 25-64 year-olds with vocational upper secondary (ISCED 3/4) attainment varies widely between countries. Over 70% of the adult population in the Czech Republic and the Slovak Republic has an upper secondary vocational education as their highest level of education, whereas in Ireland, Spain and Turkey, less than 10% of the adult population has this specific orientation. A large portion of the differences between countries on this measure hinges on the relative importance of upper secondary education to other educational levels, particularly tertiary education.

On average across countries, 31% of the adult population, and slightly less (30%) among the younger age group, has attained a vocational upper secondary (ISCED 3/4) education. The change in the proportion of individuals with vocational education in the younger cohorts varies among countries. Chart A7.5 shows the difference between the proportion of those with a vocational upper secondary education among 25-34 year-olds and the total 25-64 year-old population, and the difference in the unemployment rate for this younger cohort compared to the total number of 25-64 year-olds.

Chart A7.5. Comparison of vocational attainment and unemployment rates between 25-34 year-olds and 25-64 year-olds (2009)

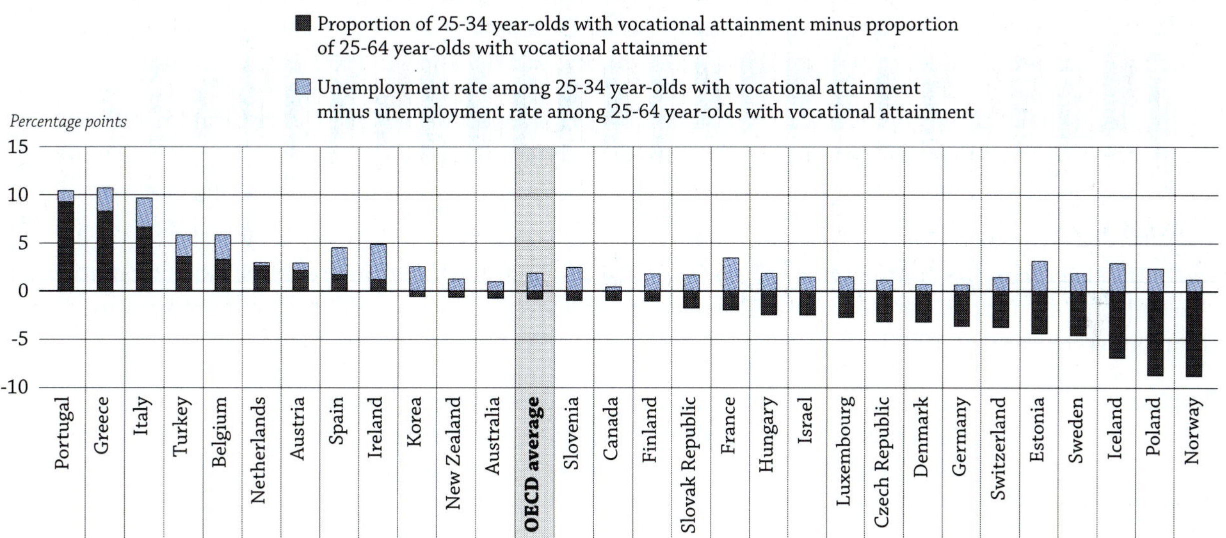

Countries are ranked in descending order of the difference between 25-34 and 25-64 year-olds with vocational education.

Source: OECD, Table A7.6, LSO network special data collection on vocational education, Learnings and Labour Transitions Working Group. See Annex 3 for notes (*www.oecd.org/edu/eag2011*).

StatLink http://dx.doi.org/10.1787/888932460496

The younger cohort with a vocational education fares well in the labour market when compared with 25-64 year-olds with upper secondary vocational education. Unemployment rates are, on average, only 1.9 percentage points higher, indicating a relatively smooth transition from education to work. This relative unemployment is somewhat higher in Estonia, France, Ireland and Italy (over three percentage points higher), whereas the unemployment rate among the younger cohort is below 0.5 percentage point of that of the total labour force in Canada and the Netherlands.

Iceland, Norway and Poland have seen less of their younger cohort attain a vocational education, but an expansion of vocational education has occurred in Greece, Italy and Portugal. Unemployment among the younger cohort relative to that of the total population with similar qualifications is generally unrelated to the expansion/contraction of vocational education, which suggests that country-specific changes in the vocational attainment of the younger cohort is largely a response to changing labour-market demands.

The notion that labour-market demands guide young people's choices is also supported by the positive relationship between the proportion of 25-34 year-olds with upper secondary vocational attainment and the difference in employment rates between young individuals with a vocational and those with a general upper secondary education (correlation 0.45). Not only do 25-34 year-olds with a vocational education do well in terms of unemployment, but their overall employment rates are 3.4 percentage points higher than that for the total 25-64 year-old population with vocational upper secondary education. Young, vocationally educated individuals also have substantially higher employment rates (8.5 percentage points) than their counterparts with a general education, indicating that investments in vocational education is money well spent in most countries.

Another picture that emerges from this new data is that labour-market outcomes among those with a vocational upper secondary education (ISCED 3/4) depend on access to higher education for those who have chosen a general track. There is a strong positive link between access – measured as the proportion of the population with general upper secondary education (ISCED 3/4) to tertiary education (ISCED 5/6) – and employment rates for those with an upper secondary vocational education.

This relationship explains over a third of the between-country variation among 25-64 year-olds and demonstrates that employment rates for those with an upper secondary vocational education improve as a larger fraction of those with a general education goes on to higher education. This relationship probably reflects either the fact that vocationally trained individuals face less competition for jobs at this skill level or that there are complementarities in the labour market between occupational and industry-specific skills and high-end skills. The relationship is stronger in the total population than among 25-34 year-olds, possibly illustrating a lowering of barriers, in recent years, for those with a vocational education to enter tertiary education.

Further refinement of the cross-country comparability of this aspect of the ISCED classification will improve the precision of estimates and open the way for greater analytical insights.

Definitions

Under the auspices of the International Labour Organization (ILO) and their conferences of labour statisticians, concepts and definitions for measuring labour force participation were established and are now used as a common reference (ILO, 1982).

Employed individuals are defined as those who, during the survey reference week: *i)* work for pay (employees) or profit (self-employed and unpaid family workers) for at least one hour; or *ii)* have a job but are temporarily not at work (through injury, illness, holiday, strike or lock-out, educational or training leave, maternity or parental leave, etc.).

The **employment rate** refers to the number of persons in employment as a percentage of the population of working age.

Unemployed individuals are defined as those who are, during the survey reference week, without work, actively seeking employment and currently available to start work.

The **unemployment rate** refers to unemployed persons as a percentage of the civil labour force.

The statistical data for Israel are supplied by and under the responsibility of the relevant Israeli authorities. The use of such data by the OECD is without prejudice to the status of the Golan Heights, East Jerusalem and Israeli settlements in the West Bank under the terms of international law.

References

The following additional material relevant to this indicator is available on line:

- ***Table A7.1b. Employment rates and educational attainment (2009)***
  StatLink http://dx.doi.org/10.1787/888932462909
- ***Table A7.2b. Unemployment rates and educational attainment (2009)***
  StatLink http://dx.doi.org/10.1787/888932462947
- ***Table A7.3b. Trends in employment rates of 25-64 year-old men, by educational attainment (1997-2009)***
  StatLink http://dx.doi.org/10.1787/888932462985
- ***Table A7.3c. Trends in employment rates of 25-64 year-old women, by educational attainment (1997-2009)***
  StatLink http://dx.doi.org/10.1787/888932463004
- ***Table A7.4b. Trends in unemployment rates of men, by educational attainment (1997-2009)***
  StatLink http://dx.doi.org/10.1787/888932463042
- ***Table A7.4c. Trends in unemployment rates of women, by educational attainment (1997-2009)***
  StatLink http://dx.doi.org/10.1787/888932463061

Table A7.1a. [1/2] Employment rates and educational attainment, by gender (2009)

Number of 25-64 year-olds in employment as a percentage of the population aged 25 to 64, by level of education attained and gender

					Upper secondary education			Tertiary education		
		Pre-primary and primary education	Lower secondary education	ISCED 3C Short	ISCED 3C Long/3B	ISCED 3A	Post-secondary non-tertiary education	Type B	Type A and advanced research programmes	All levels of education
		(1)	(2)	(3)	(4)	(5)	(6)	(7)	(8)	(9)
OECD Australia	Men	65.5	80.6	a	89.6	83.2	90.4	88.1	89.4	85.0
	Women	41.2	62.5	a	72.3	67.1	82.5	77.1	81.5	70.4
Austria	Men	x(2)	64.1	79.2	80.7	79.4	88.0	86.6	91.2	81.1
	Women	x(2)	50.0	58.5	70.9	75.2	81.2	84.5	82.7	69.6
Belgium	Men	47.2	66.4	a	79.4	80.5	85.5	87.3	87.1	76.2
	Women	26.1	46.4	a	63.7	67.3	75.5	81.4	81.7	63.3
Canada	Men	52.3	67.3	a	x(5)	77.3	79.2	84.1	84.8	78.9
	Women	34.8	50.1	a	x(5)	67.4	73.0	79.0	79.9	71.9
Chile	Men	x(2)	83.2	x(5)	88.4	87.3	a	86.5	84.7	85.7
	Women	x(2)	36.6	x(5)	57.6	49.6	a	67.9	72.6	51.6
Czech Republic	Men	c	55.4	a	81.5	88.0	x(5)	x(8)	91.0	83.4
	Women	c	39.6	a	60.9	69.1	x(5)	x(8)	76.9	64.1
Denmark	Men	63.6	70.7	83.5	82.7	79.1	89.1	87.1	89.9	81.9
	Women	31.1	58.8	67.5	76.9	73.2	71.3	82.6	86.6	75.6
Estonia	Men	c	55.1	a	65.8	73.3	75.9	82.1	89.8	73.8
	Women	c	42.8	a	55.9	71.4	68.3	77.0	82.6	72.2
Finland	Men	46.7	71.6	a	a	76.3	93.7	82.2	89.4	76.4
	Women	42.4	61.2	a	a	72.4	93.6	82.6	82.6	73.8
France	Men	47.5	73.8	a	83.4	80.0	c	89.5	85.2	78.3
	Women	37.2	57.7	a	69.0	72.3	c	81.8	80.0	67.0
Germany	Men	55.8	67.9	a	80.7	64.0	86.0	88.3	90.5	81.3
	Women	35.1	51.5	a	70.1	55.3	79.2	82.2	82.1	69.5
Greece	Men	74.3	83.3	82.0	86.8	82.0	85.3	83.9	87.8	82.0
	Women	36.6	46.7	63.3	59.7	50.6	66.1	75.1	78.5	54.6
Hungary	Men	16.3	47.7	a	70.5	76.6	80.8	85.2	83.7	70.5
	Women	7.7	34.0	a	54.9	62.9	65.5	76.1	75.0	57.0
Iceland	Men	79.4	80.7	84.2	87.5	82.2	88.9	84.9	90.4	85.9
	Women	c	72.9	77.7	81.7	71.8	78.8	88.6	86.6	79.1
Ireland	Men	49.0	68.2	71.5	a	77.1	75.0	83.8	87.3	74.3
	Women	29.2	44.2	53.8	a	61.5	63.0	75.1	81.3	62.3
Israel	Men	55.6	64.0	a	80.1	73.9	a	85.7	87.6	77.0
	Women	18.8	41.9	a	63.2	61.8	a	72.8	81.9	64.3
Italy	Men	49.1	75.0	76.0	82.5	82.4	86.8	81.1	85.0	76.6
	Women	15.5	40.9	56.4	60.2	64.1	71.6	65.2	74.9	51.6
Japan	Men	x(5)	x(5)	x(5)	x(5)	85.8	a	92.0	92.4	88.7
	Women	x(5)	x(5)	x(5)	x(5)	60.8	a	64.9	69.9	63.3
Korea	Men	73.8	79.6	a	85.8	82.2	a	89.2	88.0	84.9
	Women	57.2	58.0	a	55.7	55.6	a	60.7	59.8	57.6
Luxembourg	Men	69.3	77.2	81.0	78.9	79.3	75.6	89.8	91.1	82.5
	Women	50.4	49.2	54.6	57.1	63.6	69.4	75.8	81.1	64.1
Mexico	Men	85.7	89.9	a	x(5)	89.8	a	x(8)	88.7	87.9
	Women	38.2	46.2	a	x(5)	57.7	a	x(8)	73.0	48.4
Netherlands	Men	68.2	81.3	x(4)	82.7	89.7	85.0	85.9	90.6	85.7
	Women	38.4	55.8	x(4)	71.9	79.8	78.4	76.1	86.6	72.2
New Zealand	Men	x(2)	74.4	86.5	86.0	88.8	89.5	88.9	90.8	86.0
	Women	x(2)	57.3	74.5	72.2	78.1	73.7	77.6	80.6	72.9
Norway	Men	c	70.6	a	86.0	84.0	91.4	88.1	92.2	84.8
	Women	c	62.3	a	79.8	78.3	81.8	93.9	88.7	79.7

Source: OECD. See Annex 3 for a description of ISCED-97 levels, ISCED-97 country mappings and national data sources *(www.oecd.org/edu/eag2011)*.
Please refer to the Reader's Guide for information concerning the symbols replacing missing data.

StatLink http://dx.doi.org/10.1787/888932462890

Table A7.1a. [2/2] Employment rates and educational attainment, by gender (2009)

Number of 25-64 year-olds in employment as a percentage of the population aged 25 to 64, by level of education attained and gender

			Pre-primary and primary education	Lower secondary education	Upper secondary education: ISCED 3C Short	Upper secondary education: ISCED 3C Long/3B	Upper secondary education: ISCED 3A	Post-secondary non-tertiary education	Tertiary education: Type B	Tertiary education: Type A and advanced research programmes	All levels of education
			(1)	(2)	(3)	(4)	(5)	(6)	(7)	(8)	(9)
OECD	Poland	Men	x(2)	53.4	a	72.8	78.1	78.0	x(8)	89.9	75.2
		Women	x(2)	31.0	a	51.5	59.1	68.6	x(8)	82.1	59.8
	Portugal	Men	73.9	83.2	x(5)	x(5)	83.8	84.1	x(8)	87.6	79.0
		Women	57.3	71.8	x(5)	x(5)	76.8	69.5	x(8)	86.1	67.8
	Slovak Republic	Men	c	42.0	x(4)	76.1	84.5	x(5)	88.7	89.4	78.6
		Women	c	27.1	x(4)	56.9	67.8	x(5)	67.0	78.4	61.5
	Slovenia	Men	34.2	66.8	a	76.0	80.1	a	86.2	93.7	78.0
		Women	21.6	48.8	a	65.6	73.1	a	82.8	90.7	70.5
	Spain	Men	56.2	72.0	a	78.3	76.3	80.3	83.1	85.4	73.6
		Women	32.0	49.3	a	61.9	65.3	c	72.5	79.9	57.6
	Sweden	Men	59.3	77.7	a	x(5)	83.9	87.2	85.4	90.4	83.7
		Women	40.4	63.0	a	x(5)	77.9	76.6	83.4	88.7	78.4
	Switzerland	Men	74.0	78.8	85.5	89.0	84.6	85.9	93.8	92.5	89.3
		Women	56.7	61.3	70.8	75.9	73.0	81.9	87.2	83.4	75.8
	Turkey	Men	69.6	74.2	a	79.8	76.1	a	x(8)	80.6	73.5
		Women	22.1	19.1	a	28.7	26.0	a	x(8)	63.1	27.2
	United Kingdom	Men	c	56.2	74.6	82.5	83.9	c	86.3	88.7	81.0
		Women	c	34.2	60.8	73.7	71.2	52.3	78.7	81.9	69.0
	United States	Men	64.7	59.6	x(5)	x(5)	72.9	x(5)	80.5	86.8	76.4
		Women	40.2	42.8	x(5)	x(5)	64.8	x(5)	75.2	77.3	67.6
	OECD average	Men	59.6	70.1	80.4	81.3	80.8	84.6	86.4	88.6	80.5
		Women	35.2	48.9	63.8	64.2	65.9	73.7	77.4	80.0	65.0
	EU21 average	Men	54.1	67.1	78.3	78.9	79.9	83.5	85.7	88.8	78.7
		Women	33.4	47.8	59.3	63.6	68.1	71.9	77.8	81.9	65.8
Other G20	Argentina		m	m	m	m	m	m	m	m	m
	Brazil	Men	83.4	87.4	x(5)	x(5)	88.8	a	x(8)	91.3	86.3
		Women	51.8	58.9	x(5)	x(5)	67.7	a	x(8)	81.5	61.2
	China		m	m	m	m	m	m	m	m	m
	India		m	m	m	m	m	m	m	m	m
	Indonesia		m	m	m	m	m	m	m	m	m
	Russian Federation		m	m	m	m	m	m	m	m	m
	Saudi Arabia		m	m	m	m	m	m	m	m	m
	South Africa		m	m	m	m	m	m	m	m	m

Source: OECD. See Annex 3 for a description of ISCED-97 levels, ISCED-97 country mappings and national data sources *(www.oecd.org/edu/eag2011)*.
Please refer to the Reader's Guide for information concerning the symbols replacing missing data.
StatLink http://dx.doi.org/10.1787/888932462890

Table A7.2a. [1/2] Unemployment rates and educational attainment, by gender (2009)

Number of 25-64 year-olds in unemployment as a percentage of the labour force aged 25 to 64, by level of education attained and gender

		Pre-primary and primary education	Lower secondary education	Upper secondary education: ISCED 3C Short	Upper secondary education: ISCED 3C Long/3B	Upper secondary education: ISCED 3A	Post-secondary non-tertiary education	Tertiary education: Type B	Tertiary education: Type A and advanced research programmes	All levels of education
		(1)	(2)	(3)	(4)	(5)	(6)	(7)	(8)	(9)
OECD Australia	Men	12.0	6.3	a	3.0	5.7	1.9	4.0	3.5	4.7
	Women	6.7	5.3	a	5.8	4.3	3.0	3.4	2.8	4.1
Austria	Men	x(2)	10.8	c	4.1	4.2	3.3	c	2.3	4.2
	Women	x(2)	7.4	c	3.4	4.0	2.1	c	3.3	3.8
Belgium	Men	15.0	9.6	a	8.0	5.3	c	3.2	4.2	6.5
	Women	15.6	11.2	a	8.5	7.0	c	2.8	5.0	6.7
Canada	Men	14.7	12.5	a	x(5)	8.9	9.0	6.8	5.3	8.0
	Women	13.6	11.2	a	x(5)	7.0	6.6	5.0	4.5	6.0
Chile	Men	x(2)	5.8	x(5)	6.8	7.0	a	9.0	6.9	6.7
	Women	x(2)	6.3	x(5)	8.2	8.2	a	10.4	6.7	7.7
Czech Republic	Men	c	23.0	a	5.5	2.9	x(8)	x(8)	2.3	4.9
	Women	c	21.0	a	9.2	4.9	x(8)	x(8)	2.0	7.1
Denmark	Men	8.4	8.4	8.2	5.4	5.1	3.6	5.3	3.8	5.6
	Women	15.2	6.3	3.9	4.3	5.1	c	4.8	3.5	4.4
Estonia	Men	c	23.9	a	16.3	17.4	16.9	11.3	5.2	15.2
	Women	c	22.5	a	c	10.7	14.1	7.8	4.7	9.5
Finland	Men	9.3	10.4	a	a	8.3	c	4.9	3.6	7.0
	Women	7.1	10.9	a	a	7.3	c	3.2	4.7	6.0
France	Men	13.7	10.3	a	5.9	7.3	c	3.9	5.6	7.1
	Women	12.2	11.9	a	8.7	6.9	c	4.7	5.4	7.9
Germany	Men	23.4	17.8	a	8.4	8.3	4.8	3.2	3.2	7.7
	Women	20.5	13.1	a	7.5	7.4	4.3	3.4	3.8	7.1
Greece	Men	6.1	7.6	7.2	6.8	5.5	7.1	5.6	4.8	6.1
	Women	11.5	15.1	c	19.7	12.5	13.6	11.7	7.4	11.6
Hungary	Men	35.0	21.4	a	9.6	6.0	6.2	c	3.4	8.9
	Women	41.3	19.6	a	11.5	6.5	8.5	c	3.4	8.7
Iceland	Men	c	10.5	c	c	c	c	c	c	6.7
	Women	c	c	c	c	c	c	c	c	4.4
Ireland	Men	19.3	18.0	c	a	13.0	16.6	9.0	5.9	12.9
	Women	8.2	8.5	c	a	6.0	9.8	5.8	4.7	6.4
Israel	Men	11.6	9.8	a	7.0	7.1	a	6.0	4.5	6.7
	Women	10.4	11.6	a	8.9	8.2	a	6.6	4.7	6.8
Italy	Men	9.9	6.6	10.6	5.0	4.4	7.6	6.1	3.9	5.6
	Women	11.2	10.7	11.3	7.7	6.6	8.7	c	6.2	7.9
Japan	Men	x(5)	x(5)	x(5)	x(5)	6.4	a	4.2	3.1	5.0
	Women	x(5)	x(5)	x(5)	x(5)	5.3	a	4.1	3.3	4.6
Korea	Men	3.6	4.4	a	4.4	4.3	a	4.0	3.8	4.1
	Women	2.1	1.9	a	3.1	2.5	a	3.5	2.5	2.6
Luxembourg	Men	6.8	c	c	2.9	3.2	c	3.6	3.0	3.3
	Women	7.5	c	c	4.2	3.7	c	3.8	5.0	4.8
Mexico	Men	4.0	4.8	a	2.2	4.6	a	1.5	4.7	4.4
	Women	2.9	4.3	a	2.1	3.8	a	3.0	3.9	3.6
Netherlands	Men	5.3	3.5	x(4)	3.2	2.3	2.4	2.7	2.0	2.7
	Women	5.8	3.9	x(4)	2.9	2.9	2.1	4.0	1.8	2.8
New Zealand	Men	x(2)	6.9	4.1	5.2	3.4	3.4	4.0	3.2	4.3
	Women	x(2)	6.5	3.5	4.7	2.8	c	3.7	2.8	3.9
Norway	Men	c	5.7	a	1.9	c	c	c	1.5	2.5
	Women	c	c	a	c	c	c	c	1.5	1.6

Source: OECD. See Annex 3 for a description of ISCED-97 levels, ISCED-97 country mappings and national data sources *(www.oecd.org/edu/eag2011)*.
Please refer to the Reader's Guide for information concerning the symbols replacing missing data.
StatLink http://dx.doi.org/10.1787/888932462928

Table A7.2a. [2/2] Unemployment rates and educational attainment, by gender (2009)

Number of 25-64 year-olds in unemployment as a percentage of the labour force aged 25 to 64, by level of education attained and gender

				Pre-primary and primary education	Lower secondary education	Upper secondary education: ISCED 3C Short	Upper secondary education: ISCED 3C Long/3B	Upper secondary education: ISCED 3A	Post-secondary non-tertiary education	Tertiary education: Type B	Tertiary education: Type A and advanced research programmes	All levels of education
				(1)	(2)	(3)	(4)	(5)	(6)	(7)	(8)	(9)
OECD	Poland	Men		x(2)	13.2	a	7.2	5.3	7.4	x(8)	3.4	6.4
		Women		x(2)	15.0	a	10.2	7.6	6.3	x(8)	3.8	7.4
	Portugal	Men		9.9	8.3	x(5)	x(5)	6.5	c	x(8)	5.8	8.5
		Women		10.7	11.9	x(5)	x(5)	9.8	c	x(8)	5.4	9.7
	Slovak Republic	Men		74.7	36.8	x(4)	11.1	6.7	a	c	3.7	9.6
		Women		c	37.3	x(4)	15.7	8.6	a	c	4.0	11.7
	Slovenia	Men		15.4	7.3	a	5.5	5.1	a	4.2	1.9	5.1
		Women		22.4	6.9	a	6.5	5.6	a	3.5	3.0	5.2
	Spain	Men		23.9	19.1	a	14.1	14.8	c	10.0	7.4	15.6
		Women		24.7	23.2	a	17.7	15.6	c	13.2	8.2	16.5
	Sweden	Men		13.0	8.0	a	x(5)	6.5	4.7	6.6	4.2	6.3
		Women		16.8	8.7	a	x(5)	6.0	6.7	4.2	3.7	5.6
	Switzerland	Men		c	7.1	c	3.2	c	c	c	2.8	3.2
		Women		c	8.4	c	3.0	c	c	c	3.6	3.8
	Turkey	Men		13.4	12.8	a	9.4	11.1	x(8)	x(8)	7.7	11.8
		Women		9.1	20.1	a	22.3	21.7	x(8)	x(8)	11.8	12.6
	United Kingdom	Men		c	13.9	9.8	6.9	5.1	c	4.9	3.5	6.5
		Women		c	12.5	6.4	4.6	5.3	c	3.9	2.7	4.8
	United States	Men		13.4	18.4	x(5)	x(5)	11.5	x(5)	8.0	4.7	9.5
		Women		14.7	14.4	x(5)	x(5)	7.7	x(5)	5.6	4.0	6.6
	OECD average	Men		15.7	12.0	8.0	6.5	6.9	6.8	5.5	4.1	6.9
		Women		13.2	12.3	6.3	8.4	7.1	7.1	5.3	4.4	6.6
	EU21 average	Men		18.1	13.9	9.0	7.4	6.8	7.3	5.6	3.9	7.4
		Women		15.4	13.9	7.2	8.9	7.1	7.6	5.5	4.4	7.4
Other G20	Argentina			m	m	m	m	m	m	m	m	m
	Brazil	Men		3.6	4.8	x(5)	x(5)	5.0	a	x(8)	2.8	4.1
		Women		7.6	10.2	x(5)	x(5)	9.7	a	x(8)	4.0	8.1
	China			m	m	m	m	m	m	m	m	m
	India			m	m	m	m	m	m	m	m	m
	Indonesia			m	m	m	m	m	m	m	m	m
	Russian Federation			m	m	m	m	m	m	m	m	m
	Saudi Arabia			m	m	m	m	m	m	m	m	m
	South Africa			m	m	m	m	m	m	m	m	m

Source: OECD. See Annex 3 for a description of ISCED-97 levels, ISCED-97 country mappings and national data sources *(www.oecd.org/edu/eag2011)*.
Please refer to the Reader's Guide for information concerning the symbols replacing missing data.
StatLink http://dx.doi.org/10.1787/888932462928

Table A7.3a. [1/2] Trends in employment rates of 25-64 year-olds, by educational attainment (1997-2009)

Number of 25-64 year-olds in employment as a percentage of the population aged 25 to 64, by level of educational attainment

			1997	1998	1999	2000	2001	2002	2003	2004	2005	2006	2007	2008	2009
OECD	Australia	Below upper secondary	59.5	59.5	59.1	60.8	59.9	60.0	61.0	60.6	62.9	63.5	63.9	61.5	**66.1**
		Upper secondary and post-secondary non-tertiary	76.1	75.9	76.2	76.7	78.0	77.8	78.7	78.8	79.8	80.4	80.5	80.9	**80.2**
		Tertiary education	83.4	83.8	82.0	82.9	83.1	83.5	83.2	83.3	84.4	84.4	84.8	83.1	**84.3**
	Austria	Below upper secondary	52.8	52.6	53.3	53.7	53.5	54.4	55.0	52.2	53.3	55.7	57.9	57.0	**55.6**
		Upper secondary and post-secondary non-tertiary	75.6	75.0	75.6	74.8	74.8	75.3	75.6	73.9	74.3	75.8	76.9	78.1	**77.6**
		Tertiary education	86.0	85.8	86.2	87.5	86.6	86.0	85.0	82.5	84.5	85.9	86.8	86.4	**86.7**
	Belgium	Below upper secondary	47.5	47.5	49.1	50.5	49.0	48.8	48.9	48.8	49.0	49.0	49.8	49.4	**48.0**
		Upper secondary and post-secondary non-tertiary	73.4	72.0	74.5	75.1	73.9	73.8	72.8	73.1	74.0	73.2	74.2	74.7	**74.0**
		Tertiary education	83.9	84.3	85.4	85.3	84.5	83.7	83.6	83.9	84.2	83.6	84.9	84.7	**84.2**
	Canada	Below upper secondary	52.5	53.5	54.4	54.7	54.4	55.0	56.4	57.0	56.4	56.9	57.3	57.7	**55.1**
		Upper secondary and post-secondary non-tertiary	73.9	74.4	75.3	76.0	75.4	75.8	76.3	76.7	76.3	76.0	76.5	76.5	**73.7**
		Tertiary education	81.7	82.3	82.4	82.7	81.9	82.0	82.1	82.2	82.2	82.6	82.9	82.6	**81.7**
	Chile	Below upper secondary	m	m	m	m	m	m	m	m	m	m	59.4	58.9	**58.3**
		Upper secondary and post-secondary non-tertiary	m	m	m	m	m	m	m	m	m	m	69.3	70.1	**69.2**
		Tertiary education	m	m	m	m	m	m	m	m	m	m	77.9	79.5	**78.0**
	Czech Republic	Below upper secondary	51.1	49.5	46.9	46.9	46.7	45.3	46.0	42.3	41.2	43.9	45.7	46.5	**43.9**
		Upper secondary and post-secondary non-tertiary	79.7	78.2	76.4	75.5	75.7	76.2	75.8	74.8	75.5	75.6	76.1	76.6	**75.1**
		Tertiary education	89.3	88.7	87.4	86.8	87.8	87.1	86.5	86.4	85.8	85.1	85.2	85.1	**84.3**
	Denmark	Below upper secondary	m	60.9	61.7	62.2	61.5	61.2	62.6	61.7	61.5	62.8	66.6	66.9	**64.6**
		Upper secondary and post-secondary non-tertiary	m	79.1	80.7	81.0	81.0	80.3	79.8	79.9	79.9	81.3	82.5	83.2	**79.7**
		Tertiary education	m	87.5	87.9	88.6	87.2	86.0	85.2	85.5	86.4	87.4	87.8	89.2	**87.4**
	Estonia	Below upper secondary	m	m	m	m	m	44.1	49.0	50.9	50.0	56.5	56.7	58.3	**47.4**
		Upper secondary and post-secondary non-tertiary	m	m	m	m	m	71.9	72.9	72.6	73.6	78.1	79.4	79.7	**71.6**
		Tertiary education	m	m	m	m	m	81.6	80.3	82.4	84.5	87.7	87.4	85.8	**82.8**
	Finland	Below upper secondary	54.7	56.2	58.6	57.3	58.2	57.7	57.9	57.1	57.9	58.4	58.6	59.3	**56.8**
		Upper secondary and post-secondary non-tertiary	72.2	73.1	74.3	74.9	75.5	74.4	74.4	74.4	75.2	75.6	76.2	77.3	**74.8**
		Tertiary education	82.6	83.2	84.7	84.4	85.1	85.1	85.0	84.2	84.1	85.0	85.2	85.6	**84.4**
	France	Below upper secondary	56.3	56.3	56.4	57.0	57.7	57.8	58.9	59.1	58.6	58.2	57.8	57.4	**56.2**
		Upper secondary and post-secondary non-tertiary	75.0	75.0	75.1	75.8	76.5	76.7	76.3	75.7	75.7	75.6	75.7	75.8	**76.5**
		Tertiary education	81.3	81.6	81.8	83.1	83.7	83.3	83.3	82.9	83.0	83.0	83.4	84.6	**83.5**
	Germany	Below upper secondary	45.7	46.1	48.7	50.6	51.8	50.9	50.2	48.6	51.6	53.8	54.6	55.3	**54.9**
		Upper secondary and post-secondary non-tertiary	68.2	67.9	69.9	70.4	70.5	70.3	69.7	69.5	70.6	72.5	74.4	75.3	**75.5**
		Tertiary education	82.3	82.2	83.0	83.4	83.4	83.6	83.0	82.7	82.9	84.3	85.5	85.8	**86.4**
	Greece	Below upper secondary	57.4	57.1	57.0	57.5	57.2	58.3	59.7	57.9	59.1	59.5	59.9	60.3	**59.7**
		Upper secondary and post-secondary non-tertiary	63.3	64.8	64.6	64.6	65.0	65.3	66.8	68.1	68.7	69.7	69.4	69.8	**68.4**
		Tertiary education	80.2	80.5	80.7	80.9	80.3	81.2	81.5	81.4	81.8	83.1	82.6	82.6	**82.2**
	Hungary	Below upper secondary	36.2	36.2	35.8	35.8	36.6	36.7	37.4	36.9	38.1	38.2	38.5	38.7	**37.4**
		Upper secondary and post-secondary non-tertiary	70.7	70.9	72.1	72.1	71.9	71.7	71.4	70.9	70.4	70.4	70.2	68.7	**67.0**
		Tertiary education	81.4	81.0	82.1	82.4	82.6	82.0	82.7	82.9	83.0	81.8	80.4	79.9	**78.8**
	Iceland	Below upper secondary	83.8	85.6	87.2	87.3	87.2	86.4	83.7	81.6	83.0	83.6	84.1	83.1	**77.1**
		Upper secondary and post-secondary non-tertiary	88.0	88.6	90.5	89.0	89.7	89.4	88.7	87.8	88.2	88.6	88.6	86.3	**82.6**
		Tertiary education	94.6	94.7	95.1	95.0	94.7	95.4	92.7	92.0	92.0	92.0	92.2	91.0	**88.3**
	Ireland	Below upper secondary	50.3	53.4	54.4	60.7	58.4	56.7	56.6	57.5	58.4	58.7	58.7	56.8	**50.0**
		Upper secondary and post-secondary non-tertiary	68.7	71.7	74.8	77.0	77.3	76.6	75.6	75.9	76.7	77.3	77.1	75.5	**69.1**
		Tertiary education	81.9	85.2	87.2	87.2	87.0	86.3	86.1	86.2	86.8	86.5	86.7	85.2	**82.0**
	Israel	Below upper secondary	m	m	m	m	m	43.5	42.7	40.4	41.2	41.8	42.7	44.8	**44.3**
		Upper secondary and post-secondary non-tertiary	m	m	m	m	m	66.6	65.9	66.4	66.6	67.5	69.2	70.0	**69.0**
		Tertiary education	m	m	m	m	m	79.1	79.3	79.2	80.3	81.2	83.0	82.8	**82.4**
	Italy	Below upper secondary	m	47.8	48.0	48.6	49.4	50.5	50.7	51.7	51.7	52.5	52.8	52.5	**51.2**
		Upper secondary and post-secondary non-tertiary	m	70.1	70.3	71.2	72.1	72.3	72.4	73.5	73.5	74.4	74.5	74.3	**73.1**
		Tertiary education	m	80.8	80.7	81.4	81.6	82.2	82.0	81.2	80.4	80.6	80.2	80.7	**79.2**
	Japan	Below upper secondary	69.4	68.8	68.2	67.1	67.6	m	m	m	m	m	m	m	**m**
		Upper secondary and post-secondary non-tertiary	75.3	75.8	74.2	73.8	74.3	71.8	71.8	72.0	72.3	73.2	74.4	74.4	**73.1**
		Tertiary education	80.7	79.5	79.2	79.0	79.9	79.2	79.2	79.3	79.4	79.8	80.1	79.7	**79.7**
	Korea	Below upper secondary	71.2	66.1	66.9	68.0	67.8	68.4	66.5	66.4	65.9	66.2	66.0	66.1	**65.3**
		Upper secondary and post-secondary non-tertiary	71.7	66.5	66.4	68.7	69.3	70.5	69.6	70.1	70.1	70.3	70.7	70.7	**69.6**
		Tertiary education	80.2	76.1	74.6	75.4	75.7	76.1	76.4	76.7	76.8	77.2	77.2	77.1	**76.1**
	Luxembourg	Below upper secondary	m	m	56.5	58.3	60.0	59.3	60.3	59.1	61.8	60.8	62.3	61.1	**61.6**
		Upper secondary and post-secondary non-tertiary	m	m	73.9	74.6	74.8	73.6	73.3	72.6	71.7	73.4	73.9	70.7	**70.2**
		Tertiary education	m	m	85.0	84.3	85.5	85.2	82.3	84.1	84.0	85.2	84.5	84.7	**85.1**

Source: OECD. See Annex 3 for notes *(www.oecd.org/edu/eag2011)*.

Please refer to the Reader's Guide for information concerning the symbols replacing missing data.

StatLink http://dx.doi.org/10.1787/888932462966

Table A7.3a. [2/2] **Trends in employment rates of 25-64 year-olds, by educational attainment (1997-2009)**

Number of 25-64 year-olds in employment as a percentage of the population aged 25 to 64, by level of educational attainment

			1997	1998	1999	2000	2001	2002	2003	2004	2005	2006	2007	2008	2009
OECD	Mexico	Below upper secondary	61.8	61.3	61.4	60.7	60.5	61.3	60.9	62.2	61.8	62.8	63.0	63.6	**61.7**
		Upper secondary and post-secondary non-tertiary	70.1	69.1	69.1	70.7	69.8	69.7	69.5	70.3	71.9	73.6	73.9	73.3	**71.9**
		Tertiary education	83.2	83.2	82.0	82.5	80.9	80.9	81.2	81.4	82.0	83.3	83.1	83.1	**81.7**
	Netherlands	Below upper secondary	m	55.3	60.7	57.6	58.8	60.7	59.4	59.4	59.5	60.6	61.9	63.7	**63.6**
		Upper secondary and post-secondary non-tertiary	m	76.8	79.5	79.4	80.0	79.8	78.8	77.9	77.9	79.1	80.3	81.5	**81.7**
		Tertiary education	m	85.4	87.2	86.3	86.3	86.5	85.9	85.3	85.6	86.4	87.7	88.3	**88.1**
	New Zealand	Below upper secondary	63.1	62.4	63.6	64.8	66.0	67.1	67.4	68.9	70.0	70.4	71.0	70.5	**69.0**
		Upper secondary and post-secondary non-tertiary	80.1	79.1	79.7	80.0	80.2	81.2	81.4	82.7	84.2	84.2	84.6	83.3	**82.4**
		Tertiary education	82.4	81.5	81.9	82.2	83.6	83.0	82.7	83.4	84.1	84.5	83.7	84.5	**84.0**
	Norway	Below upper secondary	66.7	67.7	67.1	65.3	63.3	64.2	64.1	62.1	64.3	64.7	66.3	66.0	**65.4**
		Upper secondary and post-secondary non-tertiary	83.3	83.9	82.9	82.7	82.7	81.5	79.6	78.8	82.4	83.1	84.0	84.4	**83.1**
		Tertiary education	90.2	90.2	90.2	89.9	89.6	89.5	88.8	89.3	88.8	89.2	90.4	90.6	**90.2**
	Poland	Below upper secondary	50.3	49.1	46.6	42.8	41.5	39.1	38.2	37.5	37.7	38.6	41.0	43.0	**41.6**
		Upper secondary and post-secondary non-tertiary	70.7	71.1	69.7	66.6	64.8	62.5	61.6	61.3	61.7	62.9	65.2	67.0	**66.3**
		Tertiary education	86.7	87.2	86.6	84.5	84.1	83.1	82.6	82.3	82.7	83.5	84.5	85.1	**85.3**
	Portugal	Below upper secondary	m	71.6	71.8	72.8	73.1	73.0	72.4	71.9	71.5	71.7	71.6	71.7	**69.0**
		Upper secondary and post-secondary non-tertiary	m	80.1	81.9	83.3	82.7	82.2	81.5	80.3	79.3	80.2	79.8	80.6	**80.1**
		Tertiary education	m	89.4	90.0	90.6	90.8	88.6	87.5	88.0	87.3	86.4	85.9	86.7	**86.7**
	Slovak Republic	Below upper secondary	38.9	37.4	33.2	30.9	30.5	28.2	28.5	26.6	26.3	28.9	29.1	32.3	**30.3**
		Upper secondary and post-secondary non-tertiary	75.9	75.1	72.5	70.6	70.2	70.5	71.2	70.3	70.8	71.9	73.2	74.8	**72.0**
		Tertiary education	89.8	88.6	87.0	85.6	86.7	86.6	87.1	83.6	84.0	84.9	84.2	85.5	**83.2**
	Slovenia	Below upper secondary	m	m	m	m	m	55.6	54.2	55.9	56.1	55.9	56.2	55.0	**53.7**
		Upper secondary and post-secondary non-tertiary	m	m	m	m	m	74.0	72.7	74.4	74.6	74.1	75.1	76.4	**74.6**
		Tertiary education	m	m	m	m	m	86.1	86.1	86.8	87.0	88.2	87.7	87.9	**88.4**
	Spain	Below upper secondary	48.2	49.5	51.0	53.8	55.1	55.7	56.6	57.6	58.6	59.8	60.5	59.1	**54.0**
		Upper secondary and post-secondary non-tertiary	66.6	67.5	69.6	72.1	71.8	71.6	72.4	73.2	74.7	75.9	76.3	75.2	**70.6**
		Tertiary education	75.5	76.3	77.6	79.7	80.7	80.8	81.6	81.9	82.4	83.4	84.4	83.6	**81.1**
	Sweden	Below upper secondary	67.2	66.4	66.5	68.0	68.8	68.2	67.5	67.0	66.1	66.9	66.6	66.2	**64.2**
		Upper secondary and post-secondary non-tertiary	78.6	79.3	79.6	81.7	81.9	81.8	81.3	80.7	81.3	81.9	83.1	83.3	**81.3**
		Tertiary education	85.0	85.5	85.6	86.7	86.9	86.5	85.8	85.4	87.3	87.3	88.6	89.2	**88.1**
	Switzerland	Below upper secondary	68.0	68.8	68.3	64.5	69.6	68.2	66.3	65.4	65.3	64.5	66.0	67.6	**67.5**
		Upper secondary and post-secondary non-tertiary	79.6	80.8	80.9	81.4	81.3	81.1	80.5	79.9	80.0	80.2	81.1	82.0	**81.7**
		Tertiary education	89.1	90.3	90.7	90.4	91.3	90.6	89.7	89.7	90.0	90.2	90.0	90.5	**89.6**
	Turkey	Below upper secondary	56.9	57.4	55.8	53.1	51.9	50.5	49.1	47.7	47.2	47.3	46.9	46.7	**46.3**
		Upper secondary and post-secondary non-tertiary	66.8	66.0	63.9	64.0	62.4	61.8	61.1	60.3	61.8	61.5	60.9	60.8	**58.3**
		Tertiary education	81.7	81.3	79.0	78.5	78.3	76.3	74.9	74.5	75.2	74.5	74.6	74.5	**73.6**
	United Kingdom	Below upper secondary	64.7	64.5	65.0	65.3	65.5	65.3	66.0	65.4	65.5	65.2	64.9	65.6	**56.9**
		Upper secondary and post-secondary non-tertiary	79.2	80.1	80.5	81.1	80.9	81.1	81.5	81.2	81.6	81.3	80.9	82.1	**78.3**
		Tertiary education	87.2	87.1	87.7	87.8	88.1	87.6	87.8	87.7	88.0	88.1	87.8	87.8	**84.5**
	United States	Below upper secondary	55.2	57.6	57.8	57.8	58.4	57.0	57.8	56.5	57.2	58.0	58.3	56.2	**52.5**
		Upper secondary and post-secondary non-tertiary	75.7	75.8	76.2	76.7	76.2	74.0	73.3	72.8	72.8	73.3	73.6	72.8	**68.9**
		Tertiary education	85.4	85.3	84.6	85.0	84.4	83.2	82.2	82.0	82.5	82.7	83.3	83.1	**80.8**
	OECD average	Below upper secondary	57.2	57.4	57.7	57.8	58.0	56.5	56.6	56.1	56.5	57.3	58.1	58.2	**56.0**
		Upper secondary and post-secondary non-tertiary	74.3	74.6	75.0	75.4	75.4	74.6	74.4	74.3	74.8	75.5	75.9	76.1	**74.2**
		Tertiary education	84.2	84.4	84.5	84.7	84.7	84.2	83.7	83.6	84.0	84.5	84.5	84.6	**83.6**
	EU21 average	Below upper secondary	51.5	53.2	53.7	54.2	54.4	53.7	54.1	53.6	54.0	55.0	55.8	56.0	**53.4**
		Upper secondary and post-secondary non-tertiary	72.7	73.8	74.5	74.8	74.8	74.4	74.2	74.0	74.4	75.2	75.9	76.2	**74.2**
		Tertiary education	83.8	84.5	84.9	85.1	85.2	84.7	84.3	84.2	84.6	85.1	85.3	85.5	**84.4**
Other G20	Argentina		m	m	m	m	m	m	m	m	m	m	m	m	**m**
	Brazil	Below upper secondary	m	m	m	m	m	m	m	m	m	m	68.8	69.4	**68.7**
		Upper secondary and post-secondary non-tertiary	m	m	m	m	m	m	m	m	m	m	76.9	77.7	**77.4**
		Tertiary education	m	m	m	m	m	m	m	m	m	m	85.8	86.0	**85.6**
	China		m	m	m	m	m	m	m	m	m	m	m	m	**m**
	India		m	m	m	m	m	m	m	m	m	m	m	m	**m**
	Indonesia		m	m	m	m	m	m	m	m	m	m	m	m	**m**
	Russian Federation		m	m	m	m	m	m	m	m	m	m	m	m	**m**
	Saudi Arabia		m	m	m	m	m	m	m	m	m	m	m	m	**m**
	South Africa		m	m	m	m	m	m	m	m	m	m	m	m	**m**

Source: OECD. See Annex 3 for notes *(www.oecd.org/edu/eag2011)*.

Please refer to the Reader's Guide for information concerning the symbols replacing missing data.

StatLink http://dx.doi.org/10.1787/888932462966

Table A7.4a. [1/2] Trends in unemployment rates of 25-64 year-olds, by educational attainment (1997-2009)

Number of 25-64 year-olds unemployed as a percentage of the labour force aged 25 to 64, by level of educational attainment

			1997	1998	1999	2000	2001	2002	2003	2004	2005	2006	2007	2008	2009
OECD	Australia	Below upper secondary	9.6	9.0	8.4	7.5	7.6	7.5	7.0	6.2	6.3	5.6	5.1	5.2	**6.6**
		Upper secondary and post-secondary non-tertiary	6.1	5.8	5.1	4.5	4.7	4.3	4.3	3.9	3.4	3.8	3.0	2.6	**4.1**
		Tertiary education	3.5	3.3	3.4	3.6	3.1	3.3	3.0	2.8	2.5	2.3	2.2	2.1	**3.3**
	Austria	Below upper secondary	6.6	6.8	5.9	6.2	6.2	6.7	7.8	7.8	8.6	7.9	7.4	6.3	**8.4**
		Upper secondary and post-secondary non-tertiary	3.3	3.7	3.2	2.9	3.0	3.4	3.4	3.8	3.9	3.7	3.3	2.9	**3.6**
		Tertiary education	2.5	1.9	1.8	1.5	1.5	1.8	2.0	2.9	2.6	2.5	2.4	1.7	**2.2**
	Belgium	Below upper secondary	12.5	13.1	12.0	9.8	8.5	10.3	10.7	11.7	12.4	12.3	11.3	10.8	**11.9**
		Upper secondary and post-secondary non-tertiary	6.7	7.4	6.6	5.3	5.5	6.0	6.7	6.9	6.9	6.7	6.2	5.7	**6.5**
		Tertiary education	3.3	3.2	3.1	2.7	2.7	3.5	3.5	3.9	3.7	3.7	3.3	3.2	**3.8**
	Canada	Below upper secondary	12.9	11.9	10.8	10.2	10.5	11.0	10.9	10.2	9.8	9.3	9.5	9.1	**12.6**
		Upper secondary and post-secondary non-tertiary	8.1	7.5	6.7	5.9	6.3	6.7	6.5	6.2	5.9	5.6	5.4	5.5	**8.1**
		Tertiary education	5.4	4.7	4.5	4.1	4.7	5.1	5.2	4.8	4.6	4.1	3.9	4.1	**5.3**
	Chile	Below upper secondary	m	m	m	m	m	m	m	m	m	m	4.6	5.2	**5.9**
		Upper secondary and post-secondary non-tertiary	m	m	m	m	m	m	m	m	m	m	6.0	6.6	**7.4**
		Tertiary education	m	m	m	m	m	m	m	m	m	m	6.0	5.5	**7.7**
	Czech Republic	Below upper secondary	12.1	14.5	18.8	19.3	19.2	18.8	18.3	23.0	24.4	22.3	19.1	17.3	**21.8**
		Upper secondary and post-secondary non-tertiary	3.4	4.6	6.5	6.7	6.2	5.6	6.0	6.4	6.2	5.5	4.3	3.3	**5.4**
		Tertiary education	1.2	1.9	2.6	2.5	2.0	1.8	2.0	2.0	2.0	2.2	1.5	1.5	**2.2**
	Denmark	Below upper secondary	m	7.0	7.0	6.9	6.2	6.4	6.7	8.2	6.5	5.5	4.2	3.5	**7.3**
		Upper secondary and post-secondary non-tertiary	m	4.6	4.1	3.9	3.7	3.7	4.4	4.8	4.0	2.7	2.5	2.2	**5.0**
		Tertiary education	m	3.3	3.0	3.0	3.6	3.9	4.7	4.4	3.7	3.2	2.9	2.3	**3.9**
	Estonia	Below upper secondary	m	m	m	m	m	19.0	14.8	15.4	13.0	11.7	8.6	9.7	**24.1**
		Upper secondary and post-secondary non-tertiary	m	m	m	m	m	10.5	9.5	9.5	8.4	5.7	4.6	5.2	**14.8**
		Tertiary education	m	m	m	m	m	5.8	6.5	5.0	3.8	3.2	2.4	2.8	**6.3**
	Finland	Below upper secondary	15.6	13.8	13.1	12.1	11.4	12.2	11.2	11.3	10.7	10.1	8.9	8.1	**9.8**
		Upper secondary and post-secondary non-tertiary	11.9	10.6	9.5	8.9	8.5	8.8	8.3	7.9	7.4	7.0	6.1	5.4	**7.7**
		Tertiary education	6.5	5.8	4.7	4.7	4.4	4.5	4.1	4.5	4.4	3.7	3.6	3.3	**4.0**
	France	Below upper secondary	15.0	14.9	15.3	13.9	11.9	11.8	10.4	10.7	11.1	11.0	10.2	9.7	**11.6**
		Upper secondary and post-secondary non-tertiary	9.6	9.6	9.2	7.9	6.9	6.8	6.6	6.7	6.6	6.6	5.9	5.5	**7.0**
		Tertiary education	7.0	6.6	6.1	5.1	4.8	5.2	5.3	5.7	5.4	5.1	4.7	4.0	**5.0**
	Germany	Below upper secondary	16.7	16.5	15.6	13.7	13.5	15.3	18.0	20.4	20.2	19.9	18.0	16.5	**16.7**
		Upper secondary and post-secondary non-tertiary	10.1	10.3	8.6	7.8	8.2	9.0	10.2	11.2	11.0	9.9	8.3	7.2	**7.5**
		Tertiary education	5.7	5.5	4.9	4.0	4.2	4.5	5.2	5.6	5.5	4.8	3.8	3.3	**3.4**
	Greece	Below upper secondary	6.5	7.7	8.8	8.2	8.2	7.8	7.2	8.7	8.3	7.2	7.0	6.8	**8.8**
		Upper secondary and post-secondary non-tertiary	9.6	10.7	11.5	11.2	10.4	10.5	10.1	10.0	9.6	8.9	8.2	7.2	**9.2**
		Tertiary education	7.3	6.8	8.0	7.5	7.2	6.8	6.5	7.4	7.1	6.3	6.1	5.7	**6.7**
	Hungary	Below upper secondary	12.6	11.4	11.1	9.9	10.0	10.5	10.6	10.8	12.4	14.8	16.0	17.3	**21.0**
		Upper secondary and post-secondary non-tertiary	6.9	6.2	5.8	5.3	4.6	4.4	4.8	5.0	6.0	6.1	5.9	6.3	**8.2**
		Tertiary education	1.7	1.7	1.4	1.3	1.2	1.5	1.4	1.9	2.3	2.2	2.6	2.3	**3.5**
	Iceland	Below upper secondary	4.4	3.2	2.0	2.6	2.6	3.2	3.3	2.5	2.3	c	c	2.5	**7.4**
		Upper secondary and post-secondary non-tertiary	2.7	c	c	c	c	c	c	c	c	c	c	c	**5.8**
		Tertiary education	c	c	c	c	c	c	c	c	c	c	c	c	**3.9**
	Ireland	Below upper secondary	14.5	11.6	9.2	5.6	5.2	5.9	6.3	6.1	6.0	5.7	6.1	8.2	**15.4**
		Upper secondary and post-secondary non-tertiary	6.5	4.5	3.5	2.3	2.4	2.8	2.9	3.0	3.1	3.2	3.5	4.8	**11.3**
		Tertiary education	4.0	3.0	1.7	1.6	1.8	2.2	2.6	2.2	2.0	2.2	2.3	3.0	**6.1**
	Israel	Below upper secondary	m	m	m	m	m	14.0	15.2	15.6	14.0	12.8	12.4	9.8	**10.8**
		Upper secondary and post-secondary non-tertiary	m	m	m	m	m	9.8	10.3	10.6	9.5	8.7	7.2	5.8	**7.7**
		Tertiary education	m	m	m	m	m	6.4	6.4	6.1	5.1	4.5	3.8	3.7	**5.2**
	Italy	Below upper secondary	m	10.8	10.6	10.0	9.2	9.0	8.8	8.2	7.8	6.9	6.3	7.4	**8.4**
		Upper secondary and post-secondary non-tertiary	m	8.1	7.9	7.2	6.6	6.4	6.1	5.4	5.2	4.6	4.1	4.6	**5.6**
		Tertiary education	m	6.9	6.9	5.9	5.3	5.3	5.3	5.3	5.7	4.8	4.2	4.3	**5.1**
	Japan	Below upper secondary	3.9	4.3	5.6	6.0	5.9	m	m	m	m	m	m	m	**m**
		Upper secondary and post-secondary non-tertiary	3.4	3.3	4.4	4.7	4.8	5.6	5.7	5.1	4.9	4.5	4.1	4.4	**5.9**
		Tertiary education	2.3	2.6	3.3	3.5	3.1	3.8	3.7	3.3	3.1	3.0	2.9	3.1	**3.6**
	Korea	Below upper secondary	1.4	6.0	5.4	3.7	3.1	2.2	2.2	2.6	2.9	2.6	2.4	2.5	**3.0**
		Upper secondary and post-secondary non-tertiary	2.4	6.8	6.4	4.1	3.6	3.0	3.3	3.5	3.8	3.5	3.3	3.3	**3.7**
		Tertiary education	2.3	4.9	4.7	3.6	3.5	3.2	3.1	2.9	2.9	2.9	2.9	2.6	**3.5**
	Luxembourg	Below upper secondary	m	m	3.4	3.1	1.7	3.8	3.3	5.7	5.1	4.9	4.1	4.8	**5.8**
		Upper secondary and post-secondary non-tertiary	m	m	1.1	1.4	1.0	1.2	2.6	3.7	3.2	3.8	2.8	4.9	**3.4**
		Tertiary education	m	m	c	c	c	1.8	4.0	3.2	3.2	2.9	3.0	2.2	**3.7**

Source: OECD. See Annex 3 for notes *(www.oecd.org/edu/eag2011)*.

Please refer to the Reader's Guide for information concerning the symbols replacing missing data.

StatLink http://dx.doi.org/10.1787/888932463023

Table A7.4a. [2/2] Trends in unemployment rates of 25-64 year-olds, by educational attainment (1997-2009)

Number of 25-64 year-olds unemployed as a percentage of the labour force aged 25 to 64, by level of educational attainment

			1997	1998	1999	2000	2001	2002	2003	2004	2005	2006	2007	2008	2009
OECD	Mexico	Below upper secondary	2.6	2.3	1.5	1.5	1.6	1.7	1.8	2.2	2.3	2.2	2.2	2.4	**4.0**
		Upper secondary and post-secondary non-tertiary	4.4	3.3	2.5	2.2	2.3	2.3	2.2	3.0	3.0	2.5	2.7	2.9	**4.2**
		Tertiary education	2.8	3.1	3.5	2.4	2.5	3.0	3.0	3.7	3.8	3.0	3.8	3.4	**4.4**
	Netherlands	Below upper secondary	m	0.9	4.3	3.9	2.9	3.0	4.5	5.5	5.8	4.8	4.0	3.4	**4.1**
		Upper secondary and post-secondary non-tertiary	m	1.7	2.3	2.3	1.6	2.0	2.8	3.8	4.1	3.5	2.7	2.1	**2.7**
		Tertiary education	m	m	1.7	1.9	1.2	2.1	2.5	2.8	2.8	2.3	1.8	1.6	**2.0**
	New Zealand	Below upper secondary	7.6	8.9	7.8	6.6	5.8	5.0	4.3	3.7	3.4	3.2	3.1	3.7	**5.9**
		Upper secondary and post-secondary non-tertiary	4.4	5.1	5.0	3.9	3.7	3.6	3.4	2.3	2.3	2.1	2.0	2.5	**3.9**
		Tertiary education	3.5	4.0	3.7	3.3	2.8	3.1	3.0	2.7	2.3	2.4	2.2	2.4	**3.3**
	Norway	Below upper secondary	4.0	2.9	2.5	2.2	3.4	3.4	3.9	4.0	7.3	4.7	3.3	3.8	**4.7**
		Upper secondary and post-secondary non-tertiary	3.1	2.4	2.5	2.6	2.7	2.9	3.6	3.8	2.6	2.1	1.3	1.3	**1.7**
		Tertiary education	1.7	1.5	1.4	1.9	1.7	2.1	2.5	2.4	2.1	1.8	1.4	1.3	**1.4**
	Poland	Below upper secondary	13.8	13.9	16.4	20.6	22.6	25.2	25.9	27.8	27.1	21.5	15.5	11.5	**13.9**
		Upper secondary and post-secondary non-tertiary	9.9	9.1	10.7	13.9	15.9	17.8	17.8	17.4	16.6	12.7	8.7	6.3	**7.2**
		Tertiary education	2.1	2.5	3.1	4.3	5.0	6.3	6.6	6.2	6.2	5.0	3.8	3.1	**3.6**
	Portugal	Below upper secondary	m	4.4	4.0	3.6	3.6	4.4	5.7	6.4	7.5	7.6	8.0	7.6	**10.1**
		Upper secondary and post-secondary non-tertiary	m	5.1	4.5	3.5	3.3	4.4	5.3	5.6	6.7	7.1	6.8	6.6	**8.2**
		Tertiary education	m	2.8	3.1	2.7	2.8	3.9	4.9	4.4	5.4	5.4	6.6	5.8	**5.6**
	Slovak Republic	Below upper secondary	22.4	24.3	30.3	36.3	38.7	42.3	44.9	47.7	49.2	44.0	41.3	36.3	**38.3**
		Upper secondary and post-secondary non-tertiary	8.5	8.8	11.9	14.3	14.8	14.2	13.5	14.6	12.7	10.0	8.5	7.4	**10.0**
		Tertiary education	2.8	3.3	4.0	4.6	4.2	3.6	3.7	4.8	4.4	2.6	3.3	3.1	**3.9**
	Slovenia	Below upper secondary	m	m	m	m	m	8.4	8.7	8.4	8.7	7.0	6.5	5.9	**7.8**
		Upper secondary and post-secondary non-tertiary	m	m	m	m	m	5.2	5.5	5.3	5.7	5.6	4.3	3.5	**5.6**
		Tertiary education	m	m	m	m	m	2.3	3.0	2.8	3.0	3.0	3.2	3.1	**3.1**
	Spain	Below upper secondary	18.9	17.0	14.7	13.7	10.2	11.2	11.3	11.0	9.3	9.0	9.0	13.2	**21.9**
		Upper secondary and post-secondary non-tertiary	16.8	15.3	12.9	10.9	8.4	9.4	9.5	9.4	7.3	6.9	6.8	9.3	**15.4**
		Tertiary education	13.7	13.1	11.1	9.5	6.9	7.7	7.7	7.3	6.1	5.5	4.8	5.8	**9.0**
	Sweden	Below upper secondary	11.9	10.4	9.0	8.0	5.9	5.8	6.1	6.5	8.5	7.3	7.0	7.1	**10.0**
		Upper secondary and post-secondary non-tertiary	9.4	7.8	6.5	5.3	4.6	4.6	5.2	5.8	6.0	5.1	4.2	4.1	**6.2**
		Tertiary education	5.2	4.4	3.9	3.0	2.6	3.0	3.9	4.3	4.5	4.2	3.4	3.3	**4.3**
	Switzerland	Below upper secondary	6.0	5.7	4.7	4.8	3.4	4.3	5.9	7.1	7.2	7.5	6.7	6.0	**7.5**
		Upper secondary and post-secondary non-tertiary	3.1	2.9	2.5	2.2	2.1	2.4	3.2	3.7	3.7	3.3	3.0	2.9	**3.2**
		Tertiary education	4.4	2.8	1.7	1.4	1.3	2.2	2.9	2.8	2.7	2.2	2.1	1.8	**2.7**
	Turkey	Below upper secondary	4.4	4.4	5.3	4.6	6.7	8.5	8.8	8.7	9.1	8.8	8.5	9.6	**12.6**
		Upper secondary and post-secondary non-tertiary	6.3	6.6	8.2	5.5	7.4	8.7	7.8	10.1	9.1	9.0	9.0	9.2	**12.6**
		Tertiary education	3.9	4.8	5.1	3.9	4.7	7.5	6.9	7.9	6.9	6.9	6.8	7.3	**9.9**
	United Kingdom	Below upper secondary	8.4	7.5	7.1	6.6	6.1	6.0	5.2	5.3	5.1	6.3	6.5	6.2	**5.8**
		Upper secondary and post-secondary non-tertiary	5.5	4.4	4.4	4.0	3.5	3.6	3.5	3.3	3.1	3.8	3.9	3.7	**3.5**
		Tertiary education	3.1	2.6	2.6	2.1	2.0	2.4	2.3	2.2	2.1	2.2	2.3	2.0	**3.3**
	United States	Below upper secondary	10.4	8.5	7.7	7.9	8.1	10.2	9.9	10.5	9.0	8.3	8.5	10.1	**15.8**
		Upper secondary and post-secondary non-tertiary	4.8	4.5	3.7	3.6	3.8	5.7	6.1	5.6	5.1	4.6	4.5	5.3	**9.8**
		Tertiary education	2.3	2.1	2.1	1.8	2.1	3.0	3.4	3.3	2.6	2.5	2.1	2.4	**4.9**
	OECD average	Below upper secondary	10.2	9.4	9.3	9.0	8.7	9.8	10.0	10.6	10.7	10.1	9.1	8.7	**11.5**
		Upper secondary and post-secondary non-tertiary	6.7	6.5	6.1	5.7	5.5	6.1	6.3	6.5	6.2	5.6	5.0	4.9	**6.8**
		Tertiary education	4.1	4.0	3.8	3.5	3.3	3.8	4.1	4.1	3.9	3.5	3.4	3.3	**4.4**
	EU21 average	Below upper secondary	13.4	11.5	11.4	11.1	10.6	11.6	11.7	12.7	12.8	11.8	10.7	10.4	**13.5**
		Upper secondary and post-secondary non-tertiary	8.4	7.4	6.9	6.6	6.3	6.7	6.9	7.1	6.8	6.1	5.3	5.2	**7.3**
		Tertiary education	4.7	4.4	4.1	3.8	3.5	3.8	4.2	4.2	4.1	3.7	3.4	3.2	**4.3**
Other G20	Argentina		m	m	m	m	m	m	m	m	m	m	m	m	**m**
	Brazil	Below upper secondary	m	m	m	m	m	m	m	m	m	m	5.6	4.7	**5.7**
		Upper secondary and post-secondary non-tertiary	m	m	m	m	m	m	m	m	m	m	7.0	6.1	**7.2**
		Tertiary education	m	m	m	m	m	m	m	m	m	m	3.3	3.3	**3.5**
	China		m	m	m	m	m	m	m	m	m	m	m	m	**m**
	India		m	m	m	m	m	m	m	m	m	m	m	m	**m**
	Indonesia		m	m	m	m	m	m	m	m	m	m	m	m	**m**
	Russian Federation		m	m	m	m	m	m	m	m	m	m	m	m	**m**
	Saudi Arabia		m	m	m	m	m	m	m	m	m	m	m	m	**m**
	South Africa		m	m	m	m	m	m	m	m	m	m	m	m	**m**

Source: OECD. See Annex 3 for notes *(www.oecd.org/edu/eag2011)*.

Please refer to the Reader's Guide for information concerning the symbols replacing missing data.

StatLink http://dx.doi.org/10.1787/888932463023

Table A7.5. [1/2] **Proportion of individuals with earnings from employment working on a full-time basis[1] (2009 or latest available year)**

			Below upper secondary education			Upper secondary and post-secondary non-tertiary education			Tertiary education			All levels of education		
			25-64	35-44	55-64	25-64	35-44	55-64	25-64	35-44	55-64	25-64	35-44	55-64
			(1)	(2)	(3)	(4)	(5)	(6)	(7)	(8)	(9)	(10)	(11)	(12)
Australia	2009	Men	**89**	94	79	**91**	93	85	**92**	95	83	**91**	94	83
		Women	**47**	43	42	**53**	51	52	**65**	56	60	**57**	52	51
		M+W	**69**	69	61	**77**	77	74	**77**	75	72	**75**	75	69
Austria	2009	Men	**58**	58	66	**75**	77	78	**79**	82	82	**74**	76	77
		Women	**37**	34	43	**42**	38	42	**56**	47	79	**44**	39	49
		M+W	**46**	43	53	**60**	58	65	**69**	66	81	**60**	58	66
Belgium			**m**	m	m	**m**	m	m	**m**	m	m	**m**	m	m
Canada	2008	Men	**59**	64	51	**66**	72	55	**68**	75	58	**61**	67	52
		Women	**37**	43	30	**46**	49	41	**52**	53	40	**46**	48	37
		M+W	**50**	56	42	**57**	61	49	**60**	64	50	**54**	58	45
Chile			**m**	m	m	**m**	m	m	**m**	m	m	**m**	m	m
Czech Republic	2009	Men	**51**	52	51	**59**	61	56	**55**	57	51	**58**	60	54
		Women	**39**	39	36	**44**	45	41	**34**	30	28	**42**	42	38
		M+W	**44**	45	43	**53**	54	50	**46**	46	43	**51**	52	48
Denmark	2009	Men	**48**	48	46	**57**	60	53	**74**	80	67	**60**	64	56
		Women	**44**	43	42	**52**	55	46	**59**	61	56	**53**	56	48
		M+W	**46**	46	44	**55**	58	50	**66**	69	62	**56**	60	52
Estonia	2009	Men	**91**	88	86	**95**	96	96	**95**	98	89	**95**	96	92
		Women	**87**	91	80	**89**	94	89	**89**	93	89	**89**	93	88
		M+W	**89**	89	83	**92**	95	92	**91**	94	89	**91**	94	90
Finland	2009	Men	**92**	95	89	**94**	96	91	**96**	97	89	**94**	96	90
		Women	**81**	82	78	**83**	84	81	**88**	87	85	**86**	85	82
		M+W	**87**	90	83	**89**	90	85	**91**	91	87	**90**	91	85
France	2006	Men	**80**	84	71	**87**	90	68	**84**	90	77	**84**	88	71
		Women	**49**	43	50	**56**	54	53	**66**	64	72	**58**	55	56
		M+W	**65**	66	59	**73**	73	62	**75**	76	75	**72**	72	64
Germany	2009	Men	**89**	96	89	**86**	90	83	**88**	89	86	**87**	90	85
		Women	**40**	37	36	**46**	38	45	**50**	42	57	**47**	40	48
		M+W	**65**	68	61	**66**	66	64	**71**	69	74	**68**	68	68
Greece	2009	Men	**80**	85	73	**88**	90	92	**87**	88	89	**85**	88	82
		Women	**65**	65	63	**73**	76	73	**83**	86	80	**75**	77	70
		M+W	**75**	77	70	**82**	85	86	**85**	87	86	**81**	83	78
Hungary	2009	Men	**81**	83	78	**87**	88	83	**90**	92	86	**87**	88	83
		Women	**78**	80	71	**84**	85	80	**91**	91	88	**85**	86	80
		M+W	**79**	82	74	**86**	87	82	**90**	91	87	**86**	87	81
Iceland			**m**	m	m	**m**	m	m	**m**	m	m	**m**	m	m
Ireland	2009	Men	**63**	61	63	**68**	71	65	**82**	86	65	**72**	74	64
		Women	**26**	29	27	**46**	44	39	**63**	59	41	**49**	47	36
		M+W	**50**	50	53	**58**	59	51	**72**	74	55	**62**	63	53
Israel	2009	Men	**88**	93	84	**91**	92	86	**86**	92	87	**88**	92	86
		Women	**54**	73	44	**66**	65	58	**63**	65	58	**64**	65	56
		M+W	**79**	89	69	**81**	81	74	**75**	78	73	**77**	80	73
Italy	2009	Men	**85**	87	77	**89**	91	89	**89**	93	88	**87**	90	83
		Women	**60**	53	60	**77**	73	84	**75**	68	91	**71**	66	74
		M+W	**76**	75	71	**84**	82	87	**82**	79	89	**81**	79	80
Japan			**m**	m	m	**m**	m	m	**m**	m	m	**m**	m	m
Korea	2008	Men	**87**	85	87	**96**	97	94	**97**	97	91	**95**	96	90
		Women	**87**	85	87	**90**	94	81	**86**	81	76	**88**	87	85
		M+W	**87**	85	87	**94**	96	91	**93**	93	88	**92**	93	88
Luxembourg	2009	Men	**90**	89	87	**94**	93	88	**91**	91	91	**92**	92	88
		Women	**46**	44	46	**54**	56	37	**63**	56	62	**55**	53	47
		M+W	**70**	68	67	**79**	79	70	**79**	75	82	**76**	75	73

Note: The length of the reference period varies from one week to one year. Self-employed are excluded in some countries. See Annex 3 for details.

1. Full-time basis refers to people who have worked all year long and at least 30 hours per week.

Source: OECD, LSO Network special data collection on full-time, full-year earnings, Economic Working Group. See Annex 3 for notes *(www.oecd.org/edu/eag2011)*.

Please refer to the Reader's Guide for information concerning the symbols replacing missing data.

StatLink http://dx.doi.org/10.1787/888932463080

Table A7.5. [2/2] Proportion of individuals with earnings from employment working on a full-time basis[1] (2009 or latest available year)

				Below upper secondary education			Upper secondary and post-secondary non-tertiary education			Tertiary education			All levels of education		
				25-64	35-44	55-64	25-64	35-44	55-64	25-64	35-44	55-64	25-64	35-44	55-64
				(1)	(2)	(3)	(4)	(5)	(6)	(7)	(8)	(9)	(10)	(11)	(12)
OECD	Mexico			**m**	m	m	**m**	m	m	**m**	m	m	**m**	m	m
	Netherlands	2008	Men	**63**	65	61	**66**	68	65	**67**	68	62	**65**	67	63
			Women	**14**	13	11	**18**	15	18	**27**	22	23	**20**	17	16
			M+W	**41**	43	39	**43**	42	47	**48**	47	49	**45**	44	45
	New Zealand	2009	Men	**72**	75	62	**72**	75	62	**75**	81	63	**73**	77	63
			Women	**57**	55	54	**58**	53	54	**63**	57	56	**60**	55	55
			M+W	**65**	65	58	**67**	66	59	**69**	68	60	**67**	67	59
	Norway			**m**	m	m	**m**	m	m	**m**	m	m	**m**	m	m
	Poland			**m**	m	m	**m**	m	m	**m**	m	m	**m**	m	m
	Portugal	2009	Men	**99**	99	99	**97**	98	97	**94**	95	89	**98**	98	98
			Women	**91**	92	86	**95**	96	94	**93**	94	89	**92**	93	87
			M+W	**95**	96	94	**96**	97	96	**94**	95	89	**95**	96	93
	Slovak Republic	2009	Men	**52**	51	56	**64**	68	60	**72**	77	68	**64**	68	60
			Women	**46**	44	45	**59**	60	60	**67**	71	67	**58**	60	57
			M+W	**49**	47	50	**62**	64	60	**70**	74	67	**61**	64	59
	Slovenia			**m**	m	m	**m**	m	m	**m**	m	m	**m**	m	m
	Spain	2008	Men	**77**	76	78	**85**	87	84	**89**	92	88	**83**	84	82
			Women	**48**	43	56	**66**	63	80	**76**	73	86	**64**	61	67
			M+W	**66**	63	71	**76**	76	83	**83**	83	87	**75**	74	77
	Sweden	2008	Men	**77**	78	71	**81**	86	68	**80**	89	71	**80**	86	69
			Women	**34**	41	32	**46**	50	39	**59**	58	56	**51**	53	44
			M+W	**62**	61	56	**65**	70	54	**68**	72	63	**66**	70	57
	Switzerland			**m**	m	m	**m**	m	m	**m**	m	m	**m**	m	m
	Turkey			**m**	m	m	**m**	m	m	**m**	m	m	**m**	m	m
	United Kingdom	2009	Men	**87**	86	83	**94**	96	87	**94**	97	83	**93**	96	85
			Women	**44**	40	45	**55**	52	57	**70**	61	66	**61**	56	57
			M+W	**67**	66	67	**76**	74	76	**82**	79	77	**78**	76	75
	United States	2009	Men	**60**	61	63	**73**	76	72	**83**	87	79	**75**	78	74
			Women	**55**	54	63	**65**	66	65	**69**	69	65	**66**	66	64
			M+W	**58**	58	63	**69**	71	68	**76**	78	73	**71**	73	70
	OECD average		Men	**76**	77	73	**81**	84	77	**84**	87	78	**81**	84	76
			Women	**53**	53	51	**61**	61	59	**67**	64	65	**62**	60	58
			M+W	**66**	67	63	**72**	73	70	**75**	76	73	**72**	73	69
Other G20	Argentina			**m**	m	m	**m**	m	m	**m**	m	m	**m**	m	m
	Brazil	2009	Men	**74**	76	74	**79**	82	79	**78**	79	76	**76**	78	75
			Women	**46**	48	41	**62**	63	57	**61**	61	55	**54**	55	45
			M+W	**63**	65	61	**71**	73	70	**69**	69	67	**66**	68	63
	China			**m**	m	m	**m**	m	m	**m**	m	m	**m**	m	m
	India			**m**	m	m	**m**	m	m	**m**	m	m	**m**	m	m
	Indonesia			**m**	m	m	**m**	m	m	**m**	m	m	**m**	m	m
	Russian Federation			**m**	m	m	**m**	m	m	**m**	m	m	**m**	m	m
	Saudi Arabia			**m**	m	m	**m**	m	m	**m**	m	m	**m**	m	m
	South Africa			**m**	m	m	**m**	m	m	**m**	m	m	**m**	m	m

Note: The length of the reference period varies from one week to one year. Self-employed are excluded in some countries. See Annex 3 for details.

1. Full-time basis refers to people who have worked all year long and at least 30 hours per week.

Source: OECD, LSO Network special data collection on full-time, full-year earnings, Economic Working Group. See Annex 3 for notes *(www.oecd.org/edu/eag2011)*.

Please refer to the Reader's Guide for information concerning the symbols replacing missing data.

StatLink http://dx.doi.org/10.1787/888932463080

Table A7.6. [1/2] Size and labour outcomes of vocational education and training (2009)

Percentage of the population whose highest level of education is upper secondary and post-secondary non-tertiary (ISCED 3/4) aged 25-64 and 25-34 years old, by orientation and work status

		% in total population		Employment rates, % E/P		Unemployment rates, % U/E+U		Inactivity rates, %	
	Age cohort	ISCED 3/4 Vocational	ISCED 3/4 General	ISCED 3/4 Vocational	ISCED 3/4 General	ISCED 3/4 Vocational	ISCED 3/4 General	ISCED 3/4 Vocational	ISCED 3/4 General
OECD **Australia**	25-34	17.2	20.9	86.4	76.6	4.4	4.5	9.6	19.7
	25-64	17.9	16.2	85.3	74.7	3.4	5.1	11.8	21.3
Austria	25-34	59.4	7.9	86.6	71.5	4.4	6.0	9.5	23.9
	25-64	57.2	5.6	77.6	77.1	3.6	4.1	19.5	19.6
Belgium	25-34	29.2	10.9	83.6	75.1	8.7	11.9	8.4	14.8
	25-64	25.9	10.8	75.2	71.2	6.2	7.1	19.9	23.3
Canada	25-34	10.9	25.0	82.7	73.7	8.7	10.5	9.5	17.6
	25-64	11.9	26.2	77.0	72.2	8.2	8.0	16.1	21.5
Chile		m	m	m	m	m	m	m	m
Czech Republic	25-34	68.6	5.3	78.1	59.3	6.6	7.7	16.4	35.7
	25-64	71.8	4.1	75.6	66.0	5.4	6.0	20.1	29.8
Denmark	25-34	35.8	3.2	84.1	66.3	5.6	7.6	10.9	28.2
	25-64	39.0	1.7	80.4	64.9	4.9	8.1	15.5	29.4
Estonia	25-34	27.2	22.3	70.6	76.6	18.7	13.2	13.2	11.8
	25-64	31.6	21.2	71.5	71.5	15.5	13.8	15.3	17.0
Finland	25-34	37.0	13.3	77.1	71.7	9.4	9.5	15.0	20.8
	25-64	38.0	6.4	74.7	74.6	7.5	8.5	19.2	18.5
France	25-34	27.4	13.2	80.2	76.9	10.5	11.1	10.4	13.5
	25-64	29.4	11.7	77.0	75.4	7.0	7.1	17.2	18.8
Germany	25-34	52.4	7.9	81.2	52.5	8.2	7.1	11.6	43.4
	25-64	56.0	3.0	76.3	60.2	7.5	8.0	17.5	34.6
Greece	25-34	20.3	25.2	79.9	68.8	12.7	11.6	8.4	22.2
	25-64	12.0	25.7	75.9	64.9	10.3	8.6	15.4	29.0
Hungary	25-34	29.5	31.5	71.4	71.7	11.9	8.4	18.9	21.7
	25-64	31.9	28.8	65.4	68.7	10.0	6.3	27.3	26.7
Iceland	25-34	15.2	18.6	78.6	69.0	8.5	9.9	14.1	23.5
	25-64	22.1	10.7	85.8	75.8	5.6	6.2	9.1	19.2
Ireland	25-34	9.7	17.0	71.0	68.3	17.9	15.6	13.6	19.1
	25-64	8.5	17.2	69.7	68.4	14.2	10.3	18.8	23.8
Israel	25-34	8.5	36.0	77.3	63.8	9.1	9.2	14.9	29.8
	25-64	10.9	26.0	75.2	66.4	7.6	7.7	18.6	28.0
Italy	25-34	33.0	11.4	76.1	55.5	8.3	11.5	17.1	37.3
	25-64	26.4	8.5	76.1	65.0	5.3	6.1	19.7	30.8
Japan		m	m	m	m	m	m	m	m
Korea	25-34	19.4	15.1	62.5	60.5	6.5	6.3	33.2	35.5
	25-64	20.0	21.2	71.5	67.8	3.9	3.5	25.6	29.8
Luxembourg	25-34	33.8	4.3	83.5	65.1	5.0	9.6	12.1	28.0
	25-64	36.5	4.6	71.0	65.1	3.4	4.1	26.5	32.1
Mexico		m	m	m	m	m	m	m	m
Netherlands	25-34	38.2	3.2	88.8	85.5	3.3	3.8	8.2	11.1
	25-64	35.6	4.3	81.6	81.6	3.0	3.4	15.9	15.6
New Zealand	25-34	22.8	9.8	80.3	78.5	5.4	5.3	15.1	17.2
	25-64	23.4	8.7	82.3	82.9	4.1	3.1	14.2	14.4
Norway	25-34	23.5	10.7	90.7	81.7	2.9	2.9	6.5	15.9
	25-64	32.3	10.2	83.9	80.9	1.7	1.8	14.7	17.7
Poland	25-34	27.4	30.7	73.6	76.3	10.4	7.8	17.9	17.3
	25-64	36.1	30.8	65.1	67.8	8.0	6.4	29.3	27.6

Source: OECD, LSO network special data collection on vocational education, Learning and Labour Transitions Working Group. See Annex 3 for notes (*www.oecd.org/edu/eag2011*).

Please refer to the Reader's Guide for information concerning the symbols replacing missing data.

StatLink http://dx.doi.org/10.1787/888932463099

Table A7.6. [2/2] Size and labour outcomes of vocational education and training (2009)

Percentage of the population whose highest level of education is upper secondary and post-secondary non-tertiary (ISCED 3/4) aged 25-64 and 25-34 years old, by orientation and work status

		Age cohort	% in total population		Employment rates, % E/P		Unemployment rates, % U/E+U		Inactivity rates, %	
			ISCED 3/4 Vocational	ISCED 3/4 General	ISCED 3/4 Vocational	ISCED 3/4 General	ISCED 3/4 Vocational	ISCED 3/4 General	ISCED 3/4 Vocational	ISCED 3/4 General
OECD	Portugal	25-34	22.8	2.0	79.6	83.5	9.6	8.2	11.9	9.1
		25-64	13.5	1.7	79.9	82.0	8.4	6.2	12.8	12.6
	Slovak Republic	25-34	69.0	5.1	75.6	61.8	11.7	12.6	14.5	29.3
		25-64	70.8	4.4	72.4	65.3	9.9	10.9	19.6	26.8
	Slovenia	25-34	53.8	9.3	85.7	66.3	8.0	7.4	6.8	28.4
		25-64	54.7	5.2	75.0	70.7	5.5	5.8	20.6	25.0
	Spain	25-34	9.7	16.2	73.3	69.3	18.6	19.2	10.0	14.2
		25-64	8.0	14.1	69.8	71.0	15.8	15.1	17.1	16.3
	Sweden	25-34	26.9	9.2	85.7	86.5	7.3	5.7	7.5	8.2
		25-64	31.5	10.7	83.0	85.9	5.4	4.5	12.2	10.0
	Switzerland	25-34	37.7	8.4	84.4	77.9	4.8	6.5	11.3	16.7
		25-64	42.5	6.5	82.2	77.2	3.1	4.4	15.2	19.2
	Turkey	25-34	12.1	12.9	66.5	58.3	14.1	17.1	22.6	29.7
		25-64	8.5	9.9	61.8	55.4	11.8	13.3	29.9	36.1
	United Kingdom		m	m	m	m	m	m	m	m
	United States		m	m	m	m	m	m	m	m
	OECD average	25-34	30.3	14.0	79.1	70.6	9.0	9.2	13.1	22.2
		25-64	31.2	12.3	75.8	71.4	7.1	7.0	18.4	23.3
Other G20	Argentina		m	m	m	m	m	m	m	m
	Brazil		m	m	m	m	m	m	m	m
	China		m	m	m	m	m	m	m	m
	India		m	m	m	m	m	m	m	m
	Indonesia		m	m	m	m	m	m	m	m
	Russian Federation		m	m	m	m	m	m	m	m
	Saudi Arabia		m	m	m	m	m	m	m	m
	South Africa		m	m	m	m	m	m	m	m

Source: OECD, LSO network special data collection on vocational education, Learning and Labour Transitions Working Group. See Annex 3 for notes (*www.oecd.org/edu/eag2011*).

Please refer to the Reader's Guide for information concerning the symbols replacing missing data.

StatLink http://dx.doi.org/10.1787/888932463099

INDICATOR A8

WHAT ARE THE EARNINGS PREMIUMS FROM EDUCATION?

- Tertiary education brings substantial economic benefits for individuals. A person with a tertiary education can expect to earn over 50% more than a person with an upper secondary or post-secondary non-tertiary education.
- In OECD countries, those who do not complete an upper secondary education could earn an average of 23% less than their counterparts who do complete that level of education.
- The earnings advantage of having a tertiary degree increases with age.
- Across all educational levels, women earn considerably less than men.

Chart A8.1. Relative earnings from employment by level of educational attainment for 25-64 year-olds (2009 or latest available year)

Upper secondary and post-secondary non-tertiary education = 100

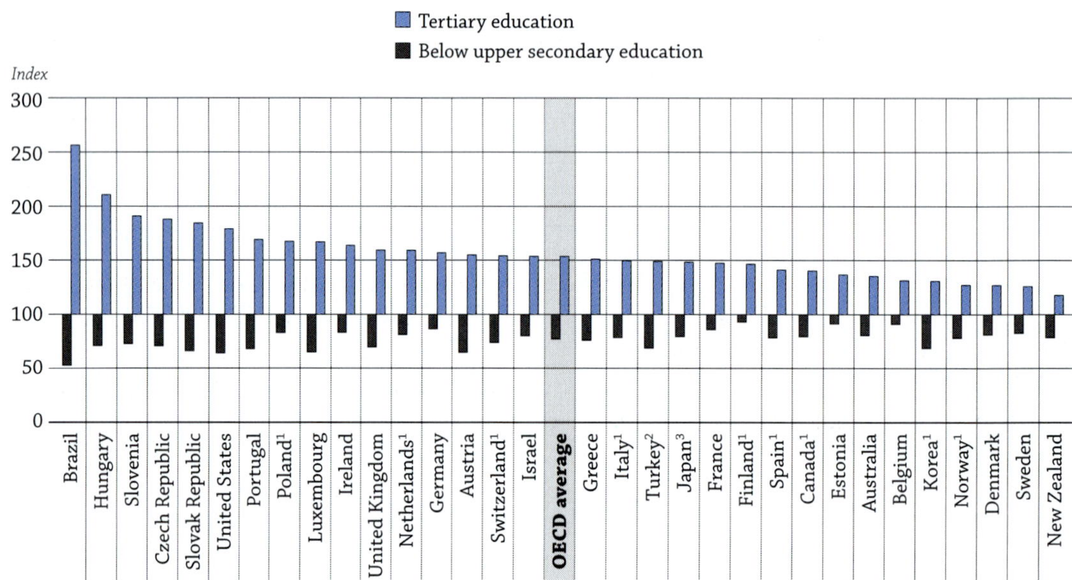

Note: Belgium, Korea and Turkey report earnings net of income tax. The Czech Republic, Hungary, Luxembourg, Poland, Portugal and Slovenia report earnings excluding data for individuals in part-time work. Hungary, Luxembourg, Poland and Slovenia also exclude data on part-year earnings.

1. Year of reference 2008.
2. Year of reference 2005.
3. Year of reference 2007.

Countries are ranked in descending order of the relative earnings of 25-64 year-olds with tertiary education.

Source: OECD. Table A8.1. See Annex 3 for notes (*www.oecd.org/edu/eag2011*).

StatLink http://dx.doi.org/10.1787/888932460515

Context

One way that labour markets provide incentives for individuals to develop and maintain skills is through earnings. The earnings premium realised by those with higher levels of education is not only an incentive to invest in education but also says something about the supply of and demand for education. High and rising earnings premiums can indicate that more highly educated individuals are in short supply; the opposite is true for low and falling premiums. Relative earnings, and trend data on the earnings premium in particular, are thus important indicators of the match between the education system and the labour market.

Other findings

- **Earnings increase with each level of education.** Those who have attained upper secondary, post-secondary non-tertiary education or tertiary education enjoy substantial earnings advantages compared with individuals of the same gender who have not completed upper secondary education. The earnings premium for tertiary education is substantial in most countries, and exceeds 50% in 17 of 32 countries.

- In Brazil, the Czech Republic, Greece, Hungary, Poland, the Slovak Republic and the United States, **men holding a degree from a university or an advanced research programme earn at least 80% more than men who have an upper secondary or post-secondary non-tertiary education**. In Brazil, Greece, Hungary, Ireland, Japan, the Slovak Republic, the United Kingdom and the United States, women have a similar advantage.

- **In Brazil, Hungary and Portugal, 40% or more of those who have completed a university or an advanced research programme earn twice as much as the median worker**. In Denmark and Norway, an individual with such a degree is as likely to fall into the lowest earnings category as the highest earnings category.

- Relative earnings for individuals with a tertiary education are higher for people in older age groups in all countries except Germany, Greece, Ireland and Turkey. **For those who have not attained an upper secondary education, the earnings disadvantage generally increases with age**.

Trends

The trend data on relative earnings suggest that the demand for tertiary-educated individuals has kept up with the increasing supply from higher educational institutions in most OECD countries. Despite an increase in the proportion of 25-64 year-olds with tertiary attainment from 21% in 1999 to 30% in 2009 (see Indicator A1), the earnings premium for those with a tertiary education has increased by 6 percentage points over the same period.

Analysis

Earnings differentials and educational attainment

Variations in relative earnings (before taxes) among countries reflect a number of factors, including the demand for skills in the labour market, minimum-wage legislation, the strength of labour unions, the coverage of collective-bargaining agreements, the supply of workers at various levels of educational attainment, and the relative incidence of part-time and seasonal work.

Still, earnings differentials are among the more straightforward indications of whether the supply of educated individuals meets demand, particularly in light of changes over time. Chart A8.2 shows a strong positive relationship between educational attainment and average earnings. In all countries, graduates of tertiary education earn more overall than graduates of upper secondary and post-secondary non-tertiary programmes.

Earnings differentials between those with tertiary education – especially tertiary-type A (largely theory-based) education and advanced research programmes – and those with upper secondary education are generally more pronounced than the differentials between upper secondary and lower secondary or below. This suggests that in many countries, upper secondary education is the level beyond which additional education implies a particularly high earnings premium. As private investment costs beyond upper secondary education rise considerably in most countries, a high earnings premium ensures that there will be an adequate supply of individuals willing to invest time and money in further education (Table A8.1).

Chart A8.2. Relative earnings from employment by level of educational attainment and gender for 25-64 year-olds (2009 or latest available year)

Upper secondary and post-secondary non-tertiary education = 100

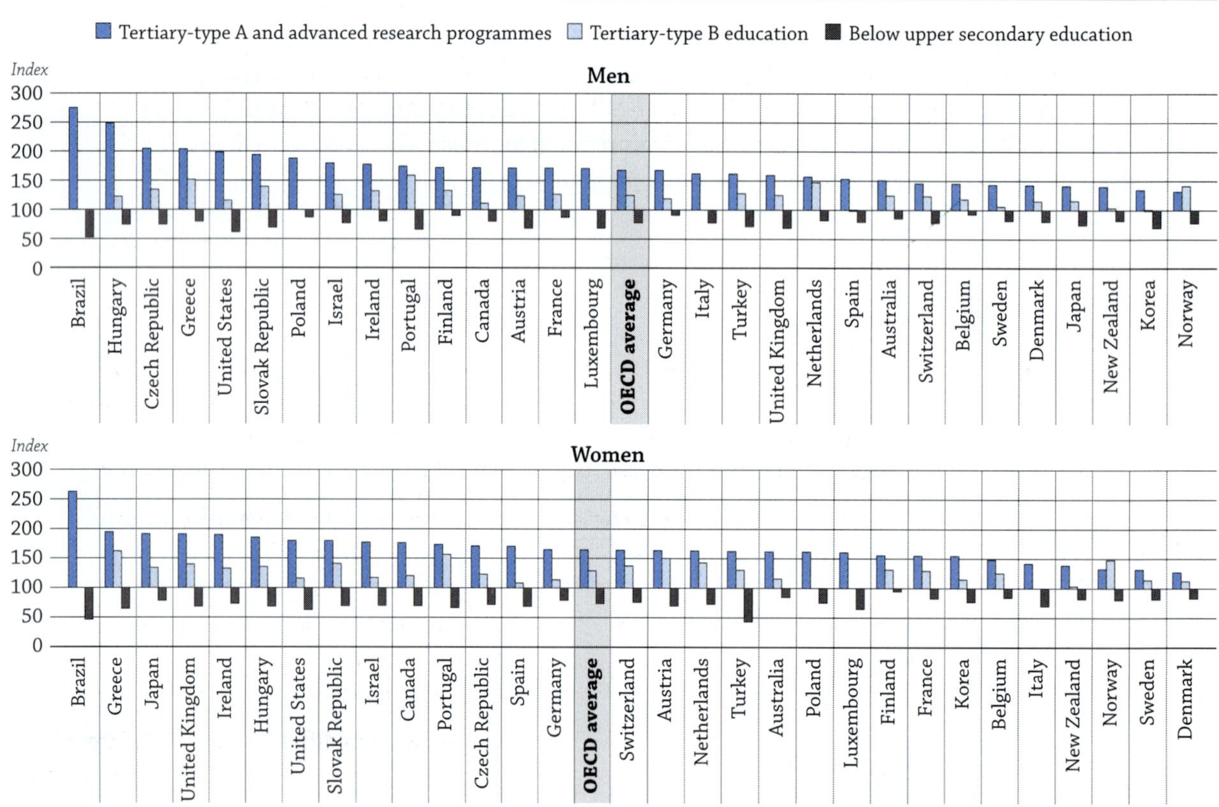

Note: Belgium, Korea and Turkey report earnings net of income tax. The Czech Republic, Hungary, Luxembourg, Poland, Portugal and Slovenia report earnings excluding data for individuals in part-time work. Hungary, Luxembourg, Poland and Slovenia also exclude data on part-year earnings.

Countries are ranked in descending order of the relative earnings of the population with a tertiary-type A (including advanced research) level of educational attainment.

Source: OECD. Table A8.1. See Annex 3 for notes (*www.oecd.org/edu/eag2011*).

StatLink http://dx.doi.org/10.1787/888932460534

Box A8.1. Earnings premiums from education in broad occupational categories

Changes in earnings premiums over time provide an overall idea of the balance between supply of and demand for skills in economies. Further insights can be derived by examining the match between education and occupations. Information about the match of higher educated individuals to skilled jobs has been published in previous editions of *Education at a Glance*, and the results suggest that people generally find jobs in line with their educational achievements. To further explore this issue, a pilot data-collection that cross-tabulates earnings by broad occupational (ISCO) and educational (ISCED) categories was conducted by the LSO network in 2011.

Following the relative-earnings methodology used in this indicator, earnings in different occupations for those with an upper secondary (ISCED 3/4) education are used as a benchmark to assess earnings premiums for those with a tertiary education. The chart below shows the tertiary earnings premium for 25-64 year-olds across four broad occupational categories for the countries that took part in the pilot (Canada, Finland, the United Kingdom and the United States).

Relative earnings of tertiary- (ISCED 5/6) to upper secondary- (3/4) educated individuals in broad occupational categories (2009 or latest available year)

25-64 year-old population

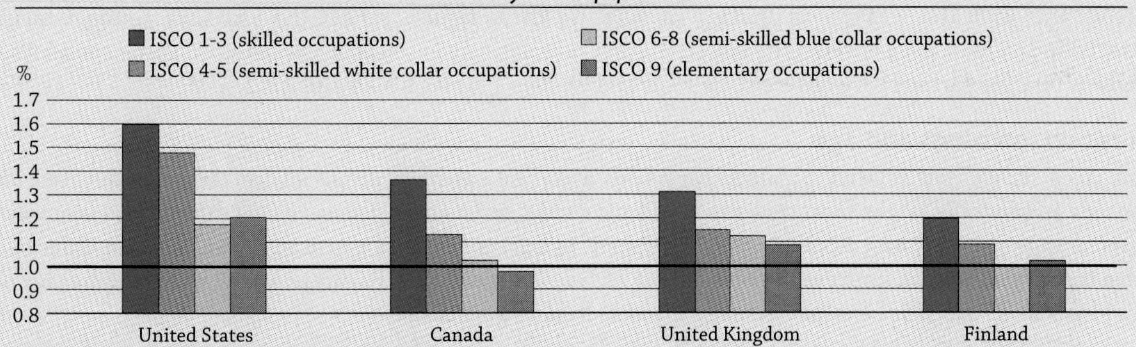

Countries are ranked in descending order of the difference in relative earnings for tertiary-educated individuals in skilled occupations.

Source: OECD, LSO network special data collection on earnings by broad occupational categories and by level of education, Economic Working Group.

StatLink http://dx.doi.org/10.1787/888932460591

Even if tertiary- and upper secondary-educated individuals are in the same occupational category, one would expect individuals with a tertiary education to be paid somewhat more than those with lower levels of attainment since they are likely to be able to do a broader range of tasks and have a skills set that allows them to better adapt to changing demands, or because they are more likely to advance in the organisation.

However, the earnings premiums for those with a tertiary education are large, too large to be motivated only by greater versatility, particularly in skilled occupations. They range from 20% in Finland to 60% in the United States, indicating large earnings and productivity differences between educational groups within similar type of jobs across the four countries. The earnings advantage for those with a tertiary education falls in occupations that are considered to be less advanced in terms of skills requirements, but are still substantial in semi-skilled, white-collar occupations, particularly in the United States.

These initial results likely indicate that those with a tertiary education work in different sectors, in larger firms, or are performing more complex tasks than those with an upper secondary education, even if they are employed in the same job category. Given that, some caution is needed in interpreting cross-country differences in the direct match between education and occupations (e.g. the proportion of higher-educated individuals in skilled jobs). A full-scale data collection would thus help to gain a deeper understanding of how well education systems are aligned to labour-market demands.

The earnings premium for men with a degree from a university or advanced research programme exceeds 100% in Brazil, the Czech Republic, Greece and Hungary. Meanwhile, women with similar degrees earn 80% or more than women with an upper secondary or post-secondary non-tertiary education in Brazil, Greece, Hungary, Ireland, Japan, the Slovak Republic, the United Kingdom and the United States.

Women who have not attained an upper secondary education are particularly disadvantaged in Brazil, Greece, Luxembourg, Turkey and the United States where their earnings represent 65% or less of those of women with an upper secondary education. In Brazil and the United States, men who have not attained an upper secondary education are in a similar situation (Table A8.1).

The relative earnings premium for those with a tertiary education has been rising in most countries over the past ten years, indicating that the demand for more educated individuals still exceeds supply in most countries. In the 19 countries with earnings data in 1999 or 2000 and 2008 or 2009, the tertiary earnings premium has increased by six percentage points over the period (Table A8.2a). In Germany, Hungary and Italy, the earnings premium has increased by over 10 percentage points; however, tertiary attainment levels are low in these countries compared to the OECD average. The earnings premium has similarly increased by over 10 percentage points in the United States despite high tertiary attainment rates (see Indicator A1).

Finland, Norway, Portugal and Sweden have seen a slight decrease in the earnings premiums for those with a tertiary education since 1999, although the premium still exceeds the OECD average in Portugal. It is unclear whether this indicates weakening demand or whether these figures reflect the fact that younger tertiary-educated individuals have entered the labour market on relatively low starting salaries. In some countries, the trends in relative earnings are different for men and women (Tables A8.2b and A8.2c).

Education, earnings and age

Table A8.1 shows how relative earnings vary with age. The earnings premium for tertiary-educated 55-64 year-olds is generally larger than that for 25-64 year-olds: on average, the earnings differential increases by 13 percentage points (Chart A8.3). Both employment opportunities and earnings advantages for older people with a tertiary education improve in most countries (see Indicator A7). Earnings are relatively higher for older individuals in all countries except Germany, Greece, Ireland and Turkey.

For those who have not attained an upper secondary education, the earnings disadvantage increases for older workers (55-64 year-olds) in all countries except Australia, Denmark, Finland, Luxembourg, the Slovak Republic, Sweden, the United Kingdom and the United States. The increase in this disadvantage is not as marked as the earnings advantage for those with a tertiary education – an indication that tertiary education is the key to higher earnings at an older age. In most countries, then, tertiary education not only improves the prospect of being employed at an older age, but is also associated with greater earnings and productivity differentials throughout the working life.

Education and gender disparities in earnings

More education does little to narrow the gender gap in earnings. Across OECD countries, the difference in full-time earnings between 25-64 year-old men and women is the smallest among those with an upper secondary and post-secondary non-tertiary education and largest among those with a tertiary education. Only in six countries are earnings of tertiary-educated women more than 75% of men's earnings. Among these countries, the earnings gap between men and women with a tertiary education is smaller than or equal to that between men and women with an upper secondary education only in Germany, New Zealand, Spain and the United Kingdom. In Brazil and Italy, women who have obtained a tertiary degree earn 65% or less of what tertiary-educated men earn (Table A8.3a).

In general, the gender gap in earnings does not narrow over the working life of women with a tertiary education. On average across OECD countries, a 55-64 year-old woman with a tertiary degree can expect to earn 72% of a man's wages – the same percentage as the earnings gender gap that exists in the total population (Table A8.3a). The gender gap in earnings is partly due to differences in occupations, the major subject of study during education, and the amount of time spent in the labour force. However, low earnings, particularly for women who have completed tertiary education, could adversely affect the labour supply and the full use of skills developed in the education system. That, in turn, could hamper economic growth.

Chart A8.3. Difference in relative earnings for 55-64 year-olds and 25-64 year-olds (2009 or latest available year)

Earnings relative to upper secondary and post-secondary non-tertiary education

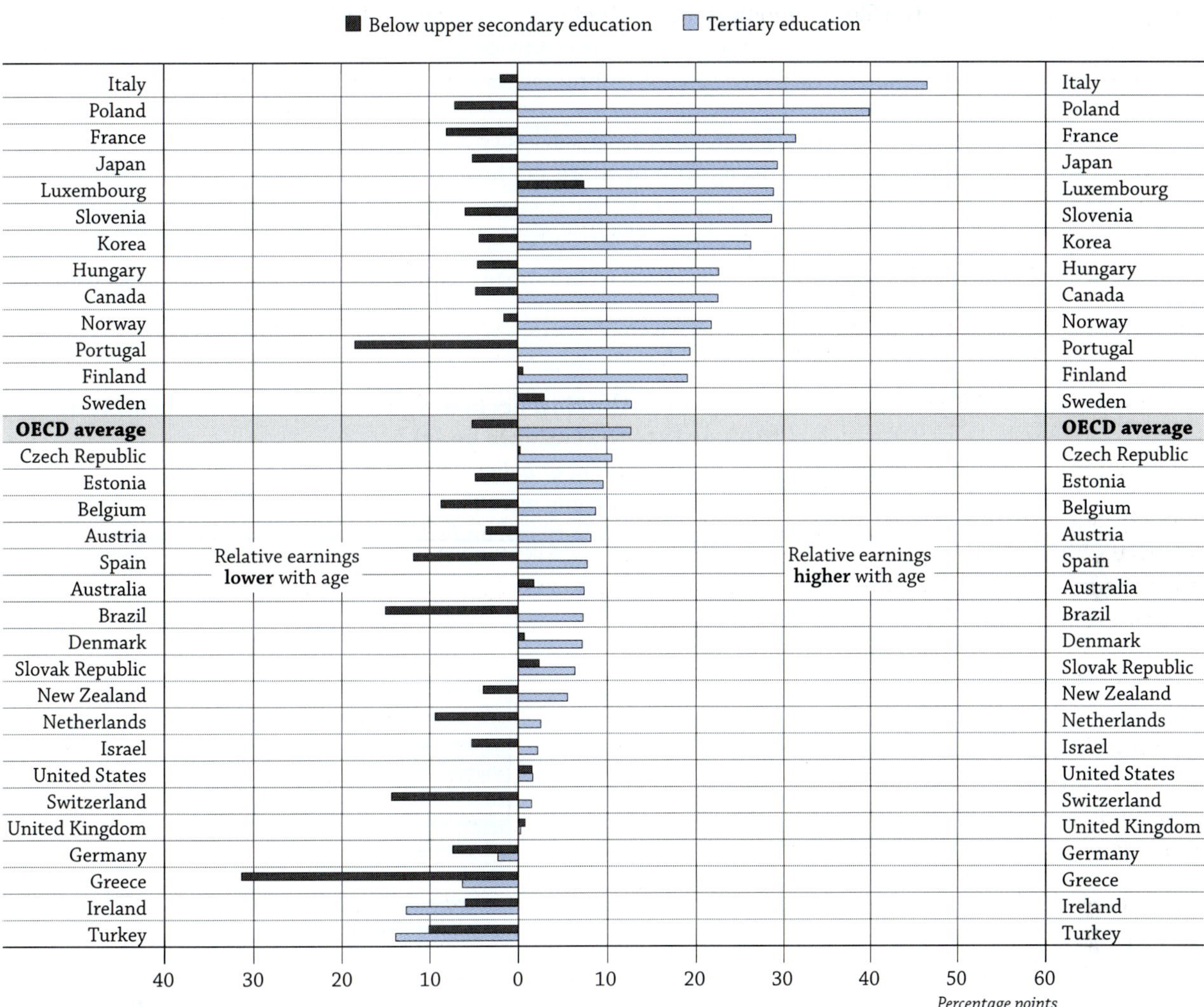

Notes: Belgium, Korea and Turkey report earnings net of income tax. The Czech Republic, Hungary, Luxembourg, Poland, Portugal and Slovenia report earnings excluding data for individuals in part-time work. Hungary, Luxembourg, Poland and Slovenia also exclude data on part-year earnings.

Countries are ranked in descending order of the difference in relative earnings for 55-64 year-olds and the total population (25-64 year-olds) at the tertiary level of education.

Source: OECD, Table A8.1. See Annex 3 for notes (*www.oecd.org/edu/eag2011*).

StatLink http://dx.doi.org/10.1787/888932460553

Distribution of earnings within levels of educational attainment

Since this indicator includes earnings from all employed individuals (except in Table A8.3a), the supply of labour in terms of hours worked influences earnings differences, in general, and the distribution in earnings, in particular. Nevertheless, data on the distribution of earnings among different educational groups can show how tightly earnings centre around the country median. In addition to providing information on equity in earnings, they indicate the risks associated with investing in education (as risk is typically measured by the variation in outcomes).

Tables A8.4a, A8.4b and A8.4c (available on line) show the distribution of earnings among 25-64 year-olds according to their level of educational attainment. Distributions are provided for the entire adult population and are also broken down for women and men. The five earnings categories range from "At or below one-half of the median" to "More than twice the median".

Chart A8.4 contrasts the results for those who do not have an upper secondary education with those who have completed a tertiary-type A or an advanced research programme by comparing the proportion of wage-earners at or below one-half of the median to those at more than twice the median. As expected, there is a large difference between these two educational categories. On average, tertiary-educated individuals are substantially more likely to earn twice as much as the median worker and are substantially less likely to be in the low-earnings category than those who have not completed an upper secondary education.

There are, however, some notable differences in how well tertiary-educated individuals fare in different countries. In Brazil, Hungary and Portugal, 40% or more of those who have completed a university or an advanced research programme earn twice as much as the median worker; in Canada, 18% of those with such a degree are found in the lowest-earnings category (at or below half of the median); and in Denmark and Norway, an individual with such a degree is as likely to fall into the lowest as the highest earnings category. This signals the risk in investing in education.

Chart A8.4. Differences in earnings distribution according to educational attainment (2009 or latest available year)

Proportion of 25-64 year-olds at or below half the median and the proportion of the population earning more than two times the median, for below upper secondary education and tertiary-type A and advanced research programmes

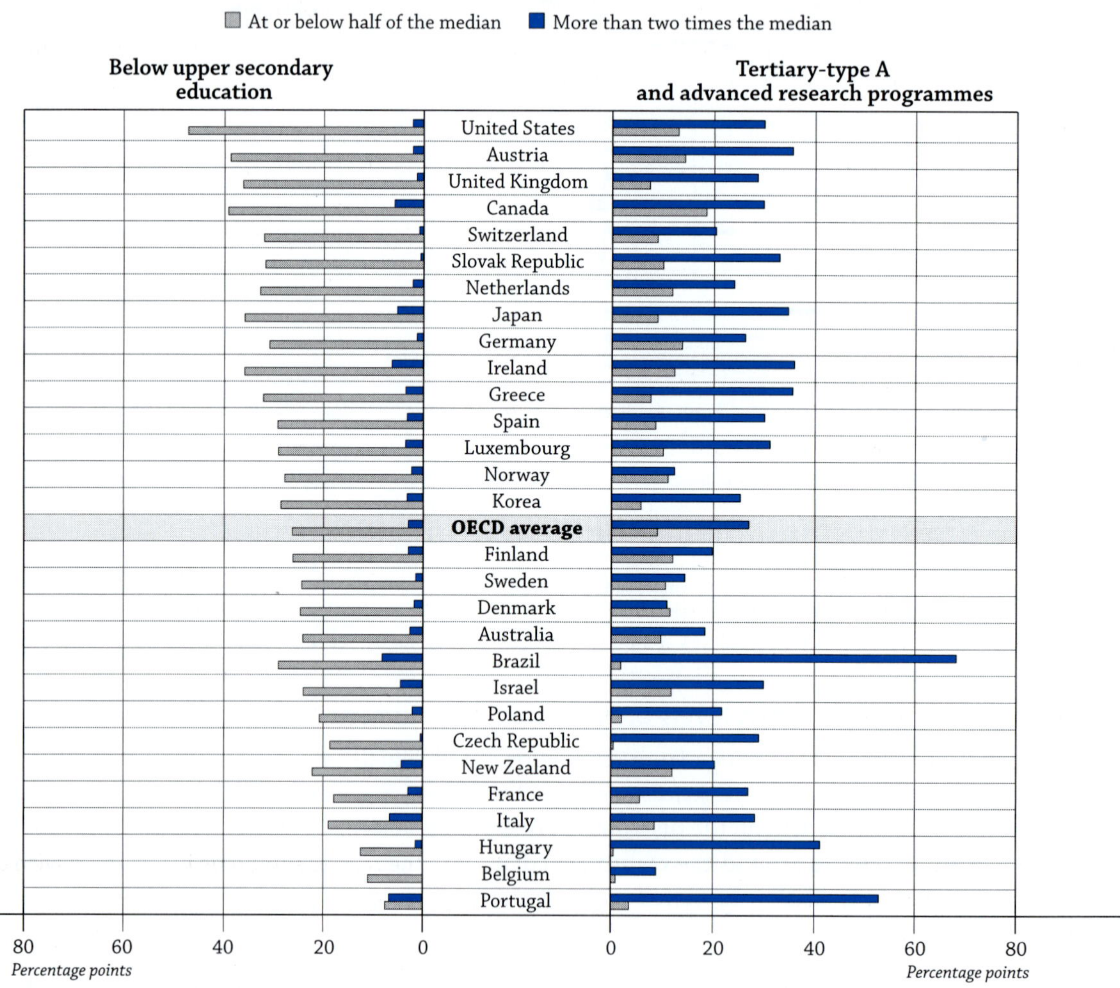

Countries are ranked in descending order of the difference in proportion of 25-64 year-olds at or below half the median and the proportion of the population earning more than two times the median, at below upper secondary education.

Source: OECD, Tables A8.4. See Annex 3 for notes (*www.oecd.org/edu/eag2011*).

StatLink http://dx.doi.org/10.1787/888932460572

Part of the reason why more highly educated individuals may fall into a low-income group is related to low earnings differentials and the supply of labour. In Denmark and Norway, the earnings premium for someone with a university or an advanced research degree is below 30% (Table A8.1). The relatively low economic reward for higher education is likely influencing the supply of labour, in terms of hours worked, and as such low earnings premiums can be detrimental to the overall supply and use of skills in those economies.

Not completing upper secondary education is associated with large earnings disadvantages in all countries. On average across OECD countries, only 3% of those who have not attained an upper secondary education earn twice the national median. In Brazil, Canada, Ireland, Italy, Japan and Portugal, this proportion is above 5%, but in no country does it exceed 10%. On average, more than 26% of those who have not completed an upper secondary education earn less than half of the median.

Definitions

For the definition of **full-time earnings**, countries were asked whether they had applied a self-designated full-time status or a threshold value of typical number of hours worked per week. Ireland, Italy, Luxembourg, Portugal, Spain, Sweden and the United Kingdom reported self-designated full-time status; the other countries defined the full-time status by the number of working hours per week. The threshold was 36 hours per week in Austria, Hungary and the Slovak Republic, 35 hours in Australia, Brazil, Canada, Estonia, Germany and the United States, and 30 hours in the Czech Republic, Greece, and New Zealand. Other participating countries did not report a minimum normal number of working hours for full-time work.

For some countries, data on **full-time, full-year earnings** are based on the European Survey on Income and Living Conditions (SILC), which uses a self-designated approach in establishing full-time status.

The **length of the reference period for earnings** also differed. Australia, New Zealand and the United Kingdom reported data on weekly earnings, while Belgium, Estonia, Finland, France, Hungary, Korea and Portugal reported monthly data. In Austria, the Czech Republic, Denmark, Germany, Greece, Israel, Italy, Luxembourg, the Netherlands, Norway, the Slovak Republic, Slovenia, Spain, Sweden and the United States, the reference period for the earnings data was 12 months.

Methodology

The indicator is based on two different data collections. One is the regular data collection that takes account of earnings from work for all individuals during the reference period, even if the individual has worked part-time or part-year. The second collects data on the earnings of those working full-time and full-year. This data collection supplies the data for Table A8.3a (gender differences in full-time earnings). The regular data collection is used for all other tables.

Earnings data in Tables A8.1, A8.2 and A8.4 (regular earnings data collection) are based on an annual reference period in Austria, Brazil, Canada, the Czech Republic, Denmark, Ireland, Italy, Korea, Luxembourg, the Netherlands, Norway, Slovenia, Spain, Sweden, Turkey and the United States. Earnings are reported weekly in Australia, New Zealand and the United Kingdom, and monthly in Belgium, Estonia, Finland, France, Hungary, Portugal and Switzerland. Data on earnings are before income tax, except for Belgium, Korea and Turkey, where earnings reported are net of income tax. Data on earnings for individuals in part-time work are also excluded in the regular data collection for the Czech Republic, Hungary, Portugal, Slovenia, and data on part-year earnings are excluded for the Czech Republic, Hungary and Portugal.

Since earnings data differ across countries in a number of ways, the results should be interpreted with caution. For example, in countries reporting annual earnings, differences in the incidence of seasonal work among individuals with different levels of educational attainment will have an effect on relative earnings that is not similarly reflected in the data for countries reporting weekly or monthly earnings.

The statistical data for Israel are supplied by and under the responsibility of the relevant Israeli authorities. The use of such data by the OECD is without prejudice to the status of the Golan Heights, East Jerusalem and Israeli settlements in the West Bank under the terms of international law.

References

The following additional material relevant to this indicator is available on line:

- *Table A8.4a Distribution of 25-64 year-olds, by level of earnings and educational attainment (2009 or latest available year)*
  StatLink http://dx.doi.org/10.1787/888932463232

- *Table A8.4b Distribution of 25-64 year-old men, by level of earnings and educational attainment (2009 or latest available year)*
  StatLink http://dx.doi.org/10.1787/888932463251

- *Table A8.4c Distribution of 25-64 year-old women, by level of earnings and educational attainment (2009 or latest available year)*
  StatLink http://dx.doi.org/10.1787/888932463270

Table A8.1. [1/2] Relative earnings of the population with income from employment (2009 or latest available year)

By level of educational attainment and gender for 25-64 year-olds, 25-34 year-olds and 55-64 year-olds (upper secondary and post-secondary non-tertiary education = 100)

			Below upper secondary education			Post-secondary non-tertiary education			Tertiary-type B education			Tertiary-type A and advanced research programmes			All tertiary education		
			25-64	25-34	55-64	25-64	25-34	55-64	25-64	25-34	55-64	25-64	25-34	55-64	25-64	25-34	55-64
			(1)	(2)	(3)	(4)	(5)	(6)	(7)	(8)	(9)	(10)	(11)	(12)	(13)	(14)	(15)
OECD Australia	2009	Men	85	78	88	103	110	100	125	100	131	151	122	163	144	117	155
		Women	85	75	88	95	107	94	116	105	118	162	151	169	148	141	150
		M+W	81	77	82	93	103	95	111	96	113	145	126	157	135	119	143
Austria	2009	Men	68	69	67	139	121	162	124	114	122	171	158	172	153	145	152
		Women	70	64	66	120	114	136	150	124	158	164	155	227	158	147	191
		M+W	65	66	61	124	111	149	133	115	130	169	151	189	155	141	163
Belgium	2009	Men	93	94	84	98	100	98	118	112	115	145	131	153	134	123	138
		Women	84	86	77	107	106	110	125	124	127	148	144	160	135	134	138
		M+W	91	92	82	101	102	100	117	113	118	146	134	163	131	124	140
Canada	2008	Men	80	82	76	111	117	102	111	109	120	172	131	208	143	120	171
		Women	70	85	68	102	107	88	121	126	121	176	183	175	147	157	144
		M+W	80	87	75	112	116	101	111	109	118	170	141	206	140	126	163
Chile			m	m	m	m	m	m	m	m	m	m	m	m	m	m	m
Czech Republic	2009	Men	75	76	78	m	m	m	134	127	131	205	163	212	201	159	210
		Women	72	73	68	m	m	m	123	119	124	171	155	175	166	148	172
		M+W	71	74	71	m	m	m	123	117	124	193	157	202	188	152	199
Denmark	2009	Men	80	78	83	92	47	115	115	119	109	143	115	153	136	116	144
		Women	83	77	85	71	43	142	112	122	107	127	123	133	125	123	130
		M+W	81	79	82	89	46	126	115	120	108	130	113	140	127	114	134
Estonia	2009	Men	88	100	84	m	m	m	m	m	m	m	m	m	142	141	144
		Women	86	89	79	m	m	m	m	m	m	m	m	m	162	170	160
		M+W	91	99	87	m	m	m	m	m	m	m	m	m	137	136	146
Finland	2008	Men	90	89	92	m	m	m	133	130	133	172	137	206	159	136	175
		Women	95	89	94	m	m	m	131	127	126	156	143	191	145	141	154
		M+W	93	92	94	m	m	m	125	117	127	160	129	204	147	127	166
France	2009	Men	87	90	84	c	c	c	127	120	149	171	143	207	154	133	193
		Women	83	86	73	c	c	c	129	127	135	155	147	168	144	139	155
		M+W	85	91	77	c	c	c	124	120	137	161	140	195	146	131	177
Germany	2009	Men	91	86	84	111	116	104	119	117	96	168	139	152	154	136	138
		Women	79	74	75	117	123	121	114	126	133	165	136	178	154	135	170
		M+W	87	82	79	109	116	105	124	118	115	168	135	167	157	133	155
Greece	2009	Men	80	85	50	106	101	97	151	133	130	204	139	251	153	133	137
		Women	65	79	35	114	104	211	162	140	165	195	182	m	163	141	165
		M+W	76	88	45	106	99	136	149	128	139	204	152	276	151	128	145
Hungary	2009	Men	75	75	73	126	118	131	123	140	111	248	210	269	247	209	268
		Women	68	71	62	115	110	118	136	136	144	186	172	198	185	171	197
		M+W	71	74	66	119	114	124	128	136	137	212	188	234	211	187	233
Iceland			m	m	m	m	m	m	m	m	m	m	m	m	m	m	m
Ireland	2009	Men	80	91	69	105	118	81	132	156	92	178	169	166	162	165	141
		Women	73	84	70	94	86	103	133	136	149	190	200	156	171	184	153
		M+W	83	88	77	101	105	91	132	146	115	180	177	172	164	168	151
Israel	2009	Men	77	91	77	146	117	139	126	111	125	180	148	181	162	137	162
		Women	70	75	63	118	126	85	117	114	116	177	161	178	159	149	156
		M+W	80	98	75	132	119	123	118	107	118	170	144	175	154	134	156
Italy	2008	Men	78	83	76	m	m	m	m	m	m	162	110	212	162	110	212
		Women	70	74	76	m	m	m	m	m	m	142	119	168	142	119	168
		M+W	79	85	77	m	m	m	m	m	m	150	109	196	150	109	196
Japan	2007	Men	74	88	71	m	m	m	116	111	126	141	126	157	139	125	154
		Women	78	73	77	m	m	m	134	134	146	191	171	225	161	155	178
		M+W	80	90	74	m	m	m	90	96	106	168	139	197	148	129	178
Korea	2008	Men	70	90	71	m	m	m	101	109	120	135	130	157	126	123	153
		Women	77	117	68	m	m	m	115	108	191	155	133	190	141	123	190
		M+W	69	98	64	m	m	m	103	106	128	143	130	161	131	122	157
Luxembourg	2009	Men	69	76	91	122	91	92	m	m	m	171	186	193	171	186	193
		Women	65	70	54	258	101	m	m	m	m	160	183	159	160	183	159
		M+W	66	76	73	146	97	104	m	m	m	162	178	191	162	178	191
Mexico			m	m	m	m	m	m	m	m	m	m	m	m	m	m	m

Note: Belgium, Korea and Turkey report earnings net of income tax. Slovenia reports earnings excluding data for individuals in part-time and/or part-year earnings.

Source: OECD. See Annex 3 for notes *(www.oecd.org/edu/eag2011).*

Please refer to the Reader's Guide for information concerning the symbols replacing missing data.

StatLink http://dx.doi.org/10.1787/888932463118

Table A8.1. [2/2] Relative earnings of the population with income from employment (2009 or latest available year)

By level of educational attainment and gender for 25-64 year-olds, 25-34 year-olds and 55-64 year-olds (upper secondary and post-secondary non-tertiary education = 100)

				Below upper secondary education			Post-secondary non-tertiary education			Tertiary-type B education			Tertiary-type A and advanced research programmes			All tertiary education		
				25-64	25-34	55-64	25-64	25-34	55-64	25-64	25-34	55-64	25-64	25-34	55-64	25-64	25-34	55-64
				(1)	(2)	(3)	(4)	(5)	(6)	(7)	(8)	(9)	(10)	(11)	(12)	(13)	(14)	(15)
OECD	Netherlands	2008	Men	82	87	79	114	120	110	147	145	130	157	139	160	156	139	158
			Women	73	75	67	117	115	112	143	137	143	163	150	161	162	149	160
			M+W	81	87	72	115	119	107	149	141	142	160	140	163	159	140	162
	New Zealand	2009	Men	82	86	76	99	103	94	104	95	101	140	120	160	127	113	136
			Women	82	76	89	95	98	83	103	103	104	139	137	160	123	127	125
			M+W	79	83	75	108	110	101	95	95	91	133	123	157	118	115	123
	Norway	2008	Men	78	75	77	118	113	126	141	127	144	132	106	150	133	107	149
			Women	80	77	76	118	112	128	148	144	148	133	126	146	133	127	146
			M+W	78	76	77	124	120	132	150	127	165	126	106	147	127	107	149
	Poland	2008	Men	87	85	82	113	107	121	m	m	m	188	160	227	188	160	227
			Women	75	83	60	119	114	119	m	m	m	161	152	176	161	152	176
			M+W	83	86	76	109	104	118	m	m	m	167	147	207	167	147	207
	Portugal	2009	Men	66	77	51	84	91	81	159	145	151	175	160	187	172	158	180
			Women	67	76	48	103	107	118	156	148	156	173	168	209	171	166	196
			M+W	68	79	50	92	98	92	157	146	154	171	161	198	169	159	188
	Slovak Republic	2009	Men	70	58	79	m	m	m	140	137	141	194	163	199	192	162	197
			Women	70	69	65	m	m	m	141	136	139	180	165	184	177	163	181
			M+W	66	61	69	m	m	m	129	125	133	188	159	194	184	158	191
	Slovenia	2009	Men	73	72	70	m	m	m	m	m	m	m	m	m	208	171	230
			Women	72	76	58	m	m	m	m	m	m	m	m	m	185	160	203
			M+W	73	76	67	m	m	m	m	m	m	m	m	m	191	156	220
	Spain	2008	Men	80	90	71	119	88	143	100	107	91	153	140	158	135	126	143
			Women	69	80	56	107	106	113	108	114	101	170	171	170	156	156	161
			M+W	78	91	67	109	92	138	105	112	95	156	149	162	141	136	149
	Sweden	2009	Men	82	78	84	123	81	126	106	96	112	143	120	158	134	114	146
			Women	81	76	85	108	84	125	114	94	122	132	129	148	127	124	138
			M+W	83	78	86	120	80	133	106	94	112	133	119	152	126	114	139
	Switzerland	2008	Men	78	88	65	103	82	128	124	124	125	146	136	142	138	133	136
			Women	76	74	65	122	119	132	137	139	118	164	142	156	156	142	145
			M+W	74	81	60	111	97	134	140	134	143	161	140	162	154	138	156
	Turkey	2005	Men	72	77	60	m	m	m	128	154	121	162	178	133	153	171	129
			Women	43	37	49	m	m	m	131	93	m	162	150	307	154	133	307
			M+W	69	70	59	m	m	m	125	131	128	157	166	138	149	156	135
	United Kingdom	2009	Men	69	71	72	m	m	m	125	117	131	160	149	163	151	144	153
			Women	68	69	73	m	m	m	140	135	146	191	189	195	176	179	178
			M+W	70	73	70	m	m	m	128	119	134	171	161	172	159	153	159
	United States	2009	Men	62	64	63	m	m	m	116	123	103	198	173	193	190	167	185
			Women	63	69	65	m	m	m	116	125	104	180	186	175	173	181	167
			M+W	64	67	66	m	m	m	113	120	102	187	170	189	179	165	181
	OECD average		Men	78	82	75	112	102	113	125	122	122	168	145	181	159	141	168
			Women	74	77	69	116	104	119	129	124	134	164	156	180	156	149	168
			M+W	77	82	72	112	103	116	123	119	124	163	144	182	153	139	166
Other G20	Argentina			m	m	m	m	m	m	m	m	m	m	m	m	m	m	m
	Brazil	2009	Men	53	58	38	m	m	m	m	m	m	275	279	265	275	279	265
			Women	47	52	34	m	m	m	m	m	m	263	262	273	263	262	273
			M+W	53	59	38	m	m	m	m	m	m	256	256	264	256	256	264
	China			m	m	m	m	m	m	m	m	m	m	m	m	m	m	m
	India			m	m	m	m	m	m	m	m	m	m	m	m	m	m	m
	Indonesia			m	m	m	m	m	m	m	m	m	m	m	m	m	m	m
	Russian Federation			m	m	m	m	m	m	m	m	m	m	m	m	m	m	m
	Saudi Arabia			m	m	m	m	m	m	m	m	m	m	m	m	m	m	m
	South Africa			m	m	m	m	m	m	m	m	m	m	m	m	m	m	m

Note: Belgium, Korea and Turkey report earnings net of income tax. Slovenia reports earnings excluding data for individuals in part-time and/or part-year earnings.

Source: OECD. See Annex 3 for notes *(www.oecd.org/edu/eag2011).*

Please refer to the Reader's Guide for information concerning the symbols replacing missing data.

StatLink http://dx.doi.org/10.1787/888932463118

Table A8.2a. [1/2] Trends in relative earnings: Total population (1999-2009)

By educational attainment, for 25-64 year-olds (upper secondary and post-secondary non-tertiary education = 100)

		1999	2000	2001	2002	2003	2004	2005	2006	2007	2008	2009
Australia	Below upper secondary	80	m	77	m	m	m	82	m	m	m	**81**
	Tertiary	134	m	133	m	m	m	134	m	m	m	**135**
Austria	Below upper secondary	m	m	m	m	m	m	71	66	67	68	**65**
	Tertiary	m	m	m	m	m	m	152	157	155	160	**155**
Belgium	Below upper secondary	m	92	m	91	89	90	89	m	m	m	**91**
	Tertiary	m	128	m	132	130	134	133	m	m	m	**131**
Canada	Below upper secondary	79	79	76	77	78	77	77	75	79	80	**m**
	Tertiary	140	144	144	138	140	137	137	139	142	140	**m**
Chile		m	m	m	m	m	m	m	m	m	m	**m**
Czech Republic	Below upper secondary	68	m	m	m	m	73	72	74	73	72	**71**
	Tertiary	179	m	m	m	m	182	181	183	183	183	**188**
Denmark	Below upper secondary	86	m	87	88	82	82	82	83	82	83	**81**
	Tertiary	124	m	124	124	127	126	125	126	125	125	**127**
Estonia	Below upper secondary	m	m	m	m	m	m	m	m	m	91	**91**
	Tertiary	m	m	m	m	m	m	m	m	m	129	**137**
Finland	Below upper secondary	96	95	95	95	94	94	94	94	94	93	**m**
	Tertiary	153	153	150	150	148	149	149	149	148	147	**m**
France	Below upper secondary	84	m	m	84	84	85	86	85	84	87	**85**
	Tertiary	150	m	m	150	146	147	144	149	150	147	**146**
Germany	Below upper secondary	79	75	m	77	87	88	88	90	91	90	**87**
	Tertiary	135	143	m	143	153	153	156	164	162	167	**157**
Greece	Below upper secondary	m	m	m	m	m	m	m	m	m	m	**76**
	Tertiary	m	m	m	m	m	m	m	m	m	m	**151**
Hungary	Below upper secondary	70	71	71	74	74	73	73	73	72	73	**71**
	Tertiary	200	194	194	205	219	217	215	219	211	210	**211**
Iceland		m	m	m	m	m	m	m	m	m	m	**m**
Ireland	Below upper secondary	m	89	m	76	m	85	86	83	77	74	**83**
	Tertiary	m	153	m	144	m	169	155	157	161	153	**164**
Israel	Below upper secondary	m	m	m	m	m	m	79	78	83	75	**80**
	Tertiary	m	m	m	m	m	m	151	151	153	152	**154**
Italy	Below upper secondary	m	78	m	78	m	79	m	76	m	79	**m**
	Tertiary	m	138	m	153	m	165	m	155	m	150	**m**
Japan	Below upper secondary	m	m	m	m	m	m	m	m	80	m	**m**
	Tertiary	m	m	m	m	m	m	m	m	148	m	**m**
Korea	Below upper secondary	m	m	m	m	67	m	m	m	69	69	**m**
	Tertiary	m	m	m	m	141	m	m	m	160	131	**m**
Luxembourg	Below upper secondary	m	m	m	78	m	m	m	74	m	m	**66**
	Tertiary	m	m	m	145	m	m	m	153	m	m	**162**
Mexico		m	m	m	m	m	m	m	m	m	m	**m**
Netherlands	Below upper secondary	m	m	m	84	m	m	m	85	m	81	**m**
	Tertiary	m	m	m	148	m	m	m	154	m	159	**m**
New Zealand	Below upper secondary	81	79	78	81	77	75	77	82	76	82	**79**
	Tertiary	120	123	120	123	123	116	120	115	117	118	**118**
Norway	Below upper secondary	84	m	79	79	78	78	78	78	79	78	**m**
	Tertiary	133	m	131	130	131	130	129	129	128	127	**m**
Poland	Below upper secondary	82	m	81	81	m	82	m	84	m	83	**m**
	Tertiary	161	m	166	172	m	179	m	173	m	167	**m**
Portugal	Below upper secondary	62	m	m	m	m	67	67	68	m	m	**68**
	Tertiary	178	m	m	m	m	178	177	177	m	m	**169**
Slovak Republic	Below upper secondary	m	m	m	m	m	m	m	m	m	69	**66**
	Tertiary	m	m	m	m	m	m	m	m	m	181	**184**
Slovenia	Below upper secondary	m	m	m	m	m	73	m	74	74	m	**73**
	Tertiary	m	m	m	m	m	198	m	193	192	m	**191**
Spain	Below upper secondary	m	m	78	m	m	85	m	m	81	78	**m**
	Tertiary	m	m	129	m	m	132	m	m	138	141	**m**

Note: Belgium, Korea and Turkey report earnings net of income tax. Slovenia reports earnings excluding data for individuals in part-time and/or part-year earnings.

Source: OECD. See Annex 3 for notes *(www.oecd.org/edu/eag2011)*.

Please refer to the Reader's Guide for information concerning the symbols replacing missing data.

StatLink http://dx.doi.org/10.1787/888932463137

Table A8.2a. [2/2] Trends in relative earnings: Total population (1999-2009)

By educational attainment, for 25-64 year-olds (upper secondary and post-secondary non-tertiary education = 100)

			1999	2000	2001	2002	2003	2004	2005	2006	2007	2008	2009
OECD	Sweden	Below upper secondary	89	m	86	87	87	87	86	85	84	83	**83**
		Tertiary	131	m	131	130	128	127	126	126	126	126	**126**
	Switzerland	Below upper secondary	75	75	76	75	74	74	75	74	75	74	**m**
		Tertiary	153	152	155	154	156	156	155	156	159	154	**m**
	Turkey	Below upper secondary	m	m	m	m	m	65	69	m	m	m	**m**
		Tertiary	m	m	m	m	m	141	149	m	m	m	**m**
	United Kingdom	Below upper secondary	69	69	70	68	69	69	71	71	70	71	**70**
		Tertiary	162	160	160	157	162	157	158	160	157	154	**159**
	United States	Below upper secondary	65	65	m	66	66	65	67	66	65	66	**64**
		Tertiary	166	172	m	172	172	172	175	176	172	177	**179**
	OECD Average	Below upper secondary	78	79	80	80	79	78	78	78	78	78	**77**
		Tertiary	151	151	145	148	148	155	151	157	154	152	**157**
Other G20	Argentina		m	m	m	m	m	m	m	m	m	m	**m**
	Brazil	Below upper secondary	m	m	m	m	m	m	m	m	51	52	**53**
		Tertiary	m	m	m	m	m	m	m	m	268	254	**256**
	China		m	m	m	m	m	m	m	m	m	m	**m**
	India		m	m	m	m	m	m	m	m	m	m	**m**
	Indonesia		m	m	m	m	m	m	m	m	m	m	**m**
	Russian Federation		m	m	m	m	m	m	m	m	m	m	**m**
	Saudi Arabia		m	m	m	m	m	m	m	m	m	m	**m**
	South Africa		m	m	m	m	m	m	m	m	m	m	**m**

Note: Belgium, Korea and Turkey report earnings net of income tax. Slovenia reports earnings excluding data for individuals in part-time and/or part-year earnings.

Source: OECD. See Annex 3 for notes *(www.oecd.org/edu/eag2011).*

Please refer to the Reader's Guide for information concerning the symbols replacing missing data.

StatLink http://dx.doi.org/10.1787/888932463137

Table A8.2b. [1/2] Trends in relative earnings: Men (1999-2009)

By educational attainment, for 25-64 year-olds (upper secondary and post-secondary non-tertiary education = 100)

			1999	2000	2001	2002	2003	2004	2005	2006	2007	2008	2009
OECD	Australia	Below upper secondary	86	m	84	m	m	m	88	m	m	m	**85**
		Tertiary	139	m	142	m	m	m	140	m	m	m	**144**
	Austria	Below upper secondary	m	m	m	m	m	m	76	72	72	71	**68**
		Tertiary	m	m	m	m	m	m	149	155	151	159	**153**
	Belgium	Below upper secondary	m	93	m	91	90	91	91	m	m	m	**93**
		Tertiary	m	128	m	132	132	137	137	m	m	m	**134**
	Canada	Below upper secondary	80	80	76	79	79	78	78	76	82	80	**m**
		Tertiary	143	149	148	142	142	139	139	142	146	143	**m**
	Chile		m	m	m	m	m	m	m	m	m	m	**m**
	Czech Republic	Below upper secondary	75	m	m	m	m	79	79	81	78	76	**75**
		Tertiary	178	m	m	m	m	193	190	194	192	193	**201**
	Denmark	Below upper secondary	87	m	87	87	82	82	82	82	81	82	**80**
		Tertiary	133	m	132	131	134	133	133	133	133	133	**136**
	Estonia	Below upper secondary	m	m	m	m	m	m	m	m	m	91	**88**
		Tertiary	m	m	m	m	m	m	m	m	m	135	**142**
	Finland	Below upper secondary	93	92	92	92	92	91	91	91	90	90	**m**
		Tertiary	167	169	163	163	160	161	162	162	161	159	**m**
	France	Below upper secondary	88	m	m	88	88	89	90	89	87	90	**87**
		Tertiary	159	m	m	159	151	154	152	157	158	155	**154**
	Germany	Below upper secondary	80	80	m	84	90	91	93	92	90	97	**91**
		Tertiary	138	141	m	140	150	149	151	163	158	163	**154**
	Greece	Below upper secondary	m	m	m	m	m	m	m	m	m	m	**80**
		Tertiary	m	m	m	m	m	m	m	m	m	m	**153**
	Hungary	Below upper secondary	73	75	75	78	77	76	76	75	74	77	**75**
		Tertiary	238	232	232	245	255	253	253	259	247	248	**247**
	Iceland		m	m	m	m	m	m	m	m	m	m	**m**
	Ireland	Below upper secondary	m	84	m	71	m	85	84	82	71	71	**80**
		Tertiary	m	138	m	141	m	171	147	149	151	156	**162**
	Israel	Below upper secondary	m	m	m	m	m	m	74	76	80	72	**77**
		Tertiary	m	m	m	m	m	m	159	166	165	164	**162**
	Italy	Below upper secondary	m	71	m	74	m	78	m	73	m	78	**m**
		Tertiary	m	143	m	162	m	188	m	178	m	162	**m**
	Japan	Below upper secondary	m	m	m	m	m	m	m	m	74	m	**m**
		Tertiary	m	m	m	m	m	m	m	m	139	m	**m**
	Korea	Below upper secondary	m	m	m	m	73	m	m	m	66	70	**m**
		Tertiary	m	m	m	m	127	m	m	m	158	126	**m**
	Luxembourg	Below upper secondary	m	m	m	79	m	m	m	74	m	m	**69**
		Tertiary	m	m	m	149	m	m	m	158	m	m	**171**
	Mexico		m	m	m	m	m	m	m	m	m	m	**m**
	Netherlands	Below upper secondary	m	m	m	84	m	m	m	87	m	82	**m**
		Tertiary	m	m	m	143	m	m	m	151	m	156	**m**
	New Zealand	Below upper secondary	87	82	81	84	80	77	83	85	78	87	**82**
		Tertiary	131	133	124	131	135	126	129	123	128	126	**127**
	Norway	Below upper secondary	85	m	80	80	79	79	78	79	79	78	**m**
		Tertiary	135	m	134	133	134	134	134	134	134	133	**m**
	Poland	Below upper secondary	85	m	85	84	m	86	m	86	m	87	**m**
		Tertiary	182	m	185	194	m	204	m	194	m	188	**m**
	Portugal	Below upper secondary	60	m	m	m	m	64	64	66	m	m	**66**
		Tertiary	180	m	m	m	m	183	183	183	m	m	**172**
	Slovak Republic	Below upper secondary	m	m	m	m	m	m	m	m	m	72	**70**
		Tertiary	m	m	m	m	m	m	m	m	m	187	**192**
	Slovenia	Below upper secondary	m	m	m	m	m	74	m	75	75	m	**73**
		Tertiary	m	m	m	m	m	217	m	210	208	m	**208**
	Spain	Below upper secondary	m	m	79	m	m	84	m	m	83	80	**m**
		Tertiary	m	m	138	m	m	132	m	m	133	135	**m**

Note: Belgium, Korea and Turkey report earnings net of income tax. Slovenia reports earnings excluding data for individuals in part-time and/or part-year earnings.

Source: OECD. See Annex 3 for notes *(www.oecd.org/edu/eag2011)*.

Please refer to the Reader's Guide for information concerning the symbols replacing missing data.

StatLink http://dx.doi.org/10.1787/888932463156

Table A8.2b. [2/2] Trends in relative earnings: Men (1999-2009)

By educational attainment, for 25-64 year-olds (upper secondary and post-secondary non-tertiary education = 100)

			1999	2000	2001	2002	2003	2004	2005	2006	2007	2008	2009
OECD	Sweden	Below upper secondary	87	m	84	85	85	85	84	83	83	82	**82**
		Tertiary	138	m	141	139	137	135	135	135	135	134	**134**
	Switzerland	Below upper secondary	80	79	84	79	78	78	80	78	77	78	**m**
		Tertiary	134	135	140	137	140	139	140	138	144	138	**m**
	Turkey	Below upper secondary	m	m	m	m	m	67	72	m	m	m	**m**
		Tertiary	m	m	m	m	m	139	153	m	m	m	**m**
	United Kingdom	Below upper secondary	76	74	73	72	71	70	72	73	69	68	**69**
		Tertiary	155	152	147	147	152	146	146	148	145	145	**151**
	United States	Below upper secondary	63	64	m	63	63	62	64	63	63	65	**62**
		Tertiary	167	178	m	178	177	179	183	183	180	188	**190**
	OECD Average	Below upper secondary	80	79	82	81	80	79	80	79	78	79	**78**
		Tertiary	157	154	152	154	152	162	156	164	158	158	**164**
Other G20	Argentina		m	m	m	m	m	m	m	m	m	m	**m**
	Brazil	Below upper secondary	m	m	m	m	m	m	m	m	51	52	**53**
		Tertiary	m	m	m	m	m	m	m	m	284	263	**275**
	China		m	m	m	m	m	m	m	m	m	m	**m**
	India		m	m	m	m	m	m	m	m	m	m	**m**
	Indonesia		m	m	m	m	m	m	m	m	m	m	**m**
	Russian Federation		m	m	m	m	m	m	m	m	m	m	**m**
	Saudi Arabia		m	m	m	m	m	m	m	m	m	m	**m**
	South Africa		m	m	m	m	m	m	m	m	m	m	**m**

Note: Belgium, Korea and Turkey report earnings net of income tax. Slovenia reports earnings excluding data for individuals in part-time and/or part-year earnings.

Source: OECD. See Annex 3 for notes *(www.oecd.org/edu/eag2011).*

Please refer to the Reader's Guide for information concerning the symbols replacing missing data.

StatLink http://dx.doi.org/10.1787/888932463156

Table A8.2c. [1/2] **Trends in relative earnings: Women (1999-2009)**

By educational attainment, for 25-64 year-olds (upper secondary and post-secondary non-tertiary education = 100)

			1999	2000	2001	2002	2003	2004	2005	2006	2007	2008	2009
OECD	Australia	Below upper secondary	89	m	84	m	m	m	88	m	m	m	**85**
		Tertiary	146	m	146	m	m	m	147	m	m	m	**148**
	Austria	Below upper secondary	m	m	m	m	m	m	74	71	73	74	**70**
		Tertiary	m	m	m	m	m	m	156	158	160	159	**158**
	Belgium	Below upper secondary	m	82	m	83	81	82	81	m	m	m	**84**
		Tertiary	m	132	m	139	132	137	134	m	m	m	**135**
	Canada	Below upper secondary	68	69	67	65	69	68	68	65	67	70	**m**
		Tertiary	144	143	148	140	147	143	142	143	145	147	**m**
	Chile		m	m	m	m	m	m	m	m	m	m	**m**
	Czech Republic	Below upper secondary	72	m	m	m	m	73	72	73	74	73	**72**
		Tertiary	170	m	m	m	m	160	161	163	165	164	**166**
	Denmark	Below upper secondary	90	m	90	90	85	85	84	84	83	84	**83**
		Tertiary	123	m	124	123	127	126	126	125	124	123	**125**
	Estonia	Below upper secondary	m	m	m	m	m	m	m	m	m	82	**86**
		Tertiary	m	m	m	m	m	m	m	m	m	146	**162**
	Finland	Below upper secondary	99	99	98	98	97	97	98	97	96	95	**m**
		Tertiary	145	146	146	146	146	146	145	146	146	145	**m**
	France	Below upper secondary	79	m	m	81	81	82	81	82	82	82	**83**
		Tertiary	145	m	m	146	146	145	142	146	147	146	**144**
	Germany	Below upper secondary	83	72	m	73	81	81	77	83	84	80	**79**
		Tertiary	123	137	m	137	145	148	151	153	159	158	**154**
	Greece	Below upper secondary	m	m	m	m	m	m	m	m	m	m	**65**
		Tertiary	m	m	m	m	m	m	m	m	m	m	**163**
	Hungary	Below upper secondary	68	71	71	71	72	71	72	72	71	71	**68**
		Tertiary	167	164	164	176	192	190	188	189	185	183	**185**
	Iceland		m	m	m	m	m	m	m	m	m	m	**m**
	Ireland	Below upper secondary	m	65	m	60	m	68	67	63	67	65	**73**
		Tertiary	m	163	m	153	m	168	178	180	185	162	**171**
	Israel	Below upper secondary	m	m	m	m	m	m	72	67	67	67	**70**
		Tertiary	m	m	m	m	m	m	157	150	155	153	**159**
	Italy	Below upper secondary	m	84	m	78	m	73	m	74	m	70	**m**
		Tertiary	m	137	m	147	m	138	m	143	m	142	**m**
	Japan	Below upper secondary	m	m	m	m	m	m	m	m	78	m	**m**
		Tertiary	m	m	m	m	m	m	m	m	161	m	**m**
	Korea	Below upper secondary	m	m	m	m	75	m	m	m	97	77	**m**
		Tertiary	m	m	m	m	176	m	m	m	167	141	**m**
	Luxembourg	Below upper secondary	m	m	m	74	m	m	m	73	m	m	**65**
		Tertiary	m	m	m	131	m	m	m	134	m	m	**160**
	Mexico		m	m	m	m	m	m	m	m	m	m	**m**
	Netherlands	Below upper secondary	m	m	m	72	m	m	m	75	m	73	**m**
		Tertiary	m	m	m	155	m	m	m	159	m	162	**m**
	New Zealand	Below upper secondary	78	86	82	86	84	83	79	89	85	83	**82**
		Tertiary	121	126	130	131	127	123	123	122	126	125	**123**
	Norway	Below upper secondary	83	m	81	81	81	81	81	81	81	80	**m**
		Tertiary	135	m	135	135	137	136	135	134	134	133	**m**
	Poland	Below upper secondary	76	m	74	73	m	74	m	76	m	75	**m**
		Tertiary	148	m	155	159	m	166	m	165	m	161	**m**
	Portugal	Below upper secondary	63	m	m	m	m	66	66	67	m	m	**67**
		Tertiary	170	m	m	m	m	173	173	173	m	m	**171**
	Slovak Republic	Below upper secondary	m	m	m	m	m	m	m	m	m	72	**70**
		Tertiary	m	m	m	m	m	m	m	m	m	176	**177**
	Slovenia	Below upper secondary	m	m	m	m	m	71	m	72	72	m	**72**
		Tertiary	m	m	m	m	m	190	m	188	187	m	**185**
	Spain	Below upper secondary	m	m	64	m	m	78	m	m	70	69	**m**
		Tertiary	m	m	125	m	m	141	m	m	149	156	**m**

Note: Belgium, Korea and Turkey report earnings net of income tax. Slovenia reports earnings excluding data for individuals in part-time and/or part-year earnings.

Source: OECD. See Annex 3 for notes (*www.oecd.org/edu/eag2011*).

Please refer to the Reader's Guide for information concerning the symbols replacing missing data.

StatLink http://dx.doi.org/10.1787/888932463175

Table A8.2c. [2/2] Trends in relative earnings: Women (1999-2009)

By educational attainment, for 25-64 year-olds (upper secondary and post-secondary non-tertiary education = 100)

			1999	2000	2001	2002	2003	2004	2005	2006	2007	2008	2009
OECD	Sweden	Below upper secondary	88	m	87	87	88	87	86	85	84	82	**81**
		Tertiary	126	m	129	129	128	127	126	126	127	126	**127**
	Switzerland	Below upper secondary	72	72	73	74	76	77	76	76	76	76	**m**
		Tertiary	146	144	148	148	151	153	148	159	156	156	**m**
	Turkey	Below upper secondary	m	m	m	m	m	46	43	m	m	m	**m**
		Tertiary	m	m	m	m	m	164	154	m	m	m	**m**
	United Kingdom	Below upper secondary	68	69	73	69	69	72	71	70	70	73	**68**
		Tertiary	178	176	187	177	182	180	181	182	181	177	**176**
	United States	Below upper secondary	61	62	m	63	66	62	63	63	61	60	**63**
		Tertiary	163	164	m	165	167	166	167	170	167	171	**173**
	OECD Average	Below upper secondary	77	75	79	77	79	75	75	75	77	75	**74**
		Tertiary	147	148	145	146	150	153	152	155	156	153	**158**
Other G20	Argentina		m	m	m	m	m	m	m	m	m	m	**m**
	Brazil	Below upper secondary	m	m	m	m	m	m	m	m	44	46	**47**
		Tertiary	m	m	m	m	m	m	m	m	270	271	**263**
	China		m	m	m	m	m	m	m	m	m	m	**m**
	India		m	m	m	m	m	m	m	m	m	m	**m**
	Indonesia		m	m	m	m	m	m	m	m	m	m	**m**
	Russian Federation		m	m	m	m	m	m	m	m	m	m	**m**
	Saudi Arabia		m	m	m	m	m	m	m	m	m	m	**m**
	South Africa		m	m	m	m	m	m	m	m	m	m	**m**

Note: Belgium, Korea and Turkey report earnings net of income tax. Slovenia reports earnings excluding data for individuals in part-time and/or part-year earnings.

Source: OECD. See Annex 3 for notes *(www.oecd.org/edu/eag2011)*.

Please refer to the Reader's Guide for information concerning the symbols replacing missing data.

StatLink http://dx.doi.org/10.1787/888932463175

Table A8.3a. Differences in earnings between women and men (2009 or latest available year)

Average annual full-time, full-year earnings of women as a percentage of men's earnings, by level of educational attainment of 25-64, 35-44 and 55-64 year-olds

			Below upper secondary education			Upper secondary and post-secondary non-tertiary education			Tertiary education			All levels of education		
			25-64	35-44	55-64	25-64	35-44	55-64	25-64	35-44	55-64	25-64	35-44	55-64
			(1)	(2)	(3)	(4)	(5)	(6)	(7)	(8)	(9)	(10)	(11)	(12)
OECD	Australia	2009	76	76	83	73	68	75	72	70	73	77	74	80
	Austria	2009	73	73	74	78	76	86	73	75	76	76	74	80
	Belgium		m	m	m	m	m	m	m	m	m	m	m	m
	Chile		m	m	m	m	m	m	m	m	m	m	m	m
	Canada	2008	65	50	61	71	67	79	70	64	56	73	66	64
	Czech Republic	2009	77	75	78	80	73	88	68	66	75	73	65	77
	Denmark	2009	83	80	83	80	78	84	77	77	77	80	79	81
	Estonia	2009	58	71	67	60	62	72	68	66	79	70	72	81
	Finland	2009	79	76	78	78	76	78	75	73	73	79	78	76
	France	2006	72	76	63	80	78	82	73	81	55	79	84	65
	Germany	2009	73	72	74	77	84	67	77	78	73	76	81	69
	Greece	2009	60	65	51	75	73	90	74	78	92	78	80	76
	Hungary	2009	82	81	85	91	85	103	67	59	74	85	78	87
	Iceland		m	m	m	m	m	m	m	m	m	m	m	m
	Ireland	2009	91	95	96	77	92	78	72	69	64	83	84	86
	Israel	2009	72	73	69	73	68	77	69	69	73	75	73	77
	Italy	2008	73	76	77	75	75	73	65	91	52	77	84	71
	Japan		m	m	m	m	m	m	m	m	m	m	m	m
	Korea	2008	62	57	59	59	55	70	67	77	77	61	61	55
	Luxembourg	2009	75	76	49	78	87	80	69	73	58	78	80	58
	Mexico		m	m	m	m	m	m	m	m	m	m	m	m
	Netherlands	2008	80	83	78	78	83	77	72	78	70	80	85	76
	New Zealand	2009	77	76	82	77	75	75	77	73	66	78	76	72
	Norway		m	m	m	m	m	m	m	m	m	m	m	m
	Poland		m	m	m	m	m	m	m	m	m	m	m	m
	Portugal	2009	74	74	73	71	71	71	69	73	69	79	79	69
	Slovak Republic	2009	73	71	73	75	71	84	68	60	76	72	66	79
	Slovenia	2009	86	84	84	88	85	102	78	78	90	93	92	110
	Spain	2008	76	73	78	78	80	86	86	85	93	88	87	90
	Sweden	2008	83	81	79	84	87	80	66	59	73	80	75	83
	Switzerland		m	m	m	m	m	m	m	m	m	m	m	m
	Turkey		m	m	m	m	m	m	m	m	m	m	m	m
	United Kingdom	2009	77	72	82	73	72	73	77	76	79	79	77	79
	United States	2009	73	72	72	73	74	72	67	68	67	72	72	67
	OECD average		75	74	74	76	76	80	72	73	72	78	77	76
Other G20	Argentina		m	m	m	m	m	m	m	m	m	m	m	m
	Brazil	2009	64	63	63	62	60	56	61	64	61	76	75	71
	China		m	m	m	m	m	m	m	m	m	m	m	m
	India		m	m	m	m	m	m	m	m	m	m	m	m
	Indonesia		m	m	m	m	m	m	m	m	m	m	m	m
	Russian Federation		m	m	m	m	m	m	m	m	m	m	m	m
	Saudi Arabia		m	m	m	m	m	m	m	m	m	m	m	m
	South Africa		m	m	m	m	m	m	m	m	m	m	m	m

Note: Korea report earnings net of income tax.
Source: OECD, LSO Network special data collection on full-time, full-year earnings, Economic Working Group. See Annex 3 for notes *(www.oecd.org/edu/eag2011)*.
Please refer to the Reader's Guide for information concerning the symbols replacing missing data.
StatLink http://dx.doi.org/10.1787/888932463194

Table A8.3b. [1/2] **Trends in differences in earnings between women and men (1999-2009)**

Average annual earnings of women as a percentage of men's earnings, by level of educational attainment of 25-64 year-olds

		1999	2000	2001	2002	2003	2004	2005	2006	2007	2008	2009
OECD												
Australia	Below upper secondary	66	m	62	m	m	m	61	m	m	m	**59**
	Upper secondary and post-secondary non-tertiary	64	m	62	m	m	m	61	m	m	m	**59**
	Tertiary	67	m	63	m	m	m	64	m	m	m	**61**
Austria	Below upper secondary	m	m	m	m	m	m	57	58	60	61	**62**
	Upper secondary and post-secondary non-tertiary	m	m	m	m	m	m	60	59	58	59	**61**
	Tertiary	m	m	m	m	m	m	62	60	62	59	**63**
Belgium	Below upper secondary	m	64	m	65	66	66	67	m	m	m	**70**
	Upper secondary and post-secondary non-tertiary	m	72	m	72	74	74	75	m	m	m	**77**
	Tertiary	m	74	m	76	74	74	73	m	m	m	**78**
Canada	Below upper secondary	51	52	51	50	52	52	53	53	52	53	**m**
	Upper secondary and post-secondary non-tertiary	60	60	59	61	59	60	61	62	63	61	**m**
	Tertiary	60	58	58	60	61	61	62	62	63	63	**m**
Chile		m	m	m	m	m	m	m	m	m	m	**m**
Czech Republic	Below upper secondary	66	m	m	m	m	74	74	73	75	75	**77**
	Upper secondary and post-secondary non-tertiary	69	m	m	m	m	80	80	80	79	78	**80**
	Tertiary	65	m	m	m	m	67	68	67	68	67	**66**
Denmark	Below upper secondary	73	m	74	75	73	74	73	72	73	74	**80**
	Upper secondary and post-secondary non-tertiary	71	m	71	73	71	71	71	71	72	72	**77**
	Tertiary	66	m	67	68	67	67	67	67	67	67	**71**
Estonia	Below upper secondary	m	m	m	m	m	m	m	m	m	54	**57**
	Upper secondary and post-secondary non-tertiary	m	m	m	m	m	m	m	m	m	59	**58**
	Tertiary	m	m	m	m	m	m	m	m	m	64	**67**
Finland	Below upper secondary	77	76	76	76	76	76	78	77	76	76	**m**
	Upper secondary and post-secondary non-tertiary	72	71	71	72	72	72	73	72	71	72	**m**
	Tertiary	62	61	63	64	66	65	65	64	65	66	**m**
France	Below upper secondary	68	m	m	70	68	68	68	68	70	68	**70**
	Upper secondary and post-secondary non-tertiary	75	m	m	77	75	74	75	74	75	74	**74**
	Tertiary	69	m	m	70	72	70	70	69	70	70	**69**
Germany	Below upper secondary	70	56	m	53	54	54	52	56	55	49	**51**
	Upper secondary and post-secondary non-tertiary	68	63	m	61	60	60	62	62	59	60	**59**
	Tertiary	60	61	m	60	58	60	62	58	59	58	**59**
Greece	Below upper secondary	m	m	m	m	m	m	m	m	m	m	**55**
	Upper secondary and post-secondary non-tertiary	m	m	m	m	m	m	m	m	m	m	**67**
	Tertiary	m	m	m	m	m	m	m	m	m	m	**71**
Hungary	Below upper secondary	84	83	83	85	89	89	88	93	87	85	**84**
	Upper secondary and post-secondary non-tertiary	89	88	88	93	95	96	93	96	91	93	**91**
	Tertiary	62	62	62	67	71	72	69	70	68	69	**68**
Iceland		m	m	m	m	m	m	m	m	m	m	**m**
Ireland	Below upper secondary	m	46	m	48	m	49	44	42	46	51	**58**
	Upper secondary and post-secondary non-tertiary	m	60	m	57	m	61	55	54	49	56	**63**
	Tertiary	m	71	m	62	m	60	67	66	60	58	**67**
Israel	Below upper secondary	m	m	m	m	m	m	57	56	52	57	**58**
	Upper secondary and post-secondary non-tertiary	m	m	m	m	m	m	59	64	63	62	**64**
	Tertiary	m	m	m	m	m	m	58	57	59	58	**62**
Italy	Below upper secondary	m	76	m	70	m	67	m	67	m	63	**m**
	Upper secondary and post-secondary non-tertiary	m	65	m	66	m	71	m	66	m	71	**m**
	Tertiary	m	62	m	60	m	52	m	53	m	62	**m**
Japan	Below upper secondary	m	m	m	m	m	m	m	m	43	m	**m**
	Upper secondary and post-secondary non-tertiary	m	m	m	m	m	m	m	m	41	m	**m**
	Tertiary	m	m	m	m	m	m	m	m	47	m	**m**
Korea	Below upper secondary	m	m	m	m	48	m	m	m	74	62	**m**
	Upper secondary and post-secondary non-tertiary	m	m	m	m	47	m	m	m	51	57	**m**
	Tertiary	m	m	m	m	65	m	m	m	54	63	**m**
Luxembourg	Below upper secondary	m	m	m	80	m	m	m	87	m	m	**61**
	Upper secondary and post-secondary non-tertiary	m	m	m	86	m	m	m	88	m	m	**65**
	Tertiary	m	m	m	75	m	m	m	75	m	m	**61**
Mexico		m	m	m	m	m	m	m	m	m	m	**m**

Note: Belgium, Korea and Turkey report earnings net of income tax. Slovenia reports earnings excluding data for individuals in part-time and/or part-year earnings.

Source: OECD. See Annex 3 for notes *(www.oecd.org/edu/eag2011)*.

Please refer to the Reader's Guide for information concerning the symbols replacing missing data.

StatLink http://dx.doi.org/10.1787/888932463213

Table A8.3b. [2/2] Trends in differences in earnings between women and men (1999-2009)

Average annual earnings of women as a percentage of men's earnings, by level of educational attainment of 25-64 year-olds

			1999	2000	2001	2002	2003	2004	2005	2006	2007	2008	2009
OECD	Netherlands	Below upper secondary	m	m	m	49	m	m	m	48	m	49	**m**
		Upper secondary and post-secondary non-tertiary	m	m	m	58	m	m	m	55	m	55	**m**
		Tertiary	m	m	m	62	m	m	m	58	m	57	**m**
	New Zealand	Below upper secondary	57	67	63	67	67	68	61	68	68	61	**67**
		Upper secondary and post-secondary non-tertiary	64	64	63	65	64	63	64	64	62	64	**67**
		Tertiary	59	61	65	65	60	62	61	64	61	64	**65**
	Norway	Below upper secondary	61	m	63	64	66	66	65	65	65	66	**m**
		Upper secondary and post-secondary non-tertiary	62	m	62	63	64	64	63	63	63	64	**m**
		Tertiary	62	m	63	64	65	65	63	63	63	64	**m**
	Poland	Below upper secondary	72	m	72	73	m	73	m	71	m	69	**m**
		Upper secondary and post-secondary non-tertiary	81	m	83	84	m	84	m	81	m	80	**m**
		Tertiary	66	m	69	68	m	68	m	69	m	68	**m**
	Portugal	Below upper secondary	71	m	m	m	m	73	73	73	m	m	**72**
		Upper secondary and post-secondary non-tertiary	69	m	m	m	m	70	71	71	m	m	**71**
		Tertiary	65	m	m	m	m	67	67	67	m	m	**71**
	Slovak Republic	Below upper secondary	m	m	m	m	m	m	m	m	m	72	**73**
		Upper secondary and post-secondary non-tertiary	m	m	m	m	m	m	m	m	m	72	**72**
		Tertiary	m	m	m	m	m	m	m	m	m	68	**67**
	Slovenia	Below upper secondary	m	m	m	m	m	84	m	82	81	m	**86**
		Upper secondary and post-secondary non-tertiary	m	m	m	m	m	88	m	86	84	m	**88**
		Tertiary	m	m	m	m	m	77	m	77	76	m	**78**
	Spain	Below upper secondary	m	m	58	m	m	63	m	m	58	60	**m**
		Upper secondary and post-secondary non-tertiary	m	m	71	m	m	68	m	m	68	69	**m**
		Tertiary	m	m	64	m	m	73	m	m	77	80	**m**
	Sweden	Below upper secondary	74	m	74	74	75	75	74	74	73	73	**74**
		Upper secondary and post-secondary non-tertiary	73	m	71	72	73	73	73	73	72	73	**74**
		Tertiary	67	m	65	67	68	69	68	68	68	69	**70**
	Switzerland	Below upper secondary	50	53	51	53	55	55	54	55	57	53	**m**
		Upper secondary and post-secondary non-tertiary	56	58	58	56	56	56	57	56	57	55	**m**
		Tertiary	61	62	61	60	61	62	60	65	62	62	**m**
	Turkey	Below upper secondary	m	m	m	m	m	52	47	m	m	m	**m**
		Upper secondary and post-secondary non-tertiary	m	m	m	m	m	75	78	m	m	m	**m**
		Tertiary	m	m	m	m	m	89	78	m	m	m	**m**
	United Kingdom	Below upper secondary	49	50	52	53	53	55	55	53	56	59	**57**
		Upper secondary and post-secondary non-tertiary	54	54	52	55	55	54	56	56	55	55	**58**
		Tertiary	62	63	66	67	66	66	69	69	69	68	**68**
	United States	Below upper secondary	59	59	m	63	67	63	63	65	64	60	**69**
		Upper secondary and post-secondary non-tertiary	61	60	m	63	64	63	65	65	66	65	**68**
		Tertiary	59	56	m	58	61	59	59	60	61	59	**62**
	OECD average	Below upper secondary	66	62	65	65	65	67	63	66	64	63	**67**
		Upper secondary and post-secondary non-tertiary	68	65	68	68	66	70	68	69	65	66	**70**
		Tertiary	63	63	64	65	65	67	66	65	64	64	**67**
Other G20	Argentina		m	m	m	m	m	m	m	m	m	m	**m**
	Brazil	Below upper secondary	m	m	m	m	m	m	m	m	49	49	**50**
		Upper secondary and post-secondary non-tertiary	m	m	m	m	m	m	m	m	58	56	**57**
		Tertiary	m	m	m	m	m	m	m	m	55	57	**55**
	China		m	m	m	m	m	m	m	m	m	m	**m**
	India		m	m	m	m	m	m	m	m	m	m	**m**
	Indonesia		m	m	m	m	m	m	m	m	m	m	**m**
	Russian Federation		m	m	m	m	m	m	m	m	m	m	**m**
	Saudi Arabia		m	m	m	m	m	m	m	m	m	m	**m**
	South Africa		m	m	m	m	m	m	m	m	m	m	**m**

Note: Belgium, Korea and Turkey report earnings net of income tax. Slovenia reports earnings excluding data for individuals in part-time and/or part-year earnings.

Source: OECD. See Annex 3 for notes *(www.oecd.org/edu/eag2011)*.

Please refer to the Reader's Guide for information concerning the symbols replacing missing data.

StatLink http://dx.doi.org/10.1787/888932463213

WHAT ARE THE INCENTIVES TO INVEST IN EDUCATION?

- On average across 25 OECD countries, the total return (net present value), both private and public, to a man who successfully completes upper secondary and tertiary education is USD 380 000.
- The net public return on an investment in tertiary education is USD 91 000 for men – almost three times the amount of public investment.
- On average, the gross earnings premium for an individual with a tertiary degree exceeds USD 300 000 for men and USD 200 000 for women across OECD countries.

Chart A9.1. Distribution of public/private costs/benefits for a woman obtaining tertiary education as part of initial education, ISCED 5/6 (2007 or latest available year)

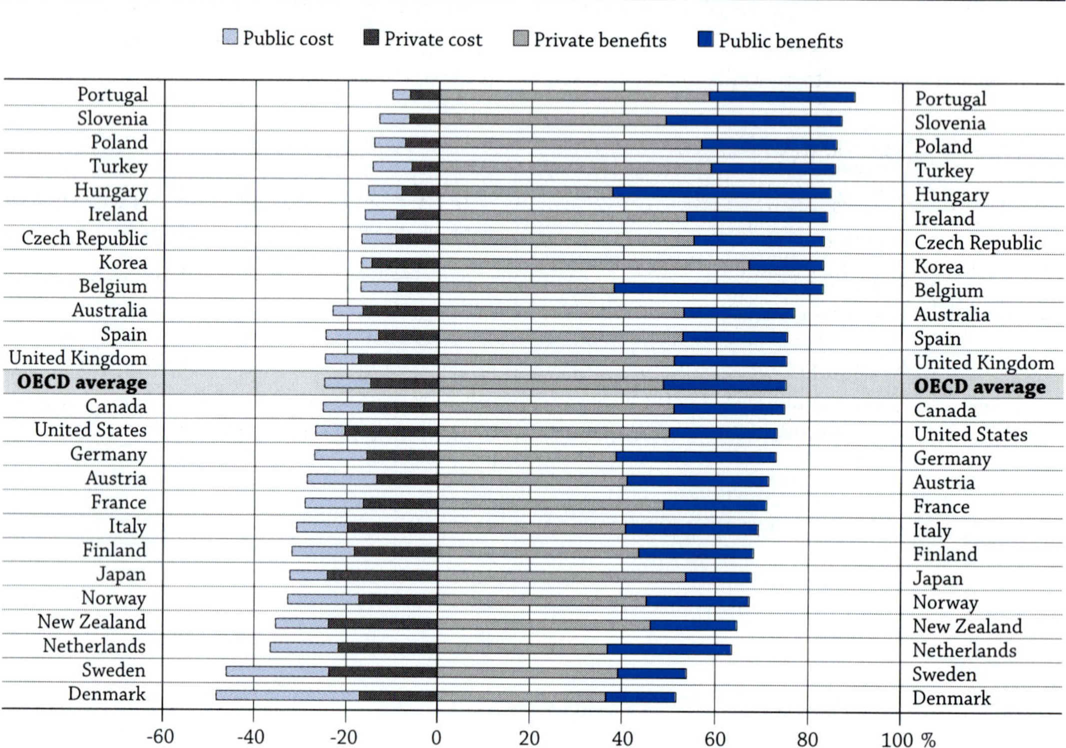

Notes: Australia, Belgium and Turkey refer to 2005; Ireland, Italy, the Netherlands, Poland, Portugal and the United Kingdom refer to 2006. All other countries refer to 2007.

Cashflows are discounted at a 3% interest rate.

Countries are ranked in descending order of the benefits (public+private) as a proportion of total (public+private), net present value for females immediately acquiring tertiary education , ISCED 5/6.

Source: OECD, Tables A9.3 and 9.4. See Annex 3 for notes (*www.oecd.org/edu/eag2011*).

StatLink http://dx.doi.org/10.1787/888932460610

Context

The financial benefits of completing higher levels of education motivate individuals to postpone consumption today for future rewards. From a policy perspective, awareness of economic incentives is crucial to understanding how individuals move through the education system. Large shifts in the demand for education can drive up earnings and returns considerably before supply catches up. This provides a strong signal, both to individuals and to the education system, of the need for additional investment.

In some countries, however, the labour market may not effectively signal demand because of rigid labour laws and structures that tend to compress wages across different educational groups. Apart from these labour-related issues, major components of the return to education are directly linked to policy: access to education, taxes and the costs of education for the individual. The economic benefits of education flow not only to individuals but also to society, in lower social transfers and in the additional taxes individuals pay once they enter the labour market. In shaping policies, it is important to consider the balance between private and public returns.

Other findings

- In Austria, Norway, Portugal, the United Kingdom and the United States, a man with an **upper secondary or post-secondary non-tertiary education can expect a gross earnings premium of more than USD 200 000** over his working life compared with a man who has not attained that level of education.
- **The value of the gross earnings premium for men and women with a tertiary education is substantial.** For example, over the course of their working lives, tertiary-educated men in Hungary, Ireland, Italy, Korea, Portugal, Slovenia and the United Kingdom can expect to earn at least USD 400 000 more than those with an upper secondary and post-secondary non-tertiary education. In the United States, this figure exceeds USD 600 000.
- On average across OECD countries with comparable data, **a woman who invests in tertiary education can expect a net gain of more than USD 100 000.** In Ireland, Korea, Portugal, Slovenia, the United Kingdom and the United States, the investment generates a net present value over USD 150 000 – a strong incentive to complete this level of education.
- **An individual invests an average of USD 50 000 to acquire a tertiary qualification,** when direct and indirect costs are taken into account. In Japan and the United States, this investment exceeds USD 100 000 in the case of a man who obtains a tertiary education.

Analysis

Financial returns on investment in education

The overall benefits of education can be assessed by estimating the economic value of the investment in education, which essentially measures the degree to which the costs of attaining higher levels of education translate into higher levels of earnings.

To understand how costs and benefits are shared between the private and public side, the calculation of benefits includes taxes, social contributions and social transfers as well as differences in the probability of finding work by educational level. The cost components include public and private direct costs, as well as foregone earnings while in school, adjusted for the probability of finding work, and for foregone taxes, social contributions and social transfers. This indicator relies on 2007 data or earlier latest available year.

In practice, raising levels of education will give rise to a complex set of fiscal effects beyond those taken into account here. As earnings generally increase with educational attainment, those individuals with higher levels of education consume more goods and services, and thus pay additional taxes on their consumption. Public returns are thus underestimated in the following calculations.

Individuals with higher earnings typically also pay more into their pension schemes and, after leaving the labour force, will have a further income advantage that is not taken into account in the calculations here. Similarly, many governments have schemes that provide loans to students at interest rates below those used in this exercise. These subsidies can often make a substantial difference in the returns to education for the individual. Given these factors, the returns on education in different countries should be assessed with caution.

Both costs and benefits are discounted back in time at a real discount rate of 3%, reflecting the fact that the calculations are made in constant prices (see Methodology section for further discussion of the discount rate). The economic benefits of tertiary education are compared to those of upper secondary education; for upper secondary education, below upper secondary education is used as a point of reference. In the calculations, women are benchmarked against women and men against men.

Incentives for the individual to invest in education

Upper secondary education or post-secondary non-tertiary education

Table A9.1 shows the value of each component and the net present value of the overall investment for a young woman and a young man attaining an upper secondary or a post-secondary non-tertiary education.

The direct costs of education for a man investing in an upper secondary or post-secondary non-tertiary education are usually negligible; the main investment cost is foregone earnings (Chart A9.2). Depending on the length of education, salary levels and the possibility of finding a job, foregone earnings vary substantially among countries. In Spain and Turkey, foregone earnings are less than USD 15 000, while in Austria, Italy and Norway, they exceed USD 35 000. Good labour-market prospects for young individuals who have not attained an upper secondary education increase the costs of further investment in education.

Gross earnings and reduced risk of unemployment over an individual's working life make up the benefit side. In most countries, men with an upper secondary or post-secondary non-tertiary education enjoy a significant earnings premium over those who have not attained that level of education. The value of reduced chances of unemployment can also be large. In the Czech Republic and Germany, the better employment prospects for men with this level of education are valued at USD 75 000 or more.

Additional education beyond compulsory schooling produces large returns from both the individual's and the public's perspective. A man who invests in upper secondary education or post-secondary non-tertiary education can expect a net gain of more than USD 78 000 during his working life over a man who has not attained that level of education. However, the amount varies significantly among countries: in the United Kingdom and the United States, this level of education generates over USD 150 000; but in Finland, Germany, Hungary, Poland and Turkey, the net benefits are less than USD 40 000 (Table A9.1).

Chart A9.2. Components of the private net present value for a man obtaining an upper secondary or post-secondary non-tertiary education, ISCED 3/4 (2007 or latest available year)

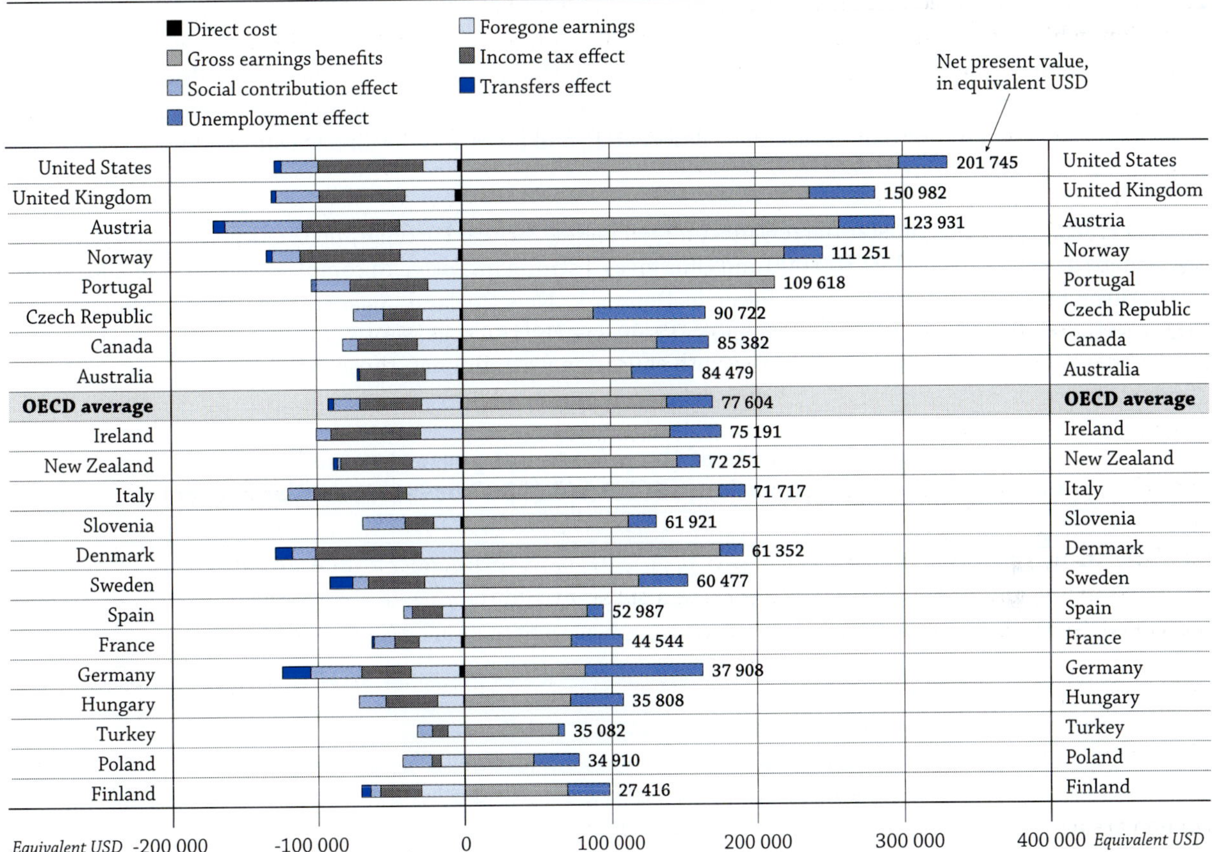

Notes: Australia, Belgium and Turkey refer to 2005; Italy, the Netherlands, Poland, Portugal and the United Kingdom refer to 2006. All other countries refer to 2007.
Cashflows are discounted at a 3% interest rate.
Countries are ranked in descending order of the net present value.
Source: OECD, Table A9.1. See Annex 3 for notes (*www.oecd.org/edu/eag2011*).
StatLink http://dx.doi.org/10.1787/888932460629

Men generally enjoy better financial returns on their upper secondary or post-secondary non-tertiary education than women, except in Hungary, Ireland, Italy, Poland and Spain. On average across OECD countries, a woman can expect a net gain of USD 63 000 over her working life. Some countries' social safety nets may work against women investing in further education and upper secondary education, in particular. In these countries, low wages for women who do not have an upper secondary education may be supplemented by social benefit schemes, removing some of the income advantage in completing an upper secondary education.

Tertiary education

The rewards to individuals with a tertiary education are, on average, twice as large as the rewards for those with an upper secondary education, reflecting the fact that an upper secondary education has become the norm in OECD countries. In some countries, individuals need to obtain tertiary education to reap the full financial rewards of education beyond compulsory schooling.

The rewards for investing in tertiary education are typically higher for men, except in Australia, Spain and Turkey, where the returns are higher for women (Table A9.3). On average across OECD countries, a woman investing in tertiary education can expect a net gain of USD 110 000, while a man can expect a net gain of almost USD 175 000.

The value of the gross earnings premium for men and women with tertiary education is substantial. Men in Hungary, Ireland, Italy, Korea, Portugal, Slovenia, the United Kingdom and the United States can expect to earn at least an additional USD 400 000 over their working lives compared to an individual with an upper secondary and post-secondary non-tertiary education.

Chart A9.3 shows the components of the returns on tertiary education for men in different countries. Compared with upper secondary and post-secondary non-tertiary education, the impact of unemployment benefits is less pronounced than the earnings differential; and taxes and the direct costs of education are more substantial.

Tertiary education brings substantial rewards for men in Italy, Korea, Portugal and the United States, where an investment generates over USD 300 000 and thus gives a strong incentive to complete this level of education. The returns on tertiary education are lower in Denmark, New Zealand, Sweden and Turkey, where a man with a tertiary education can expect a net gain of between USD 56 000 and USD 74000 over his working life.

Chart A9.3. Components of the private net present value for a man obtaining tertiary education, ISCED 5/6 (2007 or latest available year)

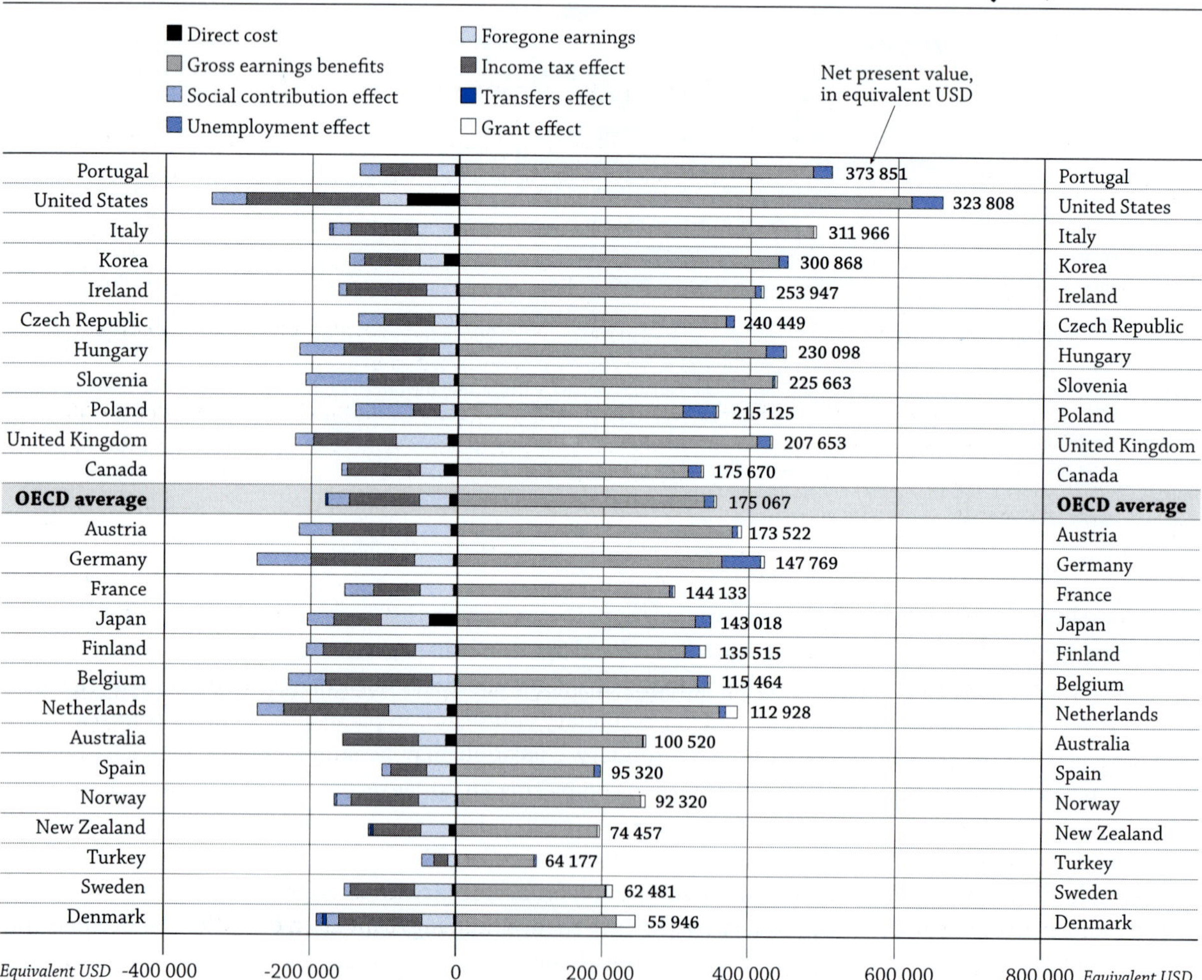

Notes: Australia, Belgium and Turkey refer to 2005; Italy, the Netherlands, Poland, Portugal and the United Kingdom refer to 2006. All other countries refer to 2007.
Cashflows are discounted at a 3% interest rate.
Countries are ranked in descending order of the net present value.
Source: OECD, Table A9.3. See Annex 3 for notes (*www.oecd.org/edu/eag2011*).
StatLink http://dx.doi.org/10.1787/888932460648

Much of the difference between countries is driven by earnings differentials. Factors such as supply and demand for highly educated individuals are important in some countries while the overall reward structure in the labour market (overall wage compression) plays an important role in other countries.

One way to mitigate weak labour market returns is to provide higher education at lower costs for the individual. Apart from subsidising the direct costs of education, a number of countries also provide students with loans and grants to improve incentives and access to education. Grants are particularly important in Austria, Denmark, Finland, the Netherlands and Sweden, where they make up more than 15% of the total investment cost (direct costs and foregone earnings). In Denmark, over 55% of the total private investment is covered by government grants.

Many countries also have favourable and substantial student loans that further lower investment costs and make investing more attractive (this will be further explored in forthcoming editions of *Education at a Glance*). Both grants and loans are particularly important tools for recruiting students from less affluent backgrounds. There is, of course, a danger in focusing only on the supply side of the investment. As younger generations become more mobile, a reward structure that does not adequately compensate more highly educated individuals could eventually lead to a loss of these individuals to countries with higher earnings potentials.

Box A9.1. **Estimating returns to education**

There are two main approaches to estimating the financial returns to education: one founded on financed-based investment theory, the other on labour economics-based econometric specification.

The basis for an investment approach is the discount rate (the time-value of money), which makes it possible to compare costs or payments (cash flows) over time. The discount rate can be estimated either by raising it to the level at which financial benefits equal costs, which is then the internal rate of return, or by setting the discount rate at a rate that takes into consideration the risk involved in the investment, which is then a net present value calculation, with the gains expressed in monetary units.

The econometric approach taken in labour economics originates from Mincer (1974). In this approach, returns to education are estimated in a regression relating earnings to years of education, labour market experience and tenure. This basic model has been extended in subsequent work to include educational levels, employment effects and additional control variables such as gender and work characteristics (part-time, firm size, contracting arrangements, utilisation of skills, etc.). The drawback of a regression approach is typically the scarcity of information beyond gross earnings to determine public and private returns, which makes it difficult to assess the actual incentives for individuals to invest in education.

Apart from availability of data, the main difference between the two approaches is that the investment approach is forward-looking (although historical data are typically used) whereas an econometric approach tries to establish the actual contribution of education to gross earnings by controlling for other factors that can influence earnings and returns. This distinction has implications for the assumptions and for the interpretation of returns to education. As the investment approach focuses on the incentives at the time of the investment decision, it is prudent not to remove the effects of (controlling for) other factors, such as work characteristics, as these are not known *ex-ante* and could be seen as part of the average returns that an individual can expect to receive when deciding to invest in education.

Depending on the impact of the control variables and how steep the earnings curves are, the results of the two approaches can diverge quite substantially. Returns may differ within discounting models, too, depending on other underlying assumptions, the size of cash flows and how these are distributed over the life span. It is therefore generally not advisable to compare rates of return from different approaches or studies.

There are some trade-offs between taxes and the direct costs of education (tuition fees) that are linked to government support for higher education. In countries with low or no tuition fees, individuals typically pay back public subsidies later in life through progressive tax schemes. In countries in which a larger portion of the investment falls on the individual, in the form of tuition fees, earnings differentials are larger and a larger portion of them accrues to the individual. In general there is a positive link, albeit a weak one, between the private direct costs of education and the overall net present value of the education.

Public rate of return on investments in education

Tables A9.2 and A9.4 show the public returns to individuals who obtain upper secondary or post-secondary non-tertiary and tertiary education as part of initial education. Chart A9.4 shows the public and private costs for men who invest in tertiary education. On average across OECD countries, over USD 85 000 is invested in a man's tertiary education, taking into account public and private spending, as well as indirect costs in the form of public and private foregone earnings and taxes. In Austria, Denmark, Japan, the Netherlands, Sweden, the United Kingdom and the United States, the value of investment costs exceeds USD 100 000 (Chart A9.4).

Chart A9.4. Public versus private investment for a man obtaining tertiary education, ISCED 5/6 (2007 or latest available year)

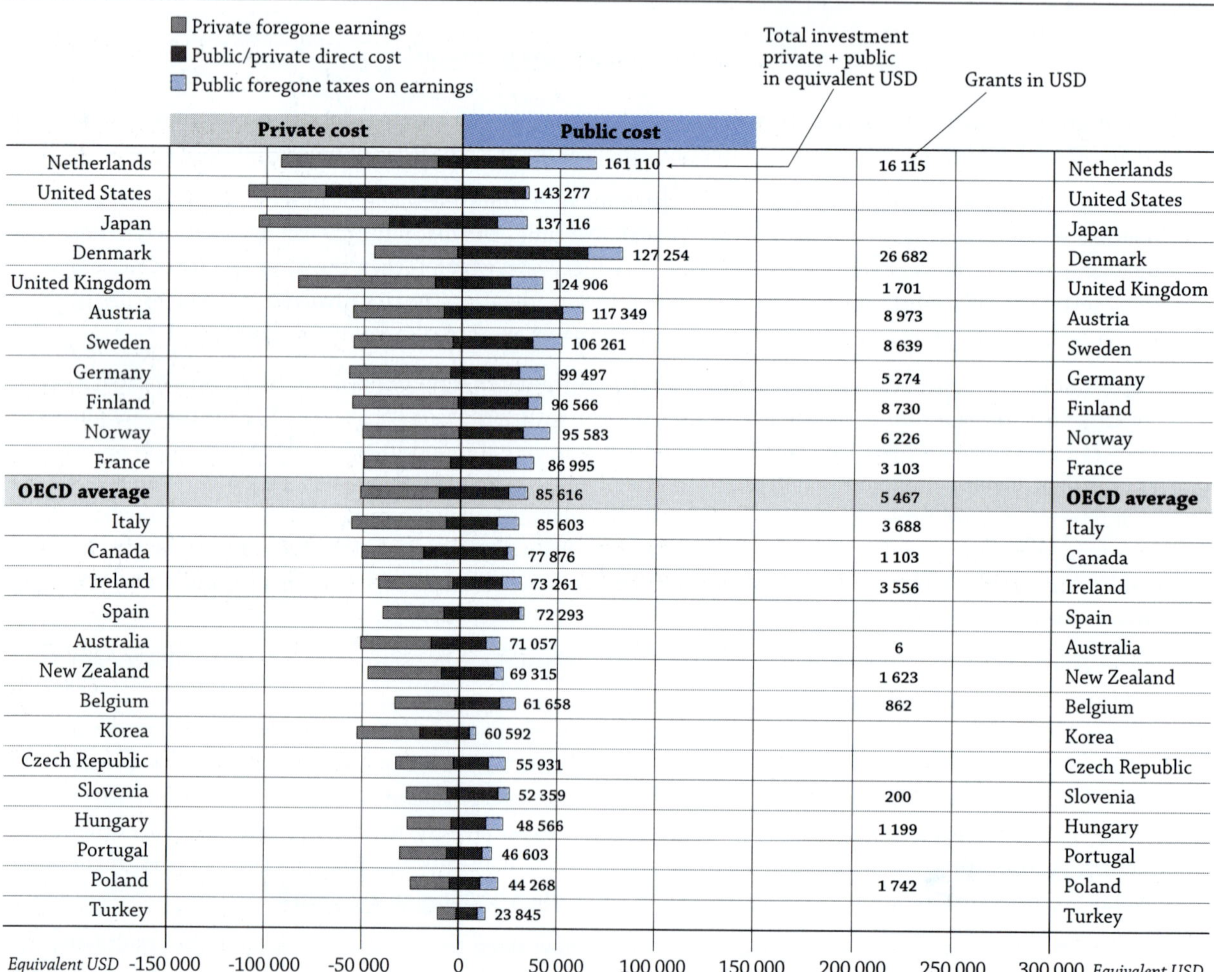

Notes: Australia, Belgium and Turkey refer to 2005; Italy, the Netherlands, Poland, Portugal and the United Kingdom refer to 2006. All other countries refer to 2007.
Cashflows are discounted at a 3% interest rate.
Countries are ranked in descending order of the total public + private cost.
Source: OECD, Tables A9.3 and A9.4. See Annex 3 for notes (*www.oecd.org/edu/eag2011*).
StatLink http://dx.doi.org/10.1787/888932460667

Direct costs for education are generally borne by the public sector, except in Australia, Japan, Korea, and the United States, where private direct costs such as tuition fees constitute over half of the overall direct investment costs. Together with foregone public earnings in the form of taxes and social contributions, direct and indirect public investment costs for a man with a tertiary education exceed USD 50 000 in Austria, Denmark, the Netherlands and Sweden. In Korea and Turkey, the total public investment cost does not exceed USD 15 000. On average among OECD countries, the total value of public investment for a man who obtains a tertiary qualification is USD 34 000 (Table A9.4).

Although public investments in tertiary education are large in many countries, private investment costs are larger in most countries. In Japan, the Netherlands, the United Kingdom and the United States, an individual invests over USD 80 000 to acquire a tertiary qualification when direct and indirect costs are taken into account. On average across OECD countries, direct costs, such as tuition fees, constitute approximately 20% of the total investment made by a tertiary graduate. In the United States, direct costs represent more than 60% of the investment, and in Canada, Japan and Korea, between 35%-40% (Table A9.3).

The decision to continue education at the tertiary level is a difficult one to take, since much is at stake, particularly for young individuals from less affluent backgrounds. To alleviate the financial burden, most countries provide grants to students. These are particularly large in Denmark (USD 25 700) and the Netherlands (USD 16 100). Note that these grants are not included in the private and public costs shown in Chart A9.4 but are displayed to illustrate the magnitude of these transfers between the private and public side. With the substantial private and public gains from tertiary investments, financial support in the form of grants and loans are important to ensure that people are not prevented from making these investments because of financial constraints.

For an individual, foregone earnings make up a substantial part of overall investment costs. In countries with lengthy tertiary education, such as Finland, Germany, the Netherlands and Sweden, foregone earnings are large (see Indicator B1). Earnings foregone also depend on expected wage levels and the probability of finding a job. As the labour market for young adults worsens (see Indicator C4) investment costs will fall. As higher-educated individuals typically fare better in the labour market in times of economic hardship, larger earnings differentials further improves the benefit side. The incentives to invest in education from both the private and public side are likely to be greater in most OECD countries in the coming years.

Investments in education also generate public returns from higher income levels in the form of income taxes, increased social insurance payments and lower social transfers. Chart A9.5 compares the public costs and economic benefits when a man invests in an upper secondary or post-secondary non-tertiary education and in tertiary education.

The public returns for a man investing in upper secondary or post-secondary non-tertiary education are positive in all countries. On average across OECD countries, this level of education generates a net return of USD 36 000; in Austria, the United Kingdom and the United States, it generates a net return of more than USD 70 000. The public returns to a woman investing in this level of education are USD 10 000 less than for a man, on average across OECD countries (Table A9.2). Nonetheless, the benefits are more than twice as large, on average, as the overall public costs for upper secondary or post-secondary non-tertiary education, for both men and women. In a few countries, students need to continue beyond upper secondary education for the public sector to reap the full benefits.

The public returns to tertiary education are substantially larger than the public returns to upper secondary or post-secondary non-tertiary education in part because a larger share of the investment costs are borne by the individuals themselves. The main contributing factors are, however, the higher taxes and social contributions that flow from the higher income levels of those with tertiary qualifications. In Belgium, Germany and the United States, these benefits exceeds USD 190 000 over an individual's working life (Chart A9.5).

On average across OECD countries, the net public return on an investment in tertiary education is over USD 90 000 for a man and USD 55 000 for a woman at this level of education. Even after taking into account student grants, the public benefits outweigh the costs by more than four times, on average. In Hungary and Korea, the benefits are 10 times larger than the public sector's initial investment in a student's tertiary education.

Chart A9.5. Public cost and benefits for a man obtaining upper secondary or post-secondary non-tertiary education and tertiary education (2007 or latest available year)

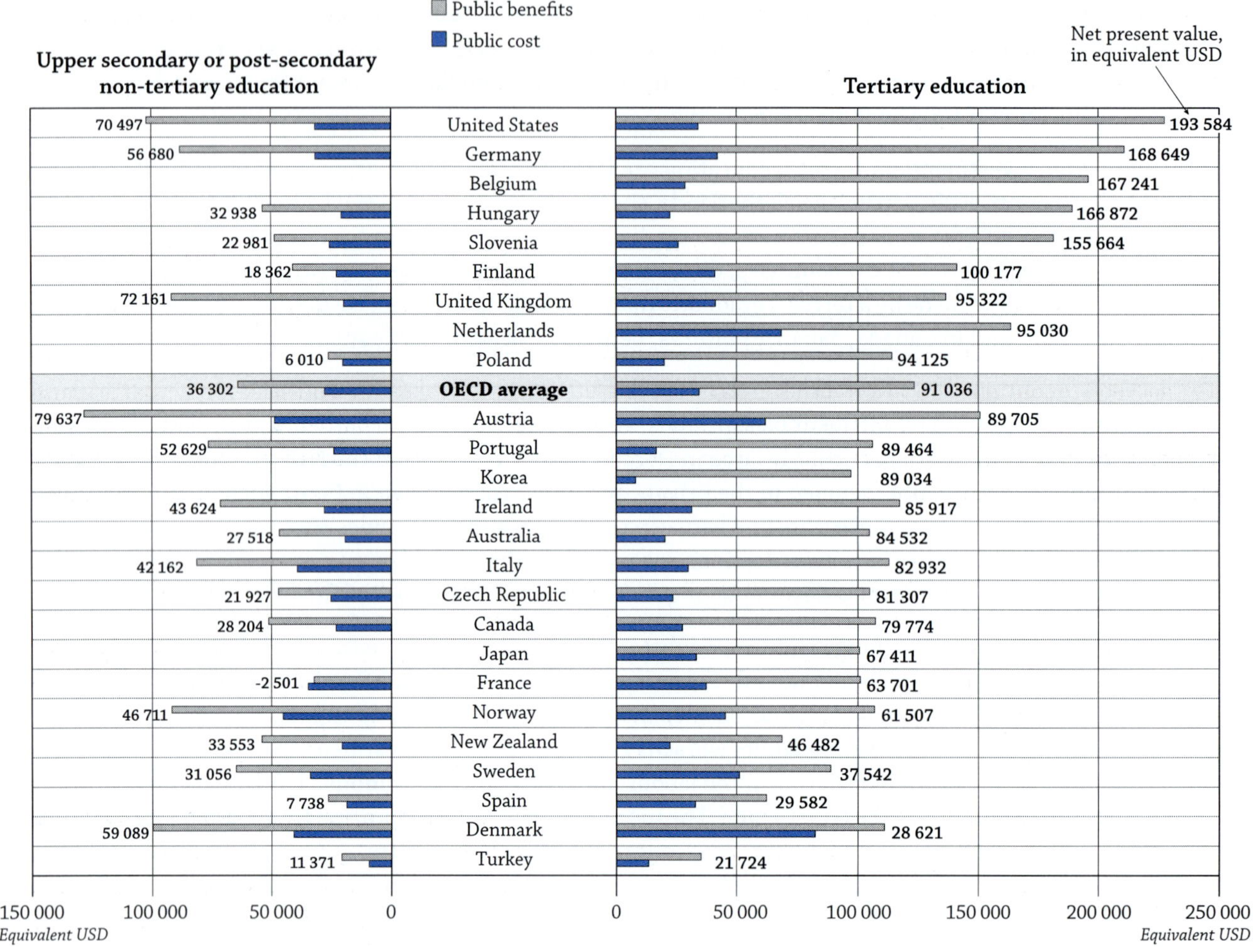

Notes: Korea is not included in the chart because of data-quality issues at that level. Japan is not included because the data at lower and upper secondary level of education are not broken down. The Netherlands are not included in the table because upper secondary education is compulsory.
Australia, Belgium and Turkey refer to 2005; Italy, the Netherlands, Poland, Portugal and the United Kingdom refer to 2006. All other countries refer to 2007.

Cashflows are discounted at a 3% interest rate.

Countries are ranked in descending order of the net present value at tertiary level of education.

Source: OECD, Tables A9.2 and A9.4. See Annex 3 for notes (*www.oecd.org/edu/eag2011*).

StatLink http://dx.doi.org/10.1787/888932460686

Returns on investments, taxation and labour-market rewards

The overall wage dispersion drives much of the returns for both the individual and the public sector. A compressed wage structure will typically generate lower returns to higher education. This is particularly true in the Nordic countries – Denmark, Norway and Sweden – and in New Zealand. The Nordic countries have generally offset the effects of this weak reward structure by providing a higher education system almost free of charge and by having a generous student-grant system; New Zealand has shared some of the direct costs with the individual and has kept income taxes low (see Indicator A10).

A number of countries have substantially larger overall income inequality, which is also reflected in the gross earnings benefits for those with tertiary education. In some countries with overall lower cost structures supply and demand appears to drive earnings differentials.

Although overall costs and income levels are low in the Czech Republic, Hungary, Poland, Portugal and Slovenia, higher education generates a substantially larger gross earnings premium over the working life than in the previous group of countries. Tertiary attainment levels in the working-age population are considerably below the OECD average (see Indicator A1), and the earnings premium has increased over the past decade in most of these countries (see Indicator A8). This suggests a short supply of higher-educated individuals, which has driven up wages and overall wage inequality over the years. As a result, the incentives are strong to make further investments, and this is also evident in the substantially higher entry rates into higher education in recent years (see Indicator A2). Given that the demand for more highly educated workers will continue to grow, it will take some time before a balance is reached.

The demand for higher-educated individuals appears to outpace the supply in other countries as well. Relative earnings have increased markedly over the past decade in Germany (by 22 percentage points), Italy and the United States (Table A8.2a). While tertiary attainment is high in the United States (41%), it is lower in Germany (26%) and substantially lower in Italy (15%) than the OECD average of 30% (Table A1.3a). To what extent the supply of higher-educated individuals matches the demand for them depends less on the overall level of tertiary-educated individuals and more on the industry structure and the pace of economic development. As a response to increasing demand and larger premiums, entry rates into tertiary education have increased in all three countries over the past 10 years, but less so in Italy and Germany where they are still below the OECD average (Table C2.2).

Given that the earnings premium and gross earnings benefits vary substantially among OECD countries, tax payments and benefits to the public sector also vary in ways that are somewhat contradictory to common perception. Because of low earnings premium in the Nordic countries, average tertiary earnings are typically below the income bracket where high marginal taxes are exercised. Instead, the largest public gains in tax and social security benefits from higher education typically occur in countries where earnings differentials are large or where average earnings levels reach high income-tax brackets.

The additional taxes and social contributions paid by those with a tertiary education are large in Belgium, Germany, Hungary, the Netherlands, Slovenia, and the United States, for example, stressing the importance for public policy to take a broad approach to strategic decisions on educational investments. Taxation and social policies also play an important role in promoting the supply of labour and are thus key to reaping the full benefits of the investments made in education.

It is important to note, however, that a number of countries have tax policies that effectively lower the actual tax paid by individuals, particularly by those in high income brackets. Tax relief for interest payments on mortgage debt have been introduced in many OECD countries to encourage homeownership. These schemes essentially favour those with higher education and high marginal taxes. The tax incentives for housing are particularly large in the Czech Republic, Denmark, Finland, Greece, the Netherlands, Norway, Sweden and the United States. For further information, see Andrews, *et al.* (2011).

Methodology

In calculating the returns to education, the approach taken here is the **net present value (NPV)** of the investment. In this framework, lifetime costs and benefits are transferred back to the start of the investment. This is done by discounting all cash flows back to the beginning of the investment with a set rate of interest (discount rate). The choice of interest rate is difficult, as it should reflect not only the overall time horizon of the investment, but also the cost of borrowing or the perceived risk of the investment. To keep things simple, and to make the interpretation of results easier, the same discount rate is applied across all OECD countries.

To arrive at a reasonable discount rate, long-term government bonds have been used as a benchmark. The average long-term interest rate across OECD countries was approximately 4.8% in 2007. Assuming that countries' central banks have succeeded in anchoring inflation expectations at or below 2% per year, a long-term nominal interest rate of 4.8% implies a real interest rate of 2.5% to 3%. The 3% real discount rate used in this indicator reflects the fact that calculations are made in constant prices. The change in the discount rate since the 2009 edition of *Education at a Glance* has a substantial impact on the net present value of education, and that must be taken into account if returns are compared across different editions of the publication.

Discounting the costs and benefits to the present value with this interest rate makes the financial returns on the overall investment and values of the different components comparable across time and countries. Using the same unit of analysis also has the advantage of making it possible to add or subtract components across different educational levels or between the private and public sectors to understand how different factors interact.

NPV calculations are based on the same method as **internal rate of return (IRR)** calculations. The main difference between the two methods lies in how the interest rate is set. For calculations developed within the IRR framework, the interest rate is raised to the level at which the economic benefits equal the cost of the investment and it pinpoints the discount rate at which the investment breaks even.

In calculating the NPV, private investment costs include after-tax foregone earnings adjusted for the probability of finding a job (unemployment rate) and direct private expenditures on education. Both of these investment streams take into account the duration of studies. On the benefit side, age-earnings profiles are used to calculate the earnings differential between different educational groups (below upper secondary education; upper secondary or post-secondary non-tertiary education; and tertiary education).

These gross earnings differentials are adjusted for differences in income taxes, social contributions and social transfers, including housing benefits and social assistance related to earnings level, to arrive at net earnings differentials. The cash flows are further adjusted for probability of finding a job (unemployment rates). The calculations are done separately for men and women to account for differences in earnings differentials and unemployment rates.

In calculating public NPV, public costs include lost tax receipts during the years of schooling (income tax and social contributions) and public expenditures, taking into account the duration of studies. Lost tax receipts are low in some countries because young individuals have low earnings levels. Public expenditures on education include direct expenditures, such as payment of teachers' salaries or spending for the construction of school buildings, purchase of textbooks, etc., and public-private transfers, such as public subsidies to households for scholarships and other grants and to other private entities for providing training at the workplace, etc. The benefits for the public sector are additional tax and social contribution receipts associated with higher earnings and savings on transfers, i.e. housing benefits and social assistance that the public sector does not have to pay because of higher levels of earnings.

It is important to consider some of the broad **conceptual limitations** on the estimates of financial returns discussed here:

- The data reported are accounting-based values only. The results no doubt differ from econometric estimates that would use the same data on the micro level rather than a lifetime stream of earnings derived from average earnings.
- The approach used here estimates future earnings for individuals with different levels of educational attainment, based on knowledge of how average present gross earnings vary by level of attainment and age. However, the relationship between different levels of educational attainment and earnings may differ in the future. Technological, economic and social changes may all alter how wage levels relate to levels of educational attainment.
- Differences in returns across countries partly reflect different institutional and non-market conditions that bear on earnings, such as institutional conditions that limit flexibility in relative earnings.
- In estimating benefits, the effect of education on the likelihood of finding employment when wanting to work is taken into account. However, this also makes the estimate sensitive to the stage in the economic cycle at which the data are collected. As more highly educated individuals typically have a stronger attachment to the labour market, the value of education generally increases in times of poor economic growth.

The calculations also involve a number of restrictive assumptions needed for international comparability. For calculating the investments in education, foregone earnings have been standardised at the level of the legal minimum wage or the equivalent in countries in which earnings data include part-time work. When no national minimum wage was available, the wage was selected from wages set in collective agreements. This assumption aims to counterbalance the very low earnings recorded for 15-24 year-olds that led to excessively high estimates in earlier editions of *Education at a Glance*. In the Czech Republic, Hungary, Japan, the Netherland, Portugal and the United Kingdom, actual earnings are used in calculating foregone earnings, as part-time work is excluded in these earnings data collections.

For the methods employed for calculating the rates of return, please see Annex 3 at *www.oecd.org/edu/eag2011*.

References

Andrews, D., Caldera Sánches, A. and A. Johansson (2011), "Housing Markets and Structural Policies in OECD Countries", *OECD Economics Department Working Papers*, No. 836, OECD, Paris.

Mincer, J. (1974), *Schooling, Experience, and Earnings*, National Bureau of Economic Research, New York.

OECD (2011), "A User's Guide to Indicator A9 – Incentives to Invest in Education" (available at *www.oecd.org/edu/eag2011*).

A9

Table A9.1. [1/2] Private net present value and internal rate of return for an individual obtaining upper secondary or post-secondary non-tertiary education as part of initial education, in equivalent USD (2007 or latest available year)

	Year	Direct cost	Foregone earnings	Total costs	Grosss earnings benefits	Income tax effect	Social contribution effect	Transfers effect	Unemployment effect	Total benefits	Net Present value	Internal rate of return
							MAN					
OECD												
Australia	2005	-2 891	-22 661	**-25 553**	114 598	-45 267	0	-1 364	42 065	**110 032**	84 479	14.4%
Austria	2007	-1 635	-40 820	**-42 456**	256 673	-66 828	-53 151	-8 227	37 919	**166 386**	123 931	12.3%
Belgium[1]												
Canada	2007	-2 642	-28 223	**-30 865**	131 999	-40 678	-10 499	0	35 426	**116 248**	85 382	12.2%
Chile		m	m	**m**	m	m	m	m	m	**m**	m	m
Czech Republic	2007	-1 870	-25 632	**-27 502**	88 484	-26 424	-20 613	0	76 777	**118 224**	90 722	14.3%
Denmark	2007	-547	-28 599	**-29 146**	174 294	-72 337	-15 813	-11 720	16 073	**90 497**	61 352	13.3%
Estonia		m	m	**m**	m	m	m	m	m	**m**	m	m
Finland	2007	-191	-29 402	**-29 592**	69 256	-27 948	-6 651	-6 392	28 744	**57 009**	27 416	7.5%
France	2007	-2 284	-28 513	**-30 797**	72 305	-16 559	-14 580	-1 082	35 258	**75 341**	44 544	8.7%
Germany	2007	-3 435	-33 027	**-36 462**	81 600	-33 742	-34 846	-19 501	80 860	**74 370**	37 908	7.4%
Greece		m	m	**m**	m	m	m	m	m	**m**	m	m
Hungary	2007	-814	-17 604	**-18 417**	71 585	-35 211	-18 296	0	36 147	**54 225**	35 808	10.9%
Iceland		m	m	**m**	m	m	m	m	m	**m**	m	m
Ireland	2006	-666	-28 309	**-28 975**	140 658	-61 467	-9 941	0	34 915	**104 166**	75 191	9.6%
Israel		m	m	**m**	m	m	m	m	m	**m**	m	m
Italy	2006	-884	-37 895	**-38 780**	173 902	-63 557	-17 786	0	17 938	**110 497**	71 717	7.2%
Japan[2]												
Korea[3]												
Luxembourg		m	m	**m**	m	m	m	m	m	**m**	m	m
Mexico		m	m	**m**	m	m	m	m	m	**m**	m	m
Netherlands[1]												
New Zealand	2007	-2 787	-32 043	**-34 830**	145 304	-49 007	-2 097	-2 992	15 872	**107 081**	72 251	9.0%
Norway	2007	-2 674	-39 641	**-42 315**	219 291	-68 618	-19 139	-4 147	26 179	**153 566**	111 251	13.2%
Poland	2006	-177	-16 120	**-16 297**	46 352	-6 124	-19 927	0	30 906	**51 207**	34 910	10.6%
Portugal	2006	-12	-23 445	**-23 456**	212 846	-53 287	-23 133	0	-3 353	**133 074**	109 618	11.5%
Slovak Republic		m	m	**m**	m	m	m	m	m	**m**	m	m
Slovenia	2007	-2 176	-18 284	**-20 460**	111 618	-19 595	-28 948	0	19 307	**82 381**	61 921	12.1%
Spain	2007	-1 348	-13 578	**-14 926**	83 112	-20 353	-5 965	0	11 119	**67 913**	52 987	9.5%
Sweden	2007	-22	-26 828	**-26 850**	118 530	-38 526	-10 616	-15 802	33 742	**87 328**	60 477	11.7%
Switzerland		m	m	**m**	m	m	m	m	m	**m**	m	m
Turkey	2005	-336	-11 218	**-11 554**	63 318	-10 584	-10 115	0	4 017	**46 637**	35 082	9.5%
United Kingdom	2006	-4 773	-34 026	**-38 799**	236 619	-58 798	-29 668	-3 350	44 978	**189 781**	150 982	13.5%
United States	2007	-2 872	-23 524	**-26 397**	297 360	-71 888	-25 293	-4 848	32 811	**228 142**	201 745	21.4%
OECD average		-1 668	-26 638	**-28 306**	138 557	-42 228	-17 956	-3 782	31 319	**105 910**	77 604	11.4%

1. Belgium and the Netherlands are not included in the table because upper secondary education is compulsory.
2. Japan is not included in the table because the data at lower and upper secondary level of education are not broken down.
3. Korea is not included in the table because of data-quality issues at that level.

Source: OECD. See Annex 3 for notes *(www.oecd.org/edu/eag2011)*.

Please refer to the Reader's Guide for information concerning the symbols replacing missing data.

StatLink http://dx.doi.org/10.1787/888932463289

Table A9.1. [2/2] **Private net present value and internal rate of return for an individual obtaining upper secondary or post-secondary non-tertiary education as part of initial education, in equivalent USD (2007 or latest available year)**

		Year	Direct cost	Foregone earnings	Total costs	Grosss earnings benefits	Income tax effect	Social contribution effect	Transfers effect	Unemployment effect	Total benefits	Net Present value	Internal rate of return
								WOMAN					
OECD	Australia	2005	-2 891	-23 380	**-26 271**	94 208	-29 950	0	-17 689	23 288	**69 857**	43 586	11.9%
	Austria	2007	-1 635	-39 437	**-41 073**	174 544	-27 749	-36 891	-24 746	24 375	**109 534**	68 461	8.9%
	Belgium[1]												
	Canada	2007	-2 642	-28 852	**-31 494**	131 145	-28 469	-13 553	-719	23 229	**111 632**	80 138	10.7%
	Chile		m	m	**m**	m	m	m	m	m	**m**	m	m
	Czech Republic	2007	-1 870	-22 236	**-24 106**	84 041	-20 163	-18 570	0	65 558	**110 866**	86 760	15.9%
	Denmark	2007	-547	-28 982	**-29 529**	131 336	-49 824	-12 498	0	14 882	**83 896**	54 366	11.1%
	Estonia		m	m	**m**	m	m	m	m	m	**m**	m	m
	Finland	2007	-191	-29 064	**-29 255**	46 963	-14 043	-4 657	-14 652	21 928	**35 538**	6 283	-1.5%
	France	2007	-2 284	-25 279	**-27 564**	57 780	-11 178	-12 193	-2 502	31 655	**63 562**	35 998	7.8%
	Germany	2007	-3 435	-33 213	**-36 648**	109 439	-29 559	-32 877	-35 152	44 706	**56 558**	19 910	5.6%
	Greece		m	m	**m**	m	m	m	m	m	**m**	m	m
	Hungary	2007	-814	-17 157	**-17 971**	73 201	-27 449	-17 656	0	30 554	**58 649**	40 678	10.9%
	Iceland		m	m	**m**	m	m	m	m	m	**m**	m	m
	Ireland	2006	-666	-28 326	**-28 993**	208 109	-25 953	-16 444	0	19 020	**184 733**	155 740	25.4%
	Israel		m	m	**m**	m	m	m	m	m	**m**	m	m
	Italy	2006	-884	-33 025	**-33 909**	137 400	-44 841	-15 224	0	28 616	**105 951**	72 042	8.5%
	Japan[2]												
	Korea[3]												
	Luxembourg		m	m	**m**	m	m	m	m	m	**m**	m	m
	Mexico		m	m	**m**	m	m	m	m	m	**m**	m	m
	Netherlands[1]												
	New Zealand	2007	-2 787	-31 353	**-34 139**	75 316	-17 930	-1 125	-12 048	10 971	**55 183**	21 044	6.3%
	Norway	2007	-2 674	-39 522	**-42 196**	131 887	-36 552	-11 685	-14 003	18 575	**88 222**	46 026	7.4%
	Poland	2006	-177	-13 249	**-13 425**	62 434	-7 066	-22 813	0	26 653	**59 207**	45 781	11.9%
	Portugal	2006	-12	-20 631	**-20 642**	150 215	-31 104	-17 731	0	10 416	**111 796**	91 153	20.8%
	Slovak Republic		m	m	**m**	m	m	m	m	m	**m**	m	m
	Slovenia	2007	-2 176	-18 557	**-20 733**	118 292	-16 877	-28 104	-708	9 009	**81 612**	60 879	11.3%
	Spain	2007	-1 348	-11 938	**-13 286**	114 657	-31 228	-8 554	0	19 656	**94 532**	81 246	13.7%
	Sweden	2007	-22	-26 139	**-26 161**	94 460	-31 299	-9 260	-20 376	38 890	**72 415**	46 253	9.6%
	Switzerland		m	m	**m**	m	m	m	m	m	**m**	m	m
	Turkey	2005	-336	-12 058	**-12 394**	75 879	-8 395	-9 432	0	-12 434	**45 618**	33 223	9.3%
	United Kingdom	2006	-4 773	-34 679	**-39 452**	211 146	-51 120	-25 797	-49 919	31 680	**115 990**	76 538	10.5%
	United States	2007	-2 872	-23 781	**-26 653**	230 500	-49 452	-20 044	-8 040	31 312	**184 276**	157 623	19.6%
	OECD average		-1 668	-25 755	**-27 424**	119 664	-28 105	-15 958	-9 550	24 407	**90 458**	63 035	11.2%

1. Belgium and the Netherlands are not included in the table because upper secondary education is compulsory.
2. Japan is not included in the table because the data at lower and upper secondary level of education are not broken down.
3. Korea is not included in the table because of data-quality issues at that level.

Source: OECD. See Annex 3 for notes *(www.oecd.org/edu/eag2011)*.

Please refer to the Reader's Guide for information concerning the symbols replacing missing data.

StatLink http://dx.doi.org/10.1787/888932463289

Table A9.2. [1/2] Public net present value and internal rate of return for an individual obtaining upper secondary or post-secondary non-tertiary education as part of initial education, in equivalent USD (2007 or latest available year)

		Year	Direct cost	Foregone taxes on earnings	Total costs	Income tax effect	Social contribution effect	Transfers effect	Unemployment effect	Total benefits	Net Present value	Internal rate of return
							MAN					
OECD	Australia	2005	-14 757	-4 357	**-19 114**	36 052	0	1 364	9 215	**46 632**	27 518	8.6%
	Austria	2007	-39 507	-9 061	**-48 568**	62 107	46 349	8 227	11 522	**128 205**	79 637	8.7%
	Belgium[1]											
	Canada	2007	-20 114	-2 859	**-22 974**	35 962	8 078	0	7 138	**51 178**	28 204	7.1%
	Chile		m	m	**m**	m	m	m	m	**m**	m	m
	Czech Republic	2007	-18 306	-6 804	**-25 110**	17 500	11 059	0	18 478	**47 037**	21 927	6.7%
	Denmark	2007	-28 705	-12 076	**-40 781**	67 770	13 925	11 720	6 455	**99 870**	59 089	8.7%
	Estonia		m	m	**m**	m	m	m	m	**m**	m	m
	Finland	2007	-19 061	-3 568	**-22 629**	22 243	4 710	6 392	7 646	**40 991**	18 362	7.6%
	France	2007	-29 063	-5 660	**-34 722**	12 887	9 800	1 082	8 452	**32 221**	-2 501	2.7%
	Germany	2007	-23 597	-7 812	**-31 410**	20 790	17 860	19 501	29 938	**88 089**	56 680	15.6%
	Greece		m	m	**m**	m	m	m	m	**m**	m	m
	Hungary	2007	-14 543	-6 026	**-20 569**	29 396	12 189	0	11 922	**53 507**	32 938	8.3%
	Iceland		m	m	**m**	m	m	m	m	**m**	m	m
	Ireland	2006	-20 729	-7 054	**-27 784**	56 783	8 256	0	6 369	**71 408**	43 624	7.1%
	Israel		m	m	**m**	m	m	m	m	**m**	m	m
	Italy	2006	-30 614	-8 568	**-39 181**	59 924	16 143	0	5 277	**81 343**	42 162	5.7%
	Japan[2]											
	Korea[3]											
	Luxembourg		m	m	**m**	m	m	m	m	**m**	m	m
	Mexico		m	m	**m**	m	m	m	m	**m**	m	m
	Netherlands[1]											
	New Zealand	2007	-16 527	-4 015	**-20 542**	45 654	1 891	2 992	3 559	**54 096**	33 553	8.0%
	Norway	2007	-34 470	-10 723	**-45 193**	63 445	17 112	4 147	7 199	**91 904**	46 711	7.7%
	Poland	2006	-12 824	-7 216	**-20 040**	4 246	11 991	0	9 813	**26 050**	6 010	4.4%
	Portugal	2006	-19 937	-3 854	**-23 791**	53 798	23 500	0	-879	**76 420**	52 629	7.7%
	Slovak Republic		m	m	**m**	m	m	m	m	**m**	m	m
	Slovenia	2007	-20 398	-5 164	**-25 562**	17 749	24 705	0	6 089	**48 543**	22 981	6.2%
	Spain	2007	-17 532	-1 048	**-18 580**	19 077	5 263	0	1 977	**26 317**	7 738	4.3%
	Sweden	2007	-26 133	-7 755	**-33 888**	31 370	8 273	15 802	9 500	**64 944**	31 056	9.7%
	Switzerland		m	m	**m**	m	m	m	m	**m**	m	m
	Turkey	2005	-4 776	-4 551	**-9 327**	9 997	9 514	0	1 188	**20 699**	11 371	6.4%
	United Kingdom	2006	-15 838	-3 817	**-19 655**	51 838	25 919	3 350	10 709	**91 815**	72 161	10.1%
	United States	2007	-30 470	-1 063	**-31 533**	66 801	22 796	4 848	7 585	**102 029**	70 497	10.4%
	OECD average		-21 805	-5 860	**-27 664**	37 399	14 254	3 782	8 531	**63 967**	36 302	7.7%

1. Belgium and the Netherlands are not included in the table because upper secondary education is compulsory.
2. Japan is not included in the table because the data at lower and upper secondary level of education are not broken down.
3. Korea is not included in the table because of data-quality issues at that level.

Source: OECD. See Annex 3 for notes *(www.oecd.org/edu/eag2011).*

Please refer to the Reader's Guide for information concerning the symbols replacing missing data.

StatLink http://dx.doi.org/10.1787/888932463308

Table A9.2. [2/2] **Public net present value and internal rate of return for an individual obtaining upper secondary or post-secondary non-tertiary education as part of initial education, in equivalent USD (2007 or latest available year)**

		Year	Direct cost	Foregone taxes on earnings	Total costs	Income tax effect	Social contribution effect	Transfers effect	Unemployment effect	Total benefits	Net Present value	Internal rate of return
		WOMAN										
OECD	Australia	2005	-14 757	-4 495	**-19 252**	25 858	0	17 689	4 092	**47 639**	28 387	17.2%
	Austria	2007	-39 507	-8 754	**-48 261**	27 007	32 530	24 746	5 103	**89 385**	41 124	7.1%
	Belgium[1]											
	Canada	2007	-20 114	-2 923	**-23 037**	26 822	12 040	719	3 161	**42 742**	19 705	5.8%
	Chile		m	m	**m**	m	m	m	m	**m**	m	m
	Czech Republic	2007	-18 306	-5 395	**-23 701**	13 867	10 427	0	14 439	**38 733**	15 032	5.9%
	Denmark	2007	-28 705	-12 238	**-40 943**	46 022	10 562	0	5 738	**62 322**	21 379	5.7%
	Estonia		m	m	**m**	m	m	m	m	**m**	m	m
	Finland	2007	-19 061	-3 527	**-22 588**	10 562	3 188	14 652	4 951	**33 353**	10 765	6.9%
	France	2007	-29 063	-5 018	**-34 081**	8 626	7 905	2 502	6 841	**25 873**	-8 207	1.8%
	Germany	2007	-23 597	-7 856	**-31 454**	25 731	23 521	35 152	13 184	**97 588**	66 134	12.5%
	Greece		m	m	**m**	m	m	m	m	**m**	m	m
	Hungary	2007	-14 543	-5 838	**-20 381**	23 484	12 493	0	9 129	**45 106**	24 725	6.9%
	Iceland		m	m	**m**	m	m	m	m	**m**	m	m
	Ireland	2006	-20 729	-7 059	**-27 788**	25 089	15 882	0	1 426	**42 396**	14 608	5.2%
	Israel		m	m	**m**	m	m	m	m	**m**	m	m
	Italy	2006	-30 614	-7 466	**-38 080**	40 842	12 613	0	6 610	**60 065**	21 984	4.8%
	Japan[2]											
	Korea[3]											
	Luxembourg		m	m	**m**	m	m	m	m	**m**	m	m
	Mexico		m	m	**m**	m	m	m	m	**m**	m	m
	Netherlands[1]		cf notes									
	New Zealand	2007	-16 527	-3 929	**-20 456**	15 897	984	12 048	2 175	**31 104**	10 648	5.7%
	Norway	2007	-34 470	-10 691	**-45 161**	33 825	10 251	14 003	4 161	**62 240**	17 079	5.3%
	Poland	2006	-12 824	-5 684	**-18 508**	5 661	15 984	0	8 235	**29 879**	11 371	5.3%
	Portugal	2006	-19 937	-2 842	**-22 779**	30 147	16 590	0	2 098	**48 835**	26 056	6.1%
	Slovak Republic		m	m	**m**	m	m	m	m	**m**	m	m
	Slovenia	2007	-20 398	-5 241	**-25 639**	16 274	26 130	708	2 577	**45 690**	20 050	5.8%
	Spain	2007	-17 532	-921	**-18 453**	29 970	7 315	0	2 496	**39 781**	21 328	6.0%
	Sweden	2007	-26 133	-7 556	**-33 689**	23 870	6 567	20 376	10 122	**60 934**	27 246	9.2%
	Switzerland		m	m	**m**	m	m	m	m	**m**	m	m
	Turkey	2005	-4 776	-4 892	**-9 668**	10 025	11 264	0	-3 463	**17 827**	8 159	5.8%
	United Kingdom	2006	-15 838	1 057	**-14 781**	46 747	23 374	49 919	6 796	**126 836**	112 055	21.9%
	United States	2007	-30 470	-1 074	**-31 544**	45 414	17 671	8 040	6 411	**77 536**	45 992	9.0%
	OECD average		-21 805	-5 350	**-27 155**	25 321	13 204	9 550	5 537	**53 613**	26 458	7.6%

1. Belgium and the Netherlands are not included in the table because upper secondary education is compulsory.
2. Japan is not included in the table because the data at lower and upper secondary level of education are not broken down.
3. Korea is not included in the table because of data-quality issues at that level.

Source: OECD. See Annex 3 for notes *(www.oecd.org/edu/eag2011)*.

Please refer to the Reader's Guide for information concerning the symbols replacing missing data.

StatLink http://dx.doi.org/10.1787/888932463308

Table A9.3. Private net present value and internal rate of return for an individual obtaining tertiary education as part of initial education, in equivalent USD (2007 or latest available year)

		Year	Direct cost	Foregone earnings	Grosss earnings benefits	Income tax effect	Social contribution effect	Transfers effect	Unemployment effect	Grants effect	Net Present value	Internal rate of return
							MAN					
OECD	Australia	2005	-14 426	-36 420	255 043	-104 749	0	0	1 067	6	100 520	9.1%
	Austria	2007	-8 806	-46 643	371 437	-115 267	-45 311	0	9 139	8 973	173 522	10.4%
	Belgium	2005	-2 133	-30 842	330 069	-146 546	-50 240	0	14 294	862	115 464	11.9%
	Canada	2007	-18 549	-31 926	315 476	-100 857	-7 420	0	17 844	1 103	175 670	11.9%
	Chile		m	m	m	m	m	m	m	m	m	m
	Czech Republic	2007	-2 844	-29 602	366 844	-69 749	-35 043	0	10 843		240 449	17.6%
	Denmark	2007	-2 330	-42 645	220 552	-114 832	-16 666	-5 084	-8 731	25 682	55 946	9.4%
	Estonia		m	m	m	m	m	m	m	m	m	m
	Finland	2007	-1 543	-54 099	312 689	-127 081	-22 749	0	19 569	8 730	135 515	11.1%
	France	2007	-5 202	-44 540	290 891	-65 381	-38 676	0	3 938	3 103	144 133	10.7%
	Germany	2007	-5 387	-51 965	362 747	-142 711	-73 358	0	53 169	5 274	147 769	11.5%
	Greece		m	m	m	m	m	m	m	m	m	m
	Hungary	2007	-3 873	-22 318	421 782	-130 630	-59 816	0	23 754	1 199	230 098	20.0%
	Iceland		m	m	m	m	m	m	m	m	m	m
	Ireland	2006	-3 759	-39 460	406 325	-110 604	-10 170	0	8 058	3 556	253 947	13.9%
	Israel		m	m	m	m	m	m	m	m	m	m
	Italy	2006	-6 977	-48 756	485 212	-92 371	-24 098	0	-4 712	3 668	311 966	11.8%
	Japan	2007	-37 215	-66 750	326 614	-64 523	-36 039	0	20 931		143 018	7.4%
	Korea	2007	-19 846	-32 639	438 338	-77 162	-19 979	0	12 156		300 868	13.6%
	Luxembourg		m	m	m	m	m	m	m	m	m	m
	Mexico		m	m	m	m	m	m	m	m	m	m
	Netherlands	2006	-12 351	-80 305	360 261	-143 665	-35 935	0	8 808	16 115	112 928	7.4%
	New Zealand	2007	-9 132	-37 956	193 122	-67 773	-2 465	-94	-2 868	1 623	74 457	8.9%
	Norway	2007	-997	-49 289	252 817	-93 575	-19 454	0	-3 407	6 226	92 320	7.3%
	Poland	2006	-4 547	-19 838	308 019	-35 830	-79 920	0	45 499	1 742	215 125	21.4%
	Portugal	2006	-5 903	-24 146	484 640	-77 432	-28 586	0	25 278		373 851	18.5%
	Slovak Republic		m	m	m	m	m	m	m	m	m	m
	Slovenia	2007	-5 895	-20 705	430 880	-97 103	-84 520	0	2 805	200	225 663	19.1%
	Spain	2007	-8 074	-31 483	188 521	-49 829	-12 490	0	8 674		95 320	9.0%
	Sweden	2007	-4 362	-50 741	204 867	-89 279	-8 060	0	1 417	8 639	62 481	7.1%
	Switzerland		m	m	m	m	m	m	m	m	m	m
	Turkey	2005	-1 061	-9 402	106 985	-18 682	-16 424	0	2 761		64 177	19.3%
	United Kingdom	2006	-13 536	-70 193	410 276	-113 696	-24 502	0	17 604	1 701	207 653	11.2%
	United States	2007	-69 907	-39 313	618 300	-180 894	-46 747	0	42 369		323 808	11.3%
	OECD average		-10 746	-40 479	338 508	-97 209	-31 947	-207	13 210	5 467	175 067	12.4%
							WOMAN					
OECD	Australia	2005	-14 426	-36 370	219 590	-72 697	0	0	14 976	6	111 078	11.3%
	Austria	2007	-8 806	-46 444	286 848	-80 191	-52 581	0	4 322	8 973	112 121	9.8%
	Belgium	2005	-2 133	-29 666	255 955	-102 599	-56 606	0	36 372	862	102 183	14.5%
	Canada	2007	-18 549	-32 640	221 289	-57 157	-17 636	0	10 678	1 103	107 088	11.1%
	Chile		m	m	m	m	m	m	m	m	m	m
	Czech Republic	2007	-2 844	-25 441	221 063	-52 199	-30 754	0	24 704		134 529	16.0%
	Denmark	2007	-2 330	-42 572	134 157	-49 751	-10 916	-4 666	1 950	25 682	51 555	11.4%
	Estonia		m	m	m	m	m	m	m	m	m	m
	Finland	2007	-1 543	-53 726	186 268	-66 033	-14 136	-2 625	19 460	8 730	76 394	9.0%
	France	2007	-5 202	-42 461	190 775	-39 009	-28 156	0	15 155	3 103	94 206	9.9%
	Germany	2007	-5 387	-52 667	243 123	-75 011	-56 960	-306	26 665	5 274	84 732	8.4%
	Greece		m	m	m	m	m	m	m	m	m	m
	Hungary	2007	-3 873	-20 252	229 315	-96 706	-42 183	0	18 694	1 199	86 195	14.3%
	Iceland		m	m	m	m	m	m	m	m	m	m
	Ireland	2007	-3 759	-39 374	373 640	-114 344	-28 582	0	11 528	3 556	202 664	17.7%
	Israel		m	m	m	m	m	m	m	m	m	m
	Italy	2006	-6 977	-45 725	181 641	-62 065	-16 963	0	1 722	3 668	55 301	7.0%
	Japan	2007	-37 215	-49 265	231 306	-20 848	-29 117	0	9 951		104 812	7.8%
	Korea	2007	-19 846	-33 982	295 653	-31 450	-21 324	-6 002	7 029		190 077	7.8%
	Luxembourg		m	m	m	m	m	m	m	m	m	m
	Mexico		m	m	m	m	m	m	m	m	m	m
	Netherlands	2006	-12 351	-77 857	249 090	-83 666	-42 675	0	14 120	16 115	62 777	6.2%
	New Zealand	2007	-9 132	-37 896	124 606	-31 672	-1 645	-4 563	2 239	1 623	43 560	7.3%
	Norway	2007	-997	-49 574	194 625	-55 174	-15 461	0	2 591	6 226	82 235	9.0%
	Poland	2006	-4 547	-15 268	182 337	-20 299	-58 532	0	44 285	1 742	129 717	20.4%
	Portugal	2006	-5 903	-20 483	355 880	-92 120	-36 253	0	9 848		210 968	18.4%
	Slovak Republic		m	m	m	m	m	m	m	m	m	m
	Slovenia	2007	-5 895	-20 090	319 493	-74 631	-74 593	0	22 535	200	167 020	17.7%
	Spain	2007	-8 074	-29 446	191 188	-50 145	-13 510	0	22 002		112 016	11.3%
	Sweden	2007	-4 362	-50 462	113 844	-33 618	-8 648	-107	9 969	8 639	35 256	5.8%
	Switzerland		m	m	m	m	m	m	m	m	m	m
	Turkey	2005	-1 061	-8 185	116 530	-21 267	-19 627	0	14 075		80 466	19.2%
	United Kingdom	2006	-13 536	-68 853	331 461	-76 300	-37 754	-343	19 056	1 701	155 432	8.8%
	United States	2007	-69 907	-40 273	372 672	-93 695	-29 957	0	18 952		157 793	8.6%
	OECD average		-10 746	-38 759	232 894	-62 106	-29 783	-744	15 315	5 467	110 007	11.5%

Source: OECD. See Annex 3 for notes *(www.oecd.org/edu/eag2011)*.

Please refer to the Reader's Guide for information concerning the symbols replacing missing data.

StatLink http://dx.doi.org/10.1787/888932463327

Table A9.4. **Public net present value and internal rate of return for an individual obtaining tertiary education as part of initial education, in equivalent USD (2007 or latest available year)**

		Year	Direct cost	Foregone taxes on earnings	Income tax effect	Social contribution effect	Transfers effect	Unemployment effect	Grants effect	Net Present value	Internal rate of return
						MAN					
OECD	Australia	2005	-13 209	-7 002	104 353	0	0	396	-6	84 532	12.4%
	Austria	2007	-51 546	-10 354	113 222	43 918	0	3 438	-8 973	89 705	6.8%
	Belgium	2005	-20 552	-8 132	142 138	48 240	0	6 407	-862	167 241	14.9%
	Canada	2007	-24 166	-3 234	97 358	6 425	0	4 494	-1 103	79 774	10.5%
	Chile		m	m	m	m	m	m	m	m	m
	Czech Republic	2007	-14 749	-8 735	68 078	33 885	0	2 828		81 307	12.9%
	Denmark	2007	-64 272	-18 007	117 724	17 609	5 084	-3 835	-25 682	28 621	4.0%
	Estonia		m	m	m	m	m	m	m	m	m
	Finland	2007	-34 358	-6 565	121 751	21 420	0	6 660	-8 730	100 177	8.9%
	France	2007	-28 412	-8 841	64 930	38 135	0	992	-3 103	63 701	7.5%
	Germany	2007	-29 854	-12 292	130 173	62 855	0	23 041	-5 274	168 649	12.6%
	Greece		m	m	m	m	m	m	m	m	m
	Hungary	2007	-13 612	-8 763	124 793	56 338	0	9 315	-1 199	166 872	21.8%
	Iceland		m	m	m	m	m	m	m	m	m
	Ireland	2006	-21 467	-9 833	109 079	9 816	0	1 878	-3 556	85 917	10.2%
	Israel		m	m	m	m	m	m	m	m	m
	Italy	2006	-18 847	-11 023	93 319	24 717	0	-1 567	-3 668	82 932	10.0%
	Japan	2007	-17 897	-15 254	62 285	33 612	0	4 665		67 411	8.4%
	Korea	2007	-5 185	-2 923	76 050	19 188	0	1 903		89 034	17.9%
	Luxembourg		m	m	m	m	m	m	m	m	m
	Mexico		m	m	m	m	m	m	m	m	m
	Netherlands	2006	-34 104	-34 351	141 871	34 115	0	3 613	-16 115	95 030	6.5%
	New Zealand	2007	-17 470	-4 756	68 519	2 502	94	-782	-1 623	46 482	9.3%
	Norway	2007	-31 963	-13 333	94 347	19 719	0	-1 036	-6 226	61 507	6.1%
	Poland	2006	-10 791	-9 092	32 030	69 015	0	14 706	-1 742	94 125	14.8%
	Portugal	2006	-11 848	-4 706	73 993	27 167	0	4 858		89 464	18.1%
	Slovak Republic		m	m	m	m	m	m	m	m	m
	Slovenia	2007	-19 911	-5 848	96 667	83 921	0	1 035	-200	155 664	16.3%
	Spain	2007	-30 308	-2 429	48 395	11 942	0	1 982		29 582	5.8%
	Sweden	2007	-36 490	-14 668	88 854	7 979	0	507	-8 639	37 542	5.1%
	Switzerland		m	m	m	m	m	m	m	m	m
	Turkey	2005	-9 567	-3 814	18 209	16 010	0	886		21 724	9.3%
	United Kingdom	2006	-24 919	-16 257	110 230	23 095	0	4 873	-1 701	95 322	10.4%
	United States	2007	-32 281	-1 776	171 718	43 611	0	12 312		193 584	15.7%
	OECD average		-24 711	-9 680	94 803	30 209	207	4 143	-5 467	91 036	11.1%
						WOMAN					
OECD	Australia	2005	-13 209	-6 993	69 331	0	0	3 366	-6	52 490	12.5%
	Austria	2007	-51 546	-10 309	79 460	51 803	0	1 509	-8 973	61 943	6.0%
	Belgium	2005	-20 552	-7 822	93 938	51 660	0	13 607	-862	129 970	17.5%
	Canada	2007	-24 166	-3 307	55 608	16 881	0	2 304	-1 103	46 218	9.2%
	Chile		m	m	m	m	m	m	m	m	m
	Czech Republic	2007	-14 749	-7 011	48 602	27 676	0	6 674		61 193	11.6%
	Denmark	2007	-64 272	-17 976	49 161	10 708	4 666	798	-25 682	-42 598	0.8%
	Estonia		m	m	m	m	m	m	m	m	m
	Finland	2007	-34 358	-6 520	61 806	12 819	2 625	5 545	-8 730	33 185	5.7%
	France	2007	-28 412	-8 428	37 259	26 098	0	3 808	-3 103	27 220	5.7%
	Germany	2007	-29 854	-12 458	70 549	51 359	306	10 063	-5 274	84 692	8.9%
	Greece		m	m	m	m	m	m	m	m	m
	Hungary	2007	-13 612	-7 539	91 824	39 014	0	8 052	-1 199	116 539	18.2%
	Iceland		m	m	m	m	m	m	m	m	m
	Ireland	2006	-21 467	-9 812	112 497	27 972	0	2 457	-3 556	108 091	12.4%
	Israel		m	m	m	m	m	m	m	m	m
	Italy	2006	-18 847	-10 338	61 193	16 803	0	1 033	-3 668	46 176	7.6%
	Japan	2007	-17 897	-10 654	20 218	27 924	0	1 822		21 414	6.2%
	Korea	2007	-5 185	-3 043	31 111	20 817	6 002	847		50 549	9.2%
	Luxembourg		m	m	m	m	m	m	m	m	m
	Mexico		m	m	m	m	m	m	m	m	m
	Netherlands	2006	-34 104	-26 483	81 979	39 014	0	5 348	-16 115	49 639	5.6%
	New Zealand	2007	-17 470	-4 749	31 220	1 616	4 563	480	-1 623	14 038	6.1%
	Norway	2007	-31 963	-13 410	54 712	15 260	0	663	-6 226	19 036	4.6%
	Poland	2006	-10 791	-6 870	17 158	47 139	0	14 534	-1 742	59 427	12.5%
	Portugal	2006	-11 848	-3 689	89 669	35 321	0	3 385		112 837	17.6%
	Slovak Republic		m	m	m	m	m	m	m	m	m
	Slovenia	2007	-19 911	-5 674	70 951	69 680	0	8 594	-200	123 439	13.4%
	Spain	2007	-30 308	-2 272	46 995	12 120	0	4 540		31 075	6.5%
	Sweden	2007	-36 490	-14 587	31 406	7 955	107	2 905	-8 639	-17 344	1.5%
	Switzerland		m	m	m	m	m	m	m	m	m
	Turkey	2005	-9 567	-3 320	19 194	17 528	0	4 171		28 006	9.1%
	United Kingdom	2006	-24 919	-8 719	73 039	36 048	343	4 967	-1 701	79 058	9.5%
	United States	2007	-32 281	-1 820	90 324	28 513	0	4 814		89 551	11.4%
	OECD average		-24 711	-8 552	59 568	27 669	744	4 651	-5 467	55 434	9.2%

Source: OECD. See Annex 3 for notes *(www.oecd.org/edu/eag2011)*.

Please refer to the Reader's Guide for information concerning the symbols replacing missing data.

StatLink http://dx.doi.org/10.1787/888932463346

INDICATOR A10

HOW EXPENSIVE ARE GRADUATES TO HIRE?

- Average annual labour costs for a tertiary worker vary substantially among OECD countries, from less than USD 20 000 in Poland to over USD 130 000 in Luxembourg.
- For workers in their prime years (45-54 year-olds), employers pay twice as much for a tertiary-educated worker, on average, as for someone without an upper secondary education.
- On average across OECD countries, an individual without an upper secondary education can expect to keep 62% of labour costs in net income while a tertiary-educated worker can expect to keep 56% of those costs.
- The most attractive wages for tertiary-educated individuals are found in Australia, Austria, Ireland, Luxembourg, the Netherlands, the United Kingdom and the United States, where average spending power exceeds USD 40 000 per year.

Chart A10.1. Net income for 45-54 year-olds as a percentage of labour costs (2009 or latest year available)

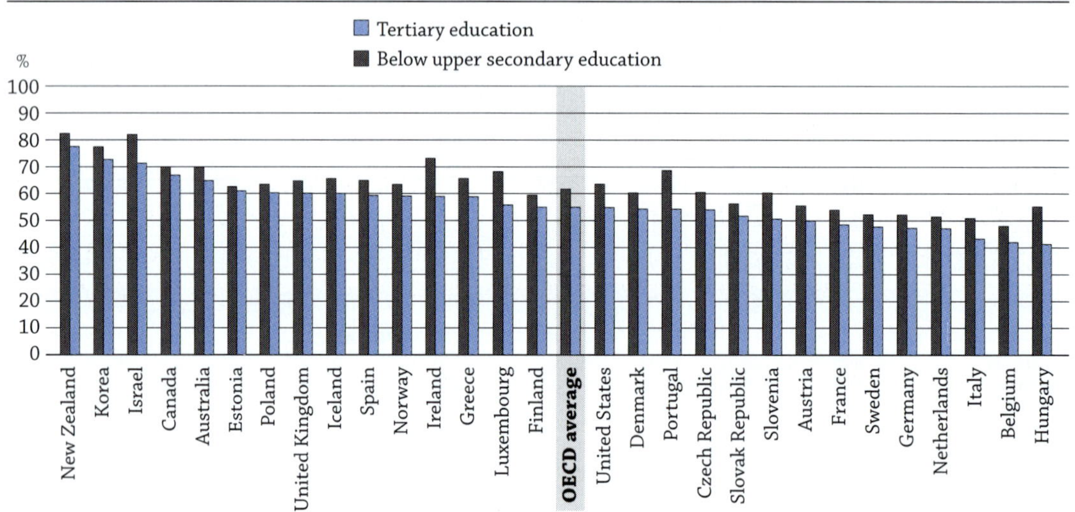

Countries are ranked in descending order of net income as a percentage of labour costs for tertiary-educated individuals.

Source: OECD, LSO Network special data collection on full-time, full-year earnings, Economic Working Group. Table A10.4. See Annex 3 for notes (*www.oecd.org/edu/eag2011*).

StatLink http://dx.doi.org/10.1787/888932460705

Context

The skills available in the labour force, and the price of those skills, determine how countries will fare in the global market. OECD countries face increasing competition in the lower and, more recently, mid-range skills segments. But even at these levels, many countries maintain a competitive advantage through technological advances, innovation and capital investments that boost productivity levels.

As services and production systems become more complex, they require workers with higher education. A highly-qualified workforce is thus important not only for jobs in the high-end skills sector, but also for maintaining an overall cost advantage in the lower skills segments. As the mobility of the global workforce increases, it becomes more important to strike the right balance between fostering overall equity in societies and offering strong economic incentives to attract and retain skilled workers.

Other findings

- **Annual labour costs increase substantially with educational attainment**. On average across the OECD area, a person without an upper secondary (ISCED 3/4) education costs USD 38 000, an individual with an upper secondary education costs USD 46 000, a tertiary-educated person costs USD 68 000 per year.

- In Austria, Denmark, Ireland, Italy, Luxembourg, the Netherlands, Norway and the United States, over the course of a year, employers pay at least USD 20 000 more than the OECD average to employ individuals with tertiary degrees. **The relative cost advantage in countries with overall low cost structures are among those with tertiary attainment**, even though within-country earnings differentials are typically large.

- On average across OECD countries, an employer can expect to pay an additional USD 25 000 per year for an experienced tertiary graduate (45-54 years old) compared to a recent graduate (25-34 years old); but that cost climbs to almost USD 40 000 for an experienced tertiary graduate over someone with similar experience who has not completed an upper secondary education. **This skills premium increases markedly if there is a short supply of highly-educated workers.**

- The difference in **average taxes and social contributions** paid on labour costs between workers with high and low levels of education is largely driven by earnings differentials. The difference is 10 percentage points or more in Hungary, Ireland, Israel, Luxembourg and Portugal, while in the Nordic countries it is typically below 5%.

- **The living standard** that accrues to an individual with a tertiary education varies substantially among OECD countries. Overall cost structures and labour-related tax policies influence net purchasing power. In Estonia, Hungary and Poland, those with a tertiary education can expect purchasing power under USD 20 000, while those in Luxembourg and the United States can expect purchasing power of more than USD 50 000.

Analysis

Labour costs by skills (educational) levels across OECD countries

This indicator is based on the earnings of individuals who work full-time, full-year, supplemented by employer cost data and employee income-tax data. A three-year average USD exchange rate is used to determine the comparative advantages and assess average tax rates for different educational groups across OECD countries. To further explore the attractiveness of labour markets across OECD countries, net income differences are also given in Purchasing Power Parities (see Table X2.1 for exchange rates).

Table A10.1 presents annual labour costs, gross earnings and net earnings based on a direct exchange-rate comparison and by a Purchasing Power Parity (PPP) adjusted comparison for three broad educational levels. Average labour costs have attracted considerable attention in cross-country comparisons in recent years. However, average labour costs say little about the price that employers need to pay for different skills levels.

Among 25-64 year-olds, annual labour costs increase sharply for both men and women with higher levels of education. On average across OECD countries, labour costs for those without an upper secondary education are USD 41 000 for men and USD 31 000 for women. Labour costs increase at the upper secondary level to USD 51 000 for men and USD 38 000 for women. The largest increase in labour costs is for highly-skilled workers: employers pay USD 77 000, on average, for a tertiary-educated man and USD 55 000 for a woman with the same level of education.

Chart A10.2 shows how the price of labour varies among countries by educational attainment. On average, annual labour costs for men and women without an upper secondary education are USD 38 000; for those with an upper secondary education, USD 46 000; and for those with a tertiary education, USD 68 000.

Chart A10.2. Deviation from the OECD mean in annual labour costs, by educational attainment

In equivalent USD for 25-64 year-old population

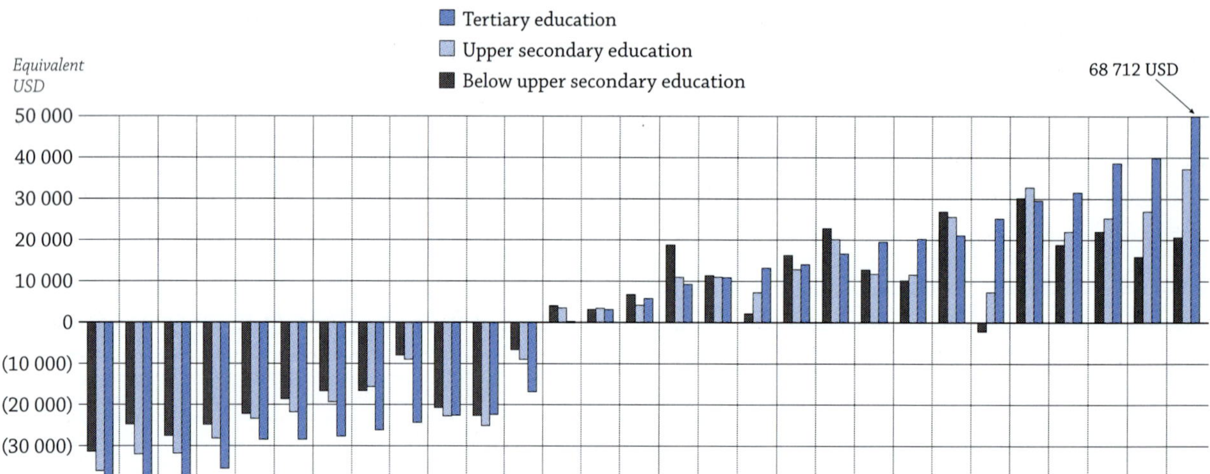

Countries are ranked in ascending order of the deviation from the OECD mean in annual labour costs of tertiary-educated individuals.

Source: OECD, LSO Network special data collection on full-time, full-year earnings, Economic Working Group. Table A10.1. See Annex 3 for notes (*www.oecd.org/edu/eag2011*).

StatLink http://dx.doi.org/10.1787/888932460724

The overall cost structure in Estonia, Hungary, Poland, Portugal and the Slovak Republic is considerably lower than in other OECD countries, and annual labour costs are at least USD 20 000 below the OECD average across all educational levels. Even though these countries have among the largest earnings differentials for tertiary-educated individuals (see Indicator A8), their relative cost advantage is still in the high-end skills segment. This suggests that earnings differentials will stay well above those in other OECD countries until a balance is reached between supply and demand.

There is a substantial cost advantage in the high-end skills market in Greece, Israel, Korea, New Zealand and Spain, where those with higher education are relatively inexpensive compared to their less-educated peers. In the Czech Republic and Slovenia, the cost advantage is similar across all educational groups. Canada, France and Iceland deviate little from the OECD average in all segments. A few countries with overall higher cost levels show decreasing labour costs as educational levels rise. From an OECD perspective, in Belgium, Denmark, Finland and Sweden, individuals with tertiary education are less expensive to employ than their counterparts with less education. A compressed wage structure and strong labour unions may explain these results to some extent.

Average labour costs for individuals with higher education increase substantially in other countries. In Austria, Ireland, Italy, Luxembourg, the Netherlands, Norway and the United States, annual labour costs are higher than the OECD average by some USD 20 000 or more, largely as a result of an overall higher cost structure and higher productivity differentials between educational categories.

Labour costs in the high-end skills segment

Given their overall high cost structure, OECD countries typically face stronger competition in the lower skills segments, where products and services are easier to imitate and where production can be shifted to low-cost countries. Their pricing power is still in the high-end skills market, even if labour costs are higher. This is also evident from other labour market-based indicators in *Education at a Glance*, which suggests that those with higher education face better job prospects (see Indicator A7) and, in many countries, also increasing premiums on their educational investments (see Indicator A8).

Employers pay an additional premium not only for education but also for labour-market experience. A comparison between tertiary labour costs for 25-34 year-old men who recently graduated and those of 45-54 year-old men with 20-30 years of experience in the labour market indicates that costs vary substantially among countries. On average across the OECD area, an employer can expect to pay an additional USD 29 000 (approximately 50% more) per year for an experienced tertiary graduate. In Italy and Portugal, employers pay 120% or more for an experienced tertiary worker, while in Estonia, new graduates are paid more than their experienced peers (Tables A10.2 and A10.4).

However, the main difference in labour costs is linked to skills levels. Chart A10.3 compares the skills premium among 45-54 year-olds (labour costs for tertiary-educated individuals compared to individuals without an upper secondary education) and tertiary attainment levels for the same age group. For a tertiary graduate, labour costs vary from over 3.5 times as much as those for an individual without an upper secondary education in Portugal, to less than 1.5 times as much in Denmark, Finland and New Zealand. The skills premium falls as the level of tertiary attainment rises.

The skills premium for experienced workers is particularly high in countries with low educational attainment. In the Czech Republic, Poland, Portugal and Slovenia, labour costs are three times as high for tertiary workers as for those without an upper secondary education, and fewer than 20% of individuals attain a tertiary education. This suggests that having too few highly educated individuals leads to upward pressure on labour costs as employers compete for a small pool of skilled workers. The labour costs for tertiary graduates in the United States are more than 2.5 times those for individuals without an upper secondary education, even though educational attainment levels are high (40%). This is likely a reflection that demand still outstrips even a relatively large supply of tertiary graduates, or that productivity differentials between these two educational categories are particularly large.

Chart A10.3. Labour cost ratio and attainment levels (2009 or latest year available)

Labour cost ratio of tertiary educated individuals (ISCED 5/6) to below upper secondary individuals (ISCED 0/1/2) and attainment levels of 45-54 year-olds

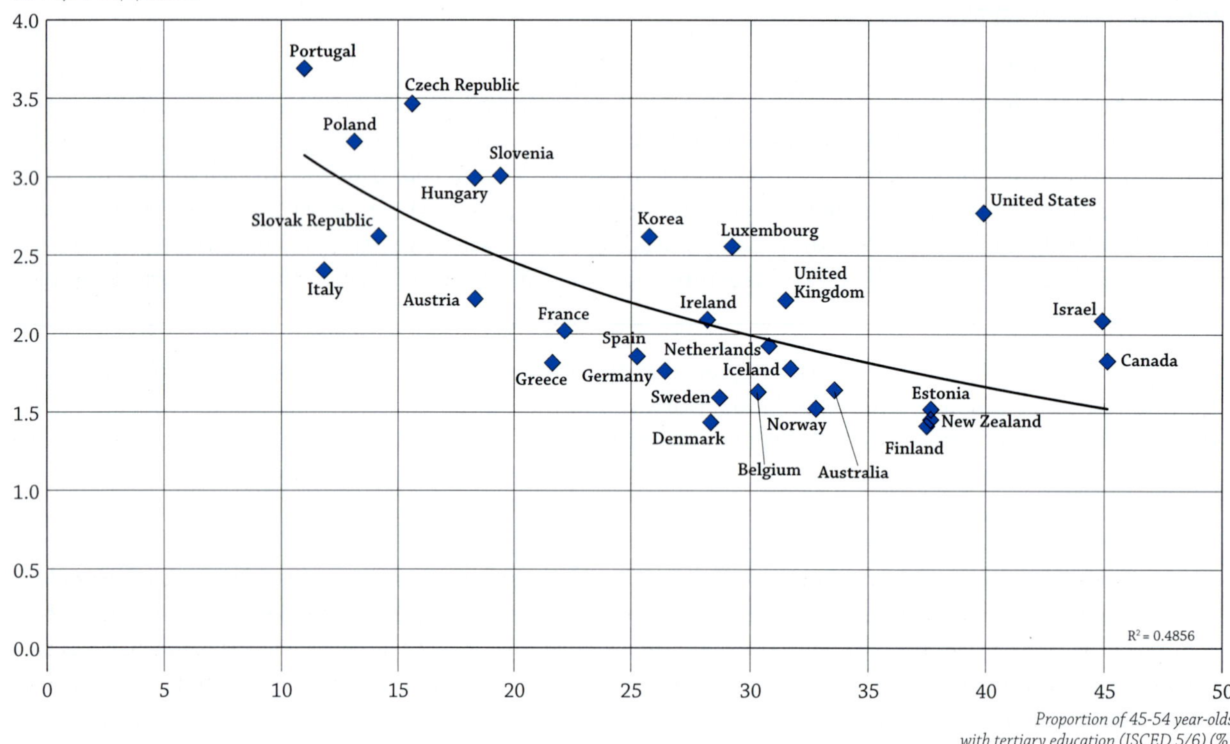

Source: OECD, LSO Network special data collection on full-time, full-year earnings, Economic Working Group. Tables A10.4 and A1.3a. See Annex 3 for notes (*www.oecd.org/edu/eag2011*).

StatLink http://dx.doi.org/10.1787/888932460743

Attractiveness of labour markets in OECD countries

Tables A10.1 through A10.5 also provide information on net earnings by ISCED levels in Purchasing Power Parity (PPP)-adjusted USD to gauge the attractiveness of labour markets from the individual's perspective. As illustrated in the introductory chart (Chart A10.1), there are substantial differences in labour-related tax policies. After accounting for employer non-tax compulsory payments, social contributions and income taxes, an individual with a tertiary education can expect to receive 70% or more of the total labour costs in Israel, Korea and New Zealand, while such an individual receives less than 50% of total labour costs in Belgium, France, Germany, Hungary, Italy, the Netherlands and Sweden.

The reward structure and overall tax rates have an impact on individuals' net income. The overall cost structure in different countries further determines the purchasing power of net earnings. Chart A10.4 shows the net annual income for a tertiary-educated individual in direct USD comparison (three-year average exchange rate) and PPP-adjusted USD. The highest net earnings are found in Ireland, Luxembourg and Norway, where those with a tertiary education can expect to receive over USD 55 000 annually (direct USD comparison).

The picture changes substantially once earnings are adjusted for the overall cost structure in countries. The highest living standards for those with a tertiary education are found in Luxembourg and the United States, where purchasing power is over USD 50 000, and in Australia, Austria, Ireland, the Netherlands and the United Kingdom, where purchasing power is USD 40 000 or more. Countries with lower overall cost structures typically gain in income comparisons from adjusting for purchasing power.

Chart A10.4. Net income in USD for 25-64 year-olds with a tertiary education (2009 or latest year available)

Unadjusted three-year average exchange rate and Purchasing Power Parity-adjusted exchange rate

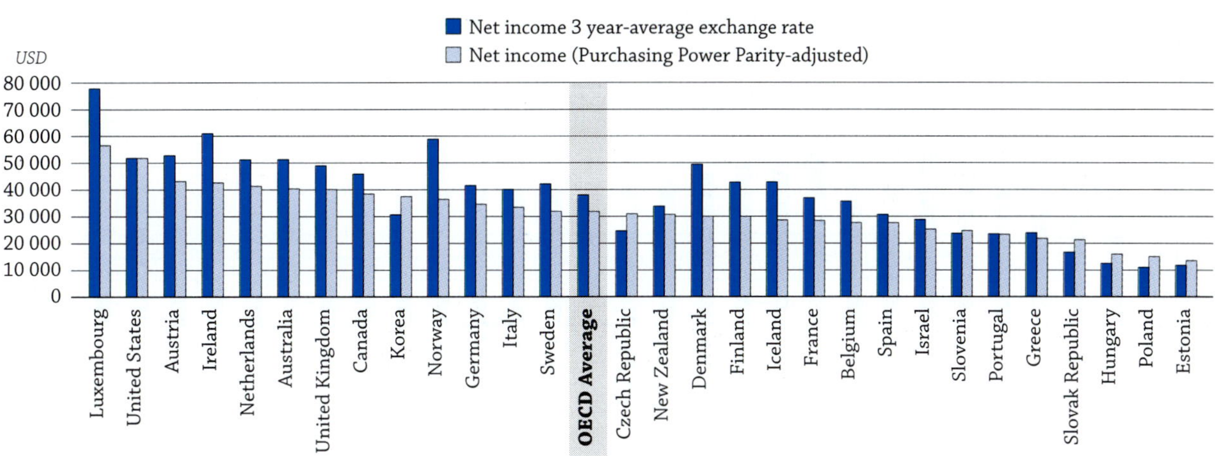

Countries are ranked in descending order of PPP-adjusted net income.

Source: OECD, LSO Network special data collection on full-time, full-year earnings, Economic Working Group. Table A10.1. See Annex 3 for notes (*www.oecd.org/edu/eag2011*).

StatLink http://dx.doi.org/10.1787/888932460762

Direct private educational costs (tuition fees) explain some of the differences between countries in the purchasing power adjustment of tertiary net earnings. Countries with low tuition fees and generous grant schemes that, in many cases, make university attendance an income-generating endeavour, are typically also the countries where the PPP adjustment has its largest impact (see, for instance, Denmark, Finland, the Netherlands, Norway and Sweden in Indicator A9).

The purchasing power adjustments for private consumption do not usually account for these public services and transfers, thus caution is needed in interpreting comparisons of PPP-adjusted income among countries. The purchasing power is somewhat lower in some countries because the net income needs to be saved (or loans to be repaid) for tertiary studies. The direct costs for a tertiary education, discounted at 3%, is more than USD 10 000 in Australia and the United Kingdom, close to USD 20 000 in Canada and Korea, and close to USD 70 000 in the United States (see Indicator A9).

With these caveats in mind, Chart A10.5 shows the PPP-adjusted net income differences by ISCED levels as a measure of the living standards people with different educational levels can expect across OECD countries.

The largest absolute gains in living standard are enjoyed by those with a tertiary education in Austria, the Czech Republic, Luxembourg, the Netherlands, the United Kingdom and the United States, where a person with a tertiary education can expect to have between USD 12 000 and USD 20 000 in additional annual spending power. On average across OECD countries, a tertiary education generates close to USD 9 000 and an upper secondary education close to USD 4 000 in additional net purchasing power every year.

The after-tax gains in purchasing power between those without an upper secondary education and those with a tertiary education is smallest in Belgium, Denmark, Estonia, Finland and Sweden, where this difference is less than USD 8 000 per year. The highest net earnings among those with low levels of education are found in Australia, Ireland, Luxembourg, the Netherlands and Norway, where an individual without an upper secondary education can expect to earn (PPP) USD 25 000 per year.

While factors other than potential earnings can spur migration flows, economic considerations are likely to become more influential as labour markets become more global, particularly for those with higher educational attainment. Chart A10.6 shows the proportion of foreign-born individuals with a tertiary degree and the purchasing power (USD) that someone with tertiary attainment can expect in different OECD countries.

Chart A10.5. Net income differences by educational attainment in PPP-adjusted USD (2009 or latest year available)

25-64 year-olds

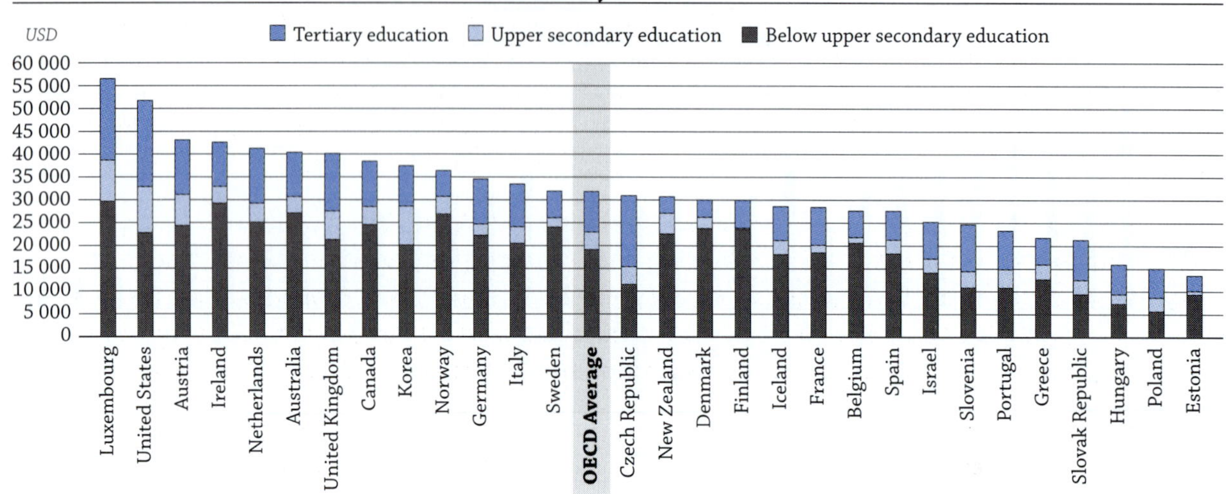

Countries are ranked in descending order of net income for those with tertiary education.

Source: OECD, LSO Network special data collection on full-time, full-year earnings, Economic Working Group. Table A10.1. See Annex 3 for notes (*www.oecd.org/edu/eag2011*).

StatLink http://dx.doi.org/10.1787/888932460781

Chart A10.6. Tertiary purchasing power (USD) and proportion of immigrants with tertiary education

Proportion of immigrants with tertiary education and annual net income for individuals with tertiary education, 25-64 year-olds

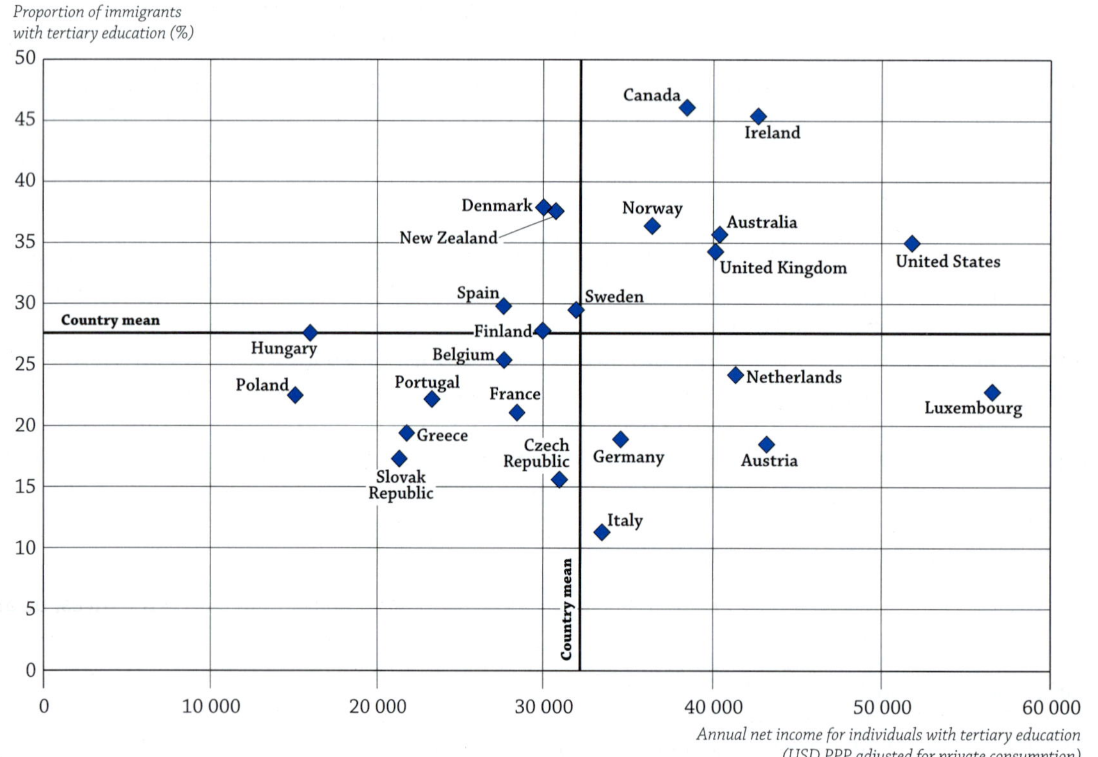

Source: OECD, LSO Network special data collection on full-time, full-year earnings, Economic Working Group. Table A10.1 and Table A10.6, available on line. See Annex 3 for notes (*www.oecd.org/edu/eag2011*).

StatLink http://dx.doi.org/10.1787/888932460800

Note that the data on educational attainment of the immigrant population is from 2003-04, and migration flows may have changed the overall composition to some extent in the past five years.

Some countries are able to attract more highly educated immigrants and/or provide the right incentives for foreign-born people to achieve higher educational attainment within the receiving country. The immigrant population in English-speaking countries are usually more skilled. Between 30% and 40% of the foreign-born population in Australia, New Zealand, the United Kingdom and the United States have a tertiary education; in Canada and Ireland, more than 45% of the immigrant population do (Table A10.6).

Immigrants in Denmark and Norway are similarly well-educated: at least 30% of them have a tertiary degree. The purchasing power of a tertiary-educated individual is above the OECD average in Austria, Germany, Italy, Luxembourg and the Netherlands, while the proportion of the immigrant population with tertiary education is low. The living standard that a tertiary-educated individual can expect to enjoy in different countries appears to play a less important role in the decision to migrate or to enter tertiary studies in the new home country.

Since education involves substantial investments, much can be gained by attracting highly skilled labour. Across OECD countries, a tertiary education cost approximately USD 80 000, after accounting for direct and indirect costs during tertiary studies (see Indicator A9). To this end, some countries have immigration policies to attract those with higher education. In general, it is becoming increasingly important to take a strategic view of education and skills in order to maintain a comparative advantage in trade and investment flows, and in the flow of people across countries.

Definitions

For the definition of **full-time earnings**, countries were asked whether they had applied a self-designated full-time status or a threshold value of typical number of hours worked per week. Ireland, Italy, Luxembourg, Portugal, Spain, Sweden and the United Kingdom reported self-designated full-time status; the other countries defined full-time status by the number of working hours per week. The threshold was 36 hours per week in Austria, Hungary and the Slovak Republic; 35 hours in Australia, Brazil, Canada, Estonia, Germany and the United States; and 30 hours in the Czech Republic, Greece and New Zealand. Other participating countries did not report a minimum normal number of working hours for full-time work. For some countries, data on **full-time, full-year earnings** are based on the European Survey on Income and Living Conditions (SILC), which uses a self-designated approach in establishing full-time status.

Not all countries were able to verify **full-time status** over the whole reference period for the earnings data. Hungary and New Zealand reported only full-time status at the time of the survey, while the surveys in the Czech Republic, Germany, Italy, Norway, the Slovak Republic and Spain verified full-time status over the whole reference period. For the other countries, full-time status was verified for a period similar to the length of the reference period, but the period may differ slightly from the reference period for earnings.

The **length of the reference period for earnings** also differed. Australia, New Zealand and the United Kingdom reported data on weekly earnings, while Belgium, Estonia, Finland, France, Hungary, Korea and Portugal reported monthly data. In Austria, the Czech Republic, Denmark, Germany, Greece, Israel, Italy, Luxembourg, the Netherlands, Norway, the Slovak Republic, Slovenia, Spain, Sweden and the United States, the reference period for the earnings data was 12 months. Earnings from full-time work can, in some instances, be affected by overtime hours worked in some countries, thus normal full-time earnings can be somewhat overstated. The full-time earnings data shown in this indicator thus differ across countries to some extent. In addition, immigration can sometimes affect earnings levels and can explain some of the differences among countries. Results should therefore be interpreted with caution.

Purchasing Power Parities (PPP) are the rates of currency conversion that equalise the purchasing power in different countries by eliminating differences in price levels between countries.

Methodology

The indicator is based on a new data collection on the earnings of individuals who work full-time and full-year, supplemented with information on employers' social contributions and non-tax compulsory payments from the OECD's *Taxing Wages Database*. Employers' social contributions (which are generally paid directly to government) and non-tax compulsory payments (which are stipulated by law but are typically paid into private insurance schemes) make up the additional compensation paid by employers on top of gross earnings. In some countries, social contributions are borne almost exclusively by the individual and paid out of the salary received. In this case, social contributions are included in gross earnings. Some countries apply a flat rate that is independent of the level of earnings while others have a progressive rate, floors or caps on social contributions, which change the level of contributions depending on the level of earnings.

OECD calculates taxes based on the Taxing Wages model. The annual *Taxing Wages* publication provides details of taxes paid on wages in all 34 OECD countries. The information contained in the report covers the personal income tax and social security contributions paid by employees and their employers, and cash benefits received by families. The results allow quantitative cross-country comparisons of labour-cost levels and the overall tax-and-benefit position of single persons and families. The 2010 edition of the *Taxing Wages Report* (OECD, 2010d) offers accurate estimates of the tax/benefit position of employees in 2009. It also shows definitive data on the tax/benefit position of employees for the year 2008 and tax burdens for the period 2000-09.

A three-year average USD exchange rate is used to take account of the comparative advantages of OECD countries from an employer's perspective. Purchasing Power Parity (for private consumption) – adjusted USD are used to compare spending power and living conditions from the individual's perspective (see Table X2.1 for exchange rates).

The education level of foreign-born 25-64 year-olds is based on data from the 2007 edition of the *International Migration Outlook*. As this data is some five years older than the earnings data, some caution is required in interpreting these data. The methodology used in this publication can differ to some extent from national sources because of, for instance, treatment of respondents with unknown educational levels.

The statistical data for Israel are supplied by and under the responsibility of the relevant Israeli authorities. The use of such data by the OECD is without prejudice to the status of the Golan Heights, East Jerusalem and Israeli settlements in the West Bank under the terms of international law.

References

OECD (2007b), *International Migration Outlook 2007*, OECD, Paris.

OECD (2010d), *Taxing Wages 2008-2009*, OECD, Paris.

The following additional material relevant to this indicator is available on line:

- ***Table A10.3. Annual labour costs, full-time gross and net earnings by ISCED levels in equivalent USD, 35-44 year-olds (2009 or latest available year)***
  StatLink http://dx.doi.org/10.1787/888932463403
- ***Table A10.5. Annual labour costs, full-time gross and net earnings by ISCED levels in equivalent USD, 55-64 year-olds (2009 or latest available year)***
  StatLink http://dx.doi.org/10.1787/888932463441
- ***Table A10.6. Education level of foreign- and native-born 25-64 year-olds in OECD countries, in percentage (2003-2004)***
  StatLink http://dx.doi.org/10.1787/888932463460

Table A10.1. [1/2] Annual labour costs, full-time gross earnings and annual net income, by ISCED levels in equivalent USD, 25-64 year-olds (2009 or latest available year)

				Annual labour costs			Gross annual full-time earnings			Annual net income			Annual net income		
				Three-year average exchange rate			Three year-average exchange rate			Three year-average exchange rate			PPP-adjusted exchange rate		
				0/1/2	3/4	5B/5A/6	0/1/2	3/4	5B/5A/6	0/1/2	3/4	5B/5A/6	0/1/2	3/4	5B/5A/6
	Year	Source	Gender	(1)	(2)	(3)	(4)	(5)	(6)	(7)	(8)	(9)	(10)	(11)	(12)
OECD Australia	2009	National	Men	53 552	61 793	89 543	46 404	53 545	77 591	36 798	41 584	56 837	28 985	32 754	44 769
			Women	40 934	44 910	64 474	35 471	38 915	55 869	29 746	31 968	43 175	23 430	25 180	34 008
			M+W	49 269	57 321	78 520	42 693	49 670	68 040	34 404	38 929	51 249	27 099	30 663	40 368
Austria	2009	National	Men	61 766	78 976	117 697	47 833	61 160	93 561	33 247	40 341	58 734	27 198	33 001	48 047
			Women	45 068	61 308	88 336	34 902	47 479	68 409	25 957	33 047	44 096	21 234	27 034	36 073
			M+W	53 804	73 291	107 502	41 667	56 758	84 077	29 771	38 061	52 762	24 354	31 136	43 162
Belgium	2009	National	Men	56 736	61 589	90 186	44 043	47 666	69 090	27 340	28 974	38 234	21 229	22 497	29 688
			Women	46 288	52 525	69 782	36 242	40 899	53 784	24 122	26 021	31 732	18 730	20 204	24 639
			M+W	54 166	59 178	81 671	42 124	45 867	62 661	26 573	28 162	35 627	20 633	21 867	27 663
Canada	2008	National	Men	46 627	55 506	77 717	41 841	50 306	71 623	32 054	37 727	51 953	26 870	31 626	43 552
			Women	30 365	39 840	55 392	27 252	35 712	50 197	22 325	28 056	37 652	18 715	23 519	31 563
			M+W	41 953	49 846	67 880	37 598	44 896	62 132	29 313	34 003	45 849	24 573	28 504	38 434
Chile				m	m	m	m	m	m	m	m	m	m	m	m
Czech Republic	2009	National	Men	17 285	22 938	50 361	12 899	17 118	37 583	10 208	13 115	27 215	12 841	16 498	34 234
			Women	13 341	18 289	34 055	9 956	13 648	25 414	8 180	10 724	18 831	10 290	13 490	23 688
			M+W	15 278	21 271	45 300	11 401	15 874	33 806	9 176	12 258	24 613	11 543	15 419	30 961
Denmark	2009	National	Men	69 973	78 538	100 461	69 566	78 131	100 054	42 057	45 599	53 749	25 572	27 725	32 681
			Women	57 858	63 125	77 094	57 451	62 718	76 686	35 171	38 188	45 062	21 385	23 219	27 398
			M+W	64 825	71 997	88 720	64 417	71 589	88 312	39 148	43 167	49 384	23 803	26 246	30 026
Estonia	2009	National	Men	15 725	17 631	24 925	11 746	13 170	18 618	9 627	10 731	14 960	11 064	12 334	17 194
			Women	9 091	10 612	16 901	6 791	7 927	12 624	5 780	6 662	10 308	6 643	7 656	11 847
			M+W	13 147	14 346	19 480	9 820	10 716	14 551	8 132	8 827	11 804	9 346	10 144	13 566
Finland	2009	National	Men	62 416	63 764	90 035	50 745	51 841	73 199	36 384	37 007	48 384	25 531	25 968	33 952
			Women	49 065	49 862	67 126	39 890	40 538	54 574	30 129	30 505	38 510	21 142	21 406	27 024
			M+W	56 688	57 290	76 893	46 088	46 577	62 515	33 724	34 008	42 720	23 665	23 864	29 977
France	2006	National	Men	51 569	54 324	83 916	36 240	38 175	58 911	26 596	27 918	41 131	20 498	21 516	31 700
			Women	32 828	40 988	61 474	26 068	30 464	43 200	20 488	22 652	31 349	15 790	17 458	24 161
			M+W	44 687	50 525	73 450	32 457	35 602	51 598	24 013	26 160	36 911	18 506	20 162	28 447
Germany	2009	National	Men	55 204	62 916	93 756	46 206	52 660	79 674	28 585	31 585	44 336	23 774	26 269	36 874
			Women	40 259	48 450	73 011	33 696	40 553	61 110	22 393	25 849	35 311	18 624	21 498	29 369
			M+W	50 688	58 084	87 175	42 425	48 616	73 764	26 767	29 721	41 556	22 262	24 719	34 562
Greece	2009	National	Men	24 316	29 506	45 779	18 988	23 041	35 748	15 950	18 735	26 740	14 547	17 086	24 388
			Women	14 596	22 253	33 648	11 397	17 377	26 275	9 574	14 597	20 772	8 732	13 313	18 945
			M+W	21 216	27 012	39 987	16 567	21 094	31 225	13 916	17 508	23 891	12 692	15 968	21 789
Hungary	2009	National	Men	11 384	15 136	37 177	8 594	11 416	27 926	6 149	7 513	14 964	7 861	9 605	19 130
			Women	9 414	13 772	24 978	7 090	10 394	18 789	5 307	7 125	10 669	6 784	9 108	13 640
			M+W	10 361	14 531	30 169	7 813	10 963	22 677	5 711	7 341	12 497	7 302	9 385	15 976
Iceland	2006	SILC	Men	45 790	54 477	87 223	40 107	47 715	76 397	29 610	34 197	51 489	19 788	22 854	34 410
			Women	34 140	38 578	54 998	29 903	33 790	48 172	23 458	25 801	34 472	15 677	17 243	23 038
			M+W	41 062	49 768	70 780	35 966	43 591	61 995	27 113	31 711	42 806	18 120	21 192	28 607
Ireland	2009	National	Men	57 668	74 764	112 853	52 070	67 507	101 899	42 309	50 029	67 490	29 546	34 937	47 130
			Women	52 343	57 739	81 435	47 262	52 135	73 530	39 080	42 342	53 042	27 290	29 568	37 040
			M+W	56 709	68 332	99 201	51 205	61 699	89 572	41 877	47 125	61 064	29 244	32 908	42 643
Israel	2009	National	Men	20 350	27 006	45 174	18 955	25 090	42 323	16 857	21 243	32 150	14 777	18 622	28 184
			Women	14 535	19 600	31 409	13 590	18 266	29 267	12 889	16 365	23 971	11 299	14 346	21 014
			M+W	19 276	24 553	39 216	17 968	22 819	36 671	16 153	19 614	28 784	14 160	17 194	25 233
Italy	2008	National	Men	51 725	64 474	105 150	37 082	46 222	75 383	26 183	31 507	46 394	21 854	26 298	38 724
			Women	37 925	48 119	68 502	27 189	34 497	49 110	20 105	24 586	32 990	16 781	20 522	27 536
			M+W	48 071	57 902	87 867	34 463	41 510	62 993	24 566	28 927	40 100	20 504	24 145	33 470
Japan				m	m	m	m	m	m	m	m	m	m	m	m
Korea	2008	National	Men	25 585	36 323	46 605	21 689	30 792	39 522	19 748	27 238	34 055	24 114	33 261	41 584
			Women	15 830	20 723	29 775	13 420	17 568	25 241	12 326	16 060	22 814	15 051	19 611	27 858
			M+W	21 263	30 679	41 506	18 025	26 007	35 186	16 470	23 434	30 668	20 111	28 615	37 449

Note: Labour costs include non-tax compulsory payments (NTCP) and employer social contributions based on OECD Taxing Wages Database (Centre for Tax Policy and Administration), except for the United States for which Bureau of Labor Statistics information is used and the United Kingdom for which EU Labour Cost Survey data is used. SILC: Statistics on Income and Living Conditions (Eurostat). USD based on three-year moving average of currency exchange rates (OECD annual exchange rates) and last three columns on net income in USD (PPP) Purchasing Power Parity-adjusted for private consumption (see Table X2.1 for exchange rates).

Source: OECD, LSO Network special data collection on full-time, full-year earnings, Economic Working Group.

Please refer to the Reader's Guide for information concerning the symbols replacing missing data.

StatLink http://dx.doi.org/10.1787/888932463365

Table A10.1. [2/2] Annual labour costs, full-time gross earnings and annual net income, by ISCED levels in equivalent USD, 25-64 year-olds (2009 or latest available year)

				Annual labour costs			Gross annual full-time earnings			Annual net income			Annual net income		
				Three-year average exchange rate			Three year-average exchange rate			Three year-average exchange rate			PPP-adjusted exchange rate		
	Year	Source	Gender	0/1/2	3/4	5B/5A/6	0/1/2	3/4	5B/5A/6	0/1/2	3/4	5B/5A/6	0/1/2	3/4	5B/5A/6
				(1)	(2)	(3)	(4)	(5)	(6)	(7)	(8)	(9)	(10)	(11)	(12)
OECD Luxembourg	2009	National	Men	63 254	88 508	153 423	55 987	78 340	135 797	43 349	55 538	85 960	31 512	40 373	62 487
			Women	47 152	69 404	106 298	41 734	61 431	94 085	34 242	46 493	63 862	24 892	33 798	46 423
			M+W	58 537	83 572	136 036	51 811	73 970	120 407	40 809	53 215	77 812	29 665	38 684	56 564
Mexico				m	m	m	m	m	m	m	m	m	m	m	m
Netherlands	2008	National	Men	61 702	74 983	114 078	48 675	59 012	91 441	31 870	37 643	54 272	25 732	30 394	43 820
			Women	48 634	58 241	83 567	38 899	46 008	65 693	26 891	30 391	41 360	21 712	24 538	33 395
			M+W	59 900	71 642	106 273	47 273	56 411	84 771	31 085	36 199	51 183	25 099	29 228	41 326
New Zealand	2009	National	Men	33 188	40 417	48 869	33 188	40 417	48 869	26 993	31 836	37 451	24 557	28 964	34 072
			Women	25 610	31 081	37 439	25 610	31 081	37 439	21 402	25 599	29 840	19 471	23 289	27 148
			M+W	29 953	37 380	43 323	29 953	37 380	43 323	24 833	29 801	33 783	22 593	27 112	30 735
Norway	2007	National	Men	74 405	87 410	115 327	65 025	76 353	100 670	46 994	54 088	67 511	29 098	33 490	41 802
			Women	56 450	63 239	78 219	49 384	55 298	68 347	36 953	40 750	49 127	22 880	25 231	30 418
			M+W	68 068	79 101	97 211	59 504	69 115	84 890	43 450	49 620	58 801	26 903	30 723	36 408
Poland	2006	SILC	Men	7 531	11 437	21 445	6 359	9 658	18 108	4 719	7 017	12 905	6 450	9 592	17 641
			Women	4 946	8 484	15 709	4 176	7 164	13 265	3 198	5 279	9 531	4 371	7 217	13 028
			M+W	6 559	10 298	18 233	5 538	8 695	15 395	4 147	6 347	11 015	5 668	8 675	15 057
Portugal	2009	National	Men	17 504	26 730	47 152	14 145	21 600	38 103	11 976	17 010	27 027	11 887	16 883	26 825
			Women	12 978	19 028	32 434	10 487	15 376	26 209	9 333	12 912	20 029	9 264	12 816	19 880
			M+W	15 697	22 953	39 210	12 684	18 548	31 685	10 866	15 011	23 497	10 785	14 899	23 322
Slovak Republic	2009	National	Men	15 601	20 446	37 840	10 729	14 062	26 132	8 547	10 884	19 352	10 949	13 944	24 791
			Women	11 342	15 401	25 942	7 801	10 592	17 855	6 492	8 450	13 558	8 317	10 826	17 369
			M+W	13 073	18 194	32 185	8 991	12 513	22 198	7 327	9 798	16 653	9 387	12 552	21 335
Slovenia	2009	National	Men	18 242	24 871	51 681	15 712	21 422	44 515	10 968	14 487	26 283	11 441	15 113	27 418
			Women	15 618	21 822	40 442	13 453	18 796	34 834	9 721	12 986	21 834	10 141	13 546	22 776
			M+W	17 179	23 602	45 089	14 797	20 329	38 836	10 369	13 866	23 673	10 817	14 464	24 695
Spain	2008	National	Men	33 502	40 846	54 198	25 790	31 444	41 723	21 552	25 544	32 475	19 400	22 993	29 232
			Women	25 366	31 874	46 609	19 528	24 537	35 881	17 125	20 660	28 535	15 415	18 597	25 686
			M+W	31 288	37 376	50 777	24 086	28 773	39 090	20 340	23 675	30 699	18 308	21 311	27 633
Sweden	2008	National	Men	62 867	70 040	101 110	43 231	48 164	69 530	32 772	36 147	47 740	24 835	27 393	36 178
			Women	52 304	58 646	67 238	35 968	40 329	46 237	27 654	30 731	34 828	20 957	23 288	26 393
			M+W	60 746	66 451	84 297	41 773	45 696	57 968	31 750	34 457	42 131	24 061	26 112	31 928
Switzerland				m	m	m	m	m	m	m	m	m	m	m	m
Turkey				m	m	m	m	m	m	m	m	m	m	m	m
United Kingdom	2009	National	Men	43 079	59 194	89 513	35 138	48 282	73 012	27 670	36 739	53 803	22 693	30 131	44 125
			Women	33 070	43 408	68 908	26 974	35 406	56 205	22 036	27 855	42 206	18 073	22 844	34 615
			M+W	40 049	53 601	80 843	32 666	43 720	65 940	25 964	33 591	48 923	21 294	27 549	40 124
United States	2009	National	Men	39 405	60 563	109 383	31 274	48 066	86 812	24 869	36 252	59 506	24 869	36 252	59 506
			Women	28 652	44 306	73 568	22 739	35 163	58 387	18 842	27 616	42 509	18 842	27 616	42 509
			M+W	35 701	53 659	92 863	28 334	42 586	73 701	22 793	32 859	51 793	22 793	32 859	51 793
OECD average			Men	41 309	50 521	77 330	34 147	41 806	63 925	25 241	29 939	42 521	20 671	24 771	35 660
			Women	31 241	38 470	55 475	26 011	31 864	45 748	20 032	23 802	32 137	16 274	19 586	26 844
			M+W	37 904	46 336	67 643	31 383	38 331	55 861	23 468	27 841	38 009	19 148	22 976	31 836
EU21 average			Men	40 907	49 600	77 273	32 942	40 004	62 381	23 717	27 813	40 102	19 353	22 883	33 631
			Women	31 404	38 731	56 357	25 569	31 346	45 418	19 190	22 765	30 877	15 551	18 664	25 758
			M+W	37 746	45 783	68 112	30 479	36 930	54 954	22 192	26 068	36 120	18 045	21 402	30 201
Other G20 Argentina				m	m	m	m	m	m	m	m	m	m	m	m
Brazil	2009	National	Men	m	m	m	5 391	9 890	25 762	m	m	m	m	m	m
			Women	m	m	m	3 476	6 125	15 602	m	m	m	m	m	m
			M+W	m	m	m	4 840	8 354	20 706	m	m	m	m	m	m
China				m	m	m	m	m	m	m	m	m	m	m	m
India				m	m	m	m	m	m	m	m	m	m	m	m
Indonesia				m	m	m	m	m	m	m	m	m	m	m	m
Russian Federation				m	m	m	m	m	m	m	m	m	m	m	m
Saudi Arabia				m	m	m	m	m	m	m	m	m	m	m	m
South Africa				m	m	m	m	m	m	m	m	m	m	m	m

Note: Labour costs include non-tax compulsory payments (NTCP) and employer social contributions based on OECD Taxing Wages Database (Centre for Tax Policy and Administration), except for the United States for which Bureau of Labor Statistics information is used and the United Kingdom for which EU Labour Cost Survey data is used. SILC: Statistics on Income and Living Conditions (Eurostat). USD based on three-year moving average of currency exchange rates (OECD annual exchange rates) and last three columns on net income in USD (PPP) Purchasing Power Parity-adjusted for private consumption (see Table X2.1 for exchange rates).

Source: OECD, LSO Network special data collection on full-time, full-year earnings, Economic Working Group.

Please refer to the Reader's Guide for information concerning the symbols replacing missing data.

StatLink http://dx.doi.org/10.1787/888932463365

Table A10.2. [1/2] Annual labour costs, full-time gross earnings and annual net income, by ISCED levels in equivalent USD, 25-34 year-olds (2009 or latest available year)

				Annual labour costs			Gross annual full-time earnings			Annual net income			Annual net income		
				Three year-average exchange rate			Three year-average exchange rate			Three year-average exchange rate			PPP-adjusted exchange rate		
				0/1/2	3/4	5B/5A/6	0/1/2	3/4	5B/5A/6	0/1/2	3/4	5B/5A/6	0/1/2	3/4	5B/5A/6
	Year	Source	Gender	(1)	(2)	(3)	(4)	(5)	(6)	(7)	(8)	(9)	(10)	(11)	(12)
OECD Australia	2009	National	Men	45 598	58 205	68 989	39 512	50 436	59 781	32 353	39 454	45 855	25 483	31 077	36 119
			Women	40 451	45 953	59 245	35 051	39 819	51 337	29 476	32 551	40 071	23 217	25 639	31 563
			M+W	44 355	54 730	64 308	38 435	47 425	55 725	31 658	37 457	43 077	24 936	29 504	33 930
Austria	2009	National	Men	53 833	62 820	92 673	41 690	48 649	71 768	29 784	33 707	45 836	24 365	27 574	37 496
			Women	41 121	50 277	69 267	31 845	38 935	53 642	24 234	28 231	36 447	19 825	23 095	29 815
			M+W	49 330	58 653	82 160	38 203	45 422	63 626	27 818	31 888	41 619	22 757	26 086	34 046
Belgium	2009	National	Men	51 406	54 826	74 146	40 063	42 617	57 043	25 644	26 796	33 201	19 912	20 806	25 779
			Women	38 849	44 510	59 633	30 940	34 914	46 206	22 253	23 713	28 315	17 279	18 412	21 986
			M+W	48 036	52 381	66 640	37 547	40 792	51 438	24 552	25 973	30 674	19 064	20 167	23 817
Canada	2008	National	Men	38 370	48 603	56 129	34 400	43 708	50 901	27 242	33 322	38 137	22 837	27 933	31 970
			Women	31 765	32 044	46 064	28 502	28 751	41 328	23 246	23 430	31 720	19 487	19 641	26 591
			M+W	36 634	43 351	51 355	32 850	38 851	46 338	26 292	30 112	34 996	22 040	25 243	29 336
Chile				m	m	m	m	m	m	m	m	m	m	m	m
Czech Republic	2009	National	Men	17 254	22 686	37 834	12 876	16 930	28 234	10 192	12 985	20 774	12 821	16 334	26 132
			Women	14 267	18 679	28 803	10 647	13 939	21 495	8 656	10 925	16 130	10 889	13 742	20 291
			M+W	16 279	21 450	34 422	12 149	16 007	25 688	9 691	12 350	19 020	12 190	15 535	23 925
Denmark	2009	National	Men	62 628	69 495	80 829	62 220	69 087	80 421	37 907	41 787	46 450	23 048	25 407	28 243
			Women	51 013	56 307	67 415	50 605	55 899	67 007	31 205	34 272	40 612	18 974	20 838	24 693
			M+W	58 847	64 127	73 747	58 440	63 719	73 340	35 743	38 754	43 817	21 733	23 563	26 642
Estonia	2009	National	Men	19 149	19 298	26 755	14 303	14 415	19 985	11 611	11 698	16 021	13 345	13 445	18 413
			Women	9 337	11 013	18 141	6 974	8 226	13 551	5 923	6 895	11 027	6 807	7 924	12 674
			M+W	15 649	16 237	21 773	11 689	12 129	16 264	9 582	9 923	13 133	11 013	11 405	15 094
Finland	2009	National	Men	57 799	58 963	73 738	46 991	47 937	59 949	34 248	34 789	41 360	24 033	24 412	29 023
			Women	46 321	46 943	59 419	37 660	38 165	48 308	28 835	29 129	35 000	20 234	20 440	24 560
			M+W	54 619	54 582	65 659	44 406	44 375	53 381	32 748	32 731	37 878	22 980	22 968	26 580
France	2006	National	Men	38 801	43 477	65 717	29 286	31 805	46 182	22 015	23 567	33 386	16 967	18 163	25 730
			Women	22 767	31 061	51 458	19 576	25 117	36 162	16 564	20 036	26 543	12 766	15 442	20 456
			M+W	33 928	39 903	58 779	26 661	29 879	41 307	20 769	22 298	30 056	16 007	17 185	23 164
Germany	2009	National	Men	42 248	53 050	70 673	35 362	44 403	59 153	23 246	27 724	34 469	19 334	23 058	28 668
			Women	35 678	44 868	62 123	29 863	37 554	51 997	20 395	24 356	31 282	16 962	20 257	26 018
			M+W	40 097	49 634	66 540	33 561	41 543	55 694	22 323	26 335	32 949	18 566	21 903	27 403
Greece	2009	National	Men	20 565	24 005	34 406	16 059	18 745	26 867	13 489	15 746	21 145	12 302	14 360	19 285
			Women	15 663	18 943	25 455	12 231	14 792	19 877	10 274	12 425	16 697	9 370	11 332	15 228
			M+W	19 677	22 263	28 970	15 365	17 384	22 622	12 907	14 603	18 471	11 771	13 318	16 846
Hungary	2009	National	Men	10 762	14 356	29 766	8 119	10 832	22 375	5 883	7 291	12 355	7 521	9 321	15 795
			Women	9 510	13 312	22 465	7 163	10 050	16 906	5 348	6 964	9 784	6 837	8 904	12 509
			M+W	10 295	13 945	25 764	7 763	10 524	19 377	5 683	7 174	10 946	7 266	9 171	13 993
Iceland	2006	SILC	Men	44 217	49 822	71 507	38 729	43 638	62 632	28 779	31 739	43 190	19 233	21 211	28 864
			Women	26 264	34 238	43 995	23 004	29 989	38 534	19 299	23 510	28 662	12 898	15 712	19 155
			M+W	39 032	44 667	55 371	34 187	39 123	48 499	26 041	29 017	34 669	17 403	19 392	23 169
Ireland	2009	National	Men	55 153	52 521	80 299	49 800	47 423	72 505	40 882	39 194	52 529	28 549	27 370	36 682
			Women	40 413	46 288	73 236	36 491	41 795	66 127	32 646	35 197	49 339	22 798	24 579	34 455
			M+W	51 712	50 030	76 485	46 693	45 174	69 061	38 675	37 597	50 806	27 008	26 255	35 479
Israel	2009	National	Men	18 259	22 103	32 990	17 032	20 566	30 767	15 485	18 007	24 946	13 575	15 785	21 869
			Women	12 844	16 157	24 542	12 008	15 100	22 809	11 389	14 107	19 606	9 984	12 366	17 188
			M+W	17 727	20 228	29 047	16 543	18 842	27 027	15 136	16 776	22 515	13 269	14 707	19 738
Italy	2008	National	Men	45 073	53 694	60 333	32 314	38 494	43 253	23 248	27 059	29 980	19 404	22 585	25 024
			Women	31 364	37 952	44 342	22 485	27 208	31 789	17 219	20 117	22 926	14 372	16 791	19 136
			M+W	41 795	47 325	52 266	29 963	33 928	37 470	21 806	24 238	26 431	18 201	20 231	22 062
Japan				m	m	m	m	m	m	m	m	m	m	m	m
Korea	2008	National	Men	23 029	25 393	32 201	19 523	21 526	27 298	17 821	19 600	24 502	21 761	23 933	29 919
			Women	22 703	20 428	25 002	19 246	17 318	21 195	17 573	15 836	19 305	21 458	19 337	23 574
			M+W	22 987	23 565	29 101	19 487	19 977	24 670	17 788	18 225	22 346	21 721	22 255	27 287

Note: Labour costs include non-tax compulsory payments (NTCP) and employer social contributions based on OECD Taxing Wages Database (Centre for Tax Policy and Administration), except for the United States for which Bureau of Labor Statistics information is used and the United Kingdom for which EU Labour Cost Survey data is used. SILC: Statistics on Income and Living Conditions (Eurostat). USD based on three-year moving average of currency exchange rates (OECD annual exchange rates) and last three columns on net income in USD (PPP) Purchasing Power Parity-adjusted for private consumption (see Table X2.1 for exchange rates).

Source: OECD, LSO Network special data collection on full-time, full-year earnings, Economic Working Group.

Please refer to the Reader's Guide for information concerning the symbols replacing missing data.

StatLink http://dx.doi.org/10.1787/888932463384

Table A10.2. [2/2] **Annual labour costs, full-time gross earnings and annual net income, by ISCED levels in equivalent USD, 25-34 year-olds (2009 or latest available year)**

		Year	Source	Gender	Annual labour costs: Three year-average exchange rate			Gross annual full-time earnings: Three year-average exchange rate			Annual net income: Three year-average exchange rate			Annual net income: PPP-adjusted exchange rate		
					0/1/2	3/4	5B/5A/6	0/1/2	3/4	5B/5A/6	0/1/2	3/4	5B/5A/6	0/1/2	3/4	5B/5A/6
					(1)	(2)	(3)	(4)	(5)	(6)	(7)	(8)	(9)	(10)	(11)	(12)
OECD	Luxembourg	2009	National	Men	47 828	62 499	118 314	42 333	55 319	104 721	34 655	42 936	69 514	25 192	31 212	50 532
				Women	37 869	53 501	86 741	33 519	47 354	76 776	28 438	37 981	54 715	20 672	27 609	39 774
				M+W	45 166	59 206	102 318	39 977	52 404	90 563	33 044	41 167	62 007	24 021	29 926	45 075
	Mexico				m	m	m	m	m	m	m	m	m	m	m	m
	Netherlands	2008	National	Men	51 710	59 763	80 449	41 175	47 165	63 266	27 983	31 025	40 002	22 594	25 050	32 298
				Women	43 345	50 838	69 208	34 985	40 529	54 517	25 012	27 674	35 139	20 195	22 344	28 372
				M+W	50 309	57 174	75 804	40 138	45 218	59 651	27 486	29 972	37 993	22 193	24 199	30 676
	New Zealand	2009	National	Men	30 422	35 132	39 235	30 422	35 132	39 235	25 163	28 295	31 044	22 893	25 742	28 243
				Women	24 283	30 955	35 996	24 283	30 955	35 996	20 354	25 515	28 873	18 517	23 213	26 268
				M+W	28 563	33 699	37 650	28 563	33 699	37 650	23 735	27 335	29 982	21 593	24 869	27 277
	Norway	2007	National	Men	65 965	79 337	88 403	57 672	69 321	77 218	42 274	49 752	54 565	26 175	30 805	33 786
				Women	49 151	56 144	67 039	43 026	49 117	58 608	32 871	36 782	42 875	20 353	22 774	26 547
				M+W	60 867	72 060	76 705	53 232	62 981	67 028	39 423	45 682	48 280	24 410	28 286	29 894
	Poland	2006	SILC	Men	8 438	9 801	16 004	7 125	8 276	13 514	5 253	6 055	9 704	7 180	8 276	13 264
				Women	5 761	6 841	12 370	4 864	5 777	10 445	3 677	4 313	7 566	5 026	5 895	10 342
				M+W	7 881	8 811	13 989	6 654	7 440	11 812	4 925	5 472	8 518	6 732	7 480	11 644
	Portugal	2009	National	Men	15 186	19 940	31 982	12 271	16 113	25 844	10 552	13 416	19 790	10 474	13 316	19 643
				Women	11 968	15 641	26 016	9 671	12 639	21 023	8 607	10 832	16 633	8 543	10 751	16 509
				M+W	13 968	17 756	28 421	11 287	14 349	22 966	9 783	12 131	17 905	9 710	12 041	17 772
	Slovak Republic	2009	National	Men	15 282	20 719	32 100	10 511	14 249	22 139	8 393	11 016	16 612	10 753	14 112	21 281
				Women	12 547	15 793	24 213	8 629	10 862	16 653	7 074	8 639	12 702	9 062	11 068	16 272
				M+W	14 230	18 939	28 507	9 787	13 026	19 639	7 886	10 157	14 830	10 102	13 013	18 998
	Slovenia	2009	National	Men	16 308	22 618	38 581	14 046	19 482	33 230	9 878	13 384	21 097	10 304	13 961	22 007
				Women	13 509	17 847	28 636	11 635	15 372	24 665	8 764	10 746	16 331	9 143	11 210	17 036
				M+W	15 694	20 785	32 421	13 518	17 902	27 925	9 764	12 401	18 185	10 185	12 936	18 970
	Spain	2008	National	Men	32 083	35 226	43 894	24 699	27 118	33 790	20 775	22 497	27 126	18 701	20 251	24 417
				Women	25 054	26 577	39 371	19 287	20 460	30 309	16 973	17 758	24 768	15 278	15 985	22 295
				M+W	30 294	31 704	41 646	23 321	24 407	32 060	19 795	20 568	25 959	17 818	18 514	23 367
	Sweden	2008	National	Men	60 168	62 307	78 106	41 375	42 846	53 711	31 471	32 508	39 947	23 849	24 635	30 272
				Women	56 400	48 339	54 424	38 784	33 241	37 426	29 641	25 731	28 683	22 462	19 499	21 736
				M+W	59 985	58 656	66 130	41 250	40 336	45 475	31 383	30 738	34 309	23 782	23 294	26 000
	Switzerland				m	m	m	m	m	m	m	m	m	m	m	m
	Turkey				m	m	m	m	m	m	m	m	m	m	m	m
	United Kingdom	2009	National	Men	37 563	50 267	72 369	30 639	41 001	59 028	24 565	31 715	44 154	20 147	26 011	36 212
				Women	30 734	40 982	61 802	25 068	33 427	50 410	20 722	26 489	38 207	16 994	21 725	31 335
				M+W	35 878	47 240	67 374	29 264	38 532	54 954	23 617	30 012	41 343	19 369	24 613	33 907
	United States	2009	National	Men	33 613	50 978	81 641	26 677	40 458	64 794	21 622	31 356	46 394	21 622	31 356	46 394
				Women	26 284	37 516	61 386	20 861	29 775	48 719	17 515	23 810	36 648	17 515	23 810	36 648
				M+W	31 416	45 947	71 415	24 933	36 466	56 678	20 391	28 536	41 473	20 391	28 536	41 473
	OECD average			Men	36 507	42 824	58 968	30 249	35 438	48 607	22 842	26 152	33 934	18 772	21 638	28 392
				Women	28 525	33 446	46 476	23 755	27 830	38 407	18 765	21 309	27 814	15 445	17 598	23 208
				M+W	34 319	39 622	52 578	28 478	32 823	43 377	21 739	24 470	30 834	17 870	20 227	25 778
	EU21 average			Men	36 154	41 540	58 998	29 203	33 472	47 475	21 508	24 138	32 164	17 657	19 984	26 962
				Women	28 261	33 167	46 883	22 996	26 965	37 871	17 736	20 115	26 612	14 499	16 564	22 166
				M+W	33 984	38 610	52 848	27 506	31 166	42 586	20 475	22 690	29 374	16 784	18 752	24 546
Other G20	Argentina				m	m	m	m	m	m	m	m	m	m	m	m
	Brazil	2009	National	Men	m	m	m	4 479	7 509	19 003	m	m	m	m	m	m
				Women	m	m	m	3 248	5 132	12 779	m	m	m	m	m	m
				M+W	m	m	m	4 158	6 517	15 668	m	m	m	m	m	m
	China				m	m	m	m	m	m	m	m	m	m	m	m
	India				m	m	m	m	m	m	m	m	m	m	m	m
	Indonesia				m	m	m	m	m	m	m	m	m	m	m	m
	Russian Federation				m	m	m	m	m	m	m	m	m	m	m	m
	Saudi Arabia				m	m	m	m	m	m	m	m	m	m	m	m
	South Africa				m	m	m	m	m	m	m	m	m	m	m	m

Note: Labour costs include non-tax compulsory payments (NTCP) and employer social contributions based on OECD Taxing Wages Database (Centre for Tax Policy and Administration), except for the United States for which Bureau of Labor Statistics information is used and the United Kingdom for which EU Labour Cost Survey data is used. SILC: Statistics on Income and Living Conditions (Eurostat). USD based on three-year moving average of currency exchange rates (OECD annual exchange rates) and last three columns on net income in USD (PPP) Purchasing Power Parity-adjusted for private consumption (see Table X2.1 for exchange rates).

Source: OECD, LSO Network special data collection on full-time, full-year earnings, Economic Working Group.

Please refer to the Reader's Guide for information concerning the symbols replacing missing data.

StatLink http://dx.doi.org/10.1787/888932463384

Table A10.4. [1/2] Annual labour costs, full-time gross earnings and annual net income, by ISCED levels in equivalent USD, 45-54 year-olds (2009 or latest available year)

				Annual labour costs			Gross annual full-time earnings			Annual net income			Annual net income		
				Three-year average exchange rate			Three-year average exchange rate			Three-year average exchange rate			PPP-adjusted exchange rate		
				0/1/2	3/4	5B/5A/6	0/1/2	3/4	5B/5A/6	0/1/2	3/4	5B/5A/6	0/1/2	3/4	5B/5A/6
	Year	Source	Gender	(1)	(2)	(3)	(4)	(5)	(6)	(7)	(8)	(9)	(10)	(11)	(12)
OECD Australia	2009	National	Men	56 719	64 114	96 536	49 148	55 556	83 650	38 572	42 961	60 381	30 382	33 840	47 561
			Women	38 969	44 491	63 641	33 768	38 552	55 146	28 648	31 734	42 681	22 565	24 996	33 619
			M+W	49 496	58 728	81 329	42 890	50 890	70 474	34 531	39 765	52 673	27 200	31 322	41 489
Austria	2009	National	Men	63 250	87 951	129 756	48 982	68 111	104 778	33 895	43 942	65 797	27 728	35 947	53 825
			Women	44 508	67 942	98 839	34 468	52 615	76 543	25 713	35 915	48 309	21 034	29 381	39 519
			M+W	52 957	80 957	117 733	41 011	62 695	93 594	29 401	41 136	58 755	24 052	33 652	48 064
Belgium	2009	National	Men	60 454	63 292	101 143	46 819	48 938	77 655	28 592	29 547	41 707	22 201	22 942	32 385
			Women	46 587	57 918	81 443	36 465	44 925	62 491	24 191	27 738	35 558	18 784	21 538	27 610
			M+W	57 549	61 714	93 841	44 650	47 760	71 947	27 614	29 016	39 393	21 441	22 530	30 587
Canada	2008	National	Men	44 973	62 367	84 692	40 331	56 864	78 464	31 073	42 242	55 936	26 048	35 411	46 890
			Women	33 867	44 886	67 041	30 379	40 253	61 330	24 595	31 022	45 311	20 617	26 006	37 984
			M+W	41 929	55 373	76 699	37 577	50 179	70 625	29 299	37 640	51 324	24 561	31 553	43 024
Chile				m	m	m	m	m	m	m	m	m	m	m	m
Czech Republic	2009	National	Men	17 017	22 307	56 461	12 699	16 647	42 135	10 070	12 790	30 352	12 668	16 089	38 180
			Women	13 089	18 051	37 090	9 768	13 471	27 679	8 051	10 602	20 391	10 127	13 337	25 651
			M+W	14 557	20 572	50 455	10 863	15 352	37 653	8 806	11 898	27 263	11 077	14 967	34 295
Denmark	2009	National	Men	72 604	82 928	111 303	72 197	82 521	110 896	43 392	47 231	57 780	26 384	28 717	35 132
			Women	59 767	66 095	81 520	59 359	65 687	81 113	36 276	39 866	46 707	22 057	24 239	28 399
			M+W	66 640	75 526	95 771	66 233	75 119	95 363	40 174	44 479	52 005	24 427	27 044	31 620
Estonia	2009	National	Men	13 281	18 124	22 131	9 921	13 538	16 531	8 210	11 017	13 341	9 435	12 662	15 332
			Women	7 971	10 592	15 362	5 954	7 912	11 475	5 131	6 650	9 416	5 897	7 643	10 822
			M+W	11 220	14 271	17 059	8 381	10 660	12 742	7 015	8 783	10 400	8 062	10 095	11 952
Finland	2009	National	Men	63 088	65 945	96 917	51 291	53 614	78 794	36 694	38 001	51 350	25 749	26 666	36 034
			Women	49 851	50 816	70 066	40 530	41 314	56 965	30 500	30 955	39 778	21 403	21 722	27 913
			M+W	57 130	58 161	80 800	46 447	47 285	65 691	33 933	34 419	44 404	23 811	24 152	31 159
France	2006	National	Men	52 007	60 919	100 542	36 547	42 810	70 530	26 806	31 083	47 836	20 659	23 956	36 867
			Women	32 744	46 006	73 817	26 023	33 167	51 854	20 466	24 498	37 059	15 773	18 880	28 561
			M+W	44 127	55 900	89 129	32 155	39 283	62 554	23 807	28 674	43 233	18 348	22 099	33 320
Germany	2009	National	Men	59 453	63 451	99 342	49 762	53 108	84 690	30 255	31 788	46 639	25 163	26 438	38 790
			Women	40 702	47 813	80 656	34 067	40 019	67 909	22 584	25 586	38 691	18 783	21 280	32 179
			M+W	53 401	58 200	94 189	44 696	48 713	80 063	27 864	29 767	44 515	23 175	24 757	37 023
Greece	2009	National	Men	28 665	32 717	48 279	22 384	25 549	37 700	18 321	20 315	27 970	16 709	18 527	25 509
			Women	16 127	23 943	37 851	12 594	18 697	29 557	10 579	15 705	22 840	9 648	14 323	20 831
			M+W	24 188	29 636	43 885	18 888	23 143	34 269	15 866	18 799	25 809	14 470	17 145	23 538
Hungary	2009	National	Men	11 866	15 431	40 098	8 962	11 638	30 115	6 355	7 597	15 992	8 124	9 712	20 445
			Women	9 338	13 861	25 894	7 032	10 461	19 475	5 274	7 150	10 992	6 743	9 141	14 052
			M+W	10 336	14 670	30 943	7 794	11 067	23 257	5 701	7 380	12 769	7 288	9 435	16 324
Iceland	2006	SILC	Men	46 545	55 553	88 694	40 768	48 658	77 686	30 008	34 765	52 265	20 055	23 234	34 929
			Women	36 713	43 613	61 691	32 157	38 200	54 034	24 817	28 460	38 006	16 585	19 020	25 400
			M+W	42 180	51 870	75 045	36 945	45 432	65 731	27 704	32 821	45 058	18 514	21 934	30 112
Ireland	2009	National	Men	59 879	104 896	134 737	54 067	94 714	121 659	43 308	63 636	77 781	30 243	44 438	54 317
			Women	50 388	65 726	97 912	45 497	59 346	88 408	37 826	45 948	60 482	26 415	32 087	42 236
			M+W	58 023	89 446	121 353	52 391	80 764	109 573	42 470	56 659	71 529	29 658	39 567	49 951
Israel	2009	National	Men	23 042	30 350	52 029	21 430	28 262	48 824	18 622	23 318	35 921	16 325	20 442	31 490
			Women	15 424	22 109	35 316	14 421	20 572	32 972	13 596	18 011	26 380	11 919	15 789	23 126
			M+W	21 408	27 304	44 677	19 927	25 373	41 851	17 551	21 440	31 876	15 386	18 795	27 944
Italy	2008	National	Men	53 969	74 492	146 289	38 691	53 404	104 876	27 180	35 196	61 436	22 686	29 377	51 279
			Women	37 032	58 018	83 495	26 549	41 594	59 858	19 712	28 978	38 507	16 453	24 187	32 141
			M+W	49 329	67 853	118 553	35 364	48 644	84 992	25 118	32 751	51 275	20 966	27 336	42 798
Japan				m	m	m	m	m	m	m	m	m	m	m	m
Korea	2008	National	Men	26 747	43 192	61 355	22 675	36 615	52 522	20 616	31 771	44 549	25 174	38 796	54 399
			Women	16 833	22 225	37 279	14 270	18 841	31 603	13 094	17 207	27 858	15 988	21 011	34 017
			M+W	21 773	36 217	57 020	18 458	30 702	48 701	16 861	27 159	41 473	20 589	33 163	50 642

Note: Labour costs include non-tax compulsory payments (NTCP) and employer social contributions based on OECD Taxing Wages Database (Centre for Tax Policy and Administration), except for the United States for which Bureau of Labor Statistics information is used and the United Kingdom for which EU Labour Cost Survey data is used. SILC: Statistics on Income and Living Conditions (Eurostat). USD based on three-year moving average of currency exchange rates (OECD annual exchange rates) and last three columns on net income in USD (PPP) Purchasing Power Parity-adjusted for private consumption (see Table X2.1 for exchange rates).

Source: OECD, LSO Network special data collection on full-time, full-year earnings, Economic Working Group.

Please refer to the Reader's Guide for information concerning the symbols replacing missing data.

StatLink http://dx.doi.org/10.1787/888932463422

Table A10.4. [2/2] **Annual labour costs, full-time gross earnings and annual net income, by ISCED levels in equivalent USD, 45-54 year-olds (2009 or latest available year)**

		Year	Source	Gender	Annual labour costs Three-year average exchange rate			Gross annual full-time earnings Three-year average exchange rate			Annual net income Three-year average exchange rate			Annual net income PPP-adjusted exchange rate		
					0/1/2	3/4	5B/5A/6	0/1/2	3/4	5B/5A/6	0/1/2	3/4	5B/5A/6	0/1/2	3/4	5B/5A/6
					(1)	(2)	(3)	(4)	(5)	(6)	(7)	(8)	(9)	(10)	(11)	(12)
OECD	Luxembourg	2009	National	Men	67 423	99 120	167 109	59 677	87 732	148 753	45 496	60 511	93 326	33 072	43 988	67 842
				Women	56 536	79 465	157 450	50 041	70 335	139 361	39 698	51 289	87 852	28 858	37 284	63 862
				M+W	64 296	95 664	164 389	56 909	84 674	146 033	43 885	58 899	91 685	31 901	42 816	66 649
	Mexico				m	m	m	m	m	m	m	m	m	m	m	m
	Netherlands	2008	National	Men	65 368	82 507	127 016	51 528	64 868	102 497	33 467	40 898	59 393	27 021	33 022	47 955
				Women	49 975	62 678	97 527	39 891	49 434	77 297	27 367	32 295	47 722	22 097	26 075	38 531
				M+W	63 095	79 195	121 311	49 759	62 290	97 622	32 477	39 456	57 135	26 222	31 857	46 131
	New Zealand	2009	National	Men	35 855	43 364	52 929	35 855	43 364	52 929	28 779	33 810	39 967	26 182	30 760	36 361
				Women	25 676	30 880	38 338	25 676	30 880	38 338	21 454	25 466	30 443	19 519	23 168	27 696
				M+W	31 032	39 003	45 149	31 032	39 003	45 149	25 566	30 888	35 007	23 259	28 101	31 848
	Norway	2007	National	Men	80 224	93 152	131 865	70 093	81 355	115 077	50 248	56 849	75 464	31 113	35 200	46 725
				Women	59 866	66 567	85 953	52 360	58 197	75 083	38 863	42 610	53 387	24 063	26 383	33 056
				M+W	72 054	83 809	109 894	62 977	73 216	95 938	45 679	52 253	64 899	28 284	32 354	40 184
	Poland	2006	SILC	Men	7 363	12 066	23 039	6 217	10 189	19 454	4 620	7 387	13 843	6 315	10 098	18 922
				Women	5 069	9 291	18 667	4 280	7 845	15 762	3 270	5 754	11 271	4 470	7 865	15 406
				M+W	6 337	10 830	20 427	5 351	9 145	17 248	4 016	6 660	12 306	5 490	9 104	16 822
	Portugal	2009	National	Men	19 089	36 306	70 426	15 426	29 338	56 910	12 950	22 079	37 640	12 853	21 914	37 360
				Women	13 564	24 762	50 139	10 961	20 010	40 516	9 755	15 969	28 354	9 683	15 850	28 143
				M+W	16 805	31 034	62 003	13 579	25 078	50 104	11 546	19 289	33 642	11 460	19 145	33 391
	Slovak Republic	2009	National	Men	15 869	19 971	40 648	10 914	13 735	28 085	8 676	10 655	20 662	11 115	13 650	26 470
				Women	11 298	15 232	26 975	7 770	10 476	18 573	6 471	8 369	14 070	8 290	10 721	18 025
				M+W	12 721	17 566	33 340	8 749	12 081	23 001	7 158	9 495	17 226	9 170	12 164	22 069
	Slovenia	2009	National	Men	19 033	25 742	58 044	16 393	22 173	49 995	11 414	14 914	28 802	11 906	15 558	30 045
				Women	16 037	24 154	48 953	13 814	20 804	42 165	9 958	14 136	25 203	10 387	14 746	26 291
				M+W	17 532	25 007	52 735	15 101	21 539	45 422	10 568	14 554	26 700	11 024	15 182	27 853
	Spain	2008	National	Men	34 250	46 743	62 240	26 366	35 984	47 914	21 962	28 605	36 649	19 769	25 748	32 989
				Women	25 613	35 770	54 724	19 718	27 536	42 127	17 245	22 795	32 747	15 523	20 519	29 477
				M+W	31 697	42 489	58 847	24 401	32 709	45 302	20 564	26 397	34 888	18 510	23 761	31 404
	Sweden	2008	National	Men	63 619	74 925	119 984	43 748	51 523	82 509	33 127	38 448	53 753	25 104	29 137	40 735
				Women	53 436	63 116	79 692	36 746	43 402	54 801	28 205	32 889	40 598	21 374	24 924	30 766
				M+W	61 212	70 881	97 566	42 094	48 743	67 092	31 974	36 545	46 554	24 230	27 695	35 279
	Switzerland				m	m	m	m	m	m	m	m	m	m	m	m
	Turkey				m	m	m	m	m	m	m	m	m	m	m	m
	United Kingdom	2009	National	Men	45 226	63 970	102 188	36 889	52 177	83 351	28 878	39 427	60 408	23 684	32 335	49 542
				Women	32 979	43 821	74 094	26 900	35 743	60 436	21 986	28 087	45 125	18 031	23 035	37 009
				M+W	40 661	55 863	90 076	33 165	45 565	73 471	26 309	34 865	54 120	21 576	28 594	44 385
	United States	2009	National	Men	42 523	65 994	123 879	33 748	52 377	98 317	26 617	38 865	66 115	26 617	38 865	66 115
				Women	28 421	46 556	80 081	22 556	36 949	63 556	18 712	28 877	45 643	18 712	28 877	45 643
				M+W	37 348	57 404	103 501	29 641	45 559	82 144	23 716	34 732	56 769	23 716	34 732	56 769
	OECD average			Men	43 083	55 582	87 920	35 639	46 047	72 665	26 145	32 402	47 347	21 396	26 809	39 808
				Women	32 013	41 600	64 190	26 690	34 388	52 980	20 484	25 330	36 255	16 614	20 829	30 275
				M+W	39 001	50 522	77 507	32 325	41 816	64 055	24 040	29 883	42 575	19 582	24 657	35 746
	EU21 average			Men	42 513	54 943	88 462	34 261	44 396	71 420	24 460	30 241	44 879	19 933	24 806	37 617
				Women	32 029	42 146	66 294	26 116	34 038	53 541	19 536	24 342	35 318	15 801	19 942	29 401
				M+W	38 753	50 259	78 781	31 333	40 586	63 666	22 679	28 091	40 743	18 398	23 004	34 029
Other G20	Argentina				m	m	m	m	m	m	m	m	m	m	m	m
	Brazil	2009	National	Men	m	m	m	5 987	12 762	31 720	m	m	m	m	m	m
				Women	m	m	m	3 614	7 765	18 667	m	m	m	m	m	m
				M+W	m	m	m	5 253	10 772	25 518	m	m	m	m	m	m
	China				m	m	m	m	m	m	m	m	m	m	m	m
	India				m	m	m	m	m	m	m	m	m	m	m	m
	Indonesia				m	m	m	m	m	m	m	m	m	m	m	m
	Russian Federation				m	m	m	m	m	m	m	m	m	m	m	m
	Saudi Arabia				m	m	m	m	m	m	m	m	m	m	m	m
	South Africa				m	m	m	m	m	m	m	m	m	m	m	m

Note: Labour costs include non-tax compulsory payments (NTCP) and employer social contributions based on OECD Taxing Wages Database (Centre for Tax Policy and Administration), except for the United States for which Bureau of Labor Statistics information is used and the United Kingdom for which EU Labour Cost Survey data is used. SILC: Statistics on Income and Living Conditions (Eurostat). USD based on three-year moving average of currency exchange rates (OECD annual exchange rates) and last three columns on net income in USD (PPP) Purchasing Power Parity-adjusted for private consumption (see Table X2.1 for exchange rates).

Source: OECD, LSO Network special data collection on full-time, full-year earnings, Economic Working Group.

Please refer to the Reader's Guide for information concerning the symbols replacing missing data.

StatLink http://dx.doi.org/10.1787/888932463422

WHAT ARE THE SOCIAL OUTCOMES OF EDUCATION?

- Adults aged 25 to 64 with higher levels of educational attainment are, on average, more satisfied with life, engaged in society and likely to report that they are in good health, even after accounting for differences in gender, age and income.
- Students in grade 8 (approximately 14 years old) who have higher levels of civic knowledge as measured by the International Civic and Citizenship Education Study (ICCS) are generally more likely to vote and be supportive of gender equality, although they are not necessarily more likely to trust civic institutions.

Chart A11.1. Proportion of adults satisfied with life, by level of education (2008)

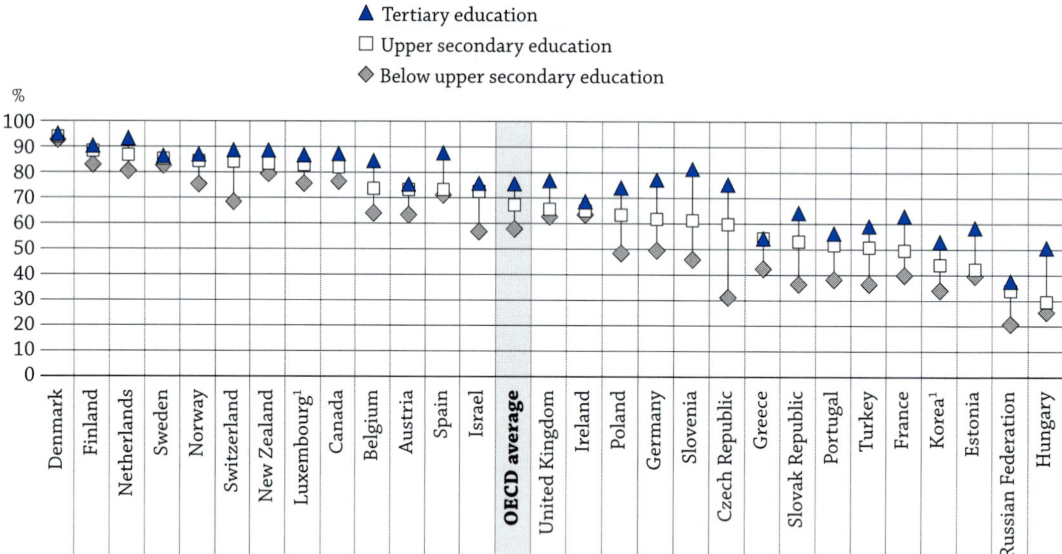

1. Year of reference 2009.

Countries are ranked in descending order of the proportion of adults aged 25-64 reporting satisfaction in life, among adults who have attained upper secondary education.

Source: OECD. Table A11.1. See Annex 3 for notes (*www.oecd.org/edu/eag2011*).

StatLink http://dx.doi.org/10.1787/888932460819

Context

There is growing interest in looking beyond the traditional economic measures of individual success, such as income, employment and GDP per capita, towards non-economic aspects of well-being and social progress, such as life satisfaction, civic engagement and health. Recent initiatives, such as the Stiglitz-Sen Commission on the Measurement of Economic Performance and Social Progress and the World Health Organization's Commission on Social Determinants of Health, have been prompted by concerns that society is not as cohesive as it should be and that citizens are not as healthy and happy as they deserve to be. Several OECD countries have seen a decline in indicators of civic engagement, such as voting, volunteering and interpersonal trust, changes that may well have significant and lasting consequences for the quality of democratic societies (OECD, 2010). The health of the population is a major concern in OECD countries, as the increasing prevalence of conditions such as obesity and depression has led to a significant reduction in the quality of life for many individuals and growing public expenditures on healthcare.

A large body of literature suggests that education is positively associated with a variety of social outcomes, such as better health, stronger civic engagement and reduced crime (OECD, 2007c; 2010e). A small but increasing number of studies further suggest that education has a positive *causal* effect on these social outcomes (see for example, Grossman, 2006 for health). There is also research suggesting that education can be a relatively cost-effective means to improve health and reduce crime (see for example Lochner and Moretti, 2004).

Other findings

- **Adults with higher levels of educational attainment are generally more likely than those with lower levels of attainment to exhibit greater satisfaction with life, stronger civic engagement (i.e. vote, volunteer, express political interest and show interpersonal trust) and better perceived health.** An individual's engagement in society and perceived health conditions appear to vary across different levels of educational attainment, even after accounting for age, gender and income differences. This suggests that education may have an impact on these outcomes by raising skills and abilities, although other factors related to the choice of education may also be at play. The differences in life satisfaction between below upper secondary and upper secondary attainment is partly driven by individual differences in income, suggesting that there may be income effects of education on life satisfaction for these individuals.

- In all the surveyed OECD countries, **students in grade 8 with higher measured levels of civic competencies** (i.e. **knowing and understanding elements and concepts of citizenship) showed higher levels of anticipated adult electoral participation and supportive attitudes towards gender equality**. However, the relationships between competencies and all the social outcomes are not necessarily positive. For example, in Chile, the Czech Republic, Greece, Italy, Mexico and the Russian Federation, the higher the level of civic knowledge, the less a student is likely to trust civic institutions. This suggests that **country contexts may shape the ways in which competencies affect people's perceptions of civic institutions**.

Analysis

Given the potentially significant cross-country differences in norms (e.g. social desirability of expressing one's satisfaction with life) and institutional contexts (e.g. eligibility and compulsory nature of voting), indicators related to social outcomes should be interpreted with caution. The main focus should be on *within-country* differences in social outcomes across levels of educational attainment and civic competencies rather than *cross-country* comparisons.

Educational attainment and social outcomes

Educational attainment is positively associated with various measures of social outcomes, including electoral participation, political interest, interpersonal trust, volunteering, self-reported good health and satisfaction with life (Charts A11.1, A11.2, Table A11.1, and Table A11.4, available on line). With the exception of electoral participation in Korea, all surveyed countries with statistically significant associations between education and these social outcomes show the relationship to be positive. In Canada, for example, only 63.4% of adults who have not attained an upper secondary education vote in national elections; but this proportion rises to 78.4% among adults with a tertiary education. These associations generally hold even after accounting for age and gender (Table A11.3 and Table A11.5 available on line).

Chart A11.2. Proportion of adults voting and volunteering, by level of education (2008)

Percentage of 25-64 year-olds, by educational attainment

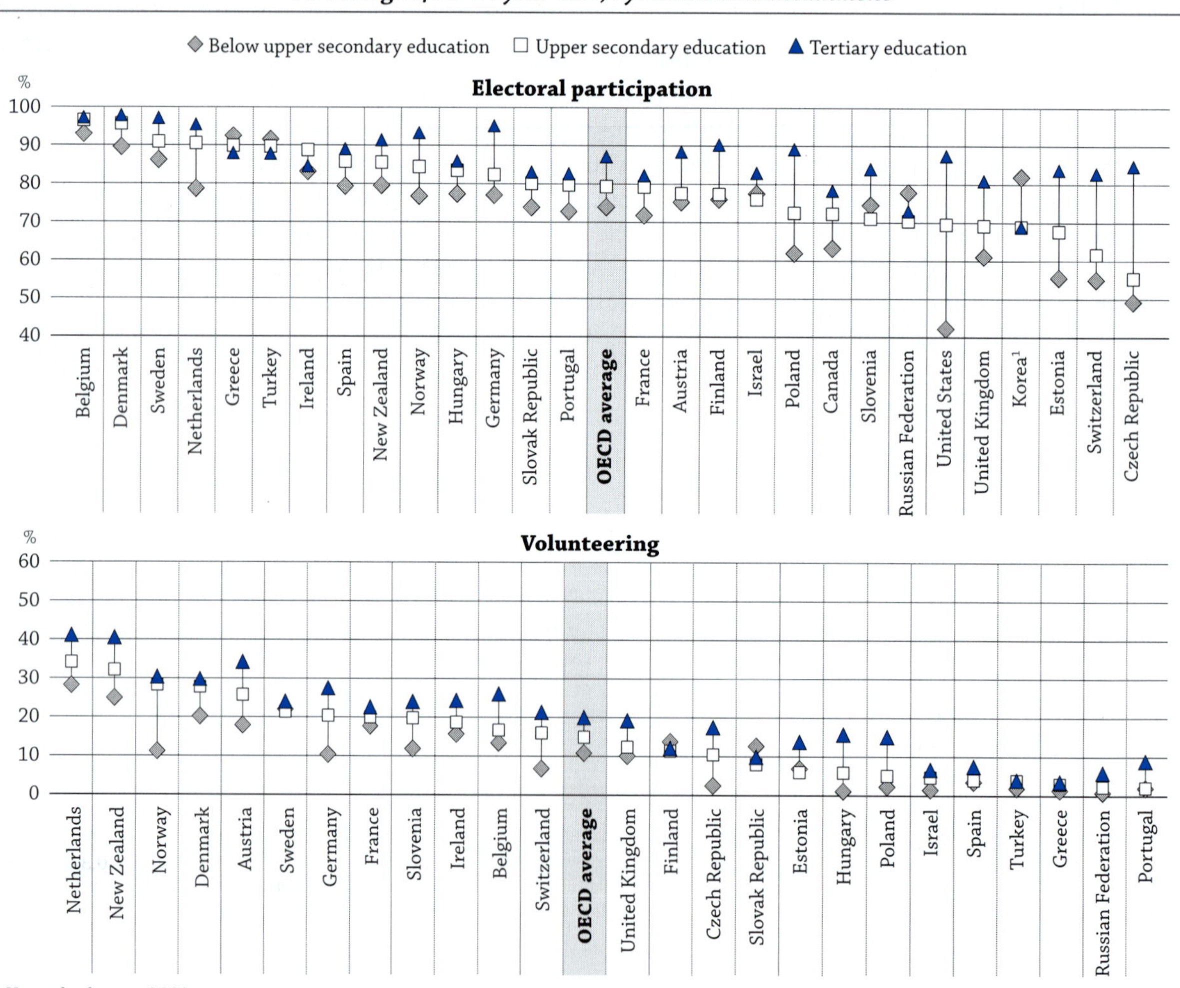

1. Year of reference 2009.

Countries are ranked in descending order of the proportion of adults aged 25-64 reporting electoral participation and volunteering among adults who have attained upper secondary education.

Source: OECD. Table A11.1. See Annex 3 for notes (*www.oecd.org/edu/eag2011*).

StatLink http://dx.doi.org/10.1787/888932460838

For most countries with statistically significant associations between education and either electoral participation or volunteering, the associations remain positive, even after accounting for differences in age, gender and income (Table A11.3). This suggests that education's contribution to civic engagement may involve fostering skills as well as raising incomes.

For many countries there is not a statistically significant relationship between education and satisfaction with life for those with lower levels of education (i.e. upper secondary or below) once differences in income are taken into account (Table A11.3). This suggests that obtaining an upper secondary education may contribute to life satisfaction largely by increasing individuals' income. However, for most countries with statistically significant association between education and satisfaction with life, the association remains significant among those who have attained tertiary education, even after accounting for age, gender and income. This indicates that higher levels of education may contribute to life satisfaction beyond their effect on income. For example, tertiary education may help individuals develop skills, social status and access to networks that could lead to greater satisfaction with life.

Civic competencies and social outcomes

Education can enhance social outcomes by helping individuals make informed and competent decisions by providing information, improving cognitive skills and strengthening socio-emotional capabilities, such as conscientiousness, self-efficacy and social skills. As such, education can help individuals follow healthier lifestyles and increase their engagement in civil society. Educational institutions such as schools can also offer an ideal environment for children to develop healthy habits and participatory attitudes and norms conducive to social cohesion. For instance, open classroom climate, practical involvement in civic matters and school ethos that promote active citizenship can foster civic participation.

Box A11.1. Relationship between "returns to civic knowledge on trust" and "perceptions of corruption"

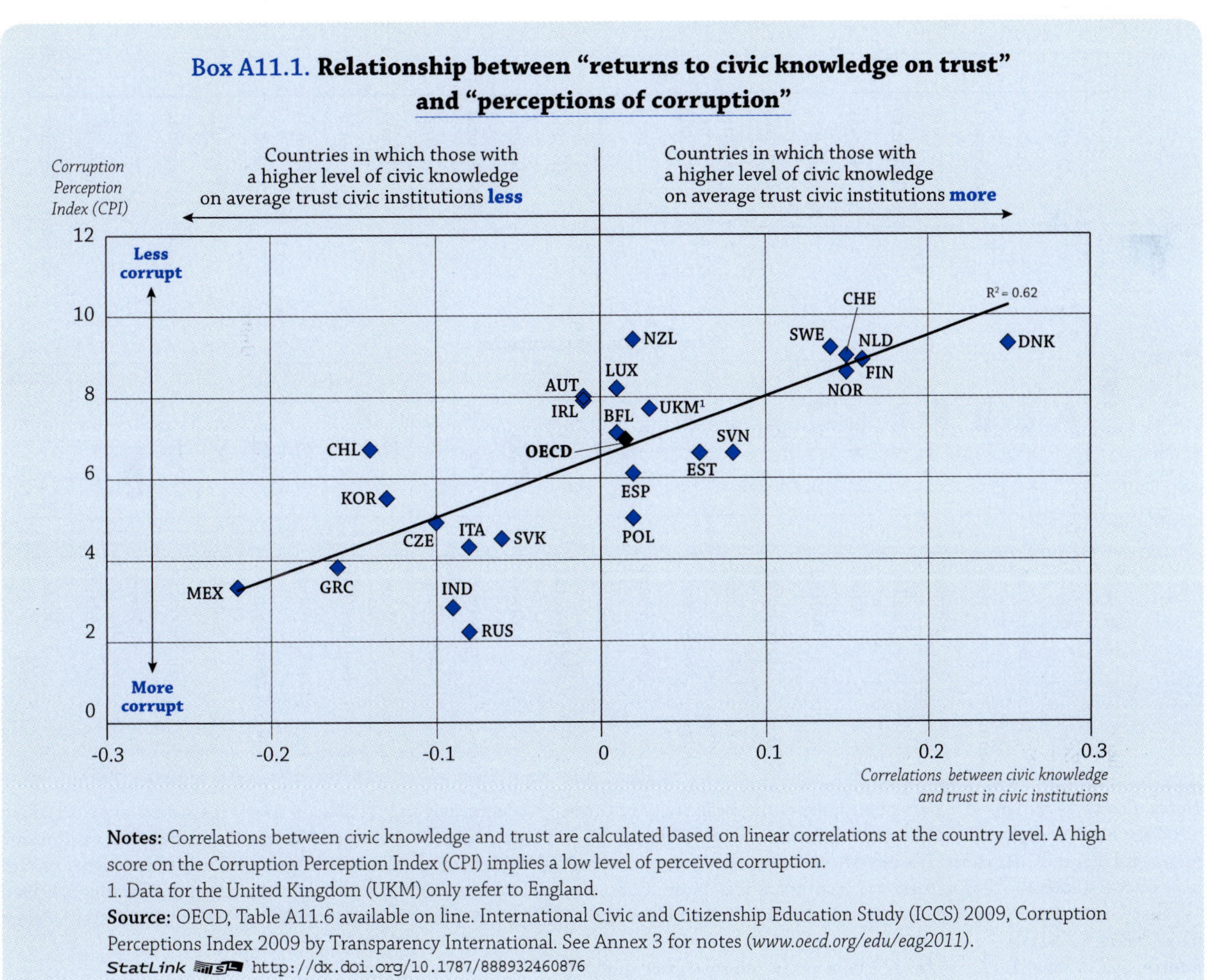

Notes: Correlations between civic knowledge and trust are calculated based on linear correlations at the country level. A high score on the Corruption Perception Index (CPI) implies a low level of perceived corruption.

1. Data for the United Kingdom (UKM) only refer to England.

Source: OECD, Table A11.6 available on line. International Civic and Citizenship Education Study (ICCS) 2009, Corruption Perceptions Index 2009 by Transparency International. See Annex 3 for notes (*www.oecd.org/edu/eag2011*).

StatLink http://dx.doi.org/10.1787/888932460876

Chart A11.3. Civic engagement, by students' level of civic knowledge (2009)

Mean scale of civic engagement among grade 8 students, by level of civic knowledge

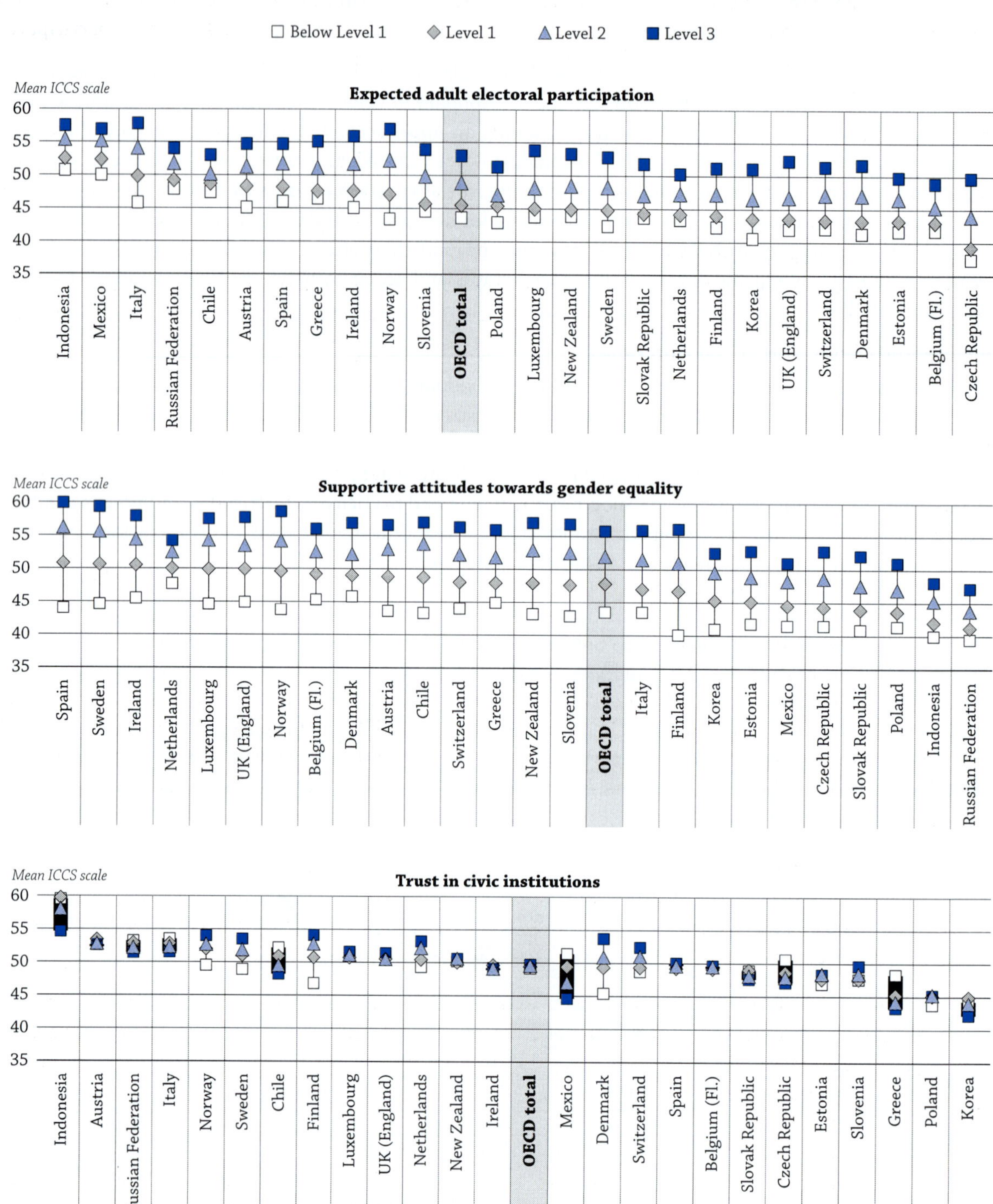

Notes: Countries are ranked in descending order of the mean scales of Grade 8 students' civic and social engagement (i.e. expect to participate in elections, have supportive attitudes towards gender equality and display trust in civic institutions) among those who have achieved Level 1 in civic knowledge. For the third panel (Trust in civic institutions), the countries highlighted in black are those in which individuals with a higher average scale of civic knowledge tend to trust civic institutions less. Mean ICCS scales are based on Rasch Partial Credit Model and the resulting weighted likelihood estimates (WLEs) were transformed into a metric with a mean of 50 and a standard deviation of 10. The Definitions section provides details of the ICCS scale.

Source: OECD. Table A11.2. See Annex 3 for notes (*www.oecd.org/edu/eag2011*).

StatLink http://dx.doi.org/10.1787/888932460857

Indeed, in all surveyed OECD countries, students in grade 8 (approximately 14 years of age) with higher levels of civic competencies show higher levels of expected adult electoral participation and supportive attitudes towards gender equality (Chart A11.3). In Norway, for example, those who are at the lowest level on a civic competency scale score only an average of 43.4 points on the ICCS scale of expected adult electoral participation, whereas those who are at the highest level on the scale score 57.0 points (Table A11.2, see Definitions below for details on the scales).

However, the relationship between competencies and social outcomes is not always positive. For example, for Chile, the Czech Republic, Greece, Italy, Mexico and the Russian Federation, the higher the level of civic knowledge, the more likely that a student has less trust in civic institutions (Chart A11.3 and Table A11.2). This may imply that national context shapes the way in which competencies affect people's perceptions about civic institutions. Indeed, in countries with a relatively high level of perceived corruption, the more civic knowledge one has, the less likely it is that one trusts civic institutions (Box A11.1). This does not necessarily imply a "negative effect" of education, however. If civic institutions are indeed corrupt in a country, a negative relationship between civic knowledge and institutional trust may indicate that the education system in that country provides a sound and critical attitude towards institutions.

Definitions

This section describes the education variables (i.e. educational attainment and civic competency) and social outcome variables. See Annex 3 (*www.oecd.org/edu/eag2011*) for detailed descriptions of the variables, including the actual questions used in each survey.

Civic knowledge means knowing about and understanding elements and concepts of citizenship as well as those of traditional civics (Schultz, 2010). The ICCS assessment is based on a 79-item test administered to lower-secondary students (8th grade) and covers issues related to civic society and systems, civic principles, civic participation and civic identities. Three-quarters of the test items involve reasoning and analysis associated with civics and citizenship, and the rest focuses on knowledge about civics and citizenship. Civic knowledge is measured on a scale with an international average of 500 points and a standard deviation of 100. There is significant variation across and within countries in civic knowledge: half of the total variance in civic knowledge was found to be at the student level, a quarter at the school level and a quarter across countries. See Schulz *et al.*, (2010) for more details on how civic knowledge is conceptualised.

Educational attainment variables in each data source are converted to three categories of educational attainment (below upper secondary education, upper secondary education and tertiary education) based on the ISCED-97 classification system. Those in the "upper secondary education" category include those who have attained post-secondary non-tertiary education (ISCED 4).

Electoral participation is captured by the percentage of adults who reported voting during the previous national election. European Social Survey (ESS) 2008, General Social Survey (GSS) 2008 for Canada and New Zealand, KEDI's Lifelong Education Survey 2009 for Korea, European Values Survey (EVS) 2008 for Luxembourg and the Current Population Survey (CPS) 2008 for the United States provide this information. The analysis in this chapter is limited to adults who are eligible to vote. Countries with compulsory voting are included in the data (i.e. Belgium, Greece, Luxembourg and Turkey). For countries with a voting-registration requirement that is not enforced or automated (e.g. Ireland, the United Kingdom and the United States), the analysis includes those who are potentially eligible (e.g. are citizens of the country) but have not registered to vote.

Expected adult electoral participation is captured by the mean ICCS scale of students' responses to questions related to adult electoral participation. They include voting in local elections, voting in national elections and obtaining information about candidates before voting in an election.

Interpersonal trust is captured by the percentage of adults who believe that most people can be trusted. ESS 2008 provides this information.

Life satisfaction is captured by the percentage of adults who reported being satisfied with life. ESS 2008, GSS 2008 for Canada and New Zealand, KEDI's Lifelong Education Survey 2009 for Korea and EVS 2009 for Luxembourg provide this information.

Political interest is captured by the percentage of adults who say they are at least fairly interested in politics. ESS 2008, KEDI's Social Capital Survey 2008 and International Social Survey Programme (ISSP) 2004 and 2006 provide this information.

Self-reported health is captured by the percentage of adults who rate their health as at least "good" on a 4- or 5-point scale. ESS 2008, KEDI's Social Capital Survey 2008, GSS for Canada and New Zealand 2008 and National Health Interview Survey (NHIS) for the United States 2008 provide this information.

Supportive attitudes towards gender equality are captured by the mean ICCS scale of students' response to questions related to attitudes towards gender equality. They include, for example, questions that ask students if they support equal opportunities to take part in government.

Trust in civic institutions is captured by the mean ICCS scale of students' responses to questions related to trust in public institutions. They include students' self-perceived trust towards public institutions such as the national government, local government, police and political parties.

Volunteering is captured by the percentage of adults who reported volunteering during the previous month (or four weeks). ESS 2008 and GSS 2008 for New Zealand provide this information.

Methodology

The indicators presented in this chapter are based on developmental work jointly conducted by the INES Network on Labour Market, Economic and Social Outcomes of Learning (LSO) and the OECD Centre for Educational Research and Innovation (CERI). The conceptual framework for the indicators was developed by CERI's Social Outcomes of Learning project (OECD 2007c; OECD 2010e) and the empirical strategies were developed by the INES LSO Network. See Annex 3 at *www.oecd.org/edu/eag2011* for details on the calculation of the indicators.

In this year's edition of *Education at a Glance* (EAG), we present six new indicators (Tables A11.1, A11.2 and A11.3) as well as updates of three indicators presented in *Education at a Glance 2009* and *2010* (Tables A11.4, A11.5 and A11.6) that can be found on line. Updated indicators are included since the primary data source, i.e. ESS 2008, recently released revised measures of educational attainment that are more comparable across countries. The new indicators were calculated using micro-data from the ESS 2008, GSS 2008 for Canada and New Zealand, EVS 2009 for Luxembourg, Lifelong Education Survey 2009 for Korea, CPS 2008 for the United States and the ICCS 2009. Updates of indicators presented in EAG 2009 and 2010 were calculated using the ESS 2008, ISSP 2006, GSS 2008 for Canada and New Zealand, KEDI Social Capital Survey for Korea 2008 and the NHIS 2008 for the United States. Surveys were selected on the basis of the following factors:

Age restriction: For surveys that cover adults (i.e. Tables A11.1, A11.3, A11.4, A11.5 and A11.6), data on adults aged 25 to 64 were used. For surveys that cover students (i.e. Tables A11.2 and A11.6), data on children enrolled in grade 8 (typically corresponding to ages 14-15) were used.

Comparability of educational attainment variables: The general principle is to use micro-data for which the distribution of educational attainment was within 10 percentage points of figures published for comparable years in *Education at a Glance*. A number of exceptions, however, were made with the recommendation of the country representatives of INES Working Party and/or INES LSO Network [i.e. Denmark (ESS), Ireland (ESS), New Zealand (ISSP), Norway (ESS) and the United Kingdom (ESS)].

Comparability of social outcomes variables: Surveys are selected on the basis of the comparability of social outcomes variables.

Country coverage: An important objective is to select surveys that represent a large number of OECD countries. This was the motivation to select the European Social Survey which covers a large number of European Union (EU) member countries and other countries for the adult population. For the ICCS, a large number of EU and other countries were included, including Austria, Belgium (Flanders), Chile, the Czech Republic, Denmark, Estonia, Finland, Greece, Indonesia, Ireland, Italy, Korea, Luxembourg, Mexico, the Netherlands, New Zealand, Norway, Poland, the Russian Federation, the Slovak Republic, Slovenia, Spain, Sweden, Switzerland and the United Kingdom (England).

Sample size: Surveys with a minimum sample of approximately 1 000 observations per country were used.

To calculate incremental differences, country-specific regression models were estimated to predict each dichotomous outcome variable (e.g. high versus low level of interest in politics) from individuals' educational attainment level, with and without control variables for age, gender and family income. In preliminary analyses, both probit and ordinary least squares (OLS) regressions were used, and were found to produce very similar estimates of incremental differences. Because OLS regression provides more readily interpretable coefficients, OLS was used for the final analysis to generate incremental differences (Tables A11.3 and A11.5).

The statistical data for Israel are supplied by and under the responsibility of the relevant Israeli authorities. The use of such data by the OECD is without prejudice to the status of the Golan Heights, East Jerusalem and Israeli settlements in the West Bank under the terms of international law.

References

Grossman, M. (2006), "Education and Nonmarket Outcomes," *Handbook of the Economics of Education*, Elsevier, Amsterdam.

Lochner, L. and E. Moretti (2004), "The Effect of Education on Crime: Evidence from Prison Inmates, Arrests, and Self-Reports", *The American Economic Review*, Vol. 94, No. 1, pp. 155-189, The American Economic Association.

OECD (2007c), *Understanding the Social Outcomes of Learning*, OECD, Paris.

OECD (2010e), *Improving Health and Social Cohesion through Education*, OECD, Paris.

Schulz, W., *et al.* (2010), *ICCS 2009 International Report: Civic knowledge, attitudes, and engagement among lower-secondary school students in 38 countries*, IEA, Amsterdam.

The following additional material relevant to this indicator is available on line:

- ***Table A11.4. Proportion of adults with self-reported good health, political interest and interpersonal trust, by level of education (2008, updated Tables A9.1, A9.2 and A9.3 in EAG 2010)***
  StatLink http://dx.doi.org/10.1787/888932463536
- ***Table A11.5. Incremental differences in adults' self-reported good health, political interest and interpersonal trust associated with an increase in the level of educational attainment (2008, updated Tables A9.4, A9.5 and A9.6 in EAG 2010)***
  StatLink http://dx.doi.org/10.1787/888932463555
- ***Table A11.6. Relationship between 'returns to civic knowledge on trust' and 'perceptions of corruption' (2009)***
  StatLink http://dx.doi.org/10.1787/888932463574

Table A11.1. Proportion of adults voting, volunteering and satisfied with life, by level of education (2008)

Percentage of 25-64 year-olds, by level of educational attainment

	Electoral participation			Volunteering			Life satisfaction			
	Below upper secondary education	Upper secondary education	Tertiary education	Below upper secondary education	Upper secondary education	Tertiary education	Below upper secondary education	Upper secondary education	Tertiary education	Data source
OECD										
Australia	m	m	m	m	m	m	m	m	m	-
Austria	75.4	77.6	88.5	17.9	25.7	34.3	63.4	73.2	75.3	ESS 2008
Belgium	93.0	96.6	97.2	13.4	16.7	26.0	64.0	73.6	84.6	ESS 2008
Chile	m	m	m	m	m	m	m	m	m	-
Canada	63.4	72.4	78.4	m	m	m	76.4	82.1	87.3	GSS 2008
Czech Republic	49.4	55.5	84.8	2.5	10.5	17.5	31.2	59.8	75.3	ESS 2008
Denmark	89.6	95.7	97.8	20.2	27.8	29.8	92.7	93.9	95.0	ESS 2008
Estonia	55.7	67.8	83.8	6.9	6.0	13.8	39.6	42.3	58.5	ESS 2008
Finland	76.1	77.4	90.3	13.8	11.4	12.1	83.0	88.4	90.4	ESS 2008
France	71.9	79.3	82.3	17.7	20.0	22.6	39.9	49.6	63.0	ESS 2008
Germany	77.1	82.4	95.2	10.4	20.4	27.5	49.5	61.8	77.2	ESS 2008
Greece	92.5	89.9	88.0	1.4	3.0	3.6	42.4	54.3	54.3	ESS 2008
Hungary	77.4	83.5	85.9	1.1	5.9	15.7	25.4	29.6	50.7	ESS 2008
Iceland	m	m	m	m	m	m	m	m	m	-
Ireland	83.2	88.8	84.6	15.7	18.7	24.3	63.5	65.0	68.6	ESS 2008
Israel	77.6	76.1	83.0	1.5	4.7	6.7	56.8	72.5	75.7	ESS 2008
Italy	m	m	m	m	m	m	m	m	m	-
Japan	m	m	m	m	m	m	m	m	m	-
Korea	82.0	69.0	69.0	m	m	m	34.0	44.0	53.0	KEDI 2009
Luxembourg	m	m	m	m	m	m	75.6	82.9	86.8	EVS 2009
Mexico	m	m	m	m	m	m	m	m	m	-
Netherlands	78.7	90.5	95.5	28.2	34.2	41.1	80.6	86.8	93.3	ESS 2008
New Zealand	79.6	85.6	91.4	24.9	32.2	40.5	79.4	83.4	88.6	GSS 2008
Norway	76.8	84.5	93.3	11.2	28.3	30.4	75.3	84.4	87.0	ESS 2008
Poland	62.1	72.6	89.1	2.3	5.1	15.1	48.4	63.4	74.0	ESS 2008
Portugal	72.9	79.8	82.7	2.0	2.1	8.9	38.2	51.7	56.3	ESS 2008
Slovak Republic	74.0	80.2	83.1	12.7	8.0	9.9	36.4	53.1	64.3	ESS 2008
Slovenia	74.7	71.1	84.0	11.9	19.8	24.0	46.0	61.3	81.4	ESS 2008
Spain	79.4	85.8	89.1	3.5	4.0	7.5	71.1	73.2	87.7	ESS 2008
Sweden	86.2	90.9	97.1	22.0	21.4	24.0	82.7	85.3	86.4	ESS 2008
Switzerland	55.1	61.8	82.9	6.8	16.0	21.3	68.4	84.2	88.7	ESS 2008
Turkey	91.5	89.7	87.8	1.9	3.9	4.0	36.4	50.8	59.1	ESS 2008
United Kingdom	61.2	69.3	81.0	10.1	12.4	19.2	62.7	65.6	76.8	ESS 2008
United States	42.4	69.6	87.5	m	m	m	m	m	m	CPS 2008
OECD average	74.0	79.4	87.2	10.8	14.9	20.0	57.9	67.3	75.5	-
EU21 average	75.3	80.8	88.4	11.2	14.4	19.8	55.8	64.8	74.4	-
Other G20										
Argentina	m	m	m	m	m	m	m	m	m	-
Brazil	m	m	m	m	m	m	m	m	m	-
China	m	m	m	m	m	m	m	m	m	-
India	m	m	m	m	m	m	m	m	m	-
Indonesia	m	m	m	m	m	m	m	m	m	-
Russian Federation	77.9	70.5	73.1	0.8	2.3	5.9	20.7	33.9	37.6	ESS 2008
Saudi Arabia	m	m	m	m	m	m	m	m	m	-
South Africa	m	m	m	m	m	m	m	m	m	-

Notes: Figures presented in the column "Below upper secondary education" describe the proportion of adults aged 25-64 who have attained below upper secondary education reporting: *a)* electoral participation; *b)* volunteering experience; and *c)* satisfaction in life. Likewise, figures presented in columns "Upper secondary education" and "Tertiary education" describe the proportion of adults who have attained upper secondary and tertiary education reporting: *a)* electoral participation; *b)* volunteering experience; and *c)* satisfaction in life. For electoral participation, the analysis is limited to adults who are eligible to vote. Countries with compulsory voting are included in the data, i.e. Belgium, Greece, Luxembourg and Turkey. For countries with a voting-registration requirement which is not enforced or automated (e.g. Ireland, the United Kingdom and the United States), the analysis includes those who are potentially eligible (e.g. are citizens of the country) but have not registered for voting.

Source: European Social Survey (ESS) 2008; General Social Survey (GSS) 2008 for Canada and New Zealand; KEDI's Lifelong Education Survey 2009 for Korea; Current Population Survey (CPS) 2008 for the United States. See Annex 3 for notes *(www.oecd.org/edu/eag2011)*.

Please refer to the Reader's Guide for information concerning the symbols replacing missing data.

StatLink http://dx.doi.org/10.1787/888932463479

Table A11.2. Civic engagement, by students' level of civic knowledge (2009)

Mean scale of civic engagement among 8th grade students, by level of civic knowledge (standard errors in parentheses)

		Expected adult electoral participation								Supportive attitudes towards gender equality								Trust in civic institutions							
		Below Level 1		Level 1		Level 2		Level 3		Below Level 1		Level 1		Level 2		Level 3		Below Level 1		Level 1		Level 2		Level 3	
		Mean	SE	Mean	SE	Mean	SE	Mean	SE	Mean	SE	Mean	SE	Mean	SE	Mean	SE	Mean	SE	Mean	SE	Mean	SE	Mean	SE
OECD	Australia	m	m	m	m	m	m	m	m	m	m	m	m	m	m	m	m	m	m	m	m	m	m	m	m
	Austria	45.1	(0.5)	48.3	(0.5)	51.3	(0.4)	54.7	(0.4)	43.6	(0.5)	48.8	(0.5)	53.0	(0.5)	56.6	(0.4)	52.6	(0.6)	53.4	(0.4)	52.8	(0.4)	52.6	(0.3)
	Belgium (Fl.)	41.8	(0.9)	43.0	(0.5)	45.4	(0.3)	48.9	(0.5)	45.3	(0.7)	49.2	(0.4)	52.6	(0.3)	56.0	(0.4)	49.6	(0.9)	49.1	(0.5)	49.5	(0.4)	49.6	(0.4)
	Canada	m	m	m	m	m	m	m	m	m	m	m	m	m	m	m	m	m	m	m	m	m	m	m	m
	Chile	47.4	(0.7)	48.7	(0.5)	50.2	(0.5)	53.0	(0.5)	43.3	(0.4)	48.7	(0.4)	53.8	(0.3)	57.0	(0.5)	52.2	(0.6)	50.9	(0.5)	49.5	(0.3)	48.2	(0.3)
	Czech Republic	37.4	(0.6)	39.2	(0.4)	44.0	(0.3)	49.7	(0.4)	41.5	(0.3)	44.3	(0.3)	48.7	(0.3)	52.8	(0.3)	50.6	(0.6)	48.6	(0.4)	47.9	(0.3)	47.1	(0.3)
	Denmark	41.3	(1.2)	43.2	(0.5)	47.1	(0.4)	51.7	(0.3)	45.8	(1.0)	49.0	(0.6)	52.2	(0.4)	56.9	(0.2)	45.4	(1.5)	49.3	(0.7)	50.9	(0.3)	53.7	(0.3)
	Estonia	41.7	(0.7)	43.2	(0.5)	46.6	(0.3)	49.8	(0.4)	41.8	(0.5)	45.1	(0.4)	48.9	(0.3)	52.8	(0.4)	46.9	(0.9)	47.6	(0.5)	48.4	(0.4)	48.3	(0.4)
	Finland	42.3	(1.8)	44.0	(0.7)	47.3	(0.3)	51.2	(0.3)	40.1	(1.7)	46.7	(0.9)	51.0	(0.6)	56.1	(0.3)	46.8	(1.9)	50.7	(0.8)	52.8	(0.3)	54.1	(0.2)
	France	m	m	m	m	m	m	m	m	m	m	m	m	m	m	m	m	m	m	m	m	m	m	m	m
	Germany	m	m	m	m	m	m	m	m	m	m	m	m	m	m	m	m	m	m	m	m	m	m	m	m
	Greece	46.5	(0.7)	47.6	(0.5)	51.1	(0.4)	55.1	(0.5)	44.9	(0.8)	47.9	(0.7)	51.8	(0.5)	55.9	(0.4)	48.3	(0.5)	45.2	(0.5)	44.2	(0.5)	43.3	(0.4)
	Hungary	m	m	m	m	m	m	m	m	m	m	m	m	m	m	m	m	m	m	m	m	m	m	m	m
	Iceland	m	m	m	m	m	m	m	m	m	m	m	m	m	m	m	m	m	m	m	m	m	m	m	m
	Ireland	45.1	(1.0)	47.6	(0.6)	51.8	(0.3)	55.9	(0.3)	45.5	(0.8)	50.5	(0.5)	54.4	(0.5)	57.9	(0.3)	49.2	(1.1)	49.6	(0.6)	49.1	(0.4)	49.1	(0.3)
	Israel	m	m	m	m	m	m	m	m	m	m	m	m	m	m	m	m	m	m	m	m	m	m	m	m
	Italy	45.8	(0.8)	49.8	(0.4)	54.1	(0.3)	57.8	(0.3)	43.5	(0.7)	47.0	(0.4)	51.5	(0.3)	55.9	(0.3)	53.5	(1.1)	52.8	(0.5)	52.3	(0.3)	51.5	(0.3)
	Japan	m	m	m	m	m	m	m	m	m	m	m	m	m	m	m	m	m	m	m	m	m	m	m	m
	Korea	40.6	(1.0)	43.5	(0.5)	46.6	(0.3)	51.1	(0.2)	41.0	(0.6)	45.3	(0.4)	49.6	(0.3)	52.5	(0.2)	44.3	(1.6)	44.9	(0.5)	44.0	(0.3)	42.2	(0.2)
	Luxembourg	43.8	(0.5)	45.0	(0.4)	48.2	(0.3)	53.8	(0.3)	44.6	(0.3)	49.9	(0.3)	54.3	(0.3)	57.5	(0.3)	51.5	(0.4)	50.7	(0.4)	51.1	(0.2)	51.6	(0.3)
	Mexico	50.0	(0.3)	52.3	(0.2)	55.2	(0.3)	56.9	(0.3)	41.5	(0.2)	44.5	(0.2)	48.3	(0.2)	51.0	(0.4)	51.4	(0.4)	49.4	(0.3)	47.0	(0.3)	44.6	(0.5)
	Netherlands	43.4	(1.4)	44.2	(0.8)	47.3	(0.6)	50.3	(0.6)	47.7	(1.5)	50.0	(0.9)	52.5	(0.6)	54.2	(1.0)	49.3	(0.9)	50.4	(0.6)	52.2	(0.5)	53.2	(0.5)
	New Zealand	43.9	(0.7)	44.9	(0.5)	48.5	(0.5)	53.3	(0.4)	43.2	(0.6)	47.9	(0.6)	52.9	(0.5)	57.0	(0.3)	50.2	(0.6)	50.0	(0.4)	50.6	(0.3)	50.6	(0.3)
	Norway	43.4	(0.9)	47.1	(0.7)	52.3	(0.4)	57.0	(0.3)	43.8	(0.7)	49.6	(0.5)	54.2	(0.4)	58.6	(0.3)	49.5	(0.8)	52.0	(0.7)	52.7	(0.4)	54.0	(0.4)
	Poland	42.9	(0.9)	45.4	(0.6)	47.1	(0.4)	51.3	(0.3)	41.4	(0.4)	43.6	(0.3)	47.0	(0.4)	51.0	(0.4)	43.8	(0.9)	45.1	(0.5)	45.3	(0.4)	45.2	(0.3)
	Portugal	m	m	m	m	m	m	m	m	m	m	m	m	m	m	m	m	m	m	m	m	m	m	m	m
	Slovak Republic	43.7	(0.9)	44.3	(0.6)	47.1	(0.4)	51.8	(0.4)	40.9	(0.6)	43.9	(0.4)	47.6	(0.3)	52.1	(0.3)	48.9	(1.3)	49.0	(0.6)	48.1	(0.4)	47.6	(0.5)
	Slovenia	44.6	(0.8)	45.7	(0.5)	49.9	(0.3)	53.9	(0.4)	42.9	(0.8)	47.6	(0.4)	52.5	(0.4)	56.8	(0.3)	47.6	(1.1)	47.6	(0.5)	48.4	(0.4)	49.6	(0.3)
	Spain	46.0	(0.8)	48.2	(0.5)	51.8	(0.3)	54.7	(0.4)	44.0	(0.7)	50.8	(0.4)	56.2	(0.3)	59.9	(0.3)	50.0	(0.8)	49.2	(0.5)	49.6	(0.3)	50.0	(0.3)
	Sweden	42.4	(0.9)	44.8	(0.5)	48.3	(0.4)	52.8	(0.3)	44.6	(0.8)	50.6	(0.6)	55.6	(0.4)	59.3	(0.3)	48.9	(1.2)	51.0	(0.5)	51.9	(0.4)	53.5	(0.3)
	Switzerland	42.1	(1.3)	43.3	(0.6)	47.2	(0.4)	51.4	(0.5)	44.0	(0.9)	48.0	(0.6)	52.2	(0.4)	56.3	(0.5)	48.7	(1.6)	49.3	(0.7)	51.0	(0.4)	52.4	(0.3)
	Turkey	m	m	m	m	m	m	m	m	m	m	m	m	m	m	m	m	m	m	m	m	m	m	m	m
	United Kingdom[1]	42.0	(0.6)	43.5	(0.6)	46.8	(0.5)	52.3	(0.5)	44.9	(0.6)	49.9	(0.6)	53.5	(0.5)	57.7	(0.3)	51.3	(0.7)	50.5	(0.4)	50.5	(0.3)	51.4	(0.4)
	United States	m	m	m	m	m	m	m	m	m	m	m	m	m	m	m	m	m	m	m	m	m	m	m	m
	OECD total	43.8	(0.2)	45.7	(0.1)	49.0	(0.1)	53.0	(0.1)	43.3	(0.2)	47.5	(0.1)	51.6	(0.1)	55.4	(0.1)	49.3	(0.2)	49.5	(0.1)	49.7	(0.1)	49.8	(0.1)
	EU21 average	43.3	(0.2)	45.1	(0.1)	48.5	(0.1)	52.7	(0.1)	43.7	(0.2)	47.9	(0.1)	52.0	(0.1)	55.9	(0.1)	49.1	(0.2)	49.4	(0.1)	49.7	(0.1)	50.1	(0.1)
Other G20	Argentina	m	m	m	m	m	m	m	m	m	m	m	m	m	m	m	m	m	m	m	m	m	m	m	m
	Brazil	m	m	m	m	m	m	m	m	m	m	m	m	m	m	m	m	m	m	m	m	m	m	m	m
	China	m	m	m	m	m	m	m	m	m	m	m	m	m	m	m	m	m	m	m	m	m	m	m	m
	India	m	m	m	m	m	m	m	m	m	m	m	m	m	m	m	m	m	m	m	m	m	m	m	m
	Indonesia	50.7	(0.3)	52.5	(0.2)	55.4	(0.3)	57.5	(0.7)	40.0	(0.2)	42.0	(0.2)	45.3	(0.3)	48.1	(0.7)	59.5	(0.4)	59.7	(0.3)	58.0	(0.4)	54.6	(0.8)
	Russian Federation	47.9	(0.7)	49.2	(0.3)	51.8	(0.3)	54.0	(0.4)	39.5	(0.3)	41.2	(0.3)	43.8	(0.2)	47.2	(0.3)	53.2	(0.7)	52.9	(0.3)	52.2	(0.3)	51.4	(0.4)
	Saudi Arabia	m	m	m	m	m	m	m	m	m	m	m	m	m	m	m	m	m	m	m	m	m	m	m	m
	South Africa	m	m	m	m	m	m	m	m	m	m	m	m	m	m	m	m	m	m	m	m	m	m	m	m

Notes: Figures presented in the column "Below Level 1" describe the mean scales of 8th grade students' civic and social engagement (i.e. expect to participate in elections, have supportive attitudes towards gender equality and display trust in civic institutions) among those who have scored "Below Level 1" in civic knowledge. Likewise, figures presented in the columns "Level 1", "Level 2" and "Level 3" describe the mean scales of students' civic and social engagement among those who have scored at "Level 1", "Level 2" and "Level 3" in civic knowledge. EU21 average represents weighted average of EU member countries that are also OECD countries. They include Austria, Belgium (Flanders), the Czech Republic, Denmark, Finland, Greece, Ireland, Italy, Luxembourg, the Netherlands, Poland, the Slovak Republic, Slovenia, Spain, Sweden and the United Kingdom (England). Mean ICCS scales are based on Rasch Partial Credit Model, and the resulting weighted likelihood estimates (WLEs) were transformed into a metric with a mean of 50 and a standard deviation of 10. Definitions provide more details of the ICCS scale.

1. Data for the United Kingdom only refer to England.

Source: International Civic and Citizenship Education Study (ICCS), 2009. See Annex 3 for notes *(www.oecd.org/edu/eag2011)*.

Please refer to the Reader's Guide for information concerning the symbols replacing missing data.

StatLink http://dx.doi.org/10.1787/888932463498

Table A11.3. Incremental differences in adult voting, volunteering and life satisfaction associated with an increase in the level of educational attainment (2008) (with and without adjustments for age, gender and income)

Percentage of 25-64 year-olds, by level of educational attainment

		Electoral participation						Volunteering						Life satisfaction						
		Difference in outcome from below upper secondary to upper secondary			Difference in outcome from upper secondary to tertiary			Difference in outcome from below upper secondary to upper secondary			Difference in outcome from upper secondary to tertiary			Difference in outcome from below upper secondary to upper secondary			Difference in outcome from upper secondary to tertiary			
		No adjustments	Adjustments for age, gender	Adjustments for age, gender, income	No adjustments	Adjustments for age, gender	Adjustments for age, gender, income	No adjustments	Adjustments for age, gender	Adjustments for age, gender, income	No adjustments	Adjustments for age, gender	Adjustments for age, gender, income	No adjustments	Adjustments for age, gender	Adjustments for age, gender, income	No adjustments	Adjustments for age, gender	Adjustments for age, gender, income	Data source
OECD	Australia	m	m	m	m	m	m	m	m	m	m	m	m	m	m	m	m	m	m	-
	Austria	2.1	7.8	7.8	11.0	11.1	-0.7	8.0	5.6	5.6	8.4	7.6	7.2	9.9	7.3	-6.7	2.1	1.9	0.6	ESS 2008
	Belgium	3.6	4.3	3.0	0.7	0.6	5.7	3.3	3.6	2.8	9.3	10.3	9.8	9.6	10.3	7.3	11.0	10.1	5.8	ESS 2008
	Canada	8.9	12.1	9.9	6.1	7.8	5.7	m	m	m	m	m	m	5.7	5.9	3.4	5.2	5.2	3.0	GSS 2008
	Chile	m	m	m	m	m	m	m	m	m	m	m	m	m	m	m	m	m	m	-
	Czech Republic	6.5	9.1	7.2	29.0	28.9	27.5	8.0	7.5	7.1	7.0	7.1	6.4	28.7	26.6	23.7	15.4	15.6	12.3	ESS 2008
	Denmark	6.1	6.4	5.5	2.1	2.0	1.5	7.6	5.8	4.2	2.0	3.9	2.9	1.2	1.1	-0.8	1.1	1.7	0.6	ESS 2008
	Estonia	11.7	11.4	9.0	19.7	19.3	17.1	-0.9	-1.4	-1.2	7.8	7.7	7.3	2.7	2.9	0.8	16.2	16.0	10.1	ESS 2008
	Finland	1.3	7.9	7.5	12.9	13.5	11.2	-2.4	-1.4	-1.6	0.7	0.8	0.1	5.4	4.8	3.7	2.0	1.9	-1.2	ESS 2008
	France	7.4	11.2	9.6	3.0	6.8	6.1	2.4	3.7	2.8	2.5	3.9	4.8	9.7	9.8	4.9	13.4	12.5	5.6	ESS 2008
	Germany	5.0	5.1	5.0	12.7	12.4	9.5	9.9	9.8	9.5	7.1	7.0	5.4	12.3	12.8	11.3	15.4	16.0	10.4	ESS 2008
	Greece	-2.6	-1.4	-2.4	-1.9	-1.7	-2.4	1.6	1.6	1.6	0.6	0.6	0.5	11.8	11.2	9.2	0.0	0.3	-1.1	ESS 2008
	Hungary	6.1	7.1	6.5	2.4	3.0	3.8	4.8	4.5	4.4	9.9	10.3	10.2	4.2	3.9	0.2	21.0	18.3	13.1	ESS 2008
	Iceland	m	m	m	m	m	m	m	m	m	m	m	m	m	m	m	m	m	m	-
	Ireland	5.6	8.2	7.6	-4.2	-0.1	-0.7	2.9	4.7	3.5	5.7	7.4	7.9	1.5	3.0	0.1	3.6	3.9	0.4	ESS 2008
	Israel	-1.4	2.8	-1.5	6.8	6.1	4.9	3.2	4.2	3.2	2.1	2.2	1.7	15.7	13.5	4.6	3.2	4.2	0.4	ESS 2008
	Italy	m	m	m	m	m	m	m	m	m	m	m	m	m	m	m	m	m	m	-
	Japan	m	m	m	m	m	m	m	m	m	m	m	m	m	m	m	m	m	m	-
	Korea	-13.3	-1.1	-1.1	0.5	5.3	5.6	m	m	m	m	m	m	9.8	12.4	11.4	9.1	10.0	7.3	KEDI 2009
	Luxembourg	m	m	m	m	m	m	m	m	m	m	m	m	7.3	8.4	5.1	3.9	4.3	0.9	EVS 2009
	Mexico	m	m	m	m	m	m	m	m	m	m	m	m	m	m	m	m	m	m	-
	Netherlands	11.8	13.0	11.1	4.9	4.7	3.2	6.0	8.6	7.4	6.9	6.3	6.3	6.2	6.3	3.2	6.5	6.4	5.4	ESS 2008
	New Zealand	6.0	8.2	7.5	5.8	5.4	4.3	7.3	8.7	8.3	8.3	8.2	7.6	4.1	4.2	2.8	5.1	5.1	3.6	GSS 2008
	Norway	7.6	10.5	7.8	8.9	10.8	9.3	17.0	17.0	15.2	2.1	3.3	3.1	9.1	8.4	3.0	2.6	2.1	-0.4	ESS 2008
	Poland	10.6	13.7	10.9	16.5	19.0	17.2	2.8	3.3	3.0	10.1	10.7	10.5	15.0	9.7	5.3	10.6	6.7	1.2	ESS 2008
	Portugal	6.9	9.9	8.7	2.9	3.9	3.0	0.2	0.3	0.3	6.8	6.8	7.4	13.5	8.9	7.1	4.6	4.9	3.0	ESS 2008
	Slovak Republic	6.2	8.7	8.7	3.1	4.3	4.3	6.1	8.6	8.6	2.7	4.0	4.0	16.7	14.5	14.5	11.2	9.6	9.6	ESS 2008
	Slovenia	-3.5	0.9	-0.4	12.9	13.6	11.6	-2.0	2.3	1.1	12.6	13.4	11.1	15.3	10.6	6.6	20.0	20.5	16.2	ESS 2008
	Spain	6.4	9.1	8.7	3.2	3.3	1.6	0.5	1.1	1.4	3.5	3.4	2.9	2.1	2.5	0.8	14.5	14.3	12.3	ESS 2008
	Sweden	4.7	7.4	7.1	6.2	6.4	5.5	-0.6	0.7	0.5	2.5	3.1	3.4	2.6	3.7	2.4	1.1	1.0	-3.1	ESS 2008
	Switzerland	6.7	10.4	8.7	21.1	20.4	18.3	9.2	9.3	10.0	5.4	4.8	5.3	15.8	15.9	12.7	4.5	5.4	1.9	ESS 2008
	Turkey	-1.9	0.2	1.6	-1.9	0.1	-0.3	-1.9	0.2	1.6	-1.9	0.1	-0.3	14.4	18.1	17.0	8.3	10.3	4.7	ESS 2008
	United Kingdom	8.1	10.4	8.9	11.7	12.0	10.9	2.3	3.0	2.3	6.9	6.8	5.4	2.9	3.0	-1.9	11.2	11.7	6.8	ESS 2008
	United States	27.2	27.7	23.4	17.8	18.0	14.1	m	m	m	m	m	m	m	m	m	m	m	m	CPS 2008
	OECD average	5.3	8.2	6.9	7.9	8.8	7.3	4.0	4.6	4.2	5.4	5.8	5.5	9.4	8.9	5.6	8.3	8.1	4.8	-
	EU21 average	5.5	7.9	6.8	7.8	8.6	7.2	3.2	3.8	3.3	5.9	6.4	6.0	8.9	8.1	4.8	9.2	8.9	5.4	-
Other G20	Argentina	m	m	m	m	m	m	m	m	m	m	m	m	m	m	m	m	m	m	-
	Brazil	m	m	m	m	m	m	m	m	m	m	m	m	m	m	m	m	m	m	-
	China	m	m	m	m	m	m	m	m	m	m	m	m	m	m	m	m	m	m	-
	India	m	m	m	m	m	m	m	m	m	m	m	m	m	m	m	m	m	m	-
	Indonesia	m	m	m	m	m	m	m	m	m	m	m	m	m	m	m	m	m	m	-
	Russian Federation	-7.4	-3.0	-1.9	2.6	2.9	2.3	1.5	1.6	1.9	3.6	3.7	3.6	13.2	11.1	8.0	3.7	3.0	1.2	ESS 2008
	Saudi Arabia	m	m	m	m	m	m	m	m	m	m	m	m	m	m	m	m	m	m	-
	South Africa	m	m	m	m	m	m	m	m	m	m	m	m	m	m	m	m	m	m	-

Notes: Calculations are based on ordinary least squares regressions among adults aged 25-64. Cells highlighted in grey are statistically significant and different from zero at the 5% level. Non-linear models (probit models) produce similar results.

Source: European Social Survey (ESS) 2008; General Social Survey (GSS) for Canada and New Zealand; KEDI's Lifelong Education Survey 2009 for Korea; Current Population Survey (CPS) 2008 for the United States. See Annex 3 for notes (*www.oecd.org/edu/eag2011*).

Please refer to the Reader's Guide for information concerning the symbols replacing missing data.

StatLink http://dx.doi.org/10.1787/888932463517

Financial and Human Resources Invested In Education

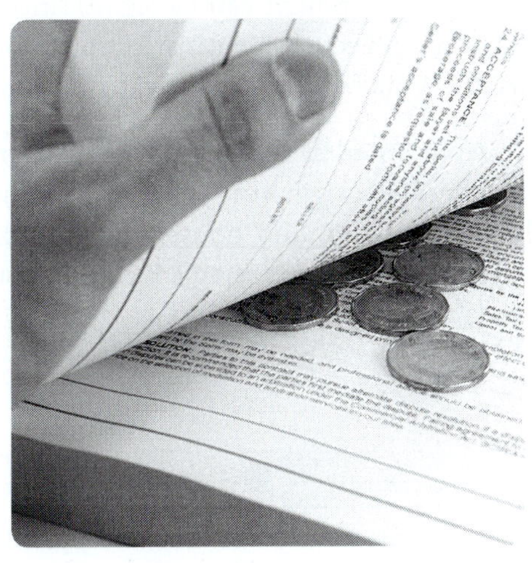

Classification of educational expenditure

Educational expenditure in this chapter is classified through three dimensions:

- The first dimension – represented by the horizontal axis in the diagram below – relates to the location where spending occurs. Spending on schools and universities, education ministries and other agencies directly involved in providing and supporting education is one component of this dimension. Spending on education outside these institutions is another.

- The second dimension – represented by the vertical axis in the diagram below – classifies the goods and services that are purchased. Not all expenditure on educational institutions can be classified as direct educational or instructional expenditure. Educational institutions in many OECD countries offer various ancillary services – such as meals, transport, housing, etc. – in addition to teaching services to support students and their families. At the tertiary level, spending on research and development can be significant. Not all spending on educational goods and services occurs within educational institutions. For example, families may purchase textbooks and materials themselves or seek private tutoring for their children.

- The third dimension – represented by the colours in the diagram below – distinguishes among the sources from which funding originates. These include the public sector and international agencies (indicated by light blue), and households and other private entities (indicated medium-blue). Where private expenditure on education is subsidised by public funds, this is indicated by cells in the grey colour.

Public sources of funds | Private sources of funds | Private funds publicly subsidised

	Spending on educational institutions (e.g. schools, universities, educational administration and student welfare services)	**Spending on education outside educational institutions** (e.g. private purchases of educational goods and services, including private tutoring)
Spending on core educational services	e.g. public spending on instructional services in educational institutions	e.g. subsidised private spending on books
	e.g. subsidised private spending on instructional services in educational institutions	e.g. private spending on books and other school materials or private tutoring
	e.g. private spending on tuition fees	
Spending on research and development	e.g. public spending on university research	
	e.g. funds from private industry for research and development in educational institutions	
Spending on educational services other than instruction	e.g. public spending on ancillary services such as meals, transport to schools, or housing on the campus	e.g. subsidised private spending on student living costs or reduced prices for transport
	e.g. private spending on fees for ancillary services	e.g. private spending on student living costs or transport

CHAPTER B

Coverage diagrams

For Indicators B1, B2 and B3

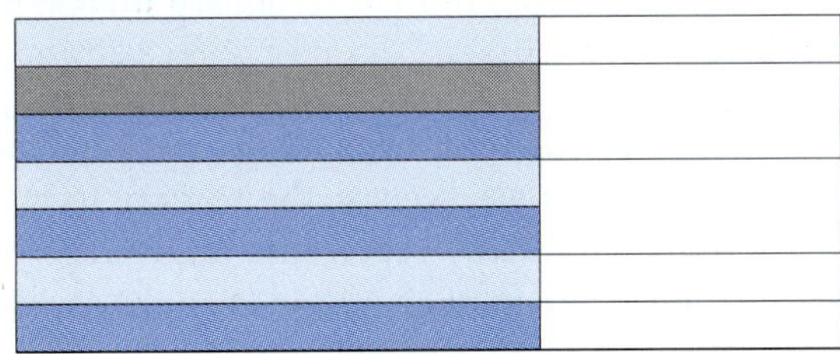

For Indicators B4 and B5

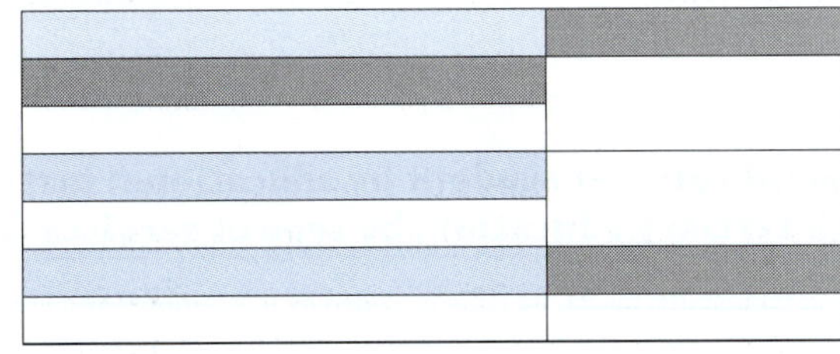

For Indicator B6

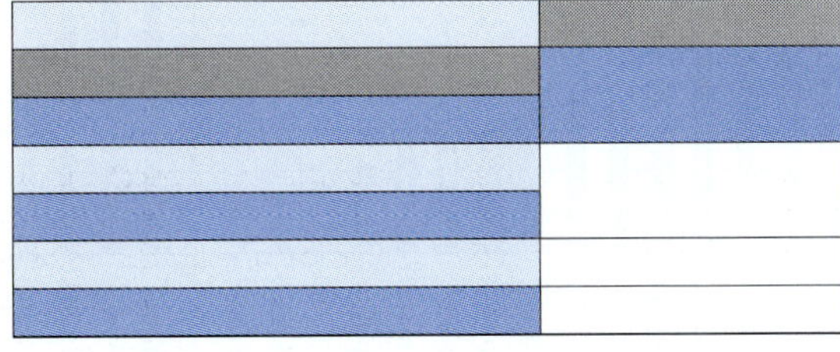

INDICATOR B1

HOW MUCH IS SPENT PER STUDENT?

- OECD countries as a whole spend USD 9 860 annually per student from primary through tertiary education: USD 7 065 per primary student, USD 8 852 per secondary student and USD 18 258 per tertiary student.
- At the primary and secondary levels, 93% of total expenditure per student goes towards core educational services. Greater differences are seen at the tertiary level, partly because expenditure on research and development (R&D) represents an average of 30% of total expenditure per student, and can account for more than 40% in Portugal, Sweden, Switzerland and the United Kingdom.
- From 2000 to 2008, expenditure per student by tertiary educational institutions increased by 14 percentage points on average in OECD countries after having remained stable between 1995 and 2000.

Chart B1.1. Annual expenditure per student by educational institutions from primary through tertiary education, by type of services (2008)

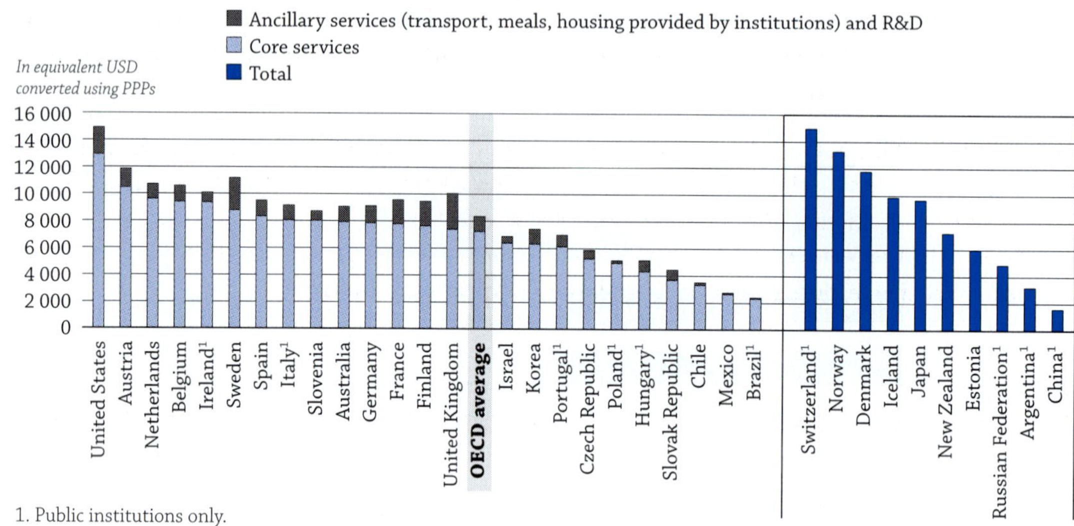

1. Public institutions only.

Countries are ranked in descending order of expenditure per student by educational institutions for core services.

Source: OECD. Argentina: UNESCO Institute for Statistics (World Education Indicators Programme). China: China Educational Finance Statistics Yearbook 2009. Table B1.2. See Annex 3 for notes (*www.oecd.org/edu/eag2011*).

StatLink http://dx.doi.org/10.1787/888932460895

How to read this chart

The amount of expenditure per student by educational institutions provides a measure of the unit costs of formal education. This chart shows annual expenditure per student by educational institutions in equivalent USD converted using purchasing power parities (PPPs), based on the full-time equivalent number of students. It distinguishes expenditure by type of services: core educational services, ancillary services and research and development. Expenditure on core educational services include all expenditure that is directly related to instruction in educational institutions. This should cover all expenditure on teachers, school buildings, teaching materials, books, and administration of schools.

Context

The demand for high-quality education, which can translate into higher costs per student, must be balanced against other demands on public expenditure and the overall burden of taxation. Policy makers must also balance the importance of improving the quality of educational services with the desirability of expanding access to educational opportunities, notably at the tertiary level. A comparative review of trends in expenditure per student by educational institutions shows that, in many OECD countries, the expansion of enrolments, particularly in tertiary education, has not always gone hand-in-hand with increased investment. In addition, some OECD countries emphasise broad access to higher education while others invest in near-universal education for children as young as three or four.

Expenditure per student by educational institutions is largely influenced by teachers' salaries (see Indicators B6 and D3), pension systems, instructional and teaching hours (see Indicators B7, D1 and D4), the cost of teaching materials and facilities, the programme provided (e.g. general or vocational), and the number of students enrolled in the education system (see Indicator C1). Policies to attract new teachers or to reduce average class size or change staffing patterns (see Indicator D2) have also contributed to changes in expenditure per student by educational institutions over time. Ancillary and R&D services can also influence the level of expenditure per student.

Other findings

- **The orientation of programmes provided to students at the secondary level influences the level of expenditure per student** in most countries. The 16 OECD countries for which data are available spend an average of USD 970 more per student in upper secondary vocational programmes than in general programmes.
- **At the primary and secondary levels there is a strong positive relationship between spending per student by educational institutions and GDP per capita. The relationship is weaker at the tertiary level.**
- On average, **OECD countries spend nearly twice as much per student at the tertiary level as at the primary level.** However, R&D activities or ancillary services can account for a significant proportion of expenditure at the tertiary level. When these are excluded, expenditure per student on core educational services at the tertiary level is still, on average, 20% higher than at the primary, secondary and post-secondary non-tertiary levels.

Trends

Expenditure per primary, secondary and post-secondary non-tertiary student by educational institutions increased in every country with available data by an average of 34% between 2000 and 2008, a period of relatively stable student numbers.

During the same period, **spending per tertiary student fell in 7 of the 30 countries** with available data, as expenditure did not keep up with expanding enrolments at this level. Chile, Israel, the Netherlands and the United States, which saw significant increases in student enrolment between 2000 and 2008, did not increase spending at the same pace; as a result, expenditure per student decreased in these countries. This is also the case in Brazil, Hungary and Switzerland, where public expenditure per student (data on private expenditure are not available) decreased during the period.

Analysis

Expenditure per student by educational institutions in equivalent USD

Spending per student from primary through tertiary education in 2008 ranged from USD 4 000 per student or less in Argentina, Brazil, Chile, China and Mexico, to more than USD 10 000 per student in Austria, Belgium, Denmark, Ireland, the Netherlands, Norway, Sweden and the United Kingdom, and up to nearly USD 15 000 in Switzerland and the United States. In 12 of 34 countries with available data, it ranged from USD 7 000 to less than USD 10 000 per student from primary through tertiary education (Chart B1.1 and Table B1.1a). Countries have different priorities for allocating their resources (see Indicator B7). For example, among the ten countries with the largest expenditure per student by educational institutions, Ireland, the Netherlands and Switzerland have the highest teachers' salaries at the secondary level after Luxembourg (see Indicator D3), while Austria, Belgium, Denmark, Norway and Sweden are among the countries with the lowest student-to-teacher ratios at the secondary level (see Indicator D2).

Even if spending per student from primary through tertiary education is similar in some OECD countries, the ways in which resources are allocated among the different levels of education vary widely. Spending per student by educational institutions in a typical OECD country (as represented by the simple mean across all OECD countries) amounts to USD 7 153 at the primary level, USD 8 972 at the secondary level and USD 13 717 at the tertiary level (Table B1.1a and Chart B1.2). At the tertiary level, the totals are affected by high expenditure in a few large OECD countries, most notably Canada and the United States.

These averages mask a broad range of expenditure per student by educational institutions. At the primary and secondary levels, expenditure per student by educational institutions varies by a factor of 6 and 10, respectively, ranging from USD 2 246 or less per student at the primary level in Brazil, Indonesia and Mexico to USD 13 648 in Luxembourg, and, at the secondary level, from USD 2 058 or less per student in Brazil and Indonesia to USD 19 898 in Luxembourg. Expenditure per tertiary student by educational institutions ranges from USD 6 560 or less in Argentina, China and the Slovak Republic to more than USD 20 000 in Canada, Sweden, Switzerland and the United States (Table B1.1a and Chart B1.2).

These comparisons are based on purchasing power parities (PPPs) for GDP, not on market exchange rates. They therefore reflect the amount of a national currency required to produce the same basket of goods and services in a given country as produced by the United States in USD.

Expenditure per student on core educational services

Expenditure on core educational services represents, on average in OECD countries, 82% of total expenditure per student from primary through tertiary education, and exceeds 95% in Brazil, Mexico and Poland. In 6 of the 25 countries for which data are available – Finland, France, Hungary, the Slovak Republic, Sweden and the United Kingdom – annual expenditure on R&D and ancillary services per student from primary through tertiary education accounts for more than 15% of the total annual expenditure per student and can influence the ranking of countries for all services combined. However, this overall picture masks large variations among the levels of education.

At the primary and secondary levels, expenditure is dominated by spending on core educational services. On average, those OECD countries for which data are available spend USD 7 617 on core educational services at the primary, secondary and post-secondary non-tertiary levels. This corresponds to 93% of the total expenditure per student by educational institutions at these levels. In 12 of the 24 countries for which data are available, ancillary services provided by these institutions account for less than 5% of the total expenditure per student. The proportion exceeds 10% of total expenditure per student in Finland, France, Hungary, Korea, the Slovak Republic, Sweden and the United Kingdom.

Chart B1.2. Annual expenditure per student by educational institutions for all services, by level of education (2008)

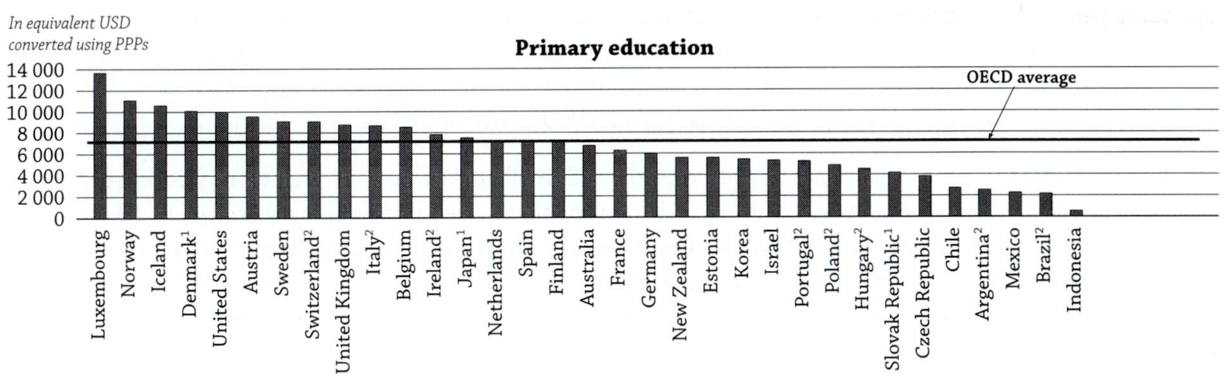

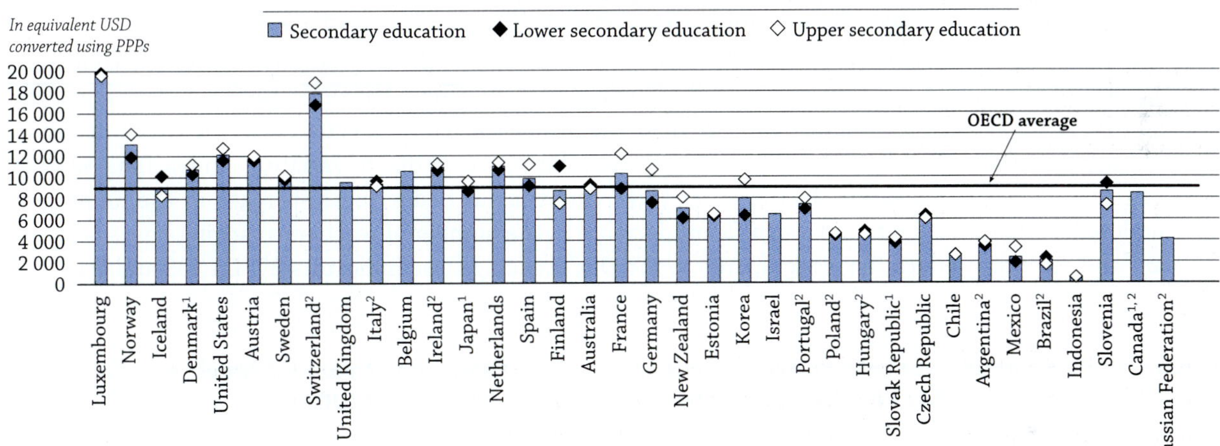

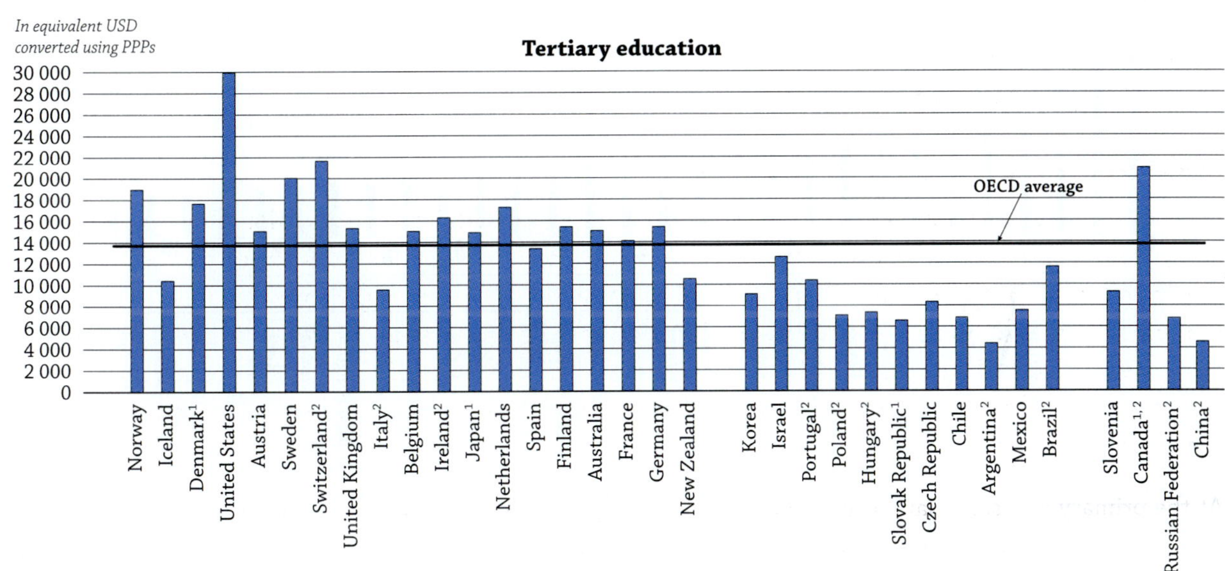

1. Some levels of education are included with others. Refer to "x" code in Table B1.1a for details.
2. Public institutions only (for Canada, in tertiary education only; for Italy, except in tertiary education).

Countries are ranked in descending order of expenditure per student by educational institutions in primary education.

Source: OECD. Argentina, Indonesia: UNESCO Institute for Statistics (World Education Indicators Programme). China: China Educational Finance Statistics Yearbook 2009. Table B1.1a. See Annex 3 for notes (*www.oecd.org/edu/eag2011*).

StatLink http://dx.doi.org/10.1787/888932460914

Greater differences are seen at the tertiary level, partly because R&D expenditure can account for a significant proportion of educational spending. The OECD countries in which most R&D is performed in tertiary education institutions tend to report higher expenditure per student than those in which a large proportion of R&D is performed in other public institutions or in industry. Excluding R&D activities and ancillary services, expenditure on core educational services in tertiary institutions is, on average, USD 9 148 per student and ranges from USD 5 000 or less in the Slovak Republic to more than USD 10 000 in Austria, Brazil, Canada, Ireland, Israel, the Netherlands, Norway and Sweden, and more than USD 23 000 in the United States (Table B1.2).

On average in OECD countries, expenditure on R&D and ancillary services at the tertiary level represents 30% and 4%, respectively, of all expenditure per student by tertiary educational institutions. In 13 of the 23 OECD countries for which data on R&D and ancillary services are available separately from total expenditure – Australia, Belgium, Canada, Finland, France, Germany, Italy, the Netherlands, Norway, Portugal, Sweden, Switzerland and the United Kingdom – expenditure on R&D and ancillary services is at least one-third of total tertiary expenditure per student by educational institutions. This can translate into significant amounts: in Canada, Germany, Norway, Sweden, Switzerland and the United Kingdom, expenditure for R&D and ancillary services amounts to more than USD 6 500 per student (Table B1.2).

Expenditure per student by educational institutions at different levels of education

Expenditure per student by educational institutions rises with the level of education in almost all countries, but the size of the differentials varies markedly (Table B1.1a and Chart B1.3). At the secondary level, the expenditure is, on average, 1.3 times greater than at the primary level. It exceeds 1.5 in the Czech Republic, France, the Netherlands and Switzerland. In Switzerland, this is mainly due to variations in teachers' salaries between these levels of education. In the other three countries, it is due to an increase in the number of instructional hours for students and a significant decrease in the number of teachers' teaching hours between primary and secondary education, as compared to the OECD average (see Indicators B7, D1, D3 and D4).

Chart B1.3. Expenditure per student by educational institutions at various levels of education for all services relative to primary education (2008)

Primary education = 100

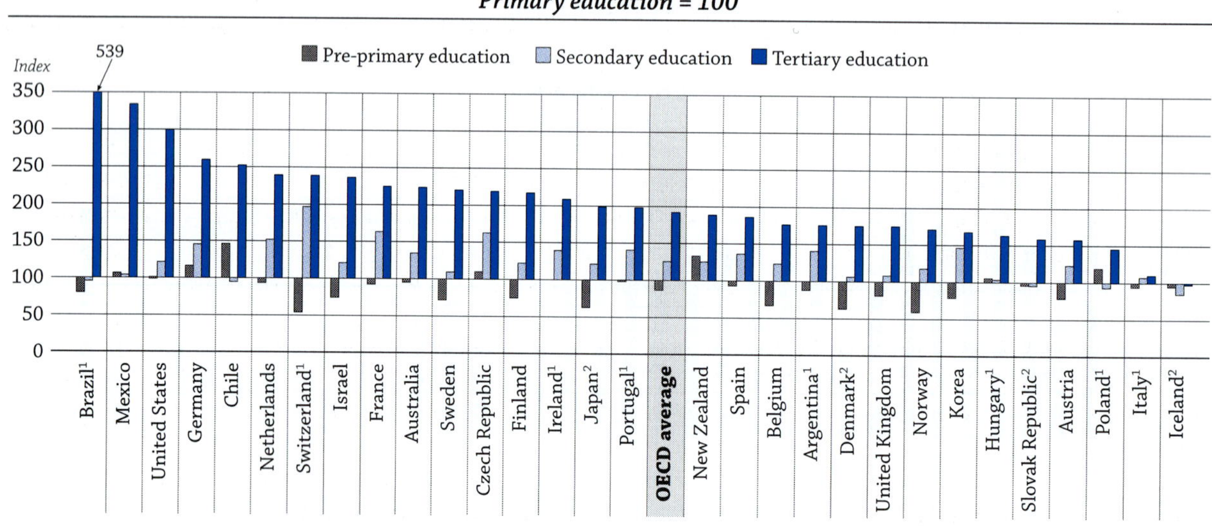

Note: A ratio of 300 for tertiary education means that expenditure per tertiary student by educational institutions is three times the expenditure per primary student by educational institutions.

A ratio of 50 for pre-primary education means that expenditure per pre-primary student by educational institutions is half the expenditure per primary student by educational institutions.

1. Public institutions only (for Italy, except in tertiary education).

2. Some levels of education are included with others. Refer to "x" code in Table B1.1a for details.

Countries are ranked in descending order of expenditure per student by educational institutions in tertiary education relative to primary education.

Source: OECD. Argentina: UNESCO Institute for Statistics (World Education Indicators Programme). Table B1.1a. See Annex 3 for notes (*www.oecd.org/edu/eag2011*).

StatLink http://dx.doi.org/10.1787/888932460933

Educational institutions in OECD countries spend, on average, 1.9 times more per tertiary student than per primary student, but spending patterns vary widely, mainly because education policies vary more at the tertiary level (see Indicator B5). For example, Iceland, Italy and Poland spend less than 1.5 times more on a tertiary student than on a primary student, but Brazil, Mexico and the United States spend about three times as much or even more (Table B1.1a and Chart B1.3).

Differences in educational expenditure per student between general and vocational programmes

In the 16 OECD countries for which data are available, expenditure per student in upper secondary vocational programmes represents, on average, USD 970 more than that per student in general programmes. The countries with large enrolments in dual-system apprenticeship programmes at the upper secondary level (e.g. Austria, France, Germany, Hungary, Luxembourg, the Netherlands and Switzerland) tend to be those with the largest difference, compared to the OECD average, between expenditure per student enrolled in general and vocational programmes. Germany, Luxembourg, the Netherlands and Switzerland spend, respectively, USD 4 567, USD 1 842, USD 3 393 and USD 8 726 more per student in vocational programmes than per student in general programmes. Exceptions to this pattern are Austria and France, which have approximately the same level of expenditure per student in the two types of programmes, and Hungary, where expenditure per student enrolled in a general programme is slightly higher than that per student in an apprenticeship programme. The latter is partly explained by the underestimation of the expenditures made by private enterprises on dual vocational programmes in Austria, France and Hungary (Box B3.1). Among the three other countries with 60% or more of upper secondary students enrolled in vocational programmes – the Czech Republic, Finland, and the Slovak Republic – all spend significantly more per student enrolled in vocational programmes than per student enrolled in general programmes (Table B1.6, Table C1.4 and Box B3.1).

Expenditure per student by educational institutions over the average duration of tertiary studies

Given that the duration and intensity of tertiary education vary from country to country, differences in annual expenditure on educational services per student (Chart B1.2) do not necessarily reflect differences in the total cost of educating the typical tertiary student. For example, if the typical duration of tertiary studies is long, comparatively low annual expenditure per student by educational institutions can result in comparatively high overall costs for tertiary education. Chart B1.4 shows the average expenditure per student throughout the course of tertiary studies. The figures account for all students for whom expenditure is incurred, including those who do not finish their studies. Although the calculations are based on a number of simplified assumptions, and therefore should be treated with caution (see Annex 3 at *www.oecd.org/edu/eag2011*), there are some notable differences between annual and aggregate expenditure in the ranking of countries.

For example, annual spending per tertiary student in Austria is about the same as in Belgium, at USD 15 043 and USD 15 020, respectively (Table B1.1a). But because of differences in the tertiary degree structure (see Indicator A3), the average duration of tertiary studies is more than one year longer in Austria than in Belgium (4.3 and 3.0 years, respectively). As a consequence, the cumulative expenditure for each tertiary student is nearly USD 20 000 less in Belgium (USD 44 911) than in Austria (USD 65 334) (Chart B1.4 and Table B1.3a).

The total cost of tertiary-type A (largely theory-based) education in Switzerland (USD 126 964) is more than twice the amount reported by other countries, with the exception of Austria, Finland, France, Germany, Japan, the Netherlands, Spain and Sweden (Table B1.3a). These figures must be interpreted bearing in mind differences in national degree structures and possible differences in the qualifications students obtain after completing their studies. Tertiary-type B (shorter and vocationally oriented) programmes tend to be less expensive than tertiary-type A programmes, largely because of their shorter duration.

Expenditure per student by educational institutions relative to GDP per capita

Since education is universal at lower levels in most of the OECD countries, spending per student by educational institutions at those levels relative to GDP per capita can be interpreted as the resources spent on the school-age population relative to a country's ability to pay. At higher levels of education, this measure is more difficult to interpret because the levels of enrolment vary sharply among countries. At the tertiary level, for example, OECD countries may rank relatively high on this measure if a large proportion of their wealth is spent on educating a relatively small number of students.

Chart B1.4. Cumulative expenditure per student by educational institutions over the average duration of tertiary studies (2008)

Annual expenditure per student by educational institutions multiplied by the average duration of studies, in equivalent USD converted using PPPs

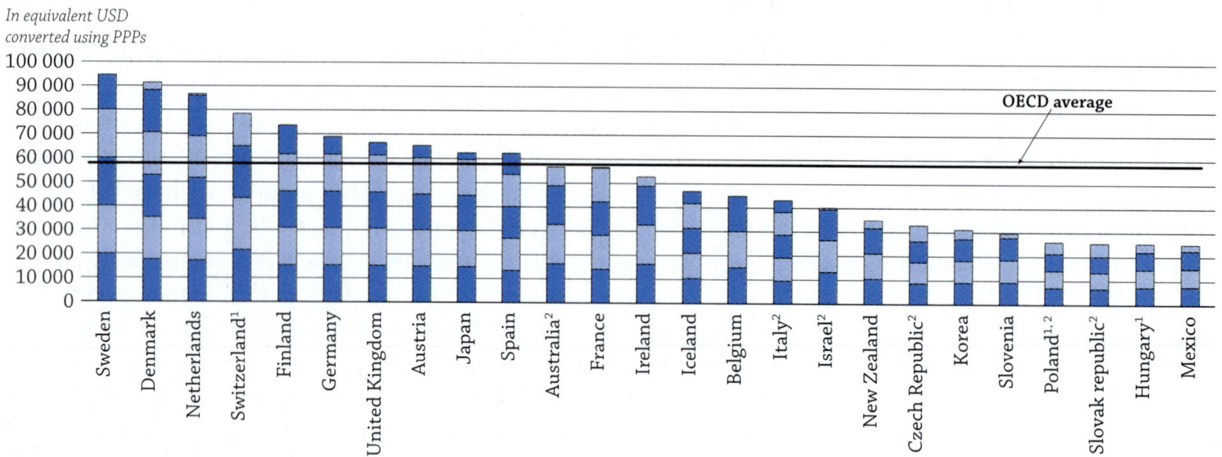

Note: Each segment of the bar represents the annual expenditure by educational institutions per student. The number of segments represents the average number of years a student remains in tertiary education.

1. Public institutions only.

2. Tertiary-type A and advanced research programmes only.

Countries are ranked in descending order of the total expenditure per student by educational institutions over the average duration of tertiary studies.

Source: OECD. Table B1.3a. See Annex 3 for notes (*www.oecd.org/edu/eag2011*).

StatLink http://dx.doi.org/10.1787/888932460952

In OECD countries, expenditure per student by educational institutions averages 21% of GDP per capita at the primary level, 26% at the secondary level and 41% at the tertiary level (Table B1.4). Countries with low levels of expenditure may nevertheless show distributions of investment relative to GDP per capita that are similar to those of countries with a high level of spending per student. For example, Korea and Portugal – countries with below OECD average expenditure per student by educational institutions at the secondary level of education and below OECD average GDP per capita – spend more per student relative to GDP per capita than the OECD average.

The relationship between GDP per capita and expenditure per student by educational institutions is complex. As one would expect, there is a clear positive relationship between the two at both primary and secondary levels of education, i.e. poorer countries tend to spend less per student than richer ones. Although the relationship is generally positive at these levels, there are variations even among countries with similar levels of GDP per capita, especially those in which it exceeds USD 30 000. Australia and Austria, for example, have similar levels of GDP per capita but spend very different proportions of it at the primary and secondary levels. In Australia, the proportions are 17% at the primary level and 23% at the secondary level (below the OECD averages of 21% and 26%, respectively), while in Austria, the proportions are among the highest, at 24% and 29%, respectively (Table B1.4 and Chart B1.5).

There is more variation in spending at the tertiary level, and the relationship between countries' relative wealth and their expenditure levels varies as well. Italy and Spain, for example, have similar levels of GDP per capita (USD 33 271 and USD 33 173, respectively) but very different levels of spending on tertiary education (USD 9 553 and USD 13 366, respectively). Globally, Canada, China, Sweden and the United States spend 50% or more of GDP per capita on each tertiary student – among the highest proportions after Brazil (Table B1.4 and Chart B1.5). Brazil spends the equivalent of 106% of GDP per capita on each tertiary student; however, it is important to bear in mind that tertiary students represent only 3% of students enrolled in all levels of education combined (Table B1.7, available on line).

Chart B1.5. Annual expenditure per student by educational institutions relative to GDP per capita (2008)

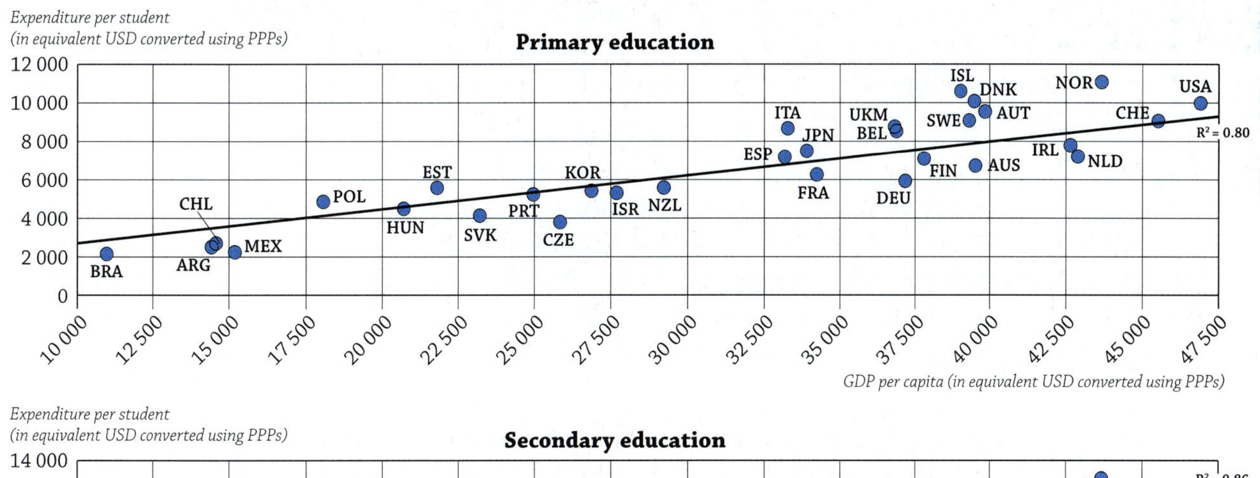

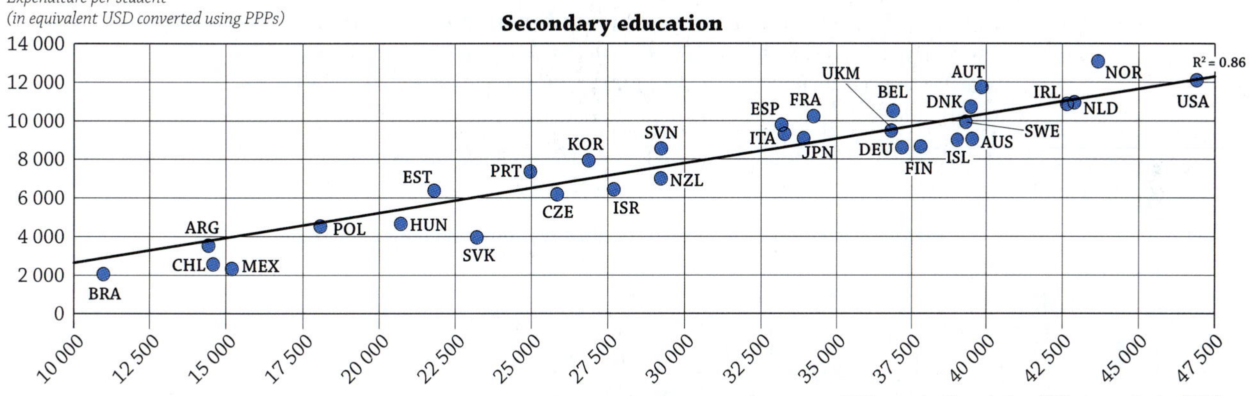

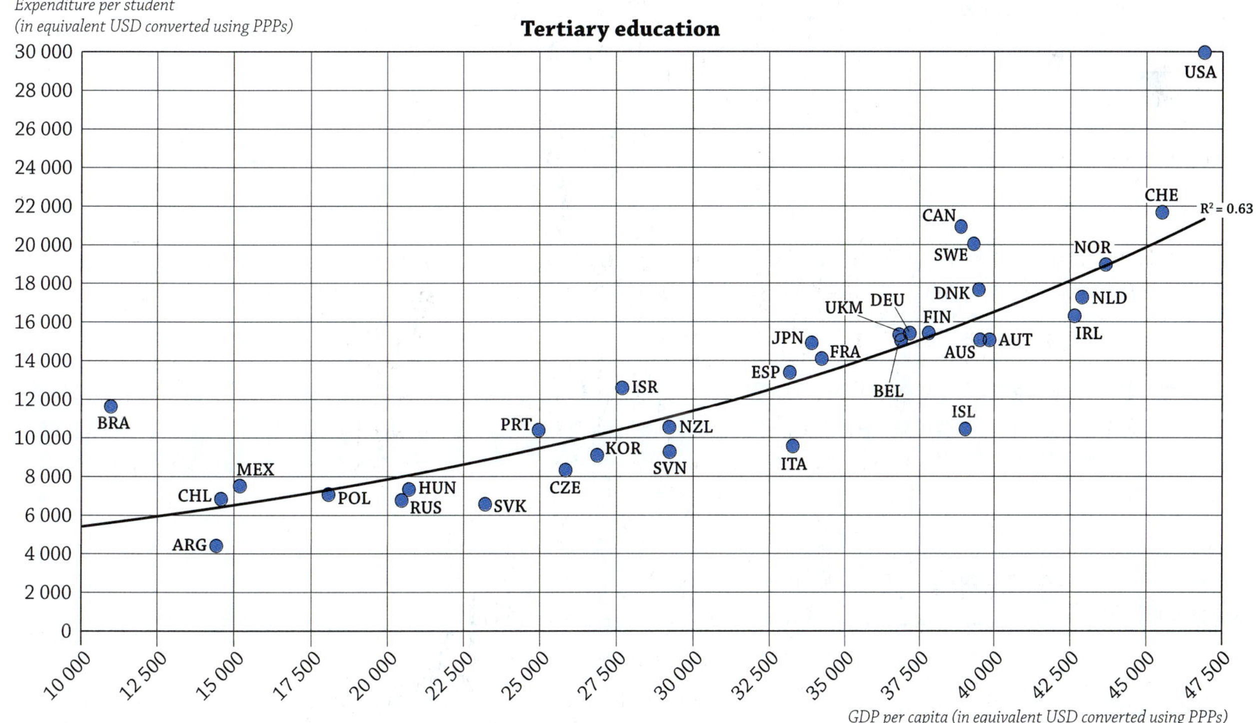

Note: Please refer to the Reader's Guide for the list of country codes used in this chart.

Source: OECD. Argentina: UNESCO Institute for Statistics (World Education Indicators Programme). Tables B1.1a, B1.4 and Annex 2. See Annex 3 for notes (*www.oecd.org/edu/eag2011*).

StatLink http://dx.doi.org/10.1787/888932460971

Change in expenditure per student by educational institutions between 1995 and 2008

Expenditure by educational institutions largely reflects changes in the size of the school-age population and in teachers' salaries. These tend to rise over time in real terms, as teachers' salaries, the main component of costs, increase in line with other workers' salaries. The size of the school-age population influences both enrolment levels and the amount of resources and organisational effort a country must invest in its education system. The larger this population, the greater the potential demand for educational services.

Expenditure per primary, secondary and post-secondary non-tertiary student by educational institutions increased in every country by an average of 54% between 1995 and 2008, when student enrolment at these levels was relatively stable. The rate of increase was similar before and after 2000; only the Czech Republic and Switzerland showed a decrease between 1995 and 2000, followed by an increase between 2000 and 2008 (Table B1.5).

Chart B1.6. Changes in the number of students and changes in expenditure per student by educational institutions, by level of education (2000, 2008)

Index of change between 2000 and 2008 (2000 = 100, 2008 constant prices)

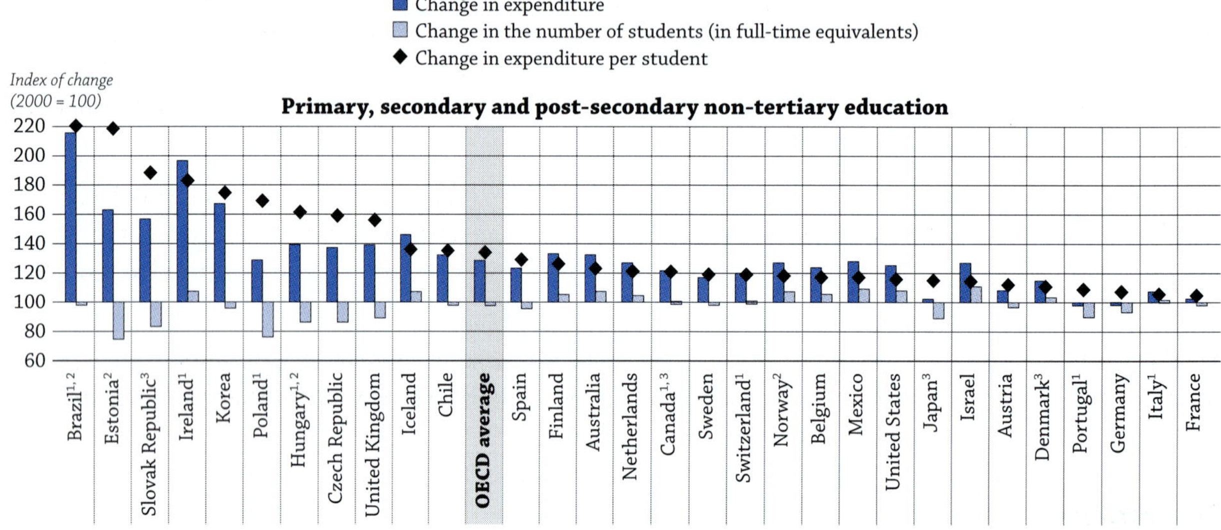

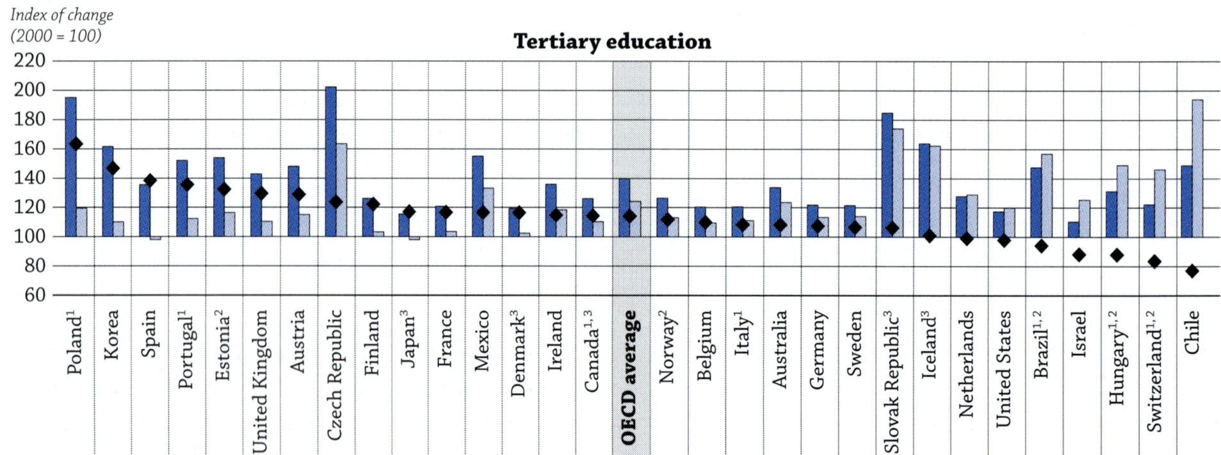

1. Public institutions only (for Canada, in tertiary education only; for Italy, except in tertiary education).
2. Public expenditure only (for Switzerland, in tertiary education only).
3. Some levels of education are included with others. Refer to "x" code in Table B1.1a for details.

Countries are ranked in descending order of the change in expenditure per student by educational institutions.

Source: OECD. Table B1.5. See Annex 3 for notes (*www.oecd.org/edu/eag2011*).

StatLink http://dx.doi.org/10.1787/888932460990

Between 2000 and 2008, in 23 of the 30 countries for which data are available, expenditure per primary, secondary and post-secondary non-tertiary student by educational institutions increased by at least 15%. The increase exceeded 40% in Brazil, the Czech Republic, Estonia, Hungary, Ireland, Korea, Poland, the Slovak Republic and the United Kingdom. In France, Germany and Italy, this expenditure increased by 7% or less between 2000 and 2008 (Table B1.5 and Chart B1.6).

In most countries, changes in enrolments do not seem to have been the main factor behind changes in expenditure at these levels. However, in the Czech Republic, Estonia, Hungary, Poland, the Slovak Republic, Spain and the United Kingdom, a decrease in enrolment of more than 5% coincided with significant increases (over 5%) in spending per student by educational institutions between 2000 and 2008. In Germany, Japan and Portugal, a similar decline in enrolment at the primary, secondary and post-secondary non-tertiary levels coincided with a decrease or only a slight increase in expenditure at those levels (Table B1.5 and Chart B1.7 available on line).

The pattern is different at the tertiary level. In some cases, spending per student fell between 1995 and 2008, as expenditure did not keep up with expanding enrolments. On average among OECD countries, expenditure per tertiary student by educational institutions remained stable from 1995 to 2000 but then increased from 2000 to 2008 (see Indicators B3 and B4). Between 2000 and 2008, the Czech Republic, Estonia, Iceland, Korea, Mexico, Poland, Portugal and the Slovak Republic increased expenditure by 50% or more and expenditure per student also increased during this period. However, the increase in expenditure per student did not completely counterbalance the decrease between 1995 and 2000 in the Czech Republic and the Slovak Republic. Nevertheless, only in Hungary was there a decrease in expenditure per student in both periods (Table B1.5).

Between 2000 and 2008, of the 30 countries for which data are available, Chile, Israel, the Netherlands and the United States recorded a decrease in expenditure per student in tertiary education. This is also the case in Brazil, Hungary and Switzerland, where public expenditure per student (data on private expenditure are not available) decreased during the period.

In all of these countries, the decline was mainly the result of a rapid increase of 20% or more in the number of tertiary students (Chart B1.6). Japan and Spain were the only countries in which the number of tertiary students decreased between 2000 and 2008 (Table B1.5 and Chart B1.6).

Definitions

Ancillary services are defined as services provided by educational institutions that are peripheral to the main educational mission. The main component of ancillary services is student welfare services. In primary, secondary and post-secondary non-tertiary education, student welfare services include such things as meals, school health services, and transportation to and from school. At the tertiary level, they include halls of residence (dormitories), dining halls, and health care.

Core educational services include all expenditure that is directly related to instruction in educational institutions. This should cover all expenditure on teachers, school buildings, teaching materials, books, and administration of schools.

Research and development (R&D) includes all expenditure on research performed at universities and other tertiary education institutions, regardless of whether the research is financed from general institutional funds or through separate grants or contracts from public or private sponsors. The classification of expenditure is based on data collected from the institutions carrying out R&D rather than on the sources of funds.

Methodology

Data refer to the financial year 2008 and are based on the UOE data collection on education statistics administered by the OECD in 2010 (for details see Annex 3 at *www.oecd.org/edu/eag2011*).

The indicator shows direct public and private expenditure by educational institutions in relation to the number of full-time equivalent students enrolled. Public subsidies for students' living expenses outside educational institutions have been excluded to ensure international comparability.

Expenditure per student by educational institutions at a particular level of education is calculated by dividing the total expenditure by educational institutions at that level by the corresponding full-time equivalent enrolment. Only educational institutions and programmes for which both enrolment and expenditure data are available are taken into account. Expenditure in national currency is converted into equivalent USD by dividing the national currency figure by the purchasing power parity (PPP) index for GDP. The PPP exchange rate is used because the market exchange rate is affected by many factors (interest rates, trade policies, expectations of economic growth, etc.) that have little to do with current relative domestic purchasing power in different OECD countries (see Annex 2 for further details).

Expenditure data for students in private educational institutions are not available for certain countries, and some other countries provide incomplete data on independent private institutions. Where this is the case, only expenditure on public and government dependent private institutions has been taken into account.

Variations in expenditure per student by educational institutions may reflect not only variations in the material resources provided to students, such as variations in student-teacher ratios, but also variations in relative salary and price levels.

Core educational services are estimated as the residual of all expenditure, that is, total expenditure on educational institutions net of expenditure on R&D and ancillary services.

The OECD total reflects the value of the indicator if the OECD region is considered as a whole (see the Reader's Guide for details).

Table B1.5 shows the changes in expenditure per student by educational institutions between the financial years 1995, 2000 and 2008. OECD countries were asked to collect 1995 and 2000 data according to the definitions and coverage of UOE 2010 data collection. All expenditure data and GDP information for 1995 and 2000 are adjusted to 2008 prices using the GDP price deflator.

Expenditure per student by educational institutions relative to GDP per capita is calculated by expressing expenditure per student by educational institutions in units of national currency as a percentage of GDP per capita, also in national currency. In cases where the educational expenditure data and the GDP data pertain to different reference periods, the expenditure data are adjusted to the same reference period as the GDP data, using inflation rates for the OECD country in question (see Annex 2).

Cumulative expenditure over the average duration of tertiary studies (Table B1.3a) is calculated by multiplying current annual expenditure by the typical duration of tertiary studies. The methodology used to estimate the typical duration of tertiary studies is described in Annex 3 (*www.oecd.org/edu/eag2011*). For estimates of the duration of tertiary education, data are based on a survey carried out in OECD countries in 2010.

The ranking of OECD countries by annual expenditure on educational services per student is affected by differences in how countries define full-time, part-time and full-time equivalent enrolment. Some OECD countries count every participant at the tertiary level as a full-time student while others determine a student's intensity of participation by the credits that he/she obtains for successful completion of specific course units during a specified reference period. OECD countries that can accurately account for part-time enrolment have higher apparent expenditure per full-time equivalent student by educational institutions than OECD countries that cannot differentiate among the different types of student attendance.

The statistical data for Israel are supplied by and under the responsibility of the relevant Israeli authorities. The use of such data by the OECD is without prejudice to the status of the Golan Heights, East Jerusalem and Israeli settlements in the West Bank under the terms of international law.

References

The following additional material relevant to this indicator is available on line:

- ***Table B1.1b. Annual expenditure per student by educational institutions for core services (2008)***
  StatLink http://dx.doi.org/10.1787/888932463612
- ***Table B1.3b. Cumulative expenditure per student by educational institutions for all services over the theoretical duration of primary and secondary studies (2008)***
  StatLink http://dx.doi.org/10.1787/888932463669
- ***Table B1.7. Distribution of expenditure (as a percentage) by educational institutions compared to the number of students enrolled at each level of education (2008)***
  StatLink http://dx.doi.org/10.1787/888932463745

B1

Table B1.1a. Annual expenditure per student by educational institutions for all services (2008)

In equivalent USD converted using PPPs for GDP, by level of education, based on full-time equivalents

		Pre-primary education (for children 3 years and older)	Primary education	Secondary education: Lower secondary education	Secondary education: Upper secondary education	Secondary education: All secondary education	Post-secondary non-tertiary education	Tertiary education (including R&D activities): Tertiary-type B education	Tertiary education (including R&D activities): Tertiary-type A & advanced research programmes	Tertiary education (including R&D activities): All tertiary education	All tertiary education excluding R&D activities	Primary to tertiary education
		(1)	(2)	(3)	(4)	(5)	(6)	(7)	(8)	(9)	(10)	(11)
OECD	Australia	6 408	6 723	9 200	8 821	9 052	6 769	8 395	16 297	15 043	9 926	**9 056**
	Austria	7 508	9 542	11 533	11 956	11 741	7 354	12 218	15 081	15 043	10 477	**11 852**
	Belgium	5 732	8 528	x(5)	x(5)	10 511	x(5)	x(9)	x(9)	15 020	9 713	**10 589**
	Canada[1, 2]	x(2)	7 648	x(2)	9 754	8 388	m	15 557	24 384	20 903	15 119	**m**
	Chile[3]	3 951	2 707	2 596	2 548	2 564	a	3 556	9 329	6 829	6 478	**3 520**
	Czech Republic	4 181	3 799	6 338	6 030	6 174	1 663	3 371	8 738	8 318	6 920	**5 895**
	Denmark	6 382	10 080	10 268	11 160	10 720	x(4, 9)	x(9)	x(9)	17 634	m	**11 788**
	Estonia	3 198	5 579	6 264	6 461	6 371	6 327	5 307	6 022	m	5 780	**5 982**
	Finland	5 334	7 092	10 950	7 461	8 659	x(5)	n	15 402	15 402	9 592	**9 463**
	France	5 787	6 267	8 816	12 087	10 231	m	11 461	14 945	14 079	9 854	**9 562**
	Germany	6 887	5 929	7 509	10 597	8 606	8 495	7 693	17 114	15 390	9 504	**9 115**
	Greece	m	m	m	m	m	m	m	m	m	m	**m**
	Hungary[2]	4 750	4 495	4 852	4 471	4 658	5 132	5 055	7 454	7 327	5 732	**5 135**
	Iceland	10 080	10 599	10 100	8 290	9 007	x(5)	x(9)	x(9)	10 429	m	**9 873**
	Ireland[2]	m	7 795	10 583	11 205	10 868	7 571	x(9)	x(9)	16 284	11 651	**10 082**
	Israel	3 953	5 314	x(5)	x(5)	6 429	5 429	9 690	13 248	12 568	m	**6 885**
	Italy[2]	8 187	8 671	9 616	9 121	9 315	m	8 944	9 556	9 553	5 959	**9 149**
	Japan	4 711	7 491	8 621	9 559	9 092	x(4, 9)	9 451	16 533	14 890	m	**9 673**
	Korea	4 281	5 420	6 307	9 666	7 931	a	5 742	10 109	9 081	7 771	**7 434**
	Luxembourg	13 460	13 648	19 791	20 002	19 898	m	m	m	m	m	**m**
	Mexico	2 391	2 246	1 853	3 277	2 333	a	x(9)	x(9)	7 504	6 298	**2 763**
	Netherlands	6 745	7 208	10 608	11 301	10 950	11 408	n	17 245	17 245	11 203	**10 704**
	New Zealand	7 431	5 582	6 071	8 025	6 994	8 796	8 594	11 125	10 526	8 815	**7 218**
	Norway	6 572	11 077	11 860	14 039	13 070	x(5)	x(9)	x(9)	18 942	11 598	**13 285**
	Poland[2]	5 792	4 855	4 424	4 613	4 525	6 184	5 079	7 089	7 063	6 038	**5 135**
	Portugal[2]	5 248	5 234	6 910	7 924	7 357	m	x(9)	x(9)	10 373	6 097	**7 005**
	Slovak Republic	3 977	4 137	3 716	4 174	3 956	x(4)	x(4)	6 560	6 560	5 671	**4 446**
	Slovenia	8 029	x(3)	9 287	7 284	8 555	x(4)	x(9)	x(9)	9 263	7 608	**8 719**
	Spain	6 708	7 184	9 108	11 113	9 792	a	10 725	13 928	13 366	9 451	**9 499**
	Sweden	6 519	9 080	9 739	10 103	9 940	6 128	7 865	20 864	20 014	10 019	**11 162**
	Switzerland[2]	4 911	9 063	16 737	18 844	17 825	x(4)	5 139	23 284	21 648	9 845	**14 977**
	Turkey	m	m	a	m	m	a	m	m	m	m	**m**
	United Kingdom	7 119	8 758	9 737	9 307	9 487	x(4)	x(9)	x(9)	15 310	8 399	**10 051**
	United States	10 070	9 982	11 551	12 690	12 097	m	x(9)	x(9)	29 910	26 908	**14 923**
	OECD average	6 210	7 153	8 498	9 396	8 972	4 780	~	~	13 717	9 349	**8 831**
	OECD total	6 254	7 065	~	~	8 852	~	~	~	18 258	15 208	**9 860**
	EU21 average	6 397	7 257	8 950	9 283	9 116	6 026	~	~	12 958	8 315	**8 702**
Other G20	Argentina[2]	2 213	2 511	3 392	3 785	3 531	a	2 878	5 123	4 411	m	**3 204**
	Brazil[2]	1 726	2 155	2 305	1 660	2 058	a	x(9)	x(9)	11 610	10 991	**2 416**
	China[2]	m	m	m	m	m	m	x(9)	x(9)	4 550	m	**1 593**
	India	m	m	m	m	m	m	m	m	m	m	**m**
	Indonesia[1]	56	534	485	477	482	a	m	636	m	m	**m**
	Russian Federation[2]	m	x(5)	x(5)	x(5)	4 071	x(5)	4 281	7 436	6 758	6 439	**4 878**
	Saudi Arabia	m	m	m	m	m	m	m	m	m	m	**m**
	South Africa	m	m	m	m	m	m	m	m	m	m	**m**
	G20 average	m	m	m	m	m	m	m	m	12 785	m	**7 217**

1. Year of reference 2007.
2. Public institutions only (for Canada, in tertiary education only; for Italy, except in tertiary education).
3. Year of reference 2009.

Source: OECD. Argentina, Indonesia: UNESCO Institute for Statistics (World Education Indicators Programme). China: China Educational Finance Statistics Yearbook 2009. See Annex 3 for notes *(www.oecd.org/edu/eag2011)*.

Please refer to the Reader's Guide for information concerning the symbols replacing missing data.

StatLink http://dx.doi.org/10.1787/888932463593

Table B1.2. Annual expenditure per student, by educational institutions on core services, ancillary services and R&D (2008)

In equivalent USD converted using PPPs for GDP, by level of education and type of service, based on full-time equivalents

	Primary, secondary and post-secondary non-tertiary education			Tertiary education				Primary to tertiary education		
	Core educational services	Ancillary services (transport, meals, housing provided by institutions)	Total	Core educational services	Ancillary services (transport, meals, housing provided by institutions)	R&D	Total	Core educational services	Ancillary services (transport, meals, housing provided by institutions) and R&D	Total
	(1)	(2)	(3)	(4)	(5)	(6)	(7)	(8)	(9)	(10)
OECD										
Australia	7 634	180	**7 814**	9 315	611	5 117	**15 043**	7 923	1 133	**9 056**
Austria	10 481	512	**10 994**	10 370	107	4 566	**15 043**	10 458	1 394	**11 852**
Belgium	9 431	275	**9 706**	9 166	546	5 308	**15 020**	9 387	1 202	**10 589**
Canada[1, 2, 3]	7 937	451	**8 388**	13 902	1 216	5 785	**20 903**	m	m	**m**
Chile[4]	2 405	230	**2 635**	6 478	x(4)	351	**6 829**	3 319	202	**3 520**
Czech Republic	4 812	424	**5 236**	6 827	94	1 397	**8 318**	5 243	652	**5 895**
Denmark[1]	10 429	a	**10 429**	x(7)	a	x(7)	**17 634**	x(10)	x(10)	**11 788**
Estonia	x(3)	x(3)	**6 054**	x(7)	x(7)	m	**5 780**	x(10)	x(10)	**5 982**
Finland	7 188	880	**8 068**	9 592	n	5 810	**15 402**	7 646	1 817	**9 463**
France	7 501	1 059	**8 559**	9 089	766	4 224	**14 079**	7 788	1 774	**9 562**
Germany	7 661	198	**7 859**	8 788	716	5 885	**15 390**	7 849	1 266	**9 115**
Greece	m	m	**m**	m	m	m	**m**	m	m	**m**
Hungary[3]	4 077	549	**4 626**	5 317	415	1 595	**7 327**	4 311	825	**5 135**
Iceland	x(3)	x(3)	**9 745**	x(7)	x(7)	x(7)	**10 429**	x(10)	x(10)	**9 873**
Ireland[3]	8 915	m	**8 915**	11 651	m	4 633	**16 284**	9 348	734	**10 082**
Israel	5 470	310	**5 780**	11 106	1 462	n	**12 568**	6 387	498	**6 885**
Italy[3, 5]	8 729	342	**9 071**	5 673	286	3 594	**9 553**	8 045	1 104	**9 149**
Japan[1]	x(3)	x(3)	**8 301**	x(7)	x(7)	x(7)	**14 890**	x(10)	x(10)	**9 673**
Korea	5 759	964	**6 723**	7 661	111	1 310	**9 081**	6 333	1 102	**7 434**
Luxembourg	16 123	786	**16 909**	m	m	m	**m**	m	m	**m**
Mexico	x(3)	x(3)	**2 284**	6 298	m	1 205	**7 504**	2 653	111	**2 763**
Netherlands	9 251	n	**9 251**	11 203	n	6 041	**17 245**	9 606	1 098	**10 704**
New Zealand	x(3)	x(3)	**6 496**	8 815	x(4)	1 711	**10 526**	x(10)	x(10)	**7 218**
Norway	x(3)	x(3)	**12 070**	11 469	129	7 344	**18 942**	x(10)	x(10)	**13 285**
Poland[3]	4 665	16	**4 682**	6 038	n	1 025	**7 063**	4 926	208	**5 135**
Portugal[3]	6 138	138	**6 276**	6 097	x(4)	4 276	**10 373**	6 130	874	**7 005**
Slovak Republic[1]	3 439	567	**4 006**	4 842	829	889	**6 560**	3 681	766	**4 446**
Slovenia	8 151	404	**8 555**	7 577	31	1 655	**9 263**	8 018	700	**8 719**
Spain	8 116	406	**8 522**	9 206	245	3 915	**13 366**	8 336	1 163	**9 499**
Sweden	8 543	981	**9 524**	10 019	n	9 995	**20 014**	8 773	2 388	**11 162**
Switzerland[3]	x(3)	x(3)	**13 775**	9 845	x(4)	11 803	**21 648**	x(10)	x(10)	**14 977**
Turkey	m	m	**m**	m	m	m	**m**	m	m	**m**
United Kingdom	7 458	1 711	**9 169**	7 024	1 375	6 911	**15 310**	7 395	2 656	**10 051**
United States	10 123	872	**10 995**	23 622	3 286	3 002	**29 910**	12 926	1 997	**14 923**
OECD average	7 617	511	**8 169**	9 148	556	4 050	**13 717**	7 238	1 116	**8 831**
EU21 average	7 953	514	**8 321**	8 146	338	4 219	**12 958**	7 467	1 213	**8 702**
Other G20										
Argentina[3]	x(3)	x(3)	**2 966**	x(7)	x(7)	x(7)	**4 411**	x(10)	x(10)	**3 204**
Brazil[3]	x(3)	x(3)	**2 098**	10 991	x(4)	619	**11 610**	2 395	21	**2 416**
China[3]	m	m	**m**	x(7)	x(7)	x(7)	**4 550**	x(10)	x(10)	**1 593**
India	m	m	**m**	m	m	m	**m**	m	m	**m**
Indonesia[2]	469	45	**514**	m	m	m	**m**	m	m	**m**
Russian Federation[3]	x(3)	x(3)	**4 071**	x(7)	x(7)	320	**6 758**	x(10)	x(10)	**4 878**
Saudi Arabia	m	m	**m**	m	m	m	**m**	m	m	**m**
South Africa	m	m	**m**	m	m	m	**m**	m	m	**m**
G20 average	m	m	**m**	m	m	m	**12 785**	m	m	**7 217**

1. Some levels of education are included with others. Refer to "x" code in Table B1.1a for details.
2. Year of reference 2007.
3. Public institutions only (for Canada, in tertiary education only; for Italy, except in tertiary education).
4. Year of reference 2009.
5. Exclude post-secondary non-tertiary education.

Source: OECD. Argentina, Indonesia: UNESCO Institute for Statistics (World Education Indicators Programme). China: China Educational Finance Statistics Yearbook 2009. See Annex 3 for notes (*www.oecd.org/edu/eag2011*).

Please refer to the Reader's Guide for information concerning the symbols replacing missing data.

StatLink http://dx.doi.org/10.1787/888932463631

Table B1.3a. **Cumulative expenditure per student by educational institutions for all services over the average duration of tertiary studies (2008)**

In equivalent USD converted using PPPS for GDP, by type of programme

		Method[1]	Average duration of tertiary studies (in years)			Cumulative expenditure per student over the average duration of tertiary studies (in USD)		
			Tertiary-type B education	Tertiary-type A and advanced research programmes	All tertiary education	Tertiary-type B education	Tertiary-type A and advanced research programmes	All tertiary education
			(1)	(2)	(3)	(4)	(5)	(6)
OECD	Australia	CM	m	3.48	**m**	m	56 714	**m**
	Austria	AF	1.89	4.80	**4.34**	23 129	72 370	**65 334**
	Belgium	CM	2.41	3.67	**2.99**	x(6)	x(6)	**44 911**
	Canada		m	m	**m**	m	m	**m**
	Chile		m	m	**m**	m	m	**m**
	Czech Republic[2]	CM	m	3.76	**m**	m	32 843	**m**
	Denmark	AF	2.51	5.97	**5.19**	x(6)	x(6)	**91 448**
	Estonia		m	m	**m**	m	m	**m**
	Finland	CM	a	4.78	**4.78**	a	73 621	**73 621**
	France[2]	CM	3.00	4.74	**4.02**	34 382	70 841	**56 597**
	Germany	CM	2.50	5.16	**4.48**	19 250	88 327	**68 913**
	Greece		m	m	**m**	m	m	**m**
	Hungary[3]	AF	1.84	3.74	**3.48**	9 278	27 877	**25 532**
	Iceland	CM	x(3)	x(3)	**4.49**	x(6)	x(6)	**46 828**
	Ireland[3]	CM	2.21	4.02	**3.24**	x(6)	x(6)	**52 760**
	Israel	CM	m	3.03	**m**	m	40 140	**m**
	Italy	AF	m	4.52	**m**	m	43 194	**m**
	Japan	CM	2.09	4.57	**4.19**	19 783	75 554	**62 385**
	Korea	CM	2.07	4.22	**3.43**	11 887	42 658	**31 149**
	Luxembourg		m	m	**m**	m	m	**m**
	Mexico	AF	1.72	3.49	**3.35**	x(6)	x(6)	**25 138**
	Netherlands	CM	m	5.02	**5.02**	m	86 568	**86 568**
	New Zealand	CM	2.22	3.90	**3.32**	19 113	43 413	**34 978**
	Norway	CM	m	m	**m**	m	m	**m**
	Poland[3]	CM	m	3.68	**m**	m	26 089	**m**
	Portugal		m	m	**m**	m	m	**m**
	Slovak Republic	AF	2.47	3.90	**3.82**	m	25 584	**m**
	Slovenia	AF	2.63	3.64	**3.21**	x(6)	x(6)	**29 718**
	Spain	CM	2.15	5.54	**4.66**	23 058	77 159	**62 287**
	Sweden	CM	2.20	4.89	**4.73**	17 302	101 970	**94 625**
	Switzerland[3]	CM	2.19	5.45	**3.62**	11 237	126 964	**78 458**
	Turkey	CM	2.73	2.37	**2.65**	m	m	**m**
	United Kingdom[2]	CM	3.52	5.86	**4.34**	x(6)	x(6)	**66 485**
	United States		m	m	**m**	m	m	**m**
	OECD average		2.23	4.33	**3.97**	~	~	**57 775**
	EU21 average		2.26	4.57	**4.16**	~	~	**62 985**
Other G20	Argentina		m	m	**m**	m	m	**m**
	Brazil		m	m	**m**	m	m	**m**
	China		m	m	**m**	m	m	**m**
	India		m	m	**m**	m	m	**m**
	Indonesia		m	m	**m**	m	m	**m**
	Russian Federation		m	m	**m**	m	m	**m**
	Saudi Arabia		m	m	**m**	m	m	**m**
	South Africa		m	m	**m**	m	m	**m**

1. Either the Chain Method (CM) or an Approximation Formula (AF) was used to estimate the duration of tertiary studies.
2. Average duration of tertiary studies is estimated based on national data.
3. Public institutions only.

Source: OECD. See Annex 3 for notes *(www.oecd.org/edu/eag2011).*

Please refer to the Reader's Guide for information concerning the symbols replacing missing data.

StatLink http://dx.doi.org/10.1787/888932463650

Table B1.4. Annual expenditure per student by educational institutions for all services relative to GDP per capita (2008)

By level of education, based on full-time equivalents

		Pre-primary education (for children 3 years and older)	Primary education	Secondary education			Post-secondary non-tertiary education	Tertiary education (including R&D activities)			All tertiary education excluding R&D activities	Primary to tertiary education
				Lower secondary education	Upper secondary education	All secondary education		Tertiary-type B education	Tertiary-type A and advanced research programmes	All tertiary education		
		(1)	(2)	(3)	(4)	(5)	(6)	(7)	(8)	(9)	(10)	(11)
OECD	Australia	16	17	23	22	23	17	21	41	38	25	**23**
	Austria	19	24	29	30	29	18	31	38	38	26	**30**
	Belgium	16	23	x(5)	x(5)	29	x(5)	x(9)	x(9)	41	26	**29**
	Canada[1, 2]	x(3)	x(3)	20	25	22	m	40	63	54	39	**29**
	Chile[3]	27	19	18	17	18	a	24	64	47	44	**24**
	Czech Republic	16	15	25	23	24	6	13	34	32	27	**23**
	Denmark	16	26	26	28	27	x(4, 9)	x(9)	x(9)	45	m	**30**
	Estonia	15	26	29	30	29	29	24	28	m	27	**27**
	Finland	14	19	29	20	23	x(5)	n	41	41	25	**25**
	France	17	18	26	35	30	m	33	44	41	29	**28**
	Germany	19	16	20	29	23	23	21	46	41	26	**25**
	Greece	m	m	m	m	m	m	m	m	m	m	**m**
	Hungary[2]	23	22	23	22	23	25	24	36	35	28	**25**
	Iceland	26	27	26	21	23	x(5)	x(9)	x(9)	27	m	**25**
	Ireland[2]	m	18	25	26	25	18	x(9)	x(9)	38	27	**24**
	Israel	14	19	x(5)	x(5)	23	20	35	48	45	m	**25**
	Italy[2]	25	26	29	27	28	m	27	29	29	18	**27**
	Japan	14	22	25	28	27	x(4, 9)	28	49	44	m	**29**
	Korea	16	20	23	36	30	a	21	38	34	29	**28**
	Luxembourg	15	15	22	22	22	m	m	m	m	m	**m**
	Mexico	16	15	12	22	15	a	x(9)	x(9)	49	41	**18**
	Netherlands	16	17	25	26	26	27	n	40	40	26	**25**
	New Zealand	25	19	21	27	24	30	29	38	36	30	**25**
	Norway	15	25	27	32	30	x(5)	x(9)	x(9)	43	27	**30**
	Poland[2]	32	27	24	26	25	34	28	39	39	33	**28**
	Portugal[2]	21	21	28	32	29	m	x(9)	x(9)	42	24	**28**
	Slovak Republic	17	18	16	18	17	x(4)	x(4)	28	28	24	**19**
	Slovenia	27	x(3)	32	25	29	x(4)	x(9)	x(9)	32	26	**30**
	Spain	20	22	27	34	30	a	32	42	40	28	**29**
	Sweden	17	23	25	26	25	16	20	53	51	25	**28**
	Switzerland[2]	11	20	37	41	39	x(4)	11	51	48	22	**33**
	Turkey	m	m	a	m	m	a	m	m	m	m	**m**
	United Kingdom	19	24	26	25	26	x(4)	x(9)	x(9)	42	23	**27**
	United States	21	21	25	27	26	m	x(9)	x(9)	64	57	**32**
	OECD average	19	21	24	27	26	15	23	42	41	29	**27**
	EU21 average	19	21	23	27	25	12	24	41	39	29	**26**
Other G20	Argentina[2]	15	17	24	26	24	a	20	36	31	m	**22**
	Brazil[2]	16	20	21	15	19	a	x(9)	x(9)	106	100	**22**
	China[2]	m	m	m	m	m	m	x(9)	x(9)	76	m	**27**
	India	m	m	m	m	m	m	m	m	m	m	**m**
	Indonesia[1]	2	14	13	13	13	a	m	17	m	m	**m**
	Russian Federation[2]	m	x(5)	x(5)	x(5)	20	x(5)	21	36	33	31	**24**
	Saudi Arabia	m	m	m	m	m	m	m	m	m	m	**m**
	South Africa	m	m	m	m	m	m	m	m	m	m	**m**
	G20 average	m	m	m	m	m	m	m	m	49	m	**26**

1. Year of reference 2007.
2. Public institutions only (for Canada, in tertiary education only. For Italy, except in tertiary education).
3. Year of reference 2009.

Source: OECD. Argentina, Indonesia: UNESCO Institute for Statistics (World Education Indicators Programme). China: China Educational Finance Statistics Yearbook 2009. See Annex 3 for notes *(www.oecd.org/edu/eag2011).*

Please refer to the Reader's Guide for information concerning the symbols replacing missing data.

StatLink http://dx.doi.org/10.1787/888932463688

Table B1.5. **Change in expenditure per student by educational institutions for all services relative to different factors, by level of education (1995, 2000, 2008)**

Index of change between 1995, 2000 and 2008 (GDP deflator 2000 = 100, constant prices)

	Primary, secondary and post-secondary non-tertiary education						Tertiary education					
	Change in expenditure (2000 = 100)		Change in the number of students (2000 = 100)		Change in expenditure per student (2000 = 100)		Change in expenditure (2000 = 100)		Change in the number of students (2000 = 100)		Change in expenditure per student (2000 = 100)	
	1995	2008	1995	2008	1995	2008	1995	2008	1995	2008	1995	2008
OECD												
Australia	81	133	94	108	**85**	**123**	90	134	83	123	**109**	**108**
Austria	93	108	m	97	**m**	**112**	97	148	91	115	**107**	**129**
Belgium	m	124	m	106	**m**	**117**	m	120	m	109	**m**	**110**
Canada[1, 2, 3]	106	122	m	101	**m**	**121**	75	126	m	110	**m**	**114**
Chile[4]	54	132	88	98	**62**	**135**	61	149	76	194	**80**	**77**
Czech Republic	116	137	107	86	**109**	**159**	101	202	64	164	**159**	**124**
Denmark[1]	84	115	96	104	**87**	**111**	91	119	96	102	**95**	**116**
Estonia[5]	78	163	96	75	**81**	**219**	69	154	60	116	**115**	**132**
Finland	89	133	93	105	**95**	**126**	90	126	89	103	**101**	**122**
France	90	103	m	98	**m**	**105**	91	121	m	103	**m**	**117**
Germany	94	100	97	93	**97**	**107**	95	122	104	113	**91**	**107**
Greece[1]	64	m	107	m	**60**	**m**	66	m	68	m	**97**	**m**
Hungary[3, 5]	100	139	105	86	**95**	**162**	78	131	58	149	**135**	**88**
Iceland	m	146	99	107	**m**	**136**	m	164	79	162	**m**	**101**
Ireland[3]	82	197	105	108	**78**	**183**	56	136	85	118	**66**	**115**
Israel	84	127	89	111	**94**	**115**	71	110	74	125	**96**	**88**
Italy[3, 6]	101	108	102	102	**99**	**106**	79	120	99	111	**80**	**108**
Japan[1]	98	103	113	89	**86**	**115**	87	115	99	99	**88**	**117**
Korea	m	167	107	96	**m**	**175**	m	162	68	110	**m**	**147**
Luxembourg	m	m	m	m	**m**	**m**	m	m	m	m	**m**	**m**
Mexico	81	128	93	109	**87**	**117**	77	155	77	133	**101**	**117**
Netherlands	82	127	97	105	**84**	**121**	95	128	96	129	**99**	**99**
New Zealand[5]	71	109	m	m	**m**	**m**	104	156	m	m	**m**	**m**
Norway[5]	83	127	89	108	**93**	**118**	93	126	100	113	**93**	**112**
Poland[3]	70	129	110	76	**64**	**169**	59	195	55	119	**107**	**163**
Portugal[3]	76	98	105	90	**72**	**109**	73	152	77	112	**96**	**136**
Slovak Republic[1]	97	157	105	83	**92**	**189**	81	185	72	174	**113**	**106**
Slovenia	m	m	m	m	**m**	**m**	m	m	m	m	**m**	**m**
Spain	99	123	119	95	**84**	**129**	72	135	100	98	**72**	**138**
Sweden	81	117	86	98	**94**	**119**	81	121	83	114	**97**	**107**
Switzerland[3, 5]	101	120	95	101	**107**	**119**	74	122	95	146	**78**	**84**
Turkey[3, 5]	57	m	m	m	**m**	**m**	55	m	m	m	**m**	**m**
United Kingdom	86	139	87	89	**99**	**156**	97	143	89	110	**109**	**130**
United States	80	125	95	108	**84**	**116**	71	117	92	120	**77**	**98**
OECD average	85	129	99	98	**87**	**134**	80	140	83	124	**98**	**114**
EU21 average	88	129	101	94	**87**	**139**	82	142	81	120	**102**	**119**
Other G20												
Argentina	m	m	m	m	**m**	**m**	m	m	m	m	**m**	**m**
Brazil[3, 5]	82	216	85	98	**96**	**221**	78	148	79	157	**98**	**94**
China	m	m	m	m	**m**	**m**	m	m	m	m	**m**	**m**
India	m	m	m	m	**m**	**m**	m	m	m	m	**m**	**m**
Indonesia	m	m	m	m	**m**	**m**	m	m	m	m	**m**	**m**
Russian Federation[5]	m	198	m	m	**m**	**m**	m	328	m	m	**m**	**m**
Saudi Arabia	m	m	m	m	**m**	**m**	m	m	m	m	**m**	**m**
South Africa	m	m	m	m	**m**	**m**	m	m	m	m	**m**	**m**

1. Some levels of education are included with others. Refer to "x" code in Table B1.1a for details.
2. Year of reference 2007 instead of 2008.
3. Public institutions only (for Canada, in tertiary education only. For Italy, except in tertiary education).
4. Year of reference 2009 instead of 2008.
5. Public expenditure only (for Switzerland, in tertiary education only).
6. Excluding post-secondary non-tertiary education.

Source: OECD. See Annex 3 for notes *(www.oecd.org/edu/eag2011)*.

Please refer to the Reader's Guide for information concerning the symbols replacing missing data.

StatLink http://dx.doi.org/10.1787/888932463707

Table B1.6. **Annual expenditure per student by educational institutions for all services, by type of programme, at the secondary level (2008)**

In equivalent USD converted using PPPs for GDP, by level of education, based on full-time equivalents

		Secondary education								
		Lower secondary education			Upper secondary education			All secondary education		
		All programmes	General programmes	Vocational/ pre-vocational programmes	All programmes	General programmes	Vocational/ pre-vocational programmes	All programmes	General programmes	Vocational/ pre-vocational programmes
		(1)	(2)	(3)	(4)	(5)	(6)	(7)	(8)	(9)
OECD	Australia	**9 200**	9 482	5 713	**8 821**	10 393	5 850	**9 052**	9 767	5 816
	Austria	**11 533**	11 533	a	**11 956**	11 729	12 031	**11 741**	11 571	12 031
	Belgium[1]	**x(7)**	x(7)	x(7)	**x(7)**	x(7)	x(7)	**10 511**	x(7)	x(7)
	Canada[1, 2]	**x(7)**	x(7)	x(7)	**x(7)**	x(7)	x(7)	**8 388**	x(7)	x(7)
	Chile[3]	**2 596**	2 596	a	**2 548**	2 689	2 273	**2 564**	2 648	2 273
	Czech Republic	**6 338**	6 318	x(1)	**6 030**	5 382	6 259	**6 174**	6 103	6 283
	Denmark	**10 268**	10 268	a	**11 160**	x(4)	x(4)	**10 720**	x(7)	x(7)
	Estonia	**6 264**	x(1)	x(1)	**6 461**	7 052	5 241	**6 371**	x(7)	x(7)
	Finland[1]	**10 950**	10 950	a	**7 461**	6 500	7 870	**8 659**	9 333	7 870
	France	**8 816**	8 816	a	**12 087**	11 807	12 518	**10 231**	9 762	12 518
	Germany	**7 509**	7 509	a	**10 597**	8 006	12 573	**8 606**	7 605	12 573
	Greece	**m**	m	m	**m**	m	m	**m**	m	m
	Hungary[4]	**4 852**	x(1)	x(1)	**4 471**	4 516	4 345	**4 658**	4 705	4 361
	Iceland[1]	**10 100**	10 100	a	**8 290**	x(4)	x(4)	**9 007**	x(7)	x(7)
	Ireland[4]	**10 583**	x(1)	x(1)	**11 205**	x(4)	x(4)	**10 868**	x(7)	x(7)
	Israel	**x(7)**	x(7)	x(7)	**x(7)**	x(7)	x(7)	**6 429**	5 187	10 389
	Italy[4]	**9 616**	x(1)	x(1)	**9 121**	x(4)	x(4)	**9 315**	x(7)	x(7)
	Japan[1]	**8 621**	8 621	a	**9 559**	x(4)	x(4)	**9 092**	x(7)	x(7)
	Korea	**6 307**	6 307	a	**9 666**	x(4)	x(4)	**7 931**	x(7)	x(7)
	Luxembourg	**19 791**	19 791	a	**20 002**	18 893	20 736	**19 898**	19 530	20 736
	Mexico	**1 853**	2 200	396	**3 277**	3 199	4 024	**2 333**	2 564	1 115
	Netherlands	**10 608**	9 490	13 409	**11 301**	8 971	12 364	**10 950**	9 335	12 677
	New Zealand	**6 071**	x(1)	x(1)	**8 025**	x(4)	x(4)	**6 994**	x(7)	x(7)
	Norway[1]	**11 860**	11 860	a	**14 039**	x(4)	x(4)	**13 070**	x(7)	x(7)
	Poland[4]	**4 424**	x(1)	x(1)	**4 613**	4 584	4 643	**4 525**	x(7)	x(7)
	Portugal[4]	**6 910**	x(1)	x(1)	**7 924**	x(4)	x(4)	**7 357**	x(7)	x(7)
	Slovak Republic[1]	**3 716**	3 716	x(6)	**4 174**	3 194	4 645	**3 956**	3 579	4 645
	Slovenia[1]	**9 287**	9 287	a	**7 284**	x(4)	x(4)	**8 555**	x(7)	x(7)
	Spain	**9 108**	x(1)	x(1)	**11 113**	x(4)	x(4)	**9 792**	x(7)	x(7)
	Sweden	**9 739**	9 778	a	**10 103**	11 080	9 424	**9 940**	10 215	9 424
	Switzerland[1, 4]	**16 737**	16 737	a	**18 844**	13 179	21 904	**17 825**	15 767	21 904
	Turkey[4]	**a**	a	a	**m**	m	m	**m**	m	m
	United Kingdom[1]	**x(7)**	x(7)	x(7)	**x(7)**	x(7)	x(7)	**9 487**	x(7)	x(7)
	United States	**11 551**	11 551	a	**12 690**	12 690	a	**12 097**	12 097	a
	OECD average	**8 498**	8 901	1 027	**9 396**	8 198	9 169	**8 972**	8 735	9 641
	EU21 average	**8 906**	9 769	1 490	**9 281**	8 476	9 387	**9 116**	9 174	10 312
Other G20	Argentina[4]	**3 392**	3 392	a	**3 785**	x(4)	x(4)	**3 531**	x(7)	x(7)
	Brazil[4]	**2 305**	2 305	a	**1 660**	x(4)	x(4)	**2 058**	x(7)	x(7)
	China	**m**	m	m	**m**	m	m	**m**	m	m
	India	**m**	m	m	**m**	m	m	**m**	m	m
	Indonesia[2]	**485**	485	a	**320**	189	131	**806**	675	131
	Russian Federation[1, 4]	**x(8)**	x(8)	a	**x(7)**	x(8)	x(9)	**4 071**	4 041	4 306
	Saudi Arabia	**m**	m	m	**m**	m	m	**m**	m	m
	South Africa	**m**	m	m	**m**	m	m	**m**	m	m

1. Some levels of education are included with others. Refer to "x" code in Table B1.1a for details.
2. Year of reference 2007.
3. Year of reference 2009.
4. Public institutions only.

Source: OECD. Argentina, Indonesia: UNESCO Institute for Statistics (World Education Indicators Programme). See Annex 3 for notes *(www.oecd.org/edu/eag2011)*.
Please refer to the Reader's Guide for information concerning the symbols replacing missing data.

StatLink http://dx.doi.org/10.1787/888932463726

INDICATOR B2

WHAT PROPORTION OF NATIONAL WEALTH IS SPENT ON EDUCATION?

- In 2008, OECD countries spent 6.1% of their collective GDP on educational institutions and this proportion exceeds 7.0% in Chile, Denmark, Iceland, Israel, Korea, Norway and the United States. Only nine of 36 countries for which data are available spend 5.0% of GDP or less.
- Between 2000 and 2008, expenditure for all levels of education combined increased at a faster rate than GDP in 25 of the 32 countries for which data are available. The increase exceeded 1.0 percentage point over the period in Brazil (from 3.5% to 5.3%), Ireland (from 4.5% to 5.6%) and Korea (from 6.1% to 7.6%).

Chart B2.1. Expenditure on educational institutions as a percentage of GDP for all levels of education (2000 and 2008) and index of change between 2000 and 2008 (2000=100, constant prices)

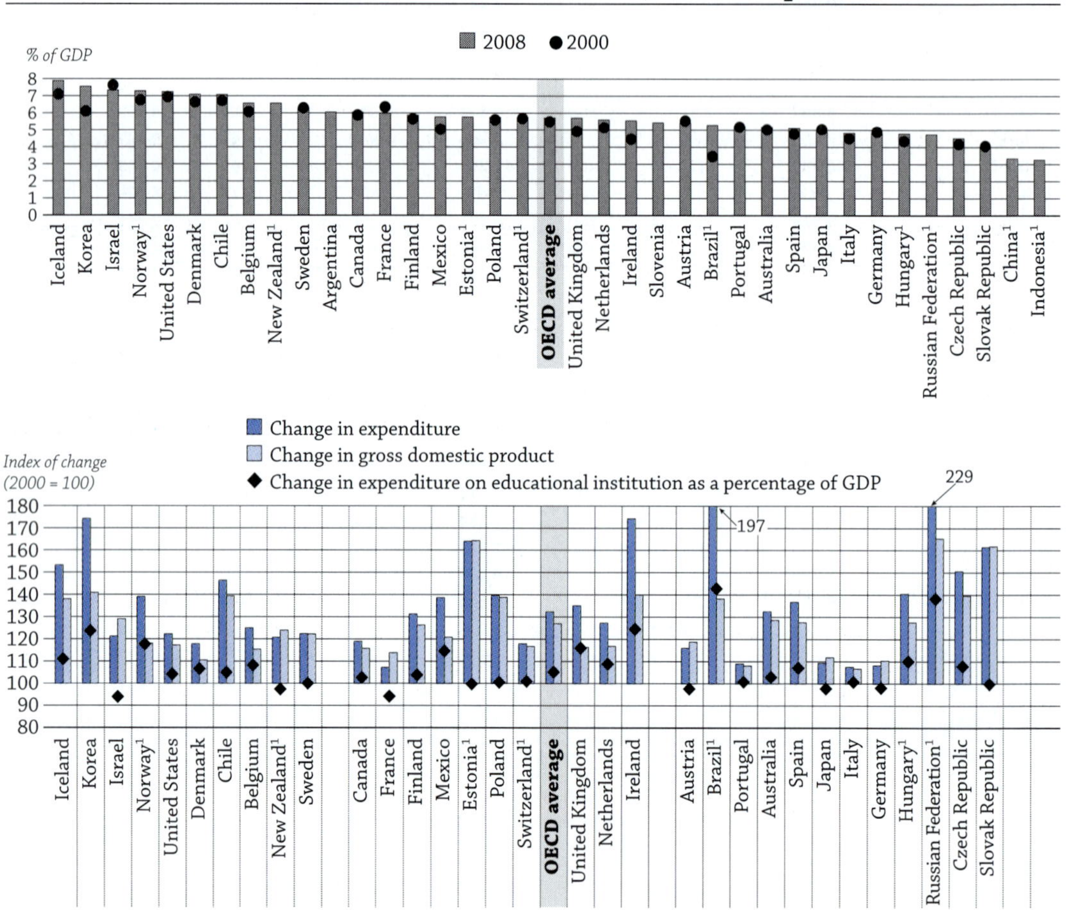

1. Public expenditure only (for Switzerland, in tertiary education only; for Norway, in primary, secondary and post-secondary non-tertiary education only; for Estonia, New Zealand and the Russian Federation, for 2000 only).

Countries are ranked in descending order of expenditure from both public and private sources on educational institutions in 2008.

Source: OECD. Argentina, Indonesia: UNESCO Institute for Statistics (World Education Indicators Programme). China: The national Statistics Bulletin on Educational Expenditure 2009. Table B2.1 and Table B2.4, available on line. See Annex 3 for notes. (*www.oecd.org/edu/eag2011*).

StatLink http://dx.doi.org/10.1787/888932461028

How to read this chart

The chart shows educational investment as the proportion of national income that countries devoted to spending on educational institutions in 2000 and 2008, and changes in overall spending on educational institutions between 2000 and 2008. It includes direct and indirect expenditure on educational institutions from both public and private sources of funds.

INDICATOR B2

Context

Expenditure on educational institutions is an investment that can help foster economic growth, enhance productivity, contribute to personal and social development, and reduce social inequality. Relative to GDP, expenditure on educational institutions indicates the priority a country gives to education. The proportion of a country's total financial resources devoted to education is the result of choices made by governments, enterprises, and individual students and their families, and is partially influenced by enrolments in education. Given that expenditure on education largely comes from public budgets, it is closely scrutinised by governments, particularly at times when governments are being urged to cut spending.

Other findings

- **Expenditure on pre-primary education accounts for 7% of combined OECD expenditure on educational institutions**, or 0.4% of the combined GDP. Differences between countries are significant. For example, while less than 0.1% of GDP is spent on pre-primary education in Australia and Indonesia, 0.8% or more is spent in Iceland, Israel and Spain.

- **Primary, secondary and post-secondary non-tertiary education accounts for 61% of combined OECD expenditure on educational institutions, or 3.7% of the combined GDP.** Relative to its GDP, Iceland spends nearly twice as much as the Slovak Republic and more than twice as much as the Russian Federation.

- **Tertiary education accounts for nearly one-third of the combined OECD expenditure on educational institutions**, or 1.9% of the combined GDP.

- **Canada, Chile, Korea and the United States spend between 2.0% and 2.7% of their GDP on tertiary institutions.** Chile, Korea and the United States also show the highest proportion of private expenditure at the tertiary level: between 1.7% and 1.9% of GDP. Relative to GDP, the United States spends over three times more on tertiary education than Brazil, Hungary, and the Slovak Republic.

Trends

Between 2000 and 2008, spending on the various levels of education evolved quite differently. From primary to post-secondary non-tertiary education, expenditure on educational institutions increased at least as much as GDP did in 17 of the 29 countries for which data are comparable for both years. In tertiary education, it increased as much as GDP did in 26 of the 29 countries with available data.

Analysis

Overall investment relative to GDP

All OECD countries invest a substantial proportion of their national resources in education. Taking into account both public and private sources of funds, in 2008 OECD countries as a whole spent 6.1% of their collective GDP on educational institutions at the pre-primary, primary, secondary and tertiary levels.

Chile, Denmark, Iceland, Israel, Korea, Norway and the United States spend the most on educational institutions: public and private spending on education represents at least 7% of GDP in these countries. In contrast, 9 of 36 countries for which data are available spend 5.0% of GDP or less: China (3.3%), the Czech Republic (4.5%), Germany (4.8%), Hungary (4.8%), Indonesia (3.3%), Italy (4.8%), Japan (4.9%), the Russian Federation (4.7%) and the Slovak Republic (4.0%).

Expenditure on educational institutions by level of education

Differences in spending on educational institutions are the greatest at the pre-primary level. Less than 0.1% of GDP is spent on pre-primary education in Australia and Indonesia, but 0.8% or more is spent in Iceland, Israel and Spain. These differences can largely be explained by enrolment rates (see Indicator C1) and starting age for primary education, but they are also sometimes a result of the extent to which this indicator covers private early childhood education. In Ireland, for example, most early childhood education is delivered in private institutions that were not covered by the Irish data for the year 2008. Moreover, high-quality early childhood education is provided not only by the educational institutions covered by this indicator but also in more informal settings. Inferences on access to and quality of early childhood education and care should therefore be made with caution (Table B2.2).

On average among OECD countries, 61% of the combined OECD expenditure goes to primary, secondary and post-secondary non-tertiary education. As enrolment in primary and lower secondary education is almost universal in OECD countries, and enrolment rates in upper secondary education are high (see Indicator C1), most of the spending on educational institutions – 3.7% of the combined OECD GDP – is directed at these levels of education (Table B2.2). Moreover, the level of national resources devoted to education depends on the age structure of the population: countries with above-average expenditure on educational institutions as a percentage of GDP are usually those with an above-average proportion of the population whose age corresponds to these levels of education. For example, in 2007, Australia, Brazil, Chile, Denmark, Iceland, Korea, Mexico, New Zealand and Norway had both an above-average proportion of their population aged 5-14 and above-average expenditure on education as a percentage of GDP (see Indicator B2 in OECD, 2010h). At the same time, significantly higher spending per student in upper secondary education means that overall investment at these levels is greater than enrolment numbers alone would suggest.

While nearly one-third of the combined OECD expenditure on educational institutions was devoted to tertiary education in 2008, the level of spending varies greatly among countries. For example, Canada, Chile, Korea and the United States spend between 2.0% and 2.7% of their GDP on tertiary institutions and, with the exception of Canada, show the highest proportion of private expenditure on tertiary education. Meanwhile, in Belgium, Brazil, Estonia, France, Iceland, Ireland, Switzerland and the United Kingdom, the proportion of GDP spent on tertiary institutions is below the OECD average, while the proportion spent on primary, secondary and post-secondary non-tertiary education is above the OECD average (Table B2.2 and Chart B2.2).

Changes in overall spending on educational institutions between 2000 and 2008

More people are completing upper secondary and tertiary education than ever before (see Indicator A1). In many countries, this growth has been accompanied by massive financial investment. For all levels of education combined, public and private investment in educational institutions increased in all countries by at least 7% between 2000 and 2008 in real terms, and increased by an average of 32% in OECD countries. From 1995 to 2008, expenditure increased by at least 14%, and by 57%, on average, in OECD countries (see Table B2.4, available on line).

Chart B2.2. Expenditure on educational institutions as a percentage of GDP (2008)

From public and private sources, by level of education and source of funds

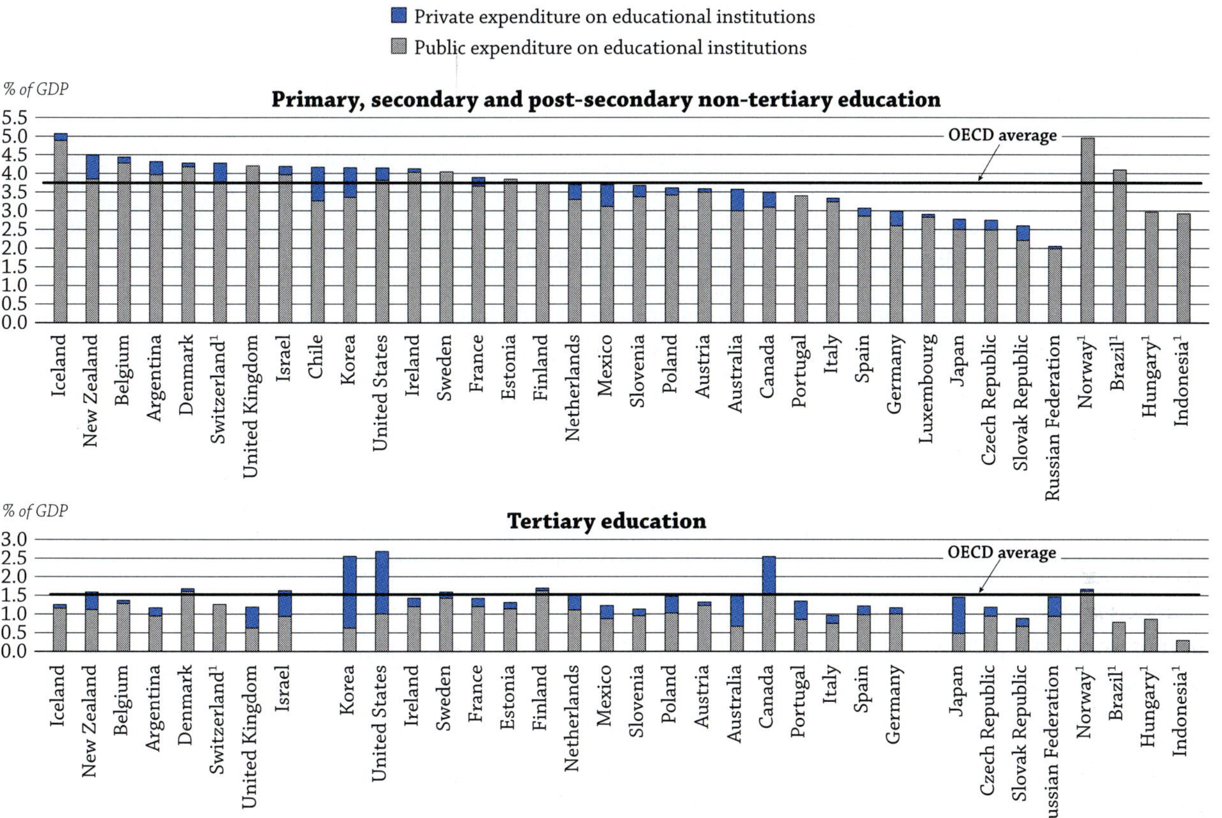

1. Public expenditure only (for Switzerland, in tertiary education only; for Norway, in primary, secondary and post-secondary non-tertiary education only).

Countries are ranked in descending order of expenditure from both public and private sources on educational institutions in primary, secondary and post-secondary non-tertiary education.

Source: OECD. Argentina, Indonesia: UNESCO Institute for Statistics (World Education Indicators Programme). Table B2.3. See Annex 3 for notes (*www.oecd.org/edu/eag2011*).

StatLink http://dx.doi.org/10.1787/888932461047

Differences among countries are partly related to variations in the size of the school-age population, as well as to trends in national income. For example, in Israel, while spending on all levels of education combined increased by more than 21% between 2000 and 2008, GDP increased by 29% over the same period, leading to a decrease in expenditure as a proportion of GDP (Chart B2.1 and Table B2.4, available on line).

Expenditure for all levels of education combined increased at a greater rate than GDP in more than three-quarters of the countries for which data are comparable for 2000 and 2008. The increase exceeded 1.0 percentage point over the period in Brazil (from 3.5% to 5.3%), Ireland (from 4.5% to 5.6%) and Korea (from 6.1% to 7.6%). However, the increase in spending on educational institutions tended to lag behind growth in GDP in Austria, France, Germany, Israel, Japan and the Slovak Republic. Among these countries, the most notable differences are found in France and Israel, where the proportion of GDP spent on educational institutions decreased by at least 0.3 percentage point between 2000 and 2008 (Table B2.1 and Chart B2.1), mainly as a result of the decrease in expenditure as a percentage of GDP at the primary, secondary and post-secondary non-tertiary level in France (decrease of 0.4 percentage point) and at the tertiary level in Israel (decrease of 0.3 percentage point).

Expenditure as a percentage of GDP also tends to increase at the different levels of education. From primary to post-secondary non-tertiary education, expenditure on educational institutions as a proportion of GDP increased from 2000 to 2008 in 17 of the 29 countries for which data are comparable for both years. This is mainly related to the stability in the number of students enrolled at these levels over this period (Tables B2.1 and B1.5).

However, the trend is more pronounced in tertiary education, where expenditure on educational institutions as a proportion of GDP decreased from 2000 to 2008 in only three countries – Ireland, Israel and Sweden. Israel is the only country where expenditure on educational institutions as a percentage of GDP decreased at primary to post-secondary non-tertiary levels as well as at the tertiary level.

Between 2000 and 2008, in 22 of the 32 countries for which data are comparable for both years, expenditure on tertiary education institutions increased at a greater rate than that for primary, secondary and post-secondary non-tertiary education. This is mainly due to governments' response to the expansion of tertiary education over this period with massive investment combined with relative stability in the number of students enrolled in lower levels of education. The exceptions to this pattern are Belgium, Brazil, Estonia, Finland, Hungary, Ireland, Israel, Korea, Norway and the United States (Table B1.5).

Expenditure on educational institutions by source of funding

Increased expenditure on educational institutions in response to growth in enrolments implies a heavier financial burden for society as a whole, one that does not, however, fall entirely on public funding. On average, of the 6.1% of the combined GDP in the OECD area devoted to education, three-quarters come from public sources for all levels of education combined (Table B2.3). Public funds are the major funding source in all countries and account for an average of 85% – and at least 97% in Finland and Sweden – of total expenditure on educational institutions. However, differences among countries in the breakdown of educational expenditure by source of funding and by level of education are great (see Indicator B3).

Definitions

Expenditure on educational institutions includes expenditure on both instructional and non-instructional educational institutions. For instructional institutions, expenditure includes teaching and public and private expenditure on ancillary services for students and families, such as housing and transport, when these services are provided by educational institutions. Spending on research and development is included in this indicator, to the extent that it is performed by educational institutions. Expenditures by businesses that provide training or instruction to students as part of dual educational programmes are also included. Non-instructional institutions provide administrative, advisory or professional services to other institutions, but do not enrol students themselves. These include national, state and local ministries or departments of education, and organisations that provide education-related services, such as vocational or psychological counselling, testing or financial aid to students.

Methodology

Data refer to the financial year 2008 and are based on the UOE data collection on education statistics administered by the OECD in 2010 (for details see Annex 3 at *www.oecd.org/edu/eag2011*).

Data on expenditure for 1995 and 2000 were obtained through a survey updated in 2010; expenditure for 1995 was adjusted to reflect the methods and definitions used in the 2010 UOE data collection. For comparisons over time, the OECD average only accounts for those OECD countries for which data are available for all reported reference years.

The OECD total reflects the value of the indicator if the OECD region is considered as a whole (see the Reader's Guide for details).

The statistical data for Israel are supplied by and under the responsibility of the relevant Israeli authorities. The use of such data by the OECD is without prejudice to the status of the Golan Heights, East Jerusalem and Israeli settlements in the West Bank under the terms of international law.

References

OECD (2010h), *Education at a Glance 2010: OECD Indicators*, OECD, Paris.

The following additional material relevant to this indicator is available on line:

- ***Table B2.4. Change in expenditure on educational institutions and in GDP (1995, 2000, 2008)***
  StatLink http://dx.doi.org/10.1787/888932463821

Table B2.1. Expenditure on educational institutions as a percentage of GDP, by level of education (1995, 2000, 2008)

From public and private sources, by year

		2008			2000			1995		
		Primary, secondary and post-secondary non-tertiary education	Tertiary education	Total all levels of education	Primary, secondary and post-secondary non-tertiary education	Tertiary education	Total all levels of education	Primary, secondary and post-secondary non-tertiary education	Tertiary education	Total all levels of education
OECD	Australia	3.6	1.5	**5.2**	3.5	1.4	**5.0**	3.4	1.6	**5.0**
	Austria	3.6	1.3	**5.4**	3.9	1.1	**5.5**	4.3	1.2	**6.2**
	Belgium	4.4	1.4	**6.6**	4.1	1.3	**6.1**	m	m	**m**
	Canada[1, 2]	3.6	2.5	**6.0**	3.3	2.3	**5.9**	4.3	2.1	**6.7**
	Chile[3]	4.2	2.2	**7.1**	4.4	2.0	**6.7**	2.9	1.5	**4.6**
	Czech Republic	2.8	1.2	**4.5**	2.8	0.8	**4.2**	3.5	0.9	**5.1**
	Denmark[2]	4.3	1.7	**7.1**	4.1	1.6	**6.6**	4.0	1.6	**6.2**
	Estonia[4]	3.9	1.3	**5.8**	3.9	1.0	**5.4**	4.2	1.0	**5.8**
	Finland	3.8	1.7	**5.9**	3.6	1.7	**5.6**	4.0	1.9	**6.3**
	France	3.9	1.4	**6.0**	4.3	1.3	**6.4**	4.5	1.4	**6.6**
	Germany	3.0	1.2	**4.8**	3.3	1.1	**4.9**	3.4	1.1	**5.1**
	Greece[2]	m	m	**m**	2.7	0.8	**3.6**	2.0	0.6	**2.6**
	Hungary[4]	3.0	0.9	**4.8**	2.7	0.8	**4.3**	3.2	0.8	**4.8**
	Iceland	5.1	1.3	**7.9**	4.8	1.1	**7.1**	m	m	**m**
	Ireland	4.1	1.4	**5.6**	2.9	1.5	**4.5**	3.8	1.3	**5.2**
	Israel	4.2	1.6	**7.3**	4.3	1.9	**7.6**	4.6	1.7	**7.8**
	Italy	3.3	1.0	**4.8**	3.2	0.9	**4.5**	3.5	0.7	**4.6**
	Japan[2]	2.8	1.5	**4.9**	3.0	1.4	**5.0**	3.1	1.3	**5.0**
	Korea	4.2	2.6	**7.6**	3.5	2.2	**6.1**	m	m	**m**
	Luxembourg	2.9	m	**m**	m	m	**m**	m	m	**m**
	Mexico	3.7	1.2	**5.8**	3.5	1.0	**5.0**	3.7	1.0	**5.1**
	Netherlands	3.7	1.5	**5.6**	3.4	1.4	**5.1**	3.4	1.6	**5.4**
	New Zealand	4.5	1.6	**6.6**	4.4	0.9	**5.6**	3.5	1.1	**4.7**
	Norway[4]	5.0	1.7	**7.3**	5.0	1.6	**6.8**	5.0	1.9	**6.9**
	Poland	3.6	1.5	**5.7**	3.9	1.1	**5.6**	3.6	0.8	**5.2**
	Portugal	3.4	1.3	**5.2**	3.8	1.0	**5.2**	3.5	0.9	**4.9**
	Slovak Republic[2]	2.6	0.9	**4.0**	2.7	0.8	**4.1**	3.1	0.7	**4.6**
	Slovenia	3.7	1.1	**5.4**	m	m	**m**	m	m	**m**
	Spain	3.1	1.2	**5.1**	3.2	1.1	**4.8**	3.8	1.0	**5.3**
	Sweden	4.0	1.6	**6.3**	4.2	1.6	**6.3**	4.1	1.5	**6.0**
	Switzerland[4]	4.3	1.3	**5.7**	4.2	1.1	**5.7**	4.6	0.9	**6.0**
	Turkey[4]	m	m	**m**	1.8	0.8	**2.5**	1.2	0.5	**1.7**
	United Kingdom	4.2	1.2	**5.7**	3.5	1.0	**4.9**	3.6	1.1	**5.2**
	United States	4.1	2.7	**7.2**	3.9	2.7	**6.9**	3.8	2.3	**6.6**
	OECD average	3.8	1.5	**5.9**	~	~	**~**	~	~	**~**
	OECD total	3.7	1.9	**6.1**	~	~	**~**	~	~	**~**
	EU21 average	3.6	1.3	**5.5**	~	~	**~**	~	~	**~**
	OECD average for countries with 1995, 2000 and 2008 data (27 countries)	3.7	1.5	**5.8**	3.7	1.3	**5.5**	3.8	1.3	**5.6**
Other G20	Argentina	4.3	1.2	**6.1**	m	m	**m**	m	m	**m**
	Brazil[4]	4.1	0.8	**5.3**	2.4	0.7	**3.5**	2.6	0.7	**3.7**
	China[4]	m	m	**3.3**	m	m	**m**	m	m	**m**
	India	m	m	**m**	m	m	**m**	m	m	**m**
	Indonesia[1, 4]	2.9	0.3	**3.3**	m	m	**m**	m	m	**m**
	Russian Federation[4]	2.1	1.5	**4.7**	1.7	0.5	**2.9**	m	m	**m**
	Saudi Arabia	m	m	**m**	m	m	**m**	m	m	**m**
	South Africa	m	m	**m**	m	m	**m**	m	m	**m**
	G20 average	m	m	**5.4**	m	m	**m**	m	m	**m**

1. Year of reference 2007 instead of 2008.
2. Some levels of education are included with others. Refer to «x» code in Table B1.1a for details.
3. Year of reference 2009 instead of 2008.
4. Public expenditure only (for Switzerland, in tertiary education only; for Norway, in primary, secondary and post-secondary non-tertiary education only; for Estonia, New Zealand and the Russian Federation, for 1995 and 2000 only).

Source: OECD. Argentina, Indonesia: UNESCO Institute for Statistics (World Education Indicators Programme).China: The national Statistics Bulletin on Educational Expenditure 2009. See Annex 3 for notes *(www.oecd.org/edu/eag2011)*.

Please refer to the Reader's Guide for information concerning the symbols replacing missing data.

StatLink http://dx.doi.org/10.1787/888932463764

Table B2.2. **Expenditure on educational institutions as a percentage of GDP, by level of education (2008)**

From public and private sources of funds[1]

		Pre-primary education (for children aged 3 and older)	Primary, secondary and post-secondary non-tertiary education				Tertiary education			All levels of education combined (including undistributed programmes)
			All primary, secondary and post-secondary non-tertiary education	Primary and lower secondary education	Upper secondary education	Post-secondary non-tertiary education	All tertiary education	Tertiary-type B education	Tertiary-type A education and advanced research programmes	
		(1)	(2)	(3)	(4)	(5)	(6)	(7)	(8)	(9)
OECD	Australia	0.1	3.6	2.7	0.7	0.1	1.5	0.1	1.3	**5.2**
	Austria	0.5	3.6	2.3	1.3	n	1.3	n	1.3	**5.4**
	Belgium[2]	0.6	4.4	1.6	2.9	x(4)	1.4	x(6)	x(6)	**6.6**
	Canada[3]	x(3)	3.5	2.1	1.4	x(7)	2.5	1.0	1.6	**6.0**
	Chile[4]	0.7	4.2	2.8	1.4	a	2.2	0.5	1.6	**7.1**
	Czech Republic	0.5	2.8	1.6	1.1	n	1.2	n	1.1	**4.5**
	Denmark	0.7	4.3	3.0	1.3	x(4, 6)	1.7	x(6)	x(6)	**7.1**
	Estonia	0.5	3.9	2.5	1.2	0.2	1.3	0.4	0.9	**5.8**
	Finland	0.4	3.8	2.3	1.4	x(4)	1.7	n	1.7	**5.9**
	France	0.7	3.9	2.5	1.4	n	1.4	0.3	1.1	**6.0**
	Germany	0.5	3.0	1.9	1.0	0.1	1.2	0.1	1.1	**4.8**
	Greece	m	m	m	m	m	m	m	m	**m**
	Hungary[5]	0.7	3.0	1.8	1.0	0.1	0.9	n	0.8	**4.8**
	Iceland	1.0	5.1	3.7	1.4	x(4)	1.3	x(6)	x(6)	**7.9**
	Ireland	n	4.1	3.0	0.9	0.2	1.4	x(6)	x(6)	**5.6**
	Israel	0.8	4.2	2.3	1.9	n	1.6	0.3	1.3	**7.3**
	Italy	0.5	3.3	2.0	1.3	n	1.0	n	1.0	**4.8**
	Japan	0.2	2.8	2.0	0.8	x(4, 6)	1.5	0.2	1.2	**4.9**
	Korea	0.2	4.2	2.7	1.5	a	2.6	0.4	2.2	**7.6**
	Luxembourg	0.5	2.9	2.0	0.9	m	m	m	m	**m**
	Mexico	0.7	3.7	2.9	0.8	a	1.2	x(6)	x(6)	**5.8**
	Netherlands	0.4	3.7	2.5	1.2	n	1.5	n	1.5	**5.6**
	New Zealand	0.5	4.5	2.8	1.5	0.2	1.6	0.3	1.3	**6.6**
	Norway[5]	0.5	5.0	3.4	1.6	x(4)	1.7	x(6)	x(6)	**7.4**
	Poland	0.7	3.6	2.5	1.1	n	1.5	n	1.5	**5.7**
	Portugal	0.4	3.4	2.4	1.0	m	1.3	x(6)	x(6)	**5.2**
	Slovak Republic	0.4	2.6	1.6	1.0	x(4)	0.9	x(4)	0.9	**4.0**
	Slovenia	0.6	3.7	2.6	1.1	x(4)	1.1	x(6)	x(6)	**5.4**
	Spain	0.8	3.1	2.4	0.7	a	1.2	0.2	1.0	**5.1**
	Sweden	0.7	4.0	2.7	1.3	n	1.6	x(6)	x(6)	**6.3**
	Switzerland[5]	0.2	4.3	2.7	1.6	x(4)	1.2	n	1.2	**5.7**
	Turkey	m	m	m	m	a	m	m	m	**m**
	United Kingdom	0.3	4.2	2.8	1.4	n	1.2	x(6)	x(6)	**5.7**
	United States	0.4	4.1	3.0	1.1	m	2.7	x(6)	x(6)	**7.2**
	OECD average	0.5	3.8	2.5	1.2	n	1.5	0.2	1.3	**5.9**
	OECD total	0.4	3.7	2.6	1.1	n	1.9	0.2	1.3	**6.1**
	EU21 average	0.5	3.6	2.3	1.2	n	1.3	0.1	1.2	**5.5**
Other G20	Argentina	0.6	4.3	3.4	0.9	a	1.2	0.3	0.8	**6.1**
	Brazil[5]	0.4	4.1	3.4	0.7	a	0.8	x(6)	x(6)	**5.3**
	China[5]	m	m	m	m	m	m	m	m	**3.3**
	India	m	m	m	m	m	m	m	m	**m**
	Indonesia[3, 5]	n	2.9	2.5	0.4	a	0.3	n	0.3	**3.3**
	Russian Federation[5]	0.7	2.1	x(2)	x(2)	x(2)	1.5	0.2	1.3	**4.7**
	Saudi Arabia	m	m	m	m	m	m	m	m	**m**
	South Africa	m	m	m	m	m	m	m	m	**m**
	G20 average	m	m	m	m	m	m	m	m	**5.4**

1. Including international sources.
2. Column 3 only refers to primary education and Column 4 refers to all secondary education.
3. Year of reference 2007.
4. Year of reference 2009.
5. Public expenditure only (for Switzerland, in tertiary education only; for Norway, in primary, secondary and post-secondary non-tertiary education only).

Source: OECD. Argentina, Indonesia: UNESCO Institute for Statistics (World Education Indicators Programme). China: The national Statistics Bulletin on Educational Expenditure 2009. See Annex 3 for notes (*www.oecd.org/edu/eag2011*).

Please refer to the Reader's Guide for information concerning the symbols replacing missing data.

StatLink http://dx.doi.org/10.1787/888932463783

Table B2.3. Expenditure on educational institutions as a percentage of GDP, by source of fund and level of education (2008)

From public and private sources of funds

		Pre-primary education			Primary, secondary and post-secondary non-tertiary education			Tertiary education			Total all levels of education		
		Public[1]	Private[2]	Total	Public[1]	Private[2]	Total	Public[1]	Private[2]	Total	Public[1]	Private[2]	Total
		(1)	(2)	(3)	(4)	(5)	(6)	(7)	(8)	(9)	(10)	(11)	(12)
OECD	Australia	0.04	0.04	**0.08**	3.0	0.6	**3.6**	0.7	0.8	**1.5**	3.7	1.4	**5.2**
	Austria	0.45	0.06	**0.51**	3.5	0.1	**3.6**	1.2	0.1	**1.3**	5.2	0.2	**5.4**
	Belgium	0.59	0.02	**0.61**	4.3	0.2	**4.4**	1.3	0.1	**1.4**	6.3	0.3	**6.6**
	Canada[3, 4]	x(4)	x(5)	**x(6)**	3.1	0.4	**3.5**	1.5	1.0	**2.5**	4.6	1.4	**6.0**
	Chile[5]	0.59	0.15	**0.74**	3.3	0.9	**4.2**	x(9)	x(9)	**2.2**	4.3	2.7	**7.1**
	Czech Republic	0.42	0.04	**0.46**	2.5	0.3	**2.8**	0.9	0.2	**1.2**	3.9	0.6	**4.5**
	Denmark[4]	0.60	0.14	**0.74**	4.2	0.1	**4.3**	1.6	0.1	**1.7**	6.5	0.6	**7.1**
	Estonia	0.53	0.01	**0.54**	3.8	n	**3.9**	1.1	0.2	**1.3**	5.5	0.2	**5.8**
	Finland	0.36	0.04	**0.40**	3.8	n	**3.8**	1.6	0.1	**1.7**	5.7	0.1	**5.9**
	France	0.63	0.04	**0.67**	3.7	0.2	**3.9**	1.2	0.2	**1.4**	5.5	0.5	**6.0**
	Germany	0.40	0.14	**0.54**	2.6	0.4	**3.0**	1.0	0.2	**1.2**	4.1	0.7	**4.8**
	Greece	m	m	**m**	m	m	**m**	m	m	**m**	m	m	**m**
	Hungary	0.69	m	**m**	3.0	m	**m**	0.9	m	**m**	4.8	m	**m**
	Iceland	0.75	0.23	**0.98**	4.9	0.2	**5.1**	1.2	0.1	**1.3**	7.2	0.7	**7.9**
	Ireland	n	n	**n**	4.0	0.1	**4.1**	1.2	0.2	**1.4**	5.2	0.3	**5.6**
	Israel	0.66	0.19	**0.84**	4.0	0.2	**4.2**	0.9	0.7	**1.6**	5.9	1.4	**7.3**
	Italy	0.48	0.03	**0.52**	3.2	0.1	**3.3**	0.8	0.2	**1.0**	4.5	0.3	**4.8**
	Japan[4]	0.09	0.12	**0.21**	2.5	0.3	**2.8**	0.5	1.0	**1.5**	3.3	1.7	**4.9**
	Korea	0.09	0.10	**0.18**	3.4	0.8	**4.2**	0.6	1.9	**2.6**	4.7	2.8	**7.6**
	Luxembourg	0.45	0.01	**0.46**	2.8	0.1	**2.9**	m	m	**m**	m	m	**m**
	Mexico	0.59	0.11	**0.70**	3.1	0.6	**3.7**	0.9	0.4	**1.2**	4.7	1.1	**5.8**
	Netherlands	0.38	n	**0.39**	3.3	0.4	**3.7**	1.1	0.4	**1.5**	4.8	0.8	**5.6**
	New Zealand	0.45	0.04	**0.49**	3.8	0.6	**4.5**	1.1	0.5	**1.6**	5.4	1.2	**6.6**
	Norway	0.42	0.08	**0.50**	5.0	m	**m**	1.6	0.1	**1.7**	7.3	m	**m**
	Poland	0.57	0.10	**0.67**	3.4	0.2	**3.6**	1.0	0.4	**1.5**	5.0	0.7	**5.7**
	Portugal	0.37	n	**0.37**	3.4	n	**3.4**	0.9	0.5	**1.3**	4.7	0.5	**5.2**
	Slovak Republic[4]	0.37	0.08	**0.44**	2.2	0.4	**2.6**	0.7	0.2	**0.9**	3.5	0.6	**4.0**
	Slovenia	0.49	0.14	**0.63**	3.4	0.3	**3.7**	1.0	0.2	**1.1**	4.8	0.6	**5.4**
	Spain	0.63	0.19	**0.82**	2.9	0.2	**3.1**	1.0	0.2	**1.2**	4.5	0.6	**5.1**
	Sweden	0.67	n	**0.67**	4.0	n	**4.0**	1.4	0.2	**1.6**	6.1	0.2	**6.3**
	Switzerland	0.19	m	**m**	3.8	0.5	**4.3**	1.3	m	**m**	5.3	m	**m**
	Turkey	m	m	**m**	m	m	**m**	m	m	**m**	m	m	**m**
	United Kingdom	0.28	n	**0.28**	4.2	n	**4.2**	0.6	0.6	**1.2**	5.1	0.6	**5.7**
	United States	0.33	0.08	**0.41**	3.8	0.3	**4.1**	1.0	1.7	**2.7**	5.1	2.1	**7.2**
	OECD average	0.44	0.07	**0.51**	3.5	0.3	**3.7**	1.0	0.5	**1.5**	5.0	0.9	**5.9**
	OECD total	0.36	0.08	**0.44**	3.4	0.3	**3.7**	0.9	1.0	**1.9**	4.7	1.4	**6.1**
	EU21 average	0.47	0.05	**0.51**	3.4	0.2	**3.6**	1.1	0.2	**1.3**	4.8	0.5	**5.5**
Other G20	Argentina	0.43	0.13	**0.57**	4.0	0.3	**4.3**	0.9	0.2	**1.2**	5.3	0.7	**6.1**
	Brazil	0.41	m	**m**	4.1	m	**m**	0.8	m	**m**	5.3	m	**m**
	China	m	m	**m**	m	m	**m**	m	m	**m**	3.3	m	**m**
	India	m	m	**m**	m	m	**m**	m	m	**m**	m	m	**m**
	Indonesia[3]	0.02	m	**m**	2.9	m	**m**	0.3	m	**m**	3.3	m	**m**
	Russian Federation	0.61	0.09	**0.70**	2.0	0.1	**2.1**	0.9	0.5	**1.5**	4.1	0.7	**4.7**
	Saudi Arabia	m	m	**m**	m	m	**m**	m	m	**m**	m	m	**m**
	South Africa	m	m	**m**	m	m	**m**	m	m	**m**	m	m	**m**
	G20 average	m	m	**m**	m	m	**m**	m	m	**m**	4.4	m	**m**

1. Including public subsidies to households attributable for educational institutions, and direct expenditure on educational institutions from international sources.
2. Net of public subsidies attributable for educational institutions.
3. Year of reference 2007.
4. Some levels of education are included with others. Refer to «x» code in Table B1.1a for details.
5. Year of reference 2009.

Source: OECD. Argentina, Indonesia: UNESCO Institute for Statistics (World Education Indicators Programme). China: The national Statistics Bulletin on Educational Expenditure 2009. See Annex 3 for notes *(www.oecd.org/edu/eag2011)*.

Please refer to the Reader's Guide for information concerning the symbols replacing missing data.

StatLink http://dx.doi.org/10.1787/888932463802

INDICATOR B3

HOW MUCH PUBLIC AND PRIVATE INVESTMENT IN EDUCATION IS THERE?

- On average in OECD countries, 83% of all funds for educational institutions come directly from public sources.
- An average of 91% of primary, secondary and post-secondary non-tertiary education in OECD countries – and never less than 80%, except in Chile, Korea and the United Kingdom – is paid for publicly.
- Compared to primary, secondary and post-secondary non-tertiary education, tertiary institutions and, to a lesser extent, pre-primary institutions, obtain the largest proportions of funds from private sources, at 31% and 19%, respectively; but these proportions vary widely between countries.
- In all countries for which comparable data are available, public funding on educational institutions, all levels combined, increased between 2000 and 2008. Private spending increased at an even greater rate in more than three-quarters of countries and, on average among OECD countries, the share of private funding for educational institutions increased between 2000 and 2008.

Chart B3.1. Share of private expenditure on educational institutions (2008)

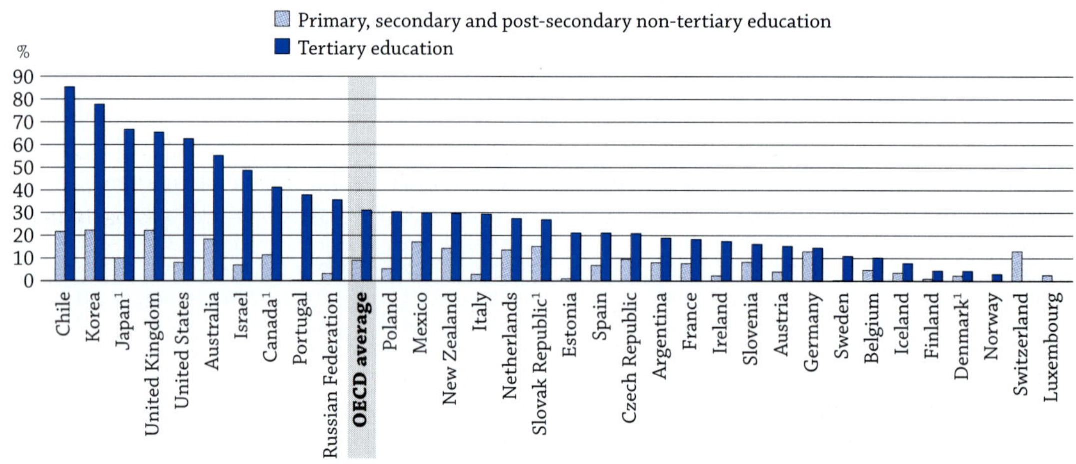

1. Some levels of education are included with others. Refer to "x" code in Table B1.1a for details.

Countries are ranked in descending order of the share of private expenditure on educational institutions for tertiary education.

Source: OECD. Argentina: UNESCO Institute for Statistics (World Education Indicators Programme). Tables B3.2a and B3.2b. See Annex 3 for notes (*www.oecd.org/edu/eag2011*).

StatLink http://dx.doi.org/10.1787/888932461066

How to read this chart

The chart shows private spending on educational institutions as a percentage of total spending on educational institutions. This includes all money transferred to educational institutions from private sources, including public funding via subsidies to households, private fees for educational services, or other private spending (e.g. on accommodation) that goes through the educational institution.

Context

The balance of private and public financing of education is an important policy issue in many OECD countries. It is particularly important for pre-primary and tertiary education, for which full or nearly full public funding is less common.

As more people participate in a wider range of educational programmes offered by increasing numbers of providers, governments are forging new partnerships to mobilise the necessary resources and to share costs and benefits more equitably. As a result, public funding more often provides only a part (albeit a very large part) of the investment in education, while the role of private sources of funding has become more important. Some stakeholders are concerned that this balance should not become so tilted as to discourage potential students from entering tertiary education.

Other findings

- Public expenditure mainly funds public institutions, but also private institutions to varying degrees. On average among OECD countries, **public expenditure on public institutions, per student, is more than twice the level of public expenditure on private institutions in pre-primary education, somewhat under twice the level in primary, secondary and post-secondary non-tertiary education, and nearly three times the level in tertiary education.**
- At the tertiary level, the **countries with the lowest amounts of public expenditure per tertiary student** in public and private institutions **are also those with the fewest students enrolled in public tertiary institutions**, except for Poland.
- In most countries for which data are available, **individual households account for most of the private expenditure on tertiary education**. Exceptions are Austria, Canada, the Czech Republic, the Slovak Republic and Sweden, where private expenditure from entities other than households is more significant than private expenditure from households.

Trends

On average among the 19 OECD countries for which trend data are available for all years **between 1995 and 2008, the share of public funding of tertiary institutions decreased slightly** from 74% in 1995, to 73% in 2000, to 68% in 2007 and to 67% in 2008. This trend is mainly influenced by non-European countries, where tuition fees are generally higher and enterprises participate more actively by providing grants to finance tertiary institutions.

Between 2000 and 2008, 20 of the 26 countries for which comparable data are available showed an **increase in the share of private funding for tertiary education**. The share increased by six percentage points, on average, and by more than ten percentage points in Austria, Portugal, the Slovak Republic and the United Kingdom. While the share of private funding for tertiary education rose substantially in some countries during the period, **this was not the case for other levels of education**.

Analysis

Public and private expenditure on educational institutions

Educational institutions in OECD countries are still mainly publicly funded, although there is a substantial and growing level of private funding at the tertiary level. On average in OECD countries, 83% of all funds for educational institutions come directly from public sources (Table B3.1).

In all OECD countries for which comparable data are available, private funding on educational institutions represents around 17% of all expenditure, on average. The proportion varies widely among countries and 11 OECD countries report a share of private funding above the OECD average. In Canada and Israel, private funds constitute nearly one-quarter of all educational expenditure, while in Australia, Chile, Japan, Korea, the United Kingdom and the United States, private funding reaches or exceeds 29% of all expenditure on education (Table B3.1).

Private spending on education for all levels of education combined increased from 2000 to 2008 and the share of private expenditure in total expenditure on educational institutions also increased, resulting in a decrease of more than eight percentage points in the share of public funding for educational institutions in Portugal, the Slovak Republic and the United Kingdom. This decrease is mainly due to a significant increase in the tuition fees charged by tertiary educational institutions over the same period (Table B3.1).

However, decreases in the share of public expenditure in total expenditure on educational institutions (and consequent increases in the share of private expenditure) have not generally gone hand-in-hand with cuts (in real terms) in public expenditure on educational institutions (Table B3.1). In fact, many of the OECD countries with the highest growth rates in private spending have also had the largest increases in public funding. This indicates that an increase in private spending tends not to replace public investment but to complement it.

However, the share of private expenditure on educational institutions varies across countries and according to the level of education.

Public and private expenditure on pre-primary, primary, secondary and post-secondary non-tertiary educational institutions

Investment in early childhood education is essential for building a strong foundation for lifelong learning and for ensuring equitable access to learning opportunities later in school. In pre-primary education, the private share of total payments to educational institutions averages around 19% – higher than the percentage for all levels of education combined. However, this proportion varies widely among countries, ranging from 5% or less in Belgium, Estonia, Luxembourg, the Netherlands and Sweden, to 25% or more in Austria and Germany, and to over 50% in Australia, Japan and Korea (Table B3.2a).

Box B3.1. Private expenditure for the work-based component of educational programmes

Many countries have some form of combined school- and work-based educational programmes (e.g. apprenticeship programmes, dual systems). The impact of reporting these programmes in the financial indicators is strong in a few countries, even if it is not significant in most countries (see Table at the end of this box). Expenditure by private employers on training apprentices (e.g. compensation of instructors and cost of instructional materials and equipment) and other participants in these programmes should be included in the financial indicators published in *Education at a Glance*. Expenditure to train company instructors is also included.

Among countries with some form of dual educational systems, only Germany, Switzerland and, to some extent, the Netherlands, conduct surveys about private expenditure by employers. In a number of countries, such as the Czech Republic, Finland, Norway, and the Slovak Republic, workplace training is directly financed by the government, or firms are reimbursed for their expenses; thus private expenditures are implicitly included in public expenditures reported in the indicators for most of these countries.

...

However, 10 of 17 countries with large dual systems – Australia, Austria, Denmark, Estonia, France, Hungary, Iceland, Luxembourg, the Russian Federation and the United Kingdom – do not include private expenditure by enterprises that relate to these programmes in the financial indicators published in *Education at a Glance*. This is mainly because of a lack of such data.

The size of the work-based component varies widely among these countries and can have a significant impact on total expenditure in some. Among countries with available data on upper secondary education, Germany, the Netherlands and Switzerland have a significant proportion of all pupils (about 20% in the Netherlands, 50% in Germany and 60% in Switzerland) enrolled in vocational education and training programmes (VET) with a work-based component. The corresponding expenditure on these programmes represents between 0.3% and 0.5% of GDP (see Indicator B2).

Further research has shown that 6% to 30% of upper secondary students (a "medium" share) are enrolled in VET programmes with a work-based component in Australia, Finland, France, Hungary, Iceland, Luxembourg, Norway, the Russian Federation, the Slovak Republic and the United Kingdom, while more than 30% of upper secondary students (a "high" proportion) in Austria, the Czech Republic, Denmark and Estonia are enrolled in such programmes. Among the group of countries with missing data on training expenditures, the impact of not reporting such expenditures is expected to be small for Australia, Denmark, Estonia, Iceland, Norway and the Slovak Republic, but is potentially important for Austria, France, Hungary, Luxembourg, the Russian Federation and the United Kingdom (see Table below).

In the financial indicators published in *Education at a Glance*, the cost of apprentices' salaries, social security contributions, and other compensation paid to students or apprentices in combined school- and work-based educational programmes is not included. Private investment in upper secondary VET programmes with a work-based component is considered to be moderate in Austria, France, Hungary, Luxembourg, the Netherlands, the Russian Federation and the United Kingdom, and large in Germany and Switzerland, where apprentices spend a substantial portion of their time in the workplace and where training is intensive (see Table below).

Level of investment by firms* in upper secondary VET programmes with a work-based component (low, medium, high) (horizontal axis) relative to the share of students (low, medium, high) enrolled in these programmes (vertical axis)

	Importance of investment by firms		
Share of dual/part-time VET to all pupils	**LOW**	**MEDIUM**	**HIGH**
HIGH (> 30%)	the Czech Republic, Denmark, Estonia	Austria	Germany, Switzerland
MEDIUM (6-30%)	Australia, Finland, Iceland, Norway, the Slovak Republic	France, Hungary Luxembourg, the Netherlands, the Russian Federation, the United Kingdom	
LOW (< 6%)	Belgium, Brazil, Canada, Chile, Greece, Ireland, Israel, Italy, Japan, Korea, Mexico, New Zealand, Poland, Portugal, Slovenia, Spain, Sweden, Turkey and the United States		

*The importance of investment by firms is an index that reflects the time that trainees spend in the workplace, the intensity of training (weekly instruction time) at the workplace, and controls for public reimbursement of such expenditure.

Public funding dominates primary, secondary and post-secondary non-tertiary education in all countries. Nevertheless, at least 10% of funding for these levels of education is private in Australia, Canada, Chile, Germany, Japan, Korea, Mexico, the Netherlands, New Zealand, the Slovak Republic, Switzerland and the United Kingdom (Table B3.2a and Chart B3.2). In most countries, the largest share of private expenditure at these levels is household expenditure, which goes mainly towards tuition. In Germany, the Netherlands and Switzerland, however, most private expenditure takes the form of contributions from the business sector to the dual system of apprenticeship in upper secondary and post-secondary non-tertiary education (see Box B3.1).

Between 2000 and 2008, 14 of the 26 countries for which comparable data are available showed a small decrease in the share of public funding for primary, secondary and post-secondary non-tertiary education. Among these countries, the increase in the private share is three percentage points or more in Canada (from 7.6% to 11.4%), Korea (from 19.2% to 22.2%), Mexico (from 13.9% to 17.1%), the Slovak Republic (from 2.4% to 15.2%) and the United Kingdom (from 11.3% to 22.1%). Significant shifts in the opposite direction, towards public funding, are evident in eight countries; however, this share of public funding increased by three percentage points or more only in Chile (from 68.4% to 78.4%, Table B3.2a).

In spite of these differences, between 2000 and 2008 the amount of public expenditure on educational institutions at these levels of education increased in all countries with comparable data, except Portugal, where the amount of private expenditure fell even more. The main reason for the decrease in Portugal is linked to the significant drop in the number of students enrolled in primary, secondary and post-secondary non-tertiary education over the same period. In contrast with general trends, increases in public expenditure for these levels of education have been accompanied by decreases in private expenditure in Chile and Sweden. However, in Sweden, less than 1% of expenditure on educational institutions was provided by private sources in 2008 (Table B3.2a).

Public and private expenditure on tertiary educational institutions

At the tertiary level, high private returns (see Indicator A9) suggest that a greater contribution to the costs of education by individuals and other private entities may be justified, as long as there are ways to ensure that funding is available to students regardless of their economic backgrounds (see Indicator B5). In all countries, the proportion of private expenditure on education is far higher for tertiary education – an average of 31% of total expenditure at this level – than it is for primary, secondary and post-secondary non-tertiary education (Tables B3.2a and B3.2b).

The proportion of expenditure on tertiary institutions covered by individuals, businesses and other private sources, including subsidised private payments, ranges from less than 5% in Denmark, Finland and Norway, to more than 40% in Australia, Canada, Israel, Japan, the United Kingdom and the United States, and to over 75% in Chile and Korea (Chart B3.2 and Table B3.2b). Among these countries, in Korea, around 80% of tertiary students are enrolled in private universities, and more than 70% of the budget comes from tuition fees.

The contribution from private entities other than households to financing educational institutions is higher for tertiary education than for other levels of education, on average across OECD countries. In Australia, Canada, the Czech Republic, Israel, Japan, Korea, the Netherlands, the Russian Federation, the Slovak Republic, Sweden, the United Kingdom and the United States, 10% or more of expenditure on tertiary institutions is covered by private entities other than households. In Sweden, these contributions are largely directed to sponsoring research and development.

In many OECD countries, greater participation in tertiary education (see Indicator C1) reflects strong individual and social demand. In 2008, an average of 69% of tertiary education in OECD countries was publicly funded. On average among the 19 OECD countries for which trend data are available for all reference years, the share of public funding for tertiary institutions decreased slightly from 74% in 1995 to 73% in 2000, to 68% in 2007 and to 67% in 2008. This trend is apparent primarily in non-European countries, where tuition fees are generally higher and enterprises participate more actively, largely through grants to tertiary institutions (Table B3.3, Chart B3.3 and Indicator B5).

Chart B3.2. Distribution of public and private expenditure on educational institutions (2008)

By level of education

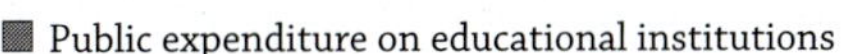

■ Public expenditure on educational institutions
■ Household expenditure
■ Expenditure of other private entities
■ All private sources, including subsidies for payments to educational institutions received from public sources

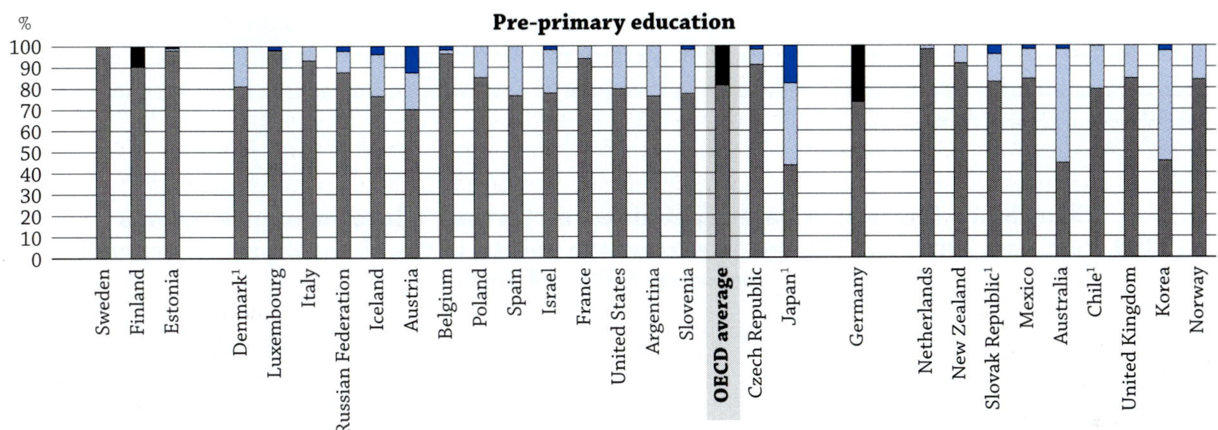

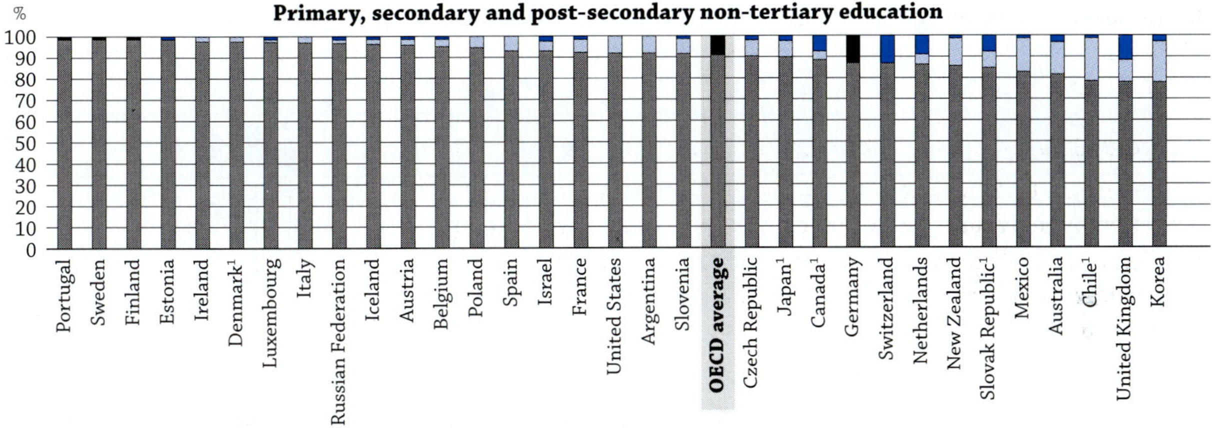

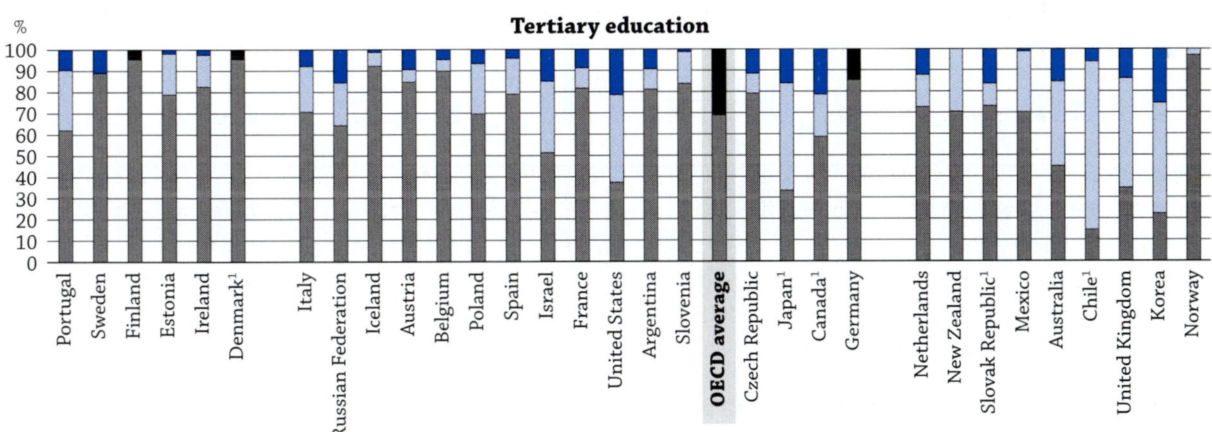

1. Some levels of education are included with others. Refer to "x" code in Table B1.1a for details.

Countries are ranked in descending order of the proportion of public expenditure on educational institutions in primary, secondary and post-secondary non-tertiary education.

Source: OECD. Argentina: UNESCO Institute for Statistics (World Education Indicators Programme). Tables B3.2a and B3.2b. See Annex 3 for notes (*www.oecd.org/edu/eag2011*).

StatLink http://dx.doi.org/10.1787/888932461085

In 14 of the 21 countries with comparable data for 1995 and 2008, the private share of educational expenditure for tertiary education increased by at least three percentage points during this period. Similarly, 20 of the 26 countries for which comparable data are available for 2000 and 2008 showed an increase in the share of private funding for tertiary education. This increase exceeded nine percentage points between 1995 and 2008 in Australia, Austria, Chile, Israel, Italy, Portugal, the Slovak Republic and the United Kingdom. Only the Czech Republic and Ireland – and, to a lesser extent, Norway and Spain – show a significant decrease in private expenditure on tertiary educational institutions (Table B3.3 and Chart B3.3). In Australia, this increase was largely due to changes to the Higher Education Contribution Scheme/Higher Education Loan Programme implemented in 1997. In Ireland, tuition fees for tertiary first-degree programmes were gradually eliminated over the past decade, leading to the reduction in the share of private spending at this level (for more details, see Indicator B5 and Annex 3).

Chart B3.3. Share of private expenditure on tertiary educational institutions (2000, 2005 and 2008) and change, in percentage points, of the share of private expenditure between 2000 and 2008

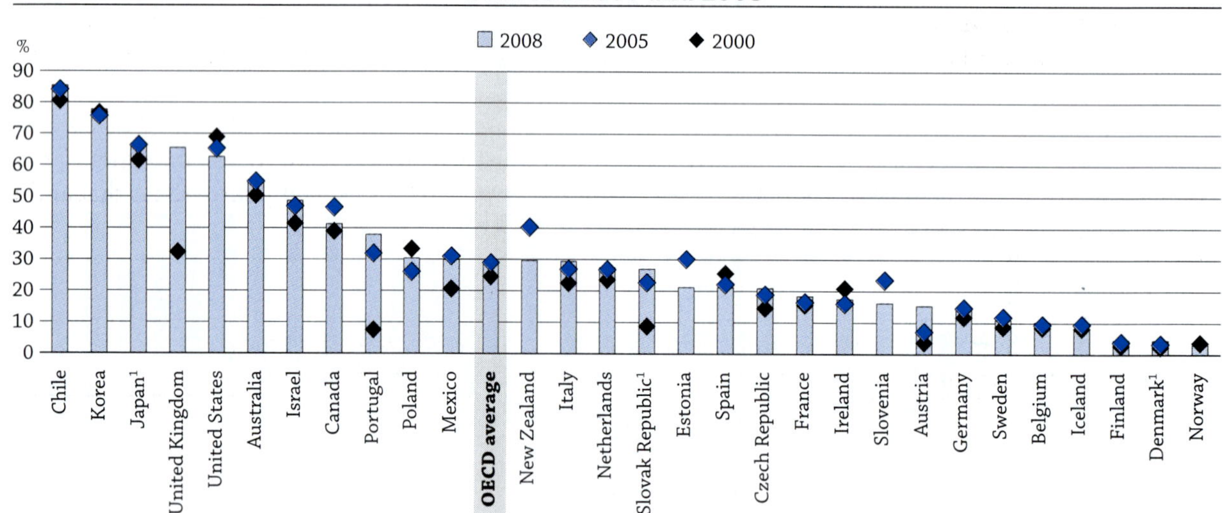

Change (in percentage points) in the proportion of private expenditure between 2000 and 2008

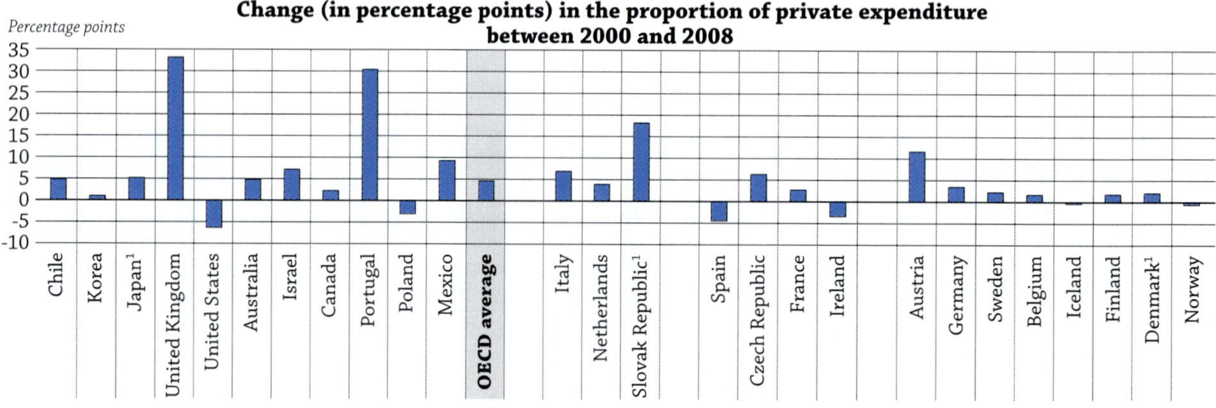

1. Some levels of education are included with others. Refer to "x" code in Table B1.1a for details.

Countries are ranked in descending order of the share of private expenditure on educational institutions in 2008.

Source: OECD. Table B3.3. See Annex 3 for notes (*www.oecd.org/edu/eag2011*).

StatLink http://dx.doi.org/10.1787/888932461104

Private expenditure on educational institutions increased generally faster than public expenditure between 2000 and 2008. Nevertheless, public investment in tertiary education has also increased in all countries for which 2000 and 2008 data are available (except Israel and Portugal), regardless of the changes in private spending (Table B3.2b). In 11 out of the 13 OECD countries with the largest increases in public expenditure on tertiary education (Austria, the Czech Republic, Estonia, Hungary, Iceland, Ireland, Mexico, New Zealand, Poland, the Slovak Republic and Spain), tertiary institutions charge low or no tuition fees and tertiary attainment is relatively low (see Indicators A1 and B5). In contrast, in Korea and the United States, where public spending has also increased significantly, there is a strong reliance on private funding of tertiary education. In New Zealand, the increase in public spending is as large, but private funding represents only 30% of expenditure on educational institutions (Table B3.2b).

Public expenditure on educational institutions per student, by type of institution

The level of public expenditure shows the degree to which governments value education. Naturally, public funds go to public institutions; but in some cases a significant part of the public budget may be devoted to private educational institutions. Table B3.4 shows public investment in educational institutions relative to the size of the education system, focusing on public expenditure, per student, on public and private educational institutions (private funds are excluded from Table B3.4, although in some countries they represent a significant share of the resources of educational institutions, especially at the tertiary level). This can be considered a measure that complements public expenditure relative to national income (see Indicator B2).

On average among OECD countries, at all levels of education, public expenditure, per student, on public institutions is about twice the public expenditure, per student, on private institutions (USD 8 027 and USD 4 071, respectively). However, the difference varies according to the level of education. Public expenditure, per student, on public institutions is more than twice that on private institutions at the pre-primary level (USD 6 281 and USD 2 474, respectively), somewhat under twice that for primary, secondary and post-secondary non-tertiary education (USD 8 111 and USD 4 572, respectively), and nearly three times that at the tertiary level (USD 10 543 and USD 3 614, respectively).

Chart B3.4. Annual public expenditure on educational institutions per student in tertiary education, by type of institution (2008)

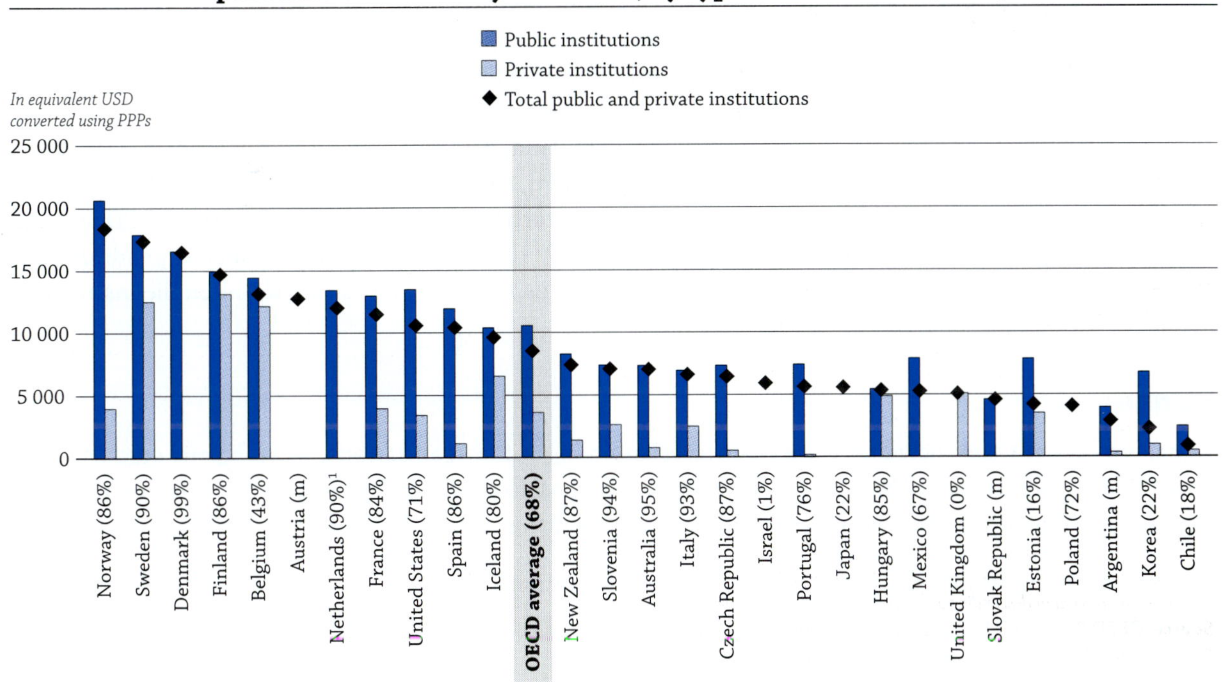

Note: The figures in brackets represent the percentage of students enrolled in public institutions in tertiary education, based on full-time equivalents.
1. Government-dependent institutions are included with public institutions.
Countries are ranked in descending order of public expenditure on public and private educational institutions per student.
Source: OECD. Argentina: UNESCO Institute for Statistics (World Education Indicators Programme). Table B3.4. See Annex 3 for notes (*www.oecd.org/edu/eag2011*).
StatLink http://dx.doi.org/10.1787/888932461123

At the pre-primary level, public expenditure per student for both public and private institutions averages USD 5 123 in OECD countries but varies from USD 2 016 or less in Argentina and Mexico to approximately USD 13 000 in Luxembourg. Public expenditure per student is usually higher for public institutions than for private institutions, but private institutions enrol fewer than 5% of pupils. In contrast, in Mexico and the Netherlands, public expenditure per student for private institutions is negligible.

Public expenditure per student for both public and private institutions for primary, secondary and post-secondary non-tertiary education (the educational level with the largest proportion of public funds, Table B3.2a) averages USD 7 354 in OECD countries, but varies from less than USD 1 900 in Mexico to approximately USD 16 000 in Luxembourg. Public expenditure per student is usually higher for public than for private institutions except in Israel and Sweden. In these two OECD countries, only 25% and 9% of pupils, respectively, are enrolled in private institutions. In Mexico and the Netherlands, the amount of public expenditure, per student, on private institutions is small or negligible, as the private sector is marginal and receives little or no public funds (Table C1.5).

At the tertiary level, public expenditure per student for both public and private institutions averages USD 8 526 in OECD countries, but varies from less than USD 1 000 in Chile to more than USD 16 000 in Denmark, Norway and Sweden, three countries in which the level of private expenditure is small or negligible. In all countries with available data, public expenditure per student is higher for public than for private institutions (Table B3.4 and Chart B3.4).

At this level, patterns in the allocation of public funds to public and private institutions differ. In Denmark and the Netherlands, at least 90% of students are enrolled in public institutions, and most public expenditure goes to these institutions. Public expenditure, per student, on public institutions is higher than the OECD average, and public expenditure per student on private institutions is negligible. In these countries, private funds complement public funds to varying degrees: private expenditure is less than 5% of expenditure for public and private educational institutions in Denmark and above 25% in the Netherlands.

In Belgium, Finland, Hungary, Iceland and Sweden, public expenditure goes to both public and private institutions, and public expenditure, per student, on private institutions represents at least 63% – and up to 90% – of the level of public expenditure, per tertiary student, on public institutions (Table B3.4). However, these countries show different participation patterns. In Finland, Hungary, Iceland and Sweden, at least 80% of students are enrolled in public institutions, whereas in Belgium, tertiary students are mainly enrolled in private institutions. In all these countries private expenditure on tertiary institutions is below the OECD average. In the remaining countries, public expenditure goes mainly to public institutions: public expenditure, per student, on private institutions is less than 46% of public expenditure, per student, on public institutions (Chart B3.1 and Table B3.2b).

Definitions

Other private entities include private businesses and non-profit organisations, e.g. religious organisations, charitable organisations and business and labour associations. Expenditure by private companies on the work-based element of school- and work-based training of apprentices and students is also taken into account.

Private spending includes all direct expenditure on educational institutions, whether partially covered by public subsidies or not. Public subsidies attributable to households, included in private spending, are shown separately.

The **public and private proportions of expenditure on educational institutions** are the percentages of total spending originating in, or generated by, the public and private sectors.

Public expenditure is related to all students at public and private institutions, whether these institutions receive public funding or not.

Methodology

Data refer to the financial year 2008 and are based on the UOE data collection on education statistics administered by the OECD in 2010 (for details see Annex 3 at *www.oecd.org/edu/eag2011*).

Not all spending on instructional goods and services occurs within educational institutions. For example, families may purchase commercial textbooks and materials or seek private tutoring for their children outside educational institutions. At the tertiary level, students' living expenses and foregone earnings can also account for a significant proportion of the costs of education. All expenditure outside educational institutions, even if publicly subsidised, is excluded from this indicator. Public subsidies for educational expenditure outside institutions are discussed in Indicators B4 and B5.

A portion of the budgets of educational institutions is related to ancillary services offered to students, including student welfare services (student meals, housing and transport). Part of the cost of these services is covered by fees collected from students and is included in the indicator.

The data on expenditure for 1995 and 2000 were obtained by a survey updated in 2010, in which expenditure for 1995 and 2000 were adjusted to the methods and definitions used in the current UOE data collection.

The statistical data for Israel are supplied by and under the responsibility of the relevant Israeli authorities. The use of such data by the OECD is without prejudice to the status of the Golan Heights, East Jerusalem and Israeli settlements in the West Bank under the terms of international law.

B3

Table B3.1. **Relative proportions of public and private expenditure on educational institutions for all levels of education (2000, 2008)**

Distribution of public and private sources of funds for educational institutions after transfers from public sources, by year

		2008					2000		Index of change between 2000 and 2008 in expenditure on educational institutions	
		Private sources								
		Public sources	Household expenditure	Expenditure of other private entities	All private sources[1]	Private: of which, subsidised	Public sources	All private sources[1]	Public sources	All private sources[1]
		(1)	(2)	(3)	(4)	(5)	(6)	(7)	(8)	(9)
OECD	Australia	**70.6**	22.8	6.7	**29.4**	1.6	73.2	26.8	128	145
	Austria	**90.8**	5.0	4.3	**9.2**	4.7	94.0	6.0	112	180
	Belgium	**94.3**	4.6	1.1	**5.7**	1.7	94.3	5.7	125	123
	Canada[2]	**76.0**	10.7	13.3	**24.0**	m	79.9	20.1	113	142
	Chile[3]	**58.6**	39.2	2.3	**41.4**	1.6	55.2	44.8	156	134
	Czech Republic	**87.3**	8.3	4.4	**12.7**	m	89.9	10.1	146	190
	Denmark	**92.2**	4.5	3.3	**7.8**	m	96.0	4.0	113	229
	Estonia	**94.7**	4.9	0.4	**5.3**	1.5	m	m	164	m
	Finland	**97.4**	x(4)	x(4)	**2.6**	n	98.0	2.0	131	167
	France	**90.0**	6.9	3.1	**10.0**	m	91.2	8.8	106	122
	Germany	**85.4**	x(4)	x(4)	**14.6**	m	86.1	13.9	107	114
	Greece	**m**	m	m	**m**	m	93.8	6.2	m	m
	Hungary	**m**	m	m	**m**	m	m	m	140	m
	Iceland	**90.9**	7.8	1.3	**9.1**	m	90.0	10.0	155	139
	Ireland	**93.8**	5.5	0.6	**6.2**	0.3	90.5	9.5	181	113
	Israel	**78.0**	16.1	5.9	**22.0**	2.4	79.8	20.2	121	135
	Italy	**91.4**	7.0	1.6	**8.6**	1.3	94.3	5.7	107	167
	Japan	**66.4**	21.3	12.3	**33.6**	m	71.0	29.0	102	127
	Korea	**59.6**	29.5	10.9	**40.4**	3.2	59.2	40.8	175	173
	Luxembourg	**m**	m	m	**m**	m	m	m	m	m
	Mexico	**80.8**	19.0	0.2	**19.2**	1.1	85.3	14.7	131	182
	Netherlands	**83.6**	7.3	9.1	**16.4**	2.0	84.1	15.9	126	131
	New Zealand	**82.4**	17.5	0.1	**17.6**	m	m	m	121	m
	Norway	**m**	m	m	**m**	m	m	m	139	m
	Poland	**87.1**	x(4)	x(4)	**12.9**	m	89.0	11.0	140	167
	Portugal	**90.5**	7.1	2.4	**9.5**	m	98.6	1.4	99	718
	Slovak Republic	**82.5**	8.6	8.8	**17.5**	2.6	96.4	3.6	136	768
	Slovenia	**88.4**	11.4	0.2	**11.6**	n	m	m	m	m
	Spain	**87.1**	11.9	1.0	**12.9**	0.4	87.4	12.6	136	141
	Sweden	**97.3**	n	2.7	**2.7**	a	97.0	3.0	122	110
	Switzerland	**m**	m	m	**m**	m	92.1	7.9	116	145
	Turkey	**m**	m	m	**m**	m	98.6	1.4	m	m
	United Kingdom	**69.5**	19.1	11.4	**30.5**	20.2	85.2	14.8	109	276
	United States	**71.0**	21.0	8.0	**29.0**	m	67.3	32.7	129	108
	OECD average	**83.5**	~	~	**16.5**	2.6	86.3	13.7	130	198
	EU21 average	**89.1**	~	~	**10.9**	2.9	92.1	7.9	128	232
Other G20	Argentina	**88.4**	9.9	1.8	**11.6**	0.1	m	m	m	m
	Brazil	**m**	m	m	**m**	m	m	m	197	m
	China	**m**	m	m	**m**	m	m	m	m	m
	India	**m**	m	m	**m**	m	m	m	m	m
	Indonesia	**m**	m	m	**m**	m	m	m	m	m
	Russian Federation	**85.8**	8.4	5.8	**14.2**	m	m	m	229	m
	Saudi Arabia	**m**	m	m	**m**	m	m	m	m	m
	South Africa	**m**	m	m	**m**	m	m	m	m	m

1. Including subsidies attributable to payments to educational institutions received from public sources.
2. Year of reference 2007 instead of 2008.
3. Year of reference 2009 instead of 2008.

Source: OECD. Argentina: UNESCO Institute for Statistics (World Education Indicators Programme). See Annex 3 for notes (*www.oecd.org/edu/eag2011*).

Please refer to the Reader's Guide for information concerning the symbols replacing missing data.

StatLink http://dx.doi.org/10.1787/888932463840

Table B3.2a. Relative proportions of public and private expenditure on educational institutions, as a percentage, by level of education (2000, 2008)

Distribution of public and private sources of funds for educational institutions after transfers from public sources, by year

	Pre-primary education (for children 3 years and older)					Primary, secondary and post-secondary non-tertiary education								
	2008					2008					2000		Index of change between 2000 and 2008 in expenditure on educational institutions	
	Public sources	Private sources			Private: of which, subsidised	Public sources	Private sources			Private: of which, subsidised	Public sources	All private sources[1]	Public sources	All private sources[1]
		Household expenditure	Expenditure of other private entities	All private sources[1]			Household expenditure	Expenditure of other private entities	All private sources[1]					
	(1)	(2)	(3)	(4)	(5)	(6)	(7)	(8)	(9)	(10)	(11)	(12)	(13)	(14)
OECD														
Australia	**44.5**	55.1	0.4	**55.5**	2.5	**81.7**	15.1	3.2	**18.3**	2.1	82.9	17.1	131	142
Austria	**70.2**	17.3	12.5	**29.8**	18.2	**95.9**	2.8	1.2	**4.1**	1.4	95.8	4.2	109	105
Belgium	**96.5**	3.3	0.2	**3.5**	0.8	**95.2**	4.6	0.2	**4.8**	1.2	94.7	5.3	125	113
Canada[2, 3]	**x(6)**	x(7)	x(8)	**x(9)**	x(6)	**88.6**	4.1	7.3	**11.4**	x(6)	92.4	7.6	117	182
Chile[4]	**79.5**	20.3	m	**20.5**	n	**78.4**	21.2	0.4	**21.6**	a	68.4	31.6	152	91
Czech Republic	**91.1**	7.4	1.6	**8.9**	m	**90.4**	7.6	2.0	**9.6**	n	91.7	8.3	136	158
Denmark[3]	**81.2**	18.8	n	**18.8**	m	**97.6**	2.4	n	**2.4**	n	97.8	2.2	115	126
Estonia	**99.0**	0.9	n	**1.0**	n	**99.0**	1.0	0.1	**1.0**	m	m	m	163	m
Finland	**90.5**	x(4)	x(4)	**9.5**	n	**99.0**	x(9)	x(9)	**1.0**	n	99.3	0.7	133	197
France	**94.0**	5.9	n	**6.0**	n	**92.3**	6.1	1.6	**7.7**	1.8	92.6	7.4	102	107
Germany	**73.5**	x(4)	x(4)	**26.5**	n	**87.1**	x(9)	x(9)	**12.9**	m	87.1	12.9	100	101
Greece	**m**	m	m	**m**	m	**m**	m	n	**m**	m	91.7	8.3	m	m
Hungary	**m**	m	m	**m**	m	**m**	m	m	**m**	n	m	m	139	m
Iceland	**76.4**	19.7	3.8	**23.6**	a	**96.4**	3.4	0.2	**3.6**	m	96.4	3.6	146	146
Ireland	**m**	m	m	**m**	m	**97.7**	2.3	m	**2.3**	m	96.0	4.0	200	115
Israel	**77.8**	20.5	1.6	**22.2**	n	**93.0**	4.6	2.4	**7.0**	1.4	94.1	5.9	126	151
Italy	**93.3**	6.7	n	**6.7**	n	**97.1**	2.9	n	**2.9**	n	97.8	2.2	110	147
Japan[3]	**43.5**	38.8	17.7	**56.5**	m	**90.0**	7.6	2.4	**10.0**	m	89.8	10.2	103	100
Korea	**45.5**	52.1	2.4	**54.5**	2.2	**77.8**	19.3	2.9	**22.2**	3.0	80.8	19.2	161	193
Luxembourg	**98.2**	1.5	0.2	**1.8**	n	**97.4**	2.0	0.6	**2.6**	m	m	m	m	m
Mexico	**84.3**	15.6	0.1	**15.7**	0.1	**82.9**	17.0	0.1	**17.1**	1.3	86.1	13.9	123	158
Netherlands	**98.4**	1.6	a	**1.6**	1.1	**86.4**	4.8	8.9	**13.6**	2.7	85.7	14.3	128	121
New Zealand	**91.6**	8.4	x(2)	**8.4**	m	**85.7**	14.2	0.1	**14.3**	m	m	m	109	m
Norway	**83.9**	16.1	m	**16.1**	n	**m**	m	m	**m**	m	m	m	127	m
Poland	**85.2**	14.8	m	**14.8**	n	**94.7**	5.3	m	**5.3**	m	95.4	4.6	128	151
Portugal	**m**	m	m	**m**	m	**99.9**	0.1	m	**0.1**	m	99.9	0.1	98	90
Slovak Republic[3]	**82.9**	13.1	4.1	**17.1**	0.8	**84.8**	7.7	7.5	**15.2**	1.5	97.6	2.4	135	992
Slovenia	**77.5**	22.4	0.1	**22.5**	n	**91.7**	8.1	0.2	**8.3**	n	m	m	m	m
Spain	**76.7**	23.3	m	**23.3**	n	**93.1**	6.9	m	**6.9**	a	93.0	7.0	124	121
Sweden	**100.0**	n	n	**n**	n	**99.9**	0.1	a	**0.1**	n	99.9	0.1	117	85
Switzerland	**m**	m	m	**m**	n	**86.9**	n	13.1	**13.1**	1.3	89.2	10.8	117	145
Turkey	**m**	m	m	**m**	m	**m**	m	m	**m**	m	m	m	m	m
United Kingdom	**84.5**	15.5	n	**15.5**	21.2	**77.9**	10.6	11.5	**22.1**	21.1	88.7	11.3	122	273
United States	**79.8**	20.2	a	**20.2**	a	**92.0**	8.0	m	**8.0**	m	91.6	8.4	126	120
OECD average	**81.5**	~	~	**18.5**	2.0	**91.0**	~	~	**9.0**	1.9	91.7	8.3	127	170
EU21 average	**87.8**	~	~	**12.2**	1.5	**93.5**	~	~	**6.5**	1.0	94.4	5.6	128	189
Other G20														
Argentina	**76.3**	23.7	n	**23.7**	0.1	**91.9**	8.1	n	**8.1**	0.1	m	m	m	m
Brazil	**m**	m	m	**m**	m	**m**	m	m	**m**	m	m	m	216	m
China	**m**	m	m	**m**	m	**m**	m	m	**m**	m	m	m	m	m
India	**m**	m	m	**m**	m	**m**	m	m	**m**	m	m	m	m	m
Indonesia	**m**	m	m	**m**	m	**m**	m	m	**m**	m	m	m	m	m
Russian Federation	**87.7**	10.0	2.3	**12.3**	m	**96.8**	1.6	1.6	**3.2**	m	m	m	198	m
Saudi Arabia	**m**	m	m	**m**	m	**m**	m	m	**m**	m	m	m	m	m
South Africa	**m**	m	m	**m**	m	**m**	m	m	**m**	m	m	m	m	m

1. Including subsidies attributable to payments to educational institutions received from public sources.
To calculate private funds net of subsidies, subtract public subsidies (Columns 5, 10) from private funds (Columns 4, 9).
To calculate total public funds, including public subsidies, add public subsidies (Columns 5, 10) to direct public funds (Columns 1, 6).
2. Year of reference 2007 instead of 2008.
3. Some levels of education are included with others. Refer to "x" code in Table B1.1a for details.
4. Year of reference 2009 instead of 2008.
Source: OECD. Argentina: UNESCO Institute for Statistics (World Education Indicators Programme). See Annex 3 for notes (*www.oecd.org/edu/eag2011*).
Please refer to the Reader's Guide for information concerning the symbols replacing missing data.
StatLink http://dx.doi.org/10.1787/888932463859

Table B3.2b. **Relative proportions of public and private expenditure on educational institutions, as a percentage, for tertiary education (2000, 2008)**

Distribution of public and private sources of funds for educational institutions after transfers from public sources, by year

		Tertiary education								
		2008					2000		Index of change between 2000 and 2008 in expenditure on educational institutions	
			Private sources							
		Public sources	Household expenditure	Expenditure of other private entities	All private sources[1]	Private: of which, subsidised	Public sources	All private sources[1]	Public sources	All private sources[1]
		(1)	(2)	(3)	(4)	(5)	(6)	(7)	(8)	(9)
OECD	Australia	**44.8**	39.8	15.4	**55.2**	0.4	49.6	50.4	121	146
	Austria	**84.7**	5.9	9.4	**15.3**	8.4	96.3	3.7	130	611
	Belgium	**89.8**	5.5	4.7	**10.2**	3.8	91.5	8.5	118	144
	Canada[2, 3]	**58.7**	19.9	21.4	**41.3**	m	61.0	39.0	121	133
	Chile[4]	**14.6**	79.3	6.1	**85.4**	7.1	19.5	80.5	112	158
	Czech Republic	**79.1**	9.4	11.5	**20.9**	m	85.4	14.6	187	289
	Denmark[3]	**95.5**	x(4)	x(4)	**4.5**	m	97.6	2.4	114	218
	Estonia	**78.8**	19.3	1.9	**21.2**	7.2	m	m	154	m
	Finland	**95.4**	x(4)	x(4)	**4.6**	n	97.2	2.8	124	209
	France	**81.7**	9.6	8.7	**18.3**	2.4	84.4	15.6	116	141
	Germany	**85.4**	x(4)	x(4)	**14.6**	m	88.2	11.8	117	150
	Greece	**m**	m	m	**m**	m	99.7	0.3	m	m
	Hungary	**m**	m	m	**m**	m	m	m	131	m
	Iceland	**92.2**	7.2	0.6	**7.8**	a	91.8	8.2	165	156
	Ireland	**82.6**	15.0	2.5	**17.4**	1.1	79.2	20.8	142	114
	Israel	**51.3**	33.7	15.0	**48.7**	6.2	58.5	41.5	97	130
	Italy	**70.7**	21.5	7.8	**29.3**	6.7	77.5	22.5	108	155
	Japan[3]	**33.3**	50.7	16.0	**66.7**	m	38.5	61.5	100	125
	Korea	**22.3**	52.1	25.6	**77.7**	2.3	23.3	76.7	155	164
	Luxembourg	**m**	m	m	**m**	m	m	m	m	m
	Mexico	**70.1**	29.5	0.4	**29.9**	1.1	79.4	20.6	137	225
	Netherlands	**72.6**	15.1	12.3	**27.4**	0.3	76.5	23.5	120	147
	New Zealand	**70.4**	29.6	m	**29.6**	m	m	m	156	m
	Norway	**96.9**	3.1	m	**3.1**	m	96.3	3.7	126	106
	Poland	**69.6**	23.7	6.7	**30.4**	m	66.6	33.4	202	176
	Portugal	**62.1**	28.3	9.6	**37.9**	m	92.5	7.5	98	739
	Slovak Republic[3]	**73.1**	10.5	16.4	**26.9**	2.0	91.2	8.8	145	557
	Slovenia	**83.8**	16.0	0.2	**16.2**	n	m	m	m	m
	Spain	**78.9**	17.0	4.2	**21.1**	1.7	74.4	25.6	144	112
	Sweden	**89.1**	n	10.9	**10.9**	a	91.3	8.7	117	151
	Switzerland	**m**	m	m	**m**	a	m	m	122	m
	Turkey	**m**	m	m	**m**	m	95.4	4.6	m	m
	United Kingdom	**34.5**	51.5	14.0	**65.5**	16.3	67.7	32.3	112	278
	United States	**37.4**	41.2	21.5	**62.6**	m	31.1	68.9	141	107
	OECD average	**68.9**	~	~	**31.1**	3.3	75.1	24.9	131	217
	EU21 average	**78.2**	~	~	**21.8**	3.0	85.7	14.3	132	262
Other G20	Argentina	**81.1**	9.6	9.3	**18.9**	0.1	m	m	m	m
	Brazil	**m**	m	m	**m**	m	m	m	148	m
	China	**m**	m	m	**m**	m	m	m	m	m
	India	**m**	m	m	**m**	m	m	m	m	m
	Indonesia	**m**	m	m	**m**	m	m	m	m	m
	Russian Federation	**64.3**	20.1	15.6	**35.7**	m	m	m	328	m
	Saudi Arabia	**m**	m	m	**m**	m	m	m	m	m
	South Africa	**m**	m	m	**m**	m	m	m	m	m

1. Including subsidies attributable to payments to educational institutions received from public sources.
To calculate private funds net of subsidies, subtract public subsidies (Column 5) from private funds (Column 4).
To calculate total public funds, including public subsidies, add public subsidies (Column 5) to direct public funds (Column 1).
2. Year of reference 2007 instead of 2008.
3. Some levels of education are included with others. Refer to «x» code in Table B1.1a for details.
4. Year of reference 2009 instead of 2008.
Source: OECD. Argentina: UNESCO Institute for Statistics (World Education Indicators Programme). See Annex 3 for notes (*www.oecd.org/edu/eag2011*).
Please refer to the Reader's Guide for information concerning the symbols replacing missing data.
StatLink http://dx.doi.org/10.1787/888932463878

Table B3.3. Trends in relative proportions of public expenditure[1] on educational institutions and index of change between 1995 and 2008 (2000 = 100), for tertiary education (1995, 2000, 2005, 2006, 2007 and 2008)

	Share of public expenditure on educational institutions (%)						Index of change between 1995 and 2008 in public expenditure on educational institutions (2000 = 100, constant prices)					
	1995	2000	2005	2006	2007	2008	1995	2000	2005	2006	2007	2008
OECD												
Australia	64.6	49.6	45.2	44.3	44.3	44.8	117	100	109	111	118	121
Austria	96.1	96.3	92.9	84.5	85.4	84.7	96	100	129	122	130	130
Belgium	m	91.5	90.6	90.6	90.3	89.8	m	100	101	108	109	118
Canada[2]	56.6	61.0	53.4	56.6	58.7	m	69	100	108	119	121	m
Chile[3]	25.1	19.5	15.9	16.1	14.4	14.6	78	100	104	98	100	112
Czech Republic	71.5	85.4	81.2	82.1	83.8	79.1	86	100	147	182	203	187
Denmark[2]	99.4	97.6	96.7	96.4	96.5	95.5	93	100	115	115	121	114
Estonia	m	m	69.9	73.1	77.1	78.8	69	100	113	120	156	154
Finland	97.8	97.2	96.1	95.5	95.7	95.4	90	100	115	117	118	124
France	85.3	84.4	83.6	83.7	84.5	81.7	93	100	106	109	115	116
Germany	89.2	88.2	85.3	85.0	84.7	85.4	96	100	102	102	105	117
Greece[2]	m	99.7	96.7	m	m	m	63	100	229	m	m	m
Hungary	80.3	76.7	78.5	77.9	m	m	78	100	125	131	131	131
Iceland[2]	m	91.8	90.5	90.2	91.0	92.2	m	100	142	137	152	165
Ireland	69.7	79.2	84.0	85.1	85.4	82.6	49	100	108	118	126	142
Israel	62.5	58.5	53.1	52.6	51.6	51.3	75	100	89	93	102	97
Italy	82.9	77.5	73.2	72.2	69.9	70.7	85	100	100	103	100	108
Japan[2]	35.1	38.5	33.7	32.2	32.5	33.3	80	100	93	95	97	100
Korea	m	23.3	24.3	23.1	20.7	22.3	m	100	132	139	134	155
Luxembourg	m	m	m	m	m	m	m	m	m	m	m	m
Mexico	77.4	79.4	69.0	67.9	71.4	70.1	75	100	119	117	134	137
Netherlands	79.4	76.5	73.3	73.4	72.4	72.6	99	100	111	111	115	120
New Zealand	m	m	59.7	63.0	65.7	70.4	104	100	119	129	140	156
Norway	93.7	96.3	m	97.0	97.0	96.9	93	100	121	120	123	126
Poland	m	66.6	74.0	70.4	71.5	69.6	89	100	193	166	172	202
Portugal	96.5	92.5	68.1	66.7	70.0	62.1	77	100	102	103	126	98
Slovak Republic[2]	95.4	91.2	77.3	82.1	76.2	73.1	86	100	127	152	138	145
Slovenia	m	m	76.5	76.9	77.2	83.8	m	m	m	m	m	m
Spain	74.4	74.4	77.9	78.2	79.0	78.9	72	100	119	125	134	144
Sweden	93.6	91.3	88.2	89.1	89.3	89.1	84	100	111	114	114	117
Switzerland	m	m	m	m	m	m	74	100	133	135	127	122
Turkey	96.3	95.4	m	m	m	m	55	100	m	137	m	m
United Kingdom	80.0	67.7	m	m	35.8	34.5	115	100	m	m	115	112
United States	37.4	31.1	34.7	34.0	31.6	37.4	85	100	132	133	137	141
OECD average	76.7	75.1	70.5	70.3	69.1	69.3	84	100	122	122	127	131
OECD average for countries with data available for all reference years	73.7	72.7	68.4	67.9	67.9	67.0	84	100	118	121	128	130
EU21 average for countries with data available for all reference years	86.8	87.0	82.7	82.4	82.3	80.4	83	100	121	126	133	136
Other G20												
Argentina	m	m	m	m	m	81.1	m	m	m	m	m	m
Brazil	m	m	m	m	m	m	78	100	118	124	126	148
China	m	m	m	m	m	m	m	m	m	m	m	m
India	m	m	m	m	m	m	m	m	m	m	m	m
Indonesia	m	m	m	m	m	m	m	m	m	m	m	m
Russian Federation	m	m	m	m	58.3	64.3	m	100	225	259	317	328
Saudi Arabia	m	m	m	m	m	m	m	m	m	m	m	m
South Africa	m	m	m	m	m	m	m	m	m	m	m	m

1. Excluding international funds in public and total expenditure on educational institutions.
2. Some levels of education are included with others. Refer to «x» code in Table B1.1a for details.
3. Year of reference 2009 instead of 2008.

Source: OECD. Argentina: UNESCO Institute for Statistics (World Education Indicators Programme). See Annex 3 for notes (*www.oecd.org/edu/eag2011*).

Please refer to the Reader's Guide for information concerning the symbols replacing missing data.

StatLink http://dx.doi.org/10.1787/888932463897

Table B3.4. **Annual public expenditure on educational institutions per student, by type of institution (2008)**

In equivalent USD converted using PPPs for GDP, by level of education and type of institution

		Pre-primary education			Primary, secondary and post-secondary non-tertiary education			Tertiary education				Total all levels of education		
		Public institutions	Private institutions	Total public and private	Public institutions	Private institutions	Total public and private	Public institutions	Private institutions	Total public and private	of which: R&D activities	Public institutions	Private institutions	Total public and private
		(1)	(2)	(3)	(4)	(5)	(6)	(7)	(8)	(9)	(10)	(11)	(12)	(13)
OECD	Australia	x(3)	x(3)	**2 848**	7 171	4 719	**6 393**	7 337	750	**7 036**	4 521	x(13)	x(13)	**6 471**
	Austria	x(3)	x(3)	**5 271**	x(6)	x(6)	**10 548**	x(9)	x(9)	**12 736**	4 566	x(13)	x(13)	**10 200**
	Belgium	5 973	5 131	**5 531**	10 253	8 543	**9 237**	14 441	12 139	**13 127**	4 236	10 537	8 608	**9 419**
	Canada[1]	x(4)	m	**m**	7 743	m	**m**	13 043	m	**m**	m	8 936	m	**m**
	Chile[2]	6 191	2 100	**3 687**	3 233	1 840	**2 436**	2 426	493	**885**	351	3 408	1 527	**2 244**
	Czech republic	3 817	3 138	**3 807**	4 865	3 034	**4 736**	7 330	531	**6 451**	1 311	5 255	2 251	**5 035**
	Denmark	5 520	1 991	**5 180**	10 756	6 382	**10 183**	16 551	a	**16 460**	x(9)	11 019	5 577	**10 446**
	Estonia	3 219	1 291	**3 162**	6 009	5 320	**5 988**	7 842	3 506	**4 207**	x(9)	5 571	3 624	**5 167**
	Finland	4 946	3 562	**4 828**	8 000	7 823	**7 988**	14 958	13 108	**14 698**	4 761	8 756	8 810	**8 760**
	France	5 758	3 230	**5 443**	8 617	5 071	**7 917**	12 943	3 956	**11 469**	3 967	8 748	4 698	**8 019**
	Germany	6 023	4 526	**m**	m	m	**m**	m	m	**m**	m	m	m	**m**
	Greece	m	m	**m**	m	m	**m**	m	m	**m**	m	m	m	**m**
	Hungary	x(3)	x(3)	**4 438**	x(3)	x(3)	**4 379**	5 425	4 877	**5 341**	1 045	4 801	4 833	**4 804**
	Iceland	8 204	3 624	**7 705**	9 544	5 392	**9 391**	10 383	6 515	**9 612**	x(9)	10 050	5 544	**9 722**
	Ireland	m	m	**m**	8 766	m	**m**	13 328	m	**m**	3 871	9 486	m	**m**
	Israel	3 842	1 984	**3 280**	5 248	5 780	**5 381**	x(9)	x(9)	**5 925**	m	5 388	5 017	**5 251**
	Italy[3]	8 074	890	**5 812**	9 005	2 249	**8 581**	6 941	2 457	**6 619**	3 379	8 513	1 651	**7 815**
	Japan	x(3)	x(3)	**2 319**	x(6)	x(6)	**7 569**	x(9)	x(9)	**5 576**	x(9)	x(13)	x(13)	**7 118**
	Korea	6 363	795	**2 030**	5 668	4 811	**5 520**	6 749	968	**2 252**	823	6 883	2 181	**5 119**
	Luxembourg	13 800	2 924	**12 979**	17 465	6 481	**15 999**	m	m	**m**	m	m	m	**m**
	Mexico	2 368	2	**2 016**	2 130	7	**1 893**	7 885	a	**5 263**	1 205	2 597	5	**2 249**
	Netherlands[4]	6 788	n	**6 760**	8 149	n	**7 936**	13 400	n	**11 996**	4 872	8 801	n	**8 477**
	New Zealand	x(3)	x(3)	**6 808**	5 842	2 519	**5 567**	8 273	1 371	**7 409**	1 711	6 378	3 685	**5 963**
	Norway	6 448	4 374	**5 516**	12 096	11 527	**12 070**	20 617	3 978	**18 353**	6 529	13 083	9 358	**12 663**
	Poland	x(3)	x(3)	**4 396**	x(6)	x(6)	**4 184**	x(9)	x(9)	**4 083**	634	x(13)	x(13)	**4 186**
	Portugal	5 248	1 850	**3 644**	6 326	3 505	**5 948**	7 397	168	**5 633**	3 108	6 535	2 226	**5 681**
	Slovak Republic	3 305	2 359	**3 276**	3 366	3 278	**3 359**	4 597	m	**4 597**	787	3 693	3 222	**3 663**
	Slovenia	6 309	1 840	**6 217**	7 740	5 029	**7 709**	7 382	2 600	**7 078**	1 293	7 496	3 333	**7 400**
	Spain	7 615	2 231	**5 674**	9 805	3 445	**7 816**	11 909	1 118	**10 404**	2 881	9 833	2 975	**7 816**
	Sweden	6 629	5 900	**6 519**	9 468	9 944	**9 517**	17 868	12 483	**17 340**	7 940	10 117	9 307	**10 027**
	Switzerland	4 911	m	**m**	11 422	m	**m**	21 648	m	**m**	m	12 327	m	**m**
	Turkey	m	m	**m**	m	m	**m**	m	m	**m**	m	m	m	**m**
	United Kingdom	7 905	1 058	**6 015**	8 308	2 362	**7 141**	a	5 077	**5 077**	5 050	8 279	3 461	**6 789**
	United States	11 499	2 104	**8 295**	12 001	675	**10 523**	13 448	3 408	**10 577**	x(9)	12 209	1 738	**10 357**
	OECD average	6 281	2 474	**5 123**	8 111	4 572	**7 354**	10 543	3 614	**8 526**	3 129	8 027	4 071	**7 069**
	EU21 average	6 474	2 586	**5 597**	8 802	4 959	**7 908**	10 332	4 730	**9 429**	3 493	8 146	4 452	**7 417**
Other G20	Argentina	2 213	734	**1 743**	2 966	1 185	**2 508**	3 943	345	**2 883**	m	3 029	1 037	**2 511**
	Brazil	1 726	m	**m**	2 098	m	**m**	11 610	m	**m**	619	2 343	m	**m**
	China	m	m	**m**	m	m	**m**	4 550	m	**m**	m	m	m	**m**
	India	m	m	**m**	m	m	**m**	m	m	**m**	m	m	m	**m**
	Indonesia	m	m	**m**	m	m	**m**	m	m	**m**	m	m	m	**m**
	Russian Federation	m	m	**m**	3 942	m	**m**	4 334	m	**m**	m	5 634	m	**m**
	Saudi Arabia	m	m	**m**	m	m	**m**	m	m	**m**	m	m	m	**m**
	South Africa	m	m	**m**	m	m	**m**	m	m	**m**	m	m	m	**m**
	G20 average	5 025	m	**m**	m	m	**m**	8 738	m	**m**	m	m	m	**m**

1. Year of reference 2007.
2. Year of reference 2009.
3. Exclude post-secondary non-tertiary education.
4. Government-dependent private institutions are included with public institutions.

Source: OECD. Argentina: UNESCO Institute for Statistics (World Education Indicators Programme). China: China Educational Finance Statistical Yearbook 2009. See Annex 3 for notes *(www.oecd.org/edu/eag2011)*.

Please refer to the Reader's Guide for information concerning the symbols replacing missing data.

StatLink http://dx.doi.org/10.1787/888932463916

WHAT IS THE TOTAL PUBLIC SPENDING ON EDUCATION?

- On average, OECD countries devote 12.9% of total public expenditure to education, but values for individual countries range from less than 10% in the Czech Republic, Italy and Japan, to more than 20% in Mexico.
- Public funding of education is a social priority, even in OECD countries with little public involvement in other areas. The proportion of public expenditure on education increased between 1995 and 2008 in 20 of the 28 countries with comparable data for both years.
- However, the main increase took place from 1995 to 2000 (by 0.9 percentage point on average in OECD countries), while public expenditure on education and on other public sectors increased in similar proportions from 2000 to 2008 (increase of the share of public funding by 0.2 percentage point on average in OECD countries).

Chart B4.1. Total public expenditure on education as a percentage of total public expenditure (1995, 2000, 2008)

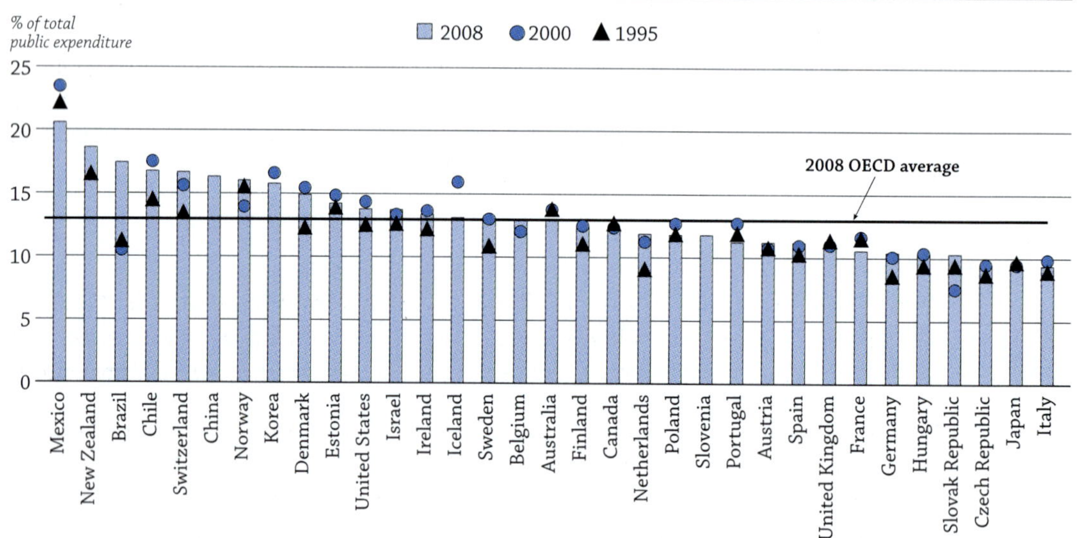

Countries are ranked in descending order of total public expenditure on education at all levels of education as a percentage of total public expenditure in 2008.

Source: OECD. China: The national Statistics Bulletin on Educational Expenditure 2009. Table B4.1. See Annex 3 for notes (*www.oecd.org/edu/eag2011*).

StatLink http://dx.doi.org/10.1787/888932461142

How to read this chart

The chart shows direct public expenditure on educational institutions plus public subsidies to households (which include subsidies for living costs such as scholarships and grants to students/households and students loans), and other private entities, as a percentage of total public expenditure, by year. Public sectors differ in size and breadth of responsibility from country to country.

Context

Public expenditure on education, as a percentage of total public expenditure, indicates the extent to which governments prioritise education in relation to other areas of investment, such as health care, social security, defence and security. If the public benefits from a particular service are greater than the private benefits, markets alone may fail to provide that service adequately and governments may need to become involved. Education is one area in which all governments intervene to fund or direct services. As there is no guarantee that markets will provide equal access to education opportunities, government funding ensures that education is not beyond the reach of some members of society.

Other findings

- In OECD countries, **public expenditure on primary, secondary and post-secondary non-tertiary education is, on average, about three times that on tertiary education.**
- The **larger share of public expenditure on education below tertiary level is mainly due to near-universal enrolment rates at those levels**, and also because private expenditure tends to be greater at the tertiary level. This ratio varies from two times or less in Canada, Finland and Norway, to five times or more in Chile, Korea and the United Kingdom. The latter figure indicates the relatively high proportion of private funds for tertiary education in these countries.
- Across OECD countries, **public funding of primary, secondary and post-secondary non-tertiary education is more decentralised than public funding for tertiary education**. On average at the primary, secondary and post-secondary non-tertiary level about 50% of the initial funding comes from central rather than regional or local government, compared with 84% for tertiary education.
- Moreover, there are greater levels of **transfers of public funds from central to regional and local levels** of government at primary, secondary and post-secondary non-tertiary level than there are at tertiary level. At primary, secondary and post-secondary non-tertiary level, 44% of public funds come from local sources after transfers between levels of government, compared to less than 30% before transfers. At the tertiary level, local sources represent less than 3% of public funds, before and after transfers between levels of government.

Trends

Since the second half of the 1990s, and especially in the aftermath of the recent financial and economic crisis, most countries have made serious efforts to consolidate public budgets. Education has to compete with a wide range of other government-funded areas for available public resources.

Between 1995 and 2008, **education took an increasing share of total public expenditure** in most countries, growing, on average in OECD countries, as fast as GDP. In Brazil, Denmark, Germany, the Netherlands, Sweden and Switzerland, there have been particularly significant shifts in public funding towards education (increase by more than 20%).

Analysis

Overall level of public resources invested in education

The share of public expenditure on education as a proportion of total public spending ranged from 10% or less in the Czech Republic, Italy and Japan to more than 20% in Mexico (Chart B4.1). As is the case with spending on education in relation to GDP per capita, these figures must be interpreted in the context of student demography and enrolment rates.

The proportion of public-sector funding of the different levels of education also varies widely among countries. In 2008, countries allocated between 6.1% (the Czech Republic) and 13.6% (Mexico) of total public expenditure to primary, secondary and post-secondary non-tertiary education and between 1.7% (Italy and the United Kingdom) and 5.5% (New Zealand) to tertiary education. On average in OECD countries, public funding of primary, secondary and post-secondary non-tertiary education is nearly three times that of tertiary education, mainly because of enrolment rates (see Indicator C1) and the demographic structure of the population or because private expenditure tends to be higher at the tertiary level (Table B4.1).

When public expenditure on education is considered as a proportion of total public spending, the relative sizes of public budgets (as measured by public spending in relation to GDP) must be taken into account. When the size of public budgets relative to GDP is compared with the proportion of public spending on education, it is evident that even in countries with relatively low rates of public spending, education is a high priority. For instance, the share of public spending allocated to education in Brazil, Chile, Mexico, New Zealand and Switzerland is among the highest (Chart B4.1), yet total public spending accounts for a relatively small proportion of GDP in these countries (Chart B4.2).

Although the overall pattern is unclear, there is some evidence to suggest that countries with high rates of public expenditure spend proportionately less on education; only one of the top ten countries for public spending on public services overall – Denmark – is among the top ten in public spending on education (Charts B4.1 and B4.2).

Chart B4.2. Total public expenditure on all services as a percentage of GDP (2000, 2008)

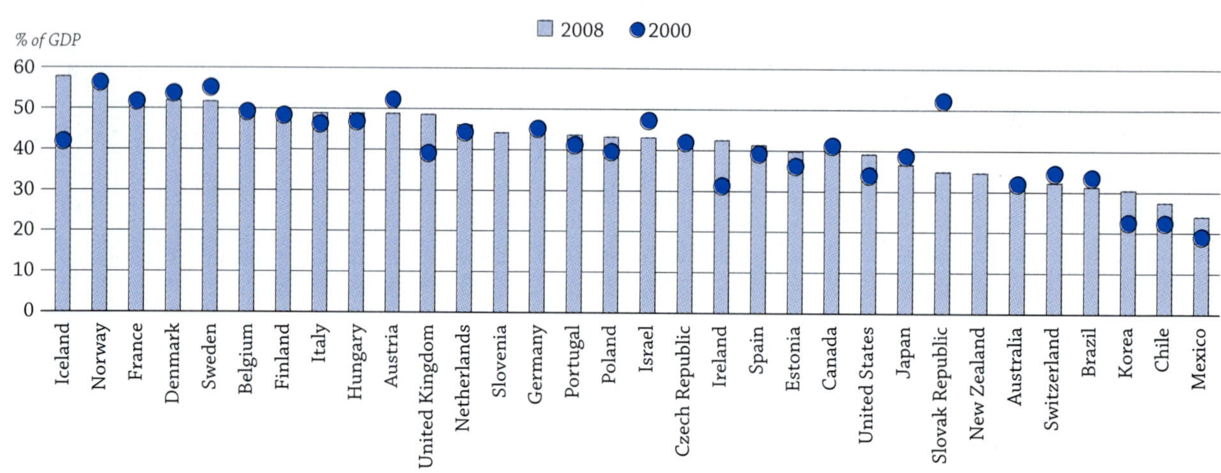

Note: This chart represents public expenditure on all services and not simply public expenditure on education.
Countries are ranked in descending order of total public expenditure as a percentage of GDP in 2008.
Source: OECD. Annex 2. See Annex 3 for notes (*www.oecd.org/edu/eag2011*).
StatLink http://dx.doi.org/10.1787/888932461161

While public expenditure on education increased from 1995 to 2008 in 20 of the 28 countries with comparable data, public expenditure on education as a percentage of GDP in these 28 countries also increased slightly, on average. Although budget consolidation has put pressure on all areas of public expenditure, particularly since 2000, the proportion of public budgets spent on education in OECD countries rose from 11.8% in 1995 to 12.9% in 2008. The greatest relative increases in the share of public expenditure on education during this period occurred in Brazil (11.2% to 17.4%), Denmark (12.3% to 14.9%), Germany (8.6% to 10.4%), the Netherlands (9.1% to 11.9%), Sweden (10.9% to 13.1%) and Switzerland (13.5% to 16.7%).

Sources of public funding invested in education

Across OECD countries, funding of primary, secondary and post-secondary non-tertiary education is more decentralised than public funding for tertiary education.

Chart B4.3. Distribution (in percentage) of initial sources of public funds for education, by level of government, for primary, secondary and post-secondary non-tertiary education (2008)

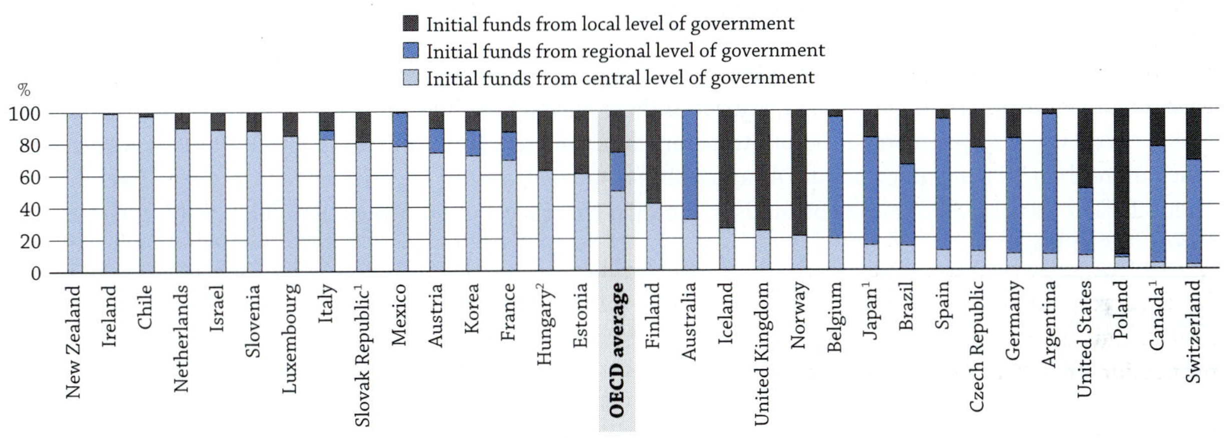

Change (in percentage points) in the proportion of educational funds received from levels of governement between initial and final purchasers of educational resources, at the primary, secondary and post-secondary non-tertiary levels (2008)

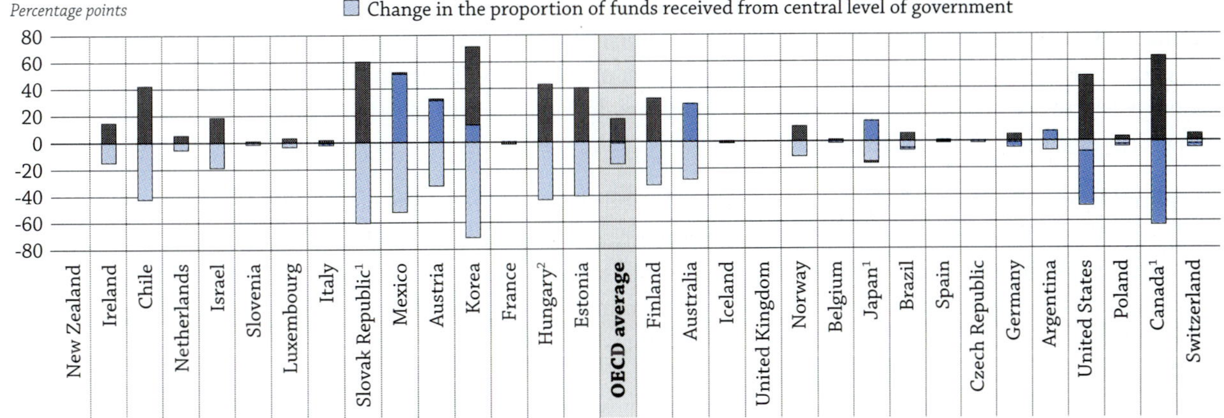

1. Some levels of education are included with others. Refer to "x" code in Table B1.1a for details.
2. Funds from the central level includes funds from the regional level of governement.

Countries are ranked in descending order of the share of initial sources of funds from the central level of government.

Source: OECD. Argentina: UNESCO Institute for Statistics (World Education Indicators Programme). Table B4.2. See Annex 3 for notes (*www.oecd.org/edu/eag2011*).

StatLink http://dx.doi.org/10.1787/888932461180

On average at the primary, secondary and post-secondary non-tertiary levels, 50% of the initial funding comes from central rather than regional or local government compared with 84% for tertiary education. Moreover, there are greater levels of transfers of funds from central to regional and local levels of government at the primary, secondary and post-secondary non-tertiary level than there are at the tertiary level, adding to the contrast in decentralisation between the levels of education. At the primary, secondary and post-secondary non-tertiary levels, 44% of public funds come from local sources after transfers between levels of government, compared to less than 30% before transfers (at the tertiary level, local sources represent less than 3% of public funds, before and after transfers between levels of government). Only New Zealand has an entirely centralised funding system below the tertiary level, while at the tertiary level, six countries (Iceland, the Netherlands, New Zealand, Norway, the Slovak Republic and the United Kingdom) operate such systems (Table B4.2 and Table B4.3, available on line).

However at the primary, secondary and post-secondary non-tertiary levels, the extent of decentralisation of public funding differs greatly among countries. For example, while in New Zealand, public funding on education comes entirely from the central level of government (before and after transfers between levels of government), in Switzerland, less than 3% of such funding comes from central sources.

In addition, the extent of public transfers between levels of government varies significantly across countries. In Austria, Chile, Estonia, Hungary, Korea, Mexico and the Slovak Republic, more than 60% of public funds come from central levels of government before transfers; but transfers from central to lower levels of government reach more than 30 percentage points. Among these countries, central government represents, after transfer, about 20% or less of public sources of funds in Estonia, Hungary and the Slovak Republic, and less than 1% in Korea (Chart B4.3).

Definitions

Public expenditure on education includes expenditure on educational institutions and subsidies for students' living costs and for other private expenditure outside institutions. It includes expenditure by all public entities, including ministries other than ministries of education, local and regional governments, and other public agencies. OECD countries differ in the ways in which they use public money for education. Public funds may flow directly to institutions or may be channelled to institutions via government programmes or via households. They may also be restricted to the purchase of educational services or be used to support student living costs.

All government sources (apart from international sources) for expenditure on education should be classified into three levels: central (national) government, regional government (province, state, *Land*, etc.), local government (municipality, district, commune, etc.). The terms "regional" and "local" apply to governments whose responsibilities are exercised within certain geographical subdivisions of a country. They do not apply to government bodies whose roles are not geographically circumscribed but are defined in terms of responsibility for particular services, functions, or categories of students.

Total public expenditure, also referred to as total public spending, corresponds to the non-repayable current and capital expenditure of all levels of government: central, regional and local. It includes direct public expenditure on educational institutions as well as public subsidies to households (e.g. scholarships and loans to students for tuition fees and student living costs) and to other private entities for education (e.g. subsidies to companies or labour organisations that operate apprenticeship programmes).

Methodology

The data refer to the financial year 2008 and are based on the UOE data collection on education statistics administered by the OECD in 2010 (for details see Annex 3 at *www.oecd.org/edu/eag2011*).

Figures for total public expenditure have been taken from the *OECD National Accounts Database* (see Annex 2) and use the System of National Accounts 1993.

Educational expenditure is expressed as a percentage of a country's total public sector expenditure and as a percentage of GDP.

Though expenditure on debt servicing (e.g. interest payments) is included in total public expenditure, it is excluded from public expenditure on education. The reason is that some countries cannot separate interest payments for education from those for other services. This means that public expenditure on education as a percentage of total public expenditure may be underestimated in countries in which interest payments represent a large proportion of total public expenditure on all services.

The statistical data for Israel are supplied by and under the responsibility of the relevant Israeli authorities. The use of such data by the OECD is without prejudice to the status of the Golan Heights, East Jerusalem and Israeli settlements in the West Bank under the terms of international law.

References

The following additional material relevant to this indicator is available on line:

- ***Table B4.3. Sources of public educational funds, before and after transfers, by level of government for tertiary education (2008)***
  StatLink http://dx.doi.org/10.1787/888932463973

- ***Table B4.4. Distribution of total public expenditure on education (2008)***
  StatLink http://dx.doi.org/10.1787/888932463992

Table B4.1. Total public expenditure on education (1995, 2000, 2008)

Direct public expenditure on educational institutions plus public subsidies to households[1] and other private entities, as a percentage of total public expenditure and as a percentage of GDP, by level of education and year

		Public expenditure[1] on education as a percentage of total public expenditure					Public expenditure[1] on education as a percentage of GDP				
		2008			2000	1995	2008			2000	1995
		Primary, secondary and post-secondary non-tertiary education	Tertiary education	All levels of education combined	All levels of education combined	All levels of education combined	Primary, secondary and post-secondary non-tertiary education	Tertiary education	All levels of education combined	All levels of education combined	All levels of education combined
OECD	Australia	9.7	3.0	**12.9**	**13.8**	**13.8**	3.1	1.0	**4.2**	**4.4**	**4.8**
	Austria	7.2	3.0	**11.2**	**10.7**	**10.8**	3.5	1.5	**5.5**	**5.6**	**6.1**
	Belgium	8.7	2.8	**12.9**	**12.0**	**m**	4.3	1.4	**6.5**	**5.9**	**m**
	Canada[2, 3]	7.8	4.5	**12.3**	**12.4**	**12.7**	3.2	1.7	**4.9**	**5.1**	**6.2**
	Chile[4]	12.3	2.2	**16.8**	**17.5**	**14.5**	3.3	0.7	**4.6**	**3.9**	**2.7**
	Czech Republic	6.1	2.3	**9.5**	**9.5**	**8.7**	2.6	1.0	**4.1**	**4.0**	**4.8**
	Denmark[3]	8.9	4.2	**14.9**	**15.4**	**12.3**	4.6	2.2	**7.7**	**8.3**	**7.3**
	Estonia	10.0	2.8	**14.2**	**14.8**	**13.9**	4.0	1.1	**5.7**	**5.4**	**5.8**
	Finland	7.9	3.9	**12.4**	**12.5**	**11.1**	3.9	1.9	**6.1**	**6.0**	**6.8**
	France	7.0	2.3	**10.6**	**11.6**	**11.5**	3.7	1.2	**5.6**	**6.0**	**6.3**
	Germany	6.5	2.8	**10.4**	**10.1**	**8.6**	2.8	1.2	**4.6**	**4.5**	**4.7**
	Greece	m	m	**m**	**7.3**	**5.6**	m	m	**m**	**3.4**	**2.6**
	Hungary	6.3	2.1	**10.4**	**10.4**	**9.4**	3.1	1.0	**5.1**	**4.9**	**5.2**
	Iceland	8.6	2.6	**13.1**	**15.9**	**m**	4.9	1.5	**7.6**	**6.7**	**m**
	Ireland	10.3	3.1	**13.4**	**13.7**	**12.2**	4.4	1.3	**5.7**	**4.3**	**5.0**
	Israel	9.2	2.2	**13.7**	**13.4**	**12.6**	4.0	0.9	**5.9**	**6.3**	**6.5**
	Italy	6.7	1.7	**9.4**	**9.8**	**9.0**	3.2	0.8	**4.6**	**4.5**	**4.7**
	Japan[3]	6.8	1.8	**9.4**	**9.5**	**9.7**	2.5	0.6	**3.4**	**3.6**	**3.6**
	Korea	11.0	2.2	**15.8**	**16.6**	**m**	3.4	0.7	**4.8**	**3.7**	**m**
	Luxembourg	7.6	m	**m**	**m**	**m**	2.8	m	**m**	**m**	**m**
	Mexico	13.6	3.9	**20.6**	**23.4**	**22.2**	3.2	0.9	**4.9**	**4.4**	**4.2**
	Netherlands	7.7	3.3	**11.9**	**11.2**	**9.1**	3.6	1.5	**5.5**	**5.0**	**5.1**
	New Zealand	11.8	5.5	**18.6**	**m**	**16.5**	4.1	1.9	**6.4**	**6.7**	**5.6**
	Norway	9.6	5.1	**16.0**	**14.0**	**15.6**	5.4	2.9	**9.0**	**7.8**	**9.3**
	Poland	8.0	2.4	**11.8**	**12.7**	**11.9**	3.5	1.0	**5.1**	**5.0**	**5.2**
	Portugal	7.9	2.2	**11.2**	**12.7**	**11.9**	3.5	0.9	**4.9**	**5.2**	**4.9**
	Slovak Republic[3]	6.6	2.2	**10.3**	**7.5**	**9.4**	2.3	0.8	**3.6**	**3.9**	**4.6**
	Slovenia	7.9	2.7	**11.8**	**m**	**m**	3.5	1.2	**5.2**	**m**	**m**
	Spain	7.1	2.6	**11.2**	**10.9**	**10.3**	2.9	1.1	**4.6**	**4.3**	**4.6**
	Sweden	8.3	3.5	**13.1**	**13.0**	**10.9**	4.3	1.8	**6.8**	**7.2**	**7.1**
	Switzerland	11.8	4.0	**16.7**	**15.6**	**13.5**	3.8	1.3	**5.4**	**5.4**	**5.7**
	Turkey	m	m	**m**	**m**	**m**	m	m	**m**	**m**	**m**
	United Kingdom	8.7	1.7	**11.1**	**11.0**	**11.4**	4.2	0.8	**5.4**	**4.3**	**5.0**
	United States	9.7	3.2	**13.8**	**14.4**	**12.5**	3.8	1.3	**5.4**	**4.9**	**4.7**
	OECD average	8.7	3.0	**12.9**	**12.7**	**11.8**	3.6	1.3	**5.4**	**5.2**	**5.3**
	EU21 average	7.8	2.7	**11.7**	**12.8**	**10.4**	3.5	1.3	**5.4**	**5.1**	**5.3**
Other G20	Argentina	m	m	**m**	**m**	**m**	4.0	1.0	**5.4**	**m**	**m**
	Brazil	13.3	2.8	**17.4**	**10.5**	**11.2**	4.2	0.9	**5.5**	**3.5**	**3.9**
	China	m	m	**16.3**	**m**	**m**	m	m	**3.3**	**m**	**m**
	India	m	m	**m**	**m**	**m**	m	m	**m**	**m**	**m**
	Indonesia[2]	m	m	**m**	**m**	**m**	3.2	0.3	**3.5**	**m**	**m**
	Russian Federation	m	m	**m**	**10.6**	**m**	2.0	0.9	**4.1**	**2.9**	**m**
	Saudi Arabia	m	m	**m**	**m**	**m**	m	m	**m**	**m**	**m**
	South Africa	m	m	**m**	**m**	**m**	m	m	**m**	**m**	**m**
	G20 average	m	m	**13.3**	**m**	**m**	m	m	**4.6**	**m**	**m**

1. Public expenditure presented in this table includes public subsidies to households for living costs (scholarships and grants to students/households and students loans), which are not spent on educational institutions. Thus the figures presented here exceed those on public spending on institutions found in Table B2.3.

2. Year of reference 2007 instead of 2008.

3. Some levels of education are included with others. Refer to «x» code in Table B1.1a for details.

4. Year of reference 2009 instead of 2008.

Source: OECD. Argentina, Indonesia: UNESCO Institute for Statistics (World Education Indicators Programme). China: The national Statistics Bulletin on Educational Expenditure 2009. See Annex 3 for notes *(www.oecd.org/edu/eag2011)*.

Please refer to the Reader's Guide for information concerning the symbols replacing missing data.

StatLink http://dx.doi.org/10.1787/888932463935

Table B4.2. **Sources of public educational funds, before and after transfers, by level of government for primary, secondary and post-secondary non-tertiary education (2008)**

		Initial funds (before transfers between levels of government)				Final funds (after transfers between levels of government)			
		Central	Regional	Local	Total	Central	Regional	Local	Total
		(1)	(2)	(3)	(4)	(5)	(6)	(7)	(8)
OECD	Australia	31.8	68.2	m	100.0	3.7	96.3	m	100.0
	Austria	73.9	15.5	10.6	100.0	41.6	47.5	10.9	100.0
	Belgium	19.7	76.1	4.2	100.0	20.9	74.9	4.2	100.0
	Canada[1, 2]	3.8	72.6	23.6	100.0	3.0	10.3	86.7	100.0
	Chile[3]	97.6	a	2.4	100.0	55.4	a	44.6	100.0
	Czech Republic	11.5	64.5	24.0	100.0	11.4	64.5	24.0	100.0
	Denmark[2]	m	m	m	100.0	42.4	n	57.6	100.0
	Estonia	60.5	a	39.5	100.0	20.2	a	79.8	100.0
	Finland	41.8	a	58.2	100.0	9.5	a	90.5	100.0
	France	69.1	17.8	13.1	100.0	68.9	18.0	13.0	100.0
	Germany	9.8	72.1	18.0	100.0	8.6	68.5	22.9	100.0
	Greece	m	m	m	m	m	m	m	m
	Hungary	62.5	x(3)	37.5	100.0	19.6	x(7)	80.4	100.0
	Iceland	26.1	a	73.9	100.0	25.8	a	74.2	100.0
	Ireland	99.5	a	0.5	100.0	84.8	a	15.2	100.0
	Israel	89.0	a	11.0	100.0	70.4	a	29.6	100.0
	Italy	82.5	5.9	11.6	100.0	81.9	4.7	13.5	100.0
	Japan[2]	15.6	67.1	17.2	100.0	0.6	82.1	17.2	100.0
	Korea	72.0	16.0	11.9	100.0	0.7	28.7	70.5	100.0
	Luxembourg	85.0	a	15.0	100.0	81.7	a	18.3	100.0
	Mexico	78.0	21.8	0.2	100.0	25.8	73.8	0.4	100.0
	Netherlands	90.0	n	10.0	100.0	84.6	n	15.4	100.0
	New Zealand	100.0	n	n	100.0	100.0	n	n	100.0
	Norway	21.3	n	78.7	100.0	10.1	n	89.9	100.0
	Poland	7.1	1.8	91.1	100.0	4.1	1.8	94.1	100.0
	Portugal	m	m	m	m	m	m	m	m
	Slovak Republic[2]	80.8	a	19.2	100.0	20.4	a	79.6	100.0
	Slovenia	88.2	a	11.8	100.0	87.1	a	12.9	100.0
	Spain	12.0	82.3	5.7	100.0	11.4	82.9	5.7	100.0
	Sweden	m	m	m	m	m	m	m	m
	Switzerland	2.8	65.0	32.2	100.0	0.2	62.5	37.3	100.0
	Turkey	m	m	m	m	m	m	m	m
	United Kingdom	24.7	a	75.3	100.0	24.7	a	75.3	100.0
	United States	8.6	41.8	49.7	100.0	0.4	1.6	98.0	100.0
	OECD average	50.5	24.6	26.7	100.0	34.0	24.8	43.5	100.0
	EU21 average	54.0	21.0	26.2	100.0	40.2	21.3	39.6	100.0
Other G20	Argentina	9.5	87.4	3.1	100.0	2.5	94.3	3.1	100.0
	Brazil	15.0	50.6	34.4	100.0	9.7	50.1	40.2	100.0
	China	m	m	m	m	m	m	m	m
	India	m	m	m	m	m	m	m	m
	Indonesia	m	m	m	m	m	m	m	m
	Russian Federation	m	m	m	m	3.0	30.4	66.6	100.0
	Saudi Arabia	m	m	m	m	m	m	m	m
	South Africa	m	m	m	m	m	m	m	m

1. Year of reference 2007.
2. Some levels of education are included with others. Refer to «x» code in Table B1.1a for details.
3. Year of reference 2009.

Source: OECD. Argentina: UNESCO Institute for Statistics (World Education Indicators Programme). See Annex 3 for notes *(www.oecd.org/edu/eag2011)*.
Please refer to the Reader's Guide for information concerning the symbols replacing missing data.

StatLink http://dx.doi.org/10.1787/888932463954

INDICATOR B5

HOW MUCH DO TERTIARY STUDENTS PAY AND WHAT PUBLIC SUBSIDIES DO THEY RECEIVE?

- In eight OECD countries, public institutions charge no tuition fees, but in one-third of countries with available data, public institutions charge annual tuition fees in excess of USD 1 500 for national students.
- In 14 of the 25 countries with available data, the tuition fees charged by public educational institutions may be different for national and international students enrolled. In 14 of the 25 countries with available data, tuition fees are also differentiated by field of education, largely because of the difference in the public cost of studies.
- An average of 21% of public spending on tertiary education is devoted to supporting students, households and other private entities. In Australia, Chile, the Netherlands, New Zealand, Norway and the United Kingdom, grants/scholarships and loans are particularly developed and public subsidies to households account for at least 29% of public tertiary education budgets.

Chart B5.1. Relationships between average tuition fees charged by public institutions and proportion of students who benefit from public loans and/or scholarships/grants in tertiary-type A education (academic year 2008-09)

For full-time national students, in USD converted using PPPs

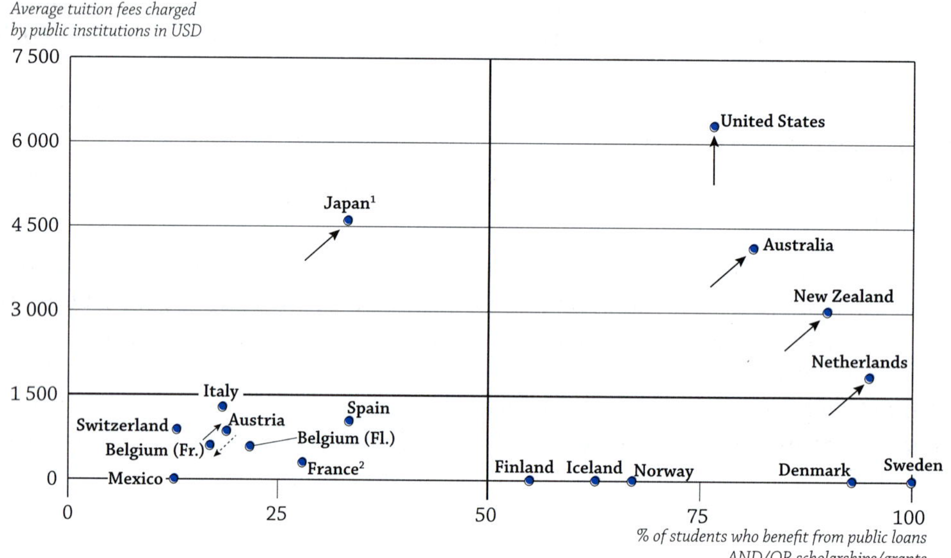

1. Tuition fees refer to public institutions but more than two-thirds of students are enrolled in private institutions.
2. Average tuition fees from USD 190 to 1 309 for university programmes dependent on the Ministry of Education.

Source: OECD. Tables B5.1 and B5.2. See Annex 3 for notes (*www.oecd.org/edu/eag2011*).

StatLink http://dx.doi.org/10.1787/888932461199

How to read this chart

This chart shows the relationships, at the tertiary-type A level of education, between annual tuition fees charged by educational institutions and public subsidies to households for students' living costs. Arrows show how the average tuition fees and the proportion of students who benefit from public subsidies have changed since 1995 further to reforms (solid arrow) and how it may alter due to changes that have been planned since 2008-09 (dash arrow).

Context

Policy decisions on tuition fees charged by educational institutions affect both the cost of tertiary education to students and the resources available to tertiary institutions. Subsidies to students and their families also serve as a way for governments to encourage participation in education – particularly among low-income students – by covering part of the cost of education and related expenses. In this way, governments can address issues of access and equality of opportunity.

The impact of such subsidies must therefore be judged, at least partly, by examining indicators of participation, retention and completion. Public subsidies to students also play an important role in indirectly financing educational institutions. Channelling funding to institutions through students may also help to increase competition among institutions. Since aid for students' living costs can serve as a substitute for income from work, public subsidies may enhance educational attainment by enabling students to work less.

Public subsidies for students come in many forms: as means-based subsidies, as family allowances for all students, as tax allowances for students or their parents, or as other household transfers. Based on a given amount of subsidies, public support, such as tax reductions or family allowances, may provide less support for low-income students than means-tested subsidies, as the former are not targeted specifically and solely to support low-income students. However, they may still help to reduce financial disparities among households with and without children in education.

Other findings

- Among the EU21 countries for which data are available, only **public institutions in Italy, the Netherlands, Portugal and the United Kingdom (government-dependent private institutions) charge annual tuition fees of more than USD 1 200** per full-time national student.

- **Low annual tuition fees** charged by public tertiary-type A (largely theory-based) institutions **are not systematically associated with a small proportion of students who benefit from public subsidies**. The tuition fees charged by public tertiary-type A institutions for national students are negligible in the Nordic countries. Yet, more than 55% of students in these countries benefit from scholarships/grants and/or public loans. Finland, Iceland, Norway and Sweden are among the eight countries with the highest entry rates to tertiary-type A education.

- **OECD countries in which students are required to pay tuition fees and can benefit from particularly large public subsidies do not have below-average levels of access to tertiary-type A education**. For example, Australia (94%) and New Zealand (78%) have some of the highest entry rates to tertiary-type A education, and the Netherlands (63%), the United Kingdom (61%) and the United States (70%) are above the OECD average (60%). Higher entry rates into tertiary-type A education in Australia and New Zealand also reflect the high proportions of international students in those countries.

Trends

Since 1995, 14 of the 25 countries with available information implemented reforms on tuition fees. Most of these reforms led to an increase in the average level of tuition fees charged by tertiary educational institutions. In all of these 14 countries except Iceland and the Slovak Republic, the reforms were combined with a change in the level of public subsidies available to students (Box B5.1 and Chart B5.1).

B5

Analysis

Annual tuition fees charged by tertiary-type A institutions for national students

The appropriate level of tuition fees charged by educational institutions has been debated for many years in OECD countries. On the one hand, high tuition fees increase the resources available to educational institutions, but they also put pressure on students – particularly students from low-income backgrounds – especially in the absence of a strong system of public subsidies to help them pay or reimburse the cost of their studies. On the other hand, very low tuition fees or free access to tertiary education puts pressure on educational institutions and governments to maintain an appropriate quality of education. This pressure has increased with the massive expansion of tertiary education in all OECD countries, and the economic crisis may make it more difficult for governments to invest more public funds in education.

Chart B5.2. Average annual tuition fees charged by tertiary-type A public institutions for full-time national students, in USD converted using PPPs (academic year 2008-09)

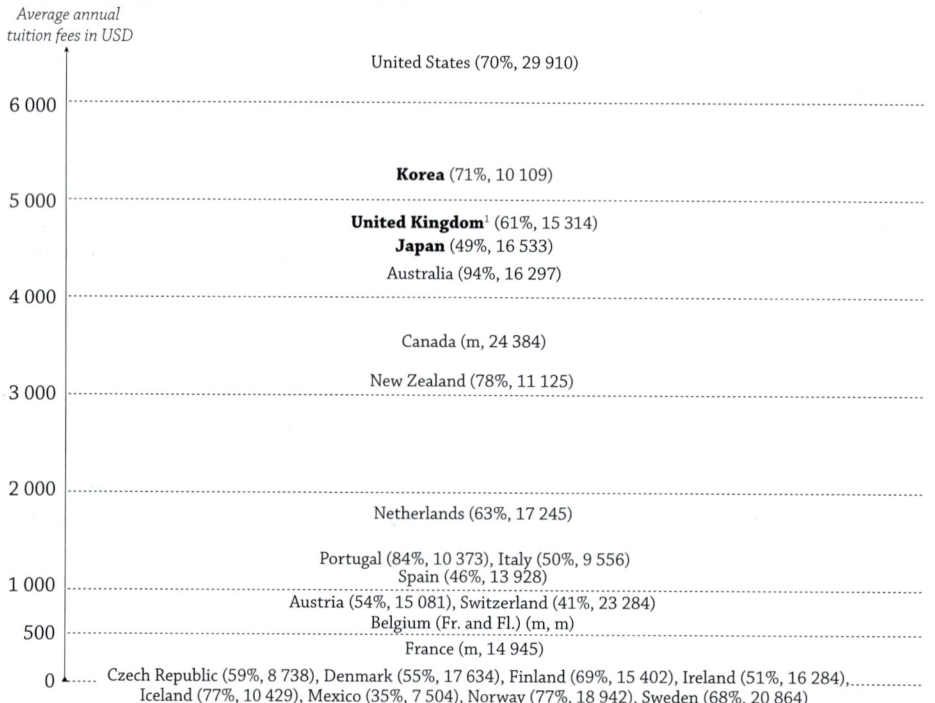

Note: This chart does not take into account grants, subsidies or loans that partially or fully offset the student's tuition fees.

1. Public institutions do not exist at this level of education and almost all students are enrolled in government-dependent private institutions.

Source: OECD. Tables B1.1a, B5.1 and Indicator C2. See Annex 3 for notes (*www.oecd.org/edu/eag2011*).

Please refer to the Reader's Guide for information concerning the symbols replacing the missing data.

StatLink http://dx.doi.org/10.1787/888932461218

How to read this chart

This chart shows the annual tuition fees charged in equivalent USD converted using PPPs. Countries in bold indicate that tuition fees refer to public institutions but more than two-thirds of students are enrolled in private institutions. The net entry rate and expenditure per student (in USD) in tertiary-type A programmes (2008) are added next to country names.

There are large differences among countries in the average tuition fees charged by tertiary-type A institutions for national students. In the five Nordic countries (Denmark, Finland, Iceland, Norway and Sweden) as well as the Czech Republic and Mexico, public institutions do not charge tuition fees. Ireland could also be included in this category as tuition fees charged by public institutions (for full-time undergraduate students from the European Union) are paid directly by the government. In contrast, in one-third of the countries with available data, public institutions (or government-dependent private institutions) charge national students annual tuition fees that exceed USD 1 500, and that reach more than USD 5 000 in Korea and the United States.

Among the EU21 countries for which data are available, only Italy, the Netherlands, Portugal and the United Kingdom have annual tuition fees that exceed USD 1 200 per full-time national student (Table B5.1 and Chart B5.2).

Differentiation of tuition fees by citizenship and field of education

National policies regarding tuition fees and financial aid to students generally cover all students studying in the country's educational institutions. Countries' policies also take international students into account. Differences between national and international students, in terms of the fees they are charged, or the financial help they may receive from the country in which they study, can, along with other factors, have an impact on the flows of international students, either by attracting students to some countries or discouraging students from studying in others (see Indicator C3).

In nearly half of the countries with available data, the tuition fees charged by public educational institutions may differ among national and international students enrolled in the same programme. In Austria, for example, the average tuition fees charged by public institutions for students who are not citizens of EU or European Economic Area (EEA) countries are twice the fees charged for citizens of these countries. Similar policies are found in Australia, Canada, Ireland, the Netherlands, New Zealand (except for foreign doctoral students), Poland (only for public institutions), the Slovak Republic, Slovenia, Switzerland, the United Kingdom and the United States, as well as in Denmark (as of 2006-07), and in Sweden (as of 2011). In these countries, the level of tuition fees varies based on citizenship or on an individual's residence (see Indicator C3 and Box C3.3).

Tuition fees are also differentiated by field of education in more than half of the countries with available data. The exceptions are Austria, Belgium (Flemish Community and French Community), Japan (in national universities), Mexico, the Netherlands, Slovenia and Switzerland, and also in the tertiary-type A educational institutions of Nordic countries that do not charge tuition fees for students, which excludes any possibility to differentiate them. The main basis for this differentiation in fees is the difference in the public cost of studies (Ireland, Italy, New Zealand, Poland and the Slovak Republic, for example). In these countries, the higher the cost of the studies, the higher the level of tuition fees charged by educational institutions.

However, in a few countries, the basis for the differentiation by field of education is the priority given to specific fields. In Australia, this type of differentiation is linked to skills shortages in the labour market. In Iceland and the United Kingdom, tuition fees vary by fields of education because of differences in both the cost of studies and labour-market opportunities (Box B5.1).

Annual tuition fees charged by private institutions

Annual tuition fees charged by private institutions vary considerably across and within countries. In most countries, private institutions charge higher tuition fees than public institutions. Finland and Sweden are the only countries with no tuition fees in either public or private institutions. Variations within countries tend to be greatest in those countries in which the largest proportions of students are enrolled in independent private tertiary-type A institutions. In contrast, in most countries tuition fees charged by institutions differ less between public and government-dependent private institutions than between public and independent private institutions. In Austria, there is no difference in the tuition fees charged by these two types of institutions. The greater level of autonomy among independent, private institutions as compared to public and government-dependent institutions partly explains this situation.

Public subsidies to households and other private entities

OECD countries spend an average of 0.5% of their GDP on public subsidies to households and other private entities for all levels of education combined. The proportion of education budgets spent on subsidies to households and private entities is much higher at the tertiary level than at the primary, secondary and post-secondary non-tertiary levels, representing less than 0.3% of GDP (against less than 0.2% at lower levels of education). At the tertiary level, the subsidies are largest in relation to GDP in Norway (1.3% of GDP), followed by New Zealand (0.8%), Denmark (0.6%), Sweden (0.5%), the United Kingdom (0.5%), the Netherlands (0.4%) and Austria (0.4%) (Table B5.3 and Table B5.4, available on line).

OECD countries spend an average of 21% of their public budgets for tertiary education on subsidies to households and other private entities (Chart B5.3). In Australia, Chile, Denmark, Japan, the Netherlands, New Zealand, Norway, Sweden and the United Kingdom, public subsidies account for more than 25% of public spending on tertiary education. Only Argentina, the Czech Republic and Poland devote less than 5% of total public spending on tertiary education on subsidies. However, in these two last countries, subsidies for students' grants are directly sent to institutions, which are responsible for distributing them among students (Table B5.3).

Country approaches to funding tertiary education

Countries differ in their approach to funding tertiary education. This section provides a taxonomy of approaches to funding tertiary education in countries with available data. Countries are grouped according to two factors. The first is the extent of cost-sharing, that is, the level of contribution required from the student and/or his or her family in tertiary-type A education. The second concerns the basis for student support at this level of education.

There is no single model for financing tertiary-type A education. Some countries in which tertiary-type A institutions charge similar tuition fees may have differences in the proportion of students benefiting from public subsidies and/or differences in the average amount of these subsidies (Tables B5.1, B5.2 and B5.3, Table B5.4 available on line, and Chart B5.1). Moreover, the arrangements regarding the tuition fees charged by tertiary educational institutions have been the subject of reforms in many OECD countries since 1995, and some countries have moved from one model to another over this period (Box B5.1 and Chart B5.1).

Box B5.1. Changes in policies on tuition fees and public subsidies to students since 1995

Since 1995, **more than half of the 25 countries with available information have undertaken reforms of their systems of tuition fees (and support for students)** and have adopted different approaches. Tuition fees have been introduced in some German federal states or have been increased since 1995 in Australia, Austria, Japan, the Netherlands, New Zealand, Portugal, the United Kingdom and the United States. Similarly, Denmark, Ireland and the Slovak Republic increased tuition fees charged for international students (only international students are charged tuition fees in these countries).

However, most countries simultaneously implemented systems to limit the variation in the level of tuition fees charged in tertiary-type A institutions for each field of education or to differentiate the fees, sometimes at the state/regional level, as tuition-fee policies vary within the country (**Canada**). These could consist in linking the level of fees to labour-market opportunities, so that fields with skills shortages have lower tuitions fees than others to attract more students (**Australia**, for example), or in setting an upper limit on tuition fees to ensure that students from socio-economically disadvantaged backgrounds have access to tertiary education (**Italy**), or even in temporarily freezing the level of fees in return for a higher government subsidy (**New Zealand**).

A few countries even reduced tuition fees: in **Austria**, tuition fees introduced in the 2001-02 academic year were suppressed for the majority of students in 2009; while in **Ireland**, tuition fees for most full-time undergraduate students have been paid by the state since 1995-96 through a transfer to public institutions. In **Hungary** (not included in the table below) a general tuition-fee system was introduced in 1996, but this obligation was abolished in 1998. Since then, there has been a special dual system in operation, in which one part of tertiary students can study free of charge by state subsidy while the other part of students can study by paying a "training contribution". The status of students is determined mainly during the application and admission procedure.

...

	Reforms have been implemented since 1995	Reforms have been combined with a change in the level of public subsidies available to students	Tertiary educational institutions differentiate tuition fees between national and international students	Tertiary educational institutions differentiate tuition fees by field of education
Australia	Yes	Yes	Yes	Yes
Austria	Yes	Yes	No	No
Belgium (Fl.)	Yes	No	Yes	No
Belgium (Fr.)	No till 2008-09	No	Yes	No
Canada	Yes	Yes	Yes	Yes
Denmark	Yes	Yes	Yes	No
Finland	No	No	No	No
France	No	No	No	Yes
Iceland	Yes	No	No	Yes
Ireland	Yes	Yes	Yes	Yes
Italy	Yes	Yes	No	Yes
Japan	Yes	Yes	No	No
Korea	Yes	Yes	No	Yes
Mexico	No	No	No	No
Netherlands	Yes	Yes	Yes	No
New Zealand	Yes	Yes	Yes	Yes
Norway	No	No	No	No
Poland	Yes	Yes	Yes	Yes
Slovak Republic	Yes	No	Yes	Yes
Slovenia	No	No	Yes	No
Spain	No	No	No	Yes
Sweden	No	No	n.a.	n.a.
Switzerland	No	No	Yes	No
United Kingdom	Yes	Yes	Yes	Yes
United States	No	No	Yes	Yes

Reforms on tuition fees are usually combined with reforms in student support. Changes in support for students usually aim to give students from disadvantaged backgrounds greater access to tertiary studies or to reduce the liquidity constraints on all students, through grants/scholarships or loans, or by introducing different rates of contributions. These kinds of systems have been developed in **Australia**, **Austria** and **Canada**. A specific loan for tuition fees has even been introduced in the **Netherlands**. In some other countries, more public funds support tertiary institutions. This is the case in **New Zealand**, where the government requires institutions to freeze their fees between 2001 and 2003, in return for proportional increases in subsidies to individuals. This limits the cost of study for students, while offering funding to institutions as a way of meeting the costs of foregoing increases in fees.

Only a few countries (the **Flemish community of Belgium**, and the **Slovak Republic**) did not change student-support systems in addition to changing their systems of tuition fees. In **Belgium (Flemish Community)**, a reform aimed to make tuition fees more flexible in 2007, based on the number of credits in which students are enrolled in the programme. In the **Slovak Republic**, the reforms aimed to allow tertiary institutions to charge tuition fees for part-time students and for students who stay longer in a programme than theoretically expected.

Model 1: Countries with no or low tuition fees but generous student-support systems

This group is composed of the Nordic countries (Denmark, Finland, Iceland, Norway and Sweden). There are no (or low) financial barriers to tertiary education and there is even a high level of student aid. At 69%, the average entry rate to tertiary-type A education for this group is above the OECD average of 60% (see Indicator C2). Tuition fees charged by public educational institutions for national students are negligible for tertiary-type A education and more than 55% of students enrolled in tertiary-type A education in this group can benefit from scholarships/grants and/or public loans to finance their studies or living expenses (Tables B5.1, B5.2 and Chart B5.1).

The level of public expenditure on tertiary education as a percentage of GDP and the level of taxation on income are also among the highest in these countries. The approach to funding tertiary education reflects these countries' deeply rooted social values, such as equality of opportunity and social equity. The notion that government should provide its citizens with tertiary education at no charge to the user is a salient feature of these countries' educational culture. In its current mode, the funding of both institutions and students in these countries is based on the principle that access to tertiary education is a right, rather than a privilege (OECD, 2008a, Chapter 4). However, Denmark decided to introduce tuition fees for international students during the past decade to increase the resources available for their tertiary institutions. This solution is also envisaged in Iceland and Sweden (Box B5.1).

Model 2: Countries with high levels of tuition fees and well-developed student-support systems

A second group includes Australia, Canada, the Netherlands, New Zealand, the United Kingdom and the United States. These countries have potentially high financial barriers to entry into tertiary-type A education, but also provide large public subsidies to students. The average entry rate to tertiary-type A education for this group of countries is, at 69%, significantly above the OECD average and higher than most countries with low tuition fees (except the Nordic countries). The Netherlands and, to a lesser extent, the United Kingdom have moved from Model 4 to this group of countries since 1995 (Chart B5.1).

Tuition fees charged by public tertiary-type A institutions exceed USD 1 500 in all these countries, and more than 75% of tertiary-type A students receive public subsidies (in Australia, the Netherlands, New Zealand and the United States, the four countries for which data are available; Tables B5.1 and B5.2). Student-support systems are well developed and mostly accommodate the needs of the entire student population, with the proportion of public subsidies in total public expenditure on tertiary education higher than the OECD average (21%) in four out of the six countries: Australia (32%), the Netherlands (29%), New Zealand (42%) and the United Kingdom (53%), and nearly at the average for Canada (17%) and the United States (20%) (Table B5.3). In this group of countries, access to tertiary-type A education is not lower than in other groups. For example, Australia and New Zealand have among the highest entry rates into tertiary-type A education (94% and 78%, respectively), partly because of the high proportion of international students enrolled in tertiary-type A education. The Netherlands (63%), the United Kingdom (61%) and the United States (70%) were also above the OECD average (60%) in 2008 (see Table C2.2). These countries spend more on core services per tertiary student than the OECD average and have a relatively high level of revenue from income tax as a percentage of GDP compared to the OECD average. The Netherlands is an outlier as its level of income taxation is below the OECD average (see Table B1.1b and OECD, 2010f).

Model 3: Countries with high levels of tuition fees but less-developed student-support systems

In Japan and Korea, most students are charged high tuition fees, but student-support systems are somewhat less developed than those in Models 1 and 2. This places a considerable financial burden on students and their families. In these two countries, tertiary-type A institutions charge high tuition fees (more than USD 4 500) but a relatively small proportion of students benefit from public subsidies (around one-third of students receive public subsidies in Japan; 15% of total public expenditure on tertiary education is allocated to public subsidies in Korea). Tertiary-type A entry rates in these two countries are 49% and 71%, respectively; Japan is below and Korea is significantly above the OECD average. In Japan, some students who excel academically but have difficulty financing their studies may benefit from reduced tuition and/or admission fees or be entirely exempted. The below-average access to tertiary-type A education is counterbalanced by an above-average entry rate into tertiary-type B (shorter and more practically oriented) programmes (see Indicator C2). These two countries are among those with the lowest levels of public expenditure allocated to tertiary education as a percentage of GDP (see Table B4.1). This partially explains the small proportion of students who benefit from public loans. However, in 2009 Japan is closer to Model 2 than it was in 1995 (Chart B5.1) because a reform was implemented to improve the student-support system. Public subsidies for students are now above the OECD average and represent 25% of total public expenditure on tertiary education. Expenditure per tertiary student is also above the OECD average (Table B5.3).

Model 4: Countries with low levels of tuition fees and less-developed student-support systems

The fourth group includes all other European countries for which data are available (Austria, Belgium, the Czech Republic, France, Ireland, Italy, Portugal, Switzerland and Spain) and Mexico. Since 1995, some reforms have also been implemented in some of these countries – mainly in Austria and Italy – to increase the level of tuition fees charged by public institutions; but all of these countries can be considered as charging moderate tuition fees compared to those in Models 2 and 3 (Chart B5.1 and Box B5.1). These countries also have relatively low financial barriers to entry into tertiary education (or no tuition-fee barriers, as in the Czech Republic, Ireland and Mexico), combined with relatively low subsidies for students, which are mainly targeted to specific groups. There is a high level of dependence on public resources for the funding of tertiary education and participation levels are typically below the OECD average. The average tertiary-type A entry rate in this group of countries is a relatively low 50%; in Belgium, this low rate is counterbalanced by high entry rates into tertiary-type B education. Similarly, expenditure per student for tertiary-type A education is also comparatively low (see Indicator B1 and Chart B5.2). While high tuition fees can raise potential barriers to student participation, this suggests that the absence of tuition fees, which is assumed to ease access to education, does not necessarily ensure high levels of access to and the quality of tertiary-type A education.

Tuition fees charged by public institutions in this group never exceed USD 1 200, and in countries for which data are available, the proportion of students who benefit from public subsidies is below 40% (Tables B5.1 and B5.2). In these countries students and their families can benefit from subsidies provided by sources other than the ministry of education (e.g. housing allowances, tax reductions and/or tax credits for education); but these are not covered in this analysis. In France, for example, housing allowances represent about 90% of scholarships/grants and about one-third of students benefit from these. Poland is notable in that some students have their studies fully subsidised by the public budget while all others pay the full costs of tuition. In other words, the burden of private contributions is borne by part of the student population rather than shared by all (see Indicator B3 in OECD, 2008b). Loan systems, such as public loans or loans guaranteed by the state, are not available or are only available to a small proportion of students in these countries (Table B5.2). At the same time, the level of public spending and the tax revenue from income as a percentage of GDP vary significantly more among this group of countries than in the other groups. Policies on tuition fees and public subsidies are not necessarily the main factors that influence students' decisions to enter tertiary-type A education.

OECD countries use different mixes of grants and loans to subsidise students' education costs

A key question in many OECD countries is whether financial subsidies for households should be provided primarily in the form of grants or loans. Governments subsidise students' living or educational costs through different mixes of these two types of subsidies. Advocates of student loans argue that loans allow available resources to be spread further: if the amount spent on grants were used to guarantee or subsidise loans instead, more aid would be available to students and overall access would increase. Loans also shift some of the cost of education to those who benefit most from educational investment. Opponents of loans argue that student loans are less effective than grants in encouraging low-income students to pursue their education. They also argue that loans may be less efficient than anticipated because of the various subsidies provided to borrowers or lenders and because of the costs of administration and servicing.

Chart B5.3. Public subsidies for education in tertiary education (2008)

Public subsidies for education to households and other private entities as a percentage of total public expenditure on education, by type of subsidy

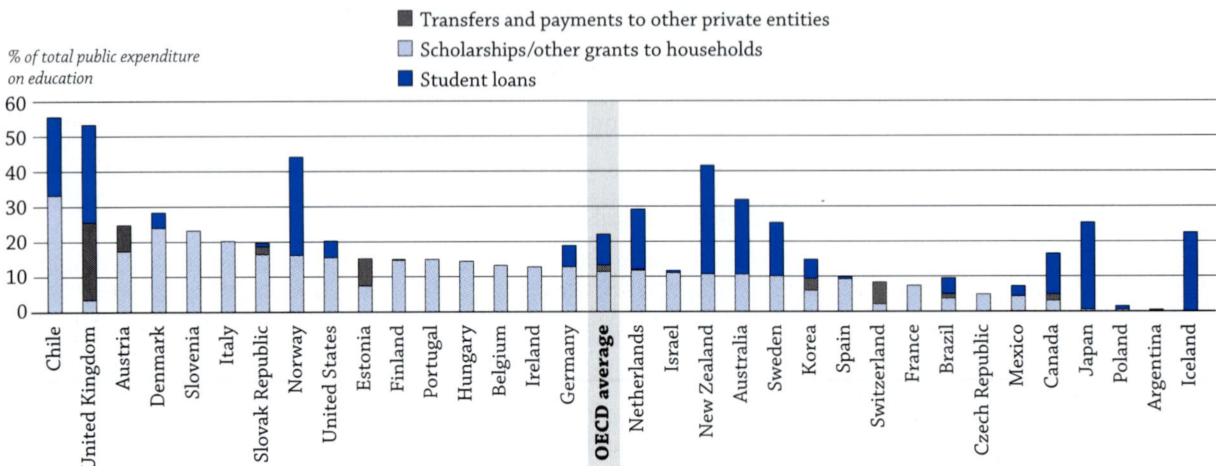

Countries are ranked in descending order of the share of scholarships/other grants to households and transfers and payments to other private entities in total public expenditure on education.

Source: OECD. Argentina: UNESCO Institute for Statistics (World Education Indicators Programme). Table B5.3. See Annex 3 for notes (*www.oecd.org/edu/eag2011*).

StatLink http://dx.doi.org/10.1787/888932461237

Chart B5.3 presents the proportion of public educational expenditure dedicated to loans, grants and scholarships, and other subsidies to households at the tertiary level. Grants and scholarships include family allowances and other specific subsidies, but exclude tax reductions that are part of the subsidy system in Australia, Belgium (Flemish Community), Canada, the Czech Republic, Finland, France, Hungary, Italy, the Netherlands, Norway, the Slovak Republic, Switzerland and the United States (see Chart B5.3 in OECD, 2006a). More than one-third of the 32 countries for which data are available rely exclusively on scholarships/grants and transfers/payments to other private entities. The other countries provide both scholarships/grants and loans to students (except Iceland, which relies only on student loans), and both subsidies are used extensively in Australia, Chile, the Netherlands, New Zealand, Norway, Sweden, the United Kingdom and the United States. In general, the largest subsidies to students are provided by the countries that offer student loans; in most cases, these countries also spend an above-average proportion of their budgets on grants and scholarships (Chart B5.3 and Table B5.3).

Definitions

Average tuition fees charged in public and private tertiary-type A institutions does not distinguish tuition fees by type of programme. This indicator gives an overview of tuition fees at this level by type of institution and shows the proportions of students who do or do not receive scholarships/grants that fully or partially cover tuition fees. Levels of tuition fees and associated proportions of students should be interpreted with caution as they are derived from the weighted average of the main tertiary-type A programmes and do not cover all educational institutions.

Public spending transferred to students, families and other private entities includes funds that may go indirectly to educational institutions, such as the subsidies that are used to cover tuition fees, and funds that do not go, even indirectly, to educational institutions, such as subsidies for students' living costs.

Public subsidies to households include: *i)* grants/scholarships (non-repayable subsidies); *ii)* public student loans, which must be repaid; *iii)* family or child allowances contingent on student status; *iv)* public subsidies in cash or in kind, specifically for housing, transport, medical expenses, books and supplies, social, recreational and other purposes; and *v)* interest-related subsidies for private loans.

However, public subsidies do not distinguish among different types of grants or loans, such as scholarships, family allowances and in-kind subsidies. Governments can also support students and their families by providing housing allowances, tax reductions and/or tax credits for education. These subsidies are not covered here. Financial aid to students in some countries may therefore be substantially underestimated.

It is also common for governments to guarantee the repayment of loans to students made by private lenders. In some OECD countries, this indirect form of subsidy is as significant as, or even more significant than, direct financial aid to students. However, for reasons of comparability, the indicator only takes into account the amounts relating to public transfers for private loans that are made to private entities, not the total value of loans generated. Some qualitative information is nevertheless presented in some of the tables to give some insight on this type of subsidy.

Student loans refer to the full volume of student loans in order to provide information on the level of support received by current students. The gross amount of loans, including scholarships and grants, provides an appropriate measure of the financial aid to current participants in education. Interest payments and repayments of principal by borrowers should be taken into account in order to assess the net cost of student loans to public and private lenders. However, such payments are usually made by former students rather than by current students and are not covered in this indicator. In most countries, moreover, loan repayments do not flow to the education authorities, and the money is not available to them to cover other educational expenditures. OECD indicators take the full amount of scholarships and loans (gross) into account when discussing financial aid to current students. Some OECD countries also have difficulty quantifying the amount of loans to students. Therefore, data on student loans should be treated with some caution.

Methodology

Data refer to the financial year 2008 and are based on the UOE data collection on education statistics administered by the OECD in 2010 (for details see Annex 3 at *www.oecd.org/edu/eag2011*).

Data on tuition fees charged by educational institutions, financial aid to students and on reforms implemented since 1995 were collected through a special survey undertaken in 2010 and refer to the academic year 2008-09. Amounts of tuition fees and amounts of loans in national currency are converted into equivalent USD by dividing the national currency by the purchasing power parity (PPP) index for GDP. Amounts of tuition fees and associated proportions of students should be interpreted with caution as they represent the weighted average of the main tertiary-type A programmes and do not cover all the educational institutions.

Public costs related to private loans guaranteed by governments are included as subsidies to other private entities. Unlike public loans, only the net cost of these loans is included.

The value of tax reductions or credits to households and students is not included.

The statistical data for Israel are supplied by and under the responsibility of the relevant Israeli authorities. The use of such data by the OECD is without prejudice to the status of the Golan Heights, East Jerusalem and Israeli settlements in the West Bank under the terms of international law.

References

OECD (2006a), *Education at a Glance 2006: OECD Indicators,* OECD, Paris.

OECD (2008a), *OECD Reviews of Tertiary Education: Tertiary Education for the Knowledge Society,* OECD, Paris.

OECD (2008b), *Education at a Glance 2008: OECD Indicators,* OECD, Paris.

OECD (2010f), *OECD Tax Statistics: Volume 2010, Issue I: Revenue Statistics,* OECD, Paris.

The following additional material relevant to this indicator is available on line:

- ***Table B5.4. Public subsidies for households and other private entities as a percentage of total public expenditure on education and GDP, for primary, secondary and post-secondary non-tertiary education (2008)***
  StatLink http://dx.doi.org/10.1787/888932464068

Table B5.1. [1/2] Estimated annual average tuition fees charged, by tertiary-type A educational institutions[1] for national students (academic year 2008-09)

In equivalent USD converted using PPPs, by type of institution, based on full-time students

Tuition fees and associated proportions of students should be interpreted with caution as they result from the weighted average of the main tertiary-type A programmes and do not cover all educational institutions. However, the figures reported can be considered as good proxies and show the difference among countries in tuition fees charged by main educational institutions and for the majority of students.

	Percentage of tertiary full-time students enrolled in tertiary-type A programmes	Percentage of tertiary-type A full-time students enrolled in:			Annual average tuition fees in USD charged by institutions (for full-time students)			
		Public institutions	Government-dependent private institutions	Independent private institutions	Public institutions	Government-dependent private institutions	Independent private institutions	Comment
		(1)	(2)	(3)	(4)	(5)	(6)	(7)
OECD								
Australia	84	97	a	3	4 140	a	8 933	93% of national students in public institutions are in subsidised places and pay an average USD 3 817 tuition fee, including HECS/HELP subsidies. There was a significant increase (~50%) in scholarships for domestic students from 2007 to 2009 as a result of government reforms aimed at doubling the number of Commonwealth Scholarships by 2012. The new scholarships were mostly targeted towards students studying national priority subjects, students who needed to relocate to study specialist subjects, and indigenous students.
Austria[2]	87	87	13	m	853	853	235 to 11 735	As of summer term 2009, tuition fees have to be paid by national students and students from EU/EEA countries when they exceed the theoretical duration of the study programme by two semesters and by students from non-EU/EEA countries (except students from least-developed countries).
Belgium (Fl.)	69	51	49	m	x(5)	545 to 618	m	Tuition fees refer to the minimum and maximum amount that institutions may charge according to the decree (indexed figures). They refer to those for students enrolled in first (bachelor) and second (master) degree programmes. The information does not refer to further degree programmes (for example a second master's degree after a first master's degree). This information refers to students without scholarships (a student with a scholarship benefits from lower tuition fees, see more details in Annex 3).
Belgium (Fr.)	m	33	67	m	599	683	m	Tuition fees charged for programmes are the same in public as in private institutions but the distribution of students differs between public and private institutions, so the weighted average is not the same.
Canada	66	100	m	m	3 774	x(4)	x(4)	
Chile	60	m	m	m	m	m	m	
Czech Republic	86	87	a	13	No tuition fees	a	m	The average fee in public institutions is negligible because fees are paid only by students studying too long (more than the standard length of the programme plus 1 year) : about 4% of students.
Denmark[3]	88	m	m	m	No tuition fees	m	a	
Estonia	62	m	m	m	a	m	m	
Finland	100	82	18	a	No tuition fees	No tuition fees	a	Excluding membership fees to student unions.
France	72	87	5	8	190 to 1 309	1 127 to 8 339	1 128 to 8 339	Tuition fees in public institutions refer to University programmes dependent from the Ministry of Education.
Germany	87	97	3	x(2)	m	m	m	There is no national nor subnational average levels of tuition fees. Since 2005, the 16 german *Länder* have been free to decide on the imposition of tuition fees. A few number of *Länder* have tuitions fees, but the level of fees differs between Länder. In some *Länder*, the higher education institutions themselves are free to decide on the imposition of study fees and the amount thereof. Most of the 16 *Länder* did not impose tuition fees for initial education.
Greece	60	m	m	m	m	m	m	
Hungary	90	m	m	m	m	m	m	There is no general tuition fee imposed. However, there is a special dual system in operation, in which one part of tertiary students can study free of charge with the help of State subsidy while the other part of students can study by paying a "training contribution" (the term "tuition fee" is not in use). The status of students is determined mainly during the application and admission procedure (with the principle that the State finances studies for the first degree by levels within a quota determined annually by the government). In 2008-09, the proportion of state-financed full-time students is 75% (19% for part-time students) – while the proportion of contribution-paying full-time students is 25% (81% for part-time students). The amount of training contributions is defined by higher education institutions but according to the current regulation it should be at least as high as the State-provided subsidy to the HEIs for the training of a student in the particular field of study.

1. Scholarships/grants that the student may receive are not taken into account.
2. Including students in advanced research programmes.
3. Tuition fees in total tertiary education.

Source: OECD. See Annex 3 for notes *(www.oecd.org/edu/eag2011)*.

Please refer to the Reader's Guide for information concerning the symbols replacing missing data.

StatLink http://dx.doi.org/10.1787/888932464011

Table B5.1. [2/2] Estimated annual average tuition fees charged, by tertiary-type A educational institutions[1] for national students (academic year 2008-09)

In equivalent USD converted using PPPs, by type of institution, based on full-time students

Tuition fees and associated proportions of students should be interpreted with caution as they result from the weighted average of the main tertiary-type A programmes and do not cover all educational institutions. However, the figures reported can be considered as good proxies and show the difference among countries in tuition fees charged by main educational institutions and for the majority of students.

		Percentage of tertiary full-time students enrolled in tertiary-type A programmes	Percentage of tertiary-type A full-time students enrolled in:			Annual average tuition fees in USD charged by institutions (for full-time students)			Comment
			Public institutions	Government-dependent private institutions	Independent private institutions	Public institutions	Government-dependent private institutions	Independent private institutions	
			(1)	(2)	(3)	(4)	(5)	(6)	(7)
	Iceland	97	79	21	n	No tuition fees	2 311 to 6 831	8 433 to 12 650	Subsidised student loans that cover tution fees are available for all students. Almost no scholarships/grants exist.
	Ireland	74	97	a	3	2 800 to 10 000	a	m	The tuition fees charged by public institutions are paid directly by the government for full-time, undergraduate students from the European Union, only. About one half of all tuition fee income is derived from households (mainly for part-time or postgraduate or non-EU students).
	Israel	76	m	m	m	a	m	m	
	Italy	98	92	a	8	1281	a	4713	The annual average tuition fees do not take into account the scholarships/grants that fully cover tuition fees but partial reductions of fees cannot be excluded.
	Japan	75	25	a	75	4 602	a	7 247	Excludes admission fees charged by the school for the first year (USD 2 398 on average).
	Korea	74	24	a	76	5 315	a	9 586	Tuition fees in first-degree programme only. Excludes admission fees to university, but includes supporting fees.
	Luxembourg	m	m	m	m	m	m	m	
	Mexico	96	66	a	34	No tuition fees	a	5 365	
	Netherlands	100	m	a	m	1 851	a	m	
	New Zealand	77	97	2	1	3 019	4 159	m	
	Norway	95	86	14	x(2)	No tuition fees	n	5 641	Student fees are representative of the dominant private ISCED 5 institution in Norway.
	Poland	96	87	a	13	n	a	1 889 to 2 537	
	Portugal[3]	96	m	m	m	1 233	4 991	m	
	Slovak Republic	96	96	a	4	Maximum 2 707	a	m	
	Slovenia	72	96	4	n	m	m	m	In public and government-dependent private institutions: first and second level full-time students do not pay tuition fees. But second cycle students who already obtained a qualification/degree equivalent to the second cycle pay tuition fees.
	Spain	81	87	a	13	1 038	a	m	
	Sweden	86	92	8	n	No tuition fees	No tuition fees	m	Excluding mandatory membership fees to student unions.
	Switzerland	83	99	m	1	879	m	7 262	
	Turkey	69	m	m	m	m	a	m	
	United Kingdom	87	a	100	n	a	4 840	m	English students from low-income households can access non-repayable grants and bursaries. Loans for tuition fees and living costs are available to all eligible students.
	United States	80	68	a	32	6 312	a	22 852	Including non-national students.
Other G20	Argentina	m	m	m	m	m	m	m	
	Brazil	90	m	m	m	m	a	m	
	China	m	m	m	m	m	m	m	
	India	m	m	m	m	m	m	m	
	Indonesia	m	m	m	m	m	m	m	
	Russian Federation	75	m	m	m	m	a	m	
	Saudi Arabia	m	m	m	m	m	m	m	
	South Africa	m	m	m	m	m	m	m	

1. Scholarships/grants that the student may receive are not taken into account.
2. Including students in advanced research programmes.
3. Tuition fees in total tertiary education.

Source: OECD. See Annex 3 for notes *(www.oecd.org/edu/eag2011)*.

Please refer to the Reader's Guide for information concerning the symbols replacing missing data.

StatLink http://dx.doi.org/10.1787/888932464011

B5

Table B5.2. **Distribution of financial aid to students compared to the amount of tuition fees charged in tertiary-type A education (academic year 2008-09)**

Based on full-time students

		Distribution of financial aid to students Percentage of students who:				Distribution of scholarships/grants in support of tuition fees Percentage of students who:			
		benefit from public loans only	benefit from scholarships/ grants only	benefit from public loans AND scholarships/ grants	DO NOT benefit from public loans OR scholarships/ grants	receive scholarships/ grants that are higher than the tuition fees	receive scholarships/ grants whose amount is equivalent to the tuition fees	receive scholarships/ grants that partially cover the tuition fees	DO NOT receive scholarships/ grants in support of tuition fees
		(1)	(2)	(3)	(4)	(5)	(6)	(7)	(8)
OECD	Australia[1]	74	1	7	19	n	n	7.3	92.7
	Austria	a	19	a	81	16.8	n	1.5	81.7
	Belgium (Fl.)[2]	a	22	a	78	21.7	x(5)	x(5)	78.3
	Belgium (Fr.)	n	17	n	83	16.9	x(5)	x(5)	83.1
	Canada	m	m	m	m	m	m	m	m
	Chile	m	m	m	m	m	m	m	m
	Czech Republic	m	m	a	m	m	m	m	m
	Denmark[2]	m	93	m	m	m	m	m	m
	Estonia	m	m	m	m	m	m	m	m
	Finland	a	55	a	45	a	a	a	a
	France[2]	a	28	a	72	24.0	4.0	a	72.0
	Germany	m	m	m	m	m	m	m	m
	Greece	m	m	m	m	m	m	m	m
	Hungary	21	35	m	m	a	a	a	100.0
	Iceland	63	m	m	37	a	a	a	100.0
	Ireland[3]	a	39	a	m	x(6)	85.5	m	14.5
	Israel	m	m	m	m	m	m	m	m
	Italy	n	18	n	82	8.2	3.1	7.0	81.7
	Japan	33	1	n	67	a	a	a	100.0
	Korea	m	m	m	m	a	1.8	38.8	59.5
	Luxembourg	m	m	m	m	m	m	m	m
	Mexico[2]	1	12	m	87	m	m	m	m
	Netherlands[3]	11	63	21	5	67.8	n	12.2	20.0
	New Zealand	51	4	35	10	m	m	m	m
	Norway[4]	12	4	52	33	m	m	m	m
	Poland	m	m	m	m	m	m	m	m
	Portugal	m	m	m	m	m	m	m	m
	Slovak Republic	m	m	m	m	m	m	m	m
	Slovenia[5]	a	21	n	m	m	m	m	m
	Spain	n	34	n	66	23.5	3.5	10.4	62.6
	Sweden	n	19	50	32	a	a	a	a
	Switzerland	2	11	m	87	m	m	m	m
	Turkey	m	m	m	m	m	m	m	m
	United Kingdom	37	8	50	6	m	m	m	42.7
	United States[2]	12	27	38	24	m	m	m	m
Other G20	Argentina	m	m	m	m	m	m	m	m
	Brazil	m	m	m	m	m	m	m	m
	China	m	m	m	m	m	m	m	m
	India	m	m	m	m	m	m	m	m
	Indonesia	m	m	m	m	m	m	m	m
	Russian Federation	m	m	m	m	m	m	m	m
	Saudi Arabia	m	m	m	m	m	m	m	m
	South Africa	m	m	m	m	m	m	m	m

1. Excludes foreign students.
2. Distribution of students in total tertiary education (only public university, including tertiary-type B in France).
3. Public institutions only.
4. Data refer to academic year 2007-08.
5. Column 2 only includes scholarships.

Source: OECD. See Annex 3 for notes *(www.oecd.org/edu/eag2011)*.

Please refer to the Reader's Guide for information concerning the symbols replacing missing data.

StatLink http://dx.doi.org/10.1787/888932464030

Table B5.3. Public subsidies for households and other private entities as a percentage of total public expenditure on education and GDP, for tertiary education (2008)

Direct public expenditure on educational institutions and subsidies for households and other private entities

			Public subsidies for education to private entities						
			Financial aid to students						
		Direct public expenditure for institutions	Scholarships/ other grants to households	Student loans	Total	Scholarships/ other grants to households attributable for educational institutions	Transfers and payments to other private entities	Total	Subsidies for education to private entities as a percentage of GDP
		(1)	(2)	(3)	(4)	(5)	(6)	(7)	(8)
OECD	Australia	**68.5**	10.6	21.3	31.9	1.0	n	**31.5**	0.31
	Austria	**75.2**	17.4	a	17.4	m	7.5	**24.8**	0.37
	Belgium	**86.8**	13.2	n	13.2	3.6	n	**13.2**	0.18
	Canada[1]	**83.5**	3.1	11.6	14.8	m	1.8	**16.5**	m
	Chile[2]	**44.4**	33.2	22.4	55.6	21.4	m	**55.6**	0.40
	Czech Republic	**95.1**	4.9	a	4.9	m	n	**4.9**	0.05
	Denmark[3]	**71.6**	24.0	4.4	28.4	n	n	**28.4**	0.62
	Estonia	**84.9**	7.4	m	7.4	m	7.7	**15.1**	0.17
	Finland	**85.1**	14.7	n	14.7	n	0.3	**14.9**	0.28
	France	**92.6**	7.4	m	7.4	m	a	**7.4**	0.09
	Germany	**81.1**	12.7	6.1	18.9	m	n	**18.9**	0.23
	Greece	**m**	m	m	m	m	m	**m**	m
	Hungary	**85.7**	14.3	n	14.3	n	n	**14.3**	0.15
	Iceland	**77.5**	n	22.5	22.5	a	n	**22.5**	0.34
	Ireland	**87.3**	12.7	n	12.7	1.2	n	**12.7**	0.17
	Israel	**88.3**	11.0	0.6	11.7	10.6	n	**11.7**	0.11
	Italy	**79.8**	20.2	n	20.2	7.5	n	**20.2**	0.17
	Japan[3]	**74.6**	0.6	24.8	25.4	m	n	**25.4**	0.16
	Korea	**85.2**	6.0	5.4	11.5	5.4	3.3	**14.8**	0.10
	Luxembourg	**m**	m	m	m	m	m	**m**	m
	Mexico	**92.8**	4.3	2.9	7.2	1.5	a	**7.2**	0.07
	Netherlands	**70.8**	11.7	17.2	28.9	a	0.3	**29.2**	0.44
	New Zealand	**58.4**	10.7	30.9	41.6	m	n	**41.6**	0.80
	Norway	**55.9**	16.2	27.9	44.1	m	n	**44.1**	1.28
	Poland	**98.4**	0.5	1.0	1.5	m	n	**1.6**	0.02
	Portugal	**85.1**	14.9	m	14.9	m	m	**14.9**	0.14
	Slovak Republic[3]	**80.3**	16.4	1.0	17.5	m	2.2	**19.7**	0.15
	Slovenia	**76.8**	23.2	n	23.2	m	n	**23.2**	0.28
	Spain	**90.1**	9.2	0.6	9.9	2.0	n	**9.9**	0.11
	Sweden	**74.6**	10.1	15.3	25.4	a	a	**25.4**	0.46
	Switzerland	**91.7**	2.1	n	2.1	m	6.2	**8.3**	0.11
	Turkey	**m**	m	m	m	m	m	**m**	m
	United Kingdom	**46.7**	3.5	27.7	31.2	x(4)	22.1	**53.3**	0.45
	United States	**79.7**	15.5	4.8	20.3	m	m	**20.3**	0.26
	OECD average	**79.0**	11.4	8.9	19.4	3.6	1.8	**21.0**	0.28
	EU21 average	**81.5**	12.6	4.6	16.4	1.6	2.2	**18.5**	0.24
Other G20	Argentina	**99.5**	0.4	n	0.4	m	0.1	**0.5**	n
	Brazil	**90.5**	3.7	4.5	8.2	x(2)	1.3	**9.5**	0.08
	China	**m**	m	m	m	m	m	**m**	m
	India	**m**	m	m	m	m	m	**m**	m
	Indonesia	**m**	m	m	m	m	m	**m**	m
	Russian Federation	**m**	m	a	m	m	m	**m**	m
	Saudi Arabia	**m**	m	m	m	m	m	**m**	m
	South Africa	**m**	m	m	m	m	m	**m**	m

1. Year of reference 2007.
2. Year of reference 2009.
3. Some levels of education are included with others. Refer to «x» code in Table B1.1a for details.

Source: OECD. Argentina: UNESCO Institute for Statistics (World Education Indicators Programme). See Annex 3 for notes *(www.oecd.org/edu/eag2011)*.
Please refer to the Reader's Guide for information concerning the symbols replacing missing data.

StatLink http://dx.doi.org/10.1787/888932464049

ON WHAT RESOURCES AND SERVICES IS EDUCATION FUNDING SPENT?

INDICATOR B6

- In primary, secondary and post-secondary non-tertiary education combined, current expenditure accounts for an average of 92% of total spending in OECD countries, and in all but five countries, more than 70% of current expenditure is allocated to staff salaries.
- At the tertiary level, OECD countries spend an average of 32% of current expenditure on purposes other than compensation of educational personnel.
- Other current expenditure and capital expenditure combined represent a bigger share of total expenditure at tertiary than at other levels, mainly because of the higher cost of facilities and equipment and the construction of new buildings in response to growing enrolments.

Chart B6.1. Distribution of current expenditure by educational institutions for primary, secondary and post-secondary non-tertiary education (2008)

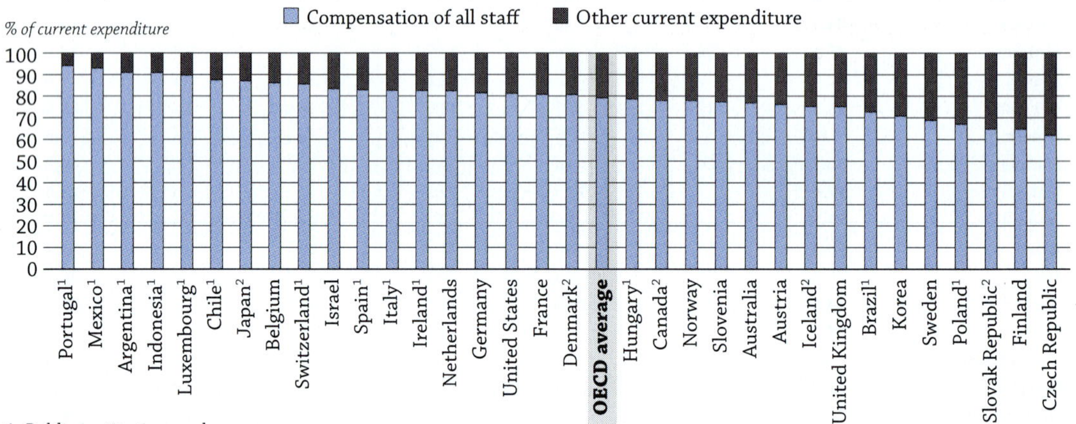

1. Public institutions only.

2. Some levels of education are included with others. Refer to "x" code in Table B1.1a for details.

Countries are ranked in descending order of the share of compensation of all staff in primary, secondary and post-secondary non-tertiary education.

Source: OECD. Argentina, Indonesia: UNESCO Institute for Statistics (World Education Indicators Programme). Table B6.2b. See Annex 3 for notes (*www.oecd.org/edu/eag2011*).

StatLink http://dx.doi.org/10.1787/888932461256

How to read this chart

The chart shows the distribution of current spending on educational institutions by resource category. This spending can be broken down into capital and current expenditure. Current expenditure comprises compensation of teachers, compensation of other staff and other current expenditures. The biggest item in current spending, teachers' salaries, is examined in greater detail in Indicator D3.

Context

Decisions taken at the system level about how resources are allocated can affect the nature of instruction and the conditions in which it is provided at the classroom level. Educational institutions offer a range of services in addition to instruction, such as meals and free transport or boarding facilities at the primary, secondary and post-secondary non-tertiary education. At the tertiary level, institutions may offer housing services and often conduct a wide range of research activities.

This indicator compares countries with respect to how they divide spending between current and capital expenditure and how they allocate current expenditure. Expenditure is affected by teachers' salaries (see Indicator D3), pension systems, the age distribution of teachers, the size of the non-teaching staff employed in education, and the degree to which expanded enrolments require the construction of new buildings.

INDICATOR B6

Other findings

- **At the primary, secondary and post-secondary non-tertiary levels of education,** OECD countries spend an average of **21% of current expenditure for purposes other than compensating education personnel**. There is little difference between primary and secondary education in terms of the proportion of current expenditure used for purposes other than compensation. In fact, the difference exceeds seven percentage points only in Ireland, Korea and Luxembourg.

- On average, **OECD countries spend 0.2% of GDP on ancillary services provided by primary, secondary and post-secondary non-tertiary institutions. This proportion exceeds 0.4% of GDP in Finland, France, Korea, Sweden and the United Kingdom.** In these five countries, as well as in Hungary and the Slovak Republic, at least 10% of total expenditure by educational institutions is allocated to ancillary services at these levels of education.

- An average of **25% of expenditure by tertiary institutions is for research and development** in OECD countries. The fact that some tertiary educational institutions spend much more than others on research and development (the proportion is above 45% in Sweden, Switzerland and the United Kingdom) helps explain large differences in total tertiary spending.

Analysis

Expenditure on instruction, research and development, and ancillary services

Below the tertiary level, most educational funding is directed to core services, such as instruction. At the tertiary level, other services – particularly those related to research and development (R&D) – can account for a significant proportion of educational spending. Differences among OECD countries in expenditure on R&D activities therefore explain a significant part of the differences in overall expenditure per tertiary-level student (Table B6.1 and Chart B6.2). For example, high levels of R&D spending (between 0.4% and 0.8% of GDP) in tertiary educational institutions in Australia, Austria, Belgium, Canada, Finland, France, Germany, Ireland, the Netherlands, Norway, Portugal, Sweden, Switzerland and the United Kingdom imply that spending on educational institutions per student in these countries would be considerably lower if the R&D component were excluded (Table B1.1a).

Chart B6.2. Expenditure on core educational services, R&D and ancillary services in tertiary educational institutions as a percentage of GDP (2008)

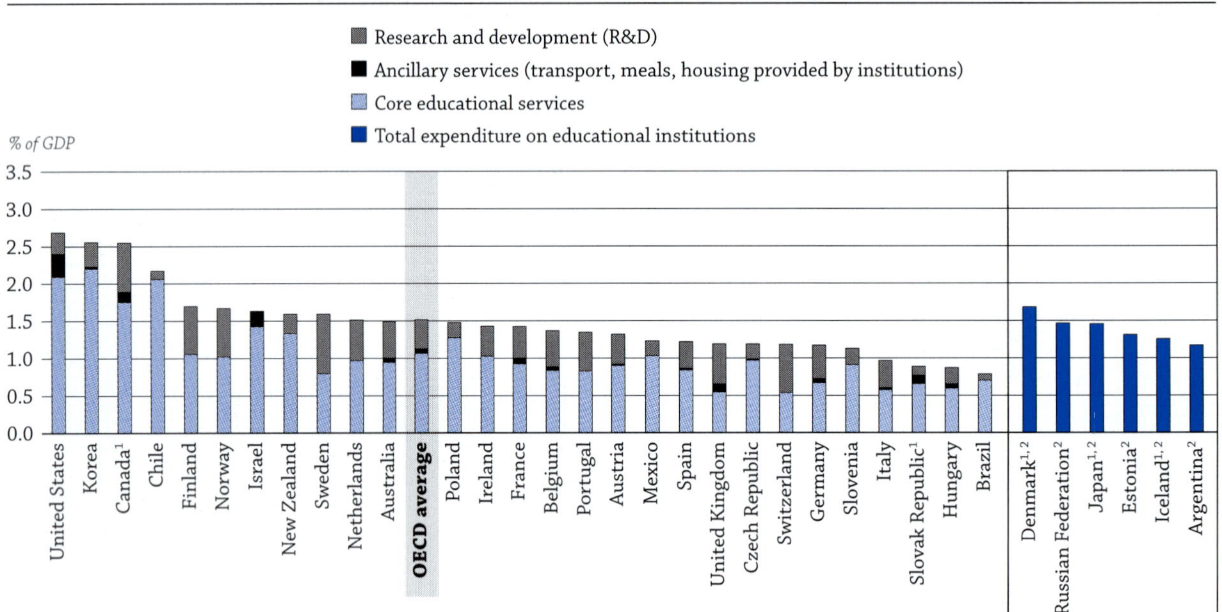

1. Some levels of education are included with others. Refer to "x" code in Table B1.1a for details.
2. Total expenditure at tertiary level including expenditure on research and development (R&D).
Countries are ranked in descending order of total expenditure on educational institutions in tertiary institutions.
Source: OECD. Argentina: UNESCO Institute for Statistics (World Education Indicators Programme). Table B6.1. See Annex 3 for notes (*www.oecd.org/edu/eag2011*).
StatLink http://dx.doi.org/10.1787/888932461275

Student welfare services

Student welfare services and, in some cases, services for the general public are an integral function of schools and universities in many OECD countries. Countries finance these ancillary services with different combinations of public expenditure, public subsidies and fees paid by students and their families.

On average in OECD countries, less than 7% of total spending by primary, secondary and post-secondary non-tertiary institutions goes towards ancillary services, but in Finland, France, Hungary, Korea, the Slovak Republic, Sweden and the United Kingdom this proportion is over 10% (Table B6.1).

Ancillary services are financed by users more often at the tertiary level than at the primary or secondary levels. On average in OECD countries, expenditure on subsidies for ancillary services at the tertiary level amounts to less than 0.10% of GDP but represents 0.14% in Canada, 0.21% in Israel, and up to 0.31% in the United States (Table B6.1).

Current and capital expenditure and the distribution of current expenditure

Educational expenditure includes both current and capital expenditure. Capital expenditure by educational institutions refers to spending on assets that last longer than one year and includes spending on the construction, renovation and major repair of buildings. Current expenditure by educational institutions includes spending on school resources used each year to operate schools.

The labour-intensive nature of instruction explains the large proportion of current spending in total educational expenditure. In primary, secondary and post-secondary non-tertiary education combined, current expenditure accounts for an average of 92% of total spending in OECD countries, and the proportion of current expenditure ranges from 82% in Luxembourg to 97% or more in Austria, Chile, Mexico and Portugal (Table B6.2b and Chart B6.3).

Chart B6.3. Distribution of current and capital expenditure on educational institutions (2008)
By resource category and level of education

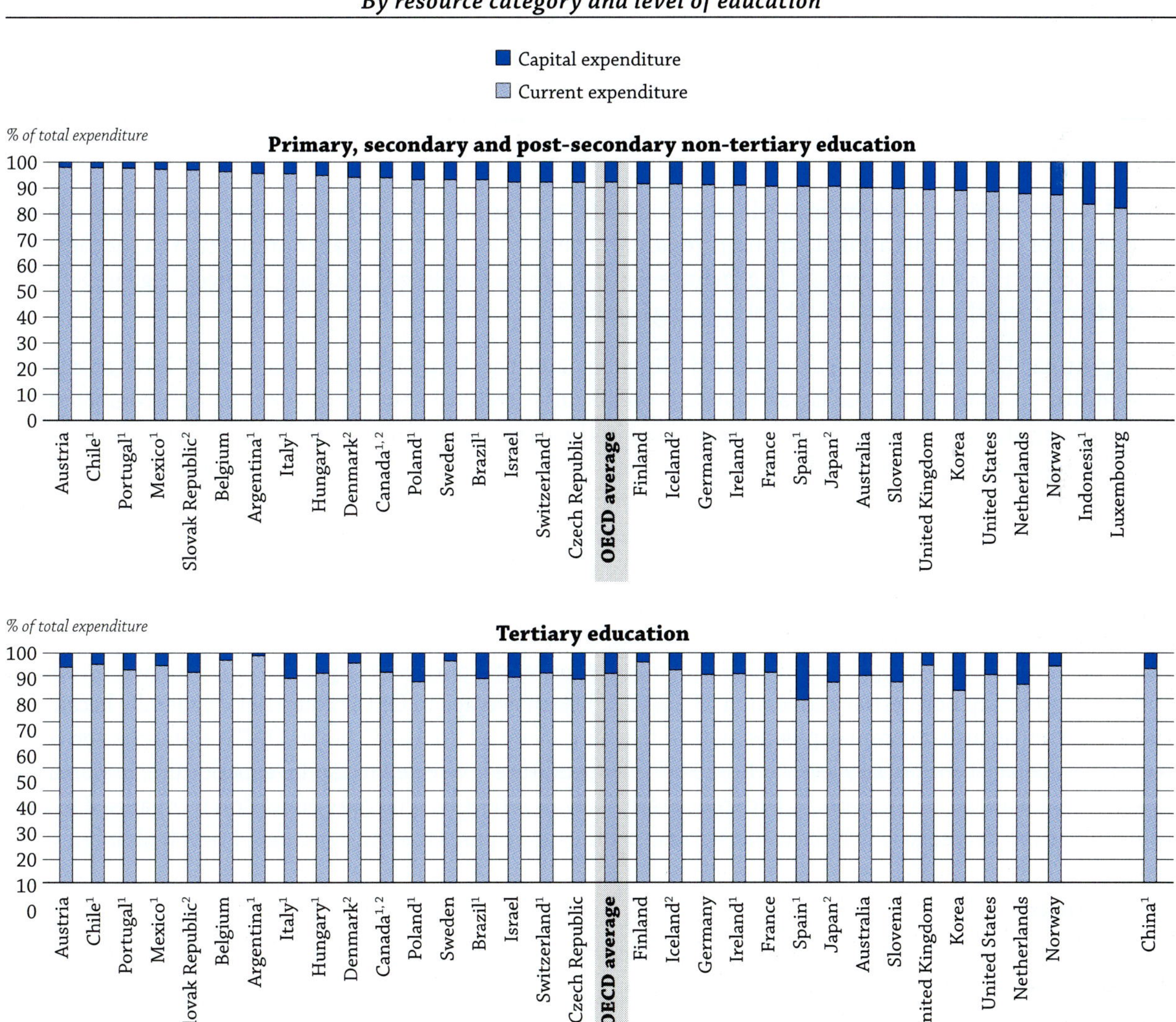

1. Public institutions only (for Canada, at the tertiary level only).
2. Some levels of education are included with others. Refer to "x" code in Table B1.1a for details.
Countries are ranked in descending order of the share of current expenditure by primary, secondary and post-secondary non-tertiary education.
Source: OECD. Argentina, Indonesia: UNESCO Institute for Statistics (World Education Indicators Programme). China: China Educational Finance Statistics Yearbook 2009. Table B6.2b. See Annex 3 for notes (*www.oecd.org/edu/eag2011*).
StatLink http://dx.doi.org/10.1787/888932461294

Proportion of current expenditure allocated to compensation of teachers and other staff, by educational institutions

Current expenditure by educational institutions can be further subdivided into three broad functional categories: compensation of teachers, compensation of other staff and other current expenditures, such as teaching materials and supplies, maintenance of school buildings, preparation of students' meals, and rental of school facilities. The amount allocated to each of these categories depends partly on current and projected changes in enrolments, on salaries of educational personnel, and on the costs of maintenance and construction of educational facilities.

The salaries of teachers and other education staff account for the largest proportion of current expenditure in all countries. In OECD countries, expenditure on compensation accounts for an average of 79% of current expenditure on primary, secondary and post-secondary non-tertiary education combined. In all countries except the Czech Republic, Finland, Poland, the Slovak Republic and Sweden, 70% or more of current expenditure at these levels is spent on staff salaries. The proportion devoted to staff compensation is over 90% in Argentina, Indonesia, Mexico and Portugal (Chart B6.1 and Table B6.2b).

Differences in the average proportion of expenditure on staff compensation between the primary and secondary levels of education exceed seven percentage points in Ireland, Korea and Luxembourg (Table B6.2a). This is mainly due to significant differences in teachers' salaries, class sizes, sizes of non-teaching staff, instruction hours received by students and teaching time of teachers between the two levels (see Indicators B7, D1, D2, D3 and D4).

OECD countries with relatively small education budgets, such as Mexico and Portugal, tend to allocate a larger proportion of current educational expenditure to staff compensation and a smaller proportion to subcontracts for services such as support services (e.g. maintenance of school buildings), ancillary services (e.g. preparation of students' meals), and rental of school buildings and other facilities.

In Argentina, Denmark, France, the United Kingdom and the United States, more than 20% of current expenditure in primary, secondary and post-secondary non-tertiary education, goes towards compensating non-teaching staff, while in Austria, Korea and Spain the figure is less than 10%. These differences are likely to reflect the degree to which education personnel, such as principals, guidance counsellors, bus drivers, school nurses, janitors and maintenance workers, are included in this category (Table B6.2b). At the tertiary level, OECD countries spend an average of 32% of current expenditure for purposes other than compensating personnel. This is due to the higher cost of facilities and equipment in higher education (Table B6.2b).

Proportion of capital expenditure

At the tertiary level, the proportion of total expenditure for capital outlays is larger than for primary, secondary and post-secondary non-tertiary education (9.1% vs. 7.9% on average in OECD countries), generally because of the greater differentiation and sophistication of teaching facilities. In 10 of the 30 OECD countries for which data are available at the tertiary level, at least 10% of expenditure is directed to capital expenditure; in Korea and Spain, it is at least 16% (Chart B6.3). Differences are likely to reflect how tertiary education is organised in each country and the degree to which the expansion in enrolments requires the construction of new buildings.

Definitions

The distinction between current and capital expenditure by educational institutions is taken from the standard definition used in national income accounting.

Current expenditure refers to spending on goods and services consumed within the current year and requiring recurrent production in order to sustain educational services. Current expenditure by educational institutions other than on compensation of personnel includes expenditure on sub-contracted services such as support services (e.g. maintenance of school buildings), ancillary services (e.g. preparation of meals for students) and rental of school buildings and other facilities. These services are obtained from outside providers, unlike the services provided by the education authorities or by the educational institutions using their own personnel.

Capital expenditure refers to spending on assets that last longer than one year, including construction, renovation or major repair of buildings and new or replacement equipment. The capital expenditure reported here represents the value of educational capital acquired or created during the year in question – that is, the amount of capital formation – regardless of whether the capital expenditure was financed from current revenue or through borrowing.

Neither current nor capital expenditure includes **debt servicing**.

Core educational services include all expenditure that is directly related to instruction in educational institutions. This should cover all expenditure on teachers, school buildings, teaching materials, books, and administration of schools.

Expenditure on R&D includes all expenditure on research performed at universities and other tertiary educational institutions, regardless of whether the research is financed from general institutional funds or through separate grants or contracts from public or private sponsors. The classification of expenditure is based on data collected from the institutions carrying out R&D rather than on the sources of funds.

Ancillary services are defined as services provided by educational institutions that are peripheral to the main educational mission. The main component of ancillary services is student welfare services. In primary, secondary and post-secondary non-tertiary education, student welfare services include such things as meals, school health services, and transportation to and from school. At the tertiary level, they include halls of residence (dormitories), dining halls, and health care.

Methodology

Data refer to the financial year 2008 and are based on the UOE data collection on education statistics administered by the OECD in 2010 (for details see Annex 3 at *www.oecd.org/edu/eag2011*).

Calculations cover expenditure by public institutions or, where available, by both public and private institutions.

Educational core services are estimated as the residual of all expenditure, that is, total expenditure on educational institutions net of expenditure on R&D and ancillary services.

The indicator does not include public and private R&D spending outside educational institutions, such as R&D spending in industry. A review of R&D spending in sectors other than education is provided in the publication *Main Science and Technology Indicators* (OECD, 2010g).

Expenditure on student welfare services provided by educational institutions only includes public subsidies for those services; expenditure by students and their families on services that are provided by institutions on a self-funding basis is not included in this indicator.

The statistical data for Israel are supplied by and under the responsibility of the relevant Israeli authorities. The use of such data by the OECD is without prejudice to the status of the Golan Heights, East Jerusalem and Israeli settlements in the West Bank under the terms of international law.

References

OECD (2010g), *Main Science and Technology Indicators,* Volume 2010, Issue 1, OECD, Paris.

Table B6.1. Expenditure on educational institutions by service category as a percentage of GDP (2008)

Expenditure on instruction, R&D and ancillary services in educational institutions and private expenditure on educational goods purchased outside educational institutions

		Primary, secondary and post-secondary non-tertiary education				Tertiary education				
		Expenditure on educational institutions				Expenditure on educational institutions				
		Core educational services	Ancillary services (transport, meals, housing provided by institutions)	Total	Private payments on instructional services/ goods outside educational institutions	Core educational services	Ancillary services (transport, meals, housing provided by institutions)	Research & development at tertiary institutions	Total	Private payments on instructional services/ goods outside educational institutions
		(1)	(2)	(3)	(4)	(5)	(6)	(7)	(8)	(9)
OECD	Australia	3.49	0.08	**3.57**	0.07	0.95	0.06	0.48	**1.49**	0.09
	Austria	3.42	0.17	**3.59**	m	0.91	0.01	0.40	**1.32**	m
	Belgium	4.31	0.13	**4.43**	0.11	0.83	0.05	0.48	**1.37**	0.17
	Canada[1, 2, 3]	3.30	0.19	**3.49**	m	1.75	0.14	0.66	**2.55**	0.10
	Chile[4]	3.86	0.31	**4.17**	m	2.06	x(5)	0.11	**2.17**	n
	Czech Republic	2.53	0.22	**2.75**	0.04	0.98	0.01	0.20	**1.19**	0.03
	Denmark[2]	x(3)	x(3)	**4.28**	0.48	x(8)	m	x(8)	**1.68**	0.62
	Estonia	x(3)	x(3)	**3.89**	m	x(8)	x(8)	n	**1.31**	m
	Finland	3.37	0.41	**3.78**	m	1.06	a	0.64	**1.70**	m
	France	3.41	0.48	**3.89**	0.16	0.92	0.08	0.42	**1.42**	0.07
	Germany	2.91	0.08	**2.99**	0.15	0.67	0.05	0.45	**1.17**	0.08
	Greece	m	m	**m**	m	m	m	m	**m**	m
	Hungary[3]	2.64	0.33	**2.97**	m	0.59	0.06	0.22	**0.87**	m
	Iceland	x(3)	x(3)	**5.07**	m	x(8)	x(8)	x(8)	**1.25**	m
	Ireland[3]	4.13	m	**4.13**	0.04	1.03	m	0.40	**1.43**	m
	Israel	3.97	0.23	**4.20**	0.26	1.42	0.21	m	**1.63**	n
	Italy[3]	3.21	0.12	**3.33**	0.37	0.57	0.03	0.36	**0.97**	0.13
	Japan[2]	x(3)	x(3)	**2.78**	0.75	x(8)	x(8)	x(8)	**1.45**	0.04
	Korea	3.59	0.56	**4.15**	m	2.20	0.03	0.33	**2.56**	m
	Luxembourg	2.77	0.14	**2.90**	0.05	m	m	m	**m**	m
	Mexico	3.70	m	**3.70**	0.18	1.03	m	0.20	**1.23**	0.04
	Netherlands	3.70	n	**3.70**	0.18	0.97	n	0.54	**1.51**	0.06
	New Zealand	x(3)	x(3)	**4.49**	n	1.33	x(8)	0.26	**1.59**	n
	Norway	x(3)	x(3)	**4.95**	m	1.02	n	0.65	**1.67**	m
	Poland[3]	3.60	0.01	**3.61**	0.26	1.27	n	0.20	**1.48**	0.05
	Portugal[3]	3.33	0.07	**3.40**	0.07	0.83	x(8)	0.52	**1.34**	m
	Slovak Republic[2]	2.23	0.37	**2.60**	0.31	0.65	0.11	0.12	**0.89**	0.21
	Slovenia	3.50	0.18	**3.68**	m	0.91	n	0.22	**1.13**	m
	Spain	2.92	0.15	**3.07**	m	0.84	0.02	0.36	**1.22**	m
	Sweden	3.63	0.42	**4.04**	m	0.80	n	0.79	**1.59**	m
	Switzerland[3]	x(3)	x(3)	**4.28**	m	0.54	x(8)	0.64	**1.18**	m
	Turkey	m	m	**m**	m	m	m	m	**m**	m
	United Kingdom	3.45	0.79	**4.24**	m	0.55	0.11	0.54	**1.19**	0.09
	United States	3.83	0.32	**4.15**	m	2.09	0.31	0.28	**2.69**	a
	OECD average	3.39	0.25	**3.76**	0.21	1.07	0.06	0.39	**1.49**	0.10
Other G20	Argentina	x(3)	x(3)	**4.31**	m	x(8)	x(8)	x(8)	**1.17**	m
	Brazil[3]	x(3)	x(3)	**4.10**	m	0.70	x(5)	0.08	**0.79**	m
	China	m	m	**m**	m	m	m	m	**m**	m
	India	m	m	**m**	m	m	m	m	**m**	m
	Indonesia	m	m	**m**	m	m	m	m	**m**	m
	Russian Federation[3]	x(3)	x(3)	**2.05**	m	x(8)	x(8)	x(8)	**1.46**	m
	Saudi Arabia	m	m	**m**	m	m	m	m	**m**	m
	South Africa	m	m	**m**	m	m	m	m	**m**	m

1. Year of reference 2007.
2. Some levels of education are included with others. Refer to "x" code in Table B1.1a for details.
3. Public institutions only (for Canada, in tertiary education only; for Italy, except in tertiary education).
4. Year of reference 2009.

Source: OECD. Argentina: UNESCO Institute for Statistics (World Education Indicators Programme). See Annex 3 for notes *(www.oecd.org/edu/eag2011)*.
Please refer to the Reader's Guide for information concerning the symbols replacing missing data.
StatLink http://dx.doi.org/10.1787/888932464087

Table B6.2a. Expenditure by educational institutions, by resource category in primary and secondary education (2008)

Distribution of total and current expenditure by educational institutions from public and private sources

	Primary education						Secondary education					
	Percentage of total expenditure		Percentage of current expenditure				Percentage of total expenditure		Percentage of current expenditure			
	Current	Capital	Compensation of teachers	Compensation of other staff	Compensation of all staff	Other current expenditure	Current	Capital	Compensation of teachers	Compensation of other staff	Compensation of all staff	Other current expenditure
	(1)	(2)	(3)	(4)	(5)	(6)	(7)	(8)	(9)	(10)	(11)	(12)
OECD												
Australia	**90.5**	**9.5**	63.7	14.2	77.8	22.2	**89.2**	**10.8**	60.0	16.2	76.2	23.8
Austria	**97.7**	**2.3**	61.5	12.4	74.0	26.0	**98.0**	**2.0**	72.2	5.1	77.3	22.7
Belgium[1]	**95.0**	**5.0**	66.1	20.2	86.3	13.7	**97.0**	**3.1**	69.7	16.3	86.0	14.0
Canada[1, 2]	**93.9**	**6.1**	62.4	15.5	77.8	22.2	**93.9**	**6.1**	62.4	15.5	77.8	22.2
Chile[3, 4]	**97.9**	**2.1**	x(5)	x(5)	88.2	11.8	**97.7**	**2.3**	x(11)	x(11)	86.6	13.4
Czech Republic	**90.4**	**9.6**	47.0	18.6	65.6	34.4	**92.5**	**7.5**	43.7	17.0	60.7	39.3
Denmark[1]	**91.9**	**8.1**	52.0	28.0	80.0	20.0	**95.7**	**4.3**	54.8	26.2	80.9	19.1
Estonia	**m**	**m**	m	m	m	m	**m**	**m**	m	m	m	m
Finland[1]	**91.2**	**8.8**	57.1	9.0	66.1	33.9	**91.6**	**8.4**	51.7	12.2	63.9	36.1
France	**93.1**	**6.9**	54.3	23.1	77.3	22.7	**89.4**	**10.6**	59.2	23.0	82.2	17.8
Germany	**92.4**	**7.6**	x(5)	x(5)	83.0	17.0	**90.7**	**9.3**	x(11)	x(11)	81.2	18.8
Greece	**m**	**m**	m	m	m	m	**m**	**m**	m	m	m	m
Hungary[3]	**96.4**	**3.6**	x(5)	x(5)	79.2	20.8	**94.3**	**5.7**	x(11)	x(11)	78.5	21.5
Iceland[1]	**89.5**	**10.5**	x(5)	x(5)	76.5	23.5	**93.3**	**6.7**	x(11)	x(11)	73.8	26.2
Ireland[3]	**86.3**	**13.7**	76.3	13.2	89.4	10.6	**95.4**	**4.6**	67.0	9.0	76.1	23.9
Israel	**91.2**	**8.8**	x(5)	x(5)	81.8	18.2	**93.1**	**6.9**	x(11)	x(11)	84.9	15.1
Italy[3]	**94.9**	**5.1**	66.4	16.9	83.3	16.7	**95.8**	**4.2**	67.5	16.0	83.5	16.5
Japan[1]	**90.6**	**9.4**	x(5)	x(5)	87.3	12.7	**90.4**	**9.6**	x(11)	x(11)	86.8	13.2
Korea	**87.5**	**12.5**	64.1	11.8	75.9	24.1	**89.7**	**10.3**	59.0	8.5	67.6	32.4
Luxembourg	**81.9**	**18.1**	87.7	6.4	94.1	5.9	**82.2**	**17.8**	73.6	13.3	86.9	13.1
Mexico[3]	**98.1**	**1.9**	85.5	8.6	94.0	6.0	**95.9**	**4.1**	74.3	17.2	91.5	8.5
Netherlands	**87.7**	**12.3**	x(5)	x(5)	84.1	15.9	**87.6**	**12.4**	x(11)	x(11)	81.3	18.7
New Zealand	**m**	**m**	m	m	m	m	**m**	**m**	m	m	m	m
Norway[1]	**87.1**	**12.9**	x(5)	x(5)	78.3	21.7	**87.3**	**12.7**	x(11)	x(11)	77.4	22.6
Poland[3]	**92.3**	**7.7**	x(5)	x(5)	68.9	31.1	**93.8**	**6.2**	x(11)	x(11)	65.5	34.5
Portugal[3]	**98.6**	**1.4**	81.5	13.6	95.2	4.8	**96.8**	**3.2**	82.8	10.5	93.3	6.7
Slovak Republic[1]	**97.0**	**3.0**	50.3	14.2	64.5	35.5	**96.9**	**3.1**	50.7	14.1	64.8	35.2
Slovenia[1]	**x(7)**	**x(8)**	x(9)	x(10)	x(11)	x(12)	**89.6**	**10.4**	x(11)	x(11)	77.2	22.8
Spain[3]	**91.3**	**8.7**	70.8	10.9	81.7	18.3	**89.9**	**10.1**	74.9	8.5	83.5	16.5
Sweden	**93.5**	**6.5**	52.9	17.7	70.6	29.4	**92.8**	**7.2**	50.2	17.2	67.4	32.6
Switzerland[1, 3]	**90.3**	**9.7**	68.6	14.8	83.4	16.6	**93.2**	**6.8**	69.7	16.8	86.6	13.4
Turkey	**m**	**m**	m	m	m	m	**m**	**m**	m	m	m	m
United Kingdom[1]	**88.1**	**11.9**	45.7	31.0	76.7	23.3	**90.0**	**10.0**	58.2	15.7	73.9	26.1
United States	**88.4**	**11.6**	55.0	26.1	81.1	18.9	**88.4**	**11.6**	55.0	26.1	81.1	18.9
OECD average	**91.9**	**8.1**	63.4	16.3	80.1	19.9	**92.4**	**7.6**	62.8	15.2	78.5	21.5
Other G20												
Argentina[3]	**94.9**	**5.1**	68.8	22.0	90.7	9.3	**96.0**	**4.0**	67.4	23.6	91.0	9.0
Brazil[3]	**93.2**	**6.8**	x(5)	x(5)	72.0	28.0	**92.9**	**7.1**	x(11)	x(11)	73.0	27.0
China[3]	**98.8**	**1.2**	m	m	m	m	**97.2**	**2.8**	m	m	m	m
India	**m**	**m**	m	m	m	m	**m**	**m**	m	m	m	m
Indonesia[2, 3]	**85.0**	**15.0**	80.8	10.7	91.5	8.5	**77.3**	**22.7**	77.6	9.7	87.3	12.7
Russian Federation	**m**	**m**	m	m	m	m	**m**	**m**	m	m	m	m
Saudi Arabia	**m**	**m**	m	m	m	m	**m**	**m**	m	m	m	m
South Africa	**m**	**m**	m	m	m	m	**m**	**m**	m	m	m	m
G20 average	**92.1**	**7.9**	m	m	m	m	**91.2**	**8.8**	m	m	m	m

1. Some levels of education are included with others. Refer to «x» code in Table B1.1a for details.
2. Year of reference 2007.
3. Public institutions only.
4. Year of reference 2009.

Source: OECD. Argentina, Indonesia: UNESCO Institute for Statistics (World Education Indicators Programme). China: China Educational Finance Statistics Yearbook 2009. See Annex 3 for notes *(www.oecd.org/edu/eag2011)*.

Please refer to the Reader's Guide for information concerning the symbols replacing missing data.

StatLink http://dx.doi.org/10.1787/888932464106

Table B6.2b. **Expenditure by educational institutions, by resource category and level of education (2008)**

Distribution of total and current expenditure by educational institutions from public and private sources

		Primary, secondary and post-secondary non-tertiary education						Tertiary education					
		Percentage of total expenditure		Percentage of current expenditure				Percentage of total expenditure		Percentage of current expenditure			
		Current	Capital	Compensation of teachers	Compensation of other staff	Compensation of all staff	Other current expenditure	Current	Capital	Compensation of teachers	Compensation of other staff	Compensation of all staff	Other current expenditure
		(1)	(2)	(3)	(4)	(5)	(6)	(7)	(8)	(9)	(10)	(11)	(12)
OECD	Australia	**89.8**	**10.2**	61.3	15.5	76.8	23.2	**89.9**	**10.1**	32.9	27.8	60.7	39.3
	Austria	**97.9**	**2.1**	68.9	7.2	76.1	23.9	**93.7**	**6.3**	60.1	2.6	62.6	37.4
	Belgium	**96.2**	**3.8**	68.4	17.7	86.1	13.9	**96.7**	**3.3**	49.4	29.2	78.6	21.4
	Canada[1, 2, 3]	**93.9**	**6.1**	62.4	15.5	77.8	22.2	**91.5**	**8.5**	37.5	26.8	64.2	35.8
	Chile[3, 4]	**97.8**	**2.2**	x(5)	x(5)	87.4	12.6	**94.9**	**5.1**	x(11)	x(11)	65.2	34.8
	Czech Republic	**92.1**	**7.9**	44.5	17.3	61.8	38.2	**88.3**	**11.7**	32.6	18.8	51.4	48.6
	Denmark[2]	**94.0**	**6.0**	53.6	27.0	80.6	19.4	**95.5**	**4.5**	55.1	26.6	81.7	18.3
	Estonia	**m**	**m**	m	m	m	m	**m**	**m**	m	m	m	m
	Finland	**91.5**	**8.5**	53.5	11.1	64.6	35.4	**95.8**	**4.2**	34.8	28.7	63.5	36.5
	France	**90.5**	**9.5**	57.6	23.0	80.6	19.4	**91.3**	**8.7**	49.0	29.3	78.2	21.8
	Germany	**91.1**	**8.9**	x(5)	x(5)	81.3	18.7	**90.4**	**9.6**	x(11)	x(11)	65.7	34.3
	Greece	**m**	**m**	m	m	m	m	**m**	**m**	m	m	m	m
	Hungary[3]	**94.7**	**5.3**	x(5)	x(5)	78.5	21.5	**91.0**	**9.0**	x(11)	x(11)	64.7	35.3
	Iceland	**91.4**	**8.6**	x(5)	x(5)	75.1	24.9	**92.4**	**7.6**	x(11)	x(11)	82.6	17.4
	Ireland[3]	**90.9**	**9.1**	71.5	10.9	82.4	17.6	**90.7**	**9.3**	45.0	28.8	73.8	26.2
	Israel	**92.1**	**7.9**	x(5)	x(5)	83.2	16.8	**89.2**	**10.8**	x(11)	x(11)	82.6	17.4
	Italy[3]	**95.4**	**4.6**	66.2	16.3	82.5	17.5	**88.8**	**11.2**	35.5	30.5	66.1	33.9
	Japan[2]	**90.5**	**9.5**	x(5)	x(5)	87.0	13.0	**87.0**	**13.0**	x(11)	x(11)	60.1	39.9
	Korea	**88.9**	**11.1**	61.0	9.8	70.7	29.3	**83.5**	**16.5**	35.4	18.1	53.5	46.5
	Luxembourg	**82.1**	**17.9**	78.9	10.7	89.7	10.4	**m**	**m**	m	m	m	m
	Mexico[3]	**97.1**	**2.9**	80.7	12.3	92.9	7.1	**94.4**	**5.6**	53.3	13.6	66.8	33.2
	Netherlands	**87.7**	**12.3**	x(5)	x(5)	82.3	17.7	**86.1**	**13.9**	x(11)	x(11)	69.9	30.1
	New Zealand	**m**	**m**	m	m	m	m	**m**	**m**	m	m	m	m
	Norway	**87.2**	**12.8**	x(5)	x(5)	77.8	22.2	**94.1**	**5.9**	x(11)	x(11)	66.7	33.3
	Poland[3]	**93.1**	**6.9**	x(5)	x(5)	67.0	33.0	**87.3**	**12.7**	x(11)	x(11)	76.7	23.3
	Portugal[3]	**97.6**	**2.4**	82.3	11.8	94.1	5.9	**92.5**	**7.5**	x(11)	x(11)	71.6	28.4
	Slovak Republic[2]	**96.9**	**3.1**	50.6	14.1	64.7	35.3	**91.4**	**8.6**	29.6	21.6	51.2	48.8
	Slovenia	**89.6**	**10.5**	x(5)	x(5)	77.2	22.8	**87.1**	**12.9**	x(11)	x(11)	67.7	32.4
	Spain[3]	**90.5**	**9.5**	73.3	9.5	82.7	17.3	**79.4**	**20.6**	55.9	21.4	77.3	22.7
	Sweden	**93.1**	**6.9**	51.3	17.4	68.7	31.3	**96.3**	**3.7**	x(11)	x(11)	63.0	37.0
	Switzerland[3]	**92.1**	**7.9**	69.3	16.1	85.4	14.6	**91.1**	**8.9**	47.0	27.8	74.9	25.1
	Turkey	**m**	**m**	m	m	m	m	**m**	**m**	m	m	m	m
	United Kingdom	**89.2**	**10.8**	53.0	22.0	75.1	24.9	**94.4**	**5.6**	44.7	38.2	82.9	17.1
	United States	**88.4**	**11.6**	55.0	26.1	81.1	18.9	**90.3**	**9.7**	26.0	36.2	62.2	37.8
	OECD average	**92.1**	**7.9**	63.2	15.6	79.0	21.0	**90.9**	**9.1**	42.6	25.1	68.5	31.5
Other G20	Argentina[3]	**95.5**	**4.5**	68.1	22.8	90.9	9.1	**98.8**	**1.2**	56.0	34.7	90.7	9.3
	Brazil[3]	**93.0**	**7.0**	x(5)	x(5)	72.6	27.4	**88.7**	**11.3**	x(11)	x(11)	77.9	22.1
	China[3]	**m**	**m**	m	m	m	m	**93.0**	**7.0**	m	m	m	m
	India	**m**	**m**	m	m	m	m	**m**	**m**	m	m	m	m
	Indonesia[1, 3]	**83.6**	**16.4**	80.3	10.6	90.8	9.2	**m**	**m**	13.1	1.0	14.1	85.9
	Russian Federation	**m**	**m**	m	m	m	m	**m**	**m**	m	m	m	m
	Saudi Arabia	**m**	**m**	m	m	m	m	**m**	**m**	m	m	m	m
	South Africa	**m**	**m**	m	m	m	m	**m**	**m**	m	m	m	m
	G20 average	**m**	**m**	m	m	m	m	**90.9**	**9.1**	m	m	m	m

1. Year of reference 2007.
2. Some levels of education are included with others. Refer to "x" code in Table B1.1a for details.
3. Public institutions only (for Canada, at the tertiary level only; for Italy, except in tertiary education).
4. Year of reference 2009.

Source: OECD. Argentina, Indonesia: UNESCO Institute for Statistics (World Education Indicators Programme). China: China Educational Finance Statistics Yearbook 2009. See Annex 3 for notes *(www.oecd.org/edu/eag2011)*.

Please refer to the Reader's Guide for information concerning the symbols replacing missing data.

StatLink http://dx.doi.org/10.1787/888932464125

WHICH FACTORS INFLUENCE THE LEVEL OF EXPENDITURE?

- Four factors (instruction time of students, teaching time of teachers, teachers' salaries and class size) influence salary cost per student; consequently, a given level of salary cost per student can result from many different combinations of these factors. Salary cost per student at the upper secondary level varies significantly among OECD countries: from USD 539 in Chile to more than ten times that amount in Luxembourg, Spain and Switzerland.
- Teachers' salaries and class size are usually the main drivers of the difference from the average salary cost per student at the primary, lower secondary and upper secondary levels. However, class size is less often the main factor when the level of education increases.

Chart B7.1. Contribution (in USD) of various factors to salary cost per student, at the upper secondary level of education (2008)

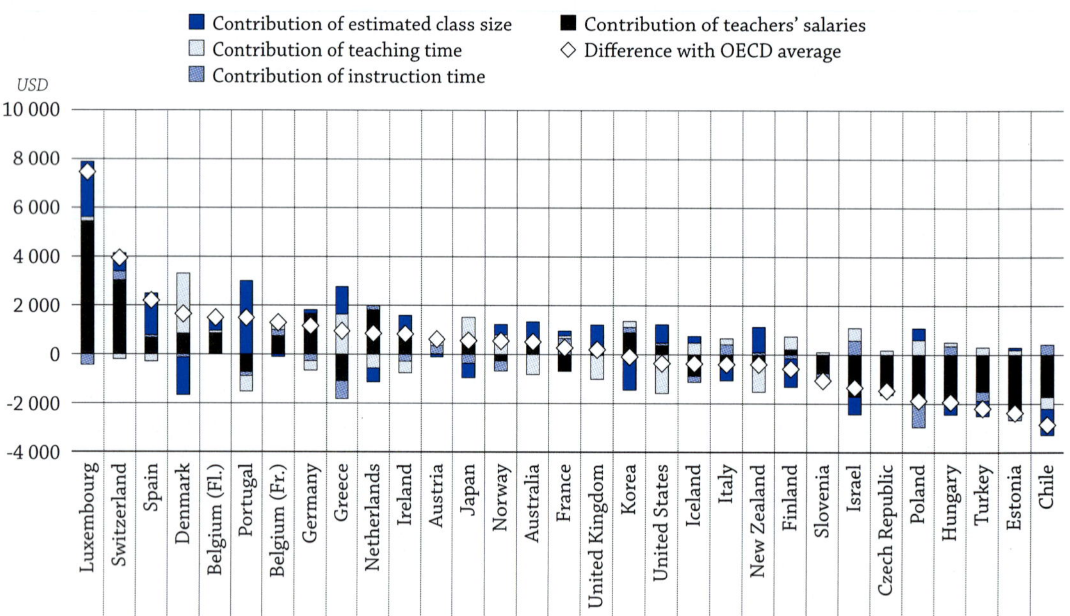

Countries are ranked in descending order of the difference between the salary cost and the OECD average.
Source: OECD. Table B7.3. See Annex 3 for notes (*www.oecd.org/edu/eag2011*).
StatLink http://dx.doi.org/10.1787/888932461313

How to read this chart
The chart shows the extent to which various factors associated with salary cost contribute to the difference, in US dollars, between a country's salary cost per student and that of the OECD average. For example, in Spain, the salary cost per student is USD 2 201 higher than the OECD average. This is because Spain has higher teachers' salaries (+USD 686) than the OECD average, annual instruction time for students close to the OECD average (+USD 94) and above-average teaching time for teachers (-USD 291) compared to the OECD average. However, Spain also has significantly smaller-than-average class size (+USD 1 711).

Context

The relationship between the resources devoted to education and the outcomes achieved has been the focus of much education policy debate in recent years as governments seek to provide more and better education for the entire population. At the same time, given the increasing pressure on public budgets, there is intense interest in ensuring that funding – public funding, in particular – is directed so as to achieve the desired outcomes as efficiently as possible.

Many factors affect the relationship between spending per student and student performance. They include the organisation and management of schooling within the system (e.g. layers of management and the distribution of decision making, the geographic dispersion of the population), the organisation of the immediate learning environment of students (e.g. class size, hours of instruction), the quality of the teaching workforce, and characteristics of the students themselves, most notably their socio-economic backgrounds.

Teachers' compensation is usually the largest part of expenditure on education and thus of expenditure per student. It is a function of instruction time of students, teaching time of teachers, teachers' salaries and the number of teachers needed to teach students, which depends on class size (Box B7.1). Differences among countries in these four factors may explain differences in the level of expenditure per student. In the same way, a given level of expenditure may result from a different combination of these factors.

Other findings

- **Similar levels of expenditure among countries in primary and secondary education can mask a variety of contrasting policy choices.** This helps to explain why there is no simple relationship between overall spending on education and the level of student performance. High spending per student cannot automatically be equated with strong performance by education systems and only 17% of the variation in 2009 PISA performance in reading results from the variation in cumulative expenditure per student aged 6 to 15.

- **In most countries, salary cost per student differs more from the OECD average as the level of education increases.** These costs are usually largest at the upper secondary level of education (in 15 of 31 OECD countries) and smallest at the primary level of education (in 20 of 31 OECD countries). This trend is most obvious in countries where the salary cost per student is furthest from the OECD average.

- Comparing salary cost to GDP per capita is a way of accounting for differences in countries' wealth. **Teachers' salaries (as a percentage of GDP per capita) are less often the main driver of the difference from the average salary cost per student when that cost is compared to GDP per capita.** In countries that show high levels of salaries and GDP per capita, such as Luxembourg and Switzerland, and in countries that show low salaries and low GDP per capita, such as the Czech Republic and Turkey, teachers' salaries are not the main driver of the difference from the average relative salary cost per student.

Analysis

Student performance and spending per student

High spending per student cannot automatically be equated with strong performance by education systems, as shown when comparing average student performance on the reading literacy scale of PISA 2009 with the cumulative spending per student between the ages of 6 and 15 in 2008 (Chart B7.2). This is not surprising, as countries might spend similar amounts on education, but not necessarily on similar policies and practices. This helps to explain why there is no simple relationship between overall spending on education and the level of student performance. However, it does not mean that the relationship would be weak if all the determinants of educational spending were analysed separately and by level of education.

Chart B7.2. Relationship between PISA performance in reading at age 15 and cumulative expenditure per student between the ages of 6 and 15 (2008, 2009)

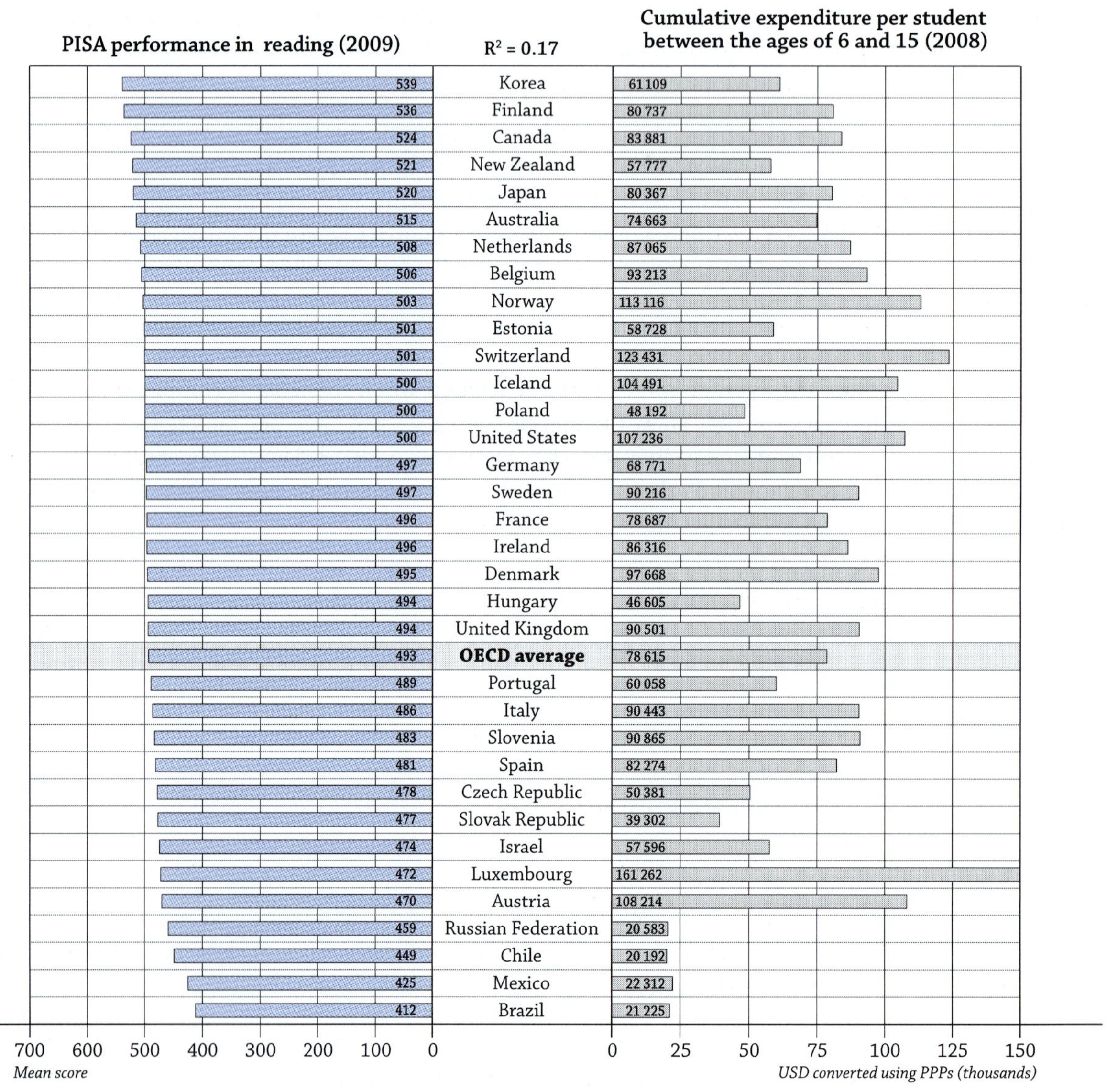

Countries are ranked in descending order of the PISA perfomance in reading of 15-year-olds.

Source: OECD, *PISA 2009 Database*. Table B1.1a. See Annex 3 for notes (*www.oecd.org/edu/eag2011*).

StatLink http://dx.doi.org/10.1787/888932461332

Globally, only 17% of the variation in 2009 PISA performance in reading literacy results from the difference in cumulative expenditure per student between the ages of 6 and 15 (Chart B7.2). Whereas the four countries with the lowest average scores in reading literacy (Brazil, Chile, Mexico and the Russian Federation) also have the lowest levels of cumulative expenditure per student, the four top-performing countries (Canada, Finland, Korea and New Zealand) are not among countries with the highest levels of cumulative expenditure per student between the ages of 6 and 15. On the contrary, the four countries with the highest levels of cumulative expenditure per student between those ages (Austria, Luxembourg, Norway and Switzerland) have an average score in reading literacy varying from slightly above the OECD average (Norway and Switzerland) to well below the OECD average (Austria and Luxembourg).

Differences in the combination of factors at the upper secondary level of education

Since four factors (instruction time of students, teaching time of teachers, teachers' salaries and class size) influence salary cost per student, a given level of salary cost per student can result from many different combinations of these factors.

For example, in both Denmark and Portugal salary costs per student at the upper secondary level are close to and well above the OECD average (USD 5 044 and USD 4 886, respectively), but these countries combine instruction time, teaching time, class size and teachers' salaries in very different ways. In Denmark, relatively large class size and, to a lesser extent, below-average instruction time reduce salary cost per student relative to the OECD average. These effects are more than counterbalanced by relatively high teachers' salaries and, most notably, below-average teaching time. Together these factors result in above-average salary cost per student. In contrast, higher-than-average salary cost per student in Portugal is almost entirely attributable to below-average class size. The impact of small class size largely outweighs the influence of below-average salaries, above-average teaching time, and below-average instruction time for students (Table B7.3 and Chart B7.1).

However, alongside such contrasts, there are also striking similarities in countries' policy choices, even if these similarities can have more or less impact compared to the OECD average and result in different levels of salary cost per student. For example, in Australia, New Zealand, the United Kingdom and the United States, salary cost per student at the upper secondary level is the result of balancing two opposing effects: above-average teaching time acts to reduce salary cost per student relative to the OECD average, and relatively small class size increases salary cost per student relative to the OECD average. However, salary cost per student resulting from this combination is above the OECD average in Australia and the United Kingdom, but below the average in New Zealand and the United States, where teaching time and class size are closer to the OECD averages than in the former two countries (Table B7.3).

Salary cost per student in primary and secondary education

Comparisons of the various levels of education show that differences in salary cost per student compared with the OECD average are largest at the upper secondary level of education in 15 of 31 OECD countries and smallest at the primary level of education in 20 of the 31 OECD countries with available data (Chart B7.3). This trend is most obvious in countries where salary cost per student is furthest from the OECD average. For example, Spain and Switzerland have two of the three highest levels of salary cost per student at the upper secondary level of education while the salary cost per student at the primary and lower secondary levels is at least USD 1 000 lower than at the upper secondary level.

At the **upper secondary level** of education, salary cost per student varies from USD 539 in Chile to around three times the OECD average (USD 3 398) in Luxembourg (USD 10 847). Teachers' salaries account for most of this difference (USD 5 440), as teachers' salaries in Luxembourg are much higher than the OECD average. In Chile, teachers' salaries also account for the large difference from the OECD average salary cost per student, although in the opposite direction (Table B7.3 and Chart B7.1).

Chart B7.3. Difference between the salary cost per student and the OECD average (in USD), by level of education (2008)

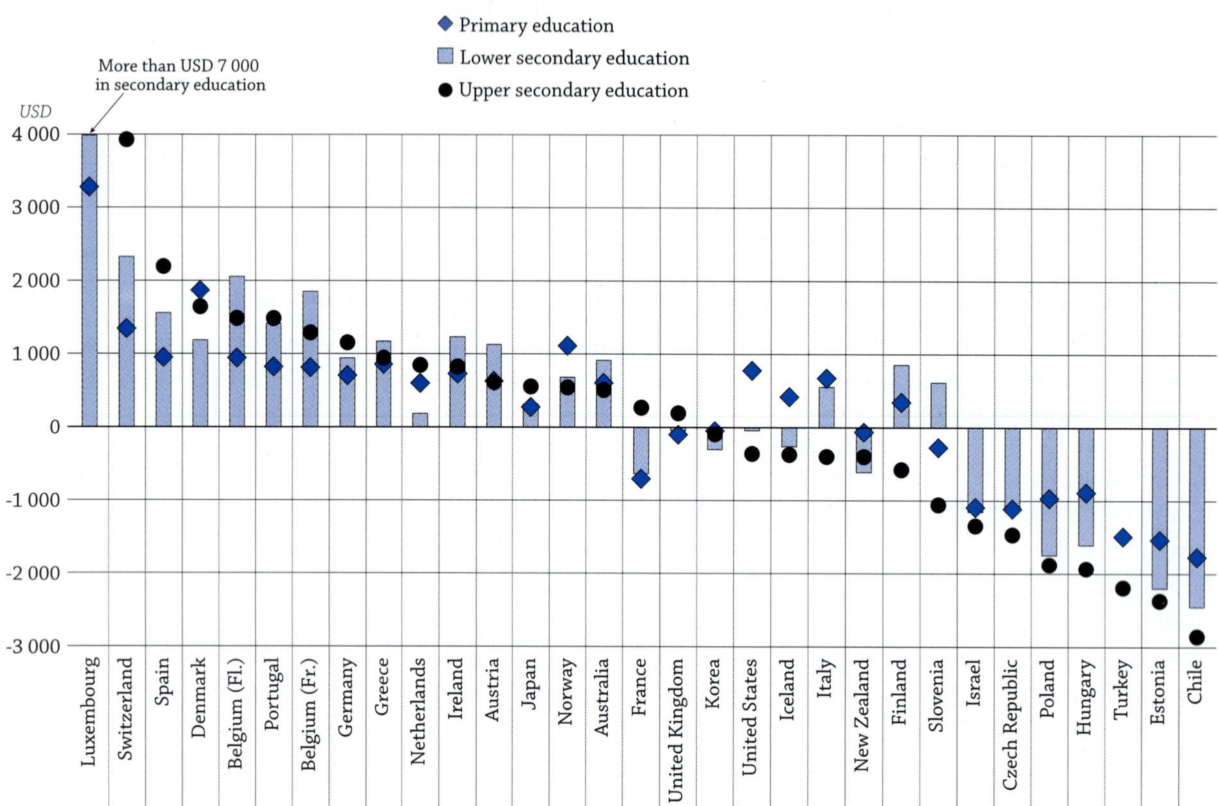

Countries are ranked in descending order of the difference between the salary cost per student and the OECD average in upper secondary education.
Source: OECD. Tables B7.1, B7.2 and B7.3. See Annex 3 for notes (*www.oecd.org/edu/eag2011*).
StatLink http://dx.doi.org/10.1787/888932461351

At the **lower secondary level** of education, salary cost per student is the highest in Luxembourg (USD 10 847, more than three times the OECD average of USD 2 991) and Switzerland (USD 5 325), but is below USD 1 500 only in Chile (USD 538, less than one-fifth of the OECD average), Estonia (USD 791), Hungary (USD 1 385), Mexico (USD 716) and Poland (USD 1 247). The differences among these countries, except for Mexico, are mostly influenced by the level of teachers' salaries (Table B7.2).

At the **primary level** of education, salary cost per student varies from less than USD 550 in Chile (USD 538) to USD 5 595 in Luxembourg, or more than twice the OECD average of USD 2 309. These differences in salary costs per student are mostly influenced by the level of teachers' salaries in these countries (Table B7.1). Teachers' salaries in Luxembourg account for more than USD 2 297 of the difference from the OECD average salary cost per student, as teachers' salaries in Luxembourg are much higher than the OECD average (USD 67 723 compared to the OECD average of USD 36 228). In contrast, in Chile, teachers' salaries account for USD 1 257 of the difference from the OECD average salary cost per student (at USD 12 976, teachers' salaries are much lower than the OECD average of USD 36 228).

Main drivers of the difference from the OECD average salary cost per student

At the **primary** level, of the four factors contributing to the salary cost per student, salary of teachers is most often the main driver of the difference from the OECD average salary cost per student (in 15 of the 32 OECD countries with available data). This is true both in countries with the highest levels of salary cost and the lowest levels of salary cost per student: below-average salaries are the main driver of the difference in seven of the eight countries with the lowest salary costs per student, and above-average salaries are the main driver in two of the three countries with the highest salary costs per student. The main driver of the difference from the OECD average varies more among countries whose salary cost per student is closer to the OECD average (Box B7.2 and Table B7.1). At this level, the second main driver of the difference is class size (in ten countries).

Box B7.1. Relationship between salary cost per student and instruction time of students, teaching time of teachers, teachers' salaries and class size

One way to analyse the factors that have an impact on expenditure per student and to measure the extent of their effects is to compare the differences between national figures and the OECD average. This analysis computes the differences in expenditure per student among countries and the OECD average, and then calculates the contribution of these different factors to the variation from the OECD average.

This exercise is based on a mathematical relationship between the different factors and follows the method presented in the Canadian publication *Education Statistics Bulletin* (2005) (see explanation in Annex 3). Educational expenditure is mathematically linked to factors related to a country's school context (number of hours of instruction time for students, number of teaching hours for teachers, estimated class size) and one factor relating to teachers (statutory salary).

Expenditure is broken down into compensation of teachers and other expenditure (defined as all expenditure other than compensation of teachers). Compensation of teachers divided by the number of students, or "the salary cost per student" (CCS), is estimated through:

$$CCS = SAL \times instT \times \frac{1}{teachT} \times \frac{1}{ClassSize} = \frac{SAL}{Ratiostud/teacher}$$

SAL: teachers' salaries (estimated by statutory salary after 15 years of experience)
instT: instruction time of students (estimated as the annual intended instruction time, in hours, for students)
teachT: teaching time of teachers (estimated as the annual number of teaching hours for teachers)
ClassSize: a proxy for class size
Ratiostud/teacher: the ratio of students to teaching staff

With the exception of class size (which is not computed at the upper secondary level, as class size is difficult to define and compare because students at this level may attend several classes depending on the subject area), values for the different variables can be obtained from the indicators published in *Education at a Glance* (Chapter D). However, for the purpose of the analysis, a "theoretical" class size or proxy class size is estimated based on the ratio of students to teaching staff and the number of teaching hours and instruction hours (Box D2.1). As a proxy, this estimated class size should be interpreted with caution. To facilitate reading, the "estimated class size" is referred to as "class size" in the text.

Using this mathematical relationship and comparing a country's values for the four factors to the OECD averages makes it possible to measure both the direct and indirect contribution of each of these four factors to the variation in salary cost per student between that country and the OECD average (for more details see Annex 3). For example, in the case where only two factors interact, if a worker receives a 10% increase in the hourly wage and increases the number of hours of work by 20%, his/her earnings will increase by 32% as a result of the direct contribution of each of these variations (0.1 + 0.2) and the indirect contribution of these variations due to the combination of the two factors (0.1 * 0.2).

To account for differences in the countries' level of wealth when comparing salary costs per student, salary cost per student, as well as teachers' salaries, can be divided by GDP per capita (on the assumption that GDP per capita is an estimate of countries' level of wealth). This makes it possible to compare countries' "relative" salary cost per student (see *Education at a Glance 2011* tables available on line).

Box B7.2. **Main driver of salary cost per student, by level of education (2008)**

	Primary education	Lower secondary education	Upper secondary education
Teachers' salary	15 countries AUS(+), CHL(-), CZE(-), EST(-), DEU(+), HUN(-), IRL(+), ISR(-), JPN(+), KOR(+), LUX(+), MEX(-), NLD(+), POL(-), CHE(+)	15 countries AUS(+), CHL(-), CZE(-), EST(-), DEU(+), HUN(-), ISL(-), IRL(+), ISR(-), JPN(+), LUX(+), NLD(+), POL(-), ESP(+), CHE(+)	18 countries BFL(+), BFR(+), CHL(-), CZE(-), EST(-), FRA(-), DEU(+), HUN(-), ISL(-), IRL(+), ISR(-), ITA(-), LUX(+), NLD(+), POL(-), SVN(-), CHE(+), TUR(-)
Instruction time	4 countries BFR(+), FIN(-), ITA(+), SVN(-)		
Teaching time	3 countries GRC(+), NZL(-), USA(-)	7 countries AUT(+), FIN(+), GRC(+), ITA(+), NZL(-), UKM(-), USA(-)	8 countries AUS(-), AUT(+), DNK(+), GRC(+), JPN(+), NZL(-), NOR(+), USA(-)
Estimated class size	10 countries AUT(+), BFL(+), DNK(+), FRA(-), ISL(+), NOR(+), PRT(+), ESP(+), TUR(-), UKM(-)	9 countries BFL(+), BFR(+), DNK(+), FRA(-), KOR(-), MEX(-), NOR(+), PRT(+), SVN(+)	5 countries FIN(-), KOR(-), PRT(+), ESP(+), UKM(+)

Note: The positive or negative signs show whether the factor increases or decreases the salary cost per student.
Source: OECD. Tables B7.1, B7.2 and B7.3. See Annex 3 for notes *(www.oecd.org/edu/eag2011)*.
Please refer to the Reader's Guide for the list of country codes used in this table.
StatLink http://dx.doi.org/10.1787/888932461370

At the **lower secondary** level, the main drivers of the difference with the OECD averages salary cost per student are more similar to the upper secondary level. At the **upper secondary** level, teachers' salaries are the main driver of the difference from the OECD average salary cost per student in 18 of the 31 OECD countries for which data are available. In eight countries with the lowest salary costs per student at this level of education, below-average teachers' salaries are the main driver (Chart B7.1); but above-average teachers' salaries are also the main driver in the two countries with the highest salary cost per student. Teaching time or class size are the main drivers of the difference from the OECD average salary cost per student in eight and five countries, respectively (Box B7.2 and Table B7.3). The higher the level of education, the greater the impact of teachers' salaries and the lower the impact of class size on the difference from the OECD average salary cost per student. For example, in Belgium (Flemish Community), France, Iceland and Turkey, the main driver of the difference from the OECD average salary cost per student is teachers' salaries at the upper secondary level and estimated class size at the primary level (Box B7.2).

When differences in countries' wealth are accounted for, comparing relative salary cost per student shows the same picture at the upper secondary level of education (Tables B7.1 continued, B7.2 continued and B7.3 continued, available on line); but relative teachers' salaries are less often the main driver of the difference from the average salary cost per student at the lowest levels, and the main driver is most often class size at each level of education (Box B7.2 continued, available on line). This is especially true in countries that have both high teachers' salaries and high GDP per capita compared to other countries, such as Luxembourg and Switzerland, and in countries that have both low teachers' salaries and low GDP per capita compared to other countries, such as Chile, the Czech Republic and Turkey.

Methodology

Cumulative spending per student is approximated by multiplying public and private expenditure on educational institutions per student in 2008 at each level of education by the theoretical duration of education at these levels between the ages of 6 and 15 in each of the countries. The results are expressed in USD using purchasing power parities.

Salary cost per student is calculated based on teachers' salaries, the number of hours of instruction for students, the number of hours of teaching for teachers and a proxy class size (see Box D2.1). In most cases, the values for these variables are derived from *Education at a Glance 2010*, and refer to the school year 2007-08 and the calendar year 2007 for indicators related to finance. However, in order to compensate for missing values for some variables, some data have been estimated on the basis of data published in previous editions of *Education at a Glance*. When it was not possible to make estimates or proxy figures were not available, the missing values have been replaced by the average for all OECD countries. Teachers' salaries in national currency are converted into equivalent USD by dividing the national currency figure by the purchasing power parity (PPP) index for GDP, so that salary cost per student is expressed in equivalent USD. Further details on the analysis of these factors are available in Annex 3 at *www.oecd.org/edu/eag2011*.

The statistical data for Israel are supplied by and under the responsibility of the relevant Israeli authorities. The use of such data by the OECD is without prejudice to the status of the Golan Heights, East Jerusalem and Israeli settlements in the West Bank under the terms of international law.

References

Education Statistics Bulletin, Ministère de l'Éducation, du Loisir et du Sport du Québec (2005), "Educational Spending Relative to the GDP in 2001: A Comparison of Quebec and the OECD Countries", *www.mels.gouv.qc.ca/stat/bulletin/bulletin_31an.pdf*.

OECD (2010h), *Education at a Glance 2010: OECD Indicators*, OECD, Paris.

The following additional material relevant to this indicator is available on line:

- ***Table B7.1. (continued) Contribution, in percentage points of GDP per capita, of various factors to salary cost per student at primary level of education (2008)***
  StatLink http://dx.doi.org/10.1787/888932464163
- ***Table B7.2. (continued) Contribution, in percentage points of GDP per capita, of various factors to salary cost per student at lower secondary level of education (2008)***
  StatLink http://dx.doi.org/10.1787/888932464201
- ***Table B7.3. (continued) Contribution, in percentage points of GDP per capita, of various factors to salary cost per student at upper secondary level of education (2008)***
  StatLink http://dx.doi.org/10.1787/888932464239
- ***Box B7.2. (continued) Main driver of salary cost per student as a percentage of GDP per capita, by level of education (2008)***
  StatLink http://dx.doi.org/10.1787/888932461389

Table B7.1. Contribution, in USD, of various factors to salary cost per student at the primary level of education (2008)

Contribution (in USD) of school factors to salary cost per student

How to read this table: In Australia, at USD 2 917, the salary cost per student exceeds the OECD average by USD 608. Above-average salaries and above-average instruction time increase the difference from the OECD average by USD 629 and USD 485, respectively, whereas above-average teaching time and above-average estimated class size decrease the difference from the average by USD 290 and USD 218, respectively. The sum of these effects results in a positive difference from the OECD average of USD 608.

		Salary cost per student	Difference from the OECD average of **USD 2 309**	Contribution of the underlying factors to the difference from the OECD average			
				Effect (in USD) of **teachers' salaries** below/above the OECD average of **USD 36 228**	Effect (in USD) of **instruction time** (for students) below/above the OECD average of **797 hours**	Effect (in USD) of **teaching time** (for teachers) below/above the OECD average of **782 hours**	Effect (in USD) of **estimated class size** below/above the OECD average of **16 students per class**
		(1)	(2) = (3) + (4) + (5) + (6)	(3)	(4)	(5)	(6)
OECD	Australia	2 917	**608**	629	485	-290	-218
	Austria	2 940	**631**	120	-213	7	718
	Belgium (Fl.)	3 256	**948**	348	145	-99	554
	Belgium (Fr.)	3 125	**816**	229	416	206	-35
	Canada	m	**m**	m	m	m	m
	Chile	538	**-1 771**	-1 257	443	-130	-827
	Czech Republic	1 198	**-1 111**	-873	-414	-144	320
	Denmark	4 182	**1 873**	494	-413	596	1 196
	Estonia	773	**-1 536**	-1 484	-441	339	50
	Finland	2 655	**346**	134	-679	360	531
	France	1 603	**-706**	-246	294	-329	-424
	Germany	3 017	**708**	1 076	-618	-79	329
	Greece	3 170	**862**	-348	-281	757	733
	Hungary	1 420	**-889**	-1 694	-516	497	823
	Iceland	2 730	**421**	-738	-262	390	1 030
	Ireland	3 041	**732**	1 075	373	-428	-288
	Israel	1 217	**-1 092**	-1 034	400	62	-519
	Italy	2 984	**675**	-370	572	163	309
	Japan	2 587	**278**	727	-291	242	-401
	Korea	2 262	**-47**	956	-616	-169	-218
	Luxembourg	5 595	**3 286**	2 297	562	213	214
	Mexico	681	**-1 628**	-851	5	-33	-750
	Netherlands	2 911	**602**	619	432	-458	10
	New Zealand	2 245	**-64**	134	487	-531	-154
	Norway	3 424	**1 115**	63	-569	154	1 467
	Poland	1 342	**-967**	-1 832	-980	866	978
	Portugal	3 135	**826**	-56	298	-246	831
	Slovak Republic	m	**m**	m	m	m	m
	Slovenia	2 033	**-276**	-266	-546	297	239
	Spain	3 263	**954**	462	124	-331	700
	Sweden	m	**m**	m	m	m	m
	Switzerland	3 657	**1 348**	1 312	-338	-372	746
	Turkey	820	**-1 489**	-876	126	317	-1 056
	United Kingdom	2 209	**-100**	477	260	-205	-632
	United States	3 090	**781**	540	563	-935	613

Source: OECD. Data from *Education at a Glance 2010 (www.oecd.org/edu/eag2010)*. See Annex 3 for notes *(www.oecd.org/edu/eag2011)*.
Please refer to the Reader's Guide for information concerning the symbols replacing missing data.

StatLink http://dx.doi.org/10.1787/888932464144

Table B7.2. Contribution, in USD, of various factors to salary cost per student at the lower secondary level of education (2008)

Contribution (in USD) of school factors to salary cost per student

		Salary cost per student	Difference from the OECD average of **USD 2 991**	Contribution of the underlying factors to the difference from the OECD average: Effect (in USD) of **teachers' salaries** below/above the OECD average of **USD 39 146**	Effect (in USD) of **instruction time** (for students) below/above the OECD average of **933 hours**	Effect (in USD) of **teaching time** (for teachers) below/above the OECD average of **707 hours**	Effect (in USD) of **estimated class size** below/above the OECD average of **17.3 students per class**
		(1)	(2) = (3) + (4) + (5) + (6)	(3)	(4)	(5)	(6)
OECD	Australia	3 909	**918**	622	279	-481	498
	Austria	4 123	**1 132**	163	95	537	337
	Belgium (Fl.)	5 053	**2 062**	193	137	65	1 666
	Belgium (Fr.)	4 848	**1 857**	28	346	249	1 234
	Canada	m	**m**	m	m	m	m
	Chile	538	**-2 453**	-1 544	254	-309	-854
	Czech Republic	1 869	**-1 122**	-1 375	-155	256	152
	Denmark	4 182	**1 190**	277	-128	308	734
	Estonia	791	**-2 200**	-1 839	-273	212	-301
	Finland	3 850	**859**	154	-405	602	508
	France	2 356	**-635**	-354	376	249	-905
	Germany	3 937	**945**	1 429	-176	-239	-69
	Greece	4 166	**1 175**	-745	-466	1 797	588
	Hungary	1 385	**-1 606**	-2 029	-117	332	209
	Iceland	2 730	**-262**	-1 054	-196	148	841
	Ireland	4 227	**1 235**	1 156	-99	-142	320
	Israel	1 838	**-1 154**	-1 342	495	413	-718
	Italy	3 547	**555**	-431	507	528	-48
	Japan	3 310	**319**	690	-229	503	-646
	Korea	2 689	**-302**	969	-214	400	-1 457
	Luxembourg	10 847	**7 855**	5 538	-177	707	1 787
	Mexico	716	**-2 275**	-784	396	-650	-1 237
	Netherlands	3 179	**188**	775	216	-186	-618
	New Zealand	2 378	**-614**	-51	147	-843	133
	Norway	3 676	**684**	-187	-407	261	1 018
	Poland	1 247	**-1 744**	-1 804	-782	708	133
	Portugal	4 407	**1 416**	-370	-112	-237	2 135
	Slovak Republic	m	**m**	m	m	m	m
	Slovenia	3 608	**617**	-676	-558	117	1 733
	Spain	4 553	**1 561**	663	316	-33	616
	Sweden	m	**m**	m	m	m	m
	Switzerland	5 325	**2 333**	2 040	-94	-823	1 210
	Turkey	a	**a**	a	a	a	a
	United Kingdom	2 981	**-10**	393	-26	-572	195
	United States	2 982	**-9**	356	150	-1 259	743

Source: OECD. Data from *Education at a Glance 2010 (www.oecd.org/edu/eag2010)*. See Annex 3 for notes *(www.oecd.org/edu/eag2011)*.
Please refer to the Reader's Guide for information concerning the symbols replacing missing data.

StatLink http://dx.doi.org/10.1787/888932464182

Table B7.3. **Contribution, in USD, of various factors to salary cost per student at the upper secondary level of education (2008)**

Contribution (in USD) of school factors to salary cost per student

		Salary cost per student	Difference from the OECD average of **USD 3 398**	Contribution of the underlying factors to the difference from the OECD average: Effect (in USD) of **teachers' salaries** below/above the OECD average of **USD 41 944**	Effect (in USD) of **instruction time** (for students) below/above the OECD average of **958 hours**	Effect (in USD) of **teaching time** (for teachers) below/above the OECD average of **649 hours**	Effect (in USD) of **estimated class size** below/above the OECD average of **18.2 students per class**
		(1)	(2) = (3) + (4) + (5) + (6)	(3)	(4)	(5)	(6)
OECD	Australia	3 909	**511**	411	128	-819	791
	Austria	4 014	**616**	21	338	362	-104
	Belgium (Fl.)	4 887	**1 489**	932	30	3	525
	Belgium (Fr.)	4 690	**1 292**	747	250	298	-2
	Canada	m	**m**	m	m	m	m
	Chile	539	**-2 859**	-1 720	418	-483	-1 074
	Czech Republic	1 932	**-1 466**	-1 502	-9	175	-131
	Denmark	5 044	**1 646**	846	-131	2 464	-1 534
	Estonia	1 026	**-2 371**	-2 375	-289	262	30
	Finland	2 819	**-579**	216	-151	522	-1 166
	France	3 671	**273**	-686	656	106	197
	Germany	4 555	**1 157**	1 655	-268	-386	157
	Greece	4 347	**949**	-1 087	-730	1 634	1 132
	Hungary	1 466	**-1 932**	-1 945	354	151	-492
	Iceland	3 024	**-374**	-875	-247	479	269
	Ireland	4 227	**829**	971	-280	-476	614
	Israel	2 053	**-1 345**	-1 704	576	511	-727
	Italy	2 998	**-400**	-554	411	247	-504
	Japan	3 956	**558**	549	-366	962	-587
	Korea	3 305	**-93**	893	213	249	-1 448
	Luxembourg	10 847	**7 449**	5 440	-434	166	2 277
	Mexico	m	**m**	m	m	m	m
	Netherlands	4 247	**849**	1 813	165	-564	-565
	New Zealand	2 997	**-401**	-287	89	-1 237	1 034
	Norway	3 943	**545**	-267	-408	798	423
	Poland	1 519	**-1 879**	-1 947	-1 008	601	476
	Portugal	4 886	**1 488**	-721	-160	-636	3 005
	Slovak Republic	m	**m**	m	m	m	m
	Slovenia	2 341	**-1 057**	-760	-155	103	-245
	Spain	5 599	**2 201**	686	94	-291	1 711
	Sweden	m	**m**	m	m	m	m
	Switzerland	7 336	**3 938**	3 036	358	-199	742
	Turkey	1 206	**-2 192**	-1 504	-370	305	-623
	United Kingdom	3 594	**197**	220	-31	-977	985
	United States	3 038	**-360**	398	74	-1 581	750

Source: OECD. Data from *Education at a Glance 2010 (www.oecd.org/edu/eag2010)*. See Annex 3 for notes *(www.oecd.org/edu/eag2011)*.
Please refer to the Reader's Guide for information concerning the symbols replacing missing data.

StatLink http://dx.doi.org/10.1787/888932464220

Chapter

Access to Education, Participation and Progression

INDICATOR C1

WHO PARTICIPATES IN EDUCATION?

- Education is universal between the ages of 5 and 14 among all OECD and other G20 countries with available data. In almost two-thirds of OECD countries, more than 70% of 3-4 year-olds are enrolled in either pre-primary or primary programmes.
- In 25 of 31 OECD countries, 80% or more of 15-19 year-olds participate in education. This is true for more than 90% of this age group in Belgium, Ireland, Poland and Slovenia.
- In Australia, Denmark, Finland, Iceland, New Zealand, Poland, Slovenia and Sweden, more than 30% of 20-29 year-olds are enrolled in education. From 1995 to 2009, enrolment rates among 20-29 year-olds increased by 8.2 percentage points in OECD countries with available and comparable data.

Chart C1.1. Enrolment rates of 20-29 year-olds (1995, 2002 and 2009)

Full-time and part-time students in public and private institutions

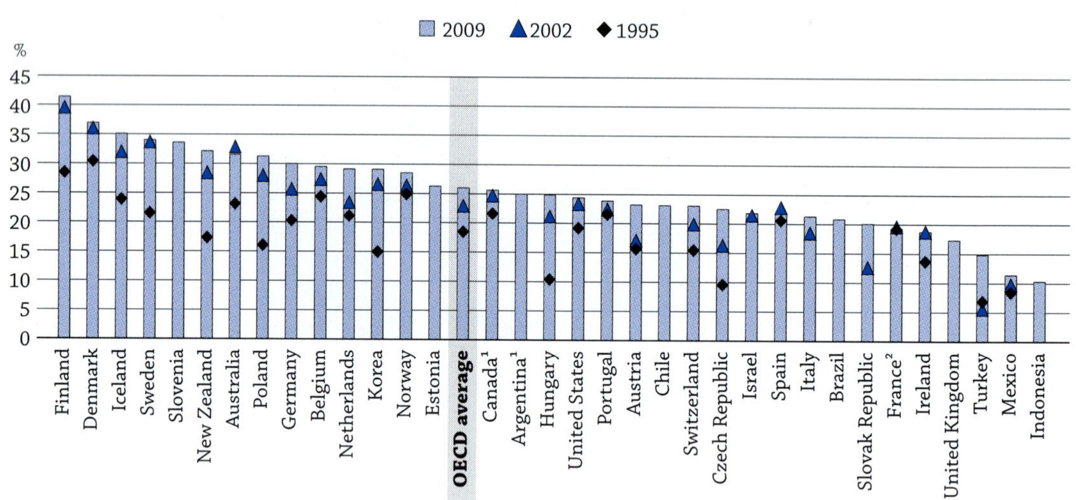

1. Year of reference 2008.

2. Excludes overseas departments for 1995.

Countries are ranked in descending order of the enrolment rates of 20-29 year-olds in 2009.

Source: OECD. Argentina and Indonesia: UNESCO Institute for Statistics (World Education Indicators Programme). Table C1.2. See Annex 3 for notes (*www.oecd.org/edu/eag2011*).

StatLink http://dx.doi.org/10.1787/888932461408

Context

According to results from PISA, children who participated in early childhood education tend to perform better in the PISA survey at age 15 than children who did not, after controlling for socio-economic background (OECD, 2010b). Over the past decade, many countries have expanded pre-primary programmes. This increased focus on early childhood education has resulted in the extension of compulsory education to lower ages in some countries, free early childhood education, and the creation of programmes that integrate care with formal pre-primary education.

Compulsory education has become virtually universal in OECD and other G20 countries. Various factors, including increased risks of unemployment and other forms of exclusion for young adults with insufficient education (see Indicator A7), have strengthened the incentive to remain in school beyond the end of compulsory education and to graduate from upper secondary education. In most OECD countries, graduation from upper secondary education is now the norm, and most upper secondary programmes prepare students for tertiary studies (see Indicator A2).

Tertiary education programmes are generally associated with better access to employment and with an improved likelihood of remaining employed in times of economic hardship (see Indicator A7), with higher earnings (see Indicator A8), and with better social outcomes, such as social engagement and self-reported health (see Indicator A11). Rates of entry into tertiary education are a partial indication of the degree to which a population is acquiring the high-level skills and knowledge valued by the labour market in today's knowledge-based societies (see Indicator C2).

As students have become more aware of the economic and social benefits of tertiary education, graduation rates for tertiary education have risen, especially for tertiary-type A (largely theory-based) programmes (see Indicator A3). These types of programmes absorb a large proportion of the available resources, as they tend to be longer than other tertiary programmes (see Indicator B1). The internationalisation of tertiary education means that some educational institutions may also have to adapt their curricula and teaching methods to a culturally and linguistically diverse student body (see Indicator C3).

Other findings

- **Virtually everyone in the OECD area has access to at least 13 years of formal education.** In Belgium, Estonia, France, Germany, Hungary, Iceland, Ireland, Italy, Japan, the Netherlands, Norway, Spain and Sweden at least 90% of students are enrolled in education for 14 years or more. Enrolment rates exceed 90% during 11 years or less of education in Argentina, Chile, Korea, Mexico and the United States; in Brazil, Indonesia and Turkey, 90% of children have access to education during only 9 years or less. Nevertheless, compulsory and free education has led to universal access to education for 7-15 year-olds in Brazil, 6-14 year-olds in Indonesia, and 7-13 year-olds in Turkey.
- **Children aged 3 to 4 are more likely to be enrolled in a pre-primary or primary programme in one of the 21 European Union countries that are members of the OECD (EU21)** than in one of the other OECD countries.

Trends

Enrolment rates in both secondary and tertiary education increased steadily in nearly all OECD countries between 1995 and 2009. In around one-third of countries with available data, and on average among OECD countries, the growth in enrolment rates for 15-19 year-olds and for 20-29 year-olds has been slowing during the past five years. In upper secondary education, this is probably because of almost universal coverage.

Analysis

Participation in early childhood education

Enrollment in pre-primary education is nearly universal in OECD countries, and PISA data confirm the importance of pre-primary education to later schooling (OECD, 2010i). In most countries, students who have attended pre-primary schools tend to perform better in school than those who have not, even after accounting for students' socio-economic background.

Early childhood education helps to build a strong foundation for lifelong learning and to ensure equitable access to later learning opportunities. Many countries have recognised this by making pre-primary education almost universal for children by the time they are three. However, institution-based pre-primary programmes covered by this indicator are not the only form of effective early childhood education available. For instance, Scandinavian countries, among others, have institution-based integrated administration of both care and pre-primary education, and data is not reported for ages under three. Inferences about access to and quality of pre-primary education and care should therefore be made with caution.

In almost half of OECD countries, full enrolment (defined here as enrolment rates exceeding 90%) begins between the ages of 5 and 7. However, in almost two-thirds of OECD countries, at least 70% of 3-4 year-olds are enrolled in either pre-primary or primary programmes (Table C1.1a). The average enrolment rate for 3-4 year-olds is more than 75% for the EU21 but only 70% for OECD countries. In Belgium, Denmark, France, Iceland, Italy, Norway and Spain, enrolment of 3-4 year-olds reached 95% or more in 2009. Turkey is the only country to enrol fewer than 9% of its 3-4 year-olds, probably because of the limited number of pre-primary schools available, most of which are private and charge fees, or because of socio-cultural factors. In Belgium (17.1%), the Russian Federation (17.6%) and Spain (24.6%), children younger than three attend pre-primary programmes attended by older children as well. The age of entry into pre-primary programmes is 2.5 years in Belgium, 1.5 years in the Russian Federation, and even younger in Spain. Children are allowed into integrated programmes of care and pre-primary starting from the age of 2 in Denmark and Iceland, which is out of the scope of data collection presented in *Education at a Glance 2011*.

Participation in compulsory education

Compulsory education includes primary and lower secondary programmes in all OECD countries and also upper secondary education in most countries. Between the ages of 5 and 14 in all OECD and other G20 countries, enrolment rates are above 90%; and in all countries except Chile, Poland, the Russian Federation and Turkey, the rates in 2009 were higher than 95% (Table C1.1a).

Participation in upper secondary education

With the continued increase in participation in upper secondary education, countries provide a more diversified pathway to students. Countries have taken various approaches to meeting these demands. Some have comprehensive secondary systems with non-selective general/academic programmes so that all students have similar opportunities for learning; others provide more diversified education programmes (academic, pre-vocational and/or vocational programmes; see the Definitions section below).

Enrolment rates for 15-19 year-olds indicate the number of individuals participating in upper secondary education. Between 1995 and 2009, there was an increase in the country average of 9.3 percentage points in the proportion of 15-19 year-olds enrolled in education in OECD countries (average annual growth of 0.7 percentage points) (Table C1.2).

Enrolment rates for 15-19 year-olds increased steadily in nearly all OECD countries between 1995 and 2005, the enrolment rate for 15-19 year-olds increased from an average of 74% in 1995 to 81% in 2005. The pace slowed in the past four years, with those rates rising to 83% in 2009. About half of countries showed variations around or below one percentage point between 2005 and 2009; in Estonia rates decreased by nearly 3 pencentage points in the same period and in Greece rates decreased by nearly 15 percentage points between 2005 and 2008. In Belgium, Ireland, Poland and Slovenia, enrolment rates reached more than 90% in 2009 (in Belgium, they had already reached this level in 1995) (Table C1.2).

Chart C1.2. Enrolment rates of 15-19 year-olds (1995, 2002 and 2009)

Full-time and part-time students in public and private institutions

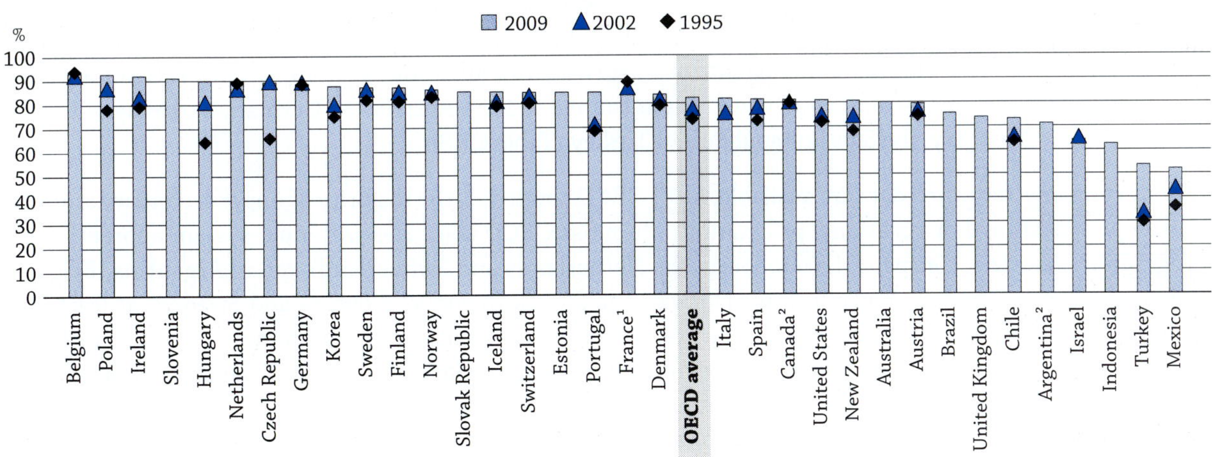

1. Excludes overseas departments for 1995.

2. Year of reference 2008.

Countries are ranked in descending order of the enrolment rates of 15-19 year-olds in 2009.

Source: OECD. Argentina and Indonesia: UNESCO Institute for Statistics (World Education Indicators Programme). Table C1.2. See Annex 3 for notes (*www.oecd.org/edu/eag2011*).

StatLink http://dx.doi.org/10.1787/888932461427

Enrolment rates in OECD countries have converged in the past 14 years. While these rates have increased by more than 20 percentage points during that period in the Czech Republic, Hungary and Turkey, and by nearly 15 points or more in Mexico, Poland and Portugal, they have remained virtually unchanged in Belgium, Canada (until 2008), Germany, Israel and the Netherlands, where a large proportion of 15-19 year-olds is enrolled in education. In France, the enrolment rate among this age group decreased from 89% to 84% during the period (Table C1.2 and Chart C1.2).

Students in upper secondary education are mainly aged between 15 and 18 years in all OECD and other G20 countries. In all countries with available data (except Argentina for 16 year-olds, Indonesia, Mexico and Turkey), at least 85% of 15-16 year-olds are enrolled in upper secondary education. Students begin to leave upper secondary education from the age of 18 in most countries; however, more than 50% of 18-year-olds are still enrolled in at this level of education. At age 19, one in four students is still enrolled in upper secondary education in OECD countries. More than 40% of 19-year-olds in Denmark, Germany, Iceland, Luxembourg, the Netherlands and Switzerland are enrolled in this level of education (Table C1.1b, available on line).

In some OECD countries, one-quarter or more of 20-year-olds are still enrolled in secondary education. This is the case in Denmark (31%), Germany (25%), Iceland (36%), the Netherlands (27%) and Slovenia (26%) (Table C1.1b, available on line). This may correspond to longer programmes, repetition of grades, late insertion into the labour market or employment being concurrent with education.

Enrollment of 15-19 year-olds girls is slightly larger than that of boys in almost all countries. The difference is greater than five percentage points in Argentina, Estonia, Israel, Portugal, Spain, the United Kingdom and the United States. However, in Switzerland and Turkey, enrolment rates for boys are greater than for girls (Table C1.1a).

Vocational and apprenticeship programmes

Vocational programmes among OECD countries offer different combinations of vocational or pre-vocational studies along with apprenticeship programmes. Upper secondary students in many education systems can enrol in vocational programmes, but some OECD countries delay vocational training until after graduation from upper secondary education. While vocational programmes are offered as advanced upper secondary education in Austria, Hungary and Spain, similar programmes are offered as post-secondary education in Canada.

Among all OECD countries, 13 countries' school systems are comprehensive, meaning that they offer a single programme of study to all 15-year-olds. Yet, even within comprehensive programmes, students can often enrol in different tracks and courses that reflect their various interests and academic goals (see the section on horizontal differentiation at the school level, below). In the remaining 19 OECD countries with stratified school systems, 15-year-olds are streamed into at least two different study programmes. Such streaming takes place at an average age of 14 but occurs as early as at the age of 10 in Austria and Germany and at age 11 in the Czech Republic, Hungary, the Slovak Republic and Turkey (Table C1.3).

Among countries for which data are available, in 13 OECD countries, the majority of upper secondary students pursue pre-vocational or vocational programmes. In most OECD countries with dual-system apprenticeship programmes (Austria, Germany, Luxembourg, the Netherlands and Switzerland) and in Argentina, Belgium, China, the Czech Republic, Finland, Italy, Norway, the Slovak Republic, Slovenia and Sweden, at least 50% of upper secondary students are enrolled in pre-vocational or vocational programmes. However, in Brazil, Canada, Chile, Estonia, Greece, Hungary, Iceland, India, Indonesia, Ireland, Israel, Japan, Korea, Mexico, New Zealand, Portugal and the United Kingdom, at least 60% of upper secondary students are enrolled in general programmes, even though pre-vocational and/or vocational programmes are offered (Table C1.3).

In many OECD countries, upper secondary vocational education is school-based. However, in Austria, the Czech Republic and Iceland, at least 40% of students in vocational education participate in programmes that combine school- and work-based elements; in Denmark, Germany, Hungary, Ireland and Switzerland, at least 75% of students in vocational education are enrolled in those kinds of programmes.

Table C1.3 includes enrolments in apprenticeship programmes that are a recognised part of countries' education systems. In most countries, except Brazil, Greece, Italy, Japan, Korea, Portugal, Spain and Sweden, some form of apprenticeship system exists. In some countries, such as Austria, Germany and Hungary, apprenticeship contracts are established between a student – not the vocational training school – and a company. The majority of countries have combined school- and work-based apprenticeship programmes. Sweden is piloting apprenticeship training as a complement to school-based education; in the United States, apprenticeship programmes exist, but they generally are not part of the formal education system.

The minimum entry requirement for apprenticeship programmes varies but is typically the completion of lower secondary education; this is true in the Czech Republic, Denmark, Finland, France, Germany, Ireland, Israel, Luxembourg, Mexico, the Netherlands, Norway, Poland, the Slovak Republic and Slovenia. In Austria, students must have completed a minimum of nine years of compulsory schooling, while in the United States students must have completed upper secondary education. In Australia, Belgium, the Netherlands, New Zealand and the United Kingdom, entry is governed (in full or in part) by age, while in New Zealand, participants must also be employed. In Turkey, the minimum requirement is completion of primary education, but entrants must be at least 14 years old and have a contract with a workplace. In the Russian Federation, there is no legal framework for entry into apprenticeship programmes.

In some countries the duration of apprenticeship programmes is standardised, ranging from one to four years in the Czech Republic, Denmark, France, Germany, Ireland, Israel, New Zealand, Norway, Poland, Slovenia and the United Kingdom. In other countries, such as Austria and Belgium, it varies according to subject, specific qualification sought, previous knowledge and/or experience.

In most countries, a student who successfully completes an apprenticeship programme is usually awarded an upper secondary or post-secondary qualification. In some countries, higher qualifications are possible (such as an Advanced Diploma in Australia).

Participation towards the end of compulsory education and beyond

Young adults with insufficient levels of education are often at greater risk of unemployment and other forms of exclusion than their more educated peers. In many OECD countries, the transition from education to employment has become longer and more complex, providing an opportunity – or creating the necessity – to combine learning and work to develop skills adapted to the labour marker (see Indicator C4).

An analysis of participation rates by level of education and single year of age shows that there is no close relationship between the end of compulsory education and the decline in enrolment rates. The age at which compulsory education ends ranges from 14 in Korea, Portugal, Slovenia and Turkey, to 18 in Belgium, Canada (in some provinces), Chile, Germany, Hungary and the Netherlands (Table C1.1a). However, the statutory age at which compulsory education ends does not always correspond to the age at which more than 90% of the student population is enrolled in school. While in most OECD and other G20 countries participation rates tend to be high to the end of compulsory education, in Belgium, Brazil, Canada, Chile, Germany, Hungary, Israel, Mexico, the Netherlands, Turkey and the United States, the rates drop below 90% before the age at which compulsory education ends (Table C1.1a and Table C1.1b available on line). In Belgium, Canada, Chile, Germany, Hungary and the Netherlands, this may be due, in part, to the fact that compulsory education ends relatively late, at age 18, and at 17 in Brazil, Israel and the United States (on average). In Belgium, and the United States, the absolute drop in enrolment at age 18 is complemented by relatively large enrolment in tertiary education, with rates above 30%.

In most OECD and other G20 countries, the sharpest decline in enrolment rates occurs not at the end of compulsory education, but at the end of upper secondary education and rates decline gradually during the last years of upper secondary education. In Argentina, Australia, Austria, Brazil, Chile, Indonesia, Israel, Mexico, Turkey and the United Kingdom, more than 20% of 15-19 year-olds are not enrolled in education (Table C1.1a and Chart C1.2).

After age 17, (or age 18 in the Czech Republic, Denmark, Estonia, Finland, Ireland, Norway, the Slovak Republic, Slovenia, Sweden and Switzerland), enrolment rates begin to decline in almost all OECD and other G20 countries. On average, enrolment rates in upper secondary education fall from 93% at age 16, to 85% at age 17, to 53% at age 18, and to 25% at age 19. In Belgium, the Czech Republic, Estonia, Finland, Hungary, Japan, Korea, Norway, Poland, the Slovak Republic, Slovenia and Sweden, 90% or more of all 17-year-olds are still enrolled at this level of education, even though, in most of these countries, compulsory education ends before a student reaches the age of 17 (Table C1.1b, available on line).

Participation of young adults in education

On average in OECD countries, 26% of 20-29 year-olds were enrolled in education, mostly tertiary education, in 2009. In Australia, Denmark, Finland, Germany, Iceland, New Zealand, Poland, Slovenia and Sweden, 30% or more of people this age were enrolled (Table C1.1a and Chart C1.1). However, tertiary enrolment rates for countries with large proportions of international students relative to population size may be overestimated. For more information on the impact of international students on entry rates and graduation rates at the tertiary education level, please refer to Indicator A3, where adjustments were made for the impact of international students.

Policies to expand education have led to greater access to tertiary education in many OECD and other G20 countries. So far, this has more than compensated for the declines in cohort sizes that, until recently, had led to predictions of stable or declining demand in several OECD countries. On average, in all OECD countries with comparable data, participation rates for 20-29 year-olds grew by 8.2 percentage points from 1995 to 2009 (an average annual growth of 0.6 percentage point). Almost all OECD and other G20 countries saw some increase in participation rates among 20-29 year-olds in this period. Growth of at least 10 percentage points was seen in the Czech Republic, Finland, Hungary, Iceland, Korea, New Zealand, Poland and Sweden. This growth was particularly significant in the Czech Republic and Hungary, which were previously at the bottom of the scale of OECD countries but recently moved up to the middle. On the other hand, France and Spain show signs of a levelling of tertiary enrolment rates (Table C1.2).

As for 15-19 year olds, the increase in enrolment rates for 20-29 year-olds has slowed in the last years. On average among OECD countries with available and comparable data, the average annual variation passed from almost 0.8 percentage points per year between 1995 and 2005 to less than 0.2 percentage points per year between 2005 and 2009. Almost one-third of countries show stable rates in the last five years (less than one percentage point of variation between 2005 and 2009) or a decrease of around two percentage points as in

Australia, Iceland, Ireland and Sweden. Among these countries, Australia, Denmark, Finland, Iceland, Norway, Poland and Sweden recorded enrolment rates of over 30% in the same period. In contrast, enrolment rates never exceeded 25% in Brazil (between 2007 and 2009), Estonia, France, Hungary, Ireland, Mexico, Spain and the United Kingdom (between 2006 and 2009). However, rates have risen by more than 2% in Austria, the Czech Republic, and the Netherlands, and by more than 4% in the Slovak Republic and Turkey between 2005 and 2009. Across OECD countries, trends in enrolment rates for 15-19 year-olds and 20-29 year-olds for all available years are highly correlated (Table C1.2 and Chart C1.1).

Gender differences

In some countries, higher levels of enrolment for young adult women are linked to improved access to education, but they can also imply a later insertion into the labour market than for men. In contrast, less access to child care and cultural barriers may lead to lower levels of participation among women.

As among 15-19 year-olds, on average in OECD, more 20-29 year-old women than men participate in education. The difference among 20-29 year-olds is higher than ten percentage points in Argentina, Estonia, Slovenia and Sweden. However, for this age group more men than women are enrolled in Germany, Indonesia, Ireland, Korea, Mexico, the Netherlands, Switzerland and Turkey; in Korea, there is a 17 percentage-point gender gap, mainly due to delayed graduation among men pursuing their mandatory military service. In all of these countries, the gender difference is reduced among 30-39 year-olds. In Ireland and Mexico, more 30-39 year-old women than men are enroled. This may be because women enter education later for family reasons. In the countries in which more 15-19 year-olds boys than girls are enrolled, such as Indonesia, Switzerland and Turkey, the trend continues among 20-29 year-olds (Table C1.1a).

Students in tertiary education are more likely to study full-time rather than part-time, whether they are enrolled in tertiary-type A or B (shorter vocationally oriented) programmes. Students may opt for part-time studies because they may also participate in the labour market at the same time, because of family constraints, particularly for women, because of preferences for different fields of education, or other reasons. On average, there is little gender difference among part-time tertiary students, although slightly more women than men tend to choose this mode of study. The picture is more diverse at the country level. In tertiary-type B programmes, designed for direct insertion into the labour market, the proportion of women in part-time enrolment is more than 10 percentage points higher than that for men in Hungary, Ireland, the Netherlands, Norway and the Slovak Republic. The opposite is true in Germany, Iceland and Switzerland, where more men than women are enroled in part-time studies than women. Gender differences are weaker in tertiary-type A programmes; however, in Hungary, Iceland, Japan, Norway, the Russian Federation and the Slovak Republic, the proportion of women in part-time studies is more than 5 percentage points greater than that for men. The inverse is true in Estonia and Finland (Table C1.5).

Participation of adults in programmes designed to allow for direct entry into the labour market

The return to or continuation of studies is an option for adults to increase and diversify their skills and make them more adaptable to the changing demands of the labour market. In times of increasing unemployment, and of a potential structural evolution in the demand for skills, some countries, such as Chile, have established specific policies to encourage adults to follow tertiary-type B studies.

The general rises in unemployment rates in OECD countries between 2008 and 2009 did not lead to a significant increase in enrolment among adults in the same period. There is also no direct correlation between growth in enrolment rates between 2008 and 2009 and the increases in unemployment rates that were seen between 2007 and 2008 in some OECD countries because other factors, such as labour force mobility within the European Union and unemployment benefits, may influence adults' decisions to return to education.

Box C1.1 shows the countries where the greatest increases in adult participation in these programmes occurred during the last year of the 2005-09 period, when all OECD countries, except Luxembourg, experienced the steepest rise in unemployment.

Box C1.1. Evolution of adult enrolment in programmes designed to prepare students for direct entry into the labour market (2008-09)

Countries where, over the period 2005-09, the highest increase in enrolment was between 2008 and 2009 and where the higher enrolment rate was attained in 2009 at ISCED 3C, 4C and 5B levels. The percentage increase in enrolment rates between 2008 and 2009 appears next to country names.

	30-34[1]	35-39[1]	Over 40[2]
Isced 3C	Netherlands 9.6%	Denmark 2.6%	-
Isced 4C	Australia 12%	Australia 10.3%	Australia 14.1%, Iceland 29.8%
Isced 5B		Australia 12.6%, Belgium 10.7%, Chile 29.5%, Israel 20.7%, New Zealand 7%, United States 17.4%	Australia 13.6%, Belgium 11.3%, Chile 23.9%, Canada 4.2%, Estonia 1.4%, New Zealand 5.5%

1. Countries with enrollment rates below 0.5% in 2009 are excluded.
2. Countries with enrollment rates below 0.1% in 2009 are excluded.

Enrollment rates are defined as students of each age group calculated as the percentage of population of the same age group.

Source: OECD. See Annex 3 for notes (*www.oecd.org/edu/eag2011*).

StatLink http://dx.doi.org/10.1787/888932464410

How to read this table
In these countries, enrolment rates among adults, over 30 years old, had their strongest increase between 2008 and 2009. This may show a greater government focus on adult education through the expansion of education programmes and may indicate more adults returning to school as the labour market adjusts. For example, in New Zealand, enrolment of 35-39 year-olds at the ISCED 5B level showed its strongest rise in the last year of the 2005-09 period.

In around one-fifth of the countries, the strongest growth in participation among 35-39 year-olds occurred between 2008 and 2009 in tertiary-type B programmes designed to lead directly into the labour market. The sharp rise in unemployment rates from 2007 to 2008 in Spain and Ireland were not mirrored in enrolment rates among adults in the following year. However, in New Zealand and the United States the increase in enrolment rates between 2008 and 2009 do reflect the increase in unemployment rates seen between 2007 and 2008. In Australia between 2008 and 2009, enrolment rates at post-secondary non-tertiary and at tertiary-type B levels showed an increase of more than 10% among 30-34 year-olds, 35-39 year-olds and among those over 40 at the same time that unemployment rates also grew (Key Short-Term Economic Indicators, *OECD Database 2011*).

The relative size of the public and the private sectors

In OECD and other G20 countries, primary and secondary education is predominantly provided by public institutions. On average, 90% of primary education students in OECD countries are enrolled in the public sector. The proportion is slightly smaller in secondary education, with 86% of lower secondary students and 81% of upper secondary students taught in public institutions. On the other hand, Indonesia has a significant share (37%) of students at the secondary level enrolled in independent private schools. Indonesia, Japan, Mexico and Portugal are the exceptions at the upper secondary level, as independent private providers (those that receive less than 50% of their funds from government sources) take in 52%, 31%, 18% and 20% of students, respectively (Table C1.4 and Indicator D5).

At the tertiary level, the pattern is quite different; private providers generally play a more significant role. For example, 38% of students enrolled in tertiary-type B programmes attend privately funded programmes, and 29% of students enrolled in tertiary-type A education and advanced research programmes attend privately funded institutions. In the United Kingdom, virtually all tertiary education is provided through government-dependent private institutions. In Israel, 66% of students enrolled in tertiary-type B programmes and 77% of students enrolled in tertiary-type A and advanced research programmes attend these kinds of institutions.

Chart C1.3. Difference in reading performance at age 15, by public and private schools

Difference in reading performance on the PISA scale between students in public and private schools (government-dependent and independent private schools)

	Percentage of students enrolled in public schools at age 15	Percentage of students enrolled in private schools at age 15: Government-dependent private	Percentage of students enrolled in private schools at age 15: Independent private	Performance difference[1]: Observed	Performance difference[1] after accounting for the socio-economic background of: Students	Performance difference[1] after accounting for the socio-economic background of: Students and schools
Netherlands[2]	35.3	64.7	0.0	13	10	3
Ireland[2]	43.4	49.5	7.1	**-35**	**-21**	**-12**
Chile	47.3	49.2	3.6	**-36**	**-22**	-5
Indonesia	57.9	14.7	27.4	**18**	**16**	**13**
Australia	61.0	23.9	15.1	**-44**	**-23**	3
Korea	64.5	18.4	17.2	-16	**-15**	**-13**
Argentina	64.7	19.9	15.3	**-87**	**-56**	**-20**
Spain	69.1	25.7	5.2	**-37**	**-19**	-7
Japan	71.4	1.9	26.7	8	**17**	**45**
Denmark	79.6	17.8	2.6	**-18**	-10	-2
OECD average	84.9	10.9	4.2	**-30**	**-14**	**7**
Israel	85.8	10.2	3.9	-30	-23	-12
Portugal	86.1	8.8	5.1	**-28**	**-16**	-4
Austria	87.4	10.8	1.8	-31	-18	9
Luxembourg	87.5	10.9	1.6	-9	-7	**-6**
Hungary	88.4	11.5	a	-15	1	**18**
Mexico[2]	89.4	0.1	10.5	**-49**	**-16**	**23**
Sweden	90.0	10.0	0.0	**-35**	**-17**	2
Shanghai-China	90.4	0.6	9.0	-20	-11	3
Slovak Republic	91.0	9.0	0.0	-24	-16	-3
Brazil	91.6	0.2	8.1	**-116**	**-87**	**-29**
United States	93.1	a	6.9	**-65**	**-31**	-1
Canada	93.6	3.5	2.9	**-50**	**-31**	-11
United Kingdom	93.7	0.0	6.3	**-62**	**-27**	**20**
Switzerland	94.0	2.3	3.7	-19	-2	28
Italy	94.7	1.9	3.3	**38**	**46**	**60**
New Zealand	95.1	0.0	4.9	**-63**	**-23**	14
Germany	96.0	4.0	0.0	-18	-4	**20**
Finland	96.1	3.9	0.0	-7	-1	1
Greece	96.6	a	3.4	**-55**	**-25**	17
Estonia	97.1	2.3	0.6	-11	-5	6
Czech Republic	97.1	2.9	a	-36	-23	5
Slovenia	97.3	2.7	0.0	**-80**	**-57**	-5
Poland	97.9	0.6	1.5	**-57**	-16	5

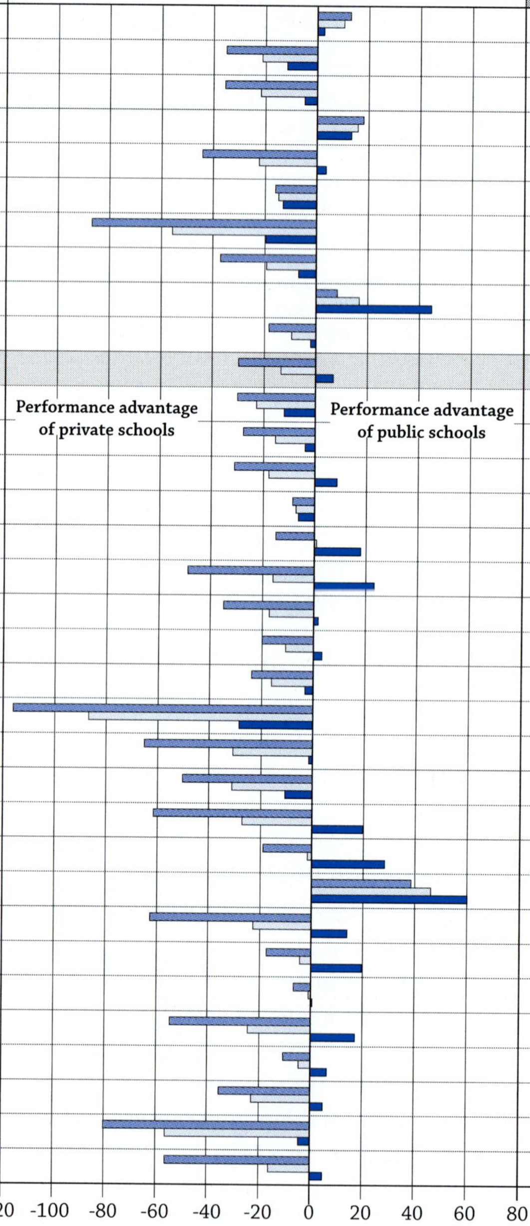

Notes: On average in OECD countries, 39 score points on the PISA scale in reading performance correspond to one school year for 15 year-old students.
1. Statistically significant differences in performance are displayed in bold.
2. Definitions of private institutions in PISA are based on the degree of government funding and also on the degree of government direction or regulation, and so may differ from those applied in *Education at a Glance 2011*.
Countries are ranked in descending order according to the percentage of students enrolled in public schools.
Source: OECD, *PISA 2009 Database*, Table IV.3.9. See Annex 3 for notes *(www.oecd.org/edu/eag2011)*.
StatLink http://dx.doi.org/10.1787/888932461446

In Estonia, 91% of students enrolled in tertiary-type A and advanced research programmes attend government-dependent private institutions. Independent private providers are more prominent at the tertiary level than at pre-tertiary levels (an average of more than 15% of tertiary students attend such institutions), particularly in Brazil, Chile, Japan and Korea, with more than 85% of students who are enrolled in tertiary-type B programmes attending such institutions (Table C1.5).

Performance in public and private institutions

School education takes place mainly in public schools, defined by PISA as schools managed directly or indirectly by a public education authority, government agency, or governing board appointed by government or elected by public franchise.

On average across the countries with a significant share of private enrolment, students in private schools outperform students in public schools in the majority of countries even if the advantage is smaller after accounting for the socio-economic background of students. In many countries and on average in OECD countries, the score advantage of students in private schools is reversed after accounting for the socio-economic background of both students and schools. In Hungary, Indonesia, Italy, Japan, Mexico, New Zealand and the United Kingdom, the performance difference after accounting for the socio-economic background of both students and schools is statistically significant in favour of public schools (Chart C1.3).

In interpreting the these data, it is important to recognise that there are many factors that affect school choice. Families may not be able to afford to send their children to independent private schools that charge high tuition fees. Even government-dependent private schools that charge no tuition fees can cater to a different clientele or apply more restrictive transfer or selection practices. One way to examine this factor is to adjust for differences in the socio-economic background of students and schools. That said, while the performance of private schools does not tend to be superior once socio-economic factors have been accounted for, in many countries these schools may still appear as an attractive alternative for parents looking to maximise the benefits for their children, including those that are conferred to students through the socio-economic level of the schools' intake (OECD, 2010i).

Definitions

Programmes at the secondary level can be subdivided into three categories, based on the degree to which they are oriented towards a specific class of occupations or trades and lead to a qualification that is relevant to the labour market:

- In **combined school- and work-based programmes**, less than 75% of the curriculum is presented in the school environment or through distance education. These programmes can be organised in conjunction with educational authorities or educational institutions and include apprenticeship programmes that involve concurrent school-based and work-based training, and programmes that involve alternating periods of attendance at educational institutions and participation in work-based training (sometimes referred to as "sandwich" programmes).
- **General education programmes** are not explicitly designed to prepare participants for specific occupations or trades, or for entry into further vocational or technical education programmes (less than 25% of programme content is vocational or technical).
- **Pre-vocational or pre-technical education programmes** are mainly designed to introduce participants to the world of work and to prepare them for entry into further vocational or technical education programmes. Successful completion of such programmes does not lead to a vocational or technical qualification that is directly relevant to the labour market (at least 25% of programme content is vocational or technical).

The degree to which a programme has a vocational or general orientation does not necessarily determine whether participants have access to tertiary education. In several OECD countries, vocationally-oriented programmes are designed to prepare students for further study at the tertiary level, and in some countries general programmes do not always provide direct access to further education.

In school-based programmes, instruction takes place (either partially or exclusively) in educational institutions. These include special training centres run by public or private authorities or enterprise-based special training centres if these qualify as educational institutions. These programmes can have an on-the-job training component involving some practical work experience at the workplace. Programmes are classified as school-based if at least 75% of the programme curriculum is presented in the school environment. This may include distance education.

Vocational or technical education programmes prepare participants for direct entry into specific occupations without further training. Successful completion of such programmes leads to a vocational or technical qualification that is relevant to the labour market.

Vocational and pre-vocational programmes are further divided into two categories (school-based and combined school- and work-based programmes) based on the amount of training provided in school as opposed to the workplace.

Methodology

Data on enrolments are for the school year 2008-09 and based on the UOE data collection on educational systems administered annually by the OECD.

Except where otherwise noted, figures are based on head counts; that is, they do not distinguish between full-time and part-time study because the concept of part-time study is not recognised by some countries. In some OECD countries, part-time education is only partially covered in the reported data.

Net enrolment rates, expressed as percentages in Tables C1.1a and C1.2, are calculated by dividing the number of students of a particular age group enrolled in all levels of education by the size of the population of that age group. In Table C1.1b, available on line, the net enrolment rate is calculated for students at a particular level of education.

In Table C1.2, data on trends in enrolment rates for the years 1995, 2000, 2001, 2002, 2003 and 2004 are based on a special survey carried out in January 2007 among OECD countries and four of six partner countries at the time (Brazil, Chile, Israel and the Russian Federation).

Data on apprenticeship programmes are based on a special survey carried out by the OECD in the autumn of 2007.

The statistical data for Israel are supplied by and under the responsibility of the relevant Israeli authorities. The use of such data by the OECD is without prejudice to the status of the Golan Heights, East Jerusalem and Israeli settlements in the West Bank under the terms of international law.

References

OECD (2006b), *Starting Strong II: Early Childhood Education And Care*, OECD, Paris.

OECD (2010b), *PISA 2009 Results: Overcoming Social Background: Equity in Learning Opportunities and Outcomes, What Students Know and Can Do: Student Performance in Reading, Mathematics and Science*, OECD, Paris.

OECD (2010i), *PISA 2009 Results: What Makes a School Successful?: Resources, Policies and Practices* (Volume IV), OECD, Paris.

OECD (2011), *Key Short-Term Economic Indicators, http://stats.oecd.org/Index.aspx?DataSetCode=KEI,* accessed 20 June 2011.

The following additional material relevant to this indicator is available on line:

- ***Table C1.1b. Transition characteristics from age 15 to 20, by level of education (2009)***
  StatLink http://dx.doi.org/10.1787/888932464277
- ***Table C1.6a. Education expectancy (2009)***
  StatLink http://dx.doi.org/10.1787/888932464372
- ***Table C1.6b. Expected years in tertiary education (2009)***
  StatLink http://dx.doi.org/10.1787/888932464391

Table C1.1a. Enrolment rates, by age (2009)

Full-time and part-time students in public and private institutions

		Ending age of compulsory education	Number of years at which over 90% of the population are enrolled	Age range at which over 90% of the population are enrolled	Students in the following age groups as a percentage of the population of the same age groups: Age 2 and under[1]	Ages 3 and 4	Ages 5 to 14	Ages 15 to19: B + G	Ages 15 to19: Boys	Ages 15 to19: Girls	Ages 20 to 29: M + W	Ages 20 to 29: Men	Ages 20 to 29: Women	Ages 30 to 39: M + W	Ages 30 to 39: Men	Ages 30 to 39: Women	Ages 40 and over
		(1)	(2)	(3)	(4)	(5)	(6)	(7)	(8)	(9)	(10)	(11)	(12)	(13)	(14)	(15)	(16)
OECD	Australia	15	12	5 - 16	a	31.8	99.3	80.0	79.2	80.8	31.5	31.2	31.9	11.7	11.1	12.3	4.6
	Austria	15	12	5 - 16	3.1	72.3	98.4	79.4	78.8	80.0	23.2	21.8	24.7	4.3	4.6	4.1	0.6
	Belgium	18	15	3 - 17	17.1	99.1	98.9	93.2	91.0	95.5	29.5	26.0	33.0	8.7	7.6	9.9	3.8
	Canada[2]	16-18	12	6 - 17	a	m	m	81.1	79.2	82.5	25.6	23.1	28.1	5.5	4.9	6.1	1.2
	Chile	18	10	6 - 15	0.1	55.9	93.2	73.0	72.5	73.5	23.1	23.0	23.2	3.8	4.0	3.6	0.7
	Czech Republic	15	13	5 - 17	5.2	72.6	98.7	89.2	88.2	90.3	22.5	19.8	25.4	3.7	3.3	4.2	0.5
	Denmark	16	13	3 - 16	a	95.5	97.6	83.6	83.3	83.9	36.9	33.1	40.8	8.0	6.9	9.2	1.5
	Estonia	15	14	4 - 17	n	90.7	100.0	84.6	82.1	87.3	26.3	21.3	31.4	6.5	4.2	8.8	0.8
	Finland	16	13	6 - 18	a	50.3	95.5	86.9	86.1	87.6	41.4	38.4	44.4	14.9	13.8	16.1	3.5
	France	16	15	3 - 17	6.1	101.4	99.8	84.0	82.7	85.3	19.2	17.4	20.9	2.6	2.1	3.1	x(13)
	Germany	18	14	4 - 17	7.4	91.9	99.4	88.5	88.1	88.9	30.0	31.0	29.0	2.7	3.1	2.3	0.1
	Greece	14-15	13	5 - 17	n	26.1	100.1	m	m	m	m	m	m	m	m	m	m
	Hungary	18	14	4 - 17	a	82.6	98.9	89.9	89.5	90.3	24.9	22.9	26.9	4.8	3.5	6.0	0.6
	Iceland	16	14	3 - 16	a	95.3	98.2	84.9	82.9	87.1	35.0	30.5	39.8	12.9	9.0	17.1	3.9
	Ireland	16	14	5 - 18	n	23.4	101.7	92.1	89.6	94.6	18.7	19.4	18.0	5.2	4.9	5.5	0.2
	Israel	17	13	4 - 16	n	89.4	96.2	64.2	61.4	67.1	21.8	19.0	24.7	5.5	6.1	5.0	1.0
	Italy	16	14	3 - 16	2.7	95.9	99.8	81.8	80.2	83.5	21.3	18.5	24.3	3.2	2.9	3.5	0.1
	Japan	15	14	4 - 17	0.1	87.8	101.0	m	m	m	m	m	m	m	m	m	m
	Korea	14	11	7 - 17	n	32.3	95.7	87.5	86.9	88.2	29.1	37.0	20.5	2.0	2.1	1.8	0.5
	Luxembourg[3]	15	12	4 - 15	1.4	82.1	95.6	m	m	m	m	m	m	m	m	m	m
	Mexico	15	11	4 - 14	n	68.1	104.6	51.9	50.7	53.1	11.4	11.6	11.2	3.9	3.3	4.4	0.7
	Netherlands	18	14	4 - 17	a	50.5	99.5	89.7	88.8	90.6	29.1	29.6	28.6	2.9	3.1	2.7	0.7
	New Zealand	16	13	4 - 16	n	90.7	100.6	80.6	78.8	82.4	32.1	31.5	32.7	12.9	11.4	14.2	5.4
	Norway	16	15	3 - 17	a	95.0	99.5	85.9	85.6	86.2	28.5	25.5	31.6	6.6	5.1	8.2	1.7
	Poland	16	13	6 - 18	1.3	47.1	94.1	92.7	92.3	93.2	31.3	30.3	32.3	4.7	3.3	6.1	x(13)
	Portugal	14	12	5 - 16	n	77.2	103.1	84.6	81.9	87.5	23.9	23.1	24.7	9.9	9.3	10.4	2.9
	Slovak Republic	16	12	6 - 17	3.3	67.2	96.1	85.1	83.7	86.5	20.1	16.6	23.7	4.2	2.8	5.7	0.7
	Slovenia	14	12	6 - 17	n	81.4	97.1	91.1	89.0	93.3	33.6	27.5	40.3	5.1	4.5	5.8	0.6
	Spain	16	14	3 - 16	24.6	98.7	100.1	81.4	78.2	84.7	21.8	19.8	23.9	4.2	4.0	4.5	1.1
	Sweden	16	15	4 - 18	a	91.2	98.7	87.0	86.5	87.5	34.0	28.5	39.7	12.9	9.1	16.8	2.7
	Switzerland	15	12	5 - 16	1.8	25.0	100.0	84.7	86.4	82.9	23.1	23.5	22.7	4.0	4.4	3.5	0.4
	Turkey	14	7	7 - 13	n	8.9	91.3	53.5	56.1	50.8	14.8	16.7	12.9	2.3	2.7	1.9	0.3
	United Kingdom	16	13	4 - 16	2.9	88.6	102.6	73.7	70.2	75.5	17.3	15.6	19.1	5.8	4.6	6.9	1.6
	United States	17	11	6 - 16	n	46.3	97.1	80.9	78.2	83.8	24.4	21.4	27.5	5.8	4.5	7.1	1.4
	OECD average	16	13	4 - 16	2.3	70.1	98.6	82.1	80.9	83.4	26.0	24.4	27.7	6.2	5.4	7.0	1.5
	EU21 average	16	13	4 - 16	3.6	75.5	98.8	86.2	84.7	87.7	26.6	24.2	29.0	6.0	5.1	6.9	1.3
Other G20	Argentina[2]	17	11	5 - 15	n	53.9	105.6	71.0	63.9	78.4	25.0	19.3	30.7	7.2	5.7	8.8	1.3
	Brazil	17	9	7 - 15	7.4	43.9	96.5	75.4	74.8	76.0	20.8	19.6	22.0	8.6	7.2	9.8	2.5
	China	m	m	m	m	m	m	m	m	m	m	m	m	m	m	m	m
	India	m	m	m	m	m	m	m	m	m	m	m	m	m	m	m	m
	Indonesia	15	9	6 - 14	n	14.4	97.2	62.4	62.6	62.3	10.3	10.6	10.0	0.1	0.1	n	n
	Russian Federation	17	8	7 - 14	17.6	70.3	93.5	m	m	m	m	m	m	m	m	m	m
	Saudi Arabia	m	m	m	m	m	m	m	m	m	m	m	m	m	m	m	m
	South Africa	m	m	m	m	m	m	m	m	m	m	m	m	m	m	m	m

Note: Ending age of compulsory education is the age at which compulsory schooling ends. For example, an ending age of 18 indicates that all students under 18 are legally obliged to participate in education. Mismatches between the coverage of the population data and the enrolment data mean that the participation rates may be underestimated for countries such as Luxembourg that are net exporters of students and may be overestimated for those that are net importers.

1. Includes only institution-based pre-primary programmes. These are not the only form of effective early childhood education available below the age of 3, therefore inferences about access to and quality of pre-primary education and care should be made with caution. In countries where an integrated system of pre-primary and care exists enrolment rate is noted as not applicable for children aged 2 and under.

2. Year of reference 2008.

3. Underestimated because a lot of resident students go to school in the neighbouring countries.

Source: OECD. Argentina and Indonesia: UNESCO Institute for Statistics (World Education Indicators Programme).
See Annex 3 for notes *(www.oecd.org/edu/eag2011).*

Please refer to the Reader's Guide for information concerning the symbols replacing missing data.

StatLink http://dx.doi.org/10.1787/888932464258

C1

Table C1.2. **Trends in enrolment rates (1995-2009)**

Full-time and part-time students in public and private institutions

		15-19 year-olds as a percentage of the population aged 15 to 19								20-29 year-olds as a percentage of the population aged 20 to 29							
		1995	2000	2002	2005	2006	2007	2008	2009	1995	2000	2002	2005	2006	2007	2008	2009
OECD	Australia	m	m	m	m	m	m	m	**80**	23	28	33	33	33	33	33	**32**
	Austria	75	77	77	80	82	79	79	**79**	16	18	17	19	20	22	22	**23**
	Belgium	94	91	92	94	95	94	92	**93**	24	25	27	29	29	28	29	**30**
	Canada	80	81	80	80	81	81	81	**m**	22	23	25	26	26	26	26	**m**
	Chile	64	66	66	74	72	74	74	**73**	m	m	m	m	m	20	21	**23**
	Czech Republic	66	81	90	90	90	90	90	**89**	10	14	16	20	20	22	21	**23**
	Denmark	79	80	82	85	83	83	84	**84**	30	35	36	38	38	38	37	**37**
	Estonia	m	m	m	87	87	85	84	**85**	m	m	m	27	27	27	26	**26**
	Finland	81	85	85	87	88	88	87	**87**	28	38	40	43	43	43	43	**41**
	France	89	87	86	85	84	84	84	**84**	19	19	20	20	20	20	19	**19**
	Germany	88	88	89	89	89	88	89	**88**	20	24	26	28	28	29	28	**30**
	Greece	62	82	83	97	93	80	83	**m**	13	16	25	24	32	27	29	**m**
	Hungary	64	78	81	87	88	89	89	**90**	10	19	21	24	25	25	25	**25**
	Iceland	79	79	81	85	85	84	84	**85**	24	31	32	37	37	36	35	**35**
	Ireland	79	81	83	89	88	90	90	**92**	14	16	19	21	20	21	18	**19**
	Israel	m	64	65	65	65	65	64	**64**	m	m	21	20	21	21	21	**22**
	Italy	m	72	76	80	81	80	82	**82**	m	17	18	20	20	21	21	**21**
	Japan	m	m	m	m	m	m	m	**m**	m	m	m	m	m	m	m	**m**
	Korea	75	79	80	86	86	87	89	**87**	15	24	27	27	28	28	28	**29**
	Luxembourg	73	74	75	72	73	74	75	**m**	m	5	6	6	9	6	10	**m**
	Mexico	36	42	44	48	49	50	52	**52**	8	9	10	11	11	11	11	**11**
	Netherlands	89	87	87	86	89	89	90	**90**	21	22	23	26	27	28	29	**29**
	New Zealand	68	72	74	74	74	75	74	**81**	17	23	28	30	29	30	29	**32**
	Norway	83	86	85	86	86	87	87	**86**	25	28	26	29	30	30	29	**29**
	Poland	78	84	87	92	93	93	93	**93**	16	24	28	31	31	31	30	**31**
	Portugal	68	71	71	73	73	77	81	**85**	22	22	22	22	21	21	23	**24**
	Slovak Republic	m	m	76	85	85	86	85	**85**	m	m	13	16	17	18	19	**20**
	Slovenia	m	m	m	91	91	91	91	**91**	m	m	m	32	33	33	33	**34**
	Spain	73	77	78	81	80	80	81	**81**	21	24	23	22	22	22	21	**22**
	Sweden	82	86	86	87	88	87	86	**87**	22	33	34	36	36	35	33	**34**
	Switzerland	80	83	83	83	84	84	85	**85**	15	19	20	22	22	23	23	**23**
	Turkey	30	28	34	41	45	47	46	**53**	7	5	6	10	11	12	13	**15**
	United Kingdom	m	m	m	m	70	71	73	**74**	m	m	m	m	17	17	17	**17**
	United States	72	73	75	79	78	80	81	**81**	19	20	23	23	23	23	23	**24**
	OECD average	73	76	78	81	81	81	81	**82**	18	22	23	25	25	25	25	**26**
	OECD average for countries with data available for all reference years	*74*	*77*	*78*	*81*	*81*	*82*	*82*	**83**	*19*	*23*	*24*	*26*	*26*	*26*	*26*	**27**
	EU21 average	77	81	82	86	85	85	85	**86**	19	22	23	25	26	25	25	**27**
Other G20	Argentina	m	m	m	m	m	m	71	**m**	m	m	m	m	m	m	25	**m**
	Brazil	m	m	m	m	m	75	76	**75**	m	m	m	m	m	21	21	**21**
	China	m	m	m	m	m	m	m	**m**	m	m	m	m	m	m	m	**m**
	India	m	m	m	m	m	m	m	**m**	m	m	m	m	m	m	m	**m**
	Indonesia	m	m	m	m	m	m	m	**62**	m	m	m	m	m	m	m	**10**
	Russian Federation	m	71	74	74	m	m	77	**m**	m	m	13	19	m	m	20	**m**
	Saudi Arabia	m	m	m	m	m	m	m	**m**	m	m	m	m	m	m	m	**m**
	South Africa	m	m	m	m	m	m	m	**m**	m	m	m	m	m	m	m	**m**

Note: Columns showing years 2001 and 2003 and 2004 are available for consultation on line (see StatLink below).

Source: OECD. Argentina and Indonesia: UNESCO Institute for Statistics (World Education Indicators Programme). See Annex 3 for notes *(www.oecd.org/edu/eag2011).*

Please refer to the Reader's Guide for information concerning the symbols replacing missing data.

StatLink http://dx.doi.org/10.1787/888932464296

Table C1.3. **Secondary enrolment patterns (2009)**

Enrolment in lower and upper secondary programmes in public and private institutions, by programme orientation and first ages of selection in the education system

		From PISA 2009: first age of differentiation in the education system	Lower secondary education			Upper secondary education			
			General	Pre-vocational	Vocational	General	Pre-vocational	Vocational	Vocational combined school and work-based
		(1)	(2)	(3)	(4)	(5)	(6)	(7)	(8)
OECD	Australia	16	**79.0**	a	21.0	**52.6**	a	47.4	m
	Austria	10	**100.0**	n	n	**22.7**	6.2	71.1	35.9
	Belgium	12	**70.5**	4.8	24.7	**27.2**	a	72.8	1.8
	Canada[1]	16	**100.0**	x(2)	x(2)	**94.5**	x(7)	5.5	a
	Chile	16	**100.0**	a	a	**66.1**	a	33.9	a
	Czech Republic	11	**99.5**	0.5	a	**26.7**	n	73.3	32.2
	Denmark	16	**100.0**	n	n	**52.7**	n	47.3	46.5
	Estonia	15	**99.0**	0.1	0.9	**67.0**	a	33.0	0.4
	Finland	16	**100.0**	a	a	**31.2**	a	68.8	14.7
	France	15	**99.7**	0.3	a	**55.8**	a	44.2	12.4
	Germany	10	**97.6**	2.4	a	**46.8**	a	53.2	45.3
	Greece	15	**100.0**	a	a	**69.1**	a	30.9	a
	Hungary	11	**99.2**	0.4	0.5	**75.5**	10.2	14.3	14.3
	Iceland	16	**100.0**	a	a	**66.1**	1.7	32.2	15.4
	Ireland	15	**97.0**	3.0	n	**65.6**	33.0	1.5	1.5
	Israel	15	**100.0**	a	a	**64.7**	a	35.3	3.6
	Italy	14	**100.0**	a	a	**41.0**	32.6	26.5	a
	Japan	15	**100.0**	a	a	**76.2**	0.9	22.8	a
	Korea	14	**100.0**	a	a	**75.6**	a	24.4	a
	Luxembourg	13	**100.0**	n	a	**38.7**	a	61.3	14.5
	Mexico	15	**81.5**	a	18.5	**90.6**	a	9.4	a
	Netherlands	12	**72.0**	21.7	6.3	**32.9**	a	67.1	21.5
	New Zealand	16	**100.0**	n	n	**60.5**	7.9	31.7	a
	Norway	16	**100.0**	a	a	**45.9**	a	54.1	16.6
	Poland	16	**99.4**	0.6	a	**52.8**	a	47.2	6.3
	Portugal	12	**83.9**	0.1	16.0	**61.6**	5.6	32.8	a
	Slovak Republic	11	**98.7**	1.3	n	**28.4**	a	71.6	27.8
	Slovenia	14	**100.0**	a	a	**35.7**	n	64.3	0.7
	Spain	16	**99.5**	a	0.5	**57.1**	a	42.9	1.7
	Sweden	16	**99.0**	n	1.0	**43.6**	1.1	55.3	n
	Switzerland	12	**100.0**	n	n	**34.5**	n	65.5	60.1
	Turkey[2]	11	**a**	a	a	**59.2**	a	40.8	n
	United Kingdom[3]	16	**100.0**	a	a	**69.5**	x(7)	30.5	m
	United States	16	**100.0**	a	a	**m**	m	m	m
	OECD average	14	**96.1**	1.1	2.8	**54.1**	3.2	42.7	12.1
	EU21 average	14	**95.9**	1.7	2.4	**47.6**	4.4	48.0	13.9
Other G20	Argentina[1]	m	**100.0**	a	a	**17.0**	a	83.0	m
	Brazil	17	**100.0**	a	n	**88.4**	a	11.6	a
	China	m	**99.8**	0.2	x(2)	**49.6**	50.4	x(5)	a
	India	m	**100.0**	a	a	**98.0**	a	2.0	m
	Indonesia	m	**100.0**	a	a	**61.7**	a	38.3	m
	Russian Federation	15	**100.0**	a	a	**51.5**	18.0	30.5	m
	Saudi Arabia	m	**m**	m	m	**m**	m	m	m
	South Africa	m	**m**	m	m	**m**	m	m	m
	G20 average	m	**99.8**	0.2	m	**62.5**	7.1	30.5	m

1. Year of reference 2008.
2. Excludes ISCED 3C.
3. Includes post-secondary non-tertiary education.

Source: OECD. Argentina, China, India, Indonesia: UNESCO Institute for Statistics (World Education Indicators Programme). See Annex 3 for notes (*www.oecd.org/edu/eag2011*).

Please refer to the Reader's Guide for information concerning the symbols replacing missing data.

StatLink http://dx.doi.org/10.1787/888932464315

Table C1.4. **Students in primary and secondary education, by type of institution or mode of enrolment (2009)**

Distribution of students, by mode of enrolment and type of institution

	Type of institution									Mode of enrolment	
	Primary			Lower secondary			Upper secondary			Primary and secondary	
	Public	Government-dependent private	Independent private	Public	Government-dependent private	Independent private	Public	Government-dependent private	Independent private	Full-time	Part-time
	(1)	(2)	(3)	(4)	(5)	(6)	(7)	(8)	(9)	(10)	(11)
OECD											
Australia	**69.5**	30.5	a	**65.8**	34.2	m	**69.7**	30.1	0.2	**84.4**	15.6
Austria	**94.4**	5.6	x(2)	**91.1**	8.9	x(5)	**89.6**	10.4	x(8)	**m**	m
Belgium[1]	**45.9**	54.1	m	**39.7**	60.3	m	**43.7**	56.3	m	**79.6**	20.4
Canada[2]	**95.0**	5.0	x(2)	**92.3**	7.7	x(5)	**94.0**	6.0	x(8)	**100.0**	a
Chile	**42.2**	51.8	6.0	**47.1**	46.9	6.0	**41.5**	51.9	6.6	**100.0**	a
Czech Republic	**98.5**	1.5	a	**97.4**	2.6	a	**85.9**	14.1	a	**100.0**	n
Denmark	**86.5**	13.2	0.3	**74.2**	25.1	0.8	**97.8**	2.1	0.1	**97.4**	2.6
Estonia	**96.0**	a	4.0	**96.9**	a	3.1	**96.2**	a	3.8	**95.8**	4.2
Finland	**98.6**	1.4	a	**95.6**	4.4	a	**86.2**	13.8	a	**100.0**	a
France	**85.1**	14.3	0.5	**78.2**	21.5	0.3	**68.6**	30.4	1.0	**m**	m
Germany	**96.1**	3.9	x(2)	**91.1**	8.9	x(5)	**92.5**	7.5	x(8)	**99.7**	0.3
Greece	**92.7**	a	7.3	**94.4**	a	5.6	**95.1**	a	4.9	**97.9**	2.1
Hungary	**91.7**	8.3	a	**90.9**	9.1	a	**80.2**	19.8	a	**95.7**	4.3
Iceland	**98.1**	1.9	n	**99.2**	0.8	n	**79.4**	20.3	0.3	**89.8**	10.2
Ireland	**99.6**	a	0.4	**100.0**	a	n	**98.3**	a	1.7	**99.9**	0.1
Israel	**m**	m	a	**m**	m	a	**m**	m	a	**100.0**	a
Italy	**93.2**	a	6.8	**96.0**	a	4.0	**91.1**	3.6	5.3	**99.1**	0.9
Japan	**98.9**	a	1.1	**92.8**	a	7.2	**69.0**	a	31.0	**98.7**	1.3
Korea	**98.6**	a	1.4	**81.6**	18.4	a	**54.3**	45.7	n	**100.0**	a
Luxembourg	**91.8**	0.4	7.9	**80.9**	10.7	8.4	**84.0**	7.2	8.8	**99.9**	0.1
Mexico	**91.7**	a	8.3	**88.7**	a	11.3	**81.5**	a	18.5	**100.0**	a
Netherlands	**m**	a	m	**m**	a	m	**m**	a	m	**99.1**	0.9
New Zealand	**87.6**	10.2	2.1	**82.9**	12.1	5.0	**72.0**	15.7	12.2	**88.4**	11.6
Norway	**97.7**	2.3	x(2)	**96.9**	3.1	x(5)	**90.5**	9.5	x(8)	**99.0**	1.0
Poland	**97.4**	0.7	1.9	**96.2**	1.1	2.7	**86.9**	1.3	11.9	**94.9**	5.1
Portugal	**88.1**	3.2	8.7	**81.2**	5.1	13.7	**75.8**	4.0	20.2	**100.0**	a
Slovak Republic	**94.2**	5.8	n	**93.6**	6.4	n	**86.4**	13.6	n	**98.8**	1.2
Slovenia	**99.7**	0.3	n	**99.9**	0.1	a	**96.2**	2.0	1.8	**94.2**	5.8
Spain	**68.5**	27.8	3.7	**67.8**	28.8	3.3	**77.5**	12.1	10.4	**92.3**	7.7
Sweden	**92.4**	7.6	n	**89.7**	10.3	n	**85.5**	14.5	n	**91.4**	8.6
Switzerland	**95.5**	1.4	3.0	**92.0**	2.8	5.2	**93.3**	2.8	3.9	**99.8**	0.2
Turkey	**97.8**	a	2.2	**a**	a	a	**97.1**	a	2.9	**m**	m
United Kingdom	**94.9**	0.1	5.0	**80.7**	13.3	6.0	**56.0**	38.1	5.9	**97.0**	3.0
United States	**90.2**	a	9.8	**90.9**	a	9.1	**91.2**	a	8.8	**100.0**	a
OECD average	**89.5**	7.6	2.9	**85.8**	10.7	3.5	**81.2**	13.1	5.7	**96.5**	3.5
EU21 average	**90.2**	7.0	2.7	**86.9**	10.3	2.8	**83.6**	11.9	4.4	**96.5**	3.5
Other G20											
Argentina[2]	**76.9**	17.8	5.3	**77.4**	17.3	5.3	**69.0**	22.6	8.3	**100.0**	a
Brazil	**87.7**	a	12.3	**89.9**	a	10.1	**85.6**	a	14.4	**m**	m
China	**93.3**	6.7	x(2)	**92.4**	7.6	x(5)	**85.4**	14.6	x(7)	**97.9**	2.1
India	**m**	m	m	**m**	m	m	**m**	m	m	**100.0**	a
Indonesia	**83.6**	a	16.4	**63.3**	a	36.7	**47.5**	a	52.5	**100.0**	a
Russian Federation	**99.4**	a	0.6	**99.5**	a	0.5	**98.8**	a	1.2	**99.9**	0.1
Saudi Arabia	**m**	m	m	**m**	m	m	**m**	m	m	**m**	m
South Africa	**m**	m	m	**m**	m	m	**m**	m	m	**m**	m
G20 average	**89.8**	4.8	5.3	**83.7**	8.4	7.9	**76.5**	12.2	11.3	**98.3**	1.7

1. Excludes independent private institutions.
2. Reference year 2008.

Source: OECD. Argentina, China, India, Indonesia: UNESCO Institute for Statistics (World Education Indicators Programme).
See Annex 3 for notes (*www.oecd.org/edu/eag2011*).

Please refer to the Reader's Guide for information concerning the symbols replacing missing data.

StatLink http://dx.doi.org/10.1787/888932464334

Table C1.5. Students in tertiary education, by type of institution or mode of enrolment (2009)

Distribution of students, by mode of enrolment, type of institution and programme destination

		Type of institution						Mode of study							
		Tertiary-type B education			Tertiary-type A and advanced research programmes			Tertiary-type B education				Tertiary-type A and advanced research programmes			
									Part-time				Part-time		
		Public	Government-dependent private	Independent private	Public	Government-dependent private	Independent private	Full-time Men + Women	M + W	Men	Women	Full-time Men + Women	M + W	Men	Women
		(1)	(2)	(3)	(4)	(5)	(6)	(7)	(8)	(9)	(10)	(11)	(12)	(13)	(14)
OECD	Australia	84.2	4.0	11.8	96.2	a	3.8	48.1	51.9	51.0	52.6	70.5	29.5	27.9	30.7
	Austria	70.3	29.7	x(2)	84.8	15.2	x(5)	m	m	m	m	m	m	m	m
	Belgium[1]	44.2	55.8	m	41.8	58.2	m	62.4	37.6	40.1	35.8	82.9	17.1	18.9	15.4
	Canada[2]	m	m	m	m	m	m	75.7	24.3	20.6	27.2	81.9	18.1	17.4	18.5
	Chile	8.9	2.6	88.5	29.0	23.2	47.8	m	m	m	m	m	m	m	m
	Czech Republic	67.3	30.3	2.4	87.1	a	12.9	88.9	11.1	13.3	10.2	97.0	3.0	1.9	3.9
	Denmark	98.9	0.5	0.6	98.2	1.8	n	62.8	37.2	33.6	41.0	90.7	9.3	8.5	9.9
	Estonia	46.6	16.9	36.5	0.2	91.2	8.6	89.7	10.3	12.6	8.9	86.0	14.0	18.1	11.5
	Finland	100.0	n	a	83.7	16.3	a	100.0	a	a	a	56.2	43.8	50.2	38.4
	France	70.0	8.4	21.6	85.0	0.8	14.2	m	m	m	m	m	m	m	m
	Germany[3]	57.5	42.5	x(2)	94.6	5.4	x(5)	87.7	12.3	23.6	7.0	95.2	4.8	5.3	4.4
	Greece	100.0	a	a	100.0	a	a	100.0	a	a	a	100.0	a	a	a
	Hungary	54.2	45.8	a	86.4	13.6	a	72.2	27.8	21.0	31.2	63.0	37.0	32.3	40.7
	Iceland	30.5	69.5	n	79.5	20.5	n	31.1	68.9	82.0	50.7	75.5	24.5	20.9	26.5
	Ireland	97.6	a	2.4	96.6	a	3.4	67.7	32.3	27.0	38.6	87.5	12.5	12.5	12.5
	Israel	33.6	66.4	a	9.3	77.4	13.3	100.0	a	a	a	81.0	18.4	17.7	20.0
	Italy	87.2	a	12.8	92.4	a	7.6	100.0	a	a	a	100.0	a	a	a
	Japan	7.8	a	92.2	24.6	a	75.4	96.9	3.1	2.2	3.6	90.7	9.3	7.2	12.4
	Korea	3.3	a	96.7	24.6	a	75.4	m	m	m	m	m	m	m	m
	Luxembourg	m	m	m	m	m	m	m	m	m	m	m	m	m	m
	Mexico	95.5	a	4.5	65.9	a	34.1	100.0	a	a	a	100.0	a	a	a
	Netherlands	m	a	m	m	a	m	34.5	65.5	56.3	72.4	85.6	14.4	13.4	15.2
	New Zealand	59.4	30.8	9.8	96.5	2.6	0.9	39.4	60.6	56.9	63.6	59.5	40.5	37.8	42.4
	Norway	43.2	56.8	x(2)	85.8	14.2	x(5)	55.6	44.4	28.0	54.1	69.4	30.6	27.3	32.6
	Poland	74.9	a	25.1	66.6	a	33.4	70.4	29.6	30.9	29.3	44.7	55.3	53.6	56.6
	Portugal	97.0	a	3.0	75.7	a	24.3	m	m	m	m	m	m	m	m
	Slovak Republic	81.9	18.1	n	86.7	n	13.3	76.0	24.0	16.7	28.1	62.1	37.9	31.4	42.1
	Slovenia	80.2	4.4	15.4	91.6	5.0	3.4	53.5	46.5	45.3	47.7	74.9	25.1	25.9	24.7
	Spain	79.7	14.6	5.7	89.7	n	10.3	95.9	4.1	2.7	5.4	71.3	28.7	30.9	26.9
	Sweden	58.4	41.6	n	93.1	6.9	n	91.6	8.4	9.7	7.3	47.4	52.6	50.4	54.1
	Switzerland	34.0	35.3	30.7	95.3	3.1	1.6	27.4	72.6	77.9	67.1	89.3	10.7	12.7	8.8
	Turkey	96.4	a	3.6	93.4	a	6.6	100.0	n	n	n	100.0	n	n	n
	United Kingdom	a	100.0	n	a	100.0	n	24.4	75.6	75.7	75.5	74.9	25.1	22.9	26.9
	United States	79.1	a	20.9	71.5	a	28.5	47.3	52.7	51.9	53.2	65.5	34.5	32.0	36.4
	OECD average	61.6	20.7	17.7	70.7	14.0	15.3	71.4	28.6	27.8	28.9	78.7	21.3	20.6	21.8
	EU21 average	71.8	20.4	7.8	76.2	15.7	8.2	75.2	24.8	24.0	25.8	77.6	22.4	22.1	22.5
Other G20	Argentina[2]	58.7	17.1	24.2	79.8	a	20.2	93.6	6.4	8.2	5.5	51.9	48.1	48.0	47.5
	Brazil	15.0	a	85.0	27.5	a	72.5	m	m	m	m	m	m	m	m
	China	m	m	m	m	m	m	70.3	29.7	31.0	28.5	75.9	24.1	24.3	24.0
	India	m	m	m	m	m	m	100.0	n	n	n	100.0	n	n	n
	Indonesia	47.9	a	52.1	38.3	a	61.7	100.0	a	a	a	100.0	a	a	a
	Russian Federation[3]	95.2	a	4.8	83.1	a	16.9	69.9	30.1	31.0	29.3	50.8	49.2	44.0	53.3
	Saudi Arabia	m	m	m	m	m	m	m	m	m	m	m	m	m	m
	South Africa	m	m	m	m	m	m	m	m	m	m	m	m	m	m
	G20 average	m	m	m	m	m	m	79.6	20.4	21.1	20.2	82.7	17.3	16.4	18.2

1. Excludes independent private institutions.
2. Year of reference 2008.
3. Excludes advanced research programmes.

Source: OECD. Argentina, China, India, Indonesia: UNESCO Institute for Statistics (World Education Indicators Programme). See Annex 3 for notes (*www.oecd.org/edu/eag2011*).

Please refer to the Reader's Guide for information concerning the symbols replacing missing data.

StatLink http://dx.doi.org/10.1787/888932464353

INDICATOR C2

HOW MANY STUDENTS WILL ENTER TERTIARY EDUCATION?

- Based on current patterns of entry, it is estimated that an average of 59% of today's young adults in OECD countries will enter tertiary-type A (largely theory-based) programmes and 19% will enter tertiary-type B (shorter, and largely vocational) programmes over their lifetimes.
- Between 1995 and 2009, entry rates for tertiary-type A programmes increased by nearly 25 percentage points, on average across OECD countries, while entry rates for tertiary-type B programmes remained stable.

Chart C2.1. Entry rates into tertiary-type A and B education (1995 and 2009)

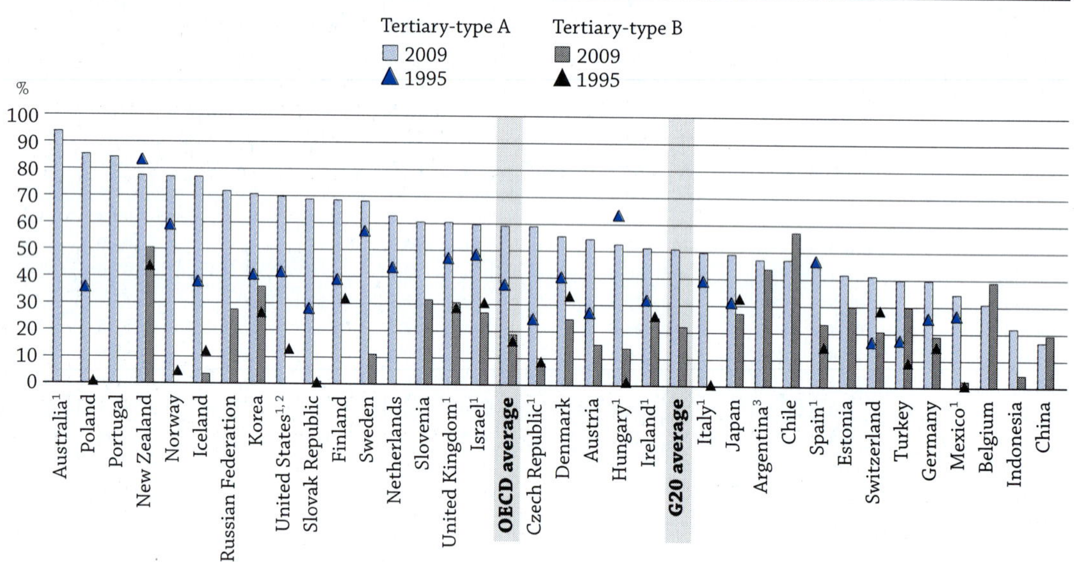

1. Year of reference 2000 instead of 1995.
2. In 2009, the entry rates for tertiary-type A programmes include the entry rates for tertiary-type B programmes.
3. Year of reference 2008 instead of 2009.

Countries are ranked in descending order of entry rates for tertiary-type A education in 2009.

Source: OECD. Argentina, China, Indonesia: UNESCO Institute for Statistics (World Education Indicators Programme). Tables C2.1, C2.2. See Annex 3 for notes (*www.oecd.org/edu/eag2011*).

StatLink http://dx.doi.org/10.1787/888932461465

Context

Entry rates estimate the proportion of people who will enter a specific type of tertiary education programme during their lifetimes. They also indicate the accessibility of tertiary education and the perceived value of attending tertiary programmes, and provide some indication of the degree to which a population is acquiring the high-level skills and knowledge valued by today's labour market. High entry and participation rates in tertiary education imply that a highly educated labour force is being developed and maintained.

In OECD countries, the belief that skills acquired through higher education are valued more than those held by people with lower educational attainment stems from the depreciation, both real and feared, of "routine" jobs that could be exported to low-wage countries or mechanised, as well as from the growing understanding that knowledge and innovation are sources of growth in high-income countries. Tertiary institutions will be challenged not only to meet growing demand by expanding the number of places offered, but also to adapt programmes and teaching methods to match the diverse needs of a new generation of students.

INDICATOR C2

Other findings

- In Australia, Iceland, Korea, New Zealand, Norway, Poland, Portugal and the Russian Federation, **entry rates into tertiary-type A programmes averaged at least 70% in 2009.**
- **The age at which young people enter tertiary-type A education varies widely among countries**, from a median age of 18.6 in Japan to 23.7 in Israel. In some countries, the age range is fairly limited and most students are relatively young (Belgium, Indonesia, Italy, Japan and Slovenia), whereas in other countries, the spectrum is much wider and includes older students (Iceland, New Zealand, Portugal and Sweden).
- In the 23 OECD countries with available data, **an estimated 2.6% of today's young adults will enter advanced research programmes.**
- **High proportions of international students influence entry rates**. In Australia, the impact of international students is so great that entry rates drop significantly when international students are excluded.

Analysis

Overall access to tertiary education

It is estimated that 59% of young adults in OECD countries will enter tertiary-type A programmes during their lifetimes if current patterns of entry continue. In several countries, at least 70% of young adults enter these kinds of programmes, while in Belgium, China, Indonesia and Mexico, at most 35% do (Chart C2.1).

The proportion of students entering tertiary-type B programmes is generally smaller, mainly because these programmes are less developed in most OECD countries. In OECD countries for which data are available, an average of 19% of young adults enters these types of programmes. Proportions range from 3% or less in Italy, Mexico, the Netherlands, Norway, Poland, Portugal and the Slovak Republic, to 30% or more in Argentina, Belgium, Estonia, Korea, the Russian Federation, Slovenia, Turkey and the United Kingdom, to at least 50% in Chile and New Zealand. Although there are relatively few of these kinds of programmes offered in the Netherlands, this is expected to change with the introduction of a new programme of associate degrees. Finland and Norway have, respectively, no or only one tertiary-type B programme in their education systems (Chart C2.1).

Belgium, Chile and China are the three countries where more students entered tertiary-type B programmes in 2009. In Belgium and Chile, broad access to tertiary-type B programmes counterbalances comparatively low entry rates into academic tertiary programmes. Other countries, most notably Israel, Slovenia and the United Kingdom, have entry rates around the OECD average for academic programmes and comparatively high rates of entry for vocational programmes. New Zealand shows entry rates for both types of programmes that are among the highest of OECD countries. However, these entry rates are inflated by a greater incidence of entry at older ages and a larger proportion of international students (see below).

On average, in all OECD countries with comparable data, the proportion of young adults entering tertiary-type A programmes in 2009 increased by 12 percentage points since 2000 and by nearly 25 percentage points since 1995. Entry rates into these programmes increased by more than 20 percentage points between 2000 and 2009 in Australia, Austria, the Czech Republic, Korea, Poland and the Slovak Republic. Finland, Hungary, New Zealand and Spain are the only OECD countries that show a decline in entry rates into these programmes; however in Hungary and Spain, the decrease is counterbalanced by a significant increase in entry rates into tertiary-type B programmes during the same period. In New Zealand, the rise and fall of entry rates between 2000 and 2009 mirrored the rise and fall of the number of international students over the same period.

Among OECD countries, overall net entry rates into tertiary-type B programmes between 1995 and 2009 have remained relatively stable except in Spain and Turkey, where they have increased by 20 percentage points. Denmark reclassified these types of programmes as tertiary-type A after 2000, which partly explains the changes observed in that country between 1995 and 2009 (Chart C2.1).

It is expected that 2.6% of today's young adults in the 23 OECD countries with comparable data will enter advanced research programmes during their lifetimes. Among all countries with available data, the proportions range from less than 1% in Argentina, Chile, Indonesia, Mexico and Turkey to at least 4% in Austria and Switzerland (Table C2.1).

Age of new entrants into tertiary-type A education

The age of new entrants into tertiary education varies among OECD countries for reasons that include differences in the typical graduation ages from upper secondary education, the intake capacity of institutions (admissions with *numerus clausus*) and the opportunity to enter the labour market before enrolling in tertiary education. People entering tertiary-type B programmes may also enter tertiary-type A programmes later in their lives.

Traditionally, students enter academic programmes immediately after having completed upper secondary education, and this remains true in many countries. For example, in Belgium, Indonesia, Ireland, Italy, Japan, Mexico, the Netherlands, and Slovenia, 80% of all first-time entrants into tertiary-type A programmes are under 23 years of age (Chart C2.2).

Chart C2.2. Age distribution of new entrants into tertiary-type A programmes (2009)

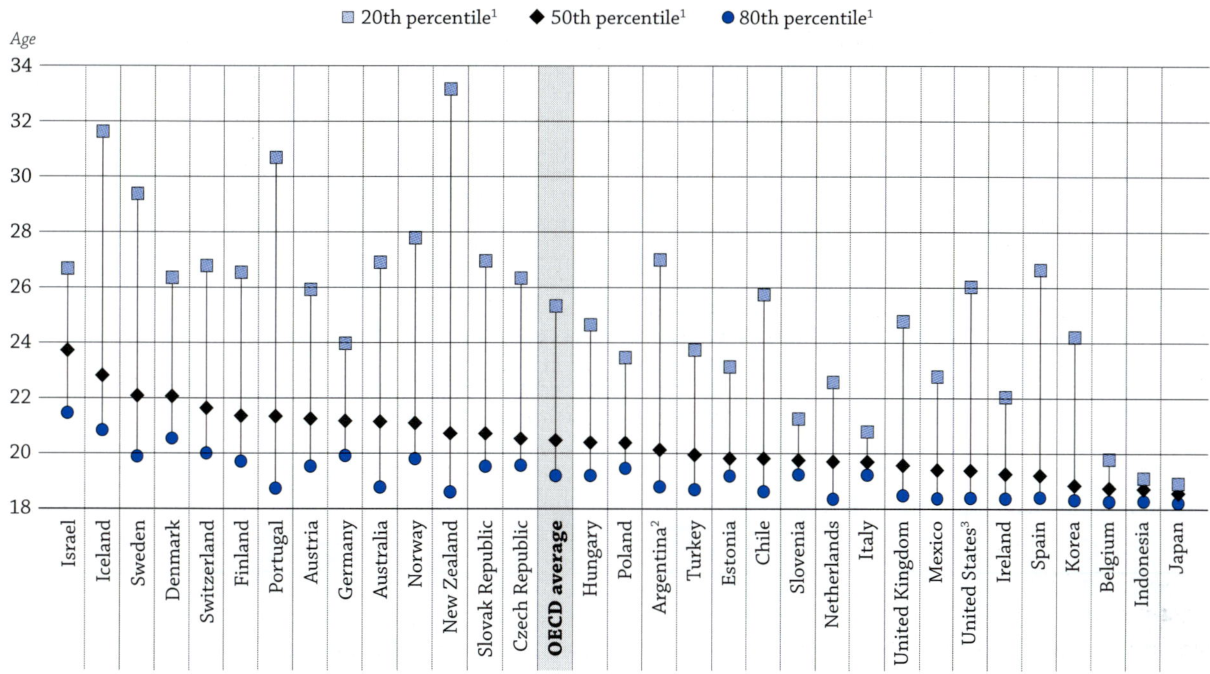

1. 20%, 50% and 80% of new entrants , respectively, are below this age.
2. Year of reference 2008.
3. The entry rates for tertiary-type A programmes include the entry rates for tertiary-type B programmes.

Countries are ranked in descending order of entry rates for tertiary-type A education in 2009 (50th percentile).

Source: OECD. Argentina, Indonesia: UNESCO Institute for Statistics (World Education Indicators Programme). Table C2.1. See Annex 3 for notes (*www.oecd.org/edu/eag2011*).

StatLink http://dx.doi.org/10.1787/888932461484

In other OECD countries, the transition from upper secondary to tertiary education may occur at a later age because of time spent in the labour force or the military. In such cases, first-time entrants into tertiary-type A programmes typically represent a much wider age range. In Denmark, Iceland, Israel and Sweden, the median age of students when they start tertiary education is 22 or older.

The proportion of older first-time entrants into these programmes may reflect the flexibility of the programmes (i.e. in the United States) and their suitability to students outside the typical age group. It may also reflect the value placed on work experience before accessing higher education, which is characteristic of the Nordic countries and is common in Australia, Hungary, New Zealand and Switzerland, where a sizeable proportion of new entrants are much older than the typical age of entry. It may also reflect some countries' mandatory military service, which postpones entry into tertiary education. For example, Israel, where more than half of students entering tertiary-type A education for the first time are 23 or older, has mandatory military service for 18-21 year-old men and 18-20 year-old women. Nevertheless, entering tertiary education at a later stage also has some consequences for the economy, such as foregone tax revenue. Some governments are encouraging students to make the most of their capacities by moving more rapidly into and through tertiary education, and are providing universities with more incentives to promote on-time completion (Table C2.1).

During the recent economic crisis, young people may have postponed their entry into the labour market and stayed in education. Some governments also developed second-chance programmes, aimed at people who left school early, to raise the skills level of the workforce and make professionalising education a real option for young people. In some countries, high entry rates may reflect a temporary phenomenon, such as university reforms, the economic crisis, or a surge in international students.

Impact of international students on entry rates into tertiary-type A programmes

By definition, all international students enrolling for the first time in a country are counted as new entrants, regardless of their previous education in other countries. To highlight the impact of international students on entry rates into tertiary-type A programmes, both unadjusted and adjusted entry rates (i.e. the entry rate when international students are excluded) are presented in Chart C2.3.

In Australia, the impact is so great – a 29 percentage-point difference – that its entry rates slip from the top to the seventh position. In Austria, Iceland, New Zealand, Norway, Sweden, Switzerland and the United Kingdom the presence of international students also affects entry rates greatly, with differences of from 9 to 20 percentage points (Table C2.1).

Chart C2.3. Entry rates into tertiary-type A education: Impact of international students (2009)

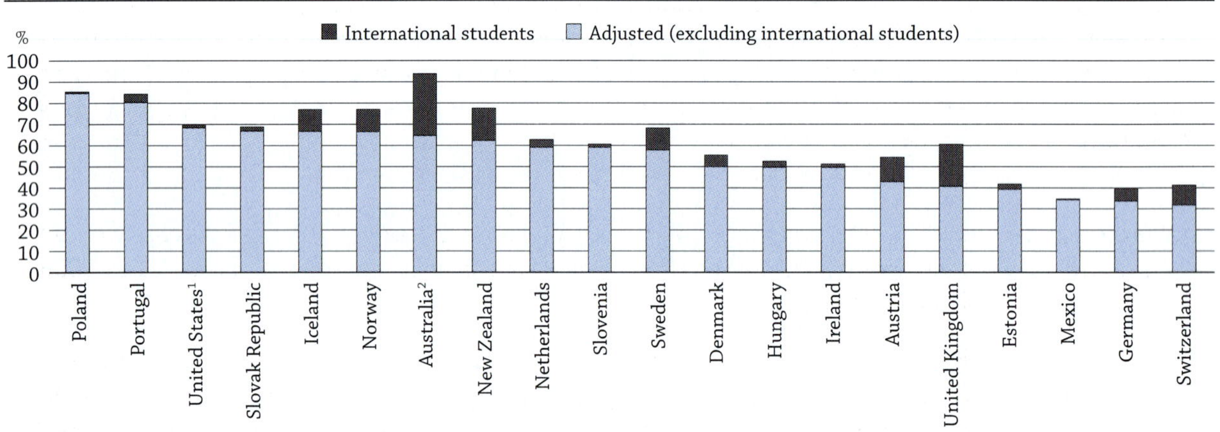

1. The entry rates at tertiary-type A level include entry rates at tertiary-type B level.
2. Year of reference 2008.

Countries are ranked in descending order of adjusted entry rates for tertiary-type A education in 2009.

Source: OECD. Table C2.1. See Annex 3 for notes (*www.oecd.org/edu/eag2011*).

StatLink http://dx.doi.org/10.1787/888932461503

Of course, the greatest impact of international students on indicators such as those on entry and graduation rates (see Indicator A3) is seen among countries with the largest proportions of international students, e.g. Australia, New Zealand and the United Kingdom. To improve the comparability of these indicators, international students should be presented separately whenever possible.

Pathways between academic and vocational programmes

In some countries, tertiary-type A and B programmes are provided by different types of institutions, but this is changing. It is increasingly common for universities or other institutions to offer both types of programmes, and the two programmes are gradually becoming more similar in terms of curriculum, orientation and learning outcomes.

Graduates from tertiary-type B programmes can often gain entry into tertiary-type A programmes, usually in the second or third year, or even into a master's programme. Adding entry rates into these two types of programmes together to obtain overall tertiary-level entry rates would thus result in overcounting. Entry is often subject to conditions, such as passing a special examination, past personal or professional achievements, and/or completion of a "bridging" programme, depending on the country or programme. In some cases, students who leave an academic programme before graduating can be successfully re-oriented towards vocational programmes.

Countries with high entry rates into tertiary education may also be those that offer pathways between the two types of programmes. There are also indications that previous schooling plays an important role in securing access to and equal opportunities in tertiary education (Box C2.1).

Box C2.1. PISA performance in reading at age 15 and access to tertiary education

In 2000, Canada launched the Youth in Transition Survey (YITS) in conjunction with the OECD Programme for International Student Assessment (PISA). Since then, the 30 000 Canadian students who participated in PISA 2000 have been interviewed every two years to collect information about their experiences in education and the labour market.

The Canadian example has demonstrated the value of linking PISA to a longitudinal follow-up and can be a model for other OECD countries that are contemplating a strategy to seek a better understanding of the social and economic impact of competencies acquired by the school-age population.

Better school performance at age 15 is associated with linear pathways through education and higher attainment, notably a university education; but the Canadian evidence on nonlinear pathways (those that shift between education and work) shows that many paths are available for young people to pursue a successful academic and professional career. Sizable proportions of university (14%) and college students (35%) worked before pursuing their post-secondary education degrees. Those at work in 2006 formed the most heterogeneous group of respondents in terms of their PISA 2000 scores.

Combining PISA and YITS, the evidence shows that, in Canada, educational attainment was associated with higher performance in PISA 2000. The vast majority of university students who were 21 in 2006 were top performers in PISA 2000, scoring at Level 4 or 5.

Generally speaking, students who completed secondary school at an older-than-average age, regardless of whether they attended post-secondary education or not, had not performed as well on the PISA survey in 2000. Also, students proceeding directly to work from school had low PISA scores. This may be indicative of the negative association between disruptions to schooling or grade repetition on both achievement and later outcomes.

Higher achievement in PISA can, to some extent, predict the transition from and to education, work and inactivity. High PISA scores are associated with completing secondary school and participating in at least some post-secondary education, even after taking other student background characteristics into account. Students in the bottom quartile of PISA reading scores were much more likely to drop out of secondary school and less likely to have completed a year beyond grade 12 than those in the top quartile. High achievers were more likely to still be in education at age 21 and also less likely to be in work. If they did work, they were more likely to return to education later. Among young men, greater proficiency in reading and mathematics had a positive association with transitions to post-secondary education, while less proficiency was associated with the transition to work. Among young women, less proficiency in mathematics had a negative relationship with transitions to work, as did low levels of education among the students' mothers. Other background characteristics, such as parents' income, did not help predict transition, but income inequality in Canada is not as great as it is in the majority of the other OECD countries.

Longitudinal multivariate analyses from PISA and YITS show the importance of the competencies measured by PISA and other student background characteristics for access to and persistence in post-secondary education and university course choice. For example, students at the top level of reading proficiency in PISA 2000 (Level 5) were twenty times more likely to attend university than those at or below Level 1, even after accounting for other background characteristics. The marks in reading that students achieved in school also contributed significantly to the likelihood of attending post-secondary education, particularly university, although that association was weaker when compared with achievement on the PISA reading survey.

...

Student background characteristics, including intergenerational transmission, also play an important role. Students with university-educated parents were 4.5 times more likely to attend university, even after adjusting for a range of other background characteristics. Furthermore, participation in university (tertiary-type A programme) was more sensitive to background characteristics than participation in college (tertiary-type B programme). Almost two-thirds of students from high-income households attended university compared with one-third from the lowest income group. Some 61% of young people born outside of Canada attended university compared to 43% of Canadian-born youth. Young women were more likely to attend university than young men. In some cases, gender differences in the choice of field of study were marked: for example, young men were five times more likely to choose pure science than young women.

Increased likelihood of participation in post-secondary education among 19-21 year-olds associated with PISA reading proficiency level at age 15 (Canada)

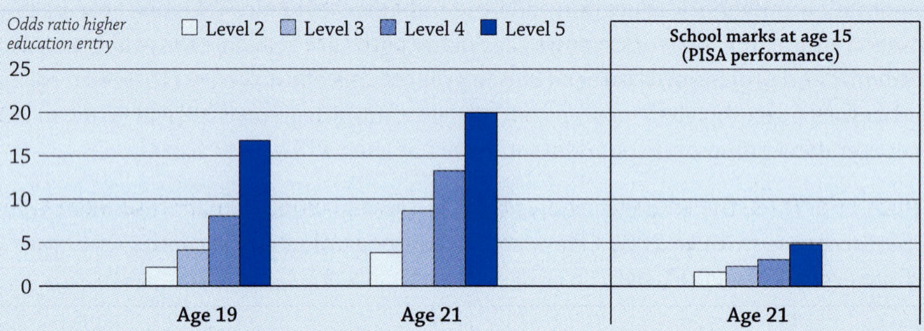

Source: OECD (2010j).
StatLink http://dx.doi.org/10.1787/888932478945

How to read this chart

The chart shows the increased likelihood of participation in post-secondary education among 19-21 year-olds associated with reading proficiency as measured by the PISA survey at age 15 (Canada), after accounting for school engagement, gender, mother tongue, place of residence, parents' education and family income (reference group PISA Level 1). The horizontal axis shows the PISA proficiency level that 15-year-old Canadians had attained in 2000. Level 2 is the baseline proficiency level and Level 5 is the top proficiency level in reading.

The lightest bar shows, for example, how many times more likely someone who attained Level 2 at age 15 was, at age 19 and 21, to have made a successful transition to university, as compared to someone who did not attain baseline PISA Level 2. The bars at the end of the chart show how school marks at age 15 can predict the subsequent success of young people.

Note: see OECD (2010j).

Definitions

Advanced research programmes (ISCED 6) are at the doctorate level.

International/foreign students enrolling for the first time in a postgraduate programme are considered first-time entrants.

New (first-time) entrants are students who enrol at the relevant level of education for the first time.

The **tertiary-level entry rate** is an estimated probability, based on current entry patterns, that a school-leaver will enter tertiary education during his or her lifetime.

Tertiary-type A programmes (ISCED 5A) are largely theory-based and designed to provide qualifications for entry into advanced research programmes and highly skilled professions.

Tertiary-type B programmes (ISCED 5B) are classified at the same level of competence as tertiary-type A programmes, but are more occupationally oriented and provide direct access to the labour market. They tend to be of shorter duration than academic programmes (typically two to three years) and are generally not designed to lead to university degrees.

Methodology

Data on trends in entry rates (Table C2.2) for the years 1995, 2000, 2001, 2002, 2003 and 2004 are based on a special survey carried out in OECD countries in January 2007.

Data on the impact of international students on tertiary entry rates are based on a special survey carried out by the OECD in December 2010.

Tables C2.1 and C2.2 show the sum of net entry rates for all ages. The net entry rate for a specific age is obtained by dividing the number of first-time entrants of that age for each type of tertiary education by the total population in the corresponding age group. The sum of net entry rates is calculated by adding the rates for each year of age. The result represents an estimate of the probability that a young person will enter tertiary education in his/her lifetime if current age-specific entry rates continue. Table C2.1 also shows the 20th, 50th and 80th percentiles of the age distribution of first-time entrants, i.e. the age below which 20%, 50% and 80% of first-time entrants are found.

Not all countries can distinguish between students entering a tertiary programme for the first time and those transferring between different levels of tertiary education or repeating or re-entering a level after an absence. Thus first-time entry rates for each level of tertiary education cannot be added to form a total tertiary-level entrance rate because it would result in counting entrants twice.

The statistical data for Israel are supplied by and under the responsibility of the relevant Israeli authorities. The use of such data by the OECD is without prejudice to the status of the Golan Heights, East Jerusalem and Israeli settlements in the West Bank under the terms of international law.

References

OECD (2010j), *Pathways to Success: How Knowledge and Skills at Age 15 Shape Future Lives in Canada*, OECD, Paris.

Table C2.1. **Entry rates into tertiary education and age distribution of new entrants (2009)**

Sum of net entry rates for each year of age, by gender and programme destination

		Tertiary-type B					Tertiary-type A									Advanced research programmes				
		Net entry rates					Net entry rates					Age at				Net entry rates				
		M+W	of which < 25	Men	Women	Adjusted from international students[1] (All age groups)	M+W	of which < 25	Men	Women	Adjusted from international students[1] (All age groups)	20th percentile[2]	50th percentile[2]	80th percentile[2]	M+W	of which < 30	Men	Women	Adjusted from international students[1] (All age groups)
		(1)	(2)	(3)	(4)	(5)	(6)	(7)	(8)	(9)	(10)	(11)	(12)	(13)	(14)	(15)	(16)	(17)	(18)
OECD	Australia	m	m	m	m	m	94	69	82	107	65	18.8	21.2	26.9	3.2	1.5	3.2	3.1	2.0
	Austria	15	8	14	16	15	54	43	48	61	43	19.5	21.3	25.9	9.1	5.7	9.0	9.1	7.2
	Belgium	39	37	33	46	m	31	30	29	33	m	18.3	18.8	19.8	m	m	m	m	m
	Canada	m	m	m	m	m	m	m	m	m	m	m	m	m	m	m	m	m	m
	Chile	57	41	58	56	m	47	35	43	52	m	18.6	19.8	25.7	0.3	0.2	0.3	0.3	m
	Czech Republic	8	7	5	12	m	59	48	51	68	m	19.6	20.5	26.3	3.5	2.7	3.8	3.1	m
	Denmark	25	13	25	24	22	55	43	44	67	50	20.5	22.1	26.4	3.2	2.1	3.4	2.9	2.5
	Estonia	30	22	23	36	30	42	35	34	50	39	19.2	19.8	23.1	2.4	1.5	2.2	2.5	2.3
	Finland	a	a	a	a	a	69	52	60	78	m	19.7	21.4	26.5	m	m	m	m	m
	France	m	m	m	m	m	m	m	m	m	m	m	m	m	m	m	m	m	m
	Germany	19	14	12	26	m	40	34	39	40	34	19.9	21.2	24.0	m	m	m	m	m
	Greece	m	m	m	m	m	m	m	m	m	m	m	m	m	m	m	m	m	m
	Hungary	14	11	10	18	14	53	44	48	57	50	19.2	20.4	24.6	1.5	1.1	1.6	1.4	1.4
	Iceland	4	n	4	3	4	77	49	58	97	67	20.8	22.8	31.6	2.3	0.7	1.7	3.0	1.7
	Ireland	25	19	30	20	25	51	45	44	58	50	18.4	19.3	22.0	m	m	m	m	m
	Israel	27	19	26	28	m	60	40	53	66	m	21.5	23.7	26.7	2.1	0.8	2.0	2.2	m
	Italy	n	n	n	n	n	50	46	42	58	m	19.2	19.7	20.8	2.3	m	2.1	2.4	m
	Japan	27	m	20	35	m	49	m	55	43	m	18.2	18.6	18.9	1.0	m	1.4	0.6	m
	Korea	36	31	33	40	m	71	60	72	69	m	18.3	18.8	24.2	2.4	0.9	2.8	1.9	m
	Luxembourg	m	m	m	m	m	m	m	m	m	m	m	m	m	m	m	m	m	m
	Mexico	2	2	3	2	2	35	29	35	35	34	18.4	19.4	22.8	0.3	0.1	0.4	0.3	0.3
	Netherlands	n	n	n	n	n	63	56	58	68	59	18.4	19.7	22.6	m	m	m	m	m
	New Zealand	50	23	45	55	41	78	51	64	91	62	18.6	20.7	33.2	2.8	1.5	3.0	2.7	1.5
	Norway	n	n	n	n	n	77	58	64	91	66	19.8	21.1	27.8	3.0	1.6	3.0	3.1	1.8
	Poland	1	1	n	1	m	85	74	76	95	85	19.5	20.4	23.5	m	m	m	m	m
	Portugal	n	n	n	n	n	84	61	74	95	80	18.7	21.3	30.7	2.9	1.1	2.5	3.3	2.5
	Slovak Republic	1	1	1	1	m	69	53	56	82	67	19.5	20.7	27.0	3.1	2.0	3.2	3.0	2.8
	Slovenia	32	22	31	32	31	61	56	48	74	59	19.2	19.8	21.3	1.5	1.0	1.2	2.0	1.3
	Spain	23	20	22	25	m	46	39	39	54	m	18.4	19.2	26.6	2.7	1.7	2.4	3.0	m
	Sweden	11	6	10	12	11	68	46	57	80	58	19.9	22.1	29.4	3.0	1.7	3.1	3.0	2.1
	Switzerland	21	10	22	20	m	41	32	40	43	32	20.0	21.6	26.8	4.9	3.7	5.4	4.4	2.5
	Turkey	30	24	33	27	m	40	34	42	38	m	18.7	20.0	23.7	0.6	0.4	0.7	0.6	m
	United Kingdom	31	9	22	40	28	61	49	53	68	41	18.5	19.6	24.8	2.6	1.6	2.8	2.4	1.4
	United States	x(6)	x(7)	x(8)	x(9)	m	70	54	62	78	68	18.4	19.4	26.0	m	m	m	m	m
	OECD average	19	13	17	21	m	59	47	52	66	m	19.2	20.5	25.3	2.6	1.6	2.7	2.6	m
	EU21 average	16	11	14	18	m	58	47	50	66	m	19.3	20.6	24.8	3.1	1.9	3.0	3.1	m
Other G20	Argentina[3]	44	27	26	62	m	47	35	41	53	m	18.8	20.1	27.0	0.5	m	0.5	0.5	m
	Brazil	m	m	m	m	m	m	m	m	m	m	m	m	m	m	m	m	m	m
	China	19	m	17	22	m	17	m	15	18	m	m	m	m	2.4	m	2.6	2.3	m
	India	m	m	m	m	m	m	m	m	m	m	m	m	m	m	m	m	m	m
	Indonesia	5	5	4	5	m	22	22	22	22	m	18.3	18.7	19.1	0.1	n	0.1	0.2	m
	Russian Federation	28	m	x(1)	x(1)	m	72	m	x(6)	x(6)	m	m	m	m	2.1	m	x(14)	x(14)	m
	Saudi Arabia	m	m	m	m	m	m	m	m	m	m	m	m	m	m	m	m	m	m
	South Africa	m	m	m	m	m	m	m	m	m	m	m	m	m	m	m	m	m	m
	G20 average	22	m	17	26	m	51	m	47	52	m	m	m	m	1.6	m	1.6	1.4	m

Note: Mismatches between the coverage of the population data and the new-entrants data mean that the entry rates for those countries that are net exporters of students may be underestimated and those that are net importers may be overestimated. The adjusted entry rates seek to compensate for that.

Please refer to Annex 1 for information on the method used to calculate entry rates (gross rates versus net rates) and the corresponding age of entry.

1. Adjusted entry rates correspond to the entry rate when international students are excluded.

2. 20%, 50% and 80% of new entrants, respectively, are below this age.

3. Year of reference 2008.

Source: OECD. Argentina, China, Indonesia: UNESCO Institute for Statistics (World Education Indicators Programme). See Annex 3 for notes (*www.oecd.org/edu/eag2011*).

Please refer to the Reader's Guide for information concerning the symbols replacing missing data.

StatLink http://dx.doi.org/10.1787/888932464429

Table C2.2. Trends in entry rates at the tertiary level (1995-2009)

	Tertiary-type 5A[1]							Tertiary-type 5B						
	1995	2000	2005	2006	2007	2008	2009	1995	2000	2005	2006	2007	2008	2009
	(1)	(2)	(7)	(8)	(9)	(10)	(11)	(12)	(13)	(18)	(19)	(20)	(21)	(22)
OECD														
Australia	m	59	82	84	86	87	**94**	m	m	m	m	m	m	**m**
Austria	27	34	37	40	42	50	**54**	m	m	9	7	7	9	**15**
Belgium	m	m	33	35	30	31	**31**	m	m	34	36	37	37	**39**
Canada	m	m	m	m	m	m	**m**	m	m	m	m	m	m	**m**
Chile	m	m	46	42	41	45	**47**	m	m	35	33	49	48	**57**
Czech Republic	m	25	41	50	54	57	**59**	m	9	8	9	8	9	**8**
Denmark	40	52	57	59	57	59	**55**	33	28	23	22	22	21	**25**
Estonia	m	m	54	41	39	42	**42**	m	m	33	32	32	31	**30**
Finland	39	71	73	76	71	70	**69**	32	a	a	a	a	a	**a**
France	m	m	m	m	m	m	**m**	m	m	m	m	m	m	**m**
Germany[2]	26	30	36	35	34	36	**40**	15	15	14	13	13	14	**19**
Greece	15	30	43	49	43	42	**m**	5	21	13	31	23	26	**m**
Hungary	m	64	68	66	63	57	**53**	m	1	11	10	11	12	**14**
Iceland	38	66	74	78	73	73	**77**	12	10	7	4	3	6	**4**
Ireland	m	32	45	40	44	46	**51**	m	26	14	21	21	20	**25**
Israel	m	48	55	56	57	60	**60**	m	31	25	26	28	26	**27**
Italy	m	39	56	56	53	51	**50**	m	1	n	n	n	n	**n**
Japan	31	40	43	45	46	48	**49**	33	32	33	32	30	29	**27**
Korea	41	45	54	59	61	71	**71**	27	51	51	50	50	38	**36**
Luxembourg	m	m	m	m	m	25	**m**	m	m	m	m	m	n	**m**
Mexico	m	27	30	31	32	34	**35**	m	1	2	2	2	2	**2**
Netherlands	44	53	59	58	60	62	**63**	n	n	n	n	n	n	**n**
New Zealand	83	95	79	72	76	72	**78**	44	52	48	49	48	46	**50**
Norway	59	67	73	70	70	71	**77**	5	5	n	n	n	n	**n**
Poland	36	65	76	78	78	83	**85**	1	1	1	1	1	1	**1**
Portugal	m	m	m	53	64	81	**84**	m	m	m	1	1	n	**n**
Slovak Republic	28	37	59	68	74	72	**69**	1	3	2	1	1	1	**1**
Slovenia	m	m	40	46	50	56	**61**	m	m	49	43	38	32	**32**
Spain	m	47	43	43	41	41	**46**	3	15	22	21	21	22	**23**
Sweden	57	67	76	76	73	65	**68**	m	7	7	10	9	10	**11**
Switzerland	17	29	37	38	39	38	**41**	29	14	16	15	16	19	**21**
Turkey	18	21	27	31	29	30	**40**	9	9	19	21	21	23	**30**
United Kingdom	m	47	51	57	55	57	**61**	m	29	28	29	30	30	**31**
United States	m	42	64	64	65	64	**70**	m	13	x(7)	x(8)	x(9)	x(10)	**x(11)**
OECD average	37	47	54	55	55	56	**59**	17	16	18	18	18	17	**19**
OECD average for countries with 1995, 2000 and 2009 data	37	50					**62**	19	19					**20**
EU21 average	35	46	53	54	54	54	**58**	11	12	15	16	15	14	**16**
Other G20														
Argentina	m	m	m	m	m	47	**m**	m	m	m	m	m	44	**m**
Brazil	m	m	m	m	m	m	**m**	m	m	m	m	m	m	**m**
China	m	m	m	m	m	m	**17**	m	m	m	m	m	m	**19**
India	m	m	m	m	m	m	**m**	m	m	m	m	m	m	**m**
Indonesia	m	m	m	m	m	m	**22**	m	m	m	m	m	m	**15**
Russian Federation	m	m	65	65	66	69	**72**	m	m	32	31	31	30	**28**
Saudi Arabia	m	m	m	m	m	m	**m**	m	m	m	m	m	m	**m**
South Africa	m	m	m	m	m	m	**m**	m	m	m	m	m	m	**m**
G20 average	m	m	m	m	m	m	**52**	m	m	m	m	m	m	**20**

Note: Columns showing entry rates for the years 2001-04 (i.e. Columns 3-6, 14-17) are available for consultation on line (see StatLink below). Please refer to Annex 1 for information on the method used to calculate entry rates (gross rates versus net rates) and the corresponding age of entry.

1. The entry rates for tertiary-type A programmes include advanced research programmes for 1995, 2000-03 (except for Belgium and Germany).

2. Break in the series between 2008 and 2009 due to a partial reallocation of vocational programmes into ISCED 2 and ISCED 5B.

Source: OECD. Argentina, China, Indonesia: UNESCO Institute for Statistics (World Education Indicators Programme). See Annex 3 for notes (*www.oecd.org/edu/eag2011*).

Please refer to the Reader's Guide for information concerning the symbols replacing missing data.

StatLink http://dx.doi.org/10.1787/888932464448

INDICATOR C3

WHO STUDIES ABROAD AND WHERE?

- In 2009, almost 3.7 million tertiary students were enrolled outside their country of citizenship.
- In descending order, Australia, the United Kingdom, Austria, Switzerland and New Zealand have the highest percentages of international students among their tertiary enrolments.
- In absolute terms, the largest numbers of international students are from China, India and Korea. Asian students represent 52% of foreign students enrolled worldwide.
- The number of foreign students enrolled in the OECD area was nearly three times the number of citizens from an OECD country studying abroad in 2009. In the 21 European countries that are members of the OECD, there were 2.6 foreign students per each European citizen enrolled abroad.
- Some 83% of all foreign students are enrolled in G20 countries, while 77% of all foreign students are enrolled in OECD countries. These proportions have remained stable during the past decade.

Chart C3.1. Evolution by region of destination in the number of students enrolled outside their country of citizenship (2000 to 2009)

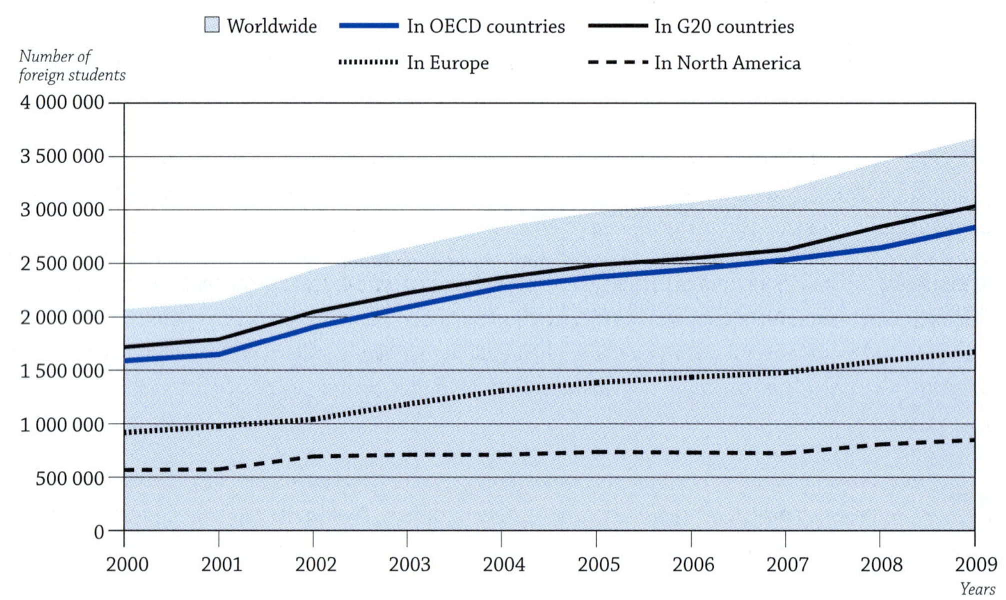

Source: OECD and UNESCO Institute for Statistics for most data on non-OECD countries. Table C3.5. See Annex 3 for notes (*www.oecd.org/edu/eag2011*).

StatLink http://dx.doi.org/10.1787/888932461522

Context

As national economies become more interconnected and participation in education expands, governments and individuals are looking to higher education to broaden students' horizons and help them to better understand the world's languages, cultures and business methods. One way for students to expand their knowledge of other societies and languages, and thus improve their prospects in globalised sectors of the labour market, such as multi-national corporations or research, is to study in tertiary education institutions in countries other than their own.

The internationalisation of tertiary education can also provide an opportunity for smaller and/or less-developed host education systems to improve the cost-efficiency of their education systems. In fact, it may allow countries to focus limited resources on educational programmes with potential economies of scale or to expand participation in tertiary education despite bottlenecks in providing it. Enrolling international students can not only help raise revenues from higher education, but it can be part of a broader strategy to recruit highly skilled immigrants.

International students tend to choose different programmes of study than local students (see Indicator A4), indicating either a degree of specialisation of countries in the programmes offered or a lack of programmes in the countries of origin.

In reading this indicator, the distinction must be made between students who have moved from their country of origin with the purpose of studying (international students) and those who are not citizens of the country where they are enrolled (foreign students) but may, in some cases, be long-term residents or, indeed, have even born in the country (see Definitions below). International students are thus a subset of foreign students.

Other findings

- **The number of tertiary students enrolled outside their country of citizenship rose by 6.4% between 2008 and 2009 while global tertiary enrolment grew by 3.3% in the same period**, a slower pace than the 8% of growth registered from 2007 to 2008 when global tertiary enrolment registered a 3.6% increase (UIS, 2011 and Table C3.5). This may reflect the fact that mobility was hampered during the period because of the financial crisis and reductions in support for studying abroad (Varghese, 2009).

- **Australia, Canada, France, Germany, the United Kingdom and the United States each receive more than 5% of all foreign students worldwide.** International students from OECD countries come mainly from Canada, France, Germany, Japan, Korea and the United States.

- **International students make up 10% or more of the enrolments in tertiary education in Australia, Austria, New Zealand, Switzerland and the United Kingdom. They also account for more than 20% of enrolments in advanced research programmes** in Australia, Austria, Belgium, Canada, Iceland, New Zealand, Sweden, Switzerland, the United Kingdom and the United States.

- In OECD countries with available data, **an average of 25% of international students who do not renew their student permits change their student status in the host country mainly for work-related reasons.**

Trends

Since 2000, the number of foreign tertiary students enrolled worldwide increased by 77%, for an average annual growth rate of 6.6%, and by 79% in the OECD area, for an average annual increase growth rate of 6.7%.

Even if their share of foreign students has slightly decreased by 2% in the past five years, European countries still lead the preferences in absolute numbers, with a share of 38% followed by North America (23%). Nevertheless, the fastest growing regions of destination are Latin America and the Caribbean, Oceania, and Asia mirroring the internationalisation of universities in an increasing set of countries (Chart C3.1).

C3

Analysis

Trends

Using a combination of OECD and UNESCO Institute for Statistics data makes it possible to examine longer-term trends and illustrates the dramatic growth in foreign enrolments (Box C3.1). Over the past three decades, the number of students enrolled outside their country of citizenship has risen dramatically, from 0.8 million worldwide in 1975 to 3.7 million in 2009, a more than fourfold increase. Growth in the internationalisation of tertiary education has accelerated during the past 34 years, mirroring the globalisation of economies and societies and also universities' expanded capacity.

The rise in the number of students enrolled abroad since 1975 stems from various factors, from an interest in promoting academic, cultural, social and political ties between countries, especially as the European Union was taking shape, to a substantial increase in global access to tertiary education, to, more recently, reduced transportation costs. The internationalisation of labour markets for highly skilled individuals gave people an incentive to gain international experience as part of their studies.

Globally, the increase in the number of foreign students can be contrasted to the increase in tertiary enrolment. According to UNESCO data, 165 million students participated in formal tertiary education around the globe in 2009; this is an increase of 65 million students since 2000 and growth of 65% (UNESCO Institute for Statistics, 2011). The number of foreign students increased during the same period from 2.1 to 3.7 million students, i.e. growth of 77%. Consequently, the proportion of foreign students among all tertiary students grew 7% from 2000 to 2009 (Chart C3.1).

Most of the new tertiary students are concentrated in countries outside the OECD area, and are likely to gradually increase the proportion of foreign students in advanced research programmes in OECD and other G20 countries in the coming years.

The growth in internationalisation of tertiary education is even greater among countries in the OECD area. In absolute terms, the number of foreign students enrolled in tertiary education more than doubled since 2000 in Australia, Canada, Chile, the Czech Republic, Estonia, Finland, Iceland, Italy, Korea, the Netherlands, New Zealand, Norway, Poland, the Russian Federation, the Slovak Republic, Slovenia and Spain. In contrast, the number of foreign students enrolled in Belgium and Turkey grew by less than 25% (Table C3.1).

Box C3.1. Long-term growth in the number of students enrolled outside their country of citizenship

Growth in internationalisation of tertiary education (1975-2009, in millions)

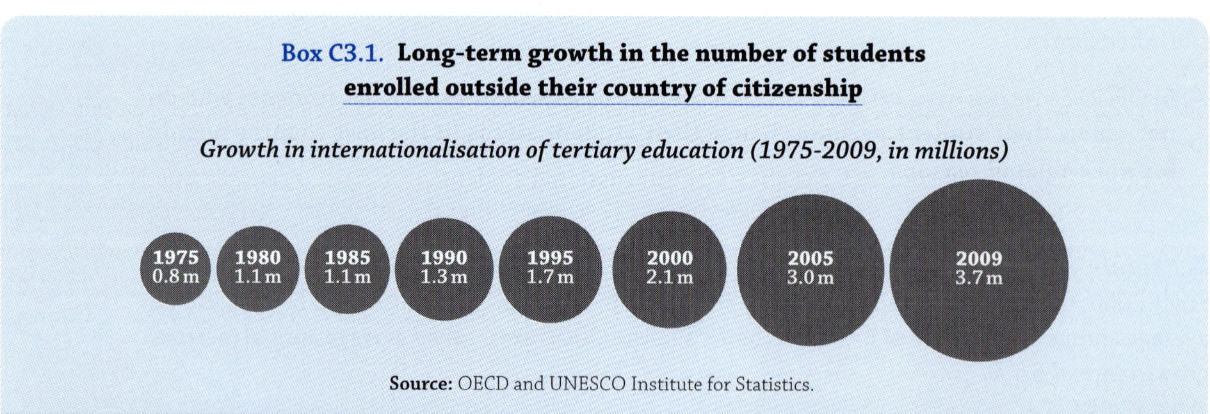

Source: OECD and UNESCO Institute for Statistics.

Data on foreign enrolment worldwide comes from both the OECD and the UNESCO Institute for Statistics (UIS). UIS provided the data on all countries for 1975-95 and most of the non-OECD countries for 2000, 2005 and 2009. The OECD provided the data on OECD countries and the other non-OECD economies in 2000 and 2009. Both sources use similar definitions, thus making their combination possible. Missing data were imputed with the closest data reports to ensure that breaks in data coverage do not result in breaks in time series.

StatLink http://dx.doi.org/10.1787/888932461617

Changes in the number of foreign students between 2000 and 2009 indicate that, on average, the number of foreign students has grown faster in the OECD area than in EU21 countries, by 189 % and 141 %, respectively (Table C3.1).

In relative terms, the percentage of international students in tertiary enrolment has also increased since 2004 in all 16 OECD countries with available data, except Canada and the Netherlands. On average, the rise in international students as a percentage of tertiary enrolment in EU21 countries between 2004 and 2009 has been higher (43%) than in the whole OECD area (32%).

Global student mobility mirrors to a great extent inter- and intra-regional migration patterns. The growth in the internationalisation of tertiary enrolment in OECD countries, and the high proportion of intra-regional student mobility show the growing importance of regional mobility over global mobility. Furthermore, student flows in European countries and in Eastern Asia and Oceania, tend to reflect the evolution of geopolitical areas (UNESCO, 2009).

Major destinations of foreign students

G20 countries attract 83% of foreign students worldwide. Some 77% of foreign students are enrolled in an OECD country. Within the OECD area, EU21 countries host the highest number of foreign students, with 38% of total foreign students. These 21 countries also host 98% of foreign students in the European Union. EU mobility policies become evident when analysing the composition of this population. Within the share of foreign students enrolled in EU21 countries, 72% of students come from another EU21 country. North America is the second most attractive region for foreign students, with a share of 23% of all foreign students. The North American region shows a more diversified profile of students than the European Union: in the United States only 4.4% of international students come from Canada, and in Canada only 9.1% of international students come from the United States (Tables C3.2, C3.3 and Chart C3.1).

In 2009, one out of two foreign students went to one of the five countries that host higher shares of students enrolled outside of their country of citizenship. The United States received the most (in absolute terms), with 18% of all foreign students worldwide, followed by the United Kingdom (10%), Australia (7%), Germany (7%) and France (7%). Although these destinations account for half of all tertiary students pursuing their studies abroad, some new players have emerged on the international education market in the past few years (Chart C3.2 and Table C3.6, available on line). Besides the five major destinations, significant numbers of foreign students were enrolled in Canada (5%), Japan (4%), the Russian Federation (4%) and Spain (2%) in 2009. The figures for Australia, the United Kingdom and the United States refer to international students (Table C3.3).

New players in the international education market

Over a nine-year period, the share of international students who chose the United States as their destination dropped from 23% to 18%. That share fell two percentage points for Germany and one percentage point for the United Kingdom. In contrast, the shares of international students who chose Australia and New Zealand as their destination grew by almost two percentage points as did that in the Russian Federation, which has become an important new player in the international education market (Chart C3.3). Some of these changes reflect the different emphases in countries' internationalisation policies, ranging from proactive marketing policies in the Asia-Pacific region to a more local and university-driven approach in the traditionally dominant United States. Note that the figures for Australia, the United Kingdom and the United States refer to international students.

Underlying factors in students' choice of a country of study

Language of instruction

The language spoken and used in instruction sometimes determines in which country a student chooses to study. Countries whose language of instruction is widely spoken and read, such as English, French, German, Russian and Spanish, are therefore leading destinations of foreign students, both in absolute and relative terms. Japan is a notable exception: despite a language of instruction that is not widespread, it enrols large numbers of foreign students, of whom 93.2 % are from Asia (Table C3.2 and Chart C3.2).

Chart C3.2. Distribution of foreign students in tertiary education, by country of destination (2009)

Percentage of foreign tertiary students reported to the OECD who are enrolled in each country of destination

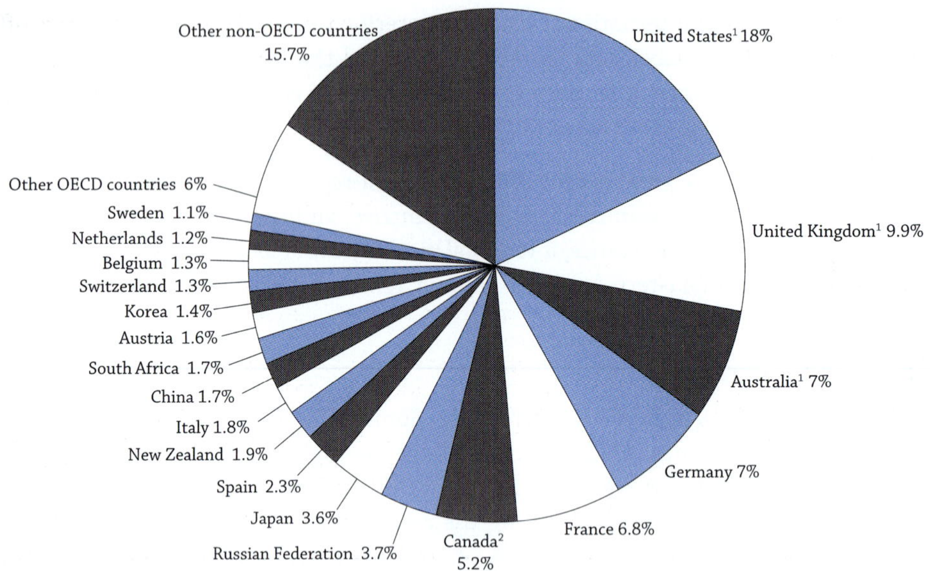

United States[1] 18%
United Kingdom[1] 9.9%
Australia[1] 7%
Germany 7%
France 6.8%
Canada[2] 5.2%
Russian Federation 3.7%
Japan 3.6%
Spain 2.3%
New Zealand 1.9%
Italy 1.8%
China 1.7%
South Africa 1.7%
Austria 1.6%
Korea 1.4%
Switzerland 1.3%
Belgium 1.3%
Netherlands 1.2%
Sweden 1.1%
Other OECD countries 6%
Other non-OECD countries 15.7%

1. Data relate to international students defined on the basis of their country of residence.
2. Year of reference 2008.

Source: OECD and UNESCO Institute for Statistics for most data on non-OECD destinations. Table C3.6, available on line. See Annex 3 for notes (*www.oecd.org/edu/eag2011*).

StatLink http://dx.doi.org/10.1787/888932461560

Chart C3.3. Trends in international education market shares (2000, 2009)

Percentage of all foreign tertiary students enrolled, by destination

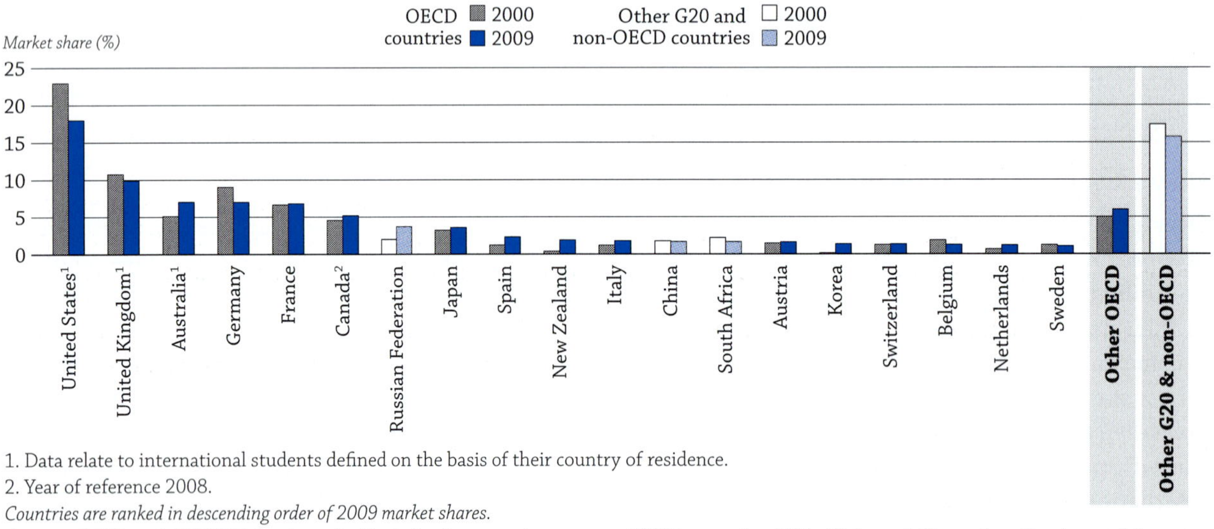

OECD countries 2000 2009
Other G20 and non-OECD countries 2000 2009
Market share (%)
25
20
15
10
5
0
United States[1]
United Kingdom[1]
Australia[1]
Germany
France
Canada[2]
Russian Federation
Japan
Spain
New Zealand
Italy
China
South Africa
Austria
Korea
Switzerland
Belgium
Netherlands
Sweden
Other OECD
Other G20 & non-OECD

1. Data relate to international students defined on the basis of their country of residence.
2. Year of reference 2008.

Countries are ranked in descending order of 2009 market shares.

Source: OECD and UNESCO Institute for Statistics for most data on non-OECD countries. Table C3.6, available on line. See Annex 3 for notes (*www.oecd.org/edu/eag2011*).

StatLink http://dx.doi.org/10.1787/888932461579

The dominance (in absolute numbers) of English-speaking destinations (Australia, Canada, New Zealand, the United Kingdom and the United States) reflects the progressive adoption of English as a global language. It may also be because students intending to study abroad are likely to have learned English in their home country and/or wish to improve their English language skills through immersion in a native English-speaking context.

The rapid increase in foreign enrolments in Australia (index change of 244), Canada (202), New Zealand (850) and the United Kingdom (163) between 2000 and 2009 can be partly attributed to linguistic considerations (Table C3.1).

Given this pattern, an increasing number of institutions in non-English-speaking countries now offers courses in English to overcome their linguistic disadvantage in attracting foreign students. This trend is especially noticeable in countries in which the use of English is widespread, such as the Nordic countries (Box C3.2).

Box C3.2. Countries offering tertiary programmes in English (2009)

Use of English in instruction	
All or nearly all programmes offered in English	Australia, Canada,[1] Ireland, New Zealand, the United Kingdom, the United States
Many programmes offered in English	Denmark, Finland, the Netherlands, Sweden
Some programmes offered in English	Belgium (Fl.),[2] the Czech Republic, France, Germany, Hungary, Iceland, Japan, Korea, Norway, Poland, Portugal, the Slovak Republic, Switzerland,[3] Turkey
No or nearly no programmes offered in English	Austria, Belgium (Fr.), Brazil, Chile, Greece, Israel, Italy, Luxembourg, Mexico,[3] the Russian Federation, Spain

Note: The extent to which a country offers a few or many programmes in English takes into account the size of the population in the country. Hence, France and Germany are classified among countries with comparatively few English programmes, although they have more English programmes than Sweden, in absolute terms.
1. In Canada, tertiary institutions are either French- (mostly Quebec) or English-speaking.
2. Master's programmes.
3. At the discretion of tertiary education institutions.
Source: OECD, compiled from brochures for prospective international students by OAD (Austria), CHES and NARIC (Czech Republic), Cirius (Denmark), CIMO (Finland), EduFrance (France), DAAD (Germany), Campus Hungary (Hungary), University of Iceland (Iceland), JPSS (Japan), NIIED (Korea), NUFFIC (Netherlands), SIU (Norway), CRASP (Poland), Swedish Institute (Sweden) and Middle-East Technical University (Turkey).

Quality of programmes

International students increasingly select their study destination based on the quality of education offered, as perceived from a wide array of information on and rankings of higher education programmes now available, both in print and on line. For instance, the high proportion of top-ranked higher education institutions in the principal destination countries and the emergence in rankings of institutions based in fast-growing student destinations draws attention to the increasing importance of the perception of quality even if a correlation between patterns of student mobility and quality judgements on individual institutions is hard to establish.

In this context, institutions of higher education are more willing to raise their standards in the quality of teaching, adapt to more diverse student populations, and are more sensitive to external perceptions.

Tuition fees and cost of living

Among most EU countries, including Austria, Belgium (Flemish Community), the Czech Republic, Denmark, Estonia, Finland, France, Germany, Ireland, Italy, the Netherlands, the Slovak Republic, Spain, Sweden and the United Kingdom, international students from other EU countries are treated as domestic students when it comes to tuition fees. This is also true in Ireland, but only on the condition that the EU student has lived in Ireland for three out of the five previous years. If this condition is satisfied, the EU student is eligible for free tuition in a given academic year. In Finland, Germany and Italy, this applies to non-EU international students as well. While there are no tuition fees in Finland and Sweden, in Germany, tuition fees are collected at all government-dependent private institutions and, in some *Bundesländer*, tuition fees have been introduced at public tertiary institutions as well. In Denmark, students from Nordic countries (Norway and Iceland) and EU countries are treated like domestic students and so pay no fees, as their education is fully subsidised.

Most international students from non-EU or non-European Economic Area (EEA) countries, however, have to pay the full tuition fee, although a limited number of talented students from non-EU/EEA countries can obtain scholarships covering all or part of their tuition fees (Box C3.3).

Box C3.3. Structure of tuition fees

Tuition fees structure	OECD and other G20 countries
Higher tuition fees for international students than for domestic students	Australia, Austria,[1] Belgium,[1,2] Canada, the Czech Republic,[1,3] Denmark,[1,3] Estonia,[1] Ireland,[3] the Netherlands,[1] New Zealand,[4] the Russian Federation, Turkey, the United Kingdom,[1] the United States[5]
Same tuition fees for international and domestic students	France, Germany, Italy, Japan, Korea, Mexico,[6] Spain
No tuition fees for either international or domestic students	Finland, Iceland, Norway, Sweden

1. For non-European Union or non-European Economic Area students.
2. In Belgium (Fl.), different tuition allowed only if institutions reach 2% of students from outside the EEA area.
3. No tuition fees for full-time domestic students in public institutions.
4. Except students in advanced research programmes, or students from Australia.
5. At public institutions, international students pay the same fees as domestic out-of-state students. However since most domestic students are enrolled in-state, international students pay higher tuition fees than most domestic students, in practice. At private universities, the fees are the same for national and international students.
6. Some institutions charge higher tuition fees for international students.

Source: OECD. Indicator B5. See Annex 3 for notes (*www.oecd.org/edu/eag2011*).

Among some non-EU countries, including Iceland, Japan, Korea, Norway and the United States, the same treatment applies to all domestic and international students. In Norway, tuition fees are the same for both domestic and international students: no fees in public institutions, but fees in some private institutions. In Iceland, all students have to pay registration fees, and students in private schools have to pay tuition fees as well. In Japan, domestic and international students are generally charged the same tuition fee, however international students with Japanese government scholarships do not have to pay tuition fees and many scholarships are available for privately financed international students. In Korea, tuition fees and subsidies for international students vary, depending on the contract between their school of origin and the school they attend in Korea. In general, most international students in Korea pay tuition fees that are somewhat lower than those paid by domestic students. In New Zealand, international students, except those in advanced research programmes, generally pay full tuition fees; however, international students from Australia receive the same subsidies as domestic students. In Australia and Canada, all international students pay full tuition fees. This is true also in the G20 country the Russian Federation, unless students are subsidised by the Russian government.

The fact that Finland, Iceland, Norway and Sweden do not have tuition fees for international students, combined with the availability of programmes taught in English, probably explains part of the robust growth in the number of foreign students enrolled in some of these countries between 2000 and 2009 (Table C3.1). However, given the absence of fees, the high unit costs of tertiary education mean that international students place a heavy financial burden on their countries of destination (see Table B1.1a). For this reason, Denmark, which previously had no tuition fees, adopted tuition fees for non-EU and non-EEA international students as of 2006-07. Similar options are being discussed in Finland and Sweden, where foreign enrolments grew by more than 126% and 55%, respectively, between 2000 and 2009.

Countries that charge their international students the full cost of education reap significant trade benefits. Several countries in the Asia-Pacific region have actually made international education an explicit part of their socio-economic development strategy and have initiated policies to attract international students on a revenue-generating or at least a cost-recovery basis. Australia and New Zealand have successfully adopted differentiated tuition fees for international students, and this has not hampered some of the strongest growth in foreign students in the past decade (Table C3.1). In Japan and Korea, with the same high tuition fees for domestic and international students, foreign enrolments nevertheless grew robustly between 2000 and 2009 (see Indicator B5). This shows that tuition costs do not necessarily discourage prospective international students as long as the quality of education provided is high and its likely returns make the investment worthwhile.

However, in choosing between similar educational opportunities, cost considerations may play a role, especially for students from developing countries. In this respect, the comparatively small rise in foreign enrolments in the United Kingdom and the United States between 2000 and 2009, and the deterioration of the United States' market share, may be attributed to the comparatively high tuition fees charged to international students in a context of fierce competition from other, primarily English-speaking, destinations offering similar educational opportunities at lower cost (Chart C3.3). Advanced research programmes in New Zealand, for example, have become more attractive since 2005, when tuitions fees for international students were reduced to the same level as those paid by domestic students (Box C3.3).

Public funding that is "portable" across borders, or student support for tertiary education, can ease the cost of studying abroad, as is evident in Belgium (Flemish Community), Chile, Finland, Iceland, the Netherlands, Norway and Sweden.

Immigration policy

As discussed below, in recent years, several OECD countries have eased their immigration policies to encourage the temporary or permanent immigration of international students (OECD, 2008). This makes these countries more attractive to students and strengthens the country's labour force. As a result, immigration considerations as well as tuition fees may also affect some students' decisions on where to study abroad (OECD, 2011a).

Other factors

Students also make their decisions on where to study based on: the academic reputation of particular institutions or programmes; the flexibility of programmes in counting time spent abroad towards degree requirements; recognition of foreign degrees; the limitations of tertiary education in the home country; restrictive university admission policies at home; geographical, trade or historical links between countries; future job opportunities; cultural aspirations; and government policies to facilitate transfer of credits between home and host institutions.

Extent of student mobility in tertiary education

The above analysis has focused on trends in absolute numbers of foreign students and their distribution by countries of destination, since time series or global aggregates on student mobility do not exist. It is also possible to measure the extent of student mobility in each country of destination by examining the proportion of international students in total tertiary enrolments. Doing so takes into account the size of different tertiary education systems and highlights those that are highly internationalised, regardless of their size and the importance of their market share.

Among countries for which data on student mobility are available, Australia, Austria, New Zealand, Switzerland and the United Kingdom show the highest levels of incoming student mobility, measured as the proportion of international students in their total tertiary enrolment. In Australia, 21.5% of tertiary students have come to the country in order to pursue their studies. Similarly, international students represent 15.1% of total tertiary enrolments in Austria, 14.6% in New Zealand, 14.9% in Switzerland and 15.3% in the United Kingdom. In contrast, incoming student mobility is less than 2% of total tertiary enrolments in Chile, Estonia, Poland and Slovenia (Table C3.1 and Chart C3.4).

Among countries for which data based on the preferred definition of international students are not available, foreign enrolments constitute a large group of tertiary students in France (11.5 %). On the other hand, foreign enrolments represent 1% or less of total tertiary enrolments in Brazil, Chile, Poland and Turkey (Table C3.1).

Chart C3.4. Student mobility in tertiary education (2009)

Percentage of international students in tertiary enrolments

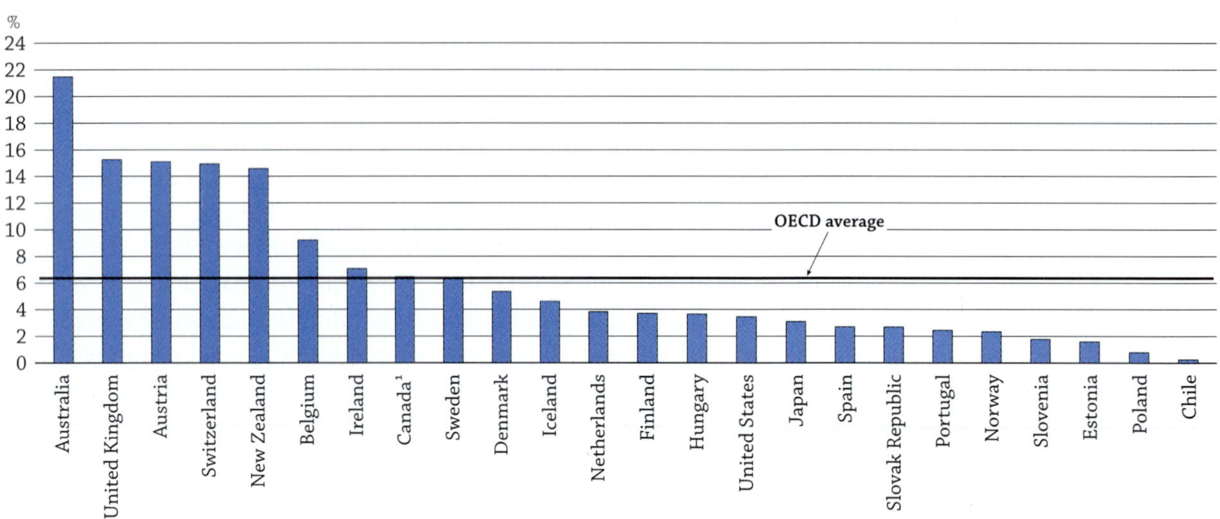

Note: The data presented in this chart are not comparable with data on foreign students in tertiary education presented in pre-2006 editions of *Education at a Glance* or elsewhere in this chapter.

1. Year of reference 2008.

Countries are ranked in descending order of the percentage of international students in tertiary education.

Source: OECD. Table C3.1. See Annex 3 for notes (*www.oecd.org/edu/eag2011*).

StatLink http://dx.doi.org/10.1787/888932461541

Proportion of international students at different levels and types of tertiary education

The proportion of international students in different types of tertiary education in each country of destination also sheds light on patterns of student mobility. With the exception of Denmark, Japan, New Zealand, Portugal and Spain, tertiary-type B (shorter and vocationally-oriented) programmes are far less internationalised than tertiary-type A (largely theory-based) programmes. With the exception of Italy, this observation also holds true for countries for which data using the preferred definition of international students are not available (Table C3.1).

Most countries show significantly higher incoming student mobility relative to total enrolments in advanced research programmes than in tertiary-type A programmes. This pattern is clear in Canada, Chile, Iceland, Japan, New Zealand, Sweden, Switzerland, the United Kingdom and the United States, as well as France, Italy and Korea, countries reporting foreign students and for which data using the preferred definition of international student are not available. This may be due to the attractiveness of advanced research programmes in these countries, or to a preference for recruiting international students at higher levels of education for their contribution to domestic research and development, or in anticipation of recruiting these students as highly qualified immigrants (Table C3.1).

Examining the proportion of international students by level and type of tertiary education reveals what kinds of programmes countries offer. In some countries, a comparatively large proportion of international students are enrolled in tertiary-type B programmes. This is the case in Belgium (26.2%), Chile (29.7%), Japan (23.7%), New Zealand (34.7%) and Spain (29.7%) (Table C3.4).

In other countries, a large proportion of international students enrol in advanced research programmes. This is particularly true in Switzerland (25.7%). This concentration can also be observed to a lesser extent in Chile (17.5%), Finland (13.5%), Japan (10%), Portugal (11.5%), the Slovak Republic (11.5%), Spain (17.2%), Sweden (16.2%) and the United States (19.4%). Among countries for which data using the preferred definition of international students are not available, 11.8% of foreign students in France are enrolled in advanced research programmes (Table C3.4). All of these countries are likely to benefit from the contribution of these high-level international students to domestic research and development. In countries that charge full tuition to foreign students, these students are also a source of revenue (Box C3.3).

Profile of international student intake in different destinations

Global balance of student mobility in OECD countries

OECD countries host more foreign students than they send abroad in tertiary education. In 2009, OECD countries hosted 2.9 foreign students per each student studying outside his or her country of origin. In absolute terms, this accounts for 2.8 million foreign students in OECD countries compared to 987 000 students outside of their OECD country of citizenship. As 93% of OECD citizens study in another OECD country, almost two-thirds of foreign students in the OECD area come from a non-OECD country (Table C3.6, available on line).

At the country level, the balance varies greatly: while in Australia there are 24 foreign students for each Australian student studying abroad, the ratio is 15 to 1 in New Zealand, and the balance is negative in Chile, Estonia, Greece, Iceland, Korea, Luxembourg, Mexico, Poland, the Slovak Republic, Slovenia and Turkey. The United Kingdom and the United States also show high ratios of foreign to national students, with more than 11 foreign students for each citizen studying abroad.

Main regions of origin

Asian students form the largest group of international students enrolled in countries reporting data to the OECD or the UNESCO Institute for Statistics: 52% of the total in all reporting destinations (51% of the total in OECD countries, and 55% of the total in non-OECD countries).

Their predominance in OECD countries is greatest in Australia, Japan and Korea, where more than 75% of international or foreign students originate from Asia. In OECD countries, the Asian group is followed by Europeans (24.4%), particularly EU21 citizens (16.9%). Students from Africa account for 10% of all international students, while those from North America account for only 3.7%. Students from Latin America and the Caribbean represent 6% of the total. Altogether, 32% of international students enrolled in the OECD area originate from another OECD country (Table C3.2).

Main countries of origin

The predominance of students from Asia and Europe is also clear when looking at individual countries of origin. Students from France (2.1%), Germany (3.6%), and Korea (4.8%) represent the largest groups of international OECD students enrolled in OECD countries, followed by students from Canada (1.8%), Japan (1.8%) and the United States (1.8%) (Table C3.2).

Among international students originating from non-member countries, students from China represent by far the largest group, with 18.2% of all international students enrolled in the OECD area (not including an additional 1.3% from Hong Kong, China) (Table C3.2). Some 21.9% of all Chinese students studying abroad head for the United States, while 14% choose Japan and 12.4% choose Australia. In OECD countries, students from China are followed by those from India (7.3%), Malaysia (1.9%), Morocco (1.6%), Viet Nam (1.5%) and the Russian Federation (1.3%). A significant number of Asian students studying abroad also come from Indonesia, the Islamic Republic of Iran, Nepal, Pakistan, Singapore and Thailand.

A large proportion of foreign students in OECD countries come from neighbouring countries. In all OECD countries, around 20% of all foreign students come from countries that share land or maritime borders with the host country. Higher levels of cross-border mobility not only reveal a particular geographic situation but may also be the consequence of cost, quality and enrolment advantages that are more apparent to students in neighbouring countries. On the other hand, higher percentages of foreign students from countries beyond the immediate borders are seen in countries that have the largest market shares in international education and in countries, such as Portugal and Spain, that have close historic and cultural ties with other countries further afield (Table 3.6, available on line).

Among OECD countries, the highest percentages of cross-border mobility are found in Korea, where 81% of foreign students come from China or Japan; in Estonia, where 77% of foreign students come from Finland, Latvia, the Russian Federation or Sweden; and in the Czech Republic, where 68% of foreign students come from Austria, Germany, Poland or the Slovak Republic. Foreign students from neighbouring countries are also strongly represented in Austria, Belgium, the Netherlands, Poland, the Russian Federation, the Slovak Republic, Slovenia and Switzerland. On the other hand, in Australia, only 5% of students come from Indonesia, New Zealand or Papua New Guinea, and only 2% come from Oceania. In Canada, just 5% of foreign students come from the United States; in Portugal, only 4% of foreign students come from Spain or Morocco; and in the United States, 8% of students come from the Bahamas, Canada, Mexico or the Russian Federation. In Portugal, around 72% of foreign students come from Angola, Brazil, Cape Verde, Guinea-Bissau, Sao Tomé and Principe or Timor-Leste – all countries where Portuguese is an official language (Table 3.6, available on line).

Destinations of citizens enrolled abroad

OECD students usually enrol in another OECD country if they are looking to pursue tertiary studies outside their country of citizenship. On average, 93% of foreign students from OECD countries are enrolled in other OECD countries. The proportion of foreign students from the other G20 countries enrolled in OECD countries is also high, with 83.5% of foreign students from Argentina, Brazil, China, India, Indonesia, the Russian Federation, Saudi Arabia and South Africa enrolled in an OECD country. Notably, students from Belgium (2%), the Czech Republic (1.7%), Iceland (0.5%), Ireland (0.7%), Luxembourg (0.2%), the Netherlands (1.9%), Norway (1.8%), and the Slovak Republic (0.7%) show an extremely low propensity to study outside of the OECD area (Table C3.3).

Language and cultural considerations, geographic proximity and similarity of education systems are all factors that students weigh when determining where they will study. Geographic considerations and differences in entry requirements are likely explanations of the concentration of students from Germany in Austria, from Belgium in France and the Netherlands, from France in Belgium, from Canada in the United States, from New Zealand in Australia, etc. Language and academic traditions also explain the propensity for English-speaking students to concentrate in other countries of the Commonwealth or in the United States, even those that are distant geographically. This is also true for other historic geopolitical areas, such as the former Soviet Union, the *Francophonie* and Latin America. Migration networks also play a role, as illustrated by the concentration of students with Portuguese citizenship in France, students from Turkey in Germany or those from Mexico in the United States.

The destinations of international students also highlight the attractiveness of specific education systems, whether because of their academic reputation or because of subsequent immigration opportunities. It is noteworthy, for example, that students from China are mostly in Australia, Canada, France, Germany, Japan, Korea, New Zealand, the United Kingdom and the United States, most of which have schemes to facilitate the immigration of international students. Similarly, students from India favour Australia, the United Kingdom and the United States. In fact, these three destinations attract 77 % of Indian citizens enrolled abroad (Table C3.3).

How many international enrolled and graduated students stay in the host countries?

Rationales for an individual to remain in the host country after studying include the different work opportunities compared to the country of origin, integration into the host country, and future career advantages when returning to the country of origin or when moving to a third country. However, insertion into the host country labour market may imply a higher risk of over-qualification for international students than for nationals.

As mentioned above, several OECD countries have eased their immigration policies to encourage the temporary or permanent immigration of international students. Australia, Canada and New Zealand, for example, make it easy for foreign students who have studied in their universities to settle by granting them additional points in those countries' immigration point system. Finland and Norway amended their naturalisation acts and now take the years of residence spent as students into account when they assess eligibility (OECD, 2010a). In France, enrolment of international students in advanced research programmes reduces the period of residence needed to be eligible for naturalisation. In many other OECD countries, working visa and temporary residence procedures have been simplified for international students and graduates.

Countries apply other measures to integrate international students. These includes local language courses, as offered in Finland and Norway, and internship programmes or work permits for part-time insertion into the labour market, as offered in Australia, the Czech Republic, Japan, Norway and Sweden.

In addition, freedom of movement of workers within Europe as well as national treatment with respect to tuition fees partly explain the high level of student mobility in Europe compared to that among the countries of North America. The North American Free Trade Agreement (NAFTA) does not permit the free movement of workers within a common labour market.

Stay rates

The number of students who remain in the country in which they have studied and the success of policies designed to retain migrants with high skills can be measured by stay rates. This year, the *OECD 2011 International Migration Outlook* (OECD 2011a) includes an indicator to measure the proportion of international students who shift from student status to another type of residence status, particularly one that allows them to work.

The stay rate is defined as the proportion of international students changing to a status other than student to the amount of students not renewing their student permits in the same year; it does not measure the rate of students who stay over the long term. Medium-term working periods abroad can be a value-added for students when returning to their country of origin. In some countries, a short-term, postdoctoral contract abroad can be decisive for acquiring a position in a university.

The estimated stay rates presented in Chart C3.5 need to be treated with some caution because of data limitations and because some students may have not completed their education at the time when they changed status. In addition, not all of these students may be staying for work reasons; some will remain because of humanitarian or family reasons. Finally, the rates exclude all students moving under a free-movement regime, such as that in the European Union. Such persons do not need a residence permit and thus do not show up in the permit statistics.

Chart C3.5. Percentage of international students changing status and staying on in selected OECD countries, 2008 or 2009

Percentage of students who have changed their status (whether for work, family or other reasons) among students who have not renewed their permits

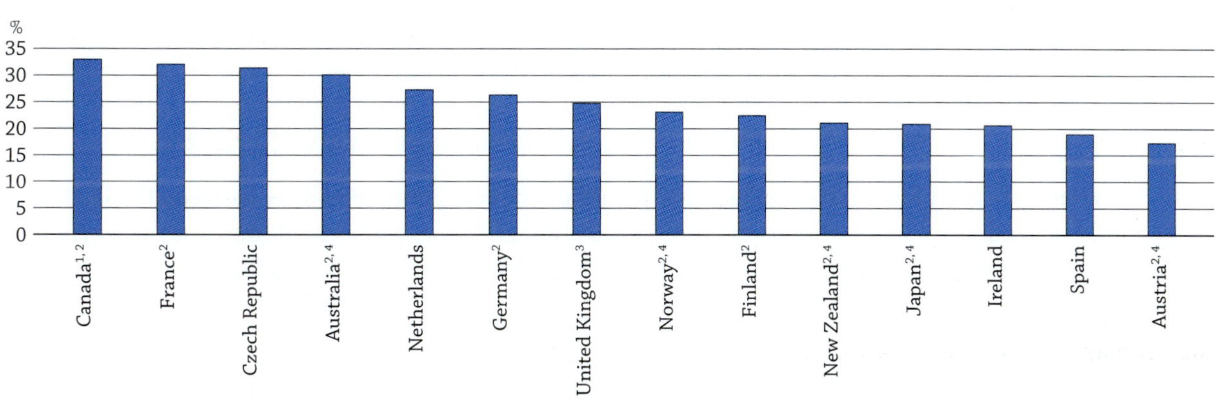

Note: For European countries, covers only students from outside the European Economic Area.

1. Data for Canada include changes from student to other temporary statuses.
2. Year of reference 2008.
3. Student stocks from visa sources.
4. Student stocks calculated from *Education at a Glance*.

Source: OECD (2011a).

StatLink http://dx.doi.org/10.1787/888932461598

The stay rate averaged 25% among international students who did not renew their student permit in 2008 or 2009, and is above 25% in Australia, Canada, the Czech Republic, France, Germany and the Netherlands. In all countries with available data, the stay rate is higher than 17% and reaches 33% in Canada. An average of 74% of students who change their status do so for work-related reasons. This is true for 80% or more of status changes in Canada, Germany, Ireland and the Netherlands. Since it is likely that a higher proportion of those who stay than those who leave actually graduate, the stay rates in this table can be considered to be the lower bounds for rates based exclusively on students who have completed their studies (Chart C3.5).

Definitions

The **country of prior education** is defined as the country in which students obtained the qualification required to enrol in their current level of education, i.e. the country in which students obtained their upper secondary or post-secondary, vocationally oriented education for international students enrolled in academically or vocationally oriented tertiary programmes, and the country in which they obtained their academically oriented tertiary education for international students enrolled in advanced research programmes. Country-specific operational definitions of international students are indicated in the tables as well as in Annex 3 (*www.oecd.org/edu/eag2011*).

Students are classified as **foreign students** if they are not citizens of the country in which the data are collected. While pragmatic and operational, this classification is inappropriate for capturing student mobility because of differing national policies regarding the naturalisation of immigrants. For instance, while Australia and Switzerland report similar intakes of foreign students relative to their tertiary enrolments (24.4 % and 21.2 %, respectively) these proportions reflect significant differences in the actual levels of student mobility (21.5 % of tertiary enrolments in Australia and 14.9 % in Switzerland) (Table C3.1).This is because Australia has a greater propensity to grant permanent residence to its immigrant populations than Switzerland does. Therefore, for student mobility and bilateral comparisons, interpretations of data based on the concept of foreign students should be made with caution.

Students are classified as **international students** if they left their country of origin and moved to another country for the purpose of study. Depending on country-specific immigration legislation, mobility arrangements, such as the free mobility of individuals within the EU and the EEA, and data availability, international students may be defined as students who are not permanent or usual residents of their country of study or alternatively as students who obtained their prior education in a different country, including another EU country.

Permanent or usual residence in the reporting country is defined according to national legislation. In practice, this means holding a student visa or permit, or electing a foreign country of domicile in the year prior to entering the education system of the country reporting data.

Methodology

Data on international and foreign students refer to the academic year 2008-09 and are based on the UOE data collection on education statistics administered by the OECD in 2010 (for details see Annex 3 at *www.oecd.org/edu/eag2011*). Additional data from the UNESCO Institute for Statistics are also included.

Data on international and foreign students are obtained from enrolments in their countries of destination. The method used for obtaining data on international and foreign students is therefore the same as that used for collecting data on total enrolments, i.e. records of regularly enrolled students in an educational programme. Domestic and international students are usually counted on a specific day or period of the year. This procedure makes it possible to measure the proportion of international enrolments in an education system, but the actual number of individuals involved may be much higher since many students study abroad for less than a full academic year, or participate in exchange programmes that do not require enrolment, such as interuniversity exchanges or short-term advanced research programmes.

Moreover, the international student body comprises some distance-learning students who are not, strictly speaking, international students. This pattern of distance enrolments is fairly common in the tertiary institutions of Australia, the United Kingdom and the United States (OECD, 2004b).

Since data on international and foreign students are obtained from tertiary enrolments in their country of destination, the data relate to incoming students rather than to students going abroad. Countries of destination covered by this indicator include all OECD and other G20 countries except Chile, Luxembourg, Mexico, the Russian Federation and Slovenia, as well as countries reporting similar data to the UNESCO Institute for Statistics. These data are used to derive global figures and to examine the destinations of students and trends in market shares.

Data on students enrolled abroad as well as trend analyses are not based on the numbers of international students, but on the number of foreign citizens on whom data consistent across countries and over time are readily available. The data do not include students enrolled in countries that did not report foreign students to the OECD or to the UNESCO Institute for Statistics. All statements on students enrolled abroad may therefore underestimate the real number of citizens studying abroad (Table C3.3), especially in cases where many citizens study in countries that do not report their foreign students to the OECD or UNESCO Institute for Statistics, such as China and India.

Estimating stay rates for international students

The stay rate is estimated as the ratio of the number of persons who have changed status (whether for work, family or other reasons) to the number of students who have not renewed their permits (see OECD 2011 for more details).

The number of students not renewing their student permit is estimated by means of the demographic equality: P2-P1=I-O, where P1 and P2 are, respectively, the stock estimates at times 1 and 2, respectively. I is the inflows and O is the outflows. In the case at hand, Pi is the number of student permits at time i, I is the number of new student permits issued during the year, and O is the number of students who have not renewed their student permit during the year. It is generally easier to obtain the Pi's and I than O. The outflow is then estimated as O=I-(P2-P1). In practice, because I tends to be larger than P2-P1, the stay rate is largely determined by the magnitude of I in the formula.

In Chart C3.5, because the change-of-status statistics are based on permit data, they do not include citizens of the European Economic Area (EEA) for European countries, who do not need a student permit to study in another country of the EEA. The number of new student permits is generally readily available from national permit statistics, obtained either on the Internet or supplied by national authorities. In some cases, the stock of permits P1 and P2 was also available. However, for a number of countries, in particular, Australia, Japan and Norway, the difference P2-P1 in the stock of student permits was proxied by the change in the number of international students, obtained from national educational authorities and published in the OECD's *Education at a Glance 2010* (OECD 2010b).

For the Czech Republic, Finland, Ireland, and Spain, all permit statistics were obtained from the online migration database of Eurostat. This was also the source for student status changes for the United Kingdom. Data for the Czech Republic, Finland, Ireland, Spain and the United Kingdom are for 2009; for all other countries, 2008.

The statistical data for Israel are supplied by and under the responsibility of the relevant Israeli authorities. The use of such data by the OECD is without prejudice to the status of the Golan Heights, East Jerusalem and Israeli settlements in the West Bank under the terms of international law.

References

The relative importance of international students in the education system affects tertiary entry and graduation rates, and may artificially increase them in some fields or levels of education (see Indicators A2 and A3). It may also affect the mix recorded between public and private expenditure (see Indicator B3).

In countries in which different tuition fees are applied to international students, student mobility may boost the financial resources of tertiary education institutions and help to finance the education system. International students may represent a heavy financial burden for countries in which tertiary tuition fees are low or non-existent, given the high level of unit costs in tertiary education (see Indicator B5).

International students enrolled in a country different from their own are only one aspect of the internationalisation of tertiary education. New forms of cross-border education have emerged in the last decade, including the mobility of educational programmes and institutions across borders. Yet, cross-border tertiary education has developed quite differently and in response to different rationales in different world regions. For a detailed analysis of these issues, as well as the trade and policy implications of the internationalisation of tertiary education, see OECD (2004).

OECD (2004b), *Internationalisation and Trade in Higher Education: Opportunities and Challenges*, OECD, Paris.

Kelo, M., U. Teichler and B. Wächter (eds.) (2005), *EURODATA: Student Mobility in European Higher Education*, Verlags and Mediengesellschaft, Bonn.

OECD (2008a), *OECD Review of Tertiary Education: Tertiary Education for the Knowledge Society,* OECD, Paris.

UNESCO (2009), *Global Education Digest 2009*, UNESCO Institute for Statistics, Montreal.

Varghese, N.V. (2009), *Globalization, economic crisis and national strategies for higher education development*, IIEP UNESCO, Paris.

OECD (2011a), *International Migration Outlook 2011*, OECD, Paris.

UNESCO Institute for Statistics (2011), *Education Database, http://www.uis.unesco.org,* accessed 1 July 2011.

The following additional material relevant to this indicator is available on line:

- ***Table C3.6. Number of foreign students in tertiary education, by country of origin and destination (2009) and market shares in international education (2000, 2009)***
  StatLink http://dx.doi.org/10.1787/888932464562

Table C3.1. International and foreign students in tertiary education (2000, 2004, 2009)

International students enrolled as a percentage of all students (international plus domestic), foreign enrolments as a percentage of all students (foreign and national) and index of change in the number of foreign students

Reading the first column: 21.5% of all students in tertiary education in Australia are international students and 14.9% of all students in tertiary education in Switzerland are international students. According to country-specific immigration legislation and data availability constraints, student mobility is either defined on the basis of students' country of residence or the country where students received their prior education. The data presented in this table on student mobility represent the best available proxy of students for each country.

Reading the sixth column: 24.4% of all students in tertiary education in Australia are not Australian citizens, and 21.2% of all students in tertiary education in Switzerland are not Swiss citizens.

		International enrolments					Foreign enrolments				
		International students as a percentage of all tertiary enrolment				Index of change in the **percentage** of international students, total tertiary (2004 = 100)	Foreign students as a percentage of all tertiary enrolment				Index of change in the **number** of foreign students, total tertiary (2000 = 100)
		Total tertiary	Tertiary-type B programmes	Tertiary-type A programmes	Advanced research programmes		Total tertiary	Tertiary-type B programmes	Tertiary-type A programmes	Advanced research programmes	
		(1)	(2)	(3)	(4)	(5)	(6)	(7)	(8)	(9)	(10)
OECD	Australia	**21.5**	19.5	21.7	26.3	129	**24.4**	19.9	24.7	36.9	244
	Austria	**15.1**	2.0	16.0	24.9	134	**19.4**	11.1	19.8	27.5	196
	Belgium	**9.2**	5.9	11.0	20.3	154	**12.6**	9.3	13.9	31.7	120
	Canada[1, 2]	**6.5**	4.0	7.0	20.2	73	**13.2**	9.8	13.7	39.2	202
	Chile	**0.3**	0.2	0.2	10.4	m	**0.9**	0.7	0.9	10.8	216
	Czech Republic	**m**	m	m	m	m	**7.3**	1.1	7.7	10.2	560
	Denmark	**5.4**	8.6	4.7	11.3	118	**9.6**	13.5	8.7	19.7	175
	Estonia	**1.6**	0.3	2.2	3.5	m	**3.7**	3.5	3.8	5.3	295
	Finland	**3.7**	n	3.4	7.1	107	**4.2**	n	3.9	9.3	226
	France	**m**	m	m	m	m	**11.5**	4.1	12.7	40.9	182
	Germany	**m**	m	9.0	m	m	**10.5**	4.0	12.0	m	137
	Greece[3]	**m**	m	m	m	m	**m**	m	m	m	m
	Hungary	**3.7**	0.4	3.9	5.8	132	**4.3**	0.5	4.5	7.0	171
	Iceland	**4.6**	0.9	4.4	22.0	m	**5.5**	0.9	5.3	23.0	231
	Ireland	**7.1**	x(1)	x(1)	x(1)	105	**7.1**	x(6)	x(6)	x(6)	175
	Israel	**m**	m	m	m	m	**m**	m	m	m	m
	Italy	**m**	m	m	m	m	**3.3**	7.1	3.2	8.2	264
	Japan	**3.1**	3.5	2.6	16.0	116	**3.4**	3.6	3.0	16.8	198
	Korea	**m**	m	m	m	m	**1.6**	0.5	1.8	6.7	1483
	Luxembourg	**m**	m	m	m	m	**m**	m	m	m	m
	Mexico	**m**	m	m	m	m	**m**	m	m	m	m
	Netherlands[3]	**3.8**	n	3.9	m	80	**7.2**	n	7.3	m	317
	New Zealand	**14.6**	18.1	12.4	34.5	m	**26.5**	27.8	25.1	49.8	850
	Norway	**2.3**	1.0	2.3	5.3	141	**8.0**	3.5	7.3	29.1	201
	Poland	**0.8**	0.1	0.8	2.4	m	**0.8**	0.1	0.8	2.4	277
	Portugal	**2.4**	7.5	2.3	6.9	m	**4.8**	8.8	4.5	12.3	169
	Slovak Republic	**2.7**	0.7	2.5	6.9	m	**2.8**	0.8	2.6	7.2	418
	Slovenia	**1.8**	0.6	2.1	9.7	m	**1.7**	1.0	1.9	8.5	253
	Spain	**2.7**	5.7	1.7	10.8	329	**4.7**	5.7	3.6	22.0	333
	Sweden	**6.4**	0.4	6.0	21.9	159	**9.4**	3.9	8.8	25.9	155
	Switzerland[3]	**14.9**	m	15.6	47.0	117	**21.2**	18.9	18.8	47.0	190
	Turkey	**m**	m	m	m	m	**0.7**	0.1	1.0	2.8	124
	United Kingdom	**15.3**	6.1	16.7	42.5	114	**20.7**	12.6	21.8	47.5	163
	United States	**3.5**	1.1	3.4	28.1	102	**m**	m	m	m	139
	OECD average	**6.4**	3.9	6.5	17.5	132	**8.7**	6.2	8.7	21.1	289
	EU21 average	**5.4**	2.7	5.7	13.4	143	**7.7**	4.8	7.9	17.9	241
Other G20	Argentina	**m**	m	m	m	m	**m**	m	m	m	m
	Brazil	**m**	m	m	m	m	**0.3**	0.2	0.3	2.0	m
	China	**m**	m	m	m	m	**m**	m	m	m	m
	India	**m**	m	m	m	m	**m**	m	m	m	m
	Indonesia	**m**	m	m	m	m	**m**	m	m	m	m
	Russian Federation[2, 3]	**m**	m	m	m	m	**1.4**	0.5	1.6	m	331
	Saudi Arabia	**m**	m	m	m	m	**m**	m	m	m	m
	South Africa	**m**	m	m	m	m	**m**	m	m	m	m

1. Year of reference 2008.
2. Excludes private institutions.
3. Percentage in total tertiary underestimated because of the exclusion of certain programmes.

Source: OECD. See Annex 3 for notes *(www.oecd.org/edu/eag2011)*.

Please refer to the Reader's Guide for information concerning the symbols replacing missing data.

StatLink http://dx.doi.org/10.1787/888932464467

Table C3.2. [1/2] Distribution of international and foreign students in tertiary education, by country of origin (2009)

Number of international and foreign students enrolled in tertiary education from a given country of origin as a percentage of all international or foreign students in the country of destination, based on head counts

The table shows for each country the proportion of international students in tertiary education who are residents of or had their prior education in a given country of origin. When data on student mobility are not available, the table shows the proportion of foreign students in tertiary education that have citizenship of a given country of origin.

Reading the third column: 0.7% of international tertiary students in Canada come from Germany, 0.1% of international tertiary students in Canada come from Greece, etc.

Reading the tenth column: 4.2% of international tertiary students in Ireland come from Germany, 0.5% of international tertiary students in Ireland come from Greece, etc.

Reading the 21th column: 34.7% of foreign tertiary students in Austria are German citizens, 0.5% of foreign tertiary students in Austria are Greek citizens, etc.

		Countries of destination																			
		OECD																			
		International students																			
		Australia	Belgium	Canada[1, 2]	Chile	Denmark	Estonia	Germany[3, 4]	Hungary	Iceland	Ireland	Netherlands[2]	New Zealand	Portugal	Slovak Republic	Slovenia	Spain[3]	Sweden	Switzerland[3]	United Kingdom	United States
	Countries of origin	(1)	(2)	(3)	(4)	(5)	(6)	(7)	(8)	(9)	(10)	(11)	(12)	(13)	(14)	(15)	(16)	(17)	(18)	(19)	(20)
OECD	Australia	a	0.1	0.3	n	0.2	n	0.2	0.1	0.6	0.6	0.1	7.7	0.2	n	n	n	0.3	0.3	0.5	0.5
	Austria	0.1	0.1	0.1	n	0.3	0.2	3.0	0.9	1.9	0.4	0.4	0.1	0.3	1.1	0.9	0.2	0.3	2.3	0.4	0.1
	Belgium	n	a	0.2	n	0.3	0.9	0.5	0.1	0.5	0.4	4.1	n	0.8	n	0.2	0.8	0.1	0.6	0.7	0.1
	Canada	1.7	0.2	a	0.3	0.4	0.2	0.3	1.0	2.4	4.7	0.2	1.3	0.3	0.1	n	0.2	0.7	1.0	1.5	4.4
	Chile	0.1	0.1	0.2	a	0.1	n	0.3	n	n	0.1	n	0.2	0.1	n	n	3.0	0.1	0.3	0.1	0.3
	Czech Republic	n	0.1	n	n	0.7	n	0.8	0.4	2.2	0.3	0.2	n	0.3	52.0	0.2	0.1	0.2	0.3	0.4	0.1
	Denmark	0.1	n	0.1	n	a	0.6	0.2	0.1	6.1	0.3	0.2	0.3	0.1	n	0.2	0.1	0.8	0.2	0.4	0.1
	Estonia	n	n	n	n	1.2	a	0.3	n	0.6	0.1	0.1	n	n	n	n	0.1	0.4	0.1	0.2	n
	Finland	0.1	0.1	0.1	n	1.1	55.4	0.4	0.2	4.6	0.4	0.5	0.1	0.1	0.1	0.2	0.1	4.8	0.2	0.5	0.1
	France	0.5	16.6	6.4	0.9	1.2	1.0	2.9	0.6	7.4	4.1	1.6	1.0	3.1	0.1	0.2	2.8	1.5	15.5	3.6	1.1
	Germany	0.8	1.0	0.7	1.1	9.6	1.7	a	11.6	13.7	4.2	59.2	3.3	1.5	5.3	0.3	2.5	3.7	27.3	3.9	1.4
	Greece	n	0.2	0.1	n	0.7	0.1	1.2	1.3	0.3	0.5	0.5	n	0.1	8.7	0.3	0.5	0.8	0.9	3.3	0.3
	Hungary	n	0.1	n	n	1.5	0.1	1.0	a	0.6	0.3	0.6	n	0.1	1.3	0.6	0.1	0.2	0.5	0.3	0.1
	Iceland	n	n	n	n	8.0	0.1	n	0.6	a	n	0.1	n	n	n	n	n	0.6	n	0.1	0.1
	Ireland	0.1	n	0.1	n	0.1	0.1	0.2	1.1	0.3	a	0.2	0.1	n	0.5	n	0.2	0.1	0.1	4.2	0.2
	Israel	0.1	0.1	0.3	0.1	0.1	0.1	0.7	5.5	n	0.1	0.2	n	0.1	1.8	n	0.1	0.1	0.2	0.2	0.5
	Italy	0.1	0.5	0.2	0.3	1.6	1.3	1.9	0.4	3.8	2.3	0.8	0.1	1.7	0.3	6.1	4.8	1.1	7.3	1.7	0.6
	Japan	1.0	0.2	1.5	n	0.1	0.3	1.0	0.7	1.9	0.5	0.2	2.0	n	0.1	n	0.2	0.6	0.6	1.1	4.4
	Korea	2.6	0.1	0.1	0.3	0.1	n	2.2	0.3	0.5	n	0.4	4.2	n	0.1	n	0.2	0.3	0.4	1.2	11.2
	Luxembourg	n	1.4	n	n	n	n	1.4	n	n	0.1	0.1	n	0.3	n	n	0.1	n	1.0	0.2	n
	Mexico	0.2	0.1	1.2	2.6	0.4	0.1	0.8	0.1	0.4	0.2	0.2	0.2	0.2	0.1	n	5.9	0.6	0.6	0.4	2.2
	Netherlands	0.1	6.5	0.2	n	0.9	0.4	0.4	0.1	2.0	0.5	a	0.2	0.3	n	n	0.5	0.6	0.6	0.9	0.3
	New Zealand	0.9	n	0.1	n	n	n	n	n	n	0.1	n	a	n	n	n	n	n	0.1	0.1	0.2
	Norway	0.5	0.1	0.2	0.1	14.9	0.5	0.2	4.9	2.6	0.5	0.5	0.4	0.1	4.1	n	0.1	1.5	0.2	0.8	0.2
	Poland	0.1	0.5	0.2	0.1	4.9	0.3	5.0	0.3	4.5	1.9	1.8	n	1.4	1.3	0.6	1.0	0.9	1.2	2.5	0.4
	Portugal	n	0.2	0.1	n	0.3	0.2	0.2	0.3	0.3	0.3	0.4	n	a	0.2	0.1	5.3	0.3	0.4	0.8	0.1
	Slovak Republic	n	0.1	n	n	0.5	n	0.5	14.5	1.3	0.2	0.3	n	n	a	0.3	0.1	0.1	0.4	0.4	0.1
	Slovenia	n	n	n	n	0.3	n	0.2	0.1	0.3	0.1	0.1	n	0.2	n	a	0.1	n	0.1	0.1	n
	Spain	0.1	0.3	0.1	0.6	1.3	0.7	2.0	0.9	5.2	1.5	1.1	0.1	4.9	0.2	0.4	a	0.8	1.4	1.6	0.6
	Sweden	0.3	0.1	0.1	0.1	12.1	0.6	0.3	2.7	4.6	0.4	0.4	0.3	0.2	1.4	0.2	0.2	a	0.6	0.9	0.5
	Switzerland	0.1	0.3	0.3	n	0.3	0.1	1.0	0.1	0.8	0.2	0.3	0.1	0.7	0.2	n	0.7	0.2	a	0.6	0.2
	Turkey	0.2	0.4	0.6	n	0.8	0.5	3.4	1.2	0.4	0.3	0.8	0.1	0.4	0.1	0.4	0.1	1.3	1.6	0.7	2.0
	United Kingdom	0.6	0.3	0.9	0.1	0.9	1.0	0.6	0.9	4.0	16.9	0.9	1.3	1.3	0.8	0.1	1.3	0.5	0.8	a	1.3
	United States	1.2	0.5	9.1	0.8	1.2	1.7	1.8	1.8	3.8	19.7	0.6	6.2	1.1	0.3	0.2	1.5	1.6	1.9	3.9	a
	Total from OECD	11.8	30.1	23.8	7.6	66.0	67.9	35.1	52.7	77.5	62.2	77.0	29.6	20.0	80.3	12.0	33.0	25.2	69.0	38.0	33.7
Other G20	Argentina	n	0.1	0.2	7.9	0.1	n	0.2	n	0.1	n	n	0.1	0.2	n	0.1	4.7	0.1	0.4	0.1	0.4
	Brazil	0.3	0.2	0.5	3.9	0.3	0.2	1.1	n	0.1	0.2	0.3	0.4	24.7	n	0.2	3.8	0.4	1.1	0.4	1.3
	China	27.3	1.3	21.4	0.6	7.0	4.8	11.8	1.4	2.4	8.7	7.3	23.5	0.4	0.3	0.3	1.2	11.4	2.1	12.9	18.8
	India	10.3	0.4	3.7	0.1	2.6	0.6	1.8	0.2	1.1	3.8	0.3	14.9	0.2	0.1	0.5	0.3	3.5	1.3	9.4	15.4
	Indonesia	4.0	0.1	0.8	n	0.1	0.2	0.8	n	0.6	0.1	1.4	0.8	0.1	n	n	0.1	0.3	0.1	0.3	1.1
	Russian Federation	0.3	0.4	0.6	0.2	0.6	5.2	5.2	1.0	2.4	0.6	0.8	0.7	0.5	0.6	1.4	1.0	1.4	1.9	0.8	0.7
	Saudi Arabia	1.4	n	1.4	n	n	n	0.1	0.3	n	0.5	n	0.9	n	1.3	n	n	0.1	n	1.4	1.9
	South Africa	0.3	0.1	0.1	n	0.1	0.1	0.1	n	n	1.2	0.2	0.3	0.5	n	n	n	0.1	0.2	0.4	0.3
	Total from other G20 countries	44.0	2.6	28.6	12.6	10.7	11.0	21.0	3.1	6.9	15.2	10.3	41.6	26.6	2.5	2.6	11.1	17.3	7.2	25.7	39.8
	Main geographic regions																				
	Total from Africa	3.0	4.5	13.2	0.2	2.8	1.7	9.2	2.6	2.2	5.7	2.4	1.0	46.7	1.3	0.5	10.3	6.0	6.1	9.7	5.5
	Total from Asia	79.1	4.6	47.2	1.4	17.8	9.8	32.6	18.5	10.3	29.3	13.2	58.7	3.6	11.0	2.5	3.6	40.3	10.2	49.1	68.4
	Total from Europe	4.2	30.2	12.4	3.8	74.6	86.0	43.0	75.7	78.7	39.0	79.7	8.7	20.4	86.8	75.3	30.9	24.7	71.4	32.4	10.8
	of which, from EU21 countries	3.1	28.1	9.8	3.3	39.4	64.5	23.0	36.5	64.1	35.2	73.4	7.2	16.8	73.3	11.2	21.1	17.2	61.8	26.8	7.7
	Total from North America	2.9	0.7	9.6	1.1	1.6	1.8	2.1	2.9	6.3	24.4	0.8	7.5	1.4	0.4	0.2	1.7	2.3	2.8	5.5	4.5
	Total from Oceania	1.8	0.1	0.4	n	0.2	n	0.2	0.1	0.6	0.7	0.1	11.0	0.3	n	n	0.1	0.3	0.4	0.6	0.8
	Total from Latin America & the Caribbean	1.3	1.0	7.8	92.4	1.2	0.6	4.3	0.2	1.9	1.0	2.4	1.2	27.5	0.5	0.9	51.4	2.4	5.1	2.2	10.1
	Not specified	7.8	58.9	9.4	1.2	1.7	n	8.6	n	n	n	1.4	12.0	n	n	20.6	2.1	23.9	4.0	0.5	n
	Total from all countries	100.0	100.0	100.0	100.0	100.0	100.0	100.0	100.0	100.0	100.0	100.0	100.0	100.0	100.0	100.0	100.0	100.0	100.0	100.0	100.0

1. Year of reference 2008.
2. Excludes private institutions.
3. Excludes tertiary-type B programmes.
4. Excludes advanced research programmes.
5. Foreign students are defined on the basis of their country of citizenship; these data are not comparable with data on international students and are therefore presented separately in the table.

Source: OECD. See Annex 3 for notes *(www.oecd.org/edu/eag2011)*.

Please refer to the Reader's Guide for information concerning the symbols replacing missing data.

StatLink http://dx.doi.org/10.1787/888932464486

Table C3.2. [2/2] Distribution of international and foreign students in tertiary education, by country of origin (2009)

Number of international and foreign students enrolled in tertiary education from a given country of origin as a percentage of all international or foreign students in the country of destination, based on head counts

The table shows for each country the proportion of international students in tertiary education who are residents of or had their prior education in a given country of origin. When data on student mobility are not available, the table shows the proportion of foreign students in tertiary education that have citizenship of a given country of origin.

Reading the third column: 0.7% of international tertiary students in Canada come from Germany, 0.1% of international tertiary students in Canada come from Greece, etc.

Reading the tenth column: 4.2% of international tertiary students in Ireland come from Germany, 0.5% of international tertiary students in Ireland come from Greece, etc.

Reading the 21th column: 34.7% of foreign tertiary students in Austria are German citizens, 0.5% of foreign tertiary students in Austria are Greek citizens, etc.

		Countries of destination														
		OECD											Other G20			
		Foreign students											Foreign students			
	Countries of origin	Austria[3,5]	Czech Republic[5]	Finland[5]	France[5]	Italy[5]	Japan[5]	Korea[5]	Norway[5]	Poland[5]	Turkey[5]	Total OECD destinations	Brazil[5]	Russian Federation[2,4,5]	Total non-OECD destinations	Total all reporting destinatio ns
		(21)	(22)	(23)	(24)	(25)	(26)	(27)	(28)	(29)	(30)	(31)	(32)	(33)	(34)	(35)
OECD	Australia	0.2	n	0.4	0.1	0.1	0.2	0.1	0.3	0.1	0.2	**0.4**	0.1	n	**0.1**	**0.3**
	Austria	a	0.1	0.3	0.2	0.3	n	n	0.3	0.3	0.2	**0.4**	0.1	n	**0.1**	**0.4**
	Belgium	0.2	n	0.2	1.2	0.3	n	n	0.2	0.1	0.1	**0.4**	0.3	n	**n**	**0.3**
	Canada	0.2	0.2	0.7	0.6	0.2	0.2	0.5	0.6	2.4	0.1	**1.8**	0.2	n	**0.1**	**1.4**
	Chile	0.1	n	0.1	0.3	0.4	n	n	0.4	n	n	**0.3**	2.6	n	**0.3**	**0.3**
	Czech Republic	1.1	a	0.4	0.3	0.3	n	n	0.3	5.5	n	**0.4**	n	n	**n**	**0.3**
	Denmark	0.2	n	0.4	0.1	0.1	n	n	4.6	0.2	0.1	**0.2**	0.1	n	**n**	**0.2**
	Estonia	0.1	n	5.4	n	0.1	n	n	0.4	0.1	n	**0.1**	n	0.4	**0.1**	**0.1**
	Finland	0.3	n	a	0.1	0.1	0.1	n	1.9	0.1	n	**0.3**	0.1	n	**0.2**	**0.2**
	France	0.9	0.3	1.3	a	1.7	0.4	0.1	1.2	0.7	0.3	**2.1**	1.9	0.1	**0.2**	**1.6**
	Germany	34.7	1.1	3.5	2.7	2.4	0.4	0.1	4.4	3.1	2.5	**3.6**	1.7	0.2	**0.3**	**2.9**
	Greece	0.5	0.7	0.5	0.7	6.5	n	n	0.2	0.2	3.9	**1.0**	n	0.2	**0.5**	**0.9**
	Hungary	2.6	0.3	0.9	0.2	0.3	0.1	n	0.2	0.4	0.1	**0.3**	n	n	**n**	**0.2**
	Iceland	0.1	n	0.1	n	n	n	n	1.6	n	n	**0.1**	n	n	**n**	**0.1**
	Ireland	0.1	0.2	0.2	0.2	0.1	n	n	0.1	0.1	n	**0.7**	n	n	**n**	**0.6**
	Israel	0.2	0.5	0.2	0.1	2.2	n	n	0.1	0.2	0.1	**0.4**	0.1	0.3	**0.9**	**0.5**
	Italy	11.4	0.1	1.3	2.1	a	0.1	n	0.7	0.4	0.1	**1.4**	1.4	n	**0.9**	**1.3**
	Japan	0.7	0.1	0.9	0.7	0.4	a	2.0	0.4	0.2	0.1	**1.8**	0.6	0.1	**0.2**	**1.4**
	Korea	0.7	0.1	0.4	1.0	0.7	18.9	a	0.3	0.2	0.1	**4.8**	1.6	0.5	**0.6**	**3.8**
	Luxembourg	1.0	n	n	0.6	0.1	n	n	n	n	n	**0.3**	n	n	**n**	**0.2**
	Mexico	0.2	n	0.7	0.7	0.5	0.1	n	0.3	0.1	n	**1.0**	0.6	n	**0.3**	**0.9**
	Netherlands	0.4	n	0.7	0.3	0.2	0.1	n	1.3	0.1	0.2	**0.4**	0.2	n	**n**	**0.3**
	New Zealand	n	n	0.1	n	n	0.1	0.1	0.1	0.1	n	**0.2**	n	n	**n**	**0.1**
	Norway	0.1	0.8	0.6	0.1	0.1	n	n	a	6.9	n	**0.5**	n	n	**n**	**0.4**
	Poland	2.8	1.2	1.7	1.2	2.2	0.1	n	1.5	a	n	**1.3**	0.1	n	**0.1**	**1.0**
	Portugal	0.2	1.3	0.3	1.1	0.2	n	n	0.3	0.3	n	**0.5**	4.2	n	**0.2**	**0.4**
	Slovak Republic	2.5	65.5	0.2	0.2	0.3	n	n	0.2	2.4	n	**1.1**	n	n	**n**	**0.9**
	Slovenia	1.3	0.1	0.1	n	0.5	n	n	n	0.1	n	**0.1**	n	n	**n**	**0.1**
	Spain	0.9	0.1	1.1	1.6	0.8	0.1	n	0.8	0.8	n	**0.9**	1.1	n	**0.1**	**0.7**
	Sweden	0.3	0.4	3.9	0.2	0.2	0.1	n	7.4	4.9	n	**0.6**	0.1	n	**0.1**	**0.5**
	Switzerland	1.3	n	0.3	0.7	1.6	0.1	n	0.3	0.1	0.1	**0.4**	0.3	n	**0.1**	**0.3**
	Turkey	4.4	0.2	0.9	0.9	0.9	0.1	0.1	0.5	0.8	a	**1.2**	n	0.3	**2.1**	**1.4**
	United Kingdom	0.4	1.3	1.5	1.0	0.4	0.3	n	1.8	0.6	0.4	**0.9**	1.7	n	**0.2**	**0.7**
	United States	0.9	0.6	1.7	1.4	0.6	1.6	1.5	2.1	5.9	0.3	**1.8**	2.5	0.1	**0.7**	**1.6**
	Total from OECD	70.9	75.4	31.2	20.8	24.8	23.4	4.9	34.9	37.1	8.8	**31.6**	21.7	2.3	**8.5**	**26.3**
Other G20	Argentina	n	n	0.1	0.3	0.6	0.1	n	0.1	n	n	**0.3**	4.7	n	**0.3**	**0.3**
	Brazil	0.2	n	0.5	1.4	1.7	0.4	0.1	0.6	0.2	n	**1.0**	a	0.1	**0.5**	**0.8**
	China	2.3	0.5	15.8	9.5	6.6	60.3	78.6	4.7	1.9	0.8	**18.2**	2.0	6.6	**10.6**	**16.5**
	India	0.6	0.4	2.4	0.5	1.1	0.4	0.8	1.1	2.1	n	**7.3**	0.1	3.1	**2.4**	**6.2**
	Indonesia	0.1	n	0.2	0.1	0.2	1.4	0.6	0.5	0.2	0.2	**1.0**	n	n	**1.4**	**1.1**
	Russian Federation	1.3	5.8	10.9	1.4	1.7	0.3	0.5	5.4	2.9	2.2	**1.3**	0.2	a	**2.5**	**1.6**
	Saudi Arabia	0.1	n	n	0.2	n	0.1	0.1	n	0.4	0.1	**1.0**	n	n	**1.2**	**1.0**
	South Africa	0.1	0.1	0.1	n	n	n	n	0.2	0.1	n	**0.2**	0.3	n	**0.1**	**0.2**
	Total from other G20 countries	4.7	6.8	30.0	13.4	12.0	62.9	80.7	12.6	7.7	3.4	**30.2**	7.4	9.9	**19.0**	**27.7**
	Main geographic regions															
	Total from Africa	1.5	1.6	19.3	42.9	11.4	0.8	0.8	10.2	4.5	2.4	**10.0**	26.3	4.3	**16.5**	**11.5**
	Total from Asia	13.1	9.8	34.8	22.1	19.4	93.2	95.4	17.3	18.8	57.3	**50.9**	6.1	60.6	**55.2**	**51.9**
	Total from Europe	82.8	86.7	40.4	21.1	56.5	2.6	1.1	42.5	67.1	25.1	**24.4**	14.0	29.6	**18.3**	**23.0**
	of which, from EU21 countries	61.8	72.9	24.0	14.1	17.1	1.9	0.4	27.9	20.2	7.9	**16.9**	13.1	1.0	**3.2**	**13.8**
	Total from North America	1.2	0.7	2.4	2.0	0.8	1.9	2.0	2.6	8.4	0.3	**3.7**	2.6	0.1	**0.8**	**3.0**
	Total from Oceania	0.2	n	0.5	0.2	0.1	0.4	0.2	0.4	0.1	0.2	**0.7**	0.8	n	**1.5**	**0.9**
	Total from Latin America & the Caribbean	1.2	0.7	2.4	5.6	9.1	1.1	0.4	2.5	1.0	0.1	**6.0**	23.8	0.6	**7.7**	**6.4**
	Not specified	n	0.5	0.2	6.2	2.7	n	n	24.5	0.1	14.6	**4.3**	26.4	4.8	**n**	**3.3**
	Total from all countries	100.0	100.0	100.0	100.0	100.0	100.0	100.0	100.0	100.0	100.0	**100.0**	100.0	100.0	**100.0**	**100.0**

1. Year of reference 2008.
2. Excludes private institutions.
3. Excludes tertiary-type B programmes.
4. Excludes advanced research programmes.
5. Foreign students are defined on the basis of their country of citizenship; these data are not comparable with data on international students and are therefore presented separately in the table.

Source: OECD. See Annex 3 for notes *(www.oecd.org/edu/eag2011).*

Please refer to the Reader's Guide for information concerning the symbols replacing missing data.

StatLink http://dx.doi.org/10.1787/888932464486

Table C3.3. [1/2] Citizens studying abroad in tertiary education, by country of destination (2009)

Number of foreign students enrolled in tertiary education in a given country of destination as a percentage of all students enrolled abroad, based on head counts

The table shows for each country the proportion of students studying abroad in tertiary education in a given country of destination.
Reading the second column: 5.8% of Czech citizens enrolled in tertiary education abroad study in Austria, 12.5% of Italian citizens enrolled in tertiary education abroad study in Austria, etc.
Reading the first row: 2.7% of Australian citizens enrolled in tertiary education abroad study in France, 28.5% of Australian citizens enrolled in tertiary education abroad study in New Zealand, etc.

	Country of origin	Australia	Austria[1]	Belgium	Canada[2, 3]	Chile	Czech Republic	Denmark	Estonia	Finland	France	Germany[4]	Greece[5]	Hungary	Iceland	Ireland[6]	Israel	Italy	Japan	Korea	Luxembourg[5]
		Countries of destination: OECD																			
		(1)	(2)	(3)	(4)	(5)	(6)	(7)	(8)	(9)	(10)	(11)	(12)	(13)	(14)	(15)	(16)	(17)	(18)	(19)	(20)
OECD	Australia	a	0.9	0.3	4.6	n	n	0.5	n	0.4	2.7	3.4	m	0.1	n	0.7	m	0.5	3.1	0.6	m
	Austria	1.8	a	0.4	1.1	n	0.2	0.4	n	0.3	3.0	52.2	m	0.9	0.1	0.4	m	1.4	0.3	0.1	m
	Belgium	0.7	1.0	a	3.2	n	0.1	0.4	0.1	0.2	24.8	8.6	m	0.2	n	0.5	m	1.7	0.4	n	m
	Canada	9.5	0.3	0.3	a	n	0.1	0.2	n	0.2	3.0	1.4	m	0.3	n	1.3	m	0.3	0.7	0.6	m
	Chile	3.4	0.3	1.1	3.3	a	0.1	0.3	n	0.2	7.1	6.3	m	n	n	0.1	m	2.3	0.3	0.1	m
	Czech Republic	0.8	5.8	0.6	1.0	n	a	1.0	n	0.4	6.5	16.4	m	0.5	0.2	0.4	m	1.6	0.4	0.1	m
	Denmark	3.1	1.5	0.7	1.9	0.1	0.1	a	0.1	0.7	2.9	7.8	m	0.2	1.2	0.6	m	1.1	0.4	0.1	m
	Estonia	0.3	1.3	0.5	0.5	n	n	5.2	a	14.9	2.2	13.8	m	0.2	0.2	0.3	m	1.2	0.4	n	m
	Finland	1.3	1.9	0.4	0.8	n	0.1	2.2	5.5	a	2.7	7.8	m	0.4	0.4	0.5	m	0.8	0.8	n	m
	France	1.8	0.8	24.3	11.6	0.1	0.2	0.4	n	0.2	a	9.4	m	0.2	0.1	0.8	m	1.6	0.8	0.1	m
	Germany	1.8	19.8	0.9	1.2	0.1	0.3	2.0	n	0.4	6.5	a	m	1.7	0.1	0.5	m	1.5	0.5	0.1	m
	Greece	0.2	0.9	1.4	0.5	n	0.7	0.4	n	0.2	5.4	16.6	a	0.5	n	0.2	m	12.4	0.1	n	m
	Hungary	0.5	17.9	1.4	1.4	n	1.1	2.6	n	1.3	6.6	25.9	m	a	0.1	0.4	m	2.4	1.0	0.1	m
	Iceland	0.9	0.8	0.1	0.9	n	0.1	46.5	0.1	0.3	0.7	2.6	m	6.0	a	0.2	m	0.3	0.7	n	m
	Ireland	1.1	0.4	0.4	1.5	n	0.3	0.3	n	0.2	2.0	2.1	m	0.8	n	a	m	0.2	0.1	n	m
	Israel	1.1	0.7	0.2	6.6	n	0.8	0.3	n	0.2	1.8	8.6	m	3.9	n	0.1	a	8.6	0.3	n	m
	Italy	0.7	12.5	3.5	0.6	n	0.1	0.6	n	0.3	9.8	14.9	m	0.1	0.1	0.5	m	a	0.3	n	m
	Japan	5.7	0.9	0.3	4.3	n	0.1	0.1	n	0.3	3.9	4.5	m	0.2	n	0.1	m	0.6	a	2.1	m
	Korea	5.3	0.4	0.1	0.3	n	n	n	n	n	1.9	4.2	m	0.1	n	n	m	0.4	19.5	a	m
	Luxembourg	0.2	7.4	20.8	0.2	n	n	0.1	n	n	18.4	34.1	m	0.1	n	0.2	m	0.4	0.1	n	a
	Mexico	1.6	0.3	0.3	6.3	0.5	n	0.2	n	0.3	6.0	5.2	m	n	n	0.1	m	1.0	0.5	n	m
	Netherlands	1.8	1.4	30.5	2.4	n	0.1	1.6	n	0.5	4.2	10.0	m	0.1	0.1	0.4	m	0.8	0.5	n	m
	New Zealand	52.7	0.2	0.1	n	n	0.1	0.3	n	0.2	1.4	1.4	m	0.1	n	0.4	m	0.1	1.9	0.7	m
	Norway	9.5	0.5	0.2	1.5	0.1	1.7	18.9	n	0.5	2.0	3.5	m	5.1	0.2	0.4	m	0.5	0.4	n	m
	Poland	0.4	4.1	1.6	1.9	n	0.9	2.5	n	0.5	7.6	33.4	m	0.2	0.1	0.6	m	3.7	0.3	n	m
	Portugal	0.5	0.8	4.6	1.6	n	2.4	0.5	n	0.2	16.4	10.0	m	0.3	n	0.2	m	0.8	0.2	n	m
	Slovak Republic	0.3	5.0	0.3	0.4	n	68.4	0.3	n	0.1	1.4	4.4	m	8.0	n	0.1	m	0.7	0.1	n	m
	Slovenia	0.8	25.4	0.9	0.6	n	0.8	1.1	n	0.6	2.8	18.5	m	0.7	0.1	0.3	m	11.2	0.5	n	m
	Spain	0.5	2.0	3.5	0.8	0.2	0.1	0.9	n	0.5	14.7	18.6	m	0.5	0.2	0.7	m	2.1	0.5	n	m
	Sweden	5.1	1.2	0.4	1.2	0.1	0.8	13.8	n	3.0	2.7	3.7	m	2.5	0.3	0.3	m	0.7	0.9	n	m
	Switzerland	2.7	6.5	1.2	3.4	0.1	0.1	0.7	n	0.3	14.5	20.1	m	0.1	0.1	0.2	m	8.6	0.6	0.1	m
	Turkey	0.6	3.6	0.5	1.3	n	0.1	0.6	n	0.2	3.2	38.2	m	0.3	n	0.1	m	0.9	0.2	0.1	m
	United Kingdom	5.2	0.8	0.8	7.6	n	1.3	1.6	n	0.6	8.1	5.9	m	0.4	0.1	6.8	m	0.8	1.3	0.1	m
	United States	5.4	1.0	0.4	18.5	0.1	0.3	0.6	n	0.4	6.4	6.5	m	0.5	0.1	4.6	m	0.8	3.8	1.4	m
	Total from OECD	3.1	4.3	3.1	3.4	0.1	2.3	1.4	0.1	0.4	5.3	11.1	m	0.8	0.1	0.8	m	1.7	3.1	0.2	m
	Total from EU21	1.5	6.9	5.5	2.9	n	4.2	1.5	0.1	0.6	6.5	11.9	m	1.1	0.1	0.9	m	2.1	0.5	n	m
Other G20	Argentina	0.7	0.2	0.4	4.2	3.2	n	0.2	n	0.1	5.7	3.1	m	n	n	n	m	3.2	0.6	0.1	m
	Brazil	2.3	0.4	0.6	3.2	0.6	n	0.3	n	0.2	10.5	7.3	m	n	n	0.1	m	3.5	1.8	0.1	m
	China	12.4	0.2	0.2	6.1	n	n	0.3	n	0.4	4.2	4.4	m	n	n	0.2	m	0.8	14.0	6.9	m
	India	12.6	0.2	0.2	4.8	n	0.1	0.2	n	0.1	0.6	1.7	m	n	n	0.2	m	0.3	0.3	0.2	m
	Indonesia	26.5	0.2	0.3	2.7	n	n	n	n	0.1	0.8	6.3	m	n	n	n	m	0.3	4.6	0.8	m
	Russian Federation	1.2	1.2	0.9	2.7	n	2.9	0.6	2.0	2.2	5.8	21.4	m	0.3	n	0.1	m	1.9	0.6	0.4	m
	Saudi Arabia	10.7	0.1	n	3.9	n	n	n	n	n	1.2	0.4	m	0.2	n	0.2	m	0.1	0.2	0.1	m
	South Africa	10.2	0.5	0.7	5.3	n	0.5	0.3	n	0.2	1.1	1.8	m	0.1	n	1.9	m	0.2	0.3	0.1	m
	Total from other G20	11.7	0.3	0.3	5.2	0.1	0.2	0.3	0.1	0.4	3.4	4.9	m	0.1	n	0.2	m	0.8	8.6	4.2	m
	Total from all countries	7.0	1.6	1.3	5.2	0.2	0.8	0.6	0.1	0.3	6.8	7.0	0.7	0.5	n	0.4	m	1.8	3.6	1.4	n

Note: The proportion of students abroad is based only on the total of students enrolled in countries reporting data to the OECD and UNESCO Institute for Statistics.

1. Excludes tertiary-type B programmes.
2. Year of reference 2008.
3. Excludes private institutions.
4. Excludes advanced research programmes.
5. Total based on the estimation by the UNESCO Institute for Statistics.
6. Excludes part-time students.

Source: OECD. See Annex 3 for notes *(www.oecd.org/edu/eag2011).*

Please refer to the Reader's Guide for information concerning the symbols replacing missing data.

StatLink http://dx.doi.org/10.1787/888932464505

Table C3.3. [2/2] Citizens studying abroad in tertiary education, by country of destination (2009)

Number of foreign students enrolled in tertiary education in a given country of destination as a percentage of all students enrolled abroad, based on head counts

The table shows for each country the proportion of students studying abroad in tertiary education in a given country of destination.
Reading the second column: 5.8% of Czech citizens enrolled in tertiary education abroad study in Austria, 12.5% of Italian citizens enrolled in tertiary education abroad study in Austria, etc.
Reading the first row: 2.7% of Australian citizens enrolled in tertiary education abroad study in France, 28.5% of Australian citizens enrolled in tertiary education abroad study in New Zealand, etc.

		Countries of destination																			
		OECD																Other G20			
	Country of origin	Mexico	Netherlands[4]	New Zealand	Norway	Poland	Portugal	Slovak Republic	Slovenia	Spain	Sweden	Switzerland	Turkey	United Kingdom	United States	Total OECD destinations	Total EU21 destinations	Brazil	Russian Federation[3,4]	Total non-OECD destinations	Total all reporting destinations
		(21)	(22)	(23)	(24)	(25)	(26)	(27)	(28)	(29)	(30)	(31)	(32)	(33)	(34)	(35)	(36)	(37)	(38)	(39)	(40)
OECD	Australia	m	0.6	28.5	0.5	0.1	0.2	n	n	0.3	0.9	0.8	0.4	15.6	29.9	**95.9**	**27.5**	0.1	n	**4.1**	**100.0**
	Austria	m	1.8	0.7	0.3	0.4	0.2	0.5	0.1	1.2	1.0	8.1	0.3	9.7	6.3	**93.4**	**74.3**	0.2	0.1	**6.6**	**100.0**
	Belgium	m	18.1	0.4	0.4	0.1	1.0	n	n	3.8	0.4	3.0	0.3	21.4	7.0	**98.0**	**82.5**	0.4	n	**2.0**	**100.0**
	Canada	m	0.3	1.6	0.2	0.9	0.2	n	n	0.3	0.4	0.7	n	11.6	63.1	**97.5**	**21.0**	0.1	0.1	**2.5**	**100.0**
	Chile	m	0.4	1.3	0.7	n	0.2	n	n	24.9	1.6	0.8	n	3.7	17.9	**76.4**	**48.6**	4.0	n	**23.6**	**100.0**
	Czech Republic	m	1.2	0.4	0.5	8.1	0.3	29.4	0.1	1.3	0.6	1.4	n	11.5	7.9	**98.3**	**85.5**	0.1	0.2	**1.7**	**100.0**
	Denmark	m	2.4	2.6	13.1	0.5	0.1	n	n	1.4	12.3	1.6	0.2	24.8	15.9	**97.3**	**57.3**	0.3	n	**2.7**	**100.0**
	Estonia	m	1.4	0.1	1.6	0.3	0.1	n	n	1.9	5.3	0.7	n	18.2	5.8	**76.7**	**67.0**	0.1	11.8	**23.3**	**100.0**
	Finland	m	2.2	0.4	3.2	0.2	0.2	n	n	1.0	28.7	1.3	n	16.7	7.4	**87.0**	**71.3**	0.1	0.5	**13.0**	**100.0**
	France	m	1.3	0.7	0.3	0.2	0.9	n	n	3.6	0.6	7.6	0.1	19.3	10.8	**97.5**	**63.7**	0.4	0.2	**2.5**	**100.0**
	Germany	m	18.3	1.7	0.7	0.5	0.3	0.3	n	2.1	1.5	11.7	0.5	13.5	9.1	**97.6**	**70.1**	0.3	0.2	**2.4**	**100.0**
	Greece	m	2.1	n	0.1	0.1	0.1	1.6	n	1.1	0.9	1.2	2.4	34.7	5.4	**89.1**	**79.2**	n	0.6	**10.9**	**100.0**
	Hungary	m	3.3	0.5	0.5	0.7	0.2	1.1	0.2	1.4	1.4	2.4	0.2	13.2	7.8	**95.8**	**81.3**	n	0.3	**4.2**	**100.0**
	Iceland	m	2.2	0.2	6.9	0.1	n	0.1	n	0.4	9.9	0.5	n	9.4	9.6	**99.5**	**79.8**	n	0.1	**0.5**	**100.0**
	Ireland	m	0.8	1.1	0.1	0.1	0.1	0.2	n	0.5	0.5	0.3	n	80.8	5.5	**99.3**	**89.5**	n	n	**0.7**	**100.0**
	Israel	m	0.9	0.3	0.1	0.2	n	0.7	n	0.7	0.2	0.4	0.1	3.6	17.6	**58.0**	**31.5**	0.1	2.2	**42.0**	**100.0**
	Italy	m	1.3	0.1	0.2	0.1	0.6	n	0.2	9.7	0.7	9.9	n	11.1	7.7	**85.8**	**66.1**	0.4	0.1	**14.2**	**100.0**
	Japan	m	0.4	2.2	0.2	0.1	n	n	n	0.3	0.4	0.5	n	8.2	61.2	**96.8**	**20.6**	0.2	0.3	**3.2**	**100.0**
	Korea	m	0.2	2.1	n	n	n	n	n	0.2	0.1	0.2	n	3.4	58.0	**96.3**	**10.8**	0.2	0.5	**3.7**	**100.0**
	Luxembourg	m	0.9	n	n	n	0.3	n	n	0.3	0.1	4.1	n	11.1	1.1	**99.8**	**94.1**	n	n	**0.2**	**100.0**
	Mexico	a	0.6	0.3	0.2	0.1	0.1	n	n	15.2	0.5	0.7	n	4.3	47.6	**92.1**	**34.4**	0.3	0.1	**7.9**	**100.0**
	Netherlands	m	a	3.0	1.4	0.1	0.5	n	n	2.3	1.8	2.7	0.2	20.0	11.5	**98.1**	**74.4**	0.2	n	**1.9**	**100.0**
	New Zealand	m	0.2	a	0.2	0.2	n	n	n	0.1	0.5	0.6	n	10.6	23.3	**95.3**	**16.0**	n	n	**4.7**	**100.0**
	Norway	m	2.5	1.2	a	8.1	n	1.8	n	0.7	8.2	0.6	n	20.9	9.2	**98.2**	**75.5**	n	0.1	**1.8**	**100.0**
	Poland	m	2.1	0.1	0.7	a	0.5	0.2	n	2.6	1.6	1.3	n	23.1	6.9	**97.3**	**85.6**	0.1	0.1	**2.7**	**100.0**
	Portugal	m	1.9	0.1	0.3	0.3	a	0.1	n	21.0	0.7	7.7	n	16.3	5.7	**92.4**	**76.4**	4.0	n	**7.6**	**100.0**
	Slovak Republic	m	0.5	0.1	0.1	1.4	0.1	a	n	0.6	0.1	0.6	n	4.5	1.8	**99.3**	**95.8**	n	0.1	**0.7**	**100.0**
	Slovenia	m	3.0	0.1	0.2	0.5	0.7	0.1	a	1.7	0.9	1.6	0.1	9.0	6.6	**88.9**	**78.2**	n	0.1	**11.1**	**100.0**
	Spain	m	3.2	0.2	0.5	0.5	2.6	n	n	a	1.3	5.6	n	21.5	14.3	**95.5**	**72.7**	0.7	0.1	**4.5**	**100.0**
	Sweden	m	1.4	0.9	8.0	5.1	0.1	0.5	n	1.5	a	1.7	0.1	19.6	19.8	**95.6**	**57.5**	0.1	0.1	**4.4**	**100.0**
	Switzerland	m	1.2	0.8	0.5	0.1	0.9	0.1	n	3.5	0.7	a	0.1	17.4	10.8	**95.4**	**76.3**	0.4	0.1	**4.6**	**100.0**
	Turkey	m	1.3	0.1	0.1	0.2	0.1	n	n	0.2	0.5	1.4	a	3.7	18.2	**75.7**	**53.7**	n	0.6	**24.3**	**100.0**
	United Kingdom	m	2.6	16.6	1.0	0.3	0.3	0.2	n	2.6	1.7	1.3	0.3	a	26.7	**95.0**	**34.7**	0.9	0.1	**5.0**	**100.0**
	United States	m	0.9	5.5	0.7	1.8	0.3	n	n	2.0	1.0	1.1	0.1	25.9	a	**90.1**	**53.4**	0.7	0.2	**9.9**	**100.0**
	Total from OECD	m	3.2	2.0	0.6	0.6	0.3	0.5	n	2.8	1.3	3.4	0.2	14.0	22.6	**92.8**	**54.1**	0.4	0.3	**7.2**	**100.0**
	Total from EU21	m	5.3	1.7	0.9	0.6	0.5	0.9	n	3.3	1.7	5.7	0.3	18.2	9.6	**95.0**	**71.8**	0.4	0.3	**5.0**	**100.0**
Other G20	Argentina	m	0.2	0.5	0.1	n	0.2	n	n	34.7	0.3	0.9	n	1.6	17.8	**78.1**	**49.9**	5.9	n	**21.9**	**100.0**
	Brazil	m	0.5	0.8	0.3	0.1	11.9	n	n	10.7	0.5	1.3	n	4.3	26.8	**88.2**	**51.0**	a	0.4	**11.8**	**100.0**
	China	m	0.6	2.5	0.1	0.1	n	n	n	0.2	0.5	0.2	n	8.3	21.9	**84.4**	**20.4**	0.1	1.6	**15.6**	**100.0**
	India	m	0.2	3.5	0.1	0.2	n	n	n	0.1	0.4	0.3	n	16.1	48.1	**90.4**	**20.7**	n	2.0	**9.6**	**100.0**
	Indonesia	m	2.7	1.2	0.2	0.1	n	n	n	0.1	0.2	0.2	0.1	2.7	19.2	**69.2**	**13.8**	n	0.2	**30.8**	**100.0**
	Russian Federation	m	0.8	0.8	1.5	0.8	0.2	0.1	0.1	1.8	1.0	1.3	0.8	4.8	7.8	**66.1**	**48.9**	0.1	a	**33.9**	**100.0**
	Saudi Arabia	m	0.1	1.1	n	0.2	n	0.2	n	0.1	n	n	0.1	15.2	36.4	**70.6**	**18.0**	n	n	**29.4**	**100.0**
	South Africa	m	1.2	21.9	0.5	0.1	1.2	n	n	0.2	0.3	0.6	n	18.5	19.6	**87.5**	**28.8**	0.5	n	**12.5**	**100.0**
	Total from other G20	m	0.6	2.6	0.2	0.1	0.4	n	n	1.1	0.5	0.3	0.1	9.7	27.2	**83.5**	**23.4**	0.1	1.4	**16.5**	**100.0**
	Total from all countries	0.1	1.2	1.9	0.5	0.5	0.5	0.2	0.1	2.3	1.1	1.3	0.6	9.9	18.0	**77.2**	**37.5**	0.4	3.7	**22.8**	**100.0**

Note: The proportion of students abroad is based only on the total of students enrolled in countries reporting data to the OECD and UNESCO Institute for Statistics.

1. Excludes tertiary-type B programmes.
2. Year of reference 2008.
3. Excludes private institutions.
4. Excludes advanced research programmes.
5. Total based on the estimation by the UNESCO Institute for Statistics.
6. Excludes part-time students.

Source: OECD. See Annex 3 for notes *(www.oecd.org/edu/eag2011)*.

Please refer to the Reader's Guide for information concerning the symbols replacing missing data.

StatLink http://dx.doi.org/10.1787/888932464505

C3

Table C3.4. **Distribution of international and foreign students in tertiary education, by level and type of tertiary education (2009)**

		Tertiary-type B programmes	Tertiary-type A programmes	Advanced research programmes	Total tertiary programmes
		(1)	(2)	(3)	(4)
		International students by level and type of tertiary education			
OECD	Australia	15.1	80.3	4.5	100
	Austria[1]	1.4	88.8	9.9	100
	Belgium	26.2	66.4	7.5	100
	Canada[2, 3]	18.9	72.2	8.9	100
	Chile	29.7	52.8	17.5	100
	Czech Republic	m	m	m	m
	Denmark	19.7	74.0	6.3	100
	Estonia	6.0	86.0	8.0	100
	Finland	n	86.5	13.5	100
	Hungary	0.9	96.3	2.8	100
	Iceland	0.4	91.7	7.9	100
	Ireland	m	m	m	100
	Israel	m	m	m	m
	Japan	23.7	66.4	10.0	100
	Luxembourg	m	m	m	m
	Mexico	m	m	m	m
	Netherlands[4]	n	100.0	m	100
	New Zealand	34.7	58.8	6.5	100
	Norway	0.2	92.7	7.1	100
	Poland	0.1	95.3	4.6	100
	Portugal	0.3	88.2	11.5	100
	Slovak Republic	0.2	88.3	11.5	100
	Slovenia	11.1	79.3	9.6	100
	Spain	29.7	53.0	17.2	100
	Sweden	0.4	83.5	16.2	100
	Switzerland[5]	m	74.3	25.7	100
	United Kingdom	8.7	81.9	9.4	100
	United States	6.8	73.7	19.4	100
Other G20	Argentina	m	m	m	m
	Brazil	m	m	m	m
	China	m	m	m	m
	India	m	m	m	m
	Indonesia	m	m	m	m
	Saudi Arabia	m	m	m	m
	South Africa	m	m	m	m
		Foreign students by level and type of tertiary education[6]			
OECD	France	9.0	79.2	11.8	100
	Germany[4]	6.9	93.1	m	100
	Greece	m	m	m	m
	Italy	0.7	94.4	4.9	100
	Korea	8.4	84.9	6.7	100
	Turkey	4.6	90.8	4.7	100
Other G20	Russian Federation[3, 4]	5.9	94.1	m	100

1. Based on the number of registrations, not head-counts.
2. Reference year 2008.
3. Excludes private institutions.
4. Excludes advanced research programmes.
5. Excludes tertiary-type B programmes.
6. Foreign students are defined on the basis of their country of citizenship, these data are not comparable with data on international students and are therefore presented separately in the table.

Source: OECD. See Annex 3 for notes *(www.oecd.org/edu/eag2011).*

Please refer to the Reader's Guide for information concerning the symbols replacing missing data.

StatLink http://dx.doi.org/10.1787/888932464524

Table C3.5. Trends in the number of foreign students enrolled outside their country of origin, by region of destination (2000 to 2009)

Number of foreign students enrolled in tertiary education outside their country of origin, head counts

Foreign students enrolled in the following destinations	Number of foreign students									
	2009	2008	2007	2006	2005	2004	2003	2002	2001	2000
Africa	129 430	131 529	124 788	116 404	108 765	108 489	104 452	101 342	94 174	100 031
Asia	395 927	369 397	337 196	316 142	296 768	271 217	237 877	220 887	190 209	197 028
Europe	1 672 422	1 587 988	1 481 430	1 435 435	1 385 763	1 308 596	1 183 742	1 040 900	978 305	918 179
North America	850 966	809 943	728 190	733 051	738 401	712 292	712 296	695 806	576 059	569 640
Latin America & the Caribbean	75 433	58 776	55 813	37 838	37 114	39 760	42 230	35 305	31 950	28 945
Oceania	335 305	298 176	283 573	258 696	251 904	240 531	219 191	202 023	136 728	118 646
Worldwide	**3 673 925**	**3 454 326**	**3 198 201**	**3 069 790**	**2 982 588**	**2 843 695**	**2 648 636**	**2 444 223**	**2 146 686**	**2 071 963**
OECD countries	2 838 027	2 646 999	2 534 414	2 446 164	2 373 011	2 272 064	2 092 527	1 904 154	1 647 622	1 588 862
EU countries	1 406 887	1 317 541	1 311 333	1 255 879	1 199 825	1 150 604	1 034 876	894 260	842 937	804 716
of which in EU21 countries	1 372 398	1 282 373	1 283 433	1 229 295	1 172 429	1 122 675	1 008 351	868 301	811 781	775 102
G20 countries	3 033 995	2 843 849	2 629 096	2 547 843	2 485 330	2 366 148	2 222 619	2 045 952	1 789 815	1 715 174

Foreign students enrolled in the following destinations	Index of change (2009)								
	2008 = 100	2007 = 100	2006 = 100	2005 = 100	2004 = 100	2003 = 100	2002 = 100	2001 = 100	2000 = 100
Africa	98	104	111	119	119	124	128	137	129
Asia	107	117	125	133	146	166	179	208	201
Europe	105	113	117	121	128	141	161	171	182
North America	105	117	116	115	119	119	122	148	149
Latin America & the Caribbean	128	135	199	203	190	179	214	236	261
Oceania	112	118	130	133	139	153	166	245	283
Worldwide	**106**	**115**	**120**	**123**	**129**	**139**	**150**	**171**	**177**
OECD countries	107	112	116	120	125	136	149	172	179
EU countries	107	107	112	117	122	136	157	167	175
of which in EU21 countries	107	107	112	117	122	136	158	169	177
G20 countries	107	115	119	122	128	137	148	170	177

Note: Figures are based on the number of foreign students enrolled in OECD and non-OECD countries reporting data to the OECD and to UNESCO Institute for Statistics, in order to provide a global picture of foreign students worldwide. The coverage of these reporting countries has evolved over time, therefore missing data have been imputed wherever necessary to ensure the comparability of time series over time. Given the inclusion of UNESCO data for non-OECD countries and the imputation of missing data, the estimates of the number of foreign students may differ from those published in previous editions of *Education at a Glance*.

Source: OECD and UNESCO Institute for Statistics for most data on non-OECD countries. See Annex 3 for notes *(www.oecd.org/edu/eag2011)*.

StatLink http://dx.doi.org/10.1787/888932464543

INDICATOR C4

TRANSITION FROM SCHOOL TO WORK: WHERE ARE THE 15-29 YEAR-OLDS?

- An average of 46% of individuals between 15 and 29 years old are still in education, 39% have left education and found a job, and 15% are neither in education or training nor employed.
- As labour market conditions worsened during the recent economic crisis, the expected number of years not in education decreased slightly, while time in unemployment and out of the labour force increased.
- The lack of an upper secondary qualification is a serious impediment to finding a job, while holding a tertiary degree increases the likelihood of being employmed, particularly during the recent economic crisis.
- Between 1999 and 2009, the number of years individuals could expect to be in education increased by an average of eight months.

Chart C4.1. Change in expected years in education and not in education, comparison of 1999-2009 change and 2008-2009 change

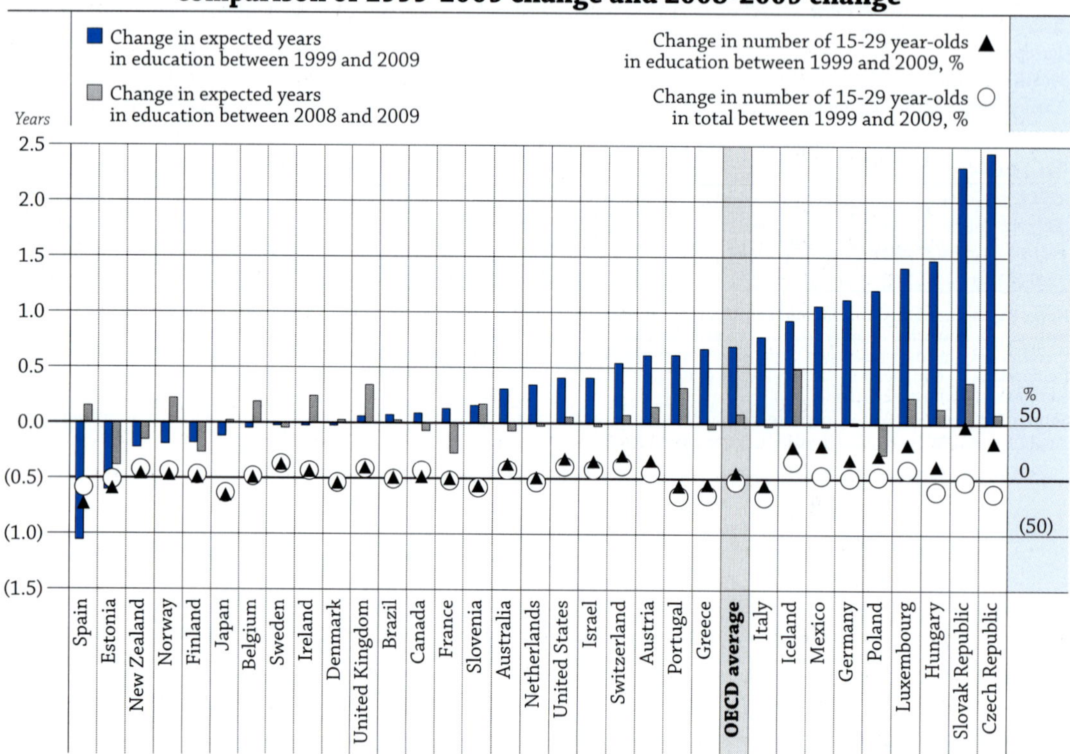

Countries are ranked in ascending order of the difference in years in education in 2009 compared with 1999.

Source: OECD. Table C4.1b, available on line. See Annex 3 for notes (*www.oecd.org/edu/eag2011*).

StatLink http://dx.doi.org/10.1787/888932461636

Context

Even in the best of times, the transition from education to work is a complex process, affected by such variables as the length and quality of the schooling received, national traditions, the state of the labour market, economic conditions and demography. For example, in Belgium and France, young people traditionally complete schooling before they look for work; while in Germany and Sweden, education and employment are usually concurrent. The ageing of the OECD population and the decline in the population of 15-29 year-olds in OECD countries favour employment among young adults.

But during a severe economic recession, some find that transition all but impossible to achieve. This edition of *Education at a Glance* includes data collected during the global downturn that began in late 2008 and shows the impact of the crisis on, among other things, the move from school to work.

High general unemployment rates make this transition substantially more difficult, as those with more work experience are favoured over new entrants into the labour force. In addition, when labour markets are poor, younger individuals tend to stay in education longer: high unemployment rates drive down the opportunity costs of education. In these circumstances, public investment in education can be a sensible way to counterbalance inactivity and invest in future economic growth by building needed skills.

To improve the transition from education to work in any economic climate, education systems must produce appropriately trained individuals to meet the requirements of the labour market and minimise the proportion of young adults who are neither in school nor in work (the NEET population: Neither in Employment nor in Education or Training).

Other findings

- **The expected years in education between the ages of 15 and 29 changes over time and varies greatly from country to country.** In Spain, expected years in education decreased from 6.7 in 1999 to 5.6 in 2009; in Germany, Luxembourg, Mexico and Poland, the expected years in education increased by more than one year, and in the Czech Republic and the Slovak Republic, expected years in education increased by more than two years.

- **On average across OECD countries, a 15-year-old in 2009 could expect to spend about 6.9 additional years in formal education.** In addition, he/she can expect to hold a job for 5.8 of the subsequent 15 years (compared to 6.1 years in 2008), to be unemployed for a total of 0.9 year (0.7 year in 2008) and to be out of the labour force, that is, neither in education nor seeking work, for 1.3 years (1.2 years in 2008).

- **In 2009, a 15-year-old girl in an OECD country could expect to spend an average of 7.1 additional years in formal education or 0.3 years more than a 15-year-old boy.** As a woman, she can expect to hold a job for 5.2 years (1.1 years less than a man), and be unemployed for less time overall (0.8 year) than a man (1.1 years). However, a woman is twice more likely than a man to be inactive, as she can expect to be completely out of the labour force for 1.9 years, compared to 0.8 year for a man (Table C4.1a).

- **On average, completion of upper secondary education reduces unemployment** among 20-24 year-olds by 7.4 percentage points (compared to 8.3 percentage points in 2008) and among 25-29 year-olds by 5.9 percentage points (5.3 percentage points in 2008). On average, completion of tertiary education reduces unemployment among 25-29 year-olds by 2.1 percentage points (compared with 0.9 percentage point in 2008) (Table C4.3). It also reduces long-term unemployment among 15-29 year-olds from 2.5% to 2.1% (Table C4.2d).

Trends

The increase in time spent in education observed between 1999 and 2009 is less the result of the economic crisis that marked the last year or so of that period than of the demographic changes occurring then. During that time, the population of young adults in OECD countries decreased by an average of 2.6%. So while the number of young adults in education fell in Greece, Italy and Portugal, for example, the total number of young adults in those countries even further.

Analysis

Young adults represent the principal source of labour with new skills. In most OECD countries, education policy seeks to encourage youth to complete at least upper secondary education. The effect of these efforts is seen in the number of additional years in education beyond compulsory schooling in which a young individual can expect to participate.

On average, a 15-year-old can expect to spend the next 15 years of his or her life as follows: 6.9 years in education, 5.8 years in a job, unemployed for a total of 0.9 year, and out of the labour force entirely (neither in education nor seeking work) for 1.3 years (Table C4.1a). Taking a look at the population of 15-29 year-olds as a whole, 46.3% are in education, 38.5% hold a job, 6.3% are unemployed, and 8.9% are outside of the labour force (Table C4.2a).

In Denmark, Finland, Iceland, Luxembourg, the Netherlands and Slovenia, a 15-year-old can expect to spend an additional eight years or more in education. In contrast, a 15-year-old in Brazil, Ireland, Japan, Mexico, Spain and Turkey can expect to spend an average of less than six more years in education.

The average number of years expected in formal education after compulsory schooling has changed considerably over the past decade. In the Czech Republic, Hungary, the Slovak Republic, and Turkey, the average number of years in education increased by at least 1.5 years, while in Estonia and Spain it decreased by at least 6 months (Table C4.1b, available on line).

In all countries except Germany, Japan, Luxembourg, Mexico, the Netherlands, New Zealand and Switzerland, young women spend more years in education than young men. In Estonia, Iceland, Norway and Slovenia, young women are likely to spend nearly one full year more in education than their male counterparts. The lowest average number of years in education for young women – 4.9 and 4.0 years in Mexico and Turkey, respectively – corresponds to the highest average number of years expected outside the labour force – 5.3 and 7.5 years, respectively (Table C4.1a).

In 2009, boys and young men between the ages of 15 and 29 are likely to have worked 6.3 years, 1.1 years longer than girls and young women. In 2008, the difference between the two was 1.3 years. This reflects the fact that young women are more likely to be outside of the labour market when not in education. Young men can expect to spend 1.9 years not in education and not employed (compared to 1.4 years in 2008), while young women can expect to spend 2.7 years not in education and not employed (compared to 2.4 years in 2008). In Brazil, Israel, Mexico and Turkey, there is a much stronger tendency for young women to spend time out of the educational system and not working, either because they are unemployed or are not in the labour force. In Canada, Denmark, Israel, Norway, Slovenia, Spain and Sweden, young men and women differ by less than 0.1 year on this measure (Table C4.1a).

The average number of years during which a young person can expect to hold a job after initial education has also changed considerably over the past decade. In 2009, 42.2% of young men between the ages of 15 and 29 were likely to be employed (representing 6.3 years), compared with 45.2% in 2008 and 48.1% in 1999 (representing 6.8 and 7.2 years, respectively) (Table C4.4b, available on line). The deterioriation in employment numbers was greater for young men than for young women: in 2009, 34.7% of women were likely to be employed (representing 5.2 years), compared with 36.2% in 2008 and 37.5% in 1999 (representing 5.4 and 5.6 years, respectively) (Table C4.4c, available on line). Conversely, the increase in the average proportion of individuals in education was greater for young women than for young men. In 2009, 45% of young men between the ages of 15 and 29 were likely to be in education, compared with 44.7% in 2008 and 41.5% in 1999. In 2009, 47.6% of women were likely to be in education, compared with 46.8% in 2008 and 37.5% in 1999.

The worsening conditions in the labour market were more severe for younger workers than older workers. Among 15-19 year-olds, the proportion of those employed fell from 8.2% in 2008 to 7.4% in 2009, representing a 10% decrease, while among 25-29 year-olds it fell from 68.5% to 66.2% during the same period, representing a 3% decrease.

Chart C4.2. Education and employment among young people (2009)

Distribution of the population by education and work status

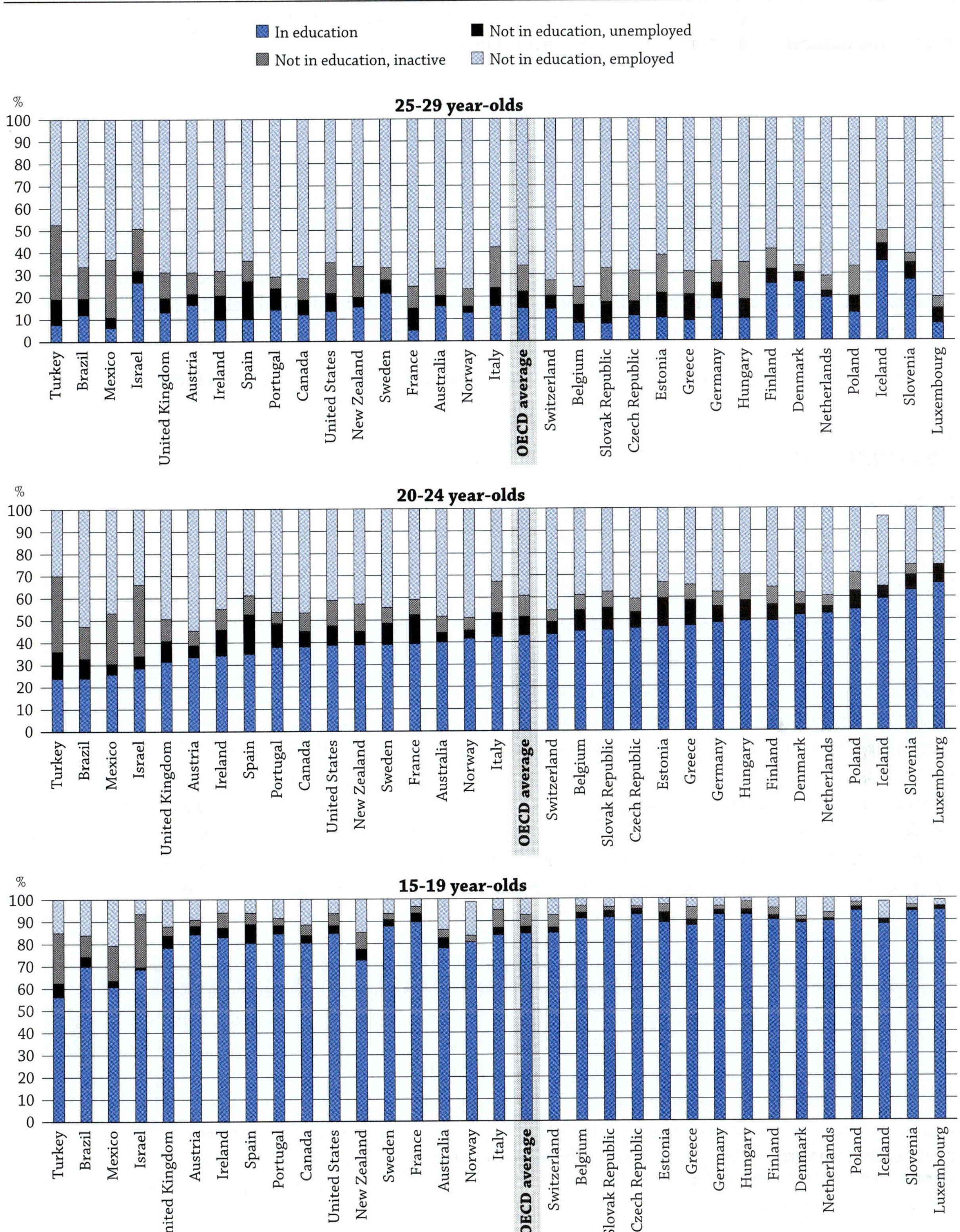

Note: Missing bars refer to cells below reliability thresholds.

Countries are ranked in ascending order of the percentage of 20-24 year-olds in education.

Source: OECD. Table C4.2a. See Annex 3 for notes (*www.oecd.org/edu/eag2011*).

StatLink http://dx.doi.org/10.1787/888932461655

Young adults leaving school and entering a difficult labour market may be unemployed or they may fall outside the labour force entirely. The average cumulative duration of unemployment varies significantly among countries, given differences in general unemployment rates and differences in levels of education.

Unemployment and non-employment among young people not in education

Non-employment is a better measure of young adults' difficulty in finding a job.

In 2009, the majority of 15-19 year-olds were still in education (84.4%, as in 2008). Those who were not (15.6%) were, in many instances, unemployed (3.1% compared to 2.4% in 2008) or out of the labour force (5.5% compared to 4.4% in 2008) or employed (7.4% compared to 8.6% in 2008). In Slovenia, 2.5% of this age group were unemployed or not in the labour force (0.9% and 1.6%, respectively) while in Turkey, 28.7% of this age group were unemployed (6.2%) or not in the labour force (22.5%). On average among OECD countries, more than half (53%) of the 15-19 year-olds not in education were not in the labour force (33%) or were unemployed (13% for less than six months and 7% for more than six months) (Table C4.2a).

Chart C4.3. Percentage of 15-19 year-olds not in education and unemployed or not in the labour force (2009)

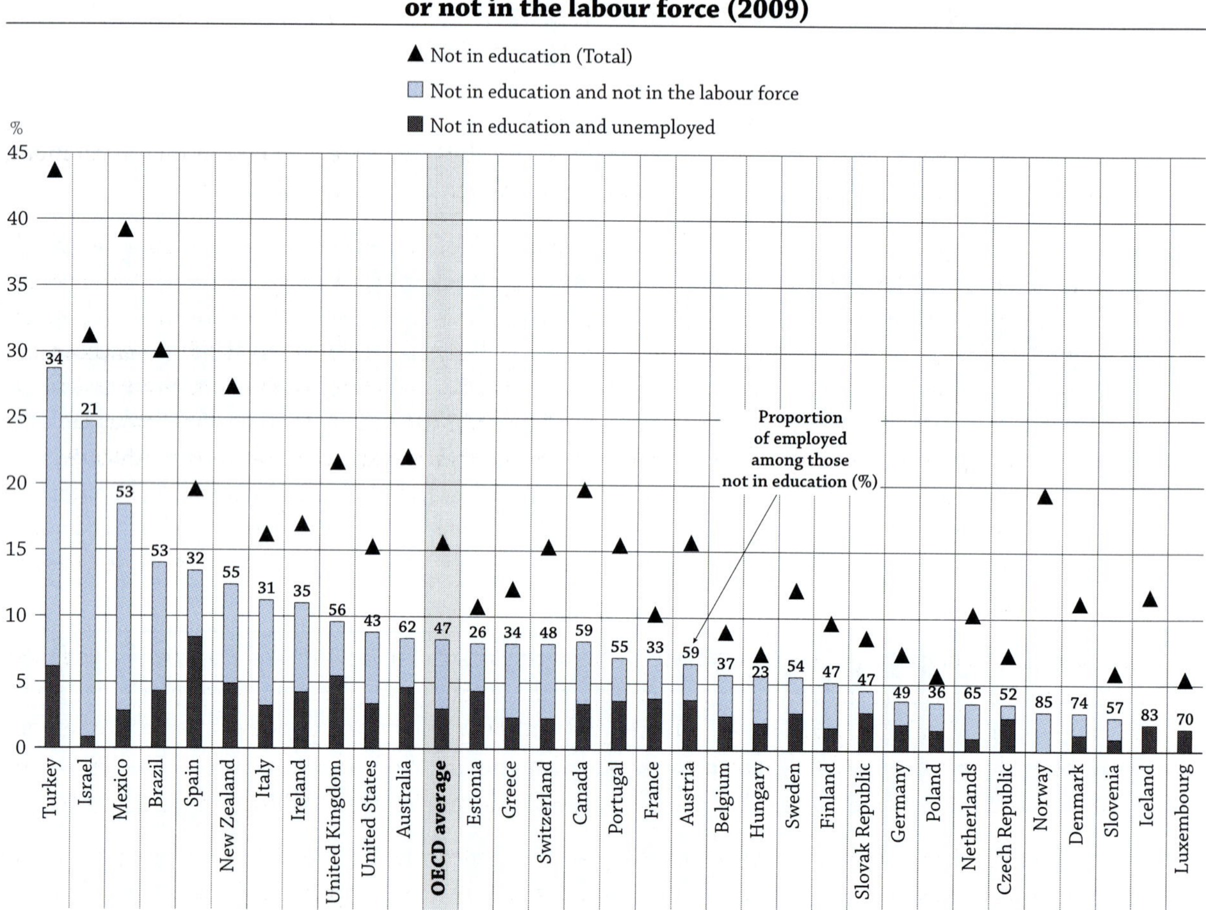

Note: Missing bars refer to cells below reliability thresholds.

Countries are ranked in descending order of the percentage of 15-19 year-olds not in education and unemployed or not in the labour force.

Source: OECD. Table C4.2a. See Annex 3 for notes (*www.oecd.org/edu/eag2011*).

StatLink http://dx.doi.org/10.1787/888932461674

Because of the expansion of upper secondary education over the years, few 15-19 year-olds are outside the education system. Those not engaged in employment, education or training are at particular risk, as they receive little or no support from welfare systems in most countries. Compared with older age groups, they are twice as likely to give up looking for work and lose contact with the labour market entirely. Inactive individuals, those out of the labour force, represent 35% of 15-19 year-olds who are not in school, 18% of 20-24 year-olds who are not in school, and 14% of 25-29 year-olds who are not in school. They are only slightly less susceptible to long-term unemployment than older cohorts: 35% of 15-19 year-olds who are not in school are unemployed for more than 6 months, as compared to 36% of 20-24 year-olds who are not in school, and 39% of 25-29 year-olds not in school (Table C4.2a).

When the labour market deteriorates, those making the transition from school to work are often the first to encounter difficulties. In these circumstances, it is often virtually impossible for young people to get a foothold in the labour market, as employers tend to prefer more experienced workers for the fewer jobs on offer. Some countries are more able than others to provide employment for young adults with relatively low levels of educational attainment (indicated by the difference between the bars and the triangles in Chart C4.2). In Denmark, Iceland and Norway, 70% or more of those young adults not in education find employment.

The transition between education and work is smoother in countries with work-study programmes at upper secondary and post-secondary non-tertiary levels of education. In Australia, Austria, Belgium, the Czech Republic, Germany, Italy, the Slovak Republic, Switzerland and the United Kingdom, which offer work-study programmes at these levels of education, young people not in school are less affected by unemployment. In these countries some 6% of young people are unemployed, compared to the OECD average of 6.3%; and 2.7% are unemployed for more than 6 months, compared to the OECD average of 2.4% (Table C4.2a).

Variation in unemployment among those not in school

Unemployment rates among young people not in school differ according to their level of educational attainment, an indication of the degree to which further education improves their economic opportunities.

On average, completing upper secondary education reduces the unemployment rate among 20-24 year-olds who are not in school by 7.4 percentage points (9.5 percentage points for young men and 5.0 percentage points for young women). Since it has become the norm in most OECD countries to complete upper secondary education (see Indicator A2), those who do not are much more likely to have difficulty finding employment when they enter the labour market. In Belgium, Canada, the Czech Republic, Estonia, France, Greece, Hungary, Ireland, the Slovak Republic, Spain, Sweden, the United Kingdom and the United States, at least 15% of 20-24 year-olds who are not in school and who have not attained an upper secondary education are unemployed. In Denmark and Mexico, that proportion is 5% or less. In Brazil and Denmark, the proportion of unemployed among 20-24 year-olds who are not in school, and who have attained an upper secondary and post-secondary non-tertiary education is greater than that of the same age group who have not attained an upper secondary education (Table C4.3).

Completing tertiary education reduces the unemployment rate among 25-29 year-olds who are not in school by an average of 2.1 percentage points (2.0 percentage points for young men, 1.9 percentage points for young women). In Australia, Denmark, Germany, the Netherlands and Sweden, the proportion of unemployed among 25-29 year-olds who are not in school, who have completed tertiary education is 3% or less. In France, Greece, Ireland, Italy, Luxembourg, Mexico, Portugal, Slovenia, Spain and Turkey, this proportion is 6% or more.

In Ireland, Spain and the United States, completing tertiary education reduces the unemployment rate among 25-29 year-olds who are not in school by five percentage points or more. In Greece, Italy, Mexico, New Zealand, Slovenia, Switzerland and Turkey, unemployment rates among 25-29 year-old upper secondary and post-secondary non-tertiary graduates who are not in education are lower than for those with tertiary qualifications in this age cohort (Table C4.3).

Individuals with a tertiary education are also less likely to become inactive. In 2009, 15.8% of young people who were not in school and who had not attained an upper secondary education were either unemployed (5.7%) or inactive (10.1%), 15.3% of those with upper secondary education were either unemployed (7%) or inactive (8.3%), and 11.7% of those with tertiary education were either unemployed (6%) or inactive (5.8%) (Table C4.2d).

C4

Chart C4.4. Proportion of 15-29 year-olds unemployed in education and not in education, by duration of unemployment (2009)

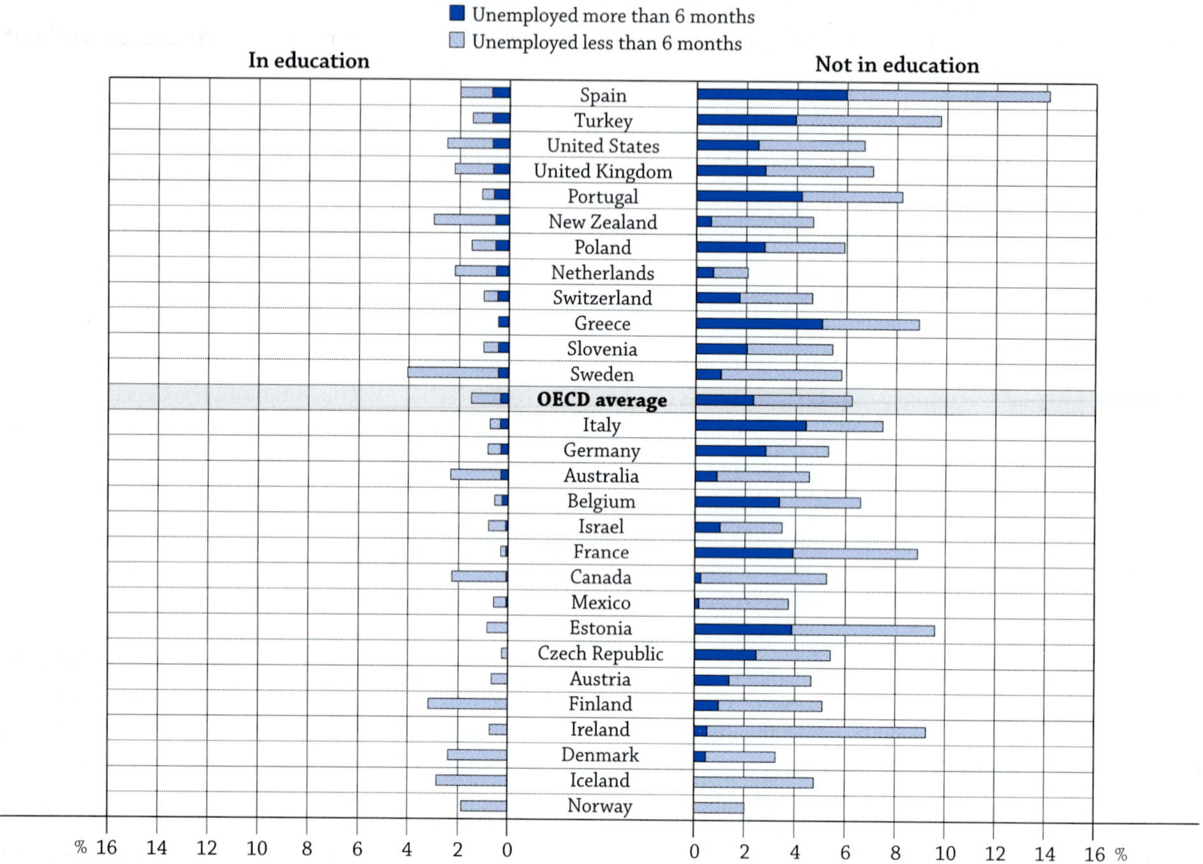

Note: Missing bars refer to cells below reliability thresholds.

Countries are ranked in descending order of the percentage of 15-29 year-olds in education and unemployed for more than 6 months.

Source: OECD. Table C4.2a. See Annex 3 for notes (*www.oecd.org/edu/eag2011*).

StatLink http://dx.doi.org/10.1787/888932461693

Overall unemployment among 15-29 year-olds in OECD countries averages 7.9% but varies considerably across countries (Table C4.2a). In Estonia, Ireland, Spain, Sweden and Turkey, between 10% and 18.1% of 15-29 year-olds are unemployed; yet the situation is very different among these countries. Anglo-Saxon and Nordic countries, which have long traditions of working students, are more likely to show unemployment among students. In Australia, Canada, Denmark, Finland, Iceland, the Netherlands, New Zealand, Sweden, the United Kingdom and the United States, unemployment among 15-29 year-olds who are still in school is at least 2.2% and up to 4% (Chart C4.4).

The nature of unemployment is also different. In Sweden, 1.4% of 15-29 year-olds, including 1% of individuals of that age group who are not in school, were unemployed for at least 6 months. In Spain, however, 6.7% of 15-29 year-olds, including 6% of individuals of that age group who are not in school, were unemployed for at least 6 months, while in Turkey, 4.6% of that age group, including 3.9% who are not in education, were unemployed for at least 6 months. On average across OECD countries, 2.8% of 15-29 year-olds are unemployed for at least 6 months.

The incidence of long-term unemployment decreases as the level of educational attainment rises. On average across OECD countries with available data, 42% of unemployed young people who are not in school and who have not completed upper secondary education are unemployed for more than 6 months. That proportion drops to 36% of unemployed young people who are not in school but who have completed upper secondary education, and to 34% of unemployed young people who are not in school but who have completed tertiary education.

Definitions

The labour-force status categories shown in this indicator are defined according to the International Labour Organization (ILO) guidelines, with one exception. For the purposes of this indicator, the term **being in education and employed** is used to describe persons in work-study programmes (see Annex 3), without reference to their ILO labour-force status during the survey reference week. This is because they may not necessarily be in the work component of their programmes during the survey reference week and may therefore not count as being employed at that point.

The category **other employed** includes individuals employed according to the ILO definition, but excludes those attending work-study programmes who are already counted as employed.

The category **not in the labour force** includes individuals who are not working and who are not unemployed, i.e. individuals who are not looking for a job.

Methodology

Data for this indicator are collected as part of the annual OECD Labour Force Survey (for certain European countries the data are from the annual European Labour Force Survey; see Annex 3) and usually refer to the first quarter, or the average of the first three months of the calendar year, thereby excluding summer employment.

The unemployment and employment rates are examined by considering their proportion in the total population, not only the labour force.

The data for Table C4.2d on unemployment for more and less than 6 months were collected with a pilot data collection by the Monitoring Transition Systems working group of the LSO Network in 2010. The data mainly refer to the national labour-force surveys for 2009. Eurostat has provided data from the EU-LFS for countries in the European Statistical System. In a few cases the Eurostat data have been replaced by national data.

The statistical data for Israel are supplied by and under the responsibility of the relevant Israeli authorities. The use of such data by the OECD is without prejudice to the status of the Golan Heights, East Jerusalem and Israeli settlements in the West Bank under the terms of international law.

References

Kelo, M., U. Teichler and B. Wächter (eds.) (2005), *EURODATA: Student Mobility in European Higher Education*, Verlags and Mediengesellschaft, Bonn.

OECD (2004b), *Internationalisation and Trade in Higher Education: Opportunities and Challenges*, OECD, Paris.

OECD (2008a), *OECD Reviews of Tertiary Education: Tertiary Education for the Knowledge Society*, OECD, Paris.

OECD (2011a), *International Migration Outlook 2010*, OECD, Paris.

The following additional material relevant to this indicator is available on line:

- ***Table C4.1b. Trends in expected years in education and not in education for 15-29 year-olds, by gender (1998-2009)***
  StatLink http://dx.doi.org/10.1787/888932464600
- ***Table C4.2b. Percentage of young men in education and not in education, by age group (2009)***
  StatLink http://dx.doi.org/10.1787/888932464638
- ***Table C4.2c. Percentage of young women in education and not in education, by age group (2009)***
  StatLink http://dx.doi.org/10.1787/888932464657
- ***Table C4.4b. Trends in the percentage of young men in education and not in education (1997-2009)***
  StatLink http://dx.doi.org/10.1787/888932464733
- ***Table C4.4c. Trends in the percentage of young women in education and not in education (1997-2009)***
  StatLink http://dx.doi.org/10.1787/888932464752

Table C4.1a. Expected years in education and not in education for 15-29 year-olds (2009)

By gender and work status

			Expected years in education			Expected years not in education			
			Not employed	Employed (including work-study programmes)	Sub-total	Employed	Unemployed	Not in the labour force	Sub-total
			(1)	(2)	(3)	(4)	(5)	(6)	(7)
OECD	Australia	Males	3.1	3.5	**6.6**	7.0	0.9	0.5	**8.4**
		Females	3.0	3.6	**6.6**	6.1	0.5	1.8	**8.4**
		M+F	3.0	3.6	**6.6**	6.6	0.7	1.2	**8.4**
	Austria	Males	3.7	2.8	**6.5**	7.1	0.8	0.7	**8.5**
		Females	4.1	2.5	**6.6**	6.5	0.6	1.3	**8.4**
		M+F	3.9	2.6	**6.5**	6.8	0.7	1.0	**8.5**
	Belgium	Males	6.4	0.5	**6.9**	6.5	1.1	0.5	**8.1**
		Females	6.6	0.6	**7.3**	5.5	0.9	1.3	**7.7**
		M+F	6.5	0.6	**7.1**	6.0	1.0	0.9	**7.9**
	Canada	Males	3.9	2.3	**6.2**	6.8	1.2	0.9	**8.8**
		Females	3.8	3.1	**6.9**	6.2	0.5	1.4	**8.1**
		M+F	3.8	2.7	**6.5**	6.5	0.9	1.1	**8.5**
	Chile		m	m	**m**	m	m	m	**m**
	Czech Republic	Males	5.0	1.7	**6.6**	7.1	0.9	0.3	**8.4**
		Females	6.2	1.4	**7.5**	4.8	0.7	2.0	**7.5**
		M+F	5.5	1.5	**7.1**	6.0	0.8	1.1	**7.9**
	Denmark	Males	3.2	5.1	**8.3**	5.7	0.6	0.3	**6.7**
		Females	3.3	5.3	**8.6**	5.4	0.3	0.7	**6.4**
		M+F	3.3	5.2	**8.4**	5.6	0.5	0.5	**6.6**
	Estonia	Males	5.4	1.1	**6.5**	5.9	1.9	0.7	**8.5**
		Females	5.7	2.0	**7.7**	4.2	1.0	2.2	**7.3**
		M+F	5.5	1.6	**7.1**	5.0	1.4	1.4	**7.9**
	Finland	Males	5.7	2.1	**7.8**	5.5	1.0	0.7	**7.2**
		Females	5.6	2.9	**8.5**	4.6	0.6	1.3	**6.5**
		M+F	5.7	2.5	**8.2**	5.0	0.8	1.0	**6.8**
	France	Males	5.4	1.1	**6.5**	6.4	1.5	0.6	**8.5**
		Females	5.9	0.8	**6.7**	5.7	1.2	1.4	**8.3**
		M+F	5.7	0.9	**6.6**	6.1	1.3	1.0	**8.4**
	Germany	Males	4.9	3.1	**8.0**	5.5	1.0	0.4	**7.0**
		Females	4.9	2.8	**7.7**	5.3	0.6	1.4	**7.3**
		M+F	4.9	3.0	**7.9**	5.4	0.8	0.9	**7.1**
	Greece	Males	5.8	0.5	**6.3**	6.9	1.2	0.6	**8.7**
		Females	6.3	0.5	**6.7**	5.0	1.5	1.8	**8.3**
		M+F	6.0	0.5	**6.5**	6.0	1.3	1.2	**8.5**
	Hungary	Males	6.7	0.3	**7.0**	5.8	1.2	1.0	**8.0**
		Females	7.1	0.3	**7.4**	4.4	0.8	2.4	**7.6**
		M+F	6.9	0.3	**7.2**	5.1	1.0	1.7	**7.8**
	Iceland	Males	4.9	3.5	**8.4**	4.9	1.1	0.6	**6.6**
		Females	4.8	5.0	**9.8**	4.2	0.5	0.6	**5.2**
		M+F	4.9	4.2	**9.1**	4.5	0.8	0.6	**5.9**
	Ireland	Males	4.4	1.2	**5.6**	6.5	2.0	0.9	**9.4**
		Females	4.3	1.4	**5.7**	6.6	0.8	1.9	**9.3**
		M+F	4.4	1.3	**5.7**	6.6	1.4	1.4	**9.3**
	Israel	Males	4.9	1.4	**6.3**	4.5	0.6	3.7	**8.7**
		Females	4.6	1.8	**6.4**	4.3	0.5	3.8	**8.6**
		M+F	4.7	1.6	**6.3**	4.4	0.6	3.7	**8.7**
	Italy	Males	6.0	0.4	**6.4**	5.9	1.2	1.5	**8.6**
		Females	6.6	0.5	**7.2**	4.2	1.1	2.6	**7.8**
		M+F	6.3	0.5	**6.8**	5.0	1.1	2.1	**8.2**
	Japan[1]	Males	5.3	0.8	**6.1**	3.2	0.4	0.3	**3.9**
		Females	4.7	0.8	**5.6**	3.4	0.4	0.6	**4.4**
		M+F	5.1	0.8	**5.9**	3.3	0.4	0.4	**4.1**
	Korea		m	m	**m**	m	m	m	**m**
	Luxembourg	Males	7.4	0.7	**8.1**	5.8	1.0	c	**6.8**
		Females	7.1	0.9	**8.0**	5.7	0.7	0.6	**7.0**
		M+F	7.2	0.8	**8.0**	5.8	0.8	0.4	**7.0**
	Mexico	Males	3.9	1.3	**5.2**	8.2	0.7	0.9	**9.8**
		Females	4.1	0.8	**4.9**	4.3	0.4	5.3	**10.1**
		M+F	4.0	1.1	**5.1**	6.2	0.6	3.1	**9.9**
OECD	Netherlands	Males	2.9	5.3	**8.2**	5.9	0.4	0.5	**6.8**
		Females	2.8	5.3	**8.1**	5.7	0.3	0.9	**6.9**
		M+F	2.9	5.3	**8.1**	5.8	0.3	0.7	**6.9**
	New Zealand	Males	3.6	3.0	**6.6**	6.7	0.8	0.9	**8.4**
		Females	3.8	2.7	**6.5**	5.4	0.7	2.4	**8.5**
		M+F	3.7	2.8	**6.6**	6.0	0.8	1.7	**8.4**
	Norway	Males	4.4	1.9	**6.3**	7.6	0.5	0.7	**8.7**
		Females	4.3	3.1	**7.4**	6.4	0.3	1.0	**7.6**
		M+F	4.4	2.5	**6.8**	7.0	0.4	0.8	**8.2**
	Poland	Males	5.9	1.5	**7.3**	6.0	1.0	0.7	**7.7**
		Females	6.4	1.4	**7.9**	4.5	0.8	1.8	**7.1**
		M+F	6.2	1.4	**7.6**	5.3	0.9	1.2	**7.4**
	Portugal	Males	5.5	0.8	**6.3**	7.1	1.1	0.5	**8.7**
		Females	5.6	0.8	**6.4**	6.4	1.4	0.9	**8.6**
		M+F	5.5	0.8	**6.3**	6.7	1.2	0.7	**8.7**
	Slovak Republic	Males	5.5	0.9	**6.4**	6.8	1.4	0.4	**8.6**
		Females	6.6	0.7	**7.3**	4.6	0.9	2.1	**7.7**
		M+F	6.0	0.8	**6.9**	5.7	1.2	1.3	**8.1**
	Slovenia	Males	5.9	2.2	**8.1**	5.6	0.9	0.4	**6.9**
		Females	6.9	2.6	**9.5**	4.2	0.7	0.7	**5.5**
		M+F	6.3	2.4	**8.7**	4.9	0.8	0.5	**6.3**
	Spain	Males	4.1	1.2	**5.3**	6.3	2.6	0.8	**9.7**
		Females	4.6	1.3	**5.9**	5.7	1.9	1.5	**9.1**
		M+F	4.4	1.2	**5.6**	6.0	2.2	1.2	**9.4**
	Sweden	Males	5.9	1.3	**7.3**	6.1	1.1	0.6	**7.7**
		Females	6.1	2.0	**8.1**	5.3	0.7	0.9	**6.9**
		M+F	6.0	1.6	**7.7**	5.7	0.9	0.8	**7.3**
	Switzerland	Males	3.1	4.1	**7.2**	6.4	0.7	0.7	**7.8**
		Females	2.9	3.9	**6.8**	6.5	0.7	1.1	**8.2**
		M+F	3.0	4.0	**7.0**	6.4	0.7	0.9	**8.0**
	Turkey	Males	4.0	0.9	**4.9**	6.5	2.1	1.5	**10.1**
		Females	3.5	0.5	**4.0**	2.7	0.8	7.5	**11.0**
		M+F	3.7	0.7	**4.4**	4.6	1.5	4.5	**10.6**
	United Kingdom	Males	4.0	1.9	**5.9**	7.1	1.4	0.7	**9.1**
		Females	4.0	2.2	**6.2**	6.1	0.7	2.0	**8.8**
		M+F	4.0	2.1	**6.1**	6.6	1.1	1.3	**8.9**
	United States	Males	4.7	1.9	**6.6**	6.2	1.2	1.0	**8.4**
		Females	4.6	2.5	**7.1**	5.1	0.8	2.0	**7.9**
		M+F	4.7	2.2	**6.9**	5.6	1.0	1.5	**8.1**
	OECD average excluding Japan	Males	4.8	1.9	**6.8**	6.3	1.1	0.8	**8.3**
		Females	5.0	2.1	**7.1**	5.2	0.8	1.9	**7.9**
		M+F	4.9	2.0	**6.9**	5.8	0.9	1.3	**8.1**
	EU21 average	Males	5.2	1.7	**6.9**	6.3	1.2	0.6	**8.1**
		Females	5.6	1.8	**7.4**	5.3	0.9	1.5	**7.6**
		M+F	5.4	1.8	**7.1**	5.8	1.0	1.1	**7.9**
Other G20	Argentina		m	m	**m**	m	m	m	**m**
	Brazil	Males	2.8	2.4	**5.2**	8.1	0.9	0.9	**9.8**
		Females	3.5	1.9	**5.5**	5.4	1.2	2.9	**9.5**
		M+F	3.2	2.2	**5.3**	6.7	1.0	1.9	**9.7**
	China		m	m	**m**	m	m	m	**m**
	India		m	m	**m**	m	m	m	**m**
	Indonesia		m	m	**m**	m	m	m	**m**
	Russian Federation		m	m	**m**	m	m	m	**m**
	Saudi Arabia		m	m	**m**	m	m	m	**m**
	South Africa		m	m	**m**	m	m	m	**m**

1. Data refer to 15-24 year-olds.

Source: OECD. See Annex 3 for notes *(www.oecd.org/edu/eag2011)*.

Please refer to the Reader's Guide for information concerning the symbols replacing missing data.

StatLink http://dx.doi.org/10.1787/888932464581

Table C4.2a. [1/3] Percentage of young people in education and not in education, by age group (2009)

By age group and work status

		In education							Not in education							
				Unemployed						Unemployed						
	Age group	Students in work-study programmes[1]	Other employed	All together	Less than 6 months	More than 6 months	Not in the labour force	Sub-total	Employed	All together	Less than 6 months	More than 6 months	Not in the labour force	Sub-total	Total in education and not in education
		(1)	(2)	(3)	(4)	(5)	(6)	(7)	(8)	(9)	(10)	(11)	(12)	(13)	(14)
OECD															
Australia	15-19	6.2	28.1	4.8	4.1	0.7	38.7	**77.9**	13.8	4.6	3.6	1.0	3.7	**22.1**	100
	20-24	4.1	21.6	2.1	1.9	c	12.2	**39.9**	48.5	4.3	3.7	0.6	7.2	**60.1**	100
	25-29	0.7	10.9	c	c	c	3.8	**15.7**	67.4	4.7	3.7	0.9	12.2	**84.3**	100
	15-29	3.6	20.1	2.3	2.0	0.3	17.9	**43.9**	43.7	4.5	3.7	0.9	7.8	**56.1**	100
Austria	15-19	25.2	4.1	0.9	c	c	54.0	**84.3**	9.2	3.8	2.5	1.3	2.7	**15.7**	100
	20-24	2.9	11.6	0.9	0.8	c	18.1	**33.5**	54.6	5.3	4.0	1.3	6.6	**66.5**	100
	25-29	c	9.9	c	c	c	5.7	**16.5**	68.9	4.9	3.2	1.6	9.7	**83.5**	100
	15-29	9.0	8.6	0.8	0.7	c	25.1	**43.6**	45.3	4.6	3.3	1.4	6.5	**56.4**	100
Belgium	15-19	1.0	2.1	c	c	m	87.9	**91.1**	3.3	2.5	1.7	0.7	3.1	**8.9**	100
	20-24	0.6	4.2	1.1	0.6	c	39.0	**44.9**	39.0	9.2	3.9	5.2	6.9	**55.1**	100
	25-29	0.7	3.1	0.5	c	c	3.5	**7.8**	75.9	8.3	4.0	4.1	8.0	**92.2**	100
	15-29	0.8	3.1	0.6	0.3	0.2	42.7	**47.2**	40.1	6.7	3.2	3.4	6.0	**52.8**	100
Canada	15-19	a	29.0	6.2	5.6	0.2	45.2	**80.3**	11.5	3.4	3.1	m	4.7	**19.7**	100
	20-24	a	18.3	1.6	1.1	m	18.2	**38.0**	46.7	7.0	6.2	0.2	8.3	**62.0**	100
	25-29	a	6.7	0.4	m	m	4.8	**11.9**	71.8	6.6	5.7	0.5	9.7	**88.1**	100
	15-29	a	17.8	2.7	2.2	0.1	22.3	**42.8**	43.9	5.7	5.0	0.2	7.6	**57.2**	100
Chile		m	m	m	m	m	m	**m**	m	m	m	m	m	**m**	m
Czech Republic	15-19	21.1	0.9	c	c	c	70.5	**92.8**	3.7	2.5	1.5	1.0	1.0	**7.2**	100
	20-24	0.9	4.7	0.5	c	c	39.9	**46.1**	40.8	7.1	3.9	3.2	6.0	**53.9**	100
	25-29	c	4.6	c	c	c	6.3	**11.2**	68.7	6.3	3.3	3.0	13.8	**88.8**	100
	15-29	6.6	3.6	0.3	0.2	c	36.7	**47.2**	40.0	5.4	2.9	2.5	7.4	**52.8**	100
Denmark	15-19	a	50.9	5.7	4.6	c	32.3	**88.8**	8.3	1.2	1.1	c	1.6	**11.2**	100
	20-24	a	34.1	2.4	2.1	c	15.3	**51.9**	38.3	4.5	3.8	c	5.3	**48.1**	100
	25-29	a	17.8	c	c	m	8.1	**26.1**	66.6	4.2	3.5	0.8	3.0	**73.9**	100
	15-29	a	34.6	2.9	2.4	c	18.8	**56.3**	37.1	3.3	2.8	0.5	3.3	**43.7**	100
Estonia	15-19	a	2.9	c	c	m	85.7	**89.2**	2.8	4.4	3.2	c	3.6	**10.8**	100
	20-24	a	19.3	c	c	c	25.6	**46.7**	33.5	12.6	6.9	5.8	7.2	**53.3**	100
	25-29	a	8.2	c	c	m	c	**10.2**	61.6	11.1	6.8	4.3	17.1	**89.8**	100
	15-29	a	10.5	1.1	0.8	c	35.8	**47.4**	33.6	9.6	5.7	3.9	9.4	**52.6**	100
Finland	15-19	a	13.8	4.8	4.4	c	71.7	**90.3**	4.5	1.7	1.5	c	3.4	**9.7**	100
	20-24	a	21.3	4.1	3.9	c	23.9	**49.3**	35.7	7.2	5.9	1.2	7.9	**50.7**	100
	25-29	a	15.2	1.4	1.4	c	8.9	**25.4**	59.1	6.5	4.9	1.5	9.0	**74.6**	100
	15-29	a	16.7	3.4	3.2	c	34.3	**54.4**	33.6	5.1	4.1	1.0	6.8	**45.6**	100
France	15-19	a	7.5	0.4	0.3	0.1	81.8	**89.7**	3.4	3.9	2.2	1.6	3.0	**10.3**	100
	20-24	a	9.2	0.5	0.3	0.1	29.6	**39.4**	40.9	13.0	6.8	6.1	6.8	**60.6**	100
	25-29	a	2.2	0.1	0.0	0.0	2.6	**4.9**	75.4	9.9	5.9	4.0	9.9	**95.1**	100
	15-29	a	6.3	0.3	0.2	0.1	37.4	**44.0**	40.5	9.0	5.0	3.9	6.6	**56.0**	100
Germany	15-19	17.7	6.7	1.4	0.7	0.6	66.9	**92.7**	3.6	2.0	0.7	1.2	1.8	**7.3**	100
	20-24	16.6	9.4	0.7	0.5	0.1	21.8	**48.5**	37.8	7.2	3.4	3.5	6.5	**51.5**	100
	25-29	2.3	7.2	0.6	0.4	0.2	8.5	**18.6**	64.5	7.1	3.2	3.7	9.8	**81.4**	100
	15-29	12.1	7.8	0.9	0.5	0.3	31.7	**52.4**	36.0	5.5	2.5	2.8	6.1	**47.6**	100
Greece	15-19	a	1.5	c	c	c	85.9	**87.9**	4.2	2.4	c	c	5.6	**12.1**	100
	20-24	a	5.1	1.4	c	c	40.6	**47.2**	34.6	11.3	5.3	6.0	6.9	**52.8**	100
	25-29	a	2.6	c	c	c	5.7	**8.9**	69.1	11.7	4.8	7.0	10.2	**91.1**	100
	15-29	a	3.1	0.8	c	0.4	39.5	**43.4**	39.8	8.9	3.9	5.0	7.9	**56.6**	100
Hungary	15-19	a	c	c	c	c	92.4	**92.7**	1.7	2.0	1.0	1.1	3.6	**7.3**	100
	20-24	a	2.5	c	c	c	46.3	**49.2**	29.9	9.1	4.0	5.2	11.8	**50.8**	100
	25-29	a	3.5	c	c	c	6.1	**9.8**	65.1	8.4	3.3	5.1	16.6	**90.2**	100
	15-29	a	2.2	0.3	c	c	45.7	**48.1**	34.1	6.7	2.8	3.9	11.0	**51.9**	100

Note: Columns 4 and 5 do not add up to Column 3 as unemployed with unknown duration are also included in Column 3.

1. Students in work-study programmes are considered to be both in education and employed, irrespective of their labour market status according to the ILO definition.

Source: OECD. See Annex 3 for notes *(www.oecd.org/edu/eag2011)*.

Please refer to the Reader's Guide for information concerning the symbols replacing missing data.

StatLink http://dx.doi.org/10.1787/888932464619

Table C4.2a. [2/3] Percentage of young people in education and not in education, by age group (2009)

By age group and work status

	Age group	In education							Not in education						Total in education and not in education
				Unemployed						Unemployed					
		Students in work-study programmes[1]	Other employed	All together	Less than 6 months	More than 6 months	Not in the labour force	Sub-total	Employed	All together	Less than 6 months	More than 6 months	Not in the labour force	Sub-total	
		(1)	(2)	(3)	(4)	(5)	(6)	(7)	(8)	(9)	(10)	(11)	(12)	(13)	(14)
OECD															
Iceland	15-19	a	30.2	c	c	m	54.2	**88.3**	8.0	2.0	c	m	c	**11.7**	100
	20-24	a	35.8	c	c	m	20.0	**59.1**	31.5	5.5	4.9	c	c	**40.9**	100
	25-29	a	19.2	c	c	m	14.9	**35.5**	50.8	7.7	7.3	m	6.0	**64.5**	100
	15-29	a	28.2	2.9	2.9	m	29.7	**60.7**	30.3	5.1	4.8	c	3.9	**39.3**	100
Ireland	15-19	a	8.6	0.8	0.8	m	73.5	**83.0**	6.0	4.3	4.1	c	6.8	**17.0**	100
	20-24	a	13.2	1.0	0.9	c	20.0	**34.2**	45.0	11.6	10.9	0.7	9.2	**65.8**	100
	25-29	a	4.9	0.5	0.5	c	4.3	**9.7**	68.2	10.9	10.2	0.7	11.1	**90.3**	100
	15-29	a	8.5	0.8	0.7	c	28.4	**37.7**	43.7	9.3	8.7	0.5	9.3	**62.3**	100
Israel	15-19	a	4.3	0.5	0.4	c	63.9	**68.8**	6.5	0.8	0.5	0.2	23.9	**31.2**	100
	20-24	a	10.9	0.9	0.8	c	16.7	**28.5**	34.0	5.4	3.5	1.5	32.0	**71.5**	100
	25-29	a	17.0	1.1	0.9	c	8.5	**26.6**	49.2	5.2	3.6	1.3	19.0	**73.4**	100
	15-29	a	10.5	0.9	0.7	0.1	30.7	**42.0**	29.3	3.7	2.5	1.0	25.0	**58.0**	100
Italy	15-19	c	0.6	0.3	0.2	0.1	82.8	**83.8**	5.0	3.2	1.2	2.1	8.0	**16.2**	100
	20-24	0.3	3.9	1.0	0.5	0.5	37.2	**42.3**	32.9	10.7	4.3	6.4	14.1	**57.7**	100
	25-29	0.2	3.9	0.8	0.5	0.3	10.8	**15.7**	57.9	8.2	3.6	4.6	18.2	**84.3**	100
	15-29	0.2	2.9	0.7	0.4	0.3	41.5	**45.3**	33.5	7.5	3.1	4.4	13.7	**54.7**	100
Japan	15-24	a	8.2	0.2	m	m	50.5	**58.8**	32.8	4.1	m	m	4.3	**41.2**	100
Korea		m	m	m	m	m	m	**m**	m	m	m	m	m	**m**	m
Luxembourg	15-19	a	5.6	1.9	c	c	87.0	**94.5**	2.8	1.7	c	c	c	**5.5**	100
	20-24	a	7.3	1.6	m	c	57.0	**66.0**	25.3	8.3	6.7	c	c	**34.0**	100
	25-29	a	3.2	0.0	m	m	4.3	**7.4**	80.7	6.8	3.0	3.8	5.1	**92.6**	100
	15-29	a	5.2	1.1	c	c	47.2	**53.5**	38.6	5.6	3.2	2.3	2.3	**46.5**	100
Mexico	15-19	a	9.4	0.7	0.7	0.0	50.7	**60.8**	20.8	2.8	2.5	0.1	15.6	**39.2**	100
	20-24	a	7.7	0.6	0.5	0.1	17.3	**25.7**	46.7	4.8	4.4	0.1	22.8	**74.3**	100
	25-29	a	3.3	0.3	0.2	0.0	2.8	**6.4**	63.2	4.5	4.1	0.2	25.9	**93.6**	100
	15-29	a	7.1	0.6	0.5	0.0	26.2	**33.9**	41.3	3.9	3.6	0.2	20.9	**66.1**	100
Netherlands	15-19	a	51.7	4.8	3.2	1.1	33.1	**89.7**	6.8	1.0	0.6	0.3	2.6	**10.3**	100
	20-24	a	37.7	1.9	1.3	0.3	12.9	**52.5**	39.6	3.0	1.9	0.9	4.9	**47.5**	100
	25-29	a	15.3	0.6	0.4	c	3.3	**19.1**	71.3	2.8	1.7	0.9	6.8	**80.9**	100
	15-29	a	35.1	2.5	1.7	0.5	16.6	**54.1**	38.9	2.2	1.4	0.7	4.8	**45.9**	100
New Zealand	15-19	a	23.5	6.6	5.2	1.0	42.5	**72.6**	15.0	4.9	3.7	0.6	7.5	**27.4**	100
	20-24	a	22.4	2.5	1.7	0.5	14.0	**38.9**	42.8	6.1	5.1	0.6	12.2	**61.1**	100
	25-29	a	9.8	0.4	c	c	5.2	**15.4**	66.5	4.2	3.4	0.6	13.9	**84.6**	100
	15-29	a	18.9	3.3	2.5	0.5	21.5	**43.7**	40.2	5.1	4.1	0.6	11.1	**56.3**	100
Norway	15-19	a	23.8	4.0	3.7	c	52.8	**80.6**	15.2	c	c	c	2.9	**19.4**	100
	20-24	a	19.3	1.7	1.7	m	20.6	**41.6**	49.0	3.7	2.9	c	5.7	**58.4**	100
	25-29	a	5.9	c	c	m	6.6	**12.7**	76.7	2.8	2.1	c	7.8	**87.3**	100
	15-29	a	16.5	2.0	1.9	c	27.1	**45.6**	46.5	2.6	2.0	c	5.4	**54.4**	100
Poland	15-19	a	3.5	0.5	0.5	c	90.3	**94.3**	2.1	1.6	1.1	0.5	2.1	**5.7**	100
	20-24	a	16.9	3.2	2.0	1.2	34.2	**54.4**	29.2	8.2	4.5	3.7	8.2	**45.6**	100
	25-29	a	8.1	0.8	0.5	0.3	3.5	**12.4**	66.8	7.4	3.7	3.6	13.4	**87.6**	100
	15-29	a	9.6	1.5	1.0	0.5	39.5	**50.7**	35.1	5.9	3.2	2.7	8.3	**49.3**	100
Portugal	15-19	a	1.8	0.8	c	c	81.9	**84.5**	8.6	3.7	2.1	1.6	3.2	**15.5**	100
	20-24	a	6.2	1.3	c	c	30.4	**37.9**	46.3	10.6	5.1	5.5	5.1	**62.1**	100
	25-29	a	7.2	1.1	c	0.8	5.9	**14.2**	71.0	9.6	4.5	5.1	5.2	**85.8**	100
	15-29	a	5.3	1.1	0.5	0.6	35.9	**42.3**	44.9	8.2	4.0	4.2	4.6	**57.7**	100

Note: Columns 4 and 5 do not add up to Column 3 as unemployed with unknown duration are also included in Column 3.

1. Students in work-study programmes are considered to be both in education and employed, irrespective of their labour market status according to the ILO definition.

Source: OECD. See Annex 3 for notes *(www.oecd.org/edu/eag2011)*.

Please refer to the Reader's Guide for information concerning the symbols replacing missing data.

StatLink http://dx.doi.org/10.1787/888932464619

Table C4.2a. [3/3] Percentage of young people in education and not in education, by age group (2009)

By age group and work status

	Age group	In education							Not in education						Total in education and not in education
		Students in work-study programmes[1]	Other employed	Unemployed			Not in the labour force	Sub-total	Employed	Unemployed			Not in the labour force	Sub-total	
				All together	Less than 6 months	More than 6 months				All together	Less than 6 months	More than 6 months			
		(1)	(2)	(3)	(4)	(5)	(6)	(7)	(8)	(9)	(10)	(11)	(12)	(13)	(14)
OECD															
Slovak Republic	15-19	10.3	c	0.1	m	c	80.9	**91.5**	4.0	2.9	0.9	1.9	1.7	**8.5**	100
	20-24	c	3.3	c	c	c	41.6	**45.3**	37.6	9.9	4.0	6.0	7.2	**54.7**	100
	25-29	a	3.1	c	c	c	4.2	**7.5**	67.6	9.8	3.1	6.7	15.1	**92.5**	100
	15-29	3.2	2.3	0.2	c	c	40.0	**45.7**	38.2	7.7	2.7	5.0	8.4	**54.3**	100
Slovenia	15-19	a	7.5	c	c	c	86.2	**94.1**	3.4	0.9	0.8	c	1.6	**5.9**	100
	20-24	a	21.3	1.6	1.0	0.6	40.0	**62.9**	25.7	6.7	4.5	2.2	4.6	**37.1**	100
	25-29	a	17.1	1.0	0.6	0.4	9.0	**27.1**	61.3	7.5	4.3	3.2	4.1	**72.9**	100
	15-29	a	16.0	1.0	0.6	0.4	41.2	**58.2**	32.7	5.4	3.4	2.0	3.6	**41.8**	100
Spain	15-19	a	14.2	6.6	1.6	0.6	59.6	**80.4**	6.2	8.4	4.3	3.9	5.0	**19.6**	100
	20-24	a	7.2	2.8	1.7	1.0	24.9	**34.9**	38.9	17.6	9.6	7.3	8.6	**65.1**	100
	25-29	a	4.8	1.4	0.8	0.5	3.7	**9.9**	63.8	17.1	9.7	6.4	9.2	**90.1**	100
	15-29	a	8.2	3.3	1.3	0.7	25.9	**37.4**	39.9	14.9	8.2	6.0	7.9	**62.6**	100
Sweden	15-19	a	11.0	7.0	6.0	c	69.9	**87.9**	6.6	2.8	2.3	c	2.7	**12.1**	100
	20-24	a	11.6	4.1	3.2	c	23.3	**39.0**	44.5	9.5	7.7	1.5	7.0	**61.0**	100
	25-29	a	10.4	1.7	1.3	c	9.4	**21.5**	67.0	6.0	4.7	1.2	5.5	**78.5**	100
	15-29	a	11.0	4.4	3.6	0.4	35.6	**51.0**	38.0	6.0	4.8	1.0	5.0	**49.0**	100
Switzerland	15-19	36.3	7.5	2.1	c	c	38.9	**84.7**	7.4	2.3	1.2	c	5.6	**15.3**	100
	20-24	12.6	14.0	1.1	c	c	15.6	**43.4**	45.9	5.5	3.6	1.9	5.2	**56.6**	100
	25-29	1.1	9.4	c	c	c	3.7	**14.3**	72.9	6.0	3.8	2.2	6.8	**85.7**	100
	15-29	16.2	10.3	1.1	0.6	0.5	18.9	**46.5**	43.0	4.6	2.9	1.7	5.9	**53.5**	100
Turkey	15-19	a	3.3	1.0	0.6	0.3	52.0	**56.3**	15.0	6.2	3.9	2.3	22.5	**43.7**	100
	20-24	a	6.0	2.7	1.5	1.3	15.1	**23.9**	30.0	12.0	7.1	4.9	34.1	**76.1**	100
	25-29	a	4.5	0.9	0.4	0.5	2.2	**7.7**	47.4	11.4	6.6	4.8	33.5	**92.3**	100
	15-29	a	4.5	1.5	0.8	0.7	23.5	**29.5**	30.9	9.7	5.8	3.9	29.8	**70.5**	100
United Kingdom	15-19	2.4	16.8	4.6	3.1	1.4	54.5	**78.3**	12.1	5.5	3.3	2.2	4.1	**21.7**	100
	20-24	0.8	12.5	1.6	1.2	0.4	16.6	**31.5**	49.3	9.2	5.6	3.6	9.9	**68.5**	100
	25-29	c	9.2	0.6	0.4	c	3.3	**13.2**	68.9	6.3	3.9	2.4	11.7	**86.8**	100
	15-29	1.1	12.8	2.2	1.6	0.6	24.3	**40.4**	43.9	7.0	4.3	2.7	8.6	**59.6**	100
United States	15-19	a	15.8	4.4	3.4	1.0	64.5	**84.7**	6.5	3.4	2.3	1.1	5.4	**15.3**	100
	20-24	a	19.2	2.2	1.6	0.6	17.4	**38.7**	41.2	8.7	5.6	3.1	11.4	**61.3**	100
	25-29	a	8.5	0.9	0.5	0.4	4.1	**13.5**	64.7	8.0	4.8	3.2	13.8	**86.5**	100
	15-29	a	14.5	2.5	1.8	0.7	28.8	**45.7**	37.4	6.7	4.2	2.5	10.2	**54.3**	100
OECD average	15-19		13.3	3.0	2.6	0.6	65.6	**84.4**	7.4	3.1	2.1	1.3	5.5	**15.6**	100
	20-24		14.1	1.7	1.4	0.6	26.0	**43.1**	39.2	8.2	5.2	3.3	10.0	**56.9**	100
	25-29		8.3	0.8	0.6	0.4	5.8	**14.7**	66.1	7.5	4.5	3.0	11.7	**85.3**	100
	15-29		11.7	1.6	1.3	0.4	31.3	**46.3**	38.5	6.3	3.9	2.4	8.9	**53.7**	100
EU21 average	15-19		11.1	2.7	2.3	0.7	72.8	**88.6**	5.2	3.0	1.9	1.5	3.4	**11.4**	100
	20-24		12.5	1.8	1.4	0.5	30.4	**45.6**	38.1	9.1	5.4	4.0	7.5	**54.4**	100
	25-29		7.7	0.8	0.6	0.4	5.8	**14.2**	67.6	8.1	4.5	3.5	10.1	**85.8**	100
	15-29		10.2	1.4	1.2	0.4	34.5	**47.6**	38.5	6.9	4.0	2.8	7.0	**52.4**	100
Other G20															
Argentina		m	m	m	m	m	m	**m**	m	m	m	m	m	**m**	m
Brazil	15-19	a	20.4	6.6	m	m	42.9	**69.9**	16.1	4.3	m	m	9.7	**30.1**	100
	20-24	a	14.1	2.8	m	m	7.0	**23.9**	52.8	8.8	m	m	14.5	**76.1**	100
	25-29	a	8.9	1.1	m	m	2.1	**12.0**	66.4	7.3	m	m	14.3	**88.0**	100
	15-29	a	14.5	3.5	m	m	17.5	**35.6**	44.9	6.8	m	m	12.8	**64.4**	100
China		m	m	m	m	m	m	**m**	m	m	m	m	m	**m**	m
India		m	m	m	m	m	m	**m**	m	m	m	m	m	**m**	m
Indonesia		m	m	m	m	m	m	**m**	m	m	m	m	m	**m**	m
Russian Federation		m	m	m	m	m	m	**m**	m	m	m	m	m	**m**	m
Saudi Arabia		m	m	m	m	m	m	**m**	m	m	m	m	m	**m**	m
South Africa		m	m	m	m	m	m	**m**	m	m	m	m	m	**m**	m

Note: Columns 4 and 5 do not add up to Column 3 as unemployed with unknown duration are also included in Column 3.

1. Students in work-study programmes are considered to be both in education and employed, irrespective of their labour market status according to the ILO definition.

Source: OECD. See Annex 3 for notes *(www.oecd.org/edu/eag2011).*

Please refer to the Reader's Guide for information concerning the symbols replacing missing data.

StatLink http://dx.doi.org/10.1787/888932464619

Table C4.2d. [1/3] Percentage of 15-29 year-olds in education and not in education, by level of education (2009)

By level of education and work status

	Level of education completed	In education							Not in education						Total in education and not in education
		Students in work-study programmes[1]	Other employed	Unemployed			Not in the labour force	Sub-total	Employed	Unemployed			Not in the labour force	Sub-total	
				All together	Less than 6 months	More than 6 months				All together	Less than 6 months	More than 6 months			
		(1)	(2)	(3)	(4)	(5)	(6)	(7)	(8)	(9)	(10)	(11)	(12)	(13)	(14)
OECD															
Australia	0/1/2	5.1	18.8	3.5	2.9	0.6	32.0	**59.4**	23.4	6.5	4.6	1.9	10.7	**40.6**	100
	3/4	4.5	22.7	2.2	2.2	c	12.9	**42.4**	47.3	3.8	3.5	0.4	6.4	**57.6**	100
	5/6	a	16.8	0.8	0.6	c	7.1	**24.7**	66.0	3.0	2.7	c	6.3	**75.3**	100
	Total	3.6	20.1	2.3	2.0	0.3	17.9	**43.9**	43.7	4.5	3.7	0.9	7.8	**56.1**	100
Austria	0/1/2	23.0	3.2	c	c	c	45.6	**72.5**	13.9	6.2	3.8	2.4	7.5	**27.5**	100
	3/4	1.3	10.7	0.9	0.8	c	14.2	**27.0**	63.1	3.8	2.9	0.9	6.1	**73.0**	100
	5/6	a	19.7	c	c	m	7.8	**28.6**	62.9	3.7	c	c	4.7	**71.4**	100
	Total	9.0	8.6	0.8	0.7	c	25.1	**43.6**	45.3	4.6	3.3	1.4	6.5	**56.4**	100
Belgium	0/1/2	1.0	1.9	c	c	c	65.5	**68.7**	15.3	6.8	3.1	3.6	9.2	**31.3**	100
	3/4	0.6	2.4	0.7	0.4	c	39.1	**42.8**	44.6	7.7	3.6	4.1	4.9	**57.2**	100
	5/6	0.9	6.4	0.7	c	c	12.2	**20.2**	72.1	4.6	2.8	1.7	3.1	**79.8**	100
	Total	0.8	3.1	0.6	0.3	0.2	42.7	**47.2**	40.1	6.7	3.2	3.4	6.0	**52.8**	100
Canada	0/1/2	a	22.7	5.6	5.1	0.3	41.0	**69.3**	16.1	5.2	4.5	0.4	9.5	**30.7**	100
	3/4	a	17.8	2.1	1.9	0.1	18.8	**38.7**	46.2	7.0	6.3	0.4	8.1	**61.3**	100
	5/6	a	13.3	0.9	0.8	m	10.3	**24.5**	66.1	4.3	3.8	0.4	5.1	**75.5**	100
	Total	a	17.8	2.7	2.5	0.1	22.3	**42.8**	43.9	5.7	5.1	0.4	7.6	**57.2**	100
Chile		m	m	m	m	m	m	**m**	m	m	m	m	m	**m**	m
Czech Republic	0/1/2	20.3	0.6	c	c	m	62.7	**83.7**	6.1	4.4	1.5	2.8	5.8	**16.3**	100
	3/4	0.5	4.0	0.3	0.3	c	25.8	**30.7**	54.5	6.3	3.7	2.5	8.5	**69.3**	100
	5/6	a	9.6	c	c	c	20.9	**31.3**	58.9	3.9	2.8	c	5.9	**68.7**	100
	Total	6.6	3.6	0.3	0.2	c	36.7	**47.2**	40.0	5.4	2.9	2.5	7.4	**52.8**	100
Denmark	0/1/2	a	43.8	4.7	3.9	c	26.3	**74.8**	19.5	2.3	2.0	c	3.4	**25.2**	100
	3/4	a	28.1	1.3	1.0	c	13.5	**42.9**	48.4	4.9	4.3	c	3.7	**57.1**	100
	5/6	a	21.9	c	c	m	6.6	**29.6**	66.8	2.0	1.6	c	1.6	**70.4**	100
	Total	a	34.6	2.9	2.4	c	18.8	**56.3**	37.1	3.3	2.8	0.5	3.3	**43.7**	100
Estonia	0/1/2	a	2.1	c	c	m	69.4	**71.8**	11.7	7.4	4.2	3.2	9.0	**28.2**	100
	3/4	a	13.3	1.9	c	c	22.0	**37.1**	42.3	14.2	8.7	5.4	6.5	**62.9**	100
	5/6	a	20.8	c	c	m	c	**24.2**	55.8	c	c	c	18.4	**75.8**	100
	Total	a	10.5	1.1	0.8	c	35.8	**47.4**	33.6	9.6	5.7	3.9	9.4	**52.6**	100
Finland	0/1/2	a	13.0	4.1	3.8	c	62.3	**79.4**	10.3	3.7	2.8	0.8	6.6	**20.6**	100
	3/4	a	20.2	3.5	3.4	c	20.3	**44.0**	42.6	6.6	5.4	1.2	6.8	**56.0**	100
	5/6	a	14.9	c	c	c	5.1	**20.9**	67.6	4.3	3.6	c	7.2	**79.1**	100
	Total	a	16.7	3.4	3.2	c	34.3	**54.4**	33.6	5.1	4.1	1.0	6.8	**45.6**	100
France	0/1/2	a	4.6	0.3	0.2	0.1	59.6	**64.4**	17.0	9.5	4.4	4.9	9.0	**35.6**	100
	3/4	a	7.5	0.4	0.3	0.1	30.2	**38.1**	45.5	10.1	6.0	4.1	6.3	**61.9**	100
	5/6	a	6.6	0.2	0.1	0.0	18.1	**24.9**	65.4	6.1	3.9	2.1	3.6	**75.1**	100
	Total	a	6.3	0.3	0.2	0.1	37.4	**44.0**	40.5	9.0	5.0	3.9	6.6	**56.0**	100
Germany	0/1/2	20.0	5.8	1.1	0.5	0.5	50.7	**77.7**	10.3	5.5	1.9	3.3	6.5	**22.3**	100
	3/4	6.7	9.4	0.7	0.5	0.1	18.9	**35.7**	52.4	6.0	3.1	2.6	6.0	**64.3**	100
	5/6	1.5	8.9	0.6	0.5	c	5.9	**16.9**	75.6	3.0	1.7	1.2	4.4	**83.1**	100
	Total	12.1	7.8	0.9	0.5	0.3	31.7	**52.4**	36.0	5.5	2.5	2.8	6.1	**47.6**	100
Greece	0/1/2	a	c	c	c	c	54.7	**55.7**	28.6	6.1	2.6	3.5	9.6	**44.3**	100
	3/4	a	4.5	1.4	c	c	39.2	**45.1**	38.4	9.2	3.8	5.3	7.4	**54.9**	100
	5/6	a	3.6	c	c	c	5.3	**9.8**	70.3	14.6	7.0	7.5	5.4	**90.2**	100
	Total	a	3.1	0.8	c	0.4	39.5	**43.4**	39.8	8.9	3.9	5.0	7.9	**56.6**	100
Hungary	0/1/2	a	c	c	c	c	71.7	**72.0**	8.9	5.8	2.3	3.5	13.3	**28.0**	100
	3/4	a	2.7	c	c	c	36.3	**39.3**	43.1	7.6	3.3	4.2	10.1	**60.7**	100
	5/6	a	5.9	c	c	c	6.6	**12.9**	73.2	5.9	2.1	3.7	8.0	**87.1**	100
	Total	a	2.2	0.3	c	c	45.7	**48.1**	34.1	6.7	2.8	3.9	11.0	**51.9**	100

Note: Columns 4 and 5 do not add up to Column 3 as unemployed with unknown duration are also included in Column 3.

1. Students in work-study programmes are considered to be both in education and employed, irrespective of their labour market status according to the ILO definition.

Source: OECD. See Annex 3 for notes *(www.oecd.org/edu/eag2011)*.

Please refer to the Reader's Guide for information concerning the symbols replacing missing data.

StatLink http://dx.doi.org/10.1787/888932464676

Table C4.2d. [2/3] **Percentage of 15-29 year-olds in education and not in education, by level of education (2009)**

By level of education and work status

		In education							Not in education						
				Unemployed						Unemployed					
	Level of education completed	Students in work-study programmes[1]	Other employed	All together	Less than 6 months	More than 6 months	Not in the labour force	Sub-total	Employed	All together	Less than 6 months	More than 6 months	Not in the labour force	Sub-total	Total in education and not in education
		(1)	(2)	(3)	(4)	(5)	(6)	(7)	(8)	(9)	(10)	(11)	(12)	(13)	(14)
OECD Iceland	0/1/2	a	28.2	3.6	3.6	m	37.2	**69.0**	20.9	5.5	4.9	c	4.6	**31.0**	100
	3/4	a	31.0	c	c	m	22.7	**56.0**	37.2	c	c	m	c	**44.0**	100
	5/6	a	21.6	c	c	m	c	**32.3**	59.4	c	c	m	c	**67.7**	100
	Total	a	28.2	2.9	2.9	m	29.7	**60.7**	30.3	5.1	4.8	c	3.9	**39.3**	100
Ireland	0/1/2	a	4.3	0.5	0.5	m	59.6	**64.4**	14.3	7.8	6.5	1.2	13.6	**35.6**	100
	3/4	a	11.7	1.1	1.0	c	20.7	**33.5**	46.3	11.3	10.9	0.4	8.9	**66.5**	100
	5/6	a	8.8	0.6	0.6	m	8.4	**17.8**	70.6	7.3	7.2	c	4.2	**82.2**	100
	Total	a	8.5	0.8	0.7	c	28.4	**37.7**	43.7	9.3	8.7	0.5	9.3	**62.3**	100
Israel	0/1/2	a	3.6	0.6	0.5	c	65.6	**69.8**	12.0	1.9	0.9	0.8	16.3	**30.2**	100
	3/4	a	13.3	1.0	0.8	c	16.9	**31.1**	31.6	4.4	3.0	1.1	32.9	**68.9**	100
	5/6	a	15.2	1.0	0.8	c	6.8	**23.0**	57.5	5.2	3.9	0.8	14.3	**77.0**	100
	Total	a	10.5	0.9	0.7	0.1	30.7	**42.0**	29.3	3.7	2.5	1.0	25.0	**58.0**	100
Italy	0/1/2	c	0.7	0.2	c	0.1	53.9	**54.9**	22.8	5.6	2.1	3.5	16.7	**45.1**	100
	3/4	0.2	4.2	1.0	0.6	0.4	33.0	**38.4**	41.6	8.8	3.6	5.3	11.2	**61.6**	100
	5/6	0.5	6.4	2.0	1.1	0.8	24.7	**33.6**	44.9	9.7	5.2	4.5	11.8	**66.4**	100
	Total	0.2	2.9	0.7	0.4	0.3	41.5	**45.3**	33.5	7.5	3.1	4.4	13.7	**54.7**	100
Japan	1/2/3	a	13.0	0.3	m	m	40.3	**53.7**	34.6	5.1	m	m	6.6	**46.3**	100
	5/6	a	m	0.0	m	m	m	**0.0**	86.7	8.4	m	m	4.9	**100.0**	100
	Total	a	8.2	0.2	m	m	50.5	**58.8**	32.8	4.1	m	m	4.3	**41.2**	100
Korea		m	m	m	m	m	m	**m**	m	m	m	m	m	**m**	m
Luxembourg	0/1/2	a	5.7	1.7	c	c	74.1	**81.5**	16.6	c	c	m	c	**18.5**	100
	3/4	a	5.9	c	m	c	38.7	**45.6**	43.6	6.9	3.3	3.6	3.9	**54.4**	100
	5/6	a	3.4	c	m	m	6.3	**9.6**	77.4	12.2	8.4	3.9	c	**90.4**	100
	Total	a	5.2	1.1	c	c	47.2	**53.5**	38.6	5.6	3.2	2.3	2.3	**46.5**	100
Mexico	0/1/2	a	5.5	0.4	0.4	0.0	26.4	**32.4**	39.6	3.6	3.3	0.1	24.5	**67.6**	100
	3/4	a	12.0	1.0	0.9	0.1	31.1	**44.2**	37.9	3.9	3.6	0.1	14.0	**55.8**	100
	5/6	a	7.9	0.5	0.5	0.0	10.7	**19.1**	65.5	7.1	6.2	0.7	8.3	**80.9**	100
	Total	a	7.1	0.6	0.5	0.0	26.2	**33.9**	41.3	3.9	3.6	0.2	20.9	**66.1**	100
Netherlands	0/1/2	a	39.8	3.8	2.5	0.9	26.6	**70.2**	20.9	2.3	1.3	0.9	6.6	**29.8**	100
	3/4	a	35.9	1.8	1.2	0.3	11.4	**49.1**	45.0	2.1	1.4	0.6	3.8	**50.9**	100
	5/6	a	24.1	1.0	0.7	c	6.2	**31.3**	64.8	1.8	1.3	0.3	2.1	**68.7**	100
	Total	a	35.1	2.5	1.7	0.5	16.6	**54.1**	38.9	2.2	1.4	0.7	4.8	**45.9**	100
New Zealand	0/1/2	a	14.0	4.5	3.6	0.7	30.2	**48.7**	29.2	6.0	4.7	0.9	16.1	**51.3**	100
	3/4	a	25.9	3.5	2.6	0.6	21.1	**50.5**	38.4	3.7	2.9	0.5	7.3	**49.5**	100
	5/6	a	15.3	1.5	0.9	c	7.7	**24.5**	60.5	5.9	5.3	c	9.2	**75.5**	100
	Total	a	18.9	3.3	2.5	0.5	21.5	**43.7**	40.2	5.1	4.1	0.6	11.1	**56.3**	100
Norway	0/1/2	a	16.9	3.1	2.8	c	37.1	**57.1**	30.5	4.1	3.0	c	8.3	**42.9**	100
	3/4	a	16.2	c	c	m	18.1	**35.5**	59.2	1.9	1.6	c	3.4	**64.5**	100
	5/6	a	18.6	c	c	m	16.0	**35.7**	60.7	c	c	c	c	**64.3**	100
	Total	a	16.5	2.0	1.9	c	27.1	**45.6**	46.5	2.6	2.0	c	5.4	**54.4**	100
Poland	0/1/2	a	3.6	0.4	0.3	c	76.8	**80.8**	8.6	3.3	1.6	1.6	7.4	**19.2**	100
	3/4	a	12.4	2.1	1.3	0.8	25.3	**39.8**	41.7	7.7	4.2	3.5	10.8	**60.2**	100
	5/6	a	13.5	1.8	1.3	0.5	7.1	**22.4**	65.5	6.5	3.6	2.9	5.6	**77.6**	100
	Total	a	9.6	1.5	1.0	0.5	39.5	**50.7**	35.1	5.9	3.2	2.7	8.3	**49.3**	100
Portugal	0/1/2	a	4.2	1.1	0.5	0.6	38.3	**43.5**	41.5	8.8	4.5	4.3	6.2	**56.5**	100
	3/4	a	6.7	c	c	c	43.2	**50.6**	39.9	6.9	3.4	3.5	2.6	**49.4**	100
	5/6	a	7.1	1.8	c	c	10.0	**19.0**	70.6	8.5	3.2	5.3	1.9	**81.0**	100
	Total	a	5.3	1.1	0.5	0.6	35.9	**42.3**	44.9	8.2	4.0	4.2	4.6	**57.7**	100

Note: Columns 4 and 5 do not add up to Column 3 as unemployed with unknown duration are also included in Column 3.

1. Students in work-study programmes are considered to be both in education and employed, irrespective of their labour market status according to the ILO definition.

Source: OECD. See Annex 3 for notes *(www.oecd.org/edu/eag2011)*.

Please refer to the Reader's Guide for information concerning the symbols replacing missing data.

StatLink http://dx.doi.org/10.1787/888932464676

Table C4.2d. [3/3] **Percentage of 15-29 year-olds in education and not in education, by level of education (2009)**

By level of education and work status

		Level of education completed	In education							Not in education						Total in education and not in education
			Students in work-study programmes[1]	Other employed	Unemployed			Not in the labour force	Sub-total	Employed	Unemployed			Not in the labour force	Sub-total	
					All together	Less than 6 months	More than 6 months				All together	Less than 6 months	More than 6 months			
			(1)	(2)	(3)	(4)	(5)	(6)	(7)	(8)	(9)	(10)	(11)	(12)	(13)	(14)
OECD	Slovak Republic	0/1/2	10.0	c	c	m	m	75.4	**85.6**	3.0	5.0	0.7	4.3	6.4	**14.4**	100
		3/4	c	2.4	0.4	c	c	26.1	**29.0**	51.7	9.7	4.0	5.8	9.5	**71.0**	100
		5/6	a	7.2	c	m	m	13.5	**20.7**	66.7	4.7	2.0	2.8	7.9	**79.3**	100
		Total	3.2	2.3	0.2	c	c	40.0	**45.7**	38.2	7.7	2.7	5.0	8.4	**54.3**	100
	Slovenia	0/1/2	a	6.6	0.5	c	c	75.4	**82.4**	9.8	3.4	1.6	1.8	4.4	**17.6**	100
		3/4	a	20.5	1.1	0.7	0.4	32.8	**54.4**	36.3	5.9	4.0	1.9	3.4	**45.6**	100
		5/6	a	15.6	1.6	c	c	3.3	**20.6**	68.6	8.1	4.8	3.3	2.7	**79.4**	100
		Total	a	16.0	1.0	0.6	0.4	41.2	**58.2**	32.7	5.4	3.4	2.0	3.6	**41.8**	100
	Spain	0/1/2	a	8.1	4.1	1.1	0.5	28.6	**40.8**	31.7	17.7	9.0	7.9	9.8	**59.2**	100
		3/4	a	7.5	2.9	1.8	1.0	32.0	**42.3**	39.1	12.6	8.1	3.9	5.9	**57.7**	100
		5/6	a	9.1	2.0	1.1	0.7	11.2	**22.4**	60.8	11.0	6.3	4.1	5.8	**77.6**	100
		Total	a	8.2	3.3	1.3	0.7	25.9	**37.4**	39.9	14.9	8.2	6.0	7.9	**62.6**	100
	Sweden	0/1/2	a	11.5	8.4	7.1	c	60.3	**80.1**	11.0	4.0	3.0	c	4.8	**19.9**	100
		3/4	a	9.8	2.8	2.1	c	16.6	**29.2**	55.1	9.7	7.8	1.5	6.0	**70.8**	100
		5/6	a	15.8	3.0	2.5	c	17.1	**35.9**	58.6	2.7	2.3	c	2.7	**64.1**	100
		Total	a	11.0	4.4	3.6	0.4	35.6	**51.0**	38.0	6.0	4.8	1.0	5.0	**49.0**	100
	Switzerland	0/1/2	35.7	5.6	1.7	c	c	31.5	**74.5**	15.1	3.8	1.7	2.1	6.7	**25.5**	100
		3/4	4.9	13.6	0.8	c	c	12.7	**32.0**	57.0	5.2	3.5	1.6	5.7	**68.0**	100
		5/6	c	12.3	c	c	c	5.9	**19.4**	70.9	5.1	3.9	c	4.5	**80.6**	100
		Total	16.2	10.3	1.1	0.6	0.5	18.9	**46.5**	43.0	4.6	2.9	1.7	5.9	**53.5**	100
	Turkey	0/1/2	a	2.6	0.8	0.5	0.3	26.5	**29.9**	26.6	8.7	5.7	2.9	34.9	**70.1**	100
		3/4	a	6.9	2.6	1.4	1.3	22.9	**32.5**	32.4	10.5	5.8	4.7	24.7	**67.5**	100
		5/6	a	10.8	2.8	1.2	1.6	5.0	**18.6**	55.3	14.6	6.2	8.4	11.5	**81.4**	100
		Total	a	4.5	1.5	0.8	0.7	23.5	**29.5**	30.9	9.7	5.8	3.9	29.8	**70.5**	100
	United Kingdom	0/1/2	1.0	4.0	1.7	1.1	0.6	43.2	**49.9**	24.4	10.0	5.1	4.9	15.7	**50.1**	100
		3/4	1.5	16.3	2.9	2.1	0.8	22.4	**43.1**	42.9	6.6	4.4	2.2	7.4	**56.9**	100
		5/6	c	13.9	0.8	0.6	c	7.5	**22.3**	69.2	4.7	3.2	1.4	3.8	**77.7**	100
		Total	1.1	12.8	2.2	1.6	0.6	24.3	**40.4**	43.9	7.0	4.3	2.7	8.6	**59.6**	100
	United States	0/1/2	a	9.2	3.2	2.5	0.7	58.0	**70.4**	14.6	4.9	3.0	2.0	10.1	**29.6**	100
		3/4	a	17.7	2.7	1.9	0.8	19.4	**39.7**	39.6	8.6	5.5	3.2	12.1	**60.3**	100
		5/6	a	14.7	1.1	0.7	c	7.9	**23.7**	65.6	4.8	3.2	1.5	5.9	**76.3**	100
		Total	a	14.5	2.5	1.8	0.7	28.8	**45.7**	37.4	6.7	4.2	2.5	10.2	**54.3**	100
	OECD average excluding Japan	0/1/2		10.4	2.5	2.2	0.5	50.5	**65.7**	18.5	5.9	3.3	2.7	10.4	**34.3**	100
		3/4		13.3	1.7	1.3	0.5	24.5	**40.0**	44.7	7.1	4.5	2.7	8.5	**60.0**	100
		5/6		12.6	1.2	0.9	0.6	9.7	**22.5**	65.6	6.3	4.0	3.0	6.2	**77.5**	100
		Total		11.7	1.6	1.3	0.4	31.3	**46.3**	38.5	6.3	3.9	2.4	8.9	**53.7**	100
	EU21 average	0/1/2		9.1	2.3	2.0	0.5	56.2	**69.3**	16.5	6.3	3.2	3.3	8.6	**30.7**	100
		3/4		11.2	1.5	1.2	0.5	26.7	**39.9**	45.6	7.8	4.8	3.1	6.7	**60.1**	100
		5/6		11.6	1.3	0.9	0.5	10.2	**22.6**	66.0	6.3	3.8	3.2	5.6	**77.4**	100
		Total		10.2	1.4	1.2	0.4	34.5	**47.6**	38.5	6.9	4.0	2.8	7.0	**52.4**	100
Other G20	Argentina		m	m	m	m	m	m	**m**	m	m	m	m	m	**m**	m
	Brazil	0/1/2	a	14.9	4.5	m	m	26.2	**45.6**	34.9	5.2	m	m	14.3	**54.4**	100
		3/4	a	14.7	2.3	m	m	6.4	**23.4**	55.7	9.3	m	m	11.6	**76.6**	100
		5/6	a	9.6	0.9	m	m	4.0	**14.5**	74.2	5.8	m	m	5.5	**85.5**	100
		Total	a	14.5	3.5	m	m	17.5	**35.6**	44.9	6.8	m	m	12.8	**64.4**	100
	China		m	m	m	m	m	m	**m**	m	m	m	m	m	**m**	m
	India		m	m	m	m	m	m	**m**	m	m	m	m	m	**m**	m
	Indonesia		m	m	m	m	m	m	**m**	m	m	m	m	m	**m**	m
	Russian Federation		m	m	m	m	m	m	**m**	m	m	m	m	m	**m**	m
	Saudi Arabia		m	m	m	m	m	m	**m**	m	m	m	m	m	**m**	m
	South Africa		m	m	m	m	m	m	**m**	m	m	m	m	m	**m**	m

Note: Columns 4 and 5 do not add up to Column 3 as unemployed with unknown duration are also included in Column 3.

1. Students in work-study programmes are considered to be both in education and employed, irrespective of their labour market status according to the ILO definition.

Source: OECD. See Annex 3 for notes *(www.oecd.org/edu/eag2011)*.

Please refer to the Reader's Guide for information concerning the symbols replacing missing data.

StatLink http://dx.doi.org/10.1787/888932464676

Table C4.3. [1/2] Percentage of the cohort population not in education and unemployed (2009)

By level of educational attainment, age group and gender

		Below upper secondary education				Upper secondary and post-secondary non-tertiary education				Tertiary education			All levels of education			
		15-19	20-24	25-29	15-29	15-19[1]	20-24	25-29	15-29	20-24[1]	25-29	15-29	15-19	20-24	25-29	15-29
		(1)	(2)	(3)	(4)	(5)	(6)	(7)	(8)	(9)	(10)	(11)	(12)	(13)	(14)	(15)
Australia	Males	5.0	13.2	17.3	**8.5**	6.3	3.9	4.0	**4.4**	4.3	3.3	**3.6**	5.3	5.7	6.1	**5.7**
	Females	2.6	8.8	5.6	**4.0**	6.2	1.6	3.1	**3.2**	2.8	2.5	**2.6**	3.9	2.9	3.2	**3.3**
	M+F	3.9	11.4	12.3	**6.5**	6.2	2.8	3.6	**3.8**	3.4	2.8	**3.0**	4.6	4.3	4.7	**4.5**
Austria	Males	3.6	18.7	12.6	**6.6**	c	5.1	4.2	**4.9**	c	c	**c**	4.1	7.1	5.1	**5.5**
	Females	3.5	c	14.1	**5.7**	c	2.3	3.1	**2.7**	c	c	**c**	3.4	3.4	4.6	**3.8**
	M+F	3.5	14.3	13.4	**6.2**	c	3.7	3.7	**3.8**	c	c	**3.7**	3.8	5.3	4.9	**4.6**
Belgium	Males	1.7	20.3	25.4	**8.5**	c	9.2	8.0	**8.0**	c	2.8	**3.1**	2.2	10.6	9.2	**7.3**
	Females	2.2	8.1	13.8	**4.9**	4.9	7.9	8.4	**7.4**	7.5	4.7	**5.6**	2.9	7.9	7.4	**6.1**
	M+F	1.9	15.4	19.9	**6.8**	4.6	8.6	8.2	**7.7**	6.1	3.9	**4.6**	2.5	9.2	8.3	**6.7**
Canada	Males	2.9	20.7	14.4	**6.8**	8.4	9.3	10.8	**9.6**	5.2	5.4	**5.3**	4.7	9.8	8.6	**7.7**
	Females	1.6	9.3	9.1	**3.1**	3.2	3.3	5.6	**3.9**	3.8	3.6	**3.6**	2.1	4.0	4.6	**3.6**
	M+F	2.3	16.2	12.3	**5.2**	5.7	6.6	8.6	**7.0**	4.3	4.4	**4.3**	3.4	7.0	6.6	**5.7**
Chile		m	m	m	**m**	m	m	m	**m**	m	m	**m**	m	m	m	**m**
Czech Republic	Males	1.3	25.1	25.2	**5.2**	12.5	7.1	5.8	**6.9**	c	c	**4.2**	2.7	8.6	6.6	**6.1**
	Females	1.3	c	18.3	**3.4**	8.2	5.1	5.8	**5.6**	c	3.4	**3.7**	2.2	5.5	6.0	**4.7**
	M+F	1.3	18.7	21.7	**4.4**	10.3	6.1	5.8	**6.3**	c	3.5	**3.9**	2.5	7.1	6.3	**5.4**
Denmark	Males	c	3.7	11.7	**3.0**	c	7.1	6.3	**7.1**	c	c	**c**	1.6	5.7	5.5	**4.3**
	Females	c	c	c	**1.5**	c	3.4	c	**2.8**	c	c	**c**	c	3.3	3.0	**2.3**
	M+F	0.8	3.5	9.0	**2.3**	c	5.1	4.0	**4.9**	c	2.0	**2.0**	1.2	4.5	4.2	**3.3**
Estonia	Males	c	29.0	c	**10.3**	c	16.6	16.6	**16.8**	c	m	**c**	6.0	18.6	12.5	**12.6**
	Females	c	c	c	**4.2**	c	6.9	18.5	**11.1**	c	c	**c**	c	6.8	9.7	**6.5**
	M+F	3.2	23.2	c	**7.4**	c	11.8	17.4	**14.2**	c	c	**c**	4.4	12.6	11.1	**9.6**
Finland	Males	c	c	13.0	**4.7**	c	9.4	6.5	**8.3**	c	4.5	**c**	c	10.1	6.7	**6.5**
	Females	c	c	16.4	**2.5**	c	3.6	6.3	**4.7**	c	4.3	**4.4**	c	4.2	6.2	**3.8**
	M+F	c	c	14.2	**3.7**	c	6.6	6.4	**6.6**	c	4.4	**4.3**	1.7	7.2	6.5	**5.1**
France	Males	3.7	34.4	17.3	**11.3**	6.6	12.1	10.4	**10.5**	4.9	6.3	**5.5**	4.3	14.9	10.0	**9.7**
	Females	2.4	24.6	14.2	**7.5**	6.4	10.0	11.8	**9.8**	7.1	6.5	**6.5**	3.4	11.2	9.7	**8.2**
	M+F	3.1	30.3	15.8	**9.5**	6.5	11.0	11.1	**10.1**	6.2	6.4	**6.1**	3.9	13.0	9.9	**9.0**
Germany	Males	2.4	15.1	21.6	**7.2**	c	6.9	7.8	**7.2**	c	2.1	**2.3**	2.5	9.2	8.7	**6.8**
	Females	1.2	7.8	11.1	**3.7**	3.5	4.5	5.1	**4.7**	3.5	3.6	**3.6**	1.4	5.2	5.6	**4.2**
	M+F	1.8	11.8	16.3	**5.5**	3.6	5.7	6.5	**6.0**	3.4	2.9	**3.0**	2.0	7.2	7.1	**5.5**
Greece	Males	c	14.9	10.4	**6.5**	c	7.8	9.4	**7.8**	c	12.4	**12.4**	c	9.6	10.5	**7.9**
	Females	c	c	c	**5.6**	c	10.2	13.2	**10.6**	24.1	13.9	**16.1**	c	13.1	13.1	**10.0**
	M+F	c	16.0	10.8	**6.1**	c	8.9	11.2	**9.2**	20.0	13.2	**14.6**	2.4	11.3	11.7	**8.9**
Hungary	Males	1.8	18.4	24.5	**7.1**	c	8.6	9.2	**8.9**	c	c	**5.7**	2.6	10.6	9.9	**7.9**
	Females	c	13.5	12.4	**4.3**	c	6.4	6.6	**6.2**	c	4.9	**6.0**	c	7.7	6.9	**5.5**
	M+F	1.5	16.3	18.2	**5.8**	c	7.5	8.0	**7.6**	11.7	4.6	**5.9**	2.0	9.1	8.4	**6.7**
Iceland	Males	c	c	c	**7.3**	m	c	c	**c**	m	c	**c**	c	c	9.7	**7.0**
	Females	c	c	c	**c**	m	c	c	**c**	m	c	**c**	c	c	c	**3.1**
	M+F	c	c	c	**5.5**	m	c	c	**c**	m	c	**c**	c	5.5	7.7	**5.1**
Ireland	Males	3.9	31.9	27.0	**12.2**	11.1	15.1	16.7	**15.1**	10.9	9.7	**10.1**	5.7	16.6	15.6	**13.1**
	Females	1.4	c	c	**2.3**	6.5	6.4	8.6	**7.2**	7.9	4.4	**5.5**	2.8	6.9	6.2	**5.5**
	M+F	2.7	22.7	18.4	**7.8**	8.7	10.8	13.0	**11.3**	9.0	6.6	**7.3**	4.3	11.6	10.9	**9.3**
Israel	Males	0.6	7.3	6.5	**2.5**	1.7	5.2	4.9	**4.4**	m	6.0	**5.0**	1.0	5.3	5.4	**3.8**
	Females	c	7.0	6.2	**1.3**	1.9	5.0	5.3	**4.4**	8.3	4.4	**5.3**	0.7	5.6	5.0	**3.7**
	M+F	0.4	7.2	6.4	**1.9**	1.8	5.1	5.1	**4.4**	6.0	5.0	**5.2**	0.8	5.4	5.2	**3.7**
Italy	Males	2.5	13.7	10.1	**6.3**	13.2	10.1	7.1	**9.0**	6.2	10.6	**9.8**	3.7	10.9	8.5	**7.8**
	Females	1.6	14.9	7.0	**4.7**	10.1	9.3	7.4	**8.6**	10.5	9.4	**9.7**	2.7	10.5	7.8	**7.1**
	M+F	2.1	14.2	8.7	**5.6**	11.5	9.7	7.2	**8.8**	9.2	9.9	**9.7**	3.2	10.7	8.2	**7.5**
Korea		m	m	m	**m**	m	m	m	**m**	m	m	**m**	m	m	m	**m**
Luxembourg	Males	c	c	m	**c**	c	5.3	8.1	**7.3**	47.6	c	**17.3**	c	11.2	5.6	**6.6**
	Females	m	m	m	**m**	m	c	7.5	**6.5**	c	7.7	**7.6**	m	5.0	7.9	**4.5**
	M+F	c	c	m	**c**	c	5.8	7.8	**6.9**	26.0	7.3	**12.2**	c	8.3	6.8	**5.6**

1. Differences between countries in these columns partly reflect the fact that the average age of graduation varies across countries. For instance, in some countries a smaller share of 15-19 year-olds attain upper secondary education simply because graduation typically occurs at 19. This means that the denominator in the ratio for the reported columns will be smaller than those for which graduation occurs at an earlier age.

Source: OECD. See Annex 3 for notes (*www.oecd.org/edu/eag2011*).

Please refer to the Reader's Guide for information concerning the symbols replacing missing data.

StatLink http://dx.doi.org/10.1787/888932464695

C4

Table C4.3. [2/2] Percentage of the cohort population not in education and unemployed (2009)

By level of educational attainment, age group and gender

		Below upper secondary education				Upper secondary and post-secondary non-tertiary education				Tertiary education			All levels of education			
		15-19	20-24	25-29	15-29	15-19[1]	20-24	25-29	15-29	20-24[1]	25-29	15-29	15-19	20-24	25-29	15-29
		(1)	(2)	(3)	(4)	(5)	(6)	(7)	(8)	(9)	(10)	(11)	(12)	(13)	(14)	(15)
OECD Mexico	Males	3.6	6.4	5.8	**4.8**	3.1	4.4	5.1	**4.4**	7.2	7.0	**7.1**	3.6	5.7	5.8	**4.9**
	Females	1.9	3.3	2.2	**2.4**	2.8	3.5	3.7	**3.4**	8.9	6.2	**7.1**	2.0	3.9	3.3	**3.0**
	M+F	2.8	4.8	3.9	**3.6**	2.9	3.9	4.4	**3.9**	8.2	6.6	**7.1**	2.8	4.8	4.5	**3.9**
Netherlands	Males	1.0	5.9	5.2	**2.7**	c	2.6	2.9	**2.5**	c	1.9	**2.0**	1.1	3.7	3.1	**2.6**
	Females	0.6	4.3	4.5	**1.8**	c	1.5	2.5	**1.8**	1.9	1.6	**1.7**	0.8	2.3	2.5	**1.9**
	M+F	0.9	5.3	4.9	**2.3**	1.2	2.0	2.7	**2.1**	2.1	1.7	**1.8**	1.0	3.0	2.8	**2.2**
New Zealand	Males	4.5	6.5	8.9	**6.1**	4.6	4.4	3.3	**4.2**	9.5	3.9	**6.5**	5.0	5.9	5.1	**5.3**
	Females	5.5	7.9	5.4	**6.0**	3.9	3.3	c	**3.2**	9.6	2.8	**5.5**	4.8	6.3	3.3	**4.8**
	M+F	5.2	7.2	7.2	**6.0**	4.3	3.8	2.8	**3.7**	9.5	3.3	**5.9**	4.9	6.1	4.2	**5.1**
Norway	Males	c	13.6	c	**5.3**	c	c	c	**c**	m	c	**c**	c	5.1	3.4	**3.2**
	Females	c	c	c	**c**	c	c	c	**c**	c	c	**c**	c	c	c	**1.9**
	M+F	c	10.7	c	**4.1**	c	c	c	**1.9**	c	c	**c**	c	3.7	2.8	**2.6**
Poland	Males	1.2	12.8	14.4	**4.1**	10.3	9.2	7.8	**8.6**	11.0	5.0	**6.0**	2.0	9.7	7.4	**6.5**
	Females	c	12.4	11.1	**2.3**	5.7	6.0	7.9	**6.7**	8.1	6.4	**6.8**	1.1	6.7	7.3	**5.3**
	M+F	0.8	12.7	13.1	**3.3**	7.8	7.6	7.8	**7.7**	9.0	5.9	**6.5**	1.6	8.2	7.4	**5.9**
Portugal	Males	4.6	14.0	8.9	**8.5**	c	4.8	5.7	**4.8**	c	7.3	**7.3**	4.4	9.7	7.8	**7.4**
	Females	3.1	13.6	15.2	**9.2**	c	8.2	12.6	**8.8**	17.3	6.5	**9.1**	3.0	11.6	11.5	**9.0**
	M+F	3.9	13.8	11.5	**8.8**	c	6.5	9.1	**6.9**	14.0	6.8	**8.5**	3.7	10.6	9.6	**8.2**
Slovak Republic	Males	2.0	28.0	39.2	**6.3**	11.5	11.1	11.4	**11.3**	c	6.2	**5.4**	3.2	12.1	11.6	**9.2**
	Females	c	c	31.6	**3.6**	15.8	7.6	7.5	**8.0**	c	c	**4.2**	2.5	7.7	7.9	**6.2**
	M+F	1.5	21.8	35.1	**5.0**	13.5	9.4	9.6	**9.7**	c	5.0	**4.7**	2.9	9.9	9.8	**7.7**
Slovenia	Males	c	15.9	17.1	**4.9**	4.9	7.1	6.6	**6.7**	c	6.4	**6.3**	1.7	8.3	7.3	**6.1**
	Females	m	9.5	c	**1.6**	c	4.4	6.6	**4.8**	c	9.2	**8.9**	c	5.0	7.8	**4.7**
	M+F	c	13.7	13.5	**3.4**	3.0	5.8	6.6	**5.9**	c	8.3	**8.1**	0.9	6.7	7.5	**5.4**
Spain	Males	9.8	29.3	27.2	**20.1**	10.4	12.2	17.3	**14.1**	11.7	11.6	**11.7**	9.9	20.1	19.5	**17.0**
	Females	6.3	25.1	20.9	**14.5**	8.2	9.8	14.5	**11.3**	11.1	10.1	**10.5**	6.8	15.0	14.6	**12.6**
	M+F	8.2	27.6	24.6	**17.7**	9.2	10.9	15.9	**12.6**	11.4	10.8	**11.0**	8.4	17.6	17.1	**14.9**
Sweden	Males	c	17.5	c	**4.7**	20.9	11.2	8.4	**11.1**	c	c	**c**	3.4	10.9	7.3	**7.1**
	Females	c	c	c	**3.3**	12.5	8.3	5.9	**8.0**	c	c	**c**	2.2	8.0	4.6	**4.8**
	M+F	c	16.1	13.9	**4.0**	16.8	9.8	7.3	**9.7**	c	2.8	**2.7**	2.8	9.5	6.0	**6.0**
Switzerland	Males	c	c	c	**3.2**	c	5.7	6.9	**6.2**	c	c	**c**	2.3	5.3	6.3	**4.7**
	Females	c	c	c	**4.4**	c	5.0	c	**4.2**	c	6.0	**6.0**	2.3	5.7	5.6	**4.6**
	M+F	2.0	6.9	13.1	**3.8**	c	5.3	5.0	**5.2**	c	5.4	**5.1**	2.3	5.5	6.0	**4.6**
Turkey	Males	8.4	21.9	20.7	**14.8**	8.6	13.3	12.2	**11.9**	18.0	13.6	**15.1**	8.5	17.4	16.7	**13.9**
	Females	2.7	4.1	2.9	**3.1**	7.9	8.9	8.8	**8.6**	17.7	12.0	**14.1**	3.6	7.3	5.8	**5.5**
	M+F	5.7	11.3	11.2	**8.7**	8.3	11.3	10.8	**10.5**	17.8	12.8	**14.6**	6.2	12.0	11.4	**9.7**
United Kingdom	Males	6.7	25.7	15.5	**13.5**	7.1	9.3	8.0	**8.2**	8.5	4.0	**5.7**	7.0	12.0	8.0	**9.0**
	Females	4.1	10.9	6.1	**6.1**	3.8	5.6	5.9	**5.0**	5.5	2.5	**3.7**	3.9	6.3	4.6	**5.0**
	M+F	5.5	19.0	11.0	**10.0**	5.4	7.5	7.0	**6.6**	6.9	3.2	**4.7**	5.5	9.2	6.3	**7.0**
United States	Males	2.2	19.7	12.7	**5.9**	8.3	10.5	11.5	**10.4**	8.5	3.5	**5.4**	4.1	11.3	8.8	**8.0**
	Females	1.2	12.5	13.4	**3.9**	5.7	6.2	8.3	**6.8**	3.7	4.6	**4.3**	2.7	6.2	7.2	**5.4**
	M+F	1.7	16.6	13.0	**4.9**	7.0	8.4	10.0	**8.6**	5.7	4.2	**4.8**	3.4	8.7	8.0	**6.7**
OECD average	Males	3.5	17.9	16.5	**7.3**	8.8	8.4	8.4	**8.3**	11.8	6.4	**7.1**	3.9	10.1	8.5	**7.5**
	Females	2.5	11.0	11.5	**4.3**	6.5	5.9	7.7	**6.2**	8.9	5.9	**6.5**	2.8	6.7	6.6	**5.2**
	M+F	2.8	14.6	13.8	**5.9**	6.9	7.2	7.8	**7.1**	9.5	5.7	**6.3**	3.2	8.2	7.5	**6.3**
EU21 average	Males	3.0	18.8	17.2	**7.2**	8.2	8.6	8.3	**8.3**	15.4	5.8	**7.0**	3.7	10.1	8.1	**7.3**
	Females	2.7	11.5	13.6	**4.4**	6.1	6.0	8.5	**6.4**	9.9	5.5	**6.3**	2.7	6.9	7.0	**5.2**
	M+F	2.5	15.5	14.9	**5.8**	6.6	7.3	8.0	**7.1**	10.5	5.3	**6.1**	3.0	8.2	7.4	**6.2**
Other G20 Argentina		m	m	m	**m**	m	m	m	**m**	m	m	**m**	m	m	m	**m**
Brazil	Males	3.2	7.8	6.1	**5.1**	12.2	8.1	6.4	**7.9**	4.3	5.3	**5.0**	4.3	7.8	6.2	**6.0**
	Females	2.9	10.4	8.5	**6.0**	13.5	12.6	11.2	**12.2**	8.5	6.4	**7.0**	4.7	11.5	9.5	**8.5**
	M+F	3.0	8.9	7.3	**5.5**	13.0	10.5	8.9	**10.2**	6.8	5.9	**6.2**	4.5	9.6	7.8	**7.3**
China		m	m	m	**m**	m	m	m	**m**	m	m	**m**	m	m	m	**m**
India		m	m	m	**m**	m	m	m	**m**	m	m	**m**	m	m	m	**m**
Indonesia		m	m	m	**m**	m	m	m	**m**	m	m	**m**	m	m	m	**m**
Russian Federation		m	m	m	**m**	m	m	m	**m**	m	m	**m**	m	m	m	**m**
Saudi Arabia		m	m	m	**m**	m	m	m	**m**	m	m	**m**	m	m	m	**m**
South Africa		m	m	m	**m**	m	m	m	**m**	m	m	**m**	m	m	m	**m**

1. Differences between countries in these columns partly reflect the fact that the average age of graduation varies across countries. For instance, in some countries a smaller share of 15-19 year-olds attain upper secondary education simply because graduation typically occurs at 19. This means that the denominator in the ratio for the reported columns will be smaller than those for which graduation occurs at an earlier age.

Source: OECD. See Annex 3 for notes *(www.oecd.org/edu/eag2011)*.

Please refer to the Reader's Guide for information concerning the symbols replacing missing data.

StatLink http://dx.doi.org/10.1787/888932464695

C4

Table C4.4a. [1/6] Trends in the percentage of young people in education and not in education (1997-2009)

By age group and work status

OECD	Age group	1997			1998			1999			2000			2001			2002			2003		
		In education	Not in education		In education	Not in education		In education	Not in education		In education	Not in education		In education	Not in education		In education	Not in education		In education	Not in education	
		Total	Employed	Not employed	Total	Employed	Not employed	Total	Employed	Not employed	Total	Employed	Not employed	Total	Employed	Not employed	Total	Employed	Not employed	Total	Employed	Not employed
		(1)	(2)	(3)	(4)	(5)	(6)	(7)	(8)	(9)	(10)	(11)	(12)	(13)	(14)	(15)	(16)	(17)	(18)	(19)	(20)	(21)
Australia	15-19	77.8	14.2	8.1	77.3	13.8	8.8	78.2	14.4	7.4	79.5	13.7	6.8	79.5	13.0	7.6	79.7	13.3	7.0	79.6	13.6	6.8
	20-24	31.5	51.0	17.5	32.7	51.3	16.0	34.9	50.6	14.5	35.9	50.9	13.3	36.5	49.6	13.9	38.7	48.1	13.2	39.7	47.0	13.3
	25-29	12.8	65.4	21.7	13.7	67.1	19.2	15.0	66.5	18.5	15.5	65.5	19.0	15.8	67.0	17.2	16.5	65.7	17.8	17.7	64.7	17.6
	15-29	39.4	44.6	16.0	40.0	45.1	14.9	41.9	44.5	13.6	42.8	44.0	13.2	43.4	43.6	13.0	44.5	42.7	12.7	45.4	42.0	12.6
Austria	15-19	m	m	m	m	m	m	m	m	m	m	m	m	m	m	m	81.5	12.1	6.3	83.6	10.7	5.6
	20-24	m	m	m	m	m	m	m	m	m	m	m	m	m	m	m	29.4	58.9	11.7	30.3	59.3	10.4
	25-29	m	m	m	m	m	m	m	m	m	m	m	m	m	m	m	10.3	77.3	12.4	12.5	75.2	12.3
	15-29	m	m	m	m	m	m	m	m	m	m	m	m	m	m	m	39.5	50.3	10.2	41.1	49.4	9.5
Belgium	15-19	88.0	c	9.0	85.3	3.9	10.8	89.4	3.7	6.8	89.9	3.6	6.5	89.7	4.1	6.2	89.6	3.6	6.8	89.1	3.8	7.1
	20-24	39.1	42.6	18.3	40.6	42.5	16.9	43.7	38.6	17.7	43.8	40.2	16.0	44.2	42.8	13.0	38.2	44.4	17.4	39.9	43.0	17.1
	25-29	7.2	74.8	17.9	9.3	72.4	18.2	14.4	67.7	17.9	11.8	72.5	15.7	15.0	69.5	15.5	5.8	77.0	17.2	8.9	72.8	18.3
	15-29	42.7	42.1	15.2	43.2	41.3	15.4	47.5	38.2	14.3	46.9	40.2	12.9	48.2	40.0	11.7	43.2	42.8	14.0	44.8	40.8	14.4
Canada	15-19	82.9	9.4	7.7	81.5	9.9	8.5	80.8	10.9	8.3	80.6	11.2	8.2	81.3	11.4	7.3	80.2	11.9	8.0	80.0	11.9	8.1
	20-24	36.8	45.3	17.9	36.7	45.4	17.8	37.1	47.2	15.7	35.7	48.5	15.7	36.5	47.9	15.7	36.4	48.3	15.3	36.7	49.0	14.3
	25-29	10.3	68.1	21.6	10.8	70.1	19.1	10.7	71.2	18.2	10.6	72.3	17.1	11.6	72.1	16.3	12.7	69.8	17.5	12.7	71.2	16.1
	15-29	44.6	40.7	14.6	44.6	41.3	14.1	44.6	42.4	13.0	44.4	43.1	12.5	45.1	42.8	12.1	45.2	42.4	12.4	45.1	43.0	11.9
Chile		m	m	m	m	m	m	m	m	m	m	m	m	m	m	m	m	m	m	m	m	m
Czech Republic	15-19	76.9	c	c	77.1	15.8	7.2	75.6	14.8	9.7	82.1	10.0	7.9	87.0	6.2	6.8	88.3	5.7	6.0	89.0	5.2	5.8
	20-24	16.3	c	c	17.1	64.3	18.5	19.6	59.8	20.6	19.7	60.0	20.3	23.1	58.9	18.1	25.7	56.2	18.1	28.7	53.3	18.0
	25-29	1.6	c	c	1.8	75.1	23.1	2.4	71.7	25.9	2.4	72.1	25.6	3.0	72.1	25.0	2.9	73.3	23.8	3.0	73.0	24.1
	15-29	32.4	c	c	31.5	52.2	16.3	30.9	50.1	19.0	31.7	49.7	18.5	33.7	48.8	17.4	34.5	48.6	16.9	35.9	47.2	16.9
Denmark	15-19	89.4	9.2	1.4	90.3	7.9	1.8	85.8	10.8	3.4	89.9	7.4	2.7	86.8	9.4	3.8	88.7	8.9	2.4	89.8	7.7	2.5
	20-24	54.1	39.4	6.5	55.0	38.0	7.0	55.8	36.6	7.6	54.8	38.6	6.6	55.3	38.1	6.6	55.3	37.4	7.3	52.1	36.1	11.8
	25-29	32.3	58.9	8.8	34.5	57.8	7.7	35.5	56.7	7.8	36.1	56.4	7.5	32.4	60.0	7.6	35.0	58.3	6.7	23.9	64.6	11.5
	15-29	56.3	37.8	5.9	58.0	36.3	5.7	56.4	37.1	6.5	57.7	36.5	5.8	55.1	38.7	6.2	57.1	37.3	5.6	52.5	38.6	8.9
Estonia	15-19	m	m	m	m	m	m	m	m	m	m	m	m	m	m	m	m	m	m	94.4	2.3	3.3
	20-24	m	m	m	m	m	m	m	m	m	m	m	m	m	m	m	m	m	m	39.7	42.3	18.0
	25-29	m	m	m	m	m	m	m	m	m	m	m	m	m	m	m	m	m	m	14.7	59.8	25.5
	15-29	m	m	m	m	m	m	m	m	m	m	m	m	m	m	m	m	m	m	51.4	33.5	15.1
Finland	15-19	m	m	m	m	m	m	m	m	m	m	m	m	m	m	m	m	m	m	88.1	5.7	6.2
	20-24	m	m	m	m	m	m	m	m	m	m	m	m	m	m	m	m	m	m	52.5	33.1	14.4
	25-29	m	m	m	m	m	m	m	m	m	m	m	m	m	m	m	m	m	m	27.2	58.7	14.1
	15-29	m	m	m	m	m	m	m	m	m	m	m	m	m	m	m	m	m	m	55.6	32.7	11.6
France	15-19	90.4	3.9	5.7	90.1	3.5	6.3	90.1	3.1	6.8	90.0	3.9	6.2	88.7	3.9	7.3	88.2	4.8	7.0	88.1	5.3	6.6
	20-24	37.0	41.7	21.3	37.2	41.6	21.2	38.5	39.4	22.1	38.8	40.7	20.5	37.3	41.5	21.2	39.4	43.0	17.6	39.5	43.4	17.1
	25-29	5.5	71.9	22.6	5.4	70.9	23.6	6.3	69.9	23.8	5.9	70.2	23.9	5.7	71.6	22.8	5.9	73.7	20.4	5.7	74.6	19.7
	15-29	42.6	40.5	16.9	42.9	39.7	17.3	43.9	38.4	17.7	43.9	39.1	17.0	43.1	39.7	17.1	44.1	40.9	15.0	44.0	41.5	14.5
Germany	15-19	89.6	5.4	5.0	m	m	m	89.5	6.0	4.5	87.4	6.8	5.7	88.5	6.4	5.1	90.1	5.2	4.7	91.2	4.1	4.7
	20-24	32.7	48.9	18.4	m	m	m	34.3	49.0	16.7	34.1	49.0	16.9	35.0	48.7	16.4	38.1	46.0	15.9	41.2	43.1	15.6
	25-29	14.1	67.3	18.5	m	m	m	13.6	68.2	18.1	12.7	69.8	17.5	13.5	68.5	18.0	16.3	66.3	17.4	17.9	63.7	18.4
	15-29	42.8	42.8	14.3	m	m	m	44.9	41.9	13.2	44.9	41.8	13.3	46.0	40.9	13.1	48.6	38.8	12.6	50.5	36.7	12.9
Greece	15-19	82.3	8.1	9.6	79.0	9.8	11.2	82.4	8.2	9.4	82.6	8.1	9.3	86.2	6.5	7.3	85.8	6.5	7.8	84.1	6.3	9.6
	20-24	31.9	40.6	27.5	26.7	44.0	29.3	29.5	43.0	27.5	30.7	43.4	25.9	36.2	39.9	23.9	34.8	41.1	24.1	37.5	40.3	22.1
	25-29	5.2	65.4	29.4	4.3	66.1	29.6	5.1	66.4	28.5	5.1	65.8	29.2	6.6	66.1	27.2	5.6	67.1	27.3	6.8	68.0	25.1
	15-29	40.9	37.3	21.8	36.3	40.3	23.4	38.9	39.3	21.8	39.0	39.4	21.5	41.4	38.7	19.9	39.6	40.1	20.3	39.6	40.8	19.6
Hungary	15-19	85.8	5.3	8.9	78.2	10.0	11.8	79.3	9.2	11.6	83.7	7.7	8.6	85.0	6.7	8.3	87.5	4.5	8.0	89.7	3.5	6.8
	20-24	28.5	42.3	29.2	26.5	45.9	27.6	28.6	47.7	23.6	32.3	45.7	22.0	35.0	45.1	20.0	36.9	42.6	20.5	40.5	39.6	19.9
	25-29	6.5	58.2	35.3	7.4	58.9	33.7	8.7	60.1	31.3	9.4	61.4	29.2	9.4	63.4	27.1	8.6	63.1	28.3	12.6	59.9	27.5
	15-29	42.6	33.7	23.7	37.7	38.0	24.2	38.3	39.5	22.2	40.7	39.1	20.2	41.5	39.7	18.9	42.1	38.4	19.5	44.7	36.5	18.8

Source: OECD. See Annex 3 for notes *(www.oecd.org/edu/eag2011).*

Please refer to the Reader's Guide for information concerning the symbols replacing missing data.

StatLink http://dx.doi.org/10.1787/888932464714

Table C4.4a. [2/6] Trends in the percentage of young people in education and not in education (1997-2009)

By age group and work status

	Age group	2004			2005			2006			2007			2008			2009		
		In education	Not in education		In education	Not in education		In education	Not in education		In education	Not in education		In education	Not in education		In education	Not in education	
		Total	Employed	Not employed	Total	Employed	Not employed	Total	Employed	Not employed	Total	Employed	Not employed	Total	Employed	Not employed	Total	Employed	Not employed
		(22)	(23)	(24)	(25)	(26)	(27)	(28)	(29)	(30)	(31)	(32)	(33)	(34)	(35)	(36)	(37)	(38)	(39)
OECD Australia	15-19	78.4	14.1	7.5	78.3	14.3	7.4	79.3	13.7	7.1	79.6	13.9	6.5	79.4	14.3	6.3	**77.9**	**13.8**	**8.3**
	20-24	39.0	48.7	12.3	39.4	49.0	11.6	39.0	49.5	11.5	39.1	50.1	10.7	39.3	50.0	10.7	**39.9**	**48.5**	**11.6**
	25-29	17.7	65.0	17.3	16.6	68.0	15.4	16.6	67.7	15.7	17.7	68.0	14.4	15.4	70.5	14.1	**15.7**	**67.4**	**16.9**
	15-29	45.4	42.3	12.3	45.0	43.5	11.4	45.1	43.5	11.4	45.4	44.1	10.5	44.4	45.2	10.4	**43.9**	**43.7**	**12.3**
Austria	15-19	83.3	9.3	7.3	84.4	8.7	6.9	85.0	8.5	6.6	85.6	9.1	5.3	84.3	10.0	5.6	**84.3**	**9.2**	**6.5**
	20-24	30.3	56.8	12.9	30.4	57.2	12.4	32.6	54.8	12.5	32.5	56.5	11.0	32.3	56.3	11.4	**33.5**	**54.6**	**11.8**
	25-29	13.0	72.6	14.4	12.0	74.6	13.4	13.7	71.0	15.3	14.2	70.4	15.4	14.6	71.7	13.7	**16.5**	**68.9**	**14.6**
	15-29	41.3	47.1	11.7	41.3	47.7	11.0	42.9	45.6	11.6	43.1	46.2	10.7	42.6	47.0	10.4	**43.6**	**45.3**	**11.1**
Belgium	15-19	92.1	3.1	4.9	90.1	3.7	6.2	88.9	4.0	7.1	91.9	2.9	5.2	90.5	4.0	5.5	**91.1**	**3.3**	**5.7**
	20-24	38.8	44.4	16.9	38.1	43.6	18.3	35.6	47.6	16.9	39.4	45.2	15.4	41.5	44.4	14.1	**44.9**	**39.0**	**16.1**
	25-29	6.0	74.3	19.7	7.4	74.9	17.7	7.2	75.3	17.5	7.2	75.5	17.2	7.7	75.8	16.5	**7.8**	**75.9**	**16.3**
	15-29	44.6	41.4	14.0	44.4	41.4	14.2	43.2	42.9	13.9	45.5	41.8	12.7	45.9	42.0	12.1	**47.2**	**40.1**	**12.7**
Canada	15-19	79.0	12.2	8.8	80.2	12.8	7.0	81.1	11.6	7.3	80.2	12.5	7.3	80.4	12.4	7.3	**80.3**	**11.5**	**8.1**
	20-24	38.2	47.6	14.2	39.2	46.3	14.4	38.4	48.6	13.0	38.5	47.8	13.7	38.9	48.0	13.1	**38.0**	**46.7**	**15.2**
	25-29	11.9	71.9	16.2	12.5	71.7	15.8	12.4	72.1	15.5	12.2	72.6	15.2	12.4	72.7	14.9	**11.9**	**71.8**	**16.3**
	15-29	44.7	43.2	12.0	45.5	43.0	11.5	43.3	44.9	11.9	43.2	44.6	12.1	43.4	44.8	11.8	**42.8**	**43.9**	**13.3**
Chile		m	m	m	m	m	m	m	m	m	m	m	m	m	m	m	**m**	**m**	**m**
Czech Republic	15-19	89.9	4.4	5.7	90.3	4.4	5.3	91.0	4.5	4.5	92.7	4.4	2.9	92.7	4.5	2.7	**92.8**	**3.7**	**3.5**
	20-24	32.3	49.2	18.5	35.9	47.5	16.6	40.0	45.8	14.1	42.1	46.9	11.0	44.8	44.7	10.6	**46.1**	**40.8**	**13.1**
	25-29	3.8	71.6	24.5	4.4	72.4	23.2	7.7	71.0	21.4	9.0	71.6	19.4	11.1	71.2	17.7	**11.2**	**68.7**	**20.1**
	15-29	37.7	45.1	17.2	39.5	44.6	15.9	42.7	43.2	14.1	44.8	43.5	11.7	46.6	42.5	10.9	**47.2**	**40.0**	**12.8**
Denmark	15-19	89.5	8.4	2.1	88.4	7.3	4.3	88.9	6.7	4.4	84.8	11.3	3.9	88.9	8.3	2.8	**88.8**	**8.3**	**2.9**
	20-24	54.0	34.8	11.3	54.4	37.2	8.3	55.3	38.8	5.9	48.0	43.8	8.2	53.2	39.1	7.7	**51.9**	**38.3**	**9.8**
	25-29	28.3	59.8	11.9	27.0	61.3	11.6	29.4	62.2	8.4	24.2	66.8	8.9	25.5	66.9	7.6	**26.1**	**66.6**	**7.3**
	15-29	55.5	35.9	8.6	55.5	36.3	8.2	58.0	35.8	6.2	52.3	40.7	7.0	56.1	37.9	6.0	**56.3**	**37.1**	**6.6**
Estonia	15-19	91.0	1.4	7.6	92.0	2.9	5.2	90.7	5.6	3.7	86.0	8.2	5.7	88.8	6.3	4.9	**89.2**	**2.8**	**8.0**
	20-24	48.6	31.9	19.5	50.9	32.7	16.3	47.6	37.0	15.4	45.4	39.3	15.3	46.5	42.8	10.7	**46.7**	**33.5**	**19.8**
	25-29	14.9	65.3	19.8	14.2	61.8	24.0	9.4	75.0	15.6	10.1	71.4	18.4	14.9	66.6	18.5	**10.2**	**61.6**	**28.2**
	15-29	53.1	31.6	15.3	54.0	31.3	14.8	50.7	37.9	11.4	48.0	38.9	13.0	49.9	38.7	11.3	**47.4**	**33.6**	**19.0**
Finland	15-19	88.9	5.2	5.9	90.2	4.5	5.2	91.8	4.6	3.6	92.2	4.3	3.5	90.3	4.6	5.1	**90.3**	**4.5**	**5.1**
	20-24	53.1	31.5	15.4	52.8	34.1	13.0	51.7	35.0	13.3	51.9	34.8	13.3	50.5	37.5	12.0	**49.3**	**35.7**	**15.1**
	25-29	25.7	58.8	15.5	25.7	60.3	14.0	25.6	60.4	13.9	27.2	59.5	13.3	29.2	58.4	12.4	**25.4**	**59.1**	**15.5**
	15-29	55.2	32.4	12.4	55.4	33.7	10.9	55.5	34.1	10.4	56.5	33.4	10.1	56.2	34.0	9.9	**54.4**	**33.6**	**12.0**
France	15-19	88.3	4.9	6.8	90.3	4.3	5.4	91.3	3.3	5.4	90.5	3.2	6.3	89.3	3.7	7.0	**89.7**	**3.4**	**6.9**
	20-24	39.3	43.1	17.6	40.0	43.3	16.7	39.9	41.3	18.8	42.5	39.7	17.8	42.1	38.9	19.0	**39.4**	**40.9**	**19.8**
	25-29	5.7	74.3	20.0	5.0	74.7	20.3	5.0	75.1	19.9	5.1	75.1	19.8	5.5	74.7	19.8	**4.9**	**75.4**	**19.7**
	15-29	44.6	40.7	14.7	45.1	40.7	14.1	45.9	39.5	14.6	46.8	38.7	14.5	46.2	38.7	15.2	**44.0**	**40.5**	**15.6**
Germany	15-19	93.4	3.0	3.6	92.9	2.7	4.4	92.4	3.3	4.2	92.2	3.6	4.2	92.4	3.9	3.7	**92.7**	**3.6**	**3.8**
	20-24	44.0	38.5	17.5	44.2	37.1	18.7	45.5	37.8	16.7	45.7	39.1	15.2	46.7	39.3	14.0	**48.5**	**37.8**	**13.7**
	25-29	17.6	62.8	19.6	18.5	60.3	21.2	18.5	61.5	20.0	18.7	62.8	18.5	19.2	63.8	17.0	**18.6**	**64.5**	**16.9**
	15-29	52.2	34.3	13.5	52.2	33.1	14.7	52.3	34.1	13.6	52.4	35.0	12.6	52.3	36.1	11.6	**52.4**	**36.0**	**11.6**
Greece	15-19	82.7	6.6	10.8	82.2	6.1	11.7	86.3	5.9	7.8	86.7	4.8	8.5	86.8	4.8	8.4	**87.9**	**4.2**	**7.9**
	20-24	34.7	41.6	23.7	40.4	38.0	21.6	44.0	37.7	18.4	47.3	35.0	17.7	48.5	34.4	17.1	**47.2**	**34.6**	**18.2**
	25-29	5.3	69.0	25.7	6.4	69.8	23.7	7.6	70.1	22.2	7.9	70.2	21.9	8.9	70.0	21.1	**8.9**	**69.1**	**22.0**
	15-29	37.3	42.0	20.7	38.6	41.7	19.7	41.4	41.6	16.9	42.8	40.5	16.8	43.7	40.1	16.2	**43.4**	**39.8**	**16.8**
Hungary	15-19	90.4	3.4	6.2	90.6	3.0	6.4	91.3	2.7	6.0	92.3	2.7	5.0	91.8	2.5	5.7	**92.7**	**1.7**	**5.6**
	20-24	43.8	37.6	18.6	46.6	34.5	18.9	47.8	33.7	18.5	49.2	33.9	16.9	48.4	33.2	18.4	**49.2**	**29.9**	**20.9**
	25-29	12.9	63.2	23.9	13.1	63.0	24.0	13.5	62.2	24.3	13.9	63.2	22.9	9.9	67.1	23.1	**9.8**	**65.1**	**25.1**
	15-29	45.2	37.8	17.1	46.3	36.5	17.2	47.3	35.6	17.0	48.6	35.7	15.6	47.2	36.5	16.3	**48.1**	**34.1**	**17.7**

Source: OECD. See Annex 3 for notes *(www.oecd.org/edu/eag2011)*.

Please refer to the Reader's Guide for information concerning the symbols replacing missing data.

StatLink http://dx.doi.org/10.1787/888932464714

Table C4.4a. [3/6] Trends in the percentage of young people in education and not in education (1997-2009)

By age group and work status

		Age group	1997			1998			1999			2000			2001			2002			2003		
			In education	Not in education		In education	Not in education		In education	Not in education		In education	Not in education		In education	Not in education		In education	Not in education		In education	Not in education	
			Total	Employed	Not employed	Total	Employed	Not employed	Total	Employed	Not employed	Total	Employed	Not employed	Total	Employed	Not employed	Total	Employed	Not employed	Total	Employed	Not employed
			(1)	(2)	(3)	(4)	(5)	(6)	(7)	(8)	(9)	(10)	(11)	(12)	(13)	(14)	(15)	(16)	(17)	(18)	(19)	(20)	(21)
OECD	Iceland	15-19	78.9	17.0	c	82.2	15.1	c	81.6	17.0	c	83.1	14.8	c	79.5	19.0	c	80.9	14.8	c	88.5	7.6	c
		20-24	51.0	42.4	6.6	47.8	45.9	6.3	44.8	48.4	6.8	48.0	47.7	c	50.3	45.6	c	53.8	40.1	6.2	57.1	35.1	7.8
		25-29	26.5	64.7	8.8	32.8	57.4	9.8	34.7	58.8	6.5	34.9	59.2	5.9	33.8	61.5	c	36.5	58.8	c	26.8	61.7	11.5
		15-29	51.1	42.3	6.6	55.3	38.6	6.1	54.5	40.7	4.8	56.0	39.9	4.1	54.7	41.8	3.4	57.0	38.0	5.1	59.0	33.5	7.6
	Ireland	15-19	m	m	m	m	m	m	79.4	15.4	5.2	80.0	15.6	4.4	80.3	15.5	4.1	81.5	13.6	4.9	81.2	13.5	5.3
		20-24	m	m	m	m	m	m	24.6	64.6	10.8	26.7	63.6	9.7	28.3	62.4	9.3	28.9	60.1	10.9	30.5	58.0	11.5
		25-29	m	m	m	m	m	m	3.1	82.4	14.5	3.3	83.4	13.3	3.3	83.1	13.5	3.6	81.4	15.0	5.0	79.7	15.3
		15-29	m	m	m	m	m	m	37.8	52.3	9.9	37.9	53.2	9.0	37.6	53.5	9.0	37.9	51.8	10.3	38.2	51.0	10.8
	Israel	15-19	m	m	m	m	m	m	m	m	m	m	m	m	m	m	m	69.4	6.0	24.6	69.0	5.7	25.2
		20-24	m	m	m	m	m	m	m	m	m	m	m	m	m	m	m	26.8	31.7	41.6	28.1	27.7	44.2
		25-29	m	m	m	m	m	m	m	m	m	m	m	m	m	m	m	19.1	52.2	28.7	19.6	52.7	27.7
		15-29	m	m	m	m	m	m	m	m	m	m	m	m	m	m	m	39.3	29.2	31.5	39.9	27.8	32.3
	Italy	15-19	m	m	m	75.4	9.5	15.2	76.9	8.3	14.8	77.1	9.8	13.1	77.6	9.8	12.6	80.8	8.7	10.5	83.8	6.9	9.3
		20-24	m	m	m	35.8	34.1	30.1	35.6	34.5	29.9	36.0	36.5	27.5	37.0	36.9	26.1	38.2	37.5	24.3	44.1	34.2	21.7
		25-29	m	m	m	16.5	54.1	29.4	17.7	53.4	28.9	17.0	56.1	26.9	16.4	58.0	25.6	15.6	59.5	24.8	22.8	54.7	22.5
		15-29	m	m	m	39.5	34.8	25.7	40.1	34.6	25.3	39.9	36.8	23.3	40.1	37.8	22.2	41.0	38.3	20.7	46.6	34.8	18.6
	Japan	15-24	58.7	33.6	7.7	60.0	32.4	7.6	60.0	31.0	9.0	62.1	29.2	8.8	62.6	28.9	8.4	58.6	32.0	9.5	58.4	31.7	9.8
	Korea		m	m	m	m	m	m	m	m	m	m	m	m	m	m	m	m	m	m	m	m	m
	Luxembourg	15-19	90.2	4.2	5.6	88.6	5.3	6.1	89.2	5.8	5.0	92.2	6.1	c	91.2	7.0	c	91.3	5.7	3.0	92.2	5.7	2.1
		20-24	35.2	54.5	10.3	40.4	50.1	9.5	47.2	43.2	9.6	42.8	48.9	8.2	46.7	44.2	9.0	47.8	45.2	7.0	46.0	45.9	8.1
		25-29	8.2	76.2	15.6	11.9	74.0	14.1	11.3	74.1	14.6	11.6	75.5	12.9	11.6	75.9	12.5	13.9	74.5	11.6	7.6	82.2	10.2
		15-29	39.1	49.7	11.2	42.1	47.5	10.5	44.1	45.5	10.4	45.3	46.6	8.1	46.7	45.1	8.2	48.5	44.0	7.5	46.1	46.9	7.0
	Mexico	15-19	49.4	31.6	19.0	46.9	33.8	19.3	49.6	32.7	17.7	47.9	33.8	18.3	50.3	31.9	17.8	53.4	29.0	17.5	54.0	28.2	17.8
		20-24	18.5	52.9	28.7	17.1	55.4	27.4	19.1	54.8	26.1	17.7	55.2	27.1	19.1	53.8	27.1	20.8	52.6	26.6	19.8	52.6	27.6
		25-29	4.9	64.8	30.3	4.2	65.2	30.6	4.9	65.0	30.1	4.0	65.8	30.2	4.1	64.9	31.0	4.6	64.8	30.6	4.2	64.8	31.0
		15-29	26.4	48.1	25.4	24.8	49.9	25.2	26.5	49.4	24.1	25.4	50.0	24.6	26.9	48.5	24.6	28.8	46.9	24.2	28.7	46.6	24.8
	Netherlands	15-19	88.9	8.2	2.8	89.7	7.6	2.7	88.2	8.9	3.0	80.6	15.7	3.7	86.5	9.9	3.6	86.7	9.5	3.8	87.0	8.7	4.3
		20-24	51.0	41.9	7.1	50.5	42.0	7.5	50.7	42.5	6.7	36.5	55.2	8.2	44.2	47.8	8.0	45.1	47.7	7.3	44.2	46.5	9.4
		25-29	23.7	64.3	12.0	24.4	64.9	10.7	25.0	65.2	9.8	5.0	83.0	12.1	15.3	73.7	11.0	16.2	71.6	12.2	16.5	71.4	12.1
		15-29	50.9	41.2	7.9	51.5	41.1	7.4	51.8	41.4	6.8	38.1	53.6	8.3	46.8	45.5	7.7	48.1	44.0	7.9	48.6	42.7	8.7
	New Zealand	15-19	m	m	m	m	m	m	m	m	m	m	m	m	m	m	m	m	m	m	m	m	m
		20-24	m	m	m	m	m	m	m	m	m	m	m	m	m	m	m	m	m	m	m	m	m
		25-29	m	m	m	m	m	m	m	m	m	m	m	m	m	m	m	m	m	m	m	m	m
		15-29	m	m	m	m	m	m	m	m	m	m	m	m	m	m	m	m	m	m	m	m	m
	Norway	15-19	87.1	11.4	1.6	92.1	6.0	1.9	91.9	6.4	c	92.4	5.9	c	85.8	11.1	3.0	85.3	11.5	3.2	86.9	10.4	2.7
		20-24	34.6	53.7	11.7	40.2	51.4	8.4	38.4	53.8	7.8	41.7	50.3	8.0	39.6	51.7	8.7	38.5	51.8	9.7	38.7	50.8	10.6
		25-29	13.6	74.1	12.2	14.4	76.1	9.6	17.2	74.4	8.3	17.5	72.1	10.4	13.9	75.9	10.2	14.2	75.0	10.7	15.4	71.9	12.7
		15-29	42.6	48.5	8.8	46.4	46.8	6.8	46.8	47.1	6.1	48.4	44.6	7.0	44.7	47.8	7.5	44.8	47.2	8.0	46.3	44.9	8.7
	Poland	15-19	90.8	3.8	5.3	91.0	4.2	4.8	93.2	2.3	4.6	92.8	2.6	4.5	91.8	2.4	5.8	95.9	1.0	3.1	95.6	1.1	3.3
		20-24	28.8	45.9	25.3	30.8	45.3	23.9	33.1	39.7	27.2	34.9	34.3	30.8	45.2	27.7	27.1	53.8	20.8	25.4	55.7	18.8	25.5
		25-29	5.4	68.7	25.9	5.7	70.5	23.8	5.4	68.0	26.6	8.0	62.9	29.1	11.4	59.9	28.7	14.9	53.3	31.8	17.3	52.4	30.2
		15-29	42.2	39.0	18.8	42.6	39.8	17.6	42.7	37.4	19.9	43.8	34.1	22.1	49.2	30.1	20.7	52.8	26.2	21.0	54.3	25.1	20.5
	Portugal	15-19	73.0	17.1	9.8	71.6	20.1	8.3	72.3	19.6	8.1	72.6	19.7	7.7	72.8	19.8	7.4	72.4	20.3	7.3	74.8	16.4	8.8
		20-24	38.4	47.4	14.2	32.4	55.7	12.0	34.9	53.2	11.9	36.5	52.6	11.0	36.3	53.3	10.4	34.7	53.3	12.0	35.2	52.5	12.3
		25-29	13.2	71.8	15.0	9.5	74.8	15.8	11.5	75.1	13.4	11.0	76.6	12.5	11.2	77.3	11.6	10.7	77.1	12.2	11.7	73.7	14.6
		15-29	43.5	43.7	12.9	36.7	51.2	12.1	38.2	50.5	11.3	38.2	51.2	10.5	38.3	51.8	9.9	37.4	51.9	10.7	38.7	49.2	12.1
	Slovak Republic	15-19	71.0	12.3	16.7	69.4	12.3	18.3	69.6	10.1	20.4	67.3	6.4	26.3	67.3	6.3	26.4	78.6	5.8	15.6	82.2	5.2	12.6
		20-24	14.5	60.0	25.5	17.4	56.3	26.3	17.4	51.2	31.4	18.1	48.8	33.1	19.4	45.7	34.9	22.1	44.0	33.9	24.0	46.4	29.6
		25-29	4.6	69.1	26.3	1.1	71.6	27.2	1.6	70.2	28.2	1.3	66.9	31.8	2.3	65.0	32.7	2.9	66.6	30.5	2.6	68.3	29.1
		15-29	31.9	45.5	22.6	31.0	45.3	23.8	30.3	43.0	26.7	29.3	40.3	30.4	29.6	39.0	31.4	34.4	38.8	26.8	36.2	39.9	23.9

Source: OECD. See Annex 3 for notes *(www.oecd.org/edu/eag2011).*

Please refer to the Reader's Guide for information concerning the symbols replacing missing data.

StatLink http://dx.doi.org/10.1787/888932464714

Table C4.4a. [4/6] Trends in the percentage of young people in education and not in education (1997-2009)

By age group and work status

	Age group	2004			2005			2006			2007			2008			2009		
		In education	Not in education		In education	Not in education		In education	Not in education		In education	Not in education		In education	Not in education		In education	Not in education	
		Total	Employed	Not employed	Total	Employed	Not employed	Total	Employed	Not employed	Total	Employed	Not employed	Total	Employed	Not employed	Total	Employed	Not employed
		(22)	(23)	(24)	(25)	(26)	(27)	(28)	(29)	(30)	(31)	(32)	(33)	(34)	(35)	(36)	(37)	(38)	(39)
OECD																			
Iceland	15-19	85.4	11.8	c	86.4	10.7	c	86.9	9.9	c	83.8	13.3	c	85.5	12.0	c	88.3	8.0	c
	20-24	56.1	37.5	6.4	53.0	37.1	10.0	53.6	41.9	c	55.8	37.8	6.4	56.7	39.8	c	59.1	31.5	9.4
	25-29	30.2	64.0	5.8	30.9	61.5	7.6	33.7	62.3	c	29.0	64.3	6.6	30.6	62.6	6.9	35.5	50.8	13.7
	15-29	57.7	37.3	5.0	57.0	36.2	6.8	58.3	37.8	3.9	56.5	38.2	5.3	57.5	38.2	4.3	60.7	30.3	9.0
Ireland	15-19	83.3	11.8	4.9	82.4	13.1	4.5	81.7	13.3	5.0	82.6	12.3	5.1	81.4	10.1	8.5	83.0	6.0	11.0
	20-24	29.0	59.4	11.6	27.7	60.0	12.3	26.5	61.7	11.8	25.9	62.0	12.1	30.2	55.3	14.6	34.2	45.0	20.8
	25-29	4.8	80.1	15.1	5.3	80.9	13.8	5.6	81.1	13.3	4.9	81.5	13.5	10.1	75.6	14.3	9.7	68.2	22.0
	15-29	37.7	51.6	10.7	36.2	53.4	10.5	34.6	55.0	10.4	33.3	55.9	10.7	36.1	51.1	12.8	37.7	43.7	18.6
Israel	15-19	68.9	5.6	25.6	68.9	6.3	24.7	69.0	6.8	24.3	68.5	5.7	25.7	70.7	7.1	22.2	68.8	6.5	24.7
	20-24	28.6	30.5	40.9	28.3	31.4	40.3	29.3	30.1	40.6	28.5	31.9	39.6	28.9	33.6	37.5	28.5	34.0	37.5
	25-29	20.9	53.9	25.3	21.4	54.3	24.2	24.8	51.8	23.4	24.5	52.0	23.5	24.0	53.1	22.9	26.6	49.2	24.2
	15-29	40.3	29.1	30.5	40.2	30.2	29.6	41.5	29.1	29.4	41.0	29.3	29.7	42.1	30.3	27.5	42.0	29.3	28.7
Italy	15-19	81.2	7.8	11.0	81.8	7.0	11.2	81.6	6.6	11.8	83.5	6.3	10.2	84.5	5.9	9.6	83.8	5.0	11.2
	20-24	37.7	38.7	23.6	38.6	37.3	24.1	40.2	37.0	22.8	41.7	35.7	22.6	42.6	35.4	22.0	42.3	32.9	24.8
	25-29	15.4	59.8	24.8	14.4	59.8	25.8	15.2	60.7	24.1	16.1	58.3	25.6	15.5	60.0	24.5	15.7	57.9	26.4
	15-29	41.2	38.3	20.5	41.5	37.5	21.1	42.7	37.2	20.1	44.5	35.5	20.0	45.3	35.5	19.2	45.3	33.5	21.2
Japan	15-24	59.1	31.7	9.2	59.7	31.5	8.8	56.7	34.2	9.1	58.4	34.0	7.6	58.6	34.0	7.4	58.8	32.8	8.4
Korea		m	m	m	m	m	m	m	m	m	m	m	m	m	m	m	m	m	m
Luxembourg	15-19	91.4	5.5	3.2	93.4	4.4	2.2	93.1	2.8	4.1	94.3	2.7	2.9	94.0	3.8	2.1	94.5	2.8	2.7
	20-24	49.1	40.8	10.1	47.4	43.3	9.3	50.3	39.4	10.3	55.1	35.6	9.2	55.9	34.3	9.8	66.0	25.3	8.7
	25-29	6.1	81.5	12.4	8.6	81.2	10.3	9.2	79.6	11.2	7.1	79.1	13.9	11.2	75.8	13.0	7.4	80.7	11.9
	15-29	46.8	44.4	8.7	48.5	44.2	7.3	49.6	41.8	8.6	49.8	41.2	8.9	51.9	39.6	8.5	53.5	38.6	7.9
Mexico	15-19	54.9	28.0	17.0	m	m	m	m	m	m	m	m	m	m	m	m	60.8	20.8	18.4
	20-24	20.3	52.3	27.4	m	m	m	m	m	m	m	m	m	m	m	m	25.7	46.7	27.6
	25-29	4.4	65.4	30.3	m	m	m	m	m	m	m	m	m	m	m	m	6.4	63.2	30.4
	15-29	29.0	46.7	24.2	32.5	42.3	25.1	32.7	43.1	24.2	33.7	43.2	23.2	33.6	43.2	23.2	33.9	41.3	24.8
Netherlands	15-19	89.2	7.5	3.3	89.2	7.0	3.9	91.7	5.2	3.0	88.1	8.3	3.6	90.7	7.2	2.1	89.7	6.8	3.6
	20-24	46.6	44.2	9.3	49.1	41.8	9.1	50.3	42.4	7.3	50.8	42.2	6.9	52.1	42.3	5.6	52.5	39.6	7.9
	25-29	16.9	71.2	11.9	18.2	70.2	11.6	18.1	71.2	10.8	19.8	70.6	9.6	18.7	73.5	7.8	19.1	71.3	9.6
	15-29	50.6	41.2	8.2	52.1	39.7	8.2	53.1	39.8	7.1	53.1	40.2	6.7	54.3	40.6	5.1	54.1	38.9	7.0
New Zealand	15-19	74.2	16.8	9.0	74.8	17.1	8.0	73.0	17.9	9.1	72.6	17.8	9.7	74.8	16.8	8.4	72.6	15.0	12.4
	20-24	38.6	46.9	14.5	38.8	46.7	14.4	37.5	48.8	13.7	38.1	47.6	14.2	38.7	46.0	15.2	38.9	42.8	18.3
	25-29	18.0	64.5	17.6	18.3	65.6	16.1	16.4	67.4	16.2	19.2	64.7	16.1	15.5	68.1	16.4	15.4	66.5	18.1
	15-29	45.1	41.4	13.5	45.7	41.7	12.6	44.0	43.2	12.8	45.0	41.9	13.1	44.7	42.2	13.1	43.7	40.2	16.1
Norway	15-19	87.2	9.9	2.8	87.4	10.1	2.5	82.1	14.5	3.4	80.6	15.8	3.7	78.3	17.7	4.0	80.6	15.2	4.2
	20-24	40.6	49.6	9.8	41.5	48.9	9.6	39.2	51.7	9.1	37.7	53.6	8.8	39.3	53.6	7.0	41.6	49.0	9.4
	25-29	15.4	71.5	13.1	15.7	72.0	12.3	12.2	76.3	11.5	12.2	77.4	10.4	12.6	78.2	9.2	12.7	76.7	10.6
	15-29	47.6	43.8	8.6	48.6	43.4	8.1	45.3	46.8	7.9	44.3	48.2	7.5	44.1	49.2	6.8	45.6	46.5	8.0
Poland	15-19	96.5	0.9	2.6	97.9	0.4	1.7	94.9	1.3	3.8	95.9	1.7	2.5	95.8	1.9	2.4	94.3	2.1	3.6
	20-24	57.5	18.4	24.1	62.7	17.2	20.1	55.1	24.2	20.7	56.4	25.2	18.3	56.8	27.6	15.6	54.4	29.2	16.4
	25-29	15.5	53.7	30.8	16.4	54.3	29.3	12.2	61.2	26.6	12.8	62.9	24.3	11.4	67.1	21.5	12.4	66.8	20.8
	15-29	53.8	25.9	20.3	55.7	26.0	18.4	52.9	29.6	17.4	53.5	31.0	15.5	52.5	33.8	13.7	50.7	35.1	14.2
Portugal	15-19	75.1	15.1	9.8	79.3	12.2	8.4	80.2	12.0	7.8	80.4	11.1	8.6	81.7	11.2	7.1	84.5	8.6	6.9
	20-24	38.7	47.8	13.5	37.4	48.4	14.1	37.7	48.9	13.3	35.5	49.3	15.2	36.5	50.0	13.5	37.9	46.3	15.7
	25-29	11.0	75.0	14.0	11.5	73.6	14.9	12.2	72.9	14.9	12.1	72.4	15.5	11.9	73.0	15.1	14.2	71.0	14.8
	15-29	38.0	49.3	12.7	38.9	48.2	12.9	39.6	48.1	12.4	39.1	47.5	13.4	40.1	47.6	12.2	42.3	44.9	12.8
Slovak Republic	15-19	87.8	4.3	7.9	90.4	3.3	6.3	90.5	2.9	6.7	90.2	4.4	5.4	90.6	3.8	5.7	91.5	4.0	4.5
	20-24	27.5	44.7	27.8	31.0	43.8	25.2	35.4	41.9	22.8	29.4	50.7	19.9	39.3	44.1	16.6	45.3	37.6	17.1
	25-29	4.5	66.6	28.9	6.1	64.9	29.0	5.7	67.9	26.4	6.8	68.0	25.2	6.5	68.7	24.7	7.5	67.6	24.9
	15-29	39.0	39.2	21.8	41.1	38.3	20.5	41.8	39.1	19.1	40.5	42.3	17.2	43.2	40.6	16.2	45.7	38.2	16.1

Source: OECD. See Annex 3 for notes *(www.oecd.org/edu/eag2011)*.
Please refer to the Reader's Guide for information concerning the symbols replacing missing data.
StatLink http://dx.doi.org/10.1787/888932464714

Table C4.4a. [5/6] Trends in the percentage of young people in education and not in education (1997-2009)

By age group and work status

	Age group	1997			1998			1999			2000			2001			2002			2003		
		In education	Not in education		In education	Not in education		In education	Not in education		In education	Not in education		In education	Not in education		In education	Not in education		In education	Not in education	
		Total	Employed	Not employed	Total	Employed	Not employed	Total	Employed	Not employed	Total	Employed	Not employed	Total	Employed	Not employed	Total	Employed	Not employed	Total	Employed	Not employed
		(1)	(2)	(3)	(4)	(5)	(6)	(7)	(8)	(9)	(10)	(11)	(12)	(13)	(14)	(15)	(16)	(17)	(18)	(19)	(20)	(21)
OECD																						
Slovenia	15-19	m	m	m	m	m	m	m	m	m	m	m	m	m	m	m	m	m	m	92.8	2.4	4.8
	20-24	m	m	m	m	m	m	m	m	m	m	m	m	m	m	m	m	m	m	56.8	30.2	13.0
	25-29	m	m	m	m	m	m	m	m	m	m	m	m	m	m	m	m	m	m	25.3	63.1	11.5
	15-29	m	m	m	m	m	m	m	m	m	m	m	m	m	m	m	m	m	m	57.2	32.8	10.0
Spain	15-19	79.2	9.9	10.9	80.2	9.9	9.8	79.3	11.3	9.4	80.6	11.4	8.0	81.4	11.6	6.9	81.9	11.0	7.2	82.6	10.1	7.3
	20-24	43.0	34.8	22.1	44.3	35.7	20.1	43.6	38.8	17.6	44.6	40.3	15.0	45.0	40.7	14.2	43.4	41.5	15.1	43.5	41.8	14.8
	25-29	15.0	54.3	30.7	15.3	57.3	27.5	15.2	59.6	25.1	16.2	62.4	21.4	17.0	63.1	19.8	16.1	64.2	19.8	15.4	65.0	19.5
	15-29	45.0	33.5	21.4	45.4	35.1	19.4	44.4	37.8	17.8	45.0	39.8	15.3	45.1	40.7	14.2	43.8	41.5	14.6	43.4	42.0	14.6
Sweden	15-19	91.1	4.3	4.6	90.9	4.3	4.7	91.5	4.9	3.7	90.6	5.8	3.6	88.4	7.3	4.3	88.4	7.0	4.6	88.7	7.0	4.2
	20-24	42.3	41.4	16.3	42.6	44.3	13.1	43.8	45.2	11.0	42.1	47.2	10.7	41.2	48.2	10.6	41.7	47.0	11.2	42.3	46.0	11.8
	25-29	21.4	64.2	14.5	24.9	65.0	10.0	22.5	68.1	9.5	21.9	68.9	9.2	22.7	70.0	7.2	22.4	69.5	8.1	22.8	67.9	9.4
	15-29	49.8	38.2	12.0	51.3	39.3	9.4	51.1	40.7	8.1	50.2	41.9	7.9	49.6	43.1	7.3	50.1	42.0	7.9	51.0	40.6	8.4
Switzerland	15-19	86.5	6.1	7.4	85.5	9.6	4.9	84.4	8.0	7.6	84.6	7.5	7.9	85.7	7.5	6.8	86.2	8.0	5.8	83.6	8.6	7.8
	20-24	30.5	59.1	10.4	34.7	54.1	11.3	35.8	55.9	8.3	37.4	56.7	5.9	39.3	52.3	8.4	37.9	52.7	9.4	35.8	51.8	12.4
	25-29	10.6	77.1	12.3	10.1	78.0	11.9	10.3	79.4	10.3	15.1	73.9	11.0	13.5	75.1	11.4	12.6	74.5	12.9	12.2	74.0	13.8
	15-29	39.4	50.3	10.2	41.6	48.9	9.5	42.9	48.4	8.7	45.1	46.6	8.3	46.4	44.7	8.9	44.3	46.2	9.5	42.7	45.8	11.4
Turkey	15-19	36.1	33.6	30.2	40.2	32.1	27.7	42.9	30.2	26.9	39.2	29.6	31.2	41.0	26.7	32.3	42.2	24.8	32.9	45.9	21.3	32.8
	20-24	13.3	38.3	48.4	13.4	44.7	42.0	13.1	45.6	41.4	12.7	43.1	44.2	12.7	43.1	44.2	14.1	40.6	45.3	15.8	36.5	47.8
	25-29	2.7	59.4	37.9	2.9	60.4	36.7	3.4	57.7	38.8	2.9	58.8	38.3	2.6	57.1	40.2	3.0	56.2	40.7	3.7	53.2	43.1
	15-29	18.9	43.2	38.0	19.9	45.0	35.1	21.1	43.7	35.2	18.5	43.7	37.8	18.8	42.4	38.9	19.6	40.8	39.6	21.7	37.2	41.1
United Kingdom	15-19	m	m	m	m	m	m	m	m	m	77.0	15.0	8.0	76.1	15.7	8.2	75.3	16.2	8.6	76.3	14.3	9.4
	20-24	m	m	m	m	m	m	m	m	m	32.4	52.2	15.4	33.5	51.7	14.8	31.0	53.7	15.3	32.6	52.1	15.3
	25-29	m	m	m	m	m	m	m	m	m	13.3	70.3	16.3	13.3	70.6	16.0	13.3	70.7	16.0	15.0	68.7	16.3
	15-29	m	m	m	m	m	m	m	m	m	40.0	46.6	13.3	40.2	46.7	13.1	39.5	47.2	13.3	41.4	44.9	13.6
United States	15-19	82.6	10.3	7.1	82.2	10.5	7.3	81.3	11.3	7.4	81.3	11.7	7.0	81.2	11.4	7.5	82.9	10.2	7.0	m	m	m
	20-24	34.3	50.7	15.1	33.0	52.6	14.4	32.8	52.1	15.1	32.5	53.1	14.4	33.9	50.5	15.6	35.0	48.5	16.5	m	m	m
	25-29	11.8	72.2	15.9	11.9	72.7	15.4	11.1	73.2	15.7	11.4	72.8	15.8	11.8	70.5	17.7	12.3	70.3	17.4	m	m	m
	15-29	43.5	43.9	12.6	43.3	44.5	12.2	43.0	44.4	12.6	43.1	44.6	12.2	44.0	42.7	13.3	45.1	41.5	13.4	m	m	m
OECD average	15-19	80.4	11.3	8.8	79.3	11.6	9.4	80.1	11.4	9.2	80.2	11.3	9.4	80.4	11.2	9.0	81.2	10.3	8.6	83.2	8.7	8.3
	20-24	33.8	46.4	19.0	34.2	47.3	18.5	34.9	47.3	17.8	34.7	48.1	17.8	36.4	46.7	17.4	36.5	45.7	17.7	38.9	43.3	17.8
	25-29	11.7	67.2	20.6	12.4	67.3	20.3	12.8	67.6	19.6	12.2	68.6	19.3	12.7	68.5	19.4	13.0	67.8	19.7	14.0	66.6	19.3
	15-29	41.3	42.2	16.0	41.2	42.8	16.0	41.8	42.8	15.4	41.4	43.5	15.1	42.2	43.0	14.8	42.6	42.1	15.2	44.5	40.3	15.2
EU21 average	15-19	84.8	7.7	7.3	82.6	8.9	8.5	83.2	8.9	7.9	83.3	9.1	7.9	83.8	8.7	7.8	85.1	8.3	6.5	86.9	7.0	6.2
	20-24	35.2	44.7	18.6	35.5	45.7	18.8	36.3	45.4	18.3	35.6	46.9	17.5	37.8	45.5	16.7	38.0	45.6	16.4	40.8	43.1	16.1
	25-29	11.7	66.6	21.0	12.3	66.7	21.0	12.4	67.3	20.3	11.3	69.1	19.6	12.4	68.7	18.9	12.2	69.1	18.6	14.1	67.5	18.4
	15-29	43.0	40.4	15.7	42.1	41.6	16.3	42.6	41.7	15.7	41.9	42.9	15.1	43.1	42.3	14.6	43.5	42.4	14.2	45.8	40.4	13.8
Other G20																						
Argentina		m	m	m	m	m	m	m	m	m	m	m	m	m	m	m	m	m	m	m	m	m
Brazil	15-19	m	m	m	m	m	m	m	m	m	m	m	m	m	m	m	m	m	m	m	m	m
	20-24	m	m	m	m	m	m	m	m	m	m	m	m	m	m	m	m	m	m	m	m	m
	25-29	m	m	m	m	m	m	m	m	m	m	m	m	m	m	m	m	m	m	m	m	m
	15-29	m	m	m	m	m	m	m	m	m	m	m	m	m	m	m	m	m	m	m	m	m
China		m	m	m	m	m	m	m	m	m	m	m	m	m	m	m	m	m	m	m	m	m
India		m	m	m	m	m	m	m	m	m	m	m	m	m	m	m	m	m	m	m	m	m
Indonesia		m	m	m	m	m	m	m	m	m	m	m	m	m	m	m	m	m	m	m	m	m
Russian Federation		m	m	m	m	m	m	m	m	m	m	m	m	m	m	m	m	m	m	m	m	m
Saudi Arabia		m	m	m	m	m	m	m	m	m	m	m	m	m	m	m	m	m	m	m	m	m
South Africa		m	m	m	m	m	m	m	m	m	m	m	m	m	m	m	m	m	m	m	m	m

Source: OECD. See Annex 3 for notes *(www.oecd.org/edu/eag2011)*.

Please refer to the Reader's Guide for information concerning the symbols replacing missing data.

StatLink http://dx.doi.org/10.1787/888932464714

Table C4.4a. [6/6] Trends in the percentage of young people in education and not in education (1997-2009)

By age group and work status

		Age group	2004			2005			2006			2007			2008			2009		
			In education	Not in education		In education	Not in education		In education	Not in education		In education	Not in education		In education	Not in education		In education	Not in education	
			Total	Employed	Not employed	Total	Employed	Not employed	Total	Employed	Not employed	Total	Employed	Not employed	Total	Employed	Not employed	Total	Employed	Not employed
			(22)	(23)	(24)	(25)	(26)	(27)	(28)	(29)	(30)	(31)	(32)	(33)	(34)	(35)	(36)	(37)	(38)	(39)
OECD	Slovenia	15-19	92.2	3.5	4.3	92.4	2.7	4.9	92.7	3.1	4.2	91.2	4.5	4.3	92.2	3.4	4.4	**94.1**	**3.4**	**2.5**
		20-24	60.9	27.9	11.2	55.7	31.3	13.0	55.8	30.5	13.7	58.7	30.9	10.4	60.6	29.2	10.3	**62.9**	**25.7**	**11.4**
		25-29	26.6	61.8	11.5	24.6	63.9	11.5	26.3	60.3	13.3	26.1	59.5	14.4	26.9	63.2	9.9	**27.1**	**61.3**	**11.6**
		15-29	58.4	32.4	9.2	55.5	34.4	10.1	55.7	33.5	10.8	56.3	33.6	10.1	57.1	34.5	8.5	**58.2**	**32.7**	**9.0**
	Spain	15-19	82.2	10.1	7.6	78.2	11.0	10.8	79.5	10.5	10.1	77.8	11.3	10.9	78.9	10.5	10.5	**80.4**	**6.2**	**13.4**
		20-24	41.3	43.2	15.6	35.1	45.5	19.4	34.5	48.6	16.9	34.5	48.2	17.2	34.0	46.5	19.4	**34.9**	**38.9**	**26.3**
		25-29	15.3	66.2	18.5	10.9	69.3	19.8	10.9	70.1	19.1	10.0	72.4	17.6	9.5	71.5	18.9	**9.9**	**63.8**	**26.3**
		15-29	42.2	43.2	14.6	37.1	45.7	17.2	37.1	47.0	15.9	36.3	48.1	15.7	36.3	46.9	16.8	**37.4**	**39.9**	**22.7**
	Sweden	15-19	89.4	5.8	4.8	89.6	5.8	4.7	87.7	7.0	5.3	86.9	7.7	5.4	87.4	8.2	4.4	**87.9**	**6.6**	**5.5**
		20-24	42.8	43.6	13.6	42.5	44.1	13.4	43.0	41.8	15.2	39.6	47.3	13.1	39.5	47.5	12.9	**39.0**	**44.5**	**16.5**
		25-29	21.5	68.0	10.5	23.6	66.5	10.0	20.9	67.5	11.6	20.2	69.2	10.6	21.7	68.7	9.5	**21.5**	**67.0**	**11.5**
		15-29	51.5	39.0	9.5	52.9	38.0	9.2	51.5	38.0	10.5	50.3	40.2	9.6	51.3	39.9	8.7	**51.0**	**38.0**	**11.0**
	Switzerland	15-19	84.9	7.9	7.2	85.3	7.2	7.5	84.4	8.0	7.6	84.4	7.5	8.2	82.9	7.7	9.4	**84.7**	**7.4**	**7.9**
		20-24	37.3	51.7	11.0	37.9	50.3	11.9	36.9	52.3	10.8	41.0	48.6	10.4	42.7	48.2	9.1	**43.4**	**45.9**	**10.7**
		25-29	15.7	72.1	12.2	12.3	75.9	11.8	14.7	73.8	11.5	12.9	75.2	11.9	14.4	75.5	10.1	**14.3**	**72.9**	**12.8**
		15-29	45.1	44.7	10.2	44.4	45.2	10.4	44.7	45.3	10.0	45.5	44.3	10.2	46.0	44.5	9.6	**46.5**	**43.0**	**10.5**
	Turkey	15-19	43.5	21.2	35.3	45.8	18.1	36.1	47.9	17.0	35.0	48.7	16.8	34.5	44.7	18.2	37.1	**56.3**	**15.0**	**28.7**
		20-24	13.0	39.1	47.8	15.4	34.9	49.7	17.3	33.9	48.8	18.6	35.1	46.3	20.0	33.9	46.1	**23.9**	**30.0**	**46.1**
		25-29	3.1	54.0	42.8	4.0	50.2	45.8	5.7	49.4	45.0	4.7	51.5	43.9	4.9	51.6	43.5	**7.7**	**47.4**	**44.9**
		15-29	19.7	38.4	41.9	22.4	34.0	43.6	24.2	33.2	42.6	24.3	34.4	41.3	23.4	34.6	42.0	**29.5**	**30.9**	**39.6**
	United Kingdom	15-19	74.3	16.7	9.0	76.0	14.6	9.3	75.7	13.4	10.9	76.2	13.0	10.7	76.5	13.7	9.8	**78.3**	**12.1**	**9.6**
		20-24	31.1	54.1	14.8	32.1	51.0	16.8	30.2	51.6	18.2	29.7	52.3	18.1	28.3	53.4	18.3	**31.5**	**49.3**	**19.1**
		25-29	14.2	69.0	16.8	13.3	70.1	16.6	14.1	69.5	16.4	12.7	71.1	16.2	12.3	71.9	15.8	**13.2**	**68.9**	**18.0**
		15-29	40.5	46.0	13.5	41.2	44.6	14.2	40.6	44.3	15.1	40.1	45.0	14.9	38.2	47.1	14.8	**40.4**	**43.9**	**15.7**
	United States	15-19	83.9	9.2	6.9	85.6	8.3	6.1	85.0	8.6	6.3	85.2	8.5	6.3	85.2	7.6	7.2	**84.7**	**6.5**	**8.8**
		20-24	35.2	47.9	16.9	36.1	48.4	15.5	35.0	49.4	15.6	35.7	48.1	16.2	36.9	45.9	17.2	**38.7**	**41.2**	**20.1**
		25-29	13.0	68.7	18.4	11.9	70.0	18.1	11.7	71.5	16.8	12.4	70.7	16.9	13.2	67.3	19.5	**13.5**	**64.7**	**21.8**
		15-29	44.8	41.3	13.9	45.2	41.7	13.1	44.4	42.7	12.8	44.8	42.1	13.1	45.3	40.1	14.6	**45.7**	**37.4**	**16.9**
	OECD average	15-19	83.0	8.9	8.3	84.5	7.8	7.9	84.5	7.8	7.8	84.2	8.3	7.7	84.4	8.2	7.6	**84.4**	**7.4**	**8.4**
		20-24	39.6	42.7	17.7	40.8	42.1	17.2	40.8	42.8	16.8	41.1	43.1	15.7	42.4	42.5	15.5	**43.1**	**39.2**	**17.7**
		25-29	14.0	67.0	19.0	14.3	67.2	18.4	14.5	67.9	18.0	14.4	68.3	17.4	14.8	68.5	16.7	**14.7**	**66.1**	**19.1**
		15-29	44.7	40.2	15.1	45.1	39.9	14.9	45.2	40.4	14.3	45.2	40.8	14.0	45.7	40.7	13.5	**46.3**	**38.5**	**15.2**
	EU21 average	15-19	87.2	6.6	6.2	87.7	6.1	6.1	87.9	6.1	6.0	87.7	6.6	5.7	88.1	6.3	5.6	**88.6**	**5.2**	**6.2**
		20-24	41.9	41.5	16.5	42.5	41.4	16.1	42.8	41.8	15.4	42.9	42.6	14.5	44.3	41.7	14.0	**45.6**	**38.1**	**16.3**
		25-29	13.6	67.8	18.6	13.6	68.0	18.4	13.7	68.9	17.4	13.6	69.1	17.3	14.4	69.3	16.3	**14.2**	**67.6**	**18.3**
		15-29	46.0	39.9	14.0	46.3	39.9	13.8	46.6	40.2	13.2	46.6	40.7	12.7	47.3	40.5	12.2	**47.6**	**38.5**	**13.9**
Other G20	Argentina		m	m	m	m	m	m	m	m	m	m	m	m	m	m	m	**m**	**m**	**m**
	Brazil	15-19	m	m	m	m	m	m	m	m	m	67.0	18.3	14.7	69.1	17.2	13.8	**69.9**	**16.1**	**14.0**
		20-24	m	m	m	m	m	m	m	m	m	24.6	52.0	23.4	23.8	53.7	22.5	**23.9**	**52.8**	**23.3**
		25-29	m	m	m	m	m	m	m	m	m	12.2	66.0	21.8	12.2	67.1	20.7	**12.0**	**66.4**	**21.6**
		15-29	m	m	m	m	m	m	m	m	m	35.1	45.0	19.9	35.4	45.7	19.0	**35.6**	**44.9**	**19.6**
	China		m	m	m	m	m	m	m	m	m	m	m	m	m	m	m	**m**	**m**	**m**
	India		m	m	m	m	m	m	m	m	m	m	m	m	m	m	m	**m**	**m**	**m**
	Indonesia		m	m	m	m	m	m	m	m	m	m	m	m	m	m	m	**m**	**m**	**m**
	Russian Federation		m	m	m	m	m	m	m	m	m	m	m	m	m	m	m	**m**	**m**	**m**
	Saudi Arabia		m	m	m	m	m	m	m	m	m	m	m	m	m	m	m	**m**	**m**	**m**
	South Africa		m	m	m	m	m	m	m	m	m	m	m	m	m	m	m	**m**	**m**	**m**

Source: OECD. See Annex 3 for notes *(www.oecd.org/edu/eag2011).*

Please refer to the Reader's Guide for information concerning the symbols replacing missing data.

StatLink http://dx.doi.org/10.1787/888932464714

INDICATOR C5

HOW MANY ADULTS PARTICIPATE IN EDUCATION AND LEARNING?

- Across the OECD, more than 40% of adults participate in formal and/or non-formal education in a given year. The proportion ranges from more than 60% in New Zealand and Sweden to less than 15% in Greece and Hungary.
- On average in the OECD area, an individual can expect to receive 988 hours of instruction in non-formal education during his or her working life, of which 715 hours are instruction in job-related non-formal education.
- Overall, 27% of adults in OECD countries have looked for information on learning possibilities in the preceding 12 months, and 87% of those seeking information found some.

Chart C5.1. Expected hours over the working life in all non-formal education and in job-related non-formal education, 2007

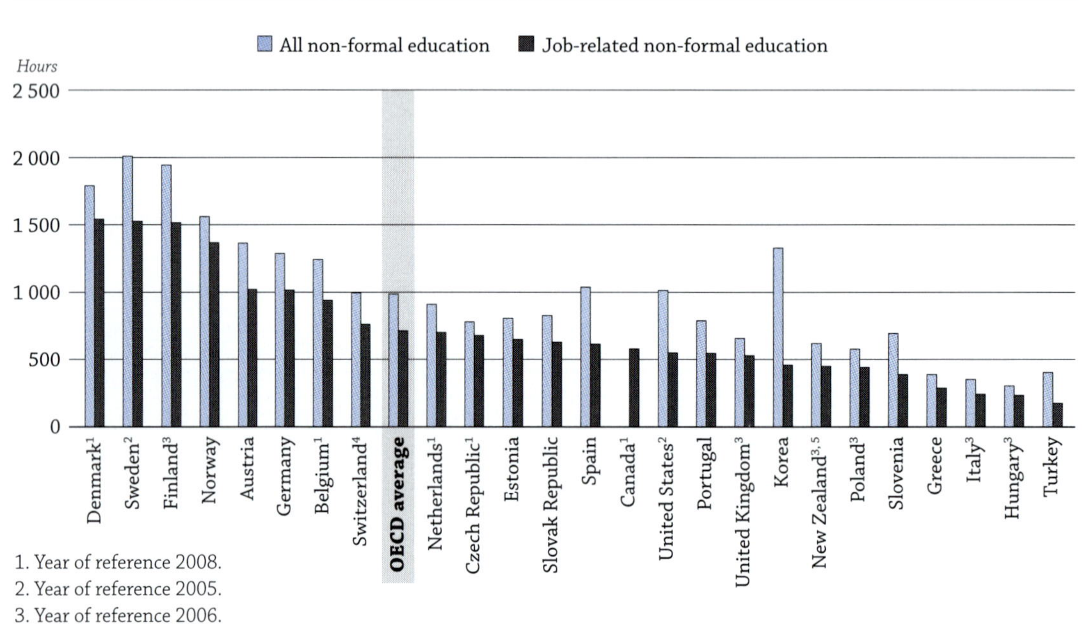

1. Year of reference 2008.
2. Year of reference 2005.
3. Year of reference 2006.
4. Year of reference 2009.
5. Excluding adults who participated only in "short seminars, lectures, workshops or special talks".

Countries are ranked in descending order of the number of expected hours in job-related non-formal education.

Source: OECD, LSO network special data collection, Adult Learning Working Group. Table C5.1a. See Annex 3 for notes (*www.oecd.org/edu/eag2011*).

StatLink http://dx.doi.org/10.1787/888932461712

Context

Investing in education and training after leaving initial education is essential for upgrading the skills of the labour force. Globalisation and the development of new technologies have broadened the international marketplace for goods and services. As a result, competition for skills is fierce, particularly in high-growth, high-technology markets. An ever-larger segment of the population must be able to adapt to changing technologies, and to learn and apply a new set of skills tailored to meet the needs of the growing services industries, in order to function effectively. Adult learning, as part of lifelong learning, is considered crucial for coping with the challenges of economic competitiveness and demographic change, and for combating unemployment, poverty and social exclusion, which marginalise a significant number of individuals in all countries.

INDICATOR C5

Other findings

- Adults with higher levels of educational attainment are more likely to participate in formal and non-formal education than adults with lower levels of attainment. They can also expect to receive more hours of instruction in non-formal education during their working lives. On average in OECD countries, **individuals with a tertiary education will receive three times as many hours of instruction in non-formal education as those with low levels of education.**

- Some adults use the formal education system to acquire additional skills. They tend to be young and highly educated. **Half of adults who have participated in formal education have also engaged in non-formal education activities** during the 12 months before the survey. A large number of adults are enrolled in formal education in Australia, Belgium, New Zealand, Sweden and the United Kingdom.

- **Younger individuals and persons with higher levels of education are more likely to look for information on learning activities**. Whereas the more highly educated are more likely to find information when they are looking for it, the information seems to be as accessible for older as for younger individuals.

Analysis

Investment in non-formal education

Given current opportunities for adult learning at various stages in life, the total number of hours of instruction in non-formal education an individual can expect to attend during his or her working life (i.e. between the ages of 25 and 64) indicates the level of investment in adult learning. The total investment, in all non-formal education exceeds 1 500 hours of instruction in Denmark, Finland, Norway and Sweden. It is less than 500 hours in Greece, Hungary, Italy and Turkey. The expected number of hours of instruction is strongly related to the overall participation rate in non-formal education.

As Chart C5.1 shows, in OECD countries, almost 75% of the expected instruction hours will be in job-related non-formal education. In the Czech Republic, Denmark and Norway, more than 86% of the expected hours are in job-related instruction, while in Korea, Slovenia, Spain, Turkey and the United States, at least 40% of hours of instruction in non-formal education are related to personal reasons.

To provide context for the expected hours of instruction in job-related non-formal education, Table C5.1a includes information on the annual average number of working hours of a full-time worker and the ratio of the expected hours of job-related non-formal education to these working hours. The investment in instruction time over the forty years of a working life equals one full working year in Denmark and slightly more than one working month in Turkey. The length of a working year varies across countries, too.

In Denmark, Finland, Norway and Sweden, the expected instruction hours represent almost a working year of investment. More than half a working year's investment in instruction hours is found in Austria, Belgium, Germany and the Netherlands. The lowest investment, the equivalent of less than one-third of a working year, is found in Greece, Hungary, Italy, Poland, Portugal, Slovenia, Turkey and the United Kingdom.

On average across the OECD, men can expect to receive about 10% more instruction hours in job-related non-formal education over their working lives than women. This advantage is considerable in Germany, Korea and the Netherlands, while in Finland, women can expect to receive 50% more hours of instruction in job-related non-formal education than men. In Denmark, Estonia, Greece, Hungary and the United States, women can also expect to receive more hours than men, albeit to a lesser degree.

In all countries except the United Kingdom, individuals with a tertiary education can expect to receive the highest number of hours of instruction in job-related non-formal education over their working lives; individuals with low levels of education will receive the lowest number of hours of instruction in job-related non-formal education over their working lives; and those who have completed their education at the upper secondary or the post-secondary non-tertiary level will fall between the two extremes in the number of instruction hours received. On average across the OECD, individuals with tertiary education will spend three times more hours of instruction than individuals with low levels of education. Only in Canada, Finland, Germany, Norway, Sweden and the United Kingdom is the advantage for highly educated individuals reduced to double (or less) the hours of instruction, while it is more than nine times that of individuals with low levels of education in Greece, Italy, Korea, Poland, the Slovak Republic, Slovenia and Turkey.

In most OECD countries, the number of expected instruction hours in job-related non-formal education rises fairly linearly as one moves from lower to higher levels of education. On average across countries, the increase in expected hours of instruction between those with ISCED 3/4 education and those without (+1.7 times) is similar to the increase in hours of instruction between those with ISCED 5/6 education and those just below (+1.9 times). This is not true for all countries: in Belgium, Hungary, Italy, the Slovak Republic, Slovenia, Switzerland and the United States, the increase in hours of instruction between those with ISCED 3/4 education and those without is double the increase in hours of instruction between those with ISCED 5/6 education and those just below. In Korea, the increase in hours of instruction between those with ISCED 3/4 education and those without (+10 times) is much greater than the increase in hours of instruction between those with ISCED 5/6 education and those with ISCED 3/4 education (+1.4 times).

Differences in investment between countries and social groups

The time spent attending non-formal education activities represents an investment in the individual's skill development for both the employer and the individual. The hours of instruction in non-formal job-related education per participant partly reflect a balance between extensive and intensive participation (Chart C5.2). The correlation between the participation rate and average hours of instruction per participant is slightly negative. The average hours of instruction per participant range from more than 80 hours in Belgium, Denmark, Hungary and Korea, to less than 40 hours in France, Italy, Slovenia and the United Kingdom. In all countries except Canada and Denmark, unemployed participants spend more time in instruction than employed participants (Table C5.2a).

Chart C5.2. Participation rate in all and in job-related non-formal education, hours of instruction per participant and per adult in job-related non-formal education, 2007

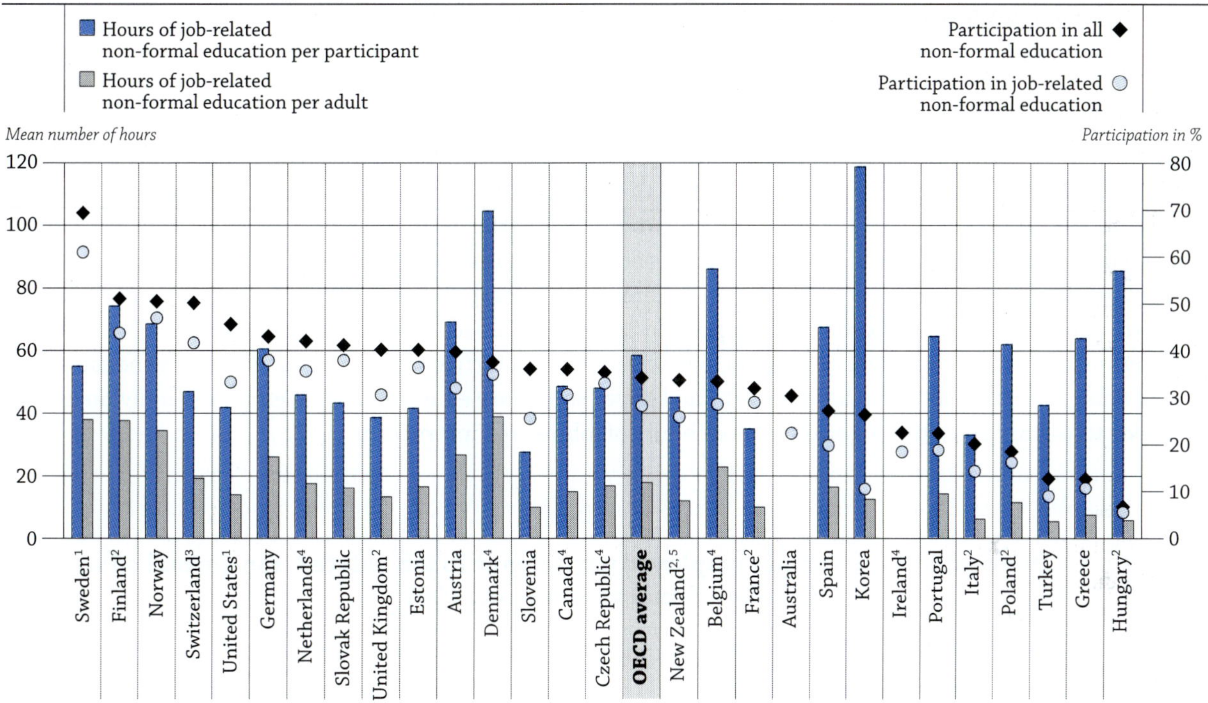

1. Year of reference 2005.
2. Year of reference 2006.
3. Year of reference 2009.
4. Year of reference 2008.
5. Excluding adults who participated only in "short seminars, lectures, workshops or special talks".

Countries are ranked in descending order of the participation rate in all non-formal education.

Source: OECD, LSO network special data collection, Adult Learning Working Group. Table C5.1a. See Annex 3 for notes (*www.oecd.org/edu/eag2011*).

StatLink http://dx.doi.org/10.1787/888932461731

The annual hours of instruction in non-formal education per adult combines the participation rate in non-formal education and the number of hours per participant. It shows the investment in each member of a certain group and can thus highlight differences and point out potential fields of expansion of investment in non-formal education. Each year, on average, OECD countries invest 25 hours of instruction in non-formal education in each 25-64 year-old; 18 of these hours are in job-related training (Chart C5.2). The investment in job-related instruction hours per adult ranges from more than 30 hours in Denmark, Finland, Norway and Sweden to less than 10 hours in Greece, Hungary, Italy and Turkey. With 10 to 15 hours invested in job-related instruction per adult, Canada, France, Korea, New Zealand, Poland, Portugal, Slovenia, the United Kingdom and the United States are below the OECD average.

There are large differences behind the average instruction hours in job-related non-formal education per adult. In all countries, 55-64 year-olds receive the fewest hours of instruction, and in 18 of the 25 countries with available data, men receive more hours of training than women (Table C5.2b, available on line). In 14 countries, the average number of instruction hours per adult decreases steadily as the age of the adult increases. In Finland and Greece, women receive more job-related non-formal training than men, and the instruction hours decrease steadily with age. In New Zealand, Portugal, Sweden and Switzerland, men attend more hours of instruction than women, but the younger age groups show a more or less equal number of instruction hours per adult, with only 55-64 year-olds receiving substantially fewer hours of instruction than younger individuals. In the United States, women receive more job-related instruction hours per adult than men, and the decrease in the number of hours of instruction by age group occurs between the second oldest and the oldest group. In Denmark and Estonia, women receive more job-related instruction hours per adult than men, and the youngest age group receives fewer hours than the next highest age group.

As older individuals and individuals with low levels of education tend to receive fewer instruction hours in job-related non-formal education, the investment in individuals with those characteristics is low: 4 hours of instruction per 55-64 year-old with a low level of education, compared to 36 hours of instruction per 25-34 year-old with a tertiary education (Table C5.2e, available on line).

Training leads to further training

The educational attainment an individual has achieved affects all aspects of adult learning. On average, the hours in job-related non-formal education vary according to the educational attainment of the employed participants, but not to a great extent (Chart C5.3). There are two distinct patterns: in the Czech Republic, Finland, Greece, Korea, Poland, the Slovak Republic, Spain, Sweden and Turkey, employed participants with a tertiary education spend considerably more hours in education (a difference of at least 27 hours), than participants who have not attained upper secondary education. The opposite is true in Canada, Denmark, Hungary, the Netherlands, Norway and the United Kingdom. In Belgium, participants with a tertiary education spend exactly the same time in education as participants who have not attained upper secondary education, while employed individuals with an upper secondary education receive the most hours of job-related instruction.

Chart C5.3. Hours of instruction per employed participant in job-related non-formal education, by educational attainment, 2007

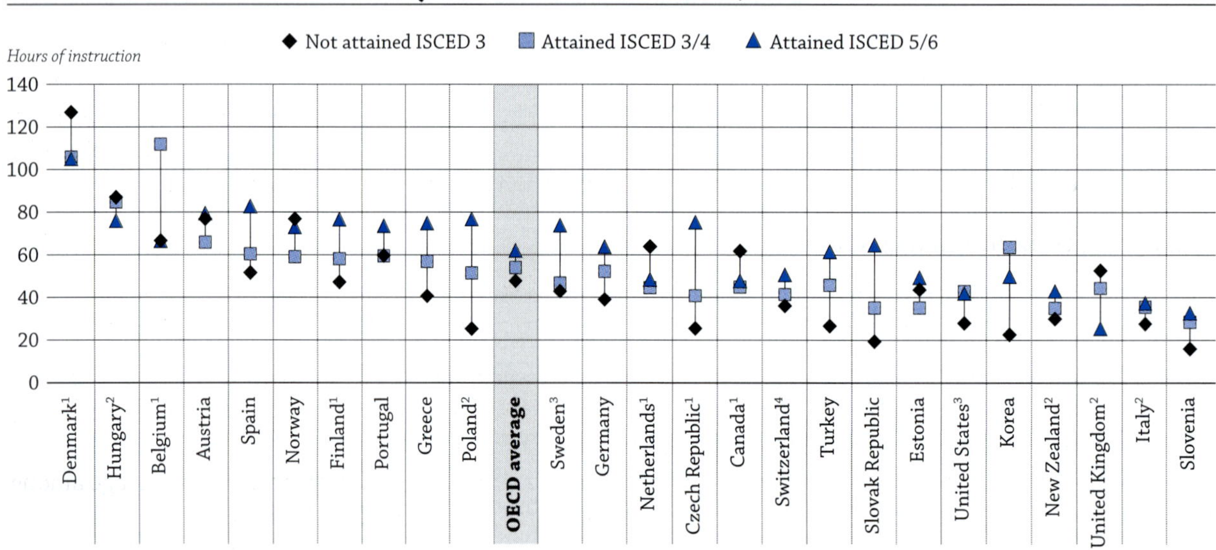

1. Year of reference 2008.
2. Year of reference 2006.
3. Year of reference 2005.
4. Year of reference 2009.

Countries are ranked in descending order of the hours of instruction for all levels of education.

Source: OECD, LSO network special data collection, Adult Learning Working Group. Table C5.2a. See Annex 3 for notes (*www.oecd.org/edu/eag2011*).

StatLink http://dx.doi.org/10.1787/888932461750

Participation in formal and non-formal education

In all countries, only a small minority of 25-64 year-olds attends institutions of formal education. Across OECD countries, an average of 8% of adults participates in formal education (Chart C5.4). Countries with a large number of adults enrolled in formal education institutions include Australia, Belgium, New Zealand, Sweden and the United Kingdom. On average, half of the participants in formal education also participate in non-formal education, an indication that these individuals take advantage of a variety of learning opportunities.

Chart C5.4. Participation in formal and/or non-formal education, 2007

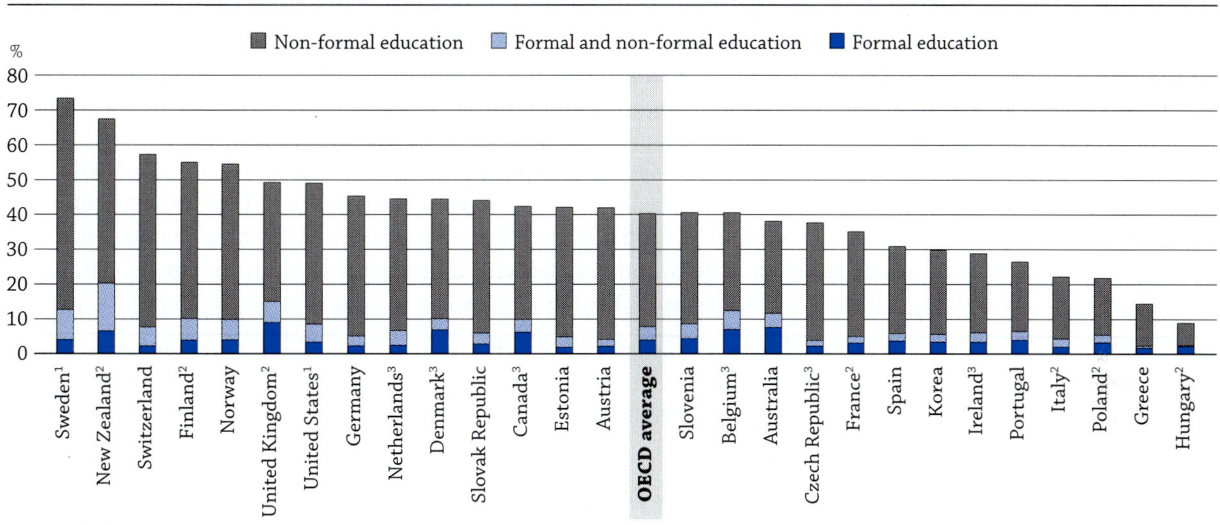

1. Year of reference 2005.
2. Year of reference 2006.
3. Year of reference 2008.

Countried are ranked in descending order of the participation rate in formal and/or nonformal education.

Source: OECD, LSO network special data collection, Adult Learning Working Group. Table C5.3a. See Annex 3 for notes (*www.oecd.org/edu/eag2011*).

StatLink http://dx.doi.org/10.1787/888932461769

On average, 13% of individuals with a tertiary education are enrolled in formal education compared with 3% of individuals with low levels of education (Table C5.3a). Younger adults are much more likely to attend formal studies (17% of 25-34 year-olds) than are older individuals (2% of 55-64 year-olds) (Table 5.3c, available on line). Across OECD countries, participation in formal education by 25-64 year-olds does not differ much by gender (Table C5.3b, available on line) or status in the labour force (Table C5.3d, available on line).

Seeking information and guidance

Effective information and counseling services can help to make education and training more accessible to a wider range of people, support learning at all ages, and empower citizens to manage their learning and work.

A special goal is to reach out to information- and assistance-deprived groups. The percentage of adults who have not participated in formal and/or non-formal education and have not looked for any information concerning learning possibilities within the 12 months prior to the survey measures the size of the population outside of both systems: the education and training system and the information and guidance system. On average among countries with comparable data, 52% of 25-64 year-olds had no contact with either the information or education systems, 41% participated in adult education, and 7% looked for information but did not participate. More than two-thirds of 25-64 year-olds remain outside both systems in Greece, Hungary, Italy, Poland and Portugal, while two-thirds of adults in Finland, the Netherlands, the Slovak Republic, Sweden, and the United Kingdom are included in both systems. The relationship between the participation rate in formal and/or non-formal education and the percentage of the population not seeking information about learning activities is negative (see charts and tables in OECD, 2010a).

In general, the results for different target groups are as expected: older individuals and those with low levels of educational attainment are more likely not to participate in these types of education and not to seek information about them, while the differences between men and women and between the employed and the general population are small in this regard.

Individuals who have looked for information were twice as likely to participate in formal and/or non-formal education as those who did not. Looking for information is an important step towards participating in adult learning. In the Netherlands, more than half the population has looked for information; in Greece, Hungary and Italy, fewer than one in ten people has (Table C5.4a). On the country level, there is a positive relationship between the rate of participation in adult learning and the rate of individuals looking for information. Independent of the extent to which they are consulted, information systems seem to be successful – except in the Netherlands. In all countries, at least 68% of those who looked for information found some; and in some countries, almost all individuals looking for information found some.

Chart C5.5 shows that individuals with a tertiary education are three times as likely to look for information as are individuals with low levels of education. The well-educated are also more likely to find information than their peers with lower levels of education. The relationships hold for all countries with available data, although they are stronger in some countries than others. Individuals with a tertiary education in Greece, Hungary, Italy, Korea and Poland are at least seven times more likely to look for information than individuals with low educational attainment; while in Australia, Belgium, Canada, Finland, France, the Netherlands and Sweden, they are less than three times as likely to look for information. In countries where these differences are large, the overall rate of looking for information tends to be lower, as does the rate of participation in adult learning.

Chart C5.5. Proportion of individuals who have looked for and found information, by educational attainment, 2007

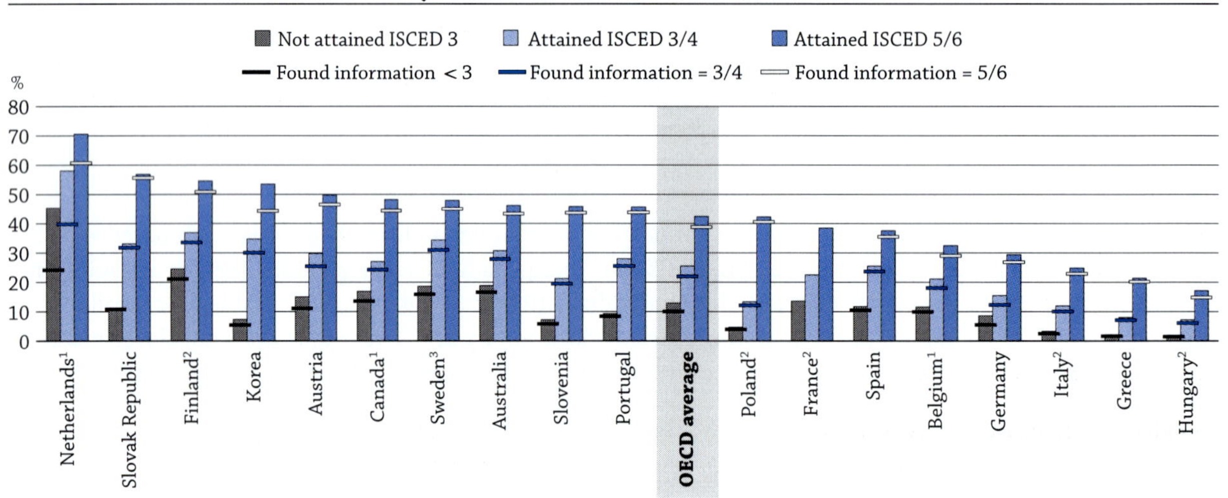

1. Year of reference 2008.
2. Year of reference 2006.
3. Year of reference 2005.

Countries are ranked in descending order of the proportion of individuals who have looked for information and have attained ISCED levels 5/6.

Source: OECD, LSO network special data collection, Adult Learning Working Group. Table C5.4a. See Annex 3 for notes (*www.oecd.org/edu/eag2011*).

StatLink http://dx.doi.org/10.1787/888932461788

Some 38% of 25-34 year-olds have looked for information on adult learning possibilities, whereas only 15% of 55-64 year-olds have. In all countries with comparable data, younger adults seek information more often than older adults: in Greece and Hungary, young people are five times more likely to look for information about education opportunities than older people, while in Australia, the Netherlands and the Slovak Republic, 25-34 year-olds are no more than two times more likely to do so. However, older people were just as successful in finding information as younger ones (Table C5.4c, available on line).

Definitions

Formal education is defined as education provided in the system of schools, colleges, universities and other formal educational institutions, and which normally constitutes a continuous "ladder" of full-time education for children and young people.

Non-formal education is defined as an organised and sustained educational activity that does not correspond exactly to the above definition of formal education. Non-formal education may therefore take place both within and outside educational institutions and cater to individuals of all ages. Depending on country contexts, it may cover educational programmes in adult literacy, basic education for out-of-school children, life skills, work skills, and general culture. The EU Adult Education Survey uses an extensive list of possible non-formal education activities, including courses, private lessons and guided, on-the-job training to prompt respondents to list all of their learning activities during the previous 12 months. Some of these learning activities might be of short duration.

Low levels of education attained refers to individuals not having attained ISCED level 3.

Middle levels of education attained refers to individuals having attained ISCED levels 3 and 4.

High levels of education attained refers to individuals having attained ISCED levels 5 and 6.

Methodology

Data for non-European countries were calculated from country-specific household surveys (see Annex 3). Data for countries in the European Statistical System come from the pilot EU Adult Education Survey (AES). The EU AES was conducted by 29 countries in the EU, EFTA and candidate countries between 2005 and 2008. The EU AES is a pilot exercise using a common framework, including a standard questionnaire, tools and quality reporting.

To calculate **expected hours in non-formal education over the working life (25-64 year-olds)**, the fictive cohort method is used, in which the total expected hours in non-formal education (NFE) equals the sum of the hours in NFE spent by the individuals of the same age at the present time. The method assumes that the behaviour of people would remain constant over time, so that the hours of participation of older people today would reflect the future hours of participation of today's young people. The result changes as the behaviour of people changes over time, so we would assume the figure to reflect these changes in behaviour.

Method of calculation:

Basic formula:

$$EXHR = \sum_{AGE=25}^{64} HR\_PER\_ADULT\_PER\_YEAR \text{ of } age, \text{ where:}$$

EXHR = EXPECTED HOURS

Ideally, one needs information on the hours spent in non-formal education by fairly narrow age bands. In the data collection, the breakdowns are in 10-year age groups (25-34, 35-44, 45-54, and 55-64). A constant number of hours is used for each of the ten years in the age group.

The modified formula is:

$$EXHR = \sum_{AGE\ GROUP=1}^{4} \frac{HOURS\_TOT}{PERSONS\_TOT} * 10, \text{ where:}$$

HOURS_TOT = Total hours in NFE for the age group
PERSONS_TOT = Total Persons in the age group

The data collection also included breakdowns by age group for gender and educational attainment.

The statistical data for Israel are supplied by and under the responsibility of the relevant Israeli authorities. The use of such data by the OECD is without prejudice to the status of the Golan Heights, East Jerusalem and Israeli settlements in the West Bank under the terms of international law.

C5

References

OECD (2007d), *Education at a Glance 2007: OECD Indicators*, OECD, Paris.

OECD (2010h), *Education at a Glance 2010: OECD Indicators*, OECD, Paris.

The following additional material relevant to this indicator is available on line:

- *Table C5.1c Participation rate, hours of instruction per participant, per adult and expected hours in all non-formal education (NFE) and in job-related NFE, by gender, 2007*
  StatLink http://dx.doi.org/10.1787/888932464809
- *Table C5.1d Participation rate and expected hours in all non-formal education, by educational attainment, 2007*
  StatLink http://dx.doi.org/10.1787/888932464828
- *Table C5.2b. Hours of instruction per participant and per adult in all non-formal education (NFE) and in job-related NFE, by gender and age group, 2007*
  StatLink http://dx.doi.org/10.1787/888932464866
- *Table C5.2c. Hours of instruction per participant and per adult in all non-formal education (NFE) and in job-related NFE, by gender and educational attainment, 2007*
  StatLink http://dx.doi.org/10.1787/888932464885
- *Table C5.2d. Hours of instruction per participant and per adult in all non-formal education (NFE) and in job-related NFE, by gender and labour force status, 2007*
  StatLink http://dx.doi.org/10.1787/888932464904
- *Table C5.2e. Hours of instruction per participant and per adult in all non-formal education (NFE) and in job-related NFE, by educational attainment and age group, 2007*
  StatLink http://dx.doi.org/10.1787/888932464923
- *Table C5.3b. Participation in formal and non-formal education by type of education and gender, 2007*
  StatLink http://dx.doi.org/10.1787/888932464961
- *Table C5.3c Participation in formal and non-formal education, by type of education and age group, 2007*
  StatLink http://dx.doi.org/10.1787/888932464980
- *Table C5.3d Participation in formal and non-formal education, by type of education and labour force status, 2007*
  StatLink http://dx.doi.org/10.1787/888932464999
- *Table C5.4b Proportion of individuals who have looked for and found information, by gender, 2007*
  StatLink http://dx.doi.org/10.1787/888932465037
- *Table C5.4c Proportion of individuals who have looked for and found information, by age group, 2007*
  StatLink http://dx.doi.org/10.1787/888932465056
- *Table C5.4d Proportion of individuals who have looked for and found information, by gender for employed persons, 2007*
  StatLink http://dx.doi.org/10.1787/888932465075

Table C5.1a. Participation rate, hours of instruction per participant, per adult and expected hours in all non-formal education (NFE) and in job-related NFE, annual hours actually worked, and ratio of hours in job-related NFE to hours worked, 2008

	All non-formal education				Job-related non-formal education				Average annual hours actually worked per worker (2009)	Ratio of hours in job-related NFE to annual hours worked
	Participation rate	Hours per participant	Hours per adult	Expected hours	Participation rate	Hours per participant	Hours per adult	Expected hours		
	(1)	(2)	(3)	(4)	(5)	(6)	(7)	(8)	(9)	(10)
OECD										
Australia	30	m	m	m	22	m	m	m	1 713	m
Austria	40	92	35	1 365	32	69	27	1 022	1 581	0.65
Belgium[1]	33	114	30	1 244	29	86	23	942	1 550	0.61
Canada[1]	36	m	m	m	31	49	15	581	1 725	0.34
Czech Republic[1]	35	55	19	781	33	48	17	680	1 891	0.36
Denmark[1]	38	121	45	1 794	35	105	39	1 542	1 544	1.00
Estonia	40	52	21	807	36	42	17	651	1 831	0.36
Finland[2]	51	95	48	1 947	44	74	38	1 517	1 672	0.91
France[2]	32	35	11	m	29	35	10	m	1 558	m
Germany	43	76	33	1 288	38	61	26	1 017	1 390	0.73
Greece	13	86	10	389	11	64	8	288	2 119	0.14
Hungary[2]	7	111	7	305	6	86	6	235	1 968	0.12
Ireland[1]	23	m	m	m	19	m	m	m	1 584	m
Italy[2]	20	48	9	353	14	33	6	244	1 773	0.14
Korea	26	132	35	1 329	11	119	13	459	2 243	0.20
Netherlands[1]	42	59	23	911	36	46	18	703	1 378	0.51
New Zealand[2, 5]	34	47	16	622	26	45	12	450	1 729	0.26
Norway	51	78	39	1 564	47	69	35	1 369	1 408	0.97
Poland[2]	19	82	15	579	16	62	12	441	1 966	0.22
Portugal	22	93	20	790	19	65	14	548	1 719	0.32
Slovak Republic	41	58	22	828	38	43	16	630	1 693	0.37
Slovenia	36	49	18	696	26	28	10	389	1 687	0.23
Spain	27	112	27	1 039	20	68	17	616	1 648	0.37
Sweden[3]	69	73	50	2 012	61	55	38	1 527	1 611	0.95
Switzerland[4]	50	46	25	996	42	47	19	763	1 640	0.47
Turkey	13	91	12	404	9	43	5	176	1 918	0.09
United Kingdom[2]	40	48	16	659	31	39	13	529	1 646	0.32
United States[3]	46	56	26	1 015	33	42	14	551	1 681	0.33
OECD average	34	76	25	988	28	58	18	715	1 710	0.44
EU21 average	34	77	24	988	29	58	19	751	1 690	0.46

1. Year of reference 2008.
2. Year of reference 2006.
3. Year of reference 2005.
4. Year of reference 2009.
5. Excludes adults who participated only in "short seminars, lectures, workshops or special talks".

Source: OECD, LSO network special data collection, Adult Learning working group. See Annex 3 for notes *(www.oecd.org/edu/eag2011)*.

Please refer to the Reader's Guide for information concerning the symbols replacing missing data.

StatLink http://dx.doi.org/10.1787/888932464771

Table C5.1b. **Participation rate and expected hours in job-related non-formal education, by educational attainment, 2007**

	Participation rate				Expected hours			
	Educational attainment				Educational attainment			
	Not attained ISCED 3	Attained ISCED 3/4	Attained ISCED 5/6	Total	Not attained ISCED 3	Attained ISCED 3/4	Attained ISCED 5/6	Total
	(1)	(2)	(3)	(4)	(5)	(6)	(7)	(8)
OECD								
Australia	14	23	30	22	m	m	m	m
Austria	13	31	57	32	635	931	1 830	1 022
Belgium[1]	11	27	47	29	416	1 089	1 166	942
Canada[1]	12	23	41	31	379	420	734	581
Czech Republic[1]	14	33	52	33	199	556	1 668	680
Denmark[1]	18	33	53	35	1 062	1 402	2 219	1 542
Estonia	15	31	54	36	315	467	1 080	651
Finland[2]	26	39	62	44	1 130	1 288	2 141	1 517
France[2]	15	28	47	29	m	m	m	m
Germany	14	38	55	38	594	953	1 477	1 017
Greece	3	11	24	11	54	224	744	288
Hungary[2]	2	5	12	6	89	232	394	235
Ireland[1]	8	14	32	19	m	m	m	m
Italy[2]	5	19	37	14	71	318	633	244
Korea	7	7	16	11	41	430	620	459
Netherlands[1]	18	34	54	36	483	615	1 025	703
New Zealand[2, 5]	14	23	36	26	226	324	692	450
Norway	33	45	62	47	1 055	1 193	1 865	1 369
Poland[2]	3	12	41	16	77	256	1 319	441
Portugal	11	31	49	19	311	794	1 496	548
Slovak Republic	12	36	51	38	70	463	1 314	630
Slovenia	7	24	46	26	56	347	745	389
Spain	10	22	35	20	282	632	1 200	616
Sweden[3]	43	61	76	61	1 084	1 276	2 355	1 527
Switzerland[4]	11	35	62	42	178	587	1 227	763
Turkey	4	15	33	9	62	246	727	176
United Kingdom[2]	21	34	38	31	603	565	467	529
United States[3]	9	23	46	33	128	387	759	551
OECD average	13	26	43	27	369	615	1 150	688
EU21 average	14	28	46	29	418	689	1 293	751

1. Year of reference 2008.
2. Year of reference 2006.
3. Year of reference 2005.
4. Year of reference 2009.
5. Excludes adults who participated only in "short seminars, lectures, workshops or special talks".
Source: OECD, LSO network special data collection, Adult Learning working group. See Annex 3 for notes *(www.oecd.org/edu/eag2011)*.
Please refer to the Reader's Guide for information concerning the symbols replacing missing data.
StatLink http://dx.doi.org/10.1787/888932464790

Table C5.2a. [1/2] **Hours of instruction per participant and per adult, in all non-formal education (NFE) and in job-related NFE, by educational attainment and labour force status, 2007**

		Not attained ISCED 3				Attained ISCED 3/4				Attained ISCED 5/6				Total			
		Hours per participant		Hours per adult		Hours per participant		Hours per adult		Hours per participant		Hours per adult		Hours per participant		Hours per adult	
	Labour force status	All NFE	Job-related NFE	All NFE	Job-related NFE	All NFE	Job-related NFE	All NFE	Job-related NFE	All NFE	Job-related NFE	All NFE	Job-related NFE	All NFE	Job-related NFE	All NFE	Job-related NFE
		1	2	3	4	5	6	7	8	9	10	11	12	13	14	15	16
OECD Austria	Employed	85	77	18	16	84	66	38	30	99	79	65	53	88	71	40	32
	Unemployed	199	180	60	55	192	147	70	53	c	c	c	c	189	153	70	57
	Not in the labour force	115	46	11	4	79	32	15	6	64	21	28	9	81	32	15	6
	Total	107	85	19	15	87	65	34	25	97	75	61	47	92	69	35	27
Belgium[1]	Employed	100	67	16	10	132	112	36	30	84	67	42	34	101	81	34	27
	Unemployed	155	92	14	8	354	257	71	52	261	234	82	74	274	204	44	33
	Not in the labour force	240	178	10	7	140	72	16	8	154	33	33	7	168	78	16	7
	Total	127	86	13	9	147	118	35	28	92	68	42	31	114	86	30	23
Canada[1]	Employed	m	62	m	10	m	45	m	12	m	48	m	21	m	48	m	17
	Unemployed	m	c	m	c	m	63	m	6	m	25	m	7	m	33	m	5
	Not in the labour force	m	37	m	c	m	303	m	5	m	68	m	4	m	110	m	3
	Total	m	61	m	7	m	48	m	11	m	48	m	19	m	49	m	15
Czech Republic[1]	Employed	26	25	7	7	45	41	19	18	88	75	57	49	54	48	25	22
	Unemployed	136	136	4	4	126	94	17	13	c	c	c	c	124	91	14	10
	Not in the labour force	101	92	1	c	53	18	3	1	81	52	12	8	61	28	3	2
	Total	30	29	4	4	46	41	16	14	88	74	50	42	55	48	19	17
Denmark[1]	Employed	158	127	43	35	119	106	45	40	111	105	64	61	121	109	51	46
	Unemployed	203	200	14	14	77	61	20	16	c	c	c	c	88	76	17	15
	Not in the labour force	174	60	27	9	89	34	9	3	84	60	18	13	136	55	20	8
	Total	162	115	37	26	117	103	40	35	109	103	59	56	121	105	45	39
Estonia	Employed	56	44	14	11	41	35	17	14	59	49	38	32	51	43	24	20
	Unemployed	c	c	c	c	64	41	10	6	c	c	c	c	72	34	12	6
	Not in the labour force	47	3	2	c	76	31	6	3	50	17	12	4	60	22	6	2
	Total	55	40	10	7	43	35	15	12	59	48	34	28	52	42	21	17
Finland[2]	Employed	65	47	28	20	71	58	37	31	94	77	70	57	81	65	48	39
	Unemployed	137	87	35	23	201	162	65	53	156	117	59	45	170	128	53	40
	Not in the labour force	297	163	43	24	167	130	45	35	153	104	65	44	184	126	49	34
	Total	98	64	33	21	89	72	41	33	100	80	69	55	95	74	48	38
France[2]	Employed	m	m	m	m	m	m	m	m	m	m	m	m	29	28	12	m
	Unemployed	m	m	m	m	m	m	m	m	m	m	m	m	111	118	32	m
	Not in the labour force	m	m	m	m	m	m	m	m	m	m	m	m	61	82	8	m
	Total	m	m	m	m	m	m	m	m	m	m	m	m	35	35	12	m
Germany	Employed	48	39	12	9	63	52	32	27	75	64	50	43	66	56	34	29
	Unemployed	206	180	27	24	156	129	45	37	109	56	42	22	153	121	40	31
	Not in the labour force	250	184	27	20	98	54	22	12	94	48	30	15	116	69	25	15
	Total	100	79	18	15	72	57	31	25	78	62	47	38	76	61	33	26
Greece	Employed	58	41	3	2	75	57	11	8	85	75	24	21	79	64	12	10
	Unemployed	98	10	2	c	173	107	19	12	173	136	35	28	168	116	18	13
	Not in the labour force	92	24	1	c	103	3	5	0	138	34	15	4	112	16	3	c
	Total	63	38	2	1	83	55	10	7	93	77	24	20	86	64	10	8
Hungary[2]	Employed	93	87	5	5	108	85	9	7	92	76	15	12	101	82	10	8
	Unemployed	291	291	2	2	268	248	17	16	84	68	14	11	238	220	11	10
	Not in the labour force	239	49	1	c	206	70	3	1	62	21	4	1	156	49	2	1
	Total	120	91	3	2	123	94	8	6	89	72	13	10	111	86	7	6
Italy[2]	Employed	40	28	4	3	46	36	13	10	46	37	22	18	45	35	11	9
	Unemployed	70	34	3	1	91	58	13	9	64	41	21	14	76	47	9	6
	Not in the labour force	48	9	2	c	59	14	8	2	63	33	15	8	56	15	4	1
	Total	42	24	3	2	49	34	12	9	48	37	21	16	48	33	9	6
Korea	Employed	54	23	10	3	109	64	18	4	129	50	45	18	118	41	30	10
	Unemployed	c	c	c	c	420	328	126	99	259	137	77	41	310	197	79	50
	Not in the labour force	85	31	15	0	143	53	39	14	124	19	50	8	130	38	38	10
	Total	67	23	11	2	141	55	29	11	136	49	48	17	132	47	35	13
Netherlands[1]	Employed	81	64	21	16	54	45	24	20	59	48	36	30	59	49	28	23
	Unemployed	c	c	c	c	c	c	c	c	c	c	c	c	95	79	32	27
	Not in the labour force	75	30	8	3	43	24	8	4	54	20	20	7	55	24	10	4
	Total	81	57	15	10	53	42	20	16	58	46	34	27	59	46	23	18

1. Year of reference 2008.
2. Year of reference 2006.
3. Year of reference 2005.
4. Year of reference 2009.

Source: OECD, LSO network special data collection, Adult Learning working group. See Annex 3 for notes *(www.oecd.org/edu/eag2011)*.

Please refer to the Reader's Guide for information concerning the symbols replacing missing data.

StatLink http://dx.doi.org/10.1787/888932464847

Table C5.2a. [2/2] Hours of instruction per participant and per adult, in all non-formal education (NFE) and in job-related NFE, by educational attainment and labour force status, 2007

		Not attained ISCED 3				Attained ISCED 3/4				Attained ISCED 5/6				Total			
		Hours per participant		Hours per adult		Hours per participant		Hours per adult		Hours per participant		Hours per adult		Hours per participant		Hours per adult	
	Labour force status	All NFE	Job-related NFE	All NFE	Job-related NFE	All NFE	Job-related NFE	All NFE	Job-related NFE	All NFE	Job-related NFE	All NFE	Job-related NFE	All NFE	Job-related NFE	All NFE	Job-related NFE
		1	2	3	4	5	6	7	8	9	10	11	12	13	14	15	16
OECD New Zealand[2]	Employed	33	30	8	6	38	35	12	9	44	43	22	17	40	38	15	12
	Unemployed	45	42	7	4	72	64	12	9	74	113	21	18	65	76	13	10
	Not in the labour force	149	91	13	6	71	54	11	4	108	63	35	23	105	66	19	11
	Total	47	42	9	6	41	37	12	8	50	50	23	18	47	45	16	12
Norway	Employed	82	77	38	35	65	59	35	32	80	73	56	51	74	68	43	39
	Unemployed	c	c	c	c	c	c	c	c	c	c	c	c	187	110	59	34
	Not in the labour force	162	103	19	12	102	65	19	12	91	48	29	15	114	69	21	13
	Total	93	79	33	28	69	61	33	29	81	72	54	48	78	69	39	35
Poland[2]	Employed	38	25	3	2	62	52	12	10	97	77	50	40	79	64	21	17
	Unemployed	151	114	6	4	106	64	8	5	163	82	38	19	127	73	11	6
	Not in the labour force	167	42	2	c	111	16	3	c	91	27	12	4	109	23	3	1
	Total	68	37	3	1	66	50	9	7	98	75	45	35	82	62	15	12
Portugal	Employed	71	60	12	10	79	60	33	25	93	74	56	44	80	64	22	18
	Unemployed	286	123	20	8	281	187	33	22	180	108	89	54	238	124	29	15
	Not in the labour force	285	2	8	c	164	21	29	4	62	5	11	1	197	9	10	0
	Total	91	60	12	8	90	60	33	22	97	74	55	41	93	65	20	14
Slovak Republic	Employed	21	19	6	6	43	35	18	15	87	65	51	38	56	44	26	21
	Unemployed	30	2	2	0	121	33	14	4	c	c	c	c	112	40	12	4
	Not in the labour force	70	c	1	c	58	21	3	1	86	27	15	5	68	22	5	2
	Total	25	16	3	2	45	35	15	12	87	64	46	34	58	43	22	16
Slovenia	Employed	21	16	3	2	41	29	16	11	49	33	33	22	44	30	19	13
	Unemployed	19	6	2	1	116	45	27	10	56	13	24	6	85	31	19	7
	Not in the labour force	121	6	7	c	68	7	13	1	60	4	23	2	72	6	12	1
	Total	40	12	4	1	49	27	16	9	50	31	32	19	49	28	18	10
Spain	Employed	80	52	14	9	103	60	31	18	108	83	45	35	100	70	29	20
	Unemployed	158	62	20	8	193	63	45	14	186	129	59	41	177	86	33	16
	Not in the labour force	156	27	14	2	144	42	23	6	202	56	50	14	165	37	19	4
	Total	101	48	14	7	113	59	31	16	117	84	46	33	112	68	27	17
Sweden[3]	Employed	55	43	35	27	60	47	45	35	90	74	83	68	70	56	54	43
	Unemployed	114	79	45	31	83	53	45	29	88	50	40	23	93	60	43	28
	Not in the labour force	108	53	26	13	73	43	28	16	108	50	62	29	93	48	35	18
	Total	64	46	33	24	62	47	42	32	92	71	78	60	73	55	50	38
Switzerland[4]	Employed	38	36	7	5	42	41	22	17	50	51	40	34	46	46	27	22
	Unemployed	89	92	22	15	68	76	27	23	77	82	39	30	74	80	29	23
	Not in the labour force	39	41	3	1	42	45	11	3	53	45	20	6	45	45	11	3
	Total	43	42	7	4	42	42	21	15	50	51	38	31	46	47	25	19
Turkey	Employed	51	27	5	3	65	46	17	12	87	62	40	28	70	46	14	9
	Unemployed	105	55	7	4	104	58	20	11	192	154	63	50	132	87	15	10
	Not in the labour force	165	18	7	1	137	26	18	3	172	32	27	5	158	22	9	1
	Total	92	25	6	2	82	42	17	9	98	63	38	25	91	43	12	5
United Kingdom[2]	Employed	65	53	22	18	50	44	19	17	32	25	15	12	45	38	18	15
	Unemployed	120	120	21	21	c	c	c	c	c	c	c	c	106	97	21	19
	Not in the labour force	60	34	8	4	53	33	13	8	66	44	16	11	60	37	11	7
	Total	66	52	16	13	50	43	18	15	36	28	16	12	48	39	16	13
United States[3]	Employed	50	28	12	4	58	43	24	13	56	42	35	22	56	42	29	17
	Unemployed	115	172	30	11	74	19	11	2	61	51	33	20	80	63	25	11
	Not in the labour force	42	30	6	1	52	48	12	3	52	35	21	4	51	38	14	3
	Total	55	39	12	3	57	43	20	10	57	42	33	19	56	42	26	14
OECD average	Employed	61	48	14	11	69	54	24	19	79	62	44	34	70	55	27	22
	Unemployed	114	83	14	10	139	94	30	20	91	64	31	20	142	98	30	19
	Not in the labour force	137	54	11	4	97	50	15	6	95	39	26	10	105	45	15	6
	Total	77	52	13	9	76	55	23	17	82	62	42	31	76	56	25	18
EU21 average	Employed	64	51	15	12	71	57	25	20	80	66	45	37	71	58	27	23
	Unemployed	132	95	16	11	145	97	29	19	84	57	28	19	142	100	27	19
	Not in the labour force	147	56	11	5	99	37	14	6	93	36	25	10	106	41	14	6
	Total	80	54	13	9	77	58	24	18	83	65	43	34	77	58	24	19

1. Year of reference 2008.
2. Year of reference 2006.
3. Year of reference 2005.
4. Year of reference 2009.

Source: OECD, LSO network special data collection, Adult Learning working group. See Annex 3 for notes *(www.oecd.org/edu/eag2011)*.

Please refer to the Reader's Guide for information concerning the symbols replacing missing data.

StatLink http://dx.doi.org/10.1787/888932464847

Table C5.3a. Participation in formal and non-formal education, by type of education and educational attainment, 2007

Participation rates

	Not attained ISCED 3						Attained ISCED 3/4						Attained ISCED 5/6						Total					
			Type of education						Type of education						Type of education						Type of education			
	Formal	Non-formal	Formal only	Formal and non-formal	Non-formal only	No participation	Formal	Non-formal	Formal only	Formal and non-formal	Non-formal only	No participation	Formal	Non-formal	Formal only	Formal and non-formal	Non-formal only	No participation	Formal	Non-formal	Formal only	Formal and non-formal	Non-formal only	No participation
	(1)	(2)	(3)	(4)	(5)	(6)	(7)	(8)	(9)	(10)	(11)	(12)	(13)	(14)	(15)	(16)	(17)	(18)	(19)	(20)	(21)	(22)	(23)	(24)
OECD																								
Australia	5	19	4	1	18	77	13	30	8	5	26	62	18	42	11	6	36	47	12	30	8	4	26	62
Austria	1	18	c	c	18	81	4	40	2	2	38	58	8	65	c	5	60	32	4	40	2	2	38	58
Belgium[1]	7	15	5	2	13	80	12	31	7	5	27	62	19	54	9	10	44	37	12	33	7	5	28	59
Canada[1]	4	14	4	c	14	82	8	27	6	2	25	68	13	47	7	6	41	46	10	36	6	4	32	58
Czech Republic[1]	1	15	c	c	14	85	3	35	2	1	33	63	10	57	5	4	53	38	4	35	2	2	34	62
Denmark[1]	7	23	7	c	22	70	10	35	6	3	32	59	13	55	8	5	49	37	10	38	7	3	34	55
Estonia	1	19	c	c	18	80	4	34	2	2	32	64	9	58	c	6	52	39	5	40	2	3	37	58
Finland[2]	4	34	c	c	31	65	12	46	5	6	40	48	13	69	4	9	60	27	10	51	4	6	45	45
France[2]	3	17	2	1	17	81	5	31	3	2	29	66	9	52	5	4	49	43	5	32	3	2	30	65
Germany	3	18	c	c	17	80	5	43	2	3	40	55	7	60	3	4	56	37	5	43	2	3	40	55
Greece	0	4	0	c	4	96	3	13	2	c	13	85	5	28	4	c	27	68	2	13	2	1	12	86
Hungary[2]	0	2	c	c	2	97	3	6	2	c	6	91	6	15	5	c	14	81	3	7	2	c	6	91
Ireland[1]	2	11	1	1	12	86	5	18	3	2	18	77	11	37	5	5	36	54	6	23	3	3	23	71
Italy[2]	1	8	c	c	8	92	6	27	3	3	24	70	14	47	5	9	38	49	4	20	2	2	18	78
Korea	0	17	c	c	17	83	6	21	c	c	18	75	7	36	4	3	32	61	6	26	3	2	24	70
Netherlands[1]	4	24	c	c	22	75	6	40	c	4	36	58	11	61	4	7	54	35	7	42	2	4	38	55
New Zealand[2]	13	40	6	7	33	54	20	56	8	12	44	36	25	78	6	19	59	16	20	61	7	14	47	33
Norway	6	36	c	c	32	62	7	48	4	4	44	48	17	66	6	11	55	28	10	51	4	6	45	45
Poland[2]	1	4	c	c	4	95	3	13	2	1	12	84	16	46	8	8	38	46	6	19	3	2	16	78
Portugal	4	13	3	1	12	84	14	37	8	6	31	54	15	58	6	8	49	36	7	22	4	3	20	74
Slovak Republic	0	14	c	c	14	86	5	38	2	3	36	59	11	57	5	6	51	38	6	41	3	3	38	56
Slovenia	2	11	c	c	11	87	9	34	5	4	30	61	14	63	4	9	54	32	9	36	4	4	32	59
Spain	2	16	1	c	15	83	7	31	5	2	29	65	13	44	7	5	38	49	6	27	4	2	25	69
Sweden[3]	6	52	4	3	50	44	9	69	3	5	64	28	25	85	5	20	65	10	13	69	4	9	61	27
Switzerland	1	20	1	1	19	79	6	52	2	4	48	46	14	75	3	11	65	21	8	55	2	6	50	43
United Kingdom[2]	8	28	5	3	26	67	17	42	10	7	35	47	21	51	12	9	42	37	15	40	9	6	34	51
United States[3]	5	21	2	3	18	77	4	35	2	2	33	63	12	58	4	8	51	37	9	46	3	5	40	51
OECD average	3	19	2	1	18	79	8	35	4	3	31	61	13	54	5	7	47	40	8	36	4	4	32	60
EU21 average	3	17	1	1	16	81	7	33	4	3	30	63	12	53	5	7	46	41	7	34	4	3	30	63

1. Year of reference 2008.
2. Year of reference 2006.
3. Year of reference 2005.

Source: OECD, LSO network special data collection, Adult Learning working group. See Annex 3 for notes *(www.oecd.org/edu/eag2011)*.

Please refer to the Reader's Guide for information concerning the symbols replacing missing data.

StatLink http://dx.doi.org/10.1787/888932464942

C5

Table C5.4a. Proportion of individuals who have looked for and found information, by educational attainment, 2007

		Persons who have looked for information				...of which have found information			
		Not attained ISCED 3	Attained ISCED 3/4	Attained ISCED 5/6	Total	Not attained ISCED 3	Attained ISCED 3/4	Attained ISCED 5/6	Total
OECD	Australia	19	31	46	32	88	91	94	92
	Austria	15	30	50	30	74	86	94	87
	Belgium[1]	12	21	32	22	86	85	89	87
	Canada[1]	17	27	48	37	80	90	92	91
	Finland[2]	25	37	55	40	86	91	93	91
	France[2]	14	23	38	24	m	m	m	m
	Germany	9	15	29	18	64	79	91	83
	Greece	2	8	21	9	78	88	94	91
	Hungary[2]	2	7	17	8	74	85	86	85
	Italy[2]	3	12	25	9	75	84	92	85
	Korea	7	35	54	39	74	86	83	84
	Netherlands[1]	45	58	71	58	53	69	86	72
	Poland[2]	5	13	42	18	84	91	96	93
	Portugal	9	28	46	17	90	91	96	92
	Slovak Republic	11	33	57	37	97	96	98	97
	Slovenia	7	21	46	24	81	92	95	93
	Spain	12	26	38	22	89	93	94	93
	Sweden[3]	19	34	48	34	85	90	94	91
	United Kingdom[2]	m	m	m	m	41	65	80	68
	OECD average	13	26	42	27	78	86	92	87
	EU21 average	13	24	41	25	77	86	92	87

1. Year of reference 2008.
2. Year of reference 2006.
3. Year of reference 2005.

Source: OECD, LSO network special data collection, Adult Learning working group. See Annex 3 for notes *(www.oecd.org/edu/eag2011)*.
Please refer to the Reader's Guide for information concerning the symbols replacing missing data.
StatLink http://dx.doi.org/10.1787/888932465018

Chapter

The Learning Environment and Organisation of Schools

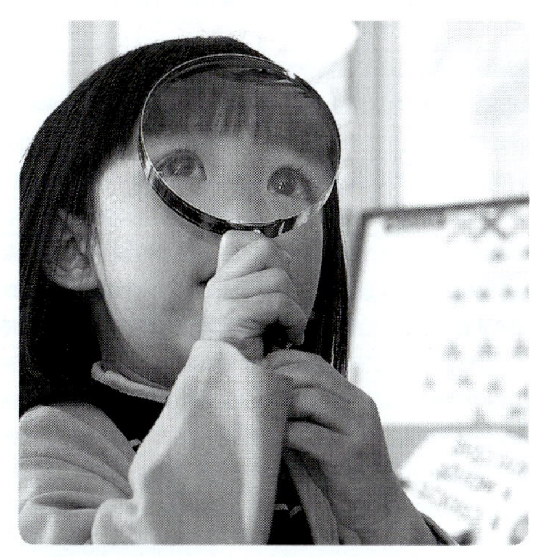

HOW MUCH TIME DO STUDENTS SPEND IN THE CLASSROOM?

- Students in OECD countries are expected to receive an average of 6 732 hours of instruction between the ages of 7 and 14, and most of that intended instruction time is compulsory.
- On average across OECD countries, instruction in reading, writing and literature, mathematics and science represents 48% of the compulsory instruction time for 9-11 year-olds and 41% for 12-14 year-olds.

Chart D1.1. Total number of intended instruction hours in public institutions between the ages of 7 and 14 (2009)

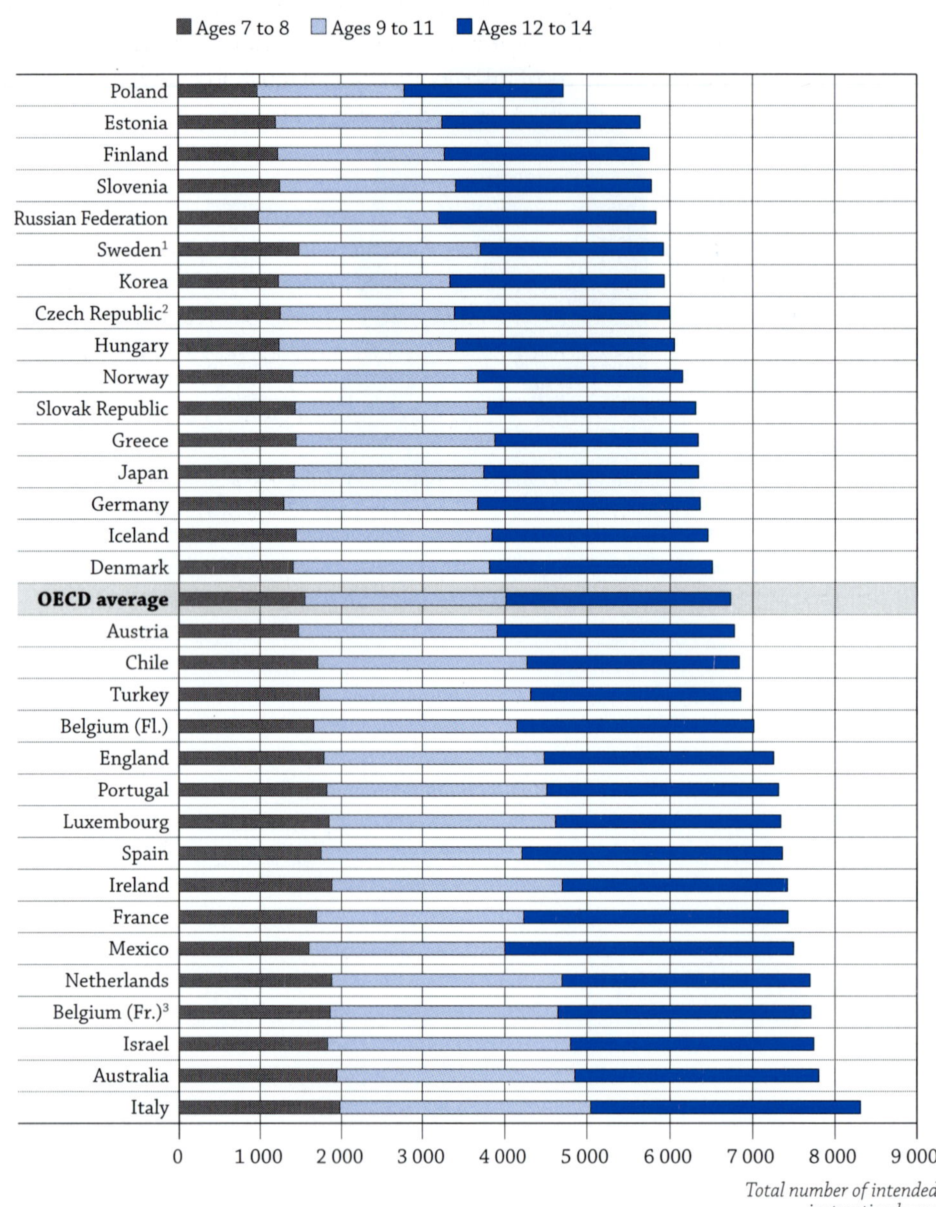

1. Estimated because breakdown by age not available.
2. Minimum number of hours per year.
3. "Ages 12-14" covers ages 12-13 only.

Countries are ranked in ascending order of the total number of intended instruction hours.

Source: OECD. Table D1.1. See Annex 3 for notes (*www.oecd.org/edu/eag2011*).

StatLink http://dx.doi.org/10.1787/888932461807

Context

Instruction time in formal classroom settings accounts for a large portion of public investment in student learning and is a central component of effective schooling. The amount of instruction time and after-school lessons available to students is an important indication of students' opportunities to learn. Matching resources with students' needs and making optimal use of time are central to education policy. The main costs of education are the use and deployment of teachers, institutional maintenance and other educational resources. The length of time during which these resources are made available to students (as partly shown in this indicator) is thus an important factor in determining how funds for education are allocated (see Indicator B7).

Countries make various choices concerning the overall amount of time devoted to instruction and which subjects should be compulsory. These choices reflect national and/or regional priorities and preferences on what material students should be taught and at what age. Countries usually have statutory or regulatory requirements regarding hours of instruction. These are most often stipulated as the minimum number of hours of instruction a school must offer and are based on the notion that sufficient teaching time is required for good learning outcomes.

Other findings

- In OECD countries, **compulsory instruction time** for 7-8 year-old students averages 749 hours per year and **intended instruction time** averages 775 hours per year. Students aged 9 to 11 receive, on average, about 44 more hours of compulsory education per year than 7-8 year-olds, while students aged 12 to 14 receive about 80 more hours per year than 9-11 year-olds. Students aged 9 to 11 receive just over 46 more hours of intended instruction per year than 7-8 year-olds, and students aged 12 to 14 receive 86 more hours per year than 9-11 year-olds.
- For 9-11 year-olds, **the proportion of the compulsory curriculum that is devoted to reading, writing and literature varies widely**, from 11% in Indonesia to 30% or more in France, Mexico and the Netherlands.

Analysis

Total intended instruction time

Total intended instruction time is an estimate of the number of hours during which students are taught both compulsory and non-compulsory parts of the curriculum as per public regulations.

Between the ages of 7 and 8, students in OECD countries are expected to receive 1 550 hours of instruction, those between the ages of 9 and 11 are expected to receive 2 462 hours, and those between the ages of 12 and 14 are expected to receive 2 720 hours. Most of this instruction time is compulsory.

While the average instruction time for students in OECD countries between the ages of 7 and 14 is 6 732 hours, formal teaching-time requirements range from 4 715 hours in Poland to 8 316 hours in Italy. During these hours, schools are obliged to offer instruction in compulsory and non-compulsory subjects. The total intended instruction time for this age range is a good indicator of students' theoretical workload in school, but it cannot be interpreted as the actual amount of instruction time students receive during the years they spend in initial education.

Annual instruction time should be examined together with the length of compulsory education. In some countries with a heavier student workload, compulsory education covers fewer years and students drop out of the school system earlier; in other countries, a more even distribution of workload and study time over more years ultimately means a larger number of total instruction hours for all. Table D1.1 shows the age range at which over 90% of the population is in education (see Indicator C1). Chart D1.1 shows the total amount of intended instruction time students should receive between the ages of 7 and 14. Intended instruction time does not capture the quality of learning opportunities provided or the level or quality of the human and material resources involved (see Indicator D2, which shows the number of teachers relative to the student population).

In some countries, intended instruction time varies considerably among regions or types of schools. In many countries, local education authorities or schools determine the number and allocation of hours of instruction. Intended instruction time can also differ from the actual instruction time. Additional teaching time is often planned for enrichment or remedial courses (Box D1.1). However, time may be lost because of student absences or a lack of qualified substitutes to replace absent teachers.

Box D1.1. **After-school lessons**

Intended instruction time only captures the time spent by students in formal classroom settings. This is only a part of the total time students spend receiving instruction. Instruction also occurs outside the classroom and/or school. Secondary school students are often encouraged to take after-school classes in subjects already taught in school to help them improve their performance in key subjects. Students can take part in after-school lessons in the form of remedial "catch-up" classes or enrichment courses, with individual tutors or in group lessons provided by school teachers, or other independent courses. These lessons can be financed publically, or can be financed by students and their families.

Findings from the 2009 PISA survey suggest that the amount of time spent in these after-school lessons differs widely among countries. On average across OECD countries, a large proportion of students reported that they attend after-school lessons for up to four hours a week: in mathematics (26%), science (17%), language-of-instruction (reading, writing and literature) (16%), and other subjects (19%). Some students even spend more than four hours a week attending after-school lessons: in mathematics (7%), language-of-instruction (5%), science (5%) and other subjects (7%). In general, after-school lessons in mathematics are most common. In Estonia, Greece, Korea, the Russian Federation and Shanghai-China, more than 45% of students spend up to 4 hours a week in after-school lessons in mathematics; an additional 20% or more of students in Korea, Indonesia and Shanghai-China spend more than 4 hours a week. A similar pattern is observed for the other subjects (Table D1.3, available on line).

Compulsory instruction time

Total compulsory instruction time is the estimated number of hours during which students are taught both the compulsory core curriculum and flexible parts of the compulsory curriculum. In OECD countries, students between the ages of 7 and 14 receive an average of 6 497 hours of compulsory instruction.

Intended instruction time is fully compulsory for all age groups between 7 and 14 years in Australia, the Czech Republic, Denmark, England, Estonia, Germany, Greece, Iceland, Israel, Japan, Korea, Luxembourg, Mexico, the Netherlands, Norway, the Russian Federation, Slovenia, Spain and Sweden. Except for Australia, England, Israel, Luxembourg, Mexico, the Netherlands and Spain, the total length of intended instruction time in these countries is less than the OECD average. Intended instruction time is also fully compulsory at age 15 in these 19 countries, except in Israel, and except in Japan, for which data are missing. In France and Ireland, although total intended instruction time is fully compulsory for 7-8 year-olds and 9-11 year-olds, it is not compulsory for the older age groups. In Finland, total intended instruction time is only fully compulsory for 7-8 year-olds.

OECD countries report an average annual total compulsory instruction time in classroom settings of 749 hours for 7-8 year-olds, 793 hours for 9-11 year-olds and 873 hours for 12-14 year-olds. Most 15-year-olds are enrolled in programmes that provide an average of 902 hours of compulsory instruction (Table D1.1).

Instruction time in reading, writing and literature, mathematics and science

In OECD countries, 9-11 year-olds do not necessarily attend separate classes for each subject they study. Students at this age spend an average of 48% of the compulsory curriculum on three basic subjects: reading, writing and literature (23%), mathematics (16%) and science (9%). On average, an additional 9% of the compulsory curriculum is devoted to modern foreign languages and 8% to social studies. Together with the arts (11%) and physical education (9%), these seven study areas form the major part of the curriculum for this age group in all OECD and other G20 countries with available data. Ancient Greek and/or Latin, technology, religion, practical and vocational skills and other subjects make up the remainder (11%) of the compulsory core curriculum for 9-11 year-olds (Table D1.2a and Chart D1.2a).

Chart D1.2a. Instruction time per subject as a percentage of total compulsory instruction time for 9-11 year-olds (2009)

Percentage of intended instruction time devoted to various subject areas within the total compulsory curriculum

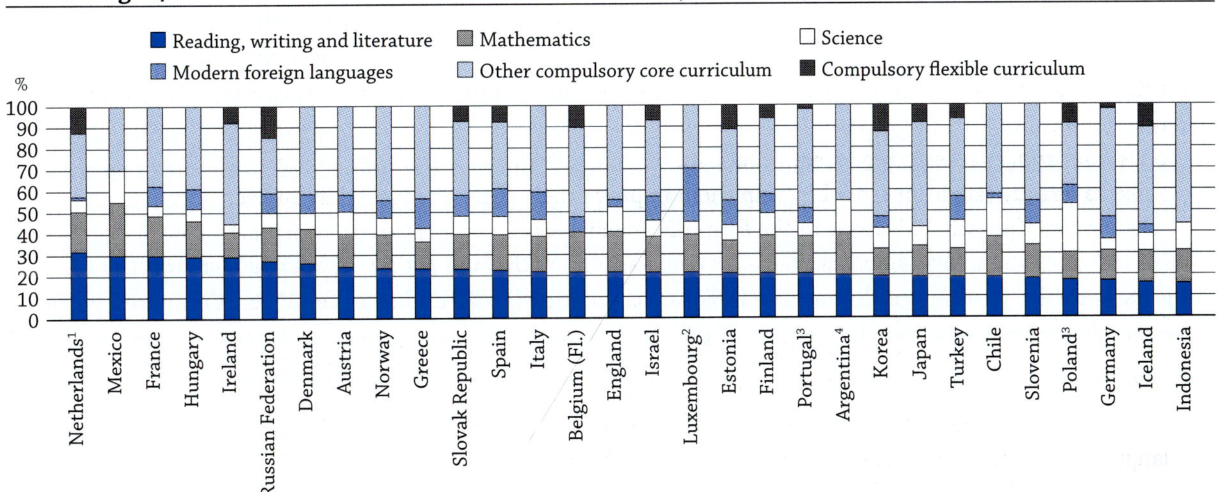

1. Includes 11-year-olds only.
2. German as a language of instruction is included in "Reading, writing and literature" in addition to the mother tongue Luxemburgish.
3. Includes 10-11 year-olds only.
4. Year of reference 2008.

Countries are ranked in descending order of the proportion of intended instruction hours devoted to reading, writing and literature.

Source: OECD. Argentina, Indonesia: UNESCO Institute for Statistics (World Education Indicators Programme). Table D1.2a. See Annex 3 for notes (*www.oecd.org/edu/eag2011*).

StatLink http://dx.doi.org/10.1787/888932461826

Chart D1.2b. Instruction time per subject as a percentage of total compulsory instruction time for 12-14 year-olds (2009)

Percentage of intended instruction time devoted to various subject areas within the total compulsory curriculum

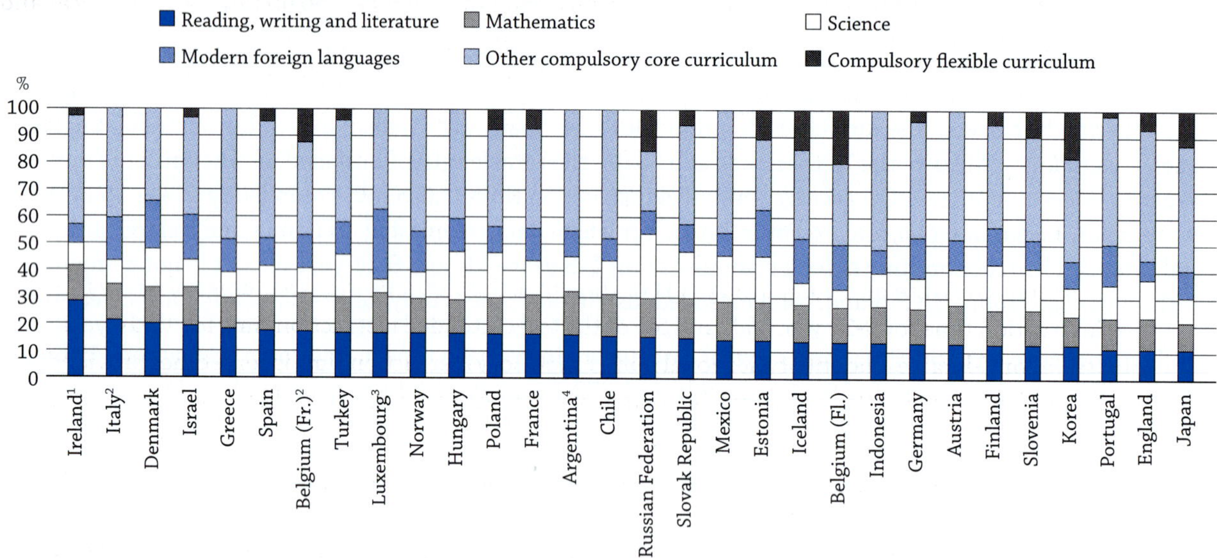

1. For 13-14 year-olds, "Arts" is included in "Non-compulsory curriculum".
2. Includes 12-13 year-olds only.
3. German as a language of instruction is included in "Reading, writing and literature" in addition to the mother tongue Luxemburgish.
4. Year of reference 2008.

Countries are ranked in descending order of the proportion of intended instruction hours devoted to reading, writing and literature.

Source: OECD. Argentina, Indonesia: UNESCO Institute for Statistics (World Education Indicators Programme). Table D1.2b. See Annex 3 for notes (*www.oecd.org/edu/eag2011*).

StatLink http://dx.doi.org/10.1787/888932461845

On average, the largest portion of the curriculum for 9-11 year-olds is devoted to reading and writing, but the differences among countries are greater than in other subjects. For example, in Indonesia, reading and writing accounts for 11% of compulsory instruction time while in France, Mexico and the Netherlands, it accounts for 30% or more of compulsory instruction time. There are also sizeable variations between countries in the time spent learning modern foreign languages. In Argentina, Chile, England, Japan, Mexico and the Netherlands, instruction in modern foreign languages accounts for 3% or less of instruction time; in Estonia, Germany, Greece, Israel, Italy, the Slovak Republic, Slovenia, Spain and Turkey it accounts for 10% or more of instruction time; and in Luxembourg, instruction in modern foreign languages accounts for 25% of total instruction time.

In OECD countries, an average of 41% of the compulsory curriculum for 12-14 year-olds is devoted to three subjects: reading, writing and literature (16%), mathematics (13%) and science (12%). Compared with the younger age group, a relatively larger part of the curriculum for this age group is devoted to modern foreign languages (13%) and social studies (12%), and somewhat less time is devoted to the arts (8%) and physical education (8%). Together, these seven study areas form the major part of the compulsory curriculum for lower secondary students in all OECD and partner countries. Ancient Greek and/or Latin, technology, religion, practical and vocational skills and other make up the remainder (12%) of the compulsory core curriculum for 12-14 year-olds (Table D1.2b and Chart D1.2b).

The allocation of time for the different subjects within the compulsory curriculum for 12-14 year-olds varies less among countries than it does for 9-11 year-olds. Again, one of the greatest variations is in the time spent teaching reading and writing, which ranges from 11% of compulsory instruction time in England, Japan and Portugal to 28% in Ireland, where reading and writing includes work in both English and Irish.

There is also substantial variation in the proportion of compulsory instruction time devoted to particular subjects for 9-11 year-olds compared to 12-14 year-olds. On average among OECD countries, the older age group spends about one-third less time studying reading, writing and literature than the younger age group. Conversely, time spent on science, social studies, modern foreign languages, technology and practical and vocational skills increases with students' age. These differences are larger in some countries than in others. For example, the percentage of compulsory instruction time devoted to reading, writing and literature for 12-14 year-olds is around one-half of that for 9-11 year-olds in England and Mexico. Yet in Ireland and Italy, the difference is less than 5%. Indonesia is the only country where the proportion of compulsory instruction time devoted to reading, writing and literature is higher for 12-14 year-olds than for 9-11 year-olds. Clearly, countries place different emphases both on subjects and on when they should be taught to students.

Among OECD countries, the non-compulsory part of the curriculum accounts for an average of 4% of the total intended instruction time for 9-11 year-olds and 5% of the total intended instruction time for 12-14 year-olds. Nevertheless, a considerable amount of additional non-compulsory instruction time is sometimes provided. For 9-11 year-olds, all intended instruction time is compulsory in most countries, but additional non-compulsory time accounts for as much as 27% of total instruction time in Chile, 20% in Hungary and Turkey, 12% in Italy and 11% in Belgium (French Community). For 12-14 year-olds, non-compulsory instruction time is a feature in Argentina, Austria, Belgium (French Community), Chile, Finland, France, Hungary, Indonesia, Ireland, Italy, Poland, Portugal, the Slovak Republic and Turkey, ranging from 3% in Portugal and the Slovak Republic to 32% in Hungary (Tables D1.2a and D1.2b).

On average among OECD countries, the flexible part of the curriculum accounts for some 4% of compulsory instruction time for 9-11 year-olds and 6% for 12-14 year-olds. Within the compulsory part of the curriculum, students have varying degrees of freedom to choose the subjects they want to study. The Czech Republic allows complete flexibility (100%) in the compulsory curriculum for 9-14 year-olds. They are followed by Australia, which allows 59% flexibility in the compulsory curriculum for 9-11 year-olds and 42% for 12-14 year-olds. Belgium, Estonia, Iceland, Japan, Korea, the Russian Federation and Slovenia allow 10% or more flexibility in the compulsory curriculum for 12-14 year-olds (Tables D1.2a and D1.2b).

Box D1.2. **Does investing in after-school classes pay off?**

Students in countries that perform well in PISA spend less time, on average, in after-school lessons and individual study, and more time in regular school lessons, than students in countries that are poor performers in PISA.

According to findings based on PISA 2006 results, learning time spent in after-school lessons and individual study is negatively related to performance. Of course, this might be because students who attend after-school classes do so for remedial purposes, rather than to enhance their school studies. Still, across countries, findings show that students tend to perform better if a high percentage of their total learning time – which includes regular school lessons, after-school lessons and individual study – is spent during normal school hours in a classroom. For example, in the high-performing countries of Australia, Finland, Japan and New Zealand, over 70% of learning in science happens during regular school science lessons. Yet time spent learning does not fully explain why students in these countries are among the best performers. In fact, in all of these countries except New Zealand, 15-year-olds spend fewer hours learning science compared to the OECD average. The same pattern is observed for mathematics and language-of-instruction learning time.

Source: OECD (2011b).

...

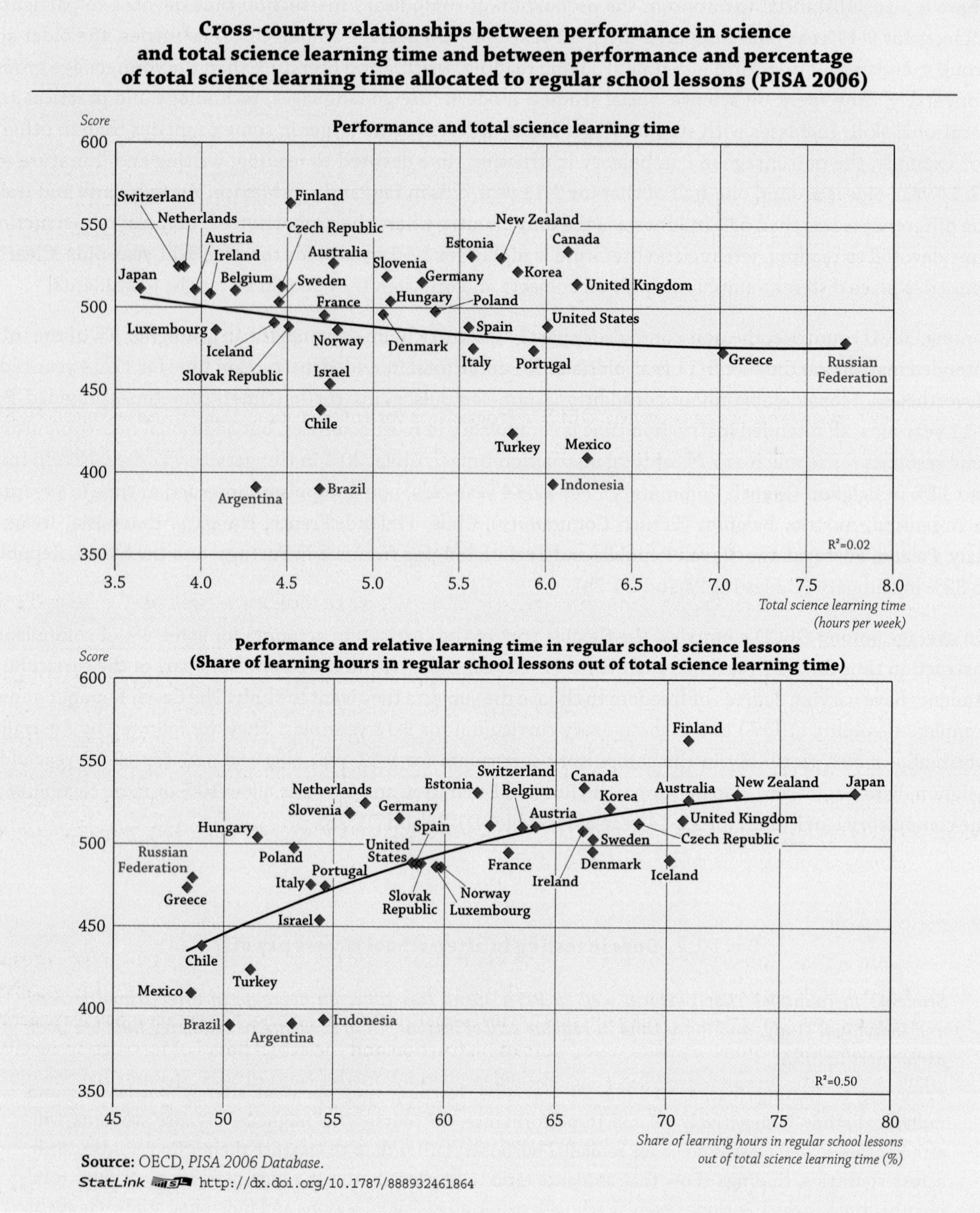

Source: OECD, *PISA 2006 Database*.

StatLink http://dx.doi.org/10.1787/888932461864

Definitions

The **compulsory curriculum** refers to the amount and allocation of instruction time that almost every public school must provide and almost all public-sector students must attend. The measurement of the time devoted to specific study areas (subjects) focuses on the minimum common core rather than on the average time spent, since the data sources (policy documents) do not allow for more precise measurement.

Instruction time for 7-15 year-olds refers to the formal number of 60-minute hours per school year organised by the school for class instruction in the reference school year 2008-09. For countries with no formal policy on instruction time, the number of hours is estimated from survey data. Hours lost when schools are closed for festivities and celebrations, such as national holidays, are excluded. Intended instruction time does not include non-compulsory time outside the school day, homework, individual tutoring, or private study done before or after school.

Instruction time for the least demanding programmes refers to programmes for students who are least likely to continue studying beyond the mandatory school age or beyond lower secondary education. Such programmes may or may not exist, depending on a country's streaming and selection policies. In many countries students are offered the same amount of instruction time in all or most programmes, but there is flexibility in the choice of subjects. Often, such choices have to be made early in the student's school career if programmes are long and differ substantially.

Intended instruction time refers to the number of hours per year during which students receive instruction in the compulsory and non-compulsory parts of the curriculum.

Language of instruction is the term the OECD's Programme for International Student Assessment (PISA) uses to denote classes in reading, writing and literature in the language in which students are taught.

The **non-compulsory part of the curriculum** refers to the average time of instruction to which students are entitled beyond the compulsory hours of instruction. These subjects often vary from school to school or from region to region and may take the form of non-compulsory (elective) subjects.

The **total compulsory curriculum** comprises the compulsory core curriculum as well as the compulsory flexible curriculum.

In Table D1.1, **typical instruction time for 15-year-olds** refers to the programme in which most students at this age are enrolled. The programme may take place in lower or upper secondary education and, in most countries, consists of a general programme. If the system channels students into different programme types at this age, the average instruction time may have been estimated for the most important mainstream programmes and weighted by the proportion of students in the grade in which most 15-year-olds are enrolled. When vocational programmes are also taken into account in typical instruction time, only the school-based part of the programme is included in the calculations.

Methodology

This indicator captures intended instruction time, as established in public regulations, as a measure of exposure to learning in formal classroom settings. It does not show the actual number of hours of instruction received by students and does not cover learning outside of the formal classroom setting. Differences may exist across countries between the regulatory minimum hours of instruction and the actual hours of instruction received by students. A study conducted by Regioplan Beleidsonderzoek in the Netherlands showed that, owing to factors such as school timetable decisions, lesson cancellations and teacher absenteeism, schools may not consistently reach the regulatory minimum instruction time (see Box D1.1 in OECD, 2007d).

The indicator also illustrates how minimum instruction times are allocated across different curricular areas. It shows the intended net hours of instruction for those grades in which the majority of students are between 7 and 15 years old. Although the data are difficult to compare among countries because of different curricular policies, they nevertheless provide an indication of how much formal instruction time is considered necessary for students to achieve the desired educational goals.

This indicator also captures the percentage of 15-year-old students who attend after-school lessons in the form of enrichment or remedial courses and the amount of time spent on them.

Data on instruction time are from the 2010 OECD-INES Survey on Teachers and the Curriculum and refer to the school year 2008-09.

The achievement scores are based on assessments administered as part of the Programme for International Student Assessment (PISA) undertaken by the Organisation for Economic Co-operation and Development (OECD). Data on after-school classes were collected during the 2006 and 2009 school year.

The target population studied for the analysis of after-school classes was 15-year-old students. Operationally, this referred to students aged between 15 years and 3 (completed) months and 16 years and 2 (completed) months at the beginning of the testing period and who were enrolled in an educational institution at the secondary level, irrespective of the grade levels or type of institutions in which they were enrolled, and of whether they participated in school full-time or part-time.

Notes on definitions and methodologies for each country are provided in Annex 3, available at *www.oecd.org/edu/eag2011*.

The statistical data for Israel are supplied by and under the responsibility of the relevant Israeli authorities. The use of such data by the OECD is without prejudice to the status of the Golan Heights, East Jerusalem and Israeli settlements in the West Bank under the terms of international law.

References

For further information about PISA 2006 and PISA 2009, see:

OECD (2011b), *Quality Time for Students: Learning In and Out of School*, OECD, Paris.

Visit *www.pisa.oecd.org*

The following additional material relevant to this indicator is available on line:

- ***Table D1.3. Percentage of 15-year-old students attending after-school lessons, by hours per week (PISA 2009)***
  StatLink http://dx.doi.org/10.1787/888932465151

Table D1.1. Compulsory and intended instruction time in public institutions (2009)

Average number of hours per year of total compulsory and non-compulsory instruction time in the curriculum for 7-8, 9-11, 12-14 and 15-year-olds

		Ending age of compulsory education	Age range at which over 90% of the population are enrolled	Average number of hours per year of total compulsory instruction time					Average number of hours per year of total intended instruction time				
				Ages 7-8	Ages 9-11	Ages 12-14	Age 15 (typical programme)	Age 15 (least demanding programme)	Ages 7-8	Ages 9-11	Ages 12-14	Age 15 (typical programme)	Age 15 (least demanding programme)
		(1)	(2)	(3)	(4)	(5)	(6)	(7)	(8)	(9)	(10)	(11)	(12)
OECD	Australia	15	5 - 16	972	971	983	964	932	972	971	983	964	932
	Austria	15	5 - 16	690	766	913	1 005	960	735	811	958	1 050	1 005
	Belgium (Fl.)	18	3 - 17	a	a	a	a	a	831	831	955	955	448
	Belgium (Fr.)[1]	18	3 - 17	840	840	960	m	m	930	930	1 020	m	m
	Canada	16 - 18	6 - 17	m	m	m	m	m	m	m	m	m	m
	Chile	18	6 - 15	675	675	709	743	743	855	855	855	945	945
	Czech Republic[2]	15	5 - 17	624	713	871	950	683	624	713	871	950	683
	Denmark	16	3 - 16	701	803	900	930	900	701	803	900	930	900
	England	16	4 - 16	893	899	925	950	a	893	899	925	950	a
	Estonia	15	4 - 17	595	683	802	840	m	595	683	802	840	m
	Finland	16	6 - 18	608	640	777	856	a	608	683	829	913	a
	France	16	3 - 17	847	847	971	1 042	a	847	847	1 065	1 147	a
	Germany	18	4 - 17	643	794	898	912	m	643	794	898	912	m
	Greece	14 - 15	5 - 17	720	812	821	798	a	720	812	821	798	a
	Hungary	18	4 - 17	555	601	671	763	763	614	724	885	1 106	1 106
	Iceland	16	3 - 16	720	800	872	888	a	720	800	872	888	a
	Ireland	16	5 - 18	941	941	848	802	713	941	941	907	891	891
	Israel	17	4 - 16	914	991	981	964	m	914	991	981	1 101	m
	Italy	16	3 - 16	891	913	1 001	1 089	m	990	1 023	1 089	1 089	m
	Japan	15	4 - 17	709	774	868	m	a	709	774	868	m	a
	Korea	14	7 - 17	612	703	867	1 020	a	612	703	867	1 020	a
	Luxembourg	15	4 - 15	924	924	908	900	900	924	924	908	900	900
	Mexico	15	4 - 14	800	800	1 167	1 058	a	800	800	1 167	1 058	a
	Netherlands	18	4 - 17	940	940	1 000	1 000	a	940	940	1 000	1 000	a
	New Zealand	16	4 - 16	m	m	m	m	m	m	m	m	m	m
	Norway	16	3 - 17	700	756	829	859	a	700	756	829	859	a
	Poland	16	6 - 18	446	563	604	595	a	486	603	644	635	a
	Portugal	14	5 - 16	875	869	908	893	m	910	898	934	945	m
	Scotland	16	4 - 16	a	a	a	a	a	a	a	a	a	a
	Slovak Republic	16	6 - 17	687	767	813	926	926	715	785	842	926	926
	Slovenia	14	6 - 17	621	721	791	908	888	621	721	791	908	888
	Spain	16	3 - 16	875	821	1 050	1 050	1 050	875	821	1 050	1 050	1 050
	Sweden[3]	16	4 - 18	741	741	741	741	a	741	741	741	741	a
	Switzerland	15	5 - 16	m	m	m	m	m	m	m	m	m	m
	Turkey	14	7 - 13	720	720	750	810	a	864	864	846	810	a
	United States	17	6 - 16	m	m	m	m	m	m	m	m	m	m
	OECD average	16	5 - 16	749	793	873	902	860	775	821	907	941	889
	EU21 average	16	4 - 17	746	790	865	897	865	767	815	902	935	880
Other G20	Argentina[4]	17	5 - 15	m	720	744	m	m	m	m	m	m	m
	Brazil	17	7 - 15	m	m	m	m	m	m	m	m	m	m
	China	m	m	531	613	793	748	m	m	m	m	m	m
	India	m	m	m	m	m	m	m	m	m	m	m	m
	Indonesia	15	6 - 14	m	551	654	m	m	m	m	m	m	m
	Russian Federation	17	7 - 14	493	737	879	912	m	493	737	879	912	m
	Saudi Arabia	m	m	m	m	m	m	m	m	m	m	m	m
	South Africa	m	m	m	m	m	m	m	m	m	m	m	m

1. "Ages 12-14" covers ages 12-13 only.
2. Minimum number of hours per year.
3. Estimated minimum numbers of hours per year because breakdown by age not available.
4. Year of reference 2008.

Source: OECD. Argentina, Indonesia: UNESCO Institute for Statistics (World Education Indicators Programme). China: The Ministry of Education, *Notes on the Experimental Curriculum of Compulsory Education*, 19 November 2001. See Annex 3 for notes *(www.oecd.org/edu/eag2011)*.

Please refer to the Reader's Guide for information concerning the symbols replacing missing data.

StatLink http://dx.doi.org/10.1787/888932465094

Table D1.2a. Instruction time per subject as a percentage of total compulsory instruction time for 9-11 year-olds (2009)

Percentage of intended instruction time devoted to various subject areas within the total compulsory curriculum

		Compulsory core curriculum															
		Reading, writing and literature	Mathematics	Science	Social studies	Modern foreign languages	Ancient Greek and/ or Latin	Technology	Arts	Physical education	Religion	Practical and vocational skills	Other	Total compulsory core curriculum	Compulsory flexible curriculum	Total compulsory curriculum	Non-compulsory curriculum
		(1)	(2)	(3)	(4)	(5)	(6)	(7)	(8)	(9)	(10)	(11)	(12)	(13)	(14)	(15)	(16)
OECD	Australia[1]	m	m	m	m	m	m	m	m	m	m	m	m	**41**	59	**100**	n
	Austria	24	16	10	3	8	n	n	18	10	8	x(12)	3	**100**	x(12)	**100**	6
	Belgium (Fl.)[1]	22	19	x(12)	x(12)	7	n	n	10	7	7	n	18	**89**	11	**100**	n
	Belgium (Fr.)[1]	x(12)	x(12)	x(12)	x(12)	5	n	x(12)	x(12)	7	7	n	81	**100**	n	**100**	11
	Canada	m	m	m	m	m	m	m	m	m	m	m	m	**m**	m	**m**	m
	Chile	19	19	18	4	2	n	9	12	9	7	n	1	**100**	n	**100**	27
	Czech Republic[1]	x(14)	x(14)	x(14)	x(14)	x(14)	n	x(14)	x(14)	x(14)	n	n	n	**x(14)**	100	**100**	n
	Denmark	26	16	7	5	9	n	n	20	10	4	n	3	**100**	n	**100**	n
	England	22	19	12	9	3	n	11	9	7	4	1	3	**100**	n	**100**	n
	Estonia	21	15	7	6	12	n	4	9	10	n	n	4	**88**	12	**100**	n
	Finland	21	18	10	2	9	n	n	19	9	5	n	n	**94**	6	**100**	7
	France	30	19	5	11	9	n	3	9	14	n	n	n	**100**	n	**100**	n
	Germany	17	14	5	6	10	n	3	14	10	6	1	10	**98**	2	**100**	n
	Greece	23	13	6	16	14	n	n	7	6	6	n	7	**100**	n	**100**	n
	Hungary	29	17	6	7	9	n	n	14	12	n	5	2	**100**	n	**100**	20
	Iceland	16	15	8	8	4	n	6	12	9	3	5	3	**89**	11	**100**	n
	Ireland	29	12	4	8	x(14)	n	n	12	4	10	n	14	**92**	8	**100**	n
	Israel	21	17	8	11	11	n	1	5	6	11	n	3	**93**	7	**100**	n
	Italy[2]	22	17	8	11	13	n	2	14	7	6	n	n	**100**	n	**100**	12
	Japan	19	15	9	9	n	n	n	10	9	n	n	21	**92**	8	**100**	m
	Korea	19	13	10	10	5	n	2	13	10	n	2	3	**87**	13	**100**	n
	Luxembourg[3]	21	18	6	2	25	n	n	11	10	7	n	n	**100**	n	**100**	n
	Mexico	30	25	15	20	n	n	n	5	5	n	n	n	**100**	n	**100**	n
	Netherlands[4]	32	19	6	6	1	n	n	9	7	5	3	n	**88**	13	**100**	n
	New Zealand	m	m	m	m	m	m	m	m	m	m	m	m	**m**	m	**m**	m
	Norway	24	16	8	9	8	n	n	15	9	8	n	3	**100**	n	**100**	n
	Poland[5]	17	13	23	8	9	n	4	4	13	n	n	n	**91**	9	**100**	7
	Portugal[5,6]	21	17	6	11	7	n	x(8)	12	6	n	n	18	**98**	2	**100**	3
	Scotland	a	a	a	a	a	a	a	a	a	a	a	a	**a**	a	**a**	a
	Slovak Republic	23	16	9	12	10	n	1	9	7	4	2	n	**93**	7	**100**	2
	Slovenia	18	16	10	8	11	n	2	11	11	n	3	10	**100**	n	**100**	n
	Spain	23	17	9	9	13	n	n	10	10	x(14)	n	3	**92**	8	**100**	n
	Sweden	m	m	m	m	m	m	m	m	m	m	m	m	**m**	m	**m**	m
	Switzerland	m	m	m	m	m	m	m	m	m	m	m	m	**m**	m	**m**	m
	Turkey	19	13	13	10	11	n	2	7	6	7	n	6	**93**	7	**100**	20
	United States	m	m	m	m	m	m	m	m	m	m	m	m	**m**	m	**m**	m
	OECD average[1]	23	16	9	8	9	n	2	11	9	4	1	4	**96**	4	**100**	4
	EU21 average[1]	23	16	8	8	9	n	2	12	9	4	1	4	**96**	4	**100**	3
Other G20	Argentina[7]	20	20	15	15	n	n	n	10	10	n	n	10	**100**	x(13)	**100**	n
	Brazil	m	m	m	m	m	m	m	m	m	m	m	m	**m**	m	**m**	m
	China	20-23	13-16	7-10	3-5	6-9	m	m	9-12	10-12	m	16-21	7-10	**m**	m	**m**	m
	India	m	m	m	m	m	m	m	m	m	m	m	m	**m**	m	**m**	m
	Indonesia	11	11	9	7	a	n	a	9	9	7	4	4	**100**	x(13)	**100**	4
	Russian Federation	27	16	7	6	9	n	7	7	7	n	n	n	**85**	15	**100**	n
	Saudi Arabia	m	m	m	m	m	m	m	m	m	m	m	m	**m**	m	**m**	m
	South Africa	m	m	m	m	m	m	m	m	m	m	m	m	**m**	m	**m**	m

1. Australia, Belgium (Fl.), Belgium (Fr.) and the Czech Republic are not included in the averages.
2. For 9 and 10 year-olds the curriculum is largely flexible, for 11-year-olds it is about the same as for 12 and 13 year-olds.
3. German as a language of instruction is included in "Reading, writing and literature" in addition to the mother tongue Luxemburgish.
4. Includes 11-year-olds only.
5. Includes 10-11 year-olds only.
6. For 9-year-olds, "Technology", "Arts" and "Practical and vocational skills" are included in "Other".
7. Year of reference 2008.

Source: OECD. Argentina, Indonesia: UNESCO Institute for Statistics (World Education Indicators Programme). China: The Ministry of Education, *Notes on the Experimental Curriculum of Compulsory Education*, 19 November 2001. See Annex 3 for notes *(www.oecd.org/edu/eag2011)*.

Please refer to the Reader's Guide for information concerning the symbols replacing missing data.

StatLink http://dx.doi.org/10.1787/888932465113

Table D1.2b. Instruction time per subject as a percentage of total compulsory instruction time for 12-14 year-olds (2009)

Percentage of intended instruction time devoted to various subject areas within the total compulsory curriculum

		Compulsory core curriculum															
		Reading, writing and literature	Mathematics	Science	Social studies	Modern foreign languages	Ancient Greek and/or Latin	Technology	Arts	Physical education	Religion	Practical and vocational skills	Other	Total compulsory core curriculum	Compulsory flexible curriculum	Total compulsory curriculum	Non-compulsory curriculum
		(1)	(2)	(3)	(4)	(5)	(6)	(7)	(8)	(9)	(10)	(11)	(12)	(13)	(14)	(15)	(16)
OECD	Australia[1]	m	m	m	m	m	m	m	m	m	m	m	m	58	42	100	n
	Austria	13	14	13	12	11	1	n	16	10	7	2	n	100	x(12)	100	5
	Belgium (Fl.)	14	13	7	9	17	n	4	4	6	6	1	n	80	20	100	n
	Belgium (Fr.)[2]	17	14	9	13	13	x(14)	3	3	9	6	n	n	88	13	100	6
	Canada	m	m	m	m	m	m	m	m	m	m	m	m	m	m	m	m
	Chile	16	16	13	13	8	n	6	11	6	6	n	5	100	n	100	19
	Czech Republic[1]	x(14)	x(14)	x(14)	x(14)	x(14)	n	x(14)	x(14)	x(14)	n	n	n	x(14)	100	100	n
	Denmark	20	13	14	9	18	n	n	11	8	3	n	3	100	n	100	n
	England	11	12	14	12	7	n	12	9	7	4	3	2	93	7	100	n
	Estonia	14	14	17	7	17	n	5	7	7	n	n	n	89	11	100	n
	Finland	13	13	17	7	14	n	n	15	7	5	4	n	95	5	100	7
	France	16	15	13	13	12	n	6	7	11	n	n	n	93	7	100	10
	Germany	13	13	11	11	15	2	4	9	9	5	2	1	96	4	100	n
	Greece	18	11	10	12	12	9	5	6	8	6	3	1	100	n	100	n
	Hungary	17	12	18	12	12	n	3	10	9	n	3	3	100	n	100	32
	Iceland	14	14	8	6	17	n	4	7	8	2	4	3	85	15	100	n
	Ireland[3]	28	13	8	17	7	n	x(16)	4	5	9	x(16)	5	97	3	100	7
	Israel	19	14	10	16	17	n	4	n	6	9	n	1	97	3	100	n
	Italy[2]	21	13	9	11	16	n	7	13	6	3	n	n	100	n	100	14
	Japan	11	10	9	9	10	n	3	7	9	n	n	18	87	13	100	m
	Korea	13	11	11	10	10	n	4	8	8	n	4	5	82	18	100	n
	Luxembourg[4]	17	15	5	10	26	n	n	10	8	6	n	3	100	n	100	n
	Mexico	14	14	17	23	9	n	n	6	6	n	9	3	100	n	100	n
	Netherlands	m	m	m	m	m	m	m	m	m	m	m	m	m	m	m	m
	New Zealand	m	m	m	m	m	m	m	m	m	m	m	m	m	m	m	m
	Norway	17	13	10	10	15	n	n	11	9	7	3	5	100	n	100	n
	Poland	16	13	17	15	10	n	4	4	13	n	n	n	92	8	100	7
	Portugal[5]	11	11	12	13	15	n	4	7	9	n	n	15	98	2	100	3
	Scotland	a	a	a	a	a	a	a	a	a	a	a	a	a	a	a	a
	Slovak Republic	15	15	17	16	10	n	n	7	7	3	3	n	94	6	100	3
	Slovenia	13	13	15	15	11	n	2	6	6	n	n	9	90	10	100	n
	Spain	17	13	11	10	10	n	5	10	7	x(14)	n	11	95	5	100	n
	Sweden	m	m	m	m	m	m	m	m	m	m	m	m	m	m	m	m
	Switzerland	m	m	m	m	m	m	m	m	m	m	m	m	m	m	m	m
	Turkey	17	13	16	11	12	n	4	4	5	5	n	8	96	4	100	13
	United States	m	m	m	m	m	m	m	m	m	m	m	m	m	m	m	m
	OECD average[1]	16	13	12	12	13	n	3	8	8	4	2	4	94	6	100	5
	EU21 average[1]	16	13	12	12	13	1	3	8	8	3	1	3	95	5	100	5
Other G20	Argentina[6]	16	16	13	19	10	n	6	10	10	n	n	n	100	x(13)	100	20
	Brazil	m	m	m	m	m	m	m	m	m	m	m	m	m	m	m	m
	China	m	m	m	m	m	m	m	m	m	m	m	m	m	m	m	m
	India	m	m	m	m	m	m	m	m	m	m	m	m	m	m	m	m
	Indonesia	13	13	13	12	9	n	4	8	8	7	6	6	100	x(13)	100	6
	Russian Federation	15	14	24	9	9	n	3	4	6	n	1	n	85	15	100	n
	Saudi Arabia	m	m	m	m	m	m	m	m	m	m	m	m	m	m	m	m
	South Africa	m	m	m	m	m	m	m	m	m	m	m	m	m	m	m	m

1. Australia and the Czech Republic are not included in the averages.
2. Includes 12-13 year-olds only.
3. For 13-14 year-olds, "Arts" is included in "Non-compulsory curriculum".
4. German as a language of instruction is included in "Reading, writing and literature" in addition to the mother tongue Luxemburgish.
5. "Technology" is included in "Arts" for 14-year-olds.
6. Year of reference 2008.

Source: OECD. Argentina, Indonesia: UNESCO Institute for Statistics (World Education Indicators Programme). See Annex 3 for notes *(www.oecd.org/edu/eag2011)*.
Please refer to the Reader's Guide for information concerning the symbols replacing missing data.
StatLink http://dx.doi.org/10.1787/888932465132

WHAT IS THE STUDENT-TEACHER RATIO AND HOW BIG ARE CLASSES?

- The average class in primary education in OECD countries has more than 21 students. Among all countries with available data, this number varies from more than 29 in Chile and China to nearly half that number in Luxembourg and the Russian Federation.
- In two-thirds of the countries with comparable data for 2000 and 2009, classes have tended to become smaller in primary education, most notably in countries that had relatively large classes in 2000, such as Korea and Turkey.
- On average in OECD countries, the number of students per class grows by two or more between primary and lower secondary education. In lower secondary education, the average class in OECD countries has about 24 students.

Chart D2.1. Average class size in primary education (2000, 2009)

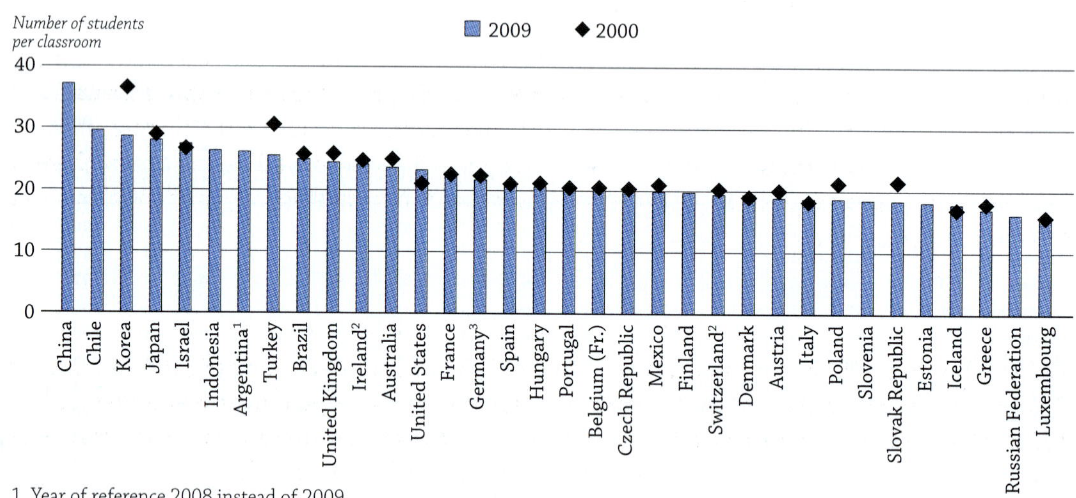

1. Year of reference 2008 instead of 2009.
2. Public institutions only.
3. Years of reference 2001 and 2009.

Countries are ranked in descending order of average class size in primary education in 2009.

Source: OECD. Argentina, China, Indonesia: UNESCO Institute for Statistics (World Education Indicators Programme). 2009 data: Table D2.1. 2000 data: Table D2.4, available on line. See Annex 3 for notes (*www.oecd.org/edu/eag2011*).

StatLink http://dx.doi.org/10.1787/888932461883

Context

Class size and student-teacher ratios are much-discussed aspects of education and, along with students' total instruction time (see Indicator D1), teachers' average working time (see Indicator D4), and the division of teachers' time between teaching and other duties, are among the determinants of the size of countries' teaching force. Together with teachers' salaries (see Indicator D3) and the age distribution of teachers (see Indicator D7, available on line), class size and student-teacher ratios also have a considerable impact on the level of current expenditure on education (see Indicator B6).

Smaller classes are often perceived as allowing teachers to focus more on the needs of individual students and reducing the amount of class time needed to deal with disruptions. Yet, while there is some evidence that smaller classes may benefit specific groups of students, such as those from disadvantaged backgrounds (Krueger, 2002), overall the evidence of the effects of differences in class size on student performance is weak. There is more evidence to support a positive relationship between smaller class size and aspects of teachers' working conditions and outcomes (e.g. allowing for greater flexibility for innovation in the classroom, improved teacher morale and job satisfaction) (Hattie, 2009; OECD, 2009).

The ratio of students to teaching staff indicates how resources for education are allocated. Smaller student-teacher ratios often have to be weighed against higher salaries for teachers, increased professional development and teacher training, greater investment in teaching technology, or more widespread use of assistant teachers and other paraprofessionals whose salaries are often considerably lower than those of qualified teachers. And as larger numbers of children with special needs are integrated into mainstream classes, more use of specialised personnel and support services may limit the resources available for reducing student-teacher ratios.

Other findings

- **The student-teacher ratio decreases between primary and secondary level in 25 of the 34 countries with available data, despite a general increase in class size between these levels**. This decrease in the student-teacher ratio reflects differences in annual instruction time for students, which tends to increase with the level of education.
- On average in OECD countries, **the availability of teaching resources relative to the number of students in secondary education is more favourable in private than in public institutions**. This is most striking in Mexico where, at the secondary level, there are nearly 17 more students per teacher in public than in private institutions. On average across OECD countries, there is fewer than one student more per class in public than in private institutions at the lower and upper secondary levels.

Trends

From 2000 to 2009, the average class size in OECD countries decreased slightly in primary school and increased very slightly in lower secondary school, and the range of class size among OECD countries seemed to have narrowed. However, class size has tended to increase in some countries that had relatively small classes in 2000, most notably in Iceland.

Analysis

Average class size in primary and lower secondary education

The average primary class in OECD countries has more than 21 students per class. When considering all countries with available data, that number varies widely: it ranges from fewer than 20 in Austria, the Czech Republic, Denmark, Estonia, Finland, Greece, Iceland, Italy, Luxembourg, Mexico, Poland, the Russian Federation, the Slovak Republic, Slovenia and Switzerland (public institutions) to more than 29 in Chile and China. At the lower secondary level, in general programmes, the average class in OECD countries has about 24 students. Among all countries with available data, that number varies from 20 or fewer in Denmark, Estonia, Finland, Iceland, Luxembourg, the Russian Federation, Slovenia, Switzerland (public institutions) and the United Kingdom to more than 35 students per class in Indonesia and Korea and to over 50 in China (Table D2.1). In one-third of OECD countries, lower secondary schools have between 22 and 25 students per class.

The number of students per class tends to increase between primary and lower secondary education. In Brazil, China, Greece, Indonesia, Israel, Japan, Korea, Mexico and Poland, the increase in average class size exceeds four students. Meanwhile, the United Kingdom and, to a lesser extent, Switzerland (public institutions only) and the United States show a drop in the number of students per class between these two levels of education (Chart D2.2).

The indicator on class size is limited to primary and lower secondary education because class size is difficult to define and compare at higher levels, where students often attend several different classes, depending on the subject area. However, data collected in the context of PISA 2009 give some insight into class size in a specific area (national language-of-instruction classes) for the grade attended by most 15-year-old students in the country (Box D2.1).

Box D2.1. National language-of-instruction class size in the grade attended by most 15-year-olds

Class size can affect how much time and attention a teacher can give to individual students, as well as the social dynamics among students. However, research on class size has generally found a weak relationship between class size and student performance (Ehrenberg, *et al.*, 2001; Piketty, 2006) or with other variables, like disciplinary climate or teacher-student relations (see *PISA 2009 Database*). Class size also seems to be more important in the earlier years of schooling than it is for 15-year-olds (Finn, 1998). However, all other things being equal, smaller classes will generally be beneficial; but PISA 2009 analysis has shown that reductions in class size are generally expensive (see also Indicator B7), and are a less efficient spending choice for improving learning outcomes than, for example, investing in the quality of teachers.

The 2009 PISA survey analysed the performance of 15-year-old students, with a focus on reading. As part of the contextual information collected, principals of institutions were asked to give the actual number of students in classes in the national language of instruction (reading, writing and literature) for the grade attended by most of the country's 15-year-old students. As the survey is representative of 15-year-olds, the size of classes is representative of class size in each country for this group of students.

Average class size, as well as the difference in class size between the smallest 10% of classes and largest 10% of classes, are shown on the chart below.

In OECD countries, the average class size corresponding to the grade attended by most of the country's 15-year-olds is 25 students. This is one more student than the class size reported in this indicator for lower secondary education. However, this difference should be interpreted with caution, owing to differences in methodology, and to differences in educational systems (15-year-olds can be enrolled in either lower or upper secondary levels). There are large differences in class size for 15-year-olds as there are at the lower secondary level, as shown in table D2.1. For the grade attended by most 15-year-olds, average class size varies from fewer than 20 students in Belgium, Denmark, Finland, Iceland and Switzerland, to nearly twice this number in Japan (37.1). Among the ten countries with the smallest class sizes for 15-year-olds, six are among the ten countries with the smallest class sizes at the lower secondary level (Denmark, Finland, Iceland, Luxembourg,

...

the Russian Federation and Switzerland). Similarly, among countries with available data for both class size in Table D2.1 and in the grade attended by most of the country's 15-year-olds, the five countries with more than 30 students in the grade attended by most of the country's 15-year-olds (Brazil, Chile, Japan, Korea and Mexico) are among the six countries with the largest class size at the lower secondary level.

Average class size in national language-of-instruction classes for 15-year-olds (2009)

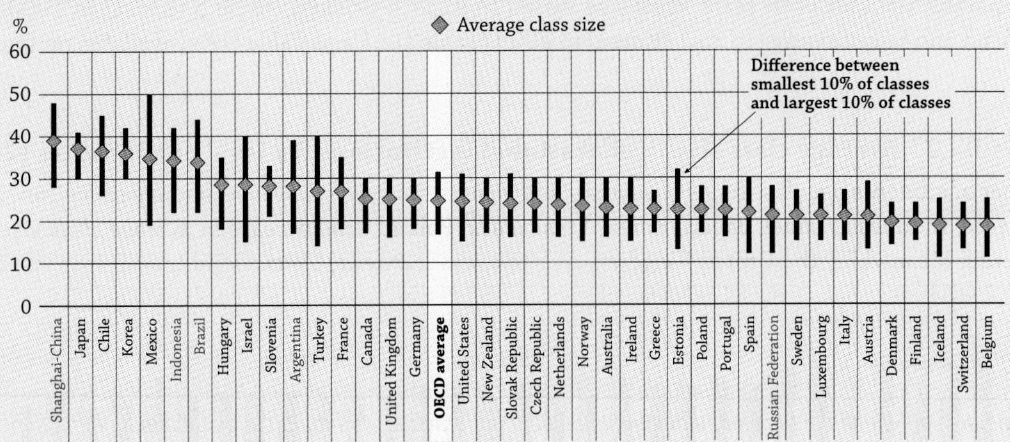

Countries are ranked in descending order of average class size in national language of instruction classes.
Source: OECD, *PISA 2009 Database*. See Annex 3 for notes (*www.oecd.org/edu/eag2011*).
StatLink http://dx.doi.org/10.1787/888932461959

Average class size in the grade attended by most 15-year-olds varies widely among countries, but the distribution of class size within each country also varies. In some countries, such as Denmark and Finland, not only is the average class size among the smallest, but within the country, the difference between the smallest 10% of classes and the largest 10% is also small (10 students or fewer). In contrast, the difference between the smallest 10% and largest 10% of classes reaches at least twice this number in Brazil, Israel and Turkey, and at least three times this number in Mexico. The average class size in the grade attended by most 15-year-olds in these four countries is larger than the OECD average. However, the extent of the variation between the smallest and largest class size in each country is not necessarily linked to average class size. In Korea, the average class size is among the largest in OECD countries; but the difference between the smallest 10% and the largest 10% of class size is about 12 students, which is less than the average across OECD countries (14.8). In Spain, the average class size of nearly 22 students is smaller than the OECD average, but there are more variations in class size than on average in OECD countries (18 and 14.8 students, respectively).

Although the data on class size at the lower secondary level do not refer to reading classes, it is interesting to look at the relationship between PISA performance in reading and average class size. The class size in the language of instruction does not seem to have a direct impact on PISA performance in reading. For example, a country like Finland has both a small average class size in the language of instruction and holds the top ranking for performance in reading among the countries taken into account. However, countries like Japan and Korea, which are also among the top five countries in PISA reading performance, have an average class size that is among the largest. Large classes do not prevent these countries from having above-average performance in reading.

However, another important feature of schools is whether they create a climate that is conducive to teaching and learning. Similar class sizes may hide differences in the disciplinary climate or in teacher-student relations that may affect the reading performance of students. Even after accounting for socio-economic background and other aspects of the learning environment measured by PISA, student performance in reading in PISA 2009 is positively related to better teacher-student relations or a better disciplinary climate. For example, whereas Japan and Chile have similar class size, differences in disciplinary climate and teacher-students relations, and in the impact of these factors on performance, may help to explain the differences in overall average performance in reading between these countries.

The size of the average primary school class in OECD countries has decreased slightly between 2000 and 2009 (21.4 students per class in 2009 as compared to 22 in 2000), even if some countries had implemented reforms on class size during that period. However, among countries with comparable data, class size decreased, and most notably (by more than three students) in countries that had larger class sizes in 2000, such as Korea and Turkey. Class size increased or was unchanged in countries that had the smallest class sizes in 2000, such as Denmark, Iceland, Italy and Luxembourg. Class size also increased between 2000 and 2009 in the United States (Chart D2.1). Variations in secondary school class size narrowed between 2000 and 2009: among countries with comparable data for both years, class size varied from 17.4 (Iceland) to 38.5 (Korea) in 2000 and from 19.5 (Iceland and Luxembourg) to 35.1 (Korea) in 2009 (Table D2.1 and Table D2.4, available on line).

Chart D2.2. Average class size in educational institutions, by level of education (2009)

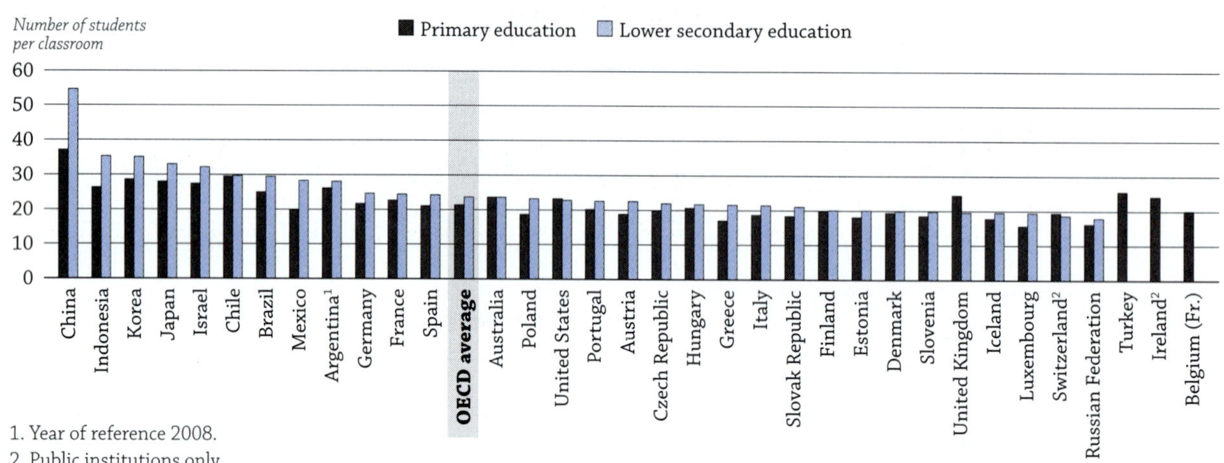

1. Year of reference 2008.
2. Public institutions only.
Countries are ranked in descending order of the average class size in lower secondary education.
Source: OECD. Argentina, China, Indonesia: UNESCO Institute for Statistics (World Education Indicators Programme). Table D2.1. See Annex 3 for notes (*www.oecd.org/edu/eag2011*).

StatLink http://dx.doi.org/10.1787/888932461902

Student-teacher ratios

The ratio of students to teaching staff compares the number of students (in full-time equivalent) to the number of teachers (in full-time equivalent) at a given level of education and in similar types of institutions. However, this ratio does not take into account the amount of instruction time for students compared to the length of a teacher's working day, nor how much time teachers spend teaching. It therefore cannot be interpreted in terms of class size (Box D2.2).

On average in OECD countries, there are 16 students for every teacher in primary schools. The student-teacher ratio ranges from 24 students or more per teacher in Brazil and Mexico, to fewer than 11 in Hungary, Italy, Norway and Poland (Chart D2.3).

Student-teacher ratios also vary, and to a larger extent, at the secondary school level, ranging from 30 students per full-time equivalent teacher in Mexico to fewer than 11 in Austria, Belgium, Iceland, Luxembourg, Norway, Portugal, the Russian Federation and Spain. On average among OECD countries, there are about 14 students per teacher at the secondary level (Table D2.2).

As the differences in student-teacher ratios indicate, there are fewer full-time equivalent students per full-time equivalent teachers at the secondary level than at the primary level of education. The student-teacher ratio decreases between primary and secondary school, despite a general increase in class size. This is true in all but nine OECD countries: Australia, Chile, Estonia, Hungary, Italy, Mexico, Poland, the United Kingdom and the United States.

Chart D2.3. Ratio of students to teaching staff in educational institutions, by level of education (2009)

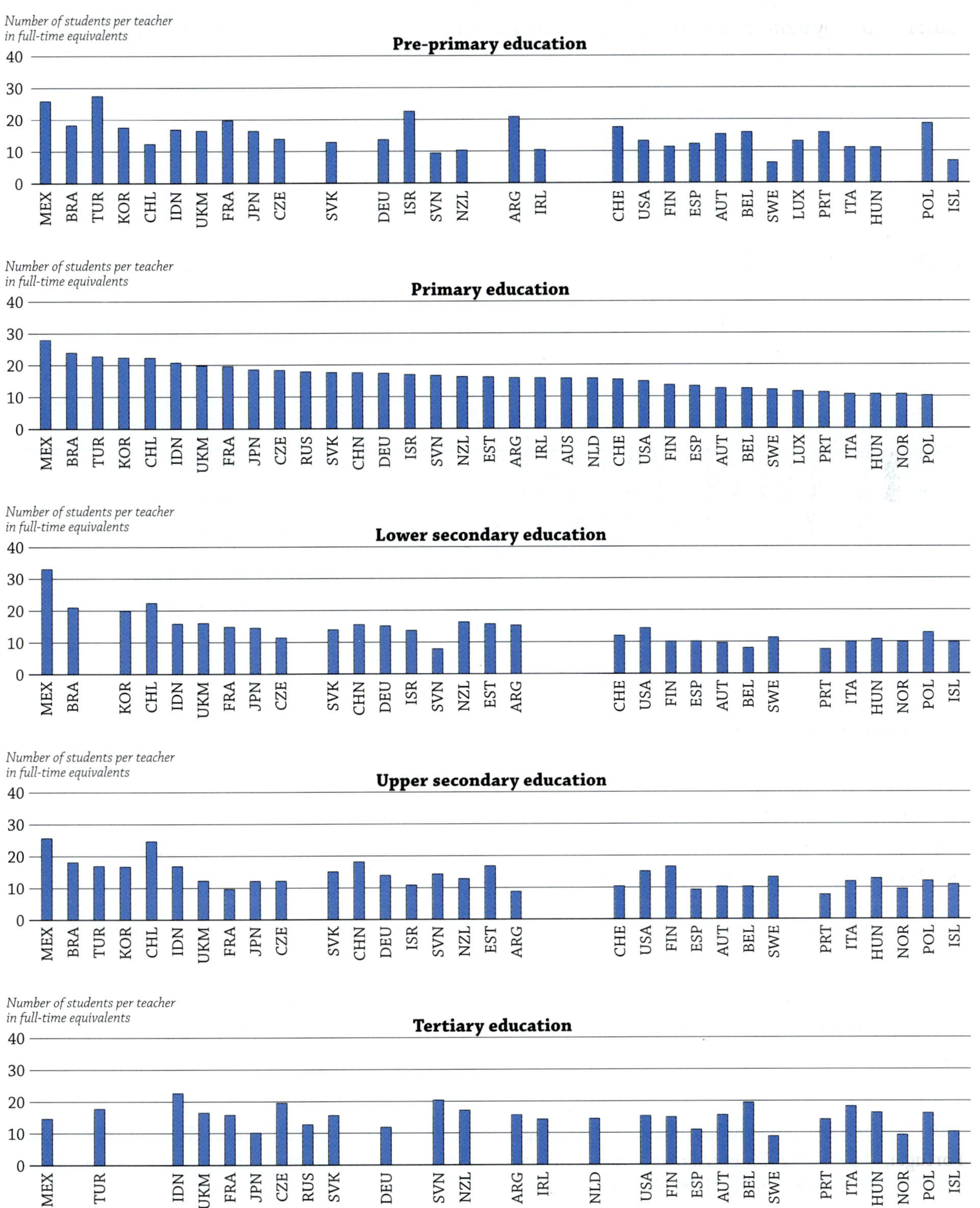

Countries are ranked in descending order of students to teaching staff ratios in primary education.

Source: OECD. Argentina, China, Indonesia: UNESCO Institute for Statistics (World Education Indicators Programme). Table D2.2. See Annex 3 for notes (*www.oecd.org/edu/eag2011*).

Please refer to the Reader's Guide for list of country codes for country names used in this chart.

StatLink http://dx.doi.org/10.1787/888932461921

Box D2.2. Relationship between class size and student-teacher ratio

The number of students per class is calculated from a number of different elements: the ratio of students to teaching staff, the number of classes or students for which a teacher is responsible, the amount of instruction time compared to the length of teachers' working days, the proportion of time teachers spend teaching, and how students are grouped within classes and team teaching.

For example, in a school of 48 full-time students and 8 full-time teachers, the student-teacher ratio is 6. If teachers' work week is estimated to be 35 hours, including 10 hours teaching, and if instruction time for each student is 40 hours per week, then, regardless of how students are grouped in the school, average class size can be estimated as follows:

Estimated class size = 6 students per teacher * (40 hours of instruction time per student/10 hours of teaching per teacher) = 24 students.

Using a different approach, the class size presented in Table D2.1 is defined as those students who are following a common course of study, based on the highest number of common courses (usually compulsory studies), and excludes teaching in subgroups. Thus, the estimated class size will be close to the average class size of Table D2.1 where teaching in subgroups is less frequent, such as in primary and lower secondary education.

Because of these definitions, similar student-teacher ratios between countries can result in different class sizes. For example, at the lower secondary level, France and Spain have similar average class sizes (24.5 students in France and 24.3 in Spain – Table D2.1), but the student-teacher ratio differs substantially, with 14.9 students per teaching staff in France compared to 10.1 in Spain (Table D2.2). The explanation may lie in the higher number of teaching hours required of teachers in Spain (713 in Spain compared with 642 in France – Table D4.1) and lower instruction time for students in Spain (Table D1.1).

This reduction in the student-teacher ratio reflects differences in annual instruction time, which tends to increase with the level of education (see Indicator D1). It may also result from delays in matching the teaching force to demographic changes, or from differences in teaching hours for teachers at different levels, which tends to decrease with the level of education, as teacher specialisation increases. The general trend is consistent among countries, but evidence is mixed as to whether smaller student-teacher ratios are more desirable from an educational perspective at higher levels of education.

For the pre-primary level, Table D2.2 shows the ratio of student to teaching staff and also the ratio of students to contact staff (teachers and teachers' aides). Some countries make extensive use of teachers' aides at the pre-primary level. Eleven countries reported smaller ratios of students to contact staff (column 1 of Table D2.2) than of students to teaching staff. For the Czech Republic, Japan, the Slovak Republic, Sweden and the United Kingdom, this difference is not substantial. However, Austria, Brazil, Chile, Germany, Ireland and Israel have larger numbers of teachers' aides. As a result, the ratios of students to contact staff are substantially lower than the ratios of students to teaching staff in these countries, particularly in Ireland and Israel.

At the tertiary level, the student-teacher ratio ranges from 20 or more students per teacher in Indonesia and Slovenia to fewer than 11 in Iceland, Japan, Norway, Spain and Sweden (Table D2.2). However, comparisons at this level should be made with caution since it is difficult to calculate full-time equivalent students and teachers on a comparable basis.

In 9 of the 13 countries with comparable data at the tertiary level, the ratio of students to teaching staff is lower in more vocationally oriented programmes (tertiary-type B) than in academic (tertiary-type A) and advanced research programmes. Turkey is the only country with a significantly higher student-teacher ratio in vocational programmes at that level (Table D2.2).

Teaching resources in public and private institutions

On average among countries for which data are available, ratios of students to teaching staff are slightly lower in private institutions than in public institutions at both lower secondary and upper secondary levels (Table D2.3). The largest differences are in Brazil and Mexico where, at the lower secondary level, there are at least ten more students per teacher in public institutions than in private institutions. At the upper secondary level in Mexico, the difference between student-teacher ratios in public and private institutions is as large as at the lower secondary level.

However, in some countries, the student-teacher ratio is lower in public institutions than in private institutions. This is most pronounced at the lower secondary level in Spain, which has some 16 students per teacher in private institutions but only 9 students per teacher in public institutions.

Among countries for which data are available, average class size does not differ between public and private institutions by more than one student per class for both primary and lower secondary education (Chart D2.4 and Table D2.1). However, there are marked differences among countries. For example, at the primary level, in Brazil, the Czech Republic, Indonesia, Poland, the Russian Federation, Turkey, the United Kingdom and the United States, average class size in public institutions is larger by four or more students per class.

Chart D2.4. Average class size in public and private institutions, by level of education (2009)

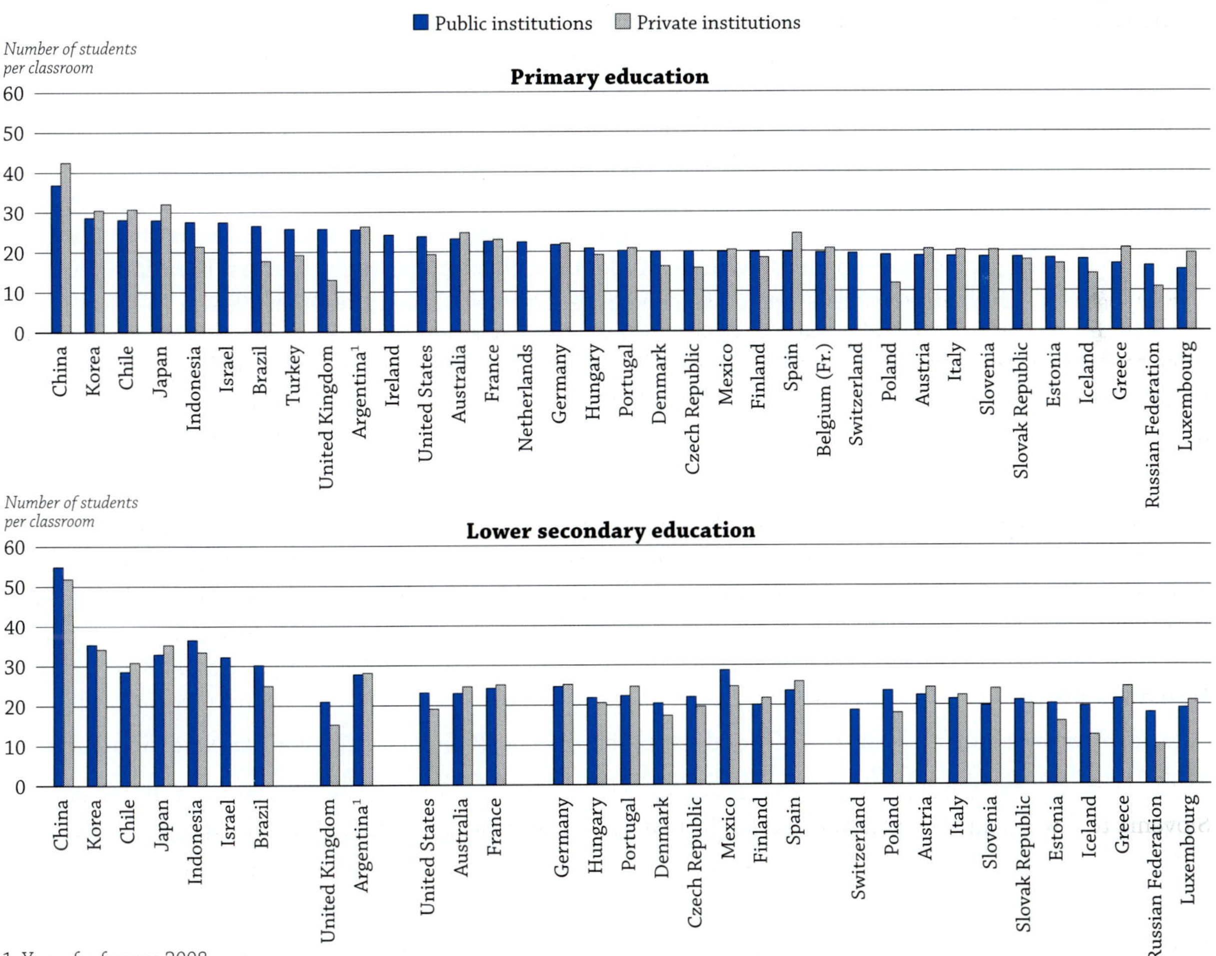

1. Year of reference 2008.

Countries are ranked in descending order of average class size in public institutions in primary education.

Source: OECD. Argentina, China, Indonesia: UNESCO Institute for Statistics (World Education Indicators Programme). Table D2.1. See Annex 3 for notes (*www.oecd.org/edu/eag2011*).

StatLink http://dx.doi.org/10.1787/888932461940

However, with the exception of Brazil and the United States, the private sector is relatively small in all of these countries, representing at most 5% of students at the primary level (see Table C1.5).

In contrast, the average class size in private institutions is larger than that in public institutions by four or more students in China, Japan, Luxembourg and Spain.

The comparison of class size between public and private institutions shows a mixed picture at the lower secondary level, where private education is more prevalent. Average class size in lower secondary schools is larger in private institutions than in public institutions in 13 OECD countries, although differences tend to be smaller than in primary education.

Countries encourage and provide resources for public and private schools for various reasons. One is to broaden the choices of schooling available to students and their families. Class size is one factor that parents often consider when deciding on a school for their children, and the difference in average class size between public and private schools could influence enrolment. Perhaps surprisingly, there are, on average, only marginal differences in class size between public and private institutions in countries where private institutions are more prevalent at primary and lower secondary levels, such as Australia, Belgium (French Community), Chile, France, Korea (lower secondary level only) and Luxembourg (see Table C1.5). Where large differences do exist, they tend to show that private institutions have more students per class than public schools. This indicates that in countries in which a substantial proportion of students and families choose private schools, class size is not a determining factor in their decision.

Definitions

Language of instruction is the term the OECD's Programme for International Student Assessment uses to denote classes in reading, writing and literature in the language in which students are taught.

Professional support for students includes professional staff who provide services to students that support their learning. In many cases, these staff originally qualified as teachers but then moved into other professional positions within the education system. This category also includes all personnel employed in education systems who provide health and social support services to students, such as guidance counsellors, librarians, doctors, dentists, nurses, psychiatrists and psychologists, and other staff with similar responsibilities.

Teachers' aides and teaching/research assistants include non-professional personnel or students who support teachers in providing instruction to students.

Teaching staff refers to professional personnel directly involved in teaching students. The classification includes classroom teachers, special-education teachers and other teachers who work with a whole class of students in a classroom, in small groups in a resource room, or in one-to-one teaching situations inside or outside a regular class. Teaching staff also includes department chairpersons whose duties include some teaching, but excludes non-professional personnel who support teachers in providing instruction to students, such as teachers' aides and other paraprofessional personnel.

Methodology

Data refer to the academic year 2008-09 and are based on the UOE data collection on education statistics administered by the OECD in 2010 (for details see Annex 3 at *www.oecd.org/edu/eag2011*).

Class size is calculated by dividing the number of students enrolled by the number of classes. In order to ensure comparability among countries, special-needs programmes are excluded. Data include only regular programmes at primary and lower secondary levels of education, and exclude teaching in sub-groups outside the regular classroom setting.

In the PISA 2009 study, class size was computed based on a questionnaire answered by principals of schools. Principals were asked to specify the size of classes according to the following nine categories: 15 students or fewer, from 16 to 20, from 21 to 25, from 26 to 30, from 31 to 35, from 36 to 40, from 41 to 45, from 46 to 50, and more than 50. From these categories, average class size was computed using the middle class size value for each category and the values 15 and 51 for the two extremes.

The **ratio of students to teaching staff** is obtained by dividing the number of full-time equivalent students at a given level of education by the number of full-time equivalent teachers at that level and in similar types of institutions.

The statistical data for Israel are supplied by and under the responsibility of the relevant Israeli authorities. The use of such data by the OECD is without prejudice to the status of the Golan Heights, East Jerusalem and Israeli settlements in the West Bank under the terms of international law.

References

Ehrenberg, R., *et al.* (2001), "Class Size and Student Achievement", *Psychological Science in the Public Interest*, Vol. 2, No. 1, pp. 1-30.

Finn, J. (1998), *Class Size and Students at Risk: What is Known? What is Next?*, US Department of Education, Office of Educational Research and Improvement, National Institute on the Education of At-Risk Students, Washington, DC.

Hattie, J. (2009), *Visible Learning; A synthesis of over 800 meta-analyses relating to achievement,* Routledge, London.

Krueger, A.B. (2002), "Economic Considerations and Class Size", *National Bureau of Economic Research Working Paper:* 8875.

OECD (2009), *Creating Effective Teaching and Learning Environments: First Results from TALIS*, OECD, Paris.

Piketty, T. and M. Valdenaire (2006), *L'Impact de la taille des classes sur la réussite scolaire dans les écoles, collèges et lycées français : Estimations à partir du panel primaire 1997 et du panel secondaire 1995*, ministère de l'Éducation nationale, de l'Enseignement supérieur et de la Recherche, Direction de l'évaluation et de la prospective, Paris.

For more information on the gender and age breakdown of teachers, see Indicator D7 available on line.

Notes on definitions and methodologies regarding this indicator for each country are presented in Annex 3 at *www.oecd.org/edu/eag2011.*

The following additional material relevant to this indicator is available on line:

- ***Table D2.4. Average class size, by type of institution and level of education (2000)***
  StatLink http://dx.doi.org/10.1787/888932465227

Table D2.1. Average class size, by type of institution and level of education (2009)

Calculations based on number of students and number of classes

		Primary education					Lower secondary education (general programmes)				
			Private institutions					Private institutions			
		Public institutions	Total private institutions	Government-dependent private institutions	Independent private institutions	Total: Public and private institutions	Public institutions	Total private institutions	Government-dependent private institutions	Independent private institutions	Total: Public and private institutions
		(1)	(2)	(3)	(4)	(5)	(6)	(7)	(8)	(9)	(10)
OECD	Australia	23.2	24.8	24.8	a	**23.7**	23.0	24.7	24.7	a	**23.7**
	Austria	18.8	20.5	x(2)	x(2)	**18.9**	22.4	24.3	x(7)	x(7)	**22.6**
	Belgium	m	m	m	m	**m**	m	m	m	m	**m**
	Belgium (Fr.)	19.6	20.7	20.7	m	**20.1**	m	m	m	m	**m**
	Canada	m	m	m	m	**m**	m	m	m	m	**m**
	Chile	28.1	30.8	32.4	22.4	**29.6**	28.6	30.8	32.2	23.9	**29.7**
	Czech Republic	20.0	15.9	15.9	a	**19.9**	22.0	19.6	19.6	a	**22.0**
	Denmark	20.0	16.3	16.3	a	**19.4**	20.5	17.3	17.3	a	**19.9**
	Estonia	18.2	16.8	a	16.8	**18.1**	20.3	15.9	a	15.9	**20.1**
	Finland	19.8	18.4	18.4	a	**19.8**	20.0	21.7	21.7	a	**20.1**
	France	22.6	23.0	x(2)	x(2)	**22.7**	24.3	25.1	25.4	14.1	**24.5**
	Germany	21.7	22.0	22.0	x(3)	**21.7**	24.6	25.2	25.2	x(8)	**24.7**
	Greece	16.8	20.7	a	20.7	**17.0**	21.5	24.5	a	24.5	**21.6**
	Hungary	20.8	19.2	19.2	a	**20.7**	21.9	20.6	20.6	a	**21.7**
	Iceland	17.9	14.3	14.3	n	**17.8**	19.6	12.4	12.4	n	**19.5**
	Ireland	24.2	m	a	m	**m**	m	m	a	m	**m**
	Israel	27.4	a	a	a	**27.4**	32.2	a	a	a	**32.2**
	Italy	18.7	20.2	a	20.2	**18.8**	21.4	22.4	a	22.4	**21.5**
	Japan	28.0	32.1	a	32.1	**28.0**	32.9	35.2	a	35.2	**33.0**
	Korea	28.6	30.5	a	30.5	**28.6**	35.3	34.1	34.1	a	**35.1**
	Luxembourg	15.3	19.4	19.7	19.4	**15.6**	19.1	21.0	21.0	21.1	**19.5**
	Mexico	19.9	20.4	a	20.4	**19.9**	28.7	24.7	a	24.7	**28.3**
	Netherlands[1]	22.4	m	m	m	**m**	m	m	m	m	**m**
	New Zealand	m	m	m	m	**m**	m	m	m	m	**m**
	Norway	a	a	a	a	**a**	a	a	a	a	**a**
	Poland	19.0	11.9	11.5	12.1	**18.7**	23.5	18.0	24.4	16.2	**23.3**
	Portugal	20.2	20.8	23.2	20.0	**20.2**	22.3	24.6	23.9	25.8	**22.6**
	Slovak Republic	18.5	17.8	17.8	n	**18.4**	21.2	20.2	20.2	n	**21.1**
	Slovenia	18.5	20.2	20.2	n	**18.5**	19.8	24.0	24.0	n	**19.8**
	Spain	19.8	24.5	24.5	24.5	**21.1**	23.5	25.8	26.0	24.2	**24.3**
	Sweden	m	m	m	n	**m**	m	m	m	n	**m**
	Switzerland	19.4	m	m	m	**m**	18.7	m	m	m	**m**
	Turkey	25.8	19.2	a	19.2	**25.6**	a	a	a	a	**a**
	United Kingdom	25.7	13.0	25.7	12.9	**24.5**	21.0	15.2	19.1	10.5	**19.6**
	United States	23.8	19.3	a	19.3	**23.3**	23.2	19.1	a	19.1	**22.8**
	OECD average	21.4	20.5	20.4	20.7	**21.4**	23.5	22.8	23.0	21.3	**23.7**
	EU21 average	20.0	19.0	19.6	18.5	**19.8**	21.9	21.7	22.0	19.8	**21.9**
Other G20	Argentina[2]	25.5	26.3	29.8	24.0	**26.2**	27.8	28.1	29.7	26.9	**28.1**
	Brazil	26.5	17.7	a	17.7	**25.0**	30.2	25.0	a	25.0	**29.5**
	China	36.9	42.5	x(2)	x(2)	**37.1**	54.9	51.8	x(7)	x(7)	**54.6**
	India	m	m	m	m	**m**	m	m	m	m	**m**
	Indonesia	27.5	21.4	a	21.4	**26.4**	36.5	33.4	a	33.4	**35.3**
	Russian Federation	16.2	10.9	a	10.9	**16.2**	18.0	10.1	a	10.1	**17.9**
	Saudi Arabia	m	m	m	m	**m**	m	m	m	m	**m**
	South Africa	m	m	m	m	**m**	m	m	m	m	**m**
	G20 average	24.7	22.9	~	~	**24.5**	26.8	24.9	~	~	**26.6**

1. Year of reference 2006.
2. Year of reference 2008.

Source: OECD. Argentina, China, Indonesia: UNESCO Institute for Statistics (World Education Indicators Programme). See Annex 3 for notes *(www.oecd.org/edu/eag2011)*.

Please refer to the Reader's Guide for information concerning the symbols replacing missing data.

StatLink http://dx.doi.org/10.1787/888932465170

Table D2.2. **Ratio of students to teaching staff in educational institutions (2009)**

By level of education, calculations based on full-time equivalents

		Pre-primary education		Primary education	Secondary education			Post-secondary non-tertiary education	Tertiary education		
		Students to contact staff (teachers and teachers' aides)	Students to teaching staff		Lower secondary education	Upper secondary education	All secondary education		Tertiary-type B	Tertiary-type A and advanced research programmes	All tertiary education
		(1)	(2)	(3)	(4)	(5)	(6)	(7)	(8)	(9)	(10)
OECD	Australia[1, 2]	m	m	15.8	x(6)	x(6)	12.0	m	m	14.4	m
	Austria	10.7	15.2	12.6	9.6	10.2	9.9	10.8	x(10)	x(10)	15.6
	Belgium[3]	15.8	15.8	12.5	8.1	10.2	9.5	x(5)	x(10)	x(10)	19.5
	Canada[4]	m	x(4)	x(4)	16.6	14.7	15.9	m	m	m	m
	Chile	9.5	12.3	22.4	22.4	24.7	23.8	a	m	23.3	m
	Czech Republic	13.6	13.8	18.4	11.5	12.2	11.8	18.9	16.2	19.9	19.6
	Denmark	m	5.5	x(4)	9.9	m	m	m	m	m	m
	Estonia	m	m	16.2	15.7	16.8	16.3	x(5)	m	m	m
	Finland	m	11.2	13.6	10.1	16.6	13.6	x(5)	n	14.9	14.9
	France[3]	19.7	19.7	19.7	14.9	9.6	12.2	x(8)	16.4	15.6	15.7
	Germany	10.6	13.6	17.4	15.1	13.9	14.8	15.0	14.1	11.5	11.9
	Greece	m	m	m	m	m	m	m	m	m	m
	Hungary	m	11.0	10.7	10.8	12.8	11.8	12.4	17.5	16.2	16.3
	Iceland	6.9	6.9	x(4)	9.9	10.9	10.2	x(5, 10)	x(10)	x(10)	10.2
	Ireland[2]	4.7	10.4	15.9	x(6)	x(6)	12.6	x(6)	x(10)	x(10)	14.3
	Israel[2]	11.6	22.6	17.0	13.7	10.8	11.9	m	m	m	m
	Italy[2]	11.0	11.0	10.7	10.0	11.8	11.0	m	7.2	18.4	18.3
	Japan	15.6	16.3	18.6	14.5	12.2	13.2	x(5, 10)	7.0	11.5	10.1
	Korea	17.5	17.5	22.5	19.9	16.7	18.2	a	m	m	m
	Luxembourg	13.0	13.0	11.6	x(6)	x(6)	9.1	m	m	m	m
	Mexico	25.9	25.9	28.1	33.0	25.6	30.1	a	13.8	14.6	14.6
	Netherlands[2]	m	x(3)	15.8	x(6)	x(6)	16.1	x(6)	x(10)	x(10)	14.4
	New Zealand	10.3	10.3	16.3	16.3	12.8	14.4	22.7	16.1	17.6	17.2
	Norway[2]	m	m	10.7	9.9	9.4	9.7	x(5)	x(10)	x(10)	9.2
	Poland	m	18.6	10.2	12.9	12.0	12.4	16.1	10.1	16.2	16.1
	Portugal	m	15.7	11.3	7.6	7.7	7.7	x(5, 10)	x(10)	x(10)	14.1
	Slovak Republic	12.7	12.8	17.7	14.0	15.1	14.5	12.7	8.2	15.7	15.6
	Slovenia	9.4	9.4	16.7	7.9	14.3	11.0	x(5)	x(10)	x(10)	20.4
	Spain	m	12.1	13.3	10.1	9.3	9.8	a	8.5	11.6	10.9
	Sweden	6.2	6.3	12.1	11.3	13.2	12.3	12.9	x(10)	x(10)	8.8
	Switzerland[1, 2]	m	17.4	15.4	12.0	10.4	11.5	m	m	m	m
	Turkey	m	27.4	22.9	a	16.9	16.9	a	58.8	13.4	17.8
	United Kingdom	15.5	16.4	19.9	16.1	12.3	13.7	x(5)	x(10)	x(10)	16.5
	United States	m	13.2	14.8	14.3	15.1	14.7	16.0	x(10)	x(10)	15.3
	OECD average	12.6	14.3	16.0	13.5	13.5	13.5	15.3	14.9	15.7	14.9
	EU21 average	11.9	12.9	14.5	11.5	12.4	12.1	14.1	12.3	15.5	15.5
Other G20	Argentina[4]	m	20.8	16.0	15.3	8.8	11.9	a	18.1	14.7	15.7
	Brazil	13.6	18.2	24.0	21.0	18.1	19.8	a	x(10)	x(10)	w
	China	m	m	17.6	15.6	18.2	16.7	m	m	m	m
	India	m	m	m	m	m	m	m	m	m	m
	Indonesia	m	16.8	20.8	15.9	16.8	16.3	a	x(10)	x(10)	22.7
	Russian Federation[2, 5]	m	m	17.9	x(6)	x(6)	8.7	x(6)	9.5	13.9	12.7
	Saudi Arabia	m	m	m	m	m	m	m	m	m	m
	South Africa	m	m	m	m	m	m	m	m	m	m
	G20 average	~	~	19.1	15.9	15.1	15.4	~	~	~	~

1. Includes only general programmes in upper secondary education.
2. Public institutions only (for Australia, for tertiary-type A and advanced research programmes only; for Ireland, at pre-primary and secondary levels only; for Israel, at pre-primary level only; for Italy, from pre-primary to secondary level; for the Russian Federation, at primary level only).
3. Excludes independent private institutions.
4. Year of reference 2008.
5. Excludes part-time personnel in public institutions at lower secondary and general upper secondary levels.

Source: OECD. Argentina, China, Indonesia: UNESCO Institute for Statistics (World Education Indicators Programme). See Annex 3 for notes *(www.oecd.org/edu/eag2011)*.

Please refer to the Reader's Guide for information concerning the symbols replacing missing data.

StatLink http://dx.doi.org/10.1787/888932465189

Table D2.3. **Ratio of students to teaching staff, by type of institution (2009)**

By level of education, calculations based on full-time equivalents

	Lower secondary education				Upper secondary education				All secondary education			
	Public	Private			Public	Private			Public	Private		
		Total private institutions	Government-dependent private institutions	Independent private institutions		Total private institutions	Government-dependent private institutions	Independent private institutions		Total private institutions	Government-dependent private institutions	Independent private institutions
	(1)	(2)	(3)	(4)	(5)	(6)	(7)	(8)	(9)	(10)	(11)	(12)
OECD												
Australia[1]	**x(9)**	**x(10)**	x(11)	a	**x(9)**	**x(10)**	x(11)	a	**12.3**	**11.7**	11.7	a
Austria	**9.5**	**11.2**	x(2)	x(2)	**10.3**	**9.5**	x(6)	x(6)	**9.8**	**10.2**	x(10)	x(10)
Belgium[2]	**7.4**	**m**	8.5	m	**10.9**	**m**	9.8	m	**9.6**	**m**	9.4	m
Canada[3, 4, 5]	**16.8**	**14.4**	x(2)	x(2)	**14.8**	**13.3**	x(6)	x(6)	**16.0**	**14.0**	x(10)	x(10)
Chile	**23.0**	**21.8**	23.0	15.8	**24.1**	**25.1**	28.2	13.6	**23.6**	**23.9**	26.3	14.3
Czech Republic	**11.5**	**10.1**	10.1	a	**11.8**	**15.0**	15.0	a	**11.6**	**14.2**	14.2	a
Denmark[4]	**10.0**	**9.9**	9.9	m	**m**	**m**	m	m	**m**	**m**	m	m
Estonia	**15.8**	**12.9**	a	12.9	**16.9**	**15.0**	a	15.0	**16.4**	**14.3**	a	14.3
Finland[6]	**10.0**	**10.6**	10.6	a	**16.2**	**19.1**	19.1	a	**13.3**	**17.2**	17.2	a
France	**14.6**	**m**	16.1	m	**9.5**	**m**	10.0	m	**12.0**	**m**	12.9	m
Germany	**15.2**	**14.3**	14.3	x(3)	**14.1**	**12.7**	12.7	x(7)	**14.9**	**13.8**	13.8	x(11)
Greece	**m**	**m**	m	m	**m**	**m**	m	m	**m**	**m**	m	m
Hungary	**10.9**	**9.9**	9.9	a	**12.8**	**12.5**	12.5	a	**11.8**	**11.6**	11.6	a
Iceland[4, 6]	**9.9**	**9.3**	9.3	n	**10.9**	**10.6**	10.6	n	**10.1**	**10.3**	10.3	n
Ireland[2]	**x(9)**	**x(10)**	a	x(12)	**x(9)**	**x(10)**	a	x(12)	**12.6**	**m**	a	m
Israel	**13.7**	**a**	a	a	**10.8**	**a**	a	a	**11.9**	**a**	a	a
Italy	**10.0**	**m**	a	m	**11.8**	**m**	a	m	**11.0**	**m**	a	m
Japan[6]	**14.7**	**13.0**	a	13.0	**11.5**	**13.9**	a	13.9	**13.1**	**13.7**	a	13.7
Korea	**19.9**	**20.0**	20.0	a	**16.2**	**17.4**	17.4	a	**18.2**	**18.1**	18.1	a
Luxembourg	**8.9**	**x(10)**	x(11)	x(12)	**9.3**	**x(10)**	x(11)	x(12)	**9.1**	**8.8**	9.2	8.4
Mexico	**35.9**	**20.3**	a	20.3	**30.6**	**15.0**	a	15.0	**34.0**	**17.5**	a	17.5
Netherlands[2]	**x(9)**	**m**	a	m	**x(9)**	**m**	a	m	**16.1**	**m**	a	m
New Zealand	**16.6**	**15.2**	16.2	13.2	**14.8**	**9.4**	14.5	6.4	**15.7**	**11.1**	15.2	7.6
Norway	**9.9**	**m**	m	m	**9.4**	**m**	m	m	**9.7**	**m**	m	m
Poland	**13.0**	**9.8**	11.3	9.2	**12.0**	**11.5**	14.0	11.1	**12.5**	**10.9**	12.7	10.5
Portugal	**7.3**	**10.3**	11.1	9.5	**8.1**	**6.5**	11.3	5.6	**7.7**	**7.6**	11.2	6.4
Slovak Republic	**14.0**	**13.3**	13.3	n	**15.4**	**13.3**	13.3	n	**14.6**	**13.3**	13.3	n
Slovenia[2]	**7.9**	**4.5**	4.5	n	**14.3**	**13.2**	x(6)	x(6)	**10.9**	**12.6**	x(10)	x(10)
Spain	**8.6**	**15.5**	15.5	15.6	**8.3**	**14.1**	14.3	13.8	**8.5**	**15.1**	15.3	14.4
Sweden	**11.2**	**12.1**	12.1	n	**13.0**	**14.7**	14.7	n	**12.1**	**13.7**	13.7	n
Switzerland[7]	**12.0**	**m**	m	m	**10.4**	**m**	m	m	**11.5**	**m**	m	m
Turkey	**a**	**a**	a	a	**17.7**	**7.5**	a	7.5	**17.7**	**7.5**	a	7.5
United Kingdom[2]	**17.6**	**11.4**	12.3	10.1	**12.8**	**11.6**	12.0	9.7	**14.9**	**11.6**	12.1	9.8
United States	**14.8**	**10.9**	a	10.9	**15.9**	**10.0**	a	10.0	**15.3**	**10.5**	a	10.5
OECD average	**13.5**	**12.8**	12.7	9.3	**13.6**	**13.2**	14.3	8.7	**13.7**	**13.0**	13.8	9.0
EU21 average	**11.3**	**11.1**	11.4	11.5	**12.2**	**13.0**	13.2	11.1	**12.1**	**12.5**	12.8	10.6
Other G20												
Argentina[3]	**14.8**	**17.0**	16.4	19.1	**7.9**	**11.5**	10.5	15.9	**11.4**	**14.0**	13.1	17.3
Brazil	**22.8**	**12.5**	a	12.5	**19.9**	**11.8**	a	11.8	**21.6**	**12.1**	a	12.1
China	**m**	**m**	m	m	**m**	**m**	m	m	**m**	**m**	m	m
India	**m**	**m**	m	m	**m**	**m**	m	m	**m**	**m**	m	m
Indonesia	**18.6**	**12.7**	a	12.7	**18.2**	**15.7**	a	15.7	**18.5**	**14.0**	a	14.0
Russian Federation	**m**	**m**	a	m	**m**	**m**	a	m	**m**	**m**	a	m
Saudi Arabia	**m**	**m**	m	m	**m**	**m**	m	m	**m**	**m**	m	m
South Africa	**m**	**m**	m	m	**m**	**m**	m	m	**m**	**m**	m	m
G20 average	**m**	**m**	m	m	**m**	**m**	m	m	**m**	**m**	m	m

1. Includes only general programmes in lower and upper secondary education.
2. Upper secondary includes post-secondary non-tertiary education.
3. Year of reference 2008.
4. Lower secondary includes primary education.
5. Lower secondary includes pre-primary education.
6. Upper secondary education includes programmes from post-secondary education.
7. Includes only general programmes in upper secondary education.

Source: OECD. Argentina, Indonesia: UNESCO Institute for Statistics (World Education Indicators Programme). See Annex 3 for notes *(www.oecd.org/edu/eag2011)*.

Please refer to the Reader's Guide for information concerning the symbols replacing missing data.

StatLink http://dx.doi.org/10.1787/888932465208

INDICATOR D3

HOW MUCH ARE TEACHERS PAID?

- The statutory salaries of teachers with at least 15 years of experience average USD 38 914 at the primary level, USD 41 701 at the lower secondary level and USD 43 711 at the upper secondary level.
- On average in OECD countries, teachers' salaries at the primary-school level amount to 77% of full-time, full-year earnings for 25-64 year-olds with a tertiary education, while teachers' salaries at the lower secondary level amount to 81% of that benchmark and teacher's salaries at the upper secondary level amount to 85% of it.

Chart D3.1. Teachers' salaries (minimum, after 10 years experience, 15 years experience, and maximum) in lower secondary education (2009)

Annual statutory teachers' salaries in public institutions in lower secondary education, in equivalent USD converted using PPPs, and the ratio of salary after 15 years of experience to earnings for full-time, full-year workers with tertiary education aged 25 to 64

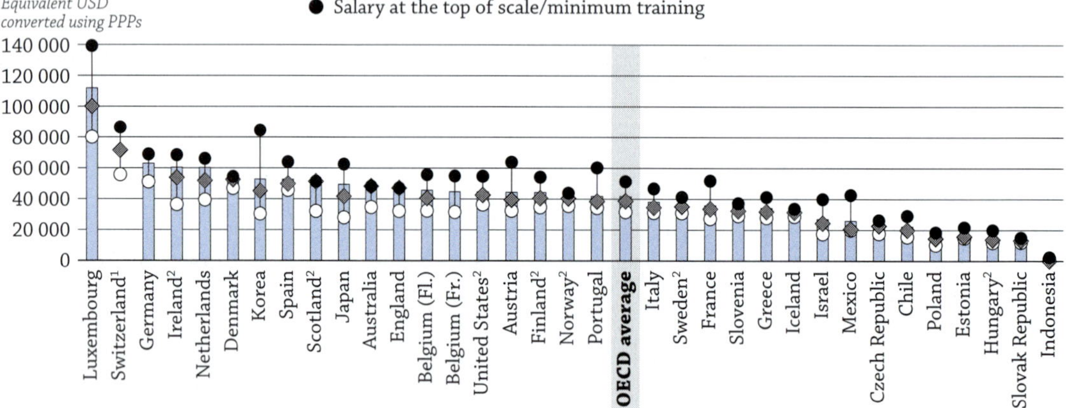

Ratio of salary after 15 years of experience/minimum training to earnings for full-time, full-year workers with tertiary education aged 25 to 64 (2009 or latest available year)

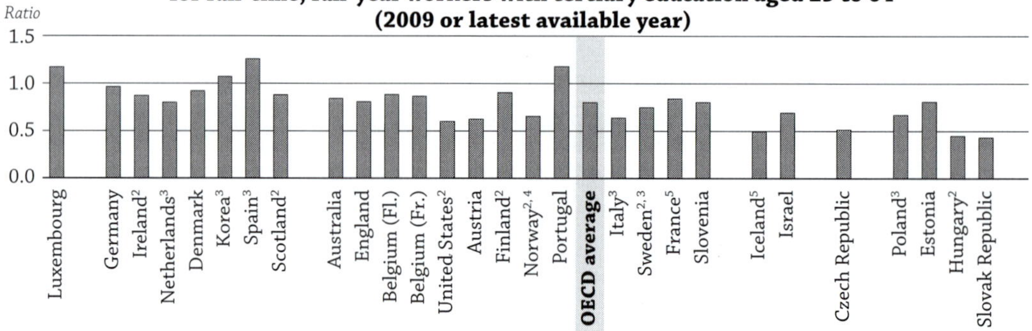

1. Salaries after 11 years of experience.
2. Actual salaries.
3. Year of reference 2008.
4. Year of reference 2007.
5. Year of reference 2006.

Countries are ranked in descending order of teachers' salaries in lower secondary education after 15 years of experience and minimum training.

Source: OECD. Indonesia: UNESCO Institute for Statistics (World Education Indicators Programme). Tables D3.1 and D3.2. See Annex 3 for notes (*www.oecd.org/edu/eag2011*).

StatLink http://dx.doi.org/10.1787/888932461978

Context

Teachers' salaries represent the largest single cost in school education. Burgeoning national debt, spurred by governments' responses to the financial crisis of late 2008, have put pressure on policy makers to reduce government expenditure – particularly on public payrolls. Since compensation and working conditions are important for attracting, developing and retaining skilled and high-quality teachers, policy makers should carefully consider teachers' salaries as they try to ensure both quality teaching and balanced education budgets (see Indicators B6 and B7).

Other findings

- In most OECD countries, **teachers' salaries increase with the level of education they teach.** For example, in Belgium, Indonesia, Luxembourg and Poland, the salary of an upper secondary school teacher with at least 15 years of experience is at least 25% higher than that of a primary school teacher with the same experience.
- **Salaries at the top of the scale are, on average, around 64% higher than starting salaries in both primary and secondary education**, and the difference tends to be greatest when it takes many years to progress through the scale. In countries where it takes 30 years or more to reach the top of the scale, the salaries at this level are an average of 80% higher than starting salaries.
- Among the 35 countries with available data, half offer an **additional payment to teachers for outstanding performance**.

Trends

Teachers' salaries rose, in real terms, in most countries with available data between 1995 and 2009. Notable exceptions are France and Switzerland, where there was a decline in teachers' salaries in real terms during that period.

Using data for countries with available data in all reference years, the growth rate in teachers' salaries was lower than the growth rate in GDP per capita in most countries between 2000 and 2008. However, from 2008 to 2009, most countries experienced an increase in teachers' salaries relative to GDP per capita. This is likely to be a result of the sharp slowdown in GDP growth in the aftermath of the financial crisis.

Analysis

Comparing teachers' salaries

Teachers' salaries are one component of teachers' total compensation. Other benefits such as regional allowances for teaching in remote regions, family allowances, reduced rates on public transport and tax allowances on the purchase of cultural materials may also form part of teachers' total remuneration. There are also large differences in taxation and social-benefits systems in OECD countries. All this should be borne in mind when comparing salaries across countries

Teachers' salaries vary widely across countries. The salaries of lower secondary school teachers with at least 15 years of experience range from less than USD 15 000 in Hungary, Indonesia and the Slovak Republic to USD 60 000 or more in Germany, Ireland and the Netherlands, and exceed USD 100 000 in Luxembourg (Table D3.1 and Chart D3.1).

In most OECD countries, teachers' salaries increase with the level of education taught. In Belgium, upper secondary school teachers with 15 years of experience earn about 30% more than both primary and lower secondary school teachers with the same experience, while in Luxembourg, both lower and upper secondary school teachers receive the same salary, which is 50% higher than that of a primary school teacher. In Chile, Iceland, Japan, Korea and Turkey, there is less than a 5% difference between upper secondary and primary school teachers' salaries and in Australia, England, Estonia, Greece, Ireland, Portugal, Scotland, the Slovak Republic and Slovenia, both primary and secondary school teachers received the same salary. In contrast, in Israel, an upper secondary school teacher earns 14% less than a primary school teacher (Table D3.1).

Differences in teachers' salaries at different education levels may influence how schools and school systems attract and retain teachers and may also influence the extent to which teachers move among education levels.

Teachers' salaries relative to earnings for workers with a tertiary education

The propensity of young people to undertake teacher training, as well as of training teachers to enter or stay in the profession will be influenced by the salaries of teachers relative to those of other occupations requiring similar levels of qualification. In all OECD countries, a tertiary qualification is required to become a teacher; so the likely alternative to teacher education is another tertiary education programme (Table D3.2 and Box D3.1). Thus, to interpret salary levels in different countries and reflect comparative labour-market conditions, teachers' salaries are compared to those of other similarly-educated professionals: 25-64 year-old full-time, full-year workers with a tertiary education (for additional information, see Indicator A10). This indicator uses the salaries of teachers with minimum qualifications and after 15 years of experience. Teachers may be of any age. The average earnings for teachers are likely to be higher than this specific statutory salary.

Teachers' salaries at the primary level amount on average to 77% of full-time, full-year earnings for 25-64 year-olds with tertiary education, 81% at the lower secondary level and 85% for upper secondary schools. The lowest relative teachers' salaries, compared to the salaries of other professionals with comparable education are found in the Slovak Republic at all levels of education, and in Hungary and Iceland for primary and lower secondary school teachers, where statutory salaries for teachers with 15 years of experience are 50% or less of what a full-time, full-year worker with a tertiary education earns, on average.

Relative salaries for teachers in primary and lower secondary education are highest in Korea, Portugal and Spain, where teachers earn more than the average salary of a worker with a tertiary education. In upper secondary education, teachers' salaries are at least 10% higher than those of comparably educated workers in Belgium, Luxembourg and Portugal, and up to 32% higher in Spain (Table D3.2 and Chart D3.1).

Teaching experience and salary scales

Salary structures define the salaries paid to teachers at different points in their careers. Deferred compensation, which rewards employees for staying in organisations or professions and for meeting established performance criteria, is also used in teachers' salary structures. OECD data on teachers' salaries are limited to information on statutory salaries at four points of the salary scale: starting salaries, salaries after 10 years of service, salaries after 15 years of experience and salaries at the top of the scale. The salaries discussed here are those of teachers who have the minimum required training. These salaries must be interpreted with caution since, in some countries, further qualifications can lead to wage increases. However, some inferences can be drawn from this data, notably the degree to which teachers' salary structures provide for salary increases at different levels of promotion and tenure.

In OECD countries, statutory salaries for lower secondary school teachers with 10 years of experience and 15 years of experience are, respectively, 24% and 35% higher, on average than starting salaries. Furthermore, salaries at the top of the salary scale, which is reached after an average of 24 years of experience, are on average 64% higher than starting salaries. However, a number of countries have relatively flat salary scales. For example, the difference between salaries at the top and bottom of the scale is less than 25% in Denmark and Iceland at the primary and lower secondary level. In Norway, the Slovak Republic and Turkey, the difference is less than 25% at all levels of education (Table D3.1).

Box D3.1. Pre-service teacher training

All OECD countries require a tertiary qualification for entry to the teaching profession at the primary level and beyond, and in most, a tertiary-type A (largely theory-based) qualification is required to become a teacher, especially at the upper secondary level. In Belgium and Luxembourg, a tertiary-type B (shorter, and largely vocational) qualification is sufficient to become a primary school teacher, while in Ireland, Japan, Poland and Portugal, both tertiary-type A and tertiary-type B qualifications are accepted. To teach lower secondary school, a tertiary-type B qualification is sufficient in Belgium, while both tertiary-type A and tertiary-type B qualifications are accepted in Ireland, Japan and Mexico. To teach at the upper secondary level, both tertiary-type A and tertiary-type B qualifications are accepted in Ireland, Mexico and Slovenia (Table D3.2).

On average, pre-service training for teachers in secondary education tends to be longer than in primary education. For primary teachers, the average length of pre-service training varies from three years in Austria, Belgium, Spain and Switzerland to five or more years in the Czech Republic, Finland, France, Germany and Slovenia. For lower secondary teachers, the average duration of pre-service training is longer than that for primary education in a third of all OECD countries. At the upper secondary level, it varies from three years (for some programmes) in England, Israel and Poland to more than six years in Germany and the Slovak Republic.

Lower secondary school teachers in Australia, Denmark, Estonia and Scotland reach the highest step on the salary scale within six to nine years. Some difficulties may arise in these countries due to weak monetary incentives as teachers approach the peak in their age-earnings profiles. However there may be some benefits to compressed pay scales. It is often argued, for example, that organisations in which there are smaller differences in salaries among employees enjoy more trust, freer flows of information and more collegiality among co-workers.

In Austria, Chile, the Czech Republic, France, Greece, Hungary, Indonesia, Israel, Italy, Japan, Korea, Luxembourg, Portugal, the Slovak Republic and Spain, lower secondary school teachers reach the top of the salary scale after at least 30 years of service (Table D3.1). While salary increases are gradual in two-thirds of the 28 OECD countries with relevant data, in the remaining one-third of countries, their salary scales include steps of uneven size. For example, in the Czech Republic and in Greece, salaries at the top of the scale are 50% higher than starting salaries, and teachers in both countries must work 32 (the Czech Republic) or 33 years (Greece) to reach the top salary.

However, most of the increase in the Czech Republic occurs during the first 10 years of service and salaries rise at a slower rate during the next 22 years, while in Greece, there are gradual salary increases throughout the career.

When considering salary structure for teachers, it is important to remember that not all teachers reach the top of the salary scale. For example, in the Netherlands, there are three different salary levels for teachers in secondary education. In 2009, only 17% of these teachers were paid according to the highest salary scale.

Statutory salaries per hour of net teaching time

The average statutory salary per teaching hour after 15 years of experience is USD 51 for primary school teachers, USD 62 for lower secondary teachers, and USD 71 for upper secondary teachers in general education. Chile, Estonia, Hungary, Indonesia, Mexico and the Slovak Republic show the lowest salaries per teaching hour – USD 30 or less. In contrast, salaries per hour reach USD 70 or more at all education levels in Denmark, Germany, Japan and Luxembourg. (Table D3.1).

As secondary school teachers are required to teach fewer hours than primary school teachers, their salaries per teaching hour are usually higher than those of teachers at lower levels of education, even in countries where statutory salaries are similar (see Indicator D4). On average among OECD countries, upper secondary school teachers' salaries per teaching hour exceed those of primary school teachers by around 34% (Table D3.1). In Chile the difference is less than 5% and in Scotland there is no difference, while it is about 100% in Denmark and Indonesia. In contrast, in England, primary school teachers' salaries per teaching hour exceed those of upper secondary school teachers by 11%.

However, the difference between primary and secondary school teachers may disappear when comparing salaries per hour of working time. In Portugal, for example, there is a 14% difference in salaries per teaching hour between primary and upper secondary school teachers, even though statutory salaries and working time are actually the same at these levels. The difference is explained by the fact that primary school teachers spend more time in teaching activities than upper secondary teachers do (see Table D4.1).

Trends since 1995

Trends in salaries in real terms

Between 2000 and 2009, teachers' salaries increased in real terms in most countries. The largest increases – of well over 50% – were seen in the Czech Republic, Estonia and Turkey. The only exceptions to this trend were Australia, France, Japan and Switzerland. Data for 1995 are only available for a small subsample of countries. All countries in this subsample saw an increase in real salaries between 1995 and 2009, except for France and Switzerland. (Table D3.3 and Chart D3.2).

Trends in relative salaries (GDP)

Comparing statutory salaries to GDP per capita facilitates standardised comparisons over time and offers a way of contextualising teacher salary levels in terms of countries' wealth. GDP per capita is related to several factors in addition to earnings, such as capital income and labour-force participation. Nevertheless, the amount countries invest in teachers relative to their available resources provides an approximate indication of the value countries place on education. According to this measure in 2009, statutory salaries for secondary teachers with 15 years of experience relative to GDP per capita are highest in Germany, Korea, Mexico (lower secondary level), Switzerland (upper secondary level) and Turkey. In primary education, the highest ratios are found in Korea and Turkey. Relative to GDP per capita, mid-career salaries are lowest in Estonia, Hungary, Indonesia and the Slovak Republic (Table D3.4).

Most countries saw a fall in teachers' salaries relative to GDP per capita during the 2000-2009 period. The fall is most noticeable in Australia, France, Japan, Korea and Switzerland but except for Australia and France, teachers' salaries relative to GDP per capita in these countries remain well above the OECD average. On the other hand, the Czech Republic, Denmark and Portugal all saw substantial increases in salaries relative to GDP per capita from 2000 to 2009 (Chart D3.3).

Chart D3.2. Changes in lower secondary teachers' salaries after 15 years of experience/minimum training (1995, 2000, 2005, 2009)

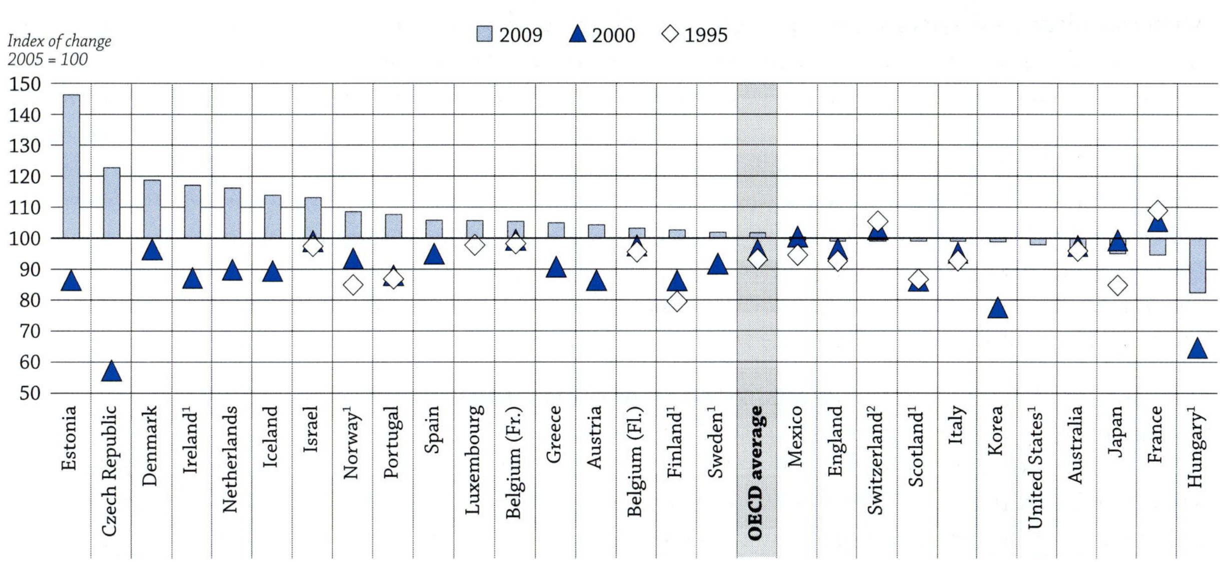

1. Actual salaries.
2. Salaries after 11 years of experience.
Countries are ranked in descending order of the index of change between 2005 and 2009 in teachers' salaries in lower secondary education after 15 years of experience.
Source: OECD. Table D3.3. See Annex 3 for notes (*www.oecd.org/edu/eag2011*).
StatLink http://dx.doi.org/10.1787/888932461997

Chart D3.3. Trends in the ratio of salaries after 15 years of experience/minimum training to GDP per capita (2000, 2005, 2009)

Ratio of annual statutory teachers' salaries in public institutions in lower secondary education after 15 years of experience to GDP per capita

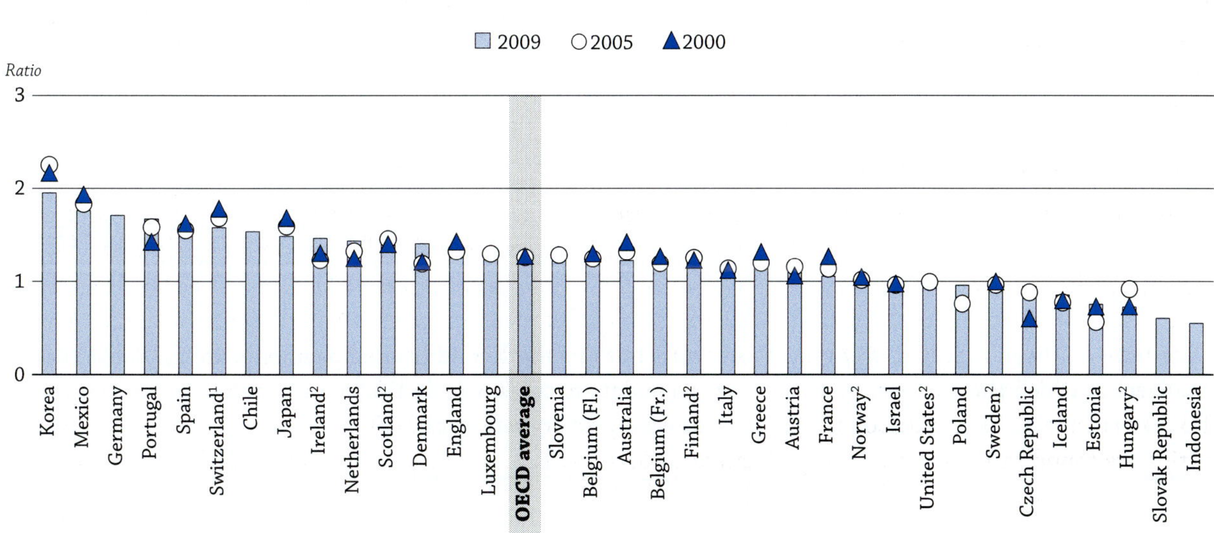

1. Salaries after 11 years of experience.
2. Actual salaries.
Countries are ranked in descending order of the ratio of salary after 15 years of experience/minimum training to GDP per capita in 2009.
Source: OECD. Indonesia: UNESCO Institute for Statistics (World Education Indicators Programme). Table D3.4. See Annex 3 for notes (*www.oecd.org/edu/eag2011*).
StatLink http://dx.doi.org/10.1787/888932462016

In most countries, GDP per capita is lower than the earnings of 25-64 year-old full-time, full-year workers with a tertiary education, thus the values of the indicator using GDP per capita are higher than those of the indicator using earnings (Table D3.2 and Table D3.4). For lower secondary school teachers, the average salary to GDP per capita across OECD countries is 1.24, while the average salary to earnings for other workers with tertiary education is 0.81. In addition, there is less variation in the latter indicator. This can be related to the fact that GDP per capita is a broad income measure and is the sum of capital income and labour income per capita in a country. However, the countries with high and low teachers' salaries relative to GDP per capita also tend to have, respectively, high and low ratios of teachers' salaries to average earnings for workers with tertiary education. Still, there are some noticeable exceptions. For example, in Korea, the indicator related to GDP per capita is high while the indicator using earnings is more in line with other countries. The opposite is true for Spain.

Box D3.2. **Effect of the financial crisis**

The financial crisis that hit the world economy in the last months of 2008 may significantly affect the salaries for civil servants and public sector workers in general. The first-order effect of the crisis was a general reduction in GDP growth in the OECD area and some countries went into a recession. The second-order effect was a large increase in national debt that put pressure on government expenditure in many countries. The combination of reduced economic growth and fiscal stress affect public-sector salaries, including teachers' salaries in many ways. A decline in GDP per capita directly increases the salary-to-GDP ratio. In addition, the likely partial effect of reduced growth and recession is to increase relative teacher salaries as wages generally react more slowly than GDP to a cyclical downturn. On the other hand, the pressure to trim government expenditure in order to reduce national debt may result in cuts in teacher and other civil-service salaries in some countries. However, in most countries, these measures were implemented after 2009.

Additional payments: Incentives and allowances

In addition to basic pay scales, school systems increasingly use schemes that offer additional payments or other rewards for teachers. These may take the form of financial remuneration and/or reduction in the number of teaching hours. Greece and Iceland, for example, offer a reduction in required teaching hours to reward experience or long service. In Portugal, teachers may receive a salary increase and a reduction in teaching time when they carry out special tasks or activities, such as training student teachers or providing guidance counselling. Together with the starting salary, these payments may influence a person's decision to enter or remain in the teaching profession. Additional payments early in a career may include family allowances and bonuses for working in certain locations, and higher initial salaries for higher-than-minimum teaching qualifications.

Data have not been collected on payment amounts but on whether additional payments are available and on the level at which the decision to award such payments is taken (Table D3.5a and Tables D3.5b, D3.5c and D3.5d available on line, and Annex 3 available at *www.oecd.org/edu/eag2011*).

Additional payments are most often awarded for particular responsibilities or working conditions, such as teaching in more disadvantaged schools, particularly those located in very poor neighbourhoods or those with a large proportion of students whose language is not the language of instruction. These schools often have difficulty attracting teachers and are more likely to have less-experienced teachers (OECD, 2005). These additional payments are provided annually in about half of the countries. Nine countries also offer additional payments, usually on an annual basis, for teachers who teach in certain fields in which there are teacher shortages.

Additional payments based on teachers' qualifications, training and performance are also common in OECD and partner countries. The most common types of payments are for an initial education qualification and/or a level of teacher certification and training that is higher than the minimum requirement. Some 65% of countries make these payments available, with half of all countries offering both types of payments. Twenty-two countries offer additional payments for the successful completion of professional development activities. In 16 of these countries, these payments help to determine the base salary, but in Korea they are only offered on an incidental basis.

Two-thirds of the 18 countries that offer an additional payment to reward outstanding teaching do so as incidental payments; 11 countries offer these payments as annual additions to teachers' salaries. In 15 of the 18 countries that offer this performance incentive, the decision to award the additional payments can be made at the school level.

Less than half of all OECD countries offer additional payments based on teachers' demographic characteristics (family status or age), and most of these are annual payments.

Definitions

An **adjustment to base salary** is defined as any difference in salary between what a particular teacher actually receives for work performed at a school and the amount that he or she would expect to receive on the basis of experience (i.e. number of years in the teaching profession). Adjustments may be temporary or permanent, and they can effectively move a teacher off the scale and to a different salary scale or to a higher step on the same salary scale.

Earnings for workers with tertiary education (Table D3.2) are average earnings for full-time, full-year workers aged 25 to 64 and with an education at ISCED 5A/5B/6 level. The relative salary indicator is calculated for the latest year with earnings data available. For countries in which teachers' salary and workers' earnings information are not available for the same year (e.g. Poland), the indicator is adjusted for inflation using the GDP deflator. Reference statistics for earnings for workers with tertiary education are provided in Annexes 2 and 3.

Salaries after 15 years of experience refer to the scheduled annual salary of a full-time classroom teacher with the minimum training necessary to be fully qualified plus 15 years of experience. The **maximum salaries** reported refer to the scheduled maximum annual salary (top of the salary scale) of a full-time classroom teacher with the minimum training to be fully qualified for the job.

Starting salaries refer to the average scheduled gross salary per year for a full-time teacher with the minimum training necessary to be fully qualified at the beginning of the teaching career.

Statutory salaries (Table D3.1) refer to scheduled salaries according to official pay scales, while **actual salaries** refer to the average annual salary earned by a full-time teacher. The salaries reported are gross (total sum paid by the employer) less the employer's contribution to social security and pension, according to existing salary scales. Salaries are "before tax", i.e. before deductions for income tax. In Table D3.1, salary per hour of net contact divides a teacher's annual statutory salary by the annual net teaching time in hours (see Table D4.1).

Methodology

Data on statutory teachers' salaries and bonuses are derived from the 2010 OECD-INES Survey on Teachers and the Curriculum. Data refer to the school year 2008-09 and are reported in accordance with formal policies for public institutions.

Statutory salaries as reported by most of the countries here must be distinguished from actual expenditures on wages by governments and from teachers' average salaries, which are also influenced by factors such as the age structure of the teaching force and the prevalence of part-time work.

Measuring the statutory salary of a full-time teacher relative to the number of hours per year that a teacher is required to spend teaching does not adjust salaries for the amount of time that teachers spend in various other teaching-related activities. Since the proportion of teachers' working time spent teaching varies across OECD countries, statutory salaries per hour of net teaching time must be interpreted with caution (see Indicator D4). However, it can provide an estimate of the cost of the actual time teachers spend in the classroom.

Gross teachers' salaries were converted using GDP and purchasing power parities (PPPs) and exchange rate data from the OECD National Accounts database. The period of reference for teachers' salaries is from 1 July 2008 to 30 June 2009. The reference date for GDP per capita and PPPs is 2008-09. As a complement to Table D3.1, which presents teachers' salaries in equivalent USD, converted using PPPs, a table with teachers' salaries in equivalent EUR converted using PPPs is included in Annex 2.

For calculation of changes in teachers' salaries (Table D3.3), the GDP deflator is used to convert salaries to 2005 prices.

Notes on definitions and methodologies for each country are provided in Annex 3 at *www.oecd.org/edu/eag2011*.

The statistical data for Israel are supplied by and under the responsibility of the relevant Israeli authorities. The use of such data by the OECD is without prejudice to the status of the Golan Heights, East Jerusalem and Israeli settlements in the West Bank under the terms of international law.

References

OECD (2005), *Teachers Matter: Attracting, Developing and Retaining Effective Teachers*, OECD, Paris.

OECD (2008c), *Improving School Leadership, Volume 1: Policy and Practices*, OECD, Paris.

The following additional material relevant to this indicator is available on line:

- ***Table D3.5b. Decisions made by school principal on payments for teachers in public institutions (2009)***
  StatLink http://dx.doi.org/10.1787/888932465341
- ***Table D3.5c. Decisions made by local or regional authority on payments for teachers in public institutions (2009)***
  StatLink http://dx.doi.org/10.1787/888932465360
- ***Table D3.5d. Decisions made by the national authority on payments for teachers in public institutions (2009)***
  StatLink http://dx.doi.org/10.1787/888932465379

Table D3.1. [1/2] Teachers' salaries (2009)

Annual statutory teachers' salaries in public institutions at starting salary, after 10 and 15 years of experience and at the top of the scale, by level of education, in equivalent USD converted using PPPs

		Primary education				Lower secondary education				Upper secondary education			
		Starting salary/ minimum training	Salary after 10 years of experience/minimum training	Salary after 15 years of experience/minimum training	Salary at top of scale/ minimum training	Starting salary/ minimum training	Salary after 10 years of experience/minimum training	Salary after 15 years of experience/minimum training	Salary at top of scale/ minimum training	Starting salary/ minimum training	Salary after 10 years of experience/minimum training	Salary after 15 years of experience/minimum training	Salary at top of scale/ minimum training
		(1)	(2)	(3)	(4)	(5)	(6)	(7)	(8)	(9)	(10)	(11)	(12)
OECD	Australia	34 664	48 233	48 233	48 233	34 664	48 233	48 233	48 233	34 664	48 233	48 233	48 233
	Austria	30 998	36 588	41 070	61 390	32 404	39 466	44 389	63 781	32 883	35 539	45 712	67 135
	Belgium (Fl.)	32 429	40 561	45 614	55 718	32 429	40 561	45 614	55 718	40 356	51 323	58 470	70 382
	Belgium (Fr.)	31 545	m	44 696	54 848	31 545	m	44 696	54 848	39 415	m	57 613	69 579
	Canada	m	m	m	m	m	m	m	m	m	m	m	m
	Chile	15 612	19 982	22 246	29 179	15 612	19 982	22 246	29 179	16 296	20 895	23 273	30 548
	Czech Republic	17 705	22 279	23 806	25 965	17 711	22 750	24 330	26 305	18 167	24 000	25 537	28 039
	Denmark	46 950	52 529	54 360	54 360	46 950	52 529	54 360	54 360	47 664	62 279	62 279	62 279
	England	32 189	47 047	47 047	47 047	32 189	47 047	47 047	47 047	32 189	47 047	47 047	47 047
	Estonia	14 881	15 758	15 758	21 749	14 881	15 758	15 758	21 749	14 881	15 758	15 758	21 749
	Finland[1]	32 692	37 632	41 415	50 461	34 707	40 550	44 294	54 181	35 743	45 444	49 237	61 089
	France	24 006	31 156	33 359	49 221	27 296	33 653	35 856	51 833	27 585	33 942	36 145	52 150
	Germany	46 446	m	57 005	61 787	51 080	m	62 930	68 861	55 743	m	68 619	77 628
	Greece	27 951	31 858	34 209	41 265	27 951	31 858	34 209	41 265	27 951	31 858	34 209	41 265
	Hungary[1]	12 045	13 838	14 902	19 952	12 045	13 838	14 902	19 952	13 572	16 211	17 894	25 783
	Iceland	28 767	31 537	32 370	33 753	28 767	31 537	32 370	33 753	26 198	30 574	32 676	34 178
	Ireland[1]	36 433	53 787	60 355	68 391	36 433	53 787	60 355	68 391	36 433	53 787	60 355	68 391
	Israel	18 935	27 262	28 929	42 425	17 530	24 407	27 112	39 942	16 715	22 344	25 013	37 874
	Italy	28 907	31 811	34 954	42 567	31 159	34 529	38 082	46 743	31 159	35 371	39 151	48 870
	Japan	27 995	41 711	49 408	62 442	27 995	41 711	49 408	62 442	27 995	41 711	49 408	64 135
	Korea	30 522	45 269	52 820	84 650	30 401	45 148	52 699	84 529	30 401	45 148	52 699	84 529
	Luxembourg	51 799	67 340	74 402	113 017	80 053	100 068	111 839	139 152	80 053	100 068	111 839	139 152
	Mexico	15 658	15 768	20 415	33 582	19 957	20 618	25 905	42 621	m	m	m	m
	Netherlands	37 974	45 064	50 370	55 440	39 400	51 830	60 174	66 042	39 400	51 830	60 174	66 042
	New Zealand	m	m	m	m	m	m	m	m	m	m	m	m
	Norway[1]	35 593	40 392	43 614	43 861	35 593	40 392	43 614	43 861	38 950	42 258	46 247	46 495
	Poland	9 186	12 809	15 568	16 221	10 340	14 520	17 732	18 479	11 676	16 585	20 290	21 149
	Portugal	34 296	38 427	41 771	60 261	34 296	38 427	41 771	60 261	34 296	38 427	41 771	60 261
	Scotland[1]	32 143	51 272	51 272	51 272	32 143	51 272	51 272	51 272	32 143	51 272	51 272	51 272
	Slovak Republic	12 139	13 352	13 964	15 054	12 139	13 352	13 964	15 054	12 139	13 352	13 964	15 054
	Slovenia	29 191	32 385	35 482	37 274	29 191	32 385	35 482	37 274	29 191	32 385	35 482	37 274
	Spain	40 896	44 576	47 182	57 067	45 721	49 807	52 654	63 942	46 609	50 823	53 759	65 267
	Sweden[1]	30 648	34 086	35 349	40 985	30 975	35 146	36 521	41 255	32 463	36 983	38 584	44 141
	Switzerland[2]	48 853	62 903	m	76 483	55 696	71 456	m	86 418	64 450	83 828	m	98 495
	Turkey	25 536	26 374	27 438	29 697	a	a	a	a	26 173	27 011	28 076	30 335
	United States[1]	36 502	42 475	44 788	51 633	36 416	42 566	44 614	54 725	36 907	43 586	47 977	54 666
	OECD average	29 767	36 127	38 914	48 154	31 687	38 683	41 701	51 317	33 044	40 319	43 711	53 651
	EU21 average	30 150	35 912	39 735	47 883	32 306	38 721	42 967	50 772	33 553	40 204	45 442	53 956
Other G20	Argentina	m	m	m	m	m	m	m	m	m	m	m	m
	Brazil	m	m	m	m	m	m	m	m	m	m	m	m
	China	m	m	m	m	m	m	m	m	m	m	m	m
	India	m	m	m	m	m	m	m	m	m	m	m	m
	Indonesia	1 564	m	1 979	2 255	1 667	m	2 255	2 450	1 930	m	2 497	2 721
	Russian Federation	m	m	m	m	m	m	m	m	m	m	m	m
	Saudi Arabia	m	m	m	m	m	m	m	m	m	m	m	m
	South Africa	m	m	m	m	m	m	m	m	m	m	m	m

1. Actual salaries.
2. Salaries after 11 years of experience for Columns 2, 6 and 10.

Source: OECD. Indonesia: UNESCO Institute for Statistics (World Education Indicators Programme). See Annex 3 for notes *(www.oecd.org/edu/eag2011)*.

Please refer to the Reader's Guide for information concerning the symbols replacing missing data.

StatLink http://dx.doi.org/10.1787/888932465246

D3

Table D3.1. [2/2] Teachers' salaries (2009)

Annual statutory teachers' salaries in public institutions at starting salary, after 10 and 15 years of experience and at the top of the scale, by level of education, in equivalent USD converted using PPPs

	Ratio of salary at top of scale to starting salary			Years from starting to top salary (lower secondary education)	Salary per hour of net contact (teaching) time after 15 years of experience			Ratio of salary per teaching hour of upper secondary to primary teachers (after 15 years of experience)
	Primary education	Lower secondary education	Upper secondary education		Primary education	Lower secondary education	Upper secondary education	
	(13)	(14)	(15)	(16)	(17)	(18)	(19)	(20)
OECD								
Australia	1.39	1.39	1.39	9	55	59	61	1.10
Austria	1.98	1.97	2.04	34	53	73	78	1.47
Belgium (Fl.)	1.72	1.72	1.74	27	57	66	91	1.60
Belgium (Fr.)	1.74	1.74	1.77	27	61	67	94	1.55
Canada	m	m	m	m	m	m	m	m
Chile	1.87	1.87	1.87	30	18	18	19	1.05
Czech Republic	1.47	1.49	1.54	32	29	39	43	1.50
Denmark	1.16	1.16	1.31	8	84	84	165	1.97
England	1.46	1.46	1.46	10	74	66	66	0.89
Estonia	1.46	1.46	1.46	7	25	25	27	1.09
Finland[1]	1.54	1.56	1.71	16	61	75	90	1.46
France	2.05	1.90	1.89	34	36	56	58	1.58
Germany	1.33	1.35	1.39	28	71	83	96	1.36
Greece	1.48	1.48	1.48	33	58	80	80	1.38
Hungary[1]	1.66	1.66	1.90	40	25	25	30	1.20
Iceland	1.17	1.17	1.30	18	53	53	60	1.12
Ireland[1]	1.88	1.88	1.88	22	64	82	82	1.29
Israel	2.24	2.28	2.27	36	37	46	48	1.30
Italy	1.47	1.50	1.57	35	46	62	63	1.37
Japan	2.23	2.23	2.29	34	70	82	99	1.41
Korea	2.77	2.78	2.78	37	63	85	87	1.38
Luxembourg	2.18	1.74	1.74	30	101	177	177	1.75
Mexico	2.14	2.14	m	14	26	25	m	m
Netherlands	1.46	1.68	1.68	17	54	80	80	1.48
New Zealand	m	m	m	m	m	m	m	m
Norway[1]	1.23	1.23	1.19	16	59	67	89	1.50
Poland	1.77	1.79	1.81	10	32	37	42	1.31
Portugal	1.76	1.76	1.76	34	48	54	54	1.14
Scotland[1]	1.60	1.60	1.60	6	60	60	60	1.00
Slovak Republic	1.24	1.24	1.24	32	17	22	23	1.35
Slovenia	1.28	1.28	1.28	13	51	51	56	1.09
Spain	1.40	1.40	1.40	38	54	74	78	1.45
Sweden[1]	1.34	1.33	1.36	a	m	m	m	m
Switzerland[2]	1.57	1.55	1.53	27	m	m	m	m
Turkey	1.16	a	1.16	a	43	a	50	1.15
United States[1]	1.41	1.50	1.48	m	41	42	46	1.12
OECD average	1.64	1.64	1.64	24	51	62	71	1.34
EU21 average	1.58	1.57	1.61	24	53	65	74	1.38
Other G20								
Argentina	m	m	m	m	m	m	m	m
Brazil	m	m	m	m	m	m	m	m
China	m	m	m	m	m	m	m	m
India	m	m	m	m	m	m	m	m
Indonesia	1.44	1.47	1.41	32	2	3	3	2.16
Russian Federation	m	m	m	m	m	m	m	m
Saudi Arabia	m	m	m	m	m	m	m	m
South Africa	m	m	m	m	m	m	m	m

1. Actual salaries.
2. Salaries after 11 years of experience for Columns 17, 18, 19 and 20 .

Source: OECD. Indonesia: UNESCO Institute for Statistics (World Education Indicators Programme). See Annex 3 for notes *(www.oecd.org/edu/eag2011)*.
Please refer to the Reader's Guide for information concerning the symbols replacing missing data.

StatLink http://dx.doi.org/10.1787/888932465246

Table D3.2. Teachers' salaries and pre-service teacher training requirements (2009)

Annual statutory teachers' salaries at 15 years of experience and system-level information on teacher training programme

		Ratio of salary after 15 years of experience (minimum training) to earnings for full-time, full-year workers with tertiary education aged 25 to 64			Duration of teacher training programme in years			ISCED type of final qualification[1]			Percentage of current teacher stock with this type of qualification		
		Primary education	Lower secondary education	Upper secondary education	Primary education	Lower secondary education	Upper secondary education	Primary education	Lower secondary education	Upper secondary education	Primary education	Lower secondary education	Upper secondary education
		(1)	(2)	(3)	(4)	(5)	(6)	(7)	(8)	(9)	(10)	(11)	(12)
OECD	Australia[2]	0.85	0.85	0.85	4	4	4	5A	5A	5A	87%	91%	x(11)
	Austria	0.58	0.63	0.65	3	5.5	5.5	5A	5A	5A	94%	95%	78%
	Belgium (Fl.)	0.89	0.89	1.14	3	3	5	5B	5B	5A, 5B	98%	97%	96%
	Belgium (Fr.)	0.87	0.87	1.12	3	3	5	5B	5B	5A	100%	m	m
	Canada	m	m	m	m	m	m	m	m	m	m	m	m
	Chile	m	m	m	m	m	m	m	m	m	m	m	m
	Czech Republic	0.51	0.52	0.55	5	5	5	5A	5A	5A	87%	88%	87%
	Denmark	0.93	0.93	1.06	4	4	6	5A	5A	5A	100%	100%	100%
	England	0.81	0.81	0.81	3, 4	3, 4	3, 4	5A	5A	5A	98%	95%	95%
	Estonia	0.82	0.82	0.82	4.5	4.5	4.5	5A	5A	5A	69%	75%	81%
	Finland[2, 3]	0.85	0.91	1.01	5	5	5	5A	5A	5A	89%	89%	93%
	France[4]	0.78	0.85	0.85	5	5	5, 6	5A	5A	5A	m	m	m
	Germany	0.88	0.97	1.06	5.5	5.5, 6.5	6.5	5A	5A	5A	m	m	m
	Greece	m	m	m	4	4	4, 5	5A	5A	5A	m	96%	98%
	Hungary[3]	0.45	0.45	0.54	4	4	5	5A	5A	5A	95%	100%	100%
	Iceland[4]	0.50	0.50	0.61	3, 4	3, 4	4	5A	5A	5A	87%	87%	78%
	Ireland[3]	0.88	0.88	0.88	3, 5.5	4, 5	4, 5	5A, 5B	5A, 5B	5A, 5B	m	m	m
	Israel	0.75	0.70	0.64	3, 4	3, 4	3, 4	5A	5A	5A	82%	92%	86%
	Italy[5]	0.59	0.64	0.66	4	4-6	4-6	5A	5A	5A	100%	100%	100%
	Japan	m	m	m	2, 4, 6	2, 4, 6	4, 6	5A+5B, 5A, 5A	5A+5B, 5A, 5A	5A	18%, 78%, 1%	7%, 91%, 2%	72%, 28%
	Korea[5]	1.08	1.08	1.08	4	4	4	5A	5A	5A	m	m	m
	Luxembourg	0.79	1.18	1.18	3, 4	5	5	5B	5A	5A	95.6%, 4.5%	100%	100%
	Mexico	m	m	m	4	4, 6	4, 6	5A	5A, 5B	5A, 5B	96%	90%	91%
	Netherlands[5]	0.67	0.81	0.81	4	4	5, 6	5A	5A	5A	100%	100%	100%
	New Zealand	m	m	m	m	m	m	m	m	m	m	m	m
	Norway[3, 6]	0.66	0.66	0.70	4	4	4	5A	5A	5A	47%	47%	21%
	Poland[5]	0.59	0.68	0.78	3, 5	3, 5	3, 5	5A, 5B	5A	5A	99%	99%	97%
	Portugal	1.19	1.19	1.19	3, 4, 6	5, 6	5, 6	5B, 5B, 5A	5A	5A	97%	91%	93%
	Scotland[3]	0.89	0.89	0.89	4, 5	4, 5	4, 5	5A	5A	5A	m	m	m
	Slovak Republic	0.44	0.44	0.44	4, 7	5, 7	5, 7	5A	5A	5A	93%, 7%	91%, 9%	87%, 13%
	Slovenia	0.81	0.81	0.81	5	5-6	5-6	5A	5A	5A, 5B	m	m	m
	Spain[5]	1.16	1.27	1.32	3	6	6	5A	5A	5A	100%	100%	100%
	Sweden[3, 5]	0.74	0.75	0.81	3.5	4.5	4.5	5A	5A	5A	84%	84%	72%
	Switzerland[7]	m	m	m	3	5	6	5A	5A	5A	m	m	m
	Turkey	m	m	m	4-5	a	4-5	5A	a	5A	90%	a	97%
	United States[3]	0.61	0.61	0.65	4	4	4	5A	5A	5A	99%	99%	99%
	OECD average	0.77	0.81	0.85									
	EU21 average	0.78	0.83	0.88									
Other G20	Argentina	m	m	m	m	m	m	m	m	m	m	m	m
	Brazil	m	m	m	m	m	m	m	m	m	m	m	m
	China	m	m	m	m	m	m	m	m	m	m	m	m
	India	m	m	m	m	m	m	m	m	m	m	m	m
	Indonesia	m	m	m	m	m	m	m	m	m	m	m	m
	Russian Federation	m	m	m	m	m	m	m	m	m	m	m	m
	Saudi Arabia	m	m	m	m	m	m	m	m	m	m	m	m
	South Africa	m	m	m	m	m	m	m	m	m	m	m	m

1. Tertiary-type A programmes are largely theory-based and are designed to provide qualifications for entry into advanced research programmes and professions with high knowledge and skill requirements. Tertiary-type B programmes are classified at the same level of competence as tertiary-type A programmes but are more occupationally oriented and usually lead directly to the labour market.
2. Year of reference 2010 for Columns 10 to 12.
3. Actual salaries for Columns 1, 2 and 3.
4. Year of reference 2006 for Columns 1, 2 and 3.
5. Year of reference 2008 for Columns 1, 2 and 3.
6. Year of reference 2007 for Columns 1, 2 and 3.
7. Salaries after 11 years of experience for Columns 1, 2 and 3.

Source: OECD. See Annex 3 for notes *(www.oecd.org/edu/eag2011)*.

Please refer to the Reader's Guide for information concerning the symbols replacing missing data.

StatLink http://dx.doi.org/10.1787/888932465265

Table D3.3. Trends in teachers' salaries between 1995 and 2009 (2005 = 100)

Index of change between 1995 and 2009 (2005 = 100) in statutory teachers' salaries after 15 years of experience/minimum training by level of education, converted to constant price levels using GDP deflators

		Primary level							Lower secondary level							Upper secondary level						
		1995	2000	2005	2006	2007	2008	2009	1995	2000	2005	2006	2007	2008	2009	1995	2000	2005	2006	2007	2008	2009
		(1)	(2)	(3)	(4)	(5)	(6)	(7)	(8)	(9)	(10)	(11)	(12)	(12)	(13)	(14)	(15)	(16)	(17)	(18)	(19)	(20)
OECD	Australia	96	98	100	94	93	96	96	96	98	100	95	95	97	96	96	98	100	95	95	97	96
	Austria	m	90	100	101	102	102	104	m	86	100	100	101	102	104	m	94	100	101	102	103	105
	Belgium (Fl.)	90	93	100	100	100	99	103	96	98	100	100	100	99	103	96	98	100	100	100	99	103
	Belgium (Fr.)	91	94	100	101	101	100	107	98	99	100	100	100	99	105	98	99	100	100	100	99	106
	Canada	m	m	m	m	m	m	m	m	m	m	m	m	m	m	m	m	m	m	m	m	m
	Chile	m	m	m	m	m	m	m	m	m	m	m	m	m	m	m	m	m	m	m	m	m
	Czech Republic	m	57	100	101	118	117	120	m	57	100	101	118	120	123	m	69	100	101	124	125	126
	Denmark	m	96	100	100	100	101	119	m	96	100	100	100	101	119	98	93	100	102	100	100	112
	England	93	97	100	101	100	100	100	93	97	100	101	100	100	100	93	97	100	101	100	100	100
	Estonia	m	86	100	108	117	135	146	m	86	100	108	117	135	146	m	86	100	108	117	135	146
	Finland[1]	82	89	100	110	110	111	113	80	86	100	100	100	101	103	83	80	100	98	97	98	100
	France	107	106	100	99	98	96	95	109	106	100	99	97	96	95	108	105	100	99	97	96	95
	Germany	w	w	w	w	w	w	w	w	w	w	w	w	w	w	w	w	w	w	w	w	w
	Greece	m	91	100	100	100	102	105	m	91	100	100	100	102	105	m	91	100	100	100	102	105
	Hungary[1]	m	65	100	98	94	93	82	m	65	100	98	94	93	82	m	65	100	94	94	89	79
	Iceland	m	89	100	104	97	103	114	m	89	100	104	97	103	114	m	90	100	108	106	103	98
	Ireland[1]	m	86	100	103	106	108	117	m	87	100	103	106	108	117	m	87	100	103	106	108	117
	Israel	97	99	100	104	114	124	135	97	99	100	103	103	112	113	99	100	100	103	103	113	107
	Italy	93	95	100	99	98	98	99	93	95	100	99	98	98	99	93	96	100	99	98	98	99
	Japan	85	99	100	101	97	95	95	85	99	100	101	97	95	95	85	99	100	101	97	95	95
	Korea	m	78	100	103	103	102	99	m	78	100	103	103	102	99	m	78	100	103	103	102	99
	Luxembourg	85	m	100	97	95	89	92	98	m	100	97	95	100	106	98	m	100	97	95	100	106
	Mexico	100	101	100	100	99	100	101	95	100	100	100	99	100	100	m	m	m	m	m	m	m
	Netherlands	m	92	100	100	102	103	107	m	90	100	100	112	112	116	m	94	100	100	83	84	87
	New Zealand	m	102	100	100	98	98	m	m	102	100	100	98	98	m	m	102	100	100	98	98	m
	Norway[1]	85	93	100	97	100	108	109	85	93	100	97	100	108	109	81	87	100	97	99	105	107
	Poland	m	m	100	m	m	131	135	m	m	100	m	m	149	154	m	m	100	m	m	172	177
	Portugal	87	88	100	99	98	97	108	87	88	100	99	98	97	108	87	88	100	99	98	97	108
	Scotland[1]	87	86	100	100	99	99	99	87	86	100	100	99	99	99	87	86	100	100	99	99	99
	Slovak Republic	m	m	m	m	m	m	m	m	m	m	m	m	m	m	m	m	m	m	m	m	m
	Slovenia	m	m	100	104	106	107	110	m	m	100	104	106	107	110	m	m	100	104	106	107	110
	Spain	106	99	100	100	98	103	106	m	95	100	100	98	100	106	108	100	100	100	98	103	106
	Sweden[1]	m	94	100	99	102	99	101	m	92	100	99	102	99	102	m	91	100	99	100	98	100
	Switzerland[2]	103	98	100	98	97	97	100	105	103	100	99	98	97	99	106	104	100	99	98	98	100
	Turkey	108	55	100	95	99	101	106	a	a	a	a	a	a	a	111	51	100	96	100	102	107
	United States[1]	m	m	100	101	101	99	99	m	m	100	101	101	98	98	m	m	100	101	101	106	105
	OECD average	94	90	100	101	101	104	107	93	91	100	100	101	104	107	96	90	100	100	101	104	107
	OECD average for countries with data available for all reference years	94	93	100	100	100	101	104	93	96	100	100	99	100	102	95	92	100	99	99	100	102
	EU21 average for countries with data available for all reference years	93	94	100	101	100	100	103	93	94	100	100	99	99	101	95	94	100	100	99	99	103
Other G20	Argentina	m	m	m	m	m	m	m	m	m	m	m	m	m	m	m	m	m	m	m	m	m
	Brazil	m	m	m	m	m	m	m	m	m	m	m	m	m	m	m	m	m	m	m	m	m
	China	m	m	m	m	m	m	m	m	m	m	m	m	m	m	m	m	m	m	m	m	m
	India	m	m	m	m	m	m	m	m	m	m	m	m	m	m	m	m	m	m	m	m	m
	Indonesia	m	m	m	m	m	m	m	m	m	m	m	m	m	m	m	m	m	m	m	m	m
	Russian Federation	m	m	m	m	m	m	m	m	m	m	m	m	m	m	m	m	m	m	m	m	m
	Saudi Arabia	m	m	m	m	m	m	m	m	m	m	m	m	m	m	m	m	m	m	m	m	m
	South Africa	m	m	m	m	m	m	m	m	m	m	m	m	m	m	m	m	m	m	m	m	m

1. Actual salaries.
2. Salaries after 11 years of experience.

Source: OECD. See Annex 3 for notes *(www.oecd.org/edu/eag2011).*

Please refer to the Reader's Guide for information concerning the symbols replacing missing data.

StatLink http://dx.doi.org/10.1787/888932465284

Table D3.4. Trends in the ratio of salaries to GDP per capita (2000-09)

Ratio of annual statutory teachers' salaries in public institutions after 15 years of experience/minimum training to GDP per capita, by level of education

		Primary level						Lower secondary level						Upper secondary level					
		2000	2005	2006	2007	2008	2009	2000	2005	2006	2007	2008	2009	2000	2005	2006	2007	2008	2009
		(1)	(2)	(3)	(4)	(5)	(6)	(7)	(8)	(9)	(10)	(11)	(12)	(12)	(13)	(14)	(15)	(16)	(17)
OECD	Australia	1.42	1.32	1.21	1.19	1.21	1.22	1.42	1.32	1.23	1.20	1.23	1.22	1.42	1.32	1.23	1.20	1.23	1.22
	Austria	1.02	1.07	1.05	1.03	1.01	1.04	1.06	1.16	1.13	1.11	1.09	1.13	1.17	1.18	1.16	1.14	1.12	1.16
	Belgium (Fl.)	1.23	1.25	1.23	1.21	1.17	1.25	1.30	1.25	1.23	1.21	1.17	1.25	1.66	1.59	1.57	1.54	1.50	1.60
	Belgium (Fr.)	1.19	1.18	1.18	1.16	1.13	1.22	1.27	1.20	1.18	1.16	1.13	1.22	1.64	1.54	1.51	1.48	1.44	1.57
	Canada	m	m	m	m	m	m	m	m	m	m	m	m	m	m	m	m	m	m
	Chile	m	m	1.01	0.94	m	1.54	m	m	1.01	0.94	m	1.54	m	m	1.05	0.98	m	1.61
	Czech Republic	0.60	0.88	0.84	0.92	0.89	0.93	0.60	0.88	0.84	0.92	0.91	0.95	0.74	0.90	0.85	0.99	0.97	0.99
	Denmark	1.21	1.19	1.17	1.14	1.15	1.41	1.21	1.19	1.17	1.14	1.15	1.41	1.42	1.45	1.45	1.39	1.39	1.61
	England	1.43	1.33	1.31	1.28	1.26	1.31	1.43	1.33	1.31	1.28	1.26	1.31	1.43	1.33	1.31	1.28	1.26	1.31
	Estonia	0.73	0.57	0.55	0.55	0.63	0.76	0.73	0.57	0.55	0.55	0.63	0.76	0.73	0.57	0.55	0.55	0.63	0.76
	Finland[1]	1.08	1.07	1.14	1.09	1.07	1.13	1.23	1.25	1.22	1.17	1.15	1.21	1.29	1.43	1.35	1.28	1.26	1.35
	France	1.18	1.05	1.03	1.00	0.97	0.98	1.27	1.14	1.11	1.07	1.05	1.06	1.27	1.14	1.12	1.08	1.06	1.06
	Germany	w	w	w	w	w	1.55	w	w	w	w	w	1.71	w	w	w	w	w	1.87
	Greece	1.32	1.20	1.16	1.11	1.11	1.16	1.32	1.20	1.16	1.11	1.11	1.16	1.32	1.20	1.16	1.11	1.11	1.16
	Hungary[1]	0.73	0.92	0.87	0.81	0.79	0.73	0.73	0.92	0.87	0.81	0.79	0.73	0.92	1.15	1.04	1.02	0.95	0.87
	Iceland	0.80	0.77	0.78	0.70	0.74	0.85	0.80	0.77	0.78	0.70	0.74	0.85	0.94	0.91	0.94	0.90	0.87	0.86
	Ireland[1]	1.29	1.23	1.23	1.23	1.27	1.47	1.31	1.23	1.23	1.23	1.27	1.47	1.31	1.23	1.23	1.23	1.27	1.47
	Israel	0.88	0.86	0.86	0.91	0.97	1.05	0.98	0.96	0.96	0.92	0.98	0.98	0.96	0.94	0.94	0.90	0.96	0.90
	Italy	1.02	1.04	1.03	1.01	1.01	1.06	1.12	1.14	1.12	1.10	1.10	1.16	1.16	1.17	1.15	1.13	1.13	1.19
	Japan	1.68	1.59	1.58	1.49	1.44	1.49	1.68	1.59	1.58	1.49	1.44	1.49	1.69	1.59	1.58	1.49	1.44	1.49
	Korea	2.17	2.26	2.22	2.13	2.04	1.96	2.17	2.25	2.22	2.12	2.03	1.95	2.17	2.25	2.22	2.12	2.03	1.95
	Luxembourg	m	0.99	0.93	0.87	0.81	0.85	m	1.30	1.22	1.14	1.18	1.28	m	1.30	1.22	1.14	1.18	1.28
	Mexico	1.53	1.44	1.39	1.34	1.33	1.39	1.94	1.83	1.77	1.71	1.69	1.76	m	m	m	m	m	m
	Netherlands	1.17	1.21	1.17	1.16	1.14	1.20	1.25	1.33	1.29	1.40	1.37	1.44	1.75	1.78	1.72	1.40	1.37	1.44
	New Zealand	1.66	1.44	1.42	1.39	1.40	m	1.66	1.44	1.42	1.39	1.40	m	1.66	1.44	1.42	1.39	1.40	m
	Norway[1]	1.05	1.02	0.95	0.94	0.98	1.00	1.05	1.02	0.95	0.94	0.98	1.00	1.05	1.09	1.02	1.00	1.04	1.06
	Poland	m	0.76	m	m	0.84	0.84	m	0.76	m	m	0.96	0.96	m	0.76	m	m	1.10	1.10
	Portugal	1.43	1.58	1.56	1.52	1.49	1.67	1.43	1.58	1.56	1.52	1.49	1.67	1.43	1.58	1.56	1.52	1.49	1.67
	Scotland[1]	1.40	1.46	1.43	1.39	1.38	1.43	1.40	1.46	1.43	1.39	1.38	1.43	1.40	1.46	1.43	1.39	1.38	1.43
	Slovak Republic	m	m	m	m	m	0.61	m	m	m	m	m	0.61	m	m	m	m	m	0.61
	Slovenia	m	1.28	1.28	1.23	1.18	1.25	m	1.28	1.28	1.23	1.18	1.25	m	1.28	1.28	1.23	1.18	1.25
	Spain	1.50	1.38	1.36	1.31	1.36	1.44	1.63	1.55	1.52	1.47	1.49	1.61	1.75	1.59	1.56	1.50	1.56	1.64
	Sweden[1]	1.00	0.94	0.90	0.90	0.87	0.93	1.00	0.96	0.92	0.92	0.89	0.96	1.07	1.04	0.99	0.98	0.95	1.01
	Switzerland[2]	1.49	1.48	1.42	1.37	1.33	1.39	1.78	1.68	1.63	1.56	1.52	1.58	2.12	1.97	1.91	1.83	1.80	1.86
	Turkey	1.24	1.94	1.73	1.73	1.74	1.88	a	a	a	a	a	a	1.15	1.96	1.77	1.77	1.79	1.92
	United States[1]	m	0.98	0.97	0.96	0.95	0.97	m	0.99	0.98	0.97	0.94	0.96	m	0.99	0.98	0.97	1.01	1.04
	OECD average	1.23	1.21	1.19	1.16	1.15	1.20	1.29	1.24	1.22	1.19	1.18	1.24	1.36	1.33	1.30	1.26	1.25	1.31
	OECD average for countries with data available for all reference years	1.22	1.23	1.20	1.17	1.17	1.24	1.27	1.26	1.23	1.20	1.19	1.26	1.34	1.36	1.32	1.28	1.27	1.33
	EU21 average for countries with data available for all reference years	1.14	1.14	1.12	1.10	1.10	1.17	1.18	1.19	1.16	1.14	1.14	1.22	1.30	1.30	1.26	1.22	1.21	1.29
Other G20	Argentina	m	m	m	m	m	m	m	m	m	m	m	m	m	m	m	m	m	m
	Brazil	m	m	m	m	m	m	m	m	m	m	m	m	m	m	m	m	m	m
	China	m	m	m	m	m	m	m	m	m	m	m	m	m	m	m	m	m	m
	India	m	m	m	m	m	m	m	m	m	m	m	m	m	m	m	m	m	m
	Indonesia	m	m	m	0.69	0.57	0.48	m	m	m	0.78	0.65	0.55	m	m	m	0.87	0.72	0.61
	Russian Federation	m	m	m	m	m	m	m	m	m	m	m	m	m	m	m	m	m	m
	Saudi Arabia	m	m	m	m	m	m	m	m	m	m	m	m	m	m	m	m	m	m
	South Africa	m	m	m	m	m	m	m	m	m	m	m	m	m	m	m	m	m	m

1. Actual salaries.
2. Salaries after 11 years of experience.

Source: OECD. Indonesia: UNESCO Institute for Statistics (World Education Indicators Programme). See Annex 3 for notes (*www.oecd.org/edu/eag2011*).

Please refer to the Reader's Guide for information concerning the symbols replacing missing data.

StatLink http://dx.doi.org/10.1787/888932465303

Table D3.5a. [1/2] Decisions on payments for teachers in public institutions (2009)

Criteria for base salary and additional payments awarded to teachers in public institutions

		Experience			Criteria based on teaching conditions/responsibilities																				
		Years of experience as a teacher			Management responsibilities in addition to teaching duties			Teaching more classes or hours than required by full-time contract			Special tasks (career guidance or counselling)			Teaching in a disadvantaged, remote or high cost area (location allowance)			Special activities (e.g. sports and drama clubs, homework clubs, summer school, etc.)			Teaching students with special educational needs (in regular schools)			Teaching courses in a particular field		
OECD	Australia	–			–										▲						▲				
	Austria	–	▲			▲			▲			▲							△						
	Belgium (Fl.)	–								△															
	Belgium (Fr.)	–											△												
	Canada	m	m	m	m	m	m	m	m	m	m	m	m	m	m	m	m	m	m	m	m	m	m	m	m
	Chile	–												–											
	Czech Republic	–	▲	△	–	▲	△		▲	△		▲	△					▲	△	–	▲	△			
	Denmark	–	▲	△	–	▲	△		▲	△		▲	△	–	▲	△		▲	△		▲	△		▲	△
	England	–	▲	△	–	▲	△							–	▲	△				–	▲	△	–	▲	△
	Estonia	–				▲	△		▲	△	–	▲	△	–	▲	△		▲	△		▲	△			
	Finland		▲		–				▲	△		▲	△	–	▲			▲	△	–			–		△
	France	–				▲	△		▲	△		▲	△	–	▲				△	–					
	Germany	–			–					△															
	Greece	–				▲				△		▲			▲										
	Hungary	–				▲			▲			▲			▲			▲			▲				
	Iceland	–	▲	△	–	▲	△		▲	△	–	▲	△					▲	△	–	▲	△			
	Ireland	–	▲	△	–	▲								–	▲										
	Israel	–			–	▲		–	▲		–	▲		–	▲		–	▲		–	▲				
	Italy	–					△			△			△		▲				△						
	Japan	–				▲			▲						▲				△		▲				
	Korea	–				▲				△						△					▲			▲	
	Luxembourg	–								△			△							–					
	Mexico	–	▲	△	–	▲		–	▲		–	▲		–	▲								–	▲	
	Netherlands	–	▲	△	–	▲	△	–	▲	△	–	▲	△	–	▲	△	–	▲	△	–	▲	△	–	▲	△
	New Zealand	m	m	m	m	m	m	m	m	m	m	m	m	m	m	m	m	m	m	m	m	m	m	m	m
	Norway	–				▲				△	–	▲	△		▲			▲	△						
	Poland	–		△					▲			▲			▲						▲				
	Portugal	–				▲				△		▲								–					
	Scotland	–													▲										
	Slovak Republic	–	▲	△		▲			▲	△		▲	△					▲	△	–	▲	△			
	Slovenia	–			–					△			△						△			△			
	Spain	–				▲									▲										
	Sweden	–			–					△				–									–		
	Switzerland	–			–					△			△						△	–					
	Turkey	–							▲			▲		–				▲							
	United States	–				▲								–	▲			▲						▲	
Other G20	Argentina	m	m	m	m	m	m	m	m	m	m	m	m	m	m	m	m	m	m	m	m	m	m	m	m
	Brazil	m	m	m	m	m	m	m	m	m	m	m	m	m	m	m	m	m	m	m	m	m	m	m	m
	China	m	m	m	m	m	m	m	m	m	m	m	m	m	m	m	m	m	m	m	m	m	m	m	m
	India	m	m	m	m	m	m	m	m	m	m	m	m	m	m	m	m	m	m	m	m	m	m	m	m
	Indonesia	m	m	m	m	m	m	m	m	m	m	m	m	m	m	m	m	m	m	m	m	m	m	m	m
	Russian Federation	–			–			–						–				▲		–				▲	
	Saudi Arabia	m	m	m	m	m	m	m	m	m	m	m	m	m	m	m	m	m	m	m	m	m	m	m	m
	South Africa	m	m	m	m	m	m	m	m	m	m	m	m	m	m	m	m	m	m	m	m	m	m	m	m

Criteria for:

– : Decisions on position in base salary scale

▲ : Decisions on supplemental payments which are paid every year

△ : Decisions on supplemental incidental payments

Source: OECD. See Annex 3 for notes *(www.oecd.org/edu/eag2011).*

Please refer to the Reader's Guide for information concerning the symbols replacing missing data.

StatLink http://dx.doi.org/10.1787/888932465322

Table D3.5a. [2/2] Decisions on payments for teachers in public institutions (2009)

Criteria for base salary and additional payments awarded to teachers in public institutions

		Criteria related to teachers' qualifications, training and performance																		Criteria based on demography						Other		
		Holding an initial educational qualification higher than the minimum qualification required to enter the teaching profession			Holding a higher than minimum level of teacher certification or training obtained during professional life			Outstanding performance in teaching			Successful completion of professional development activities			Reaching high scores in the qualification examination			Holding an educational qualification in multiple subjects			Family status (married, number of children)			Age (independent of years of teaching experience)					
OECD	Australia	–			–																▲							
	Austria									△											▲						▲	
	Belgium (Fl.)	–				▲																					▲	
	Belgium (Fr.)	–			–																						▲	△
	Canada	m	m	m	m	m	m	m	m	m	m	m	m	m	m	m	m	m	m	m	m	m	m	m	m	m	m	m
	Chile				–					△	–							▲								–		
	Czech Republic							–	▲	△													–		△			
	Denmark	–	▲	△	–	▲	△		▲	△	–	▲	△				–	▲	△									
	England	–	▲	△				–	▲	△																		
	Estonia	–			–				▲	△	–							▲	△									
	Finland	–			–	▲			▲			▲					–											
	France										–										▲							
	Germany																			–			–					
	Greece	–				▲															▲					–		
	Hungary	–			–					△	–							▲									▲	
	Iceland	–	▲	△	–	▲	△					▲	△			△			△				–	▲				
	Ireland	–	▲		–	▲																						
	Israel	–			–							▲								–	▲		–	▲				
	Italy																			–								
	Japan																				▲						▲	
	Korea												△									△		▲				
	Luxembourg				–						–										▲		–					
	Mexico	–	▲		–	▲		–	▲		–	▲		–	▲													
	Netherlands	–	▲	△	–	▲	△	–	▲	△	–	▲	△	–	▲	△	–	▲	△									
	New Zealand	m	m	m	m	m	m	m	m	m	m	m	m	m	m	m	m	m	m	m	m	m	m	m	m	m	m	m
	Norway	–	▲			▲			▲			▲			▲			▲						▲				
	Poland	–	▲	△					▲	△	–					△											▲	△
	Portugal	–			–						–			–							▲							
	Scotland				–																							
	Slovak Republic								▲	△	–	▲													△			
	Slovenia		▲			▲				△	–																	△
	Spain					▲					–																	
	Sweden	–			–			–			–			–														
	Switzerland																				▲						▲	
	Turkey	–				▲		–		△		▲									▲						▲	
	United States	–	▲		–	▲				△	–	▲																
Other G20	Argentina	m	m	m	m	m	m	m	m	m	m	m	m	m	m	m	m	m	m	m	m	m	m	m	m	m	m	m
	Brazil	m	m	m	m	m	m	m	m	m	m	m	m	m	m	m	m	m	m	m	m	m	m	m	m	m	m	m
	China	m	m	m	m	m	m	m	m	m	m	m	m	m	m	m	m	m	m	m	m	m	m	m	m	m	m	m
	India	m	m	m	m	m	m	m	m	m	m	m	m	m	m	m	m	m	m	m	m	m	m	m	m	m	m	m
	Indonesia	m	m	m	m	m	m	m	m	m	m	m	m	m	m	m	m	m	m	m	m	m	m	m	m	m	m	m
	Russian Federation	–			–				▲		–			–														
	Saudi Arabia	m	m	m	m	m	m	m	m	m	m	m	m	m	m	m	m	m	m	m	m	m	m	m	m	m	m	m
	South Africa	m	m	m	m	m	m	m	m	m	m	m	m	m	m	m	m	m	m	m	m	m	m	m	m	m	m	m

Criteria for:

– : Decisions on position in base salary scale

▲ : Decisions on supplemental payments which are paid every year

△ : Decisions on supplemental incidental payments

Source: OECD. See Annex 3 for notes *(www.oecd.org/edu/eag2011)*.

Please refer to the Reader's Guide for information concerning the symbols replacing missing data.

StatLink http://dx.doi.org/10.1787/888932465322

HOW MUCH TIME DO TEACHERS SPEND TEACHING?

- The number of teaching hours in public schools averages 779 hours per year in primary, 701 in lower secondary and 656 in upper secondary.
- The average teaching time remained largely unchanged between 2000 and 2009 at all levels of education.

INDICATOR D4

Chart D4.1. Number of teaching hours per year in lower secondary education in 2000, 2005 and 2009

Net statutory contact time in hours per year in public institutions

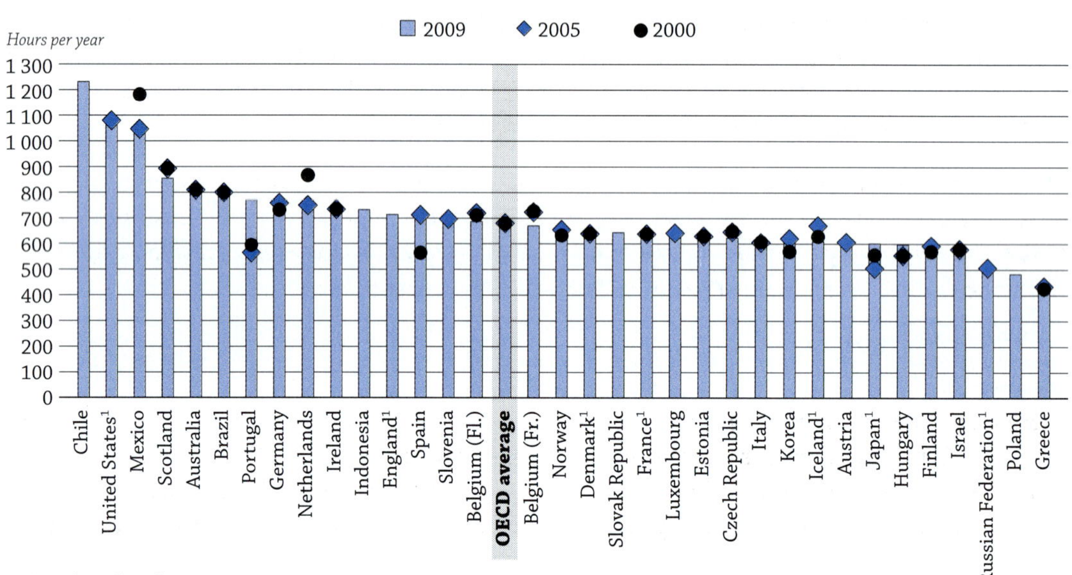

1. Actual teaching hours.

Countries are ranked in descending order of the number of teaching hours per year in lower secondary education in 2009.

Source: OECD. Indonesia: UNESCO Institute for Statistics (World Education Indicators Programme). Table D4.2. See Annex 3 for notes (*www.oecd.org/edu/eag2011*).

StatLink http://dx.doi.org/10.1787/888932462035

Context

Although statutory working hours and teaching hours only partly determine teachers' actual workload, they do give valuable insight into the demands placed on teachers in different countries. Together with teachers' salaries (see Indicator D3) and average class size (see Indicator D2), this indicator presents some key measures regarding the working lives of teachers. Teaching hours and the extent of non-teaching duties may also affect the attractiveness of the teaching profession.

The proportion of working time spent teaching provides information on the amount of time available for activities such as lesson preparation, correction, in-service training and staff meetings. A large proportion of working time spent teaching may indicate that less time is devoted to tasks such as student assessment and lesson preparation.

In addition to class size and the ratio of students to teaching staff (see Indicator D2), students' hours of instruction (see Indicator D1) and teachers' salaries (see Indicator D3), the amount of time teachers spend teaching also affects the financial resources countries need to allocate to education (see Indicator B7).

Other findings

- **The average number of teaching hours in public primary schools is 779 per year**, but ranges from less than 600 in Greece, Hungary and Poland to over 1 000 hours in Chile, Indonesia and the United States.
- **The number of teaching hours in public lower secondary schools averages 701 hours per year**, but ranges from less than 500 hours in Greece and Poland to over 1 000 hours in Argentina, Chile, Mexico and the United States.
- **The average number of teaching hours in public upper secondary general education is 656 per year**, but ranges from 377 in Denmark to 1 368 in Argentina.
- The **composition of teachers' annual teaching time**, in terms of weeks and days of instruction and hours of teaching time, varies considerably. As a result, the average number of hours per day that teachers teach also varies widely, ranging, at the lower secondary level, from three hours or less per day in Greece, Japan, Korea, Poland and the Russian Federation, to more than five hours in Argentina, Chile, Mexico and the United States.
- **Regulations concerning teachers' required working time** vary significantly. In most countries, teachers are formally required to work a specific number of hours per year. In some, teaching time is only specified by the number of lessons per week and assumptions may be made about the amount of non-teaching time required per lesson, at school or elsewhere.

Trends

In most OECD countries with available data, teaching time remained largely unchanged between 2000 and 2009. However the number of teaching hours changed dramatically in a few countries. It decreased by more than 30% in Denmark at the upper secondary level, while it increased by more than 25% in the Czech Republic at the primary level and in Portugal and Spain at the secondary level.

Analysis

Teaching time in primary education

In both primary and secondary education, countries vary in terms of the number of teaching hours per year required of the average public school teacher. Teachers are usually required to teach more hours in primary education than in secondary education.

Annual teaching hours in primary schools range from less than 600 hours in Greece, Hungary and Poland to 900 or more in France, Ireland, the Netherlands and the United States, to over 1 200 in Chile and Indonesia (Chart D4.2 and Table D4.1).

There is no set rule on how teaching time is distributed throughout the year. In Spain, for example, teachers must teach 880 hours per year, 101 hours more than the OECD average, yet the teaching hours are spread over fewer days of instruction than the OECD average because teachers in Spain teach an average of five hours per day compared to the OECD average of 4.2 hours. In contrast, primary teachers in Korea must complete a very large number of days of instruction – more than five days a week, on average – but their average teaching time per day is only 3.8 hours. Chile and Indonesia also provide an interesting contrast. They have the highest net teaching times in hours, 1 232 and 1 255 respectively, but teachers in Indonesia must complete 60 days of instruction more than teachers in Chile. The difference between the two is explained by the number of hours taught per day of instruction. Primary school teachers in Chile complete fewer days of instruction than teachers in Indonesia, but each of these days includes an average of 6.5 hours of teaching compared to 5 hours in Indonesia. Chile's teachers must provide one-and-a-half hours more teaching time per day of instruction than Indonesia's teachers; and this difference is combined with a substantial difference in the number of days of instruction they must complete each year.

In most countries, teaching time in primary schools remained about the same between 2000 and 2009. However, in the Czech Republic, primary teachers were required to teach 28% more hours, and in Japan 11% more hours, in 2009 than in 2000. In Scotland, net teaching time in primary education dropped by 10% between 2000 and 2009 (Table D4.2).

Teaching time in secondary education

Lower secondary school teachers teach an average of 701 hours per year. The teaching time ranges from less than 600 hours in Finland, Greece, Hungary, Israel, Poland and the Russian Federation to more than 1 000 hours in Argentina, Chile, Mexico and the United States (Chart D4.1 and Table D4.1).

The teaching time in upper secondary general education is usually lighter than that in lower secondary education. A teacher of general subjects has an average teaching load of 656 hours per year, ranging from 377 hours in Denmark to 800 or more in Brazil (800), Mexico (843) and Scotland (855) and over 1 000 hours in Argentina (1 368), Chile (1 232) and the United States (1 051) (Chart D4.2 and Table D4.1).

As is the case for primary school teachers, the number of hours of teaching time and the number of days of instruction for secondary school teachers vary. As a result, the average number of hours per day that teachers teach also varies widely, ranging, at the lower secondary level, from three hours or less per day in Greece, Japan, Korea, Poland and the Russian Federation, to more than five hours in Mexico and the United States and more than six hours in Argentina and Chile.

Similarly, at the upper secondary general level, teachers in Denmark, Finland, Greece, Israel, Japan, Korea, Norway, Poland and the Russian Federation teach for three hours or less per day, on average, compared to more than five hours in Argentina, Chile and the United States. Including breaks between classes in teaching time in some countries, but not in others, may explain some of these differences.

About half of the OECD countries for which data are available saw at least a 5% change, most often as an increase, in the amount of teaching time, in either lower and upper secondary schools, between 2000 and 2009. Secondary school teachers were required to teach over 25% more in 2009 than in 2000 in Portugal and Spain (up to 50% more in Portugal at the upper secondary level). In contrast, in Denmark, teaching time dropped by 33% in upper secondary education between 2005 and 2009 (Table D4.2).

Differences in teaching time between levels of education

In most countries, primary teachers are required to teach more hours per year than secondary school teachers. In the Czech Republic, France, Greece, Israel and Korea, the annual teaching time is at least 30% higher for primary school teachers than for lower secondary school teachers and up to 71% higher in Indonesia. In contrast, the difference does not exceed 3% in Poland and the United States and there is no difference in Brazil, Chile, Denmark, Estonia, Hungary, Iceland, Scotland and Slovenia. Argentina, England and Mexico are the only countries in which the teaching load for primary school teachers is lighter than that for lower secondary school teachers (Table D4.1 and Chart D4.2).

Chart D4.2. Number of teaching hours per year, by level of education (2009)

Net statutory contact time in hours per year in public institutions

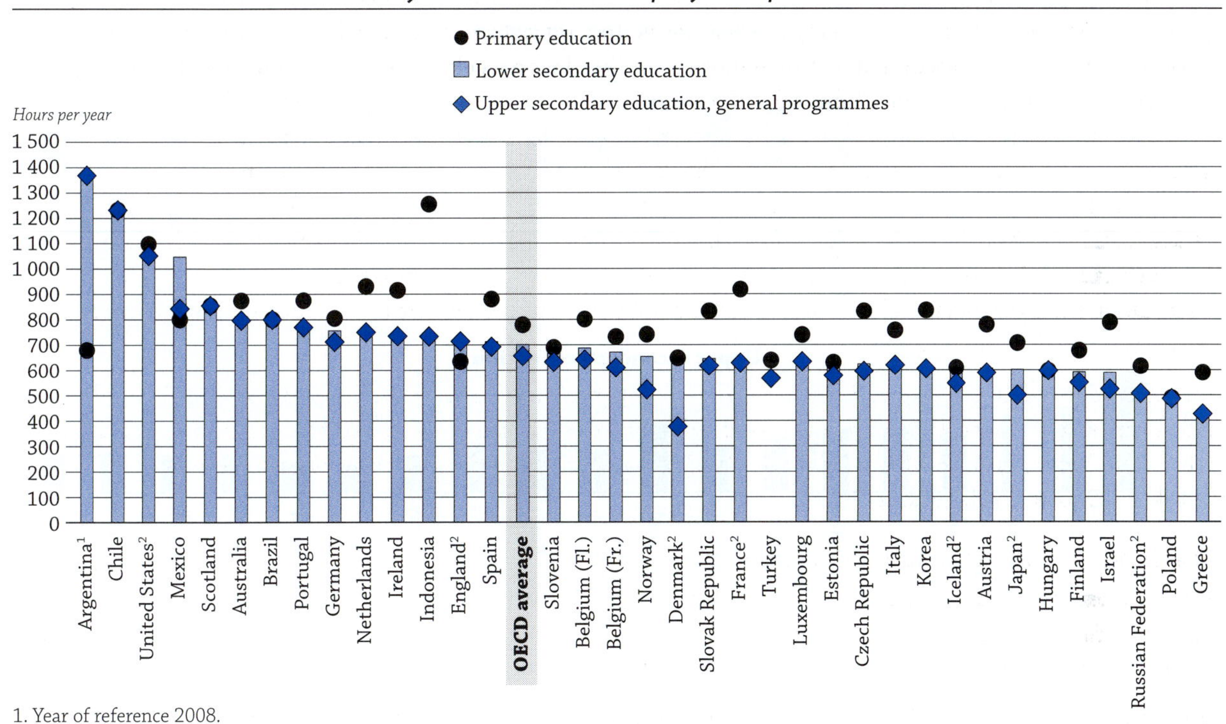

1. Year of reference 2008.
2. Actual teaching hours.

Countries are ranked in descending order of the number of teaching hours per year in lower secondary education.

Source: OECD. Argentina, Indonesia: UNESCO Institute for Statistics (World Education Indicators Programme). Table D4.1. See Annex 3 for notes (*www.oecd.org/edu/eag2011*).

StatLink http://dx.doi.org/10.1787/888932462054

In most countries teaching time at the lower and upper secondary levels are similar. However, in Japan, Mexico and Norway, the annual required teaching time at the lower secondary level is at least 20% higher than at the upper secondary level and over 70% higher in Denmark.

Teachers' working time

How teachers' hours of work are regulated varies considerably from country to country. While some countries formally regulate contact time only, others also set total working hours. In some countries, time is allocated for teaching and non-teaching activities within the formally established working time.

In most countries, teachers are formally required to work a specified number of hours per week, including teaching and non-teaching time, to earn their full-time salary. Within this framework, however, countries differ in how they allocate time for each activity (Chart D4.3). The number of hours for teaching is usually specified, except in Sweden; but some countries also regulate the time a teacher has to be present in the school.

Chart D4.3. Percentage of teachers' working time spent teaching, by level of education (2009)

Net teaching time as a percentage of total statutory working time

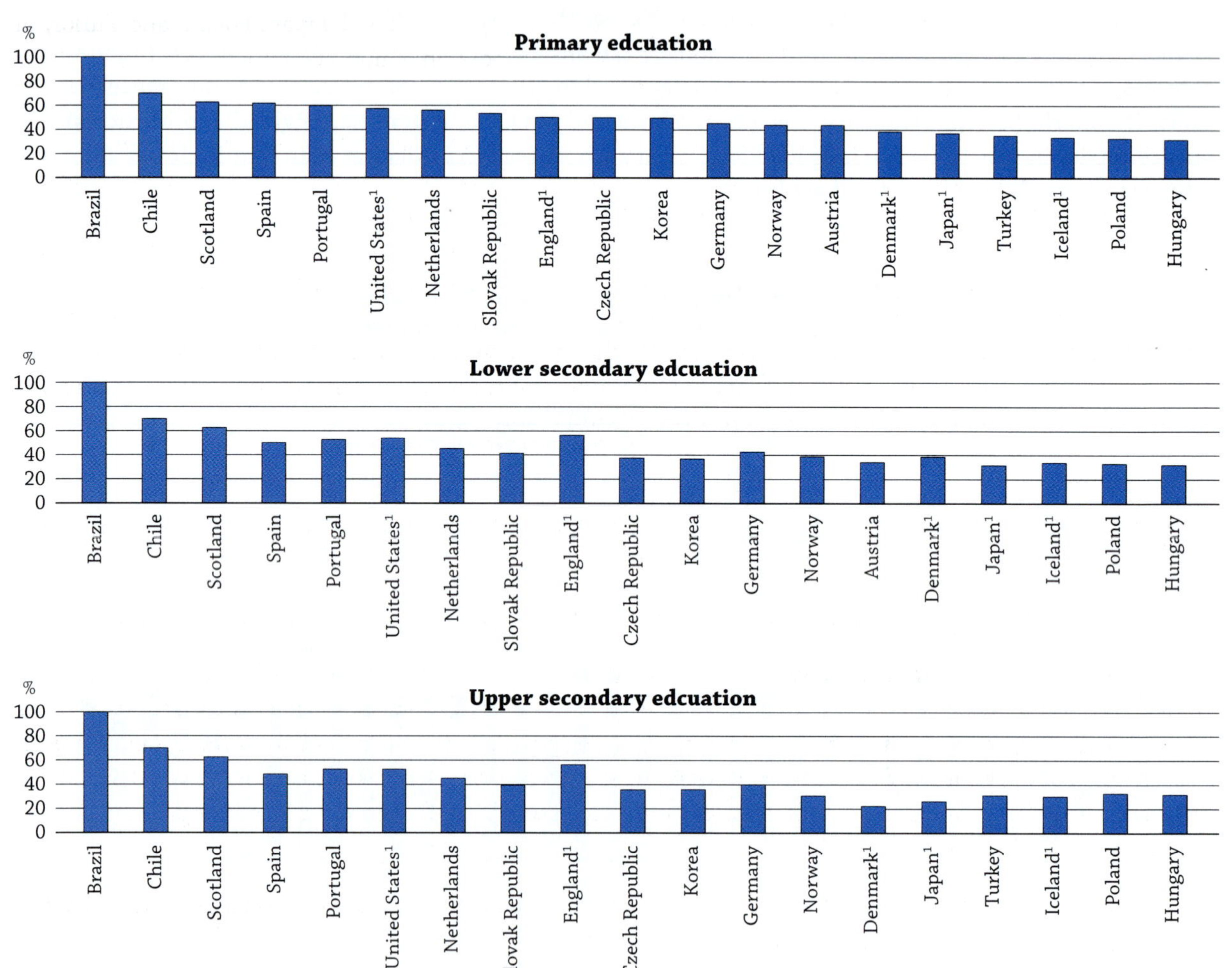

1. Actual teaching and working time.

Countries are ranked in descending order of the percentage of teachers' working time spent teaching in primary education.

Source: OECD. Table D4.1. See Annex 3 for notes (*www.oecd.org/edu/eag2011*).

StatLink http://dx.doi.org/10.1787/888932462073

Australia, Belgium (Flemish Community for primary education), Brazil, Chile, Denmark, England, Estonia, Greece, Iceland, Ireland, Israel, Luxembourg, Mexico, Norway, Portugal, Spain, Sweden, Turkey and the United States all specify the time during which teachers are required to be available at school, for both teaching and non-teaching activities.

Greece reduces teaching hours according to how many years a teacher has served. At the secondary level, teachers are required to teach 21 hours per week. After 6 years, this drops to 19 hours and after 12 years to 18 hours. After 20 years of service, teachers are required to teach 16 hours a week – more than 25% less than teachers who have just started their careers. However, the remaining hours of teachers' working time must be spent at school.

In Austria (primary and lower secondary education), the Czech Republic, Germany, Hungary, Japan, Korea, the Netherlands, Poland and Scotland, teachers' total annual working time, at school or elsewhere, is specified, but the allocation of time spent at school and time spent elsewhere is not. In some countries, the number of hours to be spent on non-teaching activities is partially specified; but what is not specified is whether teachers have to spend the non-teaching hours at school.

Non-teaching time

In the 20 countries that specify both teaching and total working time, the percentage of teachers' working time spent teaching ranges from less than 40% in Denmark, Hungary, Iceland, Japan, Poland and Turkey at all levels of education, to 100% in Brazil. In 12 countries, the proportion of non-teaching time is higher at the secondary level than at the primary level (Chart D4.3).

In Belgium (French Community), Finland, France, Italy, the Russian Federation and Slovenia, there are no formal requirements regarding time spent on non-teaching activities in primary and secondary education. However, this does not mean that teachers are given total freedom to carry out other tasks. In Austria, provisions concerning teaching time are based on the assumption that teachers' duties, including preparing lessons and tests, marking and correcting papers, overseeing examinations and handling administrative tasks, total 40 hours per week. In Belgium (Flemish Community), the additional non-teaching hours at school are set at the school level. There are no regulations regarding the time devoted to preparing lessons, correcting tests, marking students' papers, etc. The government defines only the minimum and maximum number of teaching periods a week (50 minutes each) at each level of education (Table D4.1).

Definitions

The **number of teaching days** is the number of teaching weeks multiplied by the number of days per week a teacher teaches, less the number of days on which the school is closed for holidays.

The **number of teaching weeks** refers to the number of weeks of instruction excluding holiday weeks.

Teaching time is defined as the number of hours per year that a full-time teacher teaches a group or class of students as set by policy. It is normally calculated as the number of teaching days per year multiplied by the number of hours a teacher teaches per day (excluding periods of time formally allowed for breaks between lessons or groups of lessons). Some countries provide estimates of teaching time based on survey data. At the primary school level, short breaks between lessons are included if the classroom teacher is responsible for the class during these breaks.

Working time refers to the normal working hours of a full-time teacher. It does not include paid overtime. According to a country's formal policy, working time can refer to:

- the time directly associated with teaching and other curricular activities for students, such as assignments and tests; and
- the time directly associated with teaching and hours devoted to other activities related to teaching, such as preparing lessons, counselling students, correcting assignments and tests, professional development, meetings with parents, staff meetings, and general school tasks.

Working time in school refers to the time teachers are required to spend working in school, including teaching and non-teaching time.

Methodology

Data are from the 2010 OECD-INES Survey on Teachers and the Curriculum and refer to the school year 2008-09.

In interpreting differences in teaching hours among countries, net contact time, as used here, does not necessarily correspond to the teaching load. Contact time is a substantial component, but preparing for classes and necessary follow-up, including correcting students' work, also need to be included when comparing teachers' workloads. Other relevant elements, such as the number of subjects taught, the number of students taught, and the number of years a teacher teaches the same students, should also be taken into account.

Notes on definitions and methodologies for each country are provided in Annex 3 at *www.oecd.org/edu/eag2011*.

The statistical data for Israel are supplied by and under the responsibility of the relevant Israeli authorities. The use of such data by the OECD is without prejudice to the status of the Golan Heights, East Jerusalem and Israeli settlements in the West Bank under the terms of international law.

Table D4.1. Organisation of teachers' working time (2009)

Number of teaching weeks, teaching days, net teaching hours, and teachers' working time over the school year, in public institutions

		Number of weeks of instruction			Number of days of instruction			Net teaching time in hours			Working time required at school in hours			Total statutory working time in hours		
		Primary education	Lower secondary education	Upper secondary education, general programmes	Primary education	Lower secondary education	Upper secondary education, general programmes	Primary education	Lower secondary education	Upper secondary education, general programmes	Primary education	Lower secondary education	Upper secondary education, general programmes	Primary education	Lower secondary education	Upper secondary education, general programmes
		(1)	(2)	(3)	(4)	(5)	(6)	(7)	(8)	(9)	(10)	(11)	(12)	(13)	(14)	(15)
OECD	Australia	40	40	40	197	197	193	874	812	797	1 201	1 204	1 186	a	a	a
	Austria	38	38	38	180	180	180	779	607	589	a	a	a	1 776	1 776	a
	Belgium (Fl.)	37	37	37	178	179	179	801	687	642	926	a	a	a	a	a
	Belgium (Fr.)	38	38	38	183	183	183	732	671	610	a	a	a	a	a	a
	Canada	m	m	m	m	m	m	m	m	m	m	m	m	m	m	m
	Chile	40	40	40	191	191	191	1 232	1 232	1 232	1 760	1 760	1 760	1 760	1 760	1 760
	Czech Republic	40	40	40	189	189	189	832	624	595	a	a	a	1 664	1 664	1 664
	Denmark[1]	42	42	42	200	200	200	648	648	377	648	648	377	1 680	1 680	1 680
	England[1]	38	38	38	190	190	190	635	714	714	1 265	1 265	1 265	1 265	1 265	1 265
	Estonia	39	39	39	175	175	175	630	630	578	1 540	1 540	1 540	a	a	a
	Finland	38	38	38	188	188	188	677	592	550	a	a	a	a	a	a
	France[1]	35	35	35	m	m	m	918	642	628	a	a	a	a	a	a
	Germany	40	40	40	193	193	193	805	756	713	a	a	a	1 775	1 775	1 775
	Greece	36	32	32	177	157	157	589	426	426	1 140	1 170	1 170	a	a	a
	Hungary	37	37	37	181	181	181	597	597	597	a	a	a	1 864	1 864	1 864
	Iceland[1]	36	36	35	176	176	171	609	609	547	1 650	1 650	1 720	1 800	1 800	1 800
	Ireland	37	33	33	183	167	167	915	735	735	1 036	735	735	a	a	a
	Israel	43	42	42	183	176	176	788	589	524	1 069	802	704	a	a	a
	Italy	39	39	39	172	172	172	757	619	619	a	a	a	a	a	a
	Japan[1]	40	40	40	201	201	198	707	602	500	a	a	a	1 899	1 899	1 899
	Korea	40	40	40	220	220	220	836	618	605	a	a	a	1 680	1 680	1 680
	Luxembourg	36	36	36	176	176	176	739	634	634	900	828	828	a	a	a
	Mexico	42	42	36	200	200	172	800	1 047	843	800	1 167	971	a	a	a
	Netherlands	40	m	m	195	m	m	930	750	750	a	a	a	1 659	1 659	1 659
	New Zealand	m	m	m	m	m	m	m	m	m	m	m	m	m	m	m
	Norway	38	38	38	190	190	190	741	654	523	1 300	1 225	1 150	1 688	1 688	1 688
	Poland	37	37	37	181	179	180	489	483	486	a	a	a	1 480	1 464	1 472
	Portugal	37	37	37	175	175	175	875	770	770	1 289	1 289	1 289	1 464	1 464	1 464
	Scotland	38	38	38	190	190	190	855	855	855	a	a	a	1 365	1 365	1 365
	Slovak Republic	38	38	38	187	187	187	832	645	617	m	m	m	1 560	1 560	1 560
	Slovenia	40	40	40	190	190	190	690	690	633	a	a	a	a	a	a
	Spain	37	37	36	176	176	171	880	713	693	1 140	1 140	1 140	1 425	1 425	1 425
	Sweden	a	a	a	a	a	a	a	a	a	1 360	1 360	1 360	1 767	1 767	1 767
	Switzerland	m	m	m	m	m	m	m	m	m	m	m	m	m	m	m
	Turkey	38	a	38	180	a	180	639	a	567	870	a	756	1 808	a	1 808
	United States[1]	36	36	36	180	180	180	1 097	1 068	1 051	1 381	1 381	1 378	1 913	1 977	1 998
	OECD average	38	38	38	186	185	183	779	701	656	1 182	1 198	1 137	1 665	1 660	1 663
	EU21 average	38	38	37	184	181	181	755	659	628	1 124	1 108	1 078	1 596	1 594	1 580
Other G20	Argentina[2]	36	36	36	170	171	171	680	1 368	1 368	m	m	m	m	m	m
	Brazil	40	40	40	200	200	200	800	800	800	800	800	800	800	800	800
	China	35	35	35	175	175	175	m	m	m	m	m	m	m	m	m
	India	m	m	m	m	m	m	m	m	m	m	m	m	m	m	m
	Indonesia	44	44	44	251	163	163	1 255	734	734	m	m	m	m	m	m
	Russian Federation[1]	34	35	35	164	169	169	615	507	507	a	a	a	a	a	a
	Saudi Arabia	m	m	m	m	m	m	m	m	m	m	m	m	m	m	m
	South Africa	m	m	m	m	m	m	m	m	m	m	m	m	m	m	m

1. Actual teaching and working time.
2. Year of reference 2008.

Source: OECD. Argentina, Indonesia: UNESCO Institute for Statistics (World Education Indicators Programme). China: The Ministry of Education, *Notes on the Experimental Curriculum of Compulsory Education*, 19 November 2001. See Annex 3 for notes *(www.oecd.org/edu/eag2011)*.

Please refer to the Reader's Guide for information concerning the symbols replacing missing data.

StatLink http://dx.doi.org/10.1787/888932465398

Table D4.2. Number of teaching hours per year (2000, 2005-09)

Net statutory contact time in hours per year in public institutions by level of education from 2000, 2005 to 2009

		Primary level						Lower secondary level						Upper secondary level					
		2000	2005	2006	2007	2008	2009	2000	2005	2006	2007	2008	2009	2000	2005	2006	2007	2008	2009
		(1)	(2)	(3)	(4)	(5)	(6)	(7)	(8)	(9)	(10)	(11)	(12)	(13)	(14)	(15)	(16)	(17)	(18)
OECD	Australia	882	888	884	877	873	874	811	810	818	815	812	812	803	810	817	813	810	797
	Austria	m	774	774	774	779	779	m	607	607	607	607	607	m	589	589	589	589	589
	Belgium (Fl.)	826	806	797	806	810	801	712	720	684	691	695	687	668	675	638	645	649	642
	Belgium (Fr.)	804	722	724	724	724	732	728	724	662	662	662	671	668	664	603	603	603	610
	Canada	m	m	m	m	m	m	m	m	m	m	m	m	m	m	m	m	m	m
	Chile	m	m	864	860	m	1 232	m	m	864	860	m	1 232	m	m	864	860	m	1 232
	Czech Republic	650	813	854	849	849	832	650	647	640	637	637	624	621	617	611	608	608	595
	Denmark[1]	640	640	648	648	648	648	640	640	648	648	648	648	560	560	364	364	364	377
	England[1]	m	m	m	631	654	635	m	m	m	714	722	714	m	m	m	714	722	714
	Estonia	630	630	630	630	630	630	630	630	630	630	630	630	578	578	578	578	578	578
	Finland	656	677	677	677	677	677	570	592	592	592	592	592	527	550	550	550	550	550
	France[1]	907	918	910	914	926	918	639	639	634	632	644	642	611	625	616	618	630	628
	Germany	783	808	810	806	805	805	732	758	758	758	756	756	690	714	714	714	715	713
	Greece	609	604	604	590	593	589	426	434	429	426	429	426	429	430	421	423	429	426
	Hungary	583	583	583	583	597	597	555	555	555	555	597	597	555	555	555	555	597	597
	Iceland[1]	629	671	671	671	671	609	629	671	671	671	671	609	464	560	560	560	560	547
	Ireland	915	915	915	915	915	915	735	735	735	735	735	735	735	735	735	735	735	735
	Israel	731	731	731	731	731	788	579	579	579	579	579	589	524	524	524	524	524	524
	Italy	744	739	735	735	735	757	608	605	601	601	601	619	608	605	601	601	601	619
	Japan[1]	635	578	m	705	709	707	557	505	m	600	603	602	478	429	m	498	500	500
	Korea	865	883	864	848	840	836	570	621	588	612	616	618	530	605	596	599	604	605
	Luxembourg	m	774	774	774	739	739	m	642	642	642	634	634	m	642	642	642	634	634
	Mexico	800	800	800	800	800	800	1 182	1 047	1 047	1 047	1 047	1 047	m	848	843	843	848	843
	Netherlands	930	930	930	930	930	930	867	750	750	750	750	750	867	750	750	750	750	750
	New Zealand	985	985	985	985	985	m	968	968	968	968	968	m	950	950	950	950	950	m
	Norway	713	741	741	741	741	741	633	656	654	654	654	654	505	524	523	523	523	523
	Poland	m	m	m	m	513	489	m	m	m	m	513	483	m	m	m	m	513	486
	Portugal	815	855	860	855	855	875	595	564	757	752	752	770	515	513	688	684	752	770
	Scotland	950	893	893	855	855	855	893	893	893	855	855	855	893	893	893	855	855	855
	Slovak Republic	m	m	m	m	m	832	m	m	m	m	m	645	m	m	m	m	m	617
	Slovenia	m	697	697	682	682	690	m	697	697	682	682	690	m	639	639	626	626	633
	Spain	880	880	880	880	880	880	564	713	713	713	713	713	548	693	693	693	693	693
	Sweden	a	a	a	a	a	a	a	a	a	a	a	a	a	a	a	a	a	a
	Switzerland	884	m	m	m	m	m	859	m	m	m	m	m	674	m	m	m	m	m
	Turkey	639	639	639	639	639	639	a	a	a	a	a	a	504	567	567	567	567	567
	United States[1]	m	1 080	1 080	1 080	1 097	1 097	m	1 080	1 080	1 080	1 068	1 068	m	1 080	1 080	1 080	1 051	1 051
	OECD average	773	781	792	780	770	779	693	696	711	706	696	701	620	653	662	657	649	656
	OECD average for countries with data available for all reference years	764	772	773	770	771	771	679	681	684	683	685	684	609	625	618	616	622	623
	EU21 average for countries with data available for all reference years	770	776	778	775	777	778	659	662	668	665	669	670	629	635	626	623	632	634
Other G20	Argentina	m	m	m	m	680	m	m	m	m	m	1 368	m	m	m	m	m	1 368	m
	Brazil	800	800	800	800	800	800	800	800	800	800	800	800	800	800	800	800	800	800
	China	m	m	m	m	m	m	m	m	m	m	m	m	m	m	m	m	m	m
	India	m	m	m	m	m	m	m	m	m	m	m	m	m	m	m	m	m	m
	Indonesia	m	m	m	m	1 260	1 255	m	m	m	m	738	734	m	m	m	m	738	734
	Russian Federation[1]	m	615	615	615	615	615	m	507	507	507	507	507	m	507	507	507	507	507
	Saudi Arabia	m	m	m	m	m	m	m	m	m	m	m	m	m	m	m	m	m	m
	South Africa	m	m	m	m	m	m	m	m	m	m	m	m	m	m	m	m	m	m

1. Actual teaching and working time.

Source: OECD. Argentina, Indonesia: UNESCO Institute for Statistics (World Education Indicators Programme). See Annex 3 for notes *(www.oecd.org/edu/eag2011)*.

Please refer to the Reader's Guide for information concerning the symbols replacing missing data.

StatLink http://dx.doi.org/10.1787/888932465417

HOW ARE SCHOOLS HELD ACCOUNTABLE?

- Most countries have a combination of mechanisms used to hold schools accountable. These mechanisms are covered in 3 broad types of accountability: Performance accountability, regulatory accountability, and market accountability.
- National examinations – a prominent component of performance accountability – are used in 23 of 35 countries at the upper secondary level, while national assessments are more common at the primary and lower secondary levels.
- While required school inspections are more common than required self-evaluations, the practice of school inspection varies considerably across countries, particularly in terms of the frequency in which schools are inspected.
- While most countries permit diverse forms of school choice, in practice, the proportion of students practicing choice is more limited.

Chart D5.1. Performance and regulatory accountability in public schools (2009)

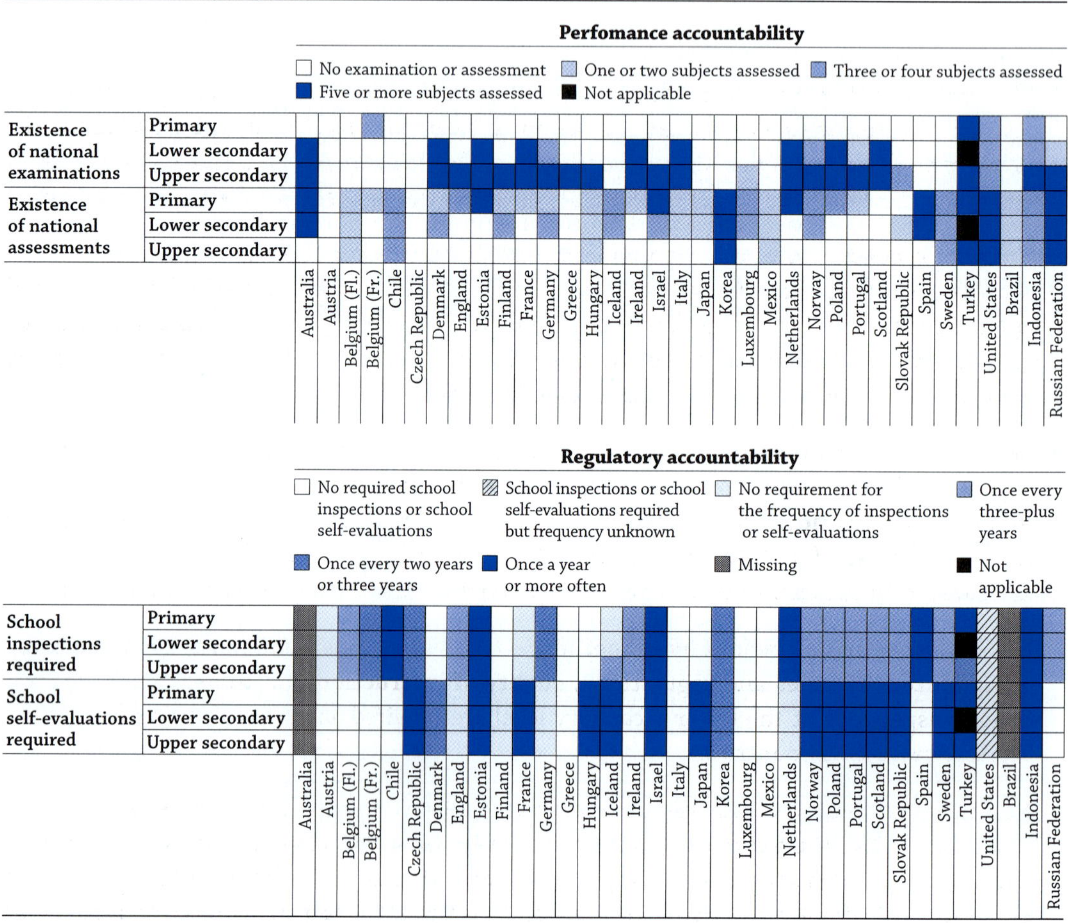

Source: OECD. Tables D5.4a, D5.4b, D5.4c, D5.6a, D5.6b, D5.6c, D5.7a, D5.7b, D5.7c, D5.10a, D5.10b and D5.10c. See Annex 3 for notes *(www.oecd.org/edu/eag2011)*.

StatLink http://dx.doi.org/10.1787/888932462092

Context

Accountability literally means "to take account of". It refers to the interaction in a hierarchical relationship between those who have power and those who are delegated authority. Those who are delegated authority have to account for what they are doing with this authority or responsibility.

INDICATOR D5

Often, the use of the word accountability refers to a system that involves collecting and sharing data, providing feedback, and making decisions based on the evidence received. Although the notion of accountability has long existed, it was only in the early 1970s that accountability was formally defined (see Levin, 1974; Tyler, 1971) and integrated into the practice of steering or governing education systems.

Accountability functions when those who are delegated authority have to account for what they are doing with this authority or responsibility. In education, elected or appointed government officials are legally responsible for ensuring that a nation's children and youth receive an education that is delivered through school systems. School administrators demonstrate accountability to higher-level education and political authorities, who delegate responsibility to them to provide instruction.

The concept of accountability has evolved over time. Today, with an increasing number of ways to measure school- and system-level performance that can also be used to compare outcomes of schools within or across countries, more attention is focused on accountability for outcomes. However, it is important to note that the use, frequency and scope of accountability mechanisms vary considerably among and within countries.

Other findings

- **National examinations**, the results of which can have a formal consequence or impact on a student's future, **are most prevalent at the upper secondary level and least prevalent at the primary level**, where only 4 of 35 countries reported the existence of a national exam at that level. Fifteen of 34 countries reported conducting national examinations at the lower secondary level.
- The key purposes of **national assessments** are to provide feedback to improve instruction and show the relative performance of students. Some 22 of 34 countries reported using national assessments at the lower secondary level. **Some 30 of 35 countries reported using national assessments in at least one subject at the primary level**. Only 11 of 35 countries reported using national assessments at the upper secondary level.
- Regulatory accountability largely considers compliance with relevant laws and regulations. **Of eight areas or domains usually covered in compliance reporting, the most common are related to information about students and student characteristics**. This was followed by safety issues, curriculum, facilities and grounds and teachers' qualifications. The three domains with the fewest countries reporting compliance data are related to school finance and governance.
- **The topics or areas covered by school inspections were most commonly reported to be compliance with rules and regulations, quality of instruction and student performance.** School inspections at the lower secondary level are required as a part of the accountability systems in 24 of 31 countries.
- Market accountability, which refers to the competitive pressures on schools, varies considerably across countries. **While most countries permit diverse forms of school choice, in practice, the proportion of students practicing choice is more limited.** Furthermore, many countries do not have the funding mechanisms, financial incentives, or support in place to ensure that there is enough school choice to create adequate competitive pressures.

Trends

Traditionally, regulatory accountability was the most common type of accountability practiced. Over the past two decades, efforts to decentralise schooling and create more site-level autonomy have lessened the importance of regulatory accountability. However, during the same period, performance and market accountability have become more important.

Analysis

Performance accountability

Performance accountability focuses on school outcomes rather than processes. It has grown in importance over time partly due to shifting interest in outcomes, as well as to the technological advances that have made it easier to test large populations of students.

The primary measures of performance accountability that are considered in this indicator relate to national examinations and national assessments used by OECD and other G20 countries. Aside from results on standardised tests, other means of capturing evidence related to school performance include data on student attainment and the success of students after leaving a particular school.

Schools are accountable to a number of stakeholder groups, including government education agencies (local, regional and national, depending on the country), parents and students, and the general public. Fair and effective measures of performance accountability take into account the needs of the students and families they serve and the resources available to serve them.

National examinations

National examinations are standardised tests that have formal consequences for students, such as an impact upon a student's eligibility to progress to a higher level of education or attainment of an officially-recognised degree.

Slightly fewer than half the 34 countries reported using national examinations at the lower secondary level (Table D5.1a). While 10 of the 15 countries that use national examinations indicated that those exams are devised and graded at the central-authority level, three countries indicated that they were devised and graded at the state-authority level. France indicated that this was done at the central- and school-authority levels, and Poland indicated the central- and provincial-authority levels. Twelve of the 15 countries reported that their national examinations were criterion-referenced tests (see Definitions, below). Two countries indicated that their examinations were norm-referenced tests (see Definitions, below). In the United States, both criterion-referenced and norm-referenced tests are allowed, and the decision to use one or the other is taken at the state level.

In 13 of 15 countries, national examinations were compulsory for public schools at the lower secondary level. In Australia and Scotland, although it is not compulsory for public schools to administer national examinations, it is done by all schools in practice. Seven of 9 countries reported that national examinations were compulsory for government-dependent private schools, and 8 of 11 countries reported that examinations were compulsory for independent private schools.

The two subjects that were most commonly covered in national examinations include math, and the national language or language-of-instruction (reading, writing and literature). To a slightly lesser extent, modern foreign languages, science and social studies were also common subjects covered in national examinations (Tables D5.6a, D5.6b and D5.6c, available on line).

In all 14 countries with available data, results from national examinations at the lower secondary level were shared with both external audiences and education authorities. In all countries, results were shared directly with students, in 13 countries results were shared directly with school administrators, and in 12 countries results from national examinations were shared directly with teachers and with parents. In only 8 of the 14 countries were the results from national examinations shared directly with the media (Table D5.1a).

Countries were asked to describe key features of the results from national examinations at the lower secondary level that were reported to external audiences. In 10 of 13 countries, the level of performance for the most recent year was reported. The performance of schools relative to other groups or populations of students was reported in 7 of 13 countries, while in 2 countries the relative growth in student achievement over two or more years (i.e. value added) was reported. In 4 of 12 countries, other indicators of school quality were presented together with results from the national examinations. In 5 of 13 countries, the results were reported to be used by education authorities to sanction or reward schools.

Only four countries reported using national examinations at the primary level (Table D5.1b, available on line). More countries (23 of 35) reported using national examinations at the upper secondary level compared with those that reported using them at the lower secondary level (Table D5.1c, available on line). National examinations were slightly more prevalent in general education programmes compared with pre-vocational/vocational programmes.

National assessments

The key purpose of assessments is to provide formative feedback to improve instruction and inform about the relative performance of students.

Two-thirds of the 34 countries reported using national assessments at the lower secondary level (Table D5.2a), and most of those indicated that national assessments are devised and graded at the central-authority level (17 of 22) or state-authority level (3 of 22). Sweden indicated that the central authorities are involved in devising assessments, while the school authorities are involved in grading them. Belgium (Flemish Community) indicated that the state authorities are involved in devising assessments. However, these tests are developed, administered, graded and analysed by a research team of a university. The Russian Federation indicated that both the central and provincial authorities were involved in doing so. Thirteen of 22 countries reported that their national assessments were criterion-referenced tests, 8 countries indicated that their assessments were norm-referenced tests, and Japan indicated that its assessments were a combination of both.

In 15 of 22 countries, national assessments were compulsory for lower secondary public schools. Ten of 14 countries reported that national assessments were compulsory for government-dependent private schools, and 5 of 13 countries reported that assessments were compulsory for independent private schools.

As with national examinations, the two subjects that were most commonly covered in national assessments were math, and the national language or language-of-instruction (reading, writing and literature). Science and modern foreign languages were also commonly covered in national assessments (Tables D5.7a, D5.7b and D5.7c, available on line).

In 21 of 22 countries, results from national assessments at the lower secondary level were shared with external audiences in additional to education authorities. In 20 countries, the results were directly shared with school administrators. In 15 countries, results were shared directly with classroom teachers. In 14 countries, results from national assessments were shared directly with parents and with students. In only 12 of the 21 countries were the results from national assessments shared directly with the media (Table D5.2a).

Countries were asked to describe key features of the results from national assessments at the lower secondary level that were reported to external audiences. In 16 of 20 countries, the level of performance for the most recent year was reported. The performance of schools relative to other groups or populations of students was reported in 14 of 20 countries, while in 6 of 21 countries the relative growth in student achievement over two or more years (i.e. value added) was reported. In 7 of 20 countries, other indicators of school quality were presented together with results from the national assessments. Four of 19 countries reported that education authorities use the results to sanction or reward schools.

Most of the 35 countries reported using national assessments at the primary level (Table D5.2b, available on line). While national examinations were prevalent at the upper secondary level, national assessments were used in fewer than a third of the 35 countries at the upper secondary level (Table D5.2c, available on line).

Regulatory accountability

A large portion of regulatory accountability, which focuses on compliance with relevant laws and regulations, typically focuses on inputs and processes within the school. It involves schools completing reports and forms for higher levels of authority – those education agencies that plan and oversee the education system. To a lesser extent, parents and students, as well as the general public, also have a need to know about the extent to which their schools comply with established laws and regulations.

Because of the nature of internal reporting, a large portion of regulatory accountability is largely hidden from public scrutiny, although some of the information that schools submit may appear in reports released to parents, students, or the general public. Countries were asked whether they report data from eight specific domains to education authorities (Table D5.3 and Tables D5.3a, D5.3b and D5.3c, available on line). Nearly all (30 of 31) countries indicated that they report data about student numbers and characteristics from public schools to regional or national authorities. Other domains in which public schools report data to regional or national authorities include teacher qualifications/credentials (23 countries), curriculum (22 countries), facilities and grounds (20 countries), safety issues (18 countries), closing budget or financial audit from previous year (18 countries), proposed budget for subsequent year (18 countries) and issues related to governance (17 countries). Table D5.3 outlines variable patterns of compliance reporting depending upon stakeholder groups.

Schools most commonly report compliance data to school boards. Government-dependent private schools are more likely to report compliance data to their school board compared with public schools. At the same time, public schools are more likely than private schools to report compliance level data to education authorities at local and regional levels. Data concerning safety issues was more commonly reported to lower-level education authorities than to regional or national authorities.

School inspection

A school inspection is a mandated, formal process of external evaluation with the aim of holding schools accountable. The practice of school inspections varies considerably among and within countries. Formal school inspection involves one or more trained inspectors to evaluate quality based on a standard procedure. The results of a school inspection are given to the school in a formal report and are used to identify strengths and weaknesses. The reports are also made available to education authorities, parents, and the public. School inspections may include evaluating such areas as student achievement, staff, administration, curriculum and the school environment. Schools may be rewarded or sanctioned based on results from these inspections.

School inspections are used as a means of external evaluation in many countries. School inspections, like other forms of external evaluations, are mandated by higher-level education or political authorities. The level of the government at which school inspections are devised and organised varies across countries from the local school board to central education authorities or governments. The education authority or government sets standards that schools must meet and regulations with which schools must comply. The government thus collects information on the extent to which those standards are met and how well the schools are complying with those regulations by appointing inspectors to evaluate schools.

School inspections are required as part of the accountability system in 24 of 31 countries at the lower secondary level. In 7 of 24 countries, school inspections are a component of a school-accreditation process, through which schools are granted recognition or credentials if they meet or exceed minimum standards. Accreditation organisations typically emphasise inputs and processes rather than outcomes. While school inspections commonly involve all schools, in 9 of 23 countries, school inspections were targeted at low-performing schools (Table D5.4a). Similar proportions of countries reported targeting primary and upper secondary level schools for inspection (Tables D5.4b and D5.4c, available on line).

Results from school inspections are most commonly used to evaluate school performance, though they are also used to evaluate school administration and to make decisions about whether or not to close schools. The results of these inspections also influence the evaluation of individual teachers. Fewer countries reported that school inspections affect decisions about remuneration and bonuses for teachers, and school budgets (Chart D5.2 and Table D5.11, available on line).

Chart D5.3 illustrates areas addressed in school inspections and self-evaluations, and shows that the areas where school inspections were most commonly reported by countries are in compliance with rules and regulations and quality of instruction.

Chart D5.2. Distribution of influence of school inspections, by domains (2009)

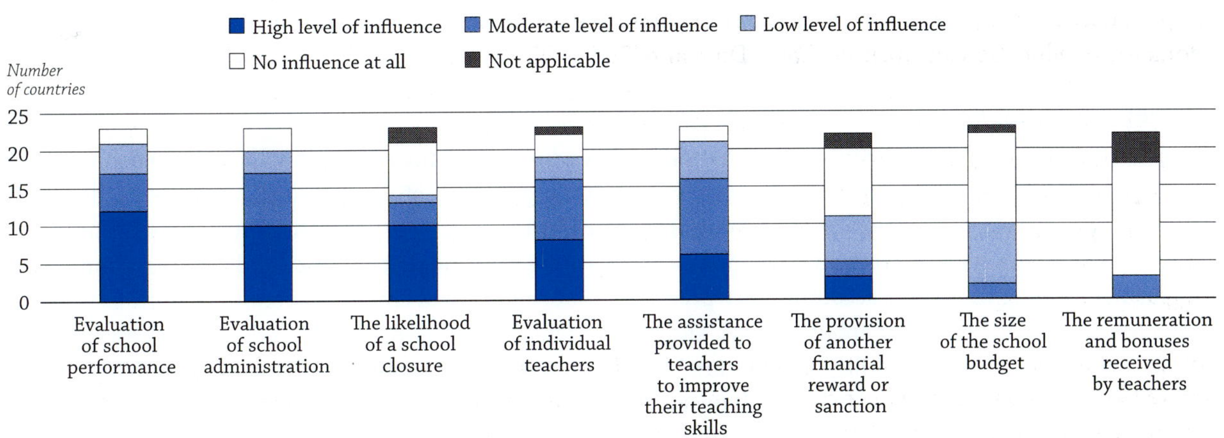

Areas are ranked in descending order of the number of countries reporting school inspections as having a high level of influence on them.
Source: OECD. Table D5.11, available on line. See Annex 3 for notes (*www.oecd.org/edu/eag2011*).
StatLink http://dx.doi.org/10.1787/888932462111

Chart D5.3. Distribution of areas addressed during school inspections and school self-evaluations at the lower secondary level (2009)

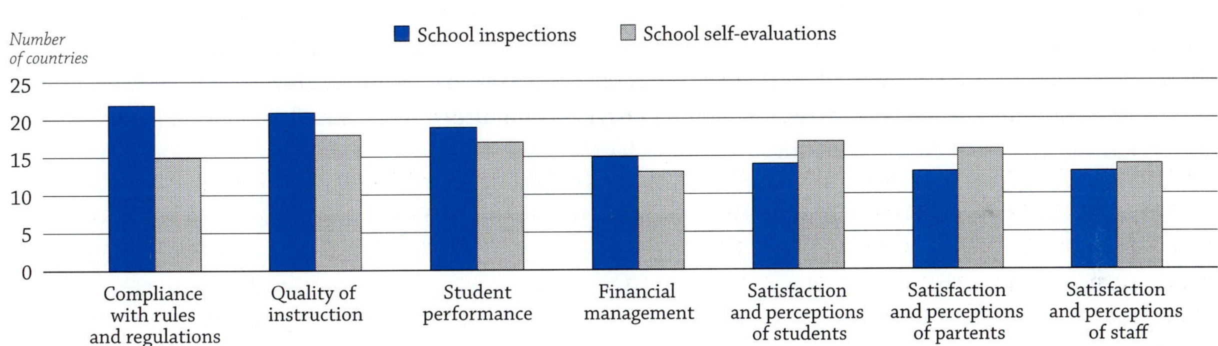

Areas are ranked in descending order of the number of countries reporting these areas as being addressed during school inspections.
Source: OECD. Table D5.4a and Table D5.10a, available on line. See Annex 3 for notes (*www.oecd.org/edu/eag2011*).
StatLink http://dx.doi.org/10.1787/888932462130

School self-evaluation

In a self-evaluation, a school systematically reviews and reflects on the quality of the instruction and education services provided and on school outcomes. Formal self-evaluation activities are mandated by external education authorities that range from local school boards to central education authorities. Results from self-evaluations can be used to inform internal audiences, or they could be used to inform school inspectors or accreditation teams. In fact, self-evaluations are often designed in connection with an external evaluation activity, such as a school inspection or a school accreditation visit. Some of the advantages of self-evaluations are that they are less costly and results can be more easily interpreted in light of the local context. The main disadvantage is that results are often seen to be less credible to external groups and more suitable to be used for improvement, rather than for accountability.

The approach to self-evaluation draws heavily on the literature on school effectiveness and improvement. This activity involves internal evaluation that is formative in nature. When schools are required to conduct self-evaluations, a set of questionnaires or tools is used to structure the activity.

Some 21 of 32 countries reported that school self-evaluation was a required part of the accountability system at the lower secondary level. Thirteen of 19 countries reported school self-evaluation was a component of the school inspection process, and 2 of 19 countries reported that it was a component of an accreditation process (Tables D5.10a, D5.10b, and D5.10c, available on line).

Market accountability

In market accountability, parents are seen as consumers who choose the school in which they wish to enroll their child. This type of accountability assumes that funding follows students, so that if parents decide to withdraw their child from one school and enroll him or her in another school, the funding would follow to the next school. As such, there would be a financial incentive for schools to attract and retain students. The proper functioning of market accountability presumes that schools will create a diversity of options, parents will have accurate information about schools, and schools will have limited ability to select or screen students. Thus, in this type of accountability, schools are largely accountable to parents and students. However, higher educational authorities might also be involved, as they might need to close failing schools.

Most countries reported having school choice, which indicates market accountability. Some 20 of 35 countries reported that families generally had the right to choose among public schools at the primary level and 19 of 34 countries at the lower secondary level. Some 20 of 33 countries reported that this was the case at the upper secondary level. Similarly, 28 of 36 countries reported that government-dependent private schools were permitted at the lower secondary level and could provide compulsory education. By definition, government-dependent private schools receive more than half of their funding from government sources. Independent private schools were permitted in 27 of 36 countries at the lower secondary level, and homeschooling at that level was permitted as a form of school choice in 24 of 35 countries. In practice, however, a very small proportion of students enroll in private schools (Table D5.5).

Data from *Education at a Glance 2010* indicate that four out of five OECD countries allow government-dependent private schools and independent private schools to provide compulsory education. In addition, 70% of OECD countries reported that homeschooling could be a legal means of providing compulsory education. Actual enrollment patterns suggest that, in practice, enrollment in government-dependent private schools exceeds 10% in only seven countries (Belgium, Chile, Denmark, France, the Netherlands, New Zealand, and Spain) and, in independent private schools, exceeds 10% only in Brazil, Mexico and Portugal. Only half of the countries reported enrollments in homeschooling, representing an average of only 0.4% of total enrollments (Table D5.2, OECD, 2010h).

Financial incentives for schools and parents that facilitated school choice and were important for the existence of a market accountability mechanism are the presence of school vouchers or scholarships, tuition tax credits, and minimal obligatory financial contributions from parents who wish to choose a school other than the one assigned for their child(ren). Furthermore, a funding mechanism that ensured that funding followed students when they leave for another public or private school was also critical to ensure that schools were negatively or positively affected when students choose to enrol or to leave (Table D5.5 and Table D5.15, available on line).

A *school voucher*, often referred to as a scholarship, is a certificate issued by the government that parents can use to pay for their child's education at a school of their choice, rather than have the child attend the public school to which he or she was assigned. In most instances, parents do not actually receive a certificate or redeemable check. Instead, schools verify that they are serving qualified students and the government provides funding to the school on the basis of the number of qualified students enrolled. Qualified students are the subgroup of students targeted by many voucher or scholarship programmes; these usually include ethnic minorities or students from low-income families. Some 13 of 29 countries reported having vouchers or scholarships that parents could use at the lower secondary level when choosing a public school. Eleven of 23 countries reported the use of vouchers to facilitate attending government-dependent private schools. Only 4 of 20 countries reported the use of vouchers to facilitate enrolment in independent private schools at the lower secondary level. At the lower secondary level, 8 of 13 countries that have vouchers or scholarships for public schools report that these are only for students from socio-economically disadvantaged backgrounds.

Seven of 11 countries that provide vouchers for government-dependent private schools provide them to disadvantaged students; and 2 of 4 countries that offer vouchers for independent private schools provide them to disadvantaged students (Table D5.5 and Table D5.14, available on line).

Tuition tax credits allow parents to deduct educational expenses, including private-school tuition, from their taxes. As a result, governments pay the costs for private schools through foregone revenues. Only 3 of 26 countries reported the use of tuition tax credits to facilitate attending government-dependent private schools at the lower secondary level. Tuition tax credits were more commonly used to facilitate enrolment in independent private schools: 6 of 24 countries reported such use of tuition tax credits at the lower secondary level. Only Estonia and the Russian Federation permit tuition tax credits for costs related to homeschooling (Table D5.5 and Table D5.16, available on line).

Perhaps most important to market accountability is a funding mechanism that ensures that funding follows the student when he or she leaves to attend a different school. This mechanism ensures that schools have an incentive to attract students, and a disincentive to lose students. In 15 of 34 countries, funding was reported to follow students who leave one public school for another at the lower secondary level within the school year. Twelve of 25 countries reported that funding directly followed students who choose to enrol in government-dependent private schools, and 6 of 12 countries reported having this mechanism in place for students who choose to enrol in independent private schools.

Countries also reported whether the funding mechanism was gradually adjusted to reflect changes in student enrolments over time. Seventeen of 35 countries reported that although funding did not directly follow the student, adjustments were made over time within the public school sector at the lower secondary level. Twelve of 25 countries reported delayed funding adjustments to reflect the movement of students among government-dependent schools, and 4 of 12 countries reported delayed funding to reflect school choice to and from independent private schools (Table D5.15, available on line).

Compulsory fees for schools at the lower secondary level are least common in public schools (2 of 35 countries), more common in government-dependent private schools (15 of 25 countries) and most common for independent private schools (all 23 countries with available data). At the lower secondary level, some 28 of 35 countries reported accepting voluntary contributions for public schools, 24 of 25 countries had voluntary contributions for government-dependent private schools, and all 21 countries with comparable data reported that independent private schools accepted voluntary contributions. The picture is similar at the primary and upper secondary levels (Table D5.5 and Table D5.17, available on line).

Tables D5.18 and D5.19 (available on line) contain data on two important components of school choice: public support for transportation, and access to information about school choice.

While countries emphasise market accountability, often the conditions required for such accountability do not exist. These conditions include – among other things – widespread school choice, where families choose and schools are restricted from selecting students, funding formulae through which money follows students, ready access to information on the choices available, and funding incentives/supports.

Definitions

A **criterion-referenced test** (CRT) assesses the extent to which students have reached the goals of a set of standards or national curriculum. Results are typically reported as cut scores, which represent a passing score or a passing point.

"Directly" sharing information or results refers to information being made available to designated groups without them having to request it. When results are available on line, they are considered as shared directly.

A **government-dependent private institution** is an institution that receives more than 50% of its core funding from government agencies or one whose teaching personnel are paid by a government agency. The term "government-dependent" refers only to the degree of a private institution's dependence on funding from government sources; it does not refer to the degree of government direction or regulation.

Homeschooling involves educating children at home, typically by parents but sometimes by tutors, in a way that meets compulsory school requirements. This should not be confused with tutoring, which supplements compulsory education.

An **independent private institution** is an institution that receives less than 50% of its core funding from government agencies and whose teaching personnel are not paid by a government agency. The term "independent" refers only to the degree of the institution's dependence on funding from government sources; it does not refer to the degree of government direction or regulation.

Market accountability refers to the competitive pressure on schools from parents and students who are seen as consumers. In other words, there is a financial incentive for schools to attract and retain students. Schools that are not accountable will lose students and funding and will eventually close.

National assessments are similar to national examinations in that they aim to measure the extent to which students have acquired a certain amount of knowledge in a given subject. National assessments may be mandatory but they do not have an impact on students' progression or certification as examinations do. Assessments are mostly used to monitor the quality of education at the system and/or school level. They also provide feedback to improve instruction and show the relative performance of students.

National examinations are standardised student tests that have a formal consequence for students, such as an impact upon a student's eligibility to progress to a higher level of education or completion of an officially recognised degree. They assess a major portion of what students are expected to know or be able to do in a given subject.

In a **norm-referenced test** (NRT), students' results are compared among their peers. Results are usually reported as a percentile rank, illustrating how many of the student's peers scored below or above.

Performance accountability focuses on school outcomes rather than processes. Aside from results on standardised tests, evidence related to school performance is included in data on student attainment and the success of students after leaving a particular school.

An institution is classified as a **private institution** if: *i)* it is controlled and managed by a non-governmental organisation (e.g. a church, trade union or business enterprise); or *ii)* most of the members of its governing board are not selected by a public agency.

An institution is classified as a **public institution** if it is: *i)* controlled and managed directly by a public education authority or agency; or *ii)* controlled and managed either by a government agency directly or by a governing body (council, committee, etc.), most of whose members are either appointed by a public authority or elected by public franchise.

Regulatory accountability refers to compliance with relevant laws and regulations: Are schools doing the things they are required to do to ensure that they are safe and effective?

Methodology

Data are from the 2010 OECD-INES Survey on School Accountability and refer to the school year 2008-09. Data on enrolments are based on the UOE data collection on educational systems administered annually by the OECD and refer to the school year 2008-09.

Notes on definitions and methodologies for each country are provided in Annex 3 at *www.oecd.org/edu/eag2011*.

The statistical data for Israel are supplied by and under the responsibility of the relevant Israeli authorities. The use of such data by the OECD is without prejudice to the status of the Golan Heights, East Jerusalem and Israeli settlements in the West Bank under the terms of international law.

References

Kogan, M. (1988), *Education Accountability: An Analytic Overview*, (2nd Ed.), Century Hutchinson, Dover.

Levin, H. (1974), "A conceptual framework for accountability in education", *School Review*, No. 82(33), pp. 363-390.

OECD (2010h), *Education at a Glance 2010: OECD Indicators*, OECD, Paris.

Tyler, R.W. (1971), "Accountability in perspective", in L.M. Lessinger and R.W. Tyler (eds.), *Accountability in Education*, Charles A. Jones, Worthington.

The following additional material relevant to this indicator is available on line:

- *Table D5.1b. National examinations at the primary level (2009)*
  StatLink http://dx.doi.org/10.1787/888932465455
- *Table D5.1c. National examinations at the upper secondary level (2009)*
  StatLink http://dx.doi.org/10.1787/888932465474
- *Table D5.2b. National assessments at the primary level (2009)*
  StatLink http://dx.doi.org/10.1787/888932465512
- *Table D5.2c. National assessments at the upper secondary level (2009)*
  StatLink http://dx.doi.org/10.1787/888932465531
- *Table D5.3a. Regulatory accountability: Domains in which public schools are expected to submit compliance-oriented reports and the groups or authorities to which these reports are submitted (2009)*
  StatLink http://dx.doi.org/10.1787/888932465569
- *Table D5.3b. Regulatory accountability: Domains in which government-dependent private schools are expected to submit compliance-oriented reports and the groups or authorities to which these reports are submitted (2009)*
  StatLink http://dx.doi.org/10.1787/888932465588
- *Table D5.3c. Regulatory accountability: Domains in which independent private schools are expected to submit compliance-oriented reports and the groups or authorities to which these reports are submitted (2009)*
  StatLink http://dx.doi.org/10.1787/888932465607
- *Table D5.4b. School inspection at the primary level (2009)*
  StatLink http://dx.doi.org/10.1787/888932465645
- *Table D5.4c. School inspection at the upper secondary level (2009)*
  StatLink http://dx.doi.org/10.1787/888932465664
- *Table D5.6a. Subjects covered in national examinations in lower secondary education (2009)*
  StatLink http://dx.doi.org/10.1787/888932465702
- *Table D5.6b. Subjects covered in national examinations in primary education (2009)*
  StatLink http://dx.doi.org/10.1787/888932465721
- *Table D5.6c. Subjects covered in national examinations in upper secondary education (2009)*
  StatLink http://dx.doi.org/10.1787/888932465740
- *Table D5.7a. Subjects covered in national assessments in lower secondary education (2009)*
  StatLink http://dx.doi.org/10.1787/888932465759
- *Table D5.7b. Subjects covered in national assessments in primary education (2009)*
  StatLink http://dx.doi.org/10.1787/888932465778
- *Table D5.7c. Subjects covered in national assessments in upper secondary education (2009)*
  StatLink http://dx.doi.org/10.1787/888932465797
- *Table D5.8. Existence and use of other forms or measures of performance accountability (2009)*
  StatLink http://dx.doi.org/10.1787/888932465816
- *Table D5.9a. Means and methods for collecting and reporting data related to regulatory accountability for public schools (2009)*
  StatLink http://dx.doi.org/10.1787/888932465835
- *Table D5.9b. Means and methods for collecting and reporting data related to regulatory accountability for government-dependent private schools (2009)*
  StatLink http://dx.doi.org/10.1787/888932465854
- *Table D5.9c. Means and methods for collecting and reporting data related to regulatory accountability for independent private schools (2009)*
  StatLink http://dx.doi.org/10.1787/888932465873

- *Table D5.10a. School self-evaluation at the lower secondary level (2009)*
  StatLink http://dx.doi.org/10.1787/888932465892
- *Table D5.10b. School self-evaluation at the primary level (2009)*
  StatLink http://dx.doi.org/10.1787/888932465911
- *Table D5.10c. School self-evaluation at the upper secondary level (2009)*
  StatLink http://dx.doi.org/10.1787/888932465930
- *Table D5.11. Possible influence of school inspections, school self-evaluations, national examinations and national assessments (2009)*
  StatLink http://dx.doi.org/10.1787/888932465949
- *Table D5.12. Freedom for parents to choose a public school for their child(ren) (2009)*
  StatLink http://dx.doi.org/10.1787/888932465968
- *Table D5.13. Criteria used by public and private schools when assigning and selecting students (2009)*
  StatLink http://dx.doi.org/10.1787/888932465987
- *Table D5.14. Availability of school vouchers (or scholarships) (2009)*
  StatLink http://dx.doi.org/10.1787/888932466006
- *Table D5.15. Extent to which public funding follows students when they leave for another public or private school (2009)*
  StatLink http://dx.doi.org/10.1787/888932466025
- *Table D5.16. Financial incentives and disincentives for school choice (2009)*
  StatLink http://dx.doi.org/10.1787/888932466044
- *Table D5.17. Compulsory and/or voluntary financial contributions from parents are permitted (2009)*
  StatLink http://dx.doi.org/10.1787/888932466063
- *Table D5.18. Use of public resources for transporting students (2009)*
  StatLink http://dx.doi.org/10.1787/888932466082
- *Table D5.19. Responsibility for informing parents about school choices available to them (2009)*
  StatLink http://dx.doi.org/10.1787/888932466101

Table D5.1a. [1/2] National examinations at the lower secondary level (2009)

			Existence	Level of government by which they are devised and graded	Based on norm-reference (N) or criterion-reference (C) test	Year first established	Public: Compulsory to administer	Public: Percentage that administer them	Government-dependent private: Compulsory to administer	Government-dependent private: Percentage that administer them	Independent private: Compulsory to administer	Independent private: Percentage that administer them	Percentage of students exempted from taking them
			(1)	(2)	(3)	(4)	(5)	(6)	(7)	(8)	(9)	(10)	(11)
OECD	Australia	All programmes	Yes	2	N	m	No	100	No	99	a	a	m
	Austria	All programmes	No	a	a	a	a	a	a	a	a	a	a
	Belgium (Fl.)	All programmes	No	a	a	a	a	a	a	a	a	a	a
	Belgium (Fr.)	All programmes	No	a	a	a	a	a	a	a	a	a	a
	Canada	All programmes	m	m	m	m	m	m	m	m	m	m	m
	Chile	All programmes	No	a	a	a	a	a	a	a	a	a	a
	Czech Republic	All programmes	No	a	a	a	a	a	a	a	a	a	a
	Denmark	All programmes	Yes	1	C	1975	Yes	100	No	95	a	a	3
	England	All programmes	No	a	a	a	a	a	a	a	a	a	a
	Estonia	General	Yes	1	C	1992	Yes	100	Yes	100	a	a	0
		Pre-voc and voc	No	a	a	a	a	a	a	a	a	a	a
	Finland	All programmes	No	a	a	a	a	a	a	a	a	a	a
	France	All programmes	Yes	1, 6	C	1988	Yes	100	Yes	100	Yes	100	0
	Germany	All programmes	Yes	2	C	1949	Yes	100	Yes	100	a	a	0
	Greece	All programmes	No	a	a	a	a	a	a	a	a	a	a
	Hungary	All programmes	No	a	a	a	a	a	a	a	a	a	a
	Iceland	All programmes	No	a	a	a	a	a	a	a	a	a	a
	Ireland	All programmes	Yes	1	C	1926	Yes	100	a	a	No	m	m
	Israel	All programmes	No	a	a	a	a	a	a	a	a	a	a
	Italy	All programmes	Yes	1	C	1962	Yes	100	a	a	Yes	100	0
	Japan	All programmes	No	a	a	a	a	a	a	a	a	a	a
	Korea	All programmes	No	a	a	a	a	a	a	a	a	a	a
	Luxembourg	All programmes	No	a	a	a	a	a	a	a	a	a	a
	Mexico	All programmes	No	a	a	a	a	a	a	a	a	a	a
	Netherlands	General	Yes	1	N	1968	Yes	100	Yes	100	Yes	100	3
		Pre-voc and voc	Yes	1	N	1968	Yes	100	Yes	100	Yes	100	6
	New Zealand	All programmes	m	m	m	m	m	m	m	m	m	m	m
	Norway	All programmes	Yes	1	C	2007	Yes	100	Yes	100	Yes	100	m
	Poland	All programmes	Yes	1, 3	C	2002	Yes	100	Yes	100	Yes	100	1.2
	Portugal	General	Yes	1	C	2005	Yes	100	Yes	100	Yes	100	0
		Pre-voc and voc	No	a	a	a	a	a	a	a	a	a	a
	Scotland	All programmes	Yes	1	C	1962	No	100	a	a	No	100	a
	Slovak Republic	All programmes	No	a	a	a	a	a	a	a	a	a	a
	Slovenia	All programmes	m	m	m	m	m	m	m	m	m	m	m
	Spain	All programmes	No	a	a	a	a	a	a	a	a	a	a
	Sweden	All programmes	No	a	a	a	a	a	a	a	a	a	a
	Switzerland	All programmes	m	m	m	m	m	m	m	m	m	m	m
	Turkey	All programmes	a	a	a	a	a	a	a	a	a	a	a
	United States	All programmes	Yes	2	m	2001	Yes	100	a	a	No	m	m
Other G20	Argentina	All programmes	m	m	m	m	m	m	m	m	m	m	m
	Brazil	All programmes	No	a	a	a	a	a	a	a	a	a	a
	China	All programmes	m	m	m	m	m	m	m	m	m	m	m
	India	All programmes	m	m	m	m	m	m	m	m	m	m	m
	Indonesia	All programmes	Yes	1	C	1982	Yes	100	a	a	Yes	100	0
	Russian Federation	All programmes	Yes	1	C	m	Yes	100	a	a	Yes	100	1-2
	Saudi Arabia	All programmes	m	m	m	m	m	m	m	m	m	m	m
	South Africa	All programmes	m	m	m	m	m	m	m	m	m	m	m

Levels of government
1: Central authority or government
2: State authorities or governments
3: Provincial/regional authorities or governments
4: Sub-regional or inter-municipal authorities or governments
5: Local authorities or governments
6: School, school board or committee

Note: Federal states or countries with highly decentralised school systems may experience regulatory differences between states, provinces or regions. Refer to Annex 3 for additional information.
Source: OECD. See Annex 3 for notes (*www.oecd.org/edu/eag2011*).
Please refer to the Reader's Guide for information concerning the symbols replacing missing data.
StatLink http://dx.doi.org/10.1787/888932465436

Table D5.1a. [2/2] **National examinations at the lower secondary level (2009)**

		How results are shared						Features used when reporting results					
		Shared with external audience in addition to education authorities	Shared directly with school administrators	Shared directly with classroom teachers	Shared directly with parents	Shared directly with students	Shared directly with media	Show level of performance for most recent year	Show "value added" or growth in student achievement based on progress of students over 2 or more years	Context sensitive	Compared with other groups or populations of students	Reported together with other indicators of school quality	Used by authorities external to the school for sanctions or rewards
		(12)	(13)	(14)	(15)	(16)	(17)	(18)	(19)	(20)	(21)	(22)	(23)
OECD Australia	All programmes	m	m	m	m	m	m	m	m	m	m	m	m
Austria	All programmes	a	a	a	a	a	a	a	a	a	a	a	a
Belgium (Fl.)	All programmes	a	a	a	a	a	a	a	a	a	a	a	a
Belgium (Fr.)	All programmes	a	a	a	a	a	a	a	a	a	a	a	a
Canada	All programmes	m	m	m	m	m	m	m	m	m	m	m	m
Chile	All programmes	a	a	a	a	a	a	a	a	a	a	a	a
Czech Republic	All programmes	a	a	a	a	a	a	a	a	a	a	a	a
Denmark	All programmes	Yes	Yes	Yes	Yes	Yes	Yes	Yes	No	No	Yes	Yes	Yes
England	All programmes	a	a	a	a	a	a	a	a	a	a	a	a
Estonia	General	Yes	Yes	Yes	Yes	Yes	Yes	Yes	No	No	Yes	Yes	No
	Pre-voc and voc	a	a	a	a	a	a	a	a	a	a	a	a
Finland	All programmes	a	a	a	a	a	a	a	a	a	a	a	a
France	All programmes	Yes	Yes	Yes	Yes	Yes	Yes	No	No	No	No	No	No
Germany	All programmes	Yes	Yes	Yes	No	Yes	No	Yes	Yes	No	No	a	No
Greece	All programmes	a	a	a	a	a	a	a	a	a	a	a	a
Hungary	All programmes	a	a	a	a	a	a	a	a	a	a	a	a
Iceland	All programmes	a	a	a	a	a	a	a	a	a	a	a	a
Ireland	All programmes	Yes	Yes	No	Yes	Yes	No	Yes	No	No	No	No	No
Israel	All programmes	a	a	a	a	a	a	a	a	a	a	a	a
Italy	All programmes	Yes	No	Yes	Yes	Yes	No	No	No	No	No	No	Yes
Japan	All programmes	a	a	a	a	a	a	a	a	a	a	a	a
Korea	All programmes	a	a	a	a	a	a	a	a	a	a	a	a
Luxembourg	All programmes	a	a	a	a	a	a	a	a	a	a	a	a
Mexico	All programmes	a	a	a	a	a	a	a	a	a	a	a	a
Netherlands	General	Yes	Yes	No	No	Yes	No	Yes	No	No	No	Yes	Yes
	Pre-voc and voc	Yes	Yes	No	No	Yes	No	Yes	No	No	No	Yes	Yes
New Zealand	All programmes	m	m	m	m	m	m	m	m	m	m	m	m
Norway	All programmes	Yes	Yes	Yes	Yes	Yes	Yes	Yes	No	No	Yes	Yes	No
Poland	All programmes	Yes	Yes	Yes	Yes	Yes	Yes	No	No	No	Yes	No	No
Portugal	General	Yes	Yes	Yes	Yes	Yes	Yes	Yes	No	No	No	No	No
	Pre-voc and voc	a	a	a	a	a	a	a	a	a	a	a	a
Scotland	All programmes	Yes	Yes	Yes	Yes	Yes	Yes	Yes	Yes	Yes	Yes	No	No
Slovak Republic	All programmes	a	a	a	a	a	a	a	a	a	a	a	a
Slovenia	All programmes	m	m	m	m	m	m	m	m	m	m	m	m
Spain	All programmes	a	a	a	a	a	a	a	a	a	a	a	a
Sweden	All programmes	a	a	a	a	a	a	a	a	a	a	a	a
Switzerland	All programmes	m	m	m	m	m	m	m	m	m	m	m	m
Turkey	All programmes	a	a	a	a	a	a	a	a	a	a	a	a
United States	All programmes	Yes	Yes	Yes	Yes	Yes	No	Yes	No	Yes	Yes	No	Yes
Other G20 Argentina	All programmes	m	m	m	m	m	m	m	m	m	m	m	m
Brazil	All programmes	a	a	a	a	a	a	a	a	a	a	a	a
China	All programmes	m	m	m	m	m	m	m	m	m	m	m	m
India	All programmes	m	m	m	m	m	m	m	m	m	m	m	m
Indonesia	All programmes	Yes	Yes	Yes	Yes	Yes	a	a	a	a	a	a	a
Russian Federation	All programmes	Yes	Yes	Yes	Yes	Yes	Yes	Yes	No	No	Yes	No	Yes
Saudi Arabia	All programmes	m	m	m	m	m	m	m	m	m	m	m	m
South Africa	All programmes	m	m	m	m	m	m	m	m	m	m	m	m

Levels of government
1: Central authority or government
2: State authorities or governments
3: Provincial/regional authorities or governments
4: Sub-regional or inter-municipal authorities or governments
5: Local authorities or governments
6: School, school board or committee

Note: Federal states or countries with highly decentralised school systems may experience regulatory differences between states, provinces or regions. Refer to Annex 3 for additional information.
Source: OECD. See Annex 3 for notes *(www.oecd.org/edu/eag2011)*.
Please refer to the Reader's Guide for information concerning the symbols replacing missing data.
StatLink http://dx.doi.org/10.1787/888932465436

D5

Table D5.2a. [1/2] National assessments at the lower secondary level (2009)

			Existence	Level of government by which they are devised and graded	Based on norm-reference (N) or criterion-reference (C) test	Year first established	Public: Compulsory to administer	Public: Percentage that administer them	Government-dependent private: Compulsory to administer	Government-dependent private: Percentage that administer them	Independent private: Compulsory to administer	Independent private: Percentage that administer them	Percentage of students exempted from taking them
			(1)	(2)	(3)	(4)	(5)	(6)	(7)	(8)	(9)	(10)	(11)
OECD	Australia	All programmes	Yes	1	N	2003	Yes	100	Yes	100	a	a	1.5
	Austria	All programmes	No	a	a	a	a	a	a	a	a	a	a
	Belgium (Fl.)	All programmes	Yes	2	C	2004	No	11.2	No	13.6	No[1]	a	m
	Belgium (Fr.)	All programmes	No	a	a	a	a	a	a	a	a	a	a
	Canada	All programmes	m	m	m	m	m	m	m	m	m	m	m
	Chile	All programmes	Yes	1	C	1988	Yes	100	Yes	100	Yes	100	7
	Czech Republic	All programmes	No	a	a	a	a	a	a	a	a	a	a
	Denmark	All programmes	Yes	1	C	2009	No	m	No	m	No	m	a
	England	All programmes	No	a	a	a	a	a	a	a	a	a	a
	Estonia	All programmes	No	a	a	a	a	a	a	a	a	a	a
	Finland	All programmes	Yes	1	C	1998	No	10-15	No	10-15	a	a	m
	France	All programmes	No	a	a	a	a	a	a	a	a	a	a
	Germany	All programmes	Yes	2	C	2007	No	100	No	100	a	a	0.7
	Greece	All programmes	No	a	a	a	a	a	a	a	a	a	a
	Hungary	All programmes	Yes	1	C	2001	Yes	100	Yes	100	a	a	0
	Iceland	All programmes	Yes	1	N	2009	Yes	100	Yes	100	a	a	10
	Ireland	All programmes	No	a	a	a	a	a	a	a	a	a	a
	Israel	All programmes	Yes	1	N	2002	Yes	100	Yes	100	m	m	5
	Italy	All programmes	Yes	1	N	2008	Yes	100	a	a	No	95	0
	Japan	All programmes	Yes	1	N, C	2007	No	100	a	a	No	55	a
	Korea	All programmes	Yes	1	C	2001	Yes	100	Yes	100	a	a	0
	Luxembourg	All programmes	Yes	1	C	2007	Yes	100	m	a	No	m	0
	Mexico	All programmes	Yes	1	C	2006	Yes	100	a	a	Yes	100	0
	Netherlands	All programmes	No	a	a	a	a	a	a	a	a	a	a
	New Zealand	All programmes	m	m	m	m	m	m	m	m	m	m	m
	Norway	All programmes	Yes	1	N	2004	Yes	100	Yes	100	Yes	100	1.7
	Poland	All programmes	No	a	a	a	a	a	a	a	a	a	a
	Portugal	All programmes	No	a	a	a	a	a	a	a	a	a	a
	Scotland	All programmes	No	a	a	a	a	a	a	a	a	a	a
	Slovak Republic	General	Yes	1	N	2004	Yes	100	Yes	100	a	a	3.01
		Pre-voc and voc	No	a	a	a	a	a	a	a	a	a	a
	Slovenia	All programmes	m	m	m	m	m	m	m	m	m	m	m
	Spain	All programmes	Yes	2	C	2007	Yes	100	Yes	100	Yes	100	0
	Sweden	All programmes	Yes	1, 6	C	1998	Yes	100	Yes	100	a	a	m
	Switzerland	All programmes	m	m	m	m	m	m	m	m	m	m	m
	Turkey	All programmes	a	a	a	a	a	a	a	a	a	a	a
	United States	All programmes	Yes	1	C	1969	No	21	a	a	No	m	a
Other G20	Argentina	All programmes	m	m	m	m	m	m	m	m	m	m	m
	Brazil	All programmes	Yes	1	N	1993	Yes	100	a	a	No	3.5	0
	China	All programmes	m	m	m	m	m	m	m	m	m	m	m
	India	All programmes	m	m	m	m	m	m	m	m	m	m	m
	Indonesia	All programmes	Yes	1	N	2008	No	2	a	a	No	2	0
	Russian Federation	All programmes	Yes	1, 3	C	m	Yes	8	a	a	Yes	8	a
	Saudi Arabia	All programmes	m	m	m	m	m	m	m	m	m	m	m
	South Africa	All programmes	m	m	m	m	m	m	m	m	m	m	m

Levels of government
1: Central authority or government
2: State authorities or governments
3: Provincial/regional authorities or governments
4: Sub-regional or inter-municipal authorities or governments
5: Local authorities or governments
6: School, school board or committee

Note: Federal states or countries with highly decentralised school systems may experience regulatory differences between states, provinces or regions. Refer to Annex 3 for additional information.

1. Independant private schools are not included in the sample for the national assessment.

Source: OECD. See Annex 3 for notes *(www.oecd.org/edu/eag2011)*.

Please refer to the Reader's Guide for information concerning the symbols replacing missing data.

StatLink http://dx.doi.org/10.1787/888932465493

Table D5.2a. [2/2] National assessments at the lower secondary level (2009)

			How results are shared						Features used when reporting results					
			Shared with external audience in addition to education authorities	Shared directly with school administrators	Shared directly with classroom teachers	Shared directly with parents	Shared directly with students	Shared directly with media	Show level of performance for most recent year	Show "value added" or growth in student achievement based on progress of students over 2 or more years	Context sensitive	Compared with other groups or populations of students	Reported together with other indicators of school quality	Used by authorities external to the school for sanctions or rewards
			(12)	(13)	(14)	(15)	(16)	(17)	(18)	(19)	(20)	(21)	(22)	(23)
OECD	Australia	All programmes	Yes	Yes	Yes	Yes	No	No	Yes	No	Yes	Yes	No	No
	Austria	All programmes	a	a	a	a	a	a	a	a	a	a	a	a
	Belgium (Fl.)	All programmes	Yes	Yes	Yes	Yes	Yes	Yes	Yes	No	Yes	Yes	No	No
	Belgium (Fr.)	All programmes	a	a	a	a	a	a	a	a	a	a	a	a
	Canada	All programmes	m	m	m	m	m	m	m	m	m	m	m	m
	Chile	All programmes	Yes	Yes	Yes	Yes	m	Yes	Yes	No	Yes	Yes	No	Yes
	Czech Republic	All programmes	a	a	a	a	a	a	a	a	a	a	a	a
	Denmark	All programmes	Yes	Yes	Yes	Yes	Yes	No	a	No	a	a	a	m
	England	All programmes	a	a	a	a	a	a	a	a	a	a	a	a
	Estonia	All programmes	a	a	a	a	a	a	a	a	a	a	a	a
	Finland	All programmes	Yes	Yes	No	No	No	No	No	Yes	No	Yes	No	No
	France	All programmes	a	a	a	a	a	a	a	a	a	a	a	a
	Germany	All programmes	Yes	Yes	Yes	No	Yes	No	Yes	Yes	Yes	No	Yes	No
	Greece	All programmes	a	a	a	a	a	a	a	a	a	a	a	a
	Hungary	All programmes	Yes	Yes	No	Yes	Yes	No	Yes	Yes	Yes	Yes	No	Yes
	Iceland	All programmes	Yes	Yes	Yes	Yes	Yes	Yes	Yes	Yes	No	Yes	No	No
	Ireland	All programmes	a	a	a	a	a	a	a	a	a	a	a	a
	Israel	All programmes	Yes	Yes	No	No	No	Yes	Yes	No	Yes	Yes	Yes	No
	Italy	All programmes	Yes	Yes	No	No	No	No	No	No	No	No	No	No
	Japan	All programmes	Yes	Yes	Yes	Yes	Yes	Yes	No	No	No	Yes	No	m
	Korea	All programmes	Yes	Yes	Yes	Yes	Yes	Yes	Yes	No	No	No	No	No
	Luxembourg	All programmes	No	a	a	a	a	a	a	a	a	a	a	a
	Mexico	All programmes	Yes	Yes	Yes	Yes	Yes	Yes	Yes	Yes	Yes	Yes	No	Yes
	Netherlands	All programmes	a	a	a	a	a	a	a	a	a	a	a	a
	New Zealand	All programmes	m	m	m	m	m	m	m	m	m	m	m	m
	Norway	All programmes	Yes	Yes	Yes	Yes	Yes	No	Yes	No	No	Yes	Yes	No
	Poland	All programmes	a	a	a	a	a	a	a	a	a	a	a	a
	Portugal	All programmes	a	a	a	a	a	a	a	a	a	a	a	a
	Scotland	All programmes	a	a	a	a	a	a	a	a	a	a	a	a
	Slovak Republic	General	Yes	Yes	No	No	Yes	No	Yes	No	No	Yes	No	No
		Pre-voc and voc	a	a	a	a	a	a	a	a	a	a	a	a
	Slovenia	All programmes	m	m	m	m	m	m	m	m	m	m	m	m
	Spain	All programmes	Yes	Yes	Yes	Yes	Yes	Yes	Yes	No	Yes	Yes	Yes	No
	Sweden	All programmes	Yes	Yes	Yes	Yes	Yes	Yes	Yes	No	Yes	No	Yes	No
	Switzerland	All programmes	m	m	m	m	m	m	m	m	m	m	m	m
	Turkey	All programmes	a	a	a	a	a	a	a	a	a	a	a	a
	United States	All programmes	Yes	Yes	Yes	Yes	Yes	Yes	Yes	No	Yes	Yes	No	No
Other G20	Argentina	All programmes	m	m	m	m	m	m	m	m	m	m	m	m
	Brazil	All programmes	Yes	Yes	Yes	Yes	Yes	Yes	Yes	No	No	No	No	No
	China	All programmes	m	m	m	m	m	m	m	m	m	m	m	m
	India	All programmes	m	m	m	m	m	m	m	m	m	m	m	m
	Indonesia	All programmes	Yes	No	No	No	No	Yes	No	Yes	Yes	Yes	Yes	No
	Russian Federation	All programmes	Yes	Yes	Yes	No	No	No	Yes	No	No	No	Yes	Yes
	Saudi Arabia	All programmes	m	m	m	m	m	m	m	m	m	m	m	m
	South Africa	All programmes	m	m	m	m	m	m	m	m	m	m	m	m

Levels of government
1: Central authority or government
2: State authorities or governments
3: Provincial/regional authorities or governments
4: Sub-regional or inter-municipal authorities or governments
5: Local authorities or governments
6: School, school board or committee

Note: Federal states or countries with highly decentralised school systems may experience regulatory differences between states, provinces or regions. Refer to Annex 3 for additional information.
1. Independant private schools are not included in the sample for the national assessment.
Source: OECD. See Annex 3 for notes *(www.oecd.org/edu/eag2011)*.
Please refer to the Reader's Guide for information concerning the symbols replacing missing data.
StatLink http://dx.doi.org/10.1787/888932465493

Table D5.3. Regulatory accountability: Domains in which public schools are expected to submit compliance-oriented reports (2009)

		School board (S) OR Municipal or local government/education authority (M)								Regional government/education authority (R) OR National government/education authority (N)								Parents and students							
		Student data	Teachers' qualifications/ credentials	Curriculum	Safety issues	Facilities and grounds	Proposed budget for subsequent year	Closing budget or financial audit from previous year	Issues related to governance	Student data	Teachers' qualifications/ credentials	Curriculum	Safety issues	Facilities and grounds	Proposed budget for subsequent year	Closing budget or financial audit from previous year	Issues related to governance	Student data	Teachers' qualifications/ credentials	Curriculum	Safety issues	Facilities and grounds	Proposed budget for subsequent year	Closing budget or financial audit from previous year	Issues related to governance
		(1)	(2)	(3)	(4)	(5)	(6)	(7)	(8)	(9)	(10)	(11)	(12)	(13)	(14)	(15)	(16)	(17)	(18)	(19)	(20)	(21)	(22)	(23)	(24)
OECD	Australia	m	m	m	m	m	m	m	m	m	m	m	m	m	m	m	m	m	m	m	m	m	m	m	m
	Austria	M	M	S/M	a	M	M	M	No	R/N	R/N	R/N	a	R/N	R/N	R/N	No	m	m	m	a	m	m	m	No
	Belgium (Fl.)	m	m	m	M	m	m	m	m	N	N	N	N	N	No	N	N	No	No	Yes	No	No	No	No	Yes
	Belgium (Fr.)	S/M	S/M	No	m	S/M	S	m	m	N	N	m	m	m	m	m	m	Yes	Yes	m	m	m	m	m	m
	Canada	m	m	m	m	m	m	m	m	m	m	m	m	m	m	m	m	m	m	m	m	m	m	m	m
	Chile	No	No	No	No	M	M	M	No	N	N	N	N	N	No	No	N	No	No	No	No	No	No	No	No
	Czech Republic	S/M	S/M	S	S	S	S/M	S/M	S	R/N	R/N	No	No	No	R/N	R/N	No	Yes	Yes	No	No	No	No	Yes	No
	Denmark	S/M	No	S/M	S/M	No	S	S	No	R/N	No	N	N	No	N	N	No	No	No	Yes	Yes	No	No	No	No
	England	S/M	S	S	S/M	S/M	S/M	S/M	S/M	N	No	No	No	No	No	No	No	No	No	No	No	No	No	No	No
	Estonia	S/M	S/M	S/M	S/M	S/M	S/M	S/M	S/M	R	R	R	R	R	R	R	R	Yes	Yes	Yes	No	Yes	Yes	Yes	Yes
	Finland	M	M	M	M	M	M	M	M	a	a	a	a	a	a	a	a	a	a	a	a	a	a	a	a
	France	S/M	S	S	S	S	S	S	S	R/N	a	a	a	a	R	R	R	Yes	a	a	a	a	No	No	No
	Germany	S/M	S/M	S/M	S/M	S/M	S/M	S/M	m	R	R	R	R	R	R	No	m	Yes	No	Yes	Yes	No	No	No	m
	Greece	M	No	No	S/M	S/M	No	S	M	R/N	R	R/N	R	R/N	No	R	R/N	No	No	Yes	Yes	No	No	No	No
	Hungary	M	M	M	M	M	M	M	M	N	No	No	No	No	No	No	No	No	No	No	No	No	No	No	No
	Iceland	S/M	S/M	S/M	S/M	S/M	S/M	S/M	S/M	N	N	N	No	No	No	No	N	No	No	Yes	No	No	No	No	No
	Ireland	S	S	S	S	S	S	S	S	N	N	N	N	No	N	N	No	No	No	No	Yes	No	No	No	No
	Israel	S/M	S/M	S	S/M	S/M	S/M	S/M	m	R/N	R/N	R/N	R/N	R	R	R	m	Yes	No	Yes	Yes	Yes	Yes	Yes	m
	Italy	M	No	S	S/M	M	S	S	No	R/N	R/N	R/N	No	R	No	No	No	No	No	No	No	No	No	No	No
	Japan	m	m	m	m	m	m	m	m	No	No	No	m	m	No	No	m	m	m	m	m	m	m	m	m
	Korea	S/M	S/M	S/M	S/M	S/M	S/M	S/M	S/M	R/N	R/N	R/N	R/N	R/N	R/N	R/N	R/N	Yes	Yes	Yes	Yes	Yes	Yes	Yes	Yes
	Luxembourg	M	M	No	M	M	M	a	M	N	N	N	N	N	N	a	N	a	a	a	a	a	a	a	a
	Mexico	S	S	No	No	S	No	No	No	R/N	R/N	R/N	No	R/N	No	No	No	No	No	No	No	No	No	No	No
	Netherlands	S	S	S	S	S	S	S	S	N	No	No	N	N	No	N	N	No	No	Yes	Yes	No	No	No	No
	New Zealand	m	m	m	m	m	m	m	m	m	m	m	m	m	m	m	m	m	m	m	m	m	m	m	m
	Norway	m	m	m	m	m	m	m	m	m	m	m	m	m	m	m	m	m	m	m	m	m	m	m	m
	Poland	S/M	S/M	S	S/M	S/M	M	S/M	S/M	R/N	R/N	No	R/N	R/N	R	R	R	No	No	Yes	No	No	No	No	No
	Portugal	S	No	S/M	S/M	S	S	S	S/M	R/N	N	N	R/N	N	N	N	R/N	No	No	Yes	Yes	No	No	No	Yes
	Scotland	No	No	No	No	No	No	No	No	R/N	R/N	R/N	R/N	R/N	R/N	No	R/N	Yes	No	No	No	No	Yes	No	No
	Slovak Republic	S/M	No	S/M	S/M	S/M	S/M	S/M	S/M	R/N	N	R/N	R/N	R/N	R/N	R/N	R/N	No	No	No	No	No	No	No	No
	Slovenia	m	m	m	m	m	m	m	m	m	m	m	m	m	m	m	m	m	m	m	m	m	m	m	m
	Spain	S/M	S/M	S/M	S/M	S/M	S/M	S/M	S/M	R/N	R/N	R/N	R/N	R/N	R/N	R/N	R/N	Yes	Yes	Yes	Yes	Yes	Yes	Yes	Yes
	Sweden	No	No	No	No	No	No	No	No	N	No	No	No	No	No	No	No	No	No	No	No	No	No	No	No
	Switzerland	m	m	m	m	m	m	m	m	m	m	m	m	m	m	m	m	m	m	m	m	m	m	m	m
	Turkey	M	No	M	No	M	M	M	No	R/N	No	R/N	No	R/N	R/N	R/N	No	No	No	No	No	No	No	No	No
	United States	S/M	S/M	S/M	S/M	S/M	S/M	S/M	S/M	R/N	R/N	R	R/N	R	R	R	R	Yes	No	No	Yes	No	Yes	Yes	No
Other G20	Argentina	m	m	m	m	m	m	m	m	m	m	m	m	m	m	m	m	m	m	m	m	m	m	m	m
	Brazil	m	m	m	m	m	m	m	m	m	m	m	m	m	m	m	m	m	m	m	m	m	m	m	m
	China	m	m	m	m	m	m	m	m	m	m	m	m	m	m	m	m	m	m	m	m	m	m	m	m
	India	m	m	m	m	m	m	m	m	m	m	m	m	m	m	m	m	m	m	m	m	m	m	m	m
	Indonesia	M	M	M	S/M	S/M	S/M	S/M	S/M	R/N	R/N	R/N	No	No	No	No	R/N	No	No	Yes	Yes	Yes	Yes	Yes	Yes
	Russian Federation	S/M	S/M	S/M	S/M	S/M	S/M	S/M	S/M	R	R	R	R	R	R	R	R	Yes	Yes	Yes	Yes	Yes	Yes	No	No
	Saudi Arabia	m	m	m	m	m	m	m	m	m	m	m	m	m	m	m	m	m	m	m	m	m	m	m	m
	South Africa	m	m	m	m	m	m	m	m	m	m	m	m	m	m	m	m	m	m	m	m	m	m	m	m

Note: Federal states or countries with highly decentralised school systems may experience regulatory differences between states, provinces or regions. Refer to Annex 3 for additional information.

Source: OECD. See Annex 3 for notes *(www.oecd.org/edu/eag2011)*.

Please refer to the Reader's Guide for information concerning the symbols replacing missing data.

StatLink http://dx.doi.org/10.1787/888932465550

Table D5.4a. [1/2] School inspection at the lower secondary level (2009)

		School inspections required as part of accountability system	Frequency of school inspections			Percentage that have inspections conducted each year			Component of school accreditation process	Extent to which they are structured	Target low performance schools	Level of the government school inspections are devised and organised	Composition of school inspection teams
			Public	Government-dependent private	Independent private	Public	Government-dependent private	Independent private					
		(1)	(2)	(3)	(4)	(5)	(6)	(7)	(8)	(9)	(10)	(11)	(12)
OECD	Australia	m	m	m	m	m	m	m	m	m	m	m	m
	Austria	Yes	1	1	a	m	m	a	No	U	No	5, 3	m
	Belgium (Fl.)	Yes	6	6	6	15	15	a	Yes	H	Yes	2	T
	Belgium (Fr.)	Yes	5	5	a	30	30	a	Yes	P	No	2	S
	Canada	m	m	m	m	m	m	m	m	m	m	m	m
	Chile	Yes	2	2	1	m	m	a	No	H	m	1, 3	T
	Czech Republic	Yes	5	5	a	33	33	a	Yes	H	No	3	S
	Denmark	No	a	a	a	a	a	a	a	a	a	a	a
	England	Yes	6	6	5	25	25	33	No	H	Yes	1	T
	Estonia	Yes	3	3	a	10	10	a	No	H	No	1	S
	Finland	No	a	a	a	a	a	a	a	a	a	a	a
	France	Yes	1	1	1	m	m	m	Yes	P	No	3	T
	Germany	Yes	4	1	a	50	a	a	No	H	No	2	T
	Greece	No	a	a	a	a	a	a	a	a	a	a	a
	Hungary	No	a	a	a	a	a	a	a	a	a	a	a
	Iceland	Yes	1	1	1	8	m	m	No	P	No	1, 5	T
	Ireland	Yes	6	a	1	10	a	0	Yes	H	Yes	1	T
	Israel	Yes	2	3	m	100	50	m	No	H	Yes	1	S
	Italy	No	a	a	a	a	a	a	a	a	a	a	a
	Japan	No	a	a	a	a	a	a	a	a	a	a	a
	Korea	Yes	5	5	a	33	33	a	No	H	Yes	3	T
	Luxembourg	a	a	a	a	a	a	a	a	a	a	a	a
	Mexico	No	a	a	a	a	a	a	a	a	a	a	a
	Netherlands	Yes	3	3	3	55	55	55	No	P, U	Yes	1	T
	New Zealand	m	m	m	m	m	m	m	m	m	m	m	m
	Norway	Yes	6	6	6	20	4	m	No	P	No	1	T
	Poland[1]	Yes	6	6	6	20	20	20	No	H	Yes	1, 3	S
	Portugal	Yes	6	1	1	25	a	a	No	H	No	1	T
	Scotland	Yes	6	6	6	16.7	16.7	16.7	No	H	No	2	T
	Slovak Republic	Yes	6	6	a	20	20	a	No	H	No	1	T
	Slovenia	m	m	m	m	m	m	m	m	m	m	m	m
	Spain	Yes	2	2	2	100	100	100	No	P	No	2	T
	Sweden	Yes	6	6	a	17[2]	17[2]	a	No	H	No	1	T
	Switzerland	m	m	m	m	m	m	m	m	m	m	m	m
	Turkey	a	a	a	a	a	a	a	a	a	a	a	a
	United States	Yes	m	a	1	m	a	m	Yes	m	Yes	2, 5, 6	B
Other G20	Argentina	m	m	m	m	m	m	m	m	m	m	m	m
	Brazil	m	m	m	m	m	m	m	m	m	m	m	m
	China	m	m	m	m	m	m	m	m	m	m	m	m
	India	m	m	m	m	m	m	m	m	m	m	m	m
	Indonesia	Yes	2	a	2	100	a	100	No	H	Yes	5	S
	Russian Federation	Yes	6	a	6	8	a	8	Yes	H	No	1, 3	T
	Saudi Arabia	m	m	m	m	m	m	m	m	m	m	m	m
	South Africa	m	m	m	m	m	m	m	m	m	m	m	m

Frequency of school inspections:
1: There are no requirement for school inspections
2: More often than once a year
3: Once a year
4: Once every two years
5: Once every three years
6: Once every three plus years

Extent to which the school inspections are structured:
H: Highly structured, similar activities completed at each school based on specific set of data collection tools
P: Partially structured
U: Unstructured, activities at each site vary and depend on the strengths and weaknesses of the school

Levels of government:
1: Central authority or government
2: State authorities or governments
3: Provincial/regional authorities or governments
4: Sub-regional or inter-municipal authorities or governments
5: Local authorities or governments
6: School, school board or committee

Composition of school inspection teams:
T: Team
S: One person
B: Mixed

Note: Federal states or countries with highly decentralised school systems may experience regulatory differences between states, provinces or regions. Refer to Annex 3 for additional information.

1. Year of reference 2010.

2. The percentage refers to the proportion of municipalities in which all schools have inspections conducted each year.

Source: OECD. See Annex 3 for notes *(www.oecd.org/edu/eag2011).*

Please refer to the Reader's Guide for information concerning the symbols replacing missing data.

StatLink http://dx.doi.org/10.1787/888932465626

Table D5.4a. [2/2] School inspection at the lower secondary level (2009)

		Areas addressed during school inspections							Sharing of results from school inspections						
		Compliance with rules and regulations	Financial management	Quality of instruction	Student performance	Satisfaction and perceptions of students	Satisfaction and perceptions of parents	Satisfaction and perceptions of staff	Shared with external audience in additional to education authorities	Shared directly with higher level education authorities	Shared directly with school administrators	Shared directly with classroom teachers	Shared directly with parents	Shared directly with students	Shared directly with media
		(13)	(14)	(15)	(16)	(17)	(18)	(19)	(20)	(21)	(22)	(23)	(24)	(25)	(26)
OECD	Australia	m	m	m	m	m	m	m	m	m	m	m	m	m	m
	Austria	m	m	m	m	m	m	m	No	m	m	m	m	m	m
	Belgium (Fl.)	Yes	No	Yes	Yes	Yes	Yes	Yes	Yes	Yes	Yes	Yes	Yes	No	Yes
	Belgium (Fr.)	Yes	No	Yes	Yes	No	No	No	Yes	No	Yes	No	No	No	No
	Canada	m	m	m	m	m	m	m	m	m	m	m	m	m	m
	Chile	Yes	Yes	No	No	No	No	No	No	a	a	a	a	a	a
	Czech Republic	Yes	Yes	Yes	No	No	No	No	Yes	Yes	Yes	Yes	Yes	Yes	Yes
	Denmark	a	a	a	a	a	a	a	a	a	a	a	a	a	a
	England	Yes	Yes	Yes	Yes	Yes	Yes	Yes	Yes	Yes	Yes	Yes	Yes	Yes	Yes
	Estonia	Yes	No	Yes	Yes	No	No	No	Yes	No	Yes	Yes	No	No	No
	Finland	a	a	a	a	a	a	a	a	a	a	a	a	a	a
	France	Yes	Yes	Yes	Yes	Yes	Yes	Yes	Yes	Yes	Yes	Yes	No	No	No
	Germany	Yes	Yes	Yes	Yes	Yes	Yes	Yes	Yes	Yes	Yes	Yes	Yes	m	No
	Greece	a	a	a	a	a	a	a	a	a	a	a	a	a	a
	Hungary	a	a	a	a	a	a	a	a	a	a	a	a	a	a
	Iceland	Yes	No	Yes	Yes	Yes	Yes	Yes	Yes	Yes	Yes	Yes	Yes	Yes	Yes
	Ireland	Yes	No	Yes	Yes	No	No	No	Yes	Yes	Yes	Yes	Yes	Yes	Yes
	Israel	Yes	Yes	Yes	No	No	Yes	Yes	Yes	Yes	Yes	No	No	No	No
	Italy	a	a	a	a	a	a	a	a	a	a	a	a	a	a
	Japan	a	a	a	a	a	a	a	a	a	a	a	a	a	a
	Korea	Yes	Yes	Yes	Yes	Yes	Yes	Yes	No	a	a	a	a	a	a
	Luxembourg	a	a	a	a	a	a	a	a	a	a	a	a	a	a
	Mexico	a	a	a	a	a	a	a	a	a	a	a	a	a	a
	Netherlands	Yes	Yes	Yes	Yes	Yes	Yes	Yes	Yes	No	Yes	No	No	No	No
	New Zealand	m	m	m	m	m	m	m	m	m	m	m	m	m	m
	Norway	Yes	Yes	No	No	Yes	No	No	Yes	Yes	Yes	Yes	Yes	Yes	Yes
	Poland[1]	Yes	Yes	Yes	Yes	Yes	Yes	Yes	Yes	Yes	Yes	Yes	Yes	Yes	Yes
	Portugal	Yes	Yes	Yes	Yes	Yes	Yes	Yes	Yes	Yes	Yes	Yes	Yes	Yes	No
	Scotland	No	No	Yes	Yes	Yes	Yes	Yes	Yes	Yes	Yes	Yes	Yes	No	Yes
	Slovak Republic	Yes	No	Yes	Yes	Yes	Yes	Yes	Yes	Yes	Yes	Yes	No	No	No
	Slovenia	m	m	m	m	m	m	m	m	m	m	m	m	m	m
	Spain	Yes	Yes	Yes	Yes	Yes	Yes	Yes	Yes	Yes	Yes	Yes	No	No	No
	Sweden	Yes	No	Yes	Yes	Yes	No	No	Yes	Yes	Yes	Yes	Yes	Yes	Yes
	Switzerland	m	m	m	m	m	m	m	m	m	m	m	m	m	m
	Turkey	a	a	a	a	a	a	a	a	a	a	a	a	a	a
	United States	Yes	Yes	Yes	Yes	No	No	No	Yes	Yes	Yes	Yes	No	No	No
Other G20	Argentina	m	m	m	m	m	m	m	m	m	m	m	m	m	m
	Brazil	m	m	m	m	m	m	m	m	m	m	m	m	m	m
	China	m	m	m	m	m	m	m	m	m	m	m	m	m	m
	India	m	m	m	m	m	m	m	m	m	m	m	m	m	m
	Indonesia	Yes	Yes	Yes	Yes	No	No	No	Yes	Yes	Yes	Yes	No	No	No
	Russian Federation	Yes	Yes	Yes	Yes	No	No	No	Yes	No	Yes	Yes	No	No	No
	Saudi Arabia	m	m	m	m	m	m	m	m	m	m	m	m	m	m
	South Africa	m	m	m	m	m	m	m	m	m	m	m	m	m	m

Frequency of school inspections:
1: There are no requirement for school inspections
2: More often than once a year
3: Once a year
4: Once every two years
5: Once every three years
6: Once every three plus years

Extent to which the school inspections are structured:
H: Highly structured, similar activities completed at each school based on specific set of data collection tools
P: Partially structured
U: Unstructured, activities at each site vary and depend on the strengths and weaknesses of the school

Levels of government:
1: Central authority or government
2: State authorities or governments
3: Provincial/regional authorities or governments
4: Sub-regional or inter-municipal authorities or governments
5: Local authorities or governments
6: School, school board or committee

Composition of school inspection teams:
T: Team
S: One person
B: Mixed

Note: Federal states or countries with highly decentralised school systems may experience regulatory differences between states, provinces or regions. Refer to Annex 3 for additional information.

1. Year of reference 2010.

2. The percentage refers to the proportion of municipalities in which all schools have inspections conducted each year.

Source: OECD. See Annex 3 for notes *(www.oecd.org/edu/eag2011).*

Please refer to the Reader's Guide for information concerning the symbols replacing missing data.

StatLink http://dx.doi.org/10.1787/888932465626

Table D5.5. [1/2] Existence of school choice options and financial incentives for school choice (2009)

By level of education

		Existence of school choice options										
		Public schools			Government-dependent private schools			Independent private schools			Homeschooling		
		Families are given a general right to enrol in any traditional public school they wish			Legally permitted to operate and provide compulsory education			Legally permitted to operate and provide compulsory education			Permitted as a legal means of providing compulsory education		
		Primary	Lower secondary	Upper secondary	Primary	Lower secondary	Upper secondary	Primary	Lower secondary	Upper secondary	Primary	Lower secondary	Upper secondary
		(1)	(2)	(3)	(4)	(5)	(6)	(7)	(8)	(9)	(10)	(11)	(12)
OECD	Australia	m	m	m	Yes	Yes	Yes	No	No	No	m	m	m
	Austria	Yes	Yes	Yes	Yes	Yes	Yes	Yes	Yes	Yes	Yes	Yes	No
	Belgium (Fl.)[1]	Yes	Yes	Yes	Yes	Yes	Yes	No	No	No	Yes	Yes	Yes
	Belgium (Fr.)[1]	Yes	Yes	Yes	Yes	Yes	Yes	No	No	No	Yes	Yes	Yes
	Canada	m	m	m	m	m	m	m	m	m	m	m	m
	Chile	Yes	Yes	Yes	Yes	Yes	Yes	Yes	Yes	Yes	No	No	No
	Czech Republic	Yes	Yes	Yes	Yes	Yes	Yes	No	No	No	Yes	No	No
	Denmark	Yes	Yes	Yes	Yes	Yes	Yes	Yes	Yes	Yes	Yes	Yes	Yes
	England	Yes	Yes	Yes	Yes	Yes	Yes	Yes	Yes	Yes	Yes	Yes	Yes
	Estonia	Yes	Yes	Yes	Yes	Yes	Yes	No	No	No	Yes	Yes	Yes
	Finland	No	No	Yes	Yes	Yes	Yes	No	No	No	Yes	Yes	Yes
	France	No	No	No	Yes	Yes	Yes	Yes	Yes	Yes	Yes	Yes	Yes
	Germany	No	No	No	Yes	Yes	Yes	Yes	Yes	Yes	No	No	No
	Greece	No	No	No	No	No	No	Yes	Yes	Yes	No	No	No
	Hungary	Yes	Yes	Yes	Yes	Yes	Yes	Yes	Yes	Yes	Yes	Yes	Yes
	Iceland	No	No	Yes	Yes	Yes	Yes	Yes	Yes	Yes	Yes	Yes	No
	Ireland	Yes	Yes	Yes	Yes	Yes	Yes	Yes	Yes	Yes	Yes	Yes	Yes
	Israel	No	No	No	Yes	Yes	Yes	Yes	Yes	Yes	Yes	Yes	Yes
	Italy	Yes	Yes	Yes	No	No	No	Yes	Yes	Yes	Yes	Yes	Yes
	Japan	No	No	No	No	No	No	Yes	Yes	Yes	No	No	No
	Korea	No	No	No	No	Yes	Yes	Yes	No	Yes	No	No	No
	Luxembourg	Yes	Yes	Yes	Yes	Yes	Yes	Yes	Yes	Yes	Yes	Yes	Yes
	Mexico	Yes	Yes	No	No	No	No	Yes	Yes	Yes	No	No	No
	Netherlands	Yes	No	No	Yes	Yes	Yes	Yes	Yes	Yes	Yes	Yes	Yes
	New Zealand[2]	Yes	Yes	m	Yes	Yes	m	Yes	Yes	m	Yes	Yes	m
	Norway	No	No	No	Yes	Yes	Yes	Yes	Yes	Yes	Yes	Yes	No
	Poland	No	No	Yes	Yes	Yes	Yes	Yes	Yes	Yes	Yes	Yes	Yes
	Portugal	Yes	Yes	Yes	Yes	Yes	Yes	Yes	Yes	Yes	Yes	Yes	Yes
	Scotland	No	No	No	Yes	Yes	Yes	Yes	Yes	Yes	Yes	Yes	Yes
	Slovak Republic	Yes	Yes	Yes	Yes	Yes	Yes	No	No	No	Yes	No	No
	Slovenia	m	m	m	m	m	m	m	m	m	m	m	m
	Spain	Yes	Yes	Yes	Yes	Yes	Yes	Yes	Yes	Yes	No	No	No
	Sweden	No	No	No	Yes	Yes	Yes	No	No	No	Yes	Yes	No
	Switzerland[2]	No	No	m	Yes	Yes	m	Yes	Yes	m	Yes	Yes	m
	Turkey	No	a	No	No	a	No	Yes	a	Yes	No	a	No
	United States	m	m	m	No	No	No	Yes	Yes	Yes	Yes	Yes	Yes
Other G20	Argentina	m	m	m	m	m	m	m	m	m	m	m	m
	Brazil	Yes	Yes	Yes	No	No	No	Yes	Yes	Yes	No	No	No
	China	m	m	m	m	m	m	m	m	m	m	m	m
	India	m	m	m	m	m	m	m	m	m	m	m	m
	Indonesia	No	No	No	No	No	No	Yes	Yes	Yes	No	No	No
	Russian Federation	Yes	Yes	Yes	No	No	No	Yes	Yes	Yes	Yes	Yes	Yes
	Saudi Arabia	m	m	m	m	m	m	m	m	m	m	m	m
	South Africa	m	m	m	m	m	m	m	m	m	m	m	m

Note: Federal states or countries with highly decentralised school systems may experience regulatory differences between states, provinces or regions. Refer to Annex 3 for additional information.

1. Independent private schools are free to arrange education but have no permission to hand out legitimate diplomas.

2. Year of reference 2008.

Source: OECD. See Annex 3 for notes *(www.oecd.org/edu/eag2011).*

Please refer to the Reader's Guide for information concerning the symbols replacing missing data.

StatLink http://dx.doi.org/10.1787/888932465683

Table D5.5. [2/2] Existence of school choice options and financial incentives for school choice (2009)

By level of education

		Financial incentives to promote school choice at the lower secondary level										
		School vouchers (also referred to as scholarships) are available and applicable			Funding follows students when they leave for another public or private school (within the school year)			Tuition tax credits are available to help families offset costs of private schooling			Obligatory financial contributions from parents		
		Public schools	Government-dependent private schools	Independent private schools	Public schools	Government-dependent private schools	Independent private schools	Government-dependent private schools	Independent private schools	Homeschooling	Public schools	Government-dependent private schools	Independent private schools
		(13)	(14)	(15)	(16)	(17)	(18)	(19)	(20)	(21)	(22)	(23)	(24)
OECD	Australia	m	m	m	m	m	m	m	m	m	m	m	m
	Austria	No	No	No	No	No	a	No	No	No	No	No	m
	Belgium (Fl.)[1]	Yes	Yes	No	No	No	a	No	m	No	Yes	Yes	m
	Belgium (Fr.)[1]	Yes	Yes	No	No	No	a	No	a	No	No	No	m
	Canada	m	m	m	m	m	m	m	m	m	m	m	m
	Chile	Yes	Yes	a	Yes	Yes	a	No	No	a	No	Yes	Yes
	Czech Republic	No	No	a	Yes	Yes	a	No	a	a	No	Yes	a
	Denmark	No	No	No	No	No	a	No	No	No	No	Yes	Yes
	England	a	a	No	No	No	a	No	No	No	No	No	Yes
	Estonia	Yes	Yes	a	Yes	Yes	a	Yes	a	Yes	No	Yes	a
	Finland	a	a	a	Yes	Yes	a	No	a	No	No	Yes	a
	France	Yes	Yes	No	Yes	Yes	No	No	No	No	No	Yes	Yes
	Germany	Yes	Yes	a	No	No	a	Yes	a	a	No	Yes	a
	Greece	No	a	No	No	a	a	a	No	a	No	a	Yes
	Hungary	No	No	a	Yes	Yes	a	No	a	No	No	Yes	a
	Iceland	No	No	a	Yes	Yes	a	No	a	No	No	No	a
	Ireland	No	a	No	Yes	a	No	a	No	No	No	a	Yes
	Israel	Yes	Yes	a	No	No	m	No	No	No	Yes	Yes	Yes
	Italy	Yes	a	No	No	a	No	a	Yes	m	No	a	Yes
	Japan	No	a	No	No	a	No	a	No	a	No	a	Yes
	Korea	No	No	a	No	No	a	No	a	a	No	No	a
	Luxembourg	No	No	No	No	No	No	No	No	No	No	Yes	Yes
	Mexico	a	a	a	No	a	a	a	No	a	No	a	Yes
	Netherlands	No	No	No	Yes	Yes	Yes	No	No	No	No	No	Yes
	New Zealand[2]	Yes	Yes	Yes	No	No	No	No	No	No	No	No	Yes
	Norway	No	No	No	No	No	a	No	No	No	No	Yes	Yes
	Poland	Yes	Yes	Yes	Yes	Yes	Yes	No	No	No	No	No	Yes
	Portugal	a	a	a	No	Yes	Yes	Yes	Yes	No	No	Yes	Yes
	Scotland	No	No	No	Yes	m	Yes	No	Yes	No	No	m	Yes
	Slovak Republic	Yes	Yes	a	Yes	Yes	a	No	a	a	No	Yes	a
	Slovenia	m	m	m	m	m	m	m	m	m	m	m	m
	Spain	Yes	Yes	a	No	No	a	No	No	a	No	No	Yes
	Sweden	No	No	a	Yes	Yes	a	No	a	No	No	No	a
	Switzerland[2]	No	No	No	No	No	a	No	No	No	No	Yes	Yes
	Turkey	a	a	a	a	a	a	a	a	a	a	a	a
	United States	a	a	Yes	m	a	Yes	a	Yes	No	No	a	Yes
Other G20	Argentina	m	m	m	m	m	m	m	m	m	m	m	m
	Brazil	a	a	a	Yes	a	a	a	Yes	a	No	a	Yes
	China	m	m	m	m	m	m	m	m	m	m	m	m
	India	m	m	m	m	m	m	m	m	m	m	m	m
	Indonesia	Yes	a	Yes	Yes	a	Yes	a	No	a	No	a	Yes
	Russian Federation	No	a	No	No	a	a	a	Yes	Yes	No	a	Yes
	Saudi Arabia	m	m	m	m	m	m	m	m	m	m	m	m
	South Africa	m	m	m	m	m	m	m	m	m	m	m	m

Note: Federal states or countries with highly decentralised school systems may experience regulatory differences between states, provinces or regions. Refer to Annex 3 for additional information.

1. Independent private schools are free to arrange education but have no permission to hand out legitimate diplomas.

2. Year of reference 2008.

Source: OECD. See Annex 3 for notes *(www.oecd.org/edu/eag2011).*

Please refer to the Reader's Guide for information concerning the symbols replacing missing data.

StatLink http://dx.doi.org/10.1787/888932465683

HOW EQUAL ARE EDUCATIONAL OUTCOMES AND OPPORTUNITIES?

- Over 40% of 15-year-old students in OECD countries scored below PISA reading proficiency Level 3. The risk of having these low reading scores was about one-and-three-quarters as large for students from socio-economically disadvantaged backgrounds, one-and-a-half times as large for immigrants as for non-immigrants, and one-and-a-half times as large for boys as for girls.
- A student whose parents have only attained low levels of education is 1.72 times more likely to score below Level 3 on the PISA reading proficiency scale.

Chart D6.1. Relationship between student vulnerability and inequality associated with parental education (PISA 2009)

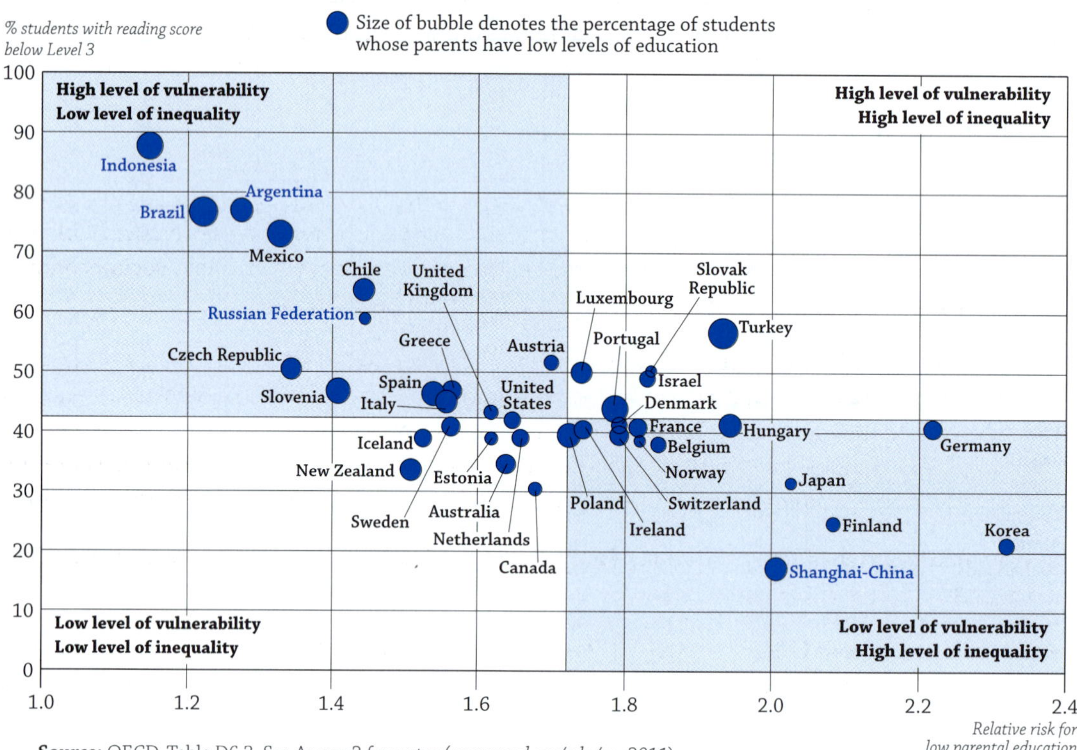

Source: OECD. Table D6.3. See Annex 3 for notes (*www.oecd.org/edu/eag2011*).

StatLink http://dx.doi.org/10.1787/888932462149

How to read this chart

This chart shows the relationship between a measure of vulnerability – 15-year-old students with reading scores below Level 3 – and an indicator of inequality – the relative risk associated with parents with low levels of education. The size of the dot for each country is proportional to the percentage of students in the country whose parents have low levels of education. A country can have a low level of inequality but not necessarily a low level of vulnerability. Chile is a good example, as the relative risk associated with parents with low levels of education is relatively small (1.4), yet Chile has a relatively high percentage of students who perform poorly in reading (64%). In New Zealand, the relative risk associated with parents who have low levels of education is also small (1.5), as in Chile, but the prevalence of 15-year-olds with poor reading performance is markedly lower (34%). Also, a country may show a relatively high level of inequality, but the difference in outcomes applies to a smaller proportion of the population. Finland and Japan are good examples, as fewer than 5% of the students in these countries have parents with low levels of education.

Context

Over the past twenty years, the demand for workers with strong literacy skills has grown, while jobs for low-skilled workers are becoming harder to find. Young people who do not acquire strong literacy skills during their primary and secondary education are considered vulnerable in that they are at greater risk of being unemployed, developing physical and mental health problems, and participating in criminal activities. The development of non-cognitive skills, such as perseverance, motivation, and social and intellectual engagement, is equally important for long-term health and well-being (Heckman, 2008). Students who fail to develop these skills adequately are also considered to be vulnerable. Willms (1997) argues that literacy itself is a defining characteristic of social class: "People become part of a culture through its language, and use that language to engage in social relations that increase their knowledge and develop their potential. Decreasing inequalities in literacy is therefore crucial for achieving tolerance, social cohesion and equality of opportunity in a modern society" (p.22).

Equality of outcomes can only be achieved if disadvantaged students have the opportunity to attend schools with high-quality resources and effective school policies and practices. Focusing on the prevalence of vulnerable students and the extent to which certain subpopulations are at greater risk of being vulnerable – having low literacy skills or being disengaged from school, for example – enables countries to set meaningful and achievable goals. The most desirable outcome for a country is to have low levels of vulnerability *and* low levels of inequality.

Other findings

- **Students from disadvantaged backgrounds are considered a potentially vulnerable group.** On average across OECD countries, these students were 1.76 times as likely to have reading scores below Level 3 as their counterparts who were in the top three quartiles on the *PISA index of economic, social and cultural status*. This relative risk associated with low socio-economic status varies among OECD countries from 1.30 to 2.26 (Table D6.3).
- **Fifteen-year-olds whose parents had low levels of education are also considered potentially vulnerable, with the relative risk associated with low levels of parents' education ranging from 1.33 to 2.32 among OECD countries.** In some countries, such as Finland, the relative risk is high, but comparatively few students have parents with low levels of education. Therefore, the reduction in vulnerability that would be gained by achieving equality for this group is small.
- **The relative risk of low proficiency in reading associated with immigrant status is 1.50 on average across OECD countries.**
- **On average across OECD countries, 15-year-old boys are about one-and-a-half times more likely to have low reading scores than 15-year-old girls.** This varies markedly among OECD countries, ranging from 1.13 to 2.57 times more likely.
- The extent to which students identify with and value schooling outcomes is a key indicator of student engagement. The prevalence of 15-year-olds who do not **value success at school** also varies considerably among countries. However, there is greater equality on this measure than in reading achievement for students from different socio-economic backgrounds, with different levels of parents' education, between immigrants and non-immigrants, and between boys and girls (Table D6.5).

Analysis

A focus on vulnerability and risk

International data on student performance allow analysts not only to examine differences among countries in their average performance, but also the prevalence of vulnerable students. In this analysis, a cut-point or benchmark for each outcome was established such that one can consider the prevalence of 15-year-olds who are considered vulnerable, such as those with "reading proficiency below Level 3" or those with "low levels of engagement".

A focus on student vulnerability and risk has at least three advantages. First, it provides a measure, easily understood by the wider community, against which goals can be set. For example, one might state that the aim of educational reforms is to reduce the prevalence of poor readers from 43% to 25% over the next ten years. This has greater meaning than saying the aim is to increase reading scores by 12 points on the PISA scale.

Second, for many countries, reducing the number of vulnerable students is more important than shifting the entire distribution of reading skills. This is because young people with poor reading skills and low levels of engagement at school are at greater risk of being unemployed and experiencing physical and mental health problems.

The third advantage is that in many countries, a substantial number of 15-year-olds score at or very close to the "floor" (or lowest level) of the test. However, the "true score" for these students may be even lower than the scores they attain on the PISA test. Depending on how many students in a country score close to the floor of the test, the *average* levels of performance is upwardly biased, while the prevalence of vulnerable students is unaffected (Nonoyama-Tarumi and Willms, 2010).

A disadvantage of using cut-points to establish vulnerability is that not all analysts or policy makers would agree on where to set the cut-point. This shortcoming can be addressed to some extent by considering two or more cut-points. For example, in this analysis, "below Level 3" refers to poor reading performance. One advantage of using "below level 3" rather than "below level 2" is that it is less sensitive to variations among countries in the percentage of students excluded from the study. Also, the majority of students scoring at Level 2 on the PISA scale lack the skills necessary for secondary-level studies. In the United States, for example, 42% of students scored below Level 3 on PISA, while 26% of public school students scored below the "Basic" level of proficiency on the Grade 8 test used for the US National Report Card. The Basic level denotes "partial mastery of prerequisite knowledge and skills that are fundamental for proficient work at each grade" (National Centre for Education Statistics, 2010). The US results suggest that about two-thirds of the students who score below Level 3 on PISA would be below the basic level of proficiency, and the remaining one-third would be at the lower end of the basic level.

Another compelling reason for focusing on a higher standard is that labour-market demands for higher literacy skills have increased over the past two decades. In their 2008 publication, Goldin and Katz describe an almost century-long "race" between education and technology: wages and economic growth depend on how well workers can keep up with changes in the complexity of job tasks.

Still, "below Level 2" is an important indicator of vulnerability as well, especially for countries with very low reading scores. About 19% of students in OECD countries had reading scores below Level 2, and in some countries the prevalence exceeded 25%. Therefore, this definition of vulnerability is considered as well (Table D6.4). The relative risk of vulnerability was about two-and-one-third times as large for students from socio-economically disadvantaged backgrounds, two times as large for immigrants as for non-immigrants, and two-and-one-fifth times as large for boys as for girls. A student whose parents have only attained low levels of education is two-and-one-quarter times more likely to score below Level 2 on the PISA reading proficiency scale.

When the analysis focuses on the prevalence of vulnerability, one can then consider various subpopulations' "risk" of being vulnerable. In this analysis, four subpopulations were considered: 15-year-old students from socio-economically disadvantaged backgrounds, that is students whose families were in the lowest quartile (bottom 25%) on the *PISA index of economic, social and cultural status* (ESCS) in their country, 15-year-old students whose parents have low levels of education, immigrants, and boys. Socio-economic disadvantage was considered in *relative* terms; that is, these students are among the 25% most disadvantaged students in their country. The results for these students are compared with those of students who are among the 25% most socio-economically advantaged students.

Box D6.1. **Summary descriptions for the seven levels of proficiency in reading**

Level	Lower score limit	Percentage of students able to perform tasks at this level or above	Characteristics of tasks
6	698	0.8%	Tasks at this level typically require the reader to make multiple inferences, comparisons and contrasts that are both detailed and precise. They require demonstration of a full and detailed understanding of one or more texts and may involve integrating information from more than one text. Tasks may require the reader to deal with unfamiliar ideas, in the presence of prominent competing information, and to generate abstract categories for interpretations. *Reflect and evaluate* tasks may require the reader to hypothesise about or critically evaluate a complex text on an unfamiliar topic, taking into account multiple criteria or perspectives, and applying sophisticated understandings from beyond the text. A salient condition for *access and retrieve* tasks at this level is precision of analysis and fine attention to detail that is inconspicuous in the texts.
5	626	7.6%	Tasks at this level that involve retrieving information require the reader to locate and organise several pieces of deeply embedded information, inferring which information in the text is relevant. Reflective tasks require critical evaluation or hypothesis, drawing on specialised knowledge. Both interpretative and reflective tasks require a full and detailed understanding of a text whose content or form is unfamiliar. For all aspects of reading, tasks at this level typically involve dealing with concepts that are contrary to expectations.
4	553	28.3%	Tasks at this level that involve retrieving information require the reader to locate and organise several pieces of embedded information. Some tasks at this level require interpreting the meaning of nuances of language in a section of text by taking into account the text as a whole. Other interpretative tasks require understanding and applying categories in an unfamiliar context. Reflective tasks at this level require readers to use formal or public knowledge to hypothesise about or critically evaluate a text. Readers must demonstrate an accurate understanding of long or complex texts whose content or form may be unfamiliar.
3	480	57.2%	Tasks at this level require the reader to locate, and in some cases recognise the relationship between, several pieces of information that must meet multiple conditions. Interpretative tasks at this level require the reader to integrate several parts of a text in order to identify a main idea, understand a relationship or construe the meaning of a word or phrase. They need to take into account many features in comparing, contrasting or categorising. Often the required information is not prominent or there is much competing information; or there are other text obstacles, such as ideas that are contrary to expectation or negatively worded. Reflective tasks at this level may require connections, comparisons, and explanations, or they may require the reader to evaluate a feature of the text. Some reflective tasks require readers to demonstrate a fine understanding of the text in relation to familiar, everyday knowledge. Other tasks do not require detailed text comprehension but require the reader to draw on less common knowledge.
2	407	81.2%	Some tasks at this level require the reader to locate one or more pieces of information, which may need to be inferred and may need to meet several conditions. Others require recognising the main idea in a text, understanding relationships, or construing meaning within a limited part of the text when the information is not prominent and the reader must make low level inferences. Tasks at this level may involve comparisons or contrasts based on a single feature in the text. Typical reflective tasks at this level require readers to make a comparison or several connections between the text and outside knowledge, by drawing on personal experience and attitudes.
1a	335	94.3%	Tasks at this level require the reader to locate one or more independent pieces of explicitly stated information; to recognise the main theme or author's purpose in a text about a familiar topic, or to make a simple connection between information in the text and common, everyday knowledge. Typically the required information in the text is prominent and there is little, if any, competing information. The reader is explicitly directed to consider relevant factors in the task and in the text.
1b	262	98.9%	Tasks at this level require the reader to locate a single piece of explicitly stated information in a prominent position in a short, syntactically simple text with a familiar context and text type, such as a narrative or a simple list. The text typically provides support to the reader, such as repetition of information, pictures or familiar symbols. There is minimal competing information. In tasks requiring interpretation the reader may need to make simple connections between adjacent pieces of information.

Source: OECD (2010a).

Low levels of parents' education were considered in *absolute* terms; that is, the subpopulation included 15-year-old students whose parents or guardians had completed less than 12 years of schooling. The results for these students are compared with students with at least one parent or guardian who had completed 12 or more years of schooling. The subpopulation of immigrants included those who were first- or second-generation immigrants. Fifteen-year-old boys were chosen as a potentially vulnerable group, because in most jurisdictions boys have lower reading scores than girls. However, the results can be readily transformed into results pertaining to girls.

A measure commonly used by epidemiologists is "relative risk". This is simply the ratio of risk in a subpopulation compared to the risk among those who are not members of that subpopulation. For example, if the prevalence of low reading scores is 60% among immigrants and 40% among non-immigrants, the relative risk for immigrants is 1.5.

Education policy can then focus on *reducing the prevalence of vulnerable students by lowering the relative risk for potentially vulnerable subpopulations.* This is different from the aim of "closing the achievement gap", which does not necessarily reduce the prevalence of vulnerability. Also, this approach allows one to gauge the "population relevance" associated with increased vulnerability among a subpopulation. Population relevance is the reduction in prevalence for the full population that would be achieved if the risk in the potentially vulnerable population (for example, immigrants) were reduced to the same prevalence as that of the non-vulnerable group (in this example, non-immigrants).

For example, in both the Netherlands and Switzerland, the relative risk for an immigrant to have reading scores below Level 3 is 1.63. In both countries, the percentage of vulnerable students – those with low reading scores – is about 39%. However, in the Netherlands, 12.1% of 15-year-olds are immigrants. If education policies reduced the risk of low reading scores for immigrants to the same level as that of non-immigrants, the overall prevalence would decrease by about 7% (the population relevance for the Netherlands). In Switzerland, 23.5% of 15-year-olds are immigrants; if education policies reduced the risk of low reading scores for immigrants to the same level as that of non-immigrants in Switzerland, the overall prevalence would decrease by about 13% (the population relevance for Switzerland) (Table D6.3).

Equality versus equity

The term "equality" is used to refer to differences in educational outcomes between high- and low-status groups, such as socio-economically advantaged and disadvantaged students. Attempts to achieve equality of outcomes usually begin by ensuring there is "equity" – a fair allocation of school resources. Thus, it is important also to consider differences between high- and low-status groups in factors known to affect educational outcomes, such as attending a school with positive student-teacher relations, certified teachers, and a strong infrastructure. After establishing cut-points or thresholds for these factors, one can use the same statistics – relative risk and population relevance – to assess whether key resources are allocated equitably.

The results show that 15-year-old students from different family backgrounds do not report substantially worse teacher-student relations: the relative risk for disadvantaged students is 1.07. The same applies for 15-year-old immigrant students, as the relative risk is 1.03. However, 15-year-old boys tend to report worse teacher-student relations, and the relative risk among them is 1.25 (Table D6.6).

The results for other school factors indicate that potentially vulnerable students tend to be in smaller, not larger, classes: the relative risk for disadvantaged 15-year-olds and for students whose parents have low levels of education are 0.66 and 0.67 (Table D6.7, available on line). However, in many countries, attending a school with poor infrastructure is an important equity issue for disadvantaged and immigrant students: the relative risks are 1.14 and 1.20, respectively (Table D6.8, available on line). In many countries, receiving instruction from uncertified teachers is an equity issue for disadvantaged students: on average across OECD countries, the relative risk is 1.12. Fifteen-year-old boys are more likely than 15-year-old girls to be taught by uncertified teachers, and their relative risk is 1.17 (Table D6.9, available on line). Students from socio-economically disadvantaged backgrounds and boys are, on average, more likely to attend a school with a climate that is not conducive to learning (Table D6.10, available on line). The factor that has the largest risk associated with all four subpopulations considered is grade repetition. On average across the OECD countries, 15-year-olds are more than twice as likely to repeat one or more grades at school if they are from disadvantaged backgrounds, have parents with a low level of education, or are immigrants. Fifteen-year-old boys are about one-and-a-half times as likely as girls to repeat one or more grades (Table D6.11, available on line).

Inclusive schools

Some school systems are more inclusive than others, although most schools welcome students of varying ability and backgrounds. The term "inclusive" is used in the broad sense to refer to schools and school systems that support diversity among all learners (UNESCO, 2000). On average, school systems with greater levels of inclusion have better overall outcomes and less inequality (Willms, 2010). This is because the students themselves are a key resource: a disadvantaged student has a better chance of success if he or she is in a school with students who have high expectations and are more intellectually engaged. When school systems are more inclusive, material resources and experienced teachers tend to be more evenly distributed among schools. Similarly, the critical factors that affect student outcomes, such as positive teacher-student relations, high expectations for students' success, and a safe school environment, are more easily achieved in inclusive school systems.

In some school systems, inequality is entrenched through the mechanisms in which students are allocated to schools, including tracks that channel students into different schools based on their prior achievement or ability, private schools, and special programmes in the public sector. Within schools, students can be selected into other programmes, such as those for students with special needs, grade repetition, split classes, ability grouping, curricular tracking, and various other types of special programmes. These processes tend to separate low- and high-performing students into different schools or different classes within schools. Willms (2010) refers to this kind of school system as *vertically* segregated. The German school system, in which students are streamed at an early age into different types of schools, is an example of a vertically segregated school system. This indicator refers to systems with low levels of vertical separation as *vertically* inclusive.

Inequality can also be embedded in school systems when there is a high level of residential segregation, especially in large cities, and when there are marked socio-economic differences between urban and rural areas. Chile and Mexico have school systems with this type of segregation. In these systems, levels of student ability can be similar within and between schools, but students from different socio-economic backgrounds are separated into different schools. Willms (2010) refers to this kind of school system as *horizontally* segregated, and this indicator refers to systems with low levels of horizontal segregation as *horizontally* inclusive.

Indices of vertical and horizontal inclusion can be derived from 2009 PISA data. The first is a measure of vertical inclusion: the proportion of variance in reading performance within schools. School systems with relatively less variation in performance *between* schools, and relatively more variation within schools, are vertically inclusive. Finland, Iceland, and Norway have high levels of *vertical* inclusion, while Germany, Hungary, Italy, the Netherlands and Turkey have low levels of *vertical* inclusion. School systems that allocate students into different types of schools based on their ability tend to have low levels of vertical inclusion (Table D6.2).

The second indicator is the proportion of variance in socio-economic background within schools. It indicates how evenly students from different backgrounds are distributed across schools. Finland, Norway, Sweden and Switzerland have high levels of horizontal inclusion, while Chile, Hungary and Mexico have low levels of horizontal inclusion. School systems in cities in which residents are separated into poor or wealthy residential areas tend to have low levels of inclusion on this measure. However, inclusive education policies can help improve horizontal inclusion (Table D6.2).

One of the best ways to achieve equality and equity is to adopt policies that increase vertical and horizontal inclusion. Increasing vertical inclusion is often difficult to achieve politically, as it can be challenging to convince parents of high-performing students that their children will fare equally well or better in mixed-ability schools. In systems with low levels of horizontal inclusion, there tend to be larger social and economic forces at play that have resulted in residential segregation or a large urban-rural socio-economic divide.

In these cases, equality and equity can be increased through a compensatory allocation of resources to schools that have a disproportionate number of students from disadvantaged families (Willms, 2008). Policies that provide greater school choice could potentially increase horizontal inclusion, but this is not necessarily the case, especially if disadvantaged parents are less able to exercise that choice (Ladd, Fiske, and Ruijs, 2009).

Definitions

Climate that is not conducive to learning is an atmosphere in the classroom with a value on the *PISA index of disciplinary climate* (DISCLIMA) that is in the bottom quarter of the OECD distribution. The cut-off point of -0.547 was calculated by taking the 25th percentile of the student distribution of DISCLIMA index in OECD countries, assigning the same weight to each OECD country. The DISCLIMA index is based on students' responses in the student questionnaire.

Grade repetition occurs when a student repeats one or more grades while in primary, lower secondary or upper secondary school. This is based on students' responses in the student questionnaire.

Immigrant students include those who were born in another country (first generation) and those who were born in the country in which they were assessed, but whose parents were born in another country (second generation). Immigrant status is based on students' responses in the student questionnaire.

Large classes are those in the top quartile of the OECD distribution. The cut-off point was calculated by taking the 75th percentile of the student distribution of class sizes in OECD countries, assigning the same weight to each OECD country. The cut-point for a large class was 30 students. The class size of students is based on students' responses in the student questionnaire.

Low levels of parents' education identifies those parents who have gone through less than 12 years of schooling. The number of years of schooling (PARED) was converted from the highest education level of parents index (HISCED), which corresponds to the higher ISCED level of either parent. The educational level of parents is based on students' responses in the student questionnaire.

Poor school infrastructure refers to those schools in the bottom quarter of the OECD distribution of the *PISA index of quality of the schools' educational resources* (SCMATEDU). The cut-off point of -0.560 was calculated by taking the 25th percentile of the student distribution on the SCMATEDU index in OECD countries, assigning the same weight to each OECD country. The SCMATEDU index is based on school principals' responses in the school principal questionnaire.

Poor student-teacher relations are those that fall in the bottom quarter of the OECD distribution on the *PISA index of teacher-student relations* (STUDREL). The cut-off point of -0.626 was calculated by taking the 25th percentile of the student distribution of STUDREL index in OECD countries, assigning the same weight to each OECD country. The STUDREL index is based on students' responses in the student questionnaire.

Socio-economically disadvantaged students are those in the bottom quarter of the OECD distribution on the *PISA index of economic, social and cultural status* (ESCS). The cut-off point was calculated by taking the 25th percentile of the student distribution of ESCS in OECD countries, assigning the same weight to each OECD country. The ESCS index is based on students' responses in the student questionnaire.

Students who were assessed by PISA were between 15 years 3 months and 16 years 2 months at the time of the assessment and had completed at least 6 years of formal schooling, regardless of the type of institution or programme they attended. The terms "15-year-olds" and "students" are used interchangeably in this indicator.

Students receiving instruction from uncertified teachers refers to those students in schools where the proportion of certified teachers is in the bottom quarter of the OECD distribution. The cut-off point of 0.889 (89.9%) was calculated by taking the 25th percentile of the student distribution of the proportion of certified teachers in OECD countries, assigning the same weight to each OECD country. This is based on school principals' responses in the school principal questionnaire.

Value school outcomes, an index reflecting how students value school outcomes, was constructed using responses to question 33 of the PISA student background questionnaire. Student responses were recoded into a 10-point scale, with higher values denoting more positive outcomes. Students' responses were classified as low if their scores were in the bottom quartile of the OECD distribution of this index. The cut-off point was calculated by taking the 25th percentile of the student distribution of this index in OECD countries, assigning the same weight to each OECD country.

Methodology

Two measures of educational equality and equity are reported: relative risk and population relevance, which in epidemiology is referred to as population attributable risk. In this report, relative risk refers to the risk associated with being a member of a potentially vulnerable sub-population (e.g. immigrant students) compared with *not* being a member of the potentially vulnerable sub-population (e.g. non-immigrant students). For example, if 40% of immigrant students had low reading scores while only 20% of non-immigrants had low reading scores, then the relative risk would be 2.0. Population relevance expresses the proportion of the total occurrence of an outcome, such as low reading scores, that is associated with membership in the potentially vulnerable population.

Consider a hypothetical population of 1 000 15-year-old students who participated in PISA. Twenty percent of the students (200) are immigrants and 30% of the population (300 students) have reading scores below Level 3. One hundred of the 200 immigrant students had low reading scores, while 200 of the 800 non-immigrant students had low reading scores. These data are displayed in Table 1.

Table 1. Low reading scores for immigrants and non-immigrants in a hypothetical population of 1 000 students with 20% immigrants

	Reading scores below Level 3	Reading scores at or above Level 3	Total
Immigrants	100	100	200
Non-immigrants	200	600	800
	300	700	N =1 000

The "risk" or prevalence of low reading scores among immigrants is 50% (100/200) while for non-immigrants it is 25% (200/800). Therefore, the relative risk is 2.0 (50/25).

The population relevance is the reduction in prevalence for the full population that would be achieved if the risk in the potentially vulnerable population (e.g. immigrants) were reduced to the same prevalence as that of the non-vulnerable group (e.g. non-immigrants). In the example for Table 1, the prevalence of low reading scores in the full population is 30% (300/1 000), while the prevalence among non-immigrants is 25%. If more equitable educational policies and practices led to a reduction in the risk for immigrants from 50% to 25% (the same prevalence as non-immigrants), then the prevalence in the full population would be reduced from 30% to 25%. This reduction of 5% represents a percentage reduction of 16.7%, which is referred to as population relevance.

Notice that the population relevance depends not only on the relative risk associated with membership in the vulnerable group, but also on the relative size of the vulnerable group. For example, consider the results in Table 2 for another hypothetical population that has only 2% immigrants.

Table 2. Low reading scores for immigrants and non-immigrants in a hypothetical population of 1 000 students with 2% immigrants

	Reading scores below Level 3	Reading scores at or above Level 3	Total
Immigrants	10	10	20
Non-immigrants	245	735	980
	255	845	N =1 000

In this example, the prevalence of low reading scores among immigrants and non-immigrants are 50% (10/20) and 25% (245/980), respectively, which are the same as those in the first example. Therefore, the relative risk is the same: 2.0. However, if the level of risk for immigrants were reduced to that of non-immigrants, the total risk would be reduced from 25.5% to 25%, or by about 2%. Thus, the population relevance is considerably lower.

The achievement scores are based on assessments of reading performance administered as part of the Programme for International Student Assessment (PISA) undertaken by the Organisation for Economic Co-operation and Development (OECD). PISA was administered most recently during the 2009 school year.

The statistical data for Israel are supplied by and under the responsibility of the relevant Israeli authorities. The use of such data by the OECD is without prejudice to the status of the Golan Heights, East Jerusalem and Israeli settlements in the West Bank under the terms of international law.

References

Goldin, C. and L. Katz (2008), *The Race Between Education and Technology*, Harvard University Press, Cambridge.

Heckman, J.J. (2008), "Schools, skills and synapses", *NBER Working Papers* No. 14064, National Bureau of Economic Research, Inc.

Ladd, H., E.B. Fiske and N. Ruijs (2009), "Parental Choice in the Netherlands: Growing Concerns about Segregation", paper prepared for the National Conference on School Choice, Duke University, Durham.

National Centre for Education Statistics (2010), *The Nation's Report Card: Reading 2009,* US Department of Education, Washington, DC.

Nonoyama-Tarumi, Y. and J.D. Willms (2010), "The relative and absolute risks of disadvantaged family background and low levels of school resources on student literacy", *Economics of Education Review,* No. 29, Vol. 2, pp. 214-224.

OECD (2010a), *PISA 2009 Results: What Students Know and Can Do: Student Performance in Reading, Mathematics and Science* (Volume I), OECD, Paris.

UNESCO (2000), *Inclusive education and education for all: A challenge and a vision,* UNESCO, Paris.

Willms, J.D. (1997), "Literacy skills and social class gradients", *Policy Options*, No. 18, Vol. 6, pp. 22-26.

Willms, J.D. (2006), *Learning Divides: Ten Policy Questions About the Performance and Equity of Schools and Schooling Systems*, UNESCO Institute for Statistics, Montreal.

Willms, J.D. (published on line September 2009; 2010), "School Composition and Contextual Effects on Student Outcomes", *Teachers College Record,* No. 112, Vol. 4, pp. 3-4.

The following additional material relevant to this indicator is available on line:

- ***Table D6.7. Student in large classes (PISA 2009)***
  StatLink http://dx.doi.org/10.1787/888932466234
- ***Table D6.8. Student attends a school with poor school infrastructure (PISA 2009)***
  StatLink http://dx.doi.org/10.1787/888932466253
- ***Table D6.9. Student receives instruction from uncertified teachers (PISA 2009)***
  StatLink http://dx.doi.org/10.1787/888932466272
- ***Table D6.10. Student attends a school with a climate that is not conducive to learning (PISA 2009)***
  StatLink http://dx.doi.org/10.1787/888932466291
- ***Table D6.11. Student has repeated one or more grades (PISA 2009)***
  StatLink http://dx.doi.org/10.1787/888932466310

Table D6.1. **Percentage of potentially vulnerable students, age 15 (PISA 2009)**

Results based on students' self-reports

		Percent of students whose parents have low levels of education[1]		Percent of immigrant students (first- and second-generation)	
		%	S.E.	%	S.E.
		(1)	(2)	(3)	(4)
OECD	Australia	14.0	(0.5)	23.2	(1.1)
	Austria	4.8	(0.4)	15.2	(1.2)
	Belgium	5.7	(0.3)	14.8	(1.1)
	Canada	3.4	(0.3)	24.4	(1.3)
	Chile	23.2	(1.2)	0.5	(0.1)
	Czech Republic	18.9	(0.7)	2.3	(0.2)
	Denmark	6.5	(0.4)	8.6	(0.4)
	Estonia	2.8	(0.3)	8.0	(0.6)
	Finland	3.9	(0.3)	2.6	(0.3)
	France	11.3	(0.7)	13.1	(1.4)
	Germany	11.7	(0.6)	17.6	(1.0)
	Greece	16.0	(1.0)	9.0	(0.8)
	Hungary	26.3	(1.2)	2.1	(0.3)
	Iceland	9.7	(0.5)	2.4	(0.2)
	Ireland	10.7	(0.6)	8.3	(0.6)
	Israel	6.8	(0.5)	19.7	(1.1)
	Italy	24.5	(0.5)	5.5	(0.3)
	Japan	1.7	(0.2)	0.3	(0.1)
	Korea	6.3	(0.4)	0.0	(0.0)
	Luxembourg	19.3	(0.6)	40.2	(0.7)
	Mexico	49.7	(0.9)	1.9	(0.2)
	Netherlands	8.5	(0.8)	12.1	(1.4)
	New Zealand	22.8	(0.8)	24.7	(1.0)
	Norway	1.9	(0.2)	6.8	(0.6)
	Poland	30.8	(0.9)	0.0	(0.0)
	Portugal	50.0	(1.3)	5.5	(0.5)
	Slovak Republic	1.6	(0.3)	0.5	(0.1)
	Slovenia	39.7	(0.9)	7.8	(0.4)
	Spain	31.4	(1.0)	9.5	(0.5)
	Sweden	12.6	(0.6)	11.7	(1.2)
	Switzerland	13.5	(0.6)	23.5	(0.9)
	Turkey	80.9	(1.2)	0.5	(0.1)
	United Kingdom	4.0	(0.4)	10.6	(1.0)
	United States	7.3	(0.7)	19.5	(1.3)
	OECD average	17.1	(0.1)	10.4	(0.1)
Other G20	Argentina	30.4	(1.3)	3.6	(0.5)
	Brazil	69.4	(0.7)	0.8	(0.1)
	Indonesia	51.3	(2.1)	0.3	(0.1)
	Russian Federation	2.0	(0.3)	12.1	(0.7)
	Shanghai-China	26.2	(1.2)	0.5	(0.1)

1. Students whose parents have less than 12 years of schooling.

Source: OECD, *PISA 2009 Database*.

Please refer to the Reader's Guide for information concerning the symbols replacing missing data.

StatLink http://dx.doi.org/10.1787/888932466120

Table D6.2. Index of social inclusion (PISA 2009)

Results based on students' performance and self-reports

		Index of vertical inclusion[1]	Index of horizontal inclusion[2]
		Proportion of student performance variance within schools	Proportion of variance in the *PISA index of social, economic and cultural status of students* (ESCS) within schools
		(1)	(2)
OECD	Australia	73.9	76.4
	Austria	44.4	69.2
	Belgium	47.5	69.8
	Canada	78.3	82.4
	Chile	45.0	48.6
	Czech Republic	51.0	75.1
	Denmark	84.1	83.6
	Estonia	78.2	81.5
	Finland	91.3	89.2
	France	w	w
	Germany	39.8	76.0
	Greece	53.9	68.0
	Hungary	33.3	54.2
	Iceland	85.9	82.8
	Ireland	71.3	76.7
	Israel	51.4	76.7
	Italy	37.9	73.9
	Japan	51.4	78.2
	Korea	65.8	74.1
	Luxembourg	56.4	73.3
	Mexico	51.9	56.2
	Netherlands	35.4	76.2
	New Zealand	75.8	78.9
	Norway	89.7	91.2
	Poland	81.2	73.3
	Portugal	66.9	73.2
	Slovak Republic	60.4	76.6
	Slovenia	42.8	75.0
	Spain	78.2	77.1
	Sweden	81.5	85.7
	Switzerland	67.4	85.4
	Turkey	33.2	63.5
	United Kingdom	70.7	81.6
	United States	64.0	70.7
	OECD average	61.4	74.8
Other G20	Argentina	39.5	59.8
	Brazil	51.6	64.7
	Indonesia	56.8	61.3
	Russian Federation	74.8	71.5
	Shanghai-China	61.6	66.3

1. The index of vertical inclusion is calculated as 100*(1-rho), where rho stands for the intra-class correlation of performance, i.e. the variance in student performance between schools, divided by the sum of variance in student performance between schools and the variance in student performance within schools.

2. The index of horizontal inclusion is calculated as 100*(1-rho), where rho stands for the intra-class correlation of socio-economic background, i.e. the variance in the *PISA index of social, economic and cultural status* of students between schools, divided by the sum of variance in students' socio-economic background between schools and the variance in students' socio-economic background within schools.

Source: OECD, *PISA 2009 Database.*

Please refer to the Reader's Guide for information concerning the symbols replacing missing data.

StatLink http://dx.doi.org/10.1787/888932466139

Table D6.3. Reading scores below PISA proficiency Level 3, age 15 (PISA 2009)

Results based on students' performance and self-reports

		Percent of students with reading scores below Level 3		Low socio-economic status (low vs. high)				Low parental education (low vs. high)				Immigrant status (immigrant vs. non-immigrant)				Gender (boys vs. girls)			
				Relative risk[1]		Population relevance[2]		Relative risk[1]		Population relevance[2]		Relative risk[1]		Population relevance[2]		Relative risk[1]		Population relevance[2]	
		%	S.E.	R.R.	S.E.	P.A.R (%)	S.E.	R.R.	S.E.	P.A.R (%)	S.E.	R.R.	S.E.	P.A.R. (%)	S.E.	R.R.	S.E.	P.A.R. (%)	S.E.
		(1)	(2)	(3)	(4)	(5)	(6)	(7)	(8)	(9)	(10)	(11)	(12)	(13)	(14)	(15)	(16)	(17)	(18)
OECD	Australia	34.7	(0.9)	1.94	(0.03)	19	(0.5)	1.64	(0.03)	8	(0.4)	0.93	(0.03)	-2	(0.7)	1.54	(0.04)	21	(1.2)
	Austria	51.7	(1.3)	1.61	(0.03)	13	(0.6)	1.70	(0.04)	3	(0.3)	1.58	(0.04)	8	(0.7)	1.39	(0.04)	16	(1.5)
	Belgium	38.0	(1.0)	2.03	(0.04)	21	(0.7)	1.85	(0.06)	5	(0.3)	1.87	(0.06)	11	(0.8)	1.34	(0.03)	15	(1.3)
	Canada	30.5	(0.7)	1.65	(0.04)	14	(0.7)	1.68	(0.07)	2	(0.2)	1.13	(0.04)	3	(0.9)	1.59	(0.03)	23	(0.7)
	Chile	63.7	(1.5)	1.44	(0.03)	10	(0.6)	1.44	(0.03)	9	(0.6)	c	c	c	c	1.15	(0.02)	7	(1.1)
	Czech Republic	50.5	(1.4)	1.59	(0.04)	13	(0.7)	1.34	(0.03)	6	(0.5)	1.12	(0.06)	0	(0.1)	1.56	(0.05)	23	(1.7)
	Denmark	41.2	(1.1)	1.82	(0.04)	17	(0.7)	1.79	(0.08)	5	(0.4)	1.82	(0.04)	7	(0.3)	1.41	(0.04)	17	(1.3)
	Estonia	39.0	(1.5)	1.50	(0.04)	11	(0.8)	1.62	(0.10)	2	(0.3)	1.43	(0.07)	3	(0.5)	1.76	(0.07)	28	(2.0)
	Finland	24.8	(0.9)	1.84	(0.07)	17	(1.2)	2.08	(0.12)	4	(0.5)	2.27	(0.17)	3	(0.5)	2.57	(0.09)	44	(1.5)
	France	40.8	(1.4)	1.92	(0.05)	19	(0.9)	1.82	(0.06)	8	(0.6)	1.67	(0.06)	8	(0.8)	1.48	(0.05)	19	(1.5)
	Germany	40.7	(1.3)	2.13	(0.08)	22	(1.2)	2.22	(0.06)	12	(0.6)	1.73	(0.05)	11	(0.7)	1.47	(0.04)	19	(1.4)
	Greece	46.9	(1.9)	1.67	(0.04)	14	(0.8)	1.57	(0.04)	8	(0.6)	1.56	(0.07)	5	(0.6)	1.54	(0.04)	21	(1.2)
	Hungary	41.3	(1.5)	2.17	(0.07)	23	(1.1)	1.94	(0.05)	20	(0.9)	0.88	(0.08)	0	(0.2)	1.48	(0.05)	19	(1.6)
	Iceland	39.0	(0.8)	1.49	(0.04)	11	(0.8)	1.53	(0.05)	5	(0.4)	1.94	(0.09)	2	(0.2)	1.62	(0.05)	23	(1.4)
	Ireland	40.5	(1.3)	1.85	(0.06)	18	(1.0)	1.74	(0.05)	7	(0.5)	1.39	(0.07)	3	(0.6)	1.47	(0.05)	19	(1.7)
	Israel	49.0	(1.3)	1.75	(0.05)	16	(0.9)	1.83	(0.05)	5	(0.3)	1.05	(0.04)	1	(0.8)	1.38	(0.04)	16	(1.3)
	Italy	45.1	(0.8)	1.69	(0.02)	15	(0.4)	1.56	(0.02)	12	(0.3)	1.69	(0.03)	4	(0.2)	1.58	(0.03)	23	(1.1)
	Japan	31.6	(1.4)	1.79	(0.05)	16	(0.8)	2.03	(0.15)	2	(0.3)	c	c	c	c	1.67	(0.09)	26	(2.7)
	Korea	21.2	(1.4)	2.26	(0.11)	24	(1.6)	2.32	(0.14)	8	(0.8)	c	c	c	c	2.07	(0.18)	36	(4.1)
	Luxembourg	50.0	(0.6)	1.84	(0.03)	17	(0.5)	1.74	(0.04)	13	(0.6)	1.50	(0.03)	17	(0.8)	1.32	(0.02)	14	(0.7)
	Mexico	73.1	(0.8)	1.30	(0.01)	7	(0.2)	1.33	(0.01)	14	(0.5)	1.33	(0.01)	1	(0.0)	1.13	(0.01)	6	(0.4)
	Netherlands	39.1	(2.7)	1.72	(0.04)	15	(0.8)	1.66	(0.07)	5	(0.6)	1.63	(0.09)	7	(1.1)	1.32	(0.04)	14	(1.4)
	New Zealand	33.7	(1.0)	1.98	(0.06)	20	(1.1)	1.51	(0.07)	10	(1.2)	1.23	(0.05)	5	(1.1)	1.67	(0.05)	25	(1.4)
	Norway	38.6	(1.2)	1.70	(0.06)	15	(1.1)	1.82	(0.10)	2	(0.2)	1.66	(0.06)	4	(0.4)	1.75	(0.06)	28	(1.5)
	Poland	39.5	(1.3)	1.75	(0.05)	16	(0.9)	1.72	(0.06)	18	(1.3)	c	c	c	c	1.81	(0.05)	29	(1.4)
	Portugal	44.0	(1.6)	1.67	(0.04)	14	(0.7)	1.79	(0.05)	28	(1.3)	1.37	(0.06)	2	(0.3)	1.50	(0.03)	20	(0.9)
	Slovak Republic	50.3	(1.3)	1.60	(0.04)	13	(0.8)	1.83	(0.08)	1	(0.2)	c	c	c	c	1.64	(0.03)	24	(1.0)
	Slovenia	46.8	(0.6)	1.65	(0.04)	14	(0.7)	1.41	(0.04)	14	(1.2)	1.48	(0.04)	4	(0.3)	1.70	(0.03)	26	(0.8)
	Spain	46.4	(1.1)	1.61	(0.04)	13	(0.7)	1.54	(0.04)	14	(1.0)	1.66	(0.03)	6	(0.3)	1.36	(0.02)	15	(0.9)
	Sweden	40.9	(1.3)	1.78	(0.04)	16	(0.8)	1.56	(0.04)	7	(0.5)	1.71	(0.05)	8	(0.8)	1.59	(0.03)	23	(0.9)
	Switzerland	39.5	(1.0)	1.81	(0.04)	17	(0.7)	1.79	(0.04)	10	(0.5)	1.63	(0.04)	13	(0.7)	1.54	(0.04)	22	(1.2)
	Turkey	56.7	(1.8)	1.56	(0.03)	12	(0.7)	1.93	(0.07)	43	(1.8)	c	c	c	c	1.43	(0.05)	18	(1.7)
	United Kingdom	43.3	(1.1)	1.75	(0.03)	16	(0.6)	1.62	(0.06)	2	(0.3)	1.19	(0.04)	2	(0.5)	1.29	(0.03)	12	(1.2)
	United States	42.0	(1.5)	1.83	(0.06)	17	(1.0)	1.65	(0.06)	4	(0.4)	1.27	(0.04)	5	(0.8)	1.28	(0.04)	12	(1.5)
	OECD average	42.8	(0.2)	1.76	(0.04)	16	(0.8)	1.72	(0.01)	9	(0.1)	1.50	(0.07)	4	(0.5)	1.54	(0.05)	21	(1.4)
Other G20	Argentina	77.0	(1.7)	1.31	(0.02)	7	(0.4)	1.27	(0.02)	8	(0.5)	1.12	(0.03)	0	(0.1)	1.13	(0.01)	5	(0.6)
	Brazil	76.7	(1.1)	1.26	(0.01)	6	(0.3)	1.22	(0.02)	13	(1.0)	1.25	(0.03)	0	(0.0)	1.10	(0.01)	5	(0.6)
	Indonesia	87.7	(1.6)	1.10	(0.02)	2	(0.4)	1.15	(0.02)	7	(0.8)	c	c	c	c	1.12	(0.01)	6	(0.6)
	Russian Federation	58.9	(1.4)	1.41	(0.03)	9	(0.6)	1.45	(0.04)	1	(0.1)	1.20	(0.04)	2	(0.4)	1.41	(0.04)	17	(1.2)
	Shanghai-China	17.3	(1.1)	2.22	(0.15)	23	(2.2)	2.01	(0.12)	21	(2.0)	c	c	c	c	2.36	(0.13)	40	(2.3)

1. Relative risk refers to the risk associated with being a member of a potentially vulnerable sub-population (e.g. immigrant students) compared with the risk associated with not being a member of the potentially vulnerable sub-population (e.g. non-immigrant students).

2. Population relevance expresses the proportion of the total prevalence of an outcome, such as low reading scores, that is associated with membership in the potentially vulnerable population.

Source: OECD, *PISA 2009 Database*.

Please refer to the Reader's Guide for information concerning the symbols replacing missing data.

StatLink http://dx.doi.org/10.1787/888932466158

Table D6.4. Reading scores below PISA proficiency Level 2, age 15 (PISA 2009)

Results based on students' performance and self-reports

	Percent of students with reading scores below Level 2		Low socio-economic status (low vs. high)				Low parental education (low vs. high)				Immigrant status (immigrant vs. non-immigrant)				Gender (boys vs. girls)			
			Relative risk[1]		Population relevance[2]		Relative risk[1]		Population relevance[2]		Relative risk[1]		Population relevance[2]		Relative risk[1]		Population relevance[2]	
	%	S.E.	R.R.	S.E.	P.A.R. (%)	S.E.	R.R.	S.E.	P.A.R. (%)	S.E.	R.R.	S.E.	P.A.R. (%)	S.E.	R.R.	S.E.	P.A.R. (%)	S.E.
	(1)	(2)	(3)	(4)	(5)	(6)	(7)	(8)	(9)	(10)	(11)	(12)	(13)	(14)	(15)	(16)	(17)	(18)
OECD																		
Australia	14.2	(0.6)	2.50	(0.08)	27	(1.1)	1.97	(0.07)	12	(0.7)	0.93	(0.05)	-2	(1.1)	2.17	(0.08)	36	(1.5)
Austria	27.6	(1.3)	2.27	(0.09)	24	(1.3)	2.52	(0.13)	7	(0.6)	2.16	(0.11)	15	(1.4)	1.74	(0.08)	27	(2.3)
Belgium	17.7	(0.9)	2.84	(0.11)	31	(1.4)	2.43	(0.16)	8	(0.8)	2.52	(0.13)	18	(1.4)	1.56	(0.08)	22	(2.5)
Canada	10.3	(0.5)	2.12	(0.10)	22	(1.6)	2.37	(0.23)	4	(0.7)	1.25	(0.07)	6	(1.6)	2.39	(0.12)	41	(2.0)
Chile	30.6	(1.5)	2.07	(0.07)	21	(1.1)	2.01	(0.07)	19	(1.2)	c	c	c	c	1.46	(0.05)	19	(1.6)
Czech Republic	23.1	(1.3)	2.09	(0.07)	21	(1.1)	1.44	(0.05)	8	(0.8)	1.43	(0.19)	1	(0.4)	2.16	(0.12)	38	(2.5)
Denmark	15.2	(0.9)	2.46	(0.12)	27	(1.6)	2.48	(0.24)	9	(1.3)	2.77	(0.18)	13	(1.2)	1.66	(0.10)	25	(2.7)
Estonia	13.3	(1.0)	1.72	(0.10)	15	(1.8)	1.88	(0.24)	2	(0.7)	1.82	(0.15)	6	(1.1)	2.58	(0.21)	45	(3.4)
Finland	8.1	(0.5)	2.18	(0.20)	23	(3.1)	2.83	(0.42)	7	(1.4)	3.92	(0.48)	7	(1.2)	4.07	(0.41)	61	(3.3)
France	19.8	(1.2)	2.68	(0.13)	30	(1.7)	2.43	(0.12)	14	(1.0)	2.19	(0.17)	14	(1.9)	1.82	(0.07)	28	(1.6)
Germany	18.5	(1.1)	3.07	(0.13)	34	(1.4)	3.29	(0.13)	21	(1.0)	2.24	(0.11)	18	(1.2)	1.89	(0.10)	31	(2.3)
Greece	21.3	(1.8)	2.37	(0.11)	25	(1.5)	2.20	(0.09)	16	(1.1)	2.05	(0.17)	9	(1.4)	2.25	(0.12)	38	(2.4)
Hungary	17.6	(1.4)	3.53	(0.22)	39	(2.2)	2.70	(0.19)	31	(2.4)	0.69	(0.14)	-1	(0.3)	2.09	(0.19)	35	(3.9)
Iceland	16.8	(0.6)	1.87	(0.11)	18	(1.9)	1.97	(0.14)	9	(1.1)	2.75	(0.23)	4	(0.5)	2.41	(0.14)	41	(2.5)
Ireland	17.2	(1.0)	2.40	(0.10)	26	(1.4)	2.05	(0.11)	10	(0.9)	1.87	(0.14)	7	(1.0)	2.06	(0.14)	35	(3.1)
Israel	26.5	(1.2)	2.22	(0.08)	23	(1.1)	2.36	(0.10)	8	(0.6)	0.99	(0.05)	0	(0.9)	1.77	(0.06)	27	(1.6)
Italy	21.0	(0.6)	2.17	(0.06)	23	(0.8)	1.86	(0.05)	18	(0.8)	2.42	(0.08)	7	(0.5)	2.28	(0.07)	40	(1.5)
Japan	13.6	(1.1)	2.02	(0.12)	20	(1.9)	2.16	(0.29)	2	(0.5)	c	c	c	c	2.36	(0.18)	41	(3.3)
Korea	5.8	(0.8)	3.49	(0.26)	38	(2.6)	3.75	(0.39)	15	(1.8)	c	c	c	c	3.65	(0.48)	58	(4.7)
Luxembourg	26.0	(0.6)	2.57	(0.12)	28	(1.6)	2.35	(0.08)	21	(1.1)	2.16	(0.07)	32	(1.4)	1.72	(0.09)	27	(2.3)
Mexico	40.1	(1.0)	1.80	(0.03)	17	(0.5)	1.82	(0.03)	29	(0.8)	2.15	(0.07)	2	(0.2)	1.36	(0.02)	15	(0.7)
Netherlands	14.3	(1.5)	1.72	(0.10)	15	(1.7)	1.77	(0.17)	6	(1.3)	1.76	(0.22)	8	(2.4)	1.67	(0.09)	25	(2.6)
New Zealand	14.3	(0.7)	2.57	(0.16)	28	(2.1)	1.68	(0.10)	13	(1.7)	1.39	(0.09)	9	(1.9)	2.64	(0.13)	46	(2.0)
Norway	15.0	(0.8)	2.32	(0.11)	25	(1.6)	2.42	(0.33)	3	(0.6)	2.26	(0.21)	8	(1.3)	2.57	(0.14)	44	(2.3)
Poland	15.0	(0.8)	2.44	(0.12)	26	(1.6)	2.20	(0.10)	27	(1.7)	c	c	c	c	3.05	(0.22)	51	(2.6)
Portugal	17.6	(1.2)	2.26	(0.12)	24	(1.7)	2.22	(0.13)	38	(2.4)	1.49	(0.13)	3	(0.7)	2.29	(0.13)	39	(2.4)
Slovak Republic	22.2	(1.2)	2.18	(0.11)	23	(1.7)	3.35	(0.22)	4	(0.5)	c	c	c	c	2.56	(0.13)	44	(2.0)
Slovenia	21.2	(0.6)	2.13	(0.07)	22	(1.1)	1.55	(0.05)	18	(1.4)	1.79	(0.12)	6	(0.8)	2.92	(0.14)	49	(1.8)
Spain	19.6	(0.9)	2.26	(0.08)	24	(1.2)	1.98	(0.08)	23	(1.5)	2.26	(0.10)	11	(0.8)	1.68	(0.06)	26	(1.6)
Sweden	17.4	(0.9)	2.61	(0.11)	29	(1.4)	2.10	(0.12)	12	(1.2)	2.51	(0.14)	15	(1.5)	2.31	(0.13)	40	(2.4)
Switzerland	16.8	(0.9)	2.49	(0.10)	27	(1.3)	2.32	(0.08)	15	(0.8)	2.30	(0.13)	23	(1.8)	1.93	(0.09)	32	(2.0)
Turkey	24.5	(1.4)	2.30	(0.12)	24	(1.8)	2.76	(0.34)	58	(4.9)	c	c	c	c	2.23	(0.13)	39	(2.6)
United Kingdom	18.4	(0.8)	2.31	(0.11)	25	(1.5)	2.03	(0.16)	4	(0.6)	1.42	(0.12)	4	(1.2)	1.65	(0.07)	24	(2.0)
United States	17.6	(1.1)	2.43	(0.14)	26	(1.9)	1.90	(0.13)	6	(0.8)	1.29	(0.09)	5	(1.5)	1.57	(0.10)	23	(3.1)
OECD average	18.8	(0.2)	2.37	(0.11)	25	(1.6)	2.27	(0.03)	15	(0.2)	2.02	(0.48)	7	(1.0)	2.19	(0.13)	36	(2.4)
Other G20																		
Argentina	51.6	(1.9)	1.68	(0.05)	15	(0.8)	1.54	(0.04)	14	(0.8)	1.31	(0.07)	1	(0.2)	1.30	(0.02)	12	(0.9)
Brazil	49.6	(1.3)	1.53	(0.02)	12	(0.4)	1.27	(0.03)	16	(1.3)	1.86	(0.09)	1	(0.1)	1.30	(0.02)	12	(0.6)
Indonesia	53.4	(2.3)	1.27	(0.03)	6	(0.7)	1.40	(0.05)	17	(1.7)	c	c	c	c	1.57	(0.05)	22	(1.4)
Russian Federation	27.4	(1.3)	1.83	(0.06)	17	(1.1)	1.87	(0.19)	2	(0.4)	1.39	(0.08)	4	(0.9)	1.95	(0.09)	32	(2.0)
Shanghai-China	4.1	(0.5)	2.64	(0.22)	29	(2.7)	2.03	(0.24)	21	(3.9)	c	c	c	c	4.19	(0.45)	61	(3.4)

1. Relative risk refers to the risk associated with being a member of a potentially vulnerable sub-population (e.g. immigrant students) compared with the risk associated with not being a member of the potentially vulnerable sub-population (e.g. non-immigrant students).

2. Population relevance expresses the proportion of the total prevalence of an outcome, such as low reading scores, that is associated with membership in the potentially vulnerable population.

Source: OECD, *PISA 2009 Database*.

Please refer to the Reader's Guide for information concerning the symbols replacing missing data.

StatLink http://dx.doi.org/10.1787/888932466177

Table D6.5. Student does not value schooling outcomes (PISA 2009)

Results based on students' self-reports

		Percent of students who do not value schooling outcomes		Low socio-economic status (low vs. high)				Low parental education (low vs. high)				Immigrant status (immigrant vs. non-immigrant)				Gender (boys vs. girls)			
				Relative risk[1]		Population relevance[2]		Relative risk[1]		Population relevance[2]		Relative risk[1]		Population relevance[2]		Relative risk[1]		Population relevance[2]	
		%	S.E.	R.R.	S.E.	P.A.R. (%)	S.E.	R.R.	S.E.	P.A.R. (%)	S.E.	R.R.	S.E.	P.A.R. (%)	S.E.	R.R.	S.E.	P.A.R. (%)	S.E.
		(1)	(2)	(3)	(4)	(5)	(6)	(7)	(8)	(9)	(10)	(11)	(12)	(13)	(14)	(15)	(16)	(17)	(18)
OECD	Australia	19.0	(0.4)	1.31	(0.03)	7	(0.6)	1.34	(0.04)	5	(0.5)	1.00	(0.03)	0	(0.6)	1.06	(0.02)	3	(1.0)
	Austria	26.3	(0.9)	1.04	(0.03)	1	(0.8)	0.95	(0.08)	0	(0.4)	0.78	(0.04)	-4	(0.7)	1.19	(0.03)	8	(1.3)
	Belgium	24.9	(0.6)	1.00	(0.03)	0	(0.7)	0.94	(0.04)	0	(0.2)	0.97	(0.03)	0	(0.5)	1.20	(0.03)	9	(1.1)
	Canada	21.7	(0.4)	1.13	(0.02)	3	(0.5)	0.97	(0.05)	0	(0.2)	0.84	(0.02)	-4	(0.6)	1.21	(0.02)	10	(0.9)
	Chile	17.9	(0.6)	0.99	(0.04)	0	(0.9)	1.00	(0.04)	0	(1.0)	c	c	c	c	0.95	(0.03)	-3	(1.6)
	Czech Republic	29.0	(0.8)	0.95	(0.02)	-1	(0.6)	0.89	(0.03)	-2	(0.6)	1.11	(0.08)	0	(0.2)	1.17	(0.03)	8	(1.3)
	Denmark	22.9	(0.7)	1.38	(0.04)	9	(0.8)	1.56	(0.07)	3	(0.4)	1.01	(0.04)	0	(0.4)	1.19	(0.04)	9	(1.5)
	Estonia	19.4	(0.7)	1.11	(0.05)	3	(1.2)	0.78	(0.19)	-1	(0.5)	0.92	(0.05)	-1	(0.4)	1.42	(0.05)	18	(1.7)
	Finland	20.0	(0.6)	1.49	(0.04)	11	(0.8)	1.40	(0.09)	2	(0.4)	0.75	(0.09)	-1	(0.3)	1.68	(0.05)	25	(1.4)
	France	22.5	(0.9)	1.22	(0.04)	5	(1.0)	1.21	(0.06)	2	(0.6)	0.92	(0.04)	-1	(0.6)	1.56	(0.05)	21	(1.4)
	Germany	30.4	(0.8)	0.85	(0.03)	-4	(0.7)	0.93	(0.04)	-1	(0.5)	0.90	(0.03)	-2	(0.6)	1.29	(0.03)	13	(1.3)
	Greece	37.4	(1.0)	0.77	(0.02)	-6	(0.5)	0.74	(0.03)	-4	(0.5)	0.72	(0.04)	-3	(0.4)	1.07	(0.03)	3	(1.1)
	Hungary	21.9	(0.8)	1.06	(0.04)	1	(1.1)	0.98	(0.04)	-1	(1.1)	0.80	(0.08)	0	(0.2)	1.28	(0.04)	12	(1.7)
	Iceland	23.1	(0.7)	1.45	(0.05)	10	(1.0)	1.45	(0.06)	4	(0.5)	0.83	(0.10)	0	(0.2)	1.36	(0.04)	15	(1.5)
	Ireland	19.5	(0.7)	1.34	(0.06)	8	(1.2)	1.19	(0.08)	2	(0.8)	0.93	(0.07)	-1	(0.6)	1.16	(0.04)	8	(1.7)
	Israel	31.0	(0.9)	0.95	(0.03)	-1	(0.7)	0.83	(0.05)	-1	(0.3)	1.19	(0.04)	4	(0.6)	1.27	(0.04)	12	(1.4)
	Italy	20.8	(0.4)	0.98	(0.02)	-1	(0.5)	0.91	(0.02)	-2	(0.4)	1.01	(0.04)	0	(0.2)	1.42	(0.03)	18	(0.9)
	Japan	45.6	(0.7)	1.10	(0.02)	3	(0.4)	0.96	(0.05)	0	(0.1)	c	c	c	c	1.13	(0.02)	6	(0.8)
	Korea	42.9	(0.9)	0.89	(0.02)	-3	(0.6)	0.91	(0.03)	-1	(0.2)	c	c	c	c	0.99	(0.02)	0	(1.1)
	Luxembourg	32.3	(0.7)	0.86	(0.02)	-4	(0.5)	0.87	(0.02)	-3	(0.5)	0.69	(0.02)	-14	(0.9)	1.32	(0.03)	14	(1.1)
	Mexico	12.6	(0.3)	1.27	(0.03)	6	(0.7)	1.26	(0.03)	11	(1.1)	2.33	(0.14)	2	(0.3)	1.54	(0.04)	21	(1.2)
	Netherlands	24.7	(0.8)	1.00	(0.03)	0	(0.7)	0.95	(0.06)	0	(0.5)	1.02	(0.06)	0	(0.7)	1.26	(0.04)	11	(1.5)
	New Zealand	17.2	(0.6)	1.44	(0.06)	10	(1.1)	1.39	(0.06)	8	(1.1)	0.84	(0.03)	-4	(0.8)	1.16	(0.05)	8	(2.0)
	Norway	33.6	(0.8)	1.26	(0.03)	6	(0.8)	1.39	(0.08)	1	(0.1)	0.88	(0.03)	-1	(0.2)	1.15	(0.03)	7	(1.1)
	Poland	37.3	(0.9)	0.89	(0.02)	-3	(0.5)	0.87	(0.02)	-4	(0.6)	c	c	c	c	1.21	(0.02)	9	(1.0)
	Portugal	12.4	(0.5)	1.13	(0.05)	3	(1.1)	0.95	(0.04)	-3	(2.0)	1.18	(0.09)	1	(0.5)	1.70	(0.07)	26	(1.8)
	Slovak Republic	25.9	(0.8)	1.01	(0.04)	0	(0.9)	0.88	(0.10)	0	(0.2)	c	c	c	c	1.40	(0.05)	16	(1.6)
	Slovenia	25.0	(0.7)	0.99	(0.04)	0	(0.9)	1.01	(0.02)	1	(0.9)	1.06	(0.05)	0	(0.4)	1.35	(0.04)	15	(1.4)
	Spain	19.7	(0.5)	1.16	(0.03)	4	(0.8)	1.08	(0.03)	3	(0.8)	1.00	(0.04)	0	(0.4)	1.55	(0.04)	22	(1.3)
	Sweden	28.3	(0.8)	1.20	(0.03)	5	(0.7)	1.15	(0.05)	2	(0.6)	0.94	(0.04)	-1	(0.5)	1.34	(0.03)	15	(1.3)
	Switzerland	28.1	(0.8)	0.98	(0.03)	0	(0.7)	0.90	(0.03)	-1	(0.4)	0.82	(0.02)	-4	(0.6)	1.37	(0.04)	16	(1.3)
	Turkey	19.8	(0.7)	0.81	(0.04)	-5	(1.0)	0.62	(0.02)	-44	(3.5)	c	c	c	c	1.28	(0.04)	13	(1.6)
	United Kingdom	18.5	(0.5)	1.52	(0.05)	11	(0.9)	1.25	(0.08)	1	(0.3)	1.04	(0.05)	0	(0.5)	0.95	(0.03)	-3	(1.5)
	United States	18.9	(0.6)	1.21	(0.03)	5	(0.7)	1.01	(0.06)	0	(0.4)	0.84	(0.03)	-3	(0.7)	1.31	(0.04)	14	(1.6)
	OECD average	25.0	(0.1)	1.11	(0.03)	2	(0.8)	1.05	(0.01)	-1	(0.2)	1.10	(0.07)	-1	(0.4)	1.28	(0.04)	12	(1.4)
Other G20	Argentina	21.7	(0.7)	0.87	(0.04)	-3	(1.0)	0.82	(0.03)	-6	(1.0)	0.86	(0.09)	0	(0.3)	1.19	(0.04)	8	(1.7)
	Brazil	12.1	(0.5)	0.90	(0.03)	-3	(0.9)	0.91	(0.03)	-7	(2.2)	1.87	(0.22)	1	(0.2)	1.38	(0.04)	15	(1.3)
	Indonesia	7.8	(0.5)	1.15	(0.07)	4	(1.6)	0.98	(0.05)	-1	(2.8)	c	c	c	c	1.49	(0.08)	19	(2.7)
	Russian Federation	15.7	(0.5)	0.92	(0.04)	-2	(1.2)	0.99	(0.14)	0	(0.3)	1.00	(0.06)	0	(0.7)	1.42	(0.05)	17	(1.8)
	Shanghai-China	35.5	(0.7)	0.94	(0.02)	-1	(0.6)	0.91	(0.02)	-2	(0.6)	c	c	c	c	1.08	(0.02)	4	(0.9)

1. Relative risk refers to the risk associated with being a member of a potentially vulnerable sub-population (e.g. immigrant students) compared with the risk associated with not being a member of the potentially vulnerable sub-population (e.g. non-immigrant students).

2. Population relevance expresses the proportion of the total prevalence of an outcome, such as low reading scores, that is associated with membership in the potentially vulnerable population.

Source: OECD, *PISA 2009 Database*.

Please refer to the Reader's Guide for information concerning the symbols replacing missing data.

StatLink http://dx.doi.org/10.1787/888932466196

Table D6.6. Student attends a school with negative student-teacher relations (PISA 2009)

Results based on students' self-reports

		Percent of students attending a school with negative student-teacher relations		Low socio-economic status (low vs. high)				Low parental education (low vs. high)				Immigrant status (immigrant vs. non-immigrant)				Gender (boys vs. girls)			
				Relative risk[1]		Population relevance[2]		Relative risk[1]		Population relevance[2]		Relative risk[1]		Population relevance[2]		Relative risk[1]		Population relevance[2]	
		%	S.E.	R.R.	S.E.	P.A.R. (%)	S.E.	R.R.	S.E.	P.A.R. (%)	S.E.	R.R.	S.E.	P.A.R. (%)	S.E.	R.R.	S.E.	P.A.R. (%)	S.E.
		(1)	(2)	(3)	(4)	(5)	(6)	(7)	(8)	(9)	(10)	(11)	(12)	(13)	(14)	(15)	(16)	(17)	(18)
OECD	Australia	19.7	(0.4)	1.43	(0.03)	10	(0.7)	1.32	(0.04)	4	(0.5)	0.83	(0.02)	-4	(0.6)	1.18	(0.02)	8	(1.0)
	Austria	29.1	(1.0)	0.96	(0.03)	-1	(0.8)	1.02	(0.09)	0	(0.4)	0.92	(0.04)	-1	(0.7)	1.18	(0.04)	8	(1.5)
	Belgium	23.2	(0.6)	0.96	(0.03)	-1	(0.7)	0.84	(0.04)	-1	(0.3)	0.99	(0.04)	0	(0.5)	1.21	(0.03)	10	(1.3)
	Canada	15.3	(0.4)	1.15	(0.03)	4	(0.6)	1.07	(0.07)	0	(0.2)	0.86	(0.03)	-3	(0.7)	1.17	(0.03)	8	(1.1)
	Chile	22.4	(0.9)	0.95	(0.03)	-1	(0.9)	0.96	(0.03)	-1	(0.8)	c	c	c	c	1.11	(0.03)	5	(1.5)
	Czech Republic	30.2	(0.9)	0.85	(0.02)	-4	(0.7)	0.86	(0.03)	-3	(0.6)	0.79	(0.06)	0	(0.1)	1.25	(0.04)	12	(1.6)
	Denmark	19.0	(0.7)	1.46	(0.04)	10	(0.8)	1.65	(0.08)	4	(0.5)	1.12	(0.04)	1	(0.4)	1.04	(0.04)	2	(1.7)
	Estonia	22.4	(0.7)	0.98	(0.03)	0	(0.9)	1.01	(0.09)	0	(0.3)	1.17	(0.06)	1	(0.5)	1.34	(0.04)	15	(1.7)
	Finland	27.8	(0.8)	1.25	(0.03)	6	(0.7)	1.23	(0.06)	1	(0.2)	0.81	(0.07)	0	(0.2)	1.18	(0.03)	8	(1.1)
	France	28.5	(0.9)	1.03	(0.03)	1	(0.8)	0.90	(0.04)	-1	(0.4)	1.16	(0.05)	2	(0.6)	1.37	(0.04)	15	(1.4)
	Germany	27.7	(0.9)	0.91	(0.03)	-2	(0.8)	0.96	(0.04)	-1	(0.5)	1.02	(0.04)	0	(0.6)	1.25	(0.04)	11	(1.4)
	Greece	32.6	(0.8)	0.86	(0.03)	-4	(0.7)	0.81	(0.03)	-3	(0.5)	0.98	(0.04)	0	(0.4)	1.29	(0.03)	12	(1.2)
	Hungary	22.1	(0.8)	0.97	(0.04)	-1	(1.0)	0.93	(0.04)	-2	(1.1)	1.04	(0.09)	0	(0.2)	1.29	(0.04)	13	(1.6)
	Iceland	21.3	(0.8)	1.25	(0.04)	6	(0.9)	1.30	(0.06)	3	(0.6)	0.51	(0.09)	-1	(0.2)	1.30	(0.04)	13	(1.5)
	Ireland	25.8	(0.9)	1.42	(0.04)	10	(0.8)	1.34	(0.05)	4	(0.5)	0.98	(0.05)	0	(0.4)	1.08	(0.04)	4	(1.7)
	Israel	28.8	(0.9)	0.92	(0.03)	-2	(0.7)	0.85	(0.04)	-1	(0.3)	1.04	(0.03)	1	(0.5)	1.33	(0.03)	14	(1.2)
	Italy	25.7	(0.4)	0.89	(0.02)	-3	(0.4)	0.88	(0.02)	-3	(0.4)	0.95	(0.03)	0	(0.2)	1.39	(0.02)	17	(0.7)
	Japan	41.4	(0.8)	1.17	(0.02)	4	(0.5)	1.32	(0.06)	1	(0.1)	c	c	c	c	1.09	(0.02)	5	(0.8)
	Korea	30.6	(0.8)	1.07	(0.03)	2	(0.7)	1.02	(0.05)	0	(0.3)	c	c	c	c	1.09	(0.03)	4	(1.3)
	Luxembourg	30.5	(0.7)	0.79	(0.02)	-6	(0.6)	0.80	(0.03)	-4	(0.6)	0.81	(0.02)	-8	(1.0)	1.31	(0.03)	14	(1.0)
	Mexico	20.1	(0.3)	0.96	(0.02)	-1	(0.5)	0.90	(0.02)	-5	(0.9)	1.64	(0.09)	1	(0.2)	1.30	(0.02)	13	(0.8)
	Netherlands	22.5	(0.8)	0.96	(0.03)	-1	(0.8)	1.06	(0.06)	0	(0.5)	1.18	(0.05)	2	(0.6)	1.10	(0.03)	5	(1.5)
	New Zealand	17.2	(0.6)	1.36	(0.05)	8	(1.1)	1.20	(0.05)	4	(1.1)	0.81	(0.03)	-5	(0.8)	1.19	(0.05)	9	(1.9)
	Norway	32.7	(0.8)	1.24	(0.03)	6	(0.6)	1.40	(0.09)	1	(0.2)	0.95	(0.04)	0	(0.2)	1.15	(0.03)	7	(1.2)
	Poland	38.2	(0.9)	1.03	(0.02)	1	(0.6)	0.92	(0.02)	-3	(0.6)	c	c	c	c	1.18	(0.02)	8	(1.0)
	Portugal	11.2	(0.5)	0.82	(0.04)	-5	(1.2)	0.82	(0.04)	-10	(2.3)	1.29	(0.11)	2	(0.6)	1.70	(0.08)	26	(2.2)
	Slovak Republic	24.7	(1.0)	1.01	(0.04)	0	(0.9)	1.09	(0.12)	0	(0.2)	c	c	c	c	1.26	(0.04)	11	(1.6)
	Slovenia	40.5	(0.6)	0.93	(0.02)	-2	(0.5)	0.92	(0.02)	-3	(0.7)	0.91	(0.03)	-1	(0.3)	0.99	(0.02)	-1	(0.9)
	Spain	26.6	(0.6)	0.97	(0.02)	-1	(0.5)	0.97	(0.02)	-1	(0.7)	0.88	(0.03)	-1	(0.3)	1.47	(0.03)	19	(1.0)
	Sweden	19.6	(0.7)	1.21	(0.05)	5	(1.2)	1.13	(0.06)	2	(0.7)	1.13	(0.06)	2	(0.6)	1.34	(0.04)	15	(1.6)
	Switzerland	21.9	(0.7)	1.03	(0.03)	1	(0.8)	1.00	(0.03)	0	(0.5)	1.12	(0.03)	3	(0.7)	1.51	(0.04)	21	(1.3)
	Turkey	16.7	(0.7)	0.87	(0.04)	-3	(1.0)	0.70	(0.03)	-31	(4.8)	c	c	c	c	1.57	(0.05)	23	(1.6)
	United Kingdom	19.0	(0.7)	1.35	(0.05)	8	(1.0)	1.25	(0.08)	1	(0.3)	0.83	(0.06)	-2	(0.7)	1.04	(0.03)	2	(1.4)
	United States	15.3	(0.5)	1.30	(0.04)	7	(1.0)	1.11	(0.07)	1	(0.5)	0.81	(0.04)	-4	(0.9)	1.20	(0.04)	9	(1.8)
	OECD average	25.0	(0.1)	1.07	(0.03)	1	(0.8)	1.05	(0.01)	-1	(0.2)	1.03	(0.06)	-1	(0.4)	1.25	(0.03)	11	(1.4)
Other G20	Argentina	23.4	(1.0)	0.59	(0.03)	-11	(1.0)	0.70	(0.03)	-10	(1.1)	0.83	(0.07)	-1	(0.2)	1.10	(0.04)	4	(1.6)
	Brazil	18.3	(0.6)	0.84	(0.03)	-4	(0.7)	0.89	(0.02)	-8	(1.9)	1.78	(0.27)	1	(0.2)	1.22	(0.03)	9	(1.3)
	Indonesia	13.1	(0.6)	0.98	(0.05)	-1	(1.2)	0.86	(0.03)	-8	(1.9)	c	c	c	c	1.15	(0.04)	7	(2.0)
	Russian Federation	19.0	(0.6)	0.90	(0.03)	-2	(0.8)	1.12	(0.12)	0	(0.2)	1.02	(0.05)	0	(0.6)	1.34	(0.04)	14	(1.5)
	Shanghai-China	14.5	(0.6)	1.41	(0.06)	9	(1.2)	1.22	(0.05)	5	(1.2)	c	c	c	c	1.23	(0.04)	10	(1.7)

1. Relative risk refers to the risk associated with being a member of a potentially vulnerable sub-population (e.g. immigrant students) compared with the risk associated with not being a member of the potentially vulnerable sub-population (e.g. non-immigrant students).

2. Population relevance expresses the proportion of the total prevalence of an outcome, such as low reading scores, that is associated with membership in the potentially vulnerable population.

Source: OECD, *PISA 2009 Database*.

Please refer to the Reader's Guide for information concerning the symbols replacing missing data.

StatLink http://dx.doi.org/10.1787/888932466215

Annex

1

Characteristics of Educational Systems

Table X1.1a. [1/2] Upper secondary graduation rate: Typical graduation ages and method used to calculate graduation rates (2009)

The typical age refers to the age of the students at the beginning of the school year; students will generally be one year older than the age indicated when they graduate at the end of the school year. The typical age is used for the gross graduation rate calculation.

		Typical graduation ages						
			Programme orientation		Educational/labour market destination			
		First-time	General programmes	Pre-vocational or vocational programmes	ISCED 3A programmes	ISCED 3B programmes	ISCED 3C short programmes[1]	ISCED 3C long programmes[1]
OECD	Australia	**17**	17	17	17	a	a	17
	Austria	**17-18**	17-18	17-19	17-18	17-19	14-15	16-17
	Belgium	**18**	18	18	18	a	18	18
	Canada	**17-18**	17-18	17-18	17-18	a	a	17-18
	Chile	**17**	17	17	17	a	a	a
	Czech Republic	**18-19**	19	18-19	19	19	a	18
	Denmark	**18-19**	18-19	20-21	18-19	a	27	20-21
	Estonia	**18**	18	18	18	18	18	a
	Finland	**19**	19	19	19	a	a	a
	France	**18-20**	18-19	17-21	18-19	19-21	17-21	18-23
	Germany	**19-20**	19-20	19-20	19-20	19-20	19-20	a
	Greece	**m**	m	m	m	a	m	m
	Hungary	**19**	19	19	19	a	18	19
	Iceland	**19**	19	17	19	19	17	19
	Ireland	**18-19**	18	19	18	a	19	18
	Israel	**17**	17	17	17	a	a	17
	Italy	**18**	18	17	18	17	16	a
	Japan	**17**	17	17	17	17	15	17
	Korea	**18**	18	18	18	a	a	18
	Luxembourg	**17-20**	17-18	17-20	17-19	18-20	16-18	17-19
	Mexico	**18**	18	18	18	a	a	18
	Netherlands	**17-19**	17	19	17	a	a	18
	New Zealand	**17-18**	17-18	17-18	18	17	17	17
	Norway	**18-20**	18	19-20	18	a	m	19-20
	Poland	**19-20**	19	20	19	a	a	19
	Portugal	**17**	17	17	m	m	m	m
	Slovak Republic	**18-19**	19	19	19	a	18	18
	Slovenia	**18**	18	16-18	18	18	16	17
	Spain	**17**	17	17	17	17	17	17
	Sweden	**18**	18	18	18	18	18	18
	Switzerland	**18-20**	18-20	18-20	18-20	18-20	17-19	18-20
	Turkey	**17**	17	17	17	a	m	a
	United Kingdom	**16**	16	16	18	18	16	16
	United States	**17**	17	m	17	m	m	m
Other G20	Argentina	**m**	17	17	17	a	a	a
	Brazil	**17-18**	17-18	18-19	17-18	18-19	a	a
	China	**17**	17	17	17	m	17	17
	India	**m**	m	m	m	m	m	m
	Indonesia	**17**	17	17	17	17	a	a
	Russian Federation	**17**	17	17	17	17	16	17
	Saudi Arabia	**m**	m	m	m	m	m	m
	South Africa	**m**	m	m	m	m	m	m

1. Duration categories for ISCED 3C – Short: at least one year shorter than ISCED 3A/3B programmes; Long: of similar duration to ISCED 3A or 3B programmes.

Source: OECD. Argentina, China, Indonesia: UNESCO Institute for Statistics (World Education Indicators Programme). See Annex 3 for notes *(www.oecd.org/edu/eag2011)*.

Please refer to the Reader's Guide for information concerning the symbols replacing missing data.

StatLink http://dx.doi.org/10.1787/888932466329

Table X1.1a. [2/2] Upper secondary graduation rate: Typical graduation ages and method used to calculate graduation rates (2009)

		Graduation rate calculation: Gross versus net						
			Programme orientation		Educational/labour market destination			
		First-time	General programmes	Pre-vocational or vocational programmes	ISCED 3A programmes	ISCED 3B programmes	ISCED 3C short programmes[1]	ISCED 3C long programmes[1]
OECD	Australia	**gross**	net	net	net	a	a	net
	Austria	**gross**	net	net	net	net	net	net
	Belgium	**gross**	net	net	net	a	net	net
	Canada	**net**	net	net	net	a	a	net
	Chile	**net**	net	net	net	a	a	a
	Czech Republic	**gross**	gross	gross	gross	gross	a	gross
	Denmark	**net**	net	net	net	a	net	net
	Estonia	**gross**	net	net	net	net	net	a
	Finland	**net**	net	net	net	a	a	a
	France	**gross**	net	net	net	net	net	net
	Germany	**gross**	gross	gross	gross	gross	gross	a
	Greece	**m**	m	m	m	m	m	m
	Hungary	**net**	net	net	net	a	m	net
	Iceland	**net**	net	net	net	net	net	net
	Ireland	**net**	net	net	net	a	net	net
	Israel	**net**	net	net	net	a	a	net
	Italy	**gross**	net	gross	net	gross	gross	a
	Japan	**gross**	gross	gross	gross	gross	m	gross
	Korea	**gross**	gross	gross	gross	a	a	gross
	Luxembourg	**net**	net	net	net	net	net	net
	Mexico	**net**	net	net	net	a	a	net
	Netherlands	**gross**	net	net	net	a	a	net
	New Zealand	**net**	net	net	net	net	net	net
	Norway	**net**	net	net	net	a	m	net
	Poland	**net**	net	net	net	a	a	net
	Portugal	**net**	net	net	m	m	m	m
	Slovak Republic	**net**	net	net	net	a	net	net
	Slovenia	**gross**	net	gross	net	gross	net	gross
	Spain	**gross**	gross	gross	gross	gross	gross	gross
	Sweden	**net**	net	net	net	n	n	net
	Switzerland	**gross**	gross	gross	gross	gross	gross	gross
	Turkey	**net**	net	net	net	a	m	a
	United Kingdom	**gross**	m	m	m	m	gross	gross
	United States	**net**	m	m	m	m	m	m
Other G20	Argentina	**m**	net	net	net	a	a	a
	Brazil	**gross**	net	net	net	net	a	a
	China	**gross**	gross	gross	gross	gross	gross	gross
	India	**m**	m	m	m	m	m	m
	Indonesia	**m**	net	net	net	net	a	a
	Russian Federation	**gross**	gross	gross	gross	gross	gross	gross
	Saudi Arabia	**m**	m	m	m	m	m	m
	South Africa	**m**	m	m	m	m	m	m

1. Duration categories for ISCED 3C – Short: at least one year shorter than ISCED 3A/3B programmes; Long: of similar duration to ISCED 3A or 3B programmes.

Source: OECD. Argentina, China, Indonesia: UNESCO Institute for Statistics (World Education Indicators Programme). See Annex 3 for notes *(www.oecd.org/edu/eag2011)*.

Please refer to the Reader's Guide for information concerning the symbols replacing missing data.

StatLink http://dx.doi.org/10.1787/888932466329

Annex 1

Table X1.1b. **Post-secondary non-tertiary graduation rates: Typical graduation ages and method used to calculate graduation rates (2009)**

The typical age refers to the age of the students at the beginning of the school year; students will generally be one year older than the age indicated when they graduate at the end of the school year. The typical age is used for the gross graduation rate calculation.

		Typical graduation ages				Graduation rate calculation: Gross versus net			
			Educational/labour market destination				Educational/labour market destination		
		First-time	ISCED 4A programmes	ISCED 4B programmes	ISCED 4C programmes	First-time graduates	ISCED 4A programmes	ISCED 4B programmes	ISCED 4C programmes
OECD	Australia	**18-20**	a	a	18-20	**net**	a	a	net
	Austria	**18-19**	18-19	19-20	23-24	**m**	net	net	net
	Belgium	**19-21**	19	19-21	19-21	**m**	net	net	net
	Canada	**m**	m	m	30-34	**m**	m	m	m
	Chile	**a**	a	a	a	**a**	a	a	a
	Czech Republic	**21**	21	a	21	**gross**	gross	a	gross
	Denmark	**21**	21	a	a	**net**	net	a	a
	Estonia	**20**	a	20	a	**m**	a	net	a
	Finland	**35-39**	a	a	35-39	**net**	a	a	net
	France	**22-25**	22-25	a	22-25	**m**	gross	a	gross
	Germany	**22**	22	22	a	**gross**	gross	gross	a
	Greece	**m**	m	m	m	**m**	m	m	m
	Hungary	**a**	a	a	20	**net**	a	a	net
	Iceland	**26**	m	m	26	**net**	n	n	net
	Ireland	**23**	a	a	23	**net**	a	a	net
	Israel	**m**	m	m	a	**m**	m	m	a
	Italy	**21**	a	a	21	**net**	a	a	net
	Japan	**18**	18	18	18	**m**	m	m	m
	Korea	**a**	a	a	a	**a**	a	a	a
	Luxembourg	**21-25**	a	a	21-25	**net**	a	a	net
	Mexico	**a**	a	a	a	**a**	a	a	a
	Netherlands	**20**	a	a	20	**m**	a	a	net
	New Zealand	**18**	18	18	18	**net**	net	net	net
	Norway	**20-22**	20-21	a	21-22	**net**	net	a	net
	Poland	**21**	a	a	21	**net**	a	a	net
	Portugal	**m**	m	m	m	**net**	m	m	m
	Slovak Republic	**21**	21	a	a	**net**	net	a	a
	Slovenia	**19-20**	19-20	19-20	a	**net**	net	net	a
	Spain	**a**	a	a	a	**a**	a	a	a
	Sweden	**21-23**	m	m	21-23	**net**	n	n	net
	Switzerland	**21-23**	21-23	21-23	a	**m**	gross	gross	a
	Turkey	**a**	a	a	a	**a**	a	a	a
	United Kingdom	**m**	m	m	m	**n**	n	n	n
	United States	**m**	m	m	m	**m**	m	m	m
Other G20	Argentina	**a**	a	a	a	**a**	a	a	a
	Brazil	**a**	a	a	a	**a**	a	a	a
	China	**m**	m	m	m	**m**	m	m	m
	India	**m**	m	m	m	**m**	m	m	m
	Indonesia	**a**	a	a	a	**a**	a	a	a
	Russian Federation	**19**	a	a	19	**m**	a	a	gross
	Saudi Arabia	**m**	m	m	m	**m**	m	m	m
	South Africa	**m**	m	m	m	**m**	m	m	m

Source: OECD. Argentina, Indonesia: UNESCO Institute for Statistics (World Education Indicators Programme). See Annex 3 for notes *(www.oecd.org/edu/eag2011)*.

Please refer to the Reader's Guide for information concerning the symbols replacing missing data.

StatLink http://dx.doi.org/10.1787/888932466348

Table X1.1c. [1/2] Tertiary graduation rate: Typical graduation ages and method used to calculate graduation rates (2009)

The typical age refers to the age of the students at the beginning of the school year; students will generally be one year older than the age indicated when they graduate at the end of the school year. The typical age is used for the gross graduation rate calculation.

		Typical graduation ages						
					Tertiary-type A (first and second degrees)			
		First-time tertiary-type B	Tertiary-type B (first degree)	First-time tertiary-type A	3 to less than 5 years	5 to 6 years	More than 6 years	Advanced research programmes
OECD	Australia	**20-21**	20-21	**21-22**	21-22	22-23	24	25-26
	Austria	**21-23**	21-23	**23-25**	22-24	24-26	a	27-29
	Belgium	**21-22**	21-22	**m**	m	m	m	27-29
	Canada	**21-24**	21-24	**22-24**	22	23-24	25	27-29
	Chile	**22-25**	22-25	**24-26**	23-26	24-26	25-27	30-34
	Czech Republic	**22-23**	22-23	**23-25**	23	25	a	28
	Denmark	**23-25**	23-25	**24**	24	26	25-29	30-34
	Estonia	**21-22**	21-22	**21-23**	21	23	a	30-34
	Finland	**30-34**	30-34	**25-29**	24	26	35-39	30-34
	France	**20-24**	20-24	**20-25**	20-23	22-25	28-31	27-29
	Germany	**21-23**	21-23	**24-27**	24-26	25-27	a	28-29
	Greece	**m**	m	**m**	m	m	m	m
	Hungary	**21**	21	**23-25**	23	25	a	30-34
	Iceland	**24**	24	**24**	24	26	n	35-39
	Ireland	**20-21**	20-21	**21**	21	23	25	27
	Israel	**m**	m	**26**	26	28-29	a	30-34
	Italy	**22-23**	22-23	**23**	23	25	a	30-34
	Japan	**19**	19	**21-23**	21	23	24	26
	Korea	**20**	20	**22-24**	22	24	a	30-34
	Luxembourg	**m**	m	**m**	m	m	m	m
	Mexico	**20**	20	**23**	23	23-26	m	24-28
	Netherlands	**m**	m	**23**	23	a	a	28-29
	New Zealand	**19-21**	19-21	**21-23**	21-23	23	24	27-28
	Norway	**21-22**	21-22	**22-27**	22-23	24-25	26-27	28-29
	Poland	**22**	22	**23-25**	23	25	a	25-29
	Portugal	**21**	21	**22**	22	23	a	30-34
	Slovak Republic	**22**	22	**23**	22-23	25	a	27
	Slovenia	**22-25**	22-25	**24-25**	24-25	24-25	a	28
	Spain	**19-20**	19-20	**22-23**	20-22	22-23	30-34	30-34
	Sweden	**22-23**	22-23	**25**	25	25	a	30-34
	Switzerland	**23-29**	23-29	**24-26**	24-26	25-27	25-27	30-34
	Turkey	**21**	21	**22-24**	22-23	25-26	30-34	30-34
	United Kingdom	**19-24**	19-24	**20-25**	20-22	22-24	23-25	25-29
	United States	**19**	19	**21**	21	23	24	26
Other G20	Argentina	**m**	20-24	**m**	20-24	25-29	a	25-29
	Brazil	**m**	m	**22-24**	22-24	m	m	30-34
	China	**m**	m	**m**	m	m	m	m
	India	**m**	m	**m**	m	m	m	m
	Indonesia	**m**	24	**m**	24	24	24	25-27
	Russian Federation	**20**	20	**22**	21	22	23	25-26
	Saudi Arabia	**m**	m	**m**	m	m	m	m
	South Africa	**m**	m	**m**	m	m	m	m

Note: Where tertiary-type A data are available by duration of programme, the graduation rate for all programmes is the sum of the graduation rates by duration of programme.

Source: OECD. Argentina, Indonesia: UNESCO Institute for Statistics (World Education Indicators Programme). See Annex 3 for notes *(www.oecd.org/edu/eag2011)*.

Please refer to the Reader's Guide for information concerning the symbols replacing missing data.

StatLink http://dx.doi.org/10.1787/888932466367

Table X1.1c. [2/2] Tertiary graduation rate: Typical graduation ages and method used to calculate graduation rates (2009)

		Graduation rate calculation: Gross versus net										
		Tertiary-type B (ISCED 5B)				Tertiary-type A (ISCED 5A)						Advanced research programmes (ISCED 6)	
		First-time		First degree		First-time		First degree		Second degree			
		Graduation rate (all students)	Graduation rate for international/ foreign students only	Graduation rate (all students)	Graduation rate for international/ foreign students only	Graduation rate (all students)	Graduation rate for international/ foreign students only	Graduation rate (all students)	Graduation rate for international/ foreign students only	Graduation rate (all students)	Graduation rate for international/ foreign students only	Graduation rate (all students)	Graduation rate for international/ foreign students only
OECD	Australia	**net**	*m*	net	*net*	**net**	*net*	net	*net*	net	*net*	net	*net*
	Austria	**net**	*m*	net	*net*	**net**	*net*	net	*net*	net	*net*	net	*net*
	Belgium	**m**	*m*	net	*net*	**m**	*m*	net	*net*	net	*net*	net	*net*
	Canada	**net**	*net*	net	*net*	**net**	*net*	net	*net*	net	*net*	net	*net*
	Chile	**m**	*m*	net	*m*	**m**	*m*	net	*m*	net	*m*	net	*m*
	Czech Republic	**net**	*m*	net	*m*	**net**	*m*	net	*m*	net	*m*	net	*m*
	Denmark	**net**	*net*	net	*net*	**net**	*net*	net	*net*	net	*net*	net	*net*
	Estonia	**m**	*m*	net	*net*	**m**	*m*	net	*net*	net	*net*	net	*net*
	Finland	**n**	*n*	n	*n*	**net**	*m*	net	*net*	net	*net*	net	*net*
	France	**m**	*m*	gross	*m*	**m**	*m*	gross	*m*	gross	*m*	gross	*m*
	Germany	**gross**	*m*	gross	*m*	**net**	*net*	net	*net*	net	*net*	net	*net*
	Greece	**m**	*m*	m	*m*	**m**	*m*	m	*m*	m	*m*	m	*m*
	Hungary	**net**	*m*	net	*m*	**net**	*m*	net	*m*	net	*m*	net	*m*
	Iceland	**net**	*net*	net	*net*	**net**	*net*	net	*net*	net	*net*	net	*net*
	Ireland	**gross**	*m*	gross	*m*	**gross**	*m*	gross	*m*	gross	*m*	gross	*m*
	Israel	**m**	*m*	m	*m*	**net**	*m*	net	*m*	net	*m*	net	*m*
	Italy	**gross**	*m*	gross	*gross*	**net**	*net*	net	*net*	m	*n*	m	*m*
	Japan	**gross**	*m*	gross	*m*	**gross**	*m*	gross	*m*	gross	*m*	gross	*m*
	Korea	**m**	*m*	net	*m*	**m**	*m*	net	*m*	net	*m*	net	*m*
	Luxembourg	**m**	*m*	m	*m*	**m**	*m*	m	*m*	m	*m*	m	*m*
	Mexico	**net**	*m*	net	*m*	**net**	*m*	net	*m*	gross	*m*	gross	*m*
	Netherlands	**n**	*n*	m	*m*	**net**	*net*	net	*net*	net	*net*	gross	*m*
	New Zealand	**net**	*net*	net	*net*	**net**	*net*	net	*net*	net	*net*	net	*net*
	Norway	**net**	*net*	net	*net*	**net**	*net*	net	*net*	net	*net*	net	*net*
	Poland	**gross**	*m*	net	*m*	**net**	*n*	net	*net*	gross	*net*	gross	*m*
	Portugal	**net**	*net*	net	*net*	**net**	*net*	net	*net*	net	*net*	net	*net*
	Slovak Republic	**net**	*m*	net	*m*	**net**	*net*	net	*net*	net	*net*	net	*net*
	Slovenia	**net**	*net*	net	*net*	**net**	*net*	net	*net*	net	*net*	net	*net*
	Spain	**net**	*m*	net	*m*	**net**	*m*	net	*gross*	net	*gross*	net	*m*
	Sweden	**net**	*net*	net	*net*	**net**	*net*	net	*net*	net	*net*	net	*net*
	Switzerland	**gross**	*m*	gross	*m*	**net**	*m*	net	*net*	net	*net*	net	*net*
	Turkey	**net**	*m*	net	*m*	**gross**	*m*	net	*m*	net	*m*	net	*m*
	United Kingdom	**net**	*net*	net	*net*	**net**	*net*	net	*net*	net	*net*	net	*net*
	United States	**gross**	*m*	gross	*m*	**gross**	*m*	gross	*m*	gross	*m*	gross	*m*
Other G20	Argentina	**m**	*m*	gross	*m*	**m**	*m*	gross	*m*	gross	*m*	gross	*m*
	Brazil	**m**	*m*	net	*m*	**m**	*m*	net	*m*	net	*m*	net	*m*
	China	**m**	*m*	m	*m*	**m**	*m*	m	*m*	m	*m*	m	*m*
	India	**m**	*m*	m	*m*	**m**	*m*	m	*m*	m	*m*	m	*m*
	Indonesia	**m**	*m*	net	*m*	**m**	*m*	net	*m*	net	*m*	net	*m*
	Russian Federation	**m**	*m*	gross	*m*	**m**	*m*	gross	*m*	gross	*m*	gross	*m*
	Saudi Arabia	**m**	*m*	m	*m*	**m**	*m*	m	*m*	m	*m*	m	*m*
	South Africa	**m**	*m*	m	*m*	**m**	*m*	m	*m*	m	*m*	m	*m*

Source: OECD. Argentina, China, Indonesia: UNESCO Institute for Statistics (World Education Indicators Programme). See Annex 3 for notes *(www.oecd.org/edu/eag2011)*.

Please refer to the Reader's Guide for information concerning the symbols replacing missing data.

StatLink http://dx.doi.org/10.1787/888932466367

Table X1.1d. Tertiary entry rate: Typical age of entry and method used to calculate entry rates (2009)

		Typical age of entry			Entry rate calculation: Gross versus net – All students			Entry rate calculation: Gross versus net – International students		
		ISCED 5A	ISCED 5B	ISCED 6	ISCED 5A	ISCED 5B	ISCED 6	ISCED 5A	ISCED 5B	ISCED 6
OECD	Australia	18	18	23	net	m	net	*net*	*m*	*net*
	Austria	19-20	20-21	25-26	net	net	net	*net*	*net*	*net*
	Belgium	18	18	m	net	net	m	*m*	*m*	*m*
	Canada	m	m	m	m	m	m	*m*	*m*	*m*
	Chile	18-19	18-19	24-28	net	net	net	*m*	*m*	*m*
	Czech Republic	19	20	25	net	net	net	*m*	*m*	*m*
	Denmark	21	21	27	net	net	net	*net*	*net*	*net*
	Estonia	19	19	24-25	net	net	net	*net*	*net*	*net*
	Finland	19	19	m	net	a	m	*m*	*a*	*m*
	France	m	m	m	m	m	m	*m*	*m*	*m*
	Germany	19-21	18-21	m	net	net	m	*net*	*m*	*m*
	Greece	m	m	m	m	m	m	*m*	*m*	*m*
	Hungary	19	19	24	net	net	net	*gross*	*gross*	*gross*
	Iceland	20	20	25	net	net	net	*net*	*net*	*net*
	Ireland	18	18	m	net	net	m	*net*	*net*	*m*
	Israel	22-24	18	27-29	net	net	net	*m*	*m*	*m*
	Italy	19	19	24	net	gross	gross	*m*	*m*	*m*
	Japan	18	18	24	net	gross	net	*m*	*m*	*m*
	Korea	18	18	24-29	net	net	net	*m*	*m*	*m*
	Luxembourg	m	m	m	m	m	m	*m*	*m*	*m*
	Mexico	18	18	24	net	net	net	*gross*	*gross*	*gross*
	Netherlands	18-19	17-18	m	net	net	m	*net*	*net*	*m*
	New Zealand	18	18	23-24	net	net	net	*net*	*net*	*net*
	Norway	19-20	19	26-27	net	net	net	*net*	*net*	*net*
	Poland	19-20	19-20	m	net	net	m	*gross*	*m*	*m*
	Portugal	18	18	22-24	net	net	net	*net*	*net*	*net*
	Slovak Republic	19	19	24	net	net	net	*net*	*m*	*net*
	Slovenia	19	19	24-26	net	net	net	*net*	*net*	*net*
	Spain	18	19-20	25	net	net	net	*m*	*m*	*m*
	Sweden	19	19	26	net	net	net	*net*	*net*	*net*
	Switzerland	19-21	19-26	25-29	net	net	net	*net*	*m*	*net*
	Turkey	18-19	18-19	25-26	net	net	net	*m*	*m*	*m*
	United Kingdom	18	18	23	net	net	net	*net*	*net*	*net*
	United States	18	18	24	net	m	m	*gross*	*m*	*m*
Other G20	Argentina	18	18	23	net	net	gross	*m*	*m*	*m*
	Brazil	m	m	m	m	m	m	*m*	*m*	*m*
	China	15-19	15-19	20-24	gross	gross	gross	*m*	*m*	*m*
	India	m	m	m	m	m	m	*m*	*m*	*m*
	Indonesia	18	18	25	net	net	net	*m*	*m*	*m*
	Russian Federation	18	18	23-24	gross	gross	gross	*m*	*m*	*m*
	Saudi Arabia	m	m	m	m	m	m	*m*	*m*	*m*
	South Africa	m	m	m	m	m	m	*m*	*m*	*m*

Source: OECD. Argentina, China, Indonesia: UNESCO Institute for Statistics (World Education Indicators Programme). See Annex 3 for notes *(www.oecd.org/edu/eag2011).*

Please refer to the Reader's Guide for information concerning the symbols replacing missing data.

StatLink http://dx.doi.org/10.1787/888932466386

Table X1.2a. **School year and financial year used for the calculation of indicators, OECD countries**

Source: OECD. See Annex 3 for notes *(www.oecd.org/edu/eag2011)*.
StatLink http://dx.doi.org/10.1787/888932466405

Table X1.2b. School year and financial year used for the calculation of indicators, other G20 countries

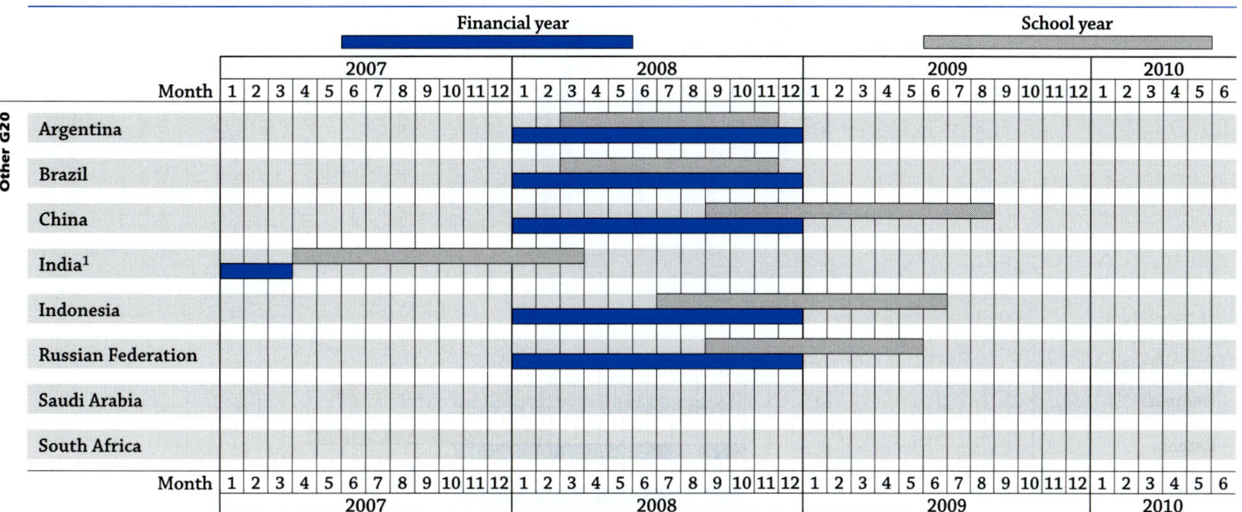

1. Financial year : from April 2006 to March 2007.

Source: OECD. Argentina, China, India, Indonesia: UNESCO Institute for Statistics (World Education Indicators Programme). See Annex 3 for notes *(www.oecd.org/edu/eag2011)*.

StatLink http://dx.doi.org/10.1787/888932466424

Table X1.3. Summary of completion requirements for upper secondary programmes

		ISCED 3A programmes				ISCED 3B programmes				ISCED 3C programmes			
		Final examination	Series of examinations during programme	Specified number of course hours, AND examination	Specified number of course hours only	Final examination	Series of examinations during programme	Specified number of course hours, AND examination	Specified number of course hours only	Final examination	Series of examinations during programme	Specified number of course hours, AND examination	Specified number of course hours only
OECD	Australia[1, 2]	N/Y	Y	Y	N	a	a	a	a	N	Y	N	N
	Austria	Y	Y	Y	N	Y	Y	Y	N	N	Y	Y	N
	Belgium (Fl.)[3]	Y	Y	N	N	a	a	a	a	Y	Y	N	N
	Belgium (Fr.)	Y	Y	N	N	a	a	a	a	Y	Y	N	N
	Canada (Québec)[1]	N	Y	Y	N					N	Y	Y	N
	Czech Republic[1]	Y	Y	Y	N	N	Y	Y	N	Y	Y	Y	N
	Denmark[1]	Y	Y	Y		a	a	a	a	Y	Y	Y	
	Finland	Y/N	Y	Y	N								
	France	Y	N	Y	N	Y	N	Y	N	Y/N	Y	N	
	Germany	Y	Y	N	N	Y	Y	N	N	Y	Y	N	N
	Greece[1]	N	Y	N	N					N	Y	N	N
	Hungary	Y	N	Y	N	a	a	a	a	Y	N	Y	N
	Iceland[1]	Y/N	Y	N	N	Y	Y	N	N	Y/N	Y	N	N
	Ireland[1]	Y	N	N	N	a	a	a	a	Y	Y	Y	N
	Israel[1]	Y/N	Y	Y	N	a	a	a	a	Y/N	Y	Y	
	Italy	Y	N	Y/N	N	Y	Y/N	Y/N	N	Y	N	Y/N	N
	Japan	N	N	Y	N	N	N	Y	N	N	N	Y	N
	Korea	N	N	N	Y					N	N	N	Y
	Luxembourg	Y	Y	Y	N	Y	Y	Y	N	Y	Y	Y	N
	Mexico	N	Y	Y	N					Y/N	Y	Y	N
	Netherlands[1]	Y	Y	Y	N	a	a	a	a	Y	Y	Y	N
	New Zealand	Y	Y	N	N								
	Norway	N	Y	Y	N	a	a	a	a	N	Y	Y	N
	Poland[1]	Y	N	Y	N	a	a	a	a	Y	N	Y	N
	Portugal	m	m	m	m	m	m	m	m	m	m	m	m
	Slovak Republic[1]	Y	N	Y	N					Y	N	Y	N
	Spain	N	Y	Y	N					Y/N	Y/N	Y/N	N
	Sweden	Y/N	Y/N	N	Y/N								
	Switzerland	Y	Y	Y		Y	Y	Y		Y		Y	
	Turkey[1]	N	N	Y	N	a	a	a	a	N	N	Y	N
	United Kingdom[1]	Y/N	Y	N	N	Y/N	Y	N	N	Y/N	Y	N	N
	United States[1]	25Y/25N	SS	SS	Y[4]	a	a	a	a	a	a	a	a

Note: Y = Yes; N = No; SS= Some states.

1. See Annex 3 Chapter A for additional notes on completion requirements *(www.oecd.org/edu/eag2011)*.

2. Completion requirements for ISCED 3A vary by state and territory. The information provided represents a generalisation of diverse requirements.

3. Covers general education only.

4. Almost all states specify levels of Carnegie credits (i.e. acquired through completion of a two-semester course in specific subjects, which vary by state).

Source: OECD. See Annex 3 for notes *(www.oecd.org/edu/eag2011)*.

Please refer to the Reader's Guide for information concerning the symbols replacing missing data.

StatLink http://dx.doi.org/10.1787/888932466443

Annex 2

Reference Statistics

Annex 2

Table X2.1. **Overview of the economic context using basic variables (reference period: calendar year 2008, 2008 current prices)**

		Total public expenditure as a percentage of GDP	GDP per capita (in equivalent USD converted using PPPs)	GDP deflator (1995 = 100)	GDP deflator (2000 = 100)	Average exchange rates between 2007 and 2009[1]	Purchasing Power Parity for private consumption (PPP) (USD = 1, 2009)[1]
OECD	Australia	32.4	39 532	151.366	137.410	1.22	1.55
	Austria	48.8	39 849	117.780	114.800	0.71	0.87
	Belgium	50.0	36 879	125.037	118.510	0.71	0.92
	Canada[2]	39.6	38 883	134.599	124.060	1.09	1.31
	Chile[3]	m	14 578	184.248	157.440	535.26	372.03
	Czech Republic	42.9	25 845	167.453	120.750	18.81	14.95
	Denmark	51.9	39 494	134.190	121.710	5.30	8.72
	Estonia	39.8	21 802	256.316	159.070	0.71	0.62
	Finland	49.3	37 795	120.407	110.630	0.71	1.01
	France	52.8	34 233	124.701	118.690	0.71	0.92
	Germany	43.8	37 171	110.092	108.980	0.71	0.85
	Greece	49.0	29 920	165.207	128.630	0.71	0.78
	Hungary	48.8	20 700	304.899	156.840	186.03	145.51
	Iceland	57.8	39 029	185.809	156.600	91.88	137.48
	Ireland	42.5	42 644	152.218	122.490	0.71	1.02
	Israel	43.0	27 690	151.992	110.650	3.88	4.42
	Italy	48.8	33 271	141.046	123.260	0.71	0.85
	Japan	36.6	33 902	88.310	91.180	104.89	126.04
	Korea	30.4	26 877	138.125	120.790	1 102.75	903.08
	Luxembourg	36.9	89 732	143.880	133.060	0.71	0.98
	Mexico	23.9	15 190	380.885	166.180	11.86	8.83
	Netherlands	46.0	42 887	137.031	122.040	0.71	0.88
	New Zealand	34.6	29 231	138.451	127.250	1.46	1.61
	Norway[4]	56.4	43 659	144.711	126.147	5.93	9.58
	Poland	43.2	18 062	209.362	123.440	2.77	2.02
	Portugal	43.6	24 962	147.457	125.250	0.71	0.72
	Slovak Republic	34.9	23 205	181.980	133.300	0.75	0.59
	Slovenia	44.1	29 241	208.225	143.550	0.71	0.68
	Spain	41.3	33 173	155.929	135.300	0.71	0.79
	Sweden	51.7	39 321	121.799	115.660	7.00	9.24
	Switzerland	32.2	45 517	112.734	110.400	1.12	1.69
	Turkey	m	14 963	5 291.775	405.350	1.38	1.12
	United Kingdom	48.6	36 817	139.534	124.060	0.56	0.69
	United States	39.1	46 901	133.228	122.530	1.00	1.00
Other G20	Argentina	m	14 426	m	m	m	m
	Brazil	31.3	10 968	279.072	184.285	1.93	m
	China	m	5 970	m	m	m	m
	India	m	2 780	m	m	m	m
	Indonesia	m	3 980	m	m	m	m
	Russian Federation	m	20 460	1 628.956	344.850	27.39	15.42
	Saudi Arabia	m	m	m	m	m	m
	South Africa	m	m	m	m	m	m

1. The average exchange rate and the Purchasing Power Parity for private consumption (PPP) are used in Indicator A10.
2. Year of reference 2007.
3. Year of reference 2009.
4. The GDP Mainland market value is used for Norway.

Source: OECD. Argentina, Indonesia: UNESCO Institute for Statistics (World Education Indicators Programme). China: *China Educational Finance Statistics Yearbook 2009*. See Annex 3 for notes *(www.oecd.org/edu/eag2011)*.

Please refer to the Reader's Guide for information concerning the symbols replacing missing data.

StatLink http://dx.doi.org/10.1787/888932466462

Table X2.2a **Basic reference statistics (reference period: calendar year 2008, 2008 current prices)[1]**

		Gross domestic product (in millions of local currency)[2]	Gross domestic product (adjusted to financial year)[3]	Total public expenditure (in millions of local currency)	Total population in thousand (mid-year estimates)	Purchasing power parity for GDP (PPP) (USD = 1)	Purchasing power parity for GDP (PPP) (Euro Zone = 1)	Purchasing power parity for private consumption (PPP) (USD = 1)
		(1)	(2)	(3)	(4)	(5)	(6)	(7)
OECD	Australia	1 253 121		405 784	21 432	1.47907	1.8297	1.530675
	Austria	283 085		138 103	8 337	0.85215	1.0541	0.875083
	Belgium	345 006		172 426	10 708	0.87365	1.0807	0.916303
	Canada[4]	1 599 608	1 547 094	612 322	33 327	1.23439	1.5270	1.301879
	Chile[5]	89 262 568		23 797 395	16 764	365.27086	451.8543	362.345326
	Czech Republic	3 688 997		1 583 380	10 430	13.68547	16.9295	14.945896
	Denmark	1 740 843		903 500	5 492	8.02595	9.9284	8.643543
	Estonia	252 015		100 270	1 341	8.62044	10.6638	0.644871
	Finland	184 649		91 121	5 313	0.91947	1.1374	1.006853
	France	1 948 511		1 028 855	64 141	0.8874	1.0977	0.92899
	Germany	2 481 200		1 085 620	82 120	0.81285	1.0055	0.859068
	Greece	235 679		115 581	11 237	0.70099	0.8672	0.755574
	Hungary	26 753 906		13 069 149	10 038	128.75482	159.2747	144.694396
	Iceland	1 477 938		853 725	319	118.5748	146.6816	123.743989
	Ireland	179 989		76 407	4 443	0.94999	1.1752	1.0715
	Israel	725 861		312 374	7 343	3.57	4.4162	4.324834
	Italy	1 567 851		765 888	59 832	0.7876	0.9743	0.853821
	Japan[6]	505 111 900	513 131 575	187 632 900	127 510	116.84581	144.5428	129.06067
	Korea	1 026 451 811		312 548 300	48 607	785.71789	971.9636	882.090515
	Luxembourg	39 640		14 618	488	0.90505	1.1196	0.974997
	Mexico	12 091 797		2 894 807	106 573	7.46953	9.2401	8.158591
	Netherlands	596 226		274 510	16 440	0.84563	1.0461	0.869952
	New Zealand	184 802		64 002	4 241	1.49071	1.8441	1.570388
	Norway[7]	1 812 173		1 022 431	4 768	8.70541	10.7689	9.538856
	Poland	1 275 432		550 652	38 116	1.85259	2.2917	2.014061
	Portugal	172 022		75 049	10 622	0.64875	0.8025	0.730549
	Slovak Republic	2 025 101		705 792	5 406	16.14361962	19.9703	0.599323
	Slovenia	37 305		16 463	2 022	0.63096	0.7805	0.683229
	Spain	1 088 124		449 238	45 593	0.71943	0.8900	0.789832
	Sweden	3 204 320		1 655 885	9 256	8.80409	10.8910	9.035758
	Switzerland	544 196		175 379	7 711	1.55051	1.9180	1.702667
	Turkey	950 534		m	71 079	0.89376	1.1056	1.093226
	United Kingdom	1 445 580	1 410 557	684 996	61 398	0.63949	0.7911	0.674537
	United States	14 296 900	14 225 375	5 567 081	304 831	1	1.2370	1
	Euro Zone					0.808		0.86
Other G20	Argentina	1 032 758		m	39 883	1.79502	2.2205	m
	Brazil	3 004 881		939 831	191 972	1.4271	1.7654	m
	China	30 065 207		m	1 327 658	3.793	4.6921	m
	India	m		m	m	m	m	m
	Indonesia	4 954 030 249		m	228 575	5445.611	6736.4328	m
	Russian Federation	41 668 034		m	142 009	14.3412	17.7406	15.071879
	Saudi Arabia	m		m	m	m	m	m
	South Africa	m		m	m	m	m	m

1. Data on GDP, PPPs and total public expenditure in countries in the Euro zone are provided in Euros.

2. GDP calculated for the fiscal year in Australia and GDP and total public expenditure calculated for the fiscal year in New Zealand.

3. For countries where GDP is not reported for the same reference period as data on educational finance, GDP is estimated as: wt-1 (GDPt - 1) + wt (GDPt), where *wt* and *wt-1* are the weights for the respective portions of the two reference periods for GDP which fall within the educational financial year. Adjustments were made in Chapter B for Canada, Japan, the United Kingdom and the United States.

4. Year of reference 2007.

5. Year of reference 2009.

6. Total public expenditure adjusted to financial year.

7. The GDP Mainland market value is used for Norway.

Source: OECD. Argentina, Indonesia: UNESCO Institute for Statistics (World Education Indicators Programme). China: *China Educational Finance Statistics Yearbook 2009*. See Annex 3 for notes *(www.oecd.org/edu/eag2011)*.

Please refer to the Reader's Guide for information concerning the symbols replacing missing data.

StatLink http://dx.doi.org/10.1787/888932466481

Table X2.2b. **Basic reference statistics (reference period: calendar year 1995 and 2000, current prices)[1]**

		Gross domestic product (in millions of local currency)		Total public expenditure (in millions of local currency)		Change in gross domestic product (2000 = 100, constant prices)		
		1995	2000	1995	2000	1995	2000	2008
		(1)	(2)	(3)	(4)	(5)	(6)	(7)
OECD	Australia	532 025	708 889	184 270	225 913	83	100	129
	Austria	174 613	207 529	98 361	108 175	86	100	119
	Belgium	207 651	252 216	108 336	123 943	87	100	115
	Canada	810 426	1 076 577	392 886	442 560	82	100	116
	Chile	28 363 879	40 679 938	5 265 291	9 058 095	82	100	139
	Czech Republic	1 466 522	2 189 169	798 790	915 413	93	100	140
	Denmark	1 019 545	1 293 964	604 404	694 479	87	100	111
	Estonia	43 283	96 380	17 866	34 815	72	100	164
	Finland	95 986	132 110	58 947	63 794	79	100	126
	France	1 194 600	1 441 372	650 325	744 253	87	100	114
	Germany	1 848 450	2 062 500	1 012 330	930 400	91	100	110
	Greece	89 555	136 281	40 783	63 627	84	100	134
	Hungary	5 746 248	13 368 903	3 197 916	6 251 647	84	100	128
	Iceland	454 013	683 747	m	286 259	79	100	138
	Ireland	53 145	105 018	21 841	32 836	63	100	140
	Israel	289 334	508 380	149 930	239 801	78	100	129
	Italy	947 339	1 191 057	497 487	550 032	91	100	107
	Japan	495 165 500	502 989 900	181 284 700	193 917 400	95	100	112
	Korea	409 653 579	603 235 999	83 399 300	135 324 800	78	100	141
	Luxembourg	15 110	22 001	5 996	8 270	74	100	135
	Mexico	2 013 954	6 020 649	384 960	1 139 998	77	100	121
	Netherlands	305 261	417 960	172 305	184 612	82	100	117
	New Zealand	94 545	117 165	31 743	m	88	100	124
	Norway[2]	806 858	1 113 893	480 575	626 569	83	100	118
	Poland	337 222	744 378	147 561	294 012	77	100	139
	Portugal	87 745	127 008	36 447	52 237	81	100	108
	Slovak Republic	582 004	939 238	282 943	489 698	85	100	162
	Slovenia	10 294	18 481	m	8 636	81	100	141
	Spain	447 205	630 263	198 730	246 542	82	100	128
	Sweden	1 809 575	2 265 447	1 175 180	1 248 029	84	100	122
	Switzerland	373 599	422 063	157 093	145 394	90	100	117
	Turkey	10 435	166 658	m	m	82	100	141
	United Kingdom	733 266	976 533	322 956	381 199	84	100	116
	United States	7 359 300	9 898 800	2 732 629	3 353 547	81	100	117
Other G20	Argentina	m	m	m	m	m	m	m
	Brazil	646 192	1 179 482	224 283	394 349	91	100	138
	China	m	m	m	m	m	m	m
	India	m	m	m	m	m	m	m
	Indonesia	m	m	m	m	m	m	m
	Russian Federation	1 428 522	7 305 646	m	2 016 630	92	100	165
	Saudi Arabia	m	m	m	m	m	m	m
	South Africa	m	m	m	m	m	m	m

1. Data on GDP, and total public expenditure in countries in the Euro zone are provided in Euros.
2. The GDP Mainland market value is used for Norway.
Source: OECD. See Annex 3 for notes *(www.oecd.org/edu/eag2011)*.
Please refer to the Reader's Guide for information concerning the symbols replacing missing data.
StatLink http://dx.doi.org/10.1787/888932466500

Table X2.3a. Teachers' salaries in national currency (2009)

		Primary education				Lower secondary education				Upper secondary education			
		Starting salary/ minimum training	Salary after 10 years of experience/ minimum training	Salary after 15 years of experience/ minimum training	Salary at top of scale/ minimum training	Starting salary/ minimum training	Salary after 10 years of experience/ minimum training	Salary after 15 years of experience/ minimum training	Salary at top of scale/ minimum training	Starting salary/ minimum training	Salary after 10 years of experience/ minimum training	Salary after 15 years of experience/ minimum training	Salary at top of scale/ minimum training
		(1)	(2)	(3)	(4)	(5)	(6)	(7)	(8)	(9)	(10)	(11)	(12)
OECD	Australia	50 807	70 696	70 696	70 696	50 807	70 696	70 696	70 696	50 807	70 696	70 696	70 696
	Austria	26 302	31 045	34 848	52 090	27 495	33 487	37 664	54 118	27 901	30 155	38 787	56 964
	Belgium (Fl.)	28 203	35 276	39 670	48 458	28 203	35 276	39 670	48 458	35 098	44 636	50 852	61 211
	Belgium (Fr.)	27 435	m	38 872	47 701	27 435	m	38 872	47 701	34 279	m	50 106	60 513
	Canada	m	m	m	m	m	m	m	m	m	m	m	m
	Chile	5 795 004	7 417 442	8 257 733	10 831 356	5 795 004	7 417 442	8 257 733	10 831 356	6 048 972	7 756 236	8 638 812	11 339 292
	Czech Republic	240 810	303 020	323 789	353 163	240 893	309 431	330 923	357 790	247 090	326 434	347 334	381 373
	Denmark	375 215	419 802	434 439	434 439	375 215	419 802	434 439	434 439	380 924	497 723	497 723	497 723
	England	20 627	30 148	30 148	30 148	20 627	30 148	30 148	30 148	20 627	30 148	30 148	30 148
	Estonia	124 696	132 048	132 048	182 246	124 696	132 048	132 048	182 246	124 696	132 048	132 048	182 246
	Finland[1]	29 905	34 424	37 884	46 159	31 748	37 093	40 518	49 562	32 696	41 570	45 040	55 881
	France	21 184	27 494	29 438	43 435	24 087	29 697	31 641	45 740	24 342	29 952	31 896	46 020
	Germany	37 589	m	46 134	50 004	41 339	m	50 929	55 729	45 113	m	55 533	62 824
	Greece	19 729	22 487	24 146	29 127	19 729	22 487	24 146	29 127	19 729	22 487	24 146	29 127
	Hungary[1]	1 547 376	1 777 740	1 914 504	2 563 236	1 547 376	1 777 740	1 914 504	2 563 236	1 743 564	2 082 672	2 298 900	3 312 288
	Iceland	3 543 514	3 884 631	3 987 224	4 157 620	3 543 514	3 884 631	3 987 224	4 157 620	3 227 000	3 766 000	4 025 000	4 210 000
	Ireland[1]	33 753	49 831	55 916	63 361	33 753	49 831	55 916	63 361	33 753	49 831	55 916	63 361
	Israel	69 313	99 796	105 899	155 303	64 171	89 345	99 247	146 215	61 187	81 794	91 563	138 644
	Italy	22 639	24 913	27 374	33 336	24 403	27 042	29 824	36 607	24 403	27 701	30 661	38 272
	Japan	3 241 000	4 829 000	5 720 000	7 229 000	3 241 000	4 829 000	5 720 000	7 229 000	3 241 000	4 829 000	5 720 000	7 425 000
	Korea	24 271 300	35 998 800	42 003 300	67 314 809	24 175 300	35 902 800	41 907 300	67 218 809	24 175 300	35 902 800	41 907 300	67 218 809
	Luxembourg	46 806	60 848	67 230	102 122	72 336	90 421	101 058	125 738	72 336	90 421	101 058	125 738
	Mexico	118 898	119 732	155 022	255 006	151 547	156 563	196 707	323 647	m	m	m	m
	Netherlands	32 156	38 160	42 654	46 947	33 364	43 890	50 955	55 924	33 364	43 890	50 955	55 924
	New Zealand	m	m	m	m	m	m	m	m	m	m	m	m
	Norway[1]	312 377	354 493	382 772	384 939	312 377	354 493	382 772	384 939	341 843	370 873	405 878	408 060
	Poland	17 054	23 781	28 902	30 115	19 196	26 958	32 920	34 308	21 678	30 790	37 670	39 264
	Portugal	21 973	24 620	26 763	38 609	21 973	24 620	26 763	38 609	21 973	24 620	26 763	38 609
	Scotland[1]	20 597	32 855	32 855	32 855	20 597	32 855	32 855	32 855	20 597	32 855	32 855	32 855
	Slovak Republic	6 325	6 957	7 276	7 844	6 325	6 957	7 276	7 844	6 325	6 957	7 276	7 844
	Slovenia	18 396	20 409	22 361	23 490	18 396	20 409	22 361	23 490	18 396	20 409	22 361	23 490
	Spain	29 257	31 890	33 754	40 826	32 709	35 632	37 669	45 744	33 344	36 359	38 459	46 692
	Sweden[1]	271 900	302 400	313 600	363 600	274 800	311 800	324 000	366 000	288 000	328 100	342 300	391 600
	Switzerland[2]	75 270	96 918	m	117 841	85 813	110 096	m	133 149	99 302	129 158	m	151 756
	Turkey	23 306	24 071	25 043	27 104	a	a	a	a	23 888	24 653	25 625	27 686
	United States[1]	36 502	42 475	44 788	51 633	36 416	42 566	44 614	54 725	36 907	43 586	47 977	54 666
Other G20	Argentina	m	m	m	m	m	m	m	m	m	m	m	m
	Brazil	m	m	m	m	m	m	m	m	m	m	m	m
	China	m	m	m	m	m	m	m	m	m	m	m	m
	India	m	m	m	m	m	m	m	m	m	m	m	m
	Indonesia	8 804 400	m	11 142 000	12 693 600	9 384 000	m	12 693 600	13 790 400	10 864 800	m	14 058 000	15 319 200
	Russian Federation	m	m	m	m	m	m	m	m	m	m	m	m
	Saudi Arabia	m	m	m	m	m	m	m	m	m	m	m	m
	South Africa	m	m	m	m	m	m	m	m	m	m	m	m

1. Actual salaries.
2. Salaries after 11 years of experience for columns 2, 6, 10.

Source: OECD. Indonesia: UNESCO Institute for Statistics (World Education Indicators Programme). See Annex 3 for notes *(www.oecd.org/edu/eag2011)*.
Please refer to the Reader's Guide for information concerning the symbols replacing missing data.

StatLink http://dx.doi.org/10.1787/888932466519

Annex 2

Table X2.3b. Teachers' salaries in equivalent euros (2009)

Annual statutory teachers' salaries in public institutions at starting salary, after 10 and 15 years of experience and at the top of the scale, by level of education, in equivalent euros converted using PPPs

		Primary education				Lower secondary education				Upper secondary education			
		Starting salary/ minimum training	Salary after 10 years of experience/ minimum training	Salary after 15 years of experience/ minimum training	Salary at top of scale/ minimum training	Starting salary/ minimum training	Salary after 10 years of experience/ minimum training	Salary after 15 years of experience/ minimum training	Salary at top of scale/ minimum training	Starting salary/ minimum training	Salary after 10 years of experience/ minimum training	Salary after 15 years of experience/ minimum training	Salary at top of scale/ minimum training
		(1)	(2)	(3)	(4)	(5)	(6)	(7)	(8)	(9)	(10)	(11)	(12)
OECD	Australia	30 435	42 349	42 349	42 349	30 435	42 349	42 349	42 349	30 435	42 349	42 349	42 349
	Austria	27 216	32 125	36 059	53 901	28 451	34 651	38 974	55 999	28 871	31 203	40 135	58 944
	Belgium (Fl.)	28 472	35 613	40 049	48 920	28 472	35 613	40 049	48 920	35 433	45 062	51 337	61 795
	Belgium (Fr.)	27 697	m	39 243	48 156	27 697	m	39 243	48 156	34 606	m	50 584	61 091
	Canada	m	m	m	m	m	m	m	m	m	m	m	m
	Chile	13 707	17 545	19 532	25 620	13 707	17 545	19 532	25 620	14 308	18 346	20 433	26 821
	Czech Republic	15 545	19 561	20 901	22 798	15 550	19 975	21 362	23 096	15 950	21 072	22 421	24 619
	Denmark	41 222	46 120	47 728	47 728	41 222	46 120	47 728	47 728	41 849	54 681	54 681	54 681
	England	28 262	41 308	41 308	41 308	28 262	41 308	41 308	41 308	28 262	41 308	41 308	41 308
	Estonia	13 066	13 836	13 836	19 096	13 066	13 836	13 836	19 096	13 066	13 836	13 836	19 096
	Finland[1]	28 704	33 041	36 362	44 305	30 473	35 603	38 890	47 571	31 382	39 900	43 231	53 636
	France	21 077	27 355	29 290	43 216	23 966	29 547	31 481	45 509	24 219	29 801	31 735	45 788
	Germany	40 780	m	50 050	54 249	44 848	m	55 252	60 460	48 942	m	60 247	68 157
	Greece	24 541	27 972	30 035	36 230	24 541	27 972	30 035	36 230	24 541	27 972	30 035	36 230
	Hungary[1]	10 575	12 150	13 084	17 518	10 575	12 150	13 084	17 518	11 916	14 234	15 711	22 637
	Iceland	25 258	27 689	28 420	29 635	25 258	27 689	28 420	29 635	23 002	26 844	28 690	30 008
	Ireland[1]	31 988	47 225	52 992	60 047	31 988	47 225	52 992	60 047	31 988	47 225	52 992	60 047
	Israel	16 625	23 936	25 400	37 249	15 391	21 429	23 804	35 069	14 676	19 618	21 961	33 254
	Italy	25 381	27 930	30 689	37 373	27 358	30 317	33 436	41 040	27 358	31 056	34 375	42 908
	Japan	24 579	36 623	43 380	54 824	24 579	36 623	43 380	54 824	24 579	36 623	43 380	56 310
	Korea	26 798	39 746	46 376	74 322	26 692	39 640	46 270	74 216	26 692	39 640	46 270	74 216
	Luxembourg	45 480	59 124	65 325	99 229	70 287	87 859	98 195	122 176	70 287	87 859	98 195	122 176
	Mexico	13 748	13 844	17 924	29 485	17 523	18 102	22 744	37 421	m	m	m	m
	Netherlands	33 341	39 566	44 225	48 677	34 593	45 507	52 832	57 984	34 593	45 507	52 832	57 984
	New Zealand	m	m	m	m	m	m	m	m	m	m	m	m
	Norway[1]	31 251	35 464	38 293	38 510	31 251	35 464	38 293	38 510	34 199	37 103	40 605	40 823
	Poland	8 065	11 247	13 668	14 242	9 078	12 749	15 569	16 225	10 252	14 561	17 815	18 569
	Portugal	30 112	33 739	36 675	52 909	30 112	33 739	36 675	52 909	30 112	33 739	36 675	52 909
	Scotland[1]	28 221	45 017	45 017	45 017	28 221	45 017	45 017	45 017	28 221	45 017	45 017	45 017
	Slovak Republic	10 658	11 723	12 260	13 218	10 658	11 723	12 260	13 218	10 658	11 723	12 260	13 218
	Slovenia	25 629	28 434	31 154	32 726	25 629	28 434	31 154	32 726	25 629	28 434	31 154	32 726
	Spain	35 907	39 138	41 426	50 105	40 143	43 731	46 231	56 141	40 923	44 623	47 200	57 304
	Sweden[1]	26 909	29 928	31 036	35 985	27 196	30 858	32 065	36 222	28 503	32 471	33 877	38 756
	Switzerland[2]	42 893	55 229	m	67 152	48 901	62 739	m	75 875	56 587	73 601	m	86 478
	Turkey	22 420	23 156	24 091	26 074	a	a	a	a	22 980	23 716	24 651	26 634
	United States[1]	32 048	37 293	39 324	45 334	31 973	37 373	39 171	48 049	32 404	38 268	42 124	47 996
	OECD average	26 512	32 177	34 624	42 784	28 262	34 511	37 164	45 664	29 472	35 968	38 957	47 740
	EU19 average	26 472	31 531	34 888	42 041	28 365	33 997	37 725	44 578	29 459	35 299	39 898	47 374
Other G20	Argentina	m	m	m	m	m	m	m	m	m	m	m	m
	Brazil	m	m	m	m	m	m	m	m	m	m	m	m
	China	m	m	m	m	m	m	m	m	m	m	m	m
	India	m	m	m	m	m	m	m	m	m	m	m	m
	Indonesia	1 373	m	1 738	1 980	1 464	m	1 980	2 151	1 694	m	2 193	2 389
	Russian Federation	m	m	m	m	m	m	m	m	m	m	m	m
	Saudi Arabia	m	m	m	m	m	m	m	m	m	m	m	m
	South Africa	m	m	m	m	m	m	m	m	m	m	m	m

1. Actual salaries.
2. Salaries after 11 years of experience.

Source: OECD. Indonesia: UNESCO Institute for Statistics (World Education Indicators Programme). See Annex 3 for notes *(www.oecd.org/edu/eag2011)*.
Please refer to the Reader's Guide for information concerning the symbols replacing missing data.

StatLink http://dx.doi.org/10.1787/888932466576

Table X2.3c. [1/2] Trends in teachers' salaries in national currency, by level of education

	Teachers' salaries in national currency after 15 years of experience/minimum training[1]										
	Primary level							Lower secondary level			
	1995	2000	2005	2006	2007	2008	2009	1995	2000	2005	2006
	(1)	(2)	(3)	(4)	(5)	(6)	(7)	(8)	(9)	(10)	(11)
OECD											
Australia	46 090	50 995	62 240	61 243	63 977	68 586	70 696	46 090	51 016	62 384	62 106
Austria	m	25 826	31 050	31 935	32 830	33 717	34 848	m	26 916	33 635	34 418
Belgium (Fl.)	27 264	29 579	35 417	36 390	37 236	37 432	39 670	29 052	31 191	35 417	36 390
Belgium (Fr.)	26 369	28 638	33 598	34 825	35 697	35 917	38 872	28 654	30 482	33 973	34 825
Canada	m	m	m	m	m	m	m	m	m	m	m
Chile	m	m	m	4 430 124	4 636 394	m	8 257 733	m	m	m	4 430 124
Czech Republic	m	125 501	250 559	254 921	302 856	309 994	323 789	m	125 501	250 559	254 921
Denmark	m	285 200	332 015	341 001	346 569	362 222	434 439	m	285 200	332 015	341 001
England	19 614	23 193	27 123	28 005	28 707	29 427	30 148	19 614	23 193	27 123	28 005
Estonia	m	48 000	68 520	78 840	94 080	117 687	132 048	m	48 000	68 520	78 840
Finland[2]	22 201	26 574	31 490	34 947	35 664	36 862	37 884	25 396	30 274	37 080	37 360
France	26 292	27 288	28 395	28 791	29 097	29 271	29 438	28 942	29 456	30 667	31 068
Germany	w	w	w	w	w	w	46 134	w	w	w	w
Greece	m	15 883	20 572	21 237	21 872	22 989	24 146	m	15 883	20 572	21 237
Hungary[2]	m	897 168	1 944 576	1 970 676	1 983 240	2 059 668	1 914 504	m	897 168	1 944 576	1 970 676
Iceland	m	1 884 000	2 573 556	2 837 950	2 830 814	3 268 766	3 987 224	m	1 884 000	2 573 556	2 837 950
Ireland[2]	m	33 370	46 591	49 421	52 177	53 221	55 916	m	33 729	46 591	49 421
Israel	46 799	68 421	73 496	77 475	86 089	94 432	105 899	52 675	76 048	82 030	86 256
Italy	17 524	20 849	25 234	25 528	25 799	26 470	27 374	19 133	22 836	27 487	27 797
Japan	5 818 000	6 645 000	6 236 000	6 235 725	5 958 000	5 753 000	5 720 000	5 818 000	6 645 000	6 236 000	6 235 725
Korea	m	26 757 000	39 712 000	40 841 220	41 387 505	42 003 300	42 003 300	m	26 661 000	39 616 000	40 745 220
Luxembourg	42 880	m	62 139	63 692	65 284	64 244	67 230	64 389	m	81 258	83 289
Mexico	34 263	86 748	124 082	130 526	137 323	145 917	155 022	41 109	109 779	157 816	166 107
Netherlands	m	29 609	37 210	37 830	39 463	40 543	42 654	m	31 692	40 880	41 612
New Zealand	m	49 450	54 979	56 628	58 327	60 660	m	m	49 450	54 979	56 628
Norway[2]	199 488	252 700	309 480	309 480	332 218	367 592	382 772	199 488	252 700	309 480	309 480
Poland	m	m	19 022	m	m	26 944	28 902	m	m	19 022	m
Portugal	14 390	17 180	22 775	23 186	23 541	23 987	26 763	14 390	17 180	22 775	23 186
Scotland[2]	20 190	22 743	29 827	30 602	31 241	32 052	32 855	20 190	22 743	29 827	30 602
Slovak Republic	m	m	m	m	m	m	7 276	m	m	m	m
Slovenia	m	m	17 939	19 025	20 005	20 911	22 361	m	m	17 939	19 025
Spain	21 085	22 701	28 122	29 347	29 934	32 193	33 754	m	24 528	31 561	32 922
Sweden[2]	m	248 300	283 200	283 200	298 800	298 800	313 600	m	248 300	290 400	290 400
Switzerland[3]	88 041	85 513	90 483	89 909	91 017	92 617	96 918	102 949	102 409	103 037	102 985
Turkey	362	2 638	17 166	17 609	19 822	22 114	25 043	a	a	a	a
United States[2]	m	m	40 734	42 404	43 633	44 172	44 788	m	m	41 090	42 775
Other G20											
Argentina	m	m	m	m	m	m	m	m	m	m	m
Brazil	m	m	m	m	m	m	m	m	m	m	m
China	m	m	m	m	m	m	m	m	m	m	m
India	m	m	m	m	m	m	m	m	m	m	m
Indonesia	m	m	m	m	11 142 000	11 142 000	11 142 000	m	m	m	m
Russian Federation	m	m	m	m	m	m	m	m	m	m	m
Saudi Arabia	m	m	m	m	m	m	m	m	m	m	m
South Africa	m	m	m	m	m	m	m	m	m	m	m

1. Data on salaries for countries now in the euro zone are shown in euros.
2. Actual salaries.
3. Salaries after 11 years of experience.

Source: OECD. Indonesia: UNESCO Institute for Statistics (World Education Indicators Programme). See Annex 3 for notes *(www.oecd.org/edu/eag2011)*.

StatLink http://dx.doi.org/10.1787/888932466538

Table X2.3c. [2/2] Trends in teachers' salaries in national currency, by level of education

		Teachers' salaries in national currency after 15 years of experience/minimum training[1]									
		Lower secondary level			Upper secondary level						
		2007	2008	2009	1995	2000	2005	2006	2007	2008	2009
		(12)	(13)	(14)	(15)	(16)	(17)	(18)	(19)	(20)	(21)
OECD	Australia	64 984	69 794	70 696	46 090	51 016	62 384	62 106	64 984	69 794	70 696
	Austria	35 467	36 455	37 664	m	29 728	34 265	35 273	36 493	37 508	38 787
	Belgium (Fl.)	37 236	37 432	39 670	37 161	39 886	45 301	46 477	47 644	47 976	50 852
	Belgium (Fr.)	35 697	35 917	38 872	36 868	39 207	43 704	44 750	45 820	46 039	50 106
	Canada	m	m	m	m	m	m	m	m	m	m
	Chile	4 636 394	m	8 257 733	m	m	m	4 638 231	4 852 425	m	8 638 812
	Czech Republic	302 856	316 173	330 923	m	152 941	255 125	258 535	323 566	337 024	347 334
	Denmark	346 569	362 222	434 439	322 000	335 000	404 229	424 212	423 426	436 926	497 723
	England	28 707	29 427	30 148	19 614	23 193	27 123	28 005	28 707	29 427	30 148
	Estonia	94 080	117 687	132 048	m	48 000	68 520	78 840	94 080	117 687	132 048
	Finland[2]	38 165	39 501	40 518	30 274	31 788	42 120	41 432	41 964	43 326	45 040
	France	31 274	31 461	31 641	28 942	29 456	30 895	31 296	31 525	31 715	31 896
	Germany	w	w	50 929	w	w	w	w	w	w	55 533
	Greece	21 872	22 989	24 146	m	15 883	20 572	21 237	21 872	22 989	24 146
	Hungary[2]	1 983 240	2 059 668	1 914 504	m	1 128 996	2 432 388	2 358 240	2 474 508	2 474 388	2 298 900
	Iceland	2 830 814	3 268 766	3 987 224	m	2 220 000	3 014 000	3 446 964	3 619 000	3 840 000	4 025 000
	Ireland[2]	52 177	53 221	55 916	m	33 729	46 591	49 421	52 177	53 221	55 916
	Israel	86 838	95 405	99 247	52 423	75 097	80 052	84 190	85 118	93 786	91 563
	Italy	28 095	28 831	29 824	19 730	23 518	28 259	28 574	28 880	29 637	30 661
	Japan	5 958 000	5 753 000	5 720 000	5 818 000	6 649 000	6 237 000	6 235 725	5 958 000	5 753 000	5 720 000
	Korea	41 291 505	41 907 300	41 907 300	m	26 661 000	39 616 000	40 745 220	41 291 505	41 907 300	41 907 300
	Luxembourg	85 371	93 772	101 058	64 389	m	81 258	83 289	85 371	93 772	101 058
	Mexico	174 854	185 616	196 707	m	m	m	m	m	m	m
	Netherlands	47 427	48 615	50 955	m	44 244	54 712	55 647	47 427	48 615	50 955
	New Zealand	58 327	60 660	m	m	49 450	54 979	56 628	58 327	60 660	m
	Norway[2]	332 218	367 592	382 772	204 840	252 700	333 492	333 492	354 059	387 383	405 878
	Poland	m	30 850	32 920	m	m	19 022	m	m	35 459	37 670
	Portugal	23 541	23 987	26 763	14 390	17 180	22 775	23 186	23 541	23 987	26 763
	Scotland[2]	31 241	32 052	32 855	20 190	22 743	29 827	30 602	31 241	32 052	32 855
	Slovak Republic	m	m	7 276	m	m	m	m	m	m	7 276
	Slovenia	20 005	20 911	22 361	m	m	17 939	19 025	20 005	20 911	22 361
	Spain	33 580	35 200	37 669	24 471	26 366	32 293	33 666	34 339	36 818	38 459
	Sweden[2]	306 300	306 300	324 000	m	264 700	313 600	313 600	326 900	326 900	342 300
	Switzerland[3]	104 157	105 874	110 096	121 198	121 629	120 602	121 187	122 259	124 936	129 158
	Turkey	a	a	a	375	2 441	17 403	18 074	20 329	22 650	25 625
	United States[2]	44 015	44 000	44 614	m	m	41 044	42 727	43 966	47 317	47 977
Other G20	Argentina	m	m	m	m	m	m	m	m	m	m
	Brazil	m	m	m	m	m	m	m	m	m	m
	China	m	m	m	m	m	m	m	m	m	m
	India	m	m	m	m	m	m	m	m	m	m
	Indonesia	11 142 000	12 693 600	12 693 600	m	m	m	m	11 142 000	14 058 000	14 058 000
	Russian Federation	m	m	m	m	m	m	m	m	m	m
	Saudi Arabia	m	m	m	m	m	m	m	m	m	m
	South Africa	m	m	m	m	m	m	m	m	m	m

1. Data on salaries for countries now in the euro zone are shown in euros.
2. Actual salaries.
3. Salaries after 11 years of experience.

Source: OECD. Indonesia: UNESCO Institute for Statistics (World Education Indicators Programme). See Annex 3 for notes *(www.oecd.org/edu/eag2011)*.

StatLink http://dx.doi.org/10.1787/888932466538

Table X2.3d. [1/3] Reference statistics used in the calculation of teachers' salaries (1995, 2000, 2005-2009)

		Purchasing power parity for GDP (PPP)[1]			Gross domestic product (GDP) (in millions of local currency, calendar year)[1]							
		2008	2009	Jan 2009	1999	2000	2004	2005	2006	2007	2008	2009
		(1)	(2)	(3)	(4)	(5)	(6)	(7)	(8)	(9)	(10)	(11)
OECD	Australia	1.48	1.45	1.47	663 867	708 889	925 864	1 000 787	1 091 327	1 181 750	1 253 121	1 272 987
	Austria	0.85	0.84	0.85	197 979	207 529	232 782	243 585	256 951	272 010	283 085	274 320
	Belgium (Fl.)[2]	0.87	0.87	0.87	238 569	252 216	290 825	302 845	318 150	335 085	345 006	339 162
	Belgium (Fr.)[2]	0.87	0.87	0.87	238 569	252 216	290 825	302 845	318 150	335 085	345 006	339 162
	Canada	1.23	1.20	1.22	982 441	1 076 577	1 290 907	1 373 845	1 450 405	1 529 589	1 599 608	1 527 259
	Chile	365.27	377.13	371.20	37 228 111	40 679 938	58 303 211	66 192 596	77 830 577	85 849 774	89 262 568	91 591 252
	Czech Republic	13.69	13.52	13.60	2 080 797	2 189 169	2 814 762	2 983 862	3 222 369	3 535 460	3 688 997	3 625 865
	Denmark	8.03	7.96	7.99	1 213 473	1 293 964	1 466 180	1 545 257	1 631 659	1 695 264	1 740 843	1 656 108
	England[3]	0.64	0.64	0.64	928 730	976 533	1 202 956	1 254 058	1 328 363	1 404 845	1 445 580	1 392 634
	Estonia	8.62	8.14	8.38	83 842	96 380	151 542	174 956	209 520	247 646	252 015	216 875
	Finland	0.92	0.91	0.91	122 222	132 110	152 148	157 307	165 643	179 702	184 649	171 315
	France	0.89	0.88	0.88	1 367 966	1 441 372	1 660 189	1 726 068	1 806 430	1 895 284	1 948 511	1 907 145
	Germany	0.81	0.81	0.81	2 012 000	2 062 500	2 210 900	2 242 200	2 326 500	2 432 400	2 481 200	2 397 100
	Greece	0.70	0.71	0.71	126 155	136 281	185 266	194 819	211 300	227 074	236 917	235 017
	Hungary	128.75	128.19	128.47	11 640 204	13 368 903	20 822 396	21 970 780	23 730 035	25 321 478	26 753 906	26 054 327
	Iceland	118.57	127.78	123.18	632 399	683 747	928 889	1 026 718	1 168 577	1 308 518	1 477 938	1 500 765
	Ireland	0.95	0.90	0.93	90 380	105 018	149 344	162 314	177 343	189 374	179 989	159 646
	Israel	3.59	3.73	3.66	458 369	508 380	568 633	602 507	651 416	690 144	725 861	768 339
	Italy	0.79	0.78	0.78	1 127 091	1 191 057	1 391 530	1 429 479	1 485 377	1 546 177	1 567 851	1 520 870
	Japan	116.85	114.70	115.77	497 628 600	502 989 900	498 328 400	501 734 400	507 364 800	515 520 400	505 111 900	474 296 000
	Korea	785.72	804.72	795.22	549 005 043	603 235 999	826 892 743	865 240 919	908 743 849	975 013 010	1 026 451 811	1 063 059 095
	Luxembourg	0.91	0.90	0.90	19 887	22 001	27 456	30 282	33 920	37 491	39 640	38 045
	Mexico	7.47	7.72	7.59	5 037 271	6 020 649	8 561 305	9 220 649	10 346 934	11 177 690	12 091 797	11 784 454
	Netherlands	0.85	0.85	0.85	386 193	417 960	491 184	513 407	540 216	571 773	596 226	571 979
	New Zealand	1.49	1.50	1.50	110 902	117 165	151 701	160 273	168 328	181 259	184 802	186 955
	Norway	8.71	8.85	8.78	1 045 340	1 113 893	1 355 314	1 451 132	1 580 665	1 724 280	1 812 173	1 846 574
	Poland	1.85	1.86	1.86	665 688	744 378	924 538	983 302	1 060 031	1 176 737	1 275 432	1 343 657
	Portugal	0.65	0.63	0.64	118 370	127 008	148 827	153 728	160 274	168 737	172 022	168 046
	Scotland[3]	0.64	0.64	0.64	928 730	976 533	1 202 956	1 254 058	1 328 363	1 404 845	1 445 580	1 392 634
	Slovak Republic	0.53	0.51	0.52	28 109	31 177	45 161	49 314	55 080	61 555	67 007	63 050
	Slovenia	0.63	0.63	0.63	16 807	18 481	27 073	28 750	31 050	34 568	37 305	35 384
	Spain	0.72	0.71	0.72	579 942	630 263	841 042	908 792	984 284	1 053 537	1 088 124	1 053 914
	Sweden	8.80	8.94	8.87	2 138 421	2 265 447	2 660 957	2 769 375	2 944 480	3 126 018	3 204 320	3 089 181
	Switzerland	1.55	1.53	1.54	402 907	422 063	451 379	463 799	490 544	521 101	544 196	535 282
	Turkey	0.89	0.93	0.91	104 596	166 658	559 033	648 932	758 391	843 178	950 534	953 974
	United States	1.00	1.00	1.00	9 301 000	9 898 800	11 812 300	12 579 700	13 336 200	13 995 000	14 296 900	14 043 900
Other G20	Argentina	m	m	m	m	m	m	m	m	m	m	m
	Brazil	m	m	m	m	m	m	m	m	m	m	m
	China	m	m	m	m	m	m	m	m	m	m	m
	India	m	m	m	m	m	m	m	m	m	m	m
	Indonesia	5 445.61	5 813.60	5 629.60	m	m	m	m	m	m	909 729	m
	Russian Federation	14.34	14.56	14.45	4 823 234	7 305 646	17 048 122	21 625 372	26 903 494	33 111 382	41 668 034	m
	Saudi Arabia	m	m	m	m	m	m	m	m	m	m	m
	South Africa	m	m	m	m	m	m	m	m	m	m	m

1. Data on PPPs and GDP for countries now in the euro zone are shown in euros.
2. Data on Gross Domestic Product and total population refer to Belgium.
3. Data on Gross Domestic Product and total population refer to the United Kingdom.

Source: OECD. Indonesia: UNESCO Institute for Statistics (World Education Indicators Programme). See Annex 3 for notes *(www.oecd.org/edu/eag2011)*.
Please refer to the Reader's Guide for information concerning the symbols replacing missing data.

StatLink http://dx.doi.org/10.1787/888932466557

Annex 2

Table X2.3d. [2/3] **Reference statistics used in the calculation of teachers' salaries (1995, 2000, 2005-2009)**

		Total population (in thousands, calendar year)							
		1999	2000	2004	2005	2006	2007	2008	2009
		(12)	(13)	(14)	(15)	(16)	(17)	(18)	(19)
OECD	Australia	19 036	19 270	20 250	20 542	20 871	21 236	21 642	22 101
	Austria	7 992	8 012	8 169	8 225	8 268	8 301	8 337	8 363
	Belgium (Fl.)[2]	10 222	10 246	10 417	10 474	10 543	10 622	10 708	10 790
	Belgium (Fr.)[2]	10 222	10 246	10 417	10 474	10 543	10 622	10 708	10 790
	Canada	30 401	30 686	31 941	32 245	32 576	32 932	33 327	33 740
	Chile	15 197	15 398	16 093	16 267	16 433	16 598	16 764	16 929
	Czech Republic	10 283	10 273	10 207	10 234	10 267	10 323	10 430	10 507
	Denmark	5 321	5 338	5 403	5 419	5 437	5 460	5 492	5 522
	England[3]	58 684	58 886	59 846	60 238	60 584	60 986	61 398	61 792
	Estonia	1 379	1 372	1 351	1 348	1 345	1 342	1 341	1 340
	Finland	5 165	5 176	5 227	5 245	5 266	5 289	5 313	5 339
	France	60 333	60 725	62 491	62 959	63 394	63 781	64 141	64 494
	Germany	82 087	82 188	82 501	82 464	82 366	82 263	82 120	81 875
	Greece	10 883	10 917	11 062	11 104	11 149	11 193	11 237	11 260
	Hungary	10 238	10 211	10 107	10 087	10 071	10 056	10 038	10 023
	Iceland	277	281	293	296	304	311	319	319
	Ireland	3 755	3 804	4 067	4 160	4 261	4 365	4 443	4 468
	Israel	6 125	6 289	6 809	6 930	7 054	7 180	7 309	7 440
	Italy	56 916	56 942	58 175	58 607	58 942	59 375	59 832	60 263
	Japan	126 667	126 926	127 787	127 768	127 770	127 771	127 510	127 328
	Korea	46 617	47 008	48 039	48 138	48 297	48 456	48 607	48 747
	Luxembourg	431	436	458	465	472	480	488	497
	Mexico	96 550	98 258	102 866	103 831	104 748	105 677	106 573	107 440
	Netherlands	15 809	15 922	16 276	16 317	16 341	16 378	16 440	16 527
	New Zealand	3 822	3 843	4 045	4 101	4 148	4 198	4 241	4 281
	Norway	4 462	4 491	4 591	4 622	4 661	4 706	4 768	4 829
	Poland	38 270	38 256	38 180	38 161	38 132	38 116	38 116	38 153
	Portugal	10 172	10 226	10 502	10 549	10 584	10 608	10 622	10 633
	Scotland[3]	58 684	58 886	59 846	60 238	60 584	60 986	61 398	61 792
	Slovak Republic	5 396	5 401	5 382	5 387	5 391	5 397	5 406	5 418
	Slovenia	1 984	1 989	1 997	2 001	2 008	2 019	2 022	2 042
	Spain	39 927	40 264	42 692	43 398	44 068	44 874	45 593	45 929
	Sweden	8 858	8 872	8 994	9 030	9 081	9 183	9 256	9 341
	Switzerland	7 167	7 209	7 454	7 501	7 558	7 619	7 711	7 799
	Turkey	63 366	64 259	67 734	68 582	69 421	70 256	71 079	71 897
	United States	279 328	282 418	293 502	296 229	299 052	302 025	304 831	307 483
Other G20	Argentina	m	m	m	m	m	m	m	m
	Brazil	m	m	m	m	m	m	m	m
	China	m	m	m	m	m	m	m	m
	India	m	m	m	m	m	m	m	m
	Indonesia	202 513	205 280	216 443	219 210	221 954	224 670	227 345	271 485
	Russian Federation	147 215	146 597	143 821	143 114	142 487	m	m	m
	Saudi Arabia	m	m	m	m	m	m	m	m
	South Africa	m	m	m	m	m	m	m	m

1. Data on PPPs and GDP for countries now in the euro zone are shown in euros.
2. Data on Gross Domestic Product and total population refer to Belgium.
3. Data on Gross Domestic Product and total population refer to the United Kingdom.

Source: OECD. Indonesia: UNESCO Institute for Statistics (World Education Indicators Programme). See Annex 3 for notes *(www.oecd.org/edu/eag2011)*.
Please refer to the Reader's Guide for information concerning the symbols replacing missing data.
StatLink http://dx.doi.org/10.1787/888932466557

Table X2.3d. [3/3] **Reference statistics used in the calculation of teachers' salaries (1995, 2000, 2005-2009)**

		GDP deflator (2005 = 100)							Reference year for 2009 salary data
		Jan 1995	Jan 2000	Jan 2005	Jan 2006	Jan 2007	Jan 2008	Jan 2009	
		(20)	(21)	(22)	(23)	(23)	(24)	(25)	(26)
OECD	Australia	77	84	100	105	110	115	118	2009
	Austria	90	93	100	102	104	106	107	2008-09
	Belgium (Fl.)[2]	86	90	100	102	105	107	109	1 Jan. 2009
	Belgium (Fr.)[2]	86	90	100	102	105	107	109	2008-09
	Canada	82	89	100	103	106	110	111	m
	Chile	64	77	100	110	120	123	126	2009
	Czech Republic	61	87	100	100	103	105	108	2008-09
	Denmark	81	89	100	102	105	108	110	2008-09
	England[3]	78	88	100	103	106	109	111	2008-09
	Estonia	45	81	100	107	117	127	132	2008-09
	Finland	86	95	100	101	103	105	106	1 Oct. 2008
	France	87	91	100	102	105	107	109	2008-09
	Germany	93	95	100	101	102	103	104	2008-09
	Greece	64	85	100	103	106	109	112	2008
	Hungary	34	71	100	103	108	114	119	2009
	Iceland	69	82	100	106	113	124	136	2008-09
	Ireland	68	83	100	103	106	105	103	2008-09
	Israel	66	94	100	102	103	104	107	2009
	Italy	75	87	100	102	104	107	110	2008-09
	Japan	110	107	100	99	98	97	96	2008-09
	Korea	74	87	100	100	101	104	107	2009
	Luxembourg	81	88	100	106	111	116	118	2008-09
	Mexico	28	69	100	106	112	118	124	2008-09
	Netherlands	78	86	100	102	104	106	107	2008-09
	New Zealand	81	88	100	103	108	112	115	m
	Norway[4]	76	87	100	103	107	110	114	1 Dec. 2008
	Poland	47	86	100	102	105	109	112	2008-09
	Portugal	73	86	100	103	106	108	109	2008-09
	Scotland[3]	78	88	100	103	106	109	111	2008-09
	Slovak Republic	57	78	100	103	105	107	108	2008-09
	Slovenia	48	76	100	102	105	109	113	2008-09
	Spain	70	82	100	104	108	111	113	2008-09
	Sweden	88	93	100	101	104	107	110	2009
	Switzerland	95	97	100	101	103	106	107	2008-09
	Turkey	2	28	100	108	117	127	138	2009
	United States	82	89	100	103	106	109	111	2008-09
Other G20	Argentina	m	m	m	m	m	m	m	m
	Brazil	m	m	m	m	m	m	m	m
	China	m	m	m	m	m	m	m	m
	India	m	m	m	m	m	m	m	m
	Indonesia	m	m	m	m	m	m	m	2008-09
	Russian Federation	5	43	100	117	134	157	m	m
	Saudi Arabia	m	m	m	m	m	m	m	m
	South Africa	m	m	m	m	m	m	m	m

1. Data on PPPs and GDP for countries now in the euro zone are shown in euros.
2. Data on Gross Domestic Product and total population refer to Belgium.
3. Data on Gross Domestic Product and total population refer to the United Kingdom.
4. The GDP Mainland market value is used for Norway.

Source: OECD. Indonesia: UNESCO Institute for Statistics (World Education Indicators Programme). See Annex 3 for notes *(www.oecd.org/edu/eag2011)*.
Please refer to the Reader's Guide for information concerning the symbols replacing missing data.

StatLink http://dx.doi.org/10.1787/888932466557

General notes

Definitions

Gross domestic product (GDP) refers to the producers' value of the gross outputs of resident producers, including distributive trades and transport, less the value of purchasers' intermediate consumption plus import duties. GDP is expressed in local money (in millions). For countries which provide this information for a reference year that is different from the calendar year (such as Australia and New Zealand), adjustments are made by linearly weighting their GDP between two adjacent national reference years to match the calendar year.

The **GDP deflator** is obtained by dividing the GDP expressed at current prices by the GDP expressed at constant prices. This provides an indication of the relative price level in a country. Data are based on the year 2000.

GDP per capita is the gross domestic product (in equivalent US dollars converted using PPPs) divided by the population.

Purchasing power parity exchange rates (PPP) are the currency exchange rates that equalise the purchasing power of different currencies.This means that a given sum of money when converted into different currencies at the PPP rates will buy the same basket of goods and services in all countries. In other words, PPPs are the rates of currency conversion which eliminate the differences in price levels among countries.Thus, when expenditure on GDP for different countries is converted into a common currency by means of PPPs, it is, in effect, expressed at the same set of international prices so that comparisons between countries reflect only differences in the volume of goods and services purchased.

Total public expenditure as used for the calculation of the education indicators, corresponds to the non-repayable current and capital expenditure of all levels of government. Current expenditure includes final consumption expenditure (e.g. compensation of employees,consumption intermediate goods and services, consumption of fixed capital,and military expenditure), property income paid, subsidies, and other current transfers paid (e.g. social security, social assistance, pensions and other welfare benefits). Capital expenditure is spending to acquire and/or improve fixed capital assets, land, intangible assets, government stocks, and non-military, non-financial assets, and spending to finance net capital transfers.

Sources

The 2010 edition of the *National Accounts of OECD Countries: Detailed Tables, Volume II.*

The theoretical framework underpinning national accounts has been provided for many years by the United Nations' publication *A System of National Accounts*, which was released in 1968. An updated version was released in 1993 (commonly referred to as SNA93).

OECD Analytical Database, March 2010.

Annex

3

Sources, Methods and Technical Notes

Annex 3 on sources and methods is available in electronic form only. It can be found at: ***www.oecd.org/edu/eag2011***

References

Andrews, D., A. Caldera Sánches and **A. Johansson** (2011), "Housing Markets and Structural Policies in OECD Countries", *OECD Economics Department Working Papers*, No. 836, OECD Publishing.

Coulombe, S., J.F. Tremblay and **S. Marchand** (2004), *Literacy Scores, Human Capital and Growth across Fourteen OECD Countries*, Statistics Canada, Ottawa.

Education, Audiovisual and Culture Executive Agency (Eurydice) (2010), *Gender Differences in Educational Outcomes: Study on the Measures Taken and the Current Situation in Europe*, Eurydice, Brussels.

Education Statistics Bulletin, Ministère de l'Éducation, du Loisir et du Sport du Québec (2005), "Educational Spending Relative to the GDP in 2001: A Comparison of Quebec and the OECD Countries", *www.mels.gouv.qc.ca/stat/bulletin/bulletin_31an.pdf*.

Ehrenberg, R. *et al.* (2001), "Class Size and Student Achievement", *Psychological Science in the Public Interest*, Vol. 2, No. 1, pp. 1-30.

Falch, T. *et al.* (2010), *Completion and Dropout in Upper Secondary Education in Norway: Causes and Consequences*, Centre for Economic Research at Norges Teknisk-Naturvitenskapelige Universitet, Trondheim.

Finn, J. (1998), "Class Size and Students at Risk: What is Known? What is Next?", US Department of Education, Office of Educational Research and Improvement, National Institute on the Education of At-Risk Students, Washington DC.

Goldin, C. and **L. Katz** (2008), *The Race Between Education and Technology*, Harvard University Press, Cambridge.

Grossman, M. (2006), "Education and Nonmarket Outcomes," *Handbook of the Economics of Education*, Elsevier, Amsterdam.

Hattie, J. (2009), *Visible Learning; A Synthesis of over 800 Meta-analyses Relating to Achievement*, Routledge, London.

Heckman, J.J. (2008), "Schools, Skills and Synapses", *NBER Working Papers*, No. 14064, National Bureau of Economic Research, Inc., Cambridge.

IFIE-ALDUCIN (2007), *Mexican National Survey to Parents Regarding the Quality of Basic Education*, IFIE- ALDUCIN, Mexico City.

Kelo, M., U. Teichler and **B. Wächter** (eds.) (2005), *EURODATA: Student Mobility in European Higher Education*, Verlags und Mediengesellschaft, Bonn.

Kogan, M. (1988), *Education Accountability: An Analytic Overview*, (2nd ed.), Century Hutchinson, Dover.

Krueger, A.B. (2002), "Economic Considerations and Class Size", *NBER Working Papers*, No. 8875, National Bureau of Economic Research, Inc., Cambridge.

Ladd, H., E.B. Fiske and **N. Ruijs** (2009), "Parental Choice in the Netherlands: Growing Concerns about Segregation", paper prepared for the National Conference on School Choice, Duke University, Durham.

Levin, H. (1974), "A Conceptual Framework for Accountability in Education", *School Review*, No. 82, Vol. 33, pp. 363-390.

Lochner, L. and **E. Moretti** (2004), "The Effect of Education on Crime: Evidence from Prison Inmates, Arrests, and Self-Reports", *The American Economic Review*, The American Economic Association, Vol. 94, No 1, pp.155-189.

Mincer, J. (1974), *Schooling, Experience, and Earnings*, National Bureau of Economic Research, New York.

National Centre for Education Statistics (2010), *The Nation's Report Card: Reading 2009*, US Department of Education, Washington, DC.

Nonoyama-Tarumi, Y. and **J.D. Willms** (2010), "The Relative and Absolute Risks of Disadvantaged Family Background and Low Levels of School Resources on Student Literacy", *Economics of Education Review*, No. 29, Vol. 2, pp. 214-224.

OECD (2004a), *OECD Handbook for Internationally Comparative Education Statistics: Concepts, Standards, Definitions and Classifications*, OECD, Paris.

OECD (2004b), *Internationalisation and Trade in Higher Education: Opportunities and Challenges*, OECD, Paris.

OECD (2005), *Teachers Matter: Attracting, Developing and Retaining Effective Teachers*, OECD, Paris.

OECD (2006a), *Education at a Glance 2006: OECD Indicators*, OECD, Paris.

OECD (2006b), *Starting Strong II: Early Childhood Education And Care*, OECD, Paris.

OECD (2007a), *PISA 2006: Science Competencies for Tomorrow's World: Volume I: Analysis*, OECD, Paris.

OECD (2007b), *International Migration Outlook 2007*, OECD, Paris.

OECD (2007c), *Understanding the Social Outcomes of Learning*, OECD, Paris.

OECD (2007d), *Education at a Glance 2007: OECD Indicators*, OECD, Paris.

OECD (2008a), *OECD Reviews of Tertiary Education: Tertiary Education for the Knowledge Society*, OECD, Paris.

OECD (2008b), *Education at a Glance 2008: OECD Indicators*, OECD, Paris.

OECD (2008c), *Improving School Leadership, Volume 1: Policy and Practices*, OECD, Paris.

OECD (2009), *Creating Effective Teaching and Learning Environments: First Results from TALIS*, OECD, Paris.

OECD (2010a), *PISA 2009 Results: What Students Know and Can Do: Student Performance in Reading, Mathematics and Science* (Volume I), OECD, Paris.

OECD (2010b), *PISA 2009 Results: Overcoming Social Background: Equity in Learning Opportunities and Outcomes* (Volume II), OECD, Paris.

OECD (2010c), *PISA 2009 Results: Learning to Learn: Student Engagement, Strategies and Practices* (Volume III), OECD, Paris.

OECD (2010d), *Taxing Wages 2008-2009*, OECD, Paris.

OECD (2010e), *Improving Health and Social Cohesion through Education*, OECD, Paris.

OECD (2010f), *OECD Tax Statistics: Volume 2010, Issue I: Revenue Statistics*, OECD, Paris.

OECD (2010g), *Main Science and Technology Indicators, Volume 2010 Issue 1*, OECD, Paris.

OECD (2010h), *Education at a Glance 2010: OECD Indicators*, OECD, Paris.

OECD (2010i), *PISA 2009 Results: What Makes a School Successful? Resources, Policies and Practices* (Volume IV), OECD, Paris.

OECD (2011j), *Pathways to Success: How Knowledge and Skills at Age 15 Shape Future Lives in Canada*, OECD, Paris.

OECD (2011a), *International Migration Outlook 2010*, OECD, Paris.

OECD (2011b), *Quality Time for Students: Learning In and Out of School*, OECD, Paris.

Piketty, T. and **M. Valdenaire** (2006), *L'Impact de la taille des classes sur la réussite scolaire dans les écoles, collèges et lycées français : Estimations à partir du panel primaire 1997 et du panel secondaire 1995*, ministère de l'Éducation nationale, de l'Enseignement supérieur et de la Recherche, Direction de l'évaluation et de la prospective, Paris.

Schulz, W. *et al.* (2010), *ICCS 2009 International Report: Civic Knowledge, Attitudes, and Engagement among Lower-secondary School Students in 38 Countries*, IEA, Amsterdam.

Tyler, R.W. (1971), "Accountability in Perspective", in L.M. Lessinger and R.W. Tyler (eds.), *Accountability in Education*, Charles A. Jones, Worthington.

UNESCO (2000), *Inclusive education and education for all: A challenge and a vision* UNESCO, Paris.

Willms, J.D. (1997), "Literacy Skills and Social Class Gradients", *Policy Options*, No. 18, Vol. 6, pp. 22-26.

Willms, J.D. (2006), *Learning Divides: Ten Policy Questions about the Performance and Equity of Schools and Schooling Systems*, UNESCO Institute for Statistics, Montreal.

Willms, J.D. (2010), "School Composition and Contextual Effects on Student Outcomes", *Teachers College Record*, No. 112, Vol. 4, pp. 3-4.

Contributors to this Publication

Many people have contributed to the development of this publication. The following lists the names of the country representatives, researchers and experts who have actively taken part in the preparatory work leading to the publication of *Education at a Glance – OECD Indicators 2011*. The OECD wishes to thank them all for their valuable efforts.

INES Working Party

Mr. Paul CMIEL (Australia)
Ms. Shannon MADDEN (Australia)
Mr. Scott MATHESON (Australia)
Ms. Margaret PEARCE (Australia)
Mr. Andreas GRIMM (Austria)
Ms. Sabine MARTINSCHITZ (Austria)
Mr. Mark NEMET (Austria)
Mr. Markus SCHWABE (Austria)
Mr. Wolfgang PAULI (Austria)
Mr. Philippe DIEU (Belgium)
Mr. Liës FEYEN (Belgium)
Ms. Nathalie JAUNIAUX (Belgium)
Mr. Guy STOFFELEN (Belgium)
Mr. Raymond VAN DE SIJPE (Belgium)
Ms. Ann VAN DRIESSCHE (Belgium)
Ms. Ana Carolina SILVA CIROTTO (Brazil)
Mr. Patrice DE BROUCKER (Canada)
Ms. Amanda HODGKINSON (Canada)
Mr. Keith LOWE (Canada)
Mr. Janusz ZIEMINSKI (Canada)
Mr. Gabriel Alonso UGARTE VERA (Chile)
Mr. Cristian Pablo YANEZ NAVARRO (Chile)
Ms. Michaela KLENHOVA (Czech Republic)
Mr. Lubomir MARTINEC (Czech Republic)
Mr. Leo Elmbirk JENSEN (Denmark)
Ms. Liv Maadele MOGENSEN (Denmark)
Ms. Karin BLIX (Denmark)
Ms. Lone SOLBJERGHOJ (Denmark)
Ms. Kristi PLOOM (Estonia)
Mr. Anders HINGEL (European Commission)
Ms. Lene MEJER (EUROSTAT, European Commission)
Mr. Fernando REIS (EUROSTAT, European Commission)
Mr. Ville HEINONEN (Finland)
Mr. Matti KYRO (Finland)
Mr. Reijo LAUKKANEN (Finland)
Ms. Riikka RAUTANEN (Finland)
Mr. Mika TUONONEN (Finland)
Mr. Matti VAISANEN (Finland)
Mr. Luc BRIERE (France)
Ms. Nadine DALSHEIMER-VAN DER TOL (France)
Ms. Florence DEFRESNE (France)
Ms. Florence LEFRESNE (France)
Ms. Valerie LIOGIER (France)
Ms. Claude MALEGUE (France)
Mr. Christophe PEPIN (France)
Ms. Pascale POULET-COULIBANDO (France)
Ms Marguerite RUDOLF (France)
Mr. Claude SAUVAGEOT (France)
Ms. Alexia STEFANOU (France)
Mr. Heinz-Werner HETMEIER (Germany)
Mr. Martin SCHULZE (Germany)
Ms. Eveline VON GAESSLER (Germany)
Ms. Roy CHOURDAKI (Greece)
Ms. Maria FASSARI (Greece)
Ms. Dimitra FARMAKIOUTOU (Greece)
Ms. Anna IMRE (Hungary)
Ms. Judit KADAR-FULOP (Hungary)
Mr. Tibor KONYVESI (Hungary)
Ms. Judit KOZMA-LUKACS (Hungary)
Mr. Laszlo LIMBACHER (Hungary)
Ms. Eva TOT (Hungary)
Mr. Gunnar ARNASON (Iceland)
Mr. Julius BJORNSSON (Iceland)
Ms. Asta URBANCIC (Iceland)
Mr. Pat McSITRIC (Ireland)
Ms. Nicola TICKNER (Ireland)
Mr. Yoav AZULAY (Israel)
Mr. Yosef GIDANIAN (Israel)
Mr. Giovanni BIONDI (Italy)
Ms. Maria Gemma DE SANCTIS (Italy)
Ms. Paola DI GIROLAMO (Italy)
Ms. Maria Teresa MORANA (Italy)
Ms. Claudia PIZZELLA (Italy)
Mr. Paolo TURCHETTI (Italy)
Mr. Jugo IMAIZUMI (Japan)
Mr. Soichi MURAKAMI (Japan)
Mr. Hiromi SASAI (Japan)
Mr. Taiji SATO (Japan)

Ms. Kumiko TANSHO-HIRABAYASHI (Japan)
Mr. Eiichi TSURUMOTO (Japan)
Mr. Eun-Bae KONG (Korea)
Ms. Jong-Hyo PARK (Korea)
Mr. Jerome LEVY (Luxembourg)
Mr. Rafael FREYRE MARTINEZ (Mexico)
Mr. Rene GOMORA CASTILLO (Mexico)
Ms. Danielle ANDARABI (Netherlands)
Mr. Egon DIETZ (Netherlands)
Ms. Linda SLIKKERVEER (Netherlands)
Mr. Marcel SMITS VAN WAESBERGHE (Netherlands)
Mr. Dick TAKKENBERG (Netherlands)
Ms. Pauline THOOLEN (Netherlands)
Ms. Anouschka VAN DER MEULEN (Netherlands)
Mr. Paul GINI (New Zealand)
Ms. Frances KELLY (New-Zealand)
Mr. David SCOTT (New-Zealand)
Ms. Marie ARNEBERG (Norway)
Mr. Terje RISBERG (Norway)
Ms. Hanna GOLASZEWSKA (Poland)
Ms. Joanna GORSKA (Poland)
Mr. Marek KOWALEWSKI (Poland)
Mr. Krzysztof MIESZKOWSKI (Poland)
Ms. Anna NOWOZYNSKA (Poland)
Ms. Beatriz GONCALVES (Portugal)
Ms. Elisa GONZALEZ (Portugal)
Mr. Joao PEREIRA DE MATOS (Portugal)
Mr. Nuno Miguel RODRIGUES (Portugal)
Mr. Joaquim SANTOS (Portugal)
Mr. Mark AGRANOVICH (Russian Federation)
Mr. Evgeny BUTKO (Russian Federation)
Ms. Anna FATEEVA (Russian Federation)
Ms. Alzbeta FERENCICOVA (Slovak Republic)
Ms. Zuzana JAKUBCOVA (Slovak Republic)
Ms. Elena REBROSOVA (Slovak Republic)
Ms. Helga KOCEVAR (Slovenia)
Ms. Tatjana SKRBEC (Slovenia)
Ms. Sagrario AVEZUELA SANCHEZ (Spain)
Ms. Isabel BLANCO NIETO (Spain)
Mr. Eduardo DE LA FUENTE (Spain)
Mr. Luis HERNAEZ GLUCK (Spain)
Mr. Jesus IBAÑEZ MILLA (Spain)
Mr. Joaquín MARTIN MUÑOZ (Spain)
Mr. Valentín RAMOS SALVADOR (Spain)
Ms. Carmen URENA URENA (Spain)
Mr. Mats BJORNSSON (Sweden)
Ms. Marie KAHLROTH (Sweden)
Mr. Kenny PETERSSON (Sweden)
Ms. Katrin HOLENSTEIN (Switzerland)
Mr. Stefan C. WOLTER (Switzerland)
Ms. Hümeyra ALTUNTAŞ (Turkey)
Ms. Nilgun DURAN (Turkey)
Mr. Ibrahim Zeki KARABIYIK (Turkey)
Mr. Michael BRUNEFORTH (UNESCO)
Mr. Albert MOTIVANS (UNESCO)
Mr. Said Ould Ahmedou VOFFAL (UNESCO)
Mr. Anthony CLARKE (United Kingdom)
Mr. Stephen HEWITT (United Kingdom)
Mr. Stephen LEMAN (United Kingdom)
Ms. Rachel DINKES (United States)
Ms. Jana KEMP (United States)
Ms. Valena White PLISKO (United States)
Mr. Thomas SNYDER (United States)

Network on Labour Market, Economic and Social Outcomes of Learning (LSO)

Lead country: Canada
Network Leader: Mr. Patrice DE BROUCKER
Mr. Paul CMIEL (Australia)
Ms. Shannon MADDEN (Australia)
Mr. Scott MATHESON (Australia)
Ms. Margaret PEARCE (Australia)
Mr. Mark NEMET (Austria)
Ms. Ariane BAYE (Belgium)
Ms. Isabelle ERAUW (Belgium)
Ms. Genevieve HINDRYCKX (Belgium)
Mr. Daniel Jaime CAPISTRANO DE OLIVEIRA (Brazil)
Ms. Ana Carolina SILVA CIROTTO (Brazil)
Mr. Patric BLOUIN (Canada)
Mr. Patrice DE BROUCKER (Canada)
Ms. Emanuelle CARRIERE (Canada)
Ms. Shannon DELBRIDGE (Canada)
Ms. Sona FORTOVA (Czech Republic)
Ms. Vendula KAŠPAROVA (Czech Republic)
Mr. Andreas GINGER-MORTENSEN (Denmark)
Ms. Liv Maadele MOGENSEN (Denmark)
Mr. Lars JAKOBSEN (EUROSTAT, European Commission)
Ms. Marta BECK-DOMZALSKA (EUROSTAT, European Commission)
Mr. Sylvain JOUHETTE (EUROSTAT, European Commission)
Ms. Irja BLOMQVIST (Finland)
Ms. Aila REPO (Finland)
Ms. Pascale POULET-COULIBANDO (France)
Ms. Christiane KRUGER-HEMMER (Germany)
Ms. Angelika TRAUB (Germany)
Mr. Angelos KARAGIANNIS (Greece)
Ms. Nicola TICKNER (Ireland)
Mr. Yosef GIDANIAN (Israel)
Mr. Haim PORTNOY (Israel)
Ms. Liana VERZICCO (Italy)

Ms. Jihee CHOI (Korea)
Ms. Jong-Hyo PARK (Korea)
Mr. Jos NOESEN (Luxembourg)
Mr. Rafael FREYRE MARTINEZ (Mexico)
Mr. Rene GOMORA CASTILLO (Mexico)
Mr. Hector ROBLES (Mexico)
Mr. Roy TJOA (Netherlands)
Mr. Francis VAN DER MOOREN (Netherlands)
Mr. Marcel SMITS VAN WAESBERGHE (Netherlands)
Mr. David SCOTT (New Zealand)
Mr. Lars NERDRUM (Norway)
Ms. Ragnhild NERSTEN (Norway)
Mr. Geir NYGARD (Norway)
Mr. Jacek MASLANKOWSKI (Poland)
Mr. Mark AGRANOVICH (Russian Federation)
Ms. Lubomira SRNANKOVA (Slovak Republic)
Ms. Raquel ALVAREZ-ESTEBAN (Spain)
Ms. Carmen UREÑA UREÑA (Spain)
Mr. Torbjorn LINDQVIST (Sweden)
Mr. Kenny PETERSSON (Sweden)
Mr. Emanuel VON ERLACH (Switzerland)
Mr. Anthony CLARKE (United Kingdom)
Mr. Stephen LEMAN (United Kingdom)
Mr. Thomas SNYDER (United States)
Ms. Kimberly TAHAN (United States)

Network for the Collection and Adjudication of System-level descriptive Information on Educational Structures, Policies and Practices (NESLI)

Lead Country: United Kingdom
Network Leader: Mr. Stephen LEMAN
Mr. Paul CMIEL (Australia)
Mr. Christian KRENTHALLER (Austria)
Mr. Francois-Gerard STOLZ (Belgium)
Mr. Raymond VAN DE SIJPE (Belgium)
Ms. Ann VAN DRIESSCHE (Belgium)
Mr. Daniel Jaime CAPISTRANO DE OLIVEIRA (Brazil)
Ms. Ana Carolina SILVA CIROTTO (Brazil)
Ms. Michaela KLENHOVA (Czech Republic)
Ms. Pavlina STASTNOVA (Czech Republic)
Mr. Jorgen Balling RASMUSSEN (Denmark)
Ms. Kristi PLOOM (Estonia)
Mr. Richard DEISS (European Commission)
Mrs. Arlette DELHAXHE (Eurydice)
Mr. Stanislav RANGUELOV (Eurydice)
Ms. Kristiina VOLMARI (Finland)
Ms. Nadine DALSHEIMER-VAN DER TOL (France)
Ms. Pia BRUGGER (Germany)
Ms. Cornelia FRANKE (Germany)
Ms. Maria FASSARI (Greece)
Ms. Dimitra FARMAKIOTOU (Greece)
Mr. Pat McSITRIC (Ireland)
Ms. Sophie ARTSEV (Israel)
Mr. Yoav AZULAY (Israel)
Ms. Gianna BARBIERI (Italy)
Ms. Ezia PALMERI (Italy)
Mr. Yasumasa SHINOHARA (Japan)
Ms. Kumiko TANSHO-HIRABAYASHI (Japan)
Ms. Jong-Hyo PARK (Korea)
Mr. Gilles HIRT (Luxembourg)
Mr. Rafael FREYRE MARTINEZ (Mexico)
Mr. Hans RUESINK (Netherlands)
Mr. Marcel SMITS VAN WAESBERGHE (Netherlands)
Mr. Cyril MAKO (New Zealand)
Mr. Kjetil HELGELAND (Norway)
Ms. Katarzyna MALEC (Poland)
Ms. Anna NOWOZYNSKA (Poland)
Mr. Nuno Miguel RODRIGUES (Portugal)
Mrs. Ana VITORINO (Portugal)
Mr. Mark AGRANOVICH (Russian Federation)
Ms. Anna FATEEVA (Russian Federation)
Mr. Valentín RAMOS SALVADOR (Spain)
Mr. Antonio DEL SASTRE (Spain)
Mr. Anders BORGSTROM (Sweden)
Ms. Helena WINTGREN (Sweden)
Ms. Rejane DEPPIERRAZ (Switzerland)
Ms. Hümeyra ALTUNTAS (Turkey)
Mr. Anthony CLARKE (United Kingdom)
Mr. Mal COOKE (United Kingdom)
Mr. Stephen LEMAN (United Kingdom)
Ms. Valena PLISKO (United States)

Other contributors to this publication

Ms. Anna BORKOWSKY (LSO consultant)
Mr. Torberg FALCH (NESLI consultant)
Mr. Henry M. LEVIN (NESLI consultant)
Mr. Jon LAUGLO (LSO consultant)
Mr. Gary MIRON (NESLI consultant)
Mr. Kenny PETERSSON (LSO consultant)
Mr. Dan SHERMAN (LSO consultant)
Mr. Bjarne STROM (NESLI consultant)
Ms. Fung-Kwan TAM (Layout)
Mr. J. Douglas WILLMS (NESLI consultant)

Related OECD Publications

PISA 2009 Results: Students On Line: Digital Technologies and Performance (Volume VI) (2011)
ISBN 978-92-64-11291-9

PISA 2009 Results: What Students Know and Can Do: Student Performance in Reading, Mathematics and Science (Volume I) (2010)
ISBN 978-92-64-09144-3

PISA 2009 Results: Overcoming Social Background: Equity in Learning Opportunities and Outcomes (Volume II) (2010)
ISBN 978-92-64-09146-7

PISA 2009 Results: Learning to Learn: Student Engagement, Strategies and Practices (Volume III) (2010)
ISBN 978-92-64-09147-4

PISA 2009 Results: What Makes a School Successful?: Resources, Policies and Practices (Volume IV) (2010)
ISBN 978-92-64-09148-1

PISA 2009 Results: Learning Trends: Changes in Student Performance Since 2000 (Volume V) (2010)
ISBN 978-92-64-09149-8

Improving Health and Social Cohesion through Education (2010)
ISBN 978-92-64-08630-2

OECD Employment Outlook 2010 (2010)
ISBN 978-92-64-08468-1

TALIS 2008 Technical Report (2010)
ISBN 978-92-64-07985-4

Taxing Wages 2008-2009 (2010)
ISBN 978-92-64-08299-1

Creating Effective Teaching and Learning Environments: First Results from TALIS (2009)
ISBN 978-92-64-05605-3

Health at a Glance 2009: OECD Indicators (2009)
ISBN 978-92-64-06153-8

OECD Science, Technology and Industry Scoreboard 2009 (2009)
ISBN 978-92-64-06371-6

OECD Reviews of Tertiary Education: Tertiary Education for the Knowledge Society (2008)
ISBN 978-92-64-04652-8

Understanding the Social Outcomes of Learning (2007)
ISBN 978-92-64-03310-8

OECD Revenue Statistics 1965-2005 (2006)
ISBN 978-92-64-02993-4

Teachers Matter: Attracting, Developing and Retaining Effective Teachers (2005)
ISBN 978-92-64-01802-0

Internationalisation and Trade in Higher Education: Opportunities and Challenges (2004)
ISBN 978-92-64-01504-3

OECD publications can be browsed or purchased at the OECD iLibrary (www.oecd-ilibrary.org).

ORGANISATION FOR ECONOMIC CO-OPERATION AND DEVELOPMENT

The OECD is a unique forum where governments work together to address the economic, social and environmental challenges of globalisation. The OECD is also at the forefront of efforts to understand and to help governments respond to new developments and concerns, such as corporate governance, the information economy and the challenges of an ageing population. The Organisation provides a setting where governments can compare policy experiences, seek answers to common problems, identify good practice and work to co-ordinate domestic and international policies.

The OECD member countries are: Australia, Austria, Belgium, Canada, Chile, the Czech Republic, Denmark, Estonia, Finland, France, Germany, Greece, Hungary, Iceland, Ireland, Israel, Italy, Japan, Korea, Luxembourg, Mexico, the Netherlands, New Zealand, Norway, Poland, Portugal, the Slovak Republic, Slovenia, Spain, Sweden, Switzerland, Turkey, the United Kingdom and the United States. The European Commission takes part in the work of the OECD.

OECD Publishing disseminates widely the results of the Organisation's statistics gathering and research on economic, social and environmental issues, as well as the conventions, guidelines and standards agreed by its members.

OECD PUBLISHING, 2, rue André-Pascal, 75775 PARIS CEDEX 16
(96 2011 04 1P) ISBN 978-92-64-11420-3 – No. 58575 2011